T0189194

Lecture Notes in Computer Science   **9528**

Commenced Publication in 1973
Founding and Former Series Editors:
Gerhard Goos, Juris Hartmanis, and Jan van Leeuwen

More information about this series at http://www.springer.com/series/7407

Guojun Wang · Albert Zomaya
Gregorio Martinez Perez · Kenli Li (Eds.)

Algorithms and Architectures for Parallel Processing

15th International Conference, ICA3PP 2015
Zhangjiajie, China, November 18–20, 2015
Proceedings, Part I

 Springer

Editors
Guojun Wang
Central South University
Changsha
China

Gregorio Martinez Perez
University of Murcia
Murcia
Spain

Albert Zomaya
The University of Sydney
Sydney, NSW
Australia

Kenli Li
Hunan University
Changsha
China

ISSN 0302-9743   ISSN 1611-3349 (electronic)
Lecture Notes in Computer Science
ISBN 978-3-319-27118-7   ISBN 978-3-319-27119-4 (eBook)
DOI 10.1007/978-3-319-27119-4

Library of Congress Control Number: 2015955380

LNCS Sublibrary: SL1 – Theoretical Computer Science and General Issues

Printed on acid-free paper

Springer International Publishing AG Switzerland is part of Springer Science+Business Media
(www.springer.com)

Welcome Message from the ICA3PP 2015 General Chairs

Welcome to the proceedings of the 15th International Conference on Algorithms and Architectures for Parallel Processing (ICA3PP 2015), which was organized by Central South University, Hunan University, National University of Defense Technology, and Jishou University.

It was our great pleasure to organize the ICA3PP 2015 conference in Zhangjiajie, China, during November 18–20, 2015. On behalf of the Organizing Committee of the conference, we would like to express our cordial gratitude to all participants who attended the conference.

ICA3PP 2015 was the 15th event in the series of conferences started in 1995 that is devoted to algorithms and architectures for parallel processing. ICA3PP is now recognized as the main regular event in the world that covers many dimensions of parallel algorithms and architectures, encompassing fundamental theoretical approaches, practical experimental projects, and commercial components and systems. The conference provides a forum for academics and practitioners from around the world to exchange ideas for improving the efficiency, performance, reliability, security, and interoperability of computing systems and applications.

ICA3PP 2015 attracted high-quality research papers highlighting the foundational work that strives to push beyond the limits of existing technologies, including experimental efforts, innovative systems, and investigations that identify weaknesses in existing parallel processing technology.

ICA3PP 2015 consisted of the main conference and six international symposia and workshops. Many individuals contributed to the success of the conference. We would like to express our special appreciation to Prof. Yang Xiang, Prof. Andrzej Goscinski, and Prof. Yi Pan, the Steering Committee chairs, for giving us the opportunity to host this prestigious conference and for their guidance with the conference organization. Special thanks to the program chairs, Prof. Albert Zomaya, Prof. Gregorio Martinez Perez, and Prof. Kenli Li, for their outstanding work on the technical program. Thanks also to the workshop chairs, Dr. Mianxiong Dong, Dr. Ryan K.L. Ko, and Dr. Md. Zakirul Alam Bhuiya, for their excellent work in organizing attractive symposia and workshops. Thanks also to the publicity chairs, Prof. Carlos Becker Westphall, Dr. Yulei Wu, Prof. Christian Callegari, Prof. Kuan-Ching Li, and Prof. James J. (Jong Hyuk) Park, for the great job in publicizing this event. We would like to give our thanks to all the members of the Organizing Committee and Program Committee as well as the external reviewers for their efforts and support. We would also like to give our thanks to the keynote speakers, Prof. John C.S. Lui, Prof. Jiannong Cao, Prof. Wanlei Zhou, and Prof. Hai Jin, for offering insightful and enlightening talks. Last but not least, we would like to thank all the authors who submitted their papers to the conference.

November 2015

Guojun Wang
Peter Mueller
Qingping Zhou

Welcome Message from the ICA3PP 2015 Program Chairs

On behalf of the Program Committee of the 15th International Conference on Algorithms and Architectures for Parallel Processing (ICA3PP 2015), we would like to welcome you to join the conference held in Zhangjiajie, China, during November 18–20, 2015.

The ICA3PP conference aims at bringing together researchers and practitioners from both academia and industry who are working on algorithms and architectures for parallel processing. The conference features keynote speeches, panel discussions, technical presentations, symposiums, and workshops, where the technical presentations from both the research community and industry cover various aspects including fundamental theoretical approaches, practical experimental projects, and commercial components and systems. ICA3PP 2015 was the next event in a series of highly successful international conferences on algorithms and architectures for parallel processing, previously held as ICA3PP 2014 (Dalian, China, August 2014), ICA3PP 2013 (Vietri sul Mare, Italy, December 2013), ICA3PP 2012 (Fukuoka, Japan, September 2012), ICA3PP 2011 (Melbourne, Australia, October 2011), ICA3PP 2010 (Busan, Korea, May 2010), ICA3PP 2009 (Taipei, Taiwan, June 2009), ICA3PP 2008 (Cyprus, June 2008), ICA3PP 2007 (Hangzhou, China, June 2007), ICA3PP 2005 (Melbourne, Australia, October 2005), ICA3PP 2002 (Beijing, China, October 2002), ICA3PP2000 (Hong Kong, China, December 2000), ICA3PP 1997 (Melbourne, Australia, December 1997), ICA3PP 1996 (Singapore, June 1996), and ICA3PP 1995 (Brisbane, Australia, April 1995).

The ICA3PP 2015 conference collected research papers on related research issues from all around the world. This year we received 602 submissions for the main conference. All submissions received at least three reviews during a high-quality review process. According to the review results, 219 papers were selected for oral presentation at the conference, giving an acceptance rate of 36.4 %.

We would like to offer our gratitude to Prof. Yang Xiang and Prof. Andrzej Goscinski from Deakin University, Australia, and Prof. Yi Pan from Georgia State University, USA, the Steering Committee chairs. Our thanks also go to the general chairs, Prof. Guojun Wang from Central South University, China, Dr. Peter Mueller from IBM Zurich Research, Switzerland, and Prof. Qingping Zhou from Jishou University, China, for their great support and good suggestions for a successful the final program. Special thanks to the workshop chairs, Dr. Mianxiong Dong from Muroran Institute of Technology, Japan, and Dr. Ryan K.L. Ko from the University of Waikato, New Zealand, and Dr. Md. Zakirul Alam Bhuiyan from Temple University, USA. In particular, we would like to give our thanks to all researchers and practitioners who submitted their manuscripts, and to the Program Committee and the external reviewers who contributed their valuable time and expertise to provide professional reviews working under a very tight schedule. Moreover, we are very grateful to our keynote speakers who kindly accepted our invitation to give insightful and prospective talks.

Finally, we believe that the conference provided a very good opportunity for participants to learn from each other. We hope you enjoy the conference proceedings.

Albert Zomaya
Gregorio Martinez Perez
Kenli Li

Welcome Message from the ICA3PP 2015 Workshop Chairs

Welcome to the proceedings of the 15th International Conference on Algorithms and Architectures for Parallel Processing (ICA3PP 2015) held in Zhangjiajie, China, during November 18–20, 2015. The program this year consisted of six symposiums/workshops covering a wide range of research topics on parallel processing technology:

(1) The 6th International Workshop on Trust, Security and Privacy for Big Data (TrustData 2015)
(2) The 5th International Symposium on Trust, Security and Privacy for Emerging Applications (TSP 2015)
(3) The Third International Workshop on Network Optimization and Performance Evaluation (NOPE 2015)
(4) The Second International Symposium on Sensor-Cloud Systems (SCS 2015)
(5) The Second International Workshop on Security and Privacy Protection in Computer and Network Systems (SPPCN 2015)
(6) The First International Symposium on Dependability in Sensor, Cloud, and Big Data Systems and Applications (DependSys 2015)

The aim of these symposiums/workshops is to provide a forum to bring together practitioners and researchers from academia and industry for discussion and presentations on the current research and future directions related to parallel processing technology. The themes and topics of these symposiums/workshops are a valuable complement to the overall scope of ICA3PP 2015 providing additional values and interests. We hope that all of the selected papers will have a good impact on future research in the respective field.

The ICA3PP 2015 workshops collected research papers on the related research issues from all around the world. This year we received 205 submissions for all workshops. All submissions received at least three reviews during a high-quality review process. According to the review results, 77 papers were selected for oral presentation at the conference, giving an acceptance rate of 37.6 %.

We offer our sincere gratitude to the workshop organizers for their hard work in designing the call for papers, assembling the Program Committee, managing the peer-review process for the selection of papers, and planning the workshop program. We are grateful to the workshop Program Committees, external reviewers, session chairs, contributing authors, and attendees. Our special thanks to the Organizing Committees of ICA3PP 2015 for their strong support, and especially to the program chairs, Prof. Albert Zomaya, Prof. Gregorio Martinez Perez, and Prof. Kenli Li, for their guidance.

Finally, we hope that you will find the proceedings interesting and stimulating.

Mianxiong Dong
Ryan K.L. Ko
Md. Zakirul Alam Bhuiyan

Welcome Message from the TrustData 2015 Program Chairs

The 6th International Workshop on Trust, Security and Privacy for Big Data (TrustData 2015) was held in Zhangjiajie, China.

TrustData aims at bringing together people from both academia and industry to present their most recent work related to trust, security, and privacy issues in big data, and to exchange ideas and thoughts in order to identify emerging research topics and define the future of big data.

TrustData 2015 was the next event in a series of highly successful international workshops, previously held as TrustData 2014 (Dalian, China, March 2012) and TrustData 2013 (Zhangjiajie, China, November, 2013).

This international workshop collected research papers on the aforementioned research issues from all around the world. Each paper was reviewed by at least three experts in the field. We feel very proud of the high participation, and although it was difficult to collect the best papers from all the submissions received, we feel we managed to have an amazing conference that was enjoyed by all participants.

We would like to offer our gratitude to the general chairs, Dr. Qin Liu and Dr. Muhammad Bashir Abdullahi, for their excellent support and invaluable suggestions for a successful final program. In particular, we would like to thank all researchers and practitioners who submitted their manuscripts, and the Program Committee members and additional reviewers for their tremendous efforts and timely reviews.

We hope you enjoy the proceedings of TrustData 2015.

Keqin Li
Avinash Srinivasan

Welcome Message from the TSP 2015 Program Chairs

On behalf of the Program Committee of the 5th International Symposium on Trust, Security and Privacy for Emerging Applications (TSP 2015), we would like to welcome you to the proceedings of the event, which was held in Zhangjiajie, China.

The symposium focuses on trust, security, and privacy issues in social networks, cloud computing, Internet of Things (IoT), wireless sensor networks, and other networking environments or system applications; it also provides a forum for presenting and discussing emerging ideas and trends in this highly challenging research area. The aim of this symposium is to provide a leading edge forum to foster interaction between researchers and developers with the trust, security, and privacy issues, and to give attendees an opportunity to network with experts in this area.

Following the success of TSP 2008 in Shanghai, China, during December 17–20, 2008, TSP 2009 in Macau SAR, China, during October 12–14, 2009, TSP 2010 in Bradford, UK, during June 29–July 1, 2010, and TSP 2013 in Zhangjiajie, China, during November 13–15, 2013, the 5th International Symposium on Trust, Security and Privacy for Emerging Applications (TSP 2015) was held in Zhangjiajie, China, during November 18–20, 2015, in conjunction with the 15th International Conference on Algorithms and Architectures for Parallel Processing (ICA3PP 2015).

The symposium collected research papers on the aforementioned research issues from all around the world. Each paper was reviewed by at least two experts in the field. We realized an amazing symposium that we hope was enjoyed by all the participants.

We would like to thank all researchers and practitioners who submitted their manuscripts, and the Program Committee members and additional reviewers for their tremendous efforts and timely reviews.

We hope you enjoy the proceedings of TSP 2015.

Imad Jawhar
Deqing Zou

Welcome Message from the NOPE 2015 Program Chair

Welcome to the proceedings of the 2015 International Workshop on Network Optimization and Performance Evaluation (NOPE 2015) held in Zhangjiajie, China, during November 18–20, 2015.

Network optimization and performance evaluation is a topic that attracts much attention in network/Internet and distributed systems. Due to the recent advances in Internet-based applications as well as WLANs, wireless home networks, wireless sensor networks, wireless mesh networks, and cloud computing, we are witnessing a variety of new technologies. However, these systems and networks are becoming very large and complex, and consuming a great amount of energy at the same time. System optimization and performance evaluation remain to be resolved before these systems become a commodity.

On behalf of the Organizing Committee, we would like to take this opportunity to express our gratitude to all reviewers who worked hard to finish reviews on time. Thanks to the publicity chairs for their efforts and support. Thanks also to all authors for their great support and contribution to the event. We would like to give our special thanks to the Organizing Committee, colleagues, and friends who worked hard behind the scenes. Without their unfailing cooperation, hard work, and dedication, this event would not have been successfully organized.

We are grateful to everyone for participating in NOPE 2015.

Gaocai Wang

Welcome Message from SCS 2015 Program Chairs

As the Program Chairs and on behalf of the Organizing Committee of the Second International Symposium on Sensor-Cloud Systems (SCS 2015), we would like to express our gratitude to all the participants who attended the symposium in Zhangjiajie, China, during November 18–20, 2015. This famous city is the location of China's first forest park (The Zhangjiajie National Forest Park) and a World Natural Heritage site (Wulingyuan Scenic Area).

The aim of SCS is to bring together researchers and practitioners working on sensor-cloud systems to present and discuss emerging ideas and trends in this highly challenging research field. It has attracted some high-quality research papers, which highlight the foundational work that strives to push beyond limits of existing technologies, including experimental efforts, innovative systems, and investigations that identify weaknesses in the existing technology services.

SCS 2015 was sponsored by the National Natural Science Foundation of China, Springer, the School of Information Science and Engineering at Central South University, and the School of Software at Central South University, and it was organized by Central South University, Hunan University, National University of Defense Technology, and Jishou University. SCS 2015 was held in conjunction with the 15th International Conference on Algorithms and Architectures for Parallel Processing (ICA3PP 2015), which highlights the latest research trends in various aspects of computer science and technology.

Many individuals contributed to the success of this international symposium. We would like to express our special appreciation to the general chairs of main conference, Prof. Guojun Wang, Prof. Peter Mueller, and Prof. Qingping Zhou, for giving us this opportunity to hold this symposium and for their guidance in the organization. Thanks also to the general chairs of this symposium, Prof. Jie Li and Prof. Dongqing Xie, for their excellent work in organizing the symposium. We would like to give our thanks to all the members of the Organizing Committee and Program Committee for their efforts and support.

Finally, we are grateful to the authors for submitting their fine work to SCS 2015 and all the participants for their attendance.

Xiaofei Xing
Md. Zakirul Alam Bhuiyan

Welcome Message from the SPPCN 2015 Program Chairs

On behalf of the Program Committee of the Second International Workshop on Security and Privacy Protection in Computer and Network Systems (SPPCN 2015), we would like to welcome you to join the proceedings of the workshop, which was held in Zhangjiajie, China.

The workshop focuses on security and privacy protection in computer and network systems, such as authentication, access control, availability, integrity, privacy, confidentiality, dependability, and sustainability issues of computer and network systems. The aim of the workshop is to provide a leading-edge forum to foster interaction between researchers and developers working on security and privacy protection in computer and network systems, and to give attendees an opportunity to network with experts in this area.

SPPCN 2015 was the next event in a series of highly successful international conferences on security and privacy protection in computer and network systems, previously held as SPPCN 2014 (Dalian, China, December 2014). The workshop collected research papers on the above research issues from all around the world. Each paper was reviewed by at least two experts in the field.

We would like to offer our gratitude to the general chair, Prof. Jian Weng, for his excellent support and contribution to the success of the final program. In particular, we would like to thank all researchers and practitioners who submitted their manuscripts, and the Program Committee members and additional reviewers for their tremendous efforts and timely reviews.

We hope all of you enjoy the proceedings of SPPCN 2015.

Mianxiong Dong
Hua Guo
Tieming Cheng
Kaimin Wei

Welcome Message from the DependSys 2015 Program Chairs

As the program chairs and on behalf of the Organizing Committee of the First International Symposium on Dependability in Sensor, Cloud, and Big Data Systems and Applications (DependSys2015), we would like to express our gratitude to all the participants attending the international symposium in Zhangjiajie, China, during November 18–20, 2015. This famous city is the location of China's first forest park (The Zhangjiajie National Forest Park) and a World Natural Heritage site (Wulingyuan Scenic Area).

DependSys is a timely event that brings together new ideas, techniques, and solutions for dependability and its issues in sensor, cloud, and big data systems and applications. As we are deep into the Information Age, we are witnessing the explosive growth of data available on the Internet. Human beings are producing quintillion bytes of data every day, which come from sensors, individual archives, social networks, Internet of Things, enterprises, and the Internet in all scales and formats. One of the most challenging issues we face is to achieve the designed system performance to an expected level, i.e., how to effectively provide dependability in sensor, cloud, and big data systems. These systems need to typically run continuously, which often tend to become inert, brittle, and vulnerable after a while.

This international symposium collected research papers on the aforementioned research issues from all around the world. Although it was the first event of DependSys, we received a large number of submissions in response to the call for papers. Each paper was reviewed by at least three experts in the field. After detailed discussions among the program chairs and general chairs, a set of quality papers was finally accepted. We are very proud of the high number of participations, and it was difficult to collect the best papers from all the submissions.

Many individuals contributed to the success of this high-caliber international symposium. We would like to express our special appreciation to the steering chairs, Prof. Jie Wu and Prof. Guojun Wang, for giving us the opportunity to hold this symposium and for their guidance in the symposium organization. In particular, we would like to give our thanks to the symposium chairs, Prof. Mohammed Atiquzzaman, Prof. Sheikh Iqbal Ahamed, and Dr. Md Zakirul Alam Bhuiyan, for their excellent support and invaluable suggestions for a successful final program. Thanks to all the Program Committee members and the additional reviewers for their tremendous efforts and timely reviews.

We hope you enjoy the proceedings of DependSys 2015.

Latifur Khan
Joarder Kamruzzaman
Al-Sakib Khan Pathan

Organization

ICA3PP 2015 Organizing and Program Committees

General Chairs

Guojun Wang	Central South University, China
Peter Mueller	IBM Zurich Research, Switzerland
Qingping Zhou	Jishou University, China

Program Chairs

Albert Zomaya	University of Sydney, Australia
Gregorio Martinez Perez	University of Murcia, Spain
Kenli Li	Hunan University, China

Steering Chairs

Andrzej Goscinski	Deakin University, Australia
Yi Pan	Georgia State University, USA
Yang Xiang	Deakin University, Australia

Workshop Chairs

Mianxiong Dong	Muroran Institute of Technology, Japan
Ryan K.L. Ko	The University of Waikato, New Zealand
Md. Zakirul Alam Bhuiyan	Central South University, China

Publicity Chairs

Carlos Becker Westphall	Federal University of Santa Catarina, Brazil
Yulei Wu	The University of Exeter, UK
Christian Callegari	University of Pisa, Italy
Kuan-Ching Li	Providence University, Taiwan
James J. (Jong Hyuk) Park	SeoulTech, Korea

Publication Chairs

Jin Zheng	Central South University, China
Wenjun Jiang	Hunan University, China

Finance Chairs

Pin Liu   Central South University, China
Wang Yang   Central South University, China

Local Arrangements Chairs

Fang Qi   Central South University, China
Qin Liu   Hunan University, China
Hongzhi Xu   Jishou University, China

Program Committee

1. Parallel and Distributed Architectures Track

Chairs

Stefano Giordano   Italian National Interuniversity Consortium
                                 for Telecommunications, Italy
Xiaofei Liao   Huazhong University of Science and Technology,
                                 China
Haikun Liu   Nanyang Technological University, Singapore

TPC Members

Marco Aldinucci   Universitá degli Studi di Torino, Italy
Yungang Bao   Chinese Academy of Sciences, China
Hui Chen   Auburn University, USA
Vladimir Getov   University of Westminster, UK
Jie Jia   Northeastern University, China
Yusen Li   Nanyang Technological University, Singapore
Zengxiang Li   Agency for Science, Technology and Research,
                                 Singapore
Xue Liu   Northeastern University, China
Yongchao Liu   Georgia Institute of Technology, USA
Salvatore Orlando   Universitá Ca' Foscari Venezia, Italy
Nicola Tonellotto   ISTI-CNR, Italy
Zeke Wang   Nanyang Technological University, Singapore
Quanqing Xu   Agency for Science, Technology and Research
                                 (A*STAR), Singapore
Ramin Yahyapour   University of Göttingen, Germany
Jidong Zhai   Tsinghua University, China
Jianlong Zhong   GraphSQL Inc., USA
Andrei Tchernykh   CICESE Research Center, Ensenada, Baja California,
                                 Mexico

2. Software Systems and Programming Track

Chairs

Xinjun Mao	National University of Defense Technology, China
Sanaa Sharafeddine	Lebanese American University, Beirut, Lebanon

TPC Members

Surendra Byna	Lawrence Berkeley National Lab, USA
Yue-Shan Chang	National Taipei University, Taiwan
Massimo Coppola	ISTI-CNR, Italy
Marco Danelutto	University of Pisa, Italy
Jose Daniel Garcia	Carlos III of Madrid University, Spain
Peter Kilpatrick	Queen's University Belfast, UK
Soo-Kyun Kim	PaiChai University, Korea
Rajeev Raje	Indiana University-Purdue University Indianapolis, USA
Salvatore Ruggieri	University of Pisa, Italy
Subhash Saini	NASA, USA
Peter Strazdins	The Australian National University, Australia
Domenico Talia	University of Calabria, Italy
Hiroyuki Tomiyama	Ritsumeikan University, Japan
Canqun Yang	National University of Defense Technology, China
Daniel Andresen	Kansas State University, USA
Sven-Bodo Scholz	Heriot-Watt University, UK
Salvatore Venticinque	Second University of Naples, Italy

3. Distributed and Network-Based Computing Track

Chairs

Casimer DeCusatis	Marist College, USA
Qi Wang	University of the West of Scotland, UK

TPC Members

Justin Baijian	Purdue University, USA
Aparicio Carranza	City University of New York, USA
Tzung-Shi Chen	National University of Tainan, Taiwan
Ciprian Dobre	University Politehnica of Bucharest, Romania
Longxiang Gao	Deakin University, Australia
Ansgar Gerlicher	Stuttgart Media University, Germany
Harald Gjermundrod	University of Nicosia, Cyprus
Christos Grecos	Independent Imaging Consultant, UK
Jia Hu	Liverpool Hope University, UK
Baback Izadi	State University of New York at New Paltz, USA
Morihiro Kuga	Kumamoto University, Japan
Mikolaj Leszczuk	AGH University of Science and Technology, Poland

Paul Lu	University of Alberta, Canada
Chunbo Luo	University of the West of Scotland, UK
Ioannis Papapanagiotou	Purdue University, USA
Michael Hobbs	Deakin University, Australia
Cosimo Anglano	Università del Piemonte Orientale, Italy
Md. ObaidurRahman	Dhaka University of Engineering and Technology, Bangladesh
Aniello Castiglione	University of Salerno, Italy
Shuhong Chen	Hunan Institute of Engineering, China

4. Big Data and Its Applications Track

Chairs

Jose M. Alcaraz Calero	University of the West of Scotland, UK
Shui Yu	Deakin University, Australia

TPC Members

Alba Amato	Second University of Naples, Italy
Tania Cerquitelli	Politecnico di Torino, Italy
Zizhong (Jeffrey) Chen	University of California at Riverside, USA
Alfredo Cuzzocrea	University of Calabria, Italy
Saptarshi Debroy	University of Missouri-Columbia, USA
Yacine Djemaiel	Communication Networks and Security, Res. Lab, Tunisia
Shadi Ibrahim	Inria, France
Hongwei Li	UESTC, China
William Liu	Auckland University of Technology, New Zealand
Xiao Liu	East China Normal University, China
Karampelas Panagiotis	Hellenic Air Force Academy, Greece
Florin Pop	University Politehnica of Bucharest, Romania
Genoveva Vargas Solar	CNRS-LIG-LAFMIA, France
Chen Wang	CSIRO ICT Centre, Australia
Chao-Tung Yang	Tunghai University, Taiwan
Peng Zhang	Stony Brook University, USA
Ling Zhen	Southeast University, China
Roger Zimmermann	National University of Singapore, Singapore
Francesco Palmieri	University of Salerno, Italy
Rajiv Ranjan	CSIRO, Canberra, Australia
Felix Cuadrado	Queen Mary University of London, UK
Nilimesh Halder	The University of Western Australia, Australia
Kuan-Chou Lai	National Taichung University of Education, Taiwan
Jaafar Gaber	UTBM, France
Eunok Paek	Hanyang University, Korea
You-Chiun Wang	National Sun Yat-sen University, Taiwan
Ke Gu	Changsha University of Technology, China

5. Parallel and Distributed Algorithms Track

Chairs

Dimitris A. Pados	The State University of New York at Buffalo, USA
Baoliu Ye	Nanjing University, China

TPC Members

George Bosilca	University of Tennessee, USA
Massimo Cafaro	University of Salento, Italy
Stefania Colonnese	Universitá degli Studi di Roma La Sapienza, Italy
Raphael Couturier	University of Franche Comte, France
Gregoire Danoy	University of Luxembourg, Luxembourg
Franco Frattolillo	Universitá del Sannio, Italy
Che-Rung Lee	National Tsing Hua University, Taiwan
Laurent Lefevre	Inria, ENS-Lyon, University of Lyon, France
Amit Majumdar	San Diego Supercomputer Center, USA
Susumu Matsumae	Saga University, Japan
George N. Karystinos	Technical University of Crete, Greece
Dana Petcu	West University of Timisoara, Romania
Francoise Sailhan	CNAM, France
Uwe Tangen	Ruhr-Universität Bochum, Germany
Wei Xue	Tsinghua University, China
Kalyan S. Perumalla	Oak Ridge National Laboratory, USA
Morris Riedel	University of Iceland, Germany
Gianluigi Folino	ICAR-CNR, Italy
Joanna Kolodziej	Cracow University of Technology, Poland
Luc Bougé	ENS Rennes, France
Hirotaka Ono	Kyushu University, Japan
Tansel Ozyer	TOBB Economics and Technology University, Turkey
Daniel Grosu	Wayne State University, USA
Tian Wang	Huaqiao University, China
Sancheng Peng	Zhaoqing University, China
Fang Qi	Central South University, China
Zhe Tang	Central South University, China
Jin Zheng	Central South University, China

6. Applications of Parallel and Distributed Computing Track

Chairs

Yu Chen	Binghamton University, State University of New York, USA
Michal Wozniak	Wroclaw University of Technology, Poland

TPC Members

Jose Alfredo F. Costa	Universidade Federal do Rio Grande do Norte, Brazil
Robert Burduk	Wroclaw University of Technology, Poland
Boguslaw Cyganek	AGH University of Science and Technology, Poland
Paolo Gasti	New York Institute of Technology, USA
Manuel Grana	University of the Basque Country, Spain
Houcine Hassan	Universidad Politecnica de Valencia, Spain
Alvaro Herrero	Universidad de Burgos, Spain
Jin Kocsis	University of Akron, USA
Esmond Ng	Lawrence Berkeley National Lab, USA
Dragan Simic	University of Novi Sad, Serbia
Ching-Lung Su	National Yunlin University of Science and Technology, Taiwan
Tomoaki Tsumura	Nagoya Institute of Technology, Japan
Krzysztof Walkowiak	Wroclaw University of Technology, Poland
Zi-Ang (John) Zhang	Binghamton University-SUNY, USA
Yunhui Zheng	IBM Research, USA
Hsi-Ya Chang	National Center for High-Performance Computing, Taiwan
Chun-Yu Lin	HTC Corp., Taiwan
Nikzad Babaii Rizvandi	The University of Sydney, Australia

7. Service Dependability and Security in Distributed and Parallel Systems Track

Chairs

Antonio Ruiz Martinez	University of Murcia, Spain
Jun Zhang	Deakin University, Australia

TPC Members

Jorge Bernal Bernabe	University of Murcia, Spain
Roberto Di Pietro	Universitá di Roma Tre, Italy
Massimo Ficco	Second University of Naples (SUN), Italy
Yonggang Huang	Beijing Institute of Technology, China
Georgios Kambourakis	University of the Aegean, Greece
Muhammad Khurram Khan	King Saud University, Saudi Arabia
Liang Luo	Southwest University, China
Barbara Masucci	Universitá di Salerno, Italy
Juan M. Marin	University of Murcia, Spain
Sabu M. Thampi	Indian Institute of Information Technology and Management – Kerala (IIITM-K), India
Fernando Pereniguez-Garcia	Catholic University of Murcia, Spain
Yongli Ren	RMIT University, Australia
Yu Wang	Deakin University, Australia
Sheng Wen	Deakin University, Australia

Mazdak Zamani	Universiti Teknologi Malaysia, Malaysia
Susan K. Donohue	University of Virginia, USA
Oana Boncalo	University Politehnica Timisoara, Romania
K.P. Lam	University of Keele, UK
George Loukas	University of Greenwich, UK
Ugo Fiore	Federico II University, Italy
Christian Esposito	University of Salerno, Italy
Arcangelo Castiglione	University of Salerno, Italy
Edward Jung	Kennesaw State University, USA
Md. Zakirul Alam Bhuiyan	Central South University, China
Xiaofei Xing	Guangzhou University, China
Qin Liu	Hunan University, China
Wenjun Jiang	Hunan University, China
Gaocai Wang	Guangxi University, China
Kaimin Wei	Jinan University, China

8. Web Services and Internet Computing Track

Chairs

Huansheng Ning	University of Science and Technology Beijing, China
Daqiang Zhang	Tongji University, China

TPC Members

Jing Chen	National Cheng Kung University, Taiwan
Eugen Dedu	University of Franche-Comte, France
Sotirios G. Ziavras	NJIT, USA
Luis Javier Garcia Villalba	Universidad Complutense de Madrid (UCM), Spain
Jaime Lloret	Universidad Politecnica de Valencia, Spain
Wei Lu	Keene University, USA
Stefano Marrone	Second University of Naples, Italy
Alejandro Masrur	Chemnitz University of Technology, Germany
Seungmin (Charlie) Rho	Sungkyul University, Korea
Giandomenico Spezzano	ICAR-CNR, Italy
Jiafu Wan	South China University of Technology, China
Yunsheng Wang	Kettering University, USA
Martine Wedlake	IBM, USA
Chung Wei-Ho	Research Center for Information Technology Innovation in Academia Sinica, Taiwan
Xingquan (Hill) Zhu	Florida Atlantic University, USA
Nikos Dimitriou	National Center for Scientific Research Demokritos, Greece
Choi Jaeho	CBNU, Chonju, Korea
Shi-Jinn Horng	National Taiwan University of Science and Technology, Taiwan

9. Performance Modeling and Evaluation Track

Chairs

Deze Zeng	China University of Geosciences, China
Bofeng Zhang	Shanghai University, China

TPC Members

Ladjel Bellatreche	ENSMA, France
Xiaoju Dong	Shanghai Jiao Tong University, China
Christian Engelman	Oak Ridge National Lab, USA
Javier Garcia Blas	University Carlos III, Spain
Mauro Iacono	Second University of Naples, Italy
Zhiyang Li	Dalian Maritime University, China
Tomas Margalef	Universitat Autonoma de Barcelona, Spain
Francesco Moscato	Second University of Naples, Italy
Heng Qi	Dalian University of Technology, China
Bing Shi	Wuhan University of Technology, China
Magdalena Szmajduch	Cracow University of Technology, Poland
Qian Wang	Wuhan University, China
Zhibo Wang	Wuhan University, China
Weigang Wu	Sun Yat-sen University, China
David E. Singh	University Carlos III of Madrid, Spain
Edmund Lai	Massey University, New Zealand
Robert J. Latham	Argonne National Laboratory, USA
Zafeirios Papazachos	Queen's University of Belfast, UK
Novella Bartolini	Sapienza University of Rome, Italy
Takeshi Nanri	Kyushu University, Japan
Mais Nijim	Texas A&M University – Kingsville, USA
Salvador Petit	Universitat Politècnica de València, Spain
Daisuke Takahashi	University of Tsukuba, Japan
Cathryn Peoples	Ulster University, Northern Ireland, UK
Hamid Sarbazi-Azad	Sharif University of Technology and IPM, Iran
Md. Abdur Razzaque	University of Dhaka, Bangladesh
Angelo Brayner	University of Fortaleza, Brazil
Sushil Prasad	Georgia State University, USA
Danilo Ardagna	Politecnico di Milano, Italy
Sun-Yuan Hsieh	National Cheng Kung University, Taiwan
Li Chaoliang	Hunan University of Commerce, China
Yongming Xie	Hunan Normal University, China
Guojun Wang	Central South University, China

Secretariats

Zhe Tang   Central South University, China
Feng Wang   Central South University, China

Webmaster

Xiangdong Lee   Central South University, China

TrustData 2015 Organizing and Program Committees

Steering Chairs

Guojun Wang   Central South University, China
Peter Mueller   IBM Zurich Research Laboratory, Switzerland

General Chairs

Qin Liu   Hunan University, China
Muhammad Bashir   Federal University of Technology, Minna, Nigeria
  Abdullahi

Program Chairs

Keqin Li   State University of New York at New Paltz, USA
Avinash Srinivasan   Temple University, USA

Publicity Chairs

Shui Yu   Deakin University, Australia
Weirong Liu   Central South University, China

Program Committee

Andrei Tchernykh   CICESE Research Center, Mexico
Baoliu Ye   Nanjing University, China
Bimal Roy   Indian Statistical Institute, India
Chang-Ai Sun   University of Science and Technology, China
Chao Song   University of Electronic Science and Technology
     of China, China
Christian Callegari   The University of Pisa, Italy
Chunhua Su   Japan Advanced Institute of Science and Technology,
     Japan
Franco Chiaraluce   Polytechnical University of Marche (UVPM), Italy
Hai Jiang   Arkansas State University, USA
Horacio Gonzalez-Velez   National College of Ireland, Ireland
Imed Romdhani   Edinburgh Napier University, UK
Jianguo Yao   Shanghai Jiao Tong University, China
Joon S. Park   Syracuse University, USA
Kevin Chan   US Army Research Laboratory, USA
Lizhe Wang   Rochester Institute of Technology, USA

TSP 2015 Organizing and Program Committees

Program Chairs

Imad Jawhar   United Arab Emirates University, UAE
Deqing Zou   Huazhong University of Science of Technology

Program Committee Members

Chao Song	University of Electronic Science and Technology, China
David Zheng	Frostburg State University, USA
Feng Li	Indiana University-Purdue University Indianapolis, USA
Haitao Lang	Beijing University of Chemical Technology, China
Huan Zhou	China Three Gorges University, China
Mingjun Xiao	University of Science and Technology of China, China
Mingwu Zhang	Hubei University of Technology, China
Shuhui Yang	Purdue University Calumet, USA
Xiaojun Hei	Huazhong University of Science and Technology, China
Xin Li	Nanjing University of Aeronautics and Astronautics, China
Xuanxia Yao	University of Science and Technology Beijing, China
Yaxiong Zhao	Google Inc., USA
Ying Dai	LinkedIn Corporation, USA
Yunsheng Wang	Kettering University, USA
Youwen Zhu	Nanjing University of Aeronautics and Astronautics, China
Yongming Xie	Changsha Medical University, China

Steering Committee

Wenjun Jiang	Hunan University, China (Chair)
Laurence T. Yang	St. Francis Xavier University, Canada
Guojun Wang	Central South University, China
Minyi Guo	Shanghai Jiao Tong University, China
Jie Li	University of Tsukuba, Japan
Jianhua Ma	Hosei University, Japan
Peter Mueller	IBM Zurich Research Laboratory, Switzerland
Indrakshi Ray	Colorado State University, USA

Kouichi Sakurai	Kyushu University, Japan
Bhavani Thuraisingham	The University of Texas at Dallas, USA
Jie Wu	Temple University, USA
Yang Xiang	Deakin University, Australia
Kun Yang	University of Essex, UK
Wanlei Zhou	Deakin University, Australia

Web Chair

Shan Peng	Central South University, China

NOPE 2015 Organizing and Program Committees

Steering Committee Chairs

Wei Li   Texas Southern University, USA
Taoshen Li   Guangxi University, China

Program Chair

Gaocai Wang   Guangxi University, China

Program Committee Members

Dieter Fiems	Ghent University, Belgium
Shuqiang Huang	Jinan University, China
Juan F. Perez	Imperial College London, UK
Haoqian Wang	Tsinghua University, China
Yitian Peng	Southeast University, China
Hongbin Chen	Guilin University of Electronic Technology, China
Jin Ye	Guangxi University, China
Junbin Liang	Hong Kong Polytechnic University, Hong Kong, SAR China
Xianfeng Liu	Hunan Normal University, China
Hao Zhang	Central South University, China
Chuyuan Wei	Beijing University of Civil Engineering and Architecture, China
Hongyun Xu	South China University of Technology, China
Zhefu Shi	University of Missouri, USA
Songfeng Lu	Huazhong University of Science and Technology, China
Yihui Deng	Jinan University, China
Lei Zhang	Beijing University of Civil Engineering and Architecture, China
Xiaoheng Deng	Central South University, China
Mingxing Luo	Southwest Jiaotong University, China
Bin Sun	Beijing University of Posts and Telecommunications, China
Zhiwei Wang	Nanjing University of Posts and Telecommunications, China
Yousheng Zhou	Chongqing University of Posts and Telecommunications, China
Daofeng Li	Guangxi University, China

SCS 2015 Organizing and Program Committees

Steering Chairs

Jie Li	Tsukuba University, Japan
Dongqing Xie	Guangzhou University, China

Program Chairs

Xiaofei Xing	Guangzhou University, China
Md. Zakirul Alam Bhuiyan	Central South University, China and Temple University, USA

Program Committee Members

Marco Aiello	University of Groningen, The Netherlands
David Chadwick	University of Kent, UK
Aparicio Carranza	City University of New York, USA
Mooi Choo Chuah	Lehigh University, USA
Yueming Deng	Hunan Normal University, China
Christos Grecos	Independent Imaging Consultant, UK
Dritan Kaleshi	University of Bristol, UK
Donghyun Kim	North Carolina Central University, USA
Santosh Kumar	University of Memphis, USA
Muthoni Masinde	University of Nairobi, Kenya
Satyjayant Mishra	New Mexico State University, USA
Nam Nguyen	Towson University, USA
Jean-Marc Seigneur	University of Geneva, Switzerland
Hamid Sharif	University of Nebraska, USA
Sheng Wen	Deakin University, Australia

Publicity Chairs

Zeyu Sun	Xi'an Jiaotong University, China
Yongming Xie	Hunan Normal University, China

SPPCN 2015 Organizing and Program Committees

General Chair

Jian Weng   Jinan University, China

Program Chairs

Mianxiong Dong	Muroran Institute of Technology, Japan
Hua Guo	Beihang University, China
Tieming Chen	Zhejiang University of Technology, China
Kaimin Wei	Jinan University, China

Program Committee

Fuchun Guo	University of Wollongong, Australia
Jianguang Han	Nanjing University of Finance and Economics, Nanjing, China
Debiao He	Wuhan University, China
Xinyi Huang	Fujian Normal University, China
Xuanya Li	Chinese Academy of Sciences, China
Fengyong Li	Shanghai University of Electric Power, China
Changlu Lin	Fujian Normal University, China
Chang Xu	Beijing Institute of Technology, China
Tao Xu	University of Jinan, China
Yanjiang Yang	I2R, Singapore
Yang Tian	Beihang University, China
Shengbao Wang	Hangzhou Normal University, China
Wei Wu	Fujian Normal University, China
Xiyong Zhang	Information Engineering University, China
Lei Zhao	Wuhan University, China

DependSys 2015 Organizing and Program Committees

Steering Committee Chairs

Jie Wu	Temple University, USA
Guojun Wang	Central South University, China

General Chairs

Mohammed Atiquzzaman	University of Oklahoma, USA
Sheikh Iqbal Ahamed	Marquette University, USA
Md. Zakirul Alam Bhuiyan	Central South University, China and Temple University, USA

Program Chairs

Latifur Khan	The University of Texas at Dallas, USA
Joarder Kamruzzaman	Federation University and Monash University, Australia
Al-Sakib Khan Pathan	International Islamic University Malaysia, Malaysia

Program Committee Members

A.B.M Shawkat Ali	The University of Fiji, Fiji
A.B.M. Alim Al Islam	Bangladesh University of Engineering and Technology, Bangladesh
A. Sohel Ferdous	University of Western Australia, Australia
A.K.M. Najmul Islam	University of Turku, Finland
Abdul Azim Mohammad	Gyeongsang National University, South Korea
Abdur Rouf Mohammad	Dhaka University of Engineering and Technology, Bangladesh
Afrand Agah	West Chester University of Pennsylvania, USA
Andreas Pashalidis	Katholieke Universiteit Leuven – iMinds, Belgium
Asaduzzaman	Chittagong University of Engineering and Technology, Bangladesh
C. Chiu Tan	Temple University, USA
Changyu Dong	University of Strathclyde, UK
Dana Petcu	West University of Timisoara, Romania
Daqiang Zhang	Tongji University, China
Farzana Rahman	James Madison University, USA
Hugo Miranda	University of Lisbon, Portugal
Jaydip Sen	National Institute of Science and Technology, India
Jianfeng Yang	Wuhan University, China
Jinkyu Jeong	Sungkyunkwan University, South Korea

Kaoru Ota	Muroran Institute of Technology, Japan
Karampelas Panagiotis	Hellenic Air Force Academy, Greece
Lien-Wu Chen	Feng Chia University, Taiwan
Liu Jialin	Texas Tech University, USA
M.M.A. Hashem	Khulna University of Engineering and Technology, Bangladesh
M. Thampi Sabu	Indian Institute of Information Technology and Management, India
Mahbub Habib Sheikh	CASED/TU Darmstadt, Germany
Mahmuda Naznin	Bangladesh University of Engineering and Technology, Bangladesh
Mamoun Alazab	Australian National University, Australia
Manuel Mazzara	Innopolis University, Russia
Md. Abdur Razzaque	University of Dhaka, Bangladesh
Md. Arafatur Rahman	University Malaysia Pahang, Malaysia
Mohammad Asad Rehman Chaudhry	University of Toronto, Canada
Md. Obaidur Rahman	Dhaka University of Engineering and Technology, Bangladesh
Md. Rafiul Hassan	King Fahd University of Petroleum and Minerals, Saudi Arabia
Md. Saiful Azad	American International University, Bangladesh
Mehran Asadi	Lincoln University of Pennsylvania, USA
Mohamad Badra	Zayed University, UAE
Mohamed Guerroumi	University of Sciences and Technology Houari Boumediene, Algeria
Mohammad Asadul Hoque	East Tennessee State University, USA
Mohammad Mehedi Hassan	King Saud University, Saudi Arabia
Mohammad Shahriar Rahman	University of Asia Pacific, Bangladesh
Mohammed Shamsul Alam	International Islamic University Chittagong, Bangladesh
Morshed Chowdhury	Deakin University, Australia
Muhammad Mostafa Monowar	King AbdulAziz University, Saudi Arabia
N. Musau Felix	Kenyatta University, Kenya
Phan Cong	Vinh Nguyen Tat Thanh University, Vietnam
Qin Liu	Hunan University, China
Ragib Hasan	University of Alabama at Birmingham, USA
Raza Hasan	Middle East College, Oman
Reaz Ahmed	University of Waterloo, Canada
Risat Mahmud Pathan	Chalmers University of Technology, Sweden
S.M. Kamruzzaman	King Saud University, Saudi Arabia
Salvatore Distefano	Politecnico di Milano, Italy
Shan Lin	Stony Brook University, USA
Shao Jie Tang	University of Texas at Dallas, USA
Sheng Wen	Deakin University, Australia

Shigeng Zhang	Central South University, China
Sk. Md. Mizanur Rahman	King Saud University, Saudi Arabia
Subrota Mondal	Hong Kong University of Science and Technology, Hong Kong, SAR China
Syed Imran Ali	Middle East College, Oman
Tanveer Ahsan	International Islamic University Chittagong, Bangladesh
Tanzima Hashem	Bangladesh University of Engineering and Technology, Bangladesh
Tao Li	The Hong Kong Polytechnic University, Hong Kong, SAR China
Tarem Ahmed	BRAC University, Bangladesh
Tian Wang	Huaqiao University, China
Tzung-Shi Chen	National University of Tainan, Taiwan
Vaskar Raychoudhury	Indian Institute of Technology Roorkee, India
Wahid Khan	University of Saskatchewan, Canada
Weigang Li	University of Brasilia, Brazil
Weigang Wu	Sun Yat-sen University, China
William Liu	Auckland University of Technology, New Zealand
Xiaofei Xing	Guangzhou University, China
Xuefeng Liu	The Hong Kong Polytechnic University, Hong Kong, SAR China
Xuyun Zhang	University of Melbourne, Australia
Yacine Djemaiel	Communication Networks and Security, Res. Lab, Tunisia
Yifan Zhang	Binghamton University, USA
Yu Wang	Deakin University, Australia

Publication Chairs

Jin Zheng	Central South University, China
Wenjun Jiang	Hunan University, China

Local Arrangements Chairs

Fang Qi	Central South University, China
Qin Liu	Hunan University, China
Hongzhi Xu	Jishou University, China

Finance Chairs

Pin Liu	Central South University, China
Wang Yang	Central South University, China

Web Chair

Min Guo	Central South University, China

Contents – Part I

Distributed and Network-Based Computing

Internet of Things and Cyber-Physical-Social Computing

Parallel and Distributed Architectures

Parallelizing Block Cryptography Algorithms on Speculative Multicores

Yaobin Wang[1,2(✉)], Hong An[2], Zhiqin Liu[1], Lei Zhang[1,2],
and Qingfeng Wang[1,2]

[1] Department of Computer Science and Technology,
Southwest University of Science and Technology, Mianyang 621010, China
{wybl982,leizh,qfwang}@mail.ustc.edu.cn,
lzq@swust.edu.cn
[2] Department of Computer Science and Technology,
University of Science and Technology of China, Hefei 230027, China
han@ustc.edu.cn

Abstract. Although block cryptography algorithms have been parallelized into different platforms, they have not yet been explored on speculative multicore architecture thoroughly, especially under CBC, CFB and OFB modes. This paper presents a study of parallelizing several block cryptography algorithms (AES, 3DES, RC5 and TWOFISH) on a novel speculative multicore architecture, including its speculative execution mechanism, architectural design and programming model. It illustrates both application and kernel level speculative speedups in these applications under all ECB, CBC, CFB and OFB modes. The experimental results show that: (1) in ECB mode, all the block cryptography algorithms perform well on speculative multicore platform. It can achieve similar speedup compared with graphics processors (GPU) while provides a more friendly programmability. (2) In CBC and CFB modes, decryption kernel in these applications still can get a promising 15.6x–25.6x speedup. (3) 32 cores' computing resources can be used efficiently in the model.

Keywords: Block cryptography · Multicore · Thread level speculation · Data dependence

1 Introduction

As we have been in the new single-chip multiprocessors (CMPs) era, how to make use of multicore computing resources to accelerate the block cryptography applications has become a common concern problem. However, the traditional block cryptography applications are written for uniprocessors and will therefore not automatically benefit from multicore designs. While these applications could be parallelized onto different multicore platforms, they usually contain data and control flow dependences that render this a daunting task.

One promising way to alleviate this problem is the thread level speculation (TLS) technology that emerges as required [1–4]. Numerous publications have shown that many applications are amenable to parallelization with TLS [5–7]. Ease of

© Springer International Publishing Switzerland 2015
G. Wang et al. (Eds.): ICA3PP 2015, Part I, LNCS 9528, pp. 3–15, 2015.
DOI: 10.1007/978-3-319-27119-4_1

programmability brought by thread level speculation could facilitate parallel computing in block cryptography obviously. Although block cryptography algorithms have been mapped into different multicore processor platforms, such as GPU [8] or FPGA [9], etc., but they have not yet been explored in thread level speculation thoroughly, especially in the CBC, CFB and OFB modes.

This paper presents a study of parallelizing several block cryptography algorithms (AES, 3DES, RC5 and TWOFISH) on a novel speculative multicore architecture, including its speculative execution mechanism, architectural design and programming model. It illustrates both application and kernel level speculative speedups in these applications under all ECB, CBC, CFB and OFB modes.

This paper makes the following three main contributions:

- A novel speculative multicore architecture is proposed to accelerate block cryptography applications.
- It demonstrates that the proposed speculative acceleration way can achieve similar speedup compared with graphics processors (GPU) while provides a more friendly programmability.
- It shows that decryption kernel in these applications still can get a promising 15.6x–25.6x speedup in CBC and CFB modes.

The rest of this paper is organized as follows. Related works are discussed in Sect. 2. Section 3 provides the speculative execution mechanism. Architectural design and programming model are described in Sects. 4 and 5, followed by experiment analysis in Sect. 6. Finally we conclude in Sect. 7.

2   Related Works

2.1   Block Cryptography Algorithms

Block cryptography algorithms have been mapped into different multicore processor platforms. T. Chen et al. from IBM implemented AES algorithm on Cell [10]. O. Harrison et al. have made their efforts to map AES algorithm into NVIDIA G80 using CUDA [8]. A similar work has been done by D. Cook [11] et al. They mapped AES cipher to the standard fixed graphics pipeline using OpenGL. A. Elbirt et al. accelerated AES and Twofish by Xilinx XCV1000 FPGA [9].

2.2   Thread Level Speculation

Numerous publications have shown that many applications are amenable to parallelization with TLS. The Wisconsin Multiscalar team achieves excellent speedups on general purpose applications, including integer applications [12]. Hydra [13] moves speculative data into each core's private space and leverage the cache coherence protocol. Prabhu and Olukotun [5] evaluate the performance potential of SPEC CPU2000 through a radical manual optimization way. Java runtime parallelizing machine (Jrpm) [14] makes an effort on speculating java programs.

2.3   Discussion

Block cryptography algorithms have been mapped into different multicore processor platforms, such as GPU or FPGA. However, speculative thread level parallelism in block cryptography applications has not yet been explored thoroughly, especially in the CBC, CFB and OFB modes.

Meanwhile, all of these related researches focused on the performance analysis in the ECB mode on the special platform. Unlike them, we make efforts to expose the potential speculative speedup in TLS and find out the reasons for unideal performance in accelerating them in CBC, CFB and OFB modes from applications themselves' perspective.

3   Speculative Execution Mechanism

3.1   Candidate Threads

Although loop iterations and subroutine calls are both good choices for candidate threads, in this paper we only choose hot loops as the candidate threads [15, 16]. The reasons are as follows: (1) the hot loops take up most of the execution time. By Amdahl's Law, high runtime ratio necessarily results in good parallel speedup. (2) Loop iterations always do the similar operations to the same data set. The data dependence between iterations is regular. They provide a runtime sequence of predictable and naturally load-balanced threads. (3) To speculate subroutine calls will bring in lots of problems for keeping the system stack safe and efficient, such as sharing the stack for different speculative threads from different cores will lead to stack error by their out of order writes.

3.2   Execution Model for Loops

The speculative execution model for loops is shown in Fig. 1. For comparing, Fig. 1(a) shows serial execution model and Fig. 1(b) shows the speculative execution model. As shown in Fig. 1, at the beginning of the speculative execution, the main processor informs all the other processors (we call it speculative processor) to load and execute different loop iterations by sending a "Loop_Start" signal to them. During the speculation, only the head processor can write to memory directly, and all the speculative processor's memory references will be cached in its own speculative buffer. If a data dependence violation occurs, the current processor delay the computation of a thread perfectly to avoid the need to rollback any of the computation. If no violation occurs, current processor commits the speculative state when all threads coming earlier in the sequential execution have committed. The next processor will become the new head processor after the current head processor committed. A new iteration will be loaded and executed after a processor committed its result into memory. When a processor found that the exit condition of the loop becomes true, it would send a "Loop_End" signal to all the other processors to finish the speculation. And only the main processor continue running the code followed the loop. It incurs little overhead in the speculation.

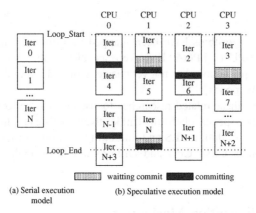

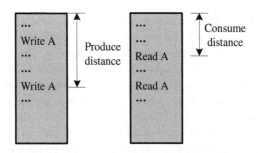

Fig. 1. Execution model for loops.

Fig. 2. Produce-distance & Consume-distance.

3.3   Analysis Method for Data Dependence Violations

The inter-thread data dependence is the most critical TLS technical factors affecting the performance. It's known that all the overheads of synchronization, conflict detection, rollback and restart are due to it. The lower the Inter-thread data dependence violations affect, the higher the performance is.

Definition 1. Produce-distance: the cycles from head of the speculative thread to the time it writes to the specific memory location.

Definition 2. Consume-distance: the cycles from head of the speculative thread to the time it reads to the specific memory location.

In speculation, the inter-thread data dependence can be abstracted as a producer/consumer model. The memory write operations play the role of producing data while the memory read operations are in charge of consuming data. To describe the data dependence violation, we introduce two terms here: "produce-distance" and "consume- distance", as shown in Fig. 2. The produce-distance means the cycles from head of the speculative thread to the time it writes to the specific memory location, and consume-distance means the cycles from head of the speculative thread to the time it reads to the specific memory location.

By definition, we can see either the produce-distance or the consume-distance is a dynamic concept, in other words, is a concept relative to program's one specific run. In different runtime environment, the different branches will be executed in the same thread. So, either of them is calculated for specific data and both of them must be calculated at running time. For thread i and its successor thread i + 1, starting at almost the same time, if the latter's consume-distance is less than the former's produce-distance, there will be a dependence violation. In this paper we select the ratio of consume-distance to produce-distance (α) to evaluate the inter-thread data dependence pattern. There will be a violation When $\alpha < 1$. Smaller ratio number means lower performance. For example, if α close to 0, it means that the speculative threads are running serially even with perfect synchronization strategy.

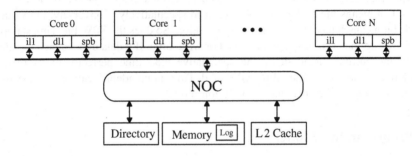

Fig. 3. Architecture model.

4   Architectural Design

4.1   Architecture Model

Figure 3 shows the basic hardware architecture model named "SMA" (Speculative Multicore Architecture simulator) in our study. It's a single-chip multiprocessors system that has much higher communication bandwidth between single cores than single-board multiprocessor system. Each core has an independent L1 data cache (dl1), a L1 instruction cache (il1) and a speculative buffer (spb). The speculative buffer is used to keep the speculative data as we mentioned. Multiple cores share a L2 cache through an ideal specific on-chip network (OCN) that can achieve only 1 cycle's link latency. And a directory-based cache coherence protocol supporting priority determination is used to support the speculation mechanism in this model. We'll discuss it further in next section.

4.2   Cache Line Support for Cache Coherence Protocal

Speculative read and write bits (R/W bits) together with timestamp mechanism proposed by us [22] is used in this model to support the directory-based cache coherence protocol. The L1 cache line structure is extended to support the speculation as shown in

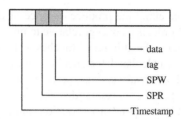

Fig. 4. Cache line in SMA.

Fig. 4. Each cache line has been added SPR (Speculative Read), SPW (Speculative Write) and Timestamp identifications. SPR is used to identify the cache line has been read speculatively. SPW shows the line has been written in speculation. If the value of SPR is 1, it means the cache line has been read speculatively. Conversely, the value 0 in SPR bit means it hasn't been read in speculation. So does the SPW bit. Timestamp is used to record the current speculative read or write time. If a data dependence violation occurs, the current thread delay the speculative read time perfectly to its relative speculative write time. The SPR, SPW and Timestamp identifications can be used together to support the speculative execution model.

5 Programming Model

From the simple programming view, SMA's programming model only does little expansion from traditional C language programming model. In this model, it is the programmers' responsibility to figure out the hot loops which they would like to parallelize, under assistance of profiler. Profiling information about the crossing-iteration data dependence probabilities could effectively guide the thread partition.

After the manual loop encapsulation, variable declaration adjustment and insertion of runtime library call, the executable code can be generated by C language compiler. The underlying platform will speculate the program automatically based on TLS runtime calls.

5.1 Loop Encapsulation

When the loop is selected as the speculative parallel goal, its loop code will be placed into a special call function. This function contains only the loop body is called encapsulation function. The loop part in the original program will be replaced by this encapsulation function. And through this function call, the program will jump to the encapsulated loop body to execute. The purpose of using the encapsulation function is to avoid the speculative threads to access the original stack frame that would bring the false sharing problem.

Figure 5 shows the Loop ~ Call conversion example. Figure 5(a) shows the original serial program source code. Figure 5(b) presents the loop encapsulation for instance, including encapsulate the loop, adjust variables' declaration and insert run-time library

```
int l=0;

for ( m = 0; m < MAX_ITERATION; m ++)
{
    l=0;
    for (n = 1; n <= 10; n++)
    {
        l += n;
    }
    if( rand[m])
    {
        p+=l;
    }
}
```

(a) Original Loop

```
void loop_function1()
{
    int m;
    int begin=lf1_begin+SMA_get_tid();
    int n=0;
    int l=0;

    for ( m = begin; m < MAX_ITERATION; m
    += NUMBER_OF_THREADS
    {
        l=0;
        for (n = 1; n <= 10; n++)
        {
            l += n;
        }
        if( rand[m])
        {
            param1.p+=l;
        }
        SMA_END_TRANSACTION;
        SMA_END_ITERATION;
    }
    SMA_halt();
}
```

(b) Loop Encapsulation

```
param1.p = 0;
lf1_begin=0;
SMA_activate        (loop_function1);
loop_function1();
SMA_wait_all();
```

(c) Loop - Call Conversion

Fig. 5. Loop ~ Call conversion example.

interface. Figure 5(c) is the final conversion example, including the system initiation and thread activation.

5.2   Variable Declaration Adjustment

In order to ensure the correctness of program execution by maintaining the original (true) data dependence between iterations, the variable declaration must be adjusted. The adjustment principle is as follows: (1) if the variable would cause violation in speculation, then it is declared as global variable; (2) If not, it can be declared as local variable. In general, programmers must ensure that the original serial semantics in speculation is right. As shown in Table 1, the variable declaration adjustment is summarized and classified. SMA would take the shown method to adjust the variables' declaration.

Table 1. Variable declaration adjustment in SMA.

Type	Cause violation	New type	Init before called	Update after return
Global	Maybe	Same	No	No
Loop index	Yes	Global /Local	Yes	Maybe
Local (Private)	No	Same	No	No
Local (Read-only)	No	Global/Local	Yes	No
Local (Shared)	Yes	Global	Yes	Yes

5.3   System Interfaces

Table 2. System Interfaces in SMA.

Interface	Function
SMA_TERMINATE_ITERATION	Iteration break macro
SMA_END_ITERATION	Iteration end macro
SMA_TERMINATE_LOOP	Loop break macro
SMA _END_THREAD	Thread end macro
SMA_init()	Init the speculation
SMA_activate(void* pc)	Activate the speculation
SMA_wait_token()	Wait for the token
SMA_release_token()	Release the token
SMA_get_tid()	Get the thread ID
SMA_wait_all()	Synchronization
SMA_halt()	Finish the loop
SMA_finalize()	Finalize the speculation

In SMA, the speculative system library functions are used as a run-time hardware and software communication interfaces that inform the underlying execution platform to take the appropriate action. Table 2 shows the functions of important system interfaces in SMA. SMA_END_ITERATION and SMA_END_TRANSACTION macros can be used in thread partition. And other system functions can be used together to support the speculation mechanism in our system.

6   Experiment Analysis

In this section we present the experimental results of parallelizing block cryptography algorithms (AES, 3DES, RC5 and TWOFISH) on speculative multicore platform in an attempt to gain insights into how well applications will map onto this accelerators. The description of benchmarks in speculation is shown in Table 3.

Table 3. Benchmark description.

Bench.	Block size	Key size	Round number	Input data size
AES	128	128 bit	10	30 M
RC5	64	128 bit	12	30 M
3DES	64	128 bit	16	30 M
Twofish	128	128 bit	16	30 M

We also trade off several important design factors in speculative multicore platform, including proper core number in speculation, speculative buffer capacity, instruction issue way, etc. We developed the speculative multicore simulator based on GEM5 [17]. The simulator configuration is shown in Table 4.

Table 4. Simulator configuration.

Configuration	Description
Core number	Variable
Processor core	Out of order, 2 issue
OCN latency	1 cycle
L1 Cache I/D	2 way, 64 KB, 64 byte line
L2 Cache	16 M, shared
L2 hit latency	6 cycles
Memory data latency	75 cycles

6.1 Speedup

Figure 6 shows the max application level speedups in all ECB, CBC, CFB and OFB modes of each benchmark by using infinite core numbers' resources in speculation. All the speedup values are based on comparing the original sequential program execution time. It's obvious that all the applications can get their best speedups in ECB mode. The best 3DES can get a nearly 14x speedup in speculation while the lowest speedup value is 10.6 for RC5. The interesting results in CBC, CFB and OFB modes are also shown in Fig. 6. The speedups of four applications in CBC and CFB modes are almost 4. And they can only get a nearly 2.1x speedup in OFB mode.

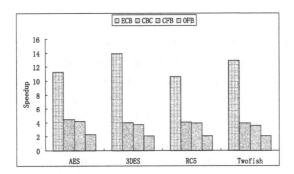

Fig. 6. Application level speedups in different modes.

For a more in-depth understanding of these results, we further examined the corresponding kernel (encryption and decryption) level speedups in Fig. 7. The EN is short for encryption kernel and DE is short for decryption kernel. Under ECB mode, speedups in these kernels are logically higher than that in application level. AES kernel can get a 17.8x speedup while the value is about 11.7 in application level. 3DES kernel gets the highest 25.6x speedup. Also, RC5 gets a lowest 15.6x kernel level speedup. In a word, it shows that all the block cryptography algorithms perform well on speculative multicore platform. It can achieve similar speedup compared with GPU while provides a more friendly programmability than other methods.

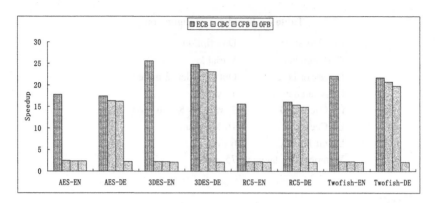

Fig. 7. Kernel level speedups in different modes.

It's also observed that these two kernels perform quite different in CBC and CFB modes. That's the reason why the application level speedup is so interesting in Fig. 6. In CBC and CFB mode, encryption kernels get much lower speedups than that in ECB mode, but the decryption kernels can still get ideal speedups in CBC and CFB mode. Then we'll discuss the speedup results further by analyzing the Inter-thread data dependence feature according to our proposed analysis method together with code analysis in next section.

Table 5. Inter-thread data dependence feature (α) in benchmarks.

Bench.	ECB	CBC	CFB	OFB
AES-EN	∞	0.48	0.44	0.39
AES-DN	∞	∞	∞	0.39
3DES-EN	∞	0.57	0.53	0.37
3DES-DN	∞	∞	∞	0.37
RC5-EN	∞	0.43	0.39	0.35
RC5-DN	∞	∞	∞	0.35
Twofish-EN	∞	0.51	0.47	0.36
Twofish-DN	∞	∞	∞	0.36

6.2   Inter-thread Data Dependence

The compared inter-thread data dependence feature (α) is shown in Table 5. This is the point that why the speedups in Fig. 7 are so different. Only in the ECB mode, all of α values in both encryption and decryption kernel are ∞, that is to say the there're no data dependence violations in speculation so that it can get an ideal result in TLS. While in CBC and CFB modes, α values for encryption kernel are about 0.5. That means the data dependence violations in speculating encryption kernel badly hurt the TLS performance. So the speedups for encryption kernel in these two models are so lower than that for decryption kernel. It's also found that all of α values in both encryption and decryption kernel are about 0.37 under OFB mode. It seems that the data dependence violations are similar in this mode. Then it would be discussed further by code analysis as follows.

Though code analysis, it's found that the input to the encryption processes of the CBC mode includes a data block called the initialization vector (IV) in addition to the plaintext. An initialization vector must be generated for each execution of the encryption operation, and the same vector is necessary for the corresponding execution of the decryption operation. In CBC encryption kernels, the input block to each forward cipher operation (except the first) depends on the result of the previous forward cipher operation, so they cannot be parallelized in speculation. But in CBC decryption kernels, the input blocks for the inverse cipher function are immediately available, so that multiple inverse cipher operations can be parallelized well in speculation. The CFB mode that is relative to CBC makes a block cipher into a self-synchronizing stream cipher. So the reason for the ideal speedup under CFB modes is similar. But in OFB mode, it makes a block cipher into a synchronous stream cipher. For either encryption or decryption kernels, they can't be performed in parallel well. The results also proved that the inter-thread data dependence feature is the key performance factor in TLS and our proposed analysis method is effective.

6.3 Core Number

The single core efficiency problem is an important design issue in multicore system. In this section, how many cores are suitable for accelerating block cryptography applications in our model are evaluated.

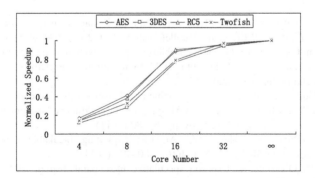

Fig. 8. Normalized Speedups in different core numbers under ECB mode.

Normalized Speedups in different core numbers under ECB mode are shown in Fig. 8. The "∞" means using infinite cores to parallelize these benchmarks. It's found that AES and RC5 can achieve about 89 % of the best performance by using 16 cores to parallelize them. However, 3DES and Twofish can get only about 78 % of the peak speedup when the core number is 16. Meanwhile, all of the four applications can achieve about 95 % of their peak speedup by using 32 cores to parallelize them. So, it's considered that the majority of block cryptography applications can use 32 cores' computing resources efficiently in the speculative thread-level parallelism.

7 Conclusions

This paper presents how to explore potential parallelism in block cryptography applications on speculative multicore architecture platform. Firstly, it introduced its speculative execution mechanism, architectural design and programming model. Secondly, it compared the application and kernel level speculative parallelism in block cryptography applications under all ECB, CBC, CFB and OFB modes. It's found that speculative multicore architecture can achieve similar speedup compared with graphics processors (GPU) while provides a more friendly programmability. Especially in CBC and CFB modes, decryption kernel in these applications still can get a promising 15.6x–25.6x speedup. Finally, it suggested 32 cores are enough to accelerate block cryptography applications in speculation.

Acknowledgement. This work is supported financially by the National Natural Science Foundation of China grants 61202044, the National Basic Research Program of China under contract 2011CB302501, the National Hi-tech Research and Development Program of China under contracts 2012AA010902, the Research Fund of Southwest University of Science and Technology 12zxwk08.

References

1. Munir, A., Ranka, S., Gordon-Ross, A.: High-performance energy-efficient multicore embedded computing. IEEE Trans. Parallel Distrib. Syst. **23**(4), 684–700 (2012)
2. Tian, C., Lin, C., Feng, M., Gupta, R.: Enhanced speculative parallelization via incremental recovery. In: Proceedings of the 16th ACM Symposium on Principles and Practice of Parallel Programming, San Antonio, TX, USA (2011)
3. Feng, M., Gupta, R., Hu, Y.: SpiceC: scalable parallelism via implicit copying and explicit commit. In: Proceedings of the 16th ACM Symposium on Principles and Practice of Parallel Programming, San Antonio, TX, USA, pp. 69–80 (2011)
4. Udupa, A., Rajan, K., Thies, W.: ALTER: exploiting breakable dependences for parallelization. ACM SIGPLAN Not. **46**(6), 480–491 (2011)
5. Prabhu, M.K., Olukotun, K.: Exposing speculative thread parallelism in SPEC2000. In: 10th ACM SIGPLAN Symposium on Principles and Practice of Parallel Programming, Chicago, IL, USA (2005)
6. Kejariwal, A., Tian, X., et al.: On the performance potential of different types of speculative thread-level parallelism. In: 20th Annual International Conference on Supercomputing, Cairns, Queensland, Australia (2006)
7. Xekalakis, P., Ioannou, N., Cintra, M.: Combining thread level speculation helper threads and runahead execution. In: 23rd International Conference on Supercomputing, pp. 410–420 (2009)

8. Harrison, O., Waldron, J.: AES encryption implementation and analysis on commodity graphics processing units. In: Paillier, P., Verbauwhede, I. (eds.) CHES 2007. LNCS, vol. 4727, pp. 209–226. Springer, Heidelberg (2007)
9. Elbirt, A.J., Yip, W., Chetwynd, B., Paar, C.: An FPGAbased performance evaluation of the AES block cipher candidate algorithm finalists. IEEE Trans. Very Large Scale Integr. Syst. **9** (4), 545–557 (2001)
10. Chen, T., Raghavan, R., Dale, J.N., Iwata, E.: Cell broadband engine architecture and its first implementation - a performance view. IBM J. Res. Dev. **51**(5), 559–572 (2007)
11. Cook, D.L., Ioannidis, J., Keromytis, A.D., Luck, J.: CryptoGraphics: secret key cryptography using graphics cards. In: Menezes, A. (ed.) CT-RSA 2005. LNCS, vol. 3376, pp. 334–350. Springer, Heidelberg (2005)
12. Sohi, G.S., Breach, S.E., Vijaykumar, T.N.: Multiscalar processors. In: 22nd Annual International Symposium on Computer Architecture (ISCA 1995), Barcelona, Spain (1995)
13. Hammond, L., Hubbert, B.A., Siu, M., Parbhu, M.K., Chen, M., Qlukotun, K.: The Stanford hydra CMP. IEEE Micro **20**(2), 71–84 (2000)
14. Chen, M.K., and Olukotun, K.: The Jrpm system for dynamically parallelizing Java programs. In: International Symposium on Computer Architecture, pp. 434–445 (2003)
15. Rul, S., Vandierendonck, H., De Bosschere, K.: Function level parallelism driven by data dependencies. ACM SIGARCH Comput. Archit. News **35**(1), 55–62 (2007)
16. Oplinger, J.T., Heine, D.L., Lam, M.S.: In search of speculative thread-level parallelism. In: PACT 1999, pp. 303–313 (1999)
17. Binkert, N., Beckmann, B., Black, G., et al.: The gem5 simulator. ACM SIGARCH Comput. Archit. News **39**(2), 1–7 (2011)
18. Johnson, T.A., Eigenmann, R., Vijaykumar, T.N.: Speculative thread decomposition through empirical optimization. In: 12th ACM SIGPLAN Symposium on Principles and Practice of Parallel Programming, pp. 205–214 (2007)
19. Tian, C., Feng, M., Gupta, R.: Speculative parallelization using state separation and multiple value prediction. ACM SIGPLAN Not. **45**(8), 63–72 (2010)
20. Raman, A., Kim, H., Mason, T.R., et al.: Speculative parallelization using software multi-threaded transactions. ACM SIGARCH Comput. Archit. News **38**(1), 65–76 (2010)
21. Liu, Y., An, H., Li, X., Leng, P., Sun, S., Chen, J.: VSCP: a cache controlling method for improving single thread performance in multicore system. In: 14th IEEE International Conference on High Performance Computing and Communications, pp. 161–168 (2012)
22. Li, G., An, H., Li, Q., Deng, B., Dai, W.: Efficient execution of speculative threads and transactions with hardware transactional memory. Future Gener. Comput. Syst. **30**, 242–253 (2014)
23. Ren, Y., An, H., Sun, T., Cong, M., Wang, Y.: Dynamic resource tuning for flexible core chip multiprocessors. In: Hsu, C.-H., Yang, L.T., Park, J.H., Yeo, S.-S. (eds.) ICA3PP 2010, Part I. LNCS, vol. 6082, pp. 32–41. Springer, Heidelberg (2010)
24. Sun, T., An, H., et al.: CRQ-based fair scheduling on composable multicore architectures. In: 26th ACM SIGARCH International Conference on Supercomputing (ICS 2012), pp. 173–184 (2012)

Performance Characterization and Optimization for Intel Xeon Phi Coprocessor

Cheng Zhang[1]([✉]), Li Liu[2], Ruizhe Li[1], and Guangwen Yang[1,2]([✉])

[1] Department of Computer Science and Technology,
Tsinghua University, Beijing 100084, China
{zhang-cheng09,lrz04}@mails.tsinghua.edu.cn

[2] Center for Earth System Science, Tsinghua University, Beijing 100084, China
{liuli-cess,ygw}@mail.tsinghua.edu.cn

Abstract. The Intel Xeon Phi is a many-core accelerator which focuses on the high performance applications. To characterize the performance of the Intel Xeon Phi, a system of dual 8-core Intel Xeon E5-2670 processors is employed as a control platform, and a subset of the PARSEC benchmark suite is selected as the benchmark applications. The first evaluation in this paper shows that the applications on the Intel Xeon Phi is averagely 2.06x slower than on the dual Intel Xeon E5-2670. The further detailed performance characterization quantifies the performance impact of various architecture parameters on the Intel Xeon Phi. To set an example for how to improve the architecture of the Intel Xeon Phi for better performance, the hardware optimization with an additional set of vector processing units is discussed and a simple emulator is developed accordingly. The evaluation results show that this optimization can provide an average speedup of 1.10.

Keywords: Intel Xeon Phi · Parallel architecture · Performance characterization · Architecture parameters · Hardware optimization

1 Introduction

Limited by power consumption and chip cooling, many-core accelerators, for example GPGPU, have gained popularity in recent years. As the architecture of the accelerators always differs from modern CPUs in many aspects, users have to pay much more efforts to rewrite the applications with other programming models like CUDA or OpenCL, which decreases the popularity of the accelerators.

To achieve better programmability and usability than GPGPU, the Intel Corporation has developed a new many-core processor product, the Intel Xeon Phi 'Knights Corner' Coprocessor (KNC), based on the Intel Many Integrated Core (MIC) architecture. As its main architecture is similar to modern multi-core CPUs, the KNC supports almost all standard program models, such as OpenMP, MPI and POSIX threads (Pthreads). Generally, the CPU applications can directly run on the KNC with a few or even no changes.

© Springer International Publishing Switzerland 2015
G. Wang et al. (Eds.): ICA3PP 2015, Part I, LNCS 9528, pp. 16–33, 2015.
DOI: 10.1007/978-3-319-27119-4_2

At the same time, there are some specific architecture designs in the KNC. For example, the KNC has 61 cores, each of which is an in-order dual-issue core with two levels of cache, supports 4 hardware threads and has a set of 512-bit wide vector processing units (VPU). These specific architecture designs make the KNC achieve higher peak performance, and result in different performance characteristics of applications, compared to CPUs.

The KNC has attracted a lot of research interests ever since it became available. Most of previous researches related to the KNC focus on optimizing applications according to the specific architectures of the KNC [1–10]. Although the KNC provides much higher peak performance than modern CPUs, the CPU applications rarely achieve performance improvement or even obtain much poorer performance when being directly run on the KNC. To achieve better application performance on the KNC than the CPUs, users have to manually optimize the program heavily according to the specific architecture features of the KNC. This dramatically harms the highlighted advantages of the KNC in programmability and usability. In other words, the KNC also suffers from the conflict between programmability and performance. On the other hand, the KNC mainly targets to the kind of applications that can scale well over one hundred threads and efficiently use the VPU [11]. If the KNC can achieve similar or even better performance than CPUs for more kinds of applications, it will be more attractive for usage.

We therefore use a subset of the parallel benchmark suite PARSEC [12,13], which are from different application domains and with different performance characteristics (VPU utilization, memory accessing, parallel scalability and so on), as the benchmark applications for this work. To provide valuable references for further improving the architecture of the KNC, we first quantify the performance characteristics of the benchmark applications with the same code on the KNC and CPU. We use dual 8-core Intel Xeon E5-2670 processors (As the codename of Intel Xeon E5-2670 is "Sandy Bridge", we call it as SNB in the following context; each SNB core is out-of-order execution, supports 2 hyper threads and has a set of 256-bit VPU), as a counterpart to the KNC.

Although the peak performance of the KNC is 3.20x higher than the dual SNB, the average performance of these benchmark applications on the KNC is 2.06x smaller than the dual SNB. To reveal why, we quantify the performance characteristics in two steps. In the first step, we analyze the single-core performance of the benchmark applications on the two systems. The single-core performance achieved on the KNC is 3.76x smaller than the dual SNB, although the peak performance of a KNC core is only 1.19x smaller than a SNB core. The causes for this result are quantified as follows:

- When vectorization is disabled, the number of micro operations executed on the KNC is 1.11x more than the dual SNB
- When vectorization is disabled, the architecture of 4 hardware threads on each KNC core significantly improves the instruction level parallelism (ILP) of the applications with a speedup of 2.21. The micro operations per cycle (MPC)

on the KNC is only 1.07, which is much smaller than 1.58, the MPC on the dual SNB. The causes for this result include:

- The usage of the two pipelines (U pipeline and V pipeline) on a KNC core is imbalanced. About 68.5 % instructions are executed by the U pipeline.
- The branch misprediction rate on the KNC is 15.8 %, which is much larger than 2.6 %, the branch misprediction rate on the dual SNB. The overhead of branch mispredictions covers 4.2 % execution time on the KNC.
- The average latencies of the memory hierarchies on the KNC are longer than the dual SNB. Meanwhile, the KNC does not have L3 cache to hide the latencies of memory accesses. On the KNC, accessing the memory hierarchies costs about 21.3 % execution time. But on the dual SNB, it costs about 19.3 % execution time.

– Although the VPU of the KNC is 2x wider than the dual SNB, the speedup achieved through vectorization on the KNC is only 1.17x higher.

In the second step, we analyze the scaling performance of the benchmark applications on the two systems when using multiple or even many cores, referencing the single-core performance on each system as the baseline. The overall speedup on the KNC is only 1.97x higher, although the KNC has 61 cores and the dual SNB has 16 cores:

– When 8 cores are used, almost the same average parallel speedup 6.36 and 6.52 is achieved on the KNC and SNB.
– When the number of cores is increased from 8 to 16, the average parallel speedup achieved on the KNC and dual SNB is 1.71 and 1.36 respectively. The lower parallel speedup on the dual SNB is because the cache-coherent Non-Uniform Memory Access architecture (ccNUMA) [14,15] introduces remote memory access with much longer latency, which results in about 21.8 % performance loss.
– Some applications cannot scale well to so many cores on the KNC. When achieving the best application performance on the KNC, the number of cores used by the benchmark applications is about 40 on average, which wastes about 1/3 cores.

The above results indicate that the application performance on the KNC can be prospectively improved through balancing the pipeline usage, improving the branch prediction architecture and improving the cache architecture. To investigate how to balance the pipeline usage, we developed a simple emulator that can well simulate the pipeline usage on the KNC with an average accuracy 98.7 %. Using this emulator, an additional set of VPU for the V pipeline is added. With this optimization, the KNC can gain a speedup of 1.104 on average.

The remainder of the paper is organized as follows. Section 2 presents the related work of Intel Xeon Phi. Section 3 describes the experiment settings in this paper. Section 4 quantifies the architecture parameters resulting in the performance differences of the two systems. Section 5 details an emulator and hardware optimizations for balancing the pipeline usage on the KNC. Section 6 discusses and concludes this work.

2   Related Work

Intel Xeon Phi is a new many-core product, which has a similar architecture with multi-core CPUs. It supports almost all standard program models such as OpenMP, MPI and POSIX threads. Previous studies have shown that transporting scientific applications and kernels to Intel Xeon Phi is relatively straightforward [16,17]. So better programmability and usability is the highlighted advantage of Intel Xeon Phi, comparing with other accelerators.

Since Intel Xeon Phi is released, a lot of researchers pay much attention on it. Existing works can be classified into two categories. The first category evaluates the basic performance parameters of the KNC using micro-benchmarks. Schmidl D. et al. showed that the maximum memory bandwidth achieved on the KNC is about 150GB/s, which is far below the theoretical memory bandwidth 352GB/s [1]. Saini S. et al. showed that the average latencies of the memory hierarchies on the KNC are longer than on the dual SNB. The average latencies of accessing L1, L2, L3 cache and main memory on the dual SNB are 4, 12, 39 and 210 cycles respectively. The average latencies of accessing L1, L2 cache and main memory on the KNC are 3, 24 and 310 cycles respectively [18]. Cramer T. et al. showed that the KNC does not introduce more overheads for OpenMP synchronization, although it has so many cores [5]. These works also demonstrated that when CPU applications directly run on the KNC without manual optimizations, the applications cannot effectively utilize the computing capability of the KNC.

The second category focuses on optimizing applications according to the architecture of the KNC [2–4,7–9]. Williams S. et al. showed that without optimization, the dual SNB outperforms the KNC by 1.45x for 3D geometric multigrid [3]. With a series of optimizations including communication-avoiding, SIMD and prefetching, the application gains about 3.8x and 1.5x improvement on the KNC and the dual SNB respectively. Finally, the KNC outperforms the dual SNB by 1.75x. Similar results can be found in [2], where a set of financial analytics benchmarks is optimized. Taking the Brownian bridge algorithm in the benchmarks as an example, with simple optimizations using pragma simd, omp and unroll, the KNC is 25 % slower than the dual SNB. With further optimizations including SIMD across paths, reducing bandwidth usage and etc., the KNC performs 2x faster than the dual SNB.

Previous works demonstrated that the application performance of the KNC over the dual SNB highly depends on deep manual optimizations which introduce significant code changes. The KNC almost cannot outperform the dual SNB when without deep manual optimizations or only with simple optimizations. This situation can make the KNC less attractive. Improving the hardware architecture is another important approach to boosting the application performance without codes changes. To improve the hardware architecture of the KNC, this paper quantified the impact of various architecture parameters on the application performance. The results revealed the potential of different hardware optimizations. Moreover, we investigated the hardware optimizations to balance the pipeline usage of the KNC.

3   Analysis Settings

In this work, the dual SNB is used as a counterpart of the KNC. This section will briefly introduce their architecture. For the purpose of performance characterization, several applications from the PARSEC [12,13] are selected as benchmarks.

3.1   Intel Xeon Phi

Figure 1 shows the micro-architecture of the Intel Xeon Phi. To deliver high computing capability, the KNC integrates 61 cores and each core has a set of 512-bit wide VPU. So the KNC can achieve 1063.84 GFLOPS (double-precision).

Each KNC core is an in-order x86 processor core, based on a modified Pentium processor design. Its instruction set is similar to Pentium, however, it does not support MMX, SSE or AVX instructions. It is dual-issued with 2 different pipelines (U and V pipeline). The U pipeline can execute all the instructions, while the V pipeline can only execute a proportion of instructions. To hide the latency exposed by the in-order execution, each core supports four hardware threads. Its instruction decoder is a two-cycle unit. A KNC core therefore cannot execute the instructions from the same hardware thread cycle by cycle. To reduce the size of the die and power consumption, the KNC core lacks state-of-the-art branch prediction units.

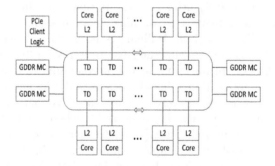

Fig. 1. Micro-architecture of Intel Xeon Phi.

3.2   Dual Intel Xeon E5-2670

For comparison, we use dual Intel Xeon E5-2670 processors as the representative of CPUs. Figure 2 shows its micro-architecture. Each SNB integrates 8 core and each core has a set of 256-bit wide VPU. So the dual SNB can achieve 332.8 GFLOPS (double precision).

Each SNB core is an out-of-order x86 processor core. It supports full x86 instruction set, MMX, SSE and AVX instruction set. The SNB core is quad-issued, i.e. 4 instructions can be issued in a cycle. Different from the KNC, the instruction decoding on the SNB only takes one cycle. To increase the performance of the SNB core, it has state-of-the-art branch prediction units.

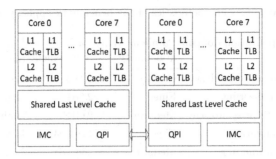

Fig. 2. Micro-architecture of dual Intel Xeon E5-2670.

3.3 PARSEC Benchmarks

PARSEC is one of the most important multi-core and multi-processor benchmark suites, which has been widely used for application-driven researches and performance measurement of real machines. As a benchmark suite, PARSEC has the following five necessary characteristics [12,13]:

- Multithreaded Applications. All applications in PARSEC are multithreaded using OpenMP, POSIX threads or Intel Threading Building Blocks (TBB).
- Emerging Workloads. New emerging applications that require higher computing capability are included by this suite.
- Diversity. PARSEC contains applications in different domains (Financial Analysis, engineering, data mining, animation, etc.) with different parallel programming models (OpenMP, Pthreads, TBB) and parallel granularities.
- State-of-the-Art Techniques. The applications in the benchmark suite implement the latest techniques (e.g., simulated annealing, deduplication, ray tracing, etc.).
- Supporting Research. This suite provides an infrastructure for research, which allows researchers to instrument and simulate the applications effectively.

In this work, a subset of PARSEC benchmark suite is selected, including blackscholes, canneal, dedup, fluidanimate, streamcluster and swaptions. Table 1 shows the characteristics of these selected 6 applications. We believe they have sufficient diversity to quantify the impact of various architecture parameters on the application performance.

Throughout this work, we use the Intel compiler version 14.0.2 with optimization level O3 to compile the benchmark applications on both the KNC and dual SNB. In our experiment, Intel Xeon Phi is used as a standalone SMP on a single chip. In this mode, the code is compiled on the dual SNB using the flags -mmic. The binary can be executed on the KNC only.

4 Performance Characterization

To motivate the detailed performance characterization, we first evaluate the overall application performance on the KNC and dual SNB. In Table 2, the left

Table 1. Key characteristics of the benchmark applications.

Application	Application domain	Parallelization granularity	Cache requirement	Data usage	
				Sharing	Exchange
blackscholes	Financial analysis	Coarse	2 MB	Low	Low
canneal	Engineering	Fine	2 GB	High	High
dedup	Enterprise storage	Medium	2 GB	High	High
fluidanimate	Animation	Fine	128 MB	Low	Medium
streamcluster	Data mining	Medium	256 MB	Low	Medium
swaptions	Financial analysis	coarse	512 KB	Low	Low

half shows the best application performance where the KNC may not be fully utilized. The right half shows the application performance for maximum usage of the cores and hardware threads on the KNC. These results reveal that the KNC is largely underutilized. The best performance of the applications on the KNC is 2.1x poorer than the dual SNB on average, although the peak performance of the KNC is 3.2x higher than the dual SNB. According to the architecture difference between the KNC and dual SNB, we conduct two major steps for detailed analysis: single-core performance analysis and scaling performance analysis with multiple or even many cores.

4.1 Single-Core Performance Analysis

Table 3 shows the execution time of the applications when using only one core on the KNC and dual SNB respectively. Although the peak performance of a KNC core is only 1.19x smaller than a SNB core, the single-core performance on

Table 2. The application performance on the two systems. Optimal means the best application performance on the two systems. Maximum means the application performance with maximum usage of the cores and hardware threads on the KNC. The thread number of fluidanimate must be 2^n. We therefore use 128 threads to run it on the KNC for maximum. The thread number of swaptions is less than 128. We therefore use 60 cores and 120 threads to run it for maximum.

Application	Optimal				Maximum	
	KNC		Dual SNB		KNC	
	Time(s)	Cores/threads	Time(s)	Cores/threads	Time(s)	Cores/threads
blackscholes	1.35	60/240	2.25	16/16	1.35	60/240
canneal	19.60	60/120	16.28	16/16	40.68	60/240
dedup	26.48	16/32	9.08	16/16	109.67	60/240
fluidanimate	100.54	32/64	56.93	16/16	131.18	60/128
streamcluster	114.93	16/32	40.90	16/16	1398.93	60/240
swaptions	41.45	60/120	13.46	16/16	41.45	60/120

the KNC is averagely 3.76x smaller than on the dual SNB. This result is because of less effective vectorization and lower ILP on the KNC.

According to Table 3, the number of micro operations on the two systems is different, and the micro operations on the KNC are 1.11x more than the dual SNB on average. This is due to the difference of instruction sets on the two systems.

Both the KNC and dual SNB provide VPU for performance acceleration. However, only two applications, i.e., blackscholes and streamcluster, can benefit from vectorization (please refer to the speedup of vectorization in Table 3). This is because there are almost no manual optimizations for vectorization and most operations cannot be automatically vectorized by the compiler in the other 4 applications. The VPU of a KNC core is 2x wider than a SNB core, while the vectorization speedup of blackscholes on the KNC is 2.5x higher than the SNB. This is because the math functions log and exp, which are frequently called in blackscholes, obtain vectorization speedup of 9.3 and 2.1 on the KNC and dual SNB respectively. The much larger vectorization speedup on the KNC is because the VPU on the KNC supports single-precision transcendental instructions for exp and log [19]. Regarding streamcluster, vectorization achieves a speedup of 1.9x on the dual SNB while almost no speedup on the KNC. This is because the most significant data structure in streamcluster is written into an array of structures (AOS), which harms the vectorization speedup obtained on the KNC [2]. On average, vectorization speedup achieved on the KNC core is only 1.17x higher than on the SNB core.

Although the KNC provides four hardware threads to exploit ILP, most of the applications, i.e., blackscholes, dedup, fluidanimate and swaptions, obtain much poorer ILP on the KNC (please refer to the micro operations per cycle in Table 3). On average, the MPC on the KNC is only 1.07, much smaller than 1.58, the MPC on the dual SNB. To reveal why much lower ILP is achieved on the KNC, we further investigate the branch prediction performance and the memory access performance on the two systems, and the pipeline usage on the KNC.

Branch Prediction Performance. Table 4 shows the branch prediction performance on the KNC and dual SNB respectively. The number of branch instructions executed is almost the same on the two systems. However, the KNC achieves much poorer branch prediction performance, with much more branch mispredictions. This is because the KNC cores lack state-of-the-art branch prediction units. The overhead of branch mispredictions on the KNC is low, due to the in-order execution and short pipelines [20]. According to our evaluation, the average overhead of a branch misprediction on the KNC is about 4 cycles. Almost 4.2 % execution time on the KNC is wasted by branch mispredictions, which further limits the MPC no more than 1.92 on average.

Memory Access Performance. To measure the overhead introduced by memory accessing, we first obtained the number of cache misses using the VTune.

Table 3. Performance parameters of the applications when only using one core on the two systems. The number of micro operations and micro operations per cycle is collected by VTune.

Application	Execution time(s) (enable vectorization)		Vectorization speedup		Number of micro operations (disable vectorization)		Micro operations per cycle (disable vectorization)	
	KNC (4 threads)	SNB (1 thread)	KNC	SNB	KNC	SNB	KNC	SNB
blackscholes	35.12	26.88	10	4	3.96e11	4.87e11	1.05	1.76
canneal	498.92	154.13	1	1	1.94e11	1.30e11	0.334	0.272
dedup	134.24	35.30	1	1	1.48e11	1.57e11	1.15	1.94
fluidanimate	1699.19	449.02	1	1	1.99e12	1.95e12	1.11	1.85
streamcluster	1006.54	270.33	1.02	1.91	1.68e12	1.63e12	1.50	1.31
swaptions	1403.05	210.12	1	1	1.93e12	1.39e12	1.25	2.33

Table 4. Performance of branch prediction, when vectorization is disabled.

Application	Branch instructions		Misprediction PKI		Overhead(%)
	KNC	SNB	KNC	SNB	KNC
blackscholes	2.71e10	2.75e10	11.50	0.60	3.53
canneal	1.31e10	1.28e10	14.02	2.99	1.16
dedup	1.32e10	1.44e10	15.11	6.05	4.40
fluidanimate	3.00e11	2.92e11	39.51	7.26	12.4
streamcluster	1.20e11	1.20e11	2.64	1.25	1.19
swaptions	1.42e11	1.36e11	9.12	1.26	2.80

Then we calculated the overhead according to the access latencies from Saini S. et al. [18], as shown in Table 5. The overhead of memory accessing is different on the two systems for each application. This is because the architecture of memory hierarchies is different. On average, about 21.3 % and 19.3 % of execution time is spent on accessing memory hierarchies on the KNC and dual SNB respectively. This overhead further limits the MPC no more than 1.50 on average.

Instruction Pipeline Usage. Table 6 shows the pipeline usage on the KNC. Most instructions are performed by the U pipeline. This is because the in-order execution and the function layout of the pipelines decreases the chances of simultaneously issuing multiple instructions. The U pipeline can execute all the instructions, while the V pipeline can execute only a part of instructions. When there is only one instruction able to be issued, it must be operated on the U pipeline. When there are two independent instructions, they can be issued and operated on the two pipelines simultaneously only when they are pairable (there are specific pairing rules to check whether the second instruction can pair up with the first instruction). So the number of micro operations executed by the

Table 5. Performance of cache hierarchies accessing, when vectorization is disabled.

Application	L1 misses PKI		L2 misses PKI		L3 misses PKI	Overhead (%)	
	KNC	SNB	KNC	SNB	SNB	KNC	SNB
blackscholes	0.09	0.08	0.013	0.014	0.013	0.22	0.39
canneal	18.7	24.6	14.3	17	15.2	77.02	64.81
dedup	10.7	11.7	0.07	0.09	0.018	24.48	21.02
fluidanimate	2.20	2.51	0.31	0.36	0.23	5.48	6.71
streamcluster	18.57	22	0.92	1.09	1.04	10.53	14.45
swaptions	8.3	7.8	0.0003	0.0004	0.00004	10	8.12

Table 6. Proportion of instructions executed by the two pipelines of the KNC core, when vectorization is disabled.

Application	Proportion of instructions executed (%)	
	U pipeline	V pipeline
blackscholes	83.3	16.7
canneal	67.2	32.8
dedup	65.8	34.2
fluidanimate	75.1	24.9
streamcluster	54.4	45.6
swaptions	65.5	34.5

V pipeline is much less than the number of micro operations executed by the U pipeline. The imbalanced usage of the U and V pipelines limits the MPC no more than 1.11 on average.

The second column in Table 7 lists out the calculated MPC on the KNC when only considering the overhead introduced by the imbalance of pipeline usage, branch mispredictions and memory accessing, which is close to the real MPC in the third column. This result demonstrates that these three factors are main causes to the smaller MPC on the KNC.

4.2   Scaling Performance Analysis with Multiple or Many Cores

In this analysis, we measured the parallel speedup of the benchmark applications on the KNC and dual SNB. The single-core performance is referenced as the baseline for calculating the parallel speedup. In other words, the parallel speedup of using only one core is 1. Table 2 shows the overall parallel speedup when fully utilizing the KNC and dual SNB respectively. On average, the overall parallel speedup on the KNC is only 1.97x higher than the dual SNB, although the number of cores on the KNC is 3.75x more than the dual SNB. According to the architecture of the KNC and dual SNB, we selected three levels to scale core number, i.e., 8, 16, and 60, for further analysis.

Table 7. Micro operations per cycle calculated and real micro operations per cycle measured on the KNC, when vectorization is disabled. When calculate micro operations per cycle, we only consider the overhead introduced by the imbalance of pipeline usage, branch misprediction and memory accessing.

Application	Micro operations per cycle	
	Calculated	Measured
blackscholes	1.16	1.05
canneal	0.338	0.334
dedup	1.10	1.15
fluidanimate	1.10	1.11
streamcluster	1.63	1.50
swaptions	1.34	1.25

For the dual SNB, the 8 cores on only one SNB processor are used in this test, to avoid the overhead introduced by the Non-Uniform Memory Access architecture. As shown in Fig. 3, similar 8-core speedup is achieved on the two systems.

As shown in Fig. 4, most applications, i.e., canneal, dedup, fluidanimate and streamcluster, obtain a lower 16-core speedup on the dual SNB. This is because the ccNUMA on the dual SNB enlarges the memory access latency. As shown in Table 1, these applications have high-level of data sharing or data exchange among threads. That is the reason why the memory access latency enlarged by the ccNUMA dramatically decreases the 16-core speedup on the dual SNB.

The above analysis shows that the KNC can make applications achieve similar or even higher parallel speedup than the dual SNB, when using the same number of cores. However, when scaling the number of cores on the KNC from 16 to 60, the applications only obtain a 1.12x speedup on average (Table 2). One important cause for this result is that the overhead introduced from load imbalance, synchronization and contention for shared resources rapidly increases with the increment of the thread number.

Regarding the highest parallel speedup, all applications except blackscholes cannot fully utilize the hardware threads and cores on the KNC. On average, the applications can effectively utilize only 40 cores and 100 threads, and obtain a 1.64x speedup when scaling the core number from 16.

5   Architecture Optimizations

The performance results in the last section show that the imbalanced usage of the U and V pipelines on the KNC dramatically limits the ILP of applications. As the imbalanced pipeline usage is due to the in-order execution and the function layout of the two pipelines, we investigated the potential benefits of hardware optimizations, i.e., improving the function layout of the pipelines, for balancing the usage of the pipelines.

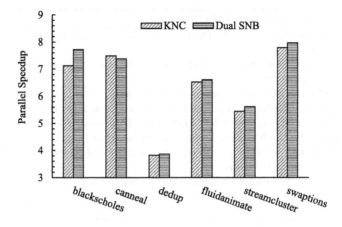

Fig. 3. Parallel speedup of 8 cores.

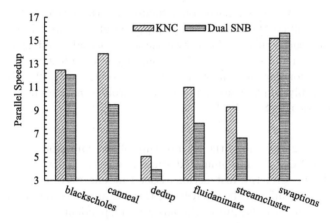

Fig. 4. Parallel speedup of 16 cores.

For evaluating the potential benefits, a simulator is required to simulate the pipeline usage on the KNC. However, there are no simulators for the KNC. Moreover, the simulators for the general multi-core processors focus on modeling the cores, memory system, network and other components, without simulating the pipeline usage, which is our concern. So the existing simulators are not suitable for our simulation.

In the following of this section, we first introduce an emulator that can accurately simulate the usage of the pipelines and next discuss several hardware optimizations for balancing the usage of the pipelines.

5.1 An Emulator for the Balance of Pipeline Usage

In order to simulate the impact of improving the function layout of the pipelines, the instructions that can be executed by the U and V pipelines respectively

---

Algorithm 1. Selecting instructions to issue

Require: Unissued instruction buffer *Unissue_insts*, Executing instruction buffer
  Executing_insts
Ensure: Instruction *instU* for the U pipeline, Instruction *instV* for the V pipeline
  1: Unset *instU* and *instV*
  2: Set *inst* to be the first instruction in *Unissue_insts*
  3: **if** *inst* does not depend on any unretired instruction in *Executing_insts* **then**
  4:     Set *instU* to be *inst* and delete *instU* from *Unissue_insts*
  5:     Set *inst* to be the first instruction in *Unissue_insts*
  6:     **if** *inst* can pair with *instU* and *inst* does not depend on any unretired instruc-
      tion in *Executing_insts* **then**
  7:         Set *instV* to be *inst* and delete *instV* from *Unissue_insts*
  8:     **end if**
  9: **end if**

---

can be changed. As the emulator only focuses on the usage of the U and V
pipelines, the events that can stall the two pipelines at the same time, e.g., branch
mispredictions, cache misses, TLB (transaction lookaside Buffer) misses, etc.,
are not considered and simulated, and the latency of each instruction is directly
from the corresponding documents of Intel Corporation [21, 22]. Although the
emulator is simply implemented, it can accurately simulate the usage of the
pipelines, as shown in Sect. 5.1.2.

Description. Figure 5 shows the architecture of the emulator. The 4 hardware
threads on a KNC core are simulated simultaneously. Following the architecture of the KNC core, the instructions issued at one cycle must be from the
same hardware thread and the 4 hardware threads are scheduled in round-robin
fashion. As a result, the hardware threads are independent to each other in the
simulation and the order of issuing instructions among the hardware threads
does not impact the balance of pipeline usage.

To trace the instructions executed by the KNC, a tool PIN is used. PIN
provides a set of APIs which enable arbitrary codes to be inserted into the
binary executable of the application to collect the execution information without
modifying the source codes [23]. It provides scalable support for multithreaded
applications [24] on heterogeneous environments. For a processor with multiple
hardware threads, it can distinguish the instructions for each hardware thread.

As a KNC core can decode 2 instructions each cycle, at most 2 instructions
can be executed at one cycle. Algorithm 1 shows how to select the instructions to
be issued. If the first unissued instruction depend on any unretired instructions,
no instructions are issued at this cycle. Otherwise, it is issued to the U pipeline.
Meanwhile, if the second unissued instruction can pair with the first instruction
and does not depend on any unretired instructions, it is issued to the V pipeline.

The KNC designs a set of pairing rules to determine whether two instructions can be issued simultaneously to the two pipelines. Each instruction has
a pairing mode in four categories (NP, PU, PV and UV) [21]. NP means the

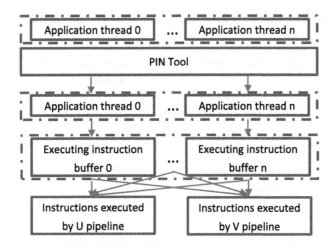

Fig. 5. Architecture of the emulator.

instruction cannot execute with any other instruction concurrently. PU means the instruction can only be issued to the U pipeline. PV means the instruction can only be issued to the V pipeline when there is another instruction to be issued simultaneously. UV means the instruction can be issued to the U or V pipeline. The change of the function layout of the pipelines can be easily achieved through modifying the pairing mode of instructions.

Evaluation. To evaluate the emulator, we built a case to simulate the balance of pipeline usage on the KNC, where the hardware optimization is disabled. Formula 1 defines the maximum instructions per cycle (MIPC), which is the upper bound of ILP determined by the imbalance of pipeline usage, where P_U is the proportion of instructions executed by the U pipeline and P_V is the proportion of instructions executed by the V pipeline. Table 8 shows the MIPC measured by the VTune and simulated by the emulator respectively. The last column in Table 8 shows the error rate of the emulator when the MIPC from the VTune is treated as the reference. The error rate ranges from 0.88 % to 2.18 % and is 1.29 % on average, which demonstrates that our emulator can accurately simulate the balance of pipeline usage.

$$MIPC = \frac{1}{max(P_U, P_V)} \tag{1}$$

5.2 Hardware Optimizations for Better Balance of Pipeline Usage

The two pipelines on a KNC core are different in functionality. Most vector instructions can be executed on the U pipeline only. A straightforward hardware optimization is to make the two pipelines have the same functionality, which

Table 8. MIPC measured by VTune and simulated by our emulator (vectorization is enabled).

Application	MIPC		Error rate of the emulator (%)
	VTune	Emulator	
blackscholes	1.140	1.130	0.88
canneal	1.487	1.504	1.14
dedup	1.520	1.544	1.58
fluidanimate	1.331	1.360	2.18
streamcluster	1.514	1.528	0.92
swaptions	1.527	1.543	1.05

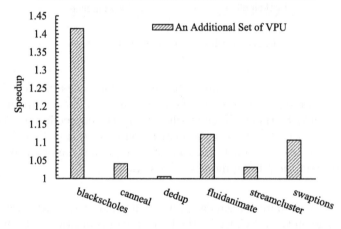

Fig. 6. Speedup of MIPC from this hardware optimization in our emulator. The baseline is the MIPC on the KNC measured by the VTune.

requires an additional set of 512-bit VPU for the V pipeline. This optimization is easily achieved by the emulator through modifying the pairing mode of the corresponding instructions from PU to UV. For other instructions with paring mode NP, PV or UV, their paring mode keeps the same. Figure 6 shows the speedup of MIPC achieved by an additional set of VPU for the V pipeline. With an additional set of VPU for the V pipeline, the balance of the pipeline usage is improved, especially for the applications blackscholes, fluidanimate and streamcluster. On average, the KNC achieves a speedup 1.121.

Figure 7 shows the performance improvement achieved from the hardware optimization, considering the overhead of branch mispredictions and memory accessing (reference to Sect. 4.1). With an additional set of VPU for the V pipeline, the KNC gains an average speedup of 1.104. So we can demonstrate that the hardware optimization can improve the real performance of the KNC effectively.

The energy per instruction (EPI) of the vector instructions with register operands is 2x of the scalar instructions and EPI of the vector instructions with other operands is almost same as the scalar instructions [25]. That is to say, the SIMD execution is energy-efficient to boost peak performance [26]. So we believe that an additional set of 512-bit VPU for V pipeline is practical.

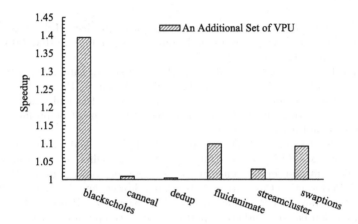

Fig. 7. Performance improvement from the hardware optimization in our emulator, when considering the overhead of branch mispredictions and memory accessing. The baseline is the performance on the KNC measured by the VTune.

6   Discussion and Conclusion

This paper aims to characterize and optimize real performance of the KNC. With the comparison between the KNC and dual SNB using real applications from the PARSEC benchmark suite, the impact of various architecture parameters on the KNC performance is quantified. To investigate the hardware optimizations for better real performance of the KNC, a simple emulator for the balance of pipeline usage is developed and several hardware optimizations are designed and evaluated. The evaluation result shows that the proposed hardware optimizations, e.g., an additional set of VPU for the V pipeline, can improve the real performance of the KNC.

If the overhead of an additional set of VPU is not affordable, one possible solution for an additional set of VPU is to split the 512-bit VPU into two identical 256-bit VPU. This solution may not improve the application performance of blackscholes, which can fully utilize the 512-bit VPU, but can prospectively improve other applications.

Acknowledgments. This work is supported in part by the Natural Science Foundation of China (no. 41275098), the National Grand Fundamental Research 973 Program of China (no. 2013CB956603), and the Tsinghua University Initiative Scientific Research Program (no. 20131089356).

References

1. Schmidl, D., Cramer, T., Wienke, S., Terboven, C., Muller, M.S.: Assessing the performance of Openmp programs on the Intel Xeon Phi. In: Euro-Par 2013 Parallel Processing, pp. 547–558 (2013)
2. Semelyanskiy, M., Sewall, J., Kalamkar, D.D., Satish, N., Dubey, P., Astafiev, N., Burylov, I., Nikolaev, A., Maidanov, S., Li, S., Kulkarni, S., Finan, C.H.: Analysis and optimization of financial analytics benchmark on modern multi- and many-core ia-based architectures. In: SC Companion: High Performance Computing, Networking, Storage and Analysis (2012)
3. Williams, S., Kalamkar, D.D., Singh, A., Deshpande, A.M., Van Straalen, B., Smelyanskiy, M., Almgren, A., Dubey, P., Shalf, J., Oliker, L.: Optimization of geometric multigrid for emerging multi-and manycore processors. In: Conference on High Performance Computing, Networking, Storage and Analysis (2012)
4. Park, J., Tang, P.T.P., Smelyanskiy, M., Kim, D., Benson, T.: Efficient backprojection-based synthetic aperture radar computation with many-core processors. In: Conference on High Performance Computing, Networking, Storage and Analysis (2012)
5. Cramer, T., Schmidl, D., Klemm, M., an Mey, D.: Openmp programming on Intel Xeon Phi coprocessors: an early performance comparison. In: Proceedings of the Many-core Applications Research Community (MARC) Symposium at RWTH Aachen University, pp. 38–44 (2012)
6. Liu, X., Smelyanskiy, M., Chow, E., Dubey, P.: Efficient sparse matrix-vector multiplication on X86-based many-core processors. In: Proceedings of the 27th International ACM Conference on International Conference on Supercomputing (ICS), Eugene, Oregon, USA (2013)
7. Pennycook, S.J., Hughes, C.J., Smelyanskiy, M., Jarvis, S.A.: Exploring Simd for molecular dynamics, using Intel Xeon processors and Intel Xeon Phi coprocessors. In: 2013 IEEE 27th International Symposium on Parallel & Distributed Processing (IPDPS). Boston, MA, USA (2013)
8. Saule, E., Kaya, K., Catalyurek, U.V.: Performance evaluation of sparse matrix multiplication kernels on Intel Xeon Phi. In: Parallel Processing and Applied Mathematics (2013)
9. Gao, T., Lu, Y., Zhang, B., Suo, G.: Using the intel many integrated core to accelerate graph traversal. Int. J. High Perform. Comput. Appl. **28**(3), 255–266 (2014)
10. Ravi, N., Yang, Y., Bao, T., Chakradhar, S.: Semi-automatic restructuring of offloadable tasks for many-core accelerators. In: Conference on High Performance Computing, Networking, Storage and Analysis (SC). Denver, USA (2013)
11. Reinders, J.: An overview of programming for Intel Xeon processors and Intel Xeon Phi coprocessors. Intel (2012)

12. Bienia, C., Kumar, S., Singh, J.P., Li, K.: The parsec benchmark suite: characterization and architectural implications. In: Proceedings of the 17th International Conference on Parallel Architectures and Compilation Techniques, pp. 72–81 (2008)
13. Bienia, C., Li, K.: Parsec 2.0: a new benchmark suite for chip-multiprocessors. In: Proceedings of the 5th Annual Workshop on Modeling, Benchmarking and Simulation (2009)
14. Molka, D., Hackenberg, D., Schone, R., Mller, M.S.: Memory performance and cache coherency effects on an Intel Nehalem multiprocessor system. In: Proceedings of the 18th International Conference on Parallel Architectures and Compilation Techniques (PACT), pp. 261–270 (2009)
15. Iyer, R., Bhuyan, L.N.: Switch cache: a framework for improving the remote memory access latency of CC-NUMA multiprocessors. In: Proceedings of 5th International Symposium on High-Performance Computer Architecture (1999)
16. Koesterke, L., Boisseau, J., Cazes, J., Milfeld, K., Stanzione, D.: Early experiences with the intel many integrated cores accelerated computing technology. In: Proceedings of the 2011 TeraGrid Conference: Extreme Digital Discovery. Salt Lake City, Utah, USA (2011)
17. Schulz, K.W., Ulerich, R., Malaya, N., Bauman, P.T., Stogner, R.H., Simmons, C.: Early experiences porting scientic applications to the many integrated core (Mic) platform. In: TACC-Intel Highly Parallel Computing Symposium. Austin, TX (2012)
18. Saini, S., Jin, H., Jespersen, D., Feng, H., Djomehri, J., Arasin, W., Hood, R., Mehrotra, P., Biswas, R.: An early performance evaluation of many integrated core architecture based SGI rackable computing system. In: Conference on High Performance Computing, Networking, Storage and Analysis (2013)
19. Rahman, R.: Intel Xeon Phi Coprocessor Architecture and Tools: the Guide for Application Developers (Experts Voice in Microprocessors). Springer, Berlin (2013)
20. Thiagarajan, S.U., Congdon, C., Naik, S., Nguyen, L.Q.: Intel Xeon Phi Coprocessor Developer's Quick Start Guide". https://software.intel.com/enus/articles/intel-xeon-phi-coprocessor-developers-quick-start-guide
21. Pentium Processor Family Developers Manual Volume 3: Architecture and Programming Manual. vol. 3, no. 241430 (1995)
22. Fang, J., Varbanescu, A.L., Sips, H., Zhang, L., Che, Y., Xu, C.: An Empirical Study of Intel Xeon Phi. arXiv preprint (2013)
23. Luk, C.K., Cohn, R., Muth, R., Patil, H., Klauser, A., Lowney, G., Wallace, S., Reddi, V.J., Hazelwood, K.: Pin: building customized program analysis tools with dynamic instrumentation. In: ACM SIGPLAN Symposium on Programming Language Design & Implementation (PLDI). Chicago, Illinois, USA (2005)
24. Hazelwood, K., Lueck, G., Cohn, R.: Scalable support for multithreaded applications on dynamic binary instrumentation systems. In: Proceedings of the 2009 International Symposium on Memory Management (ISMM), Dublin, Ireland (2009)
25. Shao, Y.S., Brooks, D.: Energy characterization and instructionlevel energy model of Intels Xeon Phi processor. In: 2013 IEEE International Symposium on Low Power Electronics and Design (2013)
26. Czechowski, K., Lee, V.M., Grochowski, E., Ronen, R., Singhal, R., Vuduc, R., Dubey, P.: Improving the energy efficiency of big cores. In: Proceedings of the 41st Annual International Symposium on Computer Architecture (2014)

EH-Code: An Extended MDS Code to Improve Single Write Performance of Disk Arrays for Correcting Triple Disk Failures

Yanbing Jiang[1], Chentao Wu[1](✉), Jie Li[1,2], and Minyi Guo[1]

[1] Shanghai Key Laboratory of Scalable Computing and Systems,
Department of Computer Science and Engineering,
Shanghai Jiao Tong University, Shanghai 200240, China
`wuct@cs.sjtu.edu.cn`
[2] Department of Computer Science, University of Tsukuba,
Tsukuba, Ibaraki 305-8577, Japan

Abstract. In the information explosion era, with the sharp increasing requirements of storage devices, concurrent multiple disk failures are not rare. In large data centers, erasure code is one of the most efficient ways to protect user data with low monetary cost. One class of erasure codes is called Maximum Distance Separable (MDS) codes, which aims to offer data protection with minimal storage overhead. However, existing Triple Disk Failure Tolerant arrays (3DFTs) based on MDS codes suffer from low single write performance, because the corresponding codes have high computational cost and low encoding performance. To address this problem, in this paper, we propose a novel MDS coding scheme called EH-Code, which is an extension of H-Code. It has three different parities, horizontal, diagonal and anti-diagonal parities, which can tolerate concurrent disk failures of any triple disks. Our mathematical analysis shows that EH-Code offers optimal storage efficiency and encoding computational complexity. Specifically, compared to STAR code, Triple-Star code and Cauchy-RS codes, EH-Code can improve the single write performance by up to 16.13 %, 14.53 % and 26.27 %, respectively.

Keywords: RAID · Erasure code · Triple disk failures · MDS Code · Performance evaluation

1   Introduction

In large distributed storage systems, massive data are stored in large amounts of redundant disks to facilitate users to access them in parallel. These redundant disks are called **R**edundant **A**rrays of **I**nexpensive (or **I**ndependent) **D**isks (**RAID**) [1]. Recently, disk arrays for correcting triple disk failures become one of the most popular choices for large data centers. It has two main reasons. On one hand, disk failures are more frequent than we expected. In previous literatures [2–4], the Annual Failure Rates (AFRs) of data disks are larger than 3 % in

© Springer International Publishing Switzerland 2015
G. Wang et al. (Eds.): ICA3PP 2015, Part I, LNCS 9528, pp. 34–49, 2015.
DOI: 10.1007/978-3-319-27119-4_3

data centers, while users only can accept 0.8 % in terms of the AFR [5]. On the other hand, with the developments of cloud storage, Triple Disk Failure Tolerant arrays (3DFTs) are highly desired because it can provide high reliability with low monetary cost [6].

In the last two decades, many famous erasure codes are proposed for disk arrays to correct triple disk failures. Typically, these codes can be categorized into two types, MDS codes [6–11] and Non-MDS codes [12–18]. MDS codes supply the maximum protection with a given amount of redundancy [10], which means the corresponding arrays have optimal storage efficiency. MDS codes are popular to implement the 3DFTs and many cloud storage systems are established based on these codes [19–21]. Compared to MDS codes, Non-MDS codes can achieve higher performance or reliability by sacrificing the storage efficiency [16,22].

Single write[1] performance is a significant aspect in storage systems [23,25–28]. In recent years, single write performance in disk arrays receives more attention due to the following reasons,

- It appears frequently in typical write intensive workloads. As shown in Table 4 (in Sect. 4), in several real I/O traces, many write requests are less than 8 KB and can be regarded as single write requests [23].
- It affects the overall performance of disk arrays. In most scenarios, the stripe write performance is determined by single write performance. Efficient single write can reduce the total number of I/O and XOR operations, which can increase the I/O throughput and decrease the I/O latency for applications.

However, existing Triple Disk Failure Tolerant arrays (3DFTs) has several limitations on single write performance. It has many reasons. First, for some MDS codes such as Reed-Solomon (RS) codes [7], the computational cost[2] over Galois Field is extremely high, which leads to low single write performance. Second, for several advanced MDS codes like STAR code [10], Triple-Star code [6] and Cauchy-RS codes [8,9], their low encoding performance[3] results in inefficient I/O process and high complexity on single write. It is because that one parity can be participated in the generation of other parities.

To address the single write performance problem, we propose a novel MDS code, named EH-Code, which can provide a disk array to tolerate concurrent disk failures of any triple disks. EH-Code is an extension of H-Code [25], which consists of three different parities, horizontal, diagonal and anti-diagonal parities.

We make the following contributions in this paper,

---

[1] In this paper, "single write" means a new write or an update to single data element [23], which is also known as "small write" in some literatures [24]. Data element refers to "data block/chunk" as well.

[2] Computational cost is the cost of mathematical calculations.

[3] Encoding performance is the speed of generating a parity by calculating the corresponding data/parity as introduced in [29].

- We propose EH-Code, which provides a disk array for correcting triple disk failures. It offers optimal storage efficiency and optimal encoding computational complexity[4].
- Our mathematical analysis and simulations show that, compared to other typical MDS codes, EH-Code achieves the higher single write performance.

This paper is organized as follows. Section 2 briefly overviews the background and related work. EH-Code is illustrated in detail in Sect. 3. The corresponding evaluations are given in Sect. 4. Finally we conclude this paper in Sect. 5.

2   Background and Our Motivation

To improve the reliability of storage systems, many erasure codes are proposed for Triple Disk Failure Tolerant arrays (3DFTs), which suffer from the single write performance problem. In this section, we discuss the background and motivation of our work. To facilitate the discussion, the related symbols in this paper are presented in Table 1.

2.1   Single Write Performance Problem in Existing MDS Codes

Reed-Solomon (RS) codes [7], Cauchy-RS codes [9], STAR code [10], Triple-Star code [6], HDD1 code [11] and STAIR Codes [31] are typical MDS codes to correct triple disk failures. However, these MDS codes have single write performance problem due to either high computational cost or low encoding performance.

(1) Caused by High Computational Cost

High computational cost can slow down the processing of single write requests in a storage system. It is caused by the complex mathematical computations in various codes such as Reed-Solomon (RS) codes [7]. They generate the parities via Galois Field computation, which has higher computational cost than XOR calculations [16, 22, 29, 32].

(2) Caused by Low Encoding Performance

Regarding to most MDS codes like STAR [10], Triple-Star [6], HDD1 [11] and Cauchy-RS [9], one parity takes part in the generation of another parity, which increases the I/O cost of single writes. We use STAR code as an example to illustrate the single write problem, which is shown in Fig. 1. From this figure, we notice that a large number of parities need to be modified, because that two special elements S_1 and S_2 participate in the generation of all diagonal and anti-diagonal parities.

We summarize the encoding performance of various MDS codes as shown in Fig. 2. $P1$, $P2$ and $P3$ represent the horizontal, diagonal and anti-diagonal parities, respectively. We use H-Code [25] as the baseline to evaluate the encoding

---

[4] Encoding computational complexity is the average number of XOR operations per data element during encoding process [30]. It can affect the encoding performance significantly.

Table 1. Symbols of EH-Code

Parameters & Symbols	Description
n	Number of disks in a disk array
p	A prime number, which is related to the disk number (n) in a disk array
i	Row ID
j	Column ID or disk ID
r	The ID of a parity chain (For a random data element $C_{i,j}$ in a horizontal, diagonal and anti-diagonal parity chain, the value of r is i, $\langle i+j \rangle_p$ and $\langle i-j \rangle_p$, respectively.)
$C_{i,j}$	An element at the ith row and jth column
f_1, f_2, f_3	Three random failed columns with IDs f_1, f_2 and f_3
h_1, h_2	Distance between two failed columns ($h_1 = f_2 - f_1$, $h_2 = f_3 - f_2$)
$\sum$ (e.g., $\sum_{j=0}^{5} C_{i,j}$)	XOR operations between/among elements ($C_{i,0} \oplus C_{i,1} \oplus \cdots \oplus C_{i,5}$)
$\langle \ \rangle$ ($\langle i \rangle_p$)	modular arithmetic ($i \bmod p$)
$S_{r,0}$	The syndrome for a horizontal parity chain which includes element $C_{r,p}$
$S_{r,1}$	The syndrome for a diagonal parity chain which includes element $C_{r,p+1}$
$S_{r,2}$	The syndrome for an anti-diagonal parity chain which includes element $C_{r,0}$
X_{i,f_1}	The sum of XOR operations of lost elements in extensional cross whose top left element is C_{i,f_1}

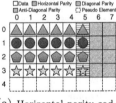

(a) Horizontal parity coding (e.g., $C_{0,5} = C_{0,0} \oplus C_{0,1} \oplus C_{0,2} \oplus C_{0,3} \oplus C_{0,4}$).

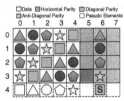

(b) Diagonal parity coding (e.g., $C_{0,6} = S_1 \oplus C_{0,0} \oplus C_{3,2} \oplus C_{2,3} \oplus C_{1,4}$, and $S_1 = C_{0,4} \oplus C_{1,3} \oplus C_{2,2} \oplus C_{3,1}$).

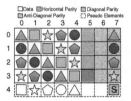

(c) Anti-diagonal parity coding (e.g., $C_{0,7} = S_2 \oplus C_{0,0} \oplus C_{1,1} \oplus C_{2,2} \oplus C_{3,3}$, and $S_2 = C_{0,1} \oplus C_{1,2} \oplus C_{2,3} \oplus C_{3,4}$).

Fig. 1. STAR code ($p = 5$, $n = 8$).

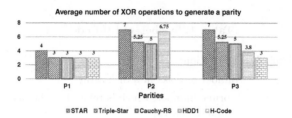

Fig. 2. Encoding performance on various MDS codes in terms of # of XOR operations ($p = 5$, 8 disks for STAR code, 7 disks for Triple-Star code, 6 disks for HDD1 code, 7 disks for Cauchy-RS and 6 disks for H-Code).

performance, which is a typical RAID-6 code with only two parities (horizontal ($P1$) and anti-diagonal ($P3$) parities) and has the optimal encoding. Obviously, compared to H-Code, most MDS codes have poor encoding performance due to their high I/O cost on the generations of vertical parities (including diagonal and anti-diagonal parities).

From the above illustration, it is clear that existing 3DFTs have low single write performance due to two primary reasons, high computational cost or low encoding performance.

2.2 Our Motivation

Table 2 summarizes the differences among existing MDS codes on single write performance. It is clear that, existing MDS codes have single write performance problem due to either high computational cost or low encoding performance. According to previous literatures [25], in RAID-6 systems, H-Code has the optimal single write performance. So in 3DFTs, an extension of H-Code is a proper way to achieve good single write performance for a storage system.

Table 2. Summary of various MDS codes on single write performance

Codes	Computational cost[1]	Encoding performance	Single write performance
Reed-Solomon	High	High	High
Cauchy-RS	Low	Low	Medium
STAR	Low	Low	Low
Triple-Star	Low	Low	Medium
HDD1	Low	Low	Medium
STAIR	High	Low	Low
EH-Code	Low	High	Very high

[1] Lower computational cost is better.

3   EH-Code

To overcome the shortages of existing erasure codes, we present an MDS coding scheme called EH-Code, which can tolerate concurrent disk failures of any triple disks. EH-Code is a solution for $p + 2$ disks, where p is a prime number.

3.1   Data/Parity Layout and Encoding of EH-Code

The data/parity layout of EH-Code is shown in Fig. 3. It is represented by a $(p-1)$-row-$(p+2)$-column matrix. By extending H-Code [25], EH-Code has four types of elements: *data elements*, *horizontal parity elements*, *diagonal parity elements* and *anti-diagonal parity elements*. In this matrix, columns p and $p + 1$ are used to store horizontal and diagonal parities, respectively. Excluding the first column (column 0) and last two columns (columns p and $p + 1$), the remaining matrix is a $(p - 1)$-row-$(p - 1)$-column square matrix. And the anti-diagonal part of the square matrix saves the anti-diagonal parities.

Assume $C_{i,j}$ $(0 \leq i \leq p - 2, 0 \leq j \leq p + 1)$ represents the element at the ith row and the jth column. The horizontal, anti-diagonal and diagonal parities are constructed by the following equations,

Horizontal Parity,

$$C_{i,p} = \sum_{j=0}^{p-1} C_{i,j} \quad (j \neq i + 1) \tag{1}$$

Anti-diagonal Parity,

$$C_{i,i+1} = \sum_{j=0}^{p-1} C_{\langle p-2-i+j \rangle_p, j} \quad (j \neq i + 1) \tag{2}$$

Diagonal Parity,

$$C_{i,p+1} = C_{i,i+1} \oplus \sum_{j=0}^{p-1} C_{\langle p+i-j \rangle_p, j} \quad (j \neq i + 1 \quad and \quad j \neq \langle p + i - j \rangle_p + 1) \tag{3}$$

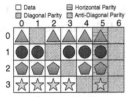

(a) Horizontal parity coding. For example, $C_{0,5} = C_{0,0} \oplus C_{0,2} \oplus C_{0,3} \oplus C_{0,4}$.

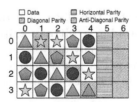

(b) Anti-diagonal parity coding. For example, $C_{0,1} = C_{3,0} \oplus C_{0,2} \oplus C_{1,3} \oplus C_{2,4}$.

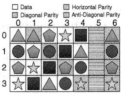

(c) Diagonal parity coding. For example, $C_{0,6} = C_{0,1} \oplus C_{0,0} \oplus C_{3,2} \oplus C_{1,4}$.

Fig. 3. EH-Code $(n = 7, p = 5)$.

Figure 3 shows an example of EH-Code for a 7-disk array ($p = 5$). It is a 4-row-7-column matrix. The last two columns (columns 5 and 6) are used for horizontal and diagonal parities, respectively. The anti-diagonal parity elements ($C_{0,1}$, $C_{1,2}$, $C_{2,3}$, etc.) are served as anti-diagonal parities.

The encoding of horizontal parity is shown in Fig. 3(a).The horizontal parity elements and the corresponding data elements are distinguished by different shapes. According to Eq. 1, we compute all horizontal elements. For example, the horizontal parity element $C_{0,5}$ can be calculated by $C_{0,0} \oplus C_{0,2} \oplus C_{0,3} \oplus C_{0,4}$. The element $C_{0,1}$ is not involved in because of $j = i + 1$.

The anti-diagonal parity encoding is given in Fig. 3(b). Based on Eq. 2, the anti-diagonal parity elements can be calculated through XOR and modular arithmetic operations. For example, to compute the anti-diagonal element $C_{0,1}$ ($i = 0$), we should get the proper data elements ($C_{\langle p-2-i+j \rangle_p, j}$) first. If $j = 0$, by using Eq. 2, $p - 2 - i + j = 3$ and then $\langle 3 \rangle_p = 3$, we get the first data element $C_{3,0}$. The following data elements which are involved in XOR operations can be calculated similarly (the following data elements are $C_{0,2}$, $C_{1,3}$ and $C_{2,4}$). Second, the corresponding anti-diagonal element ($C_{0,1}$) is constructed by performing an XOR operation on these data elements, i.e., $C_{0,1} = C_{3,0} \oplus C_{0,2} \oplus C_{1,3} \oplus C_{2,4}$.

The encoding of diagonal parity is shown in Fig. 3(c). We can compute the diagonal parity elements by using Eq. 3, which is the same as anti-diagonal parity. For example, the diagonal parity element $C_{0,6}$ can be calculated by $C_{0,1} \oplus C_{0,0} \oplus C_{3,2} \oplus C_{1,4}$.

3.2   Construction Process

Based on the above data/parity layout and encoding scheme, the construction process of EH-Code is straightforward.

- Label all data elements.
- Calculate horizontal, anti-diagonal and diagonal parity elements using Eqs. 1–3.

3.3   Proof of Correctness

In this subsection, we prove that **the data in a disk array based on EH-Code can be recovered under arbitrary triple disk failures.** To simplify the proving process, here we only discuss the scenario of one stripe. The reconstruction of multiple stripes is just a matter of scale and similar to the reconstruction of one stripe. In a stripe, we have the following theorem.

Theorem 1. *A $(p-1)$-row-$(p+2)$-column stripe constructed according to the formal description of EH-Code can be reconstructed under arbitrary triple disk failures.*

Proof. Due to the page limit, we only list the equations used in the reconstruction of EH-Code, which can be derived and proved in a way similar in previous literatures [6,10,25].

Table 3. Cases to calculate the sum of 2-tuples

Constraint condition of k	Distance d of 2-tuple elements	Corresponding equation to calculate the sum of 2-tuples
$\langle k \cdot h_1 + h_2 \rangle_p = 0$	$d = \langle k \cdot h_1 - h_2 \rangle_p$	$C_{\langle i+k\cdot h_1 \rangle_p, f_2} + C_{\langle i+h_2 \rangle_p, f_2} = \sum_{j=0}^{k-1} X_{\langle i+j\cdot h_1 \rangle_p, f_1}$
$\langle k \cdot h_1 - h_2 \rangle_p = 0$	$d = \langle k \cdot h_1 + h_2 \rangle_p$	$C_{i, f_2} + C_{\langle i+k\cdot h_1 + h_2 \rangle_p, f_2} = \sum_{j=0}^{k-1} X_{\langle i+j\cdot h_1 \rangle_p, f_1}$
$\langle k \cdot h_2 + h_1 \rangle_p = 0$	$d = \langle k \cdot h_2 - h_1 \rangle_p$	$C_{\langle i+h_1 \rangle_p, f_2} + C_{\langle i+k\cdot h_2 \rangle_p, f_2} = \sum_{j=0}^{k-1} X_{\langle i+j\cdot h_2 \rangle_p, f_1}$
$\langle k \cdot h_2 - h_1 \rangle_p = 0$	$d = \langle k \cdot h_2 + h_1 \rangle_p$	$C_{i, f_2} + C_{\langle i+h_1 + k\cdot h_2 \rangle_p, f_2} = \sum_{j=0}^{k-1} X_{\langle i+j\cdot h_2 \rangle_p, f_1}$

Equations 4 and 5 are used to calculate syndromes[5] $S_{r,0}$, $S_{r,1}$ and $S_{r,2}$.

$$C_{p-1,j} = \sum_{i=0}^{p-2} C_{i,j} \quad (j = p \quad or \quad p+1) \tag{4}$$

$$S_{r,0} = C_{r,p} \oplus \sum_{j=0}^{p-1} C_{r,j} \quad S_{r,1} = C_{r,p+1} \oplus \sum_{j=0}^{p-1} C_{\langle p+r-j \rangle_p, j} \quad S_{r,2} = \sum_{j=0}^{p-1} C_{\langle p+r+j \rangle_p, j} \tag{5}$$

where $0 \leq r \leq p-1$ and $j \neq f_1, f_2$ or f_3.

Equation 6 is to get 4-tuples[6].

$$X_{i,f_1} = S_{i,0} \oplus S_{\langle i+f_3-f_1 \rangle_p, 0} \oplus S_{\langle i+f_3 \rangle_p, 1} \oplus S_{\langle i-f_1 \rangle_p, 2}$$
$$= C_{i,f_2} \oplus C_{\langle i+h_1, f_2 \rangle_p} \oplus C_{\langle i+h_2, f_2 \rangle_p} \oplus C_{\langle i+h_1+h_2, f_2 \rangle_p} \tag{6}$$

Equations for reducing 4-tuples to 2-tuples are summarized in Table 3.

3.4 Reconstruction Process

We design the related reconstruction algorithm as shown in Algorithm 1.

3.5 Basic Property of EH-Code

EH-Code offers optimal storage efficiency and encoding computational complexity.

---

[5] Syndrome is the sum of XOR operations of the surviving parity element and its corresponding data elements for particular parity direction [10], which equals to the sum of all lost elements along a same parity chain through XOR operations.

[6] n-tuple: There are n data elements in one tuple, which can be calculated through XOR operations.

Algorithm 1. Reconstruction algorithm of EH-code

Step 1: Identify the triple failure columns:f_1, f_2 and f_3 ($f_1 < f_2 < f_3$).
Step 2: Start reconstruction process and recover the failed columns.
switch $0 \leq f_1 < f_2 < f_3 \leq p+1$ **do**

    case 1: $f_3 = p+1, 0 \leq f_1 < f_2 \leq p$ *(Column $p+1$ is lost)*
        (1): Recover f_1 and f_2 by using the reconstruction algorithm of H-Code [25];
        (2): Recover f_3 according to Eq. 3.

    case 2: *Column $p+1$ is saved*
        case 2-1: $f_3 = p, 0 \leq f_1 < f_2 \leq p-1$ *(Column p fails)*
        (1): Recover f_1 and f_2.
        case *starting point is* $C_{\langle f_1-1\rangle_p, f_1}$
            repeat
                (1): Compute the corresponding lost data in column f_2;
                (2): Then compute the corresponding lost data in column f_1.
            until *at the endpoint of* $C_{\langle f_2-1\rangle_p, f_2}$;
        (2): Recover column f_3 using Eq. 1.

        case 2-2: $0 \leq f_1 < f_2 < f_3 \leq p-1$ *(Column p is saved.)*
        (1): Calculate all syndromes according to Eqs. 4 and 5;
        (2): Compute p sets of X_{i,f_1} ($0 \leq i \leq p-1$) to get 4-tuples in column f_2 based on Eq. 6;
        (3): According to Table 3, find the smallest k and put the k into its corresponding formula, then figure out 2-tuples from 4-tuples in column f_2;
        (4): Based on Lemma 3 in STAR code [10], start from $C_{\langle f_2-1\rangle_p, f_2}$ to recover column f_2 with a fixed distance d;
        (5): Recover columns f_1 and f_3 by using the reconstruction algorithm of H-Code [25].

(a) Optimal Storage Efficiency of EH-Code:

From the proof of EH-Code's correctness, EH-Code is an MDS code. All MDS codes have optimal storage efficiency [6,8,10,31], so does EH-Code.

(b) Optimal Encoding Computational Complexity of EH-Code:

We have the following theorem for the optimal encoding computational complexity for an erasure code correcting triple disk failures.

Theorem 2. *The optimal encoding computational complexity of an erasure code tolerating triple disk failures is $\frac{3x-(i\cdot j-x)}{x}$ XOR operations per data element (Suppose there are $i\cdot j$ blocks in one stripe and x of them are data blocks).*

Proof. Proof of this theorem in detail is similar to that in RAID-6 codes such as P-Code [30].

Based on Eqs. 1–3, the XOR operation number of parity elements are all $(p-2)\cdot(p-1)$. So the encoding computational complexity of EH-Code is $\frac{3\cdot(p-2)\cdot(p-1)}{(p-1)\cdot(p-1)} = \frac{3p-6}{p-1}$ XOR operations per data element on average. According to Theorem 2, $\frac{3x-(i\cdot j-x)}{x} = \frac{3\cdot(p-1)\cdot(p-1)-((p-1)\cdot(p+2))}{(p-1)\cdot(p-1)} = \frac{3p-6}{p-1}$. Obviously, EH-Code has optimal encoding computational complexity.

4   Performance Evaluation

In this section, we give our evaluations of the write performance among EH-Code and other typical MDS codes in 3DFTs.

4.1 Evaluation Methodology

(1) Comparison among Various MDS Codes: We compare EH-Code with following MDS codes:

(a) **Codes for $p+1$ disks:** HDD1 code [11];

(b) **Codes for $p+2$ disks:** EH-Code, Triple-Star code [6] and Cauchy-RS codes [9];

(c) **Codes for $p+3$ disks:** STAR code [10].

(2) Traces: We choose both a synthetic workload and real traces as below (These traces are shown in Table 4).

(a) uniform synthetic workload: The uniform synthetic workload can be described as a uniform sequence of single writes. For EH-Code shown in Fig. 3 (which has $(p-1)^2$ total data elements in one stripe), the uniform sequence of single writes can be denoted by: $C_{0,0}, C_{0,1}, \ldots$, the last single write in this sequence is $C_{p-2,p-2}$. Each data element occurs only once and is written only once.

(b) MSR Cambridge Traces: MSR Cambridge Traces [33] are one week block I/O traces of enterprise servers at Microsoft Research Cambridge in 2007. From MSR Cambridge Traces, We choose two traces ($src2\_0$ and $prxy\_0$) in this evaluation.

(c) Financial 1 Trace: Financial 1 [34] is an I/O trace from OLTP (On-Line Transaction Processing) applications running at a large financial institution in 2002.

Table 4. Summary of different I/O traces

Trace	# of requests(K)	IOPS	Write%	Avg. request length(KB)
src2_0	1557	22.29	88.66	7.21
prxy_0	12518	207.60	96.94	4.76
Financial1	5334	122.00	76.84	3.38

(3) Metrics: We compare EH-Code and typical codes above by using the following metrics, and the first two metrics are calculated based on the sequence in the uniform synthetic workload.

(a) Avg. Number of I/O Operations of A Single Write (O_{avg}): It is the average number of I/O operations of all single writes in the sequence. The smaller the value of O_{avg}, the lower the cost of a single write and the higher the performance. Assume $N(C_{i,j})$ is used to represent the number of I/O operations of writing single data element $C_{i,j}$. If we use EH-Code ($(p-1)^2$ in each stripe) as an example and running the uniform synthetic workload, O_{avg} can be computed by,

$$O_{avg} = \frac{\sum_{i=0}^{p-2} \sum_{j=0}^{p-1} N(C_{i,j})}{(p-1)^2} \quad (j \neq i+1) \tag{7}$$

(b) Max. Number of I/O Operations of A Single Write (O_{max}): It is the maximum number of I/O operations of all single writes in the sequence. O_{max} can be calculated by,

$$O_{max} = \max\left[N(C_{i,j})\right] \tag{8}$$

(c) Average Response Time: It means the average time used between the arrival and completion of request for traces, which is an important measurement to evaluate the write performance of erasure codes.

4.2 Numerical Results

In this subsection, we give the numerical results of EH-Code compared to other popular codes using the uniform synthetic workload.

(a) Avg. Number of I/O Operations of A Single Write: It is evaluated by using various MDS codes as shown in Fig. 4(a). EH-Code has the lowest I/O cost for each single write request. We summarize the results about the improvements of EH-Code as shown in Table 5. Compared to STAR code, Triple-Star code, HDD1 code and Cauchy-RS codes, EH-Code reduces average number of I/O operations by up to 36.50 %. When p becomes larger, EH-Code achieves higher enhancement.

(b) Max. Number of I/O Operations of A Single Write: Next, we examine the maximum number of I/O operations of a single write as presented in Fig. 4(b). It is clear that EH-Code reduces 76.19 % cost on parity modifications compared to STAR code.

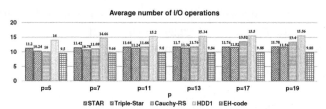

(a) Avg. number of I/O operations of a single write

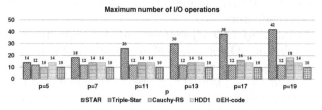

(b) Max. number of I/O operations of a single write

Fig. 4. The comparison on average &maximum number of I/O operations of a single write by using MDS codes (under uniform synthetic workload).

Table 5. Improvement of EH-Code over other MDS codes in terms of Avg. Number of I/O operations of a single write

p	STAR	Triple-Star	Cauchy-RS	HDD1
$p = 5$	15.18 %	7.23 %	5.00 %	32.14 %
$p = 7$	15.41 %	10.39 %	12.82 %	34.11 %
$p = 11$	15.81 %	12.81 %	15.95 %	35.53 %
$p = 13$	15.90 %	13.38 %	16.33 %	35.85 %
$p = 17$	15.99 %	14.24 %	26.92 %	36.26 %
$p = 19$	16.13 %	14.53 %	26.27 %	36.50 %

4.3   Simulation Results

In this subsection, we give the simulation results of average number of I/O operations and average response time (by using three real traces) to demonstrate the advantages of EH-Code on write performance. These results reflect the overall write performance by using MDS codes, including single write, partial stripe write and full stripe write performance.

We use Disksim as the simulator in our evaluation. It is an efficient and highly-configurable disk simulator for a typical storage system [35]. In Disksim, we set some proper values of parameters for each stripe. For example, the stripe unit size is set to 8 K, which means the size of an element is 8 KB, and the stripe size is approximately 256 KB, which is configured by disk arrays [36] (e.g., as shown in Fig. 3, the stripe size is 28*8 KB = 224 KB).

(a) Avg. Number of I/O Operations of A Write Request: As shown in Fig. 5, the average number of I/O operations for EH-Code is the lowest. Compared to other erasure codes, EH-Code reduces I/O cost by up to 34.22 %.

(b) Average Response Time: Figure 6 shows the results of average response time under different I/O workloads. It is clear that EH-Code achieves the best write performance among all MDS codes. Particularly, compared to STAR code and HDD1, EH-Code decreases the average response time by up to 45 %.

4.4   Analysis

The above evaluations demonstrate that EH-Code outperforms other MDS codes in terms of single write performance. The reasons that EH-Code has the lowest single write cost are: First, EH-Code uses XOR operations to generate parities, which is a cost-efficient way to save computational cost. Second, we utilize a similar layout as H-Code [25], which can sharply increase the encoding performance. Third, EH-Code has three special parity chains, which guarantee high encoding performance by avoiding the usage of intermediate parity chains (e.g., $S1$ and $S2$ in STAR code [10]).

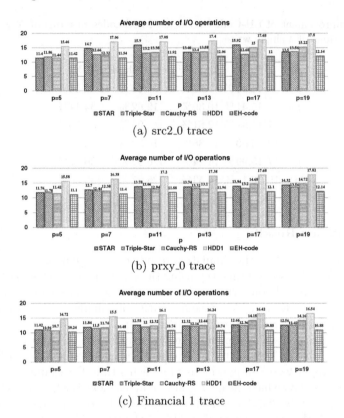

Fig. 5. Avg. number of I/O operations of a write request under various workloads by using MDS codes.

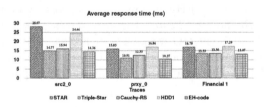

Fig. 6. Average response time of a disk array by using different MDS codes under various I/O workloads (when $p = 7$).

5   Conclusions

In this paper, we propose EH-Code which is a novel MDS code to enhance the write performance for Triple Disk Failure Tolerant arrays (3DFTs). As an extension of H-Code, EH-Code contains three types of parities: horizontal, diagonal and anti-diagonal parities to provide the reliability for 3DFTs. EH-Code has several properties, such as optimal storage efficiency and optimal encoding computational complexity, etc. In our mathematical analysis and simulations, compared to STAR code, Triple-Star code and Cauchy-RS codes, EH-Code improves the single write performance by up to 16.13 %, 14.53 % and 26.27 %, respectively.

Acknowledgments. We thank anonymous reviewers for their insightful comments. This work is partially sponsored by the National 863 Program of China (No. 2015AA015302), the National 973 Program of China No.2015CB352403), the National Natural Science Foundation of China (NSFC) (No. 61332001, No. 61303012, No. 61261160502, No. 61272099, and No. 61572323), the Shanghai Natural Science Foundation (No. 13ZR1421900), the Scientific Research Foundation for the Returned Overseas Chinese Scholars, the EU FP7 CLIMBER project (No. PIRSES-GA-2012-318939), and the CCF-Tencent Open Fund.

References

1. Patterson, D., Gibson, G., Katz, R.: A case for redundant arrays of inexpensive disks (RAID). In: Proceedings of the ACM SIGMOD 1988, Chicago, June 1988
2. Schroeder, B., Gibson, G.: Disk failures in the real world: what does an MTTF of 1, 000, 000 hours mean to you? In: Proceedings of the USENIX FAST 2007, San Jose, February 2007
3. Pinheiro, E., Weber, W., Barroso, L.: Failure trends in a large disk drive population. In: Proceedings of the USENIX FAST 2007, San Jose, February 2007
4. Ma, A., Douglis, F., Lu, G., Sawyer, D., Chandra, S., Hsu, W.: Raidshield: characterizing, monitoring, and proactively protecting against disk failures. In: Proceedings of the USENIX FAST 2015, Santa Clara, February 2015
5. Western Digital Technologies, Inc., Thermal Reliability: Cool-Running WD Hard Drives Demonstrate Exceptional Reliability in High Duty Cycle Environments, August 2005. http://www.wdc.com/wdproducts/library/other/2579-001134.pdf/
6. Wang, Y., Li, G., Zhong, X.: Triple-Star: a coding scheme with optimal encoding complexity for tolerating triple disk failures in RAID. Int. J. Innovative Comput. Inf. Control **8**(3), 1731 (2012)
7. Reed, I., Solomon, G.: Polynomial codes over certain finite fields. J. Soc. Ind. Appl. Math. **8**(2), 300–304 (1960)
8. Blomer, J., Kalfane, M., Karp, R., Karpinski, M., Luby, M., Zuckerman, D.: An XOR-based Erasure-Resilient coding scheme. Technical Report TR-95-048, International Computer Science Institute, August 1995
9. Plank, J., Xu, L.: Optimizing cauchy reed-solomon codes for fault-tolerant network storage applications. In: Proceedings of the IEEE NCA 2006, Cambridge, July 2006
10. Huang, C., Xu, L.: STAR: an efficient coding scheme for correcting triple storage node failures. IEEE Trans. Comput. **57**(7), 889–901 (2008)
11. Tau, C., Wang, T.: Efficient parity placement schemes for tolerating triple disk failures in RAID architectures. In: Proceedings of the AINA 2003, Xi'an, March 2003
12. Tang, D., Wang, X., Cao, S., Chen, Z.: A new class of highly fault tolerant erasure code for the disk array. In: Proceedings of the PEITS 2008, Guang Zhou, August 2008
13. Hafner, J.: WEAVER codes: highly fault tolerant erasure codes for storage systems. In Proceedings of the USENIX FAST 2005, San Francisco, December 2005

14. Hafner, J.: HoVer erasure codes for disk arrays. In: Proceedings of the IEEE/IFIP DSN 2006, Philadelphia, June 2006
15. Huang, C., Chen, M., Li, J.: Pyramid codes: flexible schemes to trade space for access efficiency in reliable data storage systems. In: Proceedings of the IEEE NCA 2007, Cambridge, July 2007
16. Huang, C., Simitci, H., Xu, Y., Ogus, A., Calder, B., Gopalan, P., Li, J., Yekhanin, S., et al.: Erasure coding in windows azure storage. In: Proceedings of the USENIX ATC 2012, Boston, June 2012
17. Blaum, M., Hafner, J., Hetzler, S.: Partial-MDS codes and their application to RAID type of architectures. IEEE Trans. Inf. THEORY **59**(7), 4510–4519 (2013)
18. Sathiamoorthy, W., Asteris, M., Papailiopoulos, D., Dimakis, A., Vadali, R., Chen, S., Borthakur, D.: Xoring elephants: novel erasure codes for big data. In: Proceedings of the VLDB 2013, Riva del Garda, August 2013
19. Calder, B., et al.: Windows azure storage: a highly available cloud storage service with strong consistency. In: Proceedings of the ACM SOSP 2011, Cascais, October 2011
20. Ford, D., Labelle, F., Popovici, F., Stokely, M., Truong, V., Barroso, L., Grimes, C., Quinlan, S.: Availability in globally distributed storage systems. In: Proceedings of the USENIX OSDI 2010, Vancouver, October 2010
21. Borthakur, D., Schmidt, R., Vadali, R., Chen, S., Kling, P.: HDFS RAID. In: Hadoop User Group Meeting (2010)
22. Subedi, P., He, X.: A comprehensive analysis of XOR-based erasure codes tolerating 3 or more concurrent failures. In; Proceedings of the IPDPSW 2013, Cambridge, May 2013
23. Wu, C., He, X., Wu, G., Wan, S., Liu, X., Cao, Q., Xie, C.: HDP code: a horizontal-diagonal parity code to optimize I/O load balancing in RAID-6. In; Proceedings of the IEEE/IFIP DSN 2011, Hong Kong, June 2011
24. Stodolsky, D., Gibson, G., Holland, M.: Parity logging overcoming the small write problem in redundant disk arrays. In: Proceedings of the ACM ISCA 1993, San Diego, May 1993
25. Wu, C., Wan, S., He, X., Cao, Q., Xie, C.: H-code: a hybrid MDS array code to optimize partial stripe writes in RAID-6. In: Proceedings of the IPDPS 2011, Anchorage, May 2011
26. Lee, S.S., Lee, B., Koh, K., Bahn, H.: A lifespan-aware reliability scheme for RAID-based flash storage. In: Proceedings of the ACM SAC 2011, TaiChung, March 2011
27. Grawinkel, M., Schafer, T., Brinkmann, A., Hagemeyer, J., Porrmann, M.: Evaluation of applied intra-disk redundancy schemes to improve single disk reliability. In: Proceedings of the IEEE MASCOTS 2011, Singapore, July 2011
28. Luo, X., Shu, J.: Summary of research for erasure code in storage system. J. Comput. Res. Dev. **49**(1), 1–11 (2012)
29. Plank, J.: The RAID-6 liberation codes. In: Proceedings of the USENIX FAST 2008, San Jose, February 2008
30. Jin, C., Jiang, H., Feng, D., Tian, L.: P-code: a new RAID-6 code with optimal properties. In: Proceedings of the ICS 2009, Yorktown Heights, June 2009
31. Li, M., Lee. P.: Stair codes: a general family of erasure codes for tolerating device and sector failures in practical storage systems. In: Proceedings of the USENIX FAST 2014, Santa Clara, February 2014
32. Plank, J., Luo, J., Schuman, C., Xu, L., Wilcox-O'Hearn, Z., et al.: A performance evaluation and examination of open-source erasure coding libraries for storage. In: Proceedings of the USENIX FAST 2009, San Francisco, February 2009

33. Narayanan, D., Donnelly, A., Rowstron, A.: Write off-loading: practical power management for enterprise storage. ACM Trans. Storage **4**(3), 10 (2008)
34. Goyal, P., Modha, D., Tewari, R.: Cachecow: providing QOS for storage system caches. In: ACM SIGMETRICS Performance Evaluation Review, San Diego (2003)
35. Bucy, J., Schindler, J., Schlosser S., Ganger, G.: The disksim simulation environment version 4.0 reference manual (cmu-pdl-08-101). Parallel Data Laboratory (2008)
36. EMC Corporation. EMC CLARiiON RAID 6 Technology: a detailed review, July 2007. http://www.emc.com/collateral/hardware/white-papers/h2891-clariion-raid-6.pdf

A Distributed Location-Based Service Discovery Protocol for Vehicular Ad-Hoc Networks

Chang Liu, Juan Luo$^{(\boxtimes)}$, and Qiu Pan

College of Computer Science and Electronic Engineering,
Hunan University, Changsha 410082, China
juanluo@hnu.edu.cn

Abstract. The Vehicular Ad-Hoc Network (VANET) is one of the most important techniques in smart cities. The service discovery protocol is a foundation stone of VANET. All the location-based requests could be replied only if the service provider has been discovered. A novel Distributed Location-based Service Discovery Protocol (DLSDP) is proposed in this paper. In this protocol, all the online vehicles are classified into three categories, the distributed directory service vehicles, the gateway vehicles and the member vehicles. The vehicles in the region of interest are organized as one or multiple spanning trees, of which the roots are chosen to be the leader vehicles that implement the function of service discovery in that interest region. The role of each vehicle and the spanning trees are refreshed for every location-based request to avoid keeping these information. Regardless of the demanded service providers are found or not, each location-based request is replied by the corresponding leader vehicle accordingly within a short time slot. Compared with the classical Vehicular Information Transfer Protocol (VITP), the performances of DLSDP are much better both in success rate and average response latency for requests.

Keywords: Distributed · Location-based · Non-infrastructure Service · Service discovery · VANET

1 Introduction

With the rapid development of sensor and wireless communication technologies, it is possible to acquire a series of services in anytime at anywhere for the user of networks [1]. And most of the services are tightly associated with their locations, so that the Location-based Services (LBSs) are shipped [2]. As a continuously growing branch of LBS system, the Vehicular Ad-Hoc Network (VANET) plays an increasingly important role in our daily lives. Distinguished to the traditional fixed networks, the topology of a given VANET is dynamic and reconstructing frequently, where the requests generated by members is location depended yet.

Due to the VANET is a kind of typical dynamic self-organization mobile network in which vehicles are considered as network nodes [3,4], movement and self-organization are main characteristics of it. Movement means that the requested

© Springer International Publishing Switzerland 2015
G. Wang et al. (Eds.): ICA3PP 2015, Part I, LNCS 9528, pp. 50–63, 2015.
DOI: 10.1007/978-3-319-27119-4_4

services are associated with the fast-moving locations of both service providers and requesters, while the self-organization indicates that the whole network is not determinate. As the mobility in an early mobile network is far slower than that in VANETs and so does the reconstruction frequency of vehicles, the essential location-based services discovery protocol, such as the ad-hoc network does not fully compatibly support them. Thus, to investigate a dedicated protocol of services discovering in VANETs is obligatory. But currently, it is rare finding that to consider both of those characteristics in the researching of service discovery protocols. In this paper, a Distributed Location-based Service Discovery Protocol (DLSDP) for VANETs is proposed, which is designed as a protocol running on the non-infrastructure VANETs offering the service discovering, and it is also considered to be the fundamentals of a practical VANET.

This rest of this paper is organized as follows. In Sect. 2, we give a bird's eye overview of the related works. In Sect. 3, we propose the system model that is the objective of our research work. In Sect. 4, we present the algorithm of DLSDP, which is the mainly innovative portion of this work. We introduce the corresponding experiment and result in Sect. 5, and conclude this paper in Sect. 6.

2   Related Work

Recently, there is much more rapid improvement on the research of vehicular networks. Although most of these works mainly focused on the applications of safe and comfortable driving [3], these studies are essentially about of how to optimize the applications and protocols [5].

Ververidis arranged an investigation on the research in service advertising, discovery, and selection for mobile ad-hoc networks and related issues, and categorized service discovery architectures [6]. As a conclusion,to support those variable applications, the service discovery is one of the foundation stones of all of these related fields. The popular architectures of service discovery are directory-based, directory-less and the hybrid of them. Although researchers have not reached a general consensus on which architecture is better, as a well accepted view, a distributed directory-based architecture could be more efficient when facing very heavy work loadings. The basic criteria for evaluating the effectiveness of service discovery architectures are service availability and latency.

In practical projects, some protocols are deployed in mobile and vehicular networks. Take an overview of research works around the service discovery protocols associated with the locations, a series of related works have been proposed [4,7–11].

An adaptive, flexible and efficient discovery of services with dynamic bloom filter is proposed by Deepa [12]. By integrating the bloom filter and the distributed service directories, better performance in the scalability, the service discovery success ratio and the average response latency are achieved. This is a type of distributed directory-based protocol, which performs a theoretic way to optimize the success rate and response latency of such a protocol.

Dikaiakos proposed a location-based service discovery protocol that is proposed for inter-vehicle communication [7], in which the Vehicular Information

Transfer Protocol (VITP) protocol [13] is introduced in. The basic idea of this protocol is to forward the request to the Region of Interest (RI) according to the location information, then the peer vehicles inside the region pick-up the request and decide whether to reply it or to forward it. Until a reply generated, the corresponding request is terminated. Obviously, this distributed protocol could not be a generalized one because of a lot of restrict constraints on the condition of replies.

A roadside infrastructure based service discovery protocol relies on a cluster-based infrastructures is performed by Kaouther [8]. The service discovery efficiency could be improved by the diversity of channels, due to this is a network layer protocol. The request is replied by the infrastructures on the side of the road in the RI. All the communications in this network depend on the roadside infrastructures completely. To establish such a massive deployment will be difficult due to the expensive cost.

A on-demand cluster-base framework is proposed to organize the moving vehicles to be multiple adaptive short-lived clusters [11], and those vehicles could be heterogeneous. The framework constructs on-demand clusters of mobile smart devices, allowing for executing MPI, short-lived, parallel tasks. And this type of dynamic cluster based parallel processing offers significant reference to the DLSDP.

Besides these research works, a lot of other instructive research productions have reference significance. A fully dynamic service schemes is developed by Zhou to construct a general user-satisfaction model according to the network transmission mechanism [3]. The objective of this work is the media application that requires a mount of fairness, instead of a kind of general service. Luo presented a smart service scheduling algorithm for VANETs with intelligent middleware [5].

Generally, as the direction of future development, a non-infrastructure depending location-based service discovery protocol is researching focus [9,12].

3   Distributed System Model

To be the definition, the **requester** is the vehicle that requires the service provided by other vehicles in a certain RI, the **objective** is the service that depends on the corresponding location, and those vehicles who offer services are the **provider**. To associate the service and the location, the requester may discover the service providers inside the RI.

The system model we proposed is a distributed directory based service sharing model. Some of the elements in a certain network have the ability to store the index of the services, these nodes are called service directory provider. For the directory stores in a series of nodes, the distributed architecture has much better scalability. But as the ubiquitous problem to a distributed system, it is hard to maintain the coherence among all the distributed segments of the directory [6,10].

To be an essential model, the system architecture contains three types of elements. They are the **Service Directory Vehicle** (SDV), **the Gateway Vehicle** (GV) and **the Member Vehicle** (MV).

- **Service Directory Vehicle**

Each vehicle discovers the neighboring vehicles within one hop range and elects one vehicle to be the directory service element in the corresponding region. The directory service vehicle maintains an index that contains the services information provided by its neighbors. As the basic principle, a SDV only contains the service information of the vehicles that are around it in a short range, that is why the model is called a **distributed** one.

- **Gateway Vehicle**

Once a vehicle has multiple service directories, this vehicle plays the role of gateway vehicle. The gateway vehicle bridges other SDVs, so that the services information could be shared over the entire network.

- **Member Vehicle**

The member vehicle by which the request is generated or the service is provided is the general node in this network.

A snapshot of this system is shown in Fig. 1, different colors identify the SDV, the GV and the MV. Any vehicle in the road is a MV, and this is the initial state for every mobile. Only if a MV needs to request a location based service, the vehicle will lead to the special procedures to change its own role.

As the prerequisite, to explore the connection between the demanded services and the corresponding location takes the first priority. In order to explore such relations, a range based model is referred [14]. For each of the location-based requests, a domain which indicates the valid range of this request is attached. According to the valid range domain, the service provider is able to determinate whether the received request should be acknowledged or not.

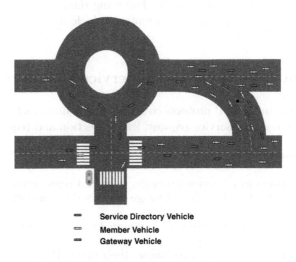

- Service Directory Vehicle
- Member Vehicle
- Gateway Vehicle

Fig. 1. System model

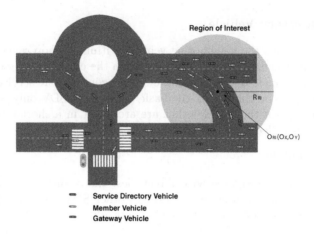

Fig. 2. Region of interest

Figure 2 gives an example of this scenario. A circular region is defined as a RI. The center coordinator is $O_{RI}(O_x, O_y)$ and the radius is R_{RI}. In the proposed model, this RI is expressed in $A(O_{RI}, R_{RI})$. And for each of the vehicle within the RI, the distance to the center is D_O.

The advantages of this architecture are obviously. Base on this architecture, any request is tightly binding with its RI and only the service provider inside the corresponding RI may reply the request. With this mechanism, service discovery is limited in a limited local scope. The global flooding and redundant reply are both avoided [11].

Besides the range request, the greedy routing strategy [14–16] is also deployed in this model. Every node forwards its package to one of its one-hop neighbors who is the closest one to the destination. Following the rules, the service request package could be transferred to the destination vehicle in unicast mode without further cost.

4   Distributed Location-Based Service Discovery Protocol

The entire process in DLSDP protocol could be broken down as four phases, and those are service register, service request, leader election and request reply.

- Service Register

When a vehicle plays as a service provider, it should register its services to its local SDV. The service registration message is defined as the follows:

$$< ProviderID, ProviderCoordinate, TimeStamp, LifePeriod, ServiceProperty >$$

where the meaning of other domains follows their name. Periodic register is necessary due to the service index is not a long-term ticket. The domain $LifePeriod$

is applied to define the service valid time. If a service provider does not refresh its registration index, the corresponding items in its directory would be discarded. The process in MV and SDV are different. The Algorithm 1 gives the detailed process of service register phase. V_i is a general vehicle in the proposed model, and S_i is the vehicle who plays the roles a SDV.

Algorithm 1. Algorithm of Service Register

PROTOCOL RUNNING AT THE VEHICLE V_i

Case A. V_i provides a location-based service that needs to be registered
Step A0 V_i sends the registration information of service to the local SDV periodically, ensuring the service to be updated timely

---

PROTOCOL RUNNING AT THE SDV S_i

Case D. S_i Receives a service registration message from a vehicle
Step D0 S_i append or update its own service information directory

---

- Service Request

As what has been shown in Fig. 3, when a requester requires the service provided by another vehicle, the vehicle (plays the role as a MV) will generate a service request that contains the information of the RI. In this protocol, the format of service request message is as below:

$$< ServiceType, ServiceName, ServiceParameter, A(O_{RI}, R_{RI}), D_O, LifePeriod >$$

It has been referred that each SDV groups its neighbors as a local sub-network. So, once a MV requests a certain LBS, it sends the request to its local SDV. For this SDV, it has two choices upon a service request. If the coordinate of this SDV is not inside the RI, the request should be forwarded. A greedy routing strategy is applied for this issue. The request is forwarding to the next GV within a one hop range. Until the request reaches the destination RI, which means a SDV inside the RI has got the request, the vehicle will initiate a leader election procedure. The leader election procedure will be described in detailed in the next segment. Algorithm 2 shows the formal statements of this phase. For vehicle V_i and S_i, define the coordinators of them are (V_{ix}, V_{iy}) and (S_{ix}, S_{iy}).

- Leader Election

This is a SDV related only phase. If a request reaches a SDV in the purposed RI, the vehicle initiates a leader election. The leader election is an atomic operation. As the result of this phase, all the vehicles in this operation has two status, the one is leading and the other is following. Leading means the SDV is elected to be the leader for this request in this RI, and the following indicates the vehicle is a

Algorithm 2. Algorithm of Service Request

PROTOCOL RUNNING AT THE VEHICLE V_i

Case B. V_i requests a LBS
Step B0 V_i generates a LBS request message, and sends the message to the SDV
    inside its scope
Step B1 Wait for a predetermined period of time
if Step B2 service reply message received **then**
    Step B2.0 GOTO Step C0
elseStep B2.1 Exit: Service not found
end if
Case C. V_i receive a LBS request message
Step C0 V_i checks whether it is inside the requested RI $A(O_{RI}, R_{RI})$
if Step C1 $(V_{ix} - O_x)^2 + (V_{iy} - O_y)^2 \geq R_{RI}^2$ **then**
    Step C1.0 V_i ignores the request due to it is not inside the demanded RI
else if Step C2 $(V_{iy} - O_x)^2 + (V_{iy} - O_y)^2 < R_{RI}^2$ **then**
    Step C2.0 generates the reply message to the local SDV
end if

PROTOCOL RUNNING AT THE SDV S_i

Case F. S_i receives a LBS request message
Step F0 S_i checks whether it is inside the requested RI $A(O_{RI}, R_{RI})$.
if Step F1 $(S_{ix} - O_x)^2 + (S_{iy} - O_y)^2 \geq R_{RI}^2$ **then**
    Step F1.0 choose a neighboring GV as next hop using greedy forwarding strategy,
        and forward message to it
else if Step F2 $(S_{ix} - O_x)^2 + (S_{iy} - O_y)^2 < R_{RI}^2$ **then**
    Step F2.0 S_i is inside the RI, start the election phase
    Step F2.1 S_i checks its current state
    Step F2.2 S_i suspends the maintenance phase of the SDV
    if Step F2.3 S_i is not in processing state, nor in leader state, nor in follower state
        then
        Step F2.3.0 S_i generates an election message
        Step F2.3.1 S_i includes its distance to the origin of RI in the election message
            and its knowledge about the requested service
        Step F2.3.2 propagate election message to the neighboring SDV
        Step F2.3.3 S_i becomes in the state processing state
        Step F2.3.4 S_i wait for the result of Leader Election procedure
    end if
end if

node who provides the directory service but is not the leader in this region. The
vehicle who initiates the election operation should send an election message of
which whose ID code and D_O is included to its neighboring SDVs. Any vehicle
who receives the election message will enter the processing state at once. After a
shot time slot, the vehicle becomes the leader only if there is no other neighboring
SDVs who received the election message closer to the center of RI. Meanwhile,
the other SDVs are the followers. Figures 4 and 5 show the election procedure.

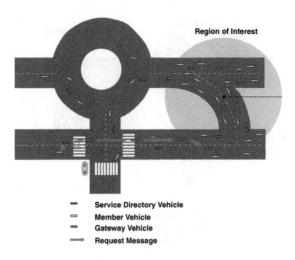

Fig. 3. Service request

In this RI, there are three SDVs. When a LBS request reaches, an election message will be broadcast among these SDVs. When the election finish, the SDV which is closest to the center of RI is the leader vehicle.

Among all of a SDV's neighboring SDVs, the one closest to the center of RI is the father node of the spanning tree. When the election operation finishes, there is at least one spanning tree which covers all the SDVs in RI. And the root of each spanning tree is a leader vehicle.

Observing these spanning tree, all the non-leaf nodes are SDVs, including leader vehicles, and all the leaf nodes are MVs who provide a certain of services. When a request has been sent to its target region, the trace of the request

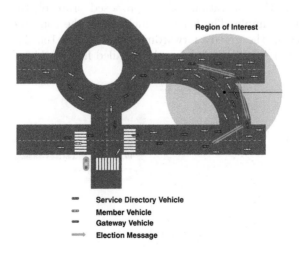

Fig. 4. Leader election

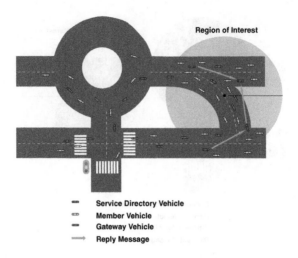

Service Directory Vehicle
Member Vehicle
Gateway Vehicle
Reply Message

Fig. 5. Election reply

and reply messages follow the tracks in Fig. 6. There might be multiple service providers who can deliver the same service, and there might be multiple replies consequently. An important function of leader vehicle is to converge those replies and release a merged single reply to the source of that request.

Algorithm 3 describes the election phase in details.

There is no need to store the information such as leader, follower and spanning tree, due to those vehicles are fast moving. Our protocol is designed to elect the leader and span that spanning tree for every single service request.

• Request Reply

Comparing with other operations of the proposed protocol, the request reply phase is relatively simple. The leader vehicle sends the converged reply to the requester following the greedy forwarding strategy [14–16]. This operation is given in Fig. 7 and Algorithm 4 shows the detailed flow of this phase.

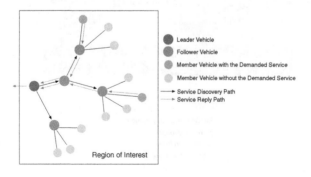

Fig. 6. Message trace in RI

Algorithm 3. Algorithm of Leader Election

PROTOCOL RUNNING AT THE SDV S_i

Case H. S_i receives an election message from its father SDV
if Step H0 S_i is inside the RI **then**
    Step H0.0 S_i checks its current state
    Step H0.1 S_i suspends the maintenance phase
    if Step H0.2 S_i is not in processing state, nor in leader state, nor in follower state
    then
        Step H0.2.0 S_i generates an election message
        Step H0.2.1 S_i includes its distance to the origin of RI in the election message
           and its acknowledgement about the requested service
        Step H0.2.2 propagate election message to the neighboring SDVs
        Step H0.2.3 S_i becomes in the processing state
    end if
end if

Case I. for each of the election period P
Step I0 S_i checks its current state
if Step I1 current state is processing state **then**
    if Step I1.0 S_i has the minimum distance to the origin of RI **then**
        Step I1.0.0 S_i enters leader state
    else if Step I1.1 S_i connects its parent SDV that is closest to the origin of RI
    then
        Step I1.1.0 S_i enters follower state
        Step I1.1.1 S_i sends its acknowledgement about the requested service to its
           parent in a local service reply message
    elseS_i S_i enters leader state
    end if
end if

Algorithm 4. Algorithm of Request Reply

PROTOCOL RUNNING AT THE SDV S_i

Case J. S_i is in the leader state and receives all local replies from its children
Step J0 S_i converges the local replies and generates a single reply
Step J1 send the service reply message

PROTOCOL RUNNING AT THE VEHICLE V_i

Case K. V_i receives a service reply
if Step K0 V_i is the service requester **then**
    Step K0.0 store service provider information
    Step K0.1 establish the connection with the provider
elseStep K1 choose a neighboring vehicle as next hop using greedy forwarding strat-
    egy, and forward message to it
end if

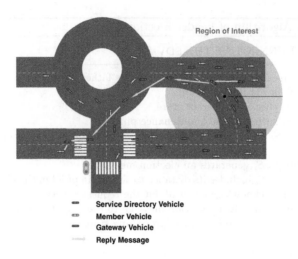

Fig. 7. Request reply

5 Simulation Results

In this section, a Matlab based experiment is designed to verify the proposed DLSDP protocol. And we implement the DLSDP protocol in the application layer in this experiment. The experimental scenario is set at a cross of a general road, which is given in the former figures in this paper [7]. As the pre-set parameters, the density of vehicles is uniform distributed and the mean value is ρ, the speed of each vehicle is in the range from $5\,\text{m/s}$ to $15\,\text{m/s}$, and the communication range is $100\,\text{m}$ that is also the 'one-hop' range. To be a probability event, the probability of straight moving of a certain vehicle is $50\,\%$, and the probability of left turn and right turn are both $25\,\%$ respectively.

The merits of such kind of protocols could be evaluated in success rate and average response latency of a dozen of requests. The success rate is the percentage of success replied requests against the total requests in a given period. And the average response latency expresses the time consuming for a number of success replied requests. These merits are all recognized and described in Sect. 2.

As a reference, VITP also provides a similar method [7]. Compared with DLSDP, VITP is consists of three phases: query phase, compute phase and reply phase. In query phase, a request is forwarded to its destination and received by a service provider. Then the Virtual Ad-Hoc Server (VAHS) resolves the request and finds a proper service provider in the compute phase. Once a preset condition is meet, the VAHS delivers the reply in this reply phase.

For the preset condition, the count of service providers who provide the same service is set to be 1, 5 or 10 in the experiment, respectively. And the count of requesters is in the range from 10 to 100 while the simulation step is 10.

Figure 8 gives the comparison between VITP and DLSDP on success rate. It is in the case that all the 10 service providers are inside the RI in Fig. 8a. The curve $VITPcnt = 1$ represents that the reply condition is meet if just one

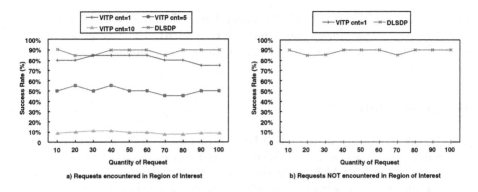

Fig. 8. Success rate vs request quantity

service provider has been discovered. Similarly, the curve $VITPcnt = 5$ and $VITPcnt = 10$ represent the reply condition is five and ten service providers have been found, respectively. The result shows that DLSDP is better than VITP on success rate. Only in terms of VITP, the success rate is inverse proportional to the reply condition, because it is more difficult to find more service providers. Figure 8b is in the case that there is no demanded service provider in RI. In VITP, there would be no reply message because the reply condition could be satisfied impossibly. By contrast, the reply is released by leader vehicle in DLSDP. The reply message will be delivered after a time slot, even there is no demanded service provider in RI. Therefore, the success rate of DLSDP is much higher than that of VITP even there is no service could be discovered.

Figure 9 is the comparison on average response latency between VITP and DLSDP protocols. Figure 9a is in the case of that all ten service providers are in the area of RI. The meanings of $VITPcnt = 1$, $VITPcnt = 5$ and $VITPcnt = 10$ are the same to that in Fig. 8. According to the curves, the average response latency in VITP is inverse proportional to the condition, and the

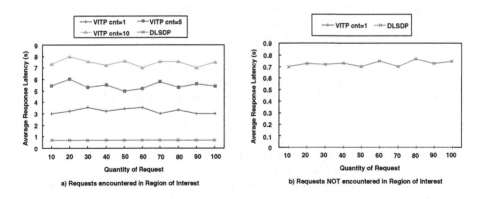

Fig. 9. Average response latency vs request quantity

average response latency of DLSDP is much shorter than that of VITP. Figure 9b is in the case of that there is no required service in RI. The average latency in DLSDP is better than that in VITP, and the reason is similar to that of the success rate.

6   Conclusion

For the VANETs, to discovery the LBS is a precondition for almost all of the location-based applications. The location-based service discovery is one of the foundation stones of VANETs. In this paper, the DLSDP is proposed to offer the non-infrastructure service. Generally, as the two key performance indicators, success rate and average response latency represent the performance of service discovery protocols. The proposed DLSDP is far beyond the widely used reference VITP on both of these performances.

Acknowledgements. This work is partially supported by Program for New Century Excellent Talents in University (NCET-12-0164); National Natural Science Foundation of China (61370094); Natural Science Foundation of Hunan (13JJ1014).

References

1. Al-Sultan, S., Al-Doori, M.M., Al-Bayatti, A.H., Zedan, H.: A comprehensive survey on vehicular ad hoc network. J. Netw. Comput. Appl. **37**, 380–392 (2014)
2. D'Roza, T., Bilchev, G.: An overview of location-based services. BT Technol. J. **21**(1), 20–27 (2003)
3. Zhou, L., Zhang, Y., Song, K., Jing, W., Vasilakos, A.V.: Distributed media services in p2p-based vehicular networks. IEEE Trans. Veh. Technol. **60**(2), 692–703 (2011)
4. Dolev, S., Gilbert, S., Lynch, N.A., Schiller, E.M., Shvartsman, M.M.A.A., Welch, J.L.: Virtual mobile nodes for mobile ad hoc networks. In: Guerraoui, R. (ed.) DISC 2004. LNCS, vol. 3274, pp. 230–244. Springer, Heidelberg (2004)
5. Luo, J., Jin, X., Wu, F.: Service scheduling algorithm in vehicle embedded middleware. In: Sun, X., Qu, W., Stojmenovic, I., Zhou, W., Li, Z., Guo, H., Min, G., Yang, T., Wu, Y., Liu, L. (eds.) ICA3PP 2014, Part II. LNCS, vol. 8631, pp. 96–107. Springer, Heidelberg (2014)
6. Ververidis, C., Polyzos, G.: Service discovery for mobile ad hoc networks: a survey of issues and techniques. IEEE Commun. Surv. Tutorials **10**(3), 30–45 (2008)
7. Dikaiakos, M., Florides, A., Nadeem, T., Iftode, L.: Location-aware services over vehicular ad-hoc networks using car-to-car communication. IEEE J. Sel. Areas Commun. **25**(8), 1590–1602 (2007)
8. Abrougui, K., Boukerche, A., Pazzi, R.: Design and evaluation of context-aware and location-based service discovery protocols for vehicular networks. IEEE Trans. Intell. Transp. Syst. **12**(3), 717–735 (2011)
9. Lenders, V., May, M., Plattner, B.: Service discovery in mobile ad hoc networks: a field theoretic approach. In: Sixth IEEE International Symposium on a World of Wireless Mobile and Multimedia Networks (WoWMoM), pp. 120–130. IEEE (2005)

10. Vodopivec, S., Bester, J., Kos, A.: A survey on clustering algorithms for vehicular ad-hoc networks. In: 2012 35th International Conference on Telecommunications and Signal Processing (TSP), pp. 52–56. IEEE (2012)
11. El-Mahdy, A., El-Shishiny, H., Algizawy, E.: Smart traffic framework based on dynamic mobile clusters. In: 2014 IEEE 3rd International Conference on Cloud Networking (CloudNet), pp. 468–474. IEEE (2014)
12. Deepa, R., Swamynathan, S.: The DBF-based semantic service discovery for mobile ad hoc networks. Can. J. Electr. Comput. Eng. **36**(3), 123–134 (2013)
13. Dikaiakos, M.D., Iqbal, S., Nadeem, T., Iftode, L.: VITP: an information transfer protocol for vehicular computing. In: Proceedings of the 2nd ACM International Workshop on Vehicular Ad Hoc Networks, pp. 30–39. ACM (2005)
14. Karp, B., Kung, H.T.: GPSR: Greedy perimeter stateless routing for wireless networks. In: Proceedings of the 6th Annual International Conference on Mobile Computing and Networking, pp. 243–254. ACM (2000)
15. Biomo, J.D.M.M., Kunz, T., St-Hilaire, M.: Routing in unmanned aerial ad hoc networks: a recovery strategy for greedy geographic forwarding failure. In: Wireless Communications and Networking Conference (WCNC), pp. 2236–2241. IEEE (2014)
16. Nguyen, N.D., Nguyen, D.T., Le Gall, M.A., Saxena, N., Choo, H.: Greedy forwarding with virtual destination strategy for geographic routing in wireless sensor networks. In: 2010 International Conference on Computational Science and Its Applications (ICCSA), pp. 217–221. IEEE (2010)
17. Turowski, K., Pousttchi, K.: Location based services. Mobile Commerce: Grundlagen und Techniken, pp. 73–80. Springer, Heidelberg (2004)
18. Kumar, N., Pathan, A.S.K., Duarte Jr, E.P., Shaikh, R.A.: Critical applications in vehicular ad hoc/sensor networks. Telecommun. Syst. **58**(4), 275–277 (2014)

Unified Virtual Memory Support for Deep CNN Accelerator on SoC FPGA

Tao Xiao[1,2]($\boxtimes$), Yuran Qiao[1,2], Junzhong Shen[1,2],
Qianming Yang[1,2], and Mei Wen[1,2]

[1] College of Computer, National University of Defense Technology,
Changsha 410073, China
xiaotao_nudt@sina.com, qiaoyuran@foxmail.com,
{shenjunzhong,yqm21249,wenmei}@nudt.edu.cn
[2] National Key Laboratory of Parallel and Distributed Processing,
National University of Defense Technology, Changsha 410073, China

Abstract. Cooperation of CPU and hardware accelerator on SoC FPGA to accomplish computational intensive tasks, provides significant advantages in performance and energy efficiency. However, current operating systems provide little support for accelerators: the OS is unaware that a computational task can be executed either on a CPU core or an accelerator, and provides no assistance in efficient management of data sharing between CPU and accelerator on the DRAM, such as zero copy, data coherence. It's also hard for current OS to allocate large contiguous physical memory space for accelerator. In this paper, we select the Xilinx ZYNQ as target and qualitatively analyze methods of sharing data. Besides using high-performance (HP) AXI interfaces of the ZYQN device, we develop a novel memory management system for FPGA-based accelerator. It provides a unified virtual space for CPU cores and accelerator so that they can access the same memory space in the operating systems user space. For a deep convolutional neural network task, our design gains up to speed-up of 5.34x compared to traditional processor-accelerator cooperation.

Keywords: Unified virtual memory · Coherence · SoC · Deep CNN · Accelerator

1 Introduction

As the energy efficiency requirement of silicon chips are growing exponentially, computer architects are seeking solutions to continue application performance scaling. An emerging solution is to use specialized functional units (such as accelerators) at different levels of a heterogeneous architecture which provides enhanced execution speed and power efficiency for specific computational workloads [1,2]. At present, in the heterogeneous architecture system, Soc FPGA has become the mainstream in the field of FPGA. SoC FPGA is composed with a hard core processor system and FPGA fabric. SoC FPGA based accelerators

© Springer International Publishing Switzerland 2015
G. Wang et al. (Eds.): ICA3PP 2015, Part I, LNCS 9528, pp. 64–76, 2015.
DOI: 10.1007/978-3-319-27119-4_5

have attracted more and more attention of researchers because they have advantages of good performance, high energy efficiency, fast development round, and capability of reconfiguration. Examples include Canny edge detection hardware accelerator [3], Sobel Filter hardware accelerator [4] and deep neural networks hardware accelerator [5,6], the operating system on the hard core manages the use of accelerator.

However, efficiently sharing of data in a SoC FPGA which contains different types of integrated computational elements is a challenging task. Current OS provides no assistance in efficient management of data sharing between CPU cores and accelerator on the DRAM, such as zero copy, data coherence. It's also difficult for current OS to allocate large contiguous physical memory space (for example, $\geq 32\,\mathrm{MB}$ or bigger) for accelerator.

In the previous work of our research group, based on a typical SoC FPGA-the Xilinx ZYNQ device, we have designed a deep convolutional neural network (CNN) accelerator. And we port a typical deep CNN framework, Caffe [7], to the accelerator system. The Caffe framework relies on many libraries of Linux, and in order to relieve the difficult of transplanting application on the hardware computation units, we install Linux operating system (kernel vision 3.14) on the ARM CPU of ZYNQ device. Thus, Caffe application can directly run on the device, and the bottleneck of data sharing is obvious. To use bandwidth efficiently, continuous accessing is preferred for deep CNN accelerator. In the Linux operating system, we can allocate large contiguous physical memory space in the kernel space for the accelerator. Normally, the maximum size we can allocate is 4096KB (using `get_free_pages` or `dma_alloc_coherent` function, and sometimes the allocation may fail) [8]. Obviously, it's not enough for the accelerator which faces big data computation.

In this paper, we focus on efficient management of data sharing between CPU cores and accelerator in SoC FPGA, and propose a unified virtual memory management system for the case deep CNN. On the view of CPU and accelerator, there is a unified virtual memory for them to share data. The main contributions of our work are summarized as follows:

- According CNN's storage requirement, we assign a portion of memory (named accelerator memory) for the accelerator specially so that the accelerator can use large contiguous physical memory space. And through mapping the accelerator memory to user space, we can avoid data copying between accelerator memory and host memory.
- We propose a strategy for data coherence between CPU and accelerator and implement it in software.
- We implement our method to our accelerator system on the Xilinx ZYNQ device with PetaLinux v2014.2. The result shows that through sharing virtual space, our method has a highest speed-up of 5.34x compared to traditional processor-accelerator cooperation for CNN kernels which execute on the accelerator.

The rest of the paper is organized as follows. Some background information is presented in Sect. 2. The system architecture proposed in this paper is described

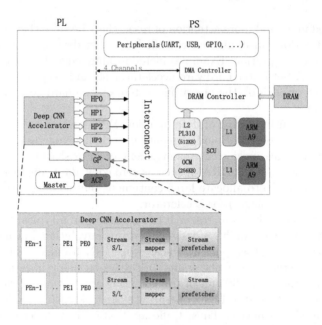

Fig. 1. A block diagram representing important elements of the Xilinx ZYNQ device. The deep CNN accelerator will be introduced in the Sect. 2.2

in Sect. 3. Section 4 presents experiment and evaluation of the method. Related work is surveyed in Sect. 5. Conclusions are offered in the Sect. 6.

2   Background

2.1   ZYNQ Architecture Description [9]

Xilinx ZYNQ device [10] contains two parts: 1-Programmable Logic (PL) which is roughly a complete FPGA fabric. 2-Programmable System (PS) which is a complete sub-system with ARM CPU cores and different peripherals [6]. A set of AXI interfaces (as shown in Fig. 1) are implemented to make the communication between PS and the PL logic possible. Basically these AXI interfaces divide into three groups:

- AXI_HP interfaces, provide PL bus masters with high bandwidth datapaths to the DRAM and OCM memories. The PL to memory interconnect routes the high-speed AXI_HP ports to two DRAM memory ports or the OCM. The AXI_HP interfaces are also referenced as AFI (AXI FIFO interface), to emphasize their buffering capabilities.
- AXI_GP interfaces, are connected directly to the ports of the master interconnect and the slave interconnect. The performance is constrained by the ports of the master and slave interconnect. These interfaces are for general-purpose use only and are not intended to achieve high performance.

– AXI_ACP interface, provides low-latency access to programmable logic masters, with optional coherency with L1 and L2 cache. This 64-bit AXI interface allows the PL to implement an AXI master that can access the L2 and OCM while maintaining memory coherency with the CPU L1 caches.

There exists a defined memory map for the ZYNQ device [10] which indicates the address range of each logic block. Every AXI slave unit, implemented on the PL will also occupy a part of this address range. It should be noted that except the CPU cores and their L1 instruction caches, the rest of the system is using physical address values.

2.2 Deep CNN Accelerator

Convolutional neural network (CNN), a well-known deep learning architecture extended from artificial neural network, has been extensively adopted in various applications, which include video surveillance, mobile robot vision, image search engine in data centers [11,12]. Inspired by the behavior of optic nerves in living creatures, a CNN design processes data with multiple layers of neuron connections to achieve high accuracy in image recognition. As a classical supervised learning algorithm, CNN employs a feedforward process for recognition and a backward path for training. The speed of feedforward computation is what our concerned with.

We port a representative deep CNN framework Caffe [7], and take the well known model, ImageNet1000, proposed by Krizhevsky et al. [13] as research case. Every time, 64 images are classified as a minibatch. The kernel of the forward process is composed with five stages, as shown in Fig. 2, we named them from stage 1 to stage 5. Stage 1 is composed with three layers: convolution layer, relu layer and pool layer, the same with stage 2 and stage 5 while stage 3 and stage 4 have only convolution layer and relu layer. Convolution layer is running on the CNN accelerator in data parallel level while relu layer and pool layer are executed on the CPU. Relu layer and pool layer will use the results of the convolution layer.

Figure 1 shows a block diagram of the deep CNN accelerator system on the ZYNQ device. Since the workload of the forward computation exists in the convolution layers, our accelerator target on the convolution layers. The accelerator architecture consists of four chains, each chain consists of one stream-prefetcher unit, one stream-mapper unit, one stream-S/L unit and several PEs (Processing elements). Stream-prefetcher unit is used to make the address stream to external memory contiguously. Stream-mapper unit is designed to handle the convolution unrolling task. Stream S/L unit and PE units are used for matrix multiplication. Because the processed data (as shown in Fig. 2) are bigger than the size of available cache (512 KB), or on-chip memory (128 KB) [10], then we select *HP Only* method (The accelerator located on HP port is responsible to perform the processing kernel alone) as memory sharing mechanism. And there is only one ACP port while there are four HP ports, HP port is the best choice when the accelerator has not only one chain. Thus, in our accelerator processing

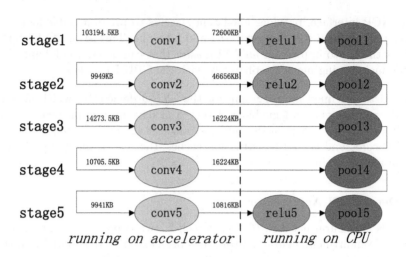

Fig. 2. The data flow diagram of Caffe. We have not concerned the full connection layers in this paper, and in order to reduce the executing time, we have remove the norm layer from the framework.

system, the PE chains are connected by a memory interface, the HP port, as shown in Fig. 1. The host CPU and the HP ports are interconnected by system bus, more specifically, both of them follow AXI protocol and shared the same physical memory space.

3   Accelerator Memory Management Design and Implementation

Our memory management system is developed as Linux kernel level driver, and the driver manages the CNN accelerator located on HP port. The driver is responsible for:

– Memory allocation and obtaining the physical address of allocated memory which will be used by CNN accelerator. Memory can be allocated in either cacheable or non-cacheable.
– Initializing, programming and triggering the CNN accelerator and handling the interrupts generated by it.
– Configuration the computation tasks on the CNN accelerator: assigning tasks and then executing the tasks on the computation units of CNN accelerator.
– Calculating the source and destination addresses for the CNN accelerator based on the status of the ongoing processing tasks.
– Interaction with user-level applications: receiving input data from user side, computation and then writing back the processed results to user-level.

In the kernel level driver, we cut a porting of memory and allocate contiguous physical memory for accelerator, we solve the data sharing problem through developing a unified virtual space and also keep coherent through flushing or invalidating cache. The detail information is described as follows:

3.1 Date Sharing in Unified Virtual Space

Since the CPU cores and accelerator share a single physical DRAM, and OS supports a virtual space, we cut a portion of memory for accelerator access (R/W) specially. Because the memory resources are very precious in the Linux operating system, thus the accelerator memory size should be suitable. We first profile the Caffe program, look out the part which we want to accelerate, and calculate the size of the data which should be stored in the accelerator memory. In the Linux boot time, we use *"mem=size"* to reserve the top of memory for accelerator and the *size* is accelerator memory's size.

And there will be one problem needed to solve: How to translate the date to the accelerator memory in the Linux operating system. Because of the Linux memory management system cannot manage the accelerator memory, when the application needs to use the accelerator, the data cannot be initialized in the user space. The data should firstly copy from user space to kernel space, as shown in the Fig. 3(a), then initialize the data in the accelerator memory so that the accelerator can access to the contiguous physical memory. But, it wastes much time when copying data.

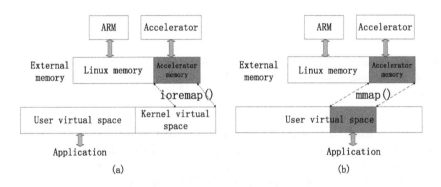

Fig. 3. Initialization of data for the accelerator

In order to realize zero copy between user space and kernel space, we use mmap function to build page table for accelerator memory, as shown in the Fig. 3(b), so that application can access to the accelerator memory through virtual address in the user space. And accelerator also can get physical address from the virtual address. In a word, CPU and accelerator can have a unified virtual memory view on the accelerator memory. In the process of mapping, we can map cacheable or non-cacheable. While mapping non-cacheable, application processes can write the data directly into the accelerator memory and accelerator can get the new data every time. But it will cause performance loss when CPU want to use the data in the accelerator memory to compute. When mapping cacheable, there will be coherent problem between CPU and accelerator, this will be discussed in Sect. 3.2.

As we known, memory management is a technology of allocation and use of memory resources when software running. In the accelerator memory, we use a linked list to manage the memory. The data which accelerator needed will be stored at accelerator memory. The request of memory is regarded as inserting a node in the linked list, and the free of memory is regarded as deleting a node in the linked list. The relationship of memory and linked list is showed as Fig. 4.

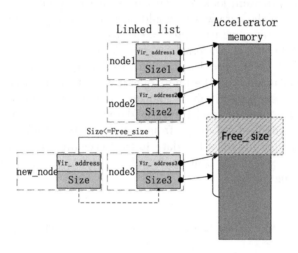

Fig. 4. Management of accelerator memory. The node of linked list is composed with virtual address and memory size, virtual address represents the starting address of the allocation memory.

When we want to allocate a contiguous physical memory space for accelerator, we call our own memory allocation function. In the allocation function, it traverses the list, if $Size \leq Free\_size$, we will insert the node in the linked list; else, we will add the node at the last of the linked list. The allocating function will return a virtual address. CPU can use the virtual address to access the accelerator memory, and accelerator can get the physical address through virtual address subtracting an offset. With this allocation strategy, it would cause fragmentation issues on applications which require executing various tasks on different times, but the current implementations of programming models do not create such tasks or handle the resources this way.

3.2 Keep Coherent Between CPU and Accelerator

Since CPU and the accelerator share a single physical DRAM, when mapping accelerator memory to user space cacheable, it causes data coherence problem in the cooperation of CPU and accelerator.

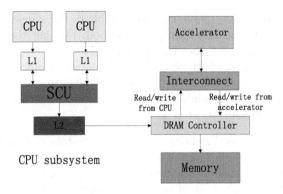

Fig. 5. A coherence architecture

Figure 5 shows the architecture of a typical embedded system needing to keep coherent. One or more CPUs, each with an L1 cache, are connected to a snoop control unit responsible for maintaining coherence between CPU's L1 caches. And L2 cache is shared among CPUs, but accelerator doesn't access the L2. The L2 cache and accelerator are connected to the memory via DRAM controller. In this system, the hardware maintains coherence between the CPUs, software must keep the L1 and L2 caches coherent with the accelerator, because the caches have no knowledge of the reads and writes between accelerator and DRAM.

Accelerator follows AXI protocol and connects accelerator memory directly without L1 cache and L2 cache between them, thus it can read/store data from accelerator memory directly through physical address. But for host processor, when it wants to load data from memory, it will find if the data is in the cache firstly. If in, it load the data from the cache directly; if not in, it will load the data from the memory. When it wants to store data, the data may not write to memory directly but in cache, thus we cannot get the data through physical address without doing something else.

Because we map the accelerator memory to the user space cacheable, when host processor initializes the accelerator memory through virtual address, some data may not write to physical space but in cache. Then, accelerator may not get the data needed. And when accelerator writes data to physical address, host processor may access to the wrong data in cache. In order to keep host processor-accelerator coherence, we should flush the cache or invalidate the cache at the right time. When accelerator wants to load the data after host processor initialization, we should flush the cache first so that all the data can write to the relevant physical address; if host processor wants to load the data handed by accelerator, we should invalidate the cache so that host processor cannot get the old data.

Process can conclude into the following steps:

- In step 1, host processor writes the data needed by accelerator into accelerator memory, the L1 cache, or the L2 cache.

- In step 2, host processor makes the data visible to the accelerator by forcing the data into main memory using this method: flushing the newly written data from all L1 and L2 caches via system API.
- In step 3, accelerator reads the data from accelerator memory, completes the computation and writes the result to the accelerator memory.
- Finally, host processor invalidates the cache of result data and reads result from accelerator memory in step 4.

But when we flush or invalidate cache with system call in the operating system, we find it no use because it doesn't flush or invalidate L2 cache. From [10], we know that L2 cache is regarded as an external device in the operating system and there are some control registers to control it. In the driver, we map the control registers to the kernel virtual space, and through assignment, we can flush or invalidate the L2 cache. In a word, before accelerator working, we flush the cache needed, and after accelerator done the work, we invalidate the cache needed, so that, we can keep host processor and accelerator coherence.

4   Experimental Results

In our work, we use the PetaLinux tools [14] provided by Xilinx to construct the embedded system. PetaLinux Tools provide a simple and fast method to build and deploy Linux-based software on Xilinx Zynq-7000 APSoC and MicroBlaze devices. We have implemented the accelerator on the ZYNQ XC7Z045 device (refer to Table 1) and port the Linux operating system on it. In the experimental work, we consider the case described in Sect. 2.2 and evaluate the performance of the proposed method.

Table 1. Information of Xilinx Board

Chip	Xilinx Zynq XC7Z045 SoC
Processor	2 ARM Cortex-A9 @800 MHz
Programmable Logic	Kintex-7
Memory	1 GB DDR3 @ 533 MHz
Memory bandwidth	3.8 GB/s full-duplex
Accelerator frequency	111 MHz

First, we compare the difference between mapping accelerator memory to kernel space and mapping accelerator memory to user space. We take the convolution layer of every stage from the Caffe application, and test the executing time of every convolution layer separately in different method. Figure 6 shows the testing results. It can be seen that the executing time of using mapping to kernel space is more than using mapping to user space for different convolution layer. The reason is that mapping accelerator memory to kernel space method needs to

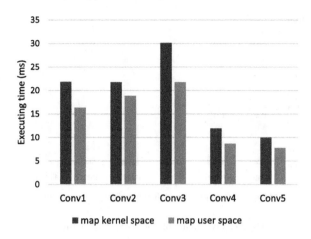

Fig. 6. The executing time of different mapping methods

copy data from user space to kernel space while mapping accelerator memory to user space method not need. And convolution layer 3 costs the more time than any other convolution layer, and the executing time of different method has the biggest difference because the convolution layer 3 has the biggest computation and needs to copy more data.

Then, we use the convolutional neural network accelerator to accelerate the kernel of CNN in two different conditions. One is that mapping the accelerator memory to the user space cacheable (labelled with *user-cacheable*); the other one is that mapping the accelerator memory to the user space non-cacheable (labelled with *user-non-cacheable*). In the test, we execute the full application in the embedded operating system and record the executing time of different layers in different stages. Table 2 presents the executing time of the different layers using different methods.

It can be seen that when we map the accelerator memory to the user space cacheable, the execution time of every stage is less than mapping non-cacheable. The execution time of conv layer in *user-cacheable* method is larger than in *user-non-cacheable* method, because in *user-cacheable* method, program needs additional flush operation to maintain coherence. The execution time of relu layer and pool layer in *user-cacheable* method is smaller than in *user-non-cacheable* method. Compared with *user-non-cacheable* method, stage 1 has the highest speed-up of 5.34x while stage 3 has the lowest speed-up of 1.39x. Therefore, compared with mapping to user space non-cacheable, we should map the accelerator memory to the user space cacheable.

Figure 7 shows the overhead of additional data preparation time, flush time and invalidation time of every stage in the total time when using the accelerator in the Caffe application. About 10 % of the total time is cost in average. It can be seen that stage 4 has the most of the additional overhead while stage 1 is the least one. In the additional overhead, flushing and invalidating cache

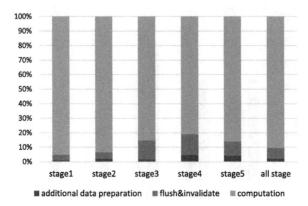

Fig. 7. Overhead of the execution time

Table 2. The executing time(ms) of different parts of kernel in the Caffe

Method	user-cacheable				user-non-cacheable				Speed-up
	conv	relu	pool	**total**	conv	relu	pool	**total**	
stage 1	2303	1203	2125	**5631**	1893	9247	18922	**30062**	5.34x
stage 2	5155	426	1007	**6588**	4785	4242	11617	**20644**	3.13x
stage 3	2781	152	0	**2933**	2613	1477	0	**4090**	1.39x
stage 4	2206	157	0	**2363**	2052	1485	0	**3537**	1.50x
stage 5	1974	107	238	**2319**	1837	985	2488	**5310**	2.29x

take up most of the time in stage 3 and stage 4, the percentage of flushing and invalidating is about 13 %.

5   Related Work

In order to solve data sharing problems between heterogeneous computation units, there were many works. AMD proposes heterogeneous uniform memory access (hUMA) in the Kaveri architecture [15]. It solves many problems in the cooperation of CPU and accelerator by modifying the underlying hardware design and instruction set. The CPU and accelerator share a single memory space and accelerator can directly access CPU memory address, allowing it to both read and write data that the CPU is also reading and writing. hUMA is also a cache coherent system, meaning that the CPU and accelerator will always see a consistent view of data in memory. Intel provides some support for shared memory on graphics through OpenCL and DirectX, but sharing is still limited to some simple cases as it missing pointer sharing, demand-based paging and true coherence in heterogeneous system architecture [16].

In [9], Sadri et al. quantified the advantages of using accelerate cache port (ACP) over the traditional method of sharing data on the DRAM. And derived the rule that if the task should be done by the hardware accelerator only (and then the CPU will just use the final result), when the processed array blocks are large, accelerator connecting through HP port always provides better results. But they are not implemented for real application. The problem of maintaining coherency between CPU caches and accelerator data in a multi-core embedded system is addressed in [17]. The paper discusses possible hardware architectures and related software solutions to tackle the problem. It concludes that the optimal solution heavily depends on the characteristics of the application. Paper [18] has described the first big.LITTLE system from ARM. The combination of a fully coherent system with Cortex-A15 and Cortex-A7 opens up new processing possibilities beyond what is possible in current high-performance mobile platforms. Koutras et al. in [19] studied memory allocations on a many-core accelerator, namely Platform 2012, and proposed a custom based memory management system to improve the performance of these operations because of the limited amount of resources.

6 Conclusion

In this paper, we develop a memory management system for the SoC FPGA-based accelerator. It provides a unified virtual memory view for CPU cores with Linux OS and accelerator. In addition, it maintains coherence between CPU and accelerator. We propose a strategy to allocate large contiguous physical memory space for requirement. The results for deep CNN is encouraging.

Acknowledgment. The authors gratefully acknowledge supports from National Nature Science Foundation of China under NSFC 61272145; National High Technology Research and Development Program of China (863 Program) under No. 2012AA012706; Research Fund for the Doctoral Program of Higher Education of China under SRFDP No. 20124307130004.

References

1. Cascaval, C., Chatterjee, S., Franke, H., Gildea, K., Pattnaik, P.: A taxonomy of accelerator architectures and their programming models. IBM J. Res. Dev. **54**(5), 473–482 (2010)
2. Menychtas, K., Shen, K., Scott, M.L.: Disengaged scheduling for fair, protected access to fast computational accelerators. In: Proceedings of the 19th International Conference on Architectural Support for Programming Languages and Operating Systems (ASPLOS 2014), pp. 301–316. ACM (2014)
3. Abdelgawad, H.M., Safar, M., Wahba, A.M.: High level synthesis of canny edge detection algorithm on zynq platform
4. Vallina, F.M., Kohn, C., Joshi, P.: Zynq all programmable soc sobel filter implementation using the vivado hls tool, vol. XAPP890, pp. 1–16 (2012)
5. Zhang, C., Li, P., Sun, G., Guan, Y., Xiao, B., Cong, J.: Optimizing fpga-based accelerator design for deep convolutional neural networks. In: Proceedings of the 2015 ACM/SIGDA International Symposium on Field-Programmable Gate Arrays, pp. 161–170. ACM (2015)

6. Gokhale, V., Jin, J., Dundar, A., Martini, B., Culurciello, E.: A 240 g-ops/s mobile coprocessor for deep neural networks. In: 2014 IEEE Conference on Computer Vision and Pattern Recognition Workshops (CVPRW), pp. 696–701 (2014)

7. Jia, Y., Shelhamer, E., Donahue, J., Karayev, S., Long, J., Girshick, R., Guadarrama, S., Darrell, T.: Caffe: convolutional architecture for fast feature embedding. In: Proceedings of the ACM International Conference on Multimedia, pp. 675–678. ACM (2014)

8. Corbet, J., Rubini, A., Kroah-Hartman, G.: Linux Device Drivers. O'Reilly Media Inc., Sebastopol (2005)

9. Sadri, M., Weis, C., Wehn, N., Benini, L.: Energy and performance exploration of accelerator coherency port using xilinx zynq. In: Proceedings of the 10th FPGA-world Conference, p. 5. ACM (2013)

10. Zynq-7000 All Programmable SoC Technical Reference Manual (UG585), Xilinx. Inc., March 2013

11. Farabet, C., Poulet, C., Han, J.Y., LeCun, Y.: Cnp: an fpga-based processor for convolutional networks. In: International Conference on Field Programmable Logic and Applications, FPL 2009, pp. 32–37. IEEE (2009)

12. Sankaradas, M., Jakkula, V., Cadambi, S., Chakradhar, S., Durdanovic, I., Cosatto, E., Graf, H.P.: A massively parallel coprocessor for convolutional neural networks. In: 20th IEEE International Conference on Application-specific Systems, Architectures and Processors, ASAP 2009, pp. 53–60. IEEE (2009)

13. Krizhevsky, A., Sutskever, I., Hinton, G.E.: Imagenet classification with deep convolutional neural networks. In: Advances in Neural Information Processing Systems, pp. 1097–1105 (2012)

14. PetaLinux Tools User Guide: Board Bringup Guide (UG980), Xilinx. Inc., June 2014

15. Rogers, P., Fellow, C.: Amd heterogeneous uniform memory access (2013)

16. Garg, I.C.: Amd kaveri review: A8-7600 and a10-7850k tested, January 2014. http://www.anandtech.com/show/7677/amd-kaveri-review-a8-7600-a10-7850k/6

17. Berg, T.: Maintaining I/O data coherence in embedded multicore systems. IEEE Micro 29(3), 10–19 (2009)

18. Greenhalgh, P.: Big. little processing with arm cortex-a15 & cortex-a7. ARM White paper (2011)

19. Koutras, I., Bartzas, A., Soudris, D.: Efficient memory allocations on a many-core accelerator. In: ARCS Workshops (ARCS), pp. 1–6. IEEE (2012)

DaSS: Dynamic Time Slice Scheduler for Virtual Machine Monitor

Ruhui Ma, Jian Li, Liwei Lin, and Haibing Guan$^{(\boxtimes)}$

Shanghai Key Laboratory of Scalable Computing and Systems,
Shanghai Jiao Tong University, Shanghai 200240, China
hbguan@sjtu.edu.cn

Abstract. I/O performance is an important factor in virtualization technology. However, the hypervisor and the scheduler brings impact on the I/O performance, since the scheduler considers I/O-intensive Virtual Machine (VM) and CPU-intensive VM as the same VM which results in scheduling latency. Most researches address this I/O problem but they do not take dynamic workload into consideration, leaving the facts that their solutions do not work well when the workload is volatile.

In this paper, we present a Dynamic time Slice Scheduler (DaSS) as a software solution which brings a significant improvement on the I/O performance. In order to maintain good flexibility and availability, DaSS requires no modification on the Guest OS but only a few changes on the VMM. We implement the prototype on Xen 4.3.0 and conduct detailed evaluations on network benchmarks. Our experimental results show that DaSS increases I/O throughput by nearly 40 %.

Keywords: Dynamic · Xen · Scheduler · VMM · I/O

1 Introduction

As the cloud computing developing rapidly, virtualization is becoming as a key technology to construct high performance and distributed computing infrastructures [1]. Virtualization technology consolidates multiple virtual machines (VMs) on a single underlying physical machine via Virtual Machine Monitor (VMM), such as Xen [2,3], KVM [4], VMware [5] and Hyper-V [6], etc., which also provides flexible resource management [7].

Unfortunately, in virtualization environment, unstable I/O processing latency perceived by applications as one of the serious challenges is still not well addressed [8]. Then we elaborate the process of causing I/O processing latency. We assume every physical CPU (pCPU) has only one core, there may be several VMs sharing one pCPU, and the CPU scheduler in the hypervisor (e.g., Xen's credit scheduler) schedules the CPU in a round robin order, with each VM given the same amount of time (e.g., 30 ms in Xen) to run in the physical CPU, ensuring fairness among the CPU-sharing VMs. In this case, a VM with a pending I/O request has to wait for its turn to access the physical CPU to

© Springer International Publishing Switzerland 2015
G. Wang et al. (Eds.): ICA3PP 2015, Part I, LNCS 9528, pp. 77–90, 2015.
DOI: 10.1007/978-3-319-27119-4_6

process the I/O request because the current VMM schedules the I/O-intensive and CPU-intensive VMs equivalently, which will lead to a high latency for each VM with I/O request. This is harmful for the I/O-intensive applications.

To reduce the I/O processing latency, some recent researches [8,9] have presented several solutions. Hu *et al.* [9] divided the physical cores into three parts: Driver Core, Fast-tick Core and General Core. They run domain 0 in Driver Core, I/O-intensive VMs in Fast-tick Core to switch them more frequently and CPU-intensive VMs in General Core without changing their frequency. Xu *et al.* [8] proposed vSlicer which ran I/O-intensive VMs and CPU-intensive VMs in the same core, but only changed the time slice of I/O-intensive VMs to accelerate their frequency by the administrator.

However, there are two issues to be addressed in these previous work mentioned. On the one hand, they do not take the CPU usage into consideration when various I/O-intensive applications executing. Xu *et al.* [8] and Hu *et al.* [9] just proposed a fixed time slice method and applied it into their corresponding system, but they did not change the size of time slice dynamically according to the class of I/O-intensive applications.

On the other, the size of time slices is controlled by the administrator, rather than I/O-intensive applications. Xu *et al.* [8] and Hu *et al.* [9] just pre-adjusted the size of time slices for I/O-intensive VMs. Indeed, the true network packages are dynamically changed, rather than stable forever. Thus, this static time-slice partitioning method used in [8,9] will cause performance degradation of I/O-intensive applications

In this paper, we propose a Dynamic time Slice Scheduler (DaSS) method that redesigns the credit scheduler in Xen to solve the two aforementioned issues. DaSS can dynamically adjust CPU the size of time slices by dividing a traditional CPU time slice (30 ms) into several small time slices. And the specific size of time slices depends on CPU usage monitoring module, which is used to monitor CPU usage of each I/O-intensive VM. In addition, DaSS can ensure that the total amount of CPU time of both I/O-intensive VMs and CPU-intensive VMs are the same, instead of sharing CPU resources of CPU-intensive VMs, thus it can ensure the fairness of scheduling.

The main contributions of this paper can be summarized as follows:

- We analyze and address the problem of I/O processing latency for Xen credit scheduler. We compare the existing solutions and point out that the fixed time slice of I/O-intensive is not suitable for dynamic workload applications. The lack of consideration of CPU usage mainly causes for the problem.
- We design a scheduling module to dynamically distinguish types (I/O-intensive or CPU-intensive) of VMs and adjust their time slice based on its type and CPU usage. Our system makes an improvement on shortening the I/O processing latency.
- We have implemented a prototype of our design named DaSS in Xen 4.3.0 and conducted extensive evaluation with network performance. Our evaluation results of network performance show that DaSS improved the performance of I/O request, and enhanced I/O throughput by nearly 40 %.

The rest of the paper is organized as follows: Sect. 2 presents a detailed analysis of the problems. Section 3 gives our design principals of DaSS. And Sect. 4 describes the prototype of DaSS based on Xen. Section 5 presents the evaluation in detail, while Sect. 6 describes the related works. In Sect. 7 we conclude our work.

2   Challenge of I/O Processing Latency

In this section, we illustrate the challenges of I/O processing latency and discuss some possible solutions.

To understand the challenge of I/O processing latency, we provide an example, in which 4 VMs are sharing one physical CPU. VM1 is an I/O-intensive VM running I/O-intensive application while VM2-VM4 is CPU-intensive VMs. VM1 acts as a server, waits for requests and makes responds back to the client. When VM1 has consumed all its credit, the scheduler selects VM2 to run, and then VM3 and VM4. When a request arrives, it has to be buffered until VM1 is re-scheduled because the credit scheduler does not boost any vCPU that has consumed up all its credits. When VM1 is re-scheduled, it can process the requests from clients. Suppose a time slice is 30 ms (as a default value in Xen), the I/O latency can be as high as 90 ms (i.e. 30 × 3) in the worst case.

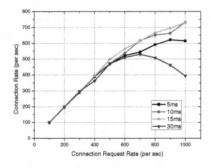

Fig. 1. Connection rate of apache server in different time slices

To address I/O processing latency, some researchers [8,9] proposed a fixed time slice by shortening the default time slice (30ms in Xen) to accelerate scheduling frequency of I/O-intensive applications. We do an experiment to show this problem in Fig. 1. We run 4 VMs in one core and one of them acts as apache server. Meanwhile, we use httperf [10] to send I/O requests to apache server, and each I/O request costs 5 KB memory page. Comparing with the I/O request— ping, this I/O request will cost much CPU resources. We can find that time slices with different length affects connection rate. Especially, the connection rate changes non-linearly, since each I/O request will cost CPU resources to transmit memory page. A long time slice (30 ms) would slow down I/O response rate, while a short time slice (5 ms) causes insufficient CPU resources to transmit a large memory page so that lots of context switches are required.

We summarize the major factors for improving the performance of whole system: time slices with reasonable length should be provided so that I/O-intensive VM is able to process different types of I/O-intensive applications efficiently.

3   Design

In this section, we figure out a clear view of our DaSS. We first introduce details of architecture and then present design of three main module of our scheduler.

3.1   Main Architecture

DaSS requires no modification in the Guest OS. All it needs is to modify VMM. The main architecture is shown in Fig. 2. We modify VMM to monitor guests' interrupt frequency and CPU usage. Two modules are introduced to handle these work: interrupt monitoring module and CPU usage monitoring module. We also modify the scheduler to achieve our design.

The interrupt monitoring module is mainly used to monitor the interrupt frequency and distinguish different types of VMs. We define two types of VMs: I/O-intensive VM (IOVM) and CPU-intensive VM (CPUVM). We also modify the scheduler to get information from the interrupt monitoring module and apply different scheduling strategy on VMs based on their types. This module would monitor the interrupt transmitted in the event channel and provide some information for scheduler to query.

The CPU usage monitoring module is response for monitoring every VM's CPU usage and calculate time slice for scheduling. The CPU usage monitoring module is added in VMM to monitor all VMs. This module is also responsible for calculating time slice based on the CPU usage. When a VM is scheduled, the scheduler would query for its time slice and apply it. Different time slices lead to different frequency of scheduling.

We make a few modifications on the credit scheduler. That is our dynamic time slice scheduler, which could query information from these two modules introduced above and apply different scheduling algorithm on different VMs. Our scheduler support dynamic time slice to adjust different workload.

3.2   Design of Scheduling Algorithm

As we mentioned above, if we reduce the default time slice, the scheduling frequency would increase and we could get fast response, but it would affect the performance of CPU-intensive tasks. On the other side, if we increase the default time slice, a good performance of CPU-intensive tasks would be achieve, but it would do harm to I/O-intensive VMs. In our design, we reduce the time slice of I/O-intensive VMs and keep the time slice of CPU-intensive VMs unchanged.

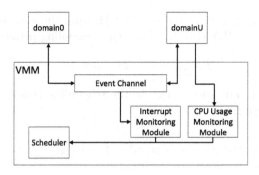

Fig. 2. Architecture of dynamic time slice scheduler

Meanwhile, we make sure that in any period the total runtime of each VM is the same no matter what type it is. Thus we obey the rule of fairness.

In our design, the scheduler could get the type information from interrupt monitoring module, which is used to judge IOVM and CPUVM. After that, we further divide the whole time slice of IOVM into a few small time slice. We show an example in Fig. 3 and assume the small time slice is 10 ms in order to facilitate the description. In Fig. 3a, suppose VM1 is a IOVM. In credit scheduler it could be scheduled once in a scheduling period, the latency could be as high as 90 ms in the worst case. But when in DaSS, the worst latency is 30 ms (one time slice of CPU-intensive VM). In Fig. 3b, VM1 and VM2 are IOVMs. Our algorithm would first schedule VM1 for 10 ms and then insert it back to the run queue. Then schedule VM2 and insert it back. From Fig. 3 we can see that in a scheduling period the total run time of each VM is the same but the scheduling frequency of IOVM increases for three times. Thus the I/O response has been improved.

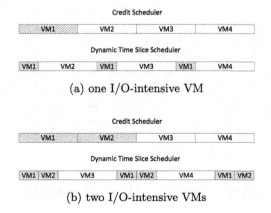

Fig. 3. An example of dynamic time slice scheduler

Suppose we have m IOVM and n CPUVM; total run time of each IOVM is T_I and that of each CPUVM is T_C. Then the scheduling period T_{period} is

$$T_{period} = m \times T_I + n \times T_C \tag{1}$$

Assume the default time slice is T_S. As the scheduling strategy of CPUVM is not changed, we can get

$$T_C = T_S \tag{2}$$

For IOVM, suppose the ith one is scheduled r_i times in a period, and run T_i' $(T_i' < T_I)$ each time, we have

$$T_I = r_i \times T_i'$$
$$T_S = r_i \times T_i' = T_I$$
$$m \times T_I = \sum_{i=1}^{m} r_i \times T_i' \tag{3}$$

Then we can get the I/O latency in the worst case:

$$T_{delay_i} = n \times T_S + \sum_{k=1 \& k \neq i}^{m} T_k' < (m + n - 1) \times T_S \tag{4}$$

We can see from the Eq. 4 that DaSS could reduce I/O latency when there are many CPU-intensive VMs.

4   Implementation

In this section, we present the details of our implementation for DaSS. We implement our prototype in Xen 4.3.0, while the ideas of our paper are generic enough to be applicable to many other virtualized environment (e.g., KVM [4], VMware [5]). In our implementation, we make some modifications in Xen credit scheduler to support different types of VMs. Decision on whether a particular VM is I/O-intensive VM or CPU-intensive VM is made by our interrupt monitoring module. And the time slice of each VM is calculated by the CPU usage monitoring module. DaSS does not depend on para-virtualization for its scheduling function. So our prototype can support Xen guests without modifications in guest OS.

Our implementation includes three main parts: the interrupt monitoring module, the CPU usage monitoring module and the scheduler. Then we introduce the details of our implementation.

4.1   Implementation of Interrupt Monitoring Module

The interrupt monitoring module is mainly response for classifying the types of VMs. In Xen virtual machine, only the hypervisor has an access to the hardware to achieve isolation. The drivers used to communicate between domain0 and domainU are frontend and backend. They use event channels to handle interrupts and I/O rings to transmit data [11]. Each domain can hold up to 1024 events. When a domainU is created, it will call *get_free_port* to send several hypercalls to VMM to apply for a free event channel port and call *grant_table_create* to allocate a free page used by I/O ring. Then the port number of the event channel will be delivered to domain0 through XenStore, which is a database used for sharing information before connection between frontend and backend is completed. Then the domain0 binds the port to a local *irq* to complete the connecting process of frontend with backend. Therefore, when an interrupts arrives, the Advanced Programmable Interrupt Controller (APIC) sends the interrupt (except for timer and serial interrupts, which are handled by hypervisor itself) to all guests registered on this IRQ. Then domain0 creates an event channel and sets the pending flag of this event channel and notify this domain regarding this interrupt.

When an interrupt comes, it enters a common entry called *common_interrupt*. After saving the content, *common_interrupt* calls *do_IRQ* to process the interrupt. For guest interrupt, *do_IRQ* calls *send_guest_pirq* to set the pending bit in event channel to notify the domainU about the interrupt.

Algorithm 1. I/O Status Monitor

Input:

    $time_i$ denotes the interval of statistic

    $time_{begin}$ denotes the beginning time of this statistic period

    $time_{now}$ denotes the time when we see an I/O interrupt

    $threshold_{high}$ denotes the threshold of I/O-intensive VM

    $threshold_{low}$ denotes the threshold of CPU-intensive VM

Output:

    get the type of I/O interrupt *Type* from the port number

1: **if** $time_{now} - timebegin < time_i$ **then**

2:    increase the count of corresponding interrupts of the domain

3: **else**

4:    clear the count record and start a new statistic period

5: **end if**

6: **if** the count of interrupts $> threshold_{high}$ **then**

7:    change the type of domain *Type* into I/O-intensive

8: **else if** the count of interrupts $< threshold_{low}$ for two continuous periods **then**

9:    change the type of domain *Type* into CPU-intensive

10: **else**

11:    do nothing

12: **end if**

13: **return** *Type*

In our prototype, we first record the port number a domainU used when it is created. Then we monitor all the interrupt transmitted in the event channel when the domainU is running. We make some modifications in function *evtchn_send* to record the interrupt frequency and store it in domain structure. In Xen-4.3.0, every domainU has its unique ID and every interrupt carries domainID and *irq* number, which we can use to trace a complete procedure of an I/O request and to decide the current type of VMs. According to our measurement, the interrupt frequency is always less than 100 times per minute for CPU-intensive VMs. But for I/O-intensive VMs, this number would become extremely high. So we choose 200 times per minute as our threshold. Once the frequency of a VM becomes more than 200 times per minute we regard it as an I/O-intensive one and when the frequency becomes less than 100 for two continuous period we change its type to CPU-intensive. The detailed algorithm implementation of I/O status monitor is shown in Algorithm 1.

4.2   Implementation of CPU Usage Monitoring Module

The CPU usage monitoring module is mainly response for monitoring CPU usage of every VM and calculating time slice for I/O-intensive VMs. In Xen virtual machine, physical CPU will set a timer when it is initialized to call *csched_vcpu_acct* every 10 ms to update credit. When updating, VMM would change the priority of VM from BOOST to UNDER and call *burn_credits* to reduce credits for non-idle VMs according to their real run time. If a VM is idle, VMM would jump over the updating procedure and put it back to the run queue.

In our prototype, we define CPU usage as the count of non-idle/total count in a updating period. The updating period is 10ms in Xen. If a VM is not running in one period, we can assume that it is idle in this period. So the ratio of count of non-idle and total count can be regarded as CPU usage. We make a simple experiment with lookbusy [12]. The result shows that the ratio we mention always equals to the parameter we set in lookbusy.

We implement the CPU usage monitoring module to count the times that a VM is scheduled in a period and calculate the CPU usage. The detailed algorithm is shown in Algorithm 2.

As shown in Sect. 2, short time slice is good for fast responding. With the reducing of time slice, overhead of context switch would increase, which would affect the efficiency of CPU used to processing I/O requests. Therefore, we should change time slice dynamically to adjust different workload. We need to dynamically change time slice for I/O-intensive VMs according to their CPU usage. In experiment we find that 1ms is good for some I/O requests who only need fast response such as ping. But for other I/O requests who need time to process, 1 ms time slice would waste many calculation resources in context switch. And the experiment shows that 20 ms is a good choice for both reducing latency and providing processing time. So our lower bound of time slice is 1 ms and upper bound is 20 ms.

We map the CPU usage to time slice from 1 ms to 20 ms. From previews experiment we find that CPU usage is stable in global but it will change constantly in a few continuous period, so we change the time slice of a VM only

---

Algorithm 2. CPU Status Monitor

Input:
    $time_i$ denotes the interval of statistic
    $time_{begin}$ denotes the beginning time of this statistic period
    $time_{now}$ denotes the time when we schedule a VCPU
Output:
    $Usage$ denotes the CPU usage of current VM
1: **if** $time_{now} - time_{begin} < time_i$ **then**
2:    increase the total schedule count in domain structure
3:    **if** the VCPU is idle **then**
4:      increase the non-idle count in domain structure
5:    **else**
6:      increase the idle count in domain structure
7:    **end if**
8:    calculate $Usage = \frac{non-idlecount}{non-idlecount+idlecount}$
9: **else**
10:   clear the count record and start a new statistic period
11: **end if**
12: **return** $Usage$

---

when its CPU usage is in a certain range. And we use aging algorithm with add some historical information to change time slices.

4.3 Implementation of Scheduler

We change the scheduling scheme in Xen based on the credit scheduler. The most important function that we modify is *csched_schedule* which is responsible for selecting the next vCPU to run from the run queue. We use two run queues to store vCPU: queue A and queue B. Queue A is used to store CPU-intensive vCPU and B is used to store I/O-intensive vCPU. When the scheduler selects the next vCPU, it would choose one from A or B according to the following rules: (a) select the head from B as the next one and put the current vCPU back to its corresponding queue; (b) until all vCPU of B have been selected or B is empty, select the head from A; (c) repeat (a) and (b) until all vCPUs have run out their credits; (d) re-allocate credits and time slice and then back to (a).

After selecting the next vCPU, the scheduler could get type and time slice of this vCPU from domain structure. Then the scheduler sets the timer with those information and begin to schedule.

5 Evaluation

In this section, we examine the detailed experimental results of our prototype DaSS. The network benchmark is used to evaluate the effectiveness of DaSS. In the experiments we mainly evaluate the following key aspects: (1) improvement on I/O processing latency; (2) overhead and cost with DaSS.

Experimental Environment Setup. We conduct our experiments on two machines which are connected via a Gigabit Ethernet switch in LAN, with each equipped with a quad-core 3.10 GHz, Intel Core i5-3450 CPU, 16 GB physical memory, one GbE network card and one 1TB SATA disk. One of the physical machines runs Ubuntu 13.10 as the host, with 64-bit Xen 4.3.0 installed. Each VM is configured with 1 vCPU, 1 GB memory and 10 GB disk.

5.1   Evaluation with Network Benchmarks

Ping RTT. We repeat a similar experiment as Sect. 2 shows, but use DaSS as the VM scheduler and compare the results with those achieved by Xen credit scheduler. We run 4 VMs in one core and one of them acts as server waiting for ping packets. Figure 4 shows the CDF of RTT of 200 ping packets. We run ping RTT evaluation under DaSS and Xen credit and find that the RTT of DaSS is less than that of Xen credit scheduler. The largest RTT of DaSS is 325ms while that of Xen credit is 600 ms. The average RTT is 42.5 ms and 73.3 ms. The results show that DaSS improve ping response for 42 %. The reason is that ping request do not need much time to process, and DaSS schedule VMs much more frequently than default scheduler.

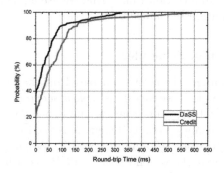

Fig. 4. CDF of RTT under default credit scheduler and DaSS

Netperf. We use netperf [13] to evaluate network performance including tcp throughput, udp throughput and tcp transaction rate. The experiment environment is similar with the evaluation of ping RTT. Figure 5a shows the test results of TCP_STREAM, which is the default test mode. In TCP_STREAM, client would send tcp packets to server to measure the throughput of transmission. We can find that the tcp throughput of DaSS varies from 100 Mbps to 120 Mbps while the throughput of credit scheduler is from 60 Mbps to 80 Mbps. Figure 5b shows the results of UDP_STREAM, which is used to measure the throughput of udp packets. The udp throughput of DaSS varies from 350 Mbps to 620 Mbps while the throughput of credit scheduler is from 300 Mbps to 500 Mbps. The reason that the throughput of DaSS is higher than that of credit scheduler is that

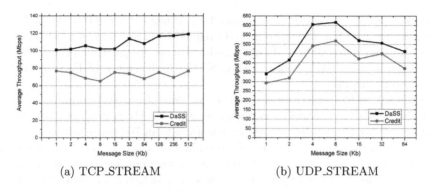

(a) TCP_STREAM   (b) UDP_STREAM

Fig. 5. Netperf test results

DaSS could schedule VMs more frequently and provide enough time to process those packets. And because of the unstableness of udp protocol, the throughput of UDP_STREAM changes significantly.

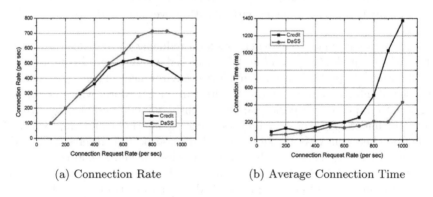

(a) Connection Rate   (b) Average Connection Time

Fig. 6. Apache test results

Apache. We also carry out experiments on real-world application to evaluate our design. We use the popular Apache web server [14] and Httperf [10] to conduct experiments. We run 4 VMs in a core and one of them is apache server which needs fast response and long time to calculate. We use httperf to send I/O requests to the server to evaluate the connection rate, response time and throughput of our system. Figure 6a hows the result of connection rate. The connection rate of both DaSS and credit scheduler grows linearly with the growth of request rate before it comes to 600 times per second. When request rate become over 600 times per second, DaSS performs better than credit scheduler. We use tcpdump to observe packets transmitted in our evaluation and find that there become lots of retransmission operations when request rate becomes higher that 600 times per second. The reason of retransmission is that with the growth of request rate, I/O requests from domain0 to domainU grow. Once the buffer of I/O ring becomes full, the following I/O requests can not be buffered and have to be dropped. For DaSS, VMs are scheduled more frequently so the buffer of I/O ring can be emptied more quickly. So the performance of DaSS is better than credit scheduler.

Then we evaluate the average connection time of our system and show the result in Fig. 6b. The average connection time gives out the time spent to establish a tcp connection. When the request rate is lower than 700 times per second, the connection time of DaSS is about 100 ms while that of credit scheduler is larger than 200 ms when the request rate becomes more than 500 times per second. That is because credit scheduler schedules VMs less frequently so I/O requests have to wait for a longer time to process. And because of retransmission, the connection time grows very quickly when request rate is over 700 times per second.

6   Related Work

We now discuss some researches related to our work. The related work is mainly about two parts: reducing virtualization overhead and modifying VMM scheduler.

In recent years, many researchers work on reducing the overhead in virtualization. For example, Chadha et al. [15] proposed a simulation-driven approach to evaluation I/O performance in virtualized environment. Their approach provided detail information about the architecture of hardware, which could help designers to improve I/O performance efficiently. vSnoop designed by Ardalan et al. [16] and vFlood designed by Gamage et al. [17] could improve TCP throughput between VMs in datacenter. They use host to receive TCP packets instead of guests. However, they cannot reduce the end-to-end latency.

Researches on VMM scheduler are mainly about modifying the scheduling strategy to improve I/O performance of VMs. Our work is focus on the modification of scheduling strategy. Kang et al. proposed MRG scheduler to improve I/O performance in MapReduce. They proposed a two-level strategy to ensure fairness between VMs. MRG sorts VMs in run-queue according to their priority and number of pending I/O requests, this strategy could reduce overhead of content switch. However, MRG works well when and only when host and guest running on the same physical CPU and it is designed for MapReduce and can not be used in other virtualization environment. Weng et al. [18] proposed a hybrid scheduling module combining two strategy to meet different requirement of workload, including high throughput and concurrent processing. This strategy schedules all virtual CPUs related to one VM together to reduce overhead of synchronization. As it needs to schedule all vCPUs together, the number of vCPUs should be less than the number of pCPUs. Bin et al. [19] proposed vSched scheduling algorithm, which is a soft real time scheduling algorithm based on real time scheduling module. But it is an application in Linux, not a scheduler in VMM.

Xu *et al.* proposed vSlicer scheduler and divided VMs into two types: latency-sensitive VM (LSVM) and non-latency-sensitive VM (NLSVM). For LSVM, they use a micro time slice instead of time slice in credit scheduler to increase the frequency of scheduling. However, they distinguish types of VMs manually, which is not suitable for real world applications. Besides, they do not provide enough to process I/O requests, so that their scheduler does not work well under dynamic workload. Guan *et al.* [20] proposed a workload-aware scheduler. This scheduler makes CPU-intensive VMs share some credits to I/O-intensive VMs, providing I/O-intensive VMs enough time to process I/O requests. This scheduler works well in high speed network environment. But it improves I/O performance by reducing time of CPU-intensive VMs, which breaks fairness in scheduling. Besides, they modified drivers in guest to distinguish CPU-intensive VMs and I/O-intensive VMs, which would lead to a poor scalability.

7   Conclusion

In this work, we mainly focus on improving the I/O processing performance. We point out that the naive designment of Xen credit scheduler has problem of I/O latency and it is not suitable for dynamic workload. Based on the discuss and analysis we carry out a software solution to overcome the issue. We propose a prototype of our design DaSS in XEN 4.3.0, where we add two new modules into VMM to monitor interrupt frequency and CPU usage and schedule VMs under different strategy. Detailed experiment proves that our design could significantly improve network performance.

Acknowledgement. This work was supported by 863 Program of China (No. 2012AA010905); The National Natural Science Foundation of China (No. 61272100, 61202374); NRF Singapore under its CREATE Program (E2S2).

References

1. Vaquero, L.M., Rodero-Merino, L., Caceres, J., Lindner, M.: A break in the clouds: towards a cloud definition. ACM SIGCOMM Comput. Commun. Rev. **39**(1), 50–55 (2008)
2. Xen. http://www.xenproject.org/
3. Barham, P., Dragovic, B., Fraser, K., Hand, S., Harris, T., Ho, A., Neugebauer, R., Pratt, I., Warfield, A.: Xen and the art of virtualization. ACM SIGOPS Oper. Syst. Rev. **37**(5), 164–177 (2003)
4. Kivity, A., Kamay, Y., Laor, D., Lublin, U., Liguori, A.: kvm: the linux virtual machine monitor. In: Proceedings of the Linux Symposium, vol. 1, pp. 225–230 (2007)
5. Waldspurger, C.A.: Memory resource management in vmware esx server. ACM SIGOPS Oper. Syst. Rev. **36**(SI), 181–194 (2002)
6. Velte, A., Velte, T.: Microsoft Virtualization with Hyper-V. McGraw-Hill Inc., New York (2009)

7. Von Laszewski, G., Wang, L., Younge, A.J., He, X.: Power-aware scheduling of virtual machines in dvfs-enabled clusters. In: Proceedings of IEEE International Conference on Cluster Computing and Workshops (CLUSTER), pp. 1–10. IEEE Press (2009)

8. Xu, C., Gamage, S., Rao, P.N., Kangarlou, A., Kompella, R.R., Xu, D.: vslicer: latency-aware virtual machine scheduling via differentiated-frequency cpu slicing. In: Proceedings of International ACM Symposium on High-Performance Parallel and Distributed Computing (HPDC), pp. 3–14. ACM Press (2012)

9. Hu, Y., Long, X., Zhang, J., He, J., Xia, L.: I/o scheduling model of virtual machine based on multi-core dynamic partitioning. In: Proceedings of International ACM Symposium on High Performance Distributed Computing (HPDC), pp. 142–154. ACM Press (2010)

10. Httperf. http://www.hpl.hp.com/research/linux/httperf/

11. Event channel. http://wiki.xen.org/wiki/Introduction_to_Xen_3.x

12. Lookbusy. http://www.devin.com/lookbusy/

13. Netperf. http://www.netperf.org/netperf/

14. Apache. http://httpd.apache.org/

15. Chadha, V., Illiikkal, R., Iyer, R., Moses, J., Newell, D., Figueiredo, R.J.: I/o processing in a virtualized platform: a simulation-driven approach. In: Proceedings of International Conference on Virtual Execution Environments (VEE), pp. 116–125. ACM Press (2007)

16. Kangarlou, A., Gamage, S., Kompella, R.R., Xu, D.: vsnoop: Improving tcp throughput in virtualized environments via acknowledgement offload. In: Proceedings of International Conference for High Performance Computing, Networking, Storage, and Analysis (SC), pp. 1–11. IEEE Computer Society (2010)

17. Gamage, S., Kangarlou, A., Kompella, R.R., Xu, D.: Opportunistic flooding to improve tcp transmit performance in virtualized clouds. In: Proceedings of ACM Symposium on Cloud Computing (SOCC), p. 24. ACM Press (2011)

18. Weng, C., Wang, Z., Li, M., Lu, X.: The hybrid scheduling framework for virtual machine systems. In: Proceedings of International Conference on Virtual Execution Environments (VEE), pp. 111–120. ACM Press (2009)

19. Lin, B., Dinda, P.A.: Vsched: mixing batch and interactive virtual machines using periodic real-time scheduling. In: Proceedings of International Conference on Supercomputing (ICS), p. 8. IEEE Computer Society (2005)

20. Guan, H., Ma, R., Li, J.: Workload-aware credit scheduler for improving network i/o performance in virtualization environment. IEEE Trans. Cloud Comput. **2**, 130–142 (2014)

Memory-Aware NoC Application Mapping Based on Adaptive Genetic Algorithm

Yizhuo Wang[✉], Zhibiao Zhang, Lifu Huang, and Weixing Ji

School of Compute Science and Technology, Beijing Institute of Technology,
Beijing 100081, China
{frankwyz,carl,leo.hlf,pass}@bit.edu.cn

Abstract. Application mapping is one of the key problems of Network-on-Chip (NoC) design. To address the application mapping on NoC with distributed memory node, this paper proposes a static mapping strategy based on adaptive genetic algorithm (AGA), which is memory-aware. This strategy solves the problem raised by the memory node through a novel encoding method, and improves the performance through dynamic adjustment on crossover probability and mutation probability. Experimental results show that our strategy saves the communication energy cost by 3 % to 6 %, compared with the mapping strategy based on standard genetic algorithm (SGA), for the task graphs studied in this paper.

Keywords: Network-on-Chip · Adaptive genetic algorithm · Application mapping · Memory-aware mapping

1 Introduction

As the development of the integrated circuit technology, the number of integrated transistors on a single chip is exponentially increasing, therefore the traditional chip interconnection approach, bus, reflects its limitations in bandwidth, energy consumption and latency, etc. To conquer the performance issues of bus, Network-on-Chip (NoC) becomes an effective interconnection method of multicore system. NoC is a modular, scalable communication architecture which interconnects various resources (processing units, memory units, etc.) with a router based network [1–3].

The application mapping on NoC-based systems is a process that partitions the target application into multiple tasks and assigns the tasks to separate processing units, given a specific NoC architecture. As the NoC application mapping directly affect the energy consumption and other performances [4] of NoC, it has become a critical step of NoC design.

For NoC-based systems which do not contain memory nodes, application mapping can adopt static mapping algorithms such as integral linear programming (LLP), genetic algorithms (GA), ant colony algorithm (ACA), or dynamic mapping algorithms such as first free (FF), nearest neighbor (NN), path load (PL), best neighbor (BN), minimum maximum channel load (MMCL), and minimum average channel load (MACL).

© Springer International Publishing Switzerland 2015
G. Wang et al. (Eds.): ICA3PP 2015, Part I, LNCS 9528, pp. 91–102, 2015.
DOI: 10.1007/978-3-319-27119-4_7

For NoC-based systems which use memory node to enable communication through it or to cope with frequent memory access [5–8], however, the traditional application mapping method may lead to decrease of system performance because the network location of the memory node is not taken into consideration during mapping. To address the above problem, this paper proposes a memory-aware application mapping strategy based on adaptive genetic algorithm. In this strategy, we convert the application characteristic graph (ACG) to the extended application characteristic graph (EACG) which contains memory node by analyzing the memory access features of the given ACG firstly. Secondly, the EACG is coded with the genetic algorithm encoding method which is improved on the encoding method in [9]. Finally, the application mapping algorithm based on an adaptive genetic algorithm [10] is carried out. Experimental results show that the proposed mapping strategy can reduce approximately 6 % of the communication energy consumption of the system.

The rest of the paper is organized as follows. Section 2 introduces the relevant researches. Section 3 gives our system model. Section 4 covers the application mapping strategy in detail. Section 5 shows the experimental results. Our conclusion is presented in Sect. 6.

2   Related Work

NoC application mapping technology can be categorized into dynamic mapping and static mapping. Dynamic mapping is online mapping strategy, which considers the current system loads at runtime. Dynamic mapping algorithms are generally studied in the literature [11–13].

As the communication overheads of dynamic mapping significantly affect system performance, static mapping strategies are generally preferred in NoC mapping [4]. Static mapping is offline mapping strategy, in which positions of the tasks are determined before system running. The major static mapping algorithms include ILP [14], BB [15], PSO [16], ACO [17], SA [18], GA [9, 19–21], etc.

These mapping algorithms merely take the computation amount and communication features as the basis for task assignment, with the control of the total communication amount as their primary goal, without considering the data access features of a specific application. For many applications, the partitioned tasks have distinct data access features. Some tasks frequently access memory, and some rarely do. It is quite clear that the memory access features should be taken into consideration when these applications are mapped to NoC system which includes independent memory module. Orsila et al. [22] bring forward a mapping strategy which is memory-aware. Lee et al. [23] connect multiport shared memory by improved crossbar switches in NoC, and assign tasks with large data access demand close to multiport shared memory so as to reduce communication overheads. At present, no adaptive genetic algorithm has been discovered which takes the memory access features of tasks into consideration in NoC application mapping.

3 System Model

3.1 Platform Model

This paper is mainly intended for multiprocessor system-on-a-chip (MPSoC) systems with 2D-Mesh NoC interconnection, which include shared memory node. As shown in Fig. 1, the shared memory node is located in the center of the network, ensuring that the average path from other nodes to the memory node is shortest.

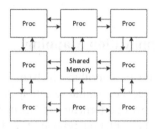

Fig. 1. Platform model

We use NoC architecture graph which is defined as Definition 1 to represent the platform model.

Definition 1: NoC Architecture Graph NAG(R, C) is a directed graph, where each vertex $r_i \in R$, represents a PE. Each directed edge $c_{i,j} \in C$ represents a physical unidirectional channel which connects an output port of r_i to an input port of r_j.

3.2 Application Model

In the literature of NoC application mapping, ACG is commonly used to model the application. This paper introduces memory task (MT) to solve the mapping problem of memory node, and introduces virtual task (VT) to solve the problem in prior work [9] that the encoding method does not consider the case that NAG nodes outnumber ACG nodes. We propose EACG on the basis of ACG by adding MT and VT to ACG. The relevant terms are defined as following.

Definition 2: Application Characteristic Graph ACG(V, E) is a directed graph, where each vertex $c_i \in V$ represents an task and each edge $e_{i,j} \in E$ represents the communication between a source task (t_i) and a destination task (t_j). Each $e_{i,j}$ is tagged with v_{ij} which represents the communication volume from t_i to t_j.

Definition 3: Memory Task (MT) is a task which originally does not exist in ACG. There is only one MT in each application. Its connection with other task indicates that the task needs to access the memory, and the weight on connecting edge indicates the amount of memory access of the task.

Definition 4: Virtual Task (VT) is a temporary task that does not exist in ACG. It is adopted to facilitate the implementation of the mapping algorithm. The communication volume from a virtual task to a normal task or another virtual task is always zero.

Definition 5: Extended Application Characteristic Graph EACG(C, E) is a directed graph, where each vertex $c_i \in V$ represents a normal task, virtual task or memory task and each edge $e_{i,j} \in E$ represents the communication between a source task (t_i) and a destination task (t_j). Each $e_{i,j}$ is tagged with v_{ij} which represents the communication volume from t_i to t_j.

4   AGA-Based NoC Application Mapping

Genetic algorithm (GA) is a heuristic algorithm which solves searching and optimization problems by mimicking the process of natural selection. Adaptive genetic algorithm is a type of algorithm which improves performance of GA by adjusting two major parameters (crossover probability and mutation probability). This paper adopts adaptive genetic algorithm to solve the problem of NoC application mapping. In the following part of this section, the two major topic of our mapping strategy will be introduced: encoding and decoding, and probability calculation. Other topics about our mapping strategy will be introduced then.

4.1   Encoding and Decoding

NoC application mapping requires that ACG nodes must share one-to-one mapping with NAG nodes. To better fulfil this constraint, Zhou et al. [9] bring forward an encoding method, which ensures that each genetic manipulation does not produce a lethal solution. But the method in [9] only considers the situation where the number of NAG nodes is the same as the number of ACG nodes, which considers neither the case where the number of ACG nodes is less than the number of NAG nodes, nor the case where there are memory nodes within the system. We made an improvement on the basis of the encoding method in [9], to address the above cases.

Next, we use an example to explain our encoding method. Let us assume mapping an application characteristic graph (shown in Fig. 2) which contains 5 tasks to a NoC topology (shown in Fig. 3) with 3 rows and 3 columns, where the grey node in the center represents the memory node (without computation capacity) and the other nodes are computation nodes.

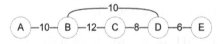

Fig. 2. Application characteristic graph

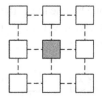

Fig. 3. NoC topology

There are two steps to convert ACG to EACG. First, we analyze the memory access features of these tasks, add an MT node to the ACG, and connect all tasks with memory access demand to the MT node, indicating they need to access memory. Each connecting edge is marked with the amount of memory access of the corresponding task. In this example, assuming the communication among D, B, and C is through a shared memory, thus an intermediate graph can be obtained as shown in Fig. 4. Second, based on the node number in NAG $c_{nag} = 9$, and node number in ACG $c_{acg} = 5$, by adding $c_{nag}-c_{acg}$ $-1 = 3$ VT onto the intermediate graph obtained in last step, we can arrive at the EACG as shown in Fig. 5, ensuring that the node number in EACG and that in NAG are equal.

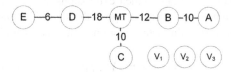

Fig. 4. Intermediate graph

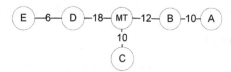

Fig. 5. Extended application characteristic graph

Chromosome represents a string of integers whose length is $c_{nag}-1$, the range of the ith integer is $[1, i]$, and the positions in the string represent the positions of the nodes in EACG other than the MT node. Assuming the chromosome in this example is (1 2 3 3 5 1 6 6). Then the first integer represents the node A, with one available position, whose value is 1. The second integer represents the node B, which has two positions, before A and after A, corresponding to value 1 and 2 respectively. In this example the value is 2 so the relative positions of A and B is BA; the third integer represents the node C, which has three positions (before A, between A and B, and after B), corresponding to 1, 2, and 3 respectively. The value is 3 in this example, which means the relative positions of A, B, C is BAC; it applies to other nodes in the same way. Thus, based on the chromosome in this example (1 2 3 3 5 1 6 6), we can obtain the relative order of nodes, V_1 B A D C E V_3 V_2. Then insert MT into the middle of the sequence, forming V_1 B A D MT C E

V_3 V_2, and put them back to NAG one by one to get the mapping result. The result graph is shown in Fig. 6(a). Finally, we remove MT and VT nodes, and the final application mapping result is shown in Fig. 6(b).

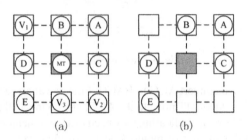

(a)   (b)

Fig. 6. A sample for application mapping

Through the above analysis, it is easy to find that the MT node is always mapped to the position of the memory node in NAG with our encoding method. In our AGA algorithm, crossover operators do not produce a lethal solution, mutation operator do not produce a lethal solution by assuring the value of ith gene is limited within the range [1, i]. In addition, the randomness of the genetic algorithm is well guaranteed.

4.2   Probability Calculation

Probability calculation is the core part of AGA algorithm. Srinivas et al. [24] give the expressions of probability calculation of an AGA algorithm. However the crossover probability and the mutation probability will be close to zero when the individual fitness is close to the population optimum according to their expressions, which leads to the insufficient crossover of excellent individuals in early stage of the algorithm. Therefore, we modified their expressions and the probability expressions used in this paper can be described as

$$P_c = \begin{cases} P_{c\_max} - \left(\dfrac{P_{c\_max} - P_{c\_min}}{f_{max} - f_{avg}} \right) \times \left(f' - f_{avg} \right), & f' > f_{avg} \\ P_{c\_max} & , f' \leq f_{avg} \end{cases} \tag{1}$$

$$P_m = \begin{cases} P_{m\_max} - \left(\dfrac{P_{m\_max} - P_{m\_min}}{f_{max} - f_{avg}} \right) \times \left(f_{max} - f \right), & f > f_{avg} \\ P_{m\_max} & , f' \leq f_{avg} \end{cases} \tag{2}$$

where P_c represents crossover probability, P_{c_max} represents maximum crossover probability, P_{c_min} represents minimum crossover probability, P_m represents mutation probability, P_{m_max} represents maximum mutation probability, P_{m_min} represents minimum mutation probability, f_{max} represents maximum fitness of population, f_{avg} represents average fitness of population, f' represents the larger fitness between two crossover individuals, and f represents the fitness of mutating individuals.

4.3   Other Topics

Population Initialization. In our algorithm, the position of MT node is always the same with the position of memory node in NAG for each individual. That is, the position of MT node has been fixed at initialization. As for the other task nodes, this paper adopts random initialization method, which only requires to ensure that the ith integer of an individual ranges from 1 to i.

Fitness Function. This paper concerns the energy consumption of the whole system. The energy consumption of the NoC-based system is mainly composed of the communication energy consumption and the computation energy consumption. The computation energy consumption does not change as the application mapping. Thus, only the communication energy consumption needs to be considered. Our optimization objective is to minimize the energy consumption overhead. Therefore we adopt the following fitness function:

$$\text{CommCost} = \sum\nolimits_{comm_{ij} \in Comm} H_{ij} \times comm_{ij} \tag{3}$$

where H_{ij} represents the Manhattan distance from node i to node j, $comm_{ij}$ represents the communication amount of this task from node i to node j.

Selection. This paper adopts the classical dual tournament as selection operator. Dual tournament selection is a method of selection based on sorting of individual fitness, which selects the one with highest fitness from two individuals each time, and repeats for N (the size of the original population) times to produce the new population. In this process, whether an individual will be selected only depends on the relative size of fitness, rather than the concrete value of fitness.

Crossover. This paper adopts uniform crossover strategy. For two parent chromosomes, their crossover probability is calculated according to the Eq. (1). If the two chromosomes are determined to be crossed according to this probability, each gene of the two chromosomes is crossed with probability of 0.5 to produce their descendant chromosome. As stated above, the ith integer of the parent chromosomes encoded with our coding method ranges between 1 and i, thus the ith integer of the descendant chromosome obtained by crossover also ranges between 1 and i. Therefore, the crossover operators will never produce a lethal solution.

Mutation. We make mutation as follows. First, the mutation probability is calculated according to the Eq. (2). Second, we check whether mutation is desired or not in accordance with the mutation probability. We randomly produce a gene position i when mutation is needed, and produce a random number between $[1, i]$. Then we assign this random number to the ith gene to produce a new chromosome. As stated above, chromosomes encoded with our method will not produce a lethal solution.

Elite Strategy. Compared with AGA algorithm in [24], our algorithm may change the optimum individual in each iteration. To avoid the degeneration of population, an elite strategy is adopted in our algorithm as follows. The optimum individual is reserved before genetic operation. If the fitness function value of the optimum individual in the current generation is not as excellent as that in the parent generation, the reserved optimum individual in the parent generation is to be substituted for the worst individual in the current generation.

5   Experiments

To evaluate our technique, we implemented the proposed AGA and the standard genetic algorithm (SGA) in C ++ under Ubuntu 14.04 platform. We compiled our programs using GNU GCC 4.8.2 and the optimization level–O3 enabled. We use TGFF [25] to generate task graphs and randomly select one of the tasks as MT for each graph. The nodes which are connected with the MT node are assumed with memory access demand. We map the graph to a 2D-Mesh topology where the NAG nodes outnumber TG nodes, using our AGA and the SGA respectively, and apply to them the same encoding method, selection method, crossover method, variation method and elite strategy. The mutation probability is fixed at 0.9, and the crossover probability is fixed at 0.05. The parameters of the AGA in our experiment are set as $P_{c\_max} = 0.9$, $P_{c\_min} = 0.5$, $P_{m\_max} = 0.2$, and $P_{m\_min} = 0.01$. The iteration number is set to 500.

5.1   Mapping Result

Figure 7 is a task graph randomly generated with TGFF, and node 1 is selected as MT (represented in grey). Figure 8 shows the result generated with our AGA mapping algorithm. The target NoC is a 5 × 5 2D-Mesh network, and the center is the memory node. We see that the MT node of the graph is mapped to the memory node of the NoC. Node 2, 4 and 6 are distributed close to the memory node. The total communication cost of the mapping result in Fig. 8 is 1219, which is optimal.

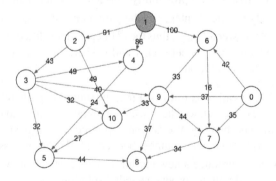

Fig. 7. Task graph generated with TGFF

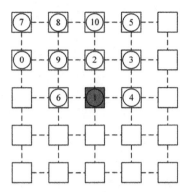

Fig. 8. Application mapping result

5.2 Performance Evaluation

We evaluate the performance of the proposed AGA and the SGA using 4 ACGs of different sizes which are randomly generated with TGFF. We run the AGA and the SGA for 100 times respectively, and report the average communication energy cost of the 100 executions in each generation of the algorithms. Figures 9, 10, 11 and 12 present the performance comparison of AGA and SGA. From Fig. 9, we see that the SGA converges to a local optimum after about 100 iterations, while the proposed AGA converges to a better local optimum after about 200 iterations. All the four figures show that AGA has better capability of premature convergence prevention than SGA.

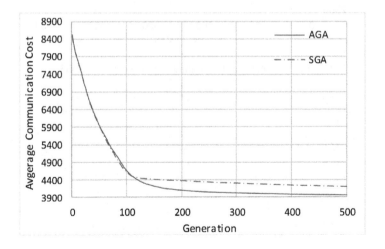

Fig. 9. Variations of the communication costs for ACG1

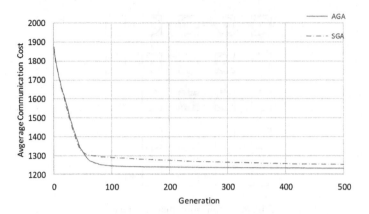

Fig. 10. Variations of the communication costs for ACG2

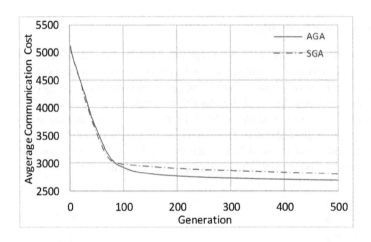

Fig. 11. Variations of the communication costs for ACG3

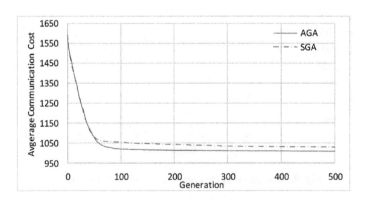

Fig. 12. Variations of the communication costs for ACG4

Table 1 reports the communication costs of the final mapping results with AGA and SGA. From the table, we see that AGA reduces the communication energy consumption by 3 % to 6 % on average, compared with SGA. In addition, we observe that the larger the size of the task graph is, the more improvement our mapping strategy can make.

Table 1. Communication costs of the mapping results with AGA and SGA

	SGA	AGA	(SGA-AGA)/SGA
ACG1	4211	3966	5.82 %
ACG2	1261	1220	3.25 %
ACG3	2802	2699	3.68 %
ACG4	1036	1004	3.09 %

6 Conclusions

In this paper, we proposed a memory-aware NoC application mapping strategy based on adaptive genetic algorithm. A novel encoding method is used in our strategy, which takes the memory access features of the tasks into consideration. The effectiveness of our strategy is demonstrated by the experiments. As future work, we plan to extend the strategy by considering more than one memory node in the network.

Acknowledgement. The authors thank the anonymous reviewers for their valuable comments on the manuscript. This work was partially supported by the National Natural Science Foundation of China under grant NSFC- 61300011.

References

1. Benini, L., De Micheli, G.: Networks on chips: a new SoC paradigm. IEEE Comput. **35**, 70–78 (2002)
2. Dally, W.J., Towles, B.: Route packets, not wires: on-chip interconnection networks. In: Proceedings of the 38th Design Automation Conference (DAC), pp. 684–689 (2001)
3. Kumar, S., Jantsch, A., Soininen, J. P., Forsell, M., Millberg, M., Oberg, J, Tiensyrja, K., Hemani, A.: A network on chip architecture and design methodology. In: Proceedings of ISVLSI, pp. 117–124 (2002)
4. Pop, R., Kumar, S.: A survey of techniques for mapping and scheduling applications to network on chip systems. Research Report, Jönköping University (2004)
5. Wang, X., Gan, G., Manzano, J., Fan, D., Guo, S.: A quantitative study of the on-chip network and memory hierarchy design for many core processor. In: Proceedings of ICPADS (2008)
6. Yoo, J., Yoo, S., Choi, K.: Multiprocessor system-on-chip designs with active memory processors for higher memory efficiency. In: Proceedings of DAC (2009)
7. Lee, S., Yoon, Y., Hwang, S.: Communication-aware task assignment algorithm for MPSoC using shared memory. J. Syst. Architect. **56**(7), 233–241 (2010)

8. Lee, J., Choi, K.: Memory-aware mapping and scheduling of tasks and communications on many-core SoC. In: ASP-DAC, pp. 419–424 (2012)
9. Zhou, W., Zhang, Y., Mao, Z.: An application specific NoC mapping for optimized delay. In: IEEE International Conference on Design and Test of Integrated Systems in Nanoscale, DTIS, vol. 45, no. 2, pp. 184–188 (2006)
10. Cheng, X., Yang, C.: Robot path planning based on adaptive isolation niche genetic algorithm. In: Proceedings of 2nd International Symposium on Intelligent Information Technology Application, pp. 151–154 (2008)
11. Chen, G., Li, F., Kandemir, M.: Compiler-directed application mapping for NoC based chip multiprocessors. In: Proceedings of LCTES, pp. 155–157 (2007)
12. Chou, C.L., Ogras, U.Y., Marculescu, R.: Energy- and performance-aware incremental mapping for NoCs with multiple voltage levels. IEEE Trans. Comput. Aided Des. Integr. Circ. Syst. 27(10), 1866–1879 (2008)
13. Carvalho, E., Moraes, F.: Congestion-aware task mapping in heterogeneous MPSoCs. In: International Symposium on SoC, pp. 1–4 (2008)
14. Ostler, C., Chatha, K.S.: An ILP formulation for system-level application mapping on network processor architecture. In: Proceedings of Design, Automation and Test in Europe (DATE), pp. 1–6 (2007)
15. Hu, J. Marculescu, R.: Energy-aware mapping for tile-based NoC architectures under performance constraints. In: Asia and South Pacific Design Automation Conference (ASP-DAC), pp. 233–239 (2003)
16. Kennedy, I., Eberhart, R.C.: Particle swarm optimization. In: Proceedings of IEEE International Conference on Neural Networks, NJ, pp. 1942–1948(1995)
17. Colorni, A., Dorigo, M., Maniezzo, V.: Distributed optimization by ant colonies. In: Actes de la Première Conférence Européenne sur la vie Artificielle. Elsevier Publishing, Paris, France (1991)
18. Harmanani, H.M., Farah, R.: A method for efficient mapping and reliable routing for NoC architectures with minimum bandwidth and area. In: IEEE International Workshop on Circuits and systems and TAISA Conference (NEWCAS-TAISA), pp. 29–32 (2008)
19. Lei, T., Kumar, S.: A two-step genetic algorithm for mapping task graphs to a network on chip architecture. In: Proceedings of the Euromicro Symposium on Digital System Design (DSD), vol. 17, no. 35, pp. 180–187 (2003)
20. Ascia, G., Catania, V., Palesi, M.: Multi-objective mapping for mesh-based NoC architectures. In: ACM International Conference on Hardware/Software Codesign and System Synthesis, vol 42, no. 12, pp. 182–187 (2004)
21. Jena, R.K., Sharma, G.K.: A multi-objective evolutionary algorithm based optimization model for Network-on-Chip synthesis. In: IEEE International Conference on Information Technology (ITNG), vol. 21, no. 4, pp. 977–982 (2007)
22. Orsila, H., Kangas, T., Salminen, E., Hamalainen, T., Hannikainen, M.: Automated memory-aware application distribution for multi-processor system-on-chips. J. Syst. Architect. 53(11), 795–815 (2007)
23. Lee, S., Yoon, Y., Hwang, S.: Communication-aware task assignment algorithm for MPSoC using shared memory. J. Syst. Architect. 56(7), 233–241 (2010)
24. Srinivas, M.: PATNAILKLM: Adaptive probabilities of crossover and mutation in genetic algorithms. IEEE Trans. Syst. 24(4), 656–667 (1994)
25. Dick, R., Rhodes, D., Wolf, W.: TGFF: task graphs for free: hardware/software codesign. In: Proceedings of the Hardware/Software Codesign, Seattle, USA (1998)

A Study on Non-volatile 3D Stacked Memory for Big Data Applications

Cheng Qian, Libo Huang$^{(\boxtimes)}$, Peng Xie, Nong Xiao, and Zhiying Wang

State Key Laboratory of High Performance Computing,
National Unversity of Defense Technology, Changsha 410073, China
{qiancheng,libohuang,xiepeng,nongxiao,zywang}@nudt.edu.cn

Abstract. Recently, big data processing has been an increasingly important field of computer applications, which has attracted a lot of attention from academia and industry. However, it worsens the memory wall problem for processor design, which means a large performance gap between processor computation and memory access. The stacked memory structure has the potential benefits for future processor design such as low latency, large capacity, and high bandwidth. Since these benefits can effectively relieve the problem of memory wall, stacked memory structure has been a promising architecture technique. Such memory structure began to use non-volatile memory (NVM) to provide a faster and larger memory, but its memory access behaviours for big data application have not been fully studied. In order to understand its memory performance better, this paper analyses the NVM 3D stacked structure using simulation method. Since flash memory is the maturest NVM media, this paper uses flash memory as the NVM part in the stacked structure to study, which results in a processor architecture with tightly connected CPU, DRAM and flash layers. In our experiment, channel number, capacity, page size and latency of read and write are test variables. Through observing the evaluation results of eight programs from big data program set, we conclude that the bandwidth and capacity have a significant effect for big data applications, and as bandwidth and capacity increasing, the Read/Write latency of flash and page size show less affection. We also point out some problems about data consistency, channel selection, read and write strategy and data granularity selection. These analysis results are useful for further study and optimization on NVM 3D stacked structure.

Keywords: Non-volatile · 3D stacked · Big data · Measurement · Memory level

1 Introduction

Nowadays, informatization has become inevitable in all aspects of society. In daily life, internet-related applications, such as online searchers, blogs, facebook and other social networking tools have been used frequently. These applications

© Springer International Publishing Switzerland 2015
G. Wang et al. (Eds.): ICA3PP 2015, Part I, LNCS 9528, pp. 103–118, 2015.
DOI: 10.1007/978-3-319-27119-4_8

result in the explosive growth of computing data, making big data processing become an increasingly important field of computer applications. Thus, it has attracted a lot of attention from academia and industry.

In order to study big data applications effectively, there are a number of benchmarks for reflecting the data features in different perspective, such as HiBench [1], CloudSuite [2], SmartCloudBench [3], CloudRank [4], DCBench [5] and so on. These benchmarks aim to reflect the characteristics from different aspects. Through analysing these benchmarks, researchers have obtained some architectural characteristics of big data applications [6]. The experimental results show that the characteristics of memory access for big data applications are quite different from that of conventional computing intensive applications. Some typical characteristics include large memory access span, scattered and random data access, unstructured data with poor spatial and temporal locality. So big data applications present a great challenge when running them on the traditional processors. Therefore, the study of processor architecture aiming at big data applications has become a research hot spot. The Eurocloud project group proposed a scale-out architecture processor in 2012 [7]. Their processor design puts many simple cores and last level cache (LLC) into a set called pod. Each pod is treated as an independent resource unit, by weakening the communication between pods and realizing resource hierarchy. Thus, the computing performance improves significantly.

However, traditional processor architectures encounter serious memory wall problem for big data applications. There is a large performance gap between processor computation and memory access. When running the big data applications this problem even worsens due to totally different memory access behaviours on conventional memory system. To relieve the memory wall problem, the 3D stacked technology has been introduced. It refers to the design of transforming the traditional 2D plane into 3D space. Different resources are distributed in different layers, and the layers are connected by Through-Silicon Via (TSV). Such structure can reduce communication latency, lower power consumption, therefore it has an outstanding advantages on memory bandwidth and access delay. Because of these characteristics, the 3D stacked storage technology is developing rapidly.

The DRAM 3D stacked structure stacks DRAM layer on the top of processor cores layer as a cache. It can achieve low-latency and high-bandwidth to improve the performance of processor's memory access [8,9]. However, its storage capacity is limited and its power consumption is relatively high. Moreover, the stored data will be lost after power failure. Since non-volatile memory (NVM) has large capacity, non-volatile and low-cost advantages, the NVM 3D stacked structure has become a new trend after stacking DRAM. HP Labs proposed Nano-store plan in 2011 [10], which studies the advantage of NVM 3D stacked and points out several research key technologies. From their principal experiments, the performance can be improved by 3X to 160X [11].

To utilize the advantages of two types of memory, DRAM layer and NVM layer are usually stacked on top of the core layer together to form a 3D hybrid storage structure. Figure 1 illustrates the block diagram of the fused NVM and DRAM stacked structure. It can meet the memory needs of big data applications with larger capacity, smaller delay, and wider bandwidth. Similar to scale-out processor's pod, DRAM and NVM layers can also be divided into multiple zones (tile) [12,13], corresponding to their core sets. Through multiple high-speed TSVs connecting computing and memory resources, the localization of computing and storage resources achieved which results in performance improvement.

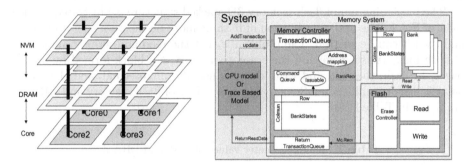

Fig. 1. NVM and DRAM stacked structure. From top to bottom there are flash layer, DRAM layer and core layer successively. Each layer has its unique organizational form (tile in core, sections in DRAM and pages in flash).

Since NVM 3D stacked structure is a new research topic, its memory access behaviours for big data application have not been fully studied. This paper attempts to use flash memory as the target storage media in the stacked structure for study, and perform measurement running big data applications. In our measurement, some representative parameters such as channel number, capacity, page size and Read/Write latency are set as test variables. The delay of the test program is chosen as the observation result metric. Through observing the evaluation results of eight programs of big data program set, we find that the bandwidth and capacity have a significant effect for big data applications. And as bandwidth and capacity increasing, the Read/Write latency of flash and page size show less affection. We also point out some problems about data consistency, channel selection, read and write strategy and data granularity selection. These analysis results are useful for further study on NVM 3D staked structure.

The rest of the paper is organized as follows: We introduce flash memory 3D stacked structure in Sect. 2. In Sect. 3, we give the evaluation methodology. After that, in Sect. 4, we test the benchmarks through changing the variables, and get some important conclusions from the experimental results. Finally, we revisit prominent prior work in Sect. 5 and conclude in Sect. 6.

2   NVM 3D Stacked Structure

NVM 3D stacked structure is usually based on DRAM memory to form mixed storage layers. The purpose is to take advantage of the DRAM's R/W speed and the NVM's capacity and non-volatile features. Flash memory is now the maturest NVM media. It has much superiorities compared to other non-volatile memory. It offers larger capacity, lower cost and can be mass produced because of mature industrial technology. Though flash also has a shortcoming on its read and write characteristics, and other NVM materials have relatively better performance on read and write operations, but they need further development to become mature. So we choose flash memory as the stacked NVM media for study in this paper.

The block diagram of flash memory 3D stacked structure is illustrated in the right of Fig. 1. The update operation of flash memory needs erase operation first and then it can be written. The problem is that the read and write granularity of flash memory is a page and the erase granularity is a block formed by many pages. In flash, the read and write delay is usually microsecond, and the erase delay is usually millisecond. Some parameter values of flash memory and DRAM are listed in Table 1 [14].

Table 1. Some parameter values of flash and DRAM

Memory	Endurance(cycles)	Read	Write	Erase	Erase Size
DRAM	10^{15}	40–60 ns	40–60 ns		
NAND flash	10^5–10^6	5–50 μs	200 μs/page	2 ms	e.g. 512 KB

As Table 1 shows, the core layer mainly makes memory requests. It has a small buffer to store data temporarily, and the buffer can get data from DRAM layer or flash memory layer. We just present one channel between layers in the figure. In fact, there are many, even hundreds of channels. They can transfer many requests and large amounts of data concurrently. It is one of the main advanced characteristics of this structure. In addition, since the read and write operation is based on the page granularity, the data transfer granularity between flash layer and other layer is also a page. In such 3D stacked structure, the data read and write operation can be proceeded as follows, the data flow can also been seen in Fig. 1.

According to the characteristics of big data applications, cores can make multiple concurrent memory access requests. Because many TSVs connected between layers in 3D stacked structure, the memory layers can respond parallel memory read and write requests. Because of flash memory's read and write operation characteristics, and the data between DRAM and flash layer should keep consistent. The mapping relation between them needs carefully design. For flash layer, the transfer unit is a page, but erase unit is a block, so data are stored in blocks. Then based on these blocks, the group-linked mapping method is used between DRAM layer, flash layer and the external memory. DRAM state table and flash state table are designed to record information about the data in the two layers. The data hit condition is judged through accessing information from two state tables. Especially, for flash state table, the erase information is also recorded for further data manage strategy.

After that, all situations can be covered as the forks following:

- If DRAM layer hits, the data can be returned directly from DRAM layer according to state table information. Then the data are returned, and the access operation is finished. If it is a write operation, the table should be updated (dirty bit).
- If flash layer hits, data are obtained from flash layer to the core layer's buffer according to state table information. Meanwhile, write the data to DRAM layer and update the DRAM state table. If it is a write operation, do it in a similar way.
- If flash layer misses, there are two situations: if it is a read operation, core layer gets data from the external memory directly and update flash layer and DRAM layer; if it is a write operation, core layer just writes data to the external memory. After that, the state tables are updated.

3   Methodology

3.1   Measurement Structures and Parameters

We choose three memory structures for memory performance comparison and analysis. The first one is an original memory structure, which does not stack any memory layer. Its memory resources include on-chip cache and off-chip memory (the external memory mentioned below). The second one is a DRAM 3D stacked structure. DRAM layer servers as the middle memory part between core layer and the external memory. The last one is the target NVM memory structure, which stacks a flash memory layer based on stacked DRAM layer. The two layers form a mixed memory structure.

Table 2. Some parameter values of flash and DRAM

Program	Data expand way
Sort	Generated (4 GB)
Wordcount	Generated (4 GB)
Grep	Generated (4 GB)
Naive Bayes	Wikipediainput (1.95 GB), expand factor: 2
SVM	Svm-data (1.95 GB), expand factor: 2
IBCF	Ibcf-data (1.95GB), expand factor: 2
FPG	Fpg-webdocs.dat (high) (1.38 GB)
HMM	Hmm-data (1.95 GB), expand factor: 2

In the original structure, if the on-chip cache misses, it would access data from the external memory. The number of channels between them is rather limited because of the limited IO pins. After stacking DRAM layer, there are usually enough channels between core layer and DRAM layer. So if DRAM layer hits, it can deal with many concurrent memory access requests, but its storage capacity is limited. To relieve this problem, we stack flash memory layer on the top of the DRAM layer, resulting in target NVM 3D memory structure. In this paper, the data in DRAM layer and flash layer are consistent, and flash layer can be treated as the expansion of DRAM layer.

Based on the three structures and the characteristics of DRAM and flash memory, we use the memory latency of chosen benchmarks as the performance metric. Several test variables are listed as follows: (1) Capacity: It is one of the most important parameters for memory structure. Many evaluation results are obtained by selecting different capacities. (2) Memory latency of flash layer: The R/W granularity of flash memory is a page, and the R/W latency is microseconds. The erase granularity of flash memory is block, and the erase latency is millisecond. Compared to the DRAM R/W latency, flash memory latency is relatively high. We choose different R/W latency to obtain its impact on the memory performance. (3) Page size: Since the R/W granularity of flash memory is page, data page is transferred from the external memory and stored in the flash layer. So it has impact on the data transmission and memory hit rate. In addition, flash memory page size has impact on the R/W latency and erase latency. Therefore, page size is an important variable. A common page size is 256 B, 512 B, 1 KB and 2 KB. Especially, 512 B and 2 KB are the most common ones. (4) The number of channels between layers: One of the important characteristics of the 3D stacked memory structure is to realize a plurality of vertical channels by TSV wires. Hence, it can support a plurality of concurrent memory access requests with high bandwidth. This would significantly improve the performance of big data applications with many threads. So the bandwidth characteristic brings by multiple channels is an important factor.

In fact, flash memory's R/W latency, capacity and page size have tightly connection with each other. Observing one test variable separately would make it simple to perform analysis. When testing multiple variables simultaneously, the practical situation including each other's influence should be considered.

3.2 Measurement Tools and Setup

In this paper, the experiment is carried out through a simulation method. We simulate DRAM layer and flash memory layer using DRAMSim2 [15] and Flash-Sim [16]. Core layer is implemented base on memory access traces, which are collected by PIN instrumentation tools [17]. We made some changes to the PIN tools, so it can return memory access traces of each program process. If there are multiple channels, the memory access requests are handled simultaneously. The memory trace collected is up to 4 GB.

We selected eight benchmarks from CloudRank-D v1.0 [4]. In CloudRank-D, there are seven workloads, which aim to reflect big data applications in a systematic way. The programs in each workload may have similar application characteristics. In our experiment, the relevant software are installed in accordance

Table 3. Some parameter values of the three structures

Parameters	Original	DRAM only	Flash added
Core frequency	1 GHz	1 GHz	1 GHz
Local Cache	32 MB	32 MB	32 MB
DRAM capacity		512 MB	512 MB
DRAM access latency		40 ns	40 ns
Flash capacity			2 GB
Flash R latency			15 us
Flash W latency			200 us
Flash erase latency			1 ms
Flash page size			2 KB
channel number(core to DRAM)		64	64
channel number(DRAM to flash)		64	64
channel number(To Ex-memory)	1	1	1
External memory access latency	70 ns	70 ns	70 ns
External memory capacity	4 GB	4 GB	4 GB

with the user manual: Hadoop version is 1.0.2, Mahout and Hive are both version 0.6. The eight programs are listed as follows. First three programs can be generated with any data size directly. Naive Bayes, SVM (Support Vector Machines), IBCF (Item based Collaboration Filtering), and HMM (Hidden Markov Model) need to be expanded. There is an original data set, and it can be expanded by multiplying by an expand factor. The information of the test programs is shown in Table 2, and the test initial conditions are listed in Table 3. In this table, core frequency and local cache show the factors of core layer. DRAM capacity (of whole DRAM layers) and access latency show the factors of DRAM layer and the rest parameters show the factors of flash layer. To show the influence of some parameters, in some cases we set the experiment environment unrealistic. All the parameters are set according to the JEDEC standard, and some detailed parameter can be seen in DRAMSim2 simulator.

4   Results and Analysis

4.1   Evaluation Results

Channels. In fact, the number of channels always means the ability of bandwidth and more channels mean greater bandwidth.In this experiment, we assume that there is only one channel between processor and external memory through IO pins in the tested three memory structures. The supported channel number of the DRAM layer is equal to that of the flash layer. That is to say, if there are 16 channels between DRAM layer and core layer, there are also 16 channels between flash layer and DRAM layer. We test the channel parameter with nine different values: 1, 4, 8, 16, 32, 64, 128, 256 and 512. Figure 2 illustrates the performance result under different channel numbers. The horizontal axis lists different channels, and colors mean different programs. The black line indicates the average value of the eight programs. The vertical axis represents the numerical value of the overall delay reduced compared to only stacking DRAM layer (the same to the following figures).

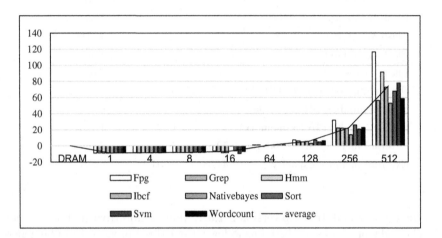

Fig. 2. Percent of memory access delay decreased under different channel number. As channels number getting more, the optimization effect is more obviously better.

As can be seen from Fig. 2, when the channel number is small, the latency is even increased by flash memory structure (it has negative values in the vertical axis). The channel number is so small that the structure's advantage of bandwidth can not be developed, and that is the reason of increment of latency when channel number is from 1 to 8. After increasing the channel number, the overall delay is decreased and changes exponentially. This is because as the number of channels increase, the advantage brought by simultaneous requests becomes more obvious. In addition, due to high capacity of flash memory, the flash layer can store a large amount of data, which is more useful for concurrent requests. This shows that the high memory bandwidth can overcome the shortage of the high latency of flash memory.

Flash Memory R/W Latency. Similarly, we assume that the number of external memory's channel is one, and the number of DRAM and flash layers channel are the same. We choose the read latency as 5 μs, 15 μs, 30 μs, 50 μs, write latency as 200 μs, and erase latency as 1 ms. We make the write latency constant because the conclusion were proven in previous work that write latency does not make great sense for write operation is far more less than read operation.

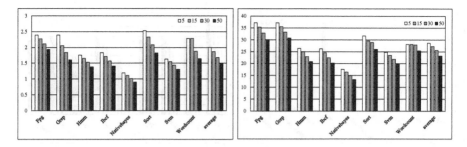

Fig. 3. Percent of memory access delay reduced with different latency. The left figure is under 64 channel configuration and the right is under 256 channel configuration. When the latency is smaller(left), the reduced ratio is bigger. In the right sub-figure, the ratio of delay reduced have smaller gap between different latency (Color figure online).

Figure 3 shows the delay reduction with different latency values. (The left figure is under 64 channel configuration and the right is under 256 channel configuration).

As can be seen from the Fig. 3, the latency has a certain effect on the overall delay. Obviously, the overall delay would decrease as the R/W latency decreases (the right-most/red column one is the shortest). However, when the number of channels reaches a certain value (256), the latency affects less. This is because the benefit of high bandwidth would fill the gap caused by the long latency in big data applications.

Capacity. Figure 4 illustrates the delay reduction with different capacity values. As can be seen from the figure, the overall delay decreases as the capacity value increases. This is mainly because more data can be stored in flash layer, and it can take advantage of bandwidth in stacked structure resulting in hit rate improvement. For FPG program, since the data size are only 1.38 GB, increasing its capacity does not have great impact. As expected, the effect brought by capacity is significant, especially when there are lots of channels.

In order to test capacity impact on the memory structure, we assume the configuration as follows: The capacities of DRAM stacked layer is 512 MB, and the capacities of flash layer is 1 GB, 2 GB, 3 GB, respectively, and the channel number is 128.

Page Size. Since the granularity of flash memory read and write operation is page, page size is an important reference variable. We choose 256 B, 512 B, 1024 B, 2048 B as page sizes to test.

Figure 5 illustrates delay reduction under 128 channels with different situations. Increasing the page size would increase data hit rate in a single page. But for some big data applications, the locality may be bad. So it does not show a great performance improvement as the page size increases. To be more specifically, we consider the relations between page size and R/W/E (read, write and erase) latency. The R/W/E latency would increase as page size increases.

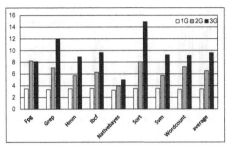

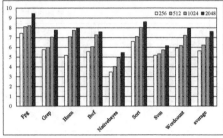

Fig. 4. Percent of memory access delay reduced with different capacities. As the capacity value increasing, the delay decreases more.

Fig. 5. Memory access delay optimization with different page sizes. A larger page size may not means a great performance improvement.

There are four configurations mixed by these factors. Suppose the page size of 256 B, its read latency is 5 μs, write latency is 200 μs and erase latency is 1 ms (256+5+1 as shown in Fig. 6). As can be seen from the figure, the latency has greater impact than the page size. But the effect is not so significant, especially when the number of channels between layers increases.

Consider All the Parameters. Considering all the parameters, Fig. 7 illustrates the evaluation results for DRAM and flash memory structure, compared to the original structure without stacked layer.

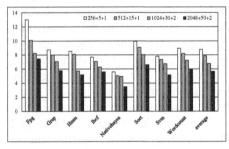

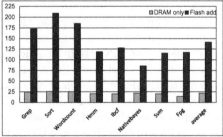

Fig. 6. Percent of memory access delay reduced in mixed situation. (256+5+1 means that the page size of 256 B, its read latency is 5 μs, write latency is 200 μs and erase latency is 1 ms. The latency has greater impact than the page size, but the effect is not so significant when the number of channels between layers increases.

Fig. 7. Percent of memory access delay reduced with the variables in Table III. When just stacking DRAM layer, the delay reduction is little due to small capacity. After adding flash layer, the delay reduction becomes obvious.

As can be seen from Fig. 7, due to different programs and different data set generation ways, the evaluation results of these programs are also different. When just stacking DRAM layer, the delay reduction is little because of small capacity. After adding flash layer, the delay reduction becomes obvious. In the condition of 128 channels, the delay reduced by the only stacking DRAM layer structure is about 20X on average. after stacking flash layer, the delay is decreased by 6.5X compared to the structure of just stacking DRAM layer.

4.2   Result Analysis

From the evaluation results described above, we can make the following analyses:

The Bandwidth Advantage of the 3D Stacked Structure Has Significant Effect for Big Data Applications. As the result of experiment about channels shows, for big data applications, scale-up enhancement of storage hierarchy by use of data locality would not improve the performance well. The more important thing is to take advantage of high bandwidth, especially when there are a lot of parallel memory access requests in scale-out applications. The high bandwidth can significantly improve the performance of memory accesses.

As the Bandwidth Increasing, the Effect of Flash Memory R/W and Erase Latency Decreases. When there are few channels, the latency of flash layer obviously impacts overall delay. But with the number of channels increasing, the high bandwidth advantage makes up for the shortage caused by the latency. In addition, the granularity of read and write is page, it can store more data in a single read, compared to DRAM read. So the latency of flash memory is not critical for big data applications.

Page Size of Flash Memory Has a Little Effect. Without considering the read latency and other effects caused by the flash memory page size, what the page size impacts most is the hit rate of a single page. However, the data locality is poor for big data applications, and data to be accessed are random. The high hit rate does not improve performance much. Hence, the effect of the page size is not so significant.

The Capacity of Flash Memory is More Important in 3D Stacked Memory Structure. For big data applications, the data are always too large to be stored in processor cache. So if the capacity of stacked layer becomes larger, it can take more advantage of high bandwidth provided by the 3D stacked structure.

From above analyses, we can see that though the access latency of flash memory is high, it can be made up by other characteristics like low energy, low cost, large capacity, and mature technology. Furthermore, as the channel number increasing, the impact of read and write latency is not significant. So the flash memory is suitable for stacked structure. However, we can also find some problems in the 3D stacked structure.

4.3 Problems

Data Consistency. In this paper, the data in DRAM layer also reside in flash layer, which should be consistent. Another situation is that the flash layer is an expansion of DRAM layer, and data in DRAM layer may not exist in flash layer. In this condition, the data in these two parts do not need to be consistent, but only need to be consistent with the external memory. In order to improve performance, it needs to analyse the programs and store the most useful data in DRAM layer, exploring its short latency benefits.

The Selection of Channel Numbers. As the data showed above, it can be easily concluded that channel number is such a precise parameter which needs carefully chosen. Too many or too few channels will both lead to a poor performance. We consider the channel number of DRAM layer and flash layer are same. In fact, they can be different. For example, 32 channels are configured for DRAM layer and 64 channels are configured for flash layer. The best number of channels is also related to the characteristic of different programs.

Flash Layer Read and Write Strategy. For flash memory, the write characteristic has impact on not only the latency of flash memory write operation, but also the lifetime of flash memory. Since the write endurance is an important factor for flash memory, its strategy of corresponding read and write operations is also important. It can partition the read area and write area in an optimized way to improve the performance. In addition, for write operation, this paper does not write data in flash layer, but write them in the external memory directly. This can also be changeable when the performance of write operation is improved. This problem can be greatly relieved if reasonable data manage strategy is applied, and it has been done in our further work.

Granularity Strategy. Data granularity transferred for flash layer is a page. It is a large size when compared to DRAM access. So the granularity for DRAM layer can be selective: a coarse-grain one (page) or a fine-grain one (small size). Usually, the coarse granularity can make a high hit ratio and the fine granularity is good for the bandwidth of useful data. So it needs more research to decide the granularity characteristics of DRAM and flash memory.

In summary, for NVM 3D stacked structure, the key points are the channel number and capacity. The R/W latency is less important for NVM in such memory structure. In addition, for taking a better advantage of fused DRAM and NVM media, the study of data management strategies according to the characteristics of the two storage media are needed. This problem can also be greatly relieved if reasonable data manage strategy is applied, and it also has been done in our further work.

5   Related Works

There are extensive studies on DRAM stacked memory structure. Djordje Jevdjic et al. introduce a data management strategy about selecting storage and access granularity. According to the characteristics of the page and block granularity of DRAM 3D stacked structure, it proposes to set different granularity for data storage and data access [18]. Using this method, the hit ratio is guaranteed and the memory performance is improved.

HMC (Hybrid memory cube) [19,20] is also based on DRAM 3D stacked structure. It can form a separate "cube" structure, integrating multiple DRAM banks and logical layer, so that the bandwidth are greatly improved, achieving 320GB/s. The communication between HMC and the processor core becomes one of the research directions. A memory-centric network (MCN) [21] refers to a plurality of processor channels connected to a local HMC, through network topology (e.g. mesh, flatted butterfly, dragonfly, etc.) to communicate among processors. Compared to the processor-centric network (PCN), bandwidth of MCN can be increased by 50 %. Meanwhile, the energy consumption is reduced. NDC (Near Data Computing) structure [22] is proposed for MapReduce applications based on HMC. The main modules of NDC are NDC hardware and Host CPU (main CPU), NDC uses NDCores and multiple DRAM banks to form a 3D Vertical Memory Slice (VMC), which makes a localization of computing resources and storage resources. This structure has advantages in execution time, bandwidth and energy consumption for MapReduce applications and is suitable for the bandwidth-needed applications that request independent computing and storage resources.

Flash memory structure usually uses a mixed structure with DRAM. Flash-cache is a hybrid storage architecture for web applications [23]. It introduces three simple and effective data management strategies based on a hybrid DRAM-flash storage structure: Use a structure to store flag information in DRAM to improve information search speed; Use a replacement policy based on wear-out characteristic to balance the flash cell erase operations, which improves memory tolerance; Offer a DMA support in the flash memory controller, to meet the needs of data transmission. These three techniques can also be used as a reference in DRAM-flash stacked structure.

Flash memory is generally used as a buffer between the main memory and the external memory. The change of the memory hierarchy leads to a corresponding change of the structure and data storage management policy. Flashtier [24] aims to propose a lightweight, consistent cache structure. According to the characteristics of flash memory divided into blocks, it unifies virtual address space, uses write-through and write-back methods to guarantee the data consistency. It also proposes a replacement strategy based on the wear balancing. In addition, aiming at the flash write characteristic, a variety of strategies have been proposed, such as ExLRU write policy [25], to improve tolerance based on different types of writing [26], a write policy for the cluster system [27]. These data management and optimization strategies are not only used in the traditional flash storage structure, but also can be a significant reference in the stacked structure.

Regarding other NVM stacked structures, Ademola Fawibe et al. proposed a DRAM-PCM hybrid main memory structure that combines the 3D stacking technology and CMM (Cache-Main Memory) structure [28]. Krishna Kavi et al. also introduces this idea to the multi-core systems [29], and do a depth analysis according to two cases: the first one is DRAM-PCM mixed CMM structure and the second one is a structure that DRAM is served as the main memory and PCM is served as the backup memory. Xiangyu Dong et al. study on MRAM storage structure that are stacked on different storage hierarchy [30]: regard the MRAM as an alternative to SRAM/DRAM L2 cache, L3 cache and the alternative of main memory. They obtain some results about the three situations, but it needs further study.

Different from existing works, this paper does an extensive study on the characteristics of flash 3D memory structure. It would be helpful for future memory structure designs.

6   Conclusion

Nowadays, big data applications are becoming increasingly important. It requires fast and large memory subsystem which decreases the impact of memory wall problem to achieve satisfactory overall performance. 3D stacked structure is a developing technology, and it has a lot of advantages, especially in communication bandwidth. Non-volatile memory is such a potential materiel for its big capacity, low cost and non-volatility. To find the key performance points of NVM 3D stacked memory system, and consider the mature technology, we select flash memory as the target storage media. We make a measurement of the flash memory stacked structure to find some conclusions that are useful for future efficient architectural design. This paper chooses some typical variables: capacity, page size, latency and the number of channels. The overall delay of eight programs in CloudRank-D v1.0 is compared. We use a simulation method and get a series of conclusions: The bandwidth advantage (channel number) has a significant effect for big data applications; with the channel number increasing, the flash memory R/W latency or erase latency effect decreases; page size of flash memory have a little impact; the capacity of flash memory is more important. Based on the evaluation result, some problems are also pointed out. These conclusions are very useful information for further study and optimization.

Acknowledgements. This research was parially funded by NSF grants (No. 61433019, No. 61472435, and No. 61572508), HPNSFC grant (No. 12JJ4070), and DFMEC grant (20114307120010).

References

1. Huang, S., Huang, J.: The HiBench benchmark suite: characterization of the MapReduce-based data analysis. In: IEEE 26th ICDEW, pp. 41–51 (2010)
2. Ferdman, M., Adileh, A.: Clearing the clouds: a study of emerging scale-out workloads on modern hardware. In: ASPLOS XVII, pp. 37–48 (2012)
3. Chhetri, M.B., Chichin, S., Vo, Q.B., et al.: Smart CloudBench - automated performance benchmarking of the cloud. In: IEEE Sixth International Conference on Cloud Computing (CLOUD), pp. 414–421 (2013)
4. Luo, C., Zhan, J., Jia, Z., Wang, L., et al.: CloudRank-D: benchmarking and ranking cloud computing systems for data processing applications. Front. Comput. Sci. **6**(4), 347–362 (2012)
5. DCBench: a Benchmark Suite for Data Center Workloads. http://prof.ict.ac.cn/DCBench/
6. Ferdman, M., Adileh, A., Kocberber, O., et al.: Clearing the clouds: a study of emerging scale-out workloads on modern hardware. ACM SIGARCH Comput. Archit. News **40**(1), 37–48 (2012). ACM
7. Lotfi-Kamran, P., Grot, B., Ferdman, M., et al.: Scale-out processors. In: Proceedings of the 39th International Symposium on Computer Architecture (ISCA) (2012)
8. Tsai, Y.-F., Xie, Y., Vijaykrishnan, N., Irwin, M.J.: Three-dimensional cache design exploration using 3DCacti. In: ICCD (2005)
9. Puttaswamy, K., Loh, G.H.: Implementing caches in a 3D technology for high performance processors. In: ICCD (2005)
10. Ranganathan, P.: From microprocessors to nanostores: rethinking data centric systems. Computer **44**, 39–48 (2011)
11. Chang, J., Ranganathan, P., Mudge, T., et al.: A limits study of benefits from nanostore-based future data-centric system architectures. In: Proceedings of the 9th Conference on Computing Frontiers, pp. 33–42. ACM (2012)
12. Guthmuller, E., Miro-Panades, I., Greiner, A.: Adaptive stackable 3D cache architecture for many-cores. In: 2012 IEEE Computer Society Annual Symposium on VLSI (ISVLSI), pp. 39–44. IEEE (2012)
13. Guthmuller, E., MiroPanades, I., Greiner, A.: Architectural exploration of a fine-grained 3D cache for high performance in a manycore context. In: 2013 IFIP/IEEE 21st International Conference on Very Large Scale Integration (VLSI-SoC), pp. 302–307. IEEE (2013)
14. Lai, S.K.: Flash memories: successes and challenges. IBM J. Res. Devel. **52**(4/5), 529–535 (2008)
15. Rosenfeld, P., Cooper-Balis, E., Jacob, B.: Dramsim2: a cycle accurate memory system simulator. Comput. Archit. Lett. **10**(1), 16–19 (2011)
16. Kim, Y., Tauras, B., Gupta, A., et al.: Flashsim: a simulator for nand flash-based solid-statedrives. In: First International Conference on Advances in System Simulation, SIMUL 2009, pp. 125–131. IEEE (2009)
17. Luk, C.K., Cohn, R., Muth, R., et al.: Pin: building customized program analysis tools with dynamic instrumentation. ACM Sigplan Not. **40**, 190–200 (2005)
18. Jevdjic, D., Volos, S., Falsafi, B.: Die-stacked DRAM caches for servers: hit ratio, latency, or bandwidth? have it all with footprint cache. In: Proceedings of the 40th ISCA ACM, pp. 404–415 (2013)
19. Pawlowski, J.T.: Hybrid memory cube (HMC). Hot Chips 23 (2011)

20. Sandhu, G.: DRAM scaling and bandwidth challenges. In: NSF Workshop on Emerging Technologies for Interconnects (2012)
21. Kim, G., Kim, J., Ahn, J.H., et al.: Memory-centric system interconnect design with hybrid memory cubes. In: Proceedings of the 22nd International Conference on Parallel Architectures and Compilation Techniques, pp. 145–156. IEEE Press (2013)
22. Pugsley, S.H., Jestes, J., et al.: NDC: Analyzing the Impact of 3D-Stacked Memory+Logic Devices on MapReduce Workloads (2013)
23. Kgil, T., Mudge, T.: FlashCache: a NAND flash memory file cache for low power webservers. In: Proceedings of the 2006 International Conference on Compilers, Architecture and Synthesis for Embedded Systems, pp. 103–112. ACM (2006)
24. Saxena, M., Swift, M.M., Zhang, Y.: Flashtier: a lightweight, consistent and durable storagecache. In: Proceedings of the 7th ACM European Conference on Computer Systems, pp. 267–280. ACM (2012)
25. Shi, L., Li, J., Xue, C.J., et al.: ExLRU: a unified write buffer cache management for flash memory. In: Proceedings of the Ninth ACM International Conference on Embedded Software, pp. 339–348. ACM (2011)
26. Yang, J., Plasson, N., et al.: HEC: improving endurance of high performance flash-based cache devices. In: Proceedings of the 6th International Systems and Storage Conference (SYSTOR 2013) (2013)
27. Caulfield, A.M., Grupp, L.M., Swanson, S.: Gordon: using flash memory to build fast, power-efficient clusters for data-intensive applications. ACM Sigplan Not. 44(3), 217–228 (2009)
28. Fawibe, A., Sherman, J., Kavi, K., Ignatowski, M., Mayhew, D.: New memory organizations for 3D DRAM and PCMs. In: Herkersdorf, A., Römer, K., Brinkschulte, U. (eds.) ARCS 2012. LNCS, vol. 7179, pp. 200–211. Springer, Heidelberg (2012)
29. Kavi, K., Pianelli, S., Pisano, G., Regina, G., Ignatowski, M.: 3D DRAM and PCMs in processor memory hierarchy. In: Maehle, E., Römer, K., Karl, W., Tovar, E. (eds.) ARCS 2014. LNCS, vol. 8350, pp. 183–195. Springer, Heidelberg (2014)
30. Dong, X., Wu, X., Sun, G., et al.: Circuit and microarchitecture evaluation of 3D stacking magnetic RAM (MRAM) as a universal memory replacement. In: 45th ACM/IEEE Design Automation Conference, DAC 2008, pp. 554–559. IEEE (2008)

Parallel Implementation of Dense Optical Flow Computation on Many-Core Processor

Wenjie Chen[1], Jin Yu[2], Weihua Zhang[3], Linhua Jiang[4], Guanhua Zhang[1], and Zhilei Chai[2(✉)]

[1] MoE Engineering Research Center for Software/Hardware Co-design Technology and Application, East China Normal University, Shanghai 200061, China
[2] School of IoT Engineering, Jiangnan University, Wuxi 214122, China
zlchai@jiangnan.edu.cn
[3] Parallel Processing Institute, Fudan University, Shanghai 200433, China
[4] Shanghai Key Lab of Modern Optical Systems,
University of Shanghai for Science and Technology, Shanghai 200093, China

Abstract. Computation of optical flow is a fundamental step in computer vision applications. However, due to its high complexity, it is difficult to compute a high-accuracy optical flow field in real time. This paper proposes a parallel computing approach for fast computation of high-accuracy optical flow field. It is specially designed for Tilera, a typical many-core processor with 36 tiles. By efficiently exploiting the advantages of the mesh architecture of Tilera, and by appropriately handling the parallelism inherent in the optical flow computation, the proposed implemention is able to significantly reduce the computation time while keep a low power consumption. Experiment shows that, for a 640×480 image, the computation time is only 0.80 seconds per frame. It is 2.56 times faster than on a typical CPU i3-3240 (3.4GHz), and the power consumption as less as 1/6. Experimental results also show that the proposed parallel approach is highly scalable for variable requirements on computation speeds and power consumptions, since it can flexibly selects a proper number of computing cores.

Keywords: Optical flow · Many-core processor · Parallel computing · High-efficiency · Tilera

1 Introduction

The relative movement between camera and objects in the scene leads to object motion in an image. The velocity field that represents the motion of object points across an image is referred to as the *optical flow (OF)* field [1]. By calculating the OF, the moving objects can be separated from the background. OF computation has been extensively studied in the areas of pattern recognition, computer vision and image processing. Numerous methods have been proposed. Horn and Schunk proposed a classic variational algorithm (HS) in [1]. Based on this, many

© Springer International Publishing Switzerland 2015
G. Wang et al. (Eds.): ICA3PP 2015, Part I, LNCS 9528, pp. 119–132, 2015.
DOI: 10.1007/978-3-319-27119-4_9

variational OF algorithms are developed, such as *Combine-Brightness-Gradient* (CBG) algorithm [2,3].

The variational OF method exploits the information of every pixel in an image to get a *dense optical flow (DOF)* field [4,5], which has several advantages: (1) can get a dense and high-accuracy OF field; (2) able to preserve motion boundaries [6]; (3) robust against noise and occlusion [7,8]; (4) suit for large-displacement OF [9,10]. However, since every pixel is needed in computation, it takes a long computation time and high power consumption. For example, for an 640×480 image, it takes 2.50 seconds to calculate the linear DOF field in our PC (*CPU: i3-3240, frequency: 3.40GHZ, memory: 4G*), which limits its application in practice. Hence, many efforts have been made to improve the computation speed, either by reducing the algorithm complexity [2,7], or by using dedicated hardware architectures.

The emerging multi-core technology provides a new possibility to speed up the computation by parallel execution of the algorithm on multiple cores, while keeping flexibility of the hardware. In this paper, we propose an optimized parallel computing approach for DOF computation. Both HS and CBG algorithm are improved and implemented on a typical many-core processor Tilera [11]. Experimental results show that for a 640×480 image, the parallelized CBG method on Tilera is 2.56 times faster than on CPU i3-3240 (3.40GHz), while the power consumption is as less as 1/6 of the normal CPU.

The rest of this paper is organized as follows. Section 2 introduces the related work on the DOF method and some acceleration techniques. Section 3 is the main part of this paper. It describes the general processing steps of DOF, then analyses different types of parallelism existing in optical flow computation and proposes our parallel optimization approach to improve computational performance on multi-core processor. Section 4 presents the experimental results, and Sect. 5 concludes this paper.

2   Related Work

2.1   Work on Optical Flow Method

The variational OF algorithms are usually posed as an energy minimization problem, with the energy function containing a data term and a smoothness term. Thus, many works have concentrated on designing a better energy function to improve the performance. For instance, the isotropic smoothness term [5,9,12,13] to preserve the motion discontinuity. Further, in [7], Bruhn proposed the *Combine-Local-Global* (CLG) model to improve the robustness to noise, which combines the advantages of both the Lucas-Kanade [14] approach and the HS approach. In [3], Brox introduced the constant gradient constraint as a complement term for the brightness constraint, which is referred to as the *Combine-Brightness-Gradient* (CBG) model. In [7], Bruhn proposed separate penalties on the brightness and gradient constraints. Zimmer [12] and Xu [13] further extended the normalized brightness and gradient constraints in DOF computation. Recently, techniques to deal with large displacements in optical flow estimation have also been proposed [9,10].

The above-mentioned variational OF models can be roughly categorized into three types, i.e., the HS Model, the CLG Model and the CBG Model. Most state-of-the-art techniques make improvements based on those models, such as the non-quadratic robust data term (NQ-D) [7], the non-quadratic robust smoothness term (NQ-S) [12,13], the multi-scale strategy [6,7], the warping strategy [3,9,10], and the segmentation strategy [15]. It should be noted that for all algorithms, there are only two energy minimization schemes, namely the linear scheme or the non-linear scheme [2].

2.2 Work on software optimization and hardware acceleration

In many applications especially in real time applications, the response time is essential. A lot of research has been made to improve the DOF algorithm to reduce the computational time without compromising the accuracy.

- *Software optimization.* In [6], Black introduced the classic multi-layer pyramid model to reduce the computational complexity. In [7], Bruhn proposed an algorithm based on multiple grids to process small images in real time. In [16], Gwosdek proposed a multi-grid red-black relaxation scheme to improve the parallelism of linear CLG model by removing the data dependency.

Beside the work on software, more efforts are focused on improving the processing speed using dedicated hardware, either by GPU or by FPGA.

- *Hardware acceleration by GPU.* Mizukami [17] realized HS algorithm on the GeForce GTX 8800. It costs 0.443 second to calculate the DOF of the image with 316×252 resolution. Gwosdek [16] implemented a better DOF on GeForce GTX 285. It costs 0.98 second per frame for image of 640×480. Sundaram [18] realized the DOF method which can handle large displacement on the GeForce GTX 480. The processing time is 1.84 seconds. More GPU implementations of DOF method are introduce on [12,13,19]. The speed-up ratio of GPU-based acceleration is very high. However, the power consumption is very high as well. For example, GeForce GTX 285 consumes 205 watt in the idle mode and 316 watt in the full speed mode. The high power consumption limits its application, especially in embedded system.

- *Hardware acceleration by FPGA.* Arribas [20] realized HS algorithm on the Altera EP20K100, for images of 50×50, the speed is 19 frames per second (fps) for 3 iterations. Martin [21] implemented HS algorithm on the Altera APEX20K, the speed is 60 fps for 256×256 images, but the iteration number is not mentioned. Rustam [22] proposed a hardware architecture by combining the integer and the fraction arithmetic functions. However, he also did not give out the number of iterations. Gultekin [19] accelerated HS algorithm on Altera Cyclone, which achieve 257 fps for images of 256×256. More instances were discussed in [21,22]. The advantages of FPGA are the flexible architecture, high speed and the lower power consumption. However, since FPGA usually uses hardware description language such as VHDL or Verilog, it is complex to develop and difficult to debug. To the best of our knowledge, only basic HS model has been implemented.

2.3   Tilera, a Many-Core Processor

Tilera is a many-core processor invented by Agarwal [11]. It has 16 to 100 cores, each core calls a *tile*. Figure 1(a) shows the architecture of 36 tiles, which are distributed with 6×6 array and connected with an extensible high-speed 2D grid network. Two independent channels are connected with two memory controllers, with up to 800 MHz memory frequency. The tile structure is shown in Fig. 1(b). It is a full function 64 bit processor with frequency of 1.2GHz. There are 3 VLIW instruction sets, and 3 instructions can be executed per cycle. Each tile has 16KB of instruction L1 cache, 8KB data L1 cache, and 16KB of hybrid L2 cache. Each tile has its own DMA and TLB to support the memory virtualization. Each tile can run an independent operating system. In addition, distributed caching and sharing system structure eliminates transmission bottlenecks and I/O contentions, and thus reduce the power consumption. The power is about 25~30 watt for a 36-tile processor. Besides, Tilera also has a good portability. It can be easily programmed using C language. Therefore, Tilera is fit for the applications that require fast response and low power consumption, such as lunar vehicles [23] and video decoding [24].

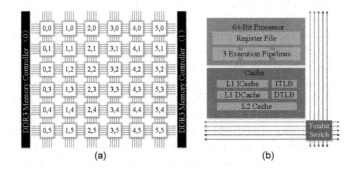

Fig. 1. The architecture of Tilera and a tile. (a)a 36-tile Tilera (b)a tile

In this paper, we use Tilera as the hardware platform to accelerate the computation of the DOF by our proposed parallel computing technique.

3   Optimization of DOF Computation

In this section, the workflow and parallelism of DOF will be analyzed and a novel approach will be designed to exploit the advantage of many-core architecture.

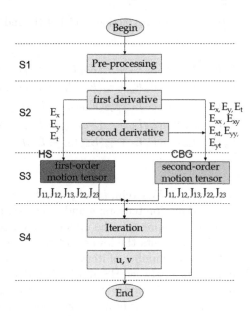

Fig. 2. Workflow diagram of HS and CBG

3.1 Workflow of HS and CBG

Figure 2 shows the workflow diagram of HS and CBG. It can be divided into four stages: preprocessing (S1), calculating the gradient (S2), constructing the motion tensor (S3) and the iteration (S4).

- *Preprocessing (S1).* S1 stage is to smooth the image sequence so as to reduce the image noise and external influence. Generally it was realized by convolution.
- *Calculating the Gradients (S2).* S2 stage is to calculate the gradient of image which has been smoothed. There are differences between HS and CBG: HS only uses the first-order gradient, while CBG algorithm uses the second-order gradient as well. The first-order gradient includes 3 dimensions: the `horizontal gradient` (E_x), the `vertical gradient` (E_y) and the `time gradient` (E_t). The second-order gradient is calculated from the first gradients with the horizontal and vertical directions, those are: E_{xx}, E_{xy}, E_{tx}, E_{ty}, and E_{yy}. Again the gradient is calculated by convolution.
- *Constructing the Motion Tensor (S3).* DOF method based on HS and CBG are required to construct 5 `motion tensors` $(J_{11}, J_{12}, J_{13}, J_{22}\ J_{23})$. This stage is to construct them based on the gradient information (Table 1). In the table, J represents the motion tensor, and γ is the weight of the data term. The main operation on this stage is matrix multiplication.
- *Iteration (S4).* This stage is to calculate OF by global iteration. For the **linear** HS and CBG scheme, only the `flow tensors` (u, v) should be updated. The iteration body employing the linear *Successive Over Relaxation*

Table 1. Motion tensors construction model of HS and CBG

HS	CBG
$J_{11} = E_x E_x$	$J_{11} = \gamma_1 E_x E_x + \gamma_2 (E_{xy} E_{xy} + E_{xx} E_{yy})$
$J_{12} = E_x E_y$	$J_{12} = \gamma_1 E_x E_y + \gamma_2 (E_{xy} E_{xx} + E_{yy} E_{xy})$
$J_{13} = E_x E_t$	$J_{13} = \gamma_1 E_x E_t + \gamma_2 (E_{xy} E_{tx} + E_{xy} E_{ty})$
$J_{22} = E_y E_y$	$J_{22} = \gamma_1 E_y E_y + \gamma_2 (E_{xy} E_{xy} + E_{yy} E_{yy})$
$J_{23} = E_y E_t$	$J_{23} = \gamma_1 E_y E_t + \gamma_2 (E_{xy} E_{tx} + E_{yy} E_{ty})$

(SOR) which is given by Eq. 1. Wherein, i and j denotes for the pixel coordinates; J is the constructed motion tensors; u and v represents horizontal and vertical flow tensor; $N_l^-(i,j)$ represents the upper and left pixels adjacent to the pixel (i,j); $N_l^+(i,j)$ represents the lower and right neighbours; ω is the weight factor of SOR; k is the number of iterations; and α is the smoothness weights of OF. The difference between HS and CBG is derived from different J. For the **non-linear** scheme, both flow tensors and motion tensors need to be updated. Although the data value of iteration schemes for motion tensors and flow tensors may be different, the data interface for them is the same (i.e. 5 motion tensors and 2 flow tensors). Hence, the non-linear iteration scheme can be implemented on the basis of the linear iteration scheme by computing non-linear factor and updating motion tensors accordingly.

$$[u]_{i,j}^{k+1} = (1-w)[u]_{i,j}^k + w \frac{\alpha\left(\sum_{(\tilde{i},\tilde{j})\in N_l^-(i,j)} \frac{[u]_{\tilde{i},\tilde{j}}^{k+1}}{h_l^2} + \sum_{(\tilde{i},\tilde{j})\in N_l^+(i,j)} \frac{[u]_{\tilde{i},\tilde{j}}^k}{h_l^2}\right) - ([J_{12}]_{i,j}[v]_{i,j}^k + [J_{13}]_{i,j})}{[J_{11}]_{i,j} + \alpha \sum_{(\tilde{i},\tilde{j})\in N_l(i,j)} \frac{1}{h_l^2}}$$

$$[v]_{i,j}^{k+1} = (1-w)[v]_{i,j}^k + w \frac{\alpha\left(\sum_{(\tilde{i},\tilde{j})\in N_l^-(i,j)} \frac{[v]_{\tilde{i},\tilde{j}}^{k+1}}{h_l^2} + \sum_{(\tilde{i},\tilde{j})\in N_l^+(i,j)} \frac{[v]_{\tilde{i},\tilde{j}}^k}{h_l^2}\right) - ([J_{12}]_{i,j}[u]_{i,j}^{k+1} + [J_{23}]_{i,j})}{[J_{22}]_{i,j} + \alpha \sum_{(\tilde{i},\tilde{j})\in N_l(i,j)} \frac{1}{h_l^2}} \tag{1}$$

3.2 Analysis of Parallelism

The parallelism of linear CBG parallel DOF can be analyzed from 3 aspects: task parallelism, data parallelism, and pipeline parallelism.

- *Task parallelism.* Fig. 3 illustrated the items to be processed and generated and their relationship during the whole procedure. it shows that dependencies is along with the operations between stages. Fortunately, within a stage, there are lots of operations can be run independently. Assuming each time two frames of images are processed, pre-smoothing of two input images ($img1$ and $img2$) can be processed simultaneously to obtain two smoothed images ($simg1$ and $simg2$) respectively. Then we can calculate the E_x and E_y according to the average value of two smoothed images (($simg1 + simg2$)/2).

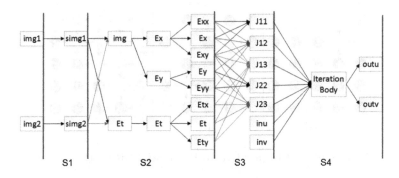

Fig. 3. Task parallelism of CBG

At the same time, we can get E_t by subtraction of two images. Moreover, as referred to Eq. 1, the 5 motion tensors can be obtained. These operations are independent and can be done simultaneously.

- *Data parallelism.* Stage S1 and S2 can be achieved by convolution, which is a typical data parallelism. For stage S3, the same instruction can be used for the calculation of every motion tensor. Therefore, these operations can be run efficiently in a parallel mode.

- *Pipeline Parallelism.* For the first three stages, there is data exchange between two adjacent stages, so they can be fully pipelined if there is any appropriate hardware. In stage S4, there are data dependencies inside and outside the iterations. Pipeline can be applied either inside or outside the iteration. These two types of pipeline can run simultaneously if sufficient hardware resources can be provided.

3.3   Optimization on iteration part

The 4 stages can be divided into two parts for optimization: the iteration part and other part.

As mentioned above, we used the SOR iteration. Figure 4(a) illustrates the regular SOR computation, which is sequential and slow. `Red-black SOR` model is an optimization for SOR parallel computation. As shown on Fig. 4(b), during one iteration, all the red points are calculated with the input of their black neighbours. Then in next iteration, black ones do. Figure 4(c) shows another model of "`Block-SOR`". The points with the same color (number) can be calculated simultaneously. Generally, the Red-black SOR model has a higher parallelism and easier to be implemented, but it has side-effect on iteration. On the contrary, Block-SOR has a relatively lower parallelism and is complicated to implement, but it has no side-effect on iteration. Moreover, it can derive some more flexible models. In this paper, we use Block-SOR model for optimization.

(1) Optimization inside each iteration. A single iteration is shown in Figure 5(a). The points (grids) connected by the same dash line can be carried out simultaneously. The number inside of the point indicates the order of

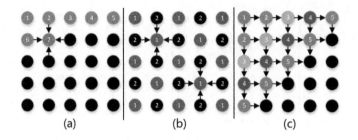

Fig. 4. SOR models. (a) SOR (b) Red-Black SOR (c) Block SOR

computation. Obviously, the parallelism is not static but increases first and then decreases. In order to cache data for each tile better, we re-design Block-SOR to a manner of "row first".("`RF-BSOR`"). As shown in Fig. 5(b), the points with the same number run in the same core. The arrows indicate the order of calculation. Figure 5(c) shows the busy state for each tile along the time. It is obviously that the load is not full on the beginning and ending.

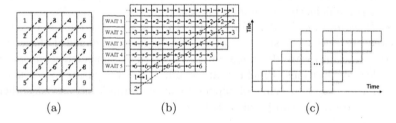

Fig. 5. Optimization inside an iteration. (a) Single iteration; (b) "Row First" Block SOR for many-core (c) Pipeline

(2) Optimization between iterations. Fortunately, as shown on Fig. 6(a), when the previous iteration moves to the second point of the second row, the new iteration on the first point begins. So the optimization between iterations can make up for the problem of non-full-load inside a iteration. Only the beginning and ending of the entire computation are not fully loaded. Similarly, we use "row first" manner. The whole iterative computation time scheme is shown in Fig. 6(b). The thick red curve indicates the boundary between two iterations.

(3) Synchronization. In the same iteration, the main problem of RF-BSOR is that one line should be handled at least one more point in advance than the next line. Otherwise, the data independency will be challenged. However, every tile of Tilera has its own program controller, so it is not feasible to predict the running speed of each tile. To solve this problem, normal CPU use **shared memory**, refer to Fig. 7(a). However, it requires frequent memory access and is very time-consuming. Tilera solve this problem by **message communication** among tiles

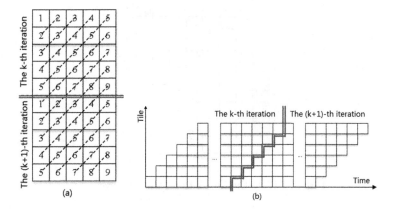

(a)   (b)

Fig. 6. Optimization between iterations. (a) Parallelism between iterations (b) Time schedule

by using the grid structure. Refer to Fig. 7(b), the points with the same number represent execution on the same tile. The horizontal arrows indicate the dependency, and the vertical arrows indicate the message communication.

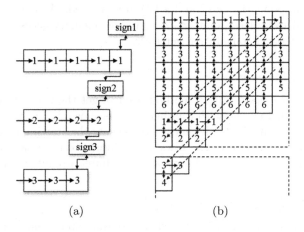

(a)   (b)

Fig. 7. Synchronization with: (a) shared memory (b) message communication

(4) Data Dependency. In SOR, computing a point is related to its 4 neighbors. The top and left points is the value of current iteration, and the right and lower points keep the value of previous iteration. The biggest problem comes from the point on the top, because it is not calculated in the same tile, and it must be updated before it takes account. On the Tilera structure, the value can be updated through the grid transfer, which can not only ensure the data correlation, but also reduce the access to DDR memory. In addition, the code can be optimized by compiler.

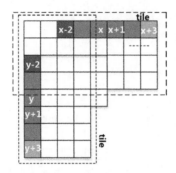

Fig. 8. Divide the image to all the tiles evenly.

3.4 Optimization on the Other Part

As mentioned previously, there are very good data parallelism and task parallelism for stage S1-S3. We combined the task parallelism and data parallelism and divided the image into tiles evenly. As shown on Fig. 8, we divided the horizontal convolution horizontally. There will be no data exchange between the tiles, and the middle data can be reused for adjacent points. For example, when x and $x+1$ is calculated, the middle four points can be reused, only the beginning and ending point (i.e. $x-2$ and $x+3$) are changed. We can set the FIFO, use point $(x+3)$ to replace point $(x-2)$ to reduce memory access. Similarly, we can divide the vertical convolution vertically.

3.5 Overall Mapping

Based on the above optimization method, we can get the whole algorithm map for every tile of Tilera along with the time axis, as shown in Fig. 9. x_n represents the starting line in the N-th tile, and y_n represents the starting column. *nrows* and *ncols* indicate the size of the rows and columns of the image respectively. In order to balance, rows and columns are distributed evenly over all tiles.

4   Evaluation

In order to evaluate the optimization effect, we did experiments on both parallelized CBG on Tilera and CBG on CPU. Here are the parameters: (1) CPU: Intel Core i3-3240, memory 4G, frequency 3.4Ghz, power 55w; (2) Tilera: TILE-Gx8036 [21], power 25–30w, system-on-chip standard Linux 2.6, PC client operating system CentOS 6.4; (3) test images: other-gray-twoframes from the standard test set of Middlebury [4].

4.1 Accuracy

Table 2 shows the AAE of both CBG computation on CPU and parallelized CBG on Tilera. From this table, we can see that Tilera has the same accuracy with CPU.

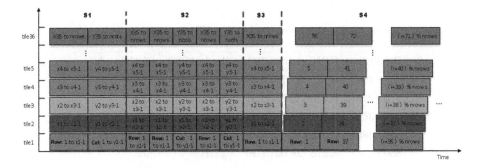

Fig. 9. Overall mapping of parallelized CBG on Tilera

Table 2. AAE of CBG computation on CPU and Tilera

Images	Resolution	SOR	Block-SOR	Red-black
RubberWhale	584×388	13.23	13.23	13.20
Grove2	640×480	14.61	14.61	14.94
Dimetrodon	584×388	22.67	22.67	22.88
Venus	420×380	23.54	23.54	23.61
Hydrangea	584×388	25.77	25.77	25.75
Grove3	640×480	27.96	27.96	28.06

4.2   Acceleration

We used "Grove2" as the test image and scaled the image size from 160×120 up to 1280×960. The computation time for CPU, one tile of Tilera, and all 36 tiles is shown in Table 3. From Fig. 10 we can see that the speed-up ratio increases along with the image size increases. The blue curve with diamond dot represents the speed-up ratio of 36-tile over 1-tile, which shows an upward trend but becomes stable on the scale of 800×600. The red curve with square dot represents the speed-up ratio of 36-tile over CPU.

4.3   Scalability

TILE-Gx8036 has 36 tiles. The acceleration effect by launching 1 to 36 tiles is shown in Fig. 11. As we can see, as the number of tiles increases, the running time is reduced and the acceleration effect enhanced.

4.4   Comparison with Other Platforms

The current mainstream parallel acceleration platform is GPU and FPGA. Table 4 lists the features of GPU, FPGA and Tilera. In general, Tilera has several advantages: (1) easy to develop; (2) low power consumption; (3) good scalability.

Table 3. Computation time under different resolution (s)

Resolution	CPU	1-tile	36-tile	1-tile:36-tile	CPU:36-tile
160×120	0.125	1.07	0.08	13.38	1.56
320×240	0.459	3.77	0.21	17.95	2.19
480×360	1.001	8.65	0.43	20.12	2.33
640×480	2.050	17.56	0.80	21.95	2.56
800×600	3.210	28.09	1.20	23.41	2.68
960×720	4.645	40.80	1.70	24.00 ·	2.68
1120×840	6.356	55.72	2.36	23.61	2.69
1280×960	8.340	72.75	3.03	24.01	2.75

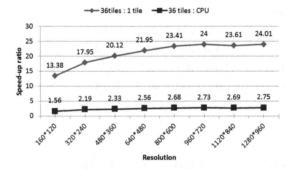

Fig. 10. The speed up effect

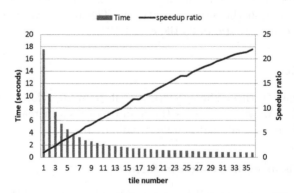

Fig. 11. Computation time and speed-up ratio along with different tiles used

Table 4. Comparison of GPU, FPGA and Tilera

	Tilera	GPU	FPGA
Programming language	C/C++	CUDA	VHDL/Verilog HDL
Main parallelism	Task Parallelism	Data parallelism	Pipeline parallelism
Complexity of developing	Easy	Easy	Hard
Power consumption	25w-30w	> 150w	< 10w
Use cases	-	[16–18]	[20–22]

5   Conclusion

In this paper, we propose a parallel computing approach to optimize the computation of the DOF using the CBG algorithm. The proposed algorithm is specially designed for Tilera, a many-core processor, such that it can efficiently exploit the advantages of the mesh architecture of Tilera, while fully exploiting the data parallelism of the CBG algorithm. In order to take the advantage of Tilera, we designed a "Row First" Block-SOR, so as to improve the parallelism inside a iteration and between iterations. The experimental results show that this approach can cut down the running time drastically, while keep the power consumption in low level. Moreover, this approach has a good scalability, the speedup ratio increases along with the tile number.

Acknowledgements. We are grateful to the support from the 863 Program of China (2015AA015304), the Shanghai Natural Science Foundation (15ZR1410000), and the program for Professor of Special Appointment (Eastern Scholar) at Shanghai Institutions of Higher Learning.

References

1. Horn, B. K., Schunck, B. G.: Determining optical flow. In: Technical Symposium East, pp. 319–331. International Society for Optics and Photonics (1981)
2. Bruhn, A.: Variational optic flow computation: accurate modelling and efficient numerics. Ph.D thesis (2006)
3. Brox, T., Bruhn, A., Papenberg, N., Weickert, J.: High accuracy optical flow estimation based on a theory for warping. In: Pajdla, T., Matas, J.G. (eds.) ECCV 2004. LNCS, vol. 3024, pp. 25–36. Springer, Heidelberg (2004)
4. Barron, J.L., Fleet, D.J., Beauchemin, S.S.: Performance of optical flow techniques. Int. J. Comput. Vis. **12**(1), 43–77 (1994)
5. Baker, S., Scharstein, D., Lewis, J.P., Roth, S., Black, M.J., Szeliski, R.: A database and evaluation methodology for optical flow. Int. J. Comput. Vis. **92**(1), 1–31 (2011)
6. Black, M.J., Anandan, P.: The robust estimation of multiple motions: parametric and piecewise-smooth flow fields. Comput. Vis. Image Underst. **63**(1), 75–104 (1996)

7. Bruhn, A., Weickert, J.: Towards ultimate motion estimation: combining highest accuracy with real-time performance. In: Tenth IEEE International Conference on Computer Vision, 2005, vol. 1, pp. 749–755 (2005)
8. Sundberg, P., Brox, T., Maire, M., Arbelaez, P., Malik, J.: Occlusion boundary detection and figure/ground assignment from optical flow. In: IEEE Conference on Computer Vision and Pattern Recognition (CVPR), 2011, (Providence, RI), pp. 2233–2240 (2011)
9. Brox, T., Bregler, C., Malik, J.: Large displacement optical flow, June 2009
10. Brox, T., Malik, J.: Large displacement optical flow: descriptor matching in variational motion estimation. IEEE Trans. Pattern Anal. Mach. Intell. **33**(3), 500–513 (2011)
11. Agarwal, A.: The tile processor: A 64-core multicore for embedded processing. In: Proceedings of HPEC Workshop (2007)
12. Zimmer, H., Bruhn, A., Weickert, J.: Optic flow in harmony. Int. J. Comput. Vis. **93**(3), 368–388 (2011)
13. Li, X., Jiaya, J., Matsushita, Y.: Motion detail preserving optical flow estimation. IEEE Trans. Pattern Anal. Mach. Intell. **34**(9), 1744–1757 (2012)
14. Lucas, B.D., Kanade, T.: An iterative image registration technique with an application to stereo vision. IJCAI **81**, 674–679 (1981)
15. Amiaz, T., Kiryati, N.: Piecewise-smooth dense optical flow via level sets. Int. J. Comput. Vis. **68**(2), 111–124 (2006)
16. Gwosdek, P., Bruhn, A., Weickert, J.: Variational optic flow on the sony playstation 3. J. Real-Time Image Process. **5**(3), 163–177 (2010)
17. Mizukami, Y., Tadamura, K.: Optical flow computation on compute unified device architecture. In: 14th International Conference on Image Analysis and Processing, 2007. ICIAP 2007, Modena, pp. 179–184 (2007)
18. Sundaram, N., Brox, T., Keutzer, K.: Dense point trajectories by GPU-accelerated large displacement optical flow (2010)
19. Gultekin, G.K., Saranli, A.: An fpga based high performance optical flow hardware design for computer vision applications. Microprocess. Microsyst. **37**(3), 270–286 (2013)
20. Arribas, P.C., Macia, F.M.H.: FPGA implementation of santos-victor optical flow algorithm for real-time image processing: an useful attempt. In: Microtechnologies for the New Millennium 2003, pp. 23–32. International Society for Optics and Photonics (2003)
21. Martn, J.L., Zuloaga, A., Cuadrado, C., Zaro, J.L., Bidarte, U.: Hardware implementation of optical flow constraint equation using FPGAs. Comput. Vis. Image Underst. **98**(3), 462–490 (2005)
22. Rustam, R., Hamid, N.H., Hussin, F.A.: FPGA-based hardware implementation of optical flow constraint equation of horn and schunck. In: 2012 4th International Conference on Intelligent and Advanced Systems (ICIAS), Kuala Lumpur, vol. 2, pp. 790–794 (2012)
23. Villalpando, C.Y., Johnson, A.E., Some, R., Oberlin, J., Goldberg, S.: Investigation of the tilera processor for real time hazard detection and avoidance on the altair lunar lander. In: 2010 IEEE Aerospace Conference, pp. 1–9. IEEE (2010)
24. Yan, C., Dai, F., Zhang, Y.: Parallel deblocking filter for H.264/AVC on the TILERA many-core systems. In: Lee, K.-T., Tsai, W.-H., Liao, H.-Y.M., Chen, T., Hsieh, J.-W., Tseng, C.-C. (eds.) MMM 2011 Part I. LNCS, vol. 6523, pp. 51–61. Springer, Heidelberg (2011)

A Power-Conserving Online Scheduling Scheme for Video Streaming Services

Yunyun Jiang, Tian Xiao, Jidong Zhai, Ying Zhao, and Wenguang Chen[(✉)]

Department of Computer Science and Technology,
Tsinghua University, Beijing 100084, China
{jiangyy09,xiaot04}@mails.tsinghua.edu.cn,
{zhaijidong,yingz,cwg}@tsinghua.edu.cn

Abstract. Video streaming is one of the most popular Internet services which may use thousands of servers. Current video streaming scheduling algorithms do not distinguish long streaming tasks from short ones which may result in sub-optimal energy consumption. In this paper, we observe that task length has strong correlations with user access profile, which can be used to predict the length of a given streaming task. Based on the predicted task length, we propose a series of heuristics algorithms that form a more power-efficient scheduling scheme. Experiments show that our approach is about 10 % to 160 % more power efficient than current scheduling approaches.

Keywords: Power-conserving · Scheduling · Video streaming service

1 Introduction

Video streaming services have gained great popularity in the past decade. Internet service providers, including both video service providers like Youtube and emerging online education services like MOOCs (Massive Open Online Courses), are facing increasing demands of video services. In a video service website, a popular TV series can bring tens of millions visits one day, and the highest access frequency can be higher than 300 times per second [1]. However, the increasing demands of video services bring great challenges to video clusters, in which, power consumption is an important one. As reported in IDC prediction report of 2013, one data center of Youtube has the power consumption nearly comparable to that of a medium-sized city [2]. Power conservation has become an important issue in video clusters.

In video clusters, different scheduling algorithms have been proposed to distribute streaming video tasks to different servers, in order to meet the increasing demands of video requests. Unfortunately, little attention has been paid to power consumption. Most scheduling algorithms distribute streaming tasks to available servers in a round-robin way. Although load balance is well achieved in these algorithms, energy can be wasted due to idle time in a large amount of servers. In contrast, a power-conserving scheduling algorithm can contribute a

© Springer International Publishing Switzerland 2015
G. Wang et al. (Eds.): ICA3PP 2015, Part I, LNCS 9528, pp. 133–154, 2015.
DOI: 10.1007/978-3-319-27119-4_10

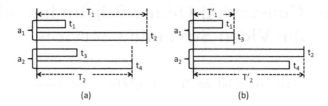

Fig. 1. An example of simple task scheduling.

lot to power saving by modulating the task assignment. For the example shown in Fig. 1, simultaneous tasks t_1, t_2, t_3 and t_4 are scheduled on two servers a_1 and a_2, each of which can process two tasks simultaneously. In Fig. 1(a), a typical traditional scheduling algorithm, which allocates tasks in the default order on servers, gets the total running time of $T_1 + T_2$. A simple power-conserving scheduling algorithm, which modulates the assignment by putting the longer tasks together, can effectively reduce the total running time to $T'_1 + T'_2$.

As shown in the example, server a_1 in Fig. 1(b) can switch to idle state after processing the two short tasks t_1 and t_3, which has an appreciable power conserving compared to server a_2 in Fig. 1(a). This inspires us to design an scheduling algorithm that isolates long streaming tasks from short ones for better power savings.

Our power-conserving scheduling mechanism mainly aims at minimizing idle time on each server by assigning tasks of similar lengths. By studying both research papers [3] and statistical data published by mainstream VoD (Video-on-Demand) websites [1,4], we have two observations: First, a video cluster has a regular busy/idle load pattern in one day, which enables server shrink to save energy. Our study shows that the number of streaming tasks increases from 6 a.m. and 5 p.m., but decreases from 2 p.m. and 8 p.m., which are consistent with people's working and resting time (details in Sect. 2 and Fig. 2). The pattern repeats every 24 h. In this pattern, when the number of streaming tasks decreases, streaming tasks can be compacted to fewer servers. This provides opportunities to shut down idle servers for power conservation. Second, streaming tasks show great variety in task lengths, and the existing long tasks could be scattered and prevents the shrink of servers. The statistical result of task lengths show that near 50 % of tasks are short tasks (less than 10 min) while few tasks are long (more than 2 h), but long tasks exist (details in Sect. 2 and Table 1). The mixture of long and short tasks scatters the long tasks to different servers in a video cluster. When the video cluster is becoming more idle, these long tasks prevent the shrink of servers, but make them underutilized and waste energy.

While it is expected to distinguish long tasks from short ones, the task length is unknown when a request comes and needs prediction. Since the task lengths are needed in online scheduling algorithms, the prediction is required to be lightweight. To this end, we propose a task length prediction algorithm by analyzing the user access profiles. We observe that the lengths of streaming tasks have strong correlations with user access profiles, e.g., user IPs and access time. This makes the task length predictable. Also, the prediction is lightweight, because the classification of user IP and access time is instant.

With the prediction of task lengths, we propose three power-conserving online scheduling algorithms for VoD Task Scheduling (VTS): Descending Greedy Algorithm (DG-VTS), Long Task Isolation Algorithm (L-VTS), and their combined version Optimized Algorithm (O-VTS). In DG-VTS, we sort all tasks in a time window (e.g., 1 s in our evaluation) with descending task length, and then assign them greedily to servers, in which case a new server is allocated only when its previous ones are saturated. While a short time window is expected in online algorithms, it limits the number of tasks that are used for sorting. With few tasks in a time window, long tasks are also assigned to a server with short tasks to saturate the server. We then propose the L-VTS algorithm. In L-VTS, we isolate very long tasks from the others, and assign them to different set of servers. This isolation prevents the very long tasks to be mixed with short tasks, which could achieve significant power saving with the simple isolation. And finally, we incorporate the two algorithms into one algorithm named O-VTS. O-VTS first isolates the long tasks from the short ones into different sets, and then sorts tasks with descending task length in each set, followed by a greedy assignment. O-VTS achieves both benefits from DG-VTS and L-VTS.

Our contributions are summarized as follows:

1. We observe that the mixture of long and short streaming tasks leads to sub-optimal energy consumption in video streaming services. And we introduce a lightweight task length prediction algorithm with user access information, by studying the correlationship of task lengths and user access information.
2. We incorporate task lengths into online scheduling and propose a series of heuristic online scheduling algorithms for video streaming services, based on the predicted task lengths.
3. We evaluate our algorithms using both real datasets from a online education video trace and a media entertainment video service website. Results show that our algorithm can save energy by at least 10 % and even up to 150 % in the real datasets.

The rest of this paper is organized as follows. Section 2 introduces the characteristics of streaming tasks in VoD system and presents the formalized description of the VTS problem model. Section 3 describes the task length prediction algorithm and verifies its accuracy and performance. Section 4 proposes the heuristic algorithms solving the problem and Sect. 5 gives the experimental results and compares the algorithms. Sections 6 and 7 will be the related work and conclusions.

2 Problem Specification

In this section, we first study the characteristics of video steaming services in details. We then give the formalization description and prove that the power-conserving online scheduling problem is NP-Complete.

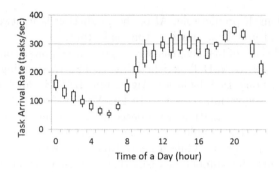

Fig. 2. Average task arrival rate in 24 h.

2.1   Task Characteristics

Task Arrival Rate. We study the task arrive rates from two platforms, XueTangX [4] and China Telecom [3]. Both of them have a regular pattern. The distribution of user accesses repeats by the cycle of 24 h. It basically turns out to increase from 6 a.m. to 8 p.m. and decrease from 8 p.m. to the next morning. This pattern conforms with the user habit of work and after-work hours. Figure 2 gives the distribution of task arrival rates in 24 h by analyzing log traces from a commercial VoD system in China Telecom [3], the bottom and top of every vertical virgule represent the minimize and maximum value of the average task number of the time region and the rectangle in the middle represents 90 % medium value of them. XuetangX [4] shows a similar pattern.

Task Lengths. We also study the characteristics of streaming task lengths. Table 1 shows the statistics of the task length distribution of statistical data [3,4]. There are two notable features of task length in VoD system: the high proportion of short tasks (less than 10 min) and the existence of extremely long tasks (more than 2 h). They both affect the scheduling strategies especially the extremely long task, which will be discussed in Sects. 4 and 5.

Power Consumption Model. From our previous work [5], we found that power consumption of each server has correlation with the number of tasks in

Table 1. Distribution of task lengths

Task length (min)	Percentage (%)	Task length (min)	Percentage (%)
0–5	36.47	5–10	12.50
10–25	18.22	25–50	20.77
50–120	11.68	>120	0.37

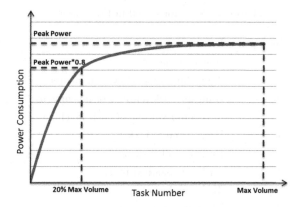

Fig. 3. Simplified Power Consumption model of the VoD system.

VoD systems. Figure 3 shows the variation of power consumption of one server with the growth of the workload scale. From the figure, we can see that the power consumption increases rapidly to nearly 0.8 times of the peak value at the first 20 % rise of the task number, and thereafter maintains at a high level throught the following 80 % task growth. Here, we define the maximum volume of each machine V as the task number that satisfies more than 95 % video playing requests with no longer than 5 s delay, which can be measured through experiments [5]. Based on this observation, we consider that, to save the power consumption of a whole VoD system, we should try to utilize each server to the best, which means to schedule as more tasks as possible on one server within its maximum volume V. In the following algorithms, we use this power-consumption/task-number model as the basis of calculation.

2.2 Problem Formalization

The power-conserving online scheduling problem for video streaming services can be defined as follows. The notations used in this paper are summarized in Table 2.

Input. Given m streaming tasks $T = \{t_1, t_2, ..., t_m\}$, a homogeneous cluster that has sufficient machines $A = \{a_1, a_2, ..., a_n\}$, each of them can process at most v tasks concurrently. The begin time and end time of task t_i is b_i and e_i, of which b_i is fixed when task arrives and e_i is calculate by adding b_i with a predicted task length. The tasks are independent so they can be assigned to any machine. A machine will be in *running* state when it has at least one task and switch to *idle* state otherwise, assuming the time cost of switching progress is constant, the power consumption of idle state is $0/s$ while that of running and switching state variates by the proportion of power consumption model with the growth of task number.

Output. The optimization target of the problem is to design an scheduling algorithm for the m tasks so that the total power consumption $Total\_PC$ of

Table 2. Notations used in this paper

Notation	Description
t_i	A streaming task
a_j	A machine in VoD system cluster
v_j	Runtime task number of machine a_j
V	Maximum volume of each machine
b_i	Begin time of task t_i
e_i	End time of task t_i
T_j	Task set assigned in a_j
m_j	Task number of T_j
d_j	Idle time of a_j
T_j_PC	Power consumption of T_j
$Total\_PC$	Total power consumption

the VoD system is minimized. That is to divide T into n disjoint subsets T_j $(j = 1, 2, 3, ..., n)$, in which each subset is assigned to one server, to make the sum of the longest running time of all servers as low as possible.

Assuming the task number of T_j is m_j, the idle time of a_j is d_j, it is worth noting that the idle time will be eliminated by the turn off/on time of the machine. Then the first and last task on a_j is t_{j1} and t_{jm_j}, the power consumption of a_j is T_j_PC, T_j_PC and $Total\_PC$ can be calculated as follows.

$$\sum_{j=1}^{n} m_j = m$$

$$Total\_PC = \sum_{j=1}^{n} T_j\_PC = \sum_{j=1}^{n} [(e_{jm_j} - b_{j1}) - d_j]$$

2.3   NP-Completeness

The VTS problem is equivalent to the wavelength assignment problem [6], which can be described as follows. In an optical linesystem with n links e_1, e_2, ..., e_n, with link e_i carrying f_i fibers. There is a demand by $[i, j]$ for $i \leq j$ if it requires links e_i, ..., e_j; the set of demands will be denoted by D. The load $l_i = l(e_i) = \lceil d_i/\mu \rceil$ on link e_i is the minimum number of fibers required to carry all the demands on link e_i, where d_i is the number of demands on link e_i and μ is the number of wavelengths. Comparing to the VTS problem, we can see that the equivalent elements respectively are the machine and the fiber, the streaming tasks and the demands, the task volume and the wavelength number. The wavelength assignment problem had been proved to be NP-complete by being reduced to an existing NP-complete problem, CIRCULAR ARC GRAPH COLORING [7]. So the VTS problem is also NP-Complete.

3   Task Length Prediction

In this section, we describe our task length prediction algorithm. The accuracy of task length prediction is important to the effectiveness of online scheduling algorithms for the VTS problem. We first define the task length and the transmission speed, and study the correlations between the task length and the user access profiles. Based on the correlations, we then propose our task length prediction algorithm. And finally, we valid our prediction algorithm using real datasets.

3.1   Definitions

Task Length. In this paper, the *Task Length* is defined as the period from the beginning of a data transmission between server and client to its end. It is worth noticing that the task length in the machine-view is different from the user-view, because no matter how long the user watch the video, the serving time of the server remain the same as the whole video has sent to the client-side. So we can represent the *Task Length* by the following formula (*VL* stands for *Video Length*, *TS* stands for *Transmission Speed*):

$$Task\ Length = VL/TS$$

Transmission Speed. The above *Video Length* in the formula is the playing time of the video ordered by user multiply by its code rate, which is measured by kilobytes and easy to acquire in database. In our online educational platform, the videos are saved as their entire segments in storage. While in some entertainment video web sites, long videos are cutted into shorter segments by about 5 to 7 min, to provide transfering too many unnecessary video data that users have not ordered, so the *Video Length* here means the length of the short video segments. Meanwhile we define the *Transmission Speed* as the data volume of the video file sent by a VoD system cluster server to client per second, it is regularly recorded in the daily log trace of the system. As the video length information already exist, the key stage of the task length prediction is the prediction of *Transmission Speed*. But at the very beginning of a streaming task, the possible average transmission speed of the video file is unknown, the only reference data are the historical log trace of the system.

3.2   Influence Factors

From the definitions we can conclude that the key technique of task length prediction is to accurately calculate the *Transmission Speed*. In this paper, we use the historical data offline training technique based on two conclusions discovered by analyzing and comparing the real dataset of log trace from XuetangX [4]:

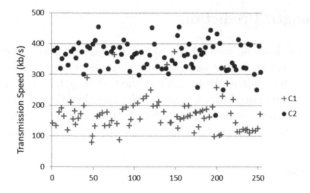

Fig. 4. The Transmission Speed Distribution of two Class C IP address fields from the long trace dataset.

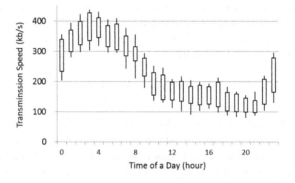

Fig. 5. The average Transmission Speed variation integrated in 24 h from the log trace dataset.

Transmission Speed Has Weak Relation with Server-Side Environment. As the location of videos' hosting server and the surrounding network environment are similar, the tasks that order different videos by the same user will get the similar transmission speed. That is why the better network environment always provides fluent watching experience no matter which video the user orders [3].

Transmission Speed Is Sensitive to the Client-Side Characteristics. We observe from the log trace analyzing that the most important influence factor is the client-side of a video-demand connection, in which the two main factors are the user's IP address field from spatial dimension and variation tendency through the free/busy time in 24 h from time dimension.

Spatial Dimension. Figure 4 shows the average *Transmission Speed* Distribution from two user-gathered Class C[1] IP address fields C1 and C2. We can see that the network environment of client side are roughly similar in the same field, while can be clearly distinguished between different ones. Besides, the tasks from the same IP address have more closer *Transmission Speed*. So we consider the IP address field as the primary influencing factor and apply it in the prediction algorithm.

Time Dimension. Figure 5 displays the average *Transmission Speed* concentrated in 24 h from the real log trace of XuetangX [4]. The bottom and top of every vertical virgule represent the minimize and maximum value of the average transmission speeds of the regions and the rectangle in the middle represents 90 % medium value of them. We can see that the *Transmission Speed* is declining from 5 a.m. to 21 p.m., then rising till the second morning, which is basically the division of working and off-working hours of the user. In addition, though the *Transmission Speed* also makes a little difference at the dimension of regional divergence, but they have nearly the same variation tendency and their absolute value do not have much difference. This also confirms that the geographical region variance is not an important influencing factors.

3.3   Prediction Algorithm

From the above observations, we can conclude that predicting *Transmission Speed* is the key point of the Task Length Prediction Algorithm. Figures 6 and 7 show the transmission speed distribution of a Class C and a Class B[2] IP address fields aggregated in 24 h from the real dataset of XuetangX. We have found that the general changing pattern can be regressed to line by being divided into three time regions, so we employ the Linear Regression method to deduce the *Transmission Speed* from its changing curve fitting from the historical data splashes. Algorithm 1 describes the key idea of the Task Length Prediction Algorithm.

We estimate the *Transmission Speed* in the following steps. Table 3 shows the equations of linear regression in the two Figures. When a streaming task generates, the predictor will first obtain the IP address of the acquiring user, the ID of the acquired video and record the begin time, then:

(i) Check the historical tasks from the offline training data base by IP address. If the IP exists, it means the user exists in the historical data, as the equation of linear regression has two parameters and there are mainly three time regions of speed changing line in one day, we need at least six splashes to compute the linear function. If the historical records are enough, we will use them to deduce the equation of linear regression and calculate the predicted *Transmission Speed* by its begin time; Otherwise the predictor will search for the former tasks that from the same class C even B IP address field for sufficient log data and deduce

---

[1] An IP address set contains 256 addresses start from 192.0.0.0 to 223.255.255.255, usually used in local area network like office buildings.

[2] An IP address set contains 65536 addresses start from 128.0.0.0 to 191.255.255.255, usually used in massive-node network like universities.

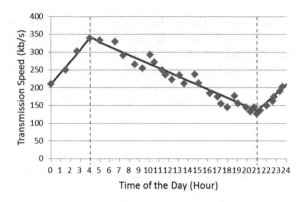

Fig. 6. The Transmission Speed Distribution of a Class C IP address fields integrated in 24 h from the log trace dataset.

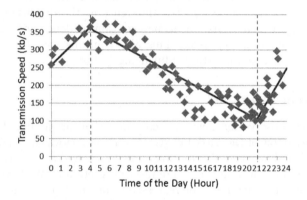

Fig. 7. The Transmission Speed Distribution of a Class B IP address fields integrated in 24 h from the log trace dataset.

the linear equation of these addresses and calculate the predicted *Transmission Speed*. If none of the above searchings have any results, mark the task's IP address as new.

(ii) Search the video information database by video ID to find each task's *Video Length*. If a task is marked as new in Step 1, the predictor will conservatively take the *Video Length* as its *Task Length*, otherwise it will divide the *Video Length* by *Transmission Speed* to calculate the *Task Length*. The end time of a task can be simply calculated by adding the begin time with *Task Length*.

3.4   Algorithm Validation

We use the datasets from the log trace of the online education platform XuetangX [4] and the entertainment video service platform of China Telecom [3]. To evaluate the performance of the prediction algorithm, we divide the log trace data into two sets: one for offline training and the other for online scheduling

Table 3. Equations of linear regression in Figs. 6 and 7

Time	Figure 6	Figure 7
0 a.m.–4 a.m	y = 32.8x + 210.7	y = 27.3x + 258.5
4 a.m.–9 p.m	y = −12.2x + 388.0	y = −17.6x + 450.9
9 p.m.–0 a.m	y = 25.9x − 390.1	y = 47.1x − 879.2

Algorithm 1. Task Length Prediction in VTS Problem.

Require:

The *IP address* of the user who starts t_i: IP_i;

The *Video ID* accessed by t_i: VID_i, video database DB;

The *begin time* of t_i: b_i, historical tasks records H;

Ensure:

Predicted Transmission Speed and Task Length of t_i;

1: /* Step 1. Transmission Speed Prediction */

2: **for** $t_j \in H \&\& b_j \in$ time region of b_i:

3:     **if** $IP_j == IP_i$:

4:         **then** mark down $t_j \in H'$, records++;

5:     **if** $records > 1$:

6:         **then** linear regression on H': $y = kx + c$;

$$TransmissionSpeed = kb_i + c$$

7:     **else if** $IP_j \in$ Class C field of IP_i:

8:         **then** mark down $t_j \in H'$, records++;

9:     **if** $records > 1$:

10:         **then** do statement 6;

11:     **else if** $IP_j \in$ Class B field of IP_i:

12:         **then** mark down $t_j \in H'$, records++;

13:     **if** $records > 1$:

14:         **then** do statement 6;

15:     **else** $IP_i = new$;

16: /* Step 2. Task Length and End Time Calculation*/

17: Search for $VideoLength$ by VID_i in DB;

18: **if** $IP_i == new$:

19:     **then** $TaskLength = VideoLength$;

20: **else** $TaskLength = VideoLength/TransmissionSpeed$.

21: $e_i = b_i + TaskLength$.

22: **return** $TaskLength$ and end time e_i of task t_i.

---

simulation. We calculate the predicted *Transmission Speed* of the tasks in the second parts by the rules extracted from the first one, then compared with their real value recorded in the original trace.

Accuracy. We choose the Goodness of Fit as the measuring standard of the prediction algorithm. The goodness of fit here is considered as the fitting degree between the predicted value and the real value. It is simplified defined as follows:

$$Goodness\ of\ Fit = TS_p/TS_r$$

The TS_p and TS_r stand for the predicted and real *Transmission Speed*. From the definition we can see that the more the value of Goodness of Fit close to 1, the better the prediction algorithm is. So we calculate the Relative Standard Deviation of all the Goodness of Fit of each task and give their mean value 0.151. It means that the prediction algorithm can give an acceptable *Transmission Speed* with the accuracy probability of 85 %. The following experiments in Sect. 5.2 show that this result is befitting enough for the scheduling algorithms.

Overhead. As the prediction information is obtained by just one or two query operations from the existing offline training data base, the overhead is almost negligible compared with the following optimization algorithms. Besides, most of the commercial VoD service web sites will play advertisements for dozens of seconds, which provides sufficient time window for the prediction and even the scheduling procedures.

The subsequent experiments of the task scheduling algorithms will show that our prediction algorithm is precise enough to provide the proper predicted task length to the optimization algorithms. But we will also explore more accurate techniques to satisfy more complex systems like scheduling multiple types of task in heterogeneous data center environments in the future.

4   Online Scheduling Algorithms

With the assistance of the task length prediction algorithm, we propose a series of heuristic algorithms to solve the online scheduling problem of video streaming services for power conserving. We firstly give an analysis of the theoretic lower bound of $Total\_PC$, then try out the most intuitive greedy algorithm and propose three optimized online algorithms to improve the solution of the greedy one. The optimized algorithms will be discussed in the later three sections. We only show the last one in Algorithm 2 due to space limitations.

4.1   Theoretic Lower Bound

A theoretic lower bound (TLB) is necessary in a mathematical model to be compared with the solutions of various algorithms. In VTS problem, we can get the exact number of tasks exist in every second if all the begin and end time of tasks are known. The least machine number needed in every second is also set by machine volume v divides task number. As the start and end time of every tasks is objectively fixed, it is easy to get the offline task length information and calculate the theoretical optimal value as the comparison standard for the later algorithms. So the total power consumption can be calculated by summarizing the power of each second which equals to the least machine number, because the power consumption is $1/s$. At the same time, the least number of machines to process the task can also be recorded after scanning the whole task arriving and leaving range.

4.2   Greedy Algorithm

Greedy algorithm is one of the simplest online scheduling strategies. It always make the best choice at present without considering the global situation. In the Greedy Algorithm for VTS problem (G-VTS), tasks are directly arranged on the first machine that has free slots.

As greedy algorithm does not take other tasks features into account when assigning the current task, it may performs poorly in most circumstances especially like task decreasing period. In this case, the former long tasks is assigned randomly in decentralized machines, with short ones ended gradually, plenty of machines could not turn to idle state, because of one or two long tasks left on them, which increases the total consumption of the cluster. In our model, the G-VTS algorithm is at least 15 % inferior to the theoretical optimal value and much more worse with a higher task decreasing ratio. Experiments show that the power waste of greedy assignment reaches up to 2 or 3 times than the Theoretic Lower Bound and sometimes even worse if the tasks are extremely long. On the basis of this characteristic, we put forward the following three algorithms.

4.3   Descending Greedy Algorithm

The Descending Greedy (DG) Algorithm is an effective optimization of the greedy algorithm in classic Multi-Processor Scheduling (MPS) problem [8]. It sorts the tasks in descending order by length before assigning them to the machines greedily. It can be proved that DG-MPS can improve the worst case solution from 2 times of the optimum to 1.5 times.

So we introduce the DG-MPS algorithm to the VTS problem and become another optimized algorithm based on G-VTS, the DG-VTS algorithm. The prediction algorithm also guarantees the practicable of the online scheduling. Different from the one in MPS, DG-VTS only sorts the tasks that arrive at the same second. As there are always dozens of tasks arrive simultaneously in normal-scaled VoD systems, the algorithm will exploit its advantage as well as in MPS problem.

4.4   Long Task Isolation Algorithm

While a short time window is expected in online algorithms, it limits the number of tasks that are used for sorting. With few tasks in a time window, long tasks are also assigned to a server with short tasks to saturate the server.

We then propose the L-VTS algorithm. The key idea of L-VTS algorithm is scheduling the long tasks in a number of specific machines, to avoid the situations when task number getting down and the long tasks keeping too many few-task-machines from idle state. As the task length has been predicted reasonably, we can trustingly make use of it to proceed the online scheduling. By restricting the long tasks scheduled in the smallest scale cluster, the power consumption waste caused by the long tasks will be reduced significantly.

According to the definitions in Sect. 2, the L-VTS algorithm firstly divides the task set into two part: normal length tasks T_s and long tasks T_l (longer than 30 min), then use G-VTS on them separately to calculate $Total\_PC_s$ and $Total\_PC_l$ respectively and adds them together to be $Total\_PC$.

4.5   Optimized Algorithm

We give the final integrated algorithm of VTS problem O-VTS in Algorithm 2. By combining the advantages of both L-VTS and DG-VTS, O-VTS algorithm will first divide the task set into normal tasks and long tasks, then schedule them separately using DG-VTS in their own cluster and get the $Total\_PC$ by the aggregation of the two parts.

It is satisfactory that the O-VTS algorithm not only has almost the same time complexity compared with the former ones but also easy to implement. The most important is that O-VTS can achieve an outstanding near optimum solution with only one more known condition (task length) than the on-line greedy algorithm. This suggests that a task length prediction based on-line scheduling for the VoD system is very promising.

5   Experimental Results

In this section, we first present the datasets we used in the evaluation. We then evaluate our proposed algorithms in both algorithm performance and complexity, in order to answer the following two questions: (1) How do our proposed algorithms perform in power conservation? (2) How much is the overhead of our proposed algorithms?

5.1   Evaluation Datasets

In the evaluation, we use both two datasets: Real-world log traces from an online education website and a media entertainment website. The first one is the log trace from a popular online education platform XuetangX [4], and the second one is generated with characteristics from mainstream video services [1] based on traces from a China Telecom VoD system [3]. Details of the two datasets are as follows:

Online Education Dataset. The online education dataset consists of a log trace covering 121 days from XuetangX [4]. We choose a part of the log trace as the offline training set and the rest part as the experimental test case. Different from the commercial entertaining VoD system, the data from XuetangX has some specialties like the single category of video type and a more specific user group. Though the real data can totally qualified for verifying our scheduling strategies, we still prepare another type of video dataset to explore the optimization scope of the algorithms.

Media Entertainment Dataset. The media entertainment dataset is generated based on a log trace covering 7 months in a VoD system with about

---

Algorithm 2. O-VTS: Optimized Algorithm of Power-Conserving Online Scheduling for Video Streaming Services.

Require:
　　The set of streaming tasks $T = \{t_1, t_2, ..., t_m\}$;
　　The set of homogeneous machines $A = \{a_1, a_2, ..., a_n\}$;
　　The maximum volume of each machine V;
　　Begin time b_i, end time e_i, predicted end time e_i' of t_i.
Ensure:
　　Assign T to A to minimize the $Total\_PC$;
 1: /* Step 1. Initialization */
 2: **for** $t_i \in T$:
 3: 　　**if** exist the set $\{t_i, ..., t_j\}$ that $b_i = ... = b_k = ... = b_j$:
 4: 　　　　**then** sort the set by e_k' in descending order;
 5: 　　**if** $(e_i' - b_i) <$ *long task threshold*:
 6: 　　　　$t_i \in T_s$;
 7: 　　**else:**
 8: 　　　　$t_i \in T_l$;
 9: Divide A into A_s and A_l by the needs of T_s and T_l.
10: /* Step 2. Assign the tasks online */
11: **for** $t_i \in T_s$, $a_j \in A_s$:
12: 　　**if** exist t_k on a_j that $e_k < b_i$:
13: 　　　　**then** $v_j = v_j - 1$;
14: 　　**if** $v_j < V$
15: 　　　　**then** $f(t_i) = a_j$, $v_j = v_j + 1$;
16: **for** $t_i \in T_l$, $a_j \in A_l$: do statement 12–15;
17: Task assignment: $f_s: T_s \to A_s$, $f_l: T_l \to A_l$, $f = f_s \cup f_l$;
18: /* Step 3. Calculate $Total\_PC$ by $f: T \to A$ */
19: **for** $a_j \in A$, scan all the m_j tasks:
20: 　　**if** exist idling time before any task that $\delta t > 0$:
21: 　　　　**then** idling time of a_j: $d_j \mathrel{+}= \delta t$;
22: Give power consumption of a_j: $T_j\_PC = (e_{jm_j}\text{-}b_{j1})\text{-}d_j$
23: The total power consumption of the cluster:

$$Total\_PC = \sum_{j=1}^{n} T_j\_PC = \sum_{j=1}^{n} [(e_{jm_j} - b_{j1}) - d_j]$$

24: **return** $f: T \to A$ and $Total\_PC$.

150,000 users deployed by China Telecom. This log trace is authentic and practical, however, its scale is not representative enough. It can be counted that there are about twenty millions tasks totally in half a year, that is about only one task per second in average. While in a mainstream VoD service website, there are always hundreds of tasks per second accessing even one popular video.

To overcome the disadvantages of this dataset, we reference both the summarized characteristics of real VoD system user behavior [1] and the statistical rules published in [3] to obtain a large-scaled series of streaming tasks as our experimental dataset. This log trace has the same quantitative variation and length distribution as practical situation so it can better reflect the algorithms' functionality in real world. The task length distribution is summarized in Table 1.

5.2   Algorithm Performance

In this section, we evaluate the performance of our proposed three algorithms, and compare them to the Greedy Algorithm and the theoretic lower bound (TLB). These algorithms are respectively evaluated using both of the two datasets.

Online Education Dataset. Figure 8 shows the normalized power consumption results given by the evaluated four algorithms and the theoretic lower bound in the first dataset. The power consumption is calculated by total running time of servers, and are normalized to that of TLB. Each algorithm has both its online and offline versions evaluated except the Greedy Algorithm, which does not need the task length information. The online algorithms use predicted task lengths, while the offline algorithms use actual task lengths in the log traces. From the figure, we have three observations:

(i) Tasks length prediction is effective, as the differences between online and offline algorithms are small. The three algorithms all have the difference around 1.5 %, which is acceptable in prediction. And it is usable in the online scheduling algorithms that are based on this prediction.

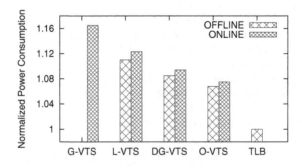

Fig. 8. Normalized power consumption of the four algorithms and their offline version. (Online Education Dataset)

(ii) The most intuitive algorithm G-VTS has the solution that is about 17 % higher than the theoretic lower bound (TLB). O-VTS and its online version obtain the best approximative result, they lower down the power consumption by nearly 10 %. It means that if the total electric charge of a VoD system is a million dollars a year, our scheduling strategy will help saving near a hundred thousand dollars.

(iii) The DG-VTS and L-VTS algorithm also outperforms the greedy solution by about 4–7%. The DG-VTS is a little better than L-VTS. This is mainly because the task length distribution of XuetangX is not as broad as commercial VoD systems and have less long tasks.

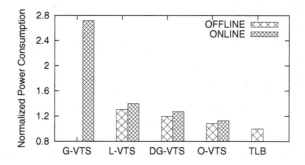

Fig. 9. Normalized power consumption of the four algorithms and their offline version. (Media Entertainment Dataset)

Media Entertainment Dataset. In the media entertainment dataset evaluation, we choose log traces in the decreasing phase of task arrivals, i.e., 8 p.m. to 6 a.m. the next day. The task length distribution is fixed according to the pattern in Table 1 and the longest task is no more than 12 h. Figure 9 shows the normalized power consumption results given by the evaluated four algorithms and the theoretic lower bound in media entertainment dataset. We can also see the significant improvement from our algorithms:

(i) The G-VTS algorithm performs so poor that it has nearly 250 % to 300 % optimization space towards the TLB.
(ii) The L-VTS and DG-VTS algorithm both can improve the greedy one in a large extent of 160 % to 180 %.
(iii) The O-VTS algorithm can optimize the VTS problem to a very satisfactory result, it only has no more than 7 % distinction compared with the TLB.

As the users who study online are usually more concentrate than the users watching news, TV series or movies online, but the teaching videos are shorter than most of the entertainment video, so the average video length and its variation range of the media entertainment website is much longer than the online education website, which has a great influence on our scheduling algorithms. That is why the second dataset has much better power consumption result than the first one.

5.3 Algorithm Complexity

We also evaluate the algorithm complexity in terms of algorithm execution time, in order to evaluate its impact on the latency of online scheduling. We use both theoretic and measured execution time in this evaluation. As the data volume of the real data set is small, all of the algorithms can be executed in tens of milliseconds, the overhead is almost negligible. So we focus on the algorithm efficiency with the media entertainment data set in this section.

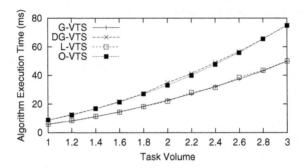

Fig. 10. Comparison of scheduling algorithms on time complexity. (X-axis is the magnification of the task volume in media entertainment dataset)

Theoretic Time Complexity. As the core of the algorithms is task assignment, we consider the time consuming of this part as the evaluation target. In the fact that all the four algorithms have the same time complexity $O(nlogn)$, because all the tasks are checked only once before choosing a machine for them in these assignment strategies. Besides, DG-VTS and O-VTS have an extra sorting procedure but still do not add the complexity dimensionality.

Measured Time Complexity. We use the data in last experiment with the 72 h longest tasks as basis and variation the task number per second and record the total execution time and assigning time to measure the relationship between calculating time and the problem scale. Figure 10 gives the charts of which x-axis is the magnification of the media entertainment dataset task number (300 tasks per second) and the y-axis is the assigning time of the algorithms, it shows that the calculating time of the four algorithms all increase linearly with the increasing of the task number.

6   Related Work

In this section, we discuss existing works that are closely related to our work in the following aspects:

VoD Systems. H. Yu et al. contributes one of the earliest comprehensive user behavior analysis in large-scale VoD system [3]. It gives a statistical introduction of streaming tasks characteristic, content access patterns and their implications based on empirical data. We get most of our test data from the order log of this work and summarize the regularities of the streaming tasks to construct the experimental benchmark. The data scale of the test set is referenced from the public index center of Sohu Video system [1], which is one of the most mainstream VoD website in China.

Task Length Prediction. Many works have been concentrated on task length prediction involving many kinds of areas. They can be as simple as the pure averaging algorithm [9], or very complicated like the exponential smoothing forecasting method [10,11]. Even the burgeoning machine learning techniques [12] are also applied into is region. Though the strategy we used in this paper is the simple averaging algorithm, it can properly provide the task length ranking informations which is accurate enough to assist the scheduling algorithms, and also, with a negligible overhead.

Task Assignment. The VoD Task Scheduling (VTS) problem can be intuitively reduced to classical Multi-Processor Scheduling (MPS) problem [8], in the fact there are at least two differences between them: a) As the VoD system is obliged to corresponding customers in a short tolerable time and stop the service when transmission completes, the streaming tasks all have fixed begin and end time; In MPS, all tasks arrive at the very beginning and can be processed at any time; b) The optimization goal of VTS is power-conserving of VoD clusters while that of MPS is minimizing the processing time on multi-processor systems.

Task assignment is also a fairly common research in many kinds of areas like MapReduce task scheduling [13–15], cloud computing QoS guarantee [12,16,17] and multi-task arrangement in MPSoC systems [18–21]. Paragon [12] is an online interference-aware scheduler in heterogeneous data center. It predicts the characteristics of the incoming workload by identifying similarities to previous applications and greedily schedules them in a interference-minimized and server utilization-maximized way. T. Liu et al. combines the task assignment problem with cache partitioning and locking for minimizing WCET (Worst-Case Execution Time) on MPSoC systems [18]. It is a typical theoretical research work with mathematical model and heuristic algorithms to give a approximate solution for an NP-Hard problem.

Power Conservation. Many research works have been conducted for power conservation from different levels, ranging from architecture level to data center level [22–26]. In VoD clusters, Y. Chai has proposed a enegery-conserving data migaration for streaming storage systems [27]. This work focuses on the energy consumption in storage systems and optimizes data migration algorithms. In comparison, our scheme focuses on the energy consumption of running servers and optimizes task scheduling algorithms.

There are also plenty of works aim at power conservation in some other platforms. J. Mars et al. provide a series of works [28,29] that contribute a lot in trading off between the performance of workloads and the cost of the platform mainly on internet searching engines. But the works are very hard to be accepted by some large-scale service providers, as they have vast amount of users, the stability of the system is far more important than operating costs. So the more slight the scheduler is, the more possible and suitable it can be applied in real systems, which is also the principle we compliant in the design of our scheduling algorithms.

7   Conclusion and Future Work

Power consumption is becoming an important design issue in video clusters with increased popularity of video services. Existing scheduling algorithms ignore the phenomena that the mixed long and short tasks could lead to sub-optimal energy consumption. In this paper, we propose a lightweight task length prediction algorithm, based on our study of correlation-ships between task lengths and user access information. With the predicted task lengths, we then propose three heuristics power-conserving online scheduling algorithms. The three algorithms are evaluated using both log traces from online education systems and media entertainment platform that follow the empirical characteristics from mainstream video service websites. Results show that our algorithms save significant energy with negligible overhead.

There are three aspects we would like to improve in the future. The first is to improve the accuracy of task length prediction with more sophisticated techniques. The second is to consider the task migration in the model, which needs to balance the power savings and migration overhead. The third is to introduce our algorithms to a more complex model with heterogeneous servers, task interference and various task types.

Acknowledgments. This work is supported by National High-tech R&D Program (863 Program, Grant No. 2012AA010903), and National Natural Science Foundation of China (Grant No. 61133006).

References

1. The index center of Sohu VoD system. http://index.tv.sohu.com
2. IDC prediction report of 2013. http://www.idc.com/research/Prediction13/
3. Hongliang, Y., Zheng, D., Zhao, B., Zheng, W.: Understanding user behavior in large-scale video-on-demand systems. In: ACM SIGOPS Operating Systems Review. ACM (2006)
4. The massive open online course platform in China. http://www.xuetangx.com/
5. Feng, S., Zhang, H., Chen, W.: Shall I use heterogeneous data centers? a case study on video on demand systems. In: Proceedings of the 15th IEEE International Conference on High Performance Computing and Communications (HPCC). IEEE (2013)

6. Winkler, P., Zhang, L.: Wavelength assignment and generalized interval graph coloring. In: Proceedings of the 14th Annual ACM-SIAM Symposium on Discrete Algorithms. SIAM (2003)
7. Garey, M.R., Johnson, D.S., Miller, G.L., Papadimitriou, C.H.: The complexity of coloring circular arcs and chords. SIAM J. Algebraic Discrete Methods 1, 216–227 (1980)
8. Kleinberg, J., Tardos, E., Li'ang, Z., Wanling, Q.: Algorithm Design. Tsinghua University Press, Beijing (2007)
9. Jackson, D.B., Snell, Q.O., Clement, M.J.: Core algorithms of the Maui scheduler. In: Feitelson, D.G., Rudolph, L. (eds.) JSSPP 2001. LNCS, vol. 2221, p. 87. Springer, Heidelberg (2001)
10. Billah, B., King, M.L., Snyder, R.D., Koehler, A.B.: Exponential smoothing model selection for forecasting. Int. J. Forecast. 22, 239–247 (2006)
11. Niu, S., Zhai, J., Ma, X., Tang, X., Chen, W.: Cost-effective cloud HPC resource provisioning by building semi-elastic virtual clusters. In: Proceedings of International Conference for High Performance Computing, Networking, Storage and Analysis (SC). ACM (2013)
12. Delimitrou, C., Kozyrakis, C: Paragon: QoS-aware scheduling for heterogeneous datacenters. In: Proceedings of the 18th International Conference on Architectural Support for Programming Languages and Operating Systems (ASPLOS). ACM (2013)
13. Isard, M., Prabhakaran, V., Currey, J., Wieder, U., Talwar, K., Goldberg, A.: Quincy: fair scheduling for distributed computing clusters. In: Proceedings of the 22nd ACM SIGOPS Symposium on Operating Systems Principles (SOSP). ACM (2009)
14. Zaharia, M., Borthakur, D., Sarma, J.S., Elmeleegy, K., Shenker, S., Stoica, I.: Delay scheduling: a simple technique for achieving locality and fairness in cluster scheduling. In: Proceedings of the 5th European Conference on Computer Systems (EuroSys). ACM (2010)
15. Ahmad, F., Chakradhar, S.T., Raghunathan, A., Vijaykumar, T.N.: Tarazu: optimizing mapreduce on heterogeneous clusters. In: ACM SIGARCH Computer Architecture News. ACM (2012)
16. Van Craeynest, K., Jaleel, A., Eeckhout, L., Narvaez, P., Emer, J.: Scheduling heterogeneous multi-cores through performance impact estimation (PIE). In: Proceedings of the 39th International Symposium on Computer Architecture (ISCA). IEEE (2012)
17. Shelepov, D., Saez Alcaide, J.C., Jeffery, S., Fedorova, A., Perez, N., Huang, Z.F., Blagodurov, S., Kumar, V.: HASS: a scheduler for heterogeneous multicore systems. ACM SIGOPS Oper. Syst. Rev. 43, 66–75 (2009)
18. Liu, T., Zhao, Y., Li, M., Xue, C.J.: Task assignment with cache partitioning and locking for WCET minimization on MPSoC. In: Proceedings of the 39th International Conference on Parallel Processing (ICPP). IEEE (2010)
19. Fedorova, A., Seltzer, M., Smith, M.D., Small, C.: CASC: a cache-aware scheduling algorithm for multithreaded chip multiprocessors. Technical report TR-2005-0142, Sun Labs (2005)
20. Fedorova, A., Seltzer, M., Smith, M.D.: Cache-fair thread scheduling for multicore processors. Technical report TR-17-06 (2006)
21. Calandrino, J.M., Anderson, J.H.: Cache-aware real-time scheduling on multicore platforms: heuristics and a case study. In: Proceedings of Euromicro Conference on Real-Time Systems (ECRTS). IEEE (2008)

22. Goiri, Í., Katsak, W., Le, K., Nguyen, T.D., Bianchini, R.: Parasol and GreenSwitch: managing datacenters powered by renewable energy. In Proceedings of the 18th International Conference on Architectural Support for Programming Languages and Operating Systems (ASPLOS). ACM (2013)

23. Shen, K., Shriraman, A., Dwarkadas, S., Zhang, X., Chen, Z.: Power containers: an OS facility for fine-grained power and energy management on multicore servers. In: Proceedings of the 18th International Conference on Architectural Support for Programming Languages and Operating Systems (ASPLOS). ACM (2013)

24. Govindan, S., Wang, D., Sivasubramaniam, A., Urgaonkar, B.: Leveraging stored energy for handling power emergencies in aggressively provisioned datacenters. In: ACM SIGARCH Computer Architecture News. ACM (2012)

25. Liu, S., Pattabiraman, K., Moscibroda, T., Zorn, B.G.: Flikker: saving DRAM refresh-power through critical data partitioning. ACM SIGPLAN Not. **47**, 213–224 (2012)

26. Ahmad, F., Vijaykumar, T.N.: Joint optimization of idle and cooling power in data centers while maintaining response time. ACM SIGPLAN Not. **45**, 243–256 (2010)

27. Chai, Y., Zhihui, D., Bader, D.A., Qin, X.: Efficient data migration to conserve energy in streaming media storage systems. IEEE Trans. Parallel Distrib. Syst. **23**(11), 2081–2093 (2012)

28. Mars, J., Tang, L., Hundt, R.: Heterogeneity in "homogeneous" warehouse-scale computers: a performance opportunity. Comput. Architect. Lett. **10**(2), 29–32 (2011)

29. Mars, J., Lingjia, T., Skadron, K., Soffa, M.L.: Increasing utilization in modern warehouse-scale computers using bubble-up. IEEE Micro **32**(3), 88–99 (2012)

Prevent Deadlock and Remove Blocking for Self-Timed Systems

Edwin H.-M. Sha[1,2], Weiwen Jiang[1(✉)], Qingfeng Zhuge[1,2], Xianzhang Chen[1], and Lei Yang[1]

[1] College of Computer Science, Chongqing University, Chongqing 400044, China
{edwinsha,jiang.wwen,qfzhuge,xzchen109,yanglary}@gmail.com
[2] Key Laboratory of Dependable Service Computing in Cyber Physical Society, Ministry of Education, Chongqing 400044, China

Abstract. In the design of distributed embedded systems, designers face two problems: how to prevent deadlock and how to improve performance. An accurate model providing abstractions for functionality and performance is important to solve these problems. Self-timed system model that conducts communications based on handshaking protocols is suitable to model these distributed embedded systems. This paper studies the fundamental properties of self-timed systems and proposes solutions of the above two problems. First, we present the necessary and sufficient conditions for a self-timed system constructed from an application to incur deadlocks; then we propose approaches to prevent any deadlocks in constructing self-timed systems. Second, we observe that the different pace of data progressing on two paths, having common source/destination nodes, may cause blocking events (not deadlock) which dramatically degrade the system performance. We establish theorems to detect blocking events and design Mixed-Integer Linear Programming (MILP) formulas to eliminate these events. Experimental results show that most self-timed systems constructed by a straightforward approach incur possible deadlocks, while our proposed methods guarantee no deadlocks. Furthermore, our proposed techniques to eliminate blocking events achieve 48.23 % performance improvements on average, compared with the straightforward approach.

Keywords: Self-timed system · DFG · Deadlock · Blocking event · Performance

1 Introduction and Related Work

As the application-specific distributed embedded system became more complicated, such as Cyber-Physical System (CPS) and Internet of Things (IoT), there are two realistic problems that trouble designers: on functionality — how to prevent deadlocks; and on performance — how to ensure a desired system throughput. As to deadlocks, we observed that the lack of buffers is the root cause of deadlocks. Thus, we insert buffers to prevent deadlocks. The problem of inserting buffers to prevent deadlock, however, is not trivial. Since the resource in

© Springer International Publishing Switzerland 2015
G. Wang et al. (Eds.): ICA3PP 2015, Part I, LNCS 9528, pp. 155–169, 2015.
DOI: 10.1007/978-3-319-27119-4_11

a CPS or an IoT system is limited, we need to minimize the number of costly buffers inserted in the system. As to performance, we found that "blocking event" in many systems dramatically degrades the system performance. The blocking event (not deadlock) is caused by the different pace of data progressing on two paths which have a common source node and a common destination node. By analyzing the fundamental property of system operations, we found that inserting buffer can eliminate the blocking event. This paper presents techniques that determine the proper amount of buffers to be inserted at the right places in the system to prevent deadlocks and increase performance.

Application-specific distributed embedded systems not only require lots of computation and communication, but also have to provide real-time performance and low cost [18]. With the increase of the system scale, computation and communication become more complicated and the system performance becomes harder to analyze. The design of distributed embedded system increasingly relies on system-level models. The self-timed system, employing hand-shaking protocol to control the communication rather than global clock, is one of the most suitable candidates to model a complex application-specific distributed embedded system. As most of previous research efforts on self-timed system focus on the circuit-level design [2,7,16,17], system-level design is still in its infancy. This paper introduces the self-timed system to model the distributed embedded system and applies the data-flow graph (DFG) to model an application. We study two fundamental problems of constructing a self-timed system from a given DFG: (1) how to construct a self-timed system fully following the behavior of the given DFG, especially ensuring deadlock-free? (2) how to eliminate blocking events in a self-timed system with the minimum amount of buffers?

The basic idea of preventing deadlocks and eliminating blocking event is to carefully insert "buffer". In self-timed system model, buffer is a self-timed unit without processing element. By inserting a proper number of buffers to appropriate positions, we can guarantee that self-timed systems have no deadlocks.

For the issue of deadlocks, deadlock prevention in the process of constructing self-timed systems is important while not well studied. Previous researches [1,7] have observed that bubble starvation in self-timed "rings" causes deadlocks, which is a special case of deadlock situations presented in the paper. We present the necessary and sufficient conditions of a general-structure self-timed system that has deadlocks, and then give techniques to prevent deadlocks.

For the issue of blocking events, to the best of authors' knowledge, no research efforts target on eliminating blocking events in a self-timed system. A similar problem is called slack matching [1,6,13,14]; however, results of these works can hardly be applied, since their system models target on circuit level and these models are not accordant with distributed embedded systems. This paper establishes theorems providing formulas to detect blocking events in a self-timed system. Based on proposed theorems, we develop MILP formulas to remove blocking events with minimum amount of buffers.

Main contributions of this paper are listed as follows.

- Study fundamental problems of how to construct a self-timed system from a given DFG;
- present the necessary and sufficient conditions for self-timed system constructed from an application to incur deadlocks;
- analyze the blocking event and establish theorems providing formulas to detect blocking events in a self-timed system;
- propose techniques to prevent deadlocks and remove blocking events.

In order to conduct comprehensive experiments, we developed a simulator using SystemC that can automatically build a self-timed system from a given DFG. Experimental results show that self-timed systems constructed by the straightforward approach incur deadlocks for many benchmarks, while our techniques guarantee no deadlocks. Furthermore, our proposed MILP approach to eliminate blocking events achieves significant improvement on performance. On average, systems constructed by the proposed techniques achieve 42% time-performance improvement, compared with those systems without deadlocks.

The rest of this paper is organized as follows. In Sect. 2, we introduce the self-timed system model. Deadlock situations are discussed in Sect. 3. Blocking issues are analyzed in Sect. 4. Experimental results are presented in Sect. 5. Section 6 concludes this paper.

2   System Model and Problem Definition

2.1   Application Definition

In this paper, an application is described as a data-flow graph (DFG), which is widely used in many fields; e.g. in program descriptions [3,12]. A **Data-Flow Graph** $G = (V, E, d, et, dt)$ is an edge-weighted directed graph, where V is the set of nodes, representing computation tasks; $E \subseteq V \times V$ is the set of edges, representing the precedence relations among task nodes. For a node $v \in V$, $et(v)$ represents the execution time of task v. For an edge $e \in E$, $e = (u, v)$, $d(e)$ represents the number of delays associated with edge e, and $dt(e)$ represents the data transmission time from node u to v.

Figures 1(a) and 1(b) are two kinds of DFGs. Their corresponding loop programs are shown in Figs. 1(c) and 1(d), respectively. DFG in Fig. 1(a) has the path structure, in which task node v_1 has no in-degree, implying that all input data of task v_1 are given (array *External* in Fig. 1(c)). While data dependencies in Fig. 1(b) form a ring-structure DFG. Two thick bars on edge (v_2, v_1) represent two delays, implying that two data items for task v_1 are given at the beginning (B[-1] and B[0] in Fig. 1(d)). These delays also represent the inter-iteration data dependencies as discussed in the following. The number attached to a node (an edge) is the execution time (data transmission time), such as $et(v_1) = 10$ $(dt(v_1, v_2) = 20)$.

An iteration is defined as executing each node in V exactly once. If the input of node v at i^{th} iteration is generated by node u at j^{th} iteration $(j < i)$, it is an inter-iteration data dependency, represented by the weighted edge with

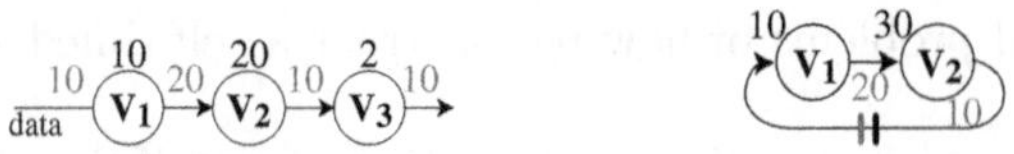

(a) Path-structure DFG   (b) Ring-structure DFG

```
given External[0..n-1];
for i = 1 to n do
    A[i]=f1(External[i]);    Task V₁
    B[i]=f2(A[i]);           Task V₂
    C[i]=f3(B[i]);           Task V₃
end
```

```
B[-1]=x;   B[0]=y;
for i = 1 to n do
    A[i]=f1(B[i-2]);    Task V₁
    B[i]=f2(A[i]);      Task V₂
end
```

(c) Behavioral description of (a)   (d) Behavioral description of (b)

Fig. 1. Two types of data-flow graphs and corresponding behavioral description

$d(u, v)$ delays, $d(u, v) = i - j$; e.g. in Fig. 1(d), input of task V_1 at i^{th} iteration is produced by task V_2 at $(i - 2)^{th}$ iteration and we have $d(V_2, V_1) = 2$. Whereas, if the input of node v is generated by node u at the same iteration, it is an inner-iteration dependency, represented by the edge without delay; e.g. input of V_2 is produced by V_1 at the same iteration in Fig. 1(d) and we have $d(V_1, V_2) = 0$. The duration time of each iteration is called *iteration period*.

For the sake of convenience, we use $u \xrightarrow{e} v$ to represent the edge e from node u to v and $v_0 \xrightarrow{p} v_k$ to represent the path p from node v_0 to v_k. The number of delays on p is $d(p)$, where $p = v_0 \xrightarrow{e_0} v_1... \xrightarrow{e_{k-1}} v_k$ and $d(p) = \sum_{i=0}^{k-1} d(e_i)$. Notice that for $v_0 \xrightarrow{p} v_k$, if $v_0 = v_k$, then p represents a cycle.

2.2   Self-Timed System Model

Since self-timed systems that do not depend on a global clock offer significant advantages, self-timed system model becomes popular. A self-timed system model is used to describe the procedure of an application that employs handshaking mechanism to communication.

A self-timed system is composed of a set of connected self-timed units. Each unit has a processing element PE, a set of input/output ports, and connected wires. Formally a self-timed unit is defined as follows.

A **Self-Timed Unit** (su) is a quintuples (PE, I, O, W, δ_r) consisting of a processing element (PE), a set of in-ports (I), a set of out-ports (O), and a set of wires (W). δ_r represents the overhead incurred by handshaking procedure. For each in-port $ip \in I$, there is an input wire from ip to PE; for each out-port $op \in O$, there is an output wire from PE to op; besides, there are $|I|$ acknowledgement wires in one su, where $|I|$ is the number of in-ports in su.

If each unit in a system contains only one in-port and one out-port, we call the system as a single-port self-timed system. Otherwise, the system is a multi-port self-timed system. In the following, we are going to formally define the single-port self-timed system model and multi-ports self-timed system model.

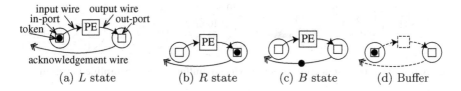

Fig. 2. Examples of the single-port self-timed unit

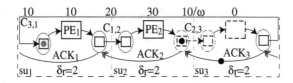

Fig. 3. Self-timed system corresponding to DFG in Fig. 1(b)

Single-Port Self-Timed System Model. Figure 2 shows examples of single-port units. Each unit contains a token (solid circle), an in-port, an out-port and three types of wires. In Fig. 2(d), the self-timed unit has no PE, representing a *self-timed buffering unit* (or called buffer). Since a buffer is directly connected to its host unit, we call the data access from PE to its buffer as local access. On the other hand, we call the data access from PE to the other PEs or their buffer as remote access. In this paper, we denote that the local access is ω times faster than remote access. In following sections, we will show that inserting buffer is an important technique to prevent "deadlocks" and "blocking events".

To model a single-port self-timed system, we define a state domain $\{L, R, B\}$ for each self-timed unit (su). According to the position of a token, each su is in a certain state at any time. In Fig. 2(a), a data item is in the in-port of su representing L state (token in Left part of su). When a data item is stored in the out-port, as shown in Fig. 2(b), the su is in R state (token in Right part of su). A token on the acknowledge wire represents B state (token on Bottom part of su), as shown in Fig. 2(c). To guarantee the correctness of a self-timed system, each unit is in one state at any time.

A **Self-Timed System** STS is a triple (SU, C, s) consisting of a set of self-timed units (SU), a set of channels (C), $C \subset SU \times SU$, and a function (s) from SU to state domain. For a channel $c_{j,k} \in C$, it connects an out-port op_j in unit su_j and an in-port ip_k in unit su_k. Correspondingly, an acknowledgement wire ACK_k in su_k is connected to the out-port op_j in su_j. For a unit $su_i \in SU$, $s(su_i)$ is the state of su_i.

Figure 3 shows an example of a self-timed system constructed according to DFG in Fig. 1(b). Nodes v_1 and v_2 are mapped on PE_1 and PE_2, respectively. Then channels and acknowledgement wire are constructed according to edges in DFG. The number above a PE (channel) represents the execution time (data transmission time). We denote $et(su_i)$ as the execution time of su_i, which equals $et(v_i)$. And $dt(su_i, su_j)$ is the data transmission time on channel $c(su_i, su_j)$,

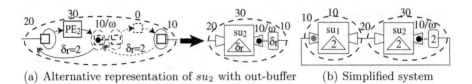

(a) Alternative representation of su_2 with out-buffer   (b) Simplified system

Fig. 4. The simplified unit with a buffer and the simplified system from Fig. 3.

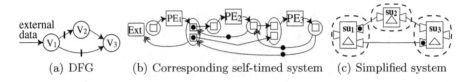

(a) DFG   (b) Corresponding self-timed system   (c) Simplified system

Fig. 5. Example of multi-ports self-timed system and the simplified system

which equals $dt(v_i, v_j)$. The number below acknowledgement wire represents the acknowledgement transmission time. Besides su_1 and su_2, an out-buffer[1], su_3, is attached to unit su_2 for preventing deadlocks (detailed discuss on the deadlock event, see Sect. 3). Initially, unit su_1 is in L state; unit su_2 is in R state; and unit su_3 is in B state.

As stated, the processes of a self-timed system can be regarded as the token-passing procedure. For three connected single-port self-timed units su_i, su_j, and su_k (as shown in Fig. 3), the state transition of su_j follows three rules.

- $L \rightarrow R$: if there exists a token in the in-port of su_j (su_j is in L state).
- $R \rightarrow B$: if there exists a token in the out-port of su_j and a token on ACK_k (su_j is in R state and su_k is in B state).
- $B \rightarrow L$: if there exists a token on ACK_j and a token in the out-port of su_i (su_j is in B state and su_i is in R state).

Considering the self-timed system in Fig. 3, PE_1 can start to fire (su_1: $L \rightarrow R$) and token in su_2 can be sent to the buffer (su_2: $R \rightarrow B$). After these transactions, one new token is produced in the out-port of su_1 and another new token is on the bottom edge of su_2. At this time, the produced token in su_1 can be sent to su_2 (su_2: $B \rightarrow L$).

For unit su_j, the transition $L \rightarrow R$ takes $et(su_i)$ time units. And the transition $R \rightarrow B$ takes $dt(su_j, su_k)$ time units. Since it takes $\delta_r(su_j)$ time units to transmit acknowledgement signal, and $dt(su_i, su_j)$ time units to receive data from su_j, the transition $B \rightarrow L$ takes $\delta_r(su_j) + dt(su_i, su_j)$ time units. Therefore, for unit su_j, the duration time of transitions $L \rightarrow R \rightarrow B \rightarrow L$ is $et(su_i) + dt(su_j, su_k) + \delta_r(su_j) + dt(su_i, su_j)$, and we call this duration time as the round period of su_j, denoted by $RP(su_j)$. For the system in Fig. 3, we have $RP(su_1) = 10 + 20 + 2 + 10 = 42$.

---

[1] There are two types of buffers: in-buffer and out-buffer. The in-buffer(out-buffer) indicates that the buffering unit is attached to the in-port(out-port) of an su.

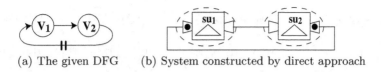

(a) The given DFG   (b) System constructed by direct approach

Fig. 6. Example of the direct approach to construct self-timed system

To simplify the representation of a self-timed system, we generally illustrate the self-time unit su_2 and its out-buffer as shown in Fig. 4(a). For the simplified unit, two things need to be noticed. (1) For any unit, if there has no tokens in both in-port and out-port, the unit is in B state. (2) Since buffer has no PE, we do not distinguish its in-port and out-port. Based on these, the simplified self-timed system in Fig. 3 is shown in Fig. 4(b).

Multi-Ports Self-Timed System Model. Single-port self-timed system model is applicable to path-structure and ring-structure applications. Whereas a more complicated application may have general-structure. For example, the DFG in Fig. 5(a) has the directed acyclic graph (DAG) structure. Figure 5 shows the corresponding self-timed system. Since the out-degree of task V_1 is 2, the corresponding unit su_1 has 2 out-ports. Similarly, for the unit su_3 on which task V_3 is mapped, it has two in-ports, connected by su_1 and su_2, respectively. According to the definition of self-timed unit, two acknowledgement wires of su_3 are connected to su_1 and su_2.

As with single-port system, processes of multi-port self-timed system can also be regraded as the token-passing procedure. Let $su_j = (PE, I, O, W, \delta_r)$ be a self-timed unit, and $STS = (SU, C, s)$ be a self-timed system. The state transition can be transmitted as follows.

When tokens arrive at every in-port of su_j, these tokens are moved to PE_j to be fired; after PE_j fired once, new tokens are generated and each out-port of su_j is filled with a token. Then, for each channel $c_{j,k}$, tokens in su_j are moved to su_k independently; only when all tokens in out-ports have been transmitted, new tokens are generated on each acknowledgement wire of su_j. At this time, for each channel $c_{i,j}$, su_j independently receives token from su_i; when su_j received a token from su_i, the token on corresponding acknowledgement wire will be removed. Notice that, data transmission between self-time units are conducted independently. As with single-port self-timed system, we can simplify the multi-port self-timed system, as shown in Fig. 5(c).

In terms of the application model and the system model, we define the **iteration period** (reciprocal of throughput) of self-timed system constructed from a DFG as the average duration in which each task in DFG is executed once.

2.3   Constructing Self-Timed System from DFG

Given a DFG and a set of self-timed units, it is important to construct a self-timed system that behaves "exactly the same with" (or called "consistent with")

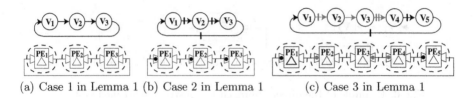

(a) Case 1 in Lemma 1   (b) Case 2 in Lemma 1   (c) Case 3 in Lemma 1

Fig. 7. Three examples of the first type of deadlock patterns

the given DFG. We define the "consistency" between a DFG and a self-timed system as follows. Let $STS = (SU, C, s)$ be a self-timed system, $G = (V, E, d, et, dt)$ be a DFG. Task node $v_i \in V$ is mapped to $su_i \in SU$. The self-timed system STS is **consistent** with DFG G, if the following condition is satisfied: $\forall e = (v_i, v_j)$, $e \in E$, input data of the unit su_j at its kth execution is produced by the unit su_i at its $(k - d(e))^{th}$ iteration.

As an example, DFG is given in Fig. 6(a). The behavior of its consistent self-timed system should meet the following two conditions. (1) The input data of task v_1 at its kth execution is produced by task v_2 at its $(k - 3)^{th}$ iteration. (2) The input data of task v_2 is produced by task v_1 at the same iteration.

According to the self-timed system model and the definition of consistency, it is natural to follow a straightforward approach (called **direct approach**) to map the DFG to a self-timed system. In the direct approach, we map each task node v_i to a self-timed unit su_i. Then we set up a channel from su_i to su_j if there exists an edge from v_i to v_j. Finally, we assign initial tokens in the self-timed system. For an edge $e = (v_i, v_j)$, if there exist n delays on e, we assign n initial tokens to the out-port of unit su_i, the in-port of unit su_j, and their internal buffers. Notice that each unit has at most one token and the total number of tokens between su_i and su_j equals n. For the DFG in Fig. 6(a), by applying the direct approach, the constructed self-timed system is shown in Fig. 6(b).

2.4   Problem Statement

We define the *Deadlock Prevention problem* as follows: Given a DFG G without deadlock cycles, the objective is to construct a self-timed system STS from G, such that STS is consistent with G and there is no possible deadlocks in STS.

We define the *Removal of Blocking Event problem* as follows: Given a deadlock-free self-timed system STS, the objective is to eliminate blocking event that degrades the system performance with the minimum number of buffers.

3   Deadlock in Self-timed System

In this section, we will show that the self-timed system constructed by the direct approach may incur deadlocks. We are going to show the necessary and sufficient conditions that a self-timed system directly constructed by DFG has deadlocks.

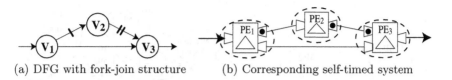

(a) DFG with fork-join structure   (b) Corresponding self-timed system

Fig. 8. Example of the second deadlock pattern

Based on the analysis, we propose an efficient algorithm to prevent deadlocks in self-timed system.

In the following, we present two patterns (sub-structure of DFG): the directly constructed system will be ended in deadlock if and only if the corresponding DFG contains any one of these patterns.

Figure 7 shows three examples of the first pattern. Lemma 1 for this pattern gives sufficient conditions of a self-timed system constructed by the direct approach that incurs deadlocks.

Lemma 1. *Let G_s be a subgraph of the given DFG, and u_i be a task node in G_s. There exists and only exists one cycle p: $u_i \overset{p}{\rightsquigarrow} u_i$. The self-timed system directly constructed according to G is in deadlock:*

1. *if $\forall (u_i \overset{e}{\rightarrow} u_{i+1}) \in p$, $d(e) = 0$, or*
2. *if $\forall (u_i \overset{e}{\rightarrow} u_{i+1}) \in p$, $d(e) \geq 1$, or*
3. *$\forall (u_i \overset{e}{\rightarrow} u_{i+1}) \in p$, s.t. $d(e) = 0$, if $d(u_{i-1}, u_i) \geq 2$, $d(u_{i+1}, u_{i+2}) \geq 1$ or $d(u_{i-1}, u_i) \geq 1$, $d(u_{i+1}, u_{i+2}) \geq 2$.*

The first condition means that the DFG has no input data (e.g. Figure 7(a)); deadlock is unavoidable in this case. The second condition indicates that each edge has at least one delay, therefore, no units in B state (e.g. Figure 7(b)). The last condition implies that for all the edges with zero delay, one of their adjacent edges has at least one delay and the other edge has at least two delays (e.g. Figure 7(c)). If a DFG meets condition 2 or 3, the system constructed by the direct approach will be ended in deadlock since no unit is in B state.

Figure 8 shows the other pattern that incurs deadlocks. The sufficient condition is formally given in Lemma 2.

Lemma 2. *Let G_s be a subgraph of the given DFG. In G_s, v_i has 0 in-degree and v_j has 0 out-degree; there exists a set of paths P, such that $\forall p \in P$ we have $v_i \overset{p}{\rightsquigarrow} v_j$; the number of paths in set P is denoted by $|P|$, and we have $|P| \geq 2$. The self-timed system directly constructed according to G is in deadlock if: $\exists p_i \in P$, such that $d(p_i) = 0$ and $\exists p_j \in P$, such that $d(p_j) \geq n(p_j) + b(p_j)$, where $n(p)$ is the number of nodes on path p, and $b(p)$ is the number of buffers inserted in STS_p (the part of self-timed system on which the path p is mapped.*

Lemma 2 means that path $v_i \overset{p_n}{\rightsquigarrow} v_j$ in the fork-join structure has no initial data, while path $v_i \overset{p_m}{\rightsquigarrow} v_j$ has $n(p_m) + b(p_m)$ data items that fill up all ports in

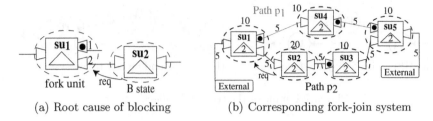

(a) Root cause of blocking   (b) Corresponding fork-join system

Fig. 9. Blocking event in self-timed system.

STS_{p_m}. In this situation, su_i cannot receive input data to fire since a data item is in its out-port; meanwhile, su_j cannot fire since the input data from p_n is not given. Thus, the system is ended in deadlock. Based on these understandings, we can prove the following theorem.

Theorem 1. *The self-timed system constructed by direct approach incurs deadlocks if and only if the pattern in Lemma 1 or Lemma 2 occurs in a given DFG.*

To prevent deadlocks and blocking events, we propose "Avoid_Deadlock" method for each pattern in above lemmas. It can be described as follows:
(1) Let STS_p be a substructure of self-timed system that has the same structure as patterns in Lemma 1. To break the deadlock, we insert $d(p) - n(p) - b(p) + 1$ extra buffers in B state at arbitrary positions of STS_p.
(2) Let STS_{fj} be a substructure of self-timed system that has the same structure as pattern in Lemma 2. To break the deadlock, we first find out the path $p \in STS_{fj}$ such that $d(p) \geq n(p) + b(p)$, and then insert at least $n(p_j) + b(p) - d(p_j) + 1$ buffers in B state to STS_p.

To find all STS_p having the same structure as patterns in Lemma 1, we employ the algorithm presented in [10]. For a DFG with v nodes, e edges, and c cycles, the time complexity of this algorithm is $O((v+e) \cdot (c+1))$. And we employ the method introduced in [11] to find the STS_{fj} having the same structure as patterns in Lemma 2. The time complexity is $O(v^3)$.

4   Blocking Event in Self-timed System

Blocking event (not deadlock) occurs in general-structure self-timed systems. It may dramatically degrade system throughput. To eliminate blocking event, we need to insert buffers to provide storage space. In the following, we first illustrate the root cause of the blocking event. Then, the conditions for a system to be blocked will be presented. Finally, we propose MILP formulations to eliminate the blocking event with the minimum number of buffers.

We continue to analyze the blocking event in the self-timed system. As shown in Fig. 9(a), su_1 is a fork unit, which has two out-ports, op_1 and op_2. In this figure, the token in op_1 is "stalled", while op_2 is empty. Unit su_2 is in B state, requesting a data token from op_2. According to token passing procedure defined in Sect. 2.2, su_1 can be fired to produce new tokens only when both op_1 and op_2 are available (empty). Since op_1 has a token, su_1 cannot be fired until the token is passed away. Therefore, the path containing $su_1 \rightarrow su_2$ is blocked.

Next, we demonstrate the negative effect of blocking events on system performance. A self-timed system with blocking event is shown in Fig. 9(b). The blocked unit su_1 finally turns into B state after 44 time units. During this period, unit su_3 first fires and the produced token is sent to su_5 (used 15 time units). Second, since all in-ports of su_5 have tokens, su_5 fires and then sends the produced data to external system (used 15 time units). Third, token in out-port of su_4 is sent to su_5, and su_4 turns to B state (used 7 time units). Finally, the stalled token in the out-port of su_1 is send to su_4, and stalled unit su_1 turns in B state (used 7 time units). On the other hand, the iteration period of the system without blocking event is 32 time units.

According to the above analysis, we define the blocking event as follows.

Definition 1. *Let STS_{f-j} be a substructure of a self-timed system, su_f and su_j be the fork unit and the join unit in STS_{f-j}, paths p_i and p_k be two paths, such that $su_f \overset{p_i}{\rightsquigarrow} su_j$ and $su_f \overset{p_k}{\rightsquigarrow} su_j$. The **blocking event** occurs if:*

1. *all units in path p_i are either in L state or R state;*
2. *a unit in path p_k requests data from the fork unit (in B state);*
3. *at least one unit in p_k is in L state or R state.*

*Under the above conditions, the fork unit cannot respond to the request from p_k in time. We call that **path p_i blocks path p_k**.*

In the following, we give the condition, under which any path p_i will not block the other path p_k.

Theorem 2. *Let STS_{f-j} be a substructure of a self-timed system, su_f and su_j be the fork unit and the join unit in STS_{f-j}, paths p_i and p_k be two paths, such that $su_f \overset{p_i}{\rightsquigarrow} su_j$ and $su_f \overset{p_k}{\rightsquigarrow} su_j$, and $data(p)$ be the number of initial data tokens on path p. Path p_i will not block p_k if the following condition is satisfied.*

$$\sum_{su_k \in p_k} [ex\,(su_k) + dt\,(su_k)] + \sum_{su_i \in p_i} [dt\,(su_i) + d_r] - dt\,(su_j) \le sp\,(p_i) \cdot IP$$

where, $sp(p_i) = n(p_i) - (data(p_i) - data(p_k))$ representing su_f can fire $sp(p_i)$ times before path p_i has been filled up, and IP is the desired iteration period.

For the self-timed system in Fig. 9(b), we have $sp(p_1) = 3 - (2 - 0) = 1$, the duration time of a token that forward propagates around p_2 is $10 + 5 + 20 + 5 + 10 + 5 + 10 + 5 = 70$ and the duration time of a token that backward propagates around p_1 is $2 + 5 + 2 + 5 + 2 + 5 = 21$. According to [8,9], the path-structure self-timed system can pipeline automatically, i.e. the desired iteration period is the maximum of round periods. Therefore, the desired iteration period is $IP = 5 + 20 + 5 + 2 = 32$, Since the inequality in Lemma 2 is not satisfied $(70 + 21 > 32 \cdot 1)$, thus, path p_1 blocks path p_2.

Based on the above theorem, we are going to formulate MILP formulations to solve the *Removal of Blocking Event problem*. We call the proposed method as "Avoid_Block" method. We first introduce notations used in MILP formulations.

(1) IP is the desired iteration period, e.g. $IP = \max_{su \in SU} (RP(su))$.

(2) For path p_i and path p_j in a fork-join structure, fj_k, $FB_k(p_i, p_j)$ represents the summation of the duration time that a token forward propagates along path p_i and the duration time that a token backward propagates along path p_j.

(3) For a fork-join structure, fj_k, SP_k equals the minimum value of $n(p_i) - [data(p_i) - data(p_j)]$, where p_i, p_j are two arbitrary paths in fj_k.

(4) The local access (PE accesses data from its local buffer) is ω times faster than remote access.

(5) δ_r is acknowledgement transmission time.

(6) For each channel c connecting units su_i and su_j in self-timed system, $dt(c)$ represents the data transmission time along channel c.

(7) For each channel c connecting units su_i and su_j in self-timed system, x_c is an integer variable, representing the number of buffers need to be inserted between su_i and su_j.

Buffer number constraint. For any channel c, the number of buffers inserted in c should be a non-negative integer as shown in Eq. 1.

$$x_c \geq 0 \qquad \forall c \in C \qquad (1)$$

Blocking event constraint. According to Theorem 2, for each fork-join structure, fj_k, in the self-timed system, we have the following condition that guarantees no blocking events in the system.

$$\sum_{c \in p_i \cup p_j} x_c \cdot \frac{dt(c)}{\omega} + (\delta_r - IP) \cdot \sum_{c \in p_j} x_{c_j} \leq SP_k \cdot IP - FB_k(p_i, p_j) \qquad \forall p_i, p_j \in fj_k \quad (2)$$

Objective Function. The objective function is to minimize the number of inserted buffers. It can be formulated as follows.

$$min = \sum_{c \in C(STS)} (x_e) \qquad (3)$$

For the self-timed system in Fig. 9(b), the optimal solution is $x_{1,2} = x_{2,3} = x_{3,5} = 0$, $x_{1,4} = 2$ and $x_{4,5} = 1$. The results imply that we need to insert 2 buffers between su_1 and su_4, and insert 1 buffer between su_4 and su_5.

5   Experiment

We develop a SystemC simulator to automatically construct self-timed systems from benchmarks. When a DFG is given, the self-timed units are generated automatically by our simulator. The simulator implements "Avoid_Deadlock" and "Avoid_Block" techniques to determine how to insert buffers in constructing a self-timed system. After a system has been constructed, we conduct the simulation and obtain the system iteration period.

Table 1. Experimental Results

Benchmark	Direct	Avoild_Deadlock		Avoid_Blocking		Improvement
	IP	IP	# Buffer	IP	# Buffer	
T50	376.68	-	-	183.79	29	51.21 %
T60	351.83	-	-	193.96	29	44.87 %
T70	435.99	-	-	266.26	42	38.93 %
T80	368.57	-	-	193.19	10	47.58 %
T90	428.57	-	-	237.32	53	44.62 %
T100	760.28	-	-	270.19	76	64.46 %
H264	26074.00	-	-	21985.00	11	15.68 %
Average Improvement						43.91 %
SD10	×	382.26	2	212.50	4	44.41 %
SD20	×	1153.34	4	385.29	37	66.59 %
SD30	×	866.64	1	598.18	18	30.98 %
DD10	×	643.63	16	257.46	21	60.00 %
DD20	×	971.23	35	260.70	40	73.16 %
DD30	×	546.10	39	245.08	47	55.12 %
latiir	×	56.65	67	35.40	70	37.51 %
Average Improvement						52.54 %

T50: Benchmark generated by TGFF with 50 nodes. SD: Sparse Delays in DFG.

DD: Dense Delays in DFG. SD and DD are benchmarks generated by SDF3.

Based on our simulator, we construct a number of self-timed systems according to real applications and multimedia benchmarks. These benchmarks are divided into two groups in terms of the structure. Benchmarks in the first group are acyclic DFGs, generated by TGFF [5]. H.264 HDTV decoder benchmark [4] is denoted by H264. In the second group, benchmarks are generated by SDF3 [15]. The "8-Stage Lattice Filter" benchmark from DSPstone [19] is denoted by lattice.

Experimental results based on the above benchmarks are shown in Table 1. Results illustrate that our proposed techniques efficiently prevent deadlock situations occurred in the self-timed system constructed by the direct approach. Since benchmarks in the first group with DAG structure have no delay and no cycle, applying direct approach on these benchmarks always obtains functional correct self-timed systems. Whereas all directly constructed self-timed systems from benchmarks in the second group are ended in deadlock (denoted by × in the column *Direct*). Column *#Buffer* in the column *Avoid_Deadlock* is the number of inserted buffer to prevent deadlocks. As shown in this table, benchmarks in *SD* category need fewer buffers than that in *DD* category. This is caused by that DFG with more delays is more likely to process the deadlock patterns presented in Sect. 3. In general, to design a deadlock-free system, designers need to understand the properties of the given applications, and our proposed techniques can detect and prevent all kinds of deadlocks.

We compare the performance of self-timed system constructed by our proposed *Avoid_Blocking* technique against the system without deadlocks that constructed by direct approach or *Avoid_Deadlock* method. For benchmarks in the first group, our *Avoid_Blocking* technique averagely achieves 43.91 % improvements, compared with the direct approach. Especially, for H.264 HDTV decoder benchmark with 51 task nodes, our approach inserts 11 buffers in the system and achieves 15.68 % improvements. For the benchmarks in the second group, *Avoid_Blocking* technique averagely achieves 52.54 % improvements, compared with *Avoid_Deadlock* method. Experimental results show that by eliminating blocking event in self-timed system, we can obtain a significant improvement on system performance.

In conclusion, our proposed *Avoid_Deadlock* method prevents all kinds of deadlocks in constructing self-timed system from a given application. Blocking events commonly exist in self-timed systems, and our *Avoid_Blocking* event can eliminate these blocking events and significantly improve the system performance. For *latiir* benchmark, *Avoid_Deadlock* method inserts 67 buffers to prevent deadlocks. Additionally, *Avoid_Blocking* technique inserts extra 3 buffers to eliminate blocking events, and achieves 37.51 % improvements.

6   Conclusion

In this paper, we focus on two fundamental problems — deadlock prevention and removal of blocking events — in constructing self-timed system. We first presented a suitable model for distributed embedded systems. Then, we gave the necessary and sufficient conditions for a self-timed system to be in deadlock and to be blocked. Finally, we proposed techniques to guarantee no deadlocks and design MILP formulas to eliminate blocking events for self-timed systems. Our experimental results show the effectiveness of the proposed techniques on constructing self-timed systems from given applications.

Acknowledgements. This work is partially supported by National 863 Program 2013AA013202, 2015AA015304, Chongqing High-Tech Research Program cstc2014yykfB40007, NSFC 61472052, NSFC 61173014.

References

1. Beerel, P.A., Lines, A., Davies, M., Kim, N.H.: Slack matching asynchronous designs. In: Proceedings of ASYNC, pp. 184–194 (2006)
2. Burns, S.M.: Performance analysis and optimization of asynchronous circuits (1991)
3. Chao, L.F., Sha, E.M.: Scheduling data-flow graphs via retiming and unfolding. IEEE Trans. Parallel Dist. Syst. **8**(12), 1259–1267 (1997)

4. Chong, J., Satish, N., Catanzaro, B.C., Ravindran, K., Keutzer, K.: Efficient parallelization of H. 264 decoding with macro block level scheduling. In: Proceedings of ICME, pp. 1874–1877 (2007)
5. Dick, R.P., Rhodes, D.L., Wolf, W.: TGFF: task graphs for free. In: Proceedings of CODES, pp. 97–101 (1998)
6. Gill, G., Singh, M.: Automated microarchitectural exploration for achieving throughput targets in pipelined asynchronous systems. In: Proceedings of ASYNC, pp. 117–127. IEEE (2010)
7. Greenstreet, M.R.: Stari: A Technique for High-bandwidth Communication. Ph.D. thesis, Princeton, NJ, USA (1993), uMI Order No. GAX93-11221
8. Jiang, W., Zhuge, Q., Chen, X., Yang, L., Yi, J., Sha, E.M.: Properties of self-timed ring architectures for deadlock-free and consistent configuration reaching maximum throughput. J. Signal Process. Syst. pp. 1–15 (2015), doi:10.1007/s11265-015-0984-6
9. Jiang, W., Zhuge, Q., Yi, J., Yang, L., Sha, E.H.: On self-timed ring for consistent mapping and maximum throughput. In: Proceedings of RTCSA, pp. 1–9 (2014)
10. Johnson, D.B.: Finding all the elementary circuits of a directed graph. SIAM J. Comput. 4(1), 77–84 (1975)
11. Kroft, D.: All paths through a maze. Proc. IEEE 55(1), 88–90 (1967)
12. Parhi, K.K., Messerschmitt, D.G.: Static rate-optimal scheduling of iterative dataflow programs via optimum unfolding. IEEE Trans. Comput. 40(2), 178–195 (1991)
13. Prakash, P., Martin, A.J.: Slack matching quasi delay-insensitive circuits. In: Proceedings of ASYNC, pp. 195–204. IEEE (2006)
14. Smirnov, A., Taubin, A.: Heuristic based throughput analysis and optimization of asynchronous pipelines. In: Proceedings of ASYNC, pp. 162–172. IEEE (2009)
15. Stuijk, S., Geilen, M., Basten, T.: SDF3: SDF for free. In: Proceedings of ACSD, vol. 6, pp. 276–278 (2006)
16. Van Berkel, C., Josephs, M.B., Nowick, S.M.: Applications of asynchronous circuits. Proc. IEEE 87(2), 223–233 (1999)
17. Williams, T.E.: Performance of iterative computation in self-timed rings. J. VLSI Signal Process. Syst. Signal, Image Video Technol. vol. 7(1–2), pp. 17–31 (1994)
18. Wolf, M.: High-Performance Embedded Computing: Applications in Cyber-Physical Systems and Mobile Computing. Morgan Kaufmann, Newnes (2014)
19. Zivojnovic, V., Velarde, J., Schlager, C., Meyr, H.: DSPstone: a DSP-oriented benchmarking methodology. In: Proceedings of ICSPAT (1994)

Improving the Memory Efficiency of In-Memory MapReduce Based HPC Systems

Cheng Pei, Xuanhua Shi$^{(\boxtimes)}$, and Hai Jin

Services Computing Technology and System Laboratory,
Cluster and Grid Computing Laboratory, School of Computer Science
and Technology, Huazhong University of Science and Technology,
Wuhan 430074, China
{peicheng,xhshi,hjin}@hust.edu.cn

Abstract. In-memory cluster computing systems based MapReduce, such as Spark, have made a great impact in addressing all kinds of big data problems. Given the overuse of memory speed, which stems from avoiding the latency caused by disk I/O operations, some process designs may cause resource inefficiency in traditional *high performance computing* (HPC) systems. Hash-based shuffle, particularly large-scale shuffle, can significantly affect job performance through excessive file operations and unreasonable use of memory. Some intermediate data unnecessarily overflow to the disk when memory usage is unevenly distributed or when memory runs out. Thus, in this study, *Write Handle Reusing* is proposed to fully utilize memory in shuffle file writing and reading. *Load Balancing Optimizer* is introduced to ensure the even distribution of data processing across all worker nodes, and *Memory-Aware Task Scheduler* that coordinates concurrency level and memory usage is also developed to prevent memory spilling. Experimental results on representative workloads demonstrate that the proposed approaches can decrease the overall job execution time and improve memory efficiency.

Keywords: MapReduce · In-memory · Hash-based shuffle · Load balancing · Task scheduler

1 Introduction

For many data-intensive applications, the high-level cluster programming models MapReduce [1] and Dryad [2] are widely adopted for processing growing volumes of data and realize scalable performance by exploiting data parallelism. The design philosophy of these models is the automatic provision of locality-aware scheduling, fault tolerance, and load balancing, all of which are embodied in some famous application systems. As a typical representative of MapReduce framework, Hadoop [3] enables a wide range of users to analyze big datasets on commodity clusters. Considering the large amount of disk I/O operations in Hadoop, some derived systems attempt to change the concrete implementation

© Springer International Publishing Switzerland 2015
G. Wang et al. (Eds.): ICA3PP 2015, Part I, LNCS 9528, pp. 170–184, 2015.
DOI: 10.1007/978-3-319-27119-4_12

of MapReduce's execution flow to obtain better performance that suits different hardware environments or some special applications. TritonSort [4] equips Hadoop clusters with abundant disks and memory to improve I/O throughput. HaLoop [5] makes the task scheduler of Hadoop loop-aware and adds various caching mechanisms for iterative programs. Meanwhile, Spark [6], which is a new representative of the MapReduce framework, absorbs several of the principles of Dryad with regard to data sharing and functional programming interface. When coupled with in-memory computing, Spark can outperform Hadoop in many aspects of applications. Spark introduces an abstraction called *resilient distributed datasets* (RDDs) [7] to persist data in memory for reuse, and retains fault tolerance for memory-resident data. Moreover, Spark is a representative of in-memory cluster computing systems. Any successful improvement in Spark inspires the development of in-memory cluster computing systems. The present study implements in Spark, an idea that is common to in-memory cluster computing systems.

The nature of compute-centric HPC systems requires large and powerful CPU equipment for computation. Memory and disks are often limited relative to CPU power. According to the published memory configurations of the top 10 supercomputers from June 2010 to November 2012, the majority of these HPC servers are equipped with less than 2 GB memory per CPU core, and some are equipped with less than 1 GB [8]. Thus, the compute-centric HPC system with a bottleneck caused by limited memory resource, rather than CPU resource, is considered in this study.

In Spark, hash-based shuffle directly writes intermediate data into separate files for each partition. Since the pressure of memory allocation and *garbage collection* (GC) on the *Java virtual machine* (JVM) are not considered, the performance deteriorates severely in cases with large amounts of mappers and reducers. The tasks of Spark are scheduled according to data locality and number of CPU cores. However, in compute-centric HPC systems, the locality-oriented scheduling techniques for MapReduce jobs can cause performance degradation [9] when data locality is maximized. In Spark, delay scheduling [10] is adopted to delay the tasks for data locality. Moreover, tasks with shuffle fetch operations have no preferred locations and are randomly assigned to worker nodes. These design characteristics may lead to load imbalance, thereby causing each worker node to process different amounts of data and to encounter various memory pressures. Furthermore, tasks are scheduled by the free CPU cores of the worker nodes without consideration of memory resource. When a worker node is left with no spare memory, intense competition for memory resource and unnecessary spill operations occur.

With the aim of achieving high performance for the in-memory cluster computing of compute-centric HPC systems, we propose three optimization techniques, which are implemented in Spark, to address the aforementioned issues by maximizing memory use. The contributions of this study are as follows:

1. We analyze the causes of performance degradation when the number of partitions increases under hash-based shuffle. We introduce *Write Handle Reusing* to surmount the deficiencies and to improve memory usage efficiency.

2. We develop algorithms, called *Load Balancing Optimizer*, based on the adjustments or resets in the preferred locations of tasks, to implement load balancing.
3. We design and implement a task scheduler, which schedules tasks according to the memory usage of tasks and the resource situation of worker nodes. The scheduler, which we called *Memory-Aware Task Scheduler*, dynamically calculates the optimal task concurrency of each worker node and minimizes expensive disk spilling.
4. We conduct extensive experiments for comparison with the original Spark platform. The experimental results show that our proposed methods dramatically improve performance in terms of the job execution time in the memory-constrained clusters.

The rest of this study is organized as follows. In Sect. 2, we provide a brief overview of in-memory MapReduce system and discuss the motivation of this research. The overall implementations of the three optimization techniques are presented in Sect. 3. Section 4 reports and analyzes the results of performance evaluations. Related work is discussed in Sect. 5. In the final section, we conclude this paper and discuss the potential future work.

2   Background and Motivation

This section provides a brief background on the approaches to design and implementation that have been adopted in existing in-memory MapReduce systems, and discusses the motivation offered by the challenges and opportunities in the job execution and memory usage mechanism of Spark.

2.1   Spark as the In-Memory MapReduce System

In-memory computing is a new concept proposed in the era of big data. Recent studies on in-memory computing focus on hardware architectures and system software. When a new hardware is introduced into the traditional architecture, an appropriate modification of the original upper system software ensues. As a distributed computing platform, Spark absorbs the essence of in-memory computing, that is, the maximization of memory speed to match CPU speed, and ideally tolerates data loss in the lineage of RDDs. However, Spark is generally a MapReduce framework like Hadoop. The differences in design and implementation between Spark and Hadoop are elaborated in the following section.

MapReduce frameworks consist of a map, shuffle, and reduce phase. The shuffle phase is commonly overshadowed by the map and reduce phases. The map phase reads data from file systems, such as HDFS, and transforms such data into key-value pairs. The reduce phase handles the values of similar keys. The shuffle phase is divided into the shuffle write and shuffle fetch. Shuffle write is the preparatory stage of the shuffle fetch in the map phase, which overlooks the process for writing shuffle files. Shuffle fetch aims to transmit the data generated by map tasks to reduce tasks in many-to-many fashion, which is often integrated as part of the reduce phase.

In earlier versions of Hadoop and Spark, map tasks directly write output data to disks, thereby creating $M \times R$ shuffle files, where M is the number of map tasks and R is the number of reduce tasks. When M and R are enormous, millions of shuffle files are created. The reading of these files then generates many random I/Os and causes a sharp decline in performance. To reduce the number of files, Hadoop creates a large in-memory buffer to cache partitioned data and spills the cached and sorted data to disks when the buffer reaches its upper limit. However, in preparation for the reduce phase, each output file of the map task in Hadoop needs to be sorted and merged into a single file, thereby requiring large disk I/O operations.

In Spark, shuffle file consolidation [11] is introduced to reduce the number of shuffle files, which creates only $C \times R$ shuffle files, where C denotes the number of CPU cores allocated to the Spark application. The few shuffle files of Spark facilitate the exploitation of strong locality benefits offered by the underlying file system. Many of the applications need not sort intermediate data. In the shuffle fetch phase, both Spark and Hadoop fetch $M \times R$ data segments or files. Spark directly stores the fetched data in memory for aggregation, whereas Hadoop stores the fetched data in disks or in memory for sorting and merging.

Similar to Hadoop's map phase, the reduce phase needs to sort and merge the fetched data through many disk I/O operations before dealing with them. However, Spark uses a hash table to aggregate values with the same partition in memory. When no spare memory is available, Spark is compelled to spill part of the data to disks. In addition, Spark leverages the distributed memory from all worker nodes to store much of the intermediate data in memory for reuse in the next stages. Spark improves overall performance by avoiding some disk I/O operations, which are otherwise unavoidable in Hadoop.

2.2 Motivation

After a shuffle file consolidation mechanism [11] is introduced into Spark, the number of shuffle files decreases and the performance improves. However, hash-based shuffle still causes performance degradation when the number of partitions reaches thousands. The job in Spark is divided into stages that run one at a time. If one stage runs slowly as a result of load imbalance, the total time of job is affected. Each stage of the job reads input data from disks or fetches data from the output of the previous stage. Whether or not the input data are distributed evenly on the cluster, Spark's scheduler assigns tasks to worker nodes based on data locality by delay scheduling [10]. If a task processes a partition without preferred locations, Spark randomly sends the task to one worker node. When processing different amounts of data, worker nodes may face different memory pressures and execute some unnecessary and expensive spill operations. Thus, the execution time of each stage can be affected by load imbalance of the data involved in the process of the worker nodes.

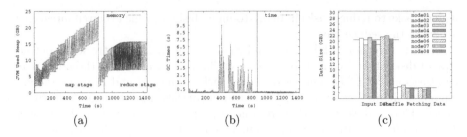

Fig. 1. (a) and (b) Illustrations of original hash-based shuffle's memory usage and GC time. (c) Data size through reading and shuffle fetching.

To analyze the reason of performance degradation caused by hash-based shuffle and to prove the existence of load imbalance, we conduct the following benchmark experiment. The experiment platform includes a cluster of nine nodes. One node functions as the master node and the remaining eight nodes as the worker nodes. Each node is equipped with two 8-core 2.6 GHz Intel Xeon E5-2670 CPUs, 32 GB memory and a 300 GB 10,000 RPM SAS disk, and runs RedHat Enterprise Linux 5 (Linux 2.6.18-308.4.1.el5). Spark version 1.1.0 is used in the experiment, running on a 160 GB dataset created by Hadoop's Random-TextWriter. The application we use is WordCount without combiner (WC), with a memory of 25 GB for each executor's JVM. We specify Netty for transferring shuffle blocks between executors and to open the option for the shuffle file consolidation mechanism.

In Spark, WC can be divided into two stages (map and reduce stages) based on the characteristics of the tasks. By adding "-XX:+PrintGCDetails -XX:+PrintGCTimeStamps" to the Java options, we obtain information on the status of memory usage and the amount of time spent on GC in one worker node. In addition, we record the size of data reading from the HDFS and fetching through the shuffle operations in all the worker nodes.

As shown in Fig. 1 (a) and (b), in the reduce stage, memory usage remains stable and little time is spent on GC. The reason for performance degradation is observable in the map stage. In the map stage, memory usage exhibits an increasing trend as time passes, and the time spent on each GC increases. When no spare memory is left, full GC occurs, indicating that the speed of memory collection by GC is lower than the speed of memory allocation. By analyzing the implementation of the hash-based shuffle write phase in the map stage, we find that each map task needs to create R file writer handles and some auxiliary objects to write data to the shuffle files. Even if the shuffle file consolidation mechanism ensures that every map task executed in the same core can share the same file group, the number of operations on the files is still $M \times R$. Each file operation needs some system calls, the write handle, 32 KB of write buffer, and some related objects. As a result, the system allocates huge memory to create objects when the number of partitions reaches thousands, which triggers a serious GC problem and increases the system overhead. From Fig. 1 (c), we observe differences in the amount of data that each worker node reads and fetches in Spark. Load imbalance of processing data can cause the data assigned to one processing node to overwhelm that node's memory capacity.

Similar to those in multi-threaded execution engines, the tasks of Spark assume the form of threads running on the worker nodes, which are conducive to sharing memory and reducing resource waste. Tasks spill to disks when the memory runs out. Spark mainly restricts memory usage to two types and sets the maximal amounts under each type. One type is used for caching data in memory, and the other type is for aggregation operations. Moreover, Spark ensures that each task on one executor can use $1/2N$ to $1/N$ of the memory for aggregation operations, where N is the number of running threads in one executor. When memory is inadequate for aggregation operations, spill operations occur. Excessive spill operations cause performance degradation. Spill operations can be avoided in two ways. One method is the creation of additional partitions to ensure each task needs less memory, although this may cause more shuffle files. The other method is the lowering of the concurrency level to let each task obtain additional memory, although in this method some stages may run very slowly when the memory is sufficient for them to compute on the previous higher concurrency level.

Motivated by the aforementioned challenges and opportunities, we propose three optimization approaches to improve memory usage efficiency. The specific details of the implementation are presented in the next section.

3   Implementation

This section presents how to implement the corresponding solutions for improving memory efficiency. The overall architecture of our approaches is shown in Fig. 2. Figure 2 is the native form of Spark, including our proposed optimization methods highlighted in red and table gridlines. *Write Handle Reusing* (WHR) is a new shuffle mechanism, which mainly optimizes the shuffle write phase, and is an option available to users. Before the tasks of a stage are submitted to the task scheduler, *Load Balancing Optimizer* (LBO) checks load imbalance and fixes it if it exists. *Memory-Aware Task Scheduler* (MATS) consists of a $feedback - sampling - decision$ mechanism, which helps the task scheduler to consider not only CPU resource but also memory resource in dispatching tasks.

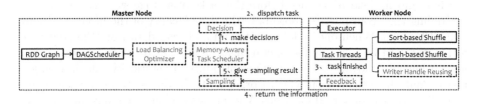

Fig. 2. Overall architecture of our approaches

3.1   Write Handle Reusing

The WHR mechanism based on the shuffle file consolidation mechanism, is designed to relieve memory pressure on the JVM and to reduce memory allocation by reusing writer handles and some related objects. In Spark, each CPU core has corresponding R partition files, called the *ShuffleWriterGroup*. When the *ShuffleWriterGroup* is used for the first time, the corresponding R partition files are opened. Then these partition files are not immediately closed after the tasks finish on the *ShuffleWriterGroup*. WHR closes the shuffle files of the worker node upon detecting that no tasks of the same stage is running on the worker node. Thus, the number of file operations is reduced to $C \times R$. Each map task running on the same core writes data to the partition files and shares the same group of writer handles, file group, and write buffer. To efficiently support fault tolerance in WHR, we follow the shuffle file consolidation; that is, we maintain the functional semantics by providing similar guarantees. After one map task finishes, its output is registered in the master node, which includes the offsets and lengths in the partition files. In WHR, the *ShuffleWriterGroup* ID is also registered, which is used for the shuffle fetch phase.

During the shuffle fetch phase in the reduce stage, the reduce task fetches the data that every map task outputs. Although the shuffle file consolidation mechanism reduces the number of shuffle files to $C \times R$, the amount of fetching data segments is still $M \times R$, and the partition files are divided into multiple parts. For fetching, however, requests for individual shuffle blocks arrive in a random order because they are requested concurrently by all executed reduce tasks. To further optimize the performance of the shuffle fetch phase, we make adjustments according to the changes in the shuffle write phase. The data in the same partition file belong to the same partition. Instead of fetching data segments, the entire partition files are pulled in WHR, which in turn reduces the number of random reads. Using the *ShuffleWriterGroup* ID, WHR transforms $M \times R$ data segments into $C \times R$ files. In the process of shuffle fetch phase, WHR checks whether or not the amount of data segments is equal to the length of the entire file for fault tolerance.

3.2   Load Balancing Optimizer

Load imbalance easily occurs when the pursuit for data locality is excessive. LBO can find and fix load imbalance before the tasks of a stage start to run. Delay scheduling then continues to coordinate the data locality of the input data and free CPU cores. When one task starts to run and read data from the HDFS or to process data by some shuffle operations, the amount of data on each worker node is known in advance. Thus, LBO is introduced to statically calculate which tasks should be executed on which worker node. In Spark, tasks are scheduled according to their preferred locations. We can achieve our desired results just by adjusting or resetting the preferred locations of the tasks. The preferred location of the input file is provided by the distributed file system. Tasks have no preferred locations when obtaining data through shuffle operations. For both cases, two different algorithms are designed. We assume that p input partition files and n worker nodes exist.

When tasks read data from the partition files on the HDFS, each task has the preferred location that LBO will adjust and reset when finding load imbalance. The corresponding algorithm of LBO is described in a following pseudo code.

Algorithm 1. Reset the Preferred Location for Input Data from HDFS

Input: The set of sizes for partition files, S; the set of preferred locations for tasks, P;
Output: The set of adjusted preferred locations for tasks, N;
 1: Initialization
 2: $sumsize = Sum(S[i])$, $averagesize = sumsize/n$, R is an empty collection;
 3: **for** $i = 1$ to p **do**
 4:     $j = P[i]$;
 5:     $N(j)$ add $(i, S[i])$;
 6: **end for**
 7: **for** $j = 1$ to n **do**
 8:     **if** $Sum(N[j]) > averagesize$ **then**
 9:         Sort $N[j]$ by the size of element;
10:         R add the redundance of $N[j]$ through choosing form small to large;
11:     **end if**
12: **end for**
13: **for** $k = 0$ to $R.length$ **do**
14:     Choose Node j which has the smallest size of partition files from N;
15:     $N[j]$ add $R[k]$;
16: **end for**
17: **for** $j = 0$ to n **do**
18:     **for** $k = 0$ to $N[j].length$ **do**
19:         $P[N[j][k].i] = j$;
20:     **end for**
21: **end for**
22: **return** N

Given that tasks run shuffle fetch operations without preferred location, LBO sets the preferred location for the tasks to pull data from every worker node. When the shuffle write phase finishes, the lengths of the partition files on each worker node are registered on the master node. The algorithm of LBO for shuffle operation takes full advantage of the data distribution to assign tasks to the worker nodes, which can make each worker node process nearly equal amounts of data and reduce network transmission. The specific steps of the LBO algorithm for tasks without preferred locations are described below.

Step 1: For each task, calculate the amount of data and their distributions.

Step 2: Divide the tasks into n groups according to the number of nodes and data size, ensuring that the data size for each group is nearly equal.

Step 3: Determine the amount of fetching data if the tasks of every group are executed on every node. Thus, a $n \times n$ matrix is created.

Step 4: Choose the largest value in the matrix to identify which group is allocated to which node. Mark the row and column at which the selected group is located to ensure that the group is not chosen next time. Goto Step 4 until no group is available.

Step 5: Set the preferred location for each task.

3.3   Memory-Aware Task Scheduler

The number of CPU cores available for tasks running on the same worker node is set by a static configuration file or parameter, which is fixed at runtime. When the tasks of a stage consume considerable amount of memory, the thread parallelism can cause fierce memory resource competitions, leading to many spill operations. Thus, we design MATS, which can dynamically adjust one worker node's concurrency level according to its current memory usage. The implementation of MATS is described below.

We let S_{mem} and S_{spill} denote the size of memory usage and the amount of data spilled to disks respectively. Spark provides approaches to obtain the values of S_{mem} and S_{spill} for each task. The upper bound of memory size S_{max} for aggregation operation and the maximal concurrency level CL_{max} are set beforehand. Thus, the equation for calculating the optimal concurrency level CL_{op} is as follows:

$$CL_{op} = \begin{cases} CL_{max} & \text{if } S_{spill} = 0 \\ S_{max}/(S_{mem} + S_{spill}) & \text{if } S_{spill} > 0 \end{cases}$$

When one task in the worker node finishes, one value of CL_{op} can be given; this value, however, does not stand for the whole worker node. Meanwhile, the master node receives much feedback information on finished tasks regarding CL_{op}. Thus, MATS establishes a $feedback - sampling - decision$ mechanism. The mechanism assigns tasks to a worker node according to the results of a sampling strategy. The strategy sets a dynamic sampling number SN and calculates the optimal concurrency level after collecting the SN values of the CL_{op}. We let $CL_{current}$ denote the current concurrency level of one worker node. The initial value of SN and $CL_{current}$ is equal to CL_{max}. Within the interval number of SN, we use CL_{sum} to add the CL_{op} returned by the finished tasks on the same worker node; the value of $CL_{current}$ is changed to CL_{op} when the CL_{op} of the feedback information is less than the $CL_{current}$. When the counter reaches SN, the values of $CL_{current}$ and SN are changed to CL_{sum}/SN.

4   Evaluation

This section presents the performance evaluation to verify the effectiveness of the improved Spark which integrates three optimization methods proposed in this paper. The environment and settings of the experiments are the same as those described in Sect. 2.2. Some special settings are described in the following sections. The performance of the improved Spark is compared with that of Spark version 1.1.0. The job configurations of the improved Spark are default and the same as those of the original Spark. In other words, we do not compare the improved Spark against the original Spark with disadvantaged configurations in the experiments.

4.1   Validation Experiments on Three Approaches

To evaluate the influence of WHR on memory and to prove the effectiveness of LBO, we conduct an experiment with conditions identical to the previously described test. Under the same experimental conditions and experimental data, we record memory usage and GC time. Similar to that from the LBO, the data size of reading from the HDFS and the shuffle fetching on each node are recorded.

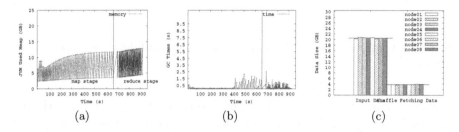

(a)   (b)   (c)

Fig. 3. (a) and (b) Illustrations of WHR's memory usage and GC time. (c) Data size through reading and shuffle fetching.

Figure 3 (a) and (b) show that the memory usage in the map stage has been reduced and is stable, and that the GC time has become shorter. Compared with the original hash-based shuffle, the maximal amount of memory usage is reduced significantly from nearly 24 GB to 13 GB. This result indicates that WHR can improve the utilization rate of memory and relieve the pressure on the JVM. WHR is capable of improving the performance because the write handles are shared in each core and the creation of large objects is reduced. According to the default value of the block size (128 MB), M and R are equal to 1440 and C is equal to 128. The improved Spark uses WHR to reuse the write handles and related objects, which can reduce the number of these objects in the map stage to $128/1440 \approx 0.089$ of the native Spark. By fetching $C \times R$ partition files instead of $M \times R$ data segments in the shuffle fetch phase, the amount of random reads is reduced. Figure 3 (c) shows that with the LBO the input and shuffle fetching data are relatively even on each node. Compared with Fig. 1 (c), the LBO changes the standard deviations of the processing input data size and fetch data size on each worker node from 0.94 to 0.19 and from 0.53 to 0.08, which makes a good load balancing. In addition, the total execution time of WC with the improved Spark is 33.3 % lower than that with the original Spark, changing from 24 min to 16 min.

To verify the effectiveness of MATS, the test application should ensure that memory resource competition and spill operations occur. Given that the aggregation operations in the reduce stage consume little memory, no disk spilling occurs in WC. Thus, we choose the PageRank (PR) proposed by the founders of Google and implemented in Spark for the comparison. The hash-based shuffle is still adopted by PR in the original Spark. PR requires some calculations of iteration and caches data in memory, which is conducive to spill operations. We set

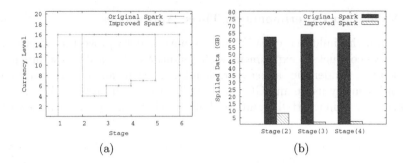

Fig. 4. (a) Average currency level of each stage. (b) Spilled data size of the middle three stages.

the number of iterations to three. The input dataset of PR is produced by the PR of HiBench, which is provided by Intel. The size of the dataset for PR is 115 GB or nearly 14 GB per worker node. The heap size of JVM in each worker node is 25 GB. To avoid serious GC problem and reduce the size of the cached data, we serialize the cached data using *org. apache. spark. serializer. KryoSerializer*. In the experiments, the data size from spill operations of all the worker nodes and the average real-time concurrency level of each worker node are recorded. The application consists of five stages. The middle three stages consume considerable memory and cause spill operations. From Fig. 4 (a) and (b), we observe that the concurrency level is dynamically changed, and it decreases when memory resource competition occurs. The total spill size in the improved Spark with MATS is much smaller than that in the original Spark by as much as 27x. The total running time of the improved version is reduced by as much as 31 %, from 96 min to 66 min, compared with the original version. MATS sacrifices concurrency to avoid expensive spill operations and additional I/O operations, which in turn reduces the amount of data spills and maximizes the use of memory. Thus, according to the results of the experiment, replacing the task scheduler with MATS to improve the overall performance is worthwhile.

The above experiments prove that the proposed three optimizations can improve the performance of in-memory MapReduce systems from different aspects. WHR plays the role to reduce overheads caused by a large number of partition. LBO tries to adjust the task scheduling to keep load balancing. MATS controls the frequency of dispatching tasks to avoid the memory resources competition. Thus, all the approaches do not affect each other in any perspectives and can work well together. For example, when the amount of input data is certain, the number of partitions is inversely proportional to the amount of single partitioned data. The memory usage is associated with the amount of data processing. So a small amount of partitions are easy to lead to memory resources competition, and a large amount of partitions cause more file operations. Users need to consider the size of the partition and the number of partitions when facing big data problems. But such thorny problems can be solved well by WHR and MATS together.

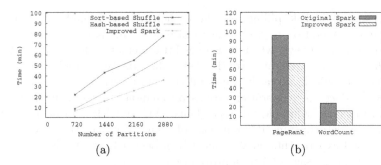

Fig. 5. (a) Performance comparison among increased number of partitions. (b) Performances relative to size of memory usage.

4.2   Increased Number of Partitions

To test the influence of the partition number in the improved Spark, we use four different partition sizes to compare execution times in the improved Spark with that in the original Spark, which separately adopts hash-based shuffle with the shuffle file consolidation mechanism and sort-based shuffle in WC. Figure 5 (a) shows that the partition sizes changes from 720 to 2880. The corresponding input data size is 80, 160, 240 and 320 GB. The hash-based shuffle performs better than the sort-based shuffle. The original Spark with the shuffle file consolidation mechanism achieves a speedup of 2.53x over the sort-based shuffle when the partition number is 720. When the partition size increases, however, the speedup drops to less than 2x. With an increase in the partition number, the hash-based shuffle runs slowly because memory is not reasonably used, thereby causing serious GC problems, and because too many file operations increase the system overhead. By contrast, the improved Spark can adapt well to different partition numbers and has good scalability. The speedup consistently remains in 2.11x or higher, reaching as high as 3.18x than the sort-based shuffle at the maximum. Compared with the hash-based shuffle, in the case with the 720 partitions, the improved Spark achieves a small speedup of 1.25x. However, when the partition number reaches 2880, the improved Spark can still decrease the run time by 36.8 % and achieve a maximal speedup of 1.58x over the hash-based shuffle. As a result of the absence of spill operations in WC, the WHR mechanism and the LBO method play important roles in the improved Spark. Therefore, the improved Spark reduces large number of memory to create objects and ensures load balancing across all the worker nodes.

4.3   Size of Memory Usage

For in-memory MapReduce systems, the size of memory usage for aggregation operations on intermediate data has a great influence on performance. In Spark, different aggregation operations consume different amounts of memory. Some aggregation operations require much memory to handle intermediate data, and therefore cause some disk spilling, especially when memory is inadequate. In WC, a *reduceByKey* operation is used to aggregate key-value pairs for summing up values with the same keys, which consumes little memory. Meanwhile, PR uses *groupByKey* operation to transform the (key, value) to (key, valuelist) and cache them in memory, which can easily cause spill operations. At every iteration of PR, the join and *reduceBykey* operations are used to handle the shuffle fetching data, which consumes considerable memory. Thus, WC and PR represent different applications which consume different size of memory usage. By analyzing the aforementioned experiments on WC and PR in Sect. 4.1, we study the effect of the size of memory usage on the improved Spark.

Figure 5 (b) shows that, in contrast to that in the original Spark, the execution time of WC in the improved Spark reaches a speedup of 1.5x, which is slightly higher than the 1.45x speedup in PR. The performance improvement of the improved Spark in PR is not as significant as that of the improved Spark in WC. This result can be explained as follows. The performance improvement from WHR and LBO can be reflected well on an application that has no spill operations, such as WC. However, the performance degradation caused by spill operation can reduce the performance improvement from WHR and LBO. Given its operations that consume large amounts of memory, PR spills some of the intermediate data to disks. Although MATS can reduce considerable data spilling, the currency level decreases, which still affects the performance improvement from the WHR and LBO. MATS can not fully compensate for the performance degradation caused by data spilling.

5   Related Work

Hash-based shuffle, which is simple yet effective, is adopted in many MapReduce systems. By reducing the number of shuffle files, the shuffle file consolidation mechanism [11] effectively solves the performance issues caused by large amounts of random I/Os in the shuffle fetch phase. However, no research has studied the relationship between hash-based shuffle and memory. The present research analyzes only the influence of hash-based shuffle on memory. By sharing some objects in file operations, the proposed WHR method releases the pressure exerted by hash-based shuffle on memory and reduces a few random I/Os. Recently, research on load balancing has attracted significant attention. Enhanced Load Balancer [9] dynamically considers the size of intermediate data generated by tasks and schedules tasks for an even distribution of intermediate data. ShuffleWatcher [12] is appropriate for multi-tenant environments and aims to reduce shuffle traffic to improve cluster performance based on network loads. In contrast to those in previous works, the proposed LBO method statically analyzes the presence of load imbalance in the processing data and adjusts the preferred location of tasks, which can help locality-oriented scheduling techniques to improve their exploitation of CPU and memory resources. With regard to research on task schedulers, Resource-Aware Adaptive Scheduler [13] is designed to dynamically adjust the number of slots and workload placement on each machine to maximize the resource utilization of the Hadoop cluster. Mammoth [8] implements a multi-threaded execution engine based on Hadoop and realizes global memory management through techniques, such as disk access serialization, multi-cache, and shuffling from memory. These previous works focus on implementing synchronization between map tasks and reduce tasks. By contrast, the proposed MATS method adapts to the multi-threaded execution engine, in which jobs are divided into stages that run one at a time. Subsequently, the tasks under each stage can share and compete for the united memory. By collecting information on the completed tasks, MATS helps the task scheduler adjust the frequency of dispatching tasks to each worker node, which can minimize expensive disk spilling caused by serious memory resource competition.

6   Conclusion and Future Work

In this study, we propose three approaches for in-memory MapReduce systems, which we implement in Spark. Through the analysis of the disadvantages of hash-based shuffle on memory usage, WHR is introduced to improve the efficiency of memory usage in the shuffle write phase and to reduce some random I/Os in the shuffle fetch phase. Moreover, LBO is designed to keep the data evenly processed on each node. When the nodes run out of memory, MATS is devised to coordinate the memory usage with the concurrency level. The results of the experiments show that the new system achieves a speedup of the job execution time from 1.25x to 3.18x over the original Spark. In addition, the improved system does not change the current Spark processing phases and can easily integrate the existing upper application techniques of Spark into the new system. Moreover, Spark applications do not need any modification to run on our improved system.

Our future work will focus on two aspects of memory. First, we will build a unified memory management system to break the restriction of static configuration on memory, which can make memory usage more efficient. Second, we will design a new execution process to reduce memory resource competitions and to avoid long GC time without changing the upper application structure of the system.

Acknowledgments. This paper is partly supported by the NSFC under grant No. 61433019 and No. 61370104, International Science & Technology Cooperation Program of China under grant No. 2015DFE12860, and Chinese Universities Scientific Fund under grant No. 2014TS008.

References

1. Dean, J., Ghemawat, S.: Mapreduce: simplified data processing on large clusters. Commun. ACM **51**(1), 107–113 (2008)
2. Isard, M., Budiu, M., Yu, Y., Birrell, A., Fetterly, D.: Dryad: Distributed data-parallel programs from sequential building blocks. In: Proceedings of the 2nd ACM European Conference on Computer Systems (EuroSys), pp. 59–72 (2007)
3. Apache hadoop. http://apache.hadoop.org

4. Rasmussen, A., Porter, G., Conley, M., Madhyastha, H.V., Mysore, R.N., Pucher, A., Vahdat, A.: Tritonsort: a balanced large-scale sorting system. In: Proceedings of USENIX Symposium on Networked Systems Design and Implementation (NSDI), pp. 29–42 (2011)

5. Bu, Y., Howe, B., Balazinska, M., Ernst, M.D.: Haloop: efficient iterative data processing on large clusters. Proc. VLDB Endowment **3**(1–2), 285–296 (2010)

6. Zaharia, M., Chowdhury, M., Franklin, M.J., Shenker, S., Stoica, I.: Spark: cluster computing with working sets. In: Proceedings of the 2nd USENIX Conference on Hot Topics in Cloud Computing (HotCloud), pp. 10–10 (2010)

7. Zaharia, M., Chowdhury, M., Das, T., Dave, A., Ma, J., McCauley, M., Franklin, M.J., Shenker, S., Stoica, I.: Resilient distributed datasets: a fault-tolerant abstraction for in-memory cluster computing. In: Proceedings of the 9th USENIX Conference on Networked Systems Design and Implementation (NSDI), pp. 2–2 (2012)

8. Shi, X., Chen, M., He, L., Xie, X., Jin, H., Chen, Y., Wu, S.: Mammoth: gearing hadoop towards memory-intensive MapReduce applications. IEEE Trans. Parallel Distrib. Syst. **26**(8), 2300–2315 (2015)

9. Wang, Y., Goldstone, R., Yu, W., Wang, T.: Characterization and optimization of memory-resident MapReduce on HPC systems. In: Proceedings of 2014 IEEE International Parallel and Distributed Processing Symposium (IPDPS), pp. 799–808 (2014)

10. Zaharia, M., Borthakur, D., Sen Sarma, J., Elmeleegy, K., Shenker, S., Stoica, I.: Delay scheduling: a simple technique for achieving locality and fairness in cluster scheduling. In: Proceedings of the 5th European Conference on Computer Systems (EuroSys), pp. 265–278 (2010)

11. Davidson, A., Or, A.: Optimizing shuffle performance in spark. Technical report, University of California, Berkeley-Department of Electrical Engineering and Computer Sciences (2013)

12. Ahmad, F., Chakradhar, S.T., Raghunathan, A., Vijaykumar, T.: ShuffleWatcher: shuffle-aware scheduling in multi-tenant MapReduce clusters. In: Proceedings of the 2014 USENIX Annual Technical Conference (ATC), pp. 1–12 (2014)

13. Polo, J., Castillo, C., Carrera, D., Becerra, Y., Whalley, I., Steinder, M., Torres, J., Ayguadé, E.: Resource-aware adaptive scheduling for MapReduce clusters. In: Kon, F., Kermarrec, A.-M. (eds.) Middleware 2011. LNCS, vol. 7049, pp. 187–207. Springer, Heidelberg (2011)

DBFS: Dual Best-First Search Mapping Algorithm for Shared-Cache Multicore Processors

Thomas Canhao Xu$^{(\boxtimes)}$ and Ville Leppänen

Department of Information Technology, University of Turku,
20014 Turku, Finland
canxu@utu.fi

Abstract. This paper proposes a task mapping algorithm for shared-cache multicore processors. The multicore system is quantitatively analysed in terms of intra-application communication latency, inter-application congestion and delay of shared-cache access. A heuristic greedy best-first search algorithm is adapted to find a compact mapping region for an application. We develop a flexible dual best-first search strategy that evaluates the network dynamically according to the current situation. Several metrics are applied to improve the quality of the mapping result. We evaluate the proposed algorithm along with others using synthetic and real applications. Results from the synthetic workloads show that the proposed algorithm achieves nearly optimal cache access delays on 64-node network under 50 % to 100 % system utilization, while the intra-application latency and inter-application congestion metrics are improved by 13.8 % and 17.2 % in a practical system configuration, compared with the incremental algorithm. We also compare our proposal with the true optimal solutions, results reveal that the algorithm can provide near-optimal results with enough search spaces. Furthermore the computation complexity of the proposed algorithm is relatively low. The data from real applications show that the average execution time of applications is reduced 13.5 % compared to the first fit algorithm.

Keywords: Multicore · Mapping · Shared cache · Best first · Parallel

1 Introduction and Related Work

Multicore systems are more and more common nowadays. Even a decade ago, when single core processors still dominated desktop computers, it was difficult to imagine that mobile phones in the near future would be equipped with octa-core processors. The driving force behind massive multicore processors is software, specifically applications that process huge amount of data. Integrating more and more cores in a chip is a hardware trend for increasing the performance of parallel applications. However the scalability of shared-bus communication is limited and it cannot handle increased number of on-chip components efficiently [4]. Network-on-Chip (NoC) concept has been proposed and emerged as

© Springer International Publishing Switzerland 2015
G. Wang et al. (Eds.): ICA3PP 2015, Part I, LNCS 9528, pp. 185–198, 2015.
DOI: 10.1007/978-3-319-27119-4_13

a promising solution for the communication infrastructure of massive multicore systems. Figure 1 illustrates a NoC with 64 nodes (n0 to n63). The nodes are interconnected by cardinal network links and routers (R). Each Processing Element (PE) is attached to a router. Each PE consists of a processor core and related L1 cache, a slice of the shared L2 cache and a Network Interface (NI). Processor cores communicate with each other by transferring messages using the network.

To execute on a NoC, applications must be mapped to different nodes of the system. *Task mapping* consists of placing the tasks in an application to different nodes of the system with a set of constraints and requirements, e.g. performance, energy cost, efficiency and network congestion. These metrics can be affected dramatically with different mapping decisions. Furthermore, applications are entering and

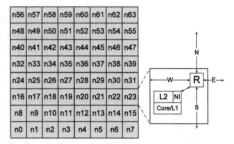

Fig. 1. A NoC with 8×8 mesh.

leaving the system at run-time, leading to dynamic and unpredictable system status. Therefore the mapping algorithm itself should be efficient and adaptive.

There are different works concerning task mapping, scheduling and management in multicore systems. For example, first fit algorithm is widely used in modern operating systems, in which the first available processor in the processor list is selected without considering other metrics. Similarly the nearest neighbor algorithm neglects all other aspects except the distance to the nearest free processor. Various mapping and scheduling algorithms for conventional computer systems are studied and discussed by different researchers [7]. Carvalho et al. investigated the performance metrics of the aforementioned algorithms and several heuristics algorithms [13]. It is shown that the proposed heuristics can reduce packet latency and channel load.

Task mapping for mesh-based on-chip networks has been studied in [6,12] and [3]. An incremental mapping algorithm is proposed in [3]. The algorithm first selects the nodes that are closest to the master node and includes these nodes in the destination mapping region which fit the size of the application. In the next step, the algorithm places the tasks to the region and tries to keep the region contiguous. The main design goal of the incremental algorithm is to improve performance and reduce energy consumption, while it is claimed that the proposed algorithm further allows multiple concurrent applications with minimal inter-application communication overhead.

The performance requirement for cache is more and more important for future applications. Lei Wang et al. have shown that applications processing huge amount of data have relatively low computation intensity but high pressure on the cache system, compared with traditional applications [16]. This implies that the performance of shared cache can be a deterministic aspect for system performance. It is noteworthy that the impact of shared-cache can be even higher in NoCs than traditional multicore systems since the cache slices are usually distributed to different nodes, leading to non-uniform access latency [20]. Previous researchers have focused on improving the compactness of the mapping, i.e. different tasks should be closer to each other [3,6], while the cache access delay is omitted. In addition, finding the optimal or near-optimal mapping is partially a problem in computational geometry [5], the effectiveness of many previous algorithms have not been well addressed. In this paper, we propose and discuss a novel heuristic task mapping by applying a dual best-first search algorithm. Results from both synthetic and real applications with various configurations support the proposed algorithm.

2   On-Chip Communication, Latency and Congestion

As aforementioned, in shared-cache multicore processors, applications generate various types of on-chip traffic. Considering the destination multicore architecture, we classify the traffic in two aspects: intra-application communication traffic and shared-cache communication traffic. Intra-application communication stands for data exchange among multiple tasks (e.g. processes and threads) in an application, while shared-cache traffic consists of fetching/storing data from/to the shared cache. Depending on the characteristics of an application, used mapping method, and the amount of concurrent applications, the network traffic may have different latency and congestion results.

Figure 2(a) illustrated a mapping of an application with 7 tasks, where the route for on-chip traffic among node 27 and other 6 nodes are shown as bold lines (refer to Fig. 1 for numbering of nodes). It is obvious that the tasks are mapped dispersedly, causing high intra-application communication overhead. An improved mapping is depicted in Fig. 2(b). The communication delay is significantly reduced since all the tasks are mapped in a congregate way. It is noteworthy that a dispersed mapping can affect other concurrent applications adversely as well, causing congestion to the network and decrease the performance of the system. Here we analyse the compactness of the mapping region. We refer to the definition of *convex hull* in computational geometry [5]. For a given set of points (processor nodes), the convex hull is the smallest convex set that contains all the points in the set. We further calculate the *area* of the convex hull in the destination mapping region. The area of the convex hull represents the *area of effect* for the mapping region, i.e. for the same application, smaller convex hull generally means lower intra-application communication overhead, and due to the smaller *area of effect*, it is expected that the possibility of congestion with multiple applications is lower. Similarly the trend of intra-application communication overhead and the possibility of congestion increases as the area of the convex hull increases. Figure 2(a) and (b) illustrated the convex hull of two different mapping methods. Apparently the area of the convex hull in Fig. 2(b) is smaller than in Fig. 2(a), meaning that different concurrent applications are more likely to interfere with each other in the mapping method of Fig. 2(a).

Notice that, generally speaking, larger convex hull means both higher intra-application communication latency and possibility of congestion among applications. However there are exceptions. Figure 2(d) shows two different mapping cases of a 12-task application, either in a 3×4 rectangle shape, or in a cross shape. The average intra-application communication latency in the cross shape mapping is lower than that in the rectangle shape (2.1111 and 2.1388), while the area of the convex hull in the rectangle shape is lower than that in the cross shape (6 and 7, refer to Sect. 3.1 for definitions of these metrics). Besides latency and congestion of intra- and inter-application communication, we further consider the access latency of the on-chip shared-cache. Figure 2(c) illustrates the minimum hop counts between node 6 and other nodes. Apparently nodes in the centre have lower average cache access delay than in the border.

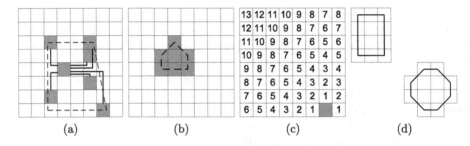

(a)   (b)   (c)   (d)

Fig. 2. (a) gray nodes are used, other nodes are free, bold lines show communication among 1 node and other 6 nodes, dotted lines shows the area of convex hull. (b) depicts an optimized mapping. (c) the access latency of all shared-cache slices for a node, numbers indicate minimum hop count to the grey node. (d) illustrates two mapping regions for a 12-task application.

We note that applications can have preference in accessing the shared-cache, e.g. due to data locality, some addresses are more frequently used than others. The problem is more severe for direct mapped cache. Fortunately modern processors mitigate this problem by implementing a set-associative cache, making the cache accesses more balanced to different parts of the cache [2]. We use 16-way set associative shared-cache in our experiment platform. Besides data locality, contention of shared resources can be another problem [15], however the problem is out of the scope of this paper.

3   The Proposed Mapping Algorithm

The aforementioned analysis suggested that, in a multicore shared-cache system with concurrent multi-task applications, the intra-application communication latency, inter-application congestion and average access delay to the shared-cache are tightly related to the mapping algorithm. In the following section, formal models are defined for the multicore platform, application and the mapping problem. We analyse several key aspects that affect application performance. A homogeneous mesh-based network is considered here to simplify the analysis.

3.1 Formal Definitions

We present formal definitions of the fundamentals of the mapping problem.

Definition 1. *A NoC $N(P(X,Y))$ consists of a mesh network $P(X,Y)$ of width X, length Y with $X{\times}Y$ nodes. Each node n_i is denoted by a coordinate (x,y), where $0{\leq}x{\leq}X-1$ and $0{\leq}y{\leq}Y-1$. The coordinate can be represented as $i=y{\times}X+x$. The Manhattan Distance between n_i and n_j is $MD(n_i, n_j)$.*

Definition 2. *A Task Graph is a directed acyclic graph, $TG = (N, E)$, where N is the set of nodes and E is the set of directed edges that associated with the graph. The amount of traffic (weight of the edge) between nodes n_i and n_j is represented as w_{n_i, n_j}. $\forall w_{n_i, n_j} \in E$.*

Definition 3. *An application $A_k(TG_k(N_k, E_k))$ consists of a list of task nodes N_k, and a list of communication volume between different nodes E_k. The application is mapped to $|N_k|$ cores for execution.*

Definition 4. *$n_{Available}$ is a set of available nodes in $P(X,Y)$.*

Definition 5. *$R_l(A_k)$ is the destination mapping region in $P(X,Y)$, consisting of a set of nodes $n_{|N_k|}$ with $|N_k|$ nodes for $A_k(TG_k(N_k, E_k))$.*

Definition 6. *$Conv_l(R_l)$ is the convex hull of R_l:*

$$Conv_l(R_l) = \left\{ \sum_{j=1}^{|N_k|} \theta_j n_j \middle| n_j \in R_l, \theta_j \in [0,1], \sum_{j=1}^{|N_k|} \theta_j = 1 \right\} \tag{1}$$

Definition 7. *Average Cache Latency (ACL_{n_i}) is the average latency for a node n_i accessing the shared last level cache. The ACL_{n_i} is calculated as:*

$$ACL_{n_i} = \frac{\sum_{j=0}^{X{\times}Y-1} MD(n_i, n_j)}{X \times Y} \tag{2}$$

Definition 8. *Average Intra-application Latency (AIL_{R_l}) is the average latency between internal nodes for an application A_k with a mapping region $R_l(A_k)$. The AIL_{R_l} is calculated as:*

$$AIL_{R_l} = \frac{\sum w_{n_i, n_j} \times MD(n_i, n_j)}{|N_k|} \tag{3}$$

Such that: $\forall i, j : n_i, n_j \in R_l(A_k)$.

Definition 9. *The Area of the Convex Hull (ACH_{Conv_l}) is the area enclosed by the convex hull $Conv_l(R_l)$.*

3.2   Application Mapping in Dynamic Systems

As we discussed in Sect. 2, application performance and system efficiency can be affected
by the intra-application latency, inter- application congestion and cache access latency.
We explain ACL, AIL and ACH with
Fig. 3(a). Application C is mapped to four
nodes n_{25}, n_{26}, n_{33} and n_{34}. We can calculate
that the ACLs of n_{25} and n_{33} are 4.75 $\left(\frac{304}{64}\right)$,
while these values for n_{26} and n_{34} are both
4.25 $\left(\frac{272}{64}\right)$. It is natural that a node has lower
ACL values in case that it has lower MD
to the geometry centre of the mesh network.
In terms of AIL, the average MD between
one node and all other nodes in the mapping
region is calculated. For simplicity here we
assume that $\forall i,j : n_i, n_j \in E_i$, $w_{n_i,n_j} = 1$.
Take n_{25} for example, $MD(n_{25}, n_{26}) = 1$,
$MD(n_{25}, n_{33}) = 1$ and $MD(n_{25}, n_{34}) = 2$,
therefore the average MD of n_{25} to other
nodes in the mapping region is 1 $\left(\frac{4}{4}\right)$. This
metric can be calculated for other 3 nodes
as well, finally by multiplying the weight of
edges, the AIL of C is the average value
of them. Both C and D are viable mapping regions for a 4-task application, however C is better in terms of the two metrics, i.e. the average ACL and AIL of D are
6.1875 and 1.625 respectively while these two
values for C are 4.625 and 1 only. In consideration of inter-application congestion, intuitively C is still more suitable than D since
it looks that C is more "compact" than D.

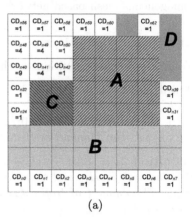

(a)

(b)

Fig. 3. (a) 4 applications $A/B/$ C/D running. (b) grey nodes are occupied, white nodes are free, $CD*$ shows the *congregate degree* of free nodes.

This is proved by ACH of two regions, where
$ACH_{Conv_C} = 1$ and $ACH_{Conv_D} = 2$. The intra-application communication in
D conflicts with mapping region A.

Finding the lowest value of one metric in ACL, ACH and AIL in a mapping
region is relatively easy. For instance, to retrieve a mapping region with optimal
ACL, all available nodes can be sorted with ACL and the required number of
nodes are output according to the sorted list. This strategy $MACL$ will be evaluated in the experiments. In case of single-task application, the $MACL$ algorithm
works well. However, as the algorithm omits the proximity of tasks, for applications with several tasks, the resulting mapping region can be fragmented, meaning higher overhead of intra-application communication and congestion among
applications [19].

To calculate the lowest AIL for an application, Demaine et al. provided an efficient algorithm that can output the optimal sum of all pairwise MD of the street grid in $\mathcal{O}(n^{7.5})$ [5]. Unfortunately the proposed algorithm works in empty system only. In a dynamic system, since the mapping space is limited and the space is fragmented by multiple concurrent applications, the problem of finding the optimal solution is proved to be NP-$Hard$ [5]. Various methods are used to achieve better compactness of the mapping region with limited cost, such as heuristic and stochastic algorithms, simulated annealing and linear programming. The proposed method is based on the proof by [5], that the shape of an optimal region is convex and near circular. Here, the AIL of a mapping region is lower in case the region is more "compact" or $congregate$. We define $congregate$ such that the shape of a region is closer to a square instead of a rectangle. For example, Fig. 3(a) illustrated two applications A and B both with 16 tasks. The AIL_{R_B} is higher than AIL_{R_A} ($AIL_{R_A} = 2.5$, $AIL_{R_B} = 3.125$). It is noteworthy that R_A is not an optimal solution in terms of AIL, the AIL of the optimal result described in [5] is 2.484, or 0.64 % less than that in R_A. We note that circular shape is closer to optimal than square, however the cost of calculating circular shape in a dynamic system can be too high. Here the $Congregate\ Degree$ is defined based on the above analysis:

Definition 10. *Congregate Degree (CD_{n_i}) is the maximum number of available nodes for n_i in the $x + y+$ (right-up) direction, in a square shape.*

It is obvious that the CD of a used node is 0, for free nodes the value is the square of an integer. For example in Fig. 3(a), $CD_{n_{40}} = 9$, meaning that for n_{40}, the maximum number of free nodes in a square shape in the right-up direction is 9 (i.e. $n_{40}, n_{41}, n_{42}, n_{48}, n_{49}, n_{50}, n_{56}, n_{57}, n_{58}$). The CDs of other unoccupied nodes are shown in the figure as well.

3.3 The Proposed Algorithm

The key idea behind the proposed algorithm is that: For an application A_k, starting from a node, continue to search and include for the remaining $|N_k| - 1$ free nodes that minimizes AIL of the mapping region (greedy best-first searching). However to achieve better AIL, ACH and ACL metrics, there is an essential problems to explore: which node is chosen to start from? Apparently nodes in the central part of the mesh network have lower ACL than nodes in the border, therefore the algorithm calculates the ACL of all nodes and explores from the node with minimum ACL (Dual Best-First Search: condition 1). The number of nodes required by an application can be equal, larger or smaller than the CD of the starting node. For that reason the region should be untouched, shrunk, or expanded accordingly. Notice that expanding operation takes time to calculate nearby nodes. Moreover, increasing the search space, i.e. the number of candidate mapping regions will increase the computation complexity as well. Each extra search will start from the second best node in the list. A variable R_{max} is defined to limit the search space. Practically, a decent algorithm should generate near-optimal result in the lowest possible search space.

In case the number of tasks in an application equals to the CD of the starting node n_i, the region will be added to the candidate region list (*Case 1, Equal → Square → Untouch*). Provided that CD_{n_i} is larger than the number of tasks in an application, and meanwhile the number of tasks can be represented by a square, then the smallest CD that is closest to the number of requested nodes is added to the candidate list (*Case 2.1, Larger → Square → Shrink*). Otherwise the square is expanded accordingly. Take a 6-task application for example, it is firstly mapped to $CD_{n_i} = 4$ when possible, then expanded with 2 nodes (*Case 2.2, Larger → Non-square → Shrink → Expand*). It is noteworthy that CD_{n_i} stands for the maximum number of free nodes in a square, while squares smaller than CD_{n_i} is evaluated to improve the overall result. The last situation, which is common in high-utilization dynamic systems, is that the CD of the starting node n_i is smaller than the number of tasks in an application. Obviously the region should be expanded in this case. However, the CD_{n_i} can be close to the number of nodes requested by the application ($CD_{n_i} = \left\lfloor \sqrt{|N|} \right\rfloor$), or it can be smaller. In the first case, the region will be expanded normally (*Case 3.1, Smaller → Close → Expand*). In the second case, remaining free nodes are searched to determine whether nodes with larger CD can be found (Dual Best-First Search: condition 2), and then the free node with $CD = \left\lfloor \sqrt{|N|} \right\rfloor$ or the free node with largest CD will be selected and expanded (*Case 3.2, Smaller → Not-close → Continue → Expand*). Finally, the candidate regions are evaluated with Normalized Average Latency (NAL):

Definition 11. *Normalized Average Latency (NAL_{R_l}) is the weighted average latency of a mapping region $R_l(A_k)$:*

$$NAL_{R_l} = \begin{cases} \dfrac{ACL_{n_i} - ACL_{min}}{ACL_{min}}, & if\ |N_k| = 1 \\ N_{ACL_{R_l}} + N_{AIL_{R_l}} + N_{ACH_{R_l}}, & if\ |N_k| > 1 \end{cases} \tag{4}$$

$$N_{ACL_{R_l}} = \frac{\frac{\sum_{n_i \in R_l} ACL_{n_i}}{|N_k|} - ACL_{min}}{ACL_{min}} \tag{5}$$

$$N_{AIL_{R_l}} = \frac{AIL_{R_l} - AIL_{min}}{AIL_{min}} \tag{6}$$

$$N_{ACH_{R_l}} = \frac{ACH_{R_l} - ACH_{min}}{ACH_{min} + 1} \tag{7}$$

where ACL_{min}, AIL_{min} and ACH_{min} represent the minimum ACL, AIL and ACH of all candidate regions.

The pseudo code of the proposed algorithm is shown in Algorithm 1. In consideration of computation complexity, the proposed algorithm is relatively low compared with performance improvements. The time taken to execute the algorithm is proportional to $n_{Available}$ and R_{max}, i.e. more free nodes leads to increased search space, where evaluating more candidate regions causes linearly

---

Algorithm 1. Pseudo code of the proposed mapping algorithm.

Input: $N(P(X,Y))$, $n_{Available}$, ACL of all nodes, R_{max}, list of candidate regions
    $R_{Candidate}$, $A(TG(N,E))$
Output: A mapping region $R(A)$ for the application

$\forall n_i \in n_{Available}$: calculate CD_{n_i} and ACL_{n_i}, sort ACL_{n_i} as ACL_{sorted}
$\forall ACL_{sorted}$ **if** $CD_{n_i} > |N|$ **then**

> Shrink the region to $\left\lfloor \sqrt{|N|} \right\rfloor$
>
> Expand the region according to the greedy best-first algorithm if $|N| > \left\lfloor \sqrt{|N|} \right\rfloor^2$
> Place the region into the candidate list $R_{Candidate}$ until reaching R_{max}
> **else if** $CD_{n_i} = |N|$ **then**
> > | Place the region into the candidate list $R_{Candidate}$ until reaching R_{max}
> **end**
>
> **else if** $CD_{n_i} < |N|$ and $CD_{n_i} = \left\lfloor \sqrt{|N|} \right\rfloor$ **then**
> > Expand the region according to the greedy best-first expanding algorithm
> > Place the region into the candidate list $R_{Candidate}$ until reaching R_{max}
> **end**
> **else**
> > Continue search with remaining nodes n_j in $n_{Available}$ with possibly larger CD
> > Expand CD_{n_j} where $CD_{n_j} = \left\lfloor \sqrt{|N|} \right\rfloor$ or $CD_{n_j} = max(CD_{n_k}, \forall n_k \in n_{Available})$
> > Place the region into the candidate list $R_{Candidate}$ until reaching R_{max}
> **end**

end
Calculate and return the region with lowest NAL in $R_{Candidate}$

---

increased time for calculation. The exact time cost will be investigated in the experiments. A possible disadvantage of the proposed algorithm is that, the available maximum CD_{n_i} may reduce quickly as applications mapped to the network, leading to fragmentation. However this is a common problem for most greedy algorithms. On the other hand, the optimization goal of the proposed algorithm is the normalized value of intra-application communication, inter-application congestion and shared-cache access, while it is possible that some applications can have unique communication patterns.

4   Experimental Evaluation

In this section, we evaluate performance of different mapping algorithms with synthetic workload and real application. Performance metrics such as ACL, AIL, ACH and time cost, as well as application performance metrics are investigated.

4.1   Synthetic Result Analysis

We first investigate various algorithms with synthetic workloads: the proposed mapping algorithm with different number of search space ($DBFS*$), the First

Fit mapping algorithm in Solaris 9 (FF), the Nearest Neighbour algorithm that always choose next node with minimum MD to the current node (NN), the incremental mapping algorithm in [3] (INC), the mapping algorithm that always choose nodes with minimum ACL ($MACL$) and random mapping ($RAND$). Tasks are generated by Task Graph Generator [14], where a set of 10,000 tasks ($1 \leq |N| \leq 16$) is generated. The tasks enter and leave the system with first-in-first-out sequence. System configurations with different node utilizations are evaluated. It is reported that the utilization of modern large-scale systems is between 50 % to 100 % [8], where the utilization can maintain 80 % to 90 % for heavy-loaded systems [9]. Therefore our experiments are based on these utilizations. In case the number of available nodes are not enough for the incoming application, the earliest application will be removed after it is finished. The results shown in Table 1 and Fig. 4 are measured by AIL, ACH and *the average ACLs of all nodes* in the mapping region.

According to Table 1, $MACL$ achieved lowest ACL in all situations. This is expected since $MACL$ always chooses nodes with lowest ACL. However the downside is obvious as well: the AIL and ACH values are among the worst. The improvement for $MACL$ under 50 % system utilization is around 13 %, while it is less noticeable as the utilization increases. The $DBFS$ achieved nearly identical ACL results regardless of the search space. The number of search space in $DBFS$ did have an impact for AIL and ACH in most cases. However the improvement is more significant for high utilized networks. For example, increasing the number of search space from 1 to 8 results as 6.5 % and 10.6 % improvements of AIL and ACH respectively under 100 % utilization. The time consumed by finding extra mapping regions increases linearly. Notice that the time spent for making each mapping decision is considerably low even for $DBFS8$ (magnitude of μs). The program execution time of real world applications is expected to be much longer comparatively. Overall, on average for 80 % and 90 % node utilizations, in comparison with INC, the AIL and ACH of

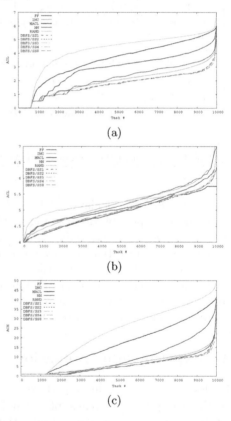

(a)

(b)

(c)

Fig. 4. Comparison of different mapping algorithms with 80 % NU. The curves show exact sorted values of AIL, ACH and ACL for 10,000 tasks.

Table 1. Result of different mapping algorithms under 64 nodes (8×8) with different Node Utilization (*NU*), the unit of time (*μs*) is the average time for each mapping decision. Simulation platform configuration: C/gcc 5.0.0, Darwin 14.0.0, Intel Haswell i5 2.7 GHz, Memory 4 GB

NU=0.5	DBFS1	DBFS8	FF	NN	INC	MACL	RAND
AIL	1.623	1.614	2.532	2.091	1.710	2.757	4.249
ACH	4.166	4.174	5.227	4.415	4.381	9.998	22.462
ACL	4.660	4.652	5.276	5.265	5.252	4.542	5.288
Time	88.6	286.4	51.3	63.2	79.0	54.4	55.0
NU=0.6	**DBFS1**	**DBFS8**	**FF**	**NN**	**INC**	**MACL**	**RAND**
AIL	1.637	1.625	2.628	2.105	1.770	3.028	4.214
ACH	4.225	4.202	6.030	4.505	4.662	11.921	22.235
ACL	4.757	4.754	5.152	5.206	5.247	4.692	5.272
Time	82.0	257.8	50.3	58.4	75.3	52.0	53.7
NU=0.7	**DBFS1**	**DBFS8**	**FF**	**NN**	**INC**	**MACL**	**RAND**
AIL	1.668	1.644	2.753	2.100	1.866	3.256	4.208
ACH	4.364	4.284	7.413	4.587	5.103	13.756	22.183
ACL	4.858	4.851	5.116	5.194	5.239	4.812	5.264
Time	76.4	213.2	47.9	54.9	68.5	48.2	50.0
NU=0.8	**DBFS1**	**DBFS8**	**FF**	**NN**	**INC**	**MACL**	**RAND**
AIL	1.756	1.701	2.842	2.122	1.967	3.516	4.203
ACH	4.851	4.586	8.154	4.818	5.576	15.815	22.065
ACL	4.978	4.977	5.114	5.217	5.217	4.949	5.264
Time	70.3	184.5	46.4	52.1	60.6	45.6	47.5
NU=0.9	**DBFS1**	**DBFS8**	**FF**	**NN**	**INC**	**MACL**	**RAND**
AIL	1.935	1.825	2.909	2.310	2.126	3.742	4.190
ACH	5.928	5.353	9.193	6.901	6.424	18.050	21.874
ACL	5.077	5.081	5.153	5.258	5.226	5.080	5.256
Time	64.1	164.0	44.0	49.6	53.5	44.2	46.0
NU=1.0	**DBFS1**	**DBFS8**	**FF**	**NN**	**INC**	**MACL**	**RAND**
AIL	2.515	2.352	2.958	2.758	2.422	4.018	4.198
ACH	9.596	8.552	9.941	9.858	9.071	20.853	21.986
ACL	5.214	5.222	5.254	5.2578	5.280	5.269	5.253
Time	58.6	135.1	42.6	45.8	48.7	42.2	45.5

*DBFS*8 have improved by 13.8 % and 17.2 %, respectively. Results from the table show that the proposed algorithm provides the best *AIL* and *ACH* among all algorithms.

Figure 4 illustrated the detailed AIL, ACH and ACL results for different mapping algorithms calculating 10,000 tasks under 80 % utilization. It is obvious that the proposed algorithm produced stable results. It provides lower AIL and ACH than other algorithms in most cases, where the ACLs are nearly identical to the minimum value in around 95 % of tasks. We notice that NN generated comparable ACH values with $DBFS$, however the AIL and ACL of NN are among the worst. Moreover, there is no significant difference between the number of search space for $DBFS$, larger search space such as 8, provides only slight performance gain in about 5 % of the cases.

4.2   Application Result Analysis

The mapping algorithms are evaluated with real applications. The experimental environment is based on a cycle-accurate NoC simulator (GEMS/Simics [10] [11]). We simulate a NoC processor with 64 (8×8) nodes. Each node consists of a dedicated router, an NI and a PE. The PE consists of a Sun UltraSPARCIII+ core with private L1 cache (split I + D, 16 KB + 16 KB, 4-way, 64-byte line, 3-cycle access delay) and a slice of the shared L2 cache (512 KB per slice, totally 16 MB, 16-way). The cache/memory architecture of the system is static non-uniform [18], and MOESI cache coherence protocol is used. Several workloads with 16 threads are selected from SPLASH-2 and PARSEC [1,17]. The system is in the state where the aforementioned 10,000 applications were executed with the corresponding mapping algorithm under 90 % utilization, i.e. the application executed here is the 10,001st. We measure execution time of applications where only $DBFS8$ is selected for simplicity. The normalized results are shown in Fig. 5.

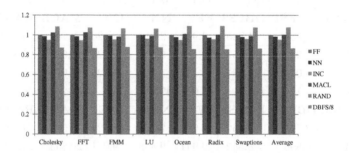

Fig. 5. Normalized average application execution time of different algorithms.

The experimental results indicated that the proposed algorithm is the best among all algorithms in terms of average application execution time. For example, compared with FF, NN and INC, the applications run 13.5 %, 12 % and 9.1 % faster, respectively. The average execution time of FF and $MACL$ are nearly the same, while as expected $RAND$ shows worst performance. The performance difference among different mapping algorithms reflected the AIL, ACH

and ACL metrics: despite the fact that INC optimizes compactness of the mapping region, the ACL is neglected. Meanwhile, the AIL and ACH are not considered in $MACL$. The application results indicated that, the continuity of the mapping region is more important than cache access delays in most of the cases. This is probably due to high system utilization, since available nodes are limited for getting low ACL values. We note the strategy of node selection is critical since region expanding algorithm relies on the selected node. A dual best-first search algorithm is used in the proposed algorithm where it is flexible to choose the starting node in various cases. However, other algorithms are inflexible comparatively: either have a fixed strategy for starting node, or have a fixed strategy for selecting the next node. The improvement of execution time differs depending on the application, applications such as Cholesky and FFT have higher intra-application communication, while for Radix and Swaptions the pressure to the shared cache is higher. Overall it is apparent that application performance is affected by different mapping methods significantly.

5   Conclusion

We proposed a greedy heuristic application mapping algorithm for shared-cache multicore processors. Performance requirements of modern data processing applications are growing constantly. We explored the on-chip communication delays of the destination system. The delays were characterised as intra-application communication latency, inter-application congestion and shared-cache access delay. We investigated an algorithm based on best-first search which optimizes all the aforementioned delays at the same time. The dual best-first search strategy explored the network dynamically and flexibly with low computation complexity. Potential disadvantages of the proposed algorithm are discussed as well. Synthetic experiments were conducted by using 64-node network with different system utilizations. Results indicated that in most cases the proposed algorithm achieved near-optimal results for all three metrics with little time overhead. We also studied the performance impact of different mappings to real applications by using a full system simulator. It is shown the average execution time of seven applications has improved by 13.5 % compared with the first fit algorithm.

References

1. Bienia, C., et al.: The parsec benchmark suite: characterization and architectural implications. In: Proceedings of 17th International Conference on Parallel Architectures and Compilation Techniques, pp. 72–81. ACM, New York, NY, USA (2008)
2. Cho, S., et al.: Managing distributed, shared l2 caches through os-level page allocation. In: Proceedings of the 39th Annual IEEE/ACM International Symposium on Microarchitecture, pp. 455–468. IEEE, Washington, DC, USA (2006)
3. Chou, C.L., et al.: Energy- and performance-aware incremental mapping for networks on chip with multiple voltage levels. IEEE Trans. Comput. Aided Des. Integr. Circ. Syst. **27**(10), 1866–1879 (2008)

4. Dally, W., et al.: Principles and Practices of Interconnection Networks. Morgan Kaufmann Publishers Inc., San Francisco (2003)
5. Demaine, E.D., et al.: Integer point sets minimizing average pairwise distance: what is the optimal shape of a town? Comput. Geom. **44**(2), 82–94 (2011)
6. Fattah, M., et al.: Mixed-criticality run-time task mapping for noc-based many-core systems. In: 2014 22nd Euromicro International Conference on Parallel, Distributed and Network-Based Processing (PDP), pp. 458–465 (2014)
7. Hakem, M., et al.: Dynamic critical path scheduling parallel programs onto multi-processors. In: Proceedings of the 19th IEEE International Parallel and Distributed Processing Symposium, p. 203.2. IEEE, Washington, DC, USA (2005)
8. Krevat, E., Castaños, J.G., Moreira, J.E.: Job scheduling for the BlueGene/L system. In: Feitelson, D.G., Rudolph, L., Schwiegelshohn, U. (eds.) JSSPP 2002. LNCS, vol. 2537, pp. 38–54. Springer, Heidelberg (2002)
9. Leung, V.J., et al.: Parallel job scheduling policies to improve fairness: A case study. In: 39th International Conference on Parallel Processing, ICPP Workshops 2010, San Diego, California, USA, pp. 346–353, 13–16 Sep 2010
10. Magnusson, P., et al.: Simics: a full system simulation platform. Computer **35**(2), 50–58 (2002)
11. Martin, M.M., et al.: Multifacet's general execution-driven multiprocessor simulator (gems) toolset. Comput. Archit. News **33**(4), 92–99 (2005)
12. Pang, K., et al.: Task mapping and mesh topology exploration for an fpga-based network on chip. Microprocess. Microsyst. **39**(3), 189–199 (2015)
13. de Souza Carvalho, E., et al.: Dynamic task mapping for MPSoCs. IEEE Des. Test Comput. **27**(5), 26–35 (2010)
14. TGG: Task graph generator (2014). http://taskgraphgen.sourceforge.net/
15. Wang, L., Wang, R., Fu, C., Luan, Z., Qian, D.: Interference-aware program scheduling for multicore processors. In: Kołodziej, J., Martino, B., Talia, D., Xiong, K. (eds.) ICA3PP 2013, Part I. LNCS, vol. 8285, pp. 436–445. Springer, Heidelberg (2013)
16. Wang, L., et al.: Bigdatabench: a big data benchmark suite from internet services. In: 2014 IEEE 20th International Symposium on High Performance Computer Architecture (HPCA), pp. 488–499 (2014)
17. Woo, S.C., et al.: The splash-2 programs: characterization and methodological considerations. In: Proceedings of the 22nd International Symposium on Computer Architecture, pp. 24–36 (1995)
18. Xu, T.C., et al.: A high-efficiency low-cost heterogeneous 3D network-on-chip design. In: Proceedings of the Fifth International Workshop on Network on Chip Architectures. NoCArc 2012, pp. 37–42. ACM, New York, NY, USA (2012)
19. Xu, T.C., et al.: Optimal placement of vertical connections in 3D network-on-chip. J. Syst. Archit. **59**(7), 441–454 (2013)
20. Zhou, X., et al.: Cache sharing management for performance fairness in chip multiprocessors. In: 18th International Conference on Parallel Architectures and Compilation Techniques 2009, PACT 2009, pp. 384–393 (2009)

HVCRouter: Energy Efficient Network-on-Chip Router with Heterogeneous Virtual Channels

Ji Wu, Xiangke Liao, Dezun Dong$^{(\boxtimes)}$, Li Wang$^{(\boxtimes)}$, and Cunlu Li

College of Computer, National University of Defense Technology,
Changsha 410073, China
{dong,liwang}@nudt.edu.cn

Abstract. The high scalability of the NoC (network-on-chip) makes it one of the best choices to meet the demand for bandwidth increasing in systems-on-chips and chip multiprocessors. However, the NoC is increasingly becoming power-constrained. A significant part of the NoC's power is consumed in the router buffer. In this paper, we propose HVCRouter, a novel NoC router design with heterogeneous virtual channels. In particular, HVCRouter incorporates a bufferless channel to respect its power efficiency at low network load. HVCRouter employs a fine-grained power gating algorithm which exploits power saving opportunities at both channel and buffer levels simultaneously, and is able to achieve high power efficiency without degrading performance at varying network utilization. Our experimental results on both synthetic and real workloads show that HVCRouter delivers similar performance with FlexiBuffer, the best in the literature. More importantly, HVCRouter consumes an average of 22.797 % less power, and results in 20.698 % lower EDP (energy delay product) than FlexiBuffer.

Keywords: Network-on-Chip router · Virtual channel · Power gating

1 Introduction

The NoC (network-on-chip) is widely considered as a first-order component of current and future multicore and manycore CMPs, due to its high flexibility and scalability to be able to effectively address the rapid increasing of core count. Unfortunately, NoCs are concerned about their excessive power consumption. For example, for Intel Terascale 80-core chip, its NoC consumes 28 % [1] of the chip power; For MIT RAW, it is up to 36 % [2,3]; In the future, NoCs in many-core processors are estimated to consume hundreds of watts of power [4] if current network implementation is naively scaled. One of the key components of an NoC router is the buffer, which is necessary to provide high performance for an NoC. However, the buffer consumes significant power (up to 30 % – 40 % of NoC power [5]). Recent studies have explored several optimizations to reduce the power consumption of router buffers. Bufferless routing [6] presents a new algorithm for routing without using buffers in router input/output ports. Bufferless routing is proved to be very effective in power saving at low network load,

© Springer International Publishing Switzerland 2015
G. Wang et al. (Eds.): ICA3PP 2015, Part I, LNCS 9528, pp. 199–213, 2015.
DOI: 10.1007/978-3-319-27119-4_14

however, because of low bandwidth and detouring, it will incur a significant performance penalty at higher network loads. Flexibuffer [7] performs power gating on buffers to reduce power consumption. Although demonstrated obvious advantages in router power saving, FlexiBuffer still incurs considerable leakage power, especially at low network load, which happens on many real-world applications for much of the time. The deficiencies of FlexiBuffer are detailed in Sect. 2.

In this paper, we propose HVCRouter, a novel NoC router design with heterogeneous virtual channels (VCs). To efficiently reduce power, HVCRouter integrates one bufferless channel to leverage its power efficiency. In addition, HVCRouter allows to power-gating not only buffers, but also channels to capture more power optimization opportunities. However, these optimizations are not achieved without a challenge. To make good use of the heterogeneous VCs, and power-gating channels as well as buffers without degrading performance at varying network loads, the channel allocation and flow control mechanisms in conventional NoC routers must be modified and carefully orchestrated as detailed in Sect. 3.

In this paper, we make the following contributions:

- We introduce a novel NoC router design with heterogeneous virtual channels. In particular, it introduces a bufferless channel to respect its power efficiency at low network utilization.
- We present a fine-grained power gating algorithm, which enables HVCRouter to adapt well to varying network loads, and achieve excellent power efficiency. To the best of our knowledge, our approach is the first to exploit power saving opportunities on NoC router at buffer-level and channel-level simultaneously.
- Our experiments show that HVCRouter achieves similar performance with FlexiBuffer, the best in the literature, consumes an average of 22.797 % less power, and provides 20.698 % lower EDP than FlexiBuffer.

The rest of the paper is organized as follows. For background information, Sect. 2 introduces the architecture of a modern NoC router, discusses bufferless routing and Flexibuffer, and motivates our work. Section 3 describes the architecture of HVCRouter. In Sect. 4, we present our approach for power gating and VC allocation. Section 5 evaluates our work. Section 6 discusses related work. In Sect. 7, we summarize and conclude the paper.

2   Background and Motivation

2.1   Router Architecture

The architecture of a typical modern virtual-channel NoC router is shown in Fig. 1. When a flit of a packet arrives at a router from one of the input virtual channels in the router's input port, the flit is hold in a buffer of that channel until it can be forwarded. The process on a flit is divided into several pipeline stages. First, route computation (RC) is performed by the routing unit to decide the output port. Second, virtual-channel allocation (VA) by the VC allocator allocates an available output virtual channel in the given output port. If all output channels are occupied, the flit is kept in the buffer and waits until there is one vacant. Third, switch allocation (SA) by the switch allocator schedules a time slot on the switch and the output channel, and forwards the flit to routed output port during this time slot. Finally, switch traversal (ST) forwards the flit to depart the current router and travel to the next router in its routing path.

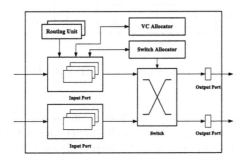

Fig. 1. The router architecture.

The buffer serves as one of the most important components in a modern NoC router, since it decouples the allocation of channel resources. Buffers within each router improve the bandwidth efficiency in the network because they enable a flit to wait until its allocated output channel and switch ready, otherwise the flit has to be dropped or misrouted, namely, sent to a less desirable destination port, thereby buffers reduce the number of dropped or misrouted packets. It is proved that more buffers result in significantly higher performance. However, buffers in the NoC occupy a significant portion of the power. On the other hand, Kim et al. [7] made the observation that even if the network is saturated, not all of the buffer resources are fully utilized.

2.2   Bufferless Routing and Flexibuffer

Recent studies have explored several optimizations to reduce the power consumption of router buffers. bufferless routing [6] presents a new algorithm for routing without using buffers in router input/output ports. When multiple flits are routed to the same output channel, an arbitration is performed as usual to choose one to get the channel. For remaining flits, bufferless routing misroutes them to other output channels and guarantees those flits will reach their destination at last. In contrast to misrouting, Mitchell et al [8] proposes another bufferless router design by dropping those losing arbitration flits, which are later retransmitted. Bufferless routing is proved to be very power efficient at low network load, however, bufferless routing suffers from poor performance and energy at higher loads because the misrouting/dropping caused by link contention leads to increased link utilization, which creates a positive feedback cycle because

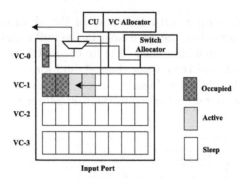

Fig. 2. The architecture of HVCRouter.

increased link utilization further increases link contention. Consequently, buffer-less networks will incur a significant performance penalty at higher network loads, and saturate at lower throughputs than buffered networks.

In contrast to eliminating buffers from routers, FlexiBuffer employs a power gating policy and adjusts the size of the active buffers adaptively. Although it demonstrates obvious advantages in terms of performance under medium-to-high network loads over bufferless routing, according to our observation, there remain optimization opportunities to be exploited. First, FlexiBuffer keeps all of the vir-tual channels active at any time, which will incur significant static power when network is lightly utilized. Second, FlexiBuffer includes buffers in each chan-nel, controls them separately, and keeps some buffers active at any time for each channel, this also introduces considerable static power, we are thereby motivated to propose a router design with heterogeneous virtual channels, and eliminate buffers from one channel to reduce static power. In addition, instead of consid-ering channels separately, our design manages channels and buffers in a global framework to allow adaptively power-gating channels as well as their buffers, if desired, to achieve higher power efficiency, without degrading performance.

3   HVCRouter Architecture

The architecture of HVCRouter is similar to the conventional design shown in Fig. 1, with the major differences in the input port and the VC allocator as highlighted in Fig. 2. HVCRouter employs a mixture of buffered and bufferless VCs, among the multiple VCs in an input port, the lowest-order one, i.e., *VC-0* is without buffers. The output of *VC-0* is connected not only to the switch as usual, but also to buffers of *VC-1* by a demultiplexer. The output selecting of the demultiplexer could be controlled by both the VC allocator and the switch allocator. When a flit coming from bufferless VC (*VC-0*) does not win the output VC arbitration during VC allocation, the VC allocator will send a signal to corresponding demultiplexer to forward the flit into the tail of buffers of *VC-1* to enable it to wait for next round of VC allocation. Similar process happens on switch allocation, if a flit in bufferless VC loses the arbitration, the switch allocator will forward it into the buffer of *VC-1* as well. This is different with the process of bufferless routing. In bufferless routing, those flits have to be dropped or misrouted, which will significantly increase the latency. This flit-inner-forwarding design will not increase notable power consumption because *VC-0* only serves at low network load, in which case, competition and arbitration rarely happen. If the load increases, HVCRouter will rely on buffered channels to service packet flow instead, and power gate *VC-0* as detailed in Sect. 4. To solve the problem of out-of-order arriving, HVCRouter receive flits in a receiver-side buffer until all flits of a packet have arrived. We adopt a bufferless channel instead of leveraging power gating to disable all buffer entries in a channel at an input port, which is based on the observation that many real-world applications have low network utilization for much of the time [6], bufferless channel suffices in those cases, and buffers' large area and high power consumption could be saved. For a buffered channel even with power-pating, transitions between power states during power-gating will increase power consumption. Besides the introduction of a bufferless VC as well as a demultiplexer logic, another notable difference for HVCRouter is the VC allocator, which integrates a control unit (CU) to be able to dynamically and adaptively turn on/off virtual channels and buffers.

4 Power-Gating and VC Allocation

4.1 Power-Gating Algorithm

The power-gating algorithm of HVCRouter introduces a state machine (as depicted in Fig. 3) with two states, characterized as follows,

- *state-0*: only *VC-0* and *VC-1* are turned on.
- *state-1*: *VC-0* is turned off, *VC-1* is turned on, other VCs may or may not be turned on.

Let us examine the power gating algorithm shown in Algorithm 1. At first, HVCRouter works at *state-0* with only *VC-0* and *VC-1* (with p active buffer entries, p is explained later) are turned on, to make use of the bufferless channel

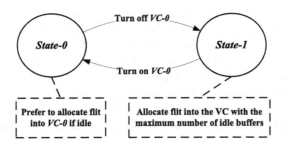

Fig. 3. The state machine of HVCRouter.

Algorithm 1. Power gating algorithm.

```
1: procedure pg_hvcrouter
2: // state-0: VC-0 and VC-1 are active
3: if current_state == 0 then
4:    if vc_occupancy(1) ≥ Q then
5:       turn_on_vc(2, p)
6:       power_gate_vc(0)
7:       current_state = 1
8:       return
9:    end if
10: end if
11: // state-1: VC-0 is power gated
12: if current_state == 1 then
13:    for i from 1 to num_vcs − 2 do
14:       if vc_occupancy(i) ≥ Q &&vc_power_gated(i + 1) == TRUE then
15:          turn_on_vc(i + 1, P)
16:       end if
17:    end for
18:    for i from num_vcs − 1 to 2 do
19:       if vc_occupancy(i) == 0 &&vc_occupancy(i − 1) < Q then
20:          power_gate_vc(i)
21:       end if
22:    end for
23:    manage_router_buffers()
24:    if vc_occupancy(1) < Q then
25:       for i = 2; i < num_vcs; i++ do
26:          if vc_power_gated(i) == FALSE then
27:             break
28:          end if
29:       end for
30:       if i == num_vcs then
31:          turn_on_vc(0, 0)
32:          current_state = 0
33:       end if
34:    end if
35: end if
```

---

to reduce the static power to a minimum at low network utilization. In Line 4, vc_occupancy(*no*) calculates the number of busy buffers (with packet flit(s) in it) in *VC-no*, to estimate the load. If the load of *VC-1* beyond a threshold, in Line 5, turn_on_vc(2, p) will turn on *VC-2* as well as its p buffer entries, here p represents the minimum number of active buffer entries needed to prevent stalls caused by the lack of available buffer entries, $p = \max(t_w, t_{crt})$, where t_w is the wake up delay of a buffer entry, and t_{crt} is the credit round-trip latency [7,9]. In Line 6, *VC-0* is power gated. As a result, the state is transited to *state-1* in Line 7.

Algorithm 2. Router buffer management.

```
 1: procedure manage_router_buffers
 2:   for i from 1 to num_vcs − 1 do
 3:     if vc_power_gated(i) == TRUE then
 4:       continue
 5:     end if
 6:     if vc_idle_buffer_num(i) ≤ P − Q &&vc_active_buffer_num(i) < BUFFER_SIZE
       then
 7:       turn_on_buffer(i, 1)
 8:     end if
 9:     if current_cycle() % T == 0 then
10:       if vc_idle_buffer_num(i) > P − Q &&vc_active_buffer_num(i) > P then
11:         power_gate_buffer(i, 1)
12:       end if
13:     end if
14: end for
```

In *state-1*, in Lines 13 − 17, the algorithm checks if some channel has encountered congestion, and turns on a higher order channel to mitigate the congestion. In Lines 18 − 22, on the contrary, the algorithm checks if some channel is idle, and its immediately lower order channel is also lightly utilized, in that case, the idle channel is power gated. In Line 23, the algorithm invokes manage_router_buffers() to perform fine-grained power gating on router buffers. As shown in Algorithm 2, for each buffered and active virtual channel, if current number of active-but-idle buffer entries is no more than $P - Q$, and there exists buffer(s) in sleep state, then one more buffer is waked up. On the contrary, if current number of active-but-idle buffer entries is more than $P - Q$, and number of active buffer entries is more than P, then one buffer is power gated. In contrast to turn on buffers, power-gating is executed less frequently (per T consecutive cycles) to avoid thrashing and reduce control overhead. Finally, in Lines 24 − 34 in Algorithm 1, if all channels except *VC-1* are power gated, and *VC-1* has a low utilization, then *VC-0* is turned on with the state transited back to *state-0*.

As the algorithm shown, when load increases, it tends to turn on more channels first, rather than more buffers in an already active channel, because more virtual channels inside a single physical channel allow other flits to use the channel bandwidth that would otherwise be left idle when a flit blocks [9], which will improve the performance.

4.2   VC Allocation

This section discusses the VC allocation policy of HVCRouter. The VC allocator allocates output channel for a flit according to the state of the corresponding input port of the downstream router. Suppose a flit in router A is waiting for VC allocation, with its routed output port being P_{A_OUT}, and the downstream router is B with corresponding input port being P_{B_IN}. If the state of P_{B_IN} is *state-0*, which implies only *VC-0* and *VC-1* are active in P_{B_IN}, then the VC allocator

Table 1. Network configuration.

Node count	64
Topology	8*8 2D MESH
VC count	4VCs per port
Buffer depth	8 flit per VC
Flit length	16 byte
Switch allocator	islip
Routing algorithm	Dimension-order
P (parameter in Algorithm 1)	3
Q (parameter in Algorithm 1)	2
T (parameter in Algorithm 2)	3

of A will check if VC-0 in P_{B_IN} is idle (A is able to know this by conventional credit based backpressured flow control [9]), and allocate the flit into VC-0 in P_{A_OUT}, otherwise, allocate it into VC-1 in P_{A_OUT}. To support power-gating router buffers, HVCRouter makes the modification to conventional credit-based flow control similar to that of FlexiBuffer. However, due to the heterogenous nature of HVCRouter, the credit count of VC-0 is initialized to 1, that of VC-1 is initialized to $p-1$ (one may be stolen by VC-0), and the others are initialized to p. If the state of P_{B_IN} is *state-1*, and supposes the input channel with the maximum number of idle buffers, i.e., maximum credits, is VC-m, then the VC allocator in A will allocate the flit into VC-m in P_{A_OUT}.

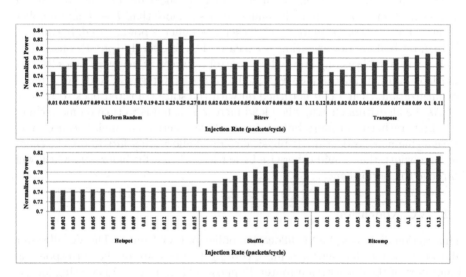

Fig. 4. Power of HVCRouter, normalized to that of FlexiBuffer, for six traffic patterns.

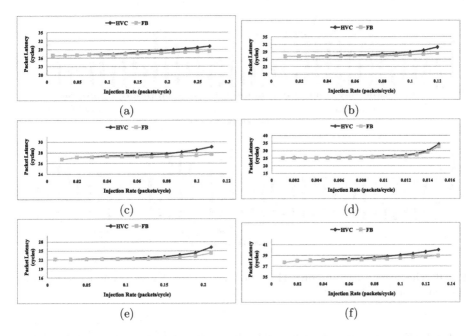

Fig. 5. Performance of HVCRouter and FlexiBuffer for (a) Uniform random (b) Bit reverse (c) Transpose (d) Hot-spot (e) Shuffle and (f) Bit complement traffic patterns.

5   Evaluation

We evaluate HVCRouter in terms of power, network latency and energy delay product by using BookSim [10] as well as DSENT [11]. Booksim is a cycle-accurate interconnection network simulator to measure network latency, and we revise it to model HVCRouter. Using the results obtained by Booksim as well as the network configuration files as input, DSENT will output the power values. The detailed network configurations used in our evaluation are listed in Table 1.

5.1   Synthetic Traffic Evaluation

Figure 4 shows the power consumption of HVCRouter for six synthetic traffic patterns, normalized to that of FlexiBuffer. It is observed that HVCRouter consumes lower power than FlexiBuffer for all the patterns under various packet injection rates. Let us examine the results in detail. All the curves demonstrate similar trend. At low injection rates, HVCRouter consumes significantly lower power than FlexiBuffer, more specifically, a maximum of 25.75 % lower for *Hotspot*. When network is lightly utilized, HVCRouter utilizes bufferless virtual channel to reduce both static and dynamic power by scheduling packets into bufferless channel whenever possible, and power gating other channels as well as buffers. As the injection rate increases, HVCRouter adaptively turns on channels and buffers to mitigate the link contention of bufferless channel. Attributing

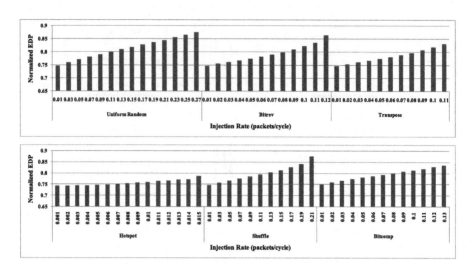

Fig. 6. The energy delay product (EDP) of HVCRouter for six traffic patterns, normalized to that of FlexiBuffer.

to the finer-grained power gating at both channel and buffer level, HVCRouter remains lower power consumption than FlexiBuffer, with an average of 22.367 % less power compared to FlexiBuffer.

The performance of HVCRouter is evaluated by measuring the packet latency. Figure 5 presents the average packet latency achieved on HVCRouter and FlexiBuffer for six traffic patterns. As the results shown, HVCRouter achieves similar performance with FlexiBuffer, with an average of 1.704 % larger packet latency than that of FlexiBuffer. The results prove that HVCRouter makes good use of the heterogeneous architecture, reacts quickly to congestion.

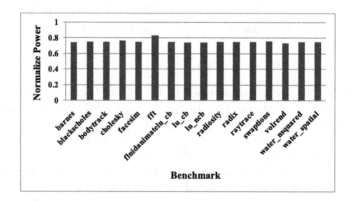

Fig. 7. Power of HVCRouter for real workload traces, normalized to that of FlexiBuffer.

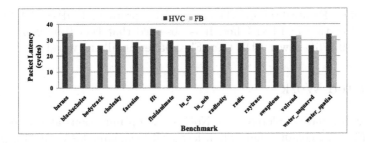

Fig. 8. Performance of HVCRouter and FlexiBuffer for real workload traces.

Figure 6 reports the energy delay product (EDP) of HVCRouter for six traffic patterns, normalized to that of FlexiBuffer. Overall, HVCRouter results in an average of 21.08 % lower EDP for all the patterns than FlexiBuffer.

5.2   Real Workload Evaluation

We also use the traffic generated by SynFull [12] for BookSim to simulate real-world workloads. SynFull introduces a synthetic traffic generation methodology that captures both application and cache coherence behavior to evaluate NoCs. Using a real-world benchmark as the input, SynFull is able to output a traffic, which could be further fed into BookSim for simulation. Currently, the traffics made publicly available by SynFull are a set of 16 traffics produced from PARSEC [13] and SPLASH-2 [14] benchmarks with the sim-small input set for 16 cores. The power and packet latency are measured with the results shown in Figs. 7 and 8, respectively. The results demonstrate that HVCRouter consumes an average of 24.83 % less power on all of the benchmarks than FlexiBuffer.

Regarding the network performance, overall, HVCRouter delivers similar performance than FlexiBuffer, with an average of 7.53 % larger latency than that

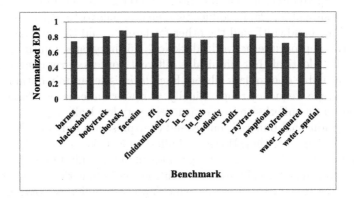

Fig. 9. The energy delay product (EDP) of HVCRouter for real workload traces, normalized to that of FlexiBuffer.

of FlexiBuffer. Figure 9 reports the energy delay product (EDP) of HVCRouter, normalized to that of FlexiBuffer. It is observed that HVCRouter provides an average of 19.176 % lower EDP than FlexiBuffer on all the workloads.

6   Related Work

Recent studies have explored some NoC power optimizations at various granularities. First, at channel and switch level, Michelogiannakis et al. [15] propose adaptive bandwidth networks (ABNs) to divide channels and switches into lanes to reduce power consumption of NoC. Second, at router level, NoRD [16] provides a power-gating bypass to decouple the node's ability for transferring packets from the powered-on/off status of the associated router, thereby increases the length of idle periods, and eliminates node-network disconnection problem. Panthre [17] adopts topology and routing reconfiguration to steer away the packets that would normally use power-gated components, to provide long intervals of uninterrupted sleep to selected units. Matsutani et al. [18] adopt look-ahead routing to hide the wake-up delay and reduce the short-term sleeps of channels. Chen et al. [19] propose a performance-aware, power reduction scheme that aims to achieve non blocking power-gating of on-chip network routers through looking ahead routing. Router Parking [20] selectively power gates routers attached to parked cores dynamically, and adopts adaptive routing to ensure the network performance. In addition, some topology dependent approaches are also proposed. Yue et al. [21] present Smart Butterfly, a core-state-aware NoC power-gating scheme based on flattened butterfly topology that utilizes the active/sleep state information of processing cores to improve power-gating effectiveness. Since Clos network has multiple alternative paths for every packet, Chen et al. [22] propose power-gating scheme MP3, which is able to achieve minimal performance penalty and save more static energy than conventional Clos network. Third, at the granularity of subnet, Balfour et al. [23] present a concentrated mesh topology with replicated sub-networks to improve area and energy efficiency in NoC. Das.R et al. [24] propose the Catnap architecture which performs power-gating on subnets in a multi-layer NoC. Mishra et al. [25] introduce two separate networks on chip, where one is optimized for bandwidth and the other for latency, and the steering of applications to the appropriate network. darkNoC [26] integrates multiple layers of architecturally identical, but physically different routers, leveraging the extra transistors available due to dark silicon. Each layer is separately optimized for a particular voltage-frequency range. Finally, at router buffer level, Moscibroda et al. [6] found that a bufferless router consumes a very low leakage power compared to that of a traditional buffered router, and they present a bufferless NoC design and a new routing algorithm. However, bufferless NoC is only applicable at low network load. Chris Fallin et al. [27] propose the minimally-buffered deflection (MinBD) router, which combines deflection routing in bufferless network with a small side buffer to reduce deflections, which improves bufferless routing to some extent. FlexiBuffer [7] reduces buffer leakage power by using fine-grained power gating and adjusting the size of the active buffers adaptively.

7 Conclusion

The router buffer makes a significant contribution to the overall NoC power. We discuss HVCRouter, a novel NoC router architecture which couples buffered and bufferless virtual channels. Employing a fine-grained power gating policy, HVCRouter consumes an average of 22.797 % less power than FlexiBuffer, the state of the art power efficient NoC router design. In terms of performance, HVCRouter matches FlexiBuffer on all the benchmarks.

Acknowledgments. We thank the anonymous reviewers for their precious feedback. We gratefully acknowledge members of Tianhe interconnect group at NUDT for many inspiring conversations early in the project. The work was partially supported by 863 Program under Grant No. 2012AA01A301, NSFC under Grant No. 61370018, 61272482, and FANEDD under Grant No. 201450.

References

1. Hoskote, Y., Vangal, S., Singh, A., Borkar, N., Borkar, S.: A 5-GHz mesh interconnect for a teraflops processor. IEEE Micro **27**(5), 51–61 (2007)
2. Taylor, M.B., Kim, J., Miller, J., Wentzlaff, D., Ghodrat, F., Greenwald, B., Hoffman, H., Johnson, P., Lee, J.-W., Lee, W., Ma, A., Saraf, A., Seneski, M., Shnidman, N., Strumpen, V., Frank, M., Amarasinghe, S., Agarwal, A.: The raw microprocessor: a computational fabric for software circuits and general-purpose programs. IEEE Micro **22**(2), 25–35 (2002)
3. Kim, J.S., Taylor, M.B., Miller, J., Wentzlaff, D.: Energy characterization of a tiled architecture processor with on-chip networks. In: Proceedings of the 2003 International Symposium on Low Power Electronics and Design, ser. ISLPED 2003, pp. 424–427. ACM, New York, NY, USA (2003)
4. Borkar, S.: Thousand core chips: a technology perspective. In: Proceedings of the 44th Annual Design Automation Conference, ser. DAC 2007, pp. 746–749. ACM, New York, NY, USA (2007)
5. Jafri, S.A.R., Hong, Y.-J., Thottethodi, M., Vijaykumar, T.N.: Adaptive flow control for robust performance and energy. In: Proceedings of the 2010 43rd Annual IEEE/ACM International Symposium on Microarchitecture, ser. MICRO '43, pp. 433–444. IEEE Computer Society, Washington, DC, USA (2010)
6. Moscibroda, T., Mutlu, O.: A case for bufferless routing in on-chip networks. In: Proceedings of the 36th Annual International Symposium on Computer Architecture, ser. ISCA 2009, pp. 196–207. ACM, New York, NY, USA (2009)
7. Kim, G., Kim, J., Yoo, S.: Flexibuffer: reducing leakage power in on-chip network routers. In: Proceedings of the 48th Design Automation Conference, ser. DAC 2011, pp. 936–941. ACM, New York, USA (2011)
8. Hayenga, M., Jerger, N.E., Lipasti, M.: Scarab: a single cycle adaptive routing and bufferless network. In: Proceedings of the 42Nd Annual IEEE/ACM International Symposium on Microarchitecture, ser. MICRO 42, pp. 244–254. ACM, New York, NY, USA (2009)
9. Dally, W.J., Towles, B.: Principles and Practices of Interconnection Networks. Morgan Kaufmann, San Francisco (2004)

10. Jiang, N., Becker, D.U., Michelogiannakis, G., Balfour, J., Towles, B., Kim, J., Dally, W.J.: A detailed and flexible cycle-accurate network-on-chip simulator. In: Proceedings of the 2013 IEEE International Symposium on Performance Analysis of Systems and Software (2013)

11. Sun, C., Chen, C.-H.O., Kurian, G., Wei, L., Miller, J., Agarwal, A., Peh, L.-S., Stojanovic, V.: Dsent - a tool connecting emerging photonics with electronics for opto-electronic networks-on-chip modeling. In: Proceedings of the 2012 IEEE/ACM Sixth International Symposium on Networks-on-Chip, ser. NOCS 2012, pp. 201–210. IEEE Computer Society, Washington, DC, USA (2012)

12. Badr, M., Jerger, N.E.: Synfull: synthetic traffic models capturing cache coherent behaviour. In: Proceeding of the 41st Annual International Symposium on Computer Architecuture, ser. ISCA 2014, pp. 109–120. IEEE Press, Piscataway, NJ, USA (2014)

13. Bienia, C.: Benchmarking modern multiprocessors. Ph.D. dissertation, aAI3445564, Princeton, NJ, USA (2011)

14. Woo, S.C., Ohara, M., Torrie, E., Singh, J.P., Gupta, A.: The splash-2 programs: characterization and methodological considerations. In: Proceedings of the 22nd Annual International Symposium on Computer Architecture, ser. ISCA 1995, pp. 24–36. ACM, New York, USA (1995)

15. Michelogiannakis, G., Shalf, J.: Variable-width datapath for on-chip network static power reduction. In: Proceedings of the 2014 IEEE/ACM Sixth International Symposium on Networks-on-Chip, ser. NOCS 2014, pp. 96–103. IEEE Computer Society, Washington, DC, USA (2014)

16. Chen, L., Pinkston, T.M.: Nord: node-router decoupling for effective power-gating of on-chip routers. In: Proceedings of the 2012 45th Annual IEEE/ACM International Symposium on Microarchitecture, ser. MICRO-45, pp. 270–281. IEEE Computer Society, Washington, DC, USA (2012)

17. Parikh, R., Das, R., Bertacco, V.: Power-aware nocs through routing and topology reconfiguration. In: Proceedings of the 51st Annual Design Automation Conference, ser. DAC 2014, pp. 162:1–162:6. ACM, New York, NY, USA (2014)

18. Matsutani, H., Koibuchi, M., Wang, D., Amano, H.: Run-time power gating of on-chip routers using look-ahead routing. In: Proceedings of the 2008 Asia and South Pacific Design Automation Conference, ser. ASP-DAC 2008, pp. 55–60. IEEE Computer Society Press, Los Alamitos, CA, USA (2008)

19. Chen, L., Zhu, D., Pedram, M., Pinkston, T.M.: Power punch: towards non-blocking power-gating of noc routers. In: Proceedings of the 2015 IEEE 21th International Symposium on High Performance Computer Architecture (HPCA), ser. HPCA 2015. IEEE Computer Society, Washington, DC, USA (2015)

20. Samih, A., Wang, R., Krishna, A., Maciocco, C., Tai, C., Solihin, Y.: Energy-efficient interconnect via router parking. In: Proceedings of the 2013 IEEE 19th International Symposium on High Performance Computer Architecture (HPCA), ser. HPCA 2013. IEEE Computer Society, Washington, DC, USA (2013)

21. Yue, D.Z.T.M.P.S., Chen, L., Pedram, M.: Smart butterfly: reducing static power dissipation of network-on-chip with core-state-awareness. In: Proceedings of the 2014 IEEE/ACM International Symposium on Low Power Electronics and Design (ISLPED), pp. 311–314 (2014)

22. Chen, L., Zhao, L., Wang, R., Pinkston, T.M.: MP3: minimizing performancepenalty for power-gating of clos network-on-chip. In: 20th IEEE International Symposium on High Performance Computer Architecture, HPCA 2014, pp. 296–307. IEEE Computer Society, Orlando, FL, USA, 15–19 Feb 2014

23. Balfour, J., Dally, W.J.: Design tradeoffs for tiled cmp on-chip networks. In: Proceedings of the 20th Annual International Conference on Supercomputing, ser. ICS 2006, pp. 187–198. ACM, New York, NY, USA (2006)
24. Das, R., Narayanasamy, S., Satpathy, S.K., Dreslinski, R.G.: Catnap: energy proportional multiple network-on-chip. In: Proceedings of the 40th Annual International Symposium on Computer Architecture, ser. ISCA 2013, pp. 320–331. ACM, New York, NY, USA (2013)
25. Mishra, A.K., Mutlu, O., Das, C.R.: A heterogeneous multiple network-on-chip design: an application-aware approach. In: The 50th Annual Design Automation Conference 2013, DAC 2013, p. 36. Austin, TX, USA, May 29–June 07 2013
26. Bokhari, H., Javaid, H., Shafique, M., Henkel, J., Parameswaran, S.: Darknoc: designing energy-efficient network-on-chip with multi-vt cells for dark silicon. In: Proceedings of the 51st Annual Design Automation Conference, ser. DAC 2014, pp. 161:1–161:6. ACM, New York, NY, USA 2014
27. Fallin, C., Nazario, G., Yu, X., Chang, K., Ausavarungnirun, R., Mutlu, O.: Minbd: minimally-buffered deflection routing for energy-efficient interconnect. In: Proceedings of the 2012 IEEE/ACM Sixth International Symposium on Networks-on-Chip, ser. NOCS 2012, pp. 1–10. IEEE Computer Society, Washington, DC, USA (2012)

Availability and Network-Aware MapReduce Task Scheduling over the Internet

Bing Tang[1]([✉]), Qi Xie[2] , Haiwu He[3], and Gilles Fedak[4]

[1] School of Computer Science and Engineering,
Hunan University of Science and Technology, Xiangtan 411201, China
btang@hnust.edu.cn
[2] College of Computer Science and Technology,
Southwest University for Nationalities, Chengdu 610041, China
qi.xie.swun@gmail.com
[3] Computer Network Information Center, Chinese Academy of Sciences,
Beijing 100190, China
haiwuhe@cstnet.cn
[4] INRIA, LIP Laboratory, University of Lyon,
46 allée d'Italie, 69364 Lyon Cedex 07, France
gilles.fedak@inria.fr

Abstract. MapReduce offers an ease-of-use programming paradigm for processing large datasets. In our previous work, we have designed a MapReduce framework called BitDew-MapReduce for desktop grid and volunteer computing environment, that allows nonexpert users to run data-intensive MapReduce jobs on top of volunteer resources over the Internet. However, network distance and resource availability have great impact on MapReduce applications running over the Internet. To address this, an availability and network-aware MapReduce framework over the Internet is proposed. Simulation results show that the MapReduce job response time could be decreased by 27.15 %, thanks to Naive Bayes Classifier-based availability prediction and landmark-based network estimation.

Keywords: MapReduce · Volunteer computing · Availability prediction · Network distance prediction · Naive Bayes Classifier

1 Introduction

In the past decade, Desktop Grid and Volunteer Computing Systems (DGVCS's) have been proved an effective solution to provide scientists with tens of TeraFLOPS from hundreds of thousands of resources [1]. DGVCS's utilize free computing, network and storage resources of idle desktop PCs distributed over Intranet or Internet environments for supporting large-scale computation and storage. DGVCS's have been one of the largest and most powerful distributed computing systems in the world, offering a high return on investment for applications from a wide range of scientific domains, including computational biology,

© Springer International Publishing Switzerland 2015
G. Wang et al. (Eds.): ICA3PP 2015, Part I, LNCS 9528, pp. 214–227, 2015.
DOI: 10.1007/978-3-319-27119-4_15

climate prediction, and high-energy physics. Through donating the idle CPU cycles or unused disk space of their desktop PCs, volunteers could participate in scientific computing or data analysis.

MapReduce is an emerging programming model for large-scale data processing [5]. Recently, there are some MapReduce implementations that are designed for large-scale parallel data processing specialized on desktop grid or volunteer resources in Intranet or Internet, such as MOON [9], P2P-MapReduce [11], VMR [4], HybridMR [16], etc. In our previous work, we also implemented a MapReduce system called BitDew-MapReduce, specifically for desktop grid environment [17].

However, because there exists node failures or dynamic node joining/leaving in desktop grid environment, MapReduce application running on desktop PCs needs to guarantees that a collection of resources is available. Resource availability is critical for the reliability and responsiveness of MapReduce services. On the other hand, for the application that data need to be transferred between nodes, such as the MapReduce application, it could potentially benefit from some level of knowledge about the relative proximity between its participating host nodes. For example, transferring data to a more closer node may save some time. Therefore, network distance and resource availability have great impact on MapReduce jobs running over Internet. To address these problems, on the basis of our previous work BitDew-MapReduce, we propose a new network and availability-aware MapReduce framework on Internet.

Given this need, our goal in this paper is to determine and evaluate predictive methods that ensure the availability of a collection of resources. In order to achieve long-term and sustained high throughput, tasks should be scheduled to high available resources. We presents how to improve job scheduling for MapReduce running on Internet, through taking advantages of resource availability prediction. In this paper, Naive Bayes Classifier (NBC) based prediction approach is applied for the MapReduce task scheduler. Furthermore, the classic binning scheme [14] whereby nodes partition themselves into bins such that nodes that fall within a given bin are relatively close to one another in terms of network latency, is also applied to the MapReduce task scheduler. We demonstrate how to integrate the availability prediction method and network distance estimation method into MapReduce framework to improve the Map/Reduce task scheduler.

2 Background and Related Work

2.1 BitDew Middleware

BitDew[1] is an open source middleware for large-scale data management on Desktop Grid, Grid and Cloud, developed by INRIA [6]. BitDew provides simple APIs to programmers for creating, accessing, storing and moving data easily even in highly dynamic and volatile environments. BitDew relies on a specific set of meta-data to drive key data management operations. The BitDew runtime environment is a flexible distributed service architecture that integrates modular

---

[1] http://bitdew.gforge.inria.fr.

P2P components such as DHTs for a distributed data catalog, and collaborative transport protocols for data distribution [3,18], asynchronous and reliable multi-protocols transfers.

Main attribute keys in BitDew and meaning of the corresponding values are as follows: (i) *replica*, which stands for replication and indicates the number of copies in the system for a particular *Data* item; (ii) *resilient*, which is a flag which indicates if the data should be scheduled to another host in case of machine crash; (iii) *lifetime*, which indicates the synchronization with existence of other *Data* in the system; (iv) *affinity*, which indicates that data with an affinity link should be placed; (v) *protocol*, which indicates the file transfer protocol to be employed when transferring files between nodes; (vi) *distrib*, which indicates the maximum number of pieces of *Data* with the same *Attribute* should be sent to particular node.

The BitDew API provides a *schedule(Data, Attribute)* function by which, a client requires a particular behavior for *Data*, according to the associated *Attribute*. (For more details on BitDew, please refer to [6].)

2.2   MapReduce on Non-dedicated Computing Resources

Several other MapReduce implementations have been realized within other systems or environments. For example, BitDew-MapReduce is specifically designed to support MapReduce applications in Desktop Grids, and exploits the BitDew middleware [10,13,17]. Implementing the MapReduce using BitDew allows to leverage on many of the needed features already provided by BitDew, such as data attribute and data scheduling.

Marozzo et al. [11] proposed P2P-MapReduce which exploits a peer-to-peer model to manage node churn, master failures, and job recovery in a decentralized but effective way, so as to provide a more reliable MapReduce middleware that can be effectively exploited in dynamic Cloud infrastructures.

Another similar work is VMR [4], a volunteer computing system able to run MapReduce applications on top of volunteer resources, spread throughout the Internet. VMR leverages users' bandwidth through the use of inter-client communication, and uses a lightweight task validation mechanism. GiGi-MR [2] is another framework that allows nonexpert users to run CPU-intensive jobs on top of volunteer resources over the Internet. Bag-of-Tasks (BoT) are executed in parallel as a set of MapReduce applications.

MOON [9] is a system designed to support MapReduce jobs on opportunistic environments. It extends Hadoop with adaptive task and data scheduling algorithms to offer reliable MapReduce services on a hybrid resource architecture, where volunteer computing systems are supplemented by a small set of dedicated nodes. The adaptive task and data scheduling algorithms in MOON distinguish between different types of MapReduce data and different types of node outages in order to place tasks and data on both volatile and dedicated nodes. Another system that shares some of the key ideas with MOON is HybridMR [16], in which MapReduce tasks are executed on top of a hybrid distributed file system composed of stable cluster nodes and volatile desktop PCs.

2.3   MapReduce Framework with Resource Prediction and Network Prediction

The problems and challenges of MapReduce on non-dedicated resources are mainly caused by resource volatile. There are also some work focusing on using node availability prediction method to enable Hadoop running on unreliable Desktop Grid or using non-dedicated computing resources. For example, ADAPT is an availability-aware MapReduce data placement strategy to improve the application performance without extra storage cost [7]. The authors introduced a stochastic model to predict the execution time of each task under interruptions. Figueiredo et al. proposed the idea of P2P-VLAN, which allows generating a "virtual local area network" from wide area network, and then ran an improved version of Hadoop on this environment, just like a real local area network [8].

As two important features, network bandwidth and network latency have great impact on application service running on Internet. The research of Internet measurement and network topology have been emerged for many years. Popular network prediction approaches include Vivaldi, GNP, IDMaps, etc. Ratnasamy et al. proposed the "binning" based method for network proximity estimation, which has proved to be simple and efficient in server selection and overlay construction [14]. Song et al. proposed a network bandwidth prediction, which will be applied in a wide-area MapReduce system [15], while the authors didn't presented any prototype or experiment results of the MapReduce system. In this paper, we use the "binning" based network distance estimation in the volunteered wide-area MapReduce system. To the best of our knowledge, it is the first MapReduce prototype system that uses network topology information for Map/Reduce scheduling in volunteer computing environment.

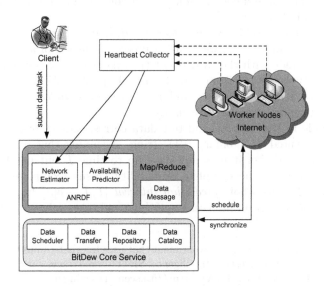

Fig. 1. Architecture of the proposed MapReduce system.

3   System Design

3.1   General Overview

In this section, we briefly introduce the general overview of the proposed MapReduce system. The architecture is shown in Fig. 1. As is shown in this figure, *Client* submit data and task, and *Worker Nodes* contribute their storage and computing resources. The main components is described as follows,

- *BitDew Core Service*, the runtime environment of BitDew which contains *Data Scheduler, Data Transfer, Data Repository, Data Catalog* service;
- *Heartbeat Collector*, collects periodical heartbeat signals from Worker Nodes;
- *Data Message*, manages all the messages during the MapReduce computation;
- *ANRDF*, the availability and network-aware resource discovery framework, including *Network Estimator* which estimates node distance using the landmark and binning scheme, and *Availability Predictor* which predicts node availability using the Naive Bayes Classifier. This framework suggests proper nodes for scheduling.

Compared with our previous work BitDew-MapReduce [17], the proposed MapReduce system in this paper exploits two techniques, availability prediction and network distance estimation, to overcome the volatility and low-speed network bandwidth between wide-area volunteer nodes.

3.2   Availability Prediction Based on Bayesian Model

Availability traces of parallel and distributed systems can be used to facilitate the design, validation, and comparison of fault-tolerant models and algorithms, such as the SETI@home traces[2]

Our prediction method is measurement-based, that is, given a set of availability traces called *training data*, we create a predictive model of availability that is tested for accuracy with the subsequent (i.e., more recent) *test data*. For the sake of simplicity we refrain from periodic model updates. We use two windows (training window and test window), and move these two windows in order to get a lot of data (training data and test data).

Each sample in the training and test data corresponds to one hour and so it can be represented as a binary (01) string. Assuming that a prediction is computed at time T (i.e. it uses any data up to time T but not beyond it), we attempt to predict the complete availability versus (complete or partial) non-availability for the whole *prediction interval* $[T, T + p]$. The value of p is designated as the *prediction interval length* (*pil*) and takes values in whole hours (i.e. 1,2,...).

---

[2] SETI@home is a global scientific experiment that uses Internet-connected computers in the Search for Extraterrestrial Intelligence. SETI@home traces can be downloaded from Failure Trace Archive (FTA), http://fta.scem.uws.edu.au/.

We compute for each node a predictive model implemented as a Naive Bayes Classifier, a classic supervised learning classifier used in data mining. A classification algorithm is usually the most suitable model type if inputs and outputs are discrete and allows the incorporation of multiple inputs and arbitrary *features*, i.e., functions of data which expose better its information content.

Features of Training Data. We denote the availability (01 string) in the training window as $e = (e_1, e_2, \cdots, e_n)^T$, where n is the number of the samples in the training window, also known as *training interval length (til)*. As an example, if the length of the training interval is in hour-scale, the training interval of 30 days is $n = 720$. Through the analysis of availability traces, we extract 6 candidate features to be used in Bayesian model, each of which can partially reflect recent availability fluctuation. The elements in the vector are organized from the oldest one to the most recent one. For example, e_n indicates the newest sample that is closest to the current moment. We summarize the 6 features as follows.

- ***Average Node Availability*** (*aveAva*)**:** It is the average node availability in the training data.
- ***Average Consecutive Availability*** (*aveAvaRun*)**:** It is the average length of a consecutive availability run.
- ***Average Consecutive Non-availability***(*aveNAvaRun*)**:** It is the average length of a consecutive non-availability run.
- ***Average Switch Times*** (*aveSwitch*)**:** It is the average number of changes of the availability status per week.
- ***Recent Availability*** (*recAvak*)**:** It is the average availability in recent k days (k=1, 2, 3, 4, 5), which is calculated by recent k days' "history bits" (24, 48, 72, 96, 120 bits in total, respectively).
- ***Compressed Length*** (*zipLen*)**:** It is the length of the training data compressed by the Lempel-Ziv-Welch (LZW) algorithm.

3.3   Network Distance Estimation Based on Binning Scheme

The classic binning scheme proposed by Ratnasamy et al. is adopted to obtain the topological information for network distance estimation in our proposed ANRDF [14]. In the *binning* scheme, nodes partition themselves into *bins* such that nodes that fall within a given bin are relatively close to one another in terms of network latency. This scheme requires a set of well-known *landmark* machines spread across the Internet. An application node measures its distance, *i.e.* round-trip time (RTT), to this set of well known landmarks and independently selects a particular bin based on these measurements.

More precisely, if $L = \{l_0, l_1, ..., l_{m-1}\}$ is the set of m landmarks, then a node A creates an ordering L_a on L, such that i appears before j in L_a if $rtt(a, l_i) < rtt(a, l_j)$ or $rtt(a, l_i) = rtt(a, l_j)$ and $l_i < l_j$. Thus, based on its delay measurements to the different landmarks, every node has an associated

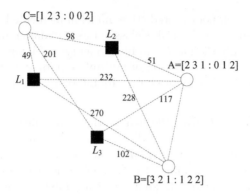

Fig. 2. Distributed binning.

ordering of landmarks. This ordering represents the "bin" the node belongs to. The rationale behind this scheme is that topologically close nodes are likely to have the same ordering and hence will belong to the same bin.

The ordering described above only makes uses of the relative distances of the landmarks from a node. The absolute values of the RTT measurements are indicated as follows: we divide the range of possible latency values into a number of *levels*. For example, we might divide the range of possible latency values into 3 levels; level 0 for latencies in the range [0, 100]ms, level 1 for latencies between [100, 200]ms and level 2 for latencies greater than 200ms. We then augment the landmark ordering of a node with a *level* vector; one level number corresponding to each landmark in the ordering. To illustrate, consider node A in Fig. 2 [14]. Its distance to landmarks l_1, l_2 and l_3 are 232ms, 51ms and 117ms respectively. Hence its ordering of landmarks is $l_2\ l_3\ l_1$. Using the 3 levels defined above, node A's level vector corresponding to its ordering of landmarks is "0 1 2". Thus, node A's bin is a vector $[V_a : V_b] = [2\ 3\ 1 : 0\ 1\ 2]$, as is shown in Fig. 2.

4   Map/Reduce Algorithm and Implementation

Our previous work introduced the architecture, runtime, and performance evaluation of BitDew-MapReduce. When the user aims to achieve a MapReduce application, the master splits all files into chunks, registers and uploads all chunks to the BitDew services, which will be scheduled and distributed to a set of workers as input data for Map task. When a worker receives data from the BitDew service node, a `data_scheduled` event is raised. At this time it determines whether the received data is treated as Map or Reduce input, and then the appropriate Map or Reduce function is called.

To initiate a MapReduce distributed computation, the Master node first creates a data *MapToken*, with an attribute whose affinity is set to the DataCollection DC. This way, *MapToken* will be scheduled to all the workers. Once the token is received by a worker, the Map function is called repeatedly to process each chunks received by the worker, creating a local $list(k, v)$.

After finishing all the Map tasks, the worker splits its local $list_m(k,v)$ into r intermediate output result files $if_{m,r}$ according to the partition function, and R, the number of reducers. For each intermediate files $if_{m,r}$, a reduce input data $ir_{m,r}$ is created. How to transmit $ir_{m,r}$ to their corresponding reducer? This is partly implemented by the master, which creates R specific data called $ReduceToken_r$, and schedules this data with the attribute $ReduceTokenAttr$. If one worker receives the token, it is selected to be a reducer. (For more details on BitDew-MapReduce, please refer to [17].)

We detail now how to integrate availability prediction and network distance estimation into our previous BitDew-MapReduce framework.

- *Measurement*: Each worker measures the RTT to each landmarks, and in the initiation of worker, it sends back the RTT value to the master. Workers periodically synchronizes with the master, in our prototype the typical synchronization interval is 10s, while it is configurable. A timeout-based approach is adopted by the worker to detect worker failure, and failure information is written to a log file which is used for generating availability traces.
- *Availability Ranking*: The availability traces are stored in the master, and the master manages a ranking list. The list is updated when a synchronization is arrived. Workers are sorted by the predicted availability in the future prediction interval length, and we also considered the stableness of each worker by average switch times (*aveSwitch*) and recent availability (*recAvak*).
- *How to Use Availability Information for Scheduling?* The worker with low availability and low stableness will stop accepting data, which makes sure that the master distributes input data and *ReduceToken* to more stable nodes.
- *Network Proximity*: The master manages all the RTT values and "bins", each node (no matter the worker or the landmark) is assigned with a bin vector. Suppose that there are two nodes n_1 and n_2 with two vectors $V_1 = [V_{1a} : V_{1b}]$ and $V_2 = [V_{2a} : V_{2b}]$, respectively. The proximity degree (or we say distance) of n_1 and n_2 can be calculated by the Euclidean distance of vector V_{1a} and V_{2a}. While if V_{1a} equals to V_{2a}, we calculate using the vector V_{1b} and V_{2b} instead. If the proximity degree is smaller than a given threshold, they are locates in the same "bin".
- *How to Use Network Information for Scheduling?* In order to avoid the load balancing problem, when a DataCollection is created and needed to be distributed to workers, a landmark is selected by random, and it also means that this landmark will "serve" this MapReduce job. The bin vector of this landmark is broadcasted to all the workers, and the workers that locate in the same bin with this landmark could accept input data. All the *ReduceToken* are also distributed to R workers that locate in the same bin. In our framework, the network feature is stronger than availability feature. Therefore, the intermediate results will be transferred to a closer node due to that both the mapper and the reducer locate in the same bin.

5   Performance Evaluation

We implemented the prototype system using BitDew middleware with Java. We conducted a simulation-based evaluation to test the performance of new MapReduce framework. Since that the landmark-based network proximity has been studied in [14], we focus on the simulation of MapReduce jobs running in a large-scale dynamic environment. Simulations are performed on an Intel Xeon E5-1650 server.

5.1   Availability Prediction

Availability Traces. We evaluate our predictive methods using real availability traces gathered from the SETI@home project. In our simulation, we used 60 days' data from real SETI@home availability traces. The SETI@home traces contain the node availability information (online or offline) of dynamic large-scale nodes over Internet (around 110 K nodes for the full traces). We generate a trace subset for our simulations by randomly selecting 1,000 nodes from the full SETI@home traces, then we perform a statistic analysis on those selected nodes, and the characteristics are presented as follows: up to around 350 nodes (approximately 35 %) are online simultaneously; and around 50 % of nodes whose availability are less than 0.7. We have used 30 days as the amount of training data for the remainder of this paper, and 4 hours as the prediction interval length.

Algorithms for Comparison. In addition to our Naive Bayes Classifier (N-BC) method, we also implemented five other prediction methods. Some of them have been shown to be effective in discrete sequence prediction. Under our formulated prediction model, we make them uniformly aim to predict availability of the future interval, based on the training data.

- *Last-State Based Method* (**LS**): The last recorded value in the training data will be used as the predicted value for the future period.
- *Simple Moving Average Method* (**SMA**): The mean value of the training data will serve as the predicted value.
- *Linear Weighted Moving Average Method* (**WMA**): The linear weighted mean value (based on Eq. (1)) will be considered as the predicted mean value for the future. Rather than the mean value, the weighted mean value weights the recent value more heavily than older ones.

$$F_{wrt}(e) = \sum_{i=1}^{n} i e_i / \sum_{i=1}^{n} i \qquad (1)$$

- *Exponential Moving Average Method* (**EMA**): This predicted value (denoted $S(t)$ at time t) is calculated based on the Eq. (2), where e_1 is the last value and α is tuned empirically to optimize accuracy.

$$S(t) = \alpha \cdot e_1 + (1 - \alpha) \cdot S(t - 1) \qquad (2)$$

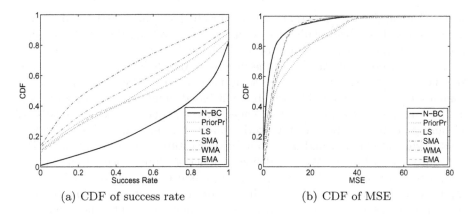

(a) CDF of success rate   (b) CDF of MSE

Fig. 3. Prediction accuracy comparison using different methods (training days = 30)

- *Prior Probability Based method* (**PriorPr**): This method uses the value with highest prior probability as the prediction for the future mean value, regardless of the evidence window.

The training period is used to fit the models. The test period is used to validate the prediction effect of different methods. In our evaluation, the size of training data is 30 days (the length of the 01 training string is 720). The key parameters used for evaluation are as follows: in the EMA method, the value of α is 0.90.

In terms of evaluating prediction accuracy, we use two metrics. First, we measure the mean squared error (MSE) between the predicted values and the true values in the prediction interval. Second, we measure success rate, which is defined as the ratio of the number of accurate predictions to total number of predictions. In general, the higher the success rate, the better, and the lower the MSE.

Figure 3(a) and 3(b) shows the cumulative distribution function (CDF) of the success rate and MSE for different prediction methods, respectively. For the success rate comparison, the curve which is more closer to the bottom-right corner is better, while for the MSE comparison, the curve which is near the top-left corner is better. Therefore, it is clear that N-BC's prediction effect is better than all the other methods. From Fig. 3(a), it is observed that SMA (Simple Moving Average Method) performs poorly, while LS (Last-State Based Method) performs poorly in Fig. 3(b). The reason why Bayesian prediction outperforms other methods is its features, which capture more complex dynamics, which have not been made by LS and SMA methods.

5.2 Simulation of the Proposed MapReduce Framework

In order to integrate the network prediction approach, BRITE is used as a topology generator, which can generate wide-area network topology according to user-predefined parameters [12]. We create a wide-area network composed of 1015 nodes. Among them, 14 nodes are supposed to be landmarks, and 1 node serves as the server. For other 1000 nodes, we assign each node an ID, and also assign each node a trace from the subset of SETI@home that we selected before.

In order to evaluate how well the proposed MapReduce performs over the Internet environment, we borrowed some ideas from GridSim, a famous Grid simulation toolkit. We build a discrete event based simulator, which loads availability traces of each node, and manages an event queue. It reads a BRITE file and generates a topological network from it. Information of this network is used to simulate latency and data transfer time estimation. We define the CPU capability for each node. We also define a model of MapReduce job, and seven parameters are configured to describe a MapReduce job, including the size of input data, the size of DFS chunk, the size of intermediate file (corresponding to Map task result of each chunk), the size of final output file, the number of Mappers, the number of Reducers, and the option of fast application pattern or slow application pattern. The fast pattern means that Mapper/Reducer time is long, while the slow pattern has short Mapper/Reducer time. We also considered the following four kinds of MapReduce jobs in the simulation:

(1) Model A: fast application, large intermediate file size;
(2) Model B: fast application, small intermediate file size;
(3) Model C: slow application, large intermediate file size;
(4) Model D: slow application, small intermediate file size.

We considered the following four scenarios when scheduling MapReduce jobs over the Internet:

(1) Scenario I: without any strategies;
(2) Scenario II: with availability prediction only;
(3) Scenario III: with network estimation only;
(4) Scenario IV: with availability prediction and network estimation together.

The main model specific parameters in BRITE topology generator are as follows: node placement is random; bandwidth distribution is exponential distribution (the value of $MaxBW$ is 8192, and the value of $MinBW$ is 30). For a MapReduce job, the input data size is set to a random value between 50GB and 200GB, and DFS chunk size is 64MB, and intermediate file size for a Mapper is set to 150MB (corresponding to large) and 50MB (corresponding to small). For fast jobs, data processing speed for a Mapper or Reducer is 10MB/GHz; while the value is 1MB/GHz for slow jobs. The CPU capacity of node is a random value between 1 GHz and 3 GHz. We start the simulator, submit 100 MapReduce jobs, and then estimate the job completion time.

Availability Prediction only. First, we compared Scenario I with Scenario II, to validate the improvement of MapReduce job completion time, when the availability prediction method is used. As we can see in Fig. 4(a), Scenarios II outperforms Scenarios I, and job completion time is decreased when using

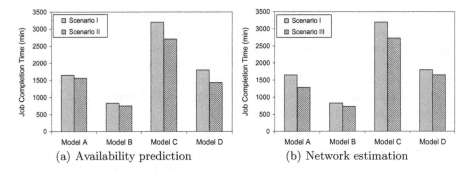

(a) Availability prediction   (b) Network estimation

Fig. 4. The improvement of MapReduce job completion time for two methods

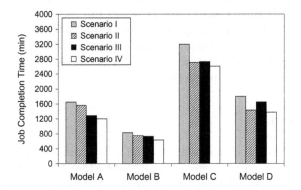

Fig. 5. Comparison of different strategies

availability prediction. With the availability prediction, task failure and task re-scheduling ratio has been decreased, especially for the Model C and Model D. For the slow MapReduce jobs, Map or Reduce task have higher possibility to be failed and needed to re-scheduled. From this figure, it is also indicated that there is also only little performance difference for Model A and Model B.

Network Estimation only. Because network distance has impact on data transfer time, we compared Scenario I with Scenario III in this evaluation, and the result is presented by Fig. 4(b). Intermediate file size and the number of landmark are two important factors for MapReduce job completion time. If the landmark-based network estimation is not used, the server doesn't consider any information or attributes of nodes and all nodes are treated equally, which may cause the problem that transferring intermediate data to a far desktop PCs. For Model A and Model C, it takes more time to transfer large intermediate file, and the job completion time is decreased by 21.93 % and 14.68 % respectively, when the network estimation method is used in Scenario III.

We also evaluated job completion time when configuring different number of landmark, and we adopted the Model A for evaluation. The number of landmark is increased from 4 to 14, and the step size is 2. As the increase of landmark number, MapReduce job completion time is also decreased from 1522 min, 1411 min, 1332 min, 1288 min, 1278 min to 1262 min, due to that with larger number of landmark, the network estimation can be more precise. While with too many landmarks, the algorithm of 'binning' is more complex. Usually, 8–12 landmarks should suffice for the current scale of the Internet [14]. Therefore, we used 10 landmarks in our previous evaluations.

Comparison of Different Strategies. We also conducted the comparison of different strategies, as we mentioned before, Scenario I, II, III and IV. For the MapReduce jobs, we evaluated all the four patterns. The comparison result is presented in Fig. 5, and Scenario IV outperforms all other scenarios. Scenario IV improves the MapReduce system and decreases the overall job response time, through combining two scheduling strategies: availability-aware and network-aware scheduling. Compared with Scenario I, the performance improvement of Scenario IV is 27.15 % for `Model A`, 24.09 % for `Model B`, 18.43 % for `Model C`, and 23.44 % for `Model D`, respectively.

6   Conclusion

In this paper, we proposed an availability and network-aware MapReduce framework on Internet. It outperforms current MapReduce framework on Internet, thanks to Naive Bayes Classifier-based availability prediction and landmark-based network estimation. The performance evaluation results were obtained by simulations. In the simulation, the real SETI@home availability traces was used for validation, and BRITE topology generator was used to generate a low-speed, wide-area network. Results show that the Bayesian method achieves higher accuracy compared with other prediction methods, and intermediate results could be transferred to a more closer nodes to perform Reduce tasks. With the resource availability prediction and network distance estimation method, the MapReduce job response time could be decreased conspicuously.

Acknowledgement. This work is supported by the "100 Talents Project" of Computer Network Information Center of Chinese Academy of Sciences under grant no. 1101002001, and the Natural Science Foundation of Hunan Province under grant no. 2015JJ3071, and Scientific Research Fund of Hunan Provincial Education Department under grant no. 12C0121, 11C0689 and 11C0535.

References

1. Anderson, D.P.: Boinc: a system for public-resource computing and storage. In: GRID, pp. 4–10. IEEE (2004)
2. Costa, F., Silva, J.N., Veiga, L., Ferreira, P.: Large-scale volunteer computing over the internet. J. Internet Serv. Appl. **3**(3), 329–346 (2012)

3. Costa, F., Silva, L.M., Fedak, G., Kelley, I.: Optimizing data distribution in desktop grid platforms. Parallel Process. Lett. **18**(3), 391–410 (2008)
4. Costa, F., Veiga, L., Ferreira, P.: Internet-scale support for map-reduce processing. J. Internet Serv. Appl. **4**(1), 1–17 (2013)
5. Dean, J., Ghemawat, S.: Mapreduce: simplified data processing on large clusters. Commun. ACM **51**(1), 107–113 (2008)
6. Fedak, G., He, H., Cappello, F.: Bitdew: a data management and distribution service with multi-protocol file transfer and metadata abstraction. J. Netw. Comput. Appl. **32**(5), 961–975 (2009)
7. Jin, H., Yang, X., Sun, X.H., Raicu, I.: Adapt: Availability-aware mapreduce data placement for non-dedicated distributed computing. In: ICDCS, pp. 516–525. IEEE (2012)
8. Lee, K., Figueiredo, R.J.O.: Mapreduce on opportunistic resources leveraging resource availability. In: CloudCom, pp. 435–442. IEEE (2012)
9. Lin, H., Ma, X., Feng, W.-C.: Reliable mapreduce computing on opportunistic resources. Cluster Comput. **15**(2), 145–161 (2012)
10. Lu, L., Jin, H., Shi, X., Fedak, G.: Assessing mapreduce for internet computing: a comparison of hadoop and bitdew-mapreduce. In: GRID, pp. 76–84. IEEE Computer Society (2012)
11. Marozzo, F., Talia, D., Trunfio, P.: P2p-mapreduce: parallel data processing in dynamic cloud environments. J. Comput. Syst. Sci. **78**(5), 1382–1402 (2012)
12. Medina, A., Lakhina, A., Matta, I., Byers, J.W.: Brite: an approach to universal topology generation. In: MASCOTS, IEEE Computer Society (2001)
13. Moca, M., Silaghi, G.C., Fedak, G.: Distributed results checking for mapreduce in volunteer computing. In: IPDPS Workshops, pp. 1847–1854. IEEE (2011)
14. Ratnasamy, S., Handley, M., Karp, R.M., Shenker, S.: Topologically-aware overlay construction and server selection. In: INFOCOM (2002)
15. Song, S., Keleher, P.J., Bhattacharjee, B., Sussman, A.: Decentralized, accurate, and low-cost network bandwidth prediction. In: INFOCOM, pp. 6–10. IEEE (2011)
16. Tang, B., He, H., Fedak, G.: Parallel data processing in dynamic hybrid computing environment using mapreduce. In: ICA3PP (2014)
17. Tang, B., Moca, M., Chevalier, S., He, H., Fedak, G.: Towards mapreduce for desktop grid computing. In: 3PGCIC, pp. 193–200. IEEE Computer Society (2010)
18. Wei, B., Fedak, G., Cappello, F.: Towards efficient data distribution on computational desktop grids with bittorrent. Future Gener. Comp. Syst. **23**(8), 983–989 (2007)

OptRS: An Optimized Algorithm Based on CRS Codes in Big Data Storage Systems

Chao Yin[1], Jianzong Wang[2,3(✉)], Haitao Lv[1], Zongmin Cui[1],
Lianglun Cheng[2], Qin Zhan[1], and Tongfang Li[1]

[1] School of Information Science and Technology, Jiujiang University,
Jiujiang 332005, Jiangxi, People's Republic of China
[2] School of Computer Science and Technology,
Guangdong University of Technology,
Guangzhou 510006, Guangdong, People's Republic of China
[3] Ping An Technology (Shenzhen) Co., Ltd,
Shenzhen 518029, Guangdong, People's Republic of China
jzwang@188.com

Abstract. It is well-known that erasure codes, such as Reed-Solomon (RS) and Cauchy RS (CRS) codes, have played an important roles in big data storage systems to both industry and academia. While RS and CRS codes provide significant saving in storage space, they can impose a huge burden of systems performance while encoding and decoding. By studying existing high reliability and space saving rate of coding technologies, it is urgent to deploy an efficient erasure coding mechanism into distributed storage systems, which is the main storage architecture in big data era.This paper puts forward an optimized algorithm named OptRS (Optimized RS), which can not only guarantee the system's reliability, but also enhance the efficiency and utilization of storage space. The dominant type of encoding and decoding inside erasure codes is matrix computation. In order to accelerate the speed of calculation, OptRS transferred the computation of matrix Galois field mapping into the XOR operation. Additionally, OptRS has developed the elimination schemes to minimize the numbers of XOR. Through theory analysis, we can conclude that OptRS algorithm improved the performance of encoding and decoding lead to shorten the computation time the same as verified by the test. The encoding efficiency with OptRS coding achieves 36.1 % and 58.2 % acceleration than using CRS and RS coding, respectively. The decoding rate by using OptRS can increase 19.3 % and 33.1 % compared with CRS and RS averagely by quantitative studying.

Keywords: Big data · Distributed storage · OptRS · Matrix calculation · Elimination schemes

1 Introduction

1.1 Background

Along with the development of data explosion and the coming of big data age, it is becoming common today that storage systems store multiple PB even ZB

G. Wang et al. (Eds.): ICA3PP 2015, Part I, LNCS 9528, pp. 228–240, 2015.
DOI: 10.1007/978-3-319-27119-4_16

of data in the form of cluster [1]. In the point of view of enterprises, loss of data could even be destructive, therefore the demand for dependability of data storage system rises up. These storage systems are expected to store the data in a reliable and available fashion in different temporary and permanent failures, which arise from unreliable components, maintenance operations and so forth.

Typically, cloud storage systems like GFS [2], HDFS [3], Amazon S3 [4] and Ceph [5], always have employed triple replication so as to ensure the data reliability. However, the tremendous expenditure of disks' purchasing are produced for a company along with the data scaling exponentially. To cut down the consumption of disks, erasure codes are imported into storage platforms. The way of erasure coding can provide higher level of reliability at lower storage cost comparing with the replication. RS codes [6] with the novel using of storage resources have proved to be the wisest choice for providing reliability warranty. It has been reported that some large-scale, distributed storage systems [7,8] has employed RS codes instead of replication to save storage capacity.

The disadvantage of RS codes comparing to replication is performance overhead. If there is data loss in replication, such as three-way replicated, the system can reconstruct by copying the missing part from one of available replicas. However, if data loss happens in the system with erasure codes, the system needs multiple blocks in the same code stripe to construct the lost block. During the processing of data reconstruction, a lot of data need to be read and calculated, which will decrease the performance of the distributed storage system dramatically. Recent research shows that it required more than 180 TB of data transferred to recover from 50 machine-unavailability events per day in Facebooks data clusters [9]. Consequently, reconstruction operations result in a large number of disk I/O and network transfers under RS codes.

The big data storage systems should minimize the burden of system resources while guaranteeing the reliability. To accelerate the data reconstruction rate in erasure codes is the main goal when designing the big data storage system. In this work, we have developed an optimized erasure coding algorithm, called OptRS, to guarantee the data reliability. This algorithm improved based on original RS and CRS [10] coding algorithms. First of all, we analyse the operating principles of RS and CRS. We have investigated that the numbers of XOR in Galois field is the most important metrics to influence the performance of decoding and encoding where the data value is coded in RS and CRS. Then the formula is leveraged to get the relations of relative rows in order to provide support to eliminate redundant rows. Secondly, by optimizing the calculating numbers of XOR, a row elimination scheme has been proposed to accelerate decoding and encoding operations. The performance of the system is also optimal by increasing the speed of matrix operations.

1.2   Contributions and Paper Organization

The main contributions of our paper are listed as below:

- (1) By analyzing the calculation rules of Vandermonde and Cauchy matrix, we have presented a coding scheme OptRS which omits the unit matrix and retains the Cauchy matrix of k rows and n columns.

- (2) The XOR operation is utilized in the computation to get the encoded values. The numbers of XOR can decrease to improve the decoding and encoding speed.
- (3) OptRS algorithm is analyzed theoretically and implemented to validate the performance of OptRS. The results show that the coding efficiency when using OptRS is 36.1 % higher than using CRS and 58.2 % higher than using RS averagely. The decoding efficiency when using OptRS is 19.3 % and 33.1 % higher than CRS and RS, respectively.

The rest of this paper is organized as follows. The architecture of the proposed big data storage system are introduced in Sect. 2. Section 3 described OptRS algorithm in detail. Section 4 gives the experimental evaluation and results. Section 5 shows related works. We make the conclusion in Sect. 6.

2   The Big Data Storage System

The overall architecture of big data storage mechanism is designed as in Fig. 1. The framework is distributed and reliable, including two kinds of nodes: Name Nodes (NNs) and Data Nodes (DNs). NNs store the metadata for all files and file paths. According to the strategy, NNs are responsible to encoded blocks and select the different DNs to control the whole system for load balancing. Keeping the user data after encoding, data nodes in the system are divided into a plurality of micro nodes, which can improve the system's parallelism extremely.

The micro node is virtual conception in the system, which is used to improve the system's parallel ability, flexibility and performance. Each micro node is equivalent to a general container, which can become the basic unit of all systems to encode and store data block and parity block. Besides storing the block, it also has much information, one is unique marker (ID), which can be used to record which code set the node belongs to. The other information is also stored in micro node to identify different characteristics, such as address, users' markers, health status, capacity use, calibration information and so on.

After name nodes have received the data submitted by the user, they will turn the data into blocks and change them into coded block with redundancy according to the users requirements. After this step, all the encoded blocks constitute a code set. Code set plays a very important role in the operation of searching users location and repairing corrupted data, so that it will be stored in name nodes. When the encoding is completed, name nodes will select the idle micro nodes to store code block in different data nodes of the system. Considering data security and load balance, we let each code set only store one micro node to store data in one data node. Data loss will not occur since each data node will keep balance even if the collapse happens in the system.

We can access the corresponding data node by its own name stored in the file when the system is damaged, and we can obtain the damaged file code set in the survived code block in order to repair the damaged data. The DHT (Distributed Hash Table) protocol is adopted for the data distribution and addressing

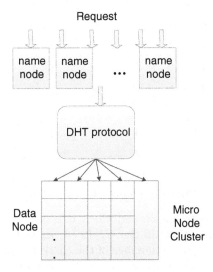

Fig. 1. The system architecture

algorithm in the storage system as demonstrated in Fig. 1. Why we use the DHT protocol but not others? As mentioned before we are in the big data age, the application scenario is the distributed storage system with massive data. Nowadays, the big storage system grouped by cheap and generic servers generally, which is different from that of designed high-end storage system. The high-end storage systems are always designed specifically, such as EMC and IBM servers, whose hardware is used to ensure the reliability of nodes and systems. The characteristics of ordinary large-scale storage system are multi nodes and large scale. There are more than tens of thousands of nodes so that node failure rate is far higher than the high-end storage systems. It is an unstable system, where erasure code and other software ensure the reliability. For this reason, DHT algorithms currently in large-scale storage systems have been widely used, such as Amazon's Dynamo [11] and Sheepdog.

3 The Proposed Schema in OptRS

3.1 OptRS Algorithm

Optimized from RS code, CRS code uses the Cauchy matrix instead of the Vandermonde matrix as the generator matrix. The Cauchy matrix can get inverse in the $O(n \wedge 2)$ time which has been proved, so that it has good property of encoding and decoding. We can conclude that the performance of coding and decoding is related with the number of 1. The more there are numbers of 1, the higher the performance of the codec is. In the process of implementing the CRS code, we can be further optimized for Cauchy matrix by matrix transformation.

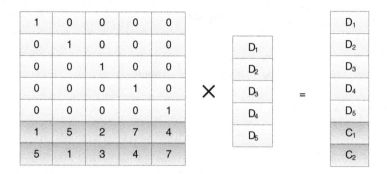

Fig. 2. The original CRS matrix

Transform coding operation through the matrix of CRS, we can obtain higher efficiency matrix. Assumptions in the $GF\left(2^{W}\right)$, let w be equal to 3, n is the number of data blocks, k is the number of the check block.

Define the Cauchy matrix with k rows and n columns, k rows data are represented as $X_1, X_2...X_k$, n columns data are represented as $Y_1, Y_2...Y_k$. The Cauchy matrix can be expressed as (1):

$$M(X,Y) = \sum_{i=1}^{k}\sum_{j=1}^{n} V(X_i, Y_j) \qquad (1)$$

where Galois field $(w = 3)$ when the value of $V(x,y)$ is expressed in matrix $M(1/(x+y))$. Let $n = 5$, $k = 2$, $X = 1, 2$, $Y = 0, 3, 4, 5, 6$, then the original CRS matrix is shown in Fig. 2.

The first n rows of the matrix constitutes a unit matrix, the last k row is Cauchy matrix. In order to accelerate the speed of matrix calculation, we make the computation of matrix Galois field mapping into the XOR operation instead of being conducted in Galois fields. We need the following operations. First, we change each data element in the $GF\left(2^{W}\right)$ to express as the form of w ∗ w. After this transformation, we change the original CRS matrix into a binary matrix $(k+w)w*nw$. Accordingly, the matrix coding and decoding operation in $GF\left(2\right)$ will have the lower computational complexity than in $GF\left(2^{W}\right)$. Figure 3 shows the transformated matrix. In order to make the graph concise, we have omitted the unit matrix, retaining only the Cauchy matrix of k rows and n columns.

The new matrix is the operation in $GF\left(2\right)$, therefore we only use the XOR operation in the computation to get the encoded values. If we want to calculate $C_{i,j}$, we only need to compute $D_{i,j}$ and all the XOR of its related rows. Each of the shaded part is 1 and the blank part is 0 in Fig. 2. We can get (2).

$$\begin{cases} C_{1,1} = D_{1,1} \oplus D_{2,1} \oplus D_{2,2} \oplus D_{3,3} \oplus D_{4,1} \oplus D_{4,2} \oplus D_{4,3} \oplus D_{5,2} \\ C_{1,2} = D_{1,2} \oplus D_{2,3} \oplus D_{3,1} \oplus D_{3,3} \oplus D_{4,1} \oplus D_{5,2} \oplus D_{5,3} \\ C_{1,3} = D_{1,3} \oplus D_{2,1} \oplus D_{3,2} \oplus D_{4,1} \oplus D_{4,2} \oplus D_{5,1} \oplus D_{5,3} \\ C_{2,1} = D_{1,1} \oplus D_{1,2} \oplus D_{2,1} \oplus D_{3,1} \oplus D_{3,3} \oplus D_{4,2} \oplus D_{5,1} \oplus D_{5,2} \oplus D_{5,3} \\ C_{2,2} = D_{1,3} \oplus D_{2,2} \oplus D_{3,1} \oplus D_{3,2} \oplus D_{3,3} \oplus D_{4,2} \oplus D_{4,3} \oplus D_{5,1} \\ C_{2,3} = D_{1,1} \oplus D_{2,3} \oplus D_{3,2} \oplus D_{3,3} \oplus D_{4,1} \oplus D_{4,3} \oplus D_{5,1} \oplus D_{5,2} \end{cases} \qquad (2)$$

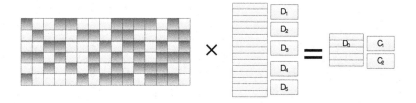

Fig. 3. The CRS matrix after transformation

Each line of the number 1 respectively in $8, 7, 7, 9, 8, 8$ matrix, the corresponding numbers of XOR operation are $7, 6, 6, 8, 7, 7$. The total numbers of XOR matrix is $\text{Num}_{xor} = 7 + 6 + 6 + 8 + 7 + 7 = 41$, this is $n = 5, k = 2, w = 3$ when calculating the number of XOR matrix. In order to improve the coding performance, we should consider how to let the numbers of XOR minimized.

3.2 Two Rows Elimination Scheme

As we can see from (2), $C_{1,1}$ and $C_{1,2}$ have the same XOR subset: $D_{3,3} \oplus D_{4,1} \oplus D_{5,2}$. When calculating $C_{1,1}$ and $C_{1,2}$, we can reduce two XOR operations. $C_{1,3}$ and $C_{2,1}$ have the same XOR subset: $D_{4,2} \oplus D_{5,1} \oplus D_{5,3}$, and we can reduce two XOR operations when calculating $C_{1,3}$ and $C_{2,1}$. Similarly, $C_{2,2}$ and $C_{2,3}$ have the same XOR subset: $D_{3,2} \oplus D_{3,3} \oplus D_{4,2} \oplus D_{5,1}$ and three XOR operations can be reduced. Through the above operations, XOR total number decreased to $\text{Num}_{xor} = 41 - 2 - 2 - 3 = 34$.

We can carry out in another way, such as comparing each of the original data. Since matrix with k lines will be changed into matrix with $k * w$ line, we can compare the first line in each K lines to reduce the XOR computation times. We will describe this method as follows using the same matrix before.

There are the same XOR subset $D_{1,1} \oplus D_{2,1} \oplus D_{3,3} \oplus D_{4,2} \oplus D_{5,2}$ in group $C_{1,1}$ and $C_{2,1}$. We can reduce 4 XOR operation when calculating $C_{1,1}$ and $C_{2,1}$. Similarly, There are the same XOR subset $D_{3,1} \oplus D_{3,3}$ and $D_{3,2} \oplus D_{4,1} \oplus D_{5,1}$ in group $C_{1,2}$, $C_{2,2}$ and $C_{1,3}$, $C_{2,3}$, that reduce the XOR operation 1 time and 2 times, respectively. Through the above operation, the total reduced numbers is $\text{Num}_{xor} = 41 - 4 - 1 - 3 = 34$ times. It is by coincidence that the results are the same from two methods.

3.3 Three Rows Elimination Scheme

Three lines elimination scheme means that we can eliminate the same values in every three lines. From Fig. 3 and Eq. (2) we can see that there are not the same XOR subset in $C_{1,1}$, $C_{1,2}$ and $C_{1,3}$. There are the same XOR subset $D_{3,3} \oplus D_{5,1}$ in $C_{2,1}$, $C_{2,2}$ and $C_{2,3}$. When calculating $C_{2,1}$, $C_{2,2}$ and $C_{2,3}$, we can reduced the XOR operation for $1*2 = 2$ times. The total numbers of reduced XOR are two times.

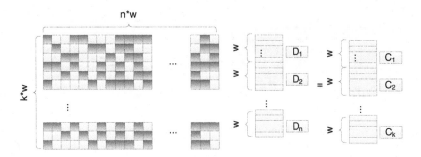

Fig. 4. The matrix code conversion schematic diagram of the expanded w

From Fig. 3 we can conclude that the total number of XOR subset will be more between the group of $C_{1,1}$, $C_{1,2}$ and $C_{2,3}$ and that of $C_{2,1}$, $C_{2,2}$ and $C_{1,3}$. According to the elimination method, there are the same XOR subset $D_{3,3} \oplus D_{4,1} \oplus D_{5,2}$ in group $C_{1,1}$, $C_{1,2}$ and $D_{4,2} \oplus D_{5,1}$ in group $C_{2,1}$, $C_{2,2}$ and $C_{1,3}$. The total XOR numbers has been reduced $2*2 + 1*2 = 6$ times.

Now we expand the value of w, not confined to 3, so that we can get the expanded matrix code conversion schematic diagram in Fig. 4.

The steps of two rows' elimination will be shown as follows. Transformation matrix as the goal, we compare every two rows, draw the same number of XOR and set the same XOR term for P_i, i means the number of lines. These steps can reduce the number of XOR P_{i-1} times. The total reduction of the number of XOR is as shown in Eq. (3).

$$Num = \begin{cases} \sum_{i=1}^{\frac{kw}{2}} p_{2i-1} - 1(kw\%2 = 1) \\ \sum_{i=1}^{\frac{kw-1}{2}} p_{2i-1} - 1(kw\%2 = 0) \end{cases} \tag{3}$$

Synthesizing all of the eliminated situations, we can get the conclusion as follows.

Inference 3.1: For data blocks n, check numbers k, in the case of $GF\left(2^W\right)$, if there are the same numbers of exclusive or in each t lines, we define the numbers as P_i, i for the number of rows, then the total numbers of XOR can be reduced is shown as Eq. (4).

$$Num = \begin{cases} (t-1) * \sum_{i=1}^{\frac{kw}{t}} p_{ti-1} - 1(kw\%t = 0) \\ (t-1) * \sum_{i=1}^{\frac{kw-1}{t}} p_{2i-1} - 1(kw\%t = 1) \\ \ldots\ldots \\ (t-1) * \sum_{i=1}^{\frac{kw-1}{t}} p_{2i-1} - 1(kw\%t = t-1) \end{cases} \tag{4}$$

All of the elimination algorithms consist of two lines, three lines to $k \times w$ lines, including hybrid lines which means the uncertain number of rows, have the 2^W elimination methods. Therefore, the eliminating problems belong to NP problem, so that it will have not the best solution. The method proposed in this paper is the realization of the approximate optimal solution. We can also eliminate three or more lines at the same time, but it will cause the reduction of the numbers of XOR. Although it can be multiplied by the coefficient, which is the elimination line numbers $h - 1$, and the optimization results achieved will be similar with two rows. In summary, we will use two elimination schemes in the following tests.

4   Evaluation Methodology

4.1   Experimental Setup

We have analyzed the OptRS in theory, we mainly discuss about the evaluation and analysis of the implementation part in the sections. The experiment is implemented on a storage platform based on the architecture described in Sect. 2. The *Namenode* of the system is installed on the machine with Intel Core i5-580, 8GB RAM and 100GB disk. This machine is connected to four storage servers with Xeon E5606 CPU, 8GB DDR3 RAM and 50GB disk.

4.2   Encoding and Decoding Time Test

We implemented the prototype system for the performance estimation of all the processes in data encoding and decoding. When encoding or decoding, Vandermonde and Cauchy codes are suitable in distributed system due to its fine fault tolerance and dispensability. Therefore these two codes will be compared with OptRS in the tests.

In the encoding process, user data is randomly generated, divided into chunks, encoded and stored. The numbers of data chunks and parity chunks are different while the time of encoding and decoding is various. Figure 5 presented encoding and decoding time in different data chunk sizes with different encoding methods. Decoding time refers to recovery time when data is corrupted here.

Figure 5 shows the encoding and decoding time pattern in a single encoding group when data chunk number is 5 and parity chunk number sets to 2. Chunks size ranging from 1M to 10M is the only variable parameter. In this figure, encoding time rises as chunk size increases. Compared to encoding time, decoding time of a single chunk has better efficiency. Simultaneously, because OptRS and CRS adopts bitmap to convert multiplication into XOR operation and requires lower encoding or decoding time than RS code, while decoding time of OptRS is obviously shorter than the CRS because of coding optimization. OptRS is more suitable to be deployed on distributed system for decoding work. It is also obvious from the figure that decoding time is less than encoding time, so encoding time in systems need attentions.

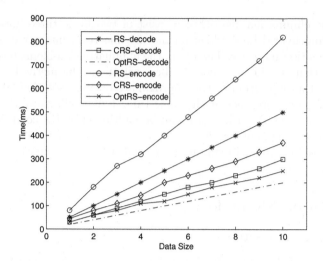

Fig. 5. Encoding and decoding time with different data size

Figure 6 shows the encoding and decoding time pattern in a 5-chunk encoding group when chunk size is 1M and parity chunk number ranges from 2 to 8. As the parity chunks in an encoding group increase, encoding time rises. More parity chunks can tolerate more faults, which means if higher fault tolerance level is needed more encoding time is required. However, the decoding time is more stable. Decoding time in RS, CRS and OptRS has no noticeable fluctuation, which indicates that increase in parity chunks numbers will not lead to decoding time increase of a single chunk. We could also indicated that OptRS performs better than RS and CRS in both encoding and decoding time, suggesting OptRS is more adaptive to efficient and time-demanding system than the others.

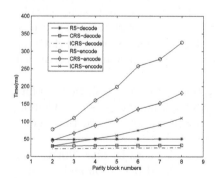

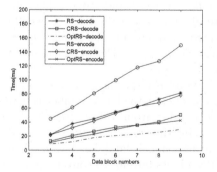

Fig. 6. Encoding and decoding time with different parity block numbers

Fig. 7. Encoding and decoding time with different data block numbers

Figure 7 shows the encoding and decoding time pattern in an encoding group when chunk size is 4M; parity chunk number is 2 and data chunk number ranges from 3 to 9. As the data chunks increase, order of magnitudes of the encoding time rises from 10 seconds to 100 seconds. OptRS code still has a lower encoding time than RS and CRS. Unlike encoding time, decoding time presents a smaller fluctuation. That indicates encoding process has larger overhead than decoding and encoding time is more susceptible by data chunk number k. OptRS remains relatively stable and high efficiency than RS, when k changes.

Figures 5, 6, 7 show different result of encoding and decoding time in an encoding group when data chunk number, parity chunk number and chunk size change. Through these comparison tests, it can be clear seen that encoding time changes when data chunk number, parity chunk number and chunk size change. The relation between recovery time of a data chunk and chunk size is the most obvious. Bigger chunk size needs more decoding time. When data chunk number in an encoding group increases, decoding recovery time increases, while the increment is less than the case when chunk size increases. In these factors, parity chunk number is the least influential one. Decoding time is less than encoding time and it fluctuates less. Besides, OptRS has a higher overall encoding and decoding efficiency in distributed system than CRS and RS. From Figs. 5, 6, 7, we can conclude that the coding efficiency when using OptRS is 36.1% higher on average than using CRS and 58.2% higher on average than using RS. The decoding efficiency when using OptRS is 19.3% higher on average than using CRS and 33.1% higher on average than using RS.

4.3 Read Performance

Normal Read. We use TPC-C benchmarks with a 1GB workload to test the normal read performance of our system. Erasure codes are RS, CRS and OptRS, respectively. We test four kinds of queries with different sizes of result sets. The results are shown in Fig. 8. The system with erasure codes outperforms triplication to some extent; the intuitive reason for this is that erasure codes only keep one copy of the original data, and the systems read performance benefits from light workloads.

Degraded Read. We test the degraded read performance of our system for a slighter workload of a 256MB file. The results are shown in Fig. 9. The first three bars represent the time to read a corrupted block when it is the only corrupted block; the second three bars show the time to read a corrupted block when there are two corrupted blocks at the same time. The last three bars display the time to read a recovered block, which can also represent the reading time when only one copy is left in triplication. OptRS tries to recover most corrupted data blocks before users read them, so the degraded reading performance can be much better than that with RS and CRS in the first two situations, or even as good as that with triplication.

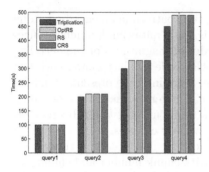

Fig. 8. Normal read performance

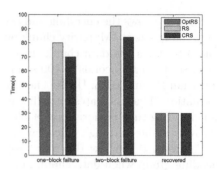

Fig. 9. Degraded read performance

5   Related Works

Erasure code has been applied in many large-scale distributed storage systems. Google Colossus [7], IBM GPFS [12] and Facebook HDFS [13] have used erasure codes in their storage system by trading off reliability and storage overhead. However, most of erasure codes used in these systems is RS or RS class codes, which usually have high recovery cost. In this section, we will review past work on erasure codes storage systems.

We have presented storage system based on random network-coding that optimize resources consumed during reconstruction in [14]. The data is only functional reconstructed to the failed data so that the system needs to read the least data to reconstruct when data loss.

There are a lot of research about Galois field. Plank et. al [15] have used fast Galois Field arithmetic in Inter SIMD field. HitchHiker [16] proposes a new encoding technique by dividing in a single Reed-Solomon code stripe into two correlated sub-stripes and improves recovery performance. Robot [17] puts forward a solution based on coding technologies in big data system that store a lot of cold data. By studying Reed-Solomon coding technologies and big data systems, Robot can not only maintain the system's reliability, but also improve the security and the utilization of storage systems.

Recently, there has been a growing focus on improving recovery performance for erasure-coded storage systems. KHAN et al. have proposed Rotated RS codes for faster recovery [18]. HACFS [19] is a new erasure-coded storage system that instead uses two different erasure codes and dynamically adapts to workload changes inside HDFS.

RS is a popular family of codes in distributed storage system, while the other popular code family is LRC [20]. The basic of LRC is using extra fragments to construct more parity. As a result, fragments in a calibration chain are less than OptRS. Reading data is lesser when experiencing a recovery. But it cost many additional calibration plates and storage.

What's more, KV Rashmiet al. [21] took minimum-storage-regeneration (MSR) codes into consideration as a superior alternative to RS codes. The product-matrix-MSR codes are built in order to minimize disk I/O consumed, while simultaneously retaining optimality in terms of both storage, reliability and network-bandwidth. MSR and the bandwidth optimization will be integrated into OptRS frameworks after inspiring some ideas in our future works.

6   Conclusions and Future Works

Big data storage systems always deploy erasure codes to substitute replication for lower storage overhead, but erasure codes bring the performance problems inevitably. This paper has presented a new code algorithm called OptRS which focuses on improving the encoding and decoding speed. In order to accelerate the speed of matrix calculation, we make the computation of the calculation of matrix Galois field mapping into the XOR operation instead of being conducted in Galois fields. By eliminate the rest rows, the OptRS method can improve performance by taking advantage of its high speed of CODEC. Test results show that it is very fast to complete CODEC by using OptRS. However, there is still much work to do in the future which mainly contains three directions. First of all, there exists much room to reduce the decoding time further. Secondly, as surveyed in related works we should care about not only lower storage costs but also recovery performance. Additionally, two different erasure codes instead of one erasure code in our system will be taken into account. Finally, we will practise OptRS after patching into HDFS and try to optimize MSR codes in the similar way.

References

1. Schmuh, F., Haskin, R.: GPFS: A shareddisk file system for large computing clusters. In: Proceedings of the 1st USENIX Conference on File and Storage Technologies (2002), Monterey, CA, USA (2002)
2. Ghemawat, S., Gobioff, H., Leung, S.-T.: The google file system. In: Proceedings of the Nineteenth ACM Symposium on Operating Systems Principles, SOSP 2003, pp. 29–43 (2003)
3. Shvachko, K., Kuang, H., Radia, S., Chansler, R.: The hadoop distributed file system. In: Proceedings of IEEE MSST 2010, Incline Village, NV, USA, May 2010
4. Amazon Simple Storage Service (S3). http://www.amazon.com/s3
5. Weil, S.A., Brandt, S.A., Miller, E.L., et al.: Ceph: a scalable, high-performance distributed file system. In: Proceedings of the 7th Conference on Operating Systems Design and Implementation (2006)
6. Reed, I.S., Solmon, G.: Polynomial codes over certain finite fields. J. Soc. Ind. Appl. Math. **8**(2), 300–304 (1960)
7. Colossus, successor to Google File System. http://static.googleusercontent.com/media/research.google.com/en/us/university/relations/facultysummit2010/storage_architecture_and_challenges.pdf/

8. Huang, C., Simitci, H., Xu, Y. et al.: Erasure coding in Windows AzureStorage. In: USENIX Annual Technical Conference (ATC) (June 2012), boston, MA,USA (2012)
9. Facebooks approach to big data storage challenge. http://www.slideshare.net/ Hadoop_Summit/facebooks-approachto-big-data-storage-challenge
10. Blomer, J., Kalfane, M., Karpinski, M., et al.: An XOR-based erasure-resilient coding scheme. Technical Report TR-95-048, International Computer Science Institute, August 1995
11. DeCandia, G., Hastorun, D., Jampani, M., et al.: Dynamo: amazon's highly available key-value store. In: ACM SIGOPS Operating Systems Review, Vol. 41(6), pp. 205–220. ACM (2007)
12. An introduction to GPFS version 3.5. http://www-03.ibm.com/systems/resources/ introduction-to-gpfs-3-5.pdf
13. Facebooks erasure coded hadoop distributed file system (HDFS-RAID). https:// github.com/facebook/hadoop-20
14. Yin, C., Xie, C., Wan, J., et al.: BMCloud: Minimizing repair bandwidth and maintenance cost in cloud storage. In: Mathematical Problems in Engineering (2013)
15. Plank, J.S., Greenan, K.M., Miller, E.L.: Screaming fast Galois Field arithmetic using Intel SIMD instructions. In: Proceedings of the 11th USENIX Conference on File and Storage Technologies (2013), San Jose, CA, USA (2013)
16. Rashmi, K.V., Shan, N.B., Gu, D., et al.: A hitchhikers guide to fast and efficient data reconstruction in erasure-coded data centers. In: Proceedings of ACM SIGCOMM14, SIGCOMM (2014)
17. Yin, C., Wang, J., Xie, C., et al.: Robot: an efficient model for big data storage systems based on erasure coding. In: Proceedings of the IEEE International Conference on Big Data, Santa Clara, CA, USA (2013)
18. Khan, O., Burns, R., Plank, J., et al.: Rethinking eerasure codes for cloud file systems: minimizing I/O for recovery and degraded reads. In: Proceedings of the 10th USENIX Conference on File and Storage Technologies, San Jose, CA, USA (2012)
19. Xia, M., Saxena, M., Blaum, M., et al.: A tale of two erasure codes in HDFS. In: the Proceedings of the 13th USENIX Conference on File and Storage Technologies, Santa Clara, CA, USA (2015)
20. Tamo, I., Barg, A.: A family of optimal locally recoverable codes. IEEE Trans. Inf. Theor. **60**(8), 4661–4676 (2014)
21. Rashmi, K.V., Nakkiran, P., Wang, J., et al.: Having your cake and eating it too: jointly optimal erasure codes for I/O, storage, and network-bandwidth. In: The Proceedings of the 13th USENIX Conference on File and Storage Technologies, Santa Clara, CA, USA (2015)

Quantum Computer Simulation on Multi-GPU Incorporating Data Locality

Pei Zhang$^{(\boxtimes)}$, Jiabin Yuan, and Xiangwen Lu

College of Computer Science and Technology,
Nanjing University of Aeronautics and Astronautics, Nanjing 211106, China
{zp_019,jbyuan,xwlv}@nuaa.edu.cn

Abstract. Quantum computer simulation (QCS) provides an effective platform for the development and validation of quantum algorithms. The exponential runtime overhead limits the simulation scale on classical computers which makes advisable the use of Graphics Processing Units. However, simulating quantum computers on multi-GPU has poor performance due to low data locality and frequent data transfer. Here, we propose a novel implemental scheme for QCS on multi-GPU. Our implementation addresses the aforementioned challenges by (i) an efficient data distribution method enhancing high data locality on each GPU global memory and (ii) an assignment function for the threads mapping to each GPU memory space achieving high bandwidth and data reuse for multiple quantum gates. Experimental results show that the simulation of 29-qubit Quantum Fourier Transform algorithm using four NVIDIA K20c GPUs gains a performance ratio of 358, compared to the sequential implementation of released libquantum, along with a parallel efficiency of 0.92.

Keywords: Quantum computer simulation · Multi-GPU · Data locality · CUDA

1 Introduction

Recently, increasing number of researchers focus on the study of quantum computation [1, 2], especially the realization of a physical quantum computer and the development of quantum algorithms. However, existing technologies still can't construct a physically stable quantum computer [3]. To provide a useful tool for the development and validation of quantum algorithms, simulating the behavior of quantum computers on a classical computer is proposed. The grand bottleneck of classical quantum computer simulation (QCS) is that the memory and arithmetic operations required on classical computers grow exponentially with scaling of quantum system [4].

Over the past years, the rapid evolution of floating-point computational capacity and memory bandwidth makes graphics processing units (GPUs) an increasing attractive platform to accelerate scientific applications. Prior single-GPU implementations for QCS, [5, 6], have achieved considerable speedup compared to the native CPU implementation. The utilization of GPU shows that the performance of applications depends strongly on the explicit exploitation of GPU memory hierarchy and DRAM bandwidth [5].

© Springer International Publishing Switzerland 2015
G. Wang et al. (Eds.): ICA3PP 2015, Part I, LNCS 9528, pp. 241–256, 2015.
DOI: 10.1007/978-3-319-27119-4_17

The main goal of our research is to present that quantum computers can be simulated more efficiently on modern heterogeneous architecture based on CPU and multi-GPU. In particular, classical QCS is a data-intensive [7] application, owing to that its arithmetic intensity is relatively low. In order to achieve the potential performance offered by multi-GPU, we identified the following two challenges to be addressed. First, during the simulation of quantum gates, there are data dependencies in the updates of different quantum states. In such a scenario, how to efficiently distribute data among different memory spaces of multi-GPU and enhance high data locality affects the performance and parallel efficiency largely. Second, how to design kernel functions to achieve high effective memory bandwidth. Since the simulation programs are memory-bound, the computation portion in each warp cannot begin until all the memory requests are finished. As for this, the exploitation of GPU L1 cache with high data reuse opportunity will improve the memory bandwidth and better overlap computation and memory accesses.

In this paper, a novel high-efficiency implemental scheme for universal QCS on the heterogeneous architecture, using Compute Unified Device Architecture (CUDA) [8] after NVIDIA, is proposed. Our implementation addresses the aforementioned challenges with two strategies. The first one involves an efficient data distribution method enhancing high data locality on each GPU global memory. The high data locality means there requires no data transfer between each GPU during kernel execution. Therefore, our scheme gains good kernel execution performance and high parallel efficiency. The second one relates to an assignment function for threads mapping to each GPU memory space (global and shared) to utilize the high-speed shared memory for multiple quantum gates. Taking memory reference locality and coalesced accesses into account, our mapping function obtains high memory bandwidth. In order to validate our implementation, Quantum Fourier Transform (QFT) [2] is adopted between classic computers and the simulation platform.

The remainder of this paper is organized as follows. We start by reviewing the related work in Sect. 2. In Sect. 3, quantum computing fundamentals and the multi-GPU system is introduced. We present our implementation scheme on multi-GPU in Sect. 4 and optimization work in Sect. 5. Experimental results are analyzed in Sect. 6. Conclusions and future work are drawn in Sect. 7.

2 Related Work

Given the necessity and challenge of classical QCS, massive parallel platforms have been exploited towards the acceleration of universal large-qubit QCS. The following is a simple introduction for some remarkable QCS based on supercomputers or GPUs.

The QCS using massive parallel computers or supercomputers enlarges the scale of qubits to some extent. At present, the most outstanding outcome is the 42-qubit Shor's algorithm performed on the JUGENE supercomputer with 262,144 processors [9], showing great scaling with the number of CPUs and problem size [4]. However, the performance ratio of the simulation is poor, and the exponential computational overhead is still a bottleneck.

In [10], a parallel GPU implementation of a simulator for QFT is present, together with a number of optimizations. Apparent speedup of over 160 times is obtained against CPU implementation, but the exploitation of GPU shared memory is insufficient. The quantum simulator described in [5] further improves the implementation on single GPU with shared memory. On a GeForce 8800GTX GPU NVIDIA platform, a 26-qubit register can be simulated up to 95 times faster than the sequential code in an Intel Core2 6400 @ 2.13 GHz. In addition to the works mentioned above, some specific quantum algorithms are implemented on GPU platform. In [11], the simulation workflow of the Grover algorithm using CUDA, along with the optimization of memory access, is studied. Experimental results show that the distinguished program on CUDA outperformed the serial program of libquantum [12] on a CPU with a speedup of up to 23 times. However, prior works of QCS are mostly on singe GPU device, resulting in limited simulation scale.

3 Background

3.1 Quantum Computing Fundamentals

The simulation of quantum computers is based on the model in [13], viewed as a family of quantum gates applied to a quantum register with a classical initial state. Due to space constraints, detailed introduction to quantum register and quantum operations can refer to [13–15].

A quantum transformation is operated on the coefficient space of a quantum register [14]. Hence, We can denote the coefficient space in its initial state before application of the transformation as $S^{in} = \left\{ a_0^{in}, a_1^{in}, \cdots, a_{2^N-1}^{in} \right\}$, and $S^{out} = \left\{ a_0^{out}, a_1^{out}, \cdots, a_{2^N-1}^{out} \right\}$ after the transformation. From the analysis of prior study [4, 5], considering a single-qubit gate operated over the qubit i of an N-qubit register, the computing of coefficient a_k^{out} depends on the coefficients of a_k^{in} and $a_{k\oplus 2^i}^{in}$. Similarly, for a two-qubit operated over the qubit i and qubit j, the computing of coefficient a_k^{out} depends on the coefficient set $\left\{ a_k^{in}, a_{k\oplus 2^i}^{in}, a_{k\oplus 2^j}^{in}, a_{k\oplus(2^i+2^j)}^{in} \right\}$.

3.2 Multi-GPU System

According to the connection method, multi-GPU systems can be classified into two types: (i) multiple GPUs within a node; (ii) multiple GPUs across multiple network nodes. Our simulation is based on the first type considering performance and price.

Typically, in the multi-GPU system, the memory spaces of CPU (called host) and different GPUs (called devices) are physically distributed, and each device has direct access to host memory. CPU is in charge of the invocation of kernel functions and data transfer between host and device. GPUs connected to the same PCI-E switch can directly use Peer-to-Peer (NVIDIA GPU Direct P2P) for memory copies. However, GPUs attached to different PCI-E switches cannot, and data should transfer through host memory. In our hardware platform, the memory throughputs of 6.02 GB/s and 6.40 GB/s for host to device and device to host transfers are measured using NVIDIA's bandwidth test program [8]. The P2P bandwidth is 4.90 GB/s measured by simpleP2P program [8]. In summary, employing multi-GPU in QCS can further speed up computation. However, the data dependencies existing in the updating of coefficients result in frequent data transfer between GPUs. Hence, the overhead of inter-GPU communication is a key concern.

4 A Novel Implemental Scheme for Multi-GPU

Given the fact that devices attached to different PCI-E switches cannot directly use P2P, an implemental scheme named P2P Scheme, is firstly proposed to address this issue. Then, we further put forward an efficient implemental scheme, named Data Locality Scheme, to eliminate the data transfer between each device.

4.1 P2P Scheme

In order to decrease the communication overhead between devices attached to different PCI-E switches, the N_d devices are partitioned into $N_d/2$ groups. Each group is made up of two devices attached to the same PCI-E switch. What we have to do is to distribute the coefficients of two states with data dependency to devices in one group.

The single-qubit gate operated over nonlocal qubit j is discussed as follows. If the coefficient $a(* \cdots * 0_j * \cdots *)$ (see definitions in Sect. 3.1) is distributed to one device, the coefficient $a(* \cdots * 1_j * \cdots *)$, in which the asterisks indicate the bits on the corresponding position are the same, will be distributed to the other device in the same group. Therefore, all the data transfer required in the updating of coefficients can be realized via P2P within each group.

An example of the simulation for 4-qubit QFT in the case of $N = 4$ and $M = 2$ is illustrated in Fig. 1. The 4 GPUs are divided into $2^{N-(M+1)} = 2^{4-(2+1)} = 2$ groups, device 0 and device 1 in Group 0, device 2 and device 3 in Group 1. At first, the coefficients of states are distributed from host to devices in the corresponding group for the gates operated over nonlocal qubits 3. Then, the update of the coefficients can be performed through P2P within groups. In general, the P2P data transfer required for a nonlocal-qubit gate is 2^4 times. After the gate on qubits 3, the coefficients should be copied back to host for reassignment. To perform the rest of quantum gates operated on the low three qubits, coefficients are sequentially distributed to each device. The simulation of quantum gate on nonlocal qubit 2 still requires P2P transfers. Afterwards, the updates for the gates operated over local qubits 1 and 0 can be performed without data transfer. At last, the coefficients are copied back to host.

It is obvious that, the main factors affecting the simulation performance reside in the 2^N data transfer during kernel execution and a round-trip data transfer of all the coefficients between host and each device for each time a nonlocal-qubit gate is performed. In addition, this scheme has a poor scalability for quantum gates on multiple nonlocal qubits. Faced with these issues, an efficient implemental scheme, inspired from the massive parallel quantum computer simulator (MPQCS) [4], is proposed.

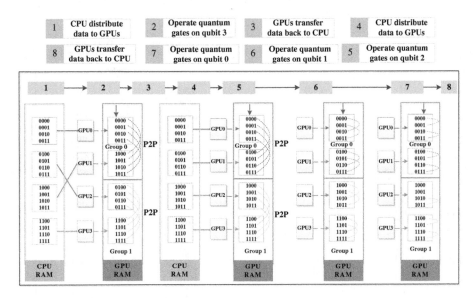

1	CPU distribute data to GPUs	2	Operate quantum gates on qubit 3	3	GPUs transfer data back to CPU	4	CPU distribute data to GPUs
8	GPUs transfer data back to CPU	7	Operate quantum gates on qubit 0	6	Operate quantum gates on qubit 1	5	Operate quantum gates on qubit 2

Fig. 1. The simulation of a 4-qubit QFT in a node with 4 GPUs implemented on P2P Scheme.

4.2   Data Locality Scheme

MPQCS is implemented on a supercomputer consisting of massively parallel processors, exploiting a swap operation to make the original nonlocal qubits local for nonlocal-qubit gates. Our implementation is different from MPQCS in memory architecture, data transfer, and computational power. In order to eliminate the data transfer between each device, we exploit the idea of swapping nonlocal qubits with local qubits, and make appropriate improvements according to the multi-GPU platform.

Data Layout. With regard to the data dependency elaborated in Sect. 4.1, we exploit an improved data layout scheme to make an original nonlocal qubit m local. What we have to do is to interchange a local qubit k in $A = (x_{M-1} \ldots x_0)$ with the nonlocal qubit m in $R = (x_{N-1} \ldots x_M)$, leaving the other qubits in place. In another word, it means changing the address of each coefficient from $A = (* \cdots * 0_k * \cdots *)$ of GPU with rank $R = (* \cdots * 1_m * \cdots *)$ to $A = (* \cdots * 1_k * \cdots *)$ of GPU with rank $R = (* \cdots * 0_m * \cdots *)$.

Similarly, this method can be extended to a multi-qubit gate, e.g. L_1-qubit $(L_1 > M)$. If all the L_1 qubits are local, there requires no data transfer between GPUs. If L_2 of them are nonlocal and $L_2 < M$, we can interchange them with L_2 local qubits at one time. But if $M < L_2 < L_1$, the interchange should be $\lceil \frac{L_2 - M}{M} \rceil$ times and exchange no more than M qubits each time. An example of swapping the nonlocal-qubit 3 and 2 with the local-qubit 1 and 0, given $N = 4$ and $M = 2$ is present in Fig. 2. Here, quantum operations on qubits 3 and 2 require no data transfer between different devices.

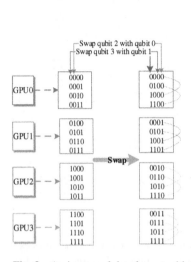

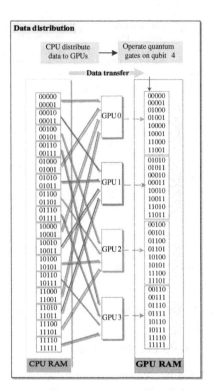

Fig. 2. An improved data layout with high data locality in device memory.

Fig. 3. The data distribution for N = 5, M = 3.

Data Distribution. To realize the high-locality data layout mentioned above, the data distribution method is discussed in two situations, quantum gates on local qubits and nonlocal qubits. For local-qubit gates, we can continuously divide 2^M coefficients into each device. But for the other, the division is not completely continuous. Assuming that there are L nonlocal qubits, mostly $L < M < N, M = N - L$, if we interchange the L nonlocal qubits with L highest local qubits, and leave the lower $N - 2L$ local qubits in place, a one-to-one mapping function is got from the address space of host to device:

$$Host(x_{N-1}\ldots x_{N-L}x_{N-L-1}\ldots x_{N-2L}x_{N-2L-1}\ldots x_0)$$
$$\rightarrow Address(x_{N-1}\ldots x_{N-L}x_{N-2L-1}\ldots x_0)\text{of GPU with } Rank(x_{N-L-1}\ldots x_{N-2L}) \tag{1}$$

Observed that the lowest $N - 2L$ local qubits remain unchanged, every 2^{N-2L} of the states are placed continuously in each device. We define the continuous states as $(N - 2L)$-order continuous batch. On the condition that each device memory can store up to 2^M coefficients, the number of batches distributed to each device is $2^M/2^{N-2L} = 2^L$, equal to the device number. Here, if we interchange the highest local qubits, the size of each continuous batch is maximum, while the number of batches distributed to each device is minimum. Fewer batches imply fewer data transfer times.

From the analysis above, we can directly distribute the 2^L continuous batches to each device. A vivid example for $N = 5, M = 3$ is present in Fig. 3. The size of each batch is $2^{5-2\times2} = 2$, and all the coefficients are divided into 2^4 batches. As each device can only accommodate 2^2 batches, the data transfer to each device is 2^2 times. After that, there is no data dependency between each device. Besides, the highest nonlocal qubits 1 and 0 on each state represent the rank of device it resides.

Implementation. On the basis of data distribution, our implementation scheme for QCS based on CPU and multi-GPU is proposed. The workflow of simulation on n GPU within a node is shown in Fig. 4. Data and computational task are averagely divided into each GPU.

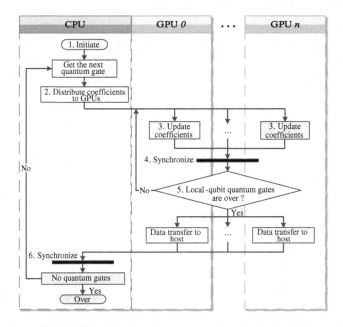

Fig. 4. The workflow of quantum computer simulation.

Some key steps are illustrated as follows:

1. The initialization of the quantum register is performed in CPU.
2. The procedure of distributing coefficients to GPUs exploits the data distribution method mentioned above. The transfer of a continuous batch between host and device is executed by a function call of *MemoryCopy*. For nonlocal-qubit gates, the data distribution makes the original nonlocal qubits local in each device memory.

3. Each quantum gate is implemented by GPU through a kernel invocation. Each working thread is arranged to compute the coefficient of one basic state. During the GPU kernel, there is no data transfer between GPUs.
4. After kernel execution, a synchronization of multi-GPU is required.
5. If there are consecutive quantum gates all operated on local qubits, they can be processed in device memory continuously.
6. After each data transfer to host, a synchronization of multi-GPU is performed on the CPU side to guarantee the data consistency.

For a better understanding of the Data Locality Scheme, the simulation of a 4-qubit QFT in a node of 4 GPUs is present in Fig. 5. Compared to the P2P Scheme in Fig. 1, Data Locality Scheme not only has no data transfer during kernel execution, but also has a good scalability for quantum gates on multiple nonlocal qubits. Moreover, for consecutive quantum gates all operated on nonlocal qubits, there just needs one round-trip data transfer between host and each device.

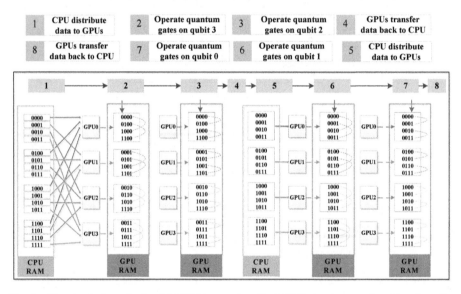

Fig. 5. The simulation of a 4-qubit QFT in a node with 4 GPUs implemented on Data Locality Scheme.

5 Bandwidth Optimization

Due to the fact that it takes several hundred clock cycles to access global memory, one of the main bottlenecks in the CUDA kernel function is the low load/store efficiency of global memory. In order to achieve high memory bandwidth, we further improve the Data Locality Scheme by exploiting the shared memory/L1 data cache with data reuse for multiple quantum gates. The challenge is to find out an assignment function for the threads mapping to each GPU memory spaces (global and shared), with taking memory reference locality and coalesced memory accesses into account. This section is organized into two subsections. First, the workflow of each thread with exploitation of shared memory on each GPU is presented. Second, the mapping function for each thread with coalesced memory accesses is illustrated in detail.

5.1 Workflow of Threads with Exploitation of Shared Memory

With reference to the exploitation of shared memory in a single GPU [4], we partition the coefficients into disjoint closed subsets. In each closed subset, the updating of coefficients for a series of quantum gates is independent from the rest of subsets. The closed subsets, as computation units, can be copied into shared memory and shared within each CUDA block. So that, each block will be in charge of processing one of such sets. According to this, the workflow of each thread is depicted as follows:

At the beginning of kernel functions, threads in a block copy the closed subset from global memory into shared memory in parallel. Then, a series of quantum gates are applied over the closed subset in shared memory. A thread-level synchronization is required between gates. Finally, each thread transfers the coefficient on shared memory back to global memory.

5.2 Mapping Function

We assume that the shared memory can store 2^r coefficients and each thread is in charge of updating one coefficient. Correspondingly, the size of each closed subset P_k is 2^r. In each closed subset, the quantum gates that can be processed are defined as operated on the $i_0, i_1, \cdots, i_m$ qubits. As illustrated in Fig. 6, each P_k is mapped to a block. In subset P_k, every 2^{r-m} coefficients resides contiguously in a row, and in each column there are the coefficients that the operation of quantum gates $i_0, i_1, \cdots, i_m$ relied on. For each GPU, the load/store of subsets P_k in global memory can be coalesced in a warp, on the condition that 2^{r-m} is bigger than the size of a warp. Therefore, a high memory bandwidth can be obtained through this mapping function.

Observed from Fig. 6, if we get the value of k, the index of other coefficients in this closed subset can be calculated out. The key problem is the mapping for a_k to the corresponding thread in each closed subset. However, the mapping in multi-GPU

$$
P_k = \left\{
\begin{array}{cccc}
a_k & a_{k+1} & \cdots & a_{k+2^c-1} \\
a_{k \oplus 2^{i_0}} & a_{k \oplus 2^{i_0}+1} & \cdots & a_{k \oplus 2^{i_0}+2^c-1} \\
a_{k \oplus 2^{i_1}} & a_{k \oplus 2^{i_1}+1} & \cdots & a_{k \oplus 2^{i_1}+2^c-1} \\
a_{k \oplus (2^{i_1}+2^{i_0})} & a_{k \oplus (2^{i_1}+2^{i_0})+1} & \cdots & a_{k \oplus (2^{i_1}+2^{i_0})+2^c-1} \\
\cdots & \cdots & \cdots & \cdots \\
a_{k \oplus (2^{i_m}+\cdots+2^{i_0})} & a_{k \oplus (2^{i_m}+\cdots+2^{i_0})+1} & \cdots & a_{k \oplus (2^{i_m}+\cdots+2^{i_0})+2^c-1}
\end{array}
\right\}
$$

$$c = r - m$$

$$\text{with } k = k \wedge \left(2^N - 1 - \sum_{u=0}^{c-1} 2^u - \sum_{t=0}^{m} 2^{i_t} \right)$$

Fig. 6. The mapping functions of a closed subset to a block.

implementation is different from single-GPU. We now illustrate the difference in two aspects. One is that unlike single-GPU implementation, the memory spaces of multiple GPUs are independent. Because of this, the quantum state of a_k should base on the global index of the corresponding thread. The other is that in case of the nonlocal-qubit gates, the order of coefficients in global memory is changed, not sequential as local qubits. Hence, we optimize the workflow of each thread, based on the method of single GPU implementation [4]. The new workflow of a thread, with thread ID Id_{thread}, block ID Id_{block}, grid ID Id_{grid} and device ID Id_{device}, is depicted in Fig. 7.

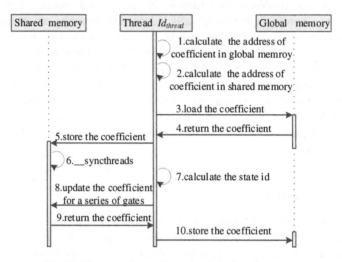

Fig. 7. The workflow of kernel using shared memory

Some key steps are elaborated as follows:

- Step 1 can be divided into three sub steps:

  (a) Calculate the global block ID:$GId_{block} = Id_{block} + Id_{grid} \times blocksPerGrid$.
  (b) Calculate the value of k via insertion of zeros in positions on bits $0, \cdots, c-1$ and $i_0, \cdots, i_m$ of the binary expression of GId_{block}.
  (c) Calculate the coefficient addresses in global memory:
  $address_{global} = k \oplus \left(2^{i_{(Id_{thread}/2^{r-m})}} + 2^{i_{((Id_{thread}/2^{r-m})-1)}} + \cdots + 2^0 \right) + 2^{Id_{thread}\%2^{r-m}}$.

- In Step 2, the address of coefficients in shared memory is equal to the thread ID: $address_{shared} = Id_{thread}$.
- Step 7 is performed in two cases. In case of local-qubit gates, the state ID Id_{state} is calculated by the equation $Id_{state} = address_{global} + Id_{device} \times 2^M$. However, in case of nonlocal-qubit gates, the order of coefficients in global memory has been changed by swapping the nonlocal qubits with local ones before kernel execution. Hence, we should extra swap back these bits in the binary expression of Id_{state}.
- In Step 8, the update of coefficients is executed in shared memory gate by gate, and a thread-level synchronization between each gate transformation is necessary.

6 Experiments

This section presents the experiment results obtained after application of the implementation scheme and optimization technics aforementioned. We analyze the results in three aspects: the simulation performance, the parallel efficiency of multi-GPU and the bandwidth of GPU global memory.

6.1 Experimental Programs

We implement QFT [2] algorithm in our QCS platform of four NVIDIA K20c @ 706 MHz GPUs and an Intel Xeon E5-2609 v2 @ 2.5 GHz CPU. The CUDA version is 6.5. The hybrid OpenMP-CUDA parallel programming model is used to parallel data transfer between host and device, and kernel executions on each device. The computational load is equally distributed to each device. In order to figure out the performance improvement of our optimization, we evaluate our simulation in three versions:

- Version 1 (V1): The algorithm is simulated according to P2P Scheme.
- Version 2 (V2): The algorithm is simulated according to Data Locality Scheme.
- Version 3 (V3): The algorithm is simulated according to Data Locality Scheme with optimization.

Programs of the three versions are separately performed on 4 GPUs, 2 GPUs and 1 GPU. The implementation with one GPU for V1 and V2 are the same, while the multi-GPU implementations are different. In the GPU implementation of V1 and V2, each block contains 512 threads and each thread computes one coefficient. However, the number of threads per block in V3 is determined by the coefficients that can be stored in shared memory. Here, we distribute 2 KB shared memory to each block, which can accommodate 256 coefficients, and thence the block size is 256 in V3.

6.2 Performance Comparisons

This subsection analyzes the performance of three implemental versions through the runtime and performance ratio compared to CPU implementation, scaling with the problem size. For comparative purposes, the CPU implementation is tested by the serial code execution of the QFT algorithm from the libquantum library [13]. The steps of serial code are the same as those of the parallel code running on the GPU.

Figure 8 shows the total runtime of the versions on different number of GPUs. We simply focus on the simulation above 22 qubits. There are two sources of overhead: data transfer between host and device, and the computation in kernel functions. For a better understanding, the total runtime is measured in four parts: data transfer from device to host (DtoH), data transfer from host to device (HtoD), kernel execution time of local-qubit gates (LocalQubit_kernel) and kernel execution time of nonlocal-qubit gates (NonlocalQubit_kernel). As shown in the Fig. 8, the total runtime grows exponentially with the increasing of qubits in spite of the GPU numbers. In Fig. 8(a), due to the limited global memory on one GPU, the largest size of qubits that can simulated is

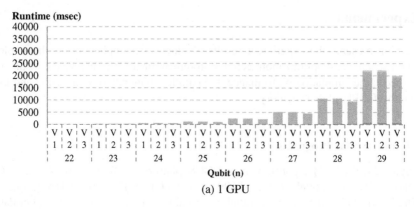

(a) 1 GPU

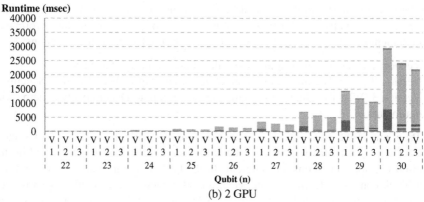

(b) 2 GPU

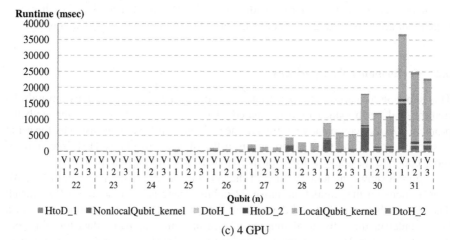

(c) 4 GPU

Fig. 8. Runtime of QFT algorithm of three versions on different number of GPUs (Color figure online)

29. Because there is no nonlocal qubit in single GPU implementation, no extra data transfer between host and device is required. With the exploitation of shared memory, V3 has a performance advantage of the kernel execution over the other two versions. In Fig. 8(b) and (c), the largest qubits that can be simulated increase with adding of GPUs. In the multi-GPU implementation, an extra round-trip data transfer between host and device is required between the nonlocal-qubit and local-qubit kernels. Obviously, the overhead on nonlocal-qubit kernel is largely decreased in V2 and V3, compared to V1. This performance improvement is achieved by the high data locality in global memory of Data Locality Scheme, which omits the P2P data transfer in P2P Scheme. In both of 4 GPUs and 2 GPUs implementations, the performance of V3 surpasses V2 through the exploitation of shared memory in kernel functions.

Performance ratio is the quotient of the total runtime of the CPU in the serial way and the GPUs in the three versions. As shown in Fig. 9, the performance ratio curves of 4 GPUs are rising most quickly with the scaling of qubits. For all simulation scales on same numbers of GPUs, V3 shows the prominent performance ratio for all qubit scales and GPU scales. In a best scenario, the performance ratio of V3 reaches 378 on 4 GPUs and 189 on 2 GPUs for the simulation of 30 qubits.

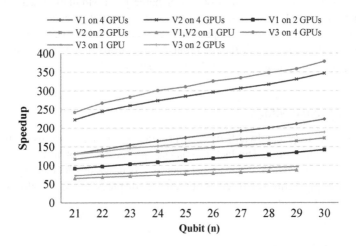

Fig. 9. Performance ratios of GPUs and CPU based programs.

6.3 Parallel Efficiency

The parallel efficiency η is calculated by: $\eta = T_{runtime}(1)/(T_{runtime}(N_d) \times N_d)$, in which $T_{runtime}(N_d)$ represents the runtime on N_d GPU. In Fig. 10, with different numbers of GPUs, the parallel efficiency of V3 and V2 is far superior to V1. This is because data are transferred by P2P between each GPU for exponential times when operating nonlocal-qubit gates in V1, while in V2 and V3, the data transfer between each GPU is eliminated through the data distribution method described in Sect. 4.2. The extra overhead caused by the data distribution method in V2 and V3 is far less than the P2P overhead in V1. Besides, the parallel efficiency of 4 GPUs in V2 and V3 is a little less

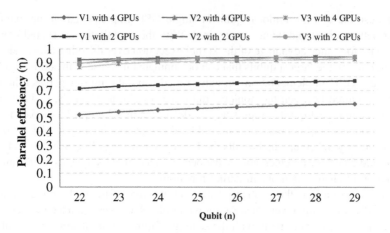

Fig. 10. Parallel efficiency on multi-GPU.

than that of 2 GPUs, which is resulting from the synchronization overhead between multiple devices. In general, Data Locality Scheme has a simulation scale advantage without optimization. In some simulation scales, the parallel efficiency of V3 is lower than that of V2. This is because, despite the kernel computation overhead in each GPU of V3 is lower than that of V2, the data transfer overheads of the two versions, which affects the parallel efficiency of multi-GPU, are still equal.

6.4   Memory Bandwidth

The effective memory bandwidth of each program is measured by using the Nsight Profiler Tools after Nvidia. The lack of coalescing access to global memory will give rise to a loss of bandwidth. The global memory bandwidth obtained by NVIDIA's bandwidth test program is 161 GB/s. Figure 11 displays the GPU global memory

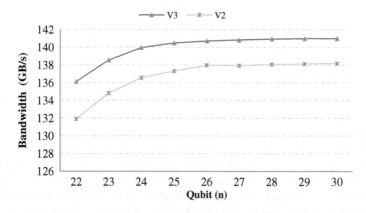

Fig. 11. Memory bandwidth of nonlocal-qubit kernel on 4 GPUs.

bandwidth in the kernel of the highest nonlocal-qubit quantum gate performed on 4 GPUs. Owing to the exploitation of shared memory with coalesced global memory access, V3 has a better performance and a higher utilization ratio of memory bandwidth.

7 Conclusion

In this paper, approaches to the simulation of an ideal quantum computer using multiple NVIDIA GPUs have been proposed and analyzed. To address the high data dependencies between different GPUs, a scheme using GPU Direct P2P transfer (P2P Scheme) is implemented. However, due to the frequent data transfer between each GPU for nonlocal-qubit gates, the P2P Scheme has a poor execution performance and low parallel efficiency. To improve this, a novel implemental scheme (Data Locality Scheme) is put forward. Additionally, in pursuit of high efficiency, the Data Locality Scheme is further improved with the memory space and memory access in kernel execution. Experimental results show that the proposed strategies are able to achieve high performance ratio and parallel efficiencies on multi-GPU implementations. In a best scenario, the performance ratio of V3, compared to the sequential implementation of libquantum, respectively reaches 378 on 4 GPUs, with parallel efficiency over 0.92, and 189 on 2 GPUs with parallel efficiency over 0.94 for 30 qubits. The memory bandwidth of 141 GB/s is measured in our 4 GPU implementation. The exponential computational overhead in quantum simulation is well amortized among streaming multi-processors in each GPU.

References

1. Steane, A.: Quantum computing. Rep. Prog. Phys. **61**(2), 117 (1998)
2. Nielsen, M.A., Chuang, I.L.: Quantum Computation and Quantum Information. Cambridge University Press, Cambridge (2010)
3. Glendinning, I., Ömer, B.: Parallelization of the QC-Lib quantum computer simulator library. In: Wyrzykowski, R., Dongarra, J., Paprzycki, M., Waśniewski, J. (eds.) PPAM 2004. LNCS, vol. 3019, pp. 461–468. Springer, Heidelberg (2004)
4. De Raedt, K., Michielsen, K., De Raedt, H., et al.: Massively parallel quantum computer simulator. Comput. Phys. Commun. **176**(2), 121–136 (2007)
5. Gutiérrez, E., Romero, S., Trenas, M.A., et al.: Quantum computer simulation using the CUDA programming model. Comput. Phys. Commun. **181**(2), 283–300 (2010)
6. Amariutei A, Caraiman S.: Parallel quantum computer simulation on the GPU. In: Proceedings of the 15th International Conference on System Theory, Control, and Computing, ICSTCC 2011, Sinaia, Romania, 14–16 October 2011, pp. 1-6. IEEE (2011)
7. Moore, R., Baru, C., Marciano, R., et al.: Data-intensive computing. In: Foster, I., Kesselman, C. (eds.) The Grid: Blueprint for a New Computing Infrastructure, pp. 105–129. Morgan Kaufmann, San Francisco (1999)
8. NVIDIA CUDA: programming guide, and SDK. http://www.nvidia.com/cuda

9. Henkel, M.: Quantum computer simulation: New world record on JUGENE, June 2010. http://archive.hpcwire.com/hpcwire/2010-06-28/quantum_computer_simulation_new_ world_record_on_jugene.html
10. Smith, A., Khavari. K.: Quantum Computer Simulation Using CUDA, University of Toronto (2009). http://www.eecg.toronto.edu/ ~ moshovos/CUDA08/arx/QFT_report.pdf
11. Lu, X., Yuan, J., Zhang, W.: Workflow of the Grover algorithm simulation incorporating CUDA and GPGPU. Comput. Phys. Commun. **184**(9), 2035–2041 (2013)
12. Butscher. B., Weimer. H.: Libquantum library. http://www.libquantum.de
13. Deutsch, D.: Quantum computational networks. Proc. Roy. Soc. Lond. A Math. Phys. Sci. **42**(1868), 73–90 (1989)
14. DiVincenzo, D.P.: Quantum computation. Science **270**(5234), 255–261 (1995)
15. Barenco, A., Bennett, C.H., Cleve, R., DiVincenzo, D.P., Margolus, N., Shor, P., et al.: Elementary gates for quantum computation. Phys. Rev. A **52**(5), 3457 (1995)

Query Execution Optimization
Based on Incremental Update
in Database Distributed Middleware

Wei Ye, Mei Wang$^{(\boxtimes)}$, and Jiajin Le

School of Computer Science and Technology, DongHua University,
Shanghai 201620, China
starskyyw@163.com, {wangmei,lejiajin}@dhu.edu.cn

Abstract. Big data is often generated incrementally in the real word. Existing incremental query optimization is mainly used in the streaming data environment. Due to the constraints of real-time streaming data applications, existing incremental execution mechanisms is difficult to directly apply to large business-oriented data in a distributed environment. This paper proposes a query execution optimization method based on incremental update in database distributed middleware. First, the proposed method defines the Reference-Graph according to tables and their foreign key relationships, based on which a data partition strategy is provided to reduce data transmission quantity during query operation. In addition, the proposed method proposes an incremental update query execution strategy and incremental intermediate result preservation mechanism in distributed environment for non-aggregate and aggregate query respectively. The combination of data partition and incremental updating strategy reduces the query execution cost and enhance the performance of complex query operation significantly. Finally, the experimental results conducted on the benchmark dataset test and verify the effectiveness of the proposed method.

Keywords: Database middleware · Distributed database · Data partition · Incremental update · Result set reuse

1 Introduction

The rapid development of information and network technology in today's society has resulted in explosive growth of data. In many fields such as Internet, scientific research, medical, commercial, manufacturing are keep generating massive amounts of data over time. The total global data has reached 2.7 ZB in 2012, and according to IDC forecast to 2020 global data store is likely to reach 35 ZB [1]. With the rapid growth of data size, the centralized database has shown its limitation in both storage and computing capability. Distributed data management has become a trend.

Traditional distributed databases provide a feasible way for distributed data storage and computing. However, since its distributed management was integrated with the database itself, it always has sophisticated implementation mechanism. And more importantly, it is hard to integrate the existing database systems in real-world

© Springer International Publishing Switzerland 2015
G. Wang et al. (Eds.): ICA3PP 2015, Part I, LNCS 9528, pp. 257–270, 2015.
DOI: 10.1007/978-3-319-27119-4_18

applications. In order to provide distributed support to MySQL, PostGreSQL and other popular open source databases, a series of database middle wares such as Amoeba [2], Cobar [3], MyCat [4] and Atlas [5] came into being. These middleware provide a flexible solution for users to build a database cluster based on the existing stand-alone centralized databases, and transfer the existing applications to "distributed cloud" smoothly, so it has shown promising application prospects and attract great attention in both academic and industrial worlds.

It should be noticed that in real practical application, data is always constantly generated in an incremental manner and then brings together to a large data scale. Same deep analysis queries are always repeated applied on the dataset to obtain the statistical information and the change trend about the data. It is very important to improve the execution efficiency of these queries. However, in the existing distributed middle wares, their query execution framework is still in a simple and direct way. That is, all the data in the current database will be applied to query execution. It is obvious that such processing framework is bound to bring a lot of redundant operation since same query analysis statement are processed repeatedly on the historical data as the new data is imported into the database, which will greatly affect the system performance. Therefore, based on Distributed Middleware, designing incremental query execution strategy is an urgent problem to be solved.

The main idea of incremental query optimization is to divide the current data into a larger base part and a smaller increment. The solution of the original query could be reconstructed according to the calculation results between the data increment and intermediate results. In this way, the problem with massive scale could be transformed into a problem based on a smaller data increment, and then the query performance will be improved significantly. Existing incremental query optimization is mainly used in the streaming data environment. However, streaming data applications have strict "real-time" constraints, while in database and data warehouse, the historical data that have been saved in the database cannot be ignored. So the incremental data partition and incremental query algorithm has big difference from the previous streaming data algorithm. Especially in distributed environment, Incremental query and update is more complicated because of the cost of data transmission and distributed data storage.

This paper proposes a query execution optimization method based on incremental update in database distributed middle-ware. First, the proposed method defines the Reference-Graph according to tables and foreign key relationships, based on which a data partition strategy is provided to reduce the data to be transmitted during query processing. In addition, the proposed method proposes an incremental update query execution and incremental intermediate result preservation mechanisms in distributed middle-ware. The strategies for non-aggregate and aggregate query are provided respectively. The combination of data partition and incremental updating strategy reduces the query execution cost and enhance the performance of complex query operation significantly. Finally, the experiments have been conducted based on the data warehouse benchmark TPC-H [6]. The experimental results have shown that compared with the traditional data division strategy, the query time could save 17 % $\sim$ 33 % by use data partitioning algorithm proposed in this paper. By reusing the historical intermediate results, in the case of the small data set increment, the query performance could be improved more than 10 times.

The remainder of this paper is organized as follows. Section 2 provides an overview of the existing work on database distributed middleware and Incremental query optimization. Section 3 introduces the proposed method including the distributed data partition algorithm and the incremental query execution strategy. Section 4 presents the experimental results. Section 5 is the summary and outlook.

2 Related Work

One kind of architecture of large data storage and application is distributed database. However, the traditional distributed database structure is complex and the distributed management was integrated with the database itself. It is difficult to integrate the existing database systems. The database distributed middleware provides a good way to solve the problems above. At present, the research of database distributed middleware mainly focuses on commercial application. The abstract structure of the database middleware is illustrated in Fig. 1:

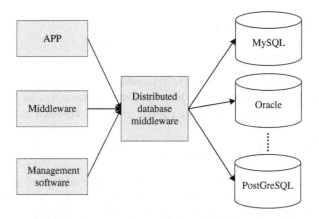

Fig. 1. Database middleware structure

Database distributed middleware take a bridge of application and the underlying database. SQL queries generated from the upper application are resolved into an independent SQL query plan by database middleware. These plans are executed by each data node and return the result to database middleware. The results are integrated by database middleware and send it back to the user.

The researches of incremental query optimization mainly focus on stream data and data mining. At incremental processing of data stream, Jin Chun et al. [7] create ARGUS system. They use Rete algorithm for execution of the SQL statement and add the query operation on incremental data which is gets good execution efficiency. However, the processing of these data does not involve the distributed storage environment. In the field of data mining, D.W. Cheung [8] et al. proposed FUP algorithm, research when transactions continue to add, how to update the association rules. The FUP algorithm in the case of doubling in the transaction, incremental computation improves the rate of nearly two times than complete calculation. Jian-Chih Ou [9] et al. process the incremental web log on data mining by using dynamic threshold method Incremental query on data mining is not general universal, so it is difficult to apply to the common query on distributed database.

Exploration in the result set reuse has many great achievements on Hadoop [10] and MapReduce [11] because of its characteristics of the storing intermediate results. Nykiel et al. [12] propose sharing MR model which can be used find the shared data among different queries. This model merges multiple tasks in order to share input and output in Hadoop platform. Elghandour et al. [13] expand data processing tool pig [14] and proposes ReStore. After user's command code is translated into MapReduce task by pig, ReStore rewrites it and save the output of task in HDFS for reuse. In addition, ReStore can decompose a single job into sub-job in order to let the result of both Map and Reduce can be reused. Because of the Master node cannot perceive the distribution of data and the special of MR computing framework, these methods cannot be used directly in a distributed database. So we need to find a more efficient method for distributed database query.

3   The Proposed Method

3.1   Query Framework

Let $T = \{A1, A2, \ldots An\}$ denotes the relational table in the database, where Ai denotes column i in table T. ΔT denotes the increment data in table T which has the same schema with table T. A common query pattern could be expressed as:

$$Q = \prod_{group\_cols, agg\_col = fun(\text{expr})} (T_1 \times T_2 \times \ldots \times T_k) \qquad (1)$$

Existing computational models often generate a large amount of redundant computation while data is produced incremental. For example, let Tm and T_n is original table, ΔT_n and ΔT_m is incremental part of Tm and Tn. A selection query operation on T_n is $\sigma(T_n + \Delta T_n) = \sigma(T_n) + \sigma(\Delta T_n)$, only need to calculate $\sigma(\Delta T_n)$, because the part $\sigma(T_n)$ has been calculated. Similarly, the join query on two tables $(T_n + \Delta T_n) \times (T_m + \Delta T_m) = T_n \times T_m + \Delta T_n \times T_m + \Delta T_m \times T_n + \Delta T_m \times \Delta T_n$, just need to calculate incremental part $\Delta Tn \times Tm + \Delta Tm \times Tn + \Delta Tm \times \Delta Tn$, the scale of ΔT_n and ΔT_m is much smaller than T_n and T_m, so it can be considered that the calculation of the time complexity is close to $O(m + n)$, which is improved greatly compared with the original complexity $O(mn)$.

So in this paper, assume at a given time, tables $T_1, T_2, \ldots, T_k$ have increments $\Delta T_1, \Delta T_2 \ldots \ldots \Delta T_k$, the query result R is reconstructed based on the following equation:

$$R = f(R_{old}, R_{increment}) \qquad (2)$$

Where R_{old} denotes the historical result, which is stored in the each data nodes in distributed middleware architecture, without the need to calculate again. $R_{increment}$ is the incremental result which is usually far less than the historical result. f is the reconstruction function. The whole query framework in distributed middleware could be illustrated by Fig. 2.

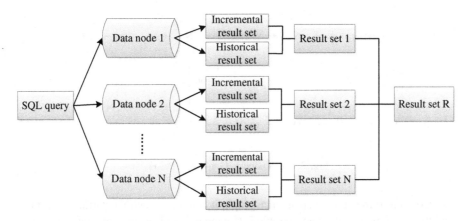

Fig. 2. The query framework

From the figure, it can be seen there are three key problems need to be addressed in the proposed framework. The first one is how to obtain the incremental result set efficiently; the second one is the result reconstruction based on the incremental and historical result sets in the each single data node. The last one is the result reconstruction of the different nodes. To address the first problem, since table T and its increments ΔT are split and distributed in the different nodes, it will take a lot of transmission cost to obtain $R_{increment}$. The effective data partition strategy will reduce such cost significantly. So at the next sections, we will first introduce the proposed data partition strategy, where the reference relationship between tables will be incorporated to generate more feasible data partition and distribution implementation. Then the result reconstruction methods will be introduced in detail.

3.2 Data Partition Strategy

Current database distributed middleware always partition each table based on itself. When data splits related to $R_{increment}$ reside in different nodes, significant overheads emerge that limit the throughput of the network and the whole systems. So in this paper, we propose to optimize the partition of data before the incremental query execution carried out based on the key-foreign key relationships.

Let take the TPC-H dataset as an example. TPC-H involves 8 tables. The dependence graph of the dataset could be obtained based on the key-foreign reference relationships as illustrated in Fig. 3. The nodes in the graph represent the tables. The alphabet in the node is the abbreviation of the table name. Between the tables, the arrow indicates the dependency and the join key.

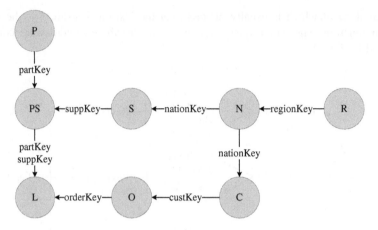

Fig. 3. Dependency Graph of TPC-H

According to the above dependence graph, it could be seen that starting from table R, all the paths eventually point to table L (Lineitem). So L is the table with maximum dependence relationship and connections with other table. So the TPC-H data set will be divided based on the attributes of table L. Other tables which depend on table L will be partitioned based on the join attributes, where tuples with the same join value will be divided into the same split. And those tuples with the same join value in the same spit are called a tuple group.

At the same time, it could be observed that in the process of partition, Table N has the reference attribute nationKey points to both table C and table S. That means there are two ways to divide N. So we need to partition the dependency graph into sub dependency graph in order to make it doesn't have one-to-many relationship or many-to-many relationship in each sub graph. The detailed information of the sub dependency graph generation is provided below.

```
Input: Dependence graph G
Output: Dependency graph set Gset
1. FOR each point V in G
2.    IF out degree of V > 1 THEN
3.       DEL all edge from V to other point
4. FOR each edge E in G
5.    put the point u, v in the same Graph Gn
6. put all sub graph Gn in Gset
7. RETURN Gset
```

According to the above algorithm, each table in the dataset will obtain the unique dependency relationship and has only one partition way. For example, the dependency graph of TPC-H in Fig. 3 could be divided as follows:

In the above two sub graphs, the out-degrees of table N and table L are zeroes. This indicates that table L and N do not refer to other tables, so we divide other tables using

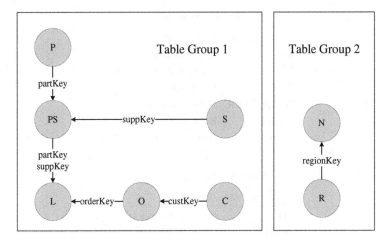

Fig. 4. Sub-dependency graph of TPC-H

the prime key of L and N. Specifically, take the left part of Fig. 4 as an example; table P, PS, O, S and C will be divided to different data node according to table L. We first divide table L into splits $\{L1, L2, \ldots Ln\}$ using hash functions based on its primary key and distribute the splits to distributed database nodes $\{D1, D2, \ldots, Dn\}$. Tuples of table O which have the same foreign key value as values in Li will be grouped into split Oi and assigned to the same data node as Li. The similar process is applied to the rest of the tables. For incremental data ΔT, use the same strategy to partition it. It is obvious that the proposed partition strategy could reduce the data transmission significantly since tuples of different tables with the same key-foreign key are located in the same data node.

3.3 Calculation of Incremental Result Set

In this section, the method to calculate the incremental result set will be presented. First, the log structure about the historical result set will be described, based on which the calculation of incremental result process will be introduced in detail.

3.3.1 Log

In order to reuse the historical query results, this method needs to write the log to save query related information. Log is stored in each data node in a distributed environment and each node has its own logs. Logs include historical query logs and data change logs. The format of the history query log is shown in Table 1. Once a query is executed, the corresponding information will be written to the log.

Data change log is used to record the change of the data in basic tables. Combined with historical data, the historical results could be updated based on the data change log and the latest query results could be generated. The format of data change log is illustrated in Table 2. When the basic table in the database is changed, we need update

Table 1. Historical query logs

Column name	Description
ID	Query record ID
SQL	Query SQL statement
TIME	Query time
DATA_NODE	Data node involved
TABLE	Basic table involved
RESULT	History result set table

Table 2. Data changing logs

Column name	Description
ID	Change records ID
TABLE	Change tables
TIME	Complete change time
COL_START	New data starting line
COL_END	New data end line
DATA_NODE	Data node involved

the historical results in the way introduced in the next section according to the corresponding log records.

3.3.2 Incremental Result Calculation

The incremental results are calculated in each data node respectively. When doing incremental updates, database middle-ware obtains the log information of the last execution of the given SQL through historical query logs. According to the time of the log to search for data change log, find if there is data change in the basic table after that time. If the basic tables during this period are not changed, incremental execution result set is null, that is $R_{increment} = NULL$. Otherwise, to perform the incremental update calculation by following steps:

Step 1: Obtain the log which records the latest query execution information from historical query logs.

Step 2: To find in the data change log according to the time of historical record and obtain the basic tables $T_1 \ldots T_m \in (T_1, T_2, \ldots, T_n)$ which is changed after this point of time.

Step 3: Assume that the Incremental of $T_k (k \in [1, n])$ is ΔT_k. According to the storage nodes of ΔT_k recorded in the data change log, the incremental join result is calculated in this data node, which is $\Delta R_k = (T_1 \times \ldots \times \Delta T_k \times \ldots T_n)$.

Step 4: Repeat step 3 until the update operations of all the basic table have been finished.

Step 5: Merge all incremental results ΔR_k and obtain the incremental results ΔR. Apply aggregate, sort and other operations to ΔR according the query demand to obtain the final result set $R_{increment}$.

3.4   Query Result Generation

According to the query framework illustrated in Fig. 2, the sub sets of each data node merge into the final result set. The result set of each sub node is merged with the historical result set R_{old} and the incremental result set $R_{increment}$. This section presents the details about the result set generation and storage.

Two kinds of merge operations mentioned above can be regarded as the same process on different data tables. The difference is that it is composed of two sub sets, or multiple sets. The merge operation of multiple subsets can be obtained by the iterative merge of two sub sets. So the method to merge two sub sets is introduced in the following. Two situations are discussed including query with and without aggregation operation.

Since the result subset is independent in non-aggregation query, for each subset, we just combine the subset of all parts directly. Assume that one subset is $R_1 = \{Tuple_{11}, Tuple_{12}, \ldots\ldots, Tuple_{1m}\}$, and another subset is $R_2 = \{Tuple_{21}, Tuple_{22}, \ldots\ldots, Tuple_{2n}\}$, then the merged result is $R = \{Tuple_{11}, Tuple_{12}, \ldots\ldots, Tuple_{1m}, Tuple_{21}, Tuple_{22}, \ldots\ldots, Tuple_{2n}\}$.

Query with aggregation operations need to identify the type of aggregation function in query, and then select the corresponding update function according to the different type. Let $T1$ denotes the increment result set, T denotes the original result set R_{old}. Commonly, $T1$ and T have the same grouping attributes and agg_col is the aggregation function column. COUNT represents the count function COUNT (*). The updates functions correspond to SUM, COUNT, AVG, MAX, MIN are shown in Table 3.

Table 3. Update function of historical result

Function name	Calculation formula
SUM	$T.agg\_col + T1.agg\_col$
COUNT	$T.agg\_col + T1.agg\_col$
AVG	$\frac{T1.agg\_col * T1.count + T.agg\_col * T.count}{T1.count + T.count}$
MAX	$Max(T1.agg\_col, T.agg\_col)$
MIN	$Min(T1.agg\_col, T.agg\_col)$

Assume the subset which need to be merged is $R_1 = \{Tuple_{11}, Tuple_{12}, \ldots\ldots, Tuple_{1k}\}$ and $R_2 = \{Tuple_{21}, Tuple_{22}, \ldots\ldots, Tuple_{2n}\}$, and the attributes in R_1 and R_2 is $(A_1, A_2, \ldots, A_n)$ where A_1 is the aggregation column. Suppose that $Tuple_{1n}.(A_2 \ldots A_n) = Tuple_{2n}.(A_2 \ldots A_n)$ and $n \in k$, obtain can get the merge result:

$$R = \{Tuple_1.(sum(A_1), A_2, \ldots A_n), Tuple_2.(sum(A_1), A_2, \ldots A_n) \\ ..Tuple_k.(sum(A_1), A_2, \ldots A_n)\} \tag{3}$$

The result set R could be obtained after each query execution, and the result set need to be stored as a historical result for the next query reuse. After query operation has been done in each data node, the historical query result set would be written for this query according the ID in historical log. The result set named RESULT_ [ID] is saved as a table at each node.

4 Experiment and Analysis

4.1 Experimental Environment

The experimental environment contains three database nodes, and a database middleware node. Each database node has a MySQL5.6 instance, the database middleware node deployment MyCat services, MyCat 1.3.02. Hardware configuration is IntelTM i7-3770CPU@3.40 GHz CPU, 8 GB RAM. The operating system is CentOS 6.5, SATA3 hard disk with the speed of 7200 rpm, Gigabit switch network. In this paper, we use the benchmark TPC-H as the test dataset. Six tables in TPC-H were divided into different data points by using key L_ORDERKEY in table L. While the table nations and region can be copied to each node as the non-changing tables. SF is used to control the scale of the original data, which is set to be 5. ΔSF is used to control the scale of incremental data. Different values of ΔSF are set to testify the performance of incremental query optimization in different situations. The experimental results have been reported when ΔSF is set to be 1, 2 and 5.

4.2 Efficiency Improvement of Data Partition

The performance of the proposed data partition method is testified in this experiment. The execution time for query Q1, Q2, Q6 Q13 by using the proposed method compared with the method with data partition in single table is illustrated in Fig. 5.

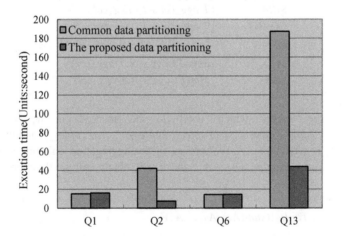

Fig. 5. The efficiency of different data partition strategies

From the figure, it is easy to see that the execution time of Q2 and Q13 by using the proposed data partition method is smaller than that by using the traditional method.

Take Q2 as example, the execution time is reduced percent. That is because there are 5 table join in Q2, and according to the division strategy in Sect. 2, tuples need to be joined are located on the same data node, which greatly reduce the data transmission quantity and improve query performance. The query uses only 17 % times of the common method. While the tables need to be joined in Q13 are only two, much less than Q2, still obtain nearly 3 times query efficiency improvement. The operation on Q1 and Q6 is about a single table, so there is no big difference on two query methods.

4.3 Incremental Query Overhead

In this section, we testify the performance of the proposed incremental query optimization method when $\Delta SF = 1$, $\Delta SF = 2$ and $\Delta SF = 5$ respectively. That is, compared to the original data scale, the incremental ratio is 20 %, 40 % and 100 %. We compare the execution time based on historical result set reuse and query directly on distributed database. Figure 6 provides the experimental results for Q2, where the results in an extreme case, that is $\Delta SF = 0$ is provided also which means there is no data change.

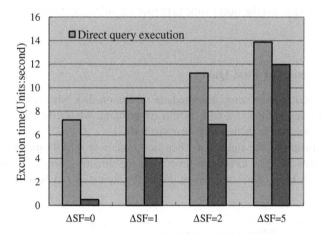

Fig. 6. Time consumption of TPC-H query-2

In Fig. 6, Q2 contains a lot of join operations, according to the steps in 2.3.3, when the increment part ΔT_k is small, the join cost could be reduced significantly. So when ΔSF is small, the advantage of incremental query optimization is more obvious. With the increase of ΔSF, a large number of join operations make the difference between incremental query and direct query operation small. We further provide the detailed results for other queries on TPC-H in Table 4.

In Table 4, query Q1 only involves one table. While it contains a large number of different types of aggregation functions, so the experimental result of Q1 readily verifies the effectiveness of the proposed incremental aggregation method. The query time is reduced to 20 %, 40 % and 55 % when ΔSF equal to 1, 2 and 5. Query Q6 is

Table 4. Time consumption of TPC-H query(Units: seccond)

Increment query		$\Delta SF = 0$	$\Delta SF = 1$	$\Delta SF = 2$	$\Delta SF = 5$
Q1	Direct query	15.822	18.356	20.875	29.871
	Incremental query	0.985	4.172	8.146	16.514
Q2	Direct query	7.259	9.102	11.245	13.875
	Incremental query	0.485	4.014	6.874	11.974
Q6	Direct query	14.301	18.125	20.754	27.481
	Incremental query	0.254	3.358	6.384	14.534
Q13	Direct query	43.906	51.879	64.875	90.145
	Incremental query	2.854	20.489	34.48	70.648

similar to Q1. While because the query results of Q6 contains only one tuple, the performance improvement is more obvious than that of Q1. The query time is reduced to 18 %, 30 % and 53 % in different incremental setting. Query Q13 contains sub query, when executing incremental query, we need to do incremental sub query update, followed with the incremental update to the entire query. The above process bring the extra I/O to write the intermediate results of sub query to disk, so the performance improvement is less and the query time is reduced to 40 %, 53 % and 77 % as shown in the table.

4.4   The Expenses of First Query

Our method need to save some intermediate results on disk when processing the first query, which bring some extra cost. In this experiment, we testify the performance of the first query execution in the proposed method.

Figure 7 illustrated the time cost when first executing 4 SQL queries based on the proposed framework. The execution time based on directly query execution has been also provided in Fig. 7 for comparison. From the figure, it can be seen that the time

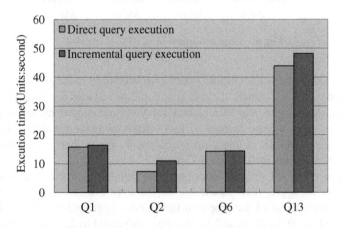

Fig. 7. Time consumption of the first query

increases about 20 % compared with directly query execution. The increased time is related to the size of result set. The result set of Q2 and Q13 are large, so take more times. The result set of Q6 only has one tuple, so the time spend is as same as directly query execution. For improving the performance of the query, the overhead of the first query could be totally acceptable.

5 Summary

This paper proposes a query execution optimization method based on incremental update in database distributed middleware. First, we provide a data partition strategy to reduce data transmission quantity during query operation. In addition, the proposed method proposes an incremental update query execution strategy and incremental intermediate result preservation mechanism in distributed environment for non-aggregate and aggregate query respectively. Finally, the experimental results conducted on the benchmark dataset test and verify the effectiveness of the proposed method. Further work is adjusting the storage of historical results according to the frequency of historical query in order to improve the efficiency of the query more.

Acknowledgments. This work was supported by the Fundamental Research Funds for the Central Universities and DHU distinguished Young Professor Program No. B201312.

References

1. Kobielus, J., Evelson, B., Karel, R., Coit, C.: In-database analytics: the heart of the predictive enterprise. Forrester Researc, Cambridge, USA (2009)
2. Amoeba Software Foundation. http://docs.hexnova.com/amoeba/index.html
3. Alibaba Group. Cobar architecture guide. http://code.alibabatech.com/docs/cobarclient/zh
4. MyCat Software Foundation. https://github.com/MyCATApache/Mycat-doc
5. QIHU 360 software Co. Atlas architecture guide. https://github.com/Qihoo360/Atlas
6. Transaction Processing Performance Council. TPC BENCHMARK H: Standard Specification Revision 2.17.0. http://www.tpc.org/tpch/spec/tpch2.17.0.pdf
7. Jin, C., Carbonell, J.G., Hayes, P.: ARGUS: Rete + DBMS = efficient persistent profile matching on large-volume data streams. In: Hacid, M.-S., Murray, N.V., Raś, Z.W., Tsumoto, S. (eds.) ISMIS 2005. LNCS (LNAI), vol. 3488, pp. 142–151. Springer, Heidelberg (2005)
8. Cheung, D.W., Han, J., Ng, V.T., Wong, C.Y.: Maintenance of discovered association rules in large databases: an incremental updating technique. In: Proceedings of the 12th International Conference on Data Engineering, pp. 106–114. IEEE Press, Piscataway (1996)
9. Ou, J.C., Lee, C.H., Chen, M.S.: Efficient algorithms for incremental Web log mining with dynamic thresholds. VLDB J. **17**(4), 827–845 (2008)
10. Borthakur, D.: The hadoop distributed file system: architecture and design. Hadoop Proj. Website **11**(2007), 21 (2007)
11. Dean, J., Ghemawat, S.: MapReduce: simplified data processing on large clusters. Commun. ACM **51**(1), 107–113 (2008)

12. Nykiel, T., Potamias, M., Mishra, C., Kollios, G., Koudas, N.: MRShare: sharing across multiple queries in MapReduce. Proc. VLDB Endowment 3(1–2), 494–505 (2010)
13. Elghandour, I., Aboulnaga, A.: Restore: Reusing results of MapReduce jobs. Proc. VLDB Endowment 5(6), 586–597 (2012)
14. Olston, C., Reed, B., Srivastava, U., Kumar, R., Tomkins, A.: Pig latin: a not-so-foreign language for data processing, In: Proceedings of the 2008 ACM SIGMOD International Conference on Management of Data, pp. 1099–1110. ACM (2008)

Distributed and Network-Based Computing

Coding-Based Cooperative Caching in Data Broadcast Environments

Houling Ji[1,2], Victor C.S. Lee[2], Chi-Yin Chow[2],
Kai Liu[3(✉)], and Guoqing Wu[1]

[1] School of Computer, Wuhan University, Wuhan 430070, China
{jihouling,wgq}@whu.edu.cn
[2] Department of Computer Science, City University of Hong Kong,
Kowloon Tong, Hong Kong
{csvlee,chiychow}@cityu.edu.hk
[3] College of Computer Science, Chongqing University, Chongqing 400000, China
liukai0807@cqu.edu.cn

Abstract. Data broadcasting has been commonly deployed in many emerging mobile applications such as intelligent transportation systems and location-based services because it is a scalable approach to disseminating information from the mobile support station (MSS) to a large population of mobile hosts (MHs). To provide timely data access and better data availability, MHs can store data items broadcast by the MSS in their local caches and share cached data items cooperatively among neighboring peers via peer-to-peer (P2P) communication. However, MHs which are not neighbors cannot cooperate even if they have each other's requested data item in their own caches. Network coding is a technique, by exploiting which multiple MHs can retrieve different requested data items from an encoded packet which encodes a number of data items broadcast by the MSS in a broadcast time unit. In this research work, we propose to apply network coding to enabling MHs which are not neighbors to cooperate indirectly. We devise two algorithms running at the MSS and MHs, respectively, for making encoding decisions and decoding requested data from encoded packets. We build the simulation model for performance evaluation and the simulation results demonstrate that the proposed solution not only increases the bandwidth efficiency of the limited downlink communication channel from the MSS to MHs but also enhances the system performance by reducing the latency in satisfying requests.

Keywords: Cooperative caching · Network coding · Data broadcast · Peer-to-peer communication

1 Introduction

Data broadcast is an effective way to disseminate data in an infrastructure network due to its scalability and flexibility. A typical infrastructure network

G. Wang et al. (Eds.): ICA3PP 2015, Part I, LNCS 9528, pp. 273–287, 2015.
DOI: 10.1007/978-3-319-27119-4_19

consists of mobile hosts (MHs) and a mobile support station (MSS). The MSS provides information access to MHs within a certain service area. Even when the number of MHs increases significantly, the data broadcast system can achieve decent performance. On-demand broadcast is one of the most promising data broadcast techniques [1]. In on-demand broadcast environments, MHs submit requests for data items to the MSS via the uplink communication channel. Outstanding requests are pended in the request queue at the MSS. In each broadcast time unit, the MSS selects the most rewarding data item to broadcast via the downlink communication channel according to a certain scheduling algorithm, such as FCFS (First Come First Served) [2], MRF (Most Requested First) [3] or RxW (Number of pending Requests Multiply Waiting time) [4], etc. Requesting MHs tune in to the downlink channel waiting for their requested data items. However, in this typical on-demand broadcast environment, the bandwidth efficiency of the downlink communication channel cannot be fully exploited because only those MHs requesting the same data item can be satisfied in one broadcast time unit.

Network coding [5], originally proposed in information theory, is a technique in which intermediate nodes can combine and forward the received data packets from multiple links [6]. It has attracted researchers' attention due to its potential for enhancing the system performance of both mobile ad hoc networks [7–10] and infrastructure networks [11–14]. Zhan et al. [14] proposed a generalized encoding framework to incorporate network coding into data scheduling algorithms for on-demand broadcast. Chen et al. [13] proposed two novel coding assisted algorithms called ADC-1 and ADC-2 which consider data scheduling, in addition to network coding. In on-demand broadcast environments, with network coding, it is possible for multiple MHs requesting different data items to be satisfied simultaneously (i.e. in one broadcast time unit) by utilizing their cached data items.

With the recent development of peer-to-peer (P2P) wireless communication technologies, a new information sharing paradigm appears. Mobile clients can not only retrieve information from the server, but also share information among peers. The peers of an MH refer to those MHs which reside in the transmission range of the MH. This kind of information sharing among peers is called cooperative caching [15]. Several cooperative caching schemes were proposed in mobile environments in the recent decade [16,17]. Ting and Chang [18] proposed an improved cooperative caching scheme called group-based cooperative caching (GCC) to enhance the performance of most group-based caching schemes by exchanging a bitmap data directory periodically among MHs. In our previous work [15,19,20], COCA (cooperative caching) and GroCoca (group-based cooperative caching) have been proposed for data dissemination in on-demand broadcast environments. In particular, COCA is a cooperative caching framework, in which P2P communication technology is used for information sharing among peers. GroCoca extends COCA based on the concept of a tightly-coupled group (TCG), which is a group of MHs that are geographically and operationally close to each other. Note that peers are not necessarily the members of the same TCG.

However, in any group-based cooperative caching schemes, it is difficult for MHs who are not neighbors to collaborate, even though they have in their caches the data items requested by others. Since network coding has the potential to exploit cached data items to serve different MHs, whether they are peers not, it is possible for network coding to bridge the gap between MHs residing out of each other's communication range and further improve the system performance of cooperative caching.

The main contributions of this paper are outlined as follows. First, we exploit the synergy between network coding and cooperative caching. On the one hand, network coding strengthens the information sharing paradigm of cooperative caching by enabling MHs residing in different groups to cooperate. Similar to the situation of cooperative caching, in case they have each other's requested data item in their own caches, the MSS can encode multiple requested data items in a single packet for broadcasting and the MHs can retrieve their own requested data items simultaneously in one broadcast time unit. Otherwise, the MSS has to broadcast the requested data items one by one in multiple broadcast time units. On the other hand, cooperative caching facilitates the operation of network coding. Consider a request submitted by an MH to the MSS. MHs in the same group of this requesting MH cannot have the requested data item in their own caches. Otherwise, they can simply share the data item with the requesting MH. Therefore, the MSS does not need to consider the cache contents of the MHs in the same group of the requesting MH in making the encoding decisions. Second, we introduce a novel system model by incorporating network coding into the cooperative caching framework. In particular, we outline the communication protocol of the system and propose two algorithms. One is running at the MSS to encode a number of requested data items in a single packet for broadcasting. The other is running at MHs for multiple MHs to decode the packet with their cached data items and retrieve different data items to satisfy their requests in a single broadcast time unit. Last, we build the simulation model for performance evaluation. The simulation results demonstrate that incorporating network coding into cooperative caching makes the data scheduling more flexible, further increases the bandwidth efficiency of the downlink communication channel, and significantly improves the system performance in terms of reducing data access latency.

The rest of this paper is organized as follows. A novel coding-based cooperative caching system is introduced and two algorithms are proposed in Sect. 2. We build the simulation model in Sect. 3. The performance evaluation is conducted in Sect. 4. Finally, we conclude this work in Sect. 5.

2   Coding-Based Cooperative Caching

In this section, we introduce a novel cooperative caching system called Coding-based Cooperative Caching, and then propose two cooperative caching algorithms. One algorithm is running at the MSS to encode and broadcast data packets to MHs, and the other algorithm is running at MHs to receive and decode data packets broadcast by the MSS.

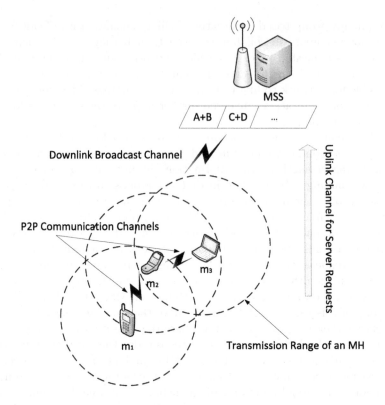

Fig. 1. System architecture

2.1 Architecture

The system architecture shown in Fig. 1 consists of one MSS and a number of MHs. Suppose there are $NumMH$ MHs $m_1, m_2, ..., m_{NumMH}$ and the MSS contains a database of $NumData$ data items $d_1, d_2, ..., d_{NumData}$. Each MH has a local cache storing data items received from either the MSS or neighbouring MHs. In the system, both the MSS and MHs have certain communication area determined by their respective transmission range. One MH can communicate with others residing in its own communication area. All the MHs are in the communication area of the MSS, which means that MHs can always communicate with the MSS wherever they move. Each MH does not manage its cache alone. Instead, multiple MHs share their cached data items cooperatively via P2P communication. There are two P2P communication paradigms: P2P broadcast and P2P point-to-point. All MHs within the transmission range of the source MH receive the broadcast message in P2P broadcast communication, while there is only one destination MH for the source MH in P2P point-to-point communication. IEEE 802.11 and CSMA/CA (Carrier Sense Multiple Access with Collision Avoidance) are adopted in the wireless communication channels to transmit data and avoid collisions.

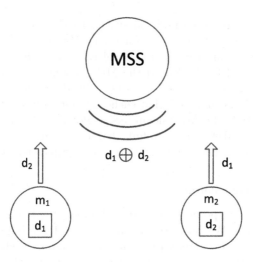

Fig. 2. A network coding example

Communication Protocol. If an MH cannot find the desired data item in its local cache, it broadcasts a request for the data item to its peers through P2P broadcast communication. The peers which cache the required data item send a *reply* message back to the requesting MH through P2P point-to-point communication. Within a timeout period, if the requesting MH receives the *reply* messages from its peers, the peer from which the MH receives the first reply is selected as a target peer. Then, the requesting MH sends a *retrieve* message, which informs the target peer to reply the data item through P2P point-to-point communication. When the target MH receives the *retrieve* message, it sends the required data item to the requesting MH. After the timeout period, if no peer sends back a *reply* message, the requesting MH will submit a request to the MSS for the data item. The MSS maintains a request queue for outstanding requests submitted by MHs. According to a certain scheduling algorithm, the MSS fetches data items from the database and makes the decision whether to encode them or not based on the information of both cached items and required items of each MH. In each broadcast time unit, the MSS broadcasts either an encoded or unencoded data item via the downlink channel to serve outstanding requests. The objective is to utilize the limited broadcast bandwidth efficiently.

The timeout period is initially set to the round-trip time of P2P communication channel such that timeout is computed by: $\frac{request\ size\ +\ reply\ size}{BW_{P2P}} \times \varphi$ initially, where BW_{P2P} is the bandwidth of P2P communication channel and φ is a congestion factor. Then, for each P2P broadcast, the requesting MH records the duration τ from the moment the requesting MH broadcasts the request to its peers to the moment a *reply* message is received for continuously adjusting the timeout period. Accordingly, the timeout period is computed by: $\bar{\tau} + \varphi' \sigma_\tau$, where $\bar{\tau}$ and σ_τ are the mean and standard deviation of τ, respectively, while φ' is the system parameter to weight the standard deviation in computing the timeout period.

Therefore, there are three possible situations that an MH may encounter when requesting a data item. (1) Local Cache Hit: If the required data item can be found in its local cache, it is a local cache hit. Otherwise, it is a local cache miss. (2) Global Cache Hit: If the MH encounters a local cache miss, it attempts to enlist its neighbouring peers for help. If any peer caches and replies the required data item, it is a global cache hit. Otherwise, it is a cache miss. (3) Server Request: If the MH encounters a global cache miss, it will send a server request to the MSS via the uplink channel. Then, the MH will tune in to the downlink broadcast channel to retrieve the required data item.

2.2   Proposed Algorithms

Network coding has the potential to further improve the bandwidth efficiency of the downlink channel. We verify this claim with the following example. Assume there is one MSS and two MHs m_1 and m_2 in the system as shown in Fig. 2. m_1 and m_2 are not peers. Suppose the MSS has a database with two data items d_1 and d_2. m_1 caches d_1 and requires d_2, while m_2 caches d_2 and requires d_1. Since both m_1 and m_2 cannot find their required data items in their own caches or from their peers, they need to submit requests for their required data items to the MSS. In the conventional broadcast strategy, the MSS needs to broadcast twice (d_1, d_2 in sequence) to satisfy both requests. In contrast, with network coding, the MSS only needs to broadcast one encoded data packet $d_1 \oplus d_2$ (bit-by-bit XOR operation) to satisfy both requests. When m_1 receives $d_1 \oplus d_2$, it can get d_2 by $d_1 \oplus (d_1 \oplus d_2)$. m_2 can get d_1 in a similar way.

First, we propose an algorithm running at the MSS (the pseudocode is shown in Algorithm 1). This algorithm is used for the MSS to schedule, encode and finally broadcast requested data items to MHs. When a request arrives at the MSS, it is inserted into the tail of the request queue. In order to illustrate the impact of network coding on the system performance, we adopt simple first-come-first-served (FCFS) scheduling algorithm at the server and encode at most two data items in a packet. The MSS seeks to maximize the number of requests to be satisfied in a broadcast unit, on the basis of satisfying the request pending at the head of the request queue first. Note that a request is satisfied if the data packet to be broadcast consists of the requested data item in an unencoded form or the requested data item is encoded with another data item which exists in the requesting MHs cache. A requested data item will be encoded with another requested data item only if the encoded packet can serve more requests.

Then, we propose an algorithm running at MHs (the pseudocode is shown in Algorithm 2). This algorithm is used for MHs to receive and decode data packets broadcast by the MSS. The MSS maintains a view of the cache content of all MHs in the system by tracing the requests submitted by MHs and data items broadcast to serve the requests. Since the cache size of MHs is limited and MHs may cache data items obtained from its peers, the data items in an MH's cache may change from time to time, leading to inconsistency between the MSS view and the real cache content of MHs. We adopt a lazy approach to minimize the maintenance cost of the view. The MSS schedules and encodes according to its

---

Algorithm 1. MSS Scheduling and Encoding Algorithm at Each Broadcast Time Unit

---

1: Fetch the request, i.e., $R(m_i, d_j)$, at the head of the request queue Q, where m_i is the MH sending the request and d_j is the data item m_i requests;
2: $MaxNum \leftarrow 0$;
3: $ClientsToSatisfy \leftarrow \phi$;
4: $DataToBroadcast \leftarrow d_j$;
5: **for** each $R(m_k, d_l) \in Q$ **do**
6:    **if** $d_l = d_j$ **then**
7:       $MaxNum \leftarrow MaxNum + 1$;
8:       $ClientsToSatisfy \leftarrow ClientsToSatisfy \cup \{m_k\}$;
9:    **end if**
10: **end for**
11: Suppose the cache content of m_i is C_i in the MSS view;
12: **for** each $d_p \in C_i$ **do**
13:    $ClientsToSatisfyEncode \leftarrow \phi$;
14:    $MaxNumEncode \leftarrow 0$;
15:    **for** each $R(m_r, d_t) \in Q$ **do**
16:       Suppose the cache content of m_r is C_r in the MSS view;
17:       **if** $d_j = d_t$ and $d_p \in C_r$ **then**
18:          $MaxNumEncode \leftarrow MaxNumEncode + 1$;
19:          $ClientsToSatisfyEncode \leftarrow ClientsToSatisfyEncode \cup \{m_r\}$;
20:       **else if** $d_p = d_t$ and $d_j \in C_r$ **then**
21:          $MaxNumEncode \leftarrow MaxNumEncode + 1$;
22:          $ClientsToSatisfyEncode \leftarrow ClientsToSatisfyEncode \cup \{m_r\}$;
23:       **end if**
24:    **end for**
25:    **if** $MaxNumEncode > MaxNum$ **then**
26:       $MaxNum \leftarrow MaxNumEncode$;
27:       $ClientsToSatisfy \leftarrow ClientsToSatisfyEncode$;
28:       $DataToBroadcast \leftarrow d_j \oplus d_p$;
29:    **end if**
30: **end for**
31: Broadcast the data packet in $DataToBroadcast$ and prefix the MH identifiers in $ClientsToSatisfy$;

---

cache view. When the MSS broadcasts an encoded packet, it prefixes a list of MH identifiers of intended recipients who should be able to decode the packet and retrieve the requested data items. If an MH in the list can decode the packet and obtain the required data item, it notifies the MSS to remove its request pending in the request queue. Otherwise, if the MH cannot decode the packet, which implies that the MSS view is inconsistent with the real cache content of MH, the MH will send the identifier of data items in its cache to the MSS to update the MSS view. The request of the MH remains in the request queue waiting for the MSS's next service.

Algorithm 2. A Requesting MH m_i's Action When Receiving Data Packet *DataToBroadcast* Broadcast by the MSS

1: Suppose the request of m_i is $R(m_i, d_j)$, pending in the request queue Q. The cache content of m_i is C_i. MHs intended to be served by the current broadcast is *ClientsToSatisfy*;
2: **if** *DataToBroadcast* is an unencoded packet, i.e., d_k **then**
3:    **if** $d_j = d_k$ **then**
4:       Obtain the requested data item d_j and and notify the MSS to remove $R(m_i, d_j)$;
5:    **else**
6:       Ignore d_k and wait for the MSS's next service;
7:    **end if**
8: **else if** *DataToBroadcast* is an encoded packet, i.e., $d_k \oplus d_p$ **then**
9:    **if** $d_j = d_k$ **and** $d_p \in C_i$ **then**
10:       Obtain the requested data item d_j by $d_p \oplus (d_k \oplus d_p)$ and notify the MSS to remove $R(m_i, d_j)$;
11:    **else if** $d_j = d_p$ **and** $d_k \in C_i$ **then**
12:       Obtain the requested data item d_j by $d_k \oplus (d_k \oplus d_p)$ and notify the MSS to remove $R(m_i, d_j)$;
13:    **else if** $m_i \in$ *ClientsToSatisfy* **then**
14:       Notify the MSS to update its view and wait for the MSS's next service;
15:    **else**
16:       Ignore $d_k \oplus d_p$ and wait for the MSS's next service;
17:    **end if**
18: **end if**

---

3   Simulation Model

We construct a simulation model as described in Sect. 2 in C++ using CSIM [21]. In our model, there is an MSS and $NumMH$ MHs. Each MH has a cache of size $CacheSize$. MHs move in an area of 3000 m × 3000 m. The service range of the MSS covers the whole area. The MSS broadcasts data items to MHs via downlink communication channel with a bandwidth of $BW_{downlink}$. MHs send requests to the MSS via uplink channel with a bandwidth of BW_{uplink}. The P2P communication channel is used for an MH to communicate with its peers with the bandwidth of BW_{P2P}.

3.1   Client Model

The MHs move in the service area of the MSS. MHs can communicate with each other within the transmission range of $TranRange$. MHs can be divided into several motion groups, each with $GroupSize$ MHs. The mobility of MHs in a group is based on the *reference point group mobility model* [22], in which there is a logical motion center as the reference for the whole group. The group mobility is based on the *random waypoint mobility model* [23]. The logical group center randomly chooses its destination and moves towards it at a speed from a uniform distribution $U(v_{min}, v_{max})$. When it reaches the destination, it rests for a second and randomly chooses another destination. Then it moves towards the destination and changes the speed according to the same uniform distribution.

The request model is a closed model, in which an MH can request another data item only after its last request has been satisfied. The size of a request is *ReqSize*. The *reply* and *retrieve* message sizes of the COCA communication protocol are *RepSize* and *RetSize* respectively. The timeout parameters are φ and φ'. The data access pattern follows the Zipf distribution, with a skewness parameter θ, where $0 \leq \theta \leq 1$. When θ equals 0, it is a uniform distribution. As θ gets larger, the accesses to data items get more skewed. The time period between two consecutive requests by an MH follows an exponential distribution with a mean of one second. Note in this paper, the local processing time at MHs is considered negligible, because the cost of decoding using bit-by-bit XOR operation is low [13].

Table 1. Default parameter settings

Parameters	Values
$NumMH$	300
$GroupSize$	3
$NumData$	1000
$TranRange$	100 m
$CacheSize$	100 data items
θ	0.6
$DataSize$	32 kb
$ReqSize, RepSize, RetSize$	512 b
$BW_{downlink}$	10 Mbps
BW_{uplink}	1 Mbps
BW_{P2P}	5 Mbps
v_{min}	1 m/s
v_{max}	5 m/s
φ, φ'	10, 3

3.2   Server Model

There is one MSS in the system, which serves the MHs in the area of $3000\,m \times 3000\,m$. The database in the MSS maintains $NumData$ data items and the size of each data item is $DataSize$. Outstanding requests are pended in the request queue at the MSS. In each broadcast tick, the MSS schedules the request with FCFS policy and encodes the requested data items with the purpose of satisfying as many requests as possible. The key parameters and their default values in the simulation are shown in Table 1.

4   Performance Evaluation

4.1   Performance Metrics

We use the following metrics to evaluate the performance of the coding-based cooperative caching.

Server Request Ratio. Server Request Ratio is the percentage of the number of server requests to the total number of requests:

$$\frac{Total\ Number\ of\ Server\ Requests}{Total\ Number\ of\ Requests} \times 100\,\%$$

Server Broadcast Productivity. Server Broadcast Productivity is the percentage of the number of server requests satisfied to the total number of packets broadcast by the MSS:

$$\frac{Total\ Number\ of\ Server\ Requests\ Satisfied}{Total\ Number\ of\ Packets\ Broadcast\ by\ the\ MSS}$$

It describes the average number of requests satisfied by one data packet.

Encoded Packet Broadcast Ratio. Encoded Packet Broadcast Ratio is the percentage of the number of encoded packets broadcast by the MSS to the total number of packets broadcast by the MSS:

$$\frac{Total\ Number\ of\ Encoded\ Packets\ Broadcast\ by\ the\ MSS}{Total\ Number\ of\ Packets\ Broadcast\ by\ the\ MSS} \times 100\,\%$$

It describes the effectiveness of network coding in the system.

Mean Request Queue Length. It describes the mean number of requests pending in the request queue.

Average Server Request Latency. It describes the waiting time from the moment an MH sends a server request to the MSS to the moment its request is finally satisfied.

Average Data Access Latency. It describes the average time period from the moment an MH wants a data item to the moment the desired data item is obtained.

4.2   Simulation Results

In this section, we present the performance results of the coding-based cooperative caching. We compare the performance of Coding-based GroCoca (denoted as GCC-NC) with non-cooperative caching scheme (denoted as NCC), non-cooperative caching scheme with network coding (denoted as NCC-NC), COCA scheme (denoted as CC), COCA scheme with network coding (denoted as CC-NC), and GroCoca (denoted as GCC). The results are collected obtained after the system reaches a steady state, in which all caches of MHs are filled with data items. The experiment continues until each MH generates over 2000 requests after the warmup period.

Effect of Cache Size. First, we study the effect of cache size on system performance by increasing the cache size from 20 to 180 data items. Figure 3(a) shows that the server request ratio decreases. This is because the local cache hit and global cache hit ratio both increase. The cache hit ratios increase because a larger cache size leads to a higher chance for MHs to obtain data items locally or from peers. As shown in Fig. 3(b), the schemes with network coding have better performance in broadcast productivity than their non-coding versions. In Fig. 3(c), the encoded packet broadcast ratio increases in NCC-NC and CC-NC because larger cache size leads to higher chance for network coding. As depicted in Fig. 3(d), the schemes with network coding have shorter request queue length than their non-coding versions because network coding can satisfy more requests in one broadcast time unit and thus abate the broadcast pressure. This also leads to less average server request latency of the schemes with network coding as shown in Fig. 3(e). In Fig. 3(f), the average data access latency decreases, because the time cost is much lower for an MH to obtain a data item from its local cache or from its peers than from the MSS. CC utilizes cooperative caching, so it has less average data access latency than NCC. GCC outperforms CC because GCC increases the chance for an MH to obtain the required data item in its TCG. All the schemes with network coding have better average data access latency than the non-coding versions because network coding can significantly reduce the server request latency.

Effect of Access Pattern. Next, we study the effect of access pattern on system performance by increasing the skewness parameter θ from 0 to 1. As θ gets larger, MHs have more common interest and so the chance for an MH to find desired data items in its local cache and its peers' caches becomes higher. Therefore, the number of requests sent to the MSS decreases, leading to the decrease of the server request ratio as shown in Fig. 4(a). The schemes with network coding have better performance in broadcast productivity than their non-coding versions as shown in Fig. 4(b). Figure 4(c) describes the encoded packet broadcast ratio decreases as θ gets larger. Skewed data access patterns degrades the efficiency of network coding. As depicted in Fig. 4(d), the schemes with network coding have shorter request queue length than their non-coding versions.

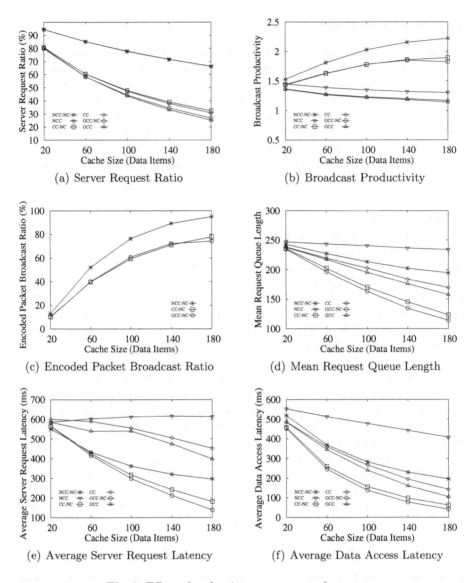

Fig. 3. Effect of cache size on system performance

So the schemes with network coding have less average server request latency as depicted in Fig. 4(e). In Fig. 4(f), the average data access latency decreases, because the server request ratio decreases and the time cost is much lower for an MH to obtain a data item from its local cache or from its peers than from the MSS. All the schemes with network coding have better average data access latency than the non-coding versions because network coding can significantly

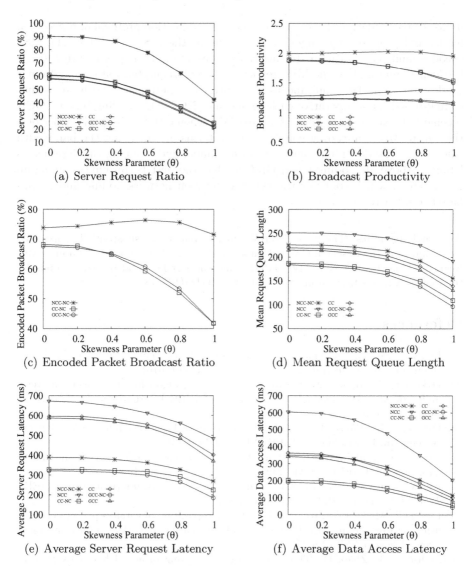

Fig. 4. Effect of access pattern on system performance

reduce the server request latency. GCC-NC has the best performance in terms of average data access latency among all the schemes.

5   Conclusion

In this paper, we have introduced a novel cooperative caching architecture by incorporating network coding into on-demand broadcast environments. MHs who are not neighbors can collaborate indirectly by utilizing their own cached data items. In particular, we have outlined the communication protocol of the system model and proposed two algorithms running at the MSS and MHs. The MSS encodes multiple data items to satisfy as many requests as possible in a single broadcast time unit, while MHs retrieve different requested data items from a single encoded packet simultaneously. Finally, the experimental results show that coding-based non-cooperative caching scheme (NCC-NC), coding-based COCA scheme (CC-NC) and coding-based GroCoca scheme (GCC-NC) all outperform their respective non-coding counterparts in terms of enhancing the bandwidth efficiency of the downlink communication channel and reducing the data access latency. Above all, coding-based GroCoca has the best performance among all the schemes, which confirms the synergy between network coding and group-based cooperative caching.

Acknowledgments. The work described in this paper was substantially supported by a grant from the Research Grants Council of the Hong Kong Special Administrative Region, China [Project No. CityU 115312] and the Fundamental Research Funds for the Central Universities (Grant No. 106112015CDJZR185518).

References

1. Liu, K., Lee, V.: On-demand broadcast for multiple-item requests in a multiple-channel environment. Inf. Sci. **180**(22), 4336–4352 (2010)
2. Dykeman, H., Ammar, M.H., Wong, J.: Scheduling algorithms for videotex systems under broadcast delivery. In: Proceedings of IEEE International Conference on Communications (ICC) (1986)
3. Dykeman, H., Wong, J.: A performance study of broadcast information delivery systems. In: Proceedings of IEEE INFOCOM (1988)
4. Aksoy, D., Franklin, M.: R× w: a scheduling approach for large-scale on-demand data broadcast. IEEE/ACM Trans. Netw. **7**(6), 846–860 (1999)
5. Ahlswede, R., Cai, N., Li, S.Y., Yeung, R.W.: Network information flow. IEEE Trans. Inf. Theory **46**(4), 1204–1216 (2000)
6. Lun, D.S., Médard, M., Koetter, R.: Efficient operation of wireless packet networks using network coding. In: Proceedings of International Workshop on Convergent Technologies (IWCT) (2005)
7. Mohseni, M., Zhao, D.: Time and power scheduling in an ad hoc network with bidirectional relaying and network coding. Wirel. Commun. Mob. Comput. **15**, 459–474 (2013)
8. Roh, H.T., Lee, J.W.: Network coding-aware flow control in wireless ad-hoc networks with multi-path routing. Wirel. Netw. **19**(5), 785–797 (2013)
9. Wu, Y., Chou, P.A., Kung, S.Y.: Minimum-energy multicast in mobile ad hoc networks using network coding. IEEE Trans. Commun. **53**(11), 1906–1918 (2005)
10. Zhang, P., Lin, C., Jiang, Y., Fan, Y., Shen, X.: A lightweight encryption scheme for network-coded mobile ad hoc networks. IEEE Trans. Parallel Distrib. Syst. **25**(9), 2211–2221 (2013)
11. Birk, Y., Kol, T.: Coding on demand by an informed source (iscod) for efficient broadcast of different supplemental data to caching clients. IEEE/ACM Trans. Netw. **14**(6), 2825–2830 (2006)

12. Ali, G., Meng, Y., Lee, V., Liu, K., Chan, E.: Performance improvement in applying network coding to on-demand scheduling algorithms for broadcasts in wireless networks. In: International Multi-Conference on Computing in the Global Information Technology (ICCGI) (2014)

13. Chen, J., Lee, V., Liu, K., Ali, G.M.N., Chan, E.: Efficient processing of requests with network coding in on-demand data broadcast environments. Inf. Sci. **232**, 27–43 (2013)

14. Zhan, C., Lee, V.C., Wang, J., Xu, Y.: Coding-based data broadcast scheduling in on-demand broadcast. IEEE Trans. Wirel. Commun. **10**(11), 3774–3783 (2011)

15. Chow, C.Y., Leong, H.V., Chan, A.T.: Grococa: group-based peer-to-peer cooperative caching in mobile environment. IEEE J. Sel. Areas Commun. **25**(1), 179–191 (2007)

16. Sailhan, F., Issarny, V.: Cooperative caching in Ad Hoc networks. In: Chen, M.-S., Chrysanthis, P.K., Sloman, M., Zaslavsky, A. (eds.) MDM 2003. LNCS, vol. 2574, pp. 13–28. Springer, Heidelberg (2003)

17. Yin, L., Cao, G.: Supporting cooperative caching in ad hoc networks. IEEE Trans. Mob. Comput. **5**(1), 77–89 (2006)

18. Ting, I.W., Chang, Y.K.: Improved group-based cooperative caching scheme for mobile ad hoc networks. J. Parallel Distrib. Comput. **73**(5), 595–607 (2013)

19. Chow, C.Y., Leong, H.V., Chan, A.: Cache signatures for peer-to-peer cooperative caching in mobile environments. In: Proceedings of International Conference on Advanced Information Networking and Applications (AINA) (2004)

20. Chow, C.Y., Leong, H.V., Chan, A.T.: Group-based cooperative cache management for mobile clients in a mobile environment. In: Proceedings of International Conference on Parallel Processing (ICPP) (2004)

21. Schwetman, H.: Csim19: a powerful tool for building system models. In: Proceedings of Conference on Winter Simulation (WSC) (2001)

22. Hong, X., Gerla, M., Pei, G., Chiang, C.C.: A group mobility model for ad hoc wireless networks. In: Proceedings ACM International Workshop on Modeling, Analysis and Simulation of Wireless and Mobile Systems (1999)

23. Broch, J., Maltz, D.A., Johnson, D.B., Hu, Y.C., Jetcheva, J.: A performance comparison of multi-hop wireless ad hoc network routing protocols. In: Proceedings of Annual ACM/IEEE International Conference on Mobile Computing and Networking (MobiCom) (1998)

Usage History-Directed Power Management for Smartphones

Xianfeng Li$^{(\boxtimes)}$, Wen Wen, and Xigui Wang

School of Electronic and Computer Engineering, Peking University,
Shenzhen 518055, China
lixianfeng@pkusz.edu.cn, {wenwen,wangxigui}@sz.pku.edu.cn

Abstract. Smartphones are now equipped with powerful application processors to meet the requirement of performance demanding apps. This often leads to over-provisioned hardware, which drains the battery quickly. To save energy for battery-powered smartphones, it is necessary to let the processor run at a power-saving state without sacrificing user experience. Android has implemented a set of CPU governors by leveraging dynamic voltage and frequency scaling (DVFS) according to the computational requirements of apps. However, they commonly adopt very conservative policies due to limited information, therefore leaving considerable energy reduction opportunities unexplored; or they are not responsive to user interactions, leading to poor user experiences. In this work, we start from an important observation on the repetitive patterns of smartphone usage for each individual user, and propose UH-DVFS, a usage history-directed DVFS framework leveraging on this observation. UH-DVFS can identify repetitive user transactions, and store their execution history information within a table. When such a user transaction is launched again, the table is consulted for an appropriate CPU frequency adaptation to reduce the energy consumption of the user transaction without sacrificing user experience. We have implemented the proposed framework on Android smartphones, and have tested it with real-world interaction-intensive apps. The results show that our framework can save energy from 10 % to 36 % without affecting the quality of user experiences.

Keywords: Smartphone · Android · Energy reduction · DVFS · User transaction

1 Introduction

The Application Processors (AP) used in today's smartphones are chasing the CPUs in PC domain to meet the increasing performance need of smartphone apps. For example, ARM Cortex A15 has adopted almost all architectural features (superscalar, out-of-order execution, branch prediction, multithreading, etc.) that were only found in traditional high-performance processors. However, unlike desktop computing, smartphones are battery-driven, and these

© Springer International Publishing Switzerland 2015
G. Wang et al. (Eds.): ICA3PP 2015, Part I, LNCS 9528, pp. 288–302, 2015.
DOI: 10.1007/978-3-319-27119-4_20

power-hungry features will drain the battery very quickly. To address this problem, some power-saving techniques, such as dynamic voltage and frequency scaling (DVFS), are commonly employed in mobile processors. The DVFS technique where the clock frequency of a processor is decreased to allow a correspongding reduction in the supply voltage [9]. According to the formula (1), where P is the dynamic power dissipated by the chip, C is the capacitance of the transistor gates, f is the operating frequency and V is the supply voltage. Here α shows the switching activity. a processor operating at a lower frequency will consume significantly less power.

$$P = \alpha C V^2 f \tag{1}$$

A difficult problem with DVFS-enabled processors is when and how to adapt the processor's frequency, such that the energy consumption is reduced without sacrificing the performance requirement of an application or system. In the context of smartphones, as the typical usage pattern is bursty user interactions, predicting the performance requirement becomes even more difficult. Therefore, exploiting the DVFS mechanism on a smartphone appropriately is a non-trivial issue. In current Android systems, a set of power management policies are enforced to make use of DVFS. However, for both the default policy named *Ondemand Governor* [10] and the *Interactive Governor*, a naive algorithm is used to adapt the processor's frequency: anytime the CPU utilization exceeds a specified threshold UP_THRESHHOLD, the CPU frequency is scaled up to the highest level. This conservative mechanism is clearly biased towards performance instead of energy, it might be the case that the computational capability is over-provisioned, and a less aggressive frequency setting might be enough for the computational requirement.

As the interactive usage of the smartphone contributes about half of its energy consumption [7], and current techniques such as the Android DVFS governors are not exploiting the energy-saving opportunities sufficiently, there is a strong need to investigate more aggressive and accurate techniques. In this work, we focus on the optimization of interactive energy consumption for smartphones, and propose a novel DVFS-based power management framework exploiting the repetitive patterns of the usage history.

Our work starts with a key concept called *user perceived transaction* (UPT), which is firstly defined in [16]. A UPT begins with a user input on the device (e.g., a screen touching or scrolling) and ends with the last display update when all the visible contents affected by this user input are drawn. Typically, an input from the end user may trigger a series of display updates, and the response time of an interactive session has a great impact on the quality of the user experience. Despite the importance of UPT latencies, there is little research that studies the tradeoff between user transaction performance and its energy consumption. By measuring the energy consumption of a smartphone at different usage scenarios, we gain two observations. First, different usage scenarios may have very different computational requirements. Second, for the same usage scenario that repeatedly happens, the UPTs exhibit very similar CPU usage patterns.

Based on these observations, we propose a usage history-directed DVFS scaling framework called UH-DVFS. The basic idea is to first capture the frequently invoked usage scenarios, and measure its computational requirement in the course of its execution, which will be recorded in a cache-like data structure, called User Transaction Table (UTT). Each time a user perceived transaction is triggered and detected, the UTT is queried for its computational requirement in its previous invocations. Upon a match, the recorded computational requirement will be used for making appropriate DVFS scaling, such that the performance can be met with the lowest possible energy consumption. We have implemented this framework on Android-powered smartphones, and have validated it with real-world interaction-intensive apps. The results show that our framework can save energy from 10 % to 36 % without affecting the quality of the user experience.

The rest of the paper is organized as follows. Section 2 surveys the related work. Section 3 describes the proposed framework in details. Section 4 evaluates the effectiveness of the framework with experimentation. Finally, Sect. 5 draws conclusions on this paper.

2   Related Work

Battery life of smartphones has been an important research topic in recent years. The first step for power and energy optimization is to understand how energy is consumed on smartphones. For this purpose, some research groups have studied usage patterns of smartphones by users to guide power optimization [6, 14]. Another thread is to study the power/energy consumption of apps and smartphone components with power modeling [12, 17] and power estimation [11] techniques. They have not only provided us with useful tools, but also have obtained some very important insights on power/energy consumption of smartphones.

For power/energy optimization, different techniques have been proposed for various hardware components of the smartphone. As our work in this paper is mainly concerned with CPU energy reduction, we only survey the related work on this component, which is one of the primary sources of energy consumption. Dynamic voltage and frequency scaling (DVFS) has been a common technique used for processor energy reduction. For example, the power management component in Linux implements some DVFS schemes like the *ondemand governor* [10], which increases the clock frequency when CPU load is above some threshold.

There are two metrics for evaluating the quality of a DVFS scaling technique: the *responsiveness* and *appropriateness*. Responsiveness means responding to the change of performance requirement in real-time, and appropriateness means that the scaled frequency is neither over-provisioned nor inadequate for the performance requirement. The techniques proposed in [8, 15] are able to adapt to the user activity quickly. They scale to the max frequency indiscriminately when the user is interacting with the phone, and lower the frequency back to the idle level while users are thinking. The problem is that they are not able to predict the frequency appropriate for the user interaction, and conservatively scale to the max frequency, which often wastes considerable energy. Another approach tries to predict the appropriate frequency with a resource-driven DVFS [5], which explores the correlation between CPU utilization and other resources. But this resource-driven scheme is unable to raise the clock frequency immediately in response to a user interaction, as it needs a time window to measure and compute the actual performance requirement. This is quite unfavorable for smartphone interactions, which are often bursty (lasting only a short amount of time). Therefore it does not satisfy the *responsiveness* metric.

Unlike these techniques, our approach meets *responsiveness* and *appropriateness* simultaneously, it can quickly scale the frequency to an appropriate level for repetitive user interactions by exploiting history information.

3   Usage History-Directed DVFS Scaling

In this paper, we propose a usage history-directed DVFS scaling framework (UH-DVFS), which run repetitive user perceived transactions with a capped frequency best matching its computational requirement estimated from past execution histories.

3.1   Key Concepts and Principles

We first lay the foundation of our work by introducing a set of important concepts, notations, and key principles backing our framework.

Activity. It is one of the primary components offered by Android application framework; an activity provides a screen with which users can interact in order to do something, such as dial the phone, take a photo, send an email, or view a map.

User Perceived Transaction (UPT). It is first introduced in [16], as shown in Fig. 1. A UPT begins with the user's manipulation of the device (e.g., a screen touching or scrolling) and ends with the last display update when all the visible contents affected by this user input are drawn. Typically, an input from the end user may trigger a series of display update, and the response time of an interactive session has a great impact on the quality of user experience. Note we also use the term **user transaction** for short in some places in this paper.

Usage Scenario. It characterizes a UPT with the activity and the corresponding user action on this activity. It can be viewed as an abstraction of a UPT, without details on the procedure of the UPT. A usage scenario can be formally represented as a tuple of $< activity, action >$.

CPU Load. It is defined as the percentage of non-idle CPU time in a duration. Modern operating systems all provide mechanisms and tools for reporting the CPU utilization in real-time. Usually a CPU load above 80 % indicates that the CPU is running very heavy tasks. CPU load is also called **CPU utilization** in the literature.

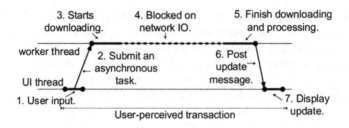

Fig. 1. An example of user perceived transaction ([16])

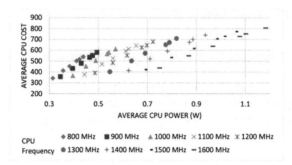

Fig. 2. Correlation between CPU cost and average CPU power ([13])

Application Cost. It is defined as the multiplication of the CPU load and the CPU frequency [4]. Intuitively, it quantifies the computational requirement of an application (or a segment of it) without the assumption of a specific frequency. Note this is only a rough estimation, as frequency is not the only aspect that decides the performance of a CPU, other factors, like the memory behavior, also has an impact. It is also called **CPU cost** in some literature [13].

Normalized CPU Load. Although CPU load is a good metric for characterizing how busy the CPU is, it does not fully exhibit the potential of the CPU. For example, a user may think that 100 % CPU load means the CPU is unable to meet the performance requirement of the application, but if this CPU load is reached with the CPU operating under a low frequency, we may easily satisfy the application by increasing the CPU frequency. Therefore, we use a more meaningful metric, called normalized CPU load, in many situations in this work. It is defined as follow (2) equation.

$$U_{norm} = U * (f_c/f_{max}) \tag{2}$$

where U is the original CPU load, f_c is the operating CPU frequency under which U is measured, f_{max} is the highest frequency offered by the CPU, and U_{norm} is the normalized CPU load. For example, if the max CPU frequency f_{max} is 1000MHz, but it runs at 300 MHz and get a 40 % CPU load, then the normalized CPU load will be calculated as $40\% \times \frac{300MHz}{1000MHz} = 0.12$ normalized CPU load.

Our work is based on the following principles.

(1) Invariance of CPU Cost. The CPU utilization roughly scales linearly with the CPU core frequency for executing the same amount of work (e.g., a UPT), therefore, the CPU cost is maintained as a constant irrespective of the CPU frequency. For example, when the CPU frequency is increased by 50%, its CPU load will decrease for about 50% compared to its original number, and the CPU cost is the same for the two settings.

(2) Correlation Between CPU Cost and Power Cost. The authors in [13] conducted a comprehensive test, and the results show that with the CPU cost unchanged, lowering the CPU frequency can result in more power efficient execution without sacrificing user experiences, as shown in Fig. 2.

3.2 Observations on CPU and Power Behaviors of UPTs

We first conduct experiments by observing the CPU and power behaviors of user perceived transactions. We connect a Xiaomi-2S smartphone's battery interface to a Monsoon power monitor to collect the power trace of the smartphone, and use a tool offered by Qualcomm to capture the CPU behavior. Figure 3 is the result on a sequence of continuous user transactions.

We first observe that the CPU frequency is adapted in a sub-second granularity, as shown in Fig. 3(b). The green line on the upper side is the trace for the actual frequency, and the blue line on the lower side shows the corresponding CPU load. As expected, the Ondemand governor of Android raises the frequency swiftly whenever it detects a high CPU load, such that sufficient CPU computation capability is provided for a heavy application load. More closely, we observe that most often, the CPU frequency simply jumps to the highest level f_{max} by the Ondemand governor of Android system. But in reality, not all user transactions need such a high frequency, therefore wasting unnecessary energy.

But on the other hand, knowing the actual computational requirements of a user transaction beforehand is a non-trivial problem. First, a user transaction is just a short burst of execution, any reactive techniques that adjust the CPU frequency according to real-time guaging of the CPU load is unrealistic. On the other hand, predictive techniques that use the information of the past execution time window will not work either, because the CPU loads of different user transactions are different, and it would be meaningless to make decisions based on the recent execution.

In stead of using reactive or native predictive methods, we propose a novel predictive method, which is based on the execution histories of the same usage scenario. This approach is based on an important observation: **the computational need for the same usage scenario is relatively stable for most usage scenarios**. As shown in Fig. 3(c), there are three usage scenarios (in color blue, red, and orange respectively). For each scenario, we repeat its user transaction for a couple of times. We can make two observations from them: first, each individual usage scenario has different CPU load; second, within the

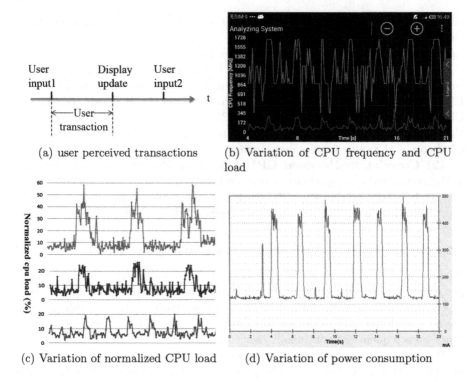

(a) user perceived transactions

(b) Variation of CPU frequency and CPU load

(c) Variation of normalized CPU load

(d) Variation of power consumption

Fig. 3. CPU and power behaviors of user perceived transactions

same usage scenario, the CPU loads of different user transactions are quite similar. Therefore, we can use the history of the same usage scenario to predict its computational requirement of its current instance.

3.3 The UH-DVFS Scaling Framework

To use the execution history of a usage scenario, the first step is to record it. As defined in Sect. 3.1, a usage scenario is characterized by a tuple $<$ $activity, action >$, where an $action$ triggered by the user is enforced on the foreground $activity$. The action can be a touch on a UI component, a scrolling of the screen, a back navigation, etc. Figure 4 shows different situations of usage scenarios with a popular app, Tencent News client.

User Transaction Table. To record these usage scenarios, we use a data structure called User Transaction Table (UTT), as shown in Fig. 5. Each entry of the UTT table is a usage scenario, i.e., a $< activity, action >$ tuple. For fast access, the UTT is designed as a hash table, where the names of the $activity$ and $action$ in combination formulate the hash index into UTT. Each time the trigger of a user transaction is identified (called $running\ user\ transaction$), The $activity$ name and $action$ name of the transaction are used to calculate a hash id, which

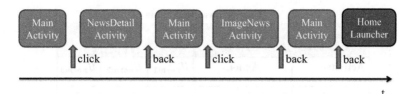

click   back   click   back   back

(a) User transactions of different Activities

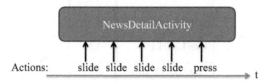

Actions: slide slide slide slide   press

(b) User transactions of the same Activity

Fig. 4. Example of usage scenarios

will be the index to access the hash table, then a comparison with the *activity* and *action* fields in the corresponding UTT entry is needed for verification. If it is a hit, then the three fields representing the most recent user transactions of this usage scenario are consulted.

Each recent user transaction field contains the normalized CPU load (as defined in Sect. 3.1) for the respective user transaction. This normalized CPU load was calculated by reading the CPU utilization data and the CPU frequency recorded by Linux/Android when the transaction was detected. We use normalized CPU load for ease of comparison among different transactions. When the three transaction fields are consulted, the maximum of them is taken for predicting the computational requirement of current transaction. Note this is a relatively conservative policy to reduce the risk of underestimation, but it is much better than blindly taking f_{max} of the CPU as the capped frequency for executing current user transaction. Then the capped frequency f_c to be used for the running user transaction can be calculated by following the formula in the definition of the normalized CPU load in Sect. 3.1: $max(U_{norm1}, U_{norm2}, U_{norm3}) = 0.8 * (f_c/f_{max})$, and we will have $f_c = max(U_{norm1}, U_{norm2}, U_{norm3}) * f_{max}/0.8$. Here 0.8 instead of 1.0 is taken to be the target CPU load for the running user transaction, as a CPU load of 1.0 means that the CPU might be too busy to meet the computational requirement, and 0.8 is a high, but safe CPU load for getting a low capped frequency.

The Framework. Based on the idea of UTT, the UH-DVFS framework is presented in Fig. 6. It consists of the application layer and the system layer. We design a background service running at the application layer, which has two basic functionalities: dynamic instrumentation and resource monitoring. To capture the user input and the corresponding foreground activity for accessing the corresponding UTT entry, a dynamic instrumentation module is designed,

User Transaction Table

Usage Scenario		Three Recent User Transactions		
Activity	Action	U_{norm1}	U_{norm2}	U_{norm3}
Activity1	Tran1(click)	0.6	0.55	0.58
	Tran2(touch slide)	0.41	0.45	0.43
	Tran3(press back)	0.33	0.35	0.31
Activity2	Tran4(click)	0.37	0.38	0.4
	Tran5(touch slide)	0.55	0.50	0.52
......				

Fig. 5. User transaction history table

which contains the code that we want to inject at runtime when the foreground application calls the API of Android Framework. The resource monitor samples the CPU load as well as the CPU frequency at 8 Hz through the file system in the kernel, and their product is normalized with respect to the max frequency. The UH-DVFS adaptor at the system layer is the key component of the framework. Its user transaction monitor captures the data of user transaction, including Activity information and user's UI manipulation events, which will be formulated as an index into the UTT for consulting its execution history. Upon a hit, the capped frequency for current running user transaction can be calcuated using the formulate described above. Otherwise, the conservative Ondemand Governor of Android will take responsibility, which will set the capped CPU frequency directly up to f_{max}. Eventually, the capped frequency f_c will be enforced on the CPU by the DVFS library and the underlying driver offered by Android kernel.

3.4   Dynamic Instrumentation

As most modules in the framework depends on the dynamic instrumentation, we elaborate on how it works. First of all, its goal is to provide facilities to capture the foreground Activity information and the user manipulation events on that Activity. In addition, we need to detect the display update to determine the user transaction interval. Figure 7 presents the overview of the instrumentation framework. With it in place, the original application will callback the instrumentation framework to get user transaction data when a call to the Android framework API for running this transaction is triggered. From the user's perspective, it appears that each time a user transaction is a launched, it simultaneously produces an output of user transaction data automatically. This instrumentation hardly has any negative effect on normal running of the original applications. It

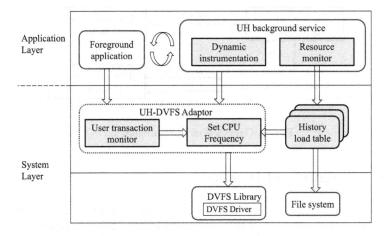

Fig. 6. The framework of UH-DVFS

simply hooks methods to the Android framework at runtime. We make use of the open source project named Xposed [3] for this purpose. In Android, Zygote is the root Java process, which is responsible for forking other Java processes. When the framework is installed, an extended app_process is copied to /system/bin. This extended startup process adds an additional jar to the classpath and calls methods from there at certain places. So we can hook or replace the method that we want to monitor and inject our own methods. We illustrate how the respective data are captured when a user transaction is triggered.

UI Operation Events. When the user interacts with the foreground activity, the UI touch events are dispatched by the method *dispatchTouchEvent* of the Activity class. Therefore, we hook this method to get motion events of the user interaction by which we can distinguish user operations between "clicking" and "sliding" on the activity.

UI Upate Events. Android system updates UI using a message queue model. Messages are placed in a queue and the UI thread loops indefinitely, processing messages from the head of the message queue. Therefore, we can detect UI update events by monitoring the message queue of the main thread, and catch the *invalidate()* invocations at the same time.

Foreground Activity Information. We need this information to identify a user transaction. Usually, an Android app consists of a set of Activities, and each one has its own life cycle. When an Activity comes into the foregound, it stays at the running state to receive user interactions. The entry point of this state transition is the *onResume()* invocation of Activity class in the Android framework. Therefore, we can inject our code at this place ,such that when any Activity invokes this API function, we can detect this Activity switching, and get the current foreground Activity in time.

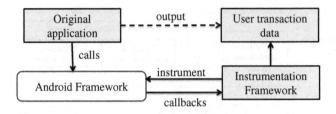

Fig. 7. Overview of instrumentation

4   Experiments and Results

To validate the effectiveness, we have implemented the framework on real smartphone devices, and use a set of popular Android apps for evaluation.

4.1   Experimental Setup

Our experiments are conducted on a Xiaomi-2S smartphone running Android 4.1
OS. It is equipped with Qualcomm Snapdragon APQ8064 CPU, which supports
14 different frequency levels. we measure the energy consumption of Xiaomi-2s
with the Power Monitor of Monsoon solutions [2], which samples power data
at a rate of 5 KHz. The experiment setup is shown in Fig. 8. The phone is connected to both the power monitor and a laptop running Windows via USB at
the same time. We disable the phone's USB battery charge to avoid any sources
of inaccuracies in the experiment. With this experimental setup, we measure the
energy consumption under the UH-DVFS framework and the default Android
DVFS governor respectively for comparison on energy efficiency. To avoid user-
introduced differences, we automate the test processes by using the Monkeyrunner [1] tool, which can record and replay the same experimental scenes
for UH-DVFS and the default DVFS governor automatically without manual
intervention.

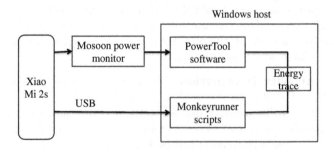

Fig. 8. Experimental setup

4.2   Energy Saving and Performance Evaluation

In this part, we evaluate the effectiveness of the proposed UH-DVFS scheme on energy savings with a set of interactive apps. The energy savings for different apps are presented in Fig. 9. It shows that our UH-DVFS approach can save the smartphone energy from 10 % to 36 % over the default Governor policy of Android. Note that this result has excluded the energy consumption of the screen, as our objective is for CPU energy reduction. We achieve this by first keeping the phone in a totally idle state with its screen on, and get the energy consumption of the screen. Then we turn the screen off, and perform the automated experiments described earlier. After obtaining the energy data, the earlier tested screen energy consumption is deducted from the overall energy consumption, and the rest amount of energy is used for comparison. Figure 9 also shows variations of energy savings for different application scenarios, because different apps have different CPU load. Usually the lower the actual application performance requirement, the higher the energy saving by our framework. This perfectly matches our objective on this work: avoid consuming unnecessary energy for application scenarios that do not need a powerful CPU setting.

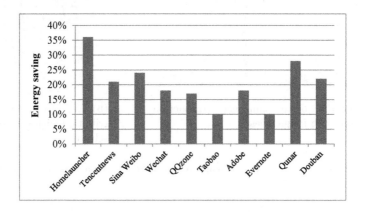

Fig. 9. Energy savings of different applications

There is one concern to be addressed: does UH-DVFS achieve energy reduction at the cost of poor performance? Or in other words, is the potential slowdown with a relatively lower capped CPU frequency sacrifing user experiences? To answer this question, we use a commonly used metric, the average frame rates (FPS,Frames Per Second) to decide whether the user experience on a user transaction is satisfied. We measured the instant frame rates using the tool Adreno Profiler offered by Qualcomm. Adreno Profiler can capture the real-time FPS whenever the phone's screen update is detected by connecting to the smartphone with adb command. We measured the average FPS by repeating the same user transaction at least ten times. Our UH-DVFS framework dynamically adjusts the capped frequency of user transactions. We take the Tencent News app as an example to study the relationship between the average FPS and the capped frequency. In the experiment, we calculate the average FPS of user transactions on Tencent News app's *MainActivity* with different capped frequencies, and the result is presented in Fig. 10. From Fig. 10(a), we can see that the average FPS begins to drop when the capped frequency is lower than 1134 M, which means the performance of user experience can not be satisfied with frequencies lower than this threshold. All frequencies higher than or equal to 1026 M make no negative impact on the quality of user experience for this usage scenario. Figure 10(b) shows the distribution of capped frequencies when Tencent News app is executed under UH-DVFS for a duration of 10 min. The result shows that the portion of capped frequencies lower than or equal to 1026 M only accounts for 7 %, which indicates that the energy saving by UH-DVSF is indeed achieved without sacrificing user experience in most cases.

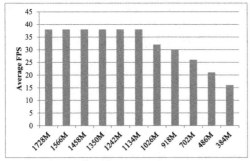

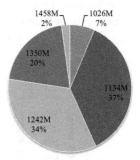

(a) Average FPS of the same user transaction with different cap frequencies

(b) Cap frequencies distribution with UTA-DVFS scheme

Fig. 10. FPS and Cap frequency measurement on the user transaction of Tencent news application

To further get an idea on how serious the average FPS is affected by CPU frequencies, we measured the average FPS under different frequencies for all the apps used earlier. The result is plotted in Fig. 11. It can be observed that the threshold frequencies meeting the quality of user experiences (e.g., 30 FPS) for different user transactions are also different, which means an adaptive DVFS scaling for different scenarios is needed.

We have measured the extra CPU overheads incurred by the UH-DVFS scheme, as it only add hooks at very few places, such as the triggering of a user transaction, it incurs very little performance overhead. According to our measurement, the CPU load of UH-DVFS is only around 1 % during an active user transaction, and it is nil during the period without user input.

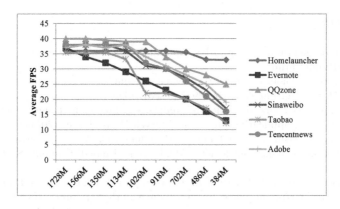

Fig. 11. Average FPS of different user transactions

5   Conclusions

Battery life is an important concern for smartphone users. Existing DVFS-based techniques for CPU energy reduction are either not responsive (sacrificing user experience), or too conservative (wasting batter power). In this paper, we propose UH-DVFS, a novel usage history-directed DVFS framework to save energy for interactive operations, which are a primary source of smartphone energy consumption. UH-DVFS is motivated by an important observation that the repetitive occurrences of the same usage scenario usually have quite stable and predictable performance behaviors. By leveraging this observation with a User Transaction Table (UTT), we are able to set the capped frequency for recurring user transactions to a lower frequency level without sacrificing user experiences. We have evaluated the effectiveness of UH-DVFS with real-world applications. Under UH-DVFS, the smartphone XiaoMi-2s achieves considerable energy reduction (ranging from 10 % to 36 %) compared to the default DVFS governor of Android. In future research, we will take account of the GPU and network together, as GPU is also a major energy-consuming component, and we believe that the integrated CPU-GPU DVFS is a new direction to study further. In addition, we will study the user transactions with more factors to refine the model, such that the refined user transactions are more stable than our current model in terms of performance.

Acknowledgments. This work is supported by the grant of Shenzhen municipal government for basic research on Information Technologies (No. JCYJ20130331144 751105).

References

1. Android monkeyrunner. http://developer.android.com/tools/help/MonkeyRunner.html
2. Monsoon power monitor. https://www.msoon.com/
3. Xposed. https://github.com/rovo89/XposedBridge
4. Bai, Y.: Memory characterization to analyze and predict multimedia performance and power in an application processor. Marvell White Paper (2011)
5. Chang, Y.-M., Hsiu, P.-C., Chang, Y.-H., Chang, C.-W.: A resource-driven dvfs scheme for smart handheld devices. ACM Trans. Embed. Comput. Syst. (TECS) **13**(3), 53 (2013)
6. Falaki, H., Mahajan, R., Kandula, S., Lymberopoulos, D., Govindan, R., Estrin, D.: Diversity in smartphone usage. In: Proceedings of the 8th International Conference on Mobile Systems, Applications, and Services, pp. 179–194, ACM (2010)
7. Kang, J.-M., Seo, S.s., Hong, J.W.-K.: Usage pattern analysis of smartphones. In: 2011, 13th Asia-Pacific Network Operations and Management Symposium (APNOMS), pp. 1–8, September 2011
8. Kim, S., Kim, H., Hwang, J., Lee, J., Seo, E.: An event-driven power management scheme for mobile consumer electronics. IEEE Trans. Consum. Electron. **59**(1), 259–266 (2013)
9. Le Sueur, E., Heiser, G.: Dynamic voltage and frequency scaling: the laws of diminishing returns. In: Proceedings of the 2010 International Conference on Power Aware Computing and Systems, pp. 1–8. USENIX Association (2010)
10. Pallipadi, V., Starikovskiy, A.: The ondemand governor. In: Proceedings of the Linux Symposium, vol. 2, pp. 215–230, sn (2006)
11. Pathak, A., Hu, Y.C., Zhang, M.: Where is the energy spent inside my app?: fine grained energy accounting on smartphones with eprof. In: Proceedings of the 7th ACM European Conference on Computer Systems, pp. 29–42, ACM (2012)
12. Pathak, A., Hu, Y.C., Zhang, M., Bahl, P., Wang, Y.-M.: Fine-grained power modeling for smartphones using system call tracing. In: Proceedings of the Sixth Conference on Computer Systems, pp. 153–168, ACM (2011)
13. Pathania, A., Jiao, Q., Prakash, A., Mitra, T.: Integrated cpu-gpu power management for 3d mobile games. In: 2014 51st ACM/EDAC/IEEE Design Automation Conference (DAC), pp. 1–6, IEEE (2014)
14. Shye, A., Scholbrock, B., Memik, G.: Into the wild: studying real user activity patterns to guide power optimizations for mobile architectures. In: Proceedings of the 42nd Annual IEEE/ACM International Symposium on Microarchitecture, pp. 168–178, ACM (2009)
15. Song, W., Sung, N., Chun, B.-G., Kim, J.: Reducing energy consumption of smartphones using user-perceived response time analysis. In: Proceedings of the 15th Workshop on Mobile Computing Systems and Applications, pp. 20, ACM (2014)
16. Zhang, L., Bild, D.R., Dick, R.P., Mao, Z.M., Dinda, P.: Panappticon: event-based tracing to measure mobile application and platform performance. In: 2013 International Conference on Hardware/Software Codesign and System Synthesis (CODES+ ISSS), pp. 1–10, IEEE (2013)
17. Zhang, L., Tiwana, B., Qian, Z., Wang, Z., Dick, R.P., Mao, Z.M., Yang, L.: Accurate online power estimation and automatic battery behavior based power model generation for smartphones. In: Proceedings of the Eighth IEEE/ACM/IFIP International Conference on Hardware/Software Codesign and System Synthesis, pp. 105–114, ACM (2010)

Application Streaming: A Mobile Application Distribution Method

Wang Yang[✉], Lei Jia, and Guojun Wang

School of Information Science and Engineering, Central South University,
Changsha 410083, China
{yangwang,jialei0396,csgjwang}@csu.edu.cn

Abstract. The traditional App Store based application distribution model is facing some challenges such as poor manageability, mobile device storage capacity limits and frequent application updates. We propose an application streaming based mobile application distribution method to address these challenges. In our method, application is installed, updated and uninstalled in server. User simply select the application to execute and it is been executed in a streaming way. This method enable manageability for mobile application distribution and more personalized mobile application experience. In addition, this method can help solve the storage capacity constraint of mobile device and the frequent application updates. We also use local cache mechanism to save network traffic and improve application loading time. Evaluation show that cache mechanism can save 84.9 % traffic compared with the non-caching streaming and 43.9 % traffic than App Store based application distribution method.

Keywords: Mobile application distribution · Transparent computing · Application streaming · Cache mechanism · Network file system

1 Introduction

In recent years, the rapid development of mobile Internet technology and the popularity of smart mobile devices have led the booming of mobile application development. The number of mobile applications worldwide has exceeded three million [1]. Mobile applications are diversified that they nearly cover every aspect of our daily life such as work, social, entertainment and so on. Development of these mobile applications made possible for people to work more efficiently and greatly enrich people's daily life. According to statistic [2], people spend more time on mobile application than desktop.

Most of the existing application distribution models are App Store based. Application developers have to submit or update their applications to different application distribution platform such as Google Play and Apple's App Store. The users need to search, download and install applications from application distribution platform before using them. However, the App Store based application distribution models are faced with the following challenges:

G. Wang et al. (Eds.): ICA3PP 2015, Part I, LNCS 9528, pp. 303–316, 2015.
DOI: 10.1007/978-3-319-27119-4_21

- Poor Manageability. In the BYOD (Bring your own device) [3] trends, employees are encouraged to bring personal owned mobile devices to their workplace to access privileged company information and applications. The manageability is required for BYOD's adoption which is not satisfied with the current application distribution model.
- Storage Capacity Constraints. The increase of mobile device storage capacity cannot keep pace with the increasing number of mobile applications. In the current application distribution model, application is treated as a minimum unit which stays in the mobile devices storage. Users have to download the entire application and install it on mobile device storage even when just use try some features of an application. So when constrained by storage, users have to manually decide which existed applications to be uninstalled to make space for the new application installation.
- Timeliness of Mobile Application Update. Mobile Application Developer update their mobile application due to adding new features, preparing bug or security vulnerabilities. However in the current application distribution model, applications are updated at user's will. This result in coexistence of many old versions of an mobile application which may bring bad user experience and even security threats. This phenomena bothers a lot of mobile application developers. They have to find way to encourage users to update the mobile applications.
- Poor Cross-Device User Experience. In traditional application distribution model, users have to install and migrate the application data manually when using a new mobile device. This process is boring and time-consuming. Consistent user experience across different mobile devices cannot be provide.

To address these challenges, we propose an application streaming based mobile application distribution method. We adopt the ideas of separation of computation and storage, streaming based code execution inspired by the idea of transparent computing [4].

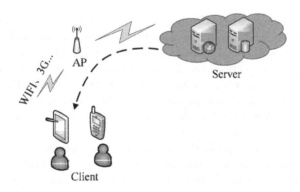

Fig. 1. Application streaming based mobile application distribution model

Figure 1 shows the application streaming based mobile application distribution method. Users can search and subscribe mobile applications according to their preference. Users don't need to consider storage capacity of mobile devices and size of mobile applications. Different from the traditional application distribution model, the subscribed application will not be installed in the mobile device. Subscribed application is actually installed in the server and present its icon to the screen of user. The application is dynamically streaming from server and cached locally in the mobile device on user's demand. When application developer update the application, server will update the mobile application in background without any user involvement. Personal data generated by users during the application usage are stored in the server. Even when the user loses or replaces his/her mobile device, these data can still be retrieved.

The rest of the paper is organized as follows: Section 2 shows some related work. Section 3 provides the system design of application streaming based mobile application distribution. Section 4 details the implementation of mobile application streaming. Section 5 evaluates the performance of application streaming in several ways. Finally, Sect. 6 make a summary and provide an outlook on future work.

2   Related Work

Transparent Computing [4] is a new computing paradigm that provide spatio-temporal extension on Von Neumann architecture. [5] proposed a distributed 4VP+ platform. Based on this platform, the operating system, application, and data are treated as resource stored in server and the client fetch resources from server in the form of data blocks through the network, implementing application streaming. Inspired on transparent computing, SMILE [6] was proposed to implement streaming management of applications and data. In SMILE, the applications and data of user are stored in server, when user click application icon on client, the applications and data will be downloaded and installed on client before he execution of application.

Application streaming is mainly implemented through the technology called application virtualization in enterprise environment. Application virtualization separates application and operating system underling logical so that application can be delivered to users as a service on demand. Currently, the main solutions of application streaming include such as XenApp [7], ThinApp [8]. But none of the above solutions targets on mobile application distribution.

Currently the most widely used network file system is NFS. [9] has proposed a mechanism called FS-Cache. It can provide a interface between local cache and network file system to achieve interpretability. [10] proposes a wireless-friendly network file system called RFS which adopts state vector to record the various operations of each file. RFS can work even when there is no network connection. It will synchronize with server according to the records of the state vector when the network connection is restored.

Now there exists several cache replacement strategies considering application access pattern. [11] proposed some strategies to optimize cache replacement

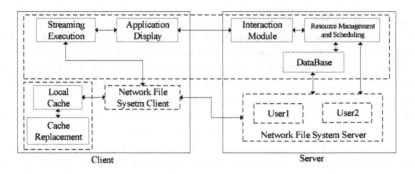

Fig. 2. System architecture

strategies such as the forecasting with bus fixes, and full associative simulation based trees to improve the hit rate of the replacement strategy. [12] proposed a self-adjusting, low-overhead adaptive cache replacement algorithm which responds to changing access pattern dynamically to improve the performance of cache replacement strategy.

Furthermore, there has been substantial prior research on the topics of partitioning and remote execution. The CloudClone [13] partition applications uses a framework that combines static program analysis with dynamic program profiling, and executes remote analysis using a virtual machine. The MAUI [14] requires programmers to annotate methods as REMOTABLE to tell the runtime process to perform remote code execution.

3   System Design

Application streaming based mobile application distribution method aims to make application distribution more timely for mobile application developers, and to remove the restrictions to users such as storage capacity of mobile device.

3.1   System Architecture

Figure 2 shows the architecture of application streaming system. The system adopts client/server model.

3.2   Client

Client includes the following components: application display module, application streaming execution module, network file system which with local cache mechanism.

– Application display module mainly displays the application icons into screen so that users can search, subscribe and use the applications that they interested in.

– Application streaming execution module. Since applications are installed on the server, when user want to use these applications, the mobile device will load applications, personal data on user's demand over the wireless network from the server through this module.
– Local cache mechanism module. Cache is designed to speed up network file system(NFS) access. Constrained by the storage capacity of mobile devices, cache replacement also is used to improve the unitization of cache storage space.

3.3 Server

Server includes the following components: interaction module, resource management and scheduling module.

– Interaction module locate on the server front-end, and listen request from the client. After receiving a request, interaction module call the resource management and scheduling module for processing. After processing by the management and scheduling module, server send response message to the client.
– Resource management and scheduling module include application installation module and management module. Application installation module take responsibility for application installation on the server while management module stored application information, user information and their relationship in the database.

4   Implementation

We implemented application streaming based on Android System. In Android System, the process of application install is as follows:

1. Extract application resources (including program files, configuration files, resource files and etc.) from the apk file and store them into the specified directory.
2. Parse configuration file to fetch the application metadata (including package name, application icon, application version, required permissions and component information etc.), and add it to PackageManager which is a package manager in Android system that used to manage installed application information.
3. Display application icon on launcher and bind intent which is generated according to the application metadata. Intent is used to describe the desired action and related data, through which we can launch the desired application component.

In traditional mode, application would be downloaded from internet and install locally, and the application resources, user data are stored in local storage. In contrast, application is installed in server in application streaming while the application resources and user data are treated as resources, stored and managed in server. When receiving user interaction, related resources could be load from the server via network on demand.

4.1   Resource Management

In the application streaming, resources are stored and managed via network file system and database in the server.

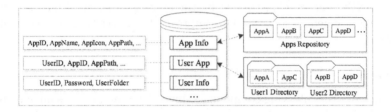

Fig. 3. Resource management

As shown in Fig. 3, resources in server mainly includes the following categories:

1. Application Repository. Application Repository includes all application installation packages in streaming distribution platform. All the packages are stored in Application Repository directory, and all the application information are stored and managed via database. The application information mainly includes application ID, application icon, application version, required permissions, component information and application storage directory etc.
2. User Information. In application streaming, server identifies different client by its user. When new user register to the platform, server will generate a personal user directory, and meanwhile store and manage user information via database. The user information mainly includes account, password and user directory etc.
3. User Applications and User Data. In application streaming, user applications and user data are stored and managed in user directory via network file system. The user directory will be mount to client via network file system when user login, and the resources in server will be loaded to client on demand when application is executed.

4.2   Application Streaming

User Interface. The user interface in client is organized to two screens. One is called Home Screen (HS) which show all the applications subscribed by user, and user can click any application icon displayed in HS to launch the application in a streaming way. The other is called Market Screen (MS) which show all the available applications that can be subscribed by user, and user can search, subscribe applications in MS.

As shown in Fig. 4, after a user login, the client can retrieve the information about the applications that have been subscribed by user. Then the client mount

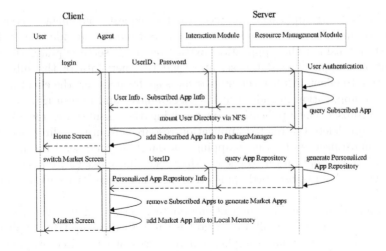

Fig. 4. User interface organization

the user directory via network file system and store subscribed applications'
metadata locally. Meanwhile, the client display all subscribed application icons
on HS.

When user switch to the MS, the client request and display the metadata of
the available applications of the markets on user's demand.

Application Subscribe/Unsubscribe, Update and Push. In the application streaming, user install and uninstall applications in the form of subscribe
and unsubscribe. As shown in Fig. 5, the client send request to server to subscribe, unsubscribe application.

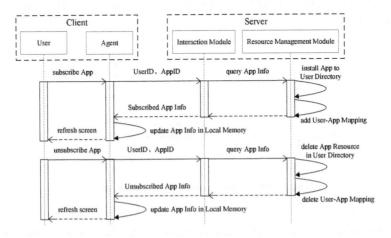

Fig. 5. Application subscribe and unsubscribe

For subscribing application, on receiving the request from client, server fetch the related apk file, extract application resources from the apk file to user directory. After finishing the application extraction, then server update the user-application mapping via database, and send the metadata of the subscribed application to client. After receiving the message from server, the client add the subscribed application metadata to PackageManager and refresh HS.

For unsubscribing application, on receiving the unsubscribe request from client, server delete the related application resources from user directory. Then server remove user-application mapping via database, and send the metadata of unsubscribed application to client. After receiving message from server, the client remove the unsubscribed application metadata from PackageManager and refresh HS.

In application streaming, application update is performed in server. For application update, server fetch all users who has subscribed the updated application and then update the related application resources in user directory and send updated application metadata to related client in real-time, and then synchronously refresh HS.

Application push is also supported by application streaming. Administrator can choose the application to be pushed to specific users from web UI, server will install application for users and send the metadata of the pushed application to correspondent client in real-time. Client will refresh HS similar to application subscription.

4.3   Application Streaming Execution

In the application streaming, the launch of application is different from traditional application distribution mode. Application icon shown on the HS is only part of application metadata that stored in client, and the other application resources are store in server rather than client. Application resources will be loaded from the server through network file system on demand when application is being executed.

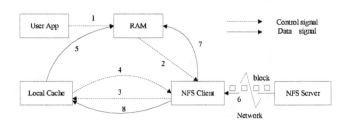

Fig. 6. Streaming execution of application

As Fig. 6 shown, the application is executed in the following way in our system.

1. User can click the application icon on HS. When application icon is clicked, the client will look for the registration information for that application locally. The application will be launched if the application resources have been loaded into system memory, otherwise it would turn to step 2.
2. If the application resources that required have not been loaded into system memory, a data request would sent to NFS client.
3. NFS client check whether application resources requested in step 2 have been cached in the local cache.
4. When application resources have been cached in the local cache, NFS client would check if the resources in the local cache is consistent with that stored in NFS client.
5. If application resources in the local cache are the same as that in NFS client, the resources would be loaded to system memory on demand and the application would be launched correctly.
6. If there has no application resources required in the local cache or the resources are inconsistent with that stored in NFS client, NFS client would load the application resources from NFS server on demand.
7. The application resources that been got from NFS server in step 6 would be loaded into system memory for application launch.
8. NFS client would also cache all the resources that loaded from NFS server into local cache so that the resources can be used again when the same application is executed.

4.4   Cache of Network File System

Network File System (NFS) implement VFS (Virtual File System) interface to upper layer, and connect down to local cache file system (CacheFiles) through the FS-Cache interface. FS-Cache is a generic cache interface layer, which defines a common interface between the file system access and caching system. CacheFiles as a cache backend implements FS-Cache interface and cache replacement algorithm.

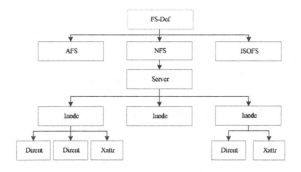

Fig. 7. FS-Cache

As a general cache interface layer, FS-Cache stores cache in a hierarchy way, as shown in Fig. 7. NFS index tree creates one branch for each server. Under the same server branch, NFS index tree creates one branch for each Inode. Each Inode contains information about the corresponding directory or file and some additional attribute fields.

When local cache size exceed a threshold in mobile device, the default replacement algorithm of CacheFiles would consider the access frequency of each cache block and discard cache blocks that have the lowest access frequency according to the inode information.

4.5 Application Distribution Platform

We implemented the application streaming client for Android Operating System on Pandaboard ES and the application streaming server in Linux server. Figure 8 shows the login interface of the client and the application distribution platform in the server.

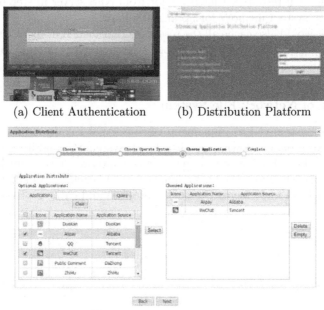

(a) Client Authentication   (b) Distribution Platform

(c) Application Distribution

Fig. 8. Application Distribution Platform

As Fig. 8(a) shown, the client is implemented as an system application (as mentioned in Sect. 4.2) in the Android OS. User use client to log in using username and password. Also, this client can send request to server according to user's choice and receive feedback message from server.

Table 1. The startup time of applications

Network	Mode	Group	Size (MB)	TdMode (ms)	SdMode (ms)	NcsdMode (ms)
Wi-Fi	Cold	Group1	24.08	19144	5045	5061
		Group2	18.94	18439	5462	5419
		Group3	59.4	20395	7502	7534
		Group4	10.42	18538	5746	5691
		Group5	13.1	14877	2386	2395
	Warm	Group1	24.08	1408	2035	5211
		Group2	18.94	2833	3517	4982
		Group3	59.4	5195	5795	7510
		Group4	10.42	4394	4746	5294
		Group5	13.1	851	1250	2376
WCDMA	Cold	Group1	24.08	24750	11436	11274
		Group2	18.94	22849	9594	10035
		Group3	59.4	34223	11127	11324
		Group4	10.42	20963	7871	7827
		Group5	13.1	17903	4798	4803
	Warm	Group1	24.08	1007	2697	11833
		Group2	18.94	2640	3591	10421
		Group3	59.4	5046	5737	10835
		Group4	10.42	4437	5298	7048
		Group5	13.1	844	1577	4686

Meanwhile, the application distribution platform implemented the management of users, resources (includes applications, data etc.) in the server. The administrator of the platform can login in, as shown in Fig. 8(b), manage application for users, and push application to specific user, as shown in Fig. 8(c).

5   Evaluation

We choose Pandaboard ES(Equipped with the Android Operating System, ARM Cortex-M3 MPCore, 1.2 GHZ Frequency, 1024 MB RAM, SD/SDIO/MMC Media Card Cage) for our evaluation, and a linux server (configuration to be added).

Firstly, we evaluate the startup time of the applications in Wi-Fi and WCDMA environment in our Streaming distribution Mode (SdMode), and compare it with Traditional distribution Mode(TdMode), Non-caching Streaming distribution Mode (NcsdMode).

- Wi-Fi(80 Mbps over a TP-link wireless router)
- WCDMA(21 Mbps over China Unicom's 3G network)

Secondly, we implement a simulator in JAVA and generate an application sequence based on statistical information that gets from Android Market. We use this simulator to analysis the network traffic.

5.1   Startup Time of Applications

We set local cache size to 400 MB and divided 20 applications into five groups(Social Communication, Multi Media, Android Game, Service Life and Phone Tool) according to the application types. We run each group twice on Wi-Fi, WCDMA. The first run, namely cold mode, is used to measure the start performance of application that load resources from server via network file system. The second run, namely warm mode, is used to measure the startup performance of application that load resources from local cache in the mobile terminal. (Note, in cold mode, TdMode includes download, install and startup of the application while SdMode includes the subscription and startup of the application).

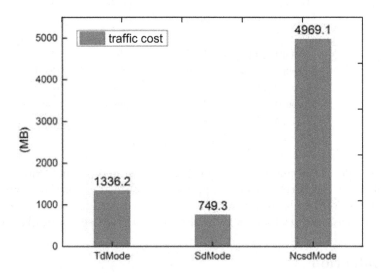

Fig. 9. Network traffic cost in different application distribution modes

Table 1 shows the application's startup time in TdMode, SdMode and Ncs-dMode. We can see: In cold mode, the startup time of application in TdMode is significantly more than that in other two modes. In warm mode, the startup performance of application does not have too much difference in SdMode and TdMode, but both of them are better than that in NcsdMode. Different network environment also bring some influence on the startup performance of application. In cold mode, the startup performance about application in Wi-Fi is significantly better than that in WCDMA. In warm mode, network environment has little effect on TdMode and SdMode, but the application will start up faster in NcsdMode.

5.2   Network Traffic Cost

Network traffic cost in TdMode mainly includes the download and update about application. While in SdMode and NcsdMode, the traffic cost will increase when application is loaded from server. In simulation, we select 24 typical applications that can be divided into 6 categories and set the local cache size to 400 MB. Then we get the statistics data about the network traffic cost during a cycle of 30 days in TdMode, SdMode and NcsdMode.

Figure 9 shows the network traffic cost during a certain time in three distribution modes. As we can see, the SdMode we propose generate less traffic than that in other two modes. And in NcsdMode, the application will generate significantly more traffic cost. Evaluation show that in SdMode, cache mechanism can save 43.9 % traffic than TdMode and 84.9 % traffic than NcsdMode which show the availability of our mode to some extent.

6   Conclusion

Concerning challenges faced by the current App Store based mobile application distribution, we propose an application streaming based mobile application distribution method. Our scheme provide application and user data as a service for mobile devices to access through wireless network.

This method enable personalized mobile application experience and manageability for mobile application distribution, solve the storage capacity constraint of mobile devices and also improve application startup time.

There are multiple extensions to this research that could be done. Firstly, the evaluation of network traffic cost is based on simulation, we will try to do experiment to verify it. Secondly, we will try to propose our cache replacement algorithm to compare with the default algorithm in the CacheFiles. Thirdly, based on the information collected through application streaming, we could provide more personalized service such as application recommendation and customization.

Acknowledgments. This work is supported in part by the National Natural Science Foundation of China under Grant Numbers 61272151, 61472451 and 61309025, the International Science & Technology Cooperation Program of China under Grant Number 2013DFB10070, the Hunan Provincial Natural Science Foundation of China under Grant Number 13JJ4016, the China Hunan Provincial Science & Technology Program under Grant Number 2012GK4106, and the "Mobile Health" Ministry of Education - China Mobile Joint Laboratory (MOE-DST No. [2012]311).

References

1. The Statistics Portal. http://www.statista.com/statistics/276623
2. Mobile App Statistics. http://www.smartinsights.com/mobile-marketing/app-marketing/mobile-app-statistics

3. Donaldson, S.E., Siegel, S.G., Williams, C.K., Aslam, A.: Enterprise cybersecurity for mobile and BYOD. Enterprise Cybersecurity: How to Build a Successful Cyberdefense Program Against Advanced Threats, pp. 119–129. Springer, Heidelberg (2015)

4. Huang, S.Z., Wu, M., Xiong, Y.: Mobile transparent computing to enable ubiquitous operating systems and applications. JACIII **18**, 32–39 (2014)

5. Zhang, Y.X., Zhou, Y.Z.: 4vp: a novel meta os approach for streaming programs in ubiquitous computing. In: 21st International Conference on Advanced Information Networking and Applications (AINA07), pp. 394–403. IEEE (2007)

6. Zhao, Y., Han, W., Xue, R., Chen, W.: Smile: streaming management of applications and data for mobile terminals. Int. J. Cloud Comput. **1**, 329–350 (2012)

7. Xenapp. http://www.citrix.com/products/xenapp/overview.html

8. VMware ThinApp. http://www.vmware.com/products/thinapp

9. Shi, L., Liu, Z., Xu, L.: BWCC: a FS-cache based cooperative caching system for network storage system. In: 2012 IEEE International Conference on Cluster Computing (CLUSTER), pp. 546–550. IEEE (2012)

10. Dong, Y., Zhu, H., Peng, J., Wang, F., Mesnier, M.P., Wang, D., Chan, S.C.: RFS: a network file system for mobile devices and the cloud. ACM SIGOPS Oper. Syst. Rev. **45**, 101–111 (2011)

11. Khatwal, R., Jain, M.K.: Application specific cache simulation analysis for application specific instruction set processor. Int. J. Comput. Appl. **90**(13), 31–44 (2014)

12. Megiddo, N., Modha, D.S.: Outperforming LRU with an adaptive replacement cache algorithm. Comput. J. **37**, 58–65 (2004)

13. Chun, B.G., Ihm, S., Maniatis, P., Naik, M., Patti, A.: Clonecloud: elastic execution between mobile device and cloud. In: Proceedings of the Sixth Conference on Computer Systems, pp. 301–314. ACM (2011)

14. Cuervo, E., Balasubramanian, A., Cho, D.K., Wolman, A., Saroiu, S., Chandra, R., Bahl, P.: Maui: making smartphones last longer with code offload. In: Proceedings of the 8th International Conference on Mobile Systems, Applications, and Services, pp. 49–62. ACM (2010)

A Clustering Algorithm Based on Rough Sets for the Recommendation Domain in Trust-Based Access Control

Bin Zhao[1,2(✉)], Jingsha He[1], Xinggang Xuan[1], Yixuan Zhang[1], and Na Huang [1]

[1] School of Software Engineering, Beijing University of Technology,
Beijing 100124, China
jnzhaobin@163.com
[2] Department of Computer Science, Jining University,
Qufu 273155, Shandong, China

Abstract. Trust-based access control (TBAC) is a hot research issue in the area of network security for open networks. Clustering of the domains of recommendation entities is a prerequisite for trust quantification and evaluation in TBAC during the interaction of network entities. In this paper, we propose a clustering algorithm using the membership function based on rough sets for recommendation domain in TBAC in which traditional K-mode, k-mean and FCM clustering techniques are utilized. First, based on a system threshold for the number of recommendation entities, the proposed algorithm derives the clustering set for the recommendation entities within a most recent minimum time window. Then, the domain for the recommendation entity of the subject is obtained by analyzing the clustering results in which the entity data samples that the object gives to a request is fixed as the initial clustering centers in order to ensure the accuracy of the recommendation domain thus formed. To evaluate the effectiveness of the proposed algorithm, we apply both the IRIS standard data sets and the UCI data sets in our experiment. And our evaluation results show that the proposed algorithm performs better in terms of efficiency and clustering accuracy compared to traditional K-mode, K-mean and FCM clustering algorithms for recommendation domain in TBAC.

Keywords: Rough set · Membership function · Clustering algorithm · Domain of recommendation entity · TBAC

1 Introduction

Rough set theory was first developed in the early 20th century [24] and has been widely used since then in representing, learning and concluding incomplete, uncertain knowledge and data. The theory has also been used as a mathematical tool to analyzing inaccurate, inconsistent, incomplete or uncertain information and to retaining key information in data analysis and reasoning to identify and

© Springer International Publishing Switzerland 2015
G. Wang et al. (Eds.): ICA3PP 2015, Part I, LNCS 9528, pp. 317–326, 2015.
DOI: 10.1007/978-3-319-27119-4_22

assess dependency relationships between data so as to find hidden knowledge. Algorithms that have been designed based on the rough set theory tend to be simple and easy to operate and implement. Therefore, it has received a great deal of attention in research areas such as machine learning, decision support systems, machine discovery, inductive reasoning and knowledge discovery in databases and pattern recognition [7,8,13].

In classical mathematics and statistical mathematics, another new discipline is fuzzy mathematical analysis methods [3,12,17], which can be used to study and deal with the phenomenon of fuzziness. Membership function in the fuzzy set theory is one of the most basic and important concept in the theory as well as in specific applications.

Nefti-Meziani et al. addressed the problem of incorporating an inclusion structure in the general class of fuzzy c-means algorithms [18]. Suleman proposed an alternative approach to fuzzy c-means clustering to eliminate the weighting exponent parameter of the conventional algorithms based on a particular convex factorization of data matrix [21]. Wang proposed type-2 fuzzy rough sets on two finite universes of discourse characterized from both the constructive and the axiomatic approaches [22]. Gautam and Ravi proposed two novel hybrid imputation methods involving particle swarm optimization based clustering method and auto-associative extreme learning machine [6]. Jain and Reddy proposed a new fuzzy graph based modeling approach for wireless sensor networks (WSNs) by taking into consideration the dynamic nature of network, volatile aspects of radio links and physical layer uncertainty [11]. Zhang et al. proposed a hybrid algorithm that combines fuzzy clustering and particle swarm optimization (PSO) for incomplete data clustering in which missing attributes are represented as intervals [23]. Sert et al. introduced a new clustering approach which is not only energy-efficient but also deployment independent for WSNs [20]. Maji and Roy presented a segmentation method, integrating judiciously the merits of rough-fuzzy computing and multiresolution image analysis techniques for documents that have both text and graphics regions [16]. Ma et al. presented an enhanced K-means clustering method for grouping fractures with meliorated initial cluster centersf [14]. Zheng investigated multiple attribute decision making (MADM) problems for evaluating college English teachers' professional competence with hesitant fuzzy uncertain linguistic information [25]. Farhadinia developed a division and subtraction formula for HFSs, IVHFSs and T-DHFSs, which provides more choices for decision makers [4].

Trust-based access control is a hot research issue in the area of network security for open networks. Clustering of the domain of recommendation entities is a prerequisite for trust quantification and evaluation in TBAC for the interaction between network entities. In this paper, we propose a clustering algorithm using the membership function based on rough sets in the recommendation domain of TBAC in combination with the traditional K-mode, k-mean and FCM clustering algorithms. First, based on a threshold on the number of recommendation entities, the proposed algorithm would obtain the set of clustered recommendation entities within a most recent minimum time window. Then, the domain of recommendation entities for the accessing subject is obtained through analyzing the clustered data results in which the entity data samples that the accessed object gives to a request is fixed as the initial clustering centers in order to ensure accurate formation of the recommendation domains. We will also perform some simulation experiment based two available data sets to demonstrate the superiority of our proposed clustering algorithm over some traditional algorithms in terms of efficiency and accuracy.

This paper is organized as follows. Section 2 introduces the related concept of rough sets and membership functions. Section 3 presents our proposed clustering algorithm using the membership function based on rough sets in the recommendation domain of TBAC along with detailed implementation steps. Section 4 presents the simulation results using the IRIS standard data sets and the UCI data sets to evaluate the efficiency and the accuracy of our proposed algorithm. Finally, Sect. 5 concludes this paper in which our future research work is also discussed.

2   Related Concepts

2.1   The Rough Set

Def. 1 Knowledge is the result of the classification on data set U of the object space, a discrete representation of the data by using the equivalence relation set R.

Def. 2 Knowledge base is the result of the classification on data set U of the object space, a discrete representation of the data by using all the equivalence relation set R, which is formalized as $K = (U, R)$.

Def. 3 Information system $S = \{U, A, V, f\}$ where
    i. U is a finite set of samples of the object space.
    ii. A is a limited set of properties for the samples of the object space and $A = A^C \cup A^D$ in which A^C is the subset of condition attributes and A^D is a subset of decision attributes.
    iii. $V = \cup_{P \in A} V_P$ where V_P is the fields of attribute P, and
    iv. $f : UA \to V$ makes each object $x_i \in U$ and attribute $q \in A$, then $f(x_i, q) = V_q$.

Def. 4 For set $P \subset A, x_i, x_j \in U, IND(P)$ specifies a set of binary relations called equivalence relations, which is defined as follows:

$$IND(P) = \{(x_i, x_j) \in U \times U | \forall p \in P, p(x_i) = p(x_j)\} \qquad (1)$$

$IND(P)$ defines the equivalent relations about property P in which for both x_i and x_j in system S, only if $p(x_i) = p(x_j)$ for all the attributes $p \in P$.

2.2   The Membership Function

Def. 5 μ_A is a mapping to a closed interval [0,1] in discourse domain, i.e.,

$$\mu_A : X \to [0, 1], x \to \mu_A \qquad (2)$$

in which we call μ_A a membership function of A since the fuzzy subset of X is determined by μ_A. Then, $\mu_A(x)$ denotes the degree of belonging to fuzzy subset A and is called the membership degree of X for A.

2.3   Clustering Algorithms

Def. 6 A clustering algorithm divides a given data set into a number of different classes as illustrated below. Let's denote N as the given data samples of data sets. We can get K classifications through division with a clustering algorithm. A classification denotes a class (cluster or group) of data samples such that $K \leq N$ and would also meet the following conditions.
  i. Each class contains at least one data sample and
  ii. Each data sample belongs to one and only one data class.

Lets denote $X = \{x_1, x_2, \ldots, x_i, \ldots, x_n\}$ as a set of N data samples in data set C and $C_1, C_2, \ldots, C_k$ as K data classifications. Then,

$$C_1 \cup C_2 \cup \ldots \cup C_k = C, C_i \cap C_j = \varnothing (0 < i \neq j \leq K) \tag{3}$$

The objective of a clustering algorithm is to make similar data samples clustered together and to maximize clustering results. Then, how to set the value of K? Firstly, the algorithm should make the first division according to the initial value of K and then change the division according to the clustering method iteratively until there is no better division. Traditional clustering algorithm is as follows: K-means [15], K-mode [9,10], FCM [19] etc.

3   The Proposed Clustering Algorithm RFCR

Both recommendation trust evaluated by the domain of the recommended entities and direction trust evaluated by the accessed object are the key consideration in trust quantification and evaluation in TBAC of network entity interactions. It is also the premier issue in recommendation trust evaluation for clustering the domain of recommended entities. Therefore, we propose a clustering algorithm using the membership function based on rough sets in the domain of recommended trust to be combined with traditional K-mode, k-means and FCM clustering algorithms. First, according to the access request from accessing subject, we get a standard sample which includes the appropriate decision attributes and authorization from the access control rules (ACR). We can then obtain the upper approximation set $\overline{P}X$ and the lower approximation set $\underline{P}X$ through corresponding entity classification in the maximum time sliding window defined. In order to follow recommendation timelines and ensure clustering accuracy, the time sliding window will be reduced until $K = N$ if $k = num(\underline{P}X)$ and the number of entity data samples in the lower approximation set $\underline{P}X$ is more than the system threshold N of the number of recommended entities.

The main idea of our algorithm is that, according to the system threshold N of the number of recommended entities, we get clustered data set S within the time sliding window. $K(2 \leq K \leq \sqrt{n})$ is determined by the standard data sample that corresponds to the access request from the accessing subject as the initial cluster centers to guarantee the clustering of the domain of the recommended entities. Then, the clustering result for the domain of the recommended entities of the accessing subject is obtained through clustering analysis.

The formula for the cluster center is as follows:

$$
v_k = \begin{cases} \dfrac{\Sigma_{X_i \in \underline{P}X} \rho(i,k) X_i}{num(\underline{P}X)}, & if\, num(\overline{P}X) = num(\underline{P}X) \\[2ex] \dfrac{num(\overline{P}X)}{(\overline{P}X) + num(\underline{P}X)} * \dfrac{\Sigma_{X_i \in \underline{P}X} \rho(i,k) X_i}{num(\underline{P}X)} + \dfrac{num(\underline{P}X)}{(\overline{P}X) + num(\underline{P}X)} * \dfrac{\Sigma_{X_i \in (\overline{P}X - \underline{P}X)} \rho(i,k) X_i}{num(\overline{P}X) - num(\underline{P}X)}, & otherwise \end{cases}
$$

(4)

The minimum value for the clustering criterion function is as follows:

$$
J_{RFCR} = \sum_{i=1}^{N} \sum_{k=1}^{C} \rho_{ki}^2 * d_{ki}
$$

(5)

where d_{ki} denotes the Euclidean distance based on the following formula:

$$
d_{ki} = \|v_k - x_i\|^2
$$

(6)

Since $m = 2$,

$$
\rho = [\sum_{j=1}^{C} (\frac{d_{ki}}{d_{ji}})^{\frac{2}{m-1}}]^{-1} = [\sum_{j=1}^{C} (\frac{d_{ki}}{d_{ji}})^2]^{-1}
$$

(7)

The detailed steps of our algorithm are described as follows:

Step1: Initialize the clustering parameters. W_{time} is the recent maximum time window. N (e.g. $N = 100$) is the threshold value of the number of data samples for the domain of recommended entities which is set by the system. We also set the fuzzy coefficient m to be 2. Both data sample set S and standard data sample $\tilde{X}$ corresponding to the access request are obtained with in W_{time}. Let's denote $\tilde{X}$ as classification K_r with center v_r in the domain of recommended entities.

Step2: According to the rough set knowledge, data samples are classified to find the upper approximation set $\overline{P}X$ and the lower approximation set $\underline{P}X$ for the corresponding classification of data samples $\tilde{X}$. If $K = num(\underline{P}X) > N$, then the time window $\tilde{W}_{time}$ narrows until $K = num(\underline{P}X) = N$ so that we can get time window $\tilde{W}_{time}$ and data sample number n and data sample set $\tilde{S}$ within $\tilde{W}_{time}$.

Step3: Obtain the maximum number $\sqrt{n}$ of cluster's subclasses.

Step4: Update clustering center classification V_k according to the effective criterion function J_{RFCR}, the upper approximation set and the lower approximation set that correspond to data samples as the initial cluster centers in the domain of recommended entities.

Step5: Calculate the effectiveness criterion function J_{RFCR} until convergence occurs, otherwise return to Step 4;

Step6: Determine the value of $K (2 \leq K \leq \sqrt{n})$ and classification centers V_k.

Step7: Output the results of clustering.

Step8: Get the domain of recommended entities for the accessing subject.

4 Experiment Results and Analysis

To verify the effectiveness of our proposed algorithm in terms of the accuracy of data clustering, the efficiency of algorithm execution and the timeliness of getting the clustering results, we perform some experiment using the IRIS standard data sets and the UCI data sets [1] and present the results.

The simulation experiment environment includes a Lenovo H3050 (CPU: dual core i3-4160, 3.6 GHZ; memory: DDR 4G; hard-disk: 500G, 7200 rpm; operating system: Windows 7) and Matlab 7.8.0 (r2009a) to run the simulation and perform data analysis.

Simulation parameter settings are as follows: M=2, $\tilde{W}_{time}$=100, n=30. The maximum number of iterations is 100. Data abstraction levels have 7 intervals based on the discrete statistics, as shown in Table 1.

Table 1. Intervals of data abstraction level

Intervals	1	2	3	4	5	6	7
Range	(0,0.14]	(0.14,0.28]	(0.28,0.42]	(0.42,0.57]	(0.57,0.71]	(0.71,0.85]	(0.85,1]

The standard formula of the data sample adopted in the simulation is as follows:

$$T_{standardization} = \begin{cases} 1, & T_{max} = T_{min} \\ \dfrac{T - T_{min}}{T_{max} - Tmin}, & T_{min} < T_{max} \end{cases} \quad (8)$$

In the above formula, T denotes the trust value of attribute variable. T_{min} denotes the minimum trust value of the attribute variable of data sample. T_{max} denotes the maximum trust value of the attribute variable of data sample. $T_{standardization}$ denotes standardized trust value and $T_{standardization} \in [0, 1]$.

4.1   Evaluation Metrics

We adopt accuracy, timeliness and efficiency as the metrics for the evaluation of the proposed clustering algorithm. The accuracy of clustering is calculated using the following formula:

$$CA = \frac{\Sigma_{k=1}^{K} a_k}{n} \quad (9)$$

where, n denotes the total number of data samples in the data set, a_k denotes the number of number k classification that are correct, K denotes the number of subclasses, CA denotes the ratio between the correct number of clustering classification and the total number of data samples in the data set. A higher CA implies a higher accuracy of clustering.

The efficiency of the algorithm is measured by the average execution time of the algorithm and the timeliness of data clustering refers to the time it takes the algorithm to reach the most recent minimum time sliding window.

Table 2. The feature of the SDSet

Data set	Number of samples	Number of attributes	Number of subclass
SDSet	7000	5	7

4.2 Simulation and Analysis of SDSet

The simulation data set (SDSet) we used contains 7000 standardized data samples to be divided into 7 subclasses. The feature of SDSet is shown in Table 2.

In the simulation experiment, we evaluate three clustering algorithms to cluster for the SDSet: k-mode, FCM and RFCR algorithms. Table 3 lists the simulation results.

Table 3. Results of k-mode, FCM and RFCR algorithms running SDSet

Clustering algorithm	k-mode	FCM	RFCR
Efficiency	0.399	0.654	0.222
Accuracy	0.8512	0.8950	0.9665

As illustrated in Table 3, the accuracy of k-mode, FCM and RFCR are 85.12 %, 89.50 % and 96.65 %, respectively, and the short average completion time shows that RFCR is much more efficient than the other two algorithms. In addition, Fig. 1a shows the accuracy of running the clustering algorithms 30 times and Fig. 1 shows the number of executions for the algorithms to converge using SDSet. From Fig. 1b, we can see that K-mode starts to converge at about the 20th time of the execution while FCM starts to converge at about the 25th time. Meanwhile, RFCR starts to converge at about the 10th time of the execution, showing its superiority over the other two algorithms in terms of

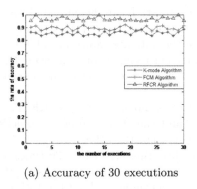

(a) Accuracy of 30 executions

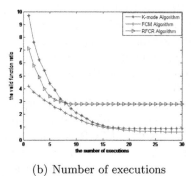

(b) Number of executions

Fig. 1. Accuracy of 30 executions and number of executions of K-mode, FCM and RFCR for convergence using SDSet

Table 4. The feature of IRIS

Data set	Number of samples	Number of attributes	Number of subclass
IRIS	150	4	3

Table 5. Results of K-mode, FCM and RFCR algorithms using IRIS

Clustering algorithm	k-mode	FCM	RFCR
Efficiency	0.168	0.255	0.111
Accuracy	0.8602	0.8933	0.9589

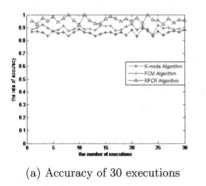
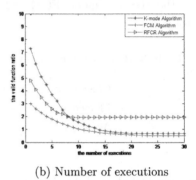

(a) Accuracy of 30 executions   (b) Number of executions

Fig. 2. Accuracy of 30 executions and number of executions of K-mode, FCM and RFCR for convergence using IRIS

execution efficiency. The above results clearly show that our RFCR is superior in both accuracy and efficiency among the three clustering algorithms.

4.3 Simulation and Analysis of IRIS

The IRIS of UCI database has been applied to study mathematical statistics [2,5]. We use the IRIS dataset that contains 150 standardized data samples to be divided into 3 subclasses. The features of the data are shown in Table 4.

We again apply the simulation for the three clustering algorithms using IRIS: K-mode, FCM and RFCR. The results on efficiency and accuracy are shown in Table 5.

As illustrated in Table 5, the accuracy of K-mode, FCM and RFCR are 86.02 %, 89.33 % and 95.89 %, respectively, and the short average completion time shows that RFCR is much more efficient than the other two algorithms. Figure 2 shows the accuracy of running the clustering algorithms 30 times and Fig. 2b shows the number of executions for the algorithms to converge using IRIS. From Fig. 2a, we can see that K-mode starts to converge at about the 15th time of the execution while FCM starts to converge at about the 20th time. Meanwhile, RFCR starts to converge at about the 8th time of the execution, showing its superiority over the other two algorithms in terms of execution efficiency. The above results clearly show that our RFCR is superior in both accuracy and efficiency among the three clustering algorithms.

5   Conclusion

In this paper, we proposed a clustering algorithm using the membership function based on rough sets in the domain of recommendation entities for TBAC and compared the performance with the traditional K-mode and FCM algorithms. Based on the access request from access control rules of ACR table, we obtain the classification of the domain of the recommended entities by clustering standard data samples in the most recent minimum time sliding window.

In our experiment simulation, we used data analysis examples from the IRIS standard data sets and UCI data sets and carried out the simulation with the Matlab software. Simulation results show that our proposed clustering algorithm using the membership function based on rough sets is better in terms of efficiency and accuracy compared to the traditional K-mode, K-mean and FCM clustering algorithms for clustering domains of recommendation entities for TBAC. Our future research will focus on determining the weights for the attributes of the recommended entities in trust evaluation.

Acknowledgments. The work in this paper has been supported by National Natural Science Foundation of China (61272500), Beijing National Science Foundation (4142008) and Shandong National Science Foundation (ZR2013FQ024).

References

1. Uci datasets (2014). http://archive.ics.uci.edu/ml/datasets.html
2. Anderson, E.: The irises of the gaspe peninsula. Bull. Am. Iris Soc. **59**, 2–5 (1935)
3. Bezdek, J.C.: Pattern recognition with fuzzy objective function algorithms. Springer Science & Business Media (2013)
4. Farhadinia, B.: Study on division and subtraction operations for hesitant fuzzy sets, interval-valued hesitant fuzzy sets and typical dual hesitant fuzzy sets. J. Intell. Fuzzy Syst. Appl. Eng. Technol. **28**(3), 1393–1402 (2015)
5. Fisher, R.A.: The use of multiple measurements in taxonomic problems. Ann. Eugenics **7**(2), 179–188 (1936)
6. Gautam, C., Ravi, V.: Data imputation via evolutionary computation, clustering and a neural network. Neurocomputing **156**, 134–142 (2015)
7. Hsieh, C.F., Cheng, K.F., Huang, Y.F.: An intrusion detection system for ad hoc networks with multi-attacks based on a support vector machine and rough set theory. J. Convergence Inf. Technol. **8**(2), 242–249 (2013)
8. Huang, G., Dong, S., Ren, J.: A minimum spanning tree clustering algorithm based on density. Adva. Inf. Sci. Serv. Sci. **5**(2), 44 (2013)
9. Huang, Z.: Clustering large data sets with mixed numeric and categorical values. In: Proceedings of the 1st Pacific-Asia Conference on Knowledge Discovery and Data Mining, (PAKDD), pp. 21–34. Singapore (1997)

10. Huang, Z.: Extensions to the k-means algorithm for clustering large data sets with categorical values. Data Min. Knowl. Disc. **2**(3), 283–304 (1998)
11. Jain, A., Reddy, B.R.: A novel method of modeling wireless sensor network using fuzzy graph and energy efficient fuzzy based k-hop clustering algorithm. Wireless Pers. Commun. **82**(1), 157–181 (2015)
12. Jiye, L., Liang, B., Fuyuan, C.: K-modes clustering algorithm based on the new distance measure. J. Comput. Res. Dev. **47**(10), 1749–1755 (2010)
13. Ling, Z., Zhong-ying, B., Kang, X., Wei, L., Guo-hui, Z.: Research of distributed intrusion detection model based on rough set in cloud computing. International Journal of Advancements in Computing Technology 5(4) (2013)
14. Ma, G., Xu, Z., Zhang, W., Li, S.: An enriched k-means clustering method for grouping fractures with meliorated initial centers. Arab. J. Geosciences **8**(4), 1881–1893 (2015)
15. MacQueen, J., et al.: Some methods for classification and analysis of multivariate observations. In: Proceedings of the Fifth Berkeley Symposium on Mathematical Statistics and Probability, vol. 1, pp. 281–297, Oakland (1967)
16. Maji, P., Roy, S.: Rough-fuzzy clustering and multiresolution image analysis for text-graphics segmentation. Appl. Soft Comput. **30**, 705–721 (2015)
17. Mitchell, T.M.: Machine Learning. wcb, New York (1997)
18. Nefti-Meziani, S., Oussalah, M., Soufian, M.: On the use of inclusion structure in fuzzy clustering algorithm in case of gaussian membership functions. J. Intell. Fuzzy Syst. Appl. Eng. Technol. **28**(4), 1477–1493 (2015)
19. Ruspini, E.H.: A new approach to clustering. Inf. Control **15**(1), 22–32 (1969)
20. Sert, S.A., Bagci, H., Yazici, A.: MOFCA: multi-objective fuzzy clustering algorithm for wireless sensor networks. Appl. Soft Comput. **30**, 151–165 (2015)
21. Suleman, A.: A convex semi-nonnegative matrix factorisation approach to fuzzy c-means clustering. Fuzzy Sets and Syst. **270**, 90–110 (2015)
22. Wang, C.Y.: Type-2 fuzzy rough sets based on extended t-norms. Inf. Sci. **305**, 165–183 (2015)
23. Zhang, L., Bing, Z., Zhang, L.: A hybrid clustering algorithm based on missing attribute interval estimation for incomplete data. Pattern Anal. Appl. **18**(2), 377–384 (2015)
24. Zhang, Q.H., Wang, G.Y., Xiao, Y.: Approximation sets of rough sets. Ruanjian Xuebao/J. Softw. **23**(7), 1745–1759 (2012)
25. Zheng, X.M.: Methods for multiple attribute decision making with hesitant fuzzy uncertain linguistic information and their application for evaluating the college english teachers' professional development competence. J. Intell. Fuzzy Syst. Appl. Eng. Technol. **28**(3), 1243–1250 (2015)

QoE Based Spectrum Allocation Optimization Using Bees Algorithm in Cognitive Radio Networks

Wenjuan Lu[1,2], Zizhong Quan[3(✉)], Quan Liu[1,2], Duzhong Zhang[1,2], and Wenjun Xu[1,2]

[1] School of Information Engineering,
Wuhan University of Technology, Wuhan 430070, China
{poeme_1990,quanliu,zhangduzhong,
xuwenjun}@whut.edu.cn
[2] Key Laboratory of Fiber Optic Sensing Technology
and Information Processing, Ministry of Education,
Wuhan University of Technology, Wuhan 430070, China
[3] School of Management, Wuhan University of Technology,
Wuhan 430070, China
zizhongquan@126.com

Abstract. Cognitive Radio is a promising technology for addressing the spectrum scarce since the growing number of wireless applications. Most of recent researches about spectrum allocation based on users' demands are channel allocation which may not effectively use spectrum holes and meanwhile, users' satisfactions are not fully matched. To satisfy users' demand better, Quality of Experience (QoE), which numerically describes users' satisfaction, is used to evaluate the spectrum allocation result; Bees algorithm is used to facilitate QoE based spectrum allocation optimization, so as to maximize the users' overall QoE while ensuring user's fairness by dynamically allocating free bandwidth to users according to their QoE requirements; Considering the network circumstance, a network model considering the Primary Users'(PU) activity, Secondary Users'(SU) diversity, spectrum characters is proposed for the QoE based spectrum optimization to adapt to network states. Evaluation performances show that the proposed spectrum allocation method outperforms the existing channel allocation methods.

Keywords: Cognitive radio · Quality of experience · Spectrum allocation · Network state

1 Introduction

The wireless network is becoming more complicated since the diversification of the wireless networks and the growing demand for different wireless applications; meanwhile, users' services are varied, such as file downloading, video steaming, etc., along with different demands. At the same time, the booming users' demands for wireless applications make the spectrum crowded and it is hard to vacant existing spectrum for

© Springer International Publishing Switzerland 2015
G. Wang et al. (Eds.): ICA3PP 2015, Part I, LNCS 9528, pp. 327–338, 2015.
DOI: 10.1007/978-3-319-27119-4_23

new applications because of the limitation and non-renewable of spectrum resources. Cognitive Radio (CR), aiming at improving spectrum utilization in time and space, is a promising technology for the challenge. Spectrum allocation, as one of the key technologies of CR which aims to effectively allocate the limited available spectrum, directly determines the spectrum utilization.

Due to the diversity of SU services, using service-oriented spectrum allocation scheme can largely improve the spectrum efficiency and users' satisfaction [1]. QoS is the main target for spectrum allocation based on service, but most works considers only the priority of SUs, which cannot measure the SUs' perceived satisfaction numerically. In contrast to QoS, the concept of QoE more directly measures SUs' satisfaction, a lot of studies on multimedia quality assessment model can estimate the QoE using the matrix Mean Opinion Score (MOS) [2].

But few works focus on QoE-based spectrum allocation which will better match the SUs' satisfaction [1]. Thus, in this paper, QoE is used to measure the SU's satisfaction in Cognitive Radio Networks (CRN). Complicated and dynamic network environment is considered in the model since there may be multiple primary networks among the Cognitive Radio Base Station (CRBS) coverage area. Bees algorithm [3] is used to facilitate QoE based spectrum allocation optimization, so as to maximize the users' overall QoE while ensuring fairness among different types of users and different users by dynamically allocating free bandwidth to users according to their QoE requirements.

The rest of the paper is organized as follows. In Sect. 2, we introduced the relevant research works of spectrum allocation based on users' demand; then in Sect. 3, the network model for CRN which considers network states is presented; then in Sect. 4, the QoE based Spectrum Allocation Model in our work is presented; and the QoE based Spectrum Allocation optimization using Bees Algorithm is then presented in Sect. 5 in detail. Evaluation performances are provided in Sect. 6, and finally, Sect. 7 concluded this paper.

2   Related Works

In this section, we introduce the relevant works. There are lots of works focus on spectrum allocation based on user's QoS. In [4], a service-oriented, multi-attribute normalization model and enhanced PSO method is proposed to efficiently satisfy user service demands and achieve better utilization and user's fairness. The authors in [5] propose a dynamic channel allocation method for video and data service, which maximize the whole network throughput and ensure different users' QoS demands. In [6, 7], queueing model is used to address the spectrum allocation, which is devised to calculate the theoretical delay, to satisfy the QoS of different SUs, in [6], the priority of SUs is arranged as a priority virtual queue, and [7] uses spectrum management for streaming and data with backup channels and ensures seamless end to end service. Another method focused on QoS is based on the fuzzy math theory to grade the spectrum quality as in [8]. These spectrum allocation methods based on user QoS are usually focus on SUs' priority, mainly consider the delay, there is no numerical matric for terminal users' perceived quality.

Few works focus on user's QoE requirement. In [9], a QoE driven spectrum allocation scheme for multimedia transmissions over centralized CRN is proposed, but the authors only consider the scenario of SUs all subscribe for multimedia service. The authors in [10] adopt MOS to measure user's satisfaction to maximize long-term satisfaction of the network and ensure the fairness among all SUs, but network environment is not considered. Bandwidth allocation is also seldom studied in CRN, but bandwidth allocation can more reasonably use spectrum resources [1] which can be validated in our work. In [11], the authors focus on scalable demands in mobile cognitive network, network state is considered on bandwidth allocation to improve SU satisfaction, but PU activities are not considered. The authors in [12] proposed a spectrum decision framework based on bandwidth allocation, a CR capacity model is proposed which describes the spectrum capacity, which will be used in our work.

But to our knowledge, none of these works considers bandwidth allocation based on users' QoE under various network states. Thus we proposed a QoE based spectrum allocation optimization algorithm to improve the overall users' QoE and at the same time ensure fairness between users.

The main contributions of our work are as follows:

- A network model is proposed for QoE based spectrum allocation to dynamically optimize overall performance, which considered the PU activity, SU diversity, spectrum characters and network states.
- A QoE based spectrum allocation optimization is facilitated based on the model using bees algorithm which maximizes the overall users' QoE demands while ensuring fairness among SUs.

3 Network Model

3.1 PU and SU Model

Suppose M free spectrum bands, the bandwidth of each spectrum is $B = \{b_m\}_{1 \times M}$, the PU's arrival in each band is a Poisson process with the arrival rate $\lambda^P = \{\lambda_m^p\}_{1 \times M}$.

The SUs are divided into two classes according to their application requests: real-time SUs (RTSU) and best-effort SUs (BESU). RTSU needs a relatively stable data rate and is sensitive to delay and data loss thus has higher priority over BESU, BESU is more scalable according to data rate and delay. So three minimum data rate requirements are defined for RTSU, R_1^{RTSU}(high), R_2^{RTSU} (normal), R_3^{RTSU}(guarantee); a data rate upper bound R^{BESU} is defined for BESU, when reached this data rate, the BESU will reach the biggest satisfaction. Suppose the number of SUs is K, including K^{RTSU} RTSUs and K^{BESU} BESUs.

Due to PU's activity and noise, the capacity for SUs in spectrums is different. Thus the normalized capacity matrix $C = \{c_{k,m}\}_{K \times M}$(bps/hz) is used for each SU according to the salon theory in (1) [12].

$$c_{k,m} = \log(1 + s_{k,m}) \tag{1}$$

Where $c_{k,m}$ is the normalized capacity for SU k in spectrum m, $s_{k,m}$ is the signal to noise ratio of SU k in spectrum m.

3.2 Network States

In our work, the network state is divided into 3 states according to the free bandwidth and RTSU number. We define the balance factor ρ_{level} which is the proportion of average required bandwidth for RTSUs when satisfies a specific rate of R_{level}^{RTSU} with the total bandwidth.

$$\rho_{level} = \frac{R_{level}^{RTSU}/c_k^{RTSU}}{\sum\limits_{m=1}^{M} b_m} \qquad level = 1, 2, 3 \qquad (2)$$

Where level = {1, 2, 3} reflects three requirement rates of RTSU, b_m is the bandwidth of spectrum m, c_k^{RTSU} is the average normalized rate of RTSU k as in (3).

$$c_k^{RTSU} = \sum\limits_{m=1}^{M} b_m \cdot \log(1 + s_{k,m}) / \sum\limits_{m=1}^{M} b_m \qquad (3)$$

Thus the network state is then defined as in (4).

$$\begin{cases} \rho_1 < 0.5 & rich - state \\ \rho_1 \geq 0.5 \& \rho_2 < 0.5 & normal - state \\ \rho_2 \geq 0.5 & pool - state \end{cases} \qquad (4)$$

In rich state, all of RTSUs will acquire the maximum data rate R_1^{RTSU}, and all of BESUs can be served. In normal state, all of RTSUs will be served, with an average rate of R_1^{RTSU}, but fairness should be ensured, so some of RTSUs will change to R_2^{RTSU}, part of BESUs will be dropped, at this stage. In the poor state, when $\rho_3 > 0.5$, then the average rate of RTSUs is set to R_2^{RTSU}, and fairness should be ensured, so some of RTSUs may change to R_3^{RTSU}. When $\rho_3 < 0.5$, the average rate of RTSUs is set to R_3^{RTSU}, some of RTSUs will be dropped, few BESUs will be served, at this stage, SU's data rate cannot be guaranteed and fairness is also low.

4   QoE Based Spectrum Allocation Model

QoE is mainly described by MOS value, which is closely related to data loss rate and data rate [2]. So first we derive the formula for data loss rate then the MOS and the problem is formulated to maximize the overall MOS, finally the fairness adjustment is described to ensure users' fairness.

4.1   Estimation of Data Loss Rate

Data loss is mainly caused by collision of PUs and SUs in CRN. Let X presents the active PUs in the network m, thus for any channel in the network, the probability when no PU arrives in unit time is:

$$P_m = P\{X(s+1) - X(s)=0\} = e^{-\lambda_m^p} \tag{5}$$

That is, the communication of SU using the spectrum m will be interrupted in unit time is $1-P_m$, suppose a constant channel switching time τ, then the possible data loss due to channel switching in unit time is:

$$D_k^{loss} = \sum_{m=1}^{M} (1-P_m) \cdot a_{k,m} \cdot c_{k,m} \cdot \tau \tag{6}$$

Where $a_{k,m}$ represents the bandwidth allocated to SU k in spectrum m, $c_{k,m}$ is the normalized capacity for SU k in spectrum m.

Considering data loss rate is the proportion of possible data loss and possible transmitted data in unit time, the data loss caused by PU activity is presented as below:

$$P_k^{loss} = \frac{D_k^{loss}}{r_k} = \frac{\sum_{m=1}^{M} \left(1-e^{-\lambda_m^p}\right) \cdot a_{k,m} \cdot c_{k,m} \cdot \tau}{\sum_{m=1}^{M} a_{k,m} \cdot c_{k,m}} \tag{7}$$

Where D_k^{loss} is the possible data loss as in (6), r_k is the maximum data rate in (8).

4.2   Problem Formulation

Suppose the final allocation matrix is $A = \{a_{k,m}\}_{K \times M}$, where $a_{k,m}$ represents the bandwidth allocated to SU k in spectrum m, given the normalized capacity for SU k $c_{k,m}$, then the maximum data rate SU k can achieve is:

$$r_k = \sum_{m=1}^{M} a_{k,m} \cdot c_{k,m} \tag{8}$$

Generally, MOS is different for different applications [2]. For RTSUs, based on the study of [9], we derive the MOS evaluation model as shown as below:

$$MOS_k^{RTSU} = \frac{c_1 + c_2 FR_k + c_3 \ln(r_k)}{1 + c_4 P_k^{loss} + c_5 \left(P_k^{loss}\right)^2} \tag{9}$$

Where $k = 1 \cdots K^{RTSU}$, P_k^{loss} is the data loss rate of RTSU k, r_k is the data rate RTSU k achieved; FR_k is the frame rate. The unknown parameters c_1 to c_5 can be obtained by a nonlinear regression analysis of the QoS parameters as in [9]. For BESUs, the MOS can be derived from the evaluation model in [2]:

$$MOS_k^{BESU} = a \cdot \log(b \cdot r_k \cdot (1 - P_k^{loss}))$$ (10)

Where $k = K^{RTSU} + 1 \cdots K$, P_k^{loss} is the data loss rate of BESU k, r_k is the data rate BESU k achieved, parameters a, b can be obtained by linear analysis in [10].

Based on the above description, to maximize the overall MOS, the optimization problem can be described as in (11).

$$\max \sum_{k=1}^{K^{RTSU}} MOS_k^{RTSU} + \sum_{k=K^{RTSU}+1}^{K^{RTSU}+K^{BESU}} MOS_k^{BESU}$$

$$s.t. \quad \sum_{m=1}^{M} a_{k,m} \cdot c_{k,m} \geq R_{level}^{RTSU} \quad level = 1,2,3 \quad k = 1, \cdots K^{RTSU}$$

$$\sum_{m=1}^{M} a_{k,m} \cdot c_{k,m} \leq R^{BESU} \quad k = K^{RTSU}+1, \cdots K^{RTSU}+K^{BESU}$$ (11)

$$\sum_{k=1}^{K^{RTSU}+K^{BESU}} a_{k,m} \leq b_m$$

Where MOS_k^{RTSU} and MOS_k^{BESU} is presented in (9) and (10), $a_{k,m}$ represents the bandwidth allocated to SU k in spectrum m, $c_{k,m}$ is the normalized capacity for SU k in spectrum m in (1), b_m is the total bandwidth of spectrum m, K^{RTSU} and K^{BESU} is the number of RTSUs and BESUs.

4.3 Fairness Adjustment

When the ratio of total bandwidth allocated to RTSUs and BESUs is greater than the threshold ζ_0, that is:

$$\zeta = \sum_{k=1}^{K^{RTSU}} \sum_{m=1}^{M} a_{k,m} / \sum_{k=K^{RTU}+1}^{K} \sum_{m=1}^{M} a_{k,m} > \zeta_0$$ (12)

Then the allocation is considered not fair, ζ is the fair coefficient, $a_{k,m}$ is the bandwidth allocated to SU k in spectrum m. We define the spectrum quality matrix as $Q_{k,m} = c_{k,m} / \lambda_m^p$. Then the spectrum and SU with the least spectrum quality will be released and reallocated to BESU to adjust the fairness. Finally the fairness is calculated as follows:

$$F^{RTSU-BESU} = \left(\sum_{k=1}^{K^{RTSU}} MOS_k^{RTSU} \cdot \sum_{k=K^{RTSU}+1}^{K^{BESU}} MOS_k^{BESU} \right)^{1/2}$$ (13)

$$F^{ALL} = \left(\prod_{k=1}^{K} (MOS_k + 10^{-4}) \right)^{1/K} \tag{14}$$

The $F^{RTSU-BESU}$ represents the fairness between RTSUs and BESUs, and F^{ALL} represents the fairness among all SUs. The larger $F^{RTSU-BESU}$ represents better fairness between RTSUs and BESUs, and larger F^{ALL} represents better fairness among all users.

5   QoE Based Spectrum Allocation Using Bees Algorithm (QoE-SABA)

Bees algorithm was firstly presented in [13], mimics the food foraging behavior of swarms of honey bees, it mainly performs a kind of exploitative neighborhood search combined with random explorative search and has good performance in continues optimization problems [14]. Bees algorithm is used in various fields, including spectrum allocation [3]. A colony of bees tries to find rich food sources to maximize the amount of nectar at the hive, include employed bees, onlooker bees and scouts.

The new food position produced by a employed bees is:

$$v_{ij} = x_{ij} + \phi_{ij}(x_{ij} - x_{kj}) \tag{15}$$

Where $i = [1 \cdots PN]$, PN is the number of solutions, $j = 1 \cdots D$, D is the dimension of a solution, k is determined randomly as its neighbor and $k \neq i$, x_{ij} is the food source, v_{ij} is the newly derived food source, ϕ_{ij} is a random number between [−1, 1].

The onlooker bee j chooses a food source i depending on the probability value associated with that food source corresponding to employed bee calculated by:

$$p_{j,i} = fit_i / \sum_{i=1}^{PN} fit_i \tag{16}$$

Where fit_i is the fitness value of solution i evaluated by its employed bee. Then, each onlooker bee uses roulette wheel to select its onlooker e_j based on the probabilities and produce a new food position from the old one using (17).

$$v_{ij} = x_{ij} + \phi_{ij}(e_j - x_{ij}) \tag{17}$$

If a position cannot be improved through a number of cycles called limit then that food source will be abandoned by scouts and randomly produce a position to replace it.

Here we also use the bees algorithm to solve our QoE based spectrum allocation problem, using MOS value as the fitness. Then the proposed QoE-based Spectrum Allocation using Bees Algorithm is as follows:

Step 1:   Generate B, λ^P, S={$s_{k,m}$}, calculate the normalized capacity matrix C, ρ_{level}, network state in (1)(2)(4), and decide the RTSU level and fairness flag

Step 2:   Initialize the sources number PN, max number of iteration t_{max}, scout bees limit, generate initial sources location $x_i = [x_{1,i}, x_{2,i}, \cdots x_{D,i}]$ to uniform distributed in the searching space, where $i = [1 \cdots PN]$, $D = K \cdot M$;

Step 3:   Check the food sources if they satisfy the constraints, if not, then adjust the food source to make it satisfy the constraints

Step 4:   Calculate the MOS of each source and rank the sources according to the MOS value, and find the current best solution

Step 5:   The employed bees, onlooker bees and scouts circle are performed in sequence according to (15) (16) (17)

Step 6:   If it reaches the predefined maximum iterations then derive the assignment matrix as mentioned in the step 4 and stop the process else go to step 3 and continue.

6   Simulation Results

The proposed QoE-SABA is compared with MOS-based Channel Allocation Greedy Algorithm (MOS-CAGA) [10] and Channel Allocation Heuristic Algorithm (CAHA) [5] and its extend Spectrum Allocation Heuristic Algorithm (SAHA).

Our simulation is conducted on MATLAB 2010. In our simulation, λ^p is randomly generated from (0, 1), users SNR are randomly generated from (10, 30) dB; we set $M = 3$, $b_m = 300$ kHz, $\zeta_0 = 1.5$, $\tau = 0.1$ s. $R_1^{RTSU} = 720$ kbps, $R_2^{RTSU} = 480$ kbps, $R_3^{RTSU} = 240$ kbps, and $R^{BESU} = 500$ kbps. Suppose when the BESU acquired the service rate R^{BESU}, then the MOS is maximum value of 5 in case of no data loss, meanwhile, we define a lower limit of 50 kbps with MOS = 1. RTSU will achieve the maximum MOS of 5 when reach R_1^{RTSU}, 4 when reach R_2^{RTSU}, 2 when reach R_3^{RTSU}, the parameters in MOS formula is calculated using nonlinear regression analysis in [9, 10], a = 2.1747, b = 0.0158, c_1 = -7.625, c_2 = –0.10068, c_3 = 2.1211, c_4 = 2.30327, c_5 = 7.21067. We set the monitoring cycle of scout bee limit to 10, bees number PN = 10. In order to compare with channel allocation algorithm, we split the spectrum into channels with bandwidth of 50 kHz, i.e. 18 free channels. For the accuracy of the results, the simulation result is the mean value of 100 simulations.

6.1   Network State of Simulation

When the number of BESU K^{BESU} is set to 10, and the RTSU number K^{RTSU} range is from 2 to 11, the network state according to RTSU number is shown in Table 1. The balance factor ρ_{level} is calculated as (2) and network state is derived from (4). As in rich state, the level of RTSU set to 720 kbps, and since spectrum resource is sufficient, it doesn't need to adjust to user fairness, thus fairness flag is set to 0; In normal state, the level of RTSU is set to 720 kbps, and needs to adjust to user fairness, and flag is 1, as a result, some level of RTSU will be changed to 480 kbps; In poor state, when $\rho_3 > 0.5$, then the level of RTSU is set to 480 kbps, and fairness should be ensured, so some level

Table 1. Network state and parameters

K^{RTSU}	ρ_1	ρ_2	ρ_3	State	R^{RTSU}	Flag
2	0.2355	0.1570	0.0785	Rich	720	0
3	0.3602	0.2401	0.1202	Rich	720	0
4	0.4783	0.3188	0.1594	Rich	720	0
5	0.5972	0.3981	0.209	Normal	720	1
6	0.7199	0.4799	0.2799	Normal	720	1
7	0.8355	0.557	0.3585	Poor	480	1
8	0.9728	0.648	0.414	Poor	480	1
9	1.0934	0.7289	0.4644	Poor	480	1
10	1.121	0.814	0.507	Poor	240	0
11	1.2075	0.902	0.5533	Poor	240	0

of RTSU may change to 240 kbps; When $\rho_3 < 0.5$, the level of RTSU is set to 240 kbps and the fairness will not be ensured.

6.2 Comparison of MOS

First, we examine our algorithm with different number of RTSUs. The number of BESU is set to 10, and the RTSU number range from 2 to 11, In Fig. 1, with the number of RTSU increasing, though the MOS is each SU will decrease as in Fig. 2, but the whole network MOS still increasing. We can see the performance of QoE-SABA outperformed the other three algorithms according to MOS, and the SAHA outperformed the CAHA, which proved that bandwidth allocation is more flexible and effective compared to channel allocation.

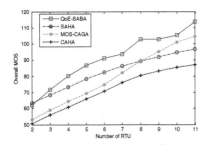

Fig. 1. Overall MOS according to number of RTSU

Fig. 2. Average MOS according to number of RTSU

6.3 Comparison of Dropping Rate

Then dropping rate and average served user number is examined with different number of RTSUs ranging from 2 to 11, the number of BESU is set to 10, and $P^{drop} = (K - K^{served})/K$, where K^{served} is the number of served SU. Figure 3 shows that the dropping rate of our proposed algorithm is low than other algorithms; when the network state is rich, the dropping rate is even 0, and doesn't shapely increase with the increase of RTSU number, which shows a relatively stable performance. Figure 4 show that the served user number is increasing with the increase of RTSU number and QoE-SABA shows a better performance.

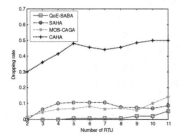
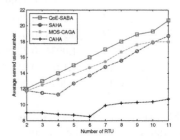

Fig. 3. Dropping rate with the number of RTSU

Fig. 4. Served user according to the number of RTSU

6.4   Comparison of User Fairness

The fairness is calculated according to (13) (14), it is actually decreasing with the number of RTSU increasing as in Fig. 5 when the number of BESU is set to 10, and the RTSU number range from 2 to 11, because when the network state is rich, each user can be better served and the fairness is high, when the network state is getting worse, the fairness and MOS is balanced and both will be lower, but our algorithm achieves better performance; while the fairness between RTSU and BESU does not change much with the RTSU increasing as shown in Fig. 6 since the network resource is constant and fairness is well ensured.

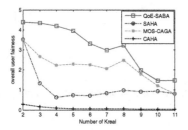
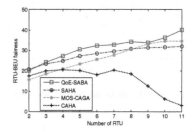

Fig. 5. Overall fairness according to number of RTSU

Fig. 6. RTSU-BESU fairness according to number of RTSU

6.5   Comparison of Data Loss Rate and Adaptive Case

P^{loss} is the average data loss rate of allocated SUs calculated by (7), the number of BESU is set to 10, with the number of RTSUs increasing from 2 to 11, the data loss rate of QoE-SABA is relatively low and shows an increasing trend but doesn't change much, which performs better according to Fig. 7. In Fig. 8, the adaptive case when algorithm parameter changing with the network state and none adaptive case when algorithm been static is compared, the result show that adaptive case will achieve better performance according to MOS, fairness, data loss rate and dropping rate which proves the effectiveness of bandwidth allocation.

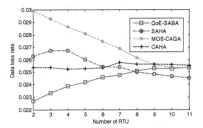

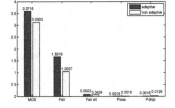

Fig. 7. Data loss rate according to the number of RTSU

Fig. 8. Comparison of adaptive and non-adaptive case

7   Conclusions

This paper proposes a QoE based spectrum allocation optimization using bees algorithm which maximize the user QoE while ensure users fairness in cognitive radio networks. A network model considers PU activity, SU diversity, spectrum characters and network states is proposed for QoE based spectrum allocation to adaptively optimize the network performance. Simulation results demonstrate that our proposed spectrum allocation algorithm can significantly improve the user MOS, fairness, dropping rate, data loss rate in a dynamic network environment and outperforms the existing MOS and throughput based channel allocation algorithm. Furthermore, the adaptive case when the parameters changed with network states is examined that demonstrate that network state should be considered in spectrum allocation algorithm. The next work will focus on online spectrum allocation based on user QoE which will be better match the real world circumstance.

Acknowledgements. This research is supported by the National Natural Science Foundation of China (Grant No. 51175389), the Keygrant Project of Chinese Ministry of Education (Grant No. 313042), and the Fundamental Research Funds for the Central Universities (Grant No. 2015III003).

References

1. Tragos, E.Z., Zeadally, S., Fragkiadakis, A.G., Siris, V.A.: Spectrum assignment in cognitive radio networks: a comprehensive survey. IEEE Commun. Surv. Tutor. **15**, 1108–1135 (2013)
2. Khan, S., Duhovnikov, S., Steinbach, E., Kellerer, W.: MOS-based multiuser multi application cross-layer optimization for mobile multimedia communication. Adv. Multimed. **2007**(Article ID 94918), 6 (2007)
3. Ghasemi, A., Masnadi-Shirazi, M.A., Biguesh, M., Qassemi, F.: Channel assignment based on bee algorithms in multi-hop cognitive radio networks. IET Commun. **8**, 2356–2365 (2014)
4. Liu, Q., Niu, H., Wenjun, X., Zhang, D.: A service-oriented spectrum allocation algorithm using enhanced PSO for cognitive radio networks. Spec. Issue Mob. Comput. Content/Serv. Oriented Netw. Archit. **74**, 81–91 (2014)
5. Zhang, X., Guo, L., Song, T., Xu, W.: Dynamic channel allocation supporting multiservice over cognitive radio networks. In: 2013 16th International Symposium on Wireless Personal Multimedia Communications (WPMC), pp. 1–5 (2013)
6. Shiang, H.-P., van der Schaar, M.: Queuing-based dynamic channel selection for heterogeneous multimedia application over cognitive radio network. IEEE Trans. Multimed. **10**, 896–909 (2008)
7. Doost-Mohammady, R., Naderi, M.Y., Chowdhury, K.R.: Spectrum allocation and QoS provisioning framework for cognitive radio with heterogeneous service classes. IEEE Trans. Wirel. Commun. **13**, 3938–3950 (2014)
8. Zhang, Y., Chen, X., Fu, L.: A demand-based spectrum allocation algorithm in cognitive radio networks. In: Sambath, S., Zhu, E. (eds.) Frontiers in Computer Education. AISC, vol. 133, pp. 1011–1018. Springer, Heidelberg (2012)
9. Jiang, T., Wang, H., Vasilakos, A.V.: QoE-driven channel allocation schemes for multimedia transmission of priority-based secondary users over cognitive radio networks. IEEE J. Sel. Areas Commun. **30**, 1215–1224 (2012)
10. He, L., Liu, B., Yao, Y., Yu, N.: MOS-based channel allocation schemes for mixed services over cognitive radio networks. In: 2013 Seventh International Conference on Image and Graphics (ICIG), pp. 832– 837 (2013)
11. Wang, J., Su, J., Wu, W.: Online spectrum allocation for cognitive cellular network supporting scalable demands. In: 2011 Sixth International ICST Conference on Cognitive Radio Oriented Wireless Networks and Communications (CROWNCOM), pp. 196–200 (2011)
12. Lee, W.-Y., Akyldiz, I.F.: A spectrum decision framework for cognitive radio network. IEEE Trans. Mob. Comput. **10**, 161–174 (2011)
13. Pham, D.T., Ghanbarzadeh, A., Koç, E., Otri, S., Rahim, S., Zaidi, M: The bees algorithm - a novel tool for complex optimization problems. In: Proceedings of Innovative Production Machines and Systems, IPROMS 2006 (2006)
14. Pham, D.T., Castellani, M.: The bees algorithm: modelling foraging behaviour to solve continuous optimization problems. Proc. Inst. Mech. Eng. C J. Mech. Eng. Sci. **223**(12), 2919–2938 (2009)

Dynamic Resource Provision for Cloud Broker with Multiple Reserved Instance Terms

Jiangtao Zhang[1,2], Shi Chen[1,3], Hejiao Huang[1,3], Xuan Wang[1,4(✉)],
and Dingzhu Du[5]

[1] School of Computer Science and Technology,
Harbin Institute of Technology Shenzhen Graduate School,
Shenzhen 518055, China
wangxuan@insun.hit.edu.cn
[2] Public Service Platform of Mobile Internet Application Security Industry,
Shenzhen 518057, China
[3] Shenzhen Key Laboratory of Internet of Information Collaboration,
Shenzhen 518055, China
[4] Shenzhen Applied Technology Engineering Laboratory for Internet Multimedia
Application, Shenzhen 518055, China
[5] Department of Computer Science, University of Texas at Dallas,
Richardson, TX 75080, USA

Abstract. Relying on the knowledge of the pricing benefit of long-term reserved resource and multiplexing gains, cloud broker strives to minimize its cost by utilizing infrastructure resources from public cloud service provider. Different reserved instance terms accompanied by different prices are provisioned by the provider. How to choose the appropriate ones from various terms to meet the dynamic user demands at the least cost is a great challenge. This paper addresses the challenge by two algorithms. Extensive real world traces driven evaluations show that the heuristic algorithm runs about twice as fast as the approximation one, while both algorithms can save almost the same resource cost up to 27 %.

Keywords: Cloud broker · Dynamic resource provision · Reserved instance terms · Cost minimization · IaaS

1 Introduction

Many public cloud service providers (CSPs) deliver infrastructure as a service (IaaS) to users. Each provider differentiates itself in terms of service area, virtual machine (VM) instance types (each instance with a fixed CPU, memory and storage etc.), prices of different sources and performance guaranteed. Especially, there are various pricing mechanisms for VM instances. The instance can be provisioned on-demand and billed at a cycle of hour (Amazon EC2 [3]), minute (Microsoft Azure [16]) or 15 min (Elasthosts [6]). Optionally, the instance can be reserved at any time in advance and then launched at any time as required [21]. The reserved instance is charged a total cost whenever it is active. For example, Amazon EC2 provides a choice of two reserved instance terms, 1 year and

© Springer International Publishing Switzerland 2015
G. Wang et al. (Eds.): ICA3PP 2015, Part I, LNCS 9528, pp. 339–356, 2015.
DOI: 10.1007/978-3-319-27119-4_24

3 years [3] and the terms are charged differently. VMware vCloud Air permits
a more flexible subscription term from 1 month to 36 months [21]. Normally,
the average price for reservation at each billing cycle is far lower than that of
the on-demand one. Furthermore, the longer the term, the lower the price. For
instance, the saving over on-demand price of Amazon m3.media instance can be
up to 29 % and 60 %, for 1-year and 3-year terms, respectively [3].

Users can rent instances from the provider directly. But limited by their
knowledge of the cloud IaaS market, it is a great pain for users to make a selection
from various instances with various prices to cut their cost. Even sometimes,
they have to bargain with more than one provider to meet the different services
or service area requirements, thus incurring more overhead. Subjectively, these
requirements drive users to seek the help of the third party and lead to the
emergence of cloud broker in recent years [11].

A cloud broker can provide on-demand instance to users with lower price.
On one hand, the broker can choose infrastructures among providers for their
"expertise and experience" offering the service. On the other hand, based on
multiplexing of relatively small requirements of individual users, the broker can
make a bulk reservation in advance at a much lower reservation price. Then offer
users on-demand instances at an intermediate price. Huge profit space exists and
entices the broker to render brokerage services objectively.

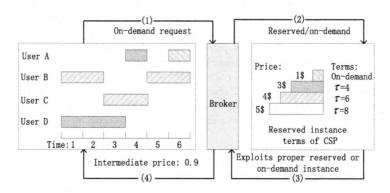

Fig. 1. Broker multiplexes the time-varying dynamic requests of four users. Then delivers on-demand services to users at a lower intermediate price by leveraging proper
reserved and on-demand instances. The left user request bar is served by the instance
bar with the same setting on the right CSP side.

Figure 1 depicts the service delivery scheme. Different users apply for on-
demand instances from time 1 to 6 (step 1). The broker tries to rent instances
from CSP to meet the requests at the least cost (step 2). CSP provides on-
demand and reserved instances with different prices and terms τ. The price for
on-demand instance is charged at each hour (billing cycle). For the reserved
scenario, the price is the total cost of τ billing cycles. Based on the number and
the lifetime of the aggregated request, the broker can exploit the pricing benefit

of long-term resource reservation and multiplexing gains (step 3). This enables the broker to offer users with a price of only 0.9\$ which is lower than the on-demand prices of CSP (step 4). In reality, the broker can earn 1.9\$, because he can charge 9.9\$ and only need to pay 8\$.

The challenge for the broker is how to exploit the price differences of on-demand and reserved resources from a cloud, so as to reduce his cost. Because every user dynamically submits his request, the aggregated request fluctuates with time. Policies for broker to rent instances from providers should be adapted accordingly. It is necessary to make the following decisions about renting instances, such as, on-demand launching or selecting an appropriate instance to reserve? How many instances and at what time to launch?

This paper aims to answer these questions. The main contributions are as follows:

1. We formulate the dynamic resource provision problem where the broker rents resources from a cloud service provider with multiple reserved instance terms.
2. A heuristic and an approximation algorithms are presented for the problem.
3. Extensive real world traces driven simulations demonstrate the effectiveness of both the algorithms. Significant resource cost saving can be achieved by using the algorithms.

The remainder of the paper is organized as follows. In Sect. 2 related work is reviewed. Section 3 formulates the problem. Section 4 and Sect. 5 present a heuristic and an approximation algorithms, respectively. They are evaluated in Sect. 6 and concluded in Sect. 7.

2 Related Work

Cloud Brokering has been proposed as a service and attracted plenty of attention in recent years [1,15]. Cost minimization and profit maximization are two main topics being explored. To minimize cost, the authors of [18] explore the possibility to optimally place VMs across multiple clouds. The capacity of each cloud and the load balance are considered. Eight heuristic algorithms which differ in diverse criteria for assigning priorities to VMs requests are presented in [17]. The authors try to maximize the profit of a broker who sublets on demand resources to customers. It is extended in [10] and a distributed simulated annealing algorithm is recommended. Different from the granularity of VMs, data center based graph clustering algorithm is presented to minimize the cost of the broker, including nodes (data centers), intra-cloud bandwidth and inter-cloud bandwidth [4]. Broker mechanism is also recommended to make cooperation decisions so as to maximize the cooperated CSPs [19].

In addition to cost and profit, quality of service is another main concern. Aiming to meet the requirements of users, a multi-objective decision strategy [2] sorts CSPs by scoring all kinds of constraints, especially on the technology heterogeneity, and then chooses the CSP with the maximum score. Reaction time minimizing and profit maximizing are explored in [13]. Based on Pareto optimum theory, the author formalizes the broker scheduling problem as a multi-objective programming and solves it by a simplified multi-objective genetic algorithm. The placement of latency sensitive application in multiple CSPs environment is also studied [5]. The problem is formulated as a mixed-integer programming subject to the resource capacity, load balance and latency. Furthermore, two policies are given to address the faulty scenario of CSP. Based on different criteria, such as performance optimization, cost minimization and energy efficiency, the scheduling function of the broker is equipped with 0-1 integer programming based algorithm to select the optimal cloud to deploy a service. Modern portfolio theory is leveraged to choose an efficient broker policy so that the tradeoff between satisfying uncertain demand and risk of not delivering satisfied services is balanced [8]. A framework is proposed to select CSPs so that the quality of service is achieved by combining their trustworthiness and competence [9]. Trustworthiness is estimated by the historical record of quality or reputation. While competence is the claimed service level. However, the aforementioned works do not take into account the price difference between on-demand and reserved resources. The dynamic property of the request is also not captured.

Reserved resources provide a great opportunity for the broker to reduce his cost. A dynamic resource reservation strategy is recommended for broker to minimize cost [22,23]. A dynamic programming is used to characterize the optimal solution. The original combinatorial problem is decomposed into a number of subproblems by using a set of recursive bellman equations and each is solved more efficiently. Two approximation algorithms are proposed for off-line and online scenarios, respectively. Especially, the off-line algorithm is proved as 2-approximate. Broker federation is explored in [14]. But all of them deem that there is only one reserved instance term. It is inconsistent with the practice of the cloud computing industry. This work explores dynamic resource provision with multiple reserved instance terms and just fills the gap.

3 Formulation

3.1 User Demand and CSP Pricing

User demand. Suppose a broker has an estimation of aggregated request up to a rather long period T. For any $t \in [1, T]$, the aggregated request at t is d_t. It is reasonable for each user should have a plan for the future request. The aggregation can be estimated based on the users' plans [14,23], or based on the historical requests. Let $L = max_t(d_t)$ is the peak request. We divide the demand d_t into L levels. Define indicator d_t^l to represent whether there is a demand at level l at billing cycle t, i.e., $d_t^l = 1$ if $d_t \geq l$, and 0 otherwise. For example, a demand curve is depicted in Fig. 2. $d_3^4 = 0$ because there is no demand at billing cycle 3 at level 4. This billing cycle is called as a vacant billing cycle. $d_5^5 = 1$, because there is a demand at billing cycle 5 at level 5. Obviously, $\sum_{l=1}^{d_t} d_t^l = d_t$.

A demand curve is called convex if for any $t_0 \in [1, T]$, there is no other $t_1 \in [1, T], t_2 \in [1, T]$, such that $t_1 < t_0 < t_2$, $\sum_{l=1}^{L} d_{t_1}^l > \sum_{l=1}^{L} d_{t_0}^l$ and $\sum_{l=1}^{L} d_{t_2}^l > \sum_{l=1}^{L} d_{t_0}^l$. For example, in Fig. 2, the curve between time 1, 3 is convex.

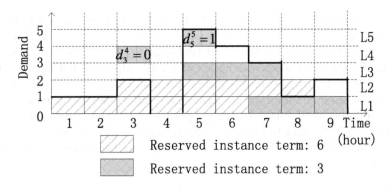

Fig. 2. Demand curve and level by level reservation with three reserved instance terms, where $\{\tau_0, \tau_1, \tau_2 \tau_3\} = \{1, 3, 6, 10\}$, $\{c_0, c_1, c_2, c_3\} = \{1, 2.5, 3.8, 6\}$. $T = 9$. At level 1, τ_1 and τ_2 will be replaced by τ_3 at last because $c_1 + c_2 > c_3$.

CSP pricing. Suppose a CSP provides J increasing reserved instance terms $\tau_1, \tau_2, ..., \tau_J$ (an instance with term τ_j is also called instance τ_j or term τ_j when there is no ambiguity, $j = 1, ..., J$), and all terms are longer than one billing cycle. The corresponding costs are $c_1, c_2, ..., c_J$, respectively. Specifically, let c_0 denotes the on-demand price, hence τ_0 is 1 which means one billing cycle. Then we have

(1) $c_0 < c_1 < ... < c_J$. Namely, the longer the term, the bigger the cost. Otherwise, the short term with bigger cost can be replaced by the long term with smaller cost. It is unnecessary to set the shorter one.

(2) $c_0/\tau_0 > c_1/\tau_1 > ... > c_J/\tau_J$. Namely, the longer the term, the cheaper the average price at each billing cycle. Otherwise, suppose for $i, j, (i < j)$, $c_i/\tau_i < c_j/\tau_j$. Then users can reserve τ_i by $\lceil \tau_j/\tau_i \rceil$ times to achieve the same resource with less cost and more capital flexibility.

3.2 Problem Formulation

Let y_{ljt} is a boolean variable which indicates whether to allocate an instance τ_j at time t to serve the demand at this time at level l. It equals 1 if this demand is served by an instance τ_j rather than τ_0, and 0 otherwise. For example, at level 2 in Fig. 2, $y_{223} = 1$ because τ_2 is reserved at time 3. All other $y_{2jt} = 0$. This problem can be formulated from the point view of levels.

$$\min \sum_{l=1}^{L} \sum_{t=1}^{T} \sum_{j=0}^{J} y_{ljt} c_j \qquad \text{(0-1ILP)}$$

$$\text{s.t.} \sum_{l=1}^{d_t} (\sum_{j=1}^{J} \sum_{i=t-\tau_j+1}^{t} y_{lji} + y_{l0t}) \geq d_t \qquad t = 1, 2, \cdots, T \qquad (1)$$

$$y_{ljt} \in \{0, 1\} \, l = 0, 1, \cdots, L, j = 0, 1, \cdots, J, t = 1, 2, \cdots, T. \qquad (2)$$

The objective is the total cost because whenever τ_j is reserved at any level, it should be charged c_j. In constraint (1), $\sum_{j=1}^{J} \sum_{i=t-\tau_j+1}^{t} y_{lji}$ is the number of instances which remain effective until time t at level l. y_{l0t} is the number of on-demand instances allocated at time t at level l. After calculating the sum of all levels, the left part of the constraint represents the number of all instances which can be used at time t. It should not be smaller than the demand d_t.

Programming 0-1ILP is a 0-1 integer programming and it belongs to one of the Karp's 21 NP-complete problems [12]. Hence it is also NP-hard.

Now, for each level l ($l = 1, 2, ..., L$), considering the following single level programming:

$$\min \sum_{t=1}^{T} \sum_{j=0}^{J} y_{ljt} c_j \qquad \text{(0-1ILPForLevel)}$$

$$\text{s.t.} \sum_{j=1}^{J} \sum_{i=t-\tau_j+1}^{t} y_{lji} + y_{l0t} \geq d_t^l \quad t = 1, 2, \cdots, T \qquad (3)$$

$$y_{ljt} \in \{0, 1\} \quad j = 0, 1, \cdots, J, t = 1, 2, \cdots, T. \qquad (4)$$

It is easy to check the feasible set of programming 0-1ILP and the intersection of the feasible set of all programming 0-1ILPForLevel are just the same. Let $f(y)$ denotes $\sum_{t=1}^{T} \sum_{j=0}^{J} y_{ljt} c_j$. Suppose y^* is the optimal solution for all programming 0-1ILPForLevel. That means, for any feasible solution of all 0-1ILPForLevel y, which is also feasible for 0-1ILP, we have $f(y) \geq f(y^*)$. So $\sum_{l=1}^{L} f(y) \geq \sum_{l=1}^{L} f(y^*)$. Thus

$$\min \sum_{l=1}^{L} f(y) \geq \min \sum_{l=1}^{L} f(y^*) = \sum_{l=1}^{L} f(y^*). \qquad (5)$$

The left part is just the optimal value of programming 0-1ILP. This motivates us to find the optimal solution of programming 0-1ILP level by level.

4   Heuristic Algorithm

4.1   Reservation Heuristic

With One Reserved Instance Term. We define $u^l = \sum_{t=1}^{T} d_t^l$, is the number of non-vacant billing cycles during period T at level l. In Fig. 2 $u^1 = 8$ because there is no demand at time 4. $u^5 = 1$.

When there is only one reserved instance term τ_1 with cost c_1, the periodic reservation mechanism is recommended [23]. Considering the simplest scenario where $T \leq \tau_1$, because any reservation remains effective in T, the problem becomes trying to reserve instances as many as possible at time 1. At level 1, if $u^1 c_0 \geq c_1$, that means compared to reserved instance with lower cost c_1, more expense is necessary if to launch u^1 on-demand instances. So we should reserve an instance τ_1. Suppose $l-1$ instances have been reserved at bottom $l-1$ levels, then the l-th instance should be reserved only if $u^l c_0 \geq c_1$, i.e., $u^l \geq c_1/c_0$. Note that u^l is non-increasing in l, we obtain a useful heuristic: reserve l instance at time 1 only if $u^l \geq c_1/c_0 > u^{l+1}$, if insufficient, launch other instances on demand. Because this heuristic finds the maximum l, for any level which is bigger than l, it is not economical any longer if adopting reservation policy.

In Fig. 3, considering the first scenario, where $T = 3 < \tau$, $d_3^3 = 0$ because there is no demand at billing cycle 3 at level 3, so even there is a reservation, it will not be used. $d_2^5 = 1$, because there is a demand at billing cycle 2 at level 5. $u^2 = 3$, $u^3 = 2$, $c_1/c_0 = 2.5$, $u^2 > c_1/c_0 > u^3$, so we reserve 2 instances at time 1.

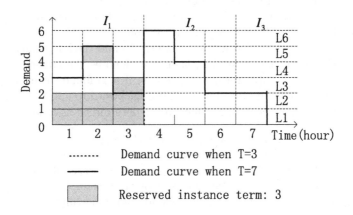

Fig. 3. Periodic reservation mechanism.

If $T > \tau_1$, T is divided into intervals and each with a length of τ_1. The upper heuristic is used in each intervals. In the upper figure, the demand curve where $T = 7$ is divided into 3 intervals.

With Multiple Reserved Instance Terms. When there are multiple reserved instance terms, it is impossible to find an appropriate term in advance to facilitate the periodic reservation. A new mechanism is necessary to address the problem. First, we give some notions to facilitate the mechanism presentation.

Length of each level. Note that the length of each level may be different. For level l, the length of this level is the number of billing cycles between the first demand time and the last demand time at level l, i.e.,

$$T^l = b_l - e_l + 1, \tag{6}$$

where $b_l = min\{t|d_t^l = 1\}, e_l = max\{t|d_t^l = 1\}$ are the first demand time and the last demand time, respectively. In Fig. 2, $[b_1, e_1] = [1, 9], T^1 = 9, [b_2, e_2] = [3, 9], T^2 = 7$.

Residue length of each level. For level l, let b' denotes the current non-vacant beginning time, then the residue length of this level is

$$T^{Rl} = e_l - b' + 1. \tag{7}$$

If beginning from b^l, $T^{Rl} = T^l$.

Note that given a level l, it is still economical to reserve a τ_j instance if

$$u_I^l c_0 \geq c_j, \tag{8}$$

where $u_I^l = \sum_{t \in I} d_t^l$, $I = [b, b + \tau_j]$. b is any given beginning time in the residue interval at this level and its initial value equals 1.

Feasible term. Given a level l with residue length T^{Rl}, a term τ_j ($j \geq 1$) is called feasible if $\tau_j \leq T^{Rl}$ and inequation (8) holds.

Beginning time update. At each level, we try to find the longest feasible term from the beginning of the level, i.e., b_l. Let b' denotes the current beginning. Suppose the longest feasible term is τ_h ($h \geq 1$) if it is found, or even τ_1 is still not feasible, then the beginning time is moved backward to find the next longest feasible term. The next beginning time can be determined as follows:

$$b = min\{t | d_t^l = 1, t \geq b' + \tau_h\}, \tag{9}$$

where $h = 1$ if there is no feasible term or τ_1 is the longest feasible term. Namely, the first demand time after the current interval. For example, in Fig. 2, at level 1, the first beginning time is 1 and the second beginning time is 7.

4.2   Level by Level Reservation Algorithm

We adopt a level by level reservation mechanism. Of course, every time the term with the lowest average price (i.e., the longest term) is preferred to others which also meet (8). If this longest term is shorter than the length of this level T^l, then the upper mechanism is repeated in the residue interval. It is detailed in Algorithm 1.

The first For loop (Lines 1–31) checks the demand level by level. At each level, If the residue length of the level is bigger than τ_1, the While loop (Lines 3–15) tries to reserve the longest term. The second For loop checks all the terms which are shorter than the residue length in a decreasing order (Lines 5–14). If a longer term is feasible, then we reserve such an instance and the related parameters are updated. Otherwise, we try the shorter instance, until we find one (Lines 7–10) or all the reservations are not economical (Lines 11–13). The beginning time is moved backward to begin a new interval try. For example, in Fig. 2, a τ_2 and then a τ_1 instance are reserved at level 1. The process is repeated until T^{Rl} is shorter than the shortest term τ_1. Then we decide whether to reserve τ_1 or serve the residue demands by on-demand instances (Lines 16–23). In Fig. 2, the demand at time 9 can only be served by an on-demand instance since there is no feasible term.

Algorithm 1. Level by level longest term preference decision (3LTPD)

Input: d_t: number of required instances at time t, $t = 1, 2, .., T$. $\tau_1, \tau_2, ..., \tau_J$: increasing reserved instance terms with increasing cost $c_1, c_2, ..., c_J$. c_0: on-demand price. L: number of levels

Output: A $T * J$ matrix $A = (A_{t,j})$: $A_{t,j}$ is the number of reserved τ_j instances at time t

1: **for** $l = 1, \cdots, L$ **do**
2:     $A \leftarrow 0$, calculate length of this level T^l (6), $T^{Rl} \leftarrow T^l$, interval beginning time $b \leftarrow min\{t : d_t^l \neq 0\}$, $b' \leftarrow b$, this level cost: $lc \leftarrow 0$
3:     **while** $T^{Rl} \geq \tau_1$ **do**
4:         Find maximum $j \leftarrow \{j : \tau_j \leq T^{Rl}\}$
5:         **for** $h = j, \cdots, 1$ **do**
6:             $I \leftarrow [b, b + \tau_h]$, reservation indicator: $resvInd \leftarrow 0$, level reservation indicator: $ind \leftarrow 0$
7:             **if** $u_I^l c_0 \geq c_h$ **then**
8:                 Reserve a τ_h instance at time b, $A_{b,h} \leftarrow A_{b,h} + 1$, update b (9) and T^{Rl} (7), $resvInd \leftarrow 1$, $ind \leftarrow ind + 1$, $lc \leftarrow lc + c_h$
9:                 break
10:             **end if**
11:             **if** $h = 1$ and $resvInd = 0$ **then**
12:                 Update b (9) and T^{Rl} (7), $lc \leftarrow lc + c_0$
13:             **end if**
14:         **end for**
15:     **end while**
16:     **if** $T^{Rl} > 0$ **then**
17:         $I \leftarrow [b, e^l]$
18:         **if** $u_I^l c_0 \geq c_1$ **then**
19:             Reserve a τ_1 instance at time b, $A_{b,1} \leftarrow A_{b,1} + 1$, $lc \leftarrow lc + c_1$
20:         **else**
21:             $lc \leftarrow lc + u_{T^{Rl}}^l c_0$
22:         **end if**
23:     **end if**
24:     **if** $lc > c_{j+1}$ **then**
25:         Cancel all reservations at this level and $A \leftarrow 0$
26:         Reserve a τ_{j+1} instance at time b', $A_{b',j+1} \leftarrow 1$
27:     **end if**
28:     **if** $ind = 0$ **then**
29:         **return**
30:     **end if**
31: **end for**

Suppose at level l, τ_j is the shortest term which is bigger than T^l. Then it is possible that the cost of τ_j is smaller than the current total cost at this level. Since it can meet the demand at this level, we will check it so as find a lower cost (Lines 24–27). As in Fig. 2, τ_1 and τ_2 at level 1 are replaced by τ_3 finally.

Because u_I^l is non-increasing of l, if no term is feasible in interval I at level l, then there is no feasible term in interval I at upper levels. It is necessary to check so that the program terminates in time (Lines 28–30), or after all levels are traversed. Any demand which cannot be served by reserved instance should be served by the on-demand instance.

It is easy to show the time complexity of 3LTPD is $O(LTJ)$. If bisearch is used to seek the longest feasible term, then $O(LTlogJ)$ time is required.

The next theorem demonstrates that for the convex demand, this algorithm can find a 2-approximation solution.

Lemma 1. *For each level, algorithm 3LTPD finds a 2-approximation solution when the demand is convex.*

Proof. Suppose there are J reserved instances with increasing terms $\tau_1, \tau_2, ..., \tau_J$ and increasing cost $c_1, c_2, ..., c_J$, where $c_1/\tau_1 > c_2/\tau_2 > ... > c_J/\tau_J$. c_0 is the on-demand price. T^l is the length of this level. Let j is the biggest one for which $\tau_j \leq T^l$. C^{Al} is the cost of level l incurred by algorithm 3LTPD and opt^l is the optimal cost of level l. When the demand is convex, then the algorithm tries to fill the level by τ_j because it is the cheapest. Suppose o^l is the number of on-demand instances to be launched. We have $C^{Al} = \lfloor T^l/\tau_j \rfloor c_j + min\{o^l c_0, c_j\}$, $opt^l \geq \lfloor T^l/\tau_j \rfloor c_j$. So $\frac{C^{Al}}{opt^l} \leq \frac{min\{\lfloor T^l/\tau_j \rfloor c_j + min\{o^l c_0, c_j\}, c_{j+1}\}}{\lfloor T^l/\tau_j \rfloor c_j} \leq \frac{min\{(\lfloor T^l/\tau_j \rfloor+1)*c_j, c_{j+1}\}}{\lfloor T^l/\tau_j \rfloor * c_j} \leq \frac{(\lfloor T^l/\tau_j \rfloor+1)*c_j}{\lfloor T^l/\tau_j \rfloor * c_j} \leq \frac{2\lfloor T^l/\tau_j \rfloor * c_j}{\lfloor T^l/\tau_j \rfloor * c_j} = 2$. The fourth inequality is due to $T^l/\tau_j \geq 1$.

Theorem 1. *For the brokering problem, algorithm 3LTPD finds a 2-approximation solution when the demand is convex.*

Proof. Let C^A is the cost of 0-1ILP incurred by 3LTPD, opt is the optimal cost of 0-1ILP and opt^l is the optimal cost of level l. Based on inequality (5), for any feasible solution y for 0-1ILP, $\sum_{l=1}^{L} f(y) \geq \sum_{l=1}^{L} f(y^*)$. So $opt \geq \sum_{l=1}^{L} opt^l$. We have $\frac{C^A}{opt} = \frac{\sum_{l=1}^{L} C^{Al}}{opt} \leq \frac{2\sum_{l=1}^{L} opt^l}{\sum_{l=1}^{L} opt^l} = 2$ where the inequality is due to Lemma 1.

5   Set Cover Based Approximation Algorithm

Given a level l, denote all non-vacant billing cycles at this level as set S^l whose element is the single non-vacant billing cycle. Taking all reserved and on-demand instances as a subset family $\tau = \{\tau_0, ..., \tau_J\}$, where each subset τ_j is attached with a cost c_j, then the cost minimization resource provision can be viewed as a cost minimization set cover problem. In this set cover problem, subset from τ can be repeatedly selected to cover S^l. Define the cost effectiveness for each τ_j at interval I as $e_j = c_j/u_I^l$ (I and u_I^l are as in inequation (8)). Then a simple algorithm based on set cover greedy algorithm (Chap. 1 of [20]) is adapted as follows. Each time it selects the feasible term (Sect. 4.1) with the lowest e_j from τ until S^l is covered. We call such term as the cheapest feasible term.

Suppose that the optimal cost of level l is opt^l. Obviously, if the optimal term is longer than T^l then cost found by Algorithm 2 is the same as opt^l. Thus Lemma 3 is established. So we only consider the case where the optimal terms are all smaller than T^l. Similar to the corresponding proof in Chap. 1 of [20], it

---

Algorithm 2. Set cover based algorithm (SCBA)

Input: A demand curve with L levels
Output: A resource provision solution
1: **for** $l = 1, \cdots, L$ **do**
2:    Select the cheapest feasible term from $b = b_l$. Update b (9). Update residue length T^{Rl} (7). Repeated this process until S^l is covered. Calculate the current overall reservation cost C.
3:    **if** Exists $\tau_j \geq T^l$ and c_j is smaller than C **then**
4:        Cancel all reservations at this level and reserve a τ_j instance at time b^l
5:    **end if**
6: **end for**

---

is easy to prove the following theorems. Number the billing cycles at level l in the sequence of covering as $1^l, ..., u^l$, we have

Lemma 2. *Given level l, for any $k \in 1^l, ..., u^l$, $e_k \leq opt^l/(u^l - k + 1)$ if the solution is not a term which is longer than T^l.*

Proof. Note that the optimal term must be feasible term, otherwise it can be replaced by any feasible ones and thus lead to a smaller cost.

Suppose opt^l is the optimal cost of level l. Because S^l can be covered by the optimal terms, during any iteration of Algorithm 2, the residue subset must can be covered by some terms with cost at most opt^l. Suppose the number of residue non-vacant billing cycles is r, then the average cost effective of the optimal terms is opt^l/r. So there must exists terms with cost effectiveness at most opt^l/r, during the iteration when k is covered, and the number of residue non-vacant billing cycles must be at most $u^l - k + 1$ elements, i.e. $r \geq u^l - k + 1$. Because in this iteration, the smallest cost effectiveness is selected, we have $e_k \leq opt^l/r \leq opt^l/(u^l - k + 1)$.

Lemma 3. *Algorithm SCBA gets a $H(u^l)-$ approximation for each level, where $H(u^l) = 1 + 1/2 + ... + 1/u^l$.*

Proof. If the solutions are some feasible terms, the cost incurred by Algorithm 2 is $\sum_{k=1}^{u^l} e_k$. Based on Lemma 2, we know the cost is at most $(1 + 1/2 + ... + 1/u^l)opt^l$. If the solution is a term which is longer than T^l, the cost is smaller than that of feasible terms found by the algorithm, and we get it.

Based on Lemma 3, similar to the proof of Theorem 1, it is easy to get

Theorem 2. *Algorithm SCBA finds a $H(m)-$ approximation for problem 0-1ILP, where $m = max_l H(u^l)$.*

Note that the only difference between 3LTPD and SCBA is the criterion to select the feasible term every time. The former selects the longest feasible term and the latter need to calculate the cost effectiveness for all feasible terms and then choose the smallest one. So SCBA will not run faster than 3LTPD as shown in experiments. For a general cost minimization set cover problem, it is proved that the greedy algorithm is tight. But maybe it is not true for the brokering problem where the set has a special structure. The next experiment demonstrates that 3LTPD can perform as well as SCBA.

6   Experimental Evaluation

6.1   Experiments Setup

Since public cloud workloads are often confidential, no real IaaS data trace is released so far. So we use Parallel Workloads Archive [7], a repository of job-level usage data from large scale parallel supercomputers, clusters and grids, to evaluate the performance of our algorithms. Four traces logs corresponding to four Intel Netbatch grid clusters, three on the west coast in the US and one in Israel, are used. Each log file contains one month's (i.e., November 2012) accounting records. The original logs are available as Intel-NetbatchX-2012-0 (where "X" is A, B, C, or D for the four different clusters). In experiments, we use A, B, C and D to represent the four data sources, respectively.

User demand and data preprocessing. Since the billing cycle is an hour, the demand at each billing cycle is rounded up, i.e., only when the lifetime of the request falling within the billing cycle is longer than 30 min, the request is counted as one demand.

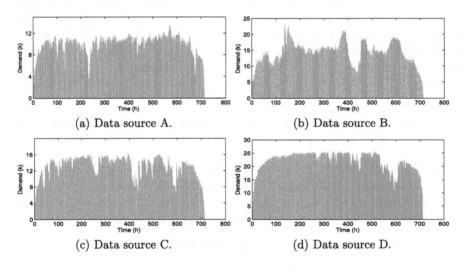

(a) Data source A.   (b) Data source B.

(c) Data source C.   (d) Data source D.

Fig. 4. Demand curves of four data sources.

The four data sources have different demand volumes and fluctuations. The corresponding demand curves are depicted in Fig. 4. The peak hourly demands are more than 13k, 23k, 16k and 25k for the four data, respectively. Figure 5 demonstrates the mean values and standard deviations. Generally speaking, data

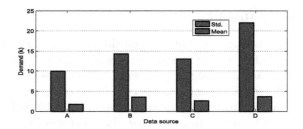

Fig. 5. Demand volume and fluctuation.

A has the smallest demand and D has the biggest demand. B and C have modest demand and B requests more than C. The fluctuation has almost the same tendency.

Parameter setting. The duration of the data trace is a month. Because there are no data at the beginning and end time of the month, we set T as the duration in which data are available, i.e., $T = 712$ h.

Table 1. Two groups of resources

CSP 1	Term	Cost ($)	Discount	CSP 2	Term	Cost ($)	Discount
τ_0	1 h	0.059	N/A	τ_0	1 h	0.059	N/A
τ_1	1 day	1.340	5 %	τ_1	5 days	6.018	15 %
τ_2	2 days	2.549	10 %	τ_2	10 days	10.62	25 %
τ_3	1 week	7.930	20 %	τ_3	20 days	16.992	40 %
τ_4	2 weeks	13.877	30 %				

Suppose there are two groups of resources represented by CSP 1 and CSP 2, each with the following terms and prices as demonstrated in Table 1. The on-demand price is borrowed from that of Amazon E2C m3.media with Windows operation system. Limited by the duration of data source, the reserved instance term is shortened accordingly. The cost discount is within the range of business CSP (about 60 % discount for 3-year term for Amazon). For convenience of comparison of the saving cost, the same on-demand price is adopted for the two groups. Note that the terms of CSP 2 are relatively longer than that of CSP 1. This setting can reveal the factors affecting the resource cost[1].

The simulation environment is set up in a Java platform. The platform is running on a PC (Lenovo Think Centre M4350t-N020Intel(R) Core(TM) i5-3470 CPU @ 3.20GHz8G RAM).

---

[1] The result under different setting demonstrates a tendency similar to the following results under this setting and hence omitted.

6.2   Experimental Results

To evaluate the cost saving of the broker and the proposed algorithms, five different schemes, including the proposed two algorithms are compared. For the scenario without broker, (1) longest preference for each user's request (abbreviated as N/B LP): select the longest reserved instance term for a continuous demand every time and traversing vacant demand is prohibited. The feasible longest term is used because obviously that the shorter term will incur more cost; (2) all demand is served by on-demand instances (abbreviated as N/B OnD). In the scenario with a broker, (1) similar as N/B LP except that it operates on the aggregated demand curve (abbreviated as W/B LP); (2) 3LTPD; (3) SCBA.

Performance Evaluation. We exploit resources from CSP 1 or CSP 2 to serve the requests from data source A, B, C and D. The resource cost is depicted in Fig. 6. In Fig. 6(b) and (d), the cost of on-demand is used as the baseline to calculate the saving percentage.

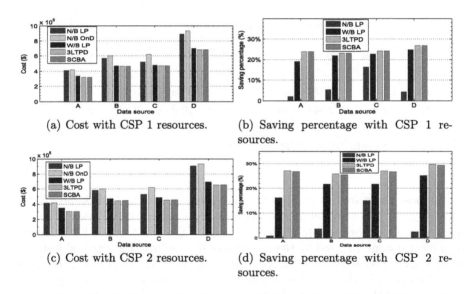

(a) Cost with CSP 1 resources.

(b) Saving percentage with CSP 1 resources.

(c) Cost with CSP 2 resources.

(d) Saving percentage with CSP 2 resources.

Fig. 6. Cost efficiency when exploiting resources from different CSP.

Since the demand volumes of four data differ, the total costs are also different. From Fig. 6(a) and (c) we can find whichever group of resources is exploited, the total costs demonstrate the similar tendency as that of the demand volume in Fig. 5. Overall, more demand incurs more cost for all five schemes.

Even when there is no broker and the demands are not multiplexed, it is still efficient to use the reserved instances as more as possible. As illustrated in Fig. 6(b) and (d), the scheme that tries the longest term (N/B LP) saves more cost. For CSP 1, it leads to an average saving up to 3.81 %. While 2.30 % for CSP 2. The reason lies in that the terms of CSP 1 are relatively shorter than that of CSP 2. When the demands are not multiplexed, the lifetime of single user's request is shorter, so the relatively longer terms of CSP 2 cannot be fully used. It reveals the effect of terms on resource cost.

However, after multiplexing by a broker, it demonstrates a contrary situation when the proposed 3LTPD is leveraged. On average, 27.23 % and 24.26 % cost are saved for CSP 2 and CSP 1, respectively. This is because that the aggregated request becomes longer and 3LTPD prefers the feasible longest term every time. Thus the relatively longer terms of CSP 2 can do better. Although W/B LP scheme also prefers the longest term, it does not use the heuristic. So, though it saves more than N/B LP, it is still not more efficient than 3LTPD. This also shows that 3LTPD can enable economical utilization of longer terms across vacant billing cycles.

The fluctuation of demand has an effect on the cost as well. Because the more volatile the demand is, the more demand valleys exist, fluctuation hinders the utilization of longer terms. It is detailed in Table 2. Note that the cost saving has the same tendency as that of the standard deviation curve in Fig. 5 when the W/B LP scheme is used: the more fluctuant, the more cost is saved. But 3LTPD can mitigate the negative effect of fluctuation. In total, the gap between cost saving for different data is reduced, though most cost is saved for data D.

Table 2. Saving percentage with broker relevant to fluctuation

Data		W/B LP (%)	3LTPD (%)		W/B LP (%)	3LTPD (%)
A	CSP 1	19.02	23.84	CSP 2	16.20	27.21
B		21.97	23.07		21.87	25.63
C		20.94	23.84		19.45	26.50
D		22.81	26.29		24.73	29.59

Figure 7 further justifies the benefit of exploiting multiple terms for 3LTPD. Herein all the terms of CSP 1 and CSP 2 are viewed as available for the algorithm and hence more candidate terms can be chosen. Figure 7(a) and (b) plot the cost and saving percentage when all terms are used. Comparing with Fig. 6, it is shown that more terms lead to more cost saving. Especially, we compare the resource cost efficiency for 3LTPD in Fig. 7(c) and (s). When all terms of both CSPs are used, up to 46 thousand dollars (5 %) are saved compared with that when only the terms of CSP 1 are used, and 19 thousand dollars (2 %) are saved compared with CSP 2. This is due to that more terms lead to higher applicability to dynamic demands.

It is noteworthy that for all data sources, although we can only prove 3LDPP is 2-approximation for the convex demand curve, 3LDPP performs almost exactly the same as SCBA for all data sources.

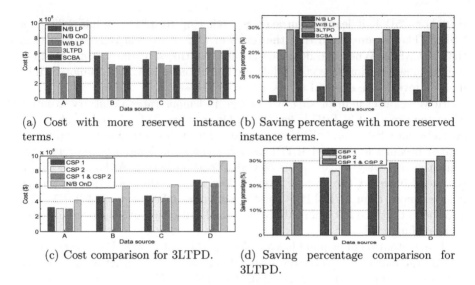

(a) Cost with more reserved instance terms.

(b) Saving percentage with more reserved instance terms.

(c) Cost comparison for 3LTPD.

(d) Saving percentage comparison for 3LTPD.

Fig. 7. Cost efficiency when more reserved instance terms are exploited.

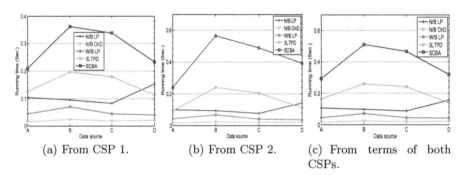

(a) From CSP 1.

(b) From CSP 2.

(c) From terms of both CSPs.

Fig. 8. Time efficiency when exploiting resources from different CSP.

Running Time Efficiency Evaluation. Running time of the algorithms is compared in Fig. 8. The running time of algorithms which exploit terms from CSP 1, CSP 2 and both of them are depicted in Fig. 8(a), (b) and (c), respectively. All the three figures show a common pattern. The on-demand algorithm takes the least time. N/B LP takes more time because it seeks the longest term each time for each user. But after multiplexing the demand of each user by the broker, the longest preference scheme (W/B LP) runs faster than N/B LP. This lies in that the broker aggregates users' request and thus reduces the number of times to find the longest term. SCBA and 3LTPD run slower than the former three schemes. Since SCBA computes the cost effectiveness for each feasible term and then selects the smallest one, 3LTPD only selects the longest feasible term, 3LTPD runs almost twice as fast as SCBA. Recall that 3LTPD and SCBA exhibit almost the same performance (Figs. 6 and 7), the superiority of 3LTPD is demonstrated.

7 Conclusion

Considering the multiple reserved instance terms, two algorithms are presented to facilitate broker to utilize infrastructure resources from public CSP at the least cost. One is heuristic and another is an approximation algorithm. Extensive traces driven evaluation demonstrates the effectiveness of both the algorithms. Our future work aims to exploit resources from multiple CSPs. In this scenario, though there are more candidate terms, there is also interoperability which impedes the multiplexing effect. How to balance the contradiction to achieve an efficient scheme is a great challenge.

Acknowledgments. This work was financially supported by National High-tech R&D Program of China (863 Program) with Grants No. 2015AA016008, National Natural Science Foundation of China with Grants No. 11371004, Shenzhen Strategic Emerging Industries Program with Grants No. JC201104210032A, No. ZDSY20120613125016389, No. JCYJ 20120613151201451 and No. JCYJ201303291532 15152 as well as Shenzhen Development and Reform Commission with Grants No. 2012720 and No. 2012900.

References

1. Amato, A., Di Martino, B., Venticinque, S.: Cloud brokering as a service. In: 2013 Eighth International Conference on P2P, Parallel, Grid, Cloud and Internet Computing (3PGCIC), pp. 9–16. IEEE (2013)
2. Amato, A., Venticinque, S.: Multi-objective decision support for brokering of cloud sla. In: 2013 27th International Conference on Advanced Information Networking and Applications Workshops (WAINA), pp. 1241–1246. IEEE (2013)
3. Amazon: Amazonvmpricing. http://aws.amazon.com/ec2/pricing/
4. Choi, T., Kim, Y., Yang, S.: Graph clustering based provisioning algorithm for optimal inter-cloud service brokering. In: 2013 15th Asia-Pacific Network Operations and Management Symposium (APNOMS), pp. 1–6. IEEE (2013)
5. Diaz-Sanchez, F., Al Zahr, S., Gagnaire, M.: An exact placement approach for optimizing cost and recovery time under faulty multi-cloud environments. In: 2013 IEEE 5th International Conference on Cloud Computing Technology and Science (CloudCom), vol. 2, pp. 138–143. IEEE (2013)
6. Elastic: Elastichostsvmpricing. http://www.elastichosts.com/pricing-information/
7. Feitelson, D.G., Tsafrir, D., Krakov, D.: Experience with using the parallel workloads archive. J. Parallel Distrib. Comput. **74**(10), 2967–2982 (2014)
8. Gaivoronski, A.A., Strasunskas, D., Nesse, P.J., Svaet, S., Su, X.: Modeling and economic analysis of the cloud brokering platform under uncertainty: choosing a risk/profit trade-off. Serv. Sci. **5**(2), 137–162 (2013)
9. Ghosh, N., Ghosh, S.K., Das, S.K.: Selcsp: a framework to facilitate selection of cloud service providers. IEEE Trans. Cloud Comput. **3**(1), 66–79 (2014)

10. Iturriaga, S., Nesmachnow, S., Dorronsoro, B., Talbi, E.G., Bouvry, P.: A parallel hybrid evolutionary algorithm for the optimization of broker virtual machines subletting in cloud systems. In: 2013 Eighth International Conference on P2P, Parallel, Grid, Cloud and Internet Computing (3PGCIC), pp. 594–599. IEEE (2013)
11. Jamcracker: Csb solutions overview. http://www.jamcracker.com/solutions
12. Karp, R.M.: Reducibility Among Combinatorial Problems. Springer, New York (1972)
13. Kessaci, Y., Melab, N., Talbi, E.G.: A pareto-based genetic algorithm for optimized assignment of vm requests on a cloud brokering environment. In: 2013 IEEE Congress on Evolutionary Computation (CEC), pp. 2496–2503. IEEE (2013)
14. Liu, K., Peng, J., Liu, W., Yao, P., Huang, Z.: Dynamic resource reservation via broker federation in cloud service: a fine-grained heuristic-based approach. In: 2014 IEEE Global Communications Conference (GLOBECOM), pp. 2338–2343, December 2014
15. Mechtri, M., Zeghlache, D., Zekri, E., Marshall, I.J.: Inter and intra cloud networking gateway as a service. In: 2013 IEEE 2nd International Conference on Cloud Networking (CloudNet), pp. 156–163. IEEE (2013)
16. Microsoft: Microsoftvmpricing. http://azure.microsoft.com/zh-cn/pricing/details/virtual-machines/#Linux
17. Nesmachnow, S., Iturriaga, S., Dorronsoro, B., Talbi, E.G., Bouvry, P.: List scheduling heuristics for virtual machine mapping in cloud systems. In: VI High Performance Computing Latin America Symposium (2013)
18. Tordsson, J., Montero, R.S., Moreno-Vozmediano, R., Llorente, I.M.: Cloud brokering mechanisms for optimized placement of virtual machines across multiple providers. Future Gener. Comput. Syst. 28(2), 358–367 (2012)
19. Truong-Huu, T., Tham, C.K.: A novel model for competition and cooperation among cloud providers. IEEE Trans. Cloud Comput. 2(3), 251–265 (2014)
20. Vazirani, V.V.: Approximation Algorithms. Springer Science & Business Media, New York (2001)
21. VMVare: Vmvarepricing. http://vcloud.vmware.com/service-offering/pricing-calculator/subscription
22. Wang, W., Niu, D., Liang, B., Li, B.: Dynamic cloud resource reservation via iaas cloud brokerage. IEEE Trans. Parallel Distrib. Syst. PP(99), 1 (2014)
23. Wang, W., Niu, D., Li, B., Liang, B.: Dynamic cloud resource reservation via cloud brokerage. In: 2013 IEEE 33rd International Conference on Distributed Computing Systems (ICDCS), pp. 400–409. IEEE (2013)

A Service Industry Perspective on Software Defined Radio Access Networks

Casimer DeCusatis[1(✉)] and Ioannis Papapanagiotou[2]

[1] School of Computer Science & Mathematics, Marist College, Poughkeepsie, NY 12603, USA
casimer.decusatis@marist.edu
[2] Computer and Information Technology, Purdue University, West Lafayette, IN 47906, USA
ipapapan@purdue.edu

Abstract. Despite the rapid growth of service science, relatively little attention has been paid to the service architecture requirements in software defined radio access networks (SDRAN). In this concept paper, we propose to repurpose cloud computing network services to address issues specific to SDRAN. In particular, a multi-level backhaul slicing approach derived from cloud computing networks is discussed as a way to mitigate interference limited networks with a frequency reuse factor of one. Experimental demonstration of the control plane implementation in a virtual cloud network is presented, and implications on service provider development and training are also discussed.

Keywords: Software defined networks · Radio access networks · SDRAN · SSME, RAN · SDN

1 Introduction

The service sector has steadily grown to become a dominant part of our global economy, particularly in developing nations [1]. The impact of the service economy is perhaps greater in the technology disciplines, where the emergence of new service offerings parallels the growth of smart cities, academic institutions, and the so-called digital knowledge economy [2]. One example is cloud computing, which has introduced the concepts of Infrastructure, Platform, Security, and Software as a service within the past five years [3]. Information technology (IT) service professionals perform tasks such as designing, installing, managing, and maintaining systems for computation, networking, and storage. Practitioners in this field are transforming legacy data centers and communication networks into next generation architectures, characterized by dynamic workloads, elastic scale-out resources, and highly virtualized infrastructure, and on-demand, self-provisioned services [3]. Collectively, these technologies are causing one of the most significant disruptions in the long history of IT [4]. The impact is evident on many large technology service providers; for example, IBM pretax income from services accounts for over 40 % of the company's total income, exceeding the contributions from selling computer hardware and software [2]. Further, IT services are the fastest growing revenue component for IBM, exceeding $60B in recent years; by contrast, hardware and

G. Wang et al. (Eds.): ICA3PP 2015, Part I, LNCS 9528, pp. 357–369, 2015.
DOI: 10.1007/978-3-319-27119-4_25

software sales *combined* barely reach half that amount [2]. Within the past decade, the field of service science has emerged to provide an inter-disciplinary framework for the development of new service offerings. Since this field is relatively new, many areas are still under investigation. In particular, the impact of next generation IT technology on the wireless communication industry, and its implications for the IT service industry, have not yet been thoroughly explored.

Wireless infrastructure is becoming increasingly complex, Driven by the need to support exponentially increasing amounts of mobile traffic over a limited amount of spectrum bandwidth, wireless infrastructure is becoming increasingly complex. As an example, major U.S. carriers such as Verizon and AT&T both have less than 100 MHz of spectrum available nationwide for LTE applications [5, 6]. This lack of available spectrum creates a number of problems for radio access network (RAN) service professionals, including architectural concerns with spectral allocation. Traditionally, a radio access network is treated as a collection of base stations, which are interconnected by backhaul links (either fiber optic cable, copper cable, or wireless backhaul links may be employed). As spectrum becomes limited, network architectures compensate by using increasingly dense designs (sometimes known as cell splitting). Such designs can force adjacent base stations to operate on the same channel. This is known as a frequency reuse factor of one, and it makes network management significantly more complex. For example, the radio resource management decisions made at one base station can affect nearby base stations (such as when a given user selects a portion of the spectrum to use for transmission at a given power level). This can lead to an interference-limited network, requiring some form of network management coordination among disparate base stations.

In principle, a dense network can improve transmission quality for each user by pushing critical infrastructure closer to the end user. Similar problems have been addressed in service provider network architectures for cloud computing. A cloud service provider (CSP), which desires to provide a mixture of services with different traffic requirements (video on demand, voice over IP, etc.), needs to determine whether to distribute network intelligence closer to the end user, or cluster it in a central location. It has been suggested [5] that all RAN base stations deployed within a given geographic area should be abstracted as if they were a single base station with a logically centralized control plane. This is the same approach used by CSPs who deploy software defined networking (SDN) in their cloud access networks. It follows that we should be able to apply some of the network architecture principles developed for CSPs to the emerging field of software defined radio access networks (SDRAN). For example, concerns with interference limited cell splitting networks may be addressed using multi-level control plane architecture for virtual slicing of a wired backhaul network between base stations, in the same way that this solution has found applications to CSP network service virtualization.

Just as server abstraction (operating system and programming languages) have superseded the requirement for all computers to be programmed in low level assembly language, SDRAN provides application programming interfaces (APIs) which automate many aspects of network management that are currently performed by low level, manual commands. This is quite different from the approach used by traditional distributed network architectures, which had no central management plane and thus were faced with significant issues when frequency reuse one networks emerged.

In this paper, we describe a conceptual framework for service offerings in SDRAN networks, based on extensions of the principles used in cloud service provider networks. We review...and propose a concept for an SDRAN system. The test bed described in this paper serves as a prototype for ongoing testing and development of SDRAN architectural principles. The specific contributions of this work include development of a test bed which demonstrates basic SDRAN principles, additional theoretical background on the SDRAN framework, and a perspective on SDRAN from the service industry, including the potential impact of SDRAN on service skills required for the networking practitioner. Following a brief overview of the service sciences and an introduction of common network service design principles, we discuss how these principles may be applied to SDRAN. We discuss abstraction and virtualization of SDRAN resources, and potential impacts on deployment time for new services and performance of software-defined network appliances. Experimental results from a 100 km metropolitan area CSP network will be presented to illustrate the benefits which can be realized using a software defined approach to the RAN. Finally, we discuss the implications of SDRAN on training programs for service practitioners, and suggest areas for future research.

2   Brief Overview of Service Science

By most estimates, the service economy has far outstripped other sectors such as agriculture and manufacturing (see Fig. 1). Many researchers and practitioners have come to challenge the conventional definition of service, as producing outcomes which are intangible, heterogeneous, instantaneous, and perishable (at least in comparison with goods and hardware). Within the past decade or so, it was recognized that this definition was inadequate for the modern service economy, in particular failing to differentiate products from services. In 2004, a more substantial definition and operational framework was introduced, known as Service Dominant Logic (SDL) [7, 8]. Within the SDL perspective on service, we can redefine service as a collaborative process between providers and recipients for the co-creation of value. The concept of value co-creation (innovation which creates value through a combination of suppliers providing new functionality and users requesting this functionality) is fundamental to this approach. There is little value in a service provider offering features which the market neither needs nor wants, and conversely there is no value creation when a user requests service features that differ from what any supplier can provide. Only through the intersection of provider and user can we realize value added services.

Concurrent with the adoption of SDL, a disciplinary framework was introduced by IBM known as Service Science, Management, and Engineering (SSME) [1, 2]. Service science is thus the application of knowledge to co-create value and the study of diverse, interconnected, complex, value co-creation systems in business. SSME advocates a multi-disciplinary, context-dependent approach that goes beyond modeling existing service offerings, and strives for radical innovation in service deployments. This discipline remains in its early stages of development, however

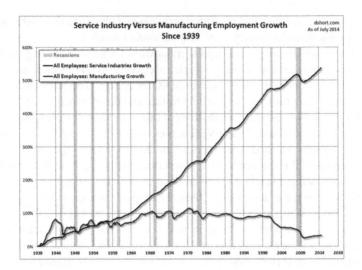

Fig. 1. Service industry employment growth over time, as compared with manufacturing and agriculture [see www.businessinsider.com]

there have been many encouraging achievements including conferences, training programs, and academic-industry liaisons.

Given the SSME focus on collaboration and multi-disciplinary innovation, the International Society for Service Innovation Professionals (ISSIP) was founded in July 2012. Consisting of nearly 1,000 individual members and over a dozen corporate and academic sponsors, ISSIP has a global mission to proliferate smart service systems and drive educational, research, professional development, and policy decisions. ISSIP has partnered with other technical societies, including the IEEE, on initiatives such as the NIST Global Smarter Cities challenge [9], which endeavors to bring leading-edge technology and services to major metropolitan areas. This includes the design and deployment of advanced communication networks as part of the urban infrastructure, such as ubiquitous, reliable, low cost wireless networks and intelligent wired communication between network service provider hubs and cloud computing centers.

Eight working groups within ISSIP focus on different facets of emerging technology In particular the software-defined networking (SDN) working group promotes research and education related to next generation communication networks. In this context, value co-creation encompasses several network design features and principles, including service reuse, network provisioning time, time to value for new network features, automation of common service tasks, optimization of service tasks, and more. The remainder of this paper will discuss a contextual framework for applying these network service industry principles to software-defined networks. Parallels between software-defined cloud networks and RANs will be presented, suggesting the benefits to be realized from SDRAN architectures.

3   Resource Allocation in SDRAN

In this section, we discuss several aspects of service management, which can be applied to a software-defined radio access network. The relative benefits of SDRAN compared with traditional approaches to radio access networks will also be described. Service reuse refers to the importance of developing new service offerings, which can be leveraged across multiple applications, or adapting an existing service offering to a new purpose. This is an important principle, since it helps control manpower costs and improves efficiency by eliminating duplication of effort. We recognize that the design principles developed for software defined networking (SDN) in a cloud computing data center may be similarly applied to the control plane of an SDRAN. In a cloud computing network, the routers within and between data center servers can be abstracted to create a single control plane, effectively treating a collection of networking resources as if they were one large switch. This same approach can be applied to the backhaul network interconnecting base stations in an SDRAN, as proposed by the SoftRAN design [5], illustrated in Fig. 2.

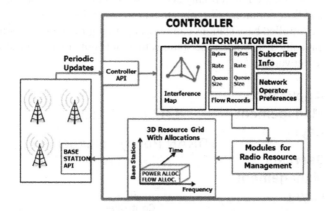

Fig. 2. Basic architecture for SDRAN controller as used in SoftRAN [5, 6]

Separation of the data plane from the management/control plane in an SDRAN, and providing a centralized network controller, offers similar benefits. For example, just as conventional data center networks consisted of routers, which make hop-by-hop decisions about traffic flow, a conventional RAN uses a distributed control plane spread across many independent devices. Coordination between these devices can be extremely difficult. Just as a cloud data center network uses the same routing hardware regardless of the application, a RAN is not application aware and has no end-to-end context for making transmission decisions between widely separated base stations. A centralized, software-defined control plane with a standardized, programmable API can address this issue. Further, a programmable network controller can be implemented as part of a modular, layered control plane architecture in both SDN and SDRAN applications. There are well known benefits to a layered control plane, including loose coupling or partial isolation between layers [9]. This allows each software layer to be developed independently of the layers above it, and optimized independently of those layers. In this approach, the underlying hardware may often be commoditized, i.e. replaced by standard x86 servers. This becomes possible, in part, because higher level functionality has been abstracted into a software control plane.

A centralized SDRAN control plane can also be made application aware through a layered software stack. A version of the CSP software architecture stack for network control [10], modified for SDRAN networks, is proposed in Fig. 3. Note that the upper level or application layer orchestration receives input from the SDRAN devices at the lower layers; this facilitates implementation of end-to-end quality of service levels. Just as essential elements of a cloud network can be abstracted to the controller, the SDRAN controller can make traffic routing decisions across many backhaul nodes at once. In a cloud computing network, for example, certain types of traffic can be isolated for special treatment. High bandwidth, long duration flows (so-called "elephant flows") can be segregated to their own sub-network to avoid congestion. Rather than have each data center switch make local routing decisions, the SDN cloud network controller owns all the routing tables for every switch in the network. Further, a controller can take into account factors, which are not normally accessible to a distributed control plane, such as the end-to-end flow duration and application or transport level traffic priorities. Similarly, SDRAN controlled base stations can select operating frequencies for traffic flows across geographically distributed base stations to avoid contention in a dynamic, interference-limited network.

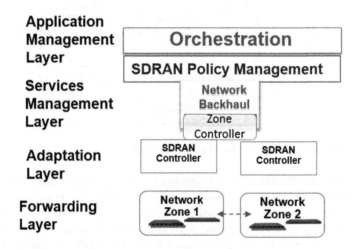

Fig. 3. Four layer software management stack for SDRAN, including centralized multi-zone network controller

Automation of common tasks is important to reducing service management costs, and to providing control of large, complex systems. Traditional data center network applications from a decade ago were statically provisioned, and did not require significant re-provisioning during their operating lifecycle. As new applications emerged (video on demand, mobile computing, big data/analytics), applications came to require dynamic re-provisioning on shorter and shorter time scales. Many cloud computing systems have long passed the point where manual provisioning alone is sufficient to keep up with application demand. Automation of the control plane has rapidly become an indispensable function for clouds, and SDRAN networks are poised to take advantage of these same benefits. Automation provides faster time to value by enabling rapid instantiation of new features and service/revenue opportunities. Consider provisioning of optical packet networks between multiple cloud data centers in a metropolitan area (about 100 km radius). Conventional data networks relying on manual provisioning of each network device along the traffic path could take days or weeks to reconfigure new services [11]. Using SDN, we have demonstrated dynamic re-provisioning of a 100 km optical network between three enterprise-class data centers in under one minute [4, 10]. If we replace the data centers with SDRAN base stations using this control plane architecture, similar improvement can be expected.

Once the network control plane is automated, we can introduce a feedback control loop to optimize performance over time. Network optimization is greatly facilitated by a centralized controller, receiving input from commodity hardware at lower layers of the management stack. In one example [4], a large Fortune 500 financial client was able to improve workload utilization on their servers and network from 10 % to over 40 %. This resulted in significant cost savings from avoiding the purchase of new equipment, more energy efficient operation of existing equipment, and improvements in service level achievements. Reduction of over-provisioning in networks has been shown to reduce energy consumption by a third or more [12]. While optimization of SDRAN is in the early stages, it is not unreasonable to expect similar performance improvements.

4   Multi-tier Virtual Network Slicing

In the previous section, we mentioned possible application performance concerns associated with centralized control of a RAN, especially for applications, which require time sensitive access to large volumes of data. We have demonstrated a dynamic bandwidth provisioning approach for service offerings in a cloud data center SDN network, which should be directly applicable to base station backhaul networks using SDRAN. Such an approach is well suited to aligning network capacity with user spectrum demands. This section will briefly describe the approach for multi-layer control planes in a software-defined nodal network, and propose a conceptual architecture for SDRAN.

To address the limitations associated with densely packed cells in an SDRAN network, a centralized controller may be employed to allocate bandwidth on the back-haul network between geographically distributed base stations. The creation of virtual sub-networks or network slices in the control plane can be extended down to the level of individual users, if desired. Each slice of the backhaul network can manage its bandwidth allocation independently of all other slices, using its own network controller (note that this does not have to be the same type of controller used to slice the backhaul network in the first place). This two level management system provides additional flexibility when optimizing overall bandwidth utilization. We have previously demonstrated such a multi-tier, network slicing management plane for cloud service providers, using a test bed at the New York State Center for Cloud Computing and Analytics [4, 10, 12] (similar principles can be applied regardless of the backhaul infrastructure). Studies of SDN vs conventionally routed data centers have shown an improvement in meeting service level conditions of up to 30 % [4]; similar improvements may be possible using SDRAN.

The test bed used for our cloud computing experiments is shown in Fig. 4, consisting of a 125 km single-mode fiber backhaul ring interconnecting three metropolitan area data centers (or base stations). The sites in this example are interconnected with a dense Wavelength Division Multiplexing (WDM) platform (Adva FSP3000), including excess, discretionary wavelength pools which can be applied to the optical packet connections. Each site also contains inexpensive demarcation point hardware (Adva XG210), which serves as a traffic monitor or traffic injection source for test purposes. The data centers (or base stations) are interconnected via 1/10 Gbps Ethernet links in this example, although other forms of connectivity could easily be used. Servers at each location host virtual machines (VMware environment), which contain software defined network (SDN) controllers and a network hypervisor for the WDM optical backhaul equipment.

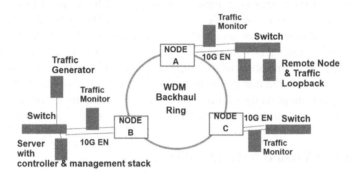

Fig. 4. Packet over optical WDM test bed using SDN and network hypervisor control

The software management plane for this test bed is illustrated in Fig. 5. We have created an extension for open source SDN controllers and the WDM network hypervisor, (a piece of software known as "Advalanche"), which performs dynamic bandwidth provisioning based on OpenFlow 1.3.1. The SDRAN centralized control plane would use a similar approach, likely a combination of Advalanche and the WDM network hypervisor to slice the backhaul network into two or more virtual network segments, each of which can be assigned to a different cell. Each cell is then able to use an open standards-based SDN controller of their choice to optimize bandwidth allocation within their slice of the network. Our test bed demonstrates the Floodlight controller in one slice, and the Open Daylight controller running at the same time in another, logically independent slice. Each tenant can also optimize their individual WDM bandwidth using Advalanche, which may be called from either Floodlight or Open Daylight; each tenant's controller can also provision network resources within a given cell. We have also created a graphical user interface which can optionally be used with the controllers and hypervisor, and which supports wireless mobile management interfaces (smartphones or tablets) that do not have good native support from the network controllers.

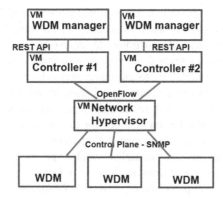

Fig. 5. Software control plane architecture for cloud service provider with two tenants

The XG210 is a small, inexpensive piece of hardware, which performs non-invasive traffic monitoring in the backhaul network. This triggers automated re-provisioning of connections in response to bandwidth requirements. We have experimentally achieved end-to-end re-provisioning in under a minute for a wide range of applications, including video on demand services and storage backup/recovery services; it is thus reasonable to expect similar performance for virtual radio base station appliances. Prior to the introduction of software-defined provisioning, an end-to-end solution as presented in this testbed would take several days or longer to be provisioned. We have shown that it is possible to implement end-to-end provisioning within a few minutes. The latency contributions of software defined provisioning are negligible compared with the achieved performance increase. Further, additional wavelengths for the affected application may be provisioned from an available wavelength pool, or by re-allocation of discretionary wavelengths from other applications (depending on existing quality of service agreements).

5   Service Professional Education

Recent interest in SDRAN is disrupting conventional radio access network architectures and administration policies. Mobile applications such as social media are driving this transformation at an accelerating pace. The emerging Internet of Things (IoT) also relies in part on an extensive network of wireless remote sensors from a variety of geographically dispersed sources, which must be collected for centralized analysis using a dynamic, next generation RAN. Applications such as the IoT are expected to invert the conventional network traffic patterns; instead of high traffic volumes and persistent flows on relatively few routers near the network core, we expect high volumes of short duration connections at the network edge. The large number of transient edge connections in the IoT will be a significant security challenge for networks without a centralized policy management system. Traditional RAN architectures are not well suited to these applications, having been designed primarily for static workloads, manual reconfiguration, and distributed, hop-by-hop management of network devices.

Since there is no single point in a conventional network which can enforce service levels, redundant connections, or network security, conventional RANs rely on highly skilled network architects and administrators to approximately translate their business requirements into a series of manual network provisioning commands. SDRAN with backhaul virtual slicing enables us to automate network resource provisioning, and through higher level orchestration creates application-aware networks. While previous sections of this paper have discussed technological improvements for SDRAN networks, these changes have even broader implications for the network service industry and for network education and certification programs. Preparing for network administrative and service roles traditionally involves complex, vendor-specific practitioner certification exams, which rely on memorizing network device configuration commands and learning how to implement hop-by-hop distributed networks. While these are valuable skills, the programming knowledge, which benefits modern software defined applications, has historically been de-emphasized for networking service practitioners [13]. This approach has begun to change. For example, to provide high availability the network administrator no longer needs to manually provision two or more redundant physical connections. Instead, using APIs in an SDRAN network, it is possible to write a script instructing the network controller to dynamically fail over traffic to a path with lower service priority, and automatically switch back once the fault had been corrected. The ability to program network infrastructure APIs is rapidly emerging as a key differentiating skill for radio network architects and administrators, and will soon become a requirement for most employers.

There are many examples of the close connection between advanced networking technologies and the services industry. Instead of building and maintaining their own private data centers, many companies are becoming increasingly reliant on cloud computing services. According to industry analysts, today 20 % of the Fortune 1000 use cloud computing for some applications, and half of them will be storing customer-sensitive data in the public cloud by 2016 [2]. A renewed emphasis on data networks for cloud computing is also disrupting conventional telecommunication companies, who are rapidly trying to transform into CSPs.

In order to promote new service offerings, processes, and business models, which reclaim value for network clients, the service profession has begun to transform networking infrastructure using SDN and NFV. Just as server abstractions (operating system and programming languages) have superseded the requirement for all computers to be programmed in low level assembly language, SDN provides application programming interfaces (APIs) which automate many aspects of network management that are currently performed by low level, manual commands. This is quite different from the approach used by traditional network switches and routers, which employ a distributed architecture (each switch only understands how to route data packets to the next hop in the network). Since there is no single point in a conventional network which can enforce service levels, redundant connections, or network security, most data centers presently rely on network architects and administrators to approximately translate their business requirements into a series of provisioning commands which are manually entered into each switch on the network. SDN enables a centralized network controller, which automates these functions and through higher level orchestration creates application-aware networks.

These changes have broad implications for the network service industry and for network education and certification programs. The programming knowledge, which benefits modern SDN deployments, has historically been de-emphasized for networking service practitioners [4]. It was felt that IT administrators didn't want or need to learn programming, which was more appropriate for traditional computer science disciplines. With the introduction of SDN/NFV, this approach to network administration education has begun to change. For example, to provide high availability the network administrator no longer needs to manually provision two or more redundant physical switches. Instead, using APIs in an SDN network, it is possible to write a script instructing the network controller to dynamically fail over traffic to a path with lower service priority, and automatically switch back once the fault had been corrected.

There have been several reports on the need to reform service education, as well as reports on the transformative power of early training curriculum redesign efforts in this field [13–15]. The need for rapid evolution in this area has never been more apparent; according to industry analysts, most of the top networking-related jobs in 2014 did not exist just a few years ago. A recent survey of 800 top service industry executives indicated that their number one obstacle in leveraging IoT and new networking technology is the lack of appropriate skills [14]. In an effort to address this skill gap for future network practitioners, the Institute for Service Industry Professionals (ISSIP) has recently formed a working group on SDN and network virtualization. The mission of this group includes promoting education related to SDN and software defined service, assessing the impact of SDN on required knowledge and skill sets, and providing guidance to a consortium of academic and industry participants.

A key principle of the service industry is value co-creation, which can be applied to industry/academic partnerships in SDN education. Academic institutions generally tend to value the creation and dissemination of knowledge, as well as the education of their students. Industry generally exists to create value for its investors and provide useful goods or services. It is thus in the interest of both parties to expand the current state of the art in key fields such as networking which enable both student job opportunities and potentially large consumer markets. We have endeavored to apply this approach to the software solutions developed at the New York State Center for Cloud Computing and Analytics, through our academic and industry partnership programs. As suggested by results from the previous sections, significant progress is being made in the re-education of the network administration workforce to accommodate trends in SDRAN.

6   Conclusion

While service science is an emerging field, it holds great promise for enabling next generation IT systems that fully exploit concepts such as resource virtualization and abstraction while providing increase velocity for service delivery. Repurposing and adapting existing service offerings to new environments are efficient ways to achieve value co-creation between service providers and their clients. Applying this approach to software defined network infrastructure for smart cities, it should be possible for SDRANs to generate value co-creation for smart city designs (that is, SDRANs can provide features which smart cities find useful and consumable). Following the principle of service re-use, we propose extending the software defined network management approach of cloud service providers to emerging SDRAN architectures. The benefits of a centralized controller, separation of the data and control planes, and abstraction of the management interface were discussed in this context. Our cloud services test bed has demonstrated reductions in service provisioning from days or weeks to minutes, reduced energy consumption by 30 %, and reduced service cost by 40 % through elimination of over-provisioning, without compromising quality of service agreements. Further, we propose adapting a multi-layer CSP management stack to virtual network slicing in the SDRAN backhaul, to mitigate problems associated with small, densely packed cells. The impact of these changes on SDRAN professional education programs was also discussed.

Future work in this area will concentrate on analytic modeling of more general problems of SDRAN network resource allocation, which are well known to both cloud service providers and RAN administrators [17]. The optimal placement of network control plane functionality (closer or further from the end user) can be modeled as a combination of locationing and dimensioning problems for a given traffic matrix. This work may be extended to specific SDRAN environments, and used to augment the application aware network orchestration discussed in this paper.

References

1. Maglio, P., Kieliszewski, C., Spohere, J. (eds.): Handbook of Service Science. Service Science: Research and Innovations in the Service Economy. Springer, New York (2010)
2. Spohrer, J.: Thinking about value: service science, management, and engineering. IBM University Programs Presentation to the Royal College of Art, 13 Jan 2015. http://www.slideshare.net/spohrer/2030-inspire-students-to-build-it-better-20150113-v3. Accessed 24 Jan 2015
3. Mell, P., Grance, T.: The NIST definition of cloud computing. NIST Special Publication 800–145, U.S. Department of Commerce, September 2011. http://csrc.nist.gov/publications/nistpubs/800-145/SP800-145.pdf. Accessed 24 Jan 2015
4. DeCusatis, C., Marty, I., Cannistra, R., Bundy, T., Sher-DeCusatis, C.J.: Software defined networking test bed for dynamic telco environments. In: Proceedings of SDN & OpenFlow World Congress, Frankfurt, Germany, 22–24 Oct 2013
5. Gudipati, A., Perry, D., Erran Li, L., Katti, S.: SoftRAN: a software defined radio access network. In: Proceedings of HotSDN, Hong Kong, China, August 2013. http://web.stanford.edu/~skatti/pubs/hotsdn13-softran.pdf. Accessed 24 Jan 2015
6. Gudipati, A., Erran Li, L., Katti, S.: RadioVisor: a slicing plane for radio access networks. In: Proceedings of HotSDN, Hong Kong, China, August 2013. http://stanford.edu/~adityag1/files/radio-visor.pdf. Accessed 24 Jan 2015
7. Vargo, S., Lusch, R.F.: Evolving to a new dominant logic for marketing. J. Market. 68(1), 1–17 (2004). http://sdlogic.net/JM_Vargo_Lusch_2004.pdf. Accessed 24 Jan 2015
8. Vargo, S., Akaka, M.A.: Service dominant logic as a foundation for service science: clarifications. J. Serv. Sci. 1(1), 32–41 (2009). http://sdlogic.net/Vargo_Akaka_2009_SS.pdf. Accessed 24 Jan 2015
9. Rhee, S.: NIST cyber-physical systems global city challenge, January 2015. http://service-science.info/archives/3691. Accessed 24 Jan 2015

10. DeCusatis, C., Cannistra, R., Hazard, L.: Managing multi-tenant services for software-defined cloud data center networks. In: Proceedings of 6th Annual IEEE International Conference on Adaptive Science & Technology (ICAST 2014), Covenant University, Nigeria, 29–31 Oct 2014
11. Manville, J.: The power of a programmable cloud. In: OFC 2012 Annual Meeting, Anaheim, CA, Paper OM2D.2, 18–22 Mar 2013
12. DeCusatis, C., Cannistra, R., Carle, B.: A demonstration of energy efficient optical networks for cloud computing using software-defined provisioning. In: Proceedings of IEEE GreenCom, 12–14 Nov 2014. http://www.ieee-onlinegreencomm.org/program.html
13. Sher-DeCusatis, C.J., DeCusatis, C.: Developing a software defined networking curriculum through industry partnership. In: Proceedings of ASEE Annual Meeting, Hartford, CT, 3–5 Apr 2014. http://asee-ne.org/proceedings/2014/index.html. Accessed 24 Jan 2015
14. Wilcox, L.C., Wilcox, M.S.: A review and evaluation of engineering education in transition. In: IEEE Proceedings of 8th International Conference on Computer Science and Education (ICCSE), Sri Lanka, 26–28 Apr 2013
15. McNickle, M.: SDN education. Tech Target Magazine, July 2013. http://searchsdn.techtarget.com/feature/SDN-education-Universities-tackle-SDN-course-content. Accessed 3 Mar 2014
16. Moghaddam, Y., Bess, C., Demirkan, H., Spohrer, J.: How to thrive as IT professionals in a converging ICT world. J. Inf. Technol. Manag. 27(3), 24–28 (2015)
17. Papapanagiotoo, I., Falkner, M., Devetsikiotis, M.: Optimal functionality placement for multiplay service provider architectures. IEEE Trans. Netw. Serv. Manag. 9(3), 359–372 (2012)

An Approach to Rapid Worker Discovery in Software Crowdsourcing

Feiya Song$^{(\boxtimes)}$, Haopeng Chen, and Ying Fu

School of Software, Shanghai Jiao Tong University, Shanghai 200240, China
{qingxueyihan, chen-hp, fyll19}@sjtu.edu.cn

Abstract. Crowdsourcing is an emerging business model which organizes distributed crowds to solve various problems through the Internet. Recently this paradigm has also flourished in software engineering domain. Despite benefits like on-demand workforce and rich expertise, a major challenge is how to discover cost-effective workers while guarantee high quality of deliveries. Current approaches to worker discovery have primarily based on workers' interest and self-evaluation which have subjective deviations. In this paper, we present a novel approach to describe each skill on the basis of feedback evaluation and estimate skill evolution dynamically. On the other side, to deal with the growing number of workforce, we use a clustering-based method to group workers with similar characteristics together to reduce search space. Our experiments show the effectiveness and efficiency of this approach.

Keywords: Crowdsourcing · Worker discovery · Sliding window analysis · Clustering · Skill degree

1 Introduction

As indicated in [1] by Jeff Howe, crowdsourcing is an online, distributed problem-solving and production model that has emerged in 2006 [2]. It rapidly mobilizes large numbers of people to accomplish tasks on a global scale [3]. With continuous development of information technology, anyone with an Internet connection can participate in this virtual workplace and contribute valuable information.

Currently there are many successful crowdsourcing platforms focusing on various contexts from micro-tasks to complex industrial problems such as Amazon Mechanical Turk [4], CrowdFlower [5] and TopCoder [6]. In the field of software engineering, crowdsourcing has also been embraced with open arms. It has been suggested as a useful approach in GUI testing [7], performance testing [8] and as a cost-effective way to outsource software development tasks. For example, American Online delegates TopCoder, a crowdsourcing community gathers global experts to work on difficult problems, to develop their communication backend software system. This project convenes more than 250,000 developers from all over the world and accomplishes within 5 months. By crowdsourcing, nearly half of the development time is reduced and the quality of delivered software also meets the industrial standard. With the increasing complexity of software requirement, traditional engineering method can

© Springer International Publishing Switzerland 2015
G. Wang et al. (Eds.): ICA3PP 2015, Part I, LNCS 9528, pp. 370–382, 2015.
DOI: 10.1007/978-3-319-27119-4_26

hardly cope with large scale development. Instead, a widely accepted trend is to take full advantage of the crowd to face future challenges.

However, software development task is a much more complex process in contrast to micro-tasks such as tagging images or transcribing audio clips, which raises some problems to be addressed. First, in many existing platforms, workers consume much energy in browsing task specifications and completing the application. For example in Upwork [9], one must submit a personal profile as well as a cover letter to the employer and accept an interview before being recognized. Besides, workers apply for tasks generally according to subjective decisions such as interest or self-evaluation, bringing in the potential risk of poor quality, over budget or unbalanced use of expertise. Last but not least, with continuous advancing of Internet technologies, the geographically distributed workforce is becoming more and more powerful. It is very time-consuming to find a suitable worker from this large number of candidates.

To solve aforementioned issues, we put forward an approach to rapid discover suitable workers in software crowdsourcing. In our approach, each worker has a skill set and each skill is evaluated according to feedback information. Next, we set up a update period to show the evolution of each skill and real-time performance. Skill descriptions are updated based on both historical and latest feedback. Last, to improve efficiency, we adopt the clustering method to divide workers into different groups and recommending suitable candidates in each group.

The remainder of the paper is structured as follows. In order to state a detailed description of aforementioned problems, we use a case to demonstrate motivations of this paper in Sect. 2. Then we outline our main idea to solve these problems in Sect. 3. Section 4 gives detailed implementations and key algorithms of our approach. Experiment results and analysis are illustrated in Sect. 5 to prove the practicability and efficiency of our approach. In Sect. 6, we compare our approach with related researches to discuss pros and cons. To make a summary, conclusion and future work is listed in Sect. 7.

2 Motivation

In this section, we take the online labor marketplace *Upwork.com* as an example to state motivations of our research. On Upwork, *jobs* are published by *clients*, *freelancers* get corresponding remuneration by completing jobs. So far, more than 1 million businesses use Upwork for top quality talent including Panasonic, Unilever etc.

For newly registered freelancers, they are required to self-evaluate their capability and add a grade label among "ENTRY", "INTERMEDIATE" and "EXPERT". However, people have different cognitions about these grades. A beginner may select a high level bring in the risk of poor quality or an expert is overmodest to choose the "INTERMEDIATE" level resulting in reduction of income and waste of expertise. On the contrary, evaluation given by clients is more objective and convinced because they know exactly whether the submitted jobs meet their requirement. They can provide evaluation based on integrity, reliability or scalability of delivered software.

"Job Success Score" in Upwork represents a worker's comprehensive performance evaluated by clients. Upwork updates this value every two weeks and looks at trends over a 24-month period. Although this kind of dynamic update method shows latest performance, it is inflexible to restrict calculation range within two weeks. For part-time freelancers, inactive or absent in several days is quite often. But when they are back, their Job Success Score, which is an important hiring reference is lost. As for feedback information given by clients, they only provide an overall evaluation despite the fact that not all skills are necessary in a single task. Therefore, a more reasonable feedback mechanism is needed to flexibly describe skill evolution.

Upwork has more than 1 million freelancers and nearly 80 thousand jobs now and the number will continue to expand in the future. Figure 1 shows a statistic chart of the worker number under "Web, Mobile & Software Development" job category. The least number that people who can do game development is more than 30,000. Although there are other optional constraints like hours billed, hourly rate, location etc., there is no screening conditions especially against skills. Users still need to search manually to find cost-effective freelancers whose skill set or subset meets their requirement.

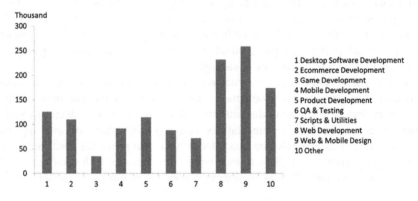

Fig. 1. Statistical chart of worker number

3 System Design

In this section, we explain the system design of a crowdsourcing platform applied our approach. Generally, two stakeholders can be identified as depicted in Fig. 2. *Employers* want to obtain results with high quality in a cost-effective manner, and *workers* provide their labor by processing tasks.

Our approach uses a *degree* property to represent the proficiency of each skill. Higher degree means much expertise while lower degree on behalf of less experience. For new workers, they need to build their personal profile in "Worker Register" module. After registration, one's capability is stored as a set consisting of many key-value pairs < *skill, degree* > in the "Worker Profile Database". Since each task needs to specify desired skill requirement in "Task Publish" module, worker's skill set or its subset exposes opportunistic behaviors to a certain task. In "Worker Clustering" module, we cluster workers with similar characteristics into the same group to reduce unnecessary search space. In "Worker Discovery" module, our method recommends

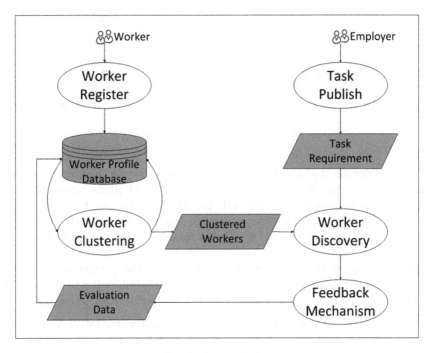

Fig. 2. System design

suitable workers for each task based on clustering results. After each completion of a task, employers evaluate each skill involved in this task through "Feedback Mechanism". We adopt the *Sliding Window Analysis* to process evaluation data and dynamically update each degree value. Detailed algorithms are illustrated in Sect. 4.

4 Key Algorithms

In this section implementation aspects particularly about algorithms are discussed. Our approach mainly focuses on the skill perspective when finding cost-effective workers. Other non-technical constraints in the task requirement such as location or available working time beyond the scope of this paper, which are all assumed to be satisfied for simplicity.

4.1 Sliding Window Analysis

As shown in Fig. 3, Sliding Window Analysis relies on bounded information to update skill degree dynamically. We set p days as the unit of a window size and assume a worker is capable of s different skills. Here are some definitions:

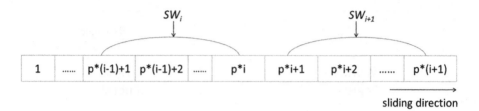

Fig. 3. Sliding window analysis

- SW_i, $i{\in}N$: denotes the i_{th} sliding window. For simplicity, we mark each day as an integer from 1. Thus the first SW includes days between $[1, p]$, the next window will slide to right by p days, namely $[p + 1, 2p]$. SW_n is $[p*(n-1) + 1, n*p]$.
- FD_{qj}, $j,q{\in}N$, $q{\in}[1, s]$: denotes the j_{th} feedback degree of skill q in a sliding window. Besides, we assume q totally get m pieces of feedback information in a window and $j{\in}[1, m]$.
- SD_{qi}, $q,i{\in}N$, $q{\in}[1, s]$: denotes the degree of skill q in the i_{th} window.
- W: the impact factor represents the influence of one's historical performance. The higher the value is, the greater impact of historical performance to current degree.

Thus, the degree of skill q in i_{th} window is calculated by the following formula:

$$SD_{qi} = W * SD_{q(i-1)} + (1 - W) * \frac{\sum_{j=1}^{m} FD_{qj}}{m} \tag{1}$$

It has to be noted that all historical evaluations, rather than only recent records, are taken into account by giving $SD_{q(i-1)}$ a certain weight. It influences one's current skill degree SD_{qi} to some extent and avoids great degree change between two windows, which is generally impossible in knowledge-intensive software tasks.

Formula (1) works well in the case that a worker has certain working time and accumulates a number of historical data. But for newly registered workers, since they have not received any feedback, we match suitable tasks to them only through their self-evaluations. Once they finish their first task, we no longer use those subjective scores. Instead, following discovery processes use the average of previous feedback scores until the number of received feedback reaches p, namely fill in the first window. Thus the sliding window analysis is ready to start after the first window is fixed.

4.2   Clustering Method

Our clustering method periodically groups workers into k clusters and each cluster consists of workers with similar characteristics.

Algorithm1: clustering method
Input: worker set $W = W_1 \cup W_2 \cup ... \cup W_k$; **center set** $C = \{C_1, C_2, ... C_k\}$;
Output: updated worker set $W' = W_1' \cup W_2' \cup ... \cup W_k'$; **updated center**
set $C' = \{C_1', C_2', ... C_k'\}$
Function:
begin
  while true
    W' **<-** W, C' **<-** C
    iter_count++ //record number of iterations
    for each worker w_i **in** W
      Distance_set$_i$ <- {distance(w$_1$,C$_1$), ...distance(w$_1$,C$_k$)}
      Nearest_center$_i$ <- min(Distance_set$_i$)

      W_{target} **<-** w_i, **Nearest_center$_i \in W_{target}$**

      //add each worker to the nearest cluster
    end for
    C' **<- Update_Centers(C')** //recalculate each center
    if
      $\forall w \in W$,**exists** $w' \in W'$ **and** $w == w'$
      $\forall w' \in W'$,**exists** $w \in W$ **and** $w' == w$
      break
    else if

      iter_count≥MAXIMUM //reach maximum iteration

      break
  end while
  Output(W', C')
end

In the above algorithm, each worker and center is both represented by a vector. Vector of worker consists of all skill degree while center is the average value in each dimension, calculated by workers belongs to this cluster. *distance()* is the Euclidean distance between two vectors. MAXIMUM is used to control the convergence of algorithm to avoid high time complexity caused by discrete data. For the first time clustering, initial parameters are selected randomly. Following processes can take previous results as inputs to improve efficiency.

Besides, since the number of skills related to software development is very large, it is redundant to use a single vector to record all skill degree for each worker. Thus, as in the case of Upwork, we classify tasks into different categories and remove unnecessary skills in this category to avoid the sparsity and cold-start problem in recommending system [10]. Considering different cognitions against classification, we don't specify categories in this paper and each crowdsourcing platform can build their own rules of classification.

4.3 Worker Discovery Method

Worker discovery is responsible for finding suitable workers for a specific task. When publishing a task, employers are required to specify detailed skill requirement according to task difficulty or quality standard. Then our method recommends top-N suitable candidates for them based on the clustering results.

```
Algorithm2: worker discovery method
Input: worker set  W = W₁ ∪ W₂ ∪ ... ∪ Wₖ; center set  C = {C₁, C₂, ... Cₖ};
task requirement R
Output: N candidates
Function:
begin
  for each center c in C
    //find the nearest center
    Dis_Cen_setᵣ <- {distance(R,c₁), ...distance(R,cₖ)}
  end for
  Nearest_cenᵢ <- min(Dis_Cen_setᵣ)

  Nearest_cluster <-  Wᵢ, Nearest_cenᵢ∈Wᵢ

  for each worker w in Nearest_cluster
    //find candidates in the nearest cluster
    Dis_setᵣ = {distance(R,w₁),...distance(R,wⱼ)}
  end for
  sort(Dis_setᵣ)
  Candidates <- top-N elements in Dis_setᵣ
  Output(Candidates)
end
```

5 Experiments and Analysis

To evaluate the effectiveness of our approach, we generate massive data set and design a series of emulational experiments. The data set is generated based on some sample data collected from Upwork and conformed to the format of real data. We set each degree value as a decimal number between [0, 1] and use Euclidean distance as comparison metrics to measure discovery results. The smaller the distance is, the more suitable of a worker to do this task.

5.1 Efficiency and Effectiveness

In this part, we first compare the time cost between proposed worker discovery method and general method. Assume the time needed to find a specific worker w from N workers is $Find(w, N)$, thus we use formula (2) to represent the time cost for non-clustering method:

$$Time_{non-clustering} = Find(w, N) \qquad (2)$$

As for clustering-based method, the time cost is consists of three parts as shown in formula (3): apportioned clustering cost, cost to find the nearest center and cost to find a worker in a cluster. Num is the total number of tasks used to apportion clustering cost, k is the number of clusters and N_c' is the worker number of the cluster containing center c.

$$Time_{clustering} = \frac{Cost_{clustering}}{Num} + Find(c, k) + Find\left(w, N_c'\right) \qquad (3)$$

We conduct several experiments on a 10,000 worker set, corresponding parameters and results are shown in Table 1. In order to clearly reflect the efficiency improvement, we set the value of $Time_{non-clustering}$ in the first experiment as the basic unit, and rest results (last three columns) are multiple values compared to it.

Table 1. Time cost

	k	Num	N	N_c'	$Cost_{clustering}$	$Time_{clustering}$	$Time_{non-clustering}$
1	10	1000	10000	917	3.61	0.10	1
2	10	1000	10000	1060	1.13	0.12	1.12
3	10	1000	10000	979	1.35	0.10	1.03
4	10	1000	10000	1122	1.35	0.12	1.09
5	10	1000	10000	983	1.58	0.10	1.02

$Cost_{clustering}$ in the first experiment is larger than others because the initial worker set is totally unorganized. Following clustering reduces this cost by taking previous outputs as inputs. Comparing $Time_{clustering}$ with $Time_{non\text{-}clustering}$, we can see that the efficiency is improved by almost 10 times. Although periodical clustering ($Cost_{clustering}$) costs certain time, this cost becomes very small after *Num* times of apportionment.

Then the effectiveness of our method is evaluated in Fig. 4. We recommend most suitable 10 workers for 5 different tasks and compare the results. "*min*" represents the distance from best matching worker while "*mean*" is the average distance of top 10 workers. As we can see, our method is capable of finding the best matching worker in most cases and only has a small rise of the average distance, which is caused by workers in the edge of a cluster. Considering the great improvement of search efficiency, the small increasement is worth of sacrificing.

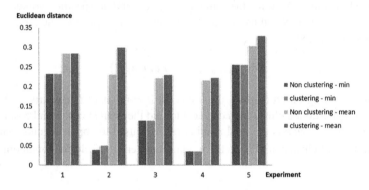

Fig. 4. Distance comparison between two methods

5.2   Analysis of Skill Description

Here we analyze the accuracy of sliding window method by comparing experiment results conducted on two different worker sets. One set is a static skill set and the other is dynamically updated based on sliding window.

Then we elaborate the design of this experiment. Assume three workers A, B, C are looking for web development tasks and their initial skill degree is listed in Table 2. Table 3 lists three tasks with detailed skill requirements. Next, we compute the suitability of these workers for each task. As we can see from Fig. 5(a), A, B and C is best matching for task 1, 2, 3 respectively.

Table 2. Initial skill degree

skill worker	JS	HTML5	jQuery	AJAX	json	CSS3	PHP	Java	MySQL
A	0.4	0.5	0.5	0.4	0.3	0.5	0.1	0.6	0.1
B	0.4	0.6	0.5	0.5	0.4	0.4	0.2	0.5	0.3
C	0.8	0.8	0.7	0.6	0.7	0.8	0.9	0.6	0.9

After a sliding window cycle, their skill degree is updated to Table 4 according to received evaluations. Generally, A is well recognized leading to the enhancement of some skills. B's skill degree drops because of relatively poor performance which fails to achieve employer's expectation. C is not active during this period, therefore all his scores change to weighted historical value. If tasks which have same requirements with task 1, 2 or 3 arrive at this point, discovery results are changed to Fig. 5(b). A is best matching for task 2 and 3, B is recommended to task 1 while C is no longer competitive for these three tasks. We can conclude from this experiment that the dynamicity of skill degree is a key factor to ensure the accuracy of worker discovery.

Table 3. Task requirement

task \ skill	JS	HTML5	jQuery	AJAX	json	CSS3	PHP	Java	MySQL
1	0.5	0.4	0.5	0.4	0.2	0.4	0	0.5	0
2	0.4	0.5	0.5	0.3	0.5	0.4	0.4	0.6	0.3
3	0.7	0.9	0.8	0.5	0.2	0.8	0.7	0.9	0.7

Table 4. Updated skill degree

worker \ skill	JS	HTML5	jQuery	AJAX	json	CSS3	PHP	Java	MySQL
A	0.5	0.5	0.5	0.4	0.5	0.5	0.3	0.6	0.1
B	0.5	0.4	0.5	0.5	0.2	0.4	0.1	0.5	0.1
C	0.6	0.6	0.6	0.5	0.6	0.6	0.7	0.5	0.7

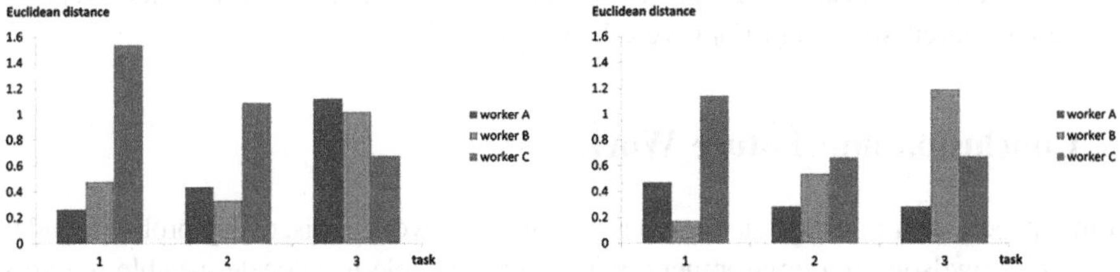

Fig. 5. (a) Distance of static worker set. (b) Distance of dynamic worker set

6 Related Work

Crowdsourcing has become a successful paradigm in the past decade. In this domain, efficient and effective worker discovery is a mandatory requirement to successfully manage this business model [11].

In the Web domain, recommendation systems [12–14] are used to suggest relevant items (news, books, movies, etc.) attracting particular users. Man-Ching Yuen etc. [15] learn from this idea and propose a task matching approach that elicits the historical preference of workers. In this way, a list of tasks sorted by the order of best matching can be provided to workers. However, their approach focuses on recommending subjectively interested tasks without taking capabilities into account, which cannot guarantee the quality of deliveries.

In order to ensure quality, requesters are suggested to employee a sufficient number of workers for micro-tasks, and adopt the answer chosen by most workers through "majority voting" [16, 17]. This method is effective to filter out noisy and unreliable answers but waste a lot of human resources. Another widely recognized solution is creating a mechanism in which requesters and workers validate each other according to reputation [18]. For example, Amazon Mechanical Turk measures the percentage of work that has been approved as a reference for following adoption of deliveries from the same worker [19]. But when dealing with software development tasks, which requires a variety of professional knowledge, a single success ratio is far from enough to represent a worker's capability. In our approach, we make full use of objective evaluations provided by different employers to measure skill level, which is more accurate and convinced.

Considering skill level changes along with experience accumulation, it is important to take into account the time aspect in the process of evaluation. This is similar to QoS (Quality of Service) information in service oriented computing(SOC) environment. In SOC, dynamic reputation of each published service is a key issue for selection [20]. New reputations are more important than old ones since old experiences may become obsolete or irrelevant with time passing by [21]. Thus in our approach, we periodically update skill levels to ensure accurate worker discovery.

The growing number of worker will generate a large amount of data inevitably. In the field of data mining, K-means is undoubtedly the most widely used partitional clustering algorithm [22]. It has the following characteristics: each cluster itself is as compact as possible and different clusters are separated as much as possible [23]. Thus in this paper, we cluster workers into different groups before worker discovery to reduce the search space and improve efficiency.

7   Conclusion and Future Work

In this paper, we presented an approach to solve the worker discovery problem under software crowdsourcing environment. Our method is able to allocate capable workers to heterogeneous software development tasks while save cost.

First, we put forward a new format to describe the proficiency of each skill. Large numbers of evaluations given by employers are collected to ensure the credibility of descriptions. During this process, Sliding Window Analysis is used to dynamically update skill degree. Then we improve the efficiency of our method by clustering workers into different groups based on their characteristics, which greatly reduces unnecessary search space. By comparing the performance and time complexity between our approach and general approach, we demonstrate that our approach is well practical and able to find suitable workers efficiently.

Our future work will focus on further improvement of the method. For example, clustering method is effective in most cases except for one situation in which workers are at the edge of a cluster. How to discover these workers correctly remains a challenge. On the other hand, employers are usually reluctant to hire newly registered workers since they do not have any convinced evaluations. How to bring them to a positive feedback loop quickly is a key factor to attract new crowdsourcing workers.

Acknowledgements. This paper is supported by the Program of University-Industry Cooperation of Shanghai under Granted No. Hu-CXY-2014-013 and the National Natural Science Foundation of China under Granted No. 61472242. This support is gratefully acknowledged. We would also like to express our sincere thanks to anonymous referees, whose comments helped clarify a number of issues.

References

1. Howe, J.: The rise of crowdsourcing. Wired Mag. **14**(6), 1–4 (2006)
2. Brabham, D.C.: Crowdsourcing as a model for problem solving an introduction and cases. Converg. Int. J. Res. N. Media Technol. **14**(1), 75–90 (2008)
3. Kittur, A., Nickerson, J.V., Bernstein, M., et al.: The future of crowd work. In: Proceedings of the 2013 Conference on Computer Supported Cooperative Work, pp. 1301–1318, ACM (2013)
4. https://www.mturk.com/
5. http://www.crowdflower.com/
6. http://www.topcoder.com/
7. Dolstra, E., Vliegendhart, R., Pouwelse, J.: Crowdsourcing gui tests. In: 2013 IEEE Sixth International Conference on Software Testing, Verification and Validation (ICST), pp. 332–341, IEEE (2013)
8. Musson, R., Richards, J., Fisher, D., et al.: Leveraging the crowd: how 48,000 users helped improve Lync performance. IEEE Softw. **30**(4), 38–45 (2013)
9. https://www.upwork.com/
10. Lam, X.N., Vu, T., Le, T.D., et al.: Addressing cold-start problem in recommendation systems. In: Proceedings of the 2nd International Conference on Ubiquitous Information Management and Communication, pp. 208–211, ACM (2008)
11. Le, V.T., Zhang, J., Johnstone, M., et al.: Dynamic control of skilled and unskilled labour task assignments. In: 2013 IEEE/ASME International Conference on Advanced Intelligent Mechatronics (AIM), pp. 955–960, IEEE (2013)
12. Ma, H., King, I., Lyu, M.R.: Effective missing data prediction for collaborative filtering. In: Proceedings of the 30th Annual International ACM SIGIR Conference on Research and Development in Information Retrieval, SIGIR 2007, pp. 39–46. ACM, New York, NY, USA (2007)
13. Xin, X., King, I., Deng, H., Lyu, M.R.: A social recommendation framework based on multi-scale continuous conditional random fields. In: Proceeding of the 18th ACM Conference on Information and Knowledge Management, CIKM 2009, pp. 1247–1256, New York, NY, USA (2009)

14. Zhou, T.C., Ma, H., King, I., Lyu, M.R.: Tagrec: leveraging tagging wisdom for recommendation. In: Proceedings of the 2009 International Conference on Computational Science and Engineering, vol. 04, pp. 194–199. IEEE Computer Society, Washington, DC, USA (2009)
15. Yuen, M.C., King, I., Leung, K.S.: Task matching in crowdsourcing. In: 2011 International Conference on and 4th International Conference on Cyber, Physical and Social Computing Internet of Things (iThings/CPSCom), pp. 409–412, IEEE (2011)
16. Yue, D., Yu, G., Shen, D., et al.: A weighted aggregation rule in crowdsourcing systems for high result accuracy. In: 2014 IEEE 12th International Conference on Dependable, Autonomic and Secure Computing (DASC), pp. 265–270, IEEE (2014)
17. Cao, C.C., She, J., Tong, Y., et al.: Whom to ask?: jury selection for decision making tasks on micro-blog services. Proc. VLDB Endow. 5(11), 1495–1506 (2012)
18. Kulkarni, A., Gutheim, P., Narula, P., et al.: Mobileworks: designing for quality in a managed crowdsourcing architecture. IEEE Internet Comput. 16(5), 28–35 (2012)
19. Doan, A., Ramakrishnan, R., Halevy, A.Y.: Crowdsourcing systems on the world-wide web. Commun. ACM 54(4), 86–96 (2011)
20. Yan, S., Zheng, X., Chen, D.: Dynamic service selection with reputation management. In: 2010 International Conference on Service Sciences (ICSS), pp. 9–16, IEEE (2010)
21. Wang, Y., Vassileva, J.: A review on trust and reputation for web service selection. In: 27th International Conference on Distributed Computing Systems Workshops 2007, ICDCSW 2007, pp. 25–25, IEEE (2007)
22. Celebi, M.E., Kingravi, H.A., Vela, P.A.: A comparative study of efficient initialization methods for the k-means clustering algorithm. Expert Syst. Appl. 40(1), 200–210 (2013)
23. Esteves, R.M., Pais, R., Rong, C.: K-means clustering in the cloud–a Mahout test. In: 2011 IEEE Workshops of International Conference on Advanced Information Networking and Applications (WAINA), pp. 514–519, IEEE (2011)

STWM: A Solution to Self-adaptive Task-Worker Matching in Software Crowdsourcing

Ying Fu$^{(\boxtimes)}$, Haopeng Chen, and Feiya Song

School of Software, Shanghai Jiao Tong University, Shanghai 200240, China
{fyll19, chen-hp, qingxueyihan}@sjtu.edu.cn

Abstract. Crowdsourcing engages a workforce to accomplish complex tasks regardless of geographical limitation and is now growing rapidly in a variety of areas. On the one hand the selection of a wide array of workers has created a competitive and flexible market that suits well the needs of different types of task publishers, on the other hand, it is hard to select workers that satisfy the requirements of the task publishers best among a large number of workers. As such, task-worker matching plays a crucial role in crowdsourcing lifecycle. In this paper, we present a solution that enables customizing task description and adaptive task matching for software crowd work. An extensible meta-model is proposed to support description of both worker skills and task requirements. Based on this meta-model, we define an algorithm that allows self-adaptive matching of the task requirements against the worker skills. Further, several workers will be chosen to form a team once a single individual doesn't meet the requirements of the task. A full experimental validation with four tasks and thousands of workers has been done showing the validation of our solution.

Keywords: Crowdsourcing · Meta-model · Task assignment · Worker matching · Team formation

1 Introduction

Crowdsourcing is a distributed problem-solving and business production model. Jeff Howe [1] defines "crowdsourcing" as "an idea of outsourcing a task that is traditionally performed by an employee to a large group of people in the form of an open call". And this model has been applied to software engineering successfully [2, 3]. Because of the popularity of Web 2.0 technology, crowdsourcing websites attract much attention at present [4]. In Amazon Mechanical Turk (or MTurk) [5], tasks range from labeling images with keywords to judging the relevance of search results to transcribing podcasts. Such "micro-task" markets typically involve short tasks which users self-select and complete for monetary gain. While more complex tasks are accomplished on professional online marketplaces such as TopCoder [6], CrowdFlower, upwork (formerly oDesk). These tasks have more professional skill requirements on the problem undertakers and usually take more time.

A well-defined task description expresses the task publisher intents clearly and makes workers understand it exactly. While how should task requirements on workers be described? What criteria should be given in the description? Tasks on some Crowd

© Springer International Publishing Switzerland 2015
G. Wang et al. (Eds.): ICA3PP 2015, Part I, LNCS 9528, pp. 383–398, 2015.
DOI: 10.1007/978-3-319-27119-4_27

marketplaces (e.g. Taskcn[1]) are described by clients entirely in natural language which is not machine-readable and makes task assignment inefficient since task and worker cannot be matched automatically. As such, workers undertaking the task are chosen by the task publisher subjectively in these marketplaces.

However, describing the task requirements and worker skills simply with tags (like upwork[2] does) is not sufficient to articulate the task publishers' needs. All the skills tagged are in the same weight and the constraints on certain skills are ignored. For instance, there are two tasks A and B. Task A requires a worker who knows both Java and Javascript well. Task B requires a worker knowing any one of them. In this scenario, the tagging approach cannot distinguish task A from task B. Moreover, the requirements of the tasks are not exhaustive and the matching rules may also vary on skills. Thus a novel and extensible description model is needed to describe the task requirements, worker skills as well as the constraints on them. Also, a worker satisfying the task skill requirements should be discovered automatically and recommended to the clients. Upwork has nearly 80 thousand jobs and 5+ million workers. It's extremely time-consuming for task publishers to search suitable workers by themselves. The searching results are usually not accurate and the number is huge. Or rather, you'll get none worker if your query conditions are too strict. Task-worker matching can help task publishers find their preferred workers easier and faster, and it can encourage more qualified workers to contribute and thus complete the task more effectively with higher quality.

Furthermore, what if there is no single suitable worker meeting all the required skills of the task? Currently, once a task publisher can't find a worker meeting all his skill requirements from the task applicants, he would cancel the task or wait until such a worker appears, which is inappropriate. While a worker team formed by several workers may completely satisfy all the skill requirements and is quite up to the task. In this case, such a worker team should be recommended to the clients.

STWM, a solution to self-adaptive task-worker matching in software crowd-sourcing is introduced in this paper. We present a meta-model for the task and worker description which is machine-readable and extensible. Task publishers will be capable to customize their requirements and task assignment rules flexibly with this model. Based on this meta-model, we propose a self-adaptive task matching algorithm. Workers possessing the skills required by the task will be discovered automatically and recommended to task publishers in a certain order according to the preference of task publishers such as ranking workers by their skill proficiency. What's more, a worker team will be formed once there is no single worker satisfying the task requirements. And if there is no worker or team found with our approach that meets the task requirements, task publisher will be informed to re-describe the task.

The rest of the paper is organized as follows. Section 2 surveys some important related work. Section 3 introduces the solutions as well as the framework and the matching and team formation algorithms we integrated. Section 4 presents the experimental results and analysis. Section 5 summarizes the paper and discusses about our future work.

---

[1] http://www.taskcn.com/.

[2] https://www.upwork.com/.

2 Related Work

Many researchers have worked on the related problem of crowdsourcing. In paper [7], Aniket Kittur et al. frame the major challenges that stand in the way of constructing a mature crowd workplace. They lay out research challenges in twelve major areas which includes the task assignment problem.

Allocating a fixed pool of workers to multiple tasks with deadlines is a classic example for task assignment. Paper [8] proposes a first come/first serve model for task assignment, and paper [9] suggests to force workers to sort queues by task volume and recency. Ideally, requesters will see their tasks completed quickly, while workers are continuously employed with tasks and matched their interests. In the worst case, workers are matched to tasks that are uninteresting or too difficult, and won't accomplish the tasks as expected. These task assignment approaches ignore the relationship between worker skills and task requirements, thus may get a undesired result. Ambati et al. [10] present classification based task recommendation approach to recommend tasks to users based on implicit modeling of skills and interests. In paper [11], Snow et al. propose worker modeling as a form of bias correction in crowd data. They estimate worker models computing accuracies on a gold standard dataset. A large labeling task can be effectively designed and carried out in this method at a fraction of the usual expense. However, these two methods only apply for micro-tasks and constraints on user and tasks are not incorporated. Labeling [12] is a commonly used technique for task matching while its limitations are also evident, such as unable to express constraint on data. Paper [13] proposes a novel idea on task matching in crowdsourcing to motivate workers to keep on working on crowdsourcing platforms in long run. This method focuses on recommending the best matching tasks to workers, which inspires us on the task matching problem of our solution.

Part of our team formation algorithm is motivated by the following researches on the team formation problem. Paper [14, 15] study the problem of team formation in social networks Both propose effective algorithms for finding a worker team possessing all the skills required by the task. And the communication overhead of the team is small. Besides, algorithm in paper [14] also takes the workload balance among the team members into consideration. Paper [16] provides a heuristic for finding near-optimal teams that yield the best tradeoff between skill coverage and team connectivity. While these papers mainly focus on the algorithm but ignore the constraints on the skills required by the task publishers.

3 Design of the Solution

3.1 Framework of STWM

As shown in Fig. 1, STWM is part of the entire task-worker matching system. STWM takes the responsibility of describing task requirements and worker capabilities, matching task and workers and supports team formation simultaneously. The whole task-worker matching system has two ports, namely Worker Registry Port and Task Publishing Port. Workers can create their profiles via Worker Registry Port and task publishers will publish a task through Task Publishing Port. And both the worker skills and the task requirements are described by our meta-model.

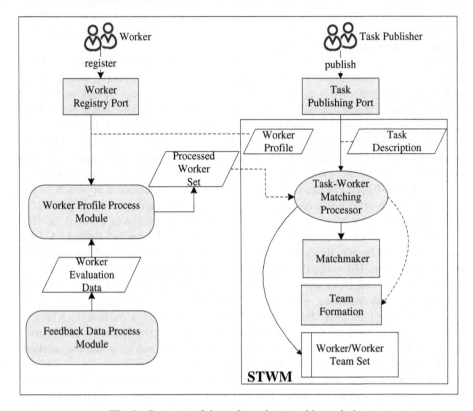

Fig. 1. Structure of the task-worker matching solution

The Feedback Data Process Module processes the feedback data periodically and produces Worker Evaluation Data. This dataset will be feedback to the Worker Profile Process Module continuously to correct the worker profile data such as the skill level which is initially given by the worker subjectively. The Worker Profile Process Module runs periodically to cluster the workers on the multiple capability dimensions and these clustered workers will be provided to the Task-Worker Matching Processor as Processed Worker Set. When a task is published, the Task-Worker Matching Processor will call the Matchmaker module to deal with this task-worker matching request, which will look for suitable workers in the Processed Worker Set and generate a worker set for the task. Particularly, if there is no worker that can meet the task requirements, then the Team Formation module will be called to handle this issue. In this paper we mainly focus on the STWM part of the entire task-worker matching framework. The Worker Profile Process Module and Feedback Data Process Module involve Bigdata storage and processing which will not be discussed in this paper.

3.2 Meta Model for Task and Worker Description

The meta model defines the way how a task requirement and worker skill should be described. Considering the diversity of task requirements, the model should be extensible and support task publishers to customize their matching rules. Our meta-model achieves these goals to a large extent. The definition is shown as below:

```
Class PropertyMetaData{                 Class Property{
    name: String                            value: <value, constraint>
    type: <type, constraint>                weight: w
    constraint: conts                       attribute: <type, value, constraint>
    match: function                     }
    composite: function
    domain: {time, space, skill, pay}
}
```

We define PropertyMetaData Class to describe the metadata of a property. They are the property name, property type, match and composite function of the property, constraint to be met in the matching and composite process, and which domain this property belongs to, currently we enumerate four domains: time, space, skill, and pay. The *constraint* in this model is a function which should be defined by RDF [17] and usually with a Boolean return value. For the match function, we provide several common operations such as "=" which means the worker property value should equal to the value of the same property of the task requirement. The other operations include "within", ">", "<", "$\neq$" etc. Obviously, it's not sufficient to express task publishers' requirements with the above operations. We provide an API for users to implement their own matching function: *Boolean match (Property P_1, Property P_2)*, in which P_1 and P_2 must be Property objects and the return value should be a Boolean.

The composition function is designed for team formation mechanism. It defines the calculation rule on the property when several workers form a team. Similarly, we also offer several calculation operation rules for composition (suppose several workers form a team Q), like "Sum" which means to sum the value of the same property P of the workers in Q, and the sum value will be treated as the value of Property P of the team Q. The other calculation operations are "Max", "Min", "$\cup$", "$\cap$" etc. And the API for the composition function is *Property composite (Set<Property> properties)*, in which the parameter is a Set consisting of the same property P of different workers in team Q and the function returns a new object of Class Property.

The Class Property includes value, weight, and an attribute consisting of type, value, and constraint. The weight attribute is used to denote the priority of different properties of the task requirements with a value out of one point. Note only the property of task requirement has this attribute. In particular, the "attribute" is designed to meet the customization need on different properties. As an instance, properties in the skill domain may have a "skill_level" attribute while properties in time domain may have an attribute named "dailyWorkHour" instead.

Following shows the metadata class definition of properties belonging to skill, time and pay domain. All extends from PropertyMetaData Class. Note, the metadata class is a singleton, all the objects of one Property Class have the same property metadata such as name, type, and domain etc. Particularly, all properties in the skill domain have an attribute "skill_level" to depict the proficiency of the skills and the upper bound is 5.

Class languageMetaData{	Class timeMetaData{	Class payMetaData{
name: language	name: time	name: pay
type:<t,String ǁ String[]>	type: <int, null>	type: <int, null >
constrain: conts	constraint: conts	constraint:conts
match: include	match: <	match: <
composite: ∪	Max	composite: Sum
domain: skill	domain:time	domain: pay
}	}	}

Let's take Class languageMetaData as an example. The constraint on *type* attribute means the type of a language object is either a String or a String Array. The match function of property language is *include*, thus the *value* of property language of a worker should include the *value* of the property language of the task requirements and meet the constraint *cons* at the same time. ∪ is the composition function which computes the union of the language property values of different workers when form a team. The value of *domain* indicates the language property belongs to skill domain. A definition of Class language is given as below:

```
Class language {
    value: <{v}, inLanguageSet(v)> //inLanguageSet(v) is defined in RDF
    weight: w
    skill_level: <double[],constraint>
}
```

language language_of_task1 {	language language_of_worker1{
value: <{java,C++,JavaScript}, null>	value:<{java, C++, sql}, null>
weight: 0.9	weight: null
skill_level: <{3.0,3.0,3.0},{>,>,>}>	skill_level: <{4.0,2.0,3.0},null>
constraint: java ǁ C++ && JavaScript	}
}	

language_of_task1 and language_of_worker1 are two instances of language class. In language_of_client1, the value for the language property in task requirements limits to java, C++, JavaScript, and no constraint on value. The weight of the language in all the skill requirements of this task is 0.9. And the constraint of *skill_level* requires the skill level on each value of p' must be greater than 3.0 in which p' is the language property of a worker. Besides, the worker has to master at least one of a programming language java or C++, and a script language JavaScript meanwhile, according to the constraint defined in the langue_of_client1 object. worker1 knows 3 programming language, java, C++ and sql, and the skill level of them is 4.0, 2.0, 3.0 respectively.

Up to now, we can use the above meta-model to describe workers and tasks as below. A worker has a set of skill properties, a time property, a space property, a pay property and an additional attribute *"score"* which is a criterion used to sort matched workers, and the value is assigned in the matching process. Considering a task basically has requirements on worker skills, the time to accomplish the task, pay for workers, and sometimes geography limitation for workers, we list the above properties respectively in the class definition instead of defining them in a property set. In addition, *skill_weight* is used to demonstrate the weight of the skill among the listed four property requirements in the task class. The sum of the weights of *"skill_requirement"* and the other three required properties is 1. Similarly, the sum of the weights of all the properties in the *skill_requirement* set is 1. For a property, the higher the weight is, the higher the priority is.

Class worker{	Class task{
Property[] skill_list;	Property[] skill_requirment;
Property time;	double skill_weight;
Property space;	Property time_requirment;
Property pay;	Property space_requirment;
double score;	Property pay_give;
}	}

3.3 Match Algorithm for Individual Worker

When a task is described using the meta-model and published, the Task-Worker Matching processor will perform the matching process to get the suitable worker set for the task publisher. The detail matching algorithm is given in Algorithm 1. Here are some definitions used in our algorithm:

Set<worker> FinalSet: workers in this set meet all the requirements of the task T.

Set<worker> PreferCandidate: workers in this set meet all the necessary requirements of the task T.

Set<worker> Candidate: workers in this set meet part of the requirements of the task T.

Set<Property> M: the set of all properties required by task T.

Set<Property> M': the set of all necessary properties required by task T.

For a property p of task T, we say it's a necessary property, if *p.domain ≠ skill and p.weight ≥ baseline_weight*. The *baseline_weight* is a positive number less than 1 given by user to define the smallest weight of a necessary property. Usually we pick *baseline_weight = 0.25* since there are four property requirements in the task class and the sum of them is 1. If *p.domain = skill*, it will be a necessary property when *p. weight ≥ avg_weight(skills)* and *T.skill_weight ≥ baseline_weight*. We denote *avg_weight(skills) = 1 ÷ T.skill_requirement.size*.

The worker set W in Algorithm 1 is produced by Worker Profile Processor. Each worker in W is mapped onto a point in a multidimensional space of which each dimension represents a property of worker, and all the workers are clustered into several subspaces of the multidimensional space. The Cluster method called in

Algorithm 1 takes task T as a parameter, and maps the task T into the same multidimensional space, then returns a worker set $\mathscr{R}$ consisting of all the workers in the subspace closest to the task T. This operation will highly reduce the searching space of workers for a certain task T.

We calculate the score of a worker with the following formula (w is an instance of Class worker, p' is the property of the worker w with the same property name as p):

$$w.score = \sum_{p \in M'} p.weight \times p'.skillLevelValue | for\ p' \in w\ and\ p'.domain = skill$$

In which, p'.skillLevelValue is the sum of required and matched values in the array of p'.skill_level. As an instance, the skillLevelValue of language_of_worker1 for task1 is $4.0 + 2.0 = 6.0$ since the value "sql" is not in the value set of property language_of_client1.

Algorithm 1. Task-worker matching algorithm

Input: Set<worker> W; task T.
Output: Set<worker> W';

```
1. function matching(Set<worker> W, task T):
2.      FinalSet, PreferCandidate, Candidate, W' ← Ø;
3.      Set<worker> R = Cluster(W, T);
4.      for each worker w in R:
5.          if for ∀p ∈ M, p.match(p')=true then
6.              FinalSet = FinalSet ∪ w;
7.          else if for ∀p ∈ M', p.match(p')=true then
8.              PreferCandidate = PreferCandidate ∪ w;
9.          else if ∃p ∈ M, p.match(p')=true then
10.             Candidate = Candidate ∪ w;
11.         endif
12.     endfor
13.     if FinalSet ≠ Ø then
14.         for each worker w in FinalSet
15.             Calculate w.score;
16.         endfor
17.         W' = Sort(T, FinalSet)
18.     else if PreferCandidate ≠ Ø then
19.         for each worker w in PreferCandidate
20.             Calculate w.score;
21.         endfor
22.         W' = Sort(T, PreferCandidate)
23.     endif
24.     return W';
25. end function
```

Usually, we will get more than one worker satisfying the task requirements, especially when the number of workers is large or the task requirements are relatively simple. In this case, we will recommend these workers to task publishers in a certain order. Currently, we sort the worker set which we get from the matching algorithm with the following sorting rules:

For a task T, we consider the property with the highest weight as the sorting priority. Firstly, T.skill_weight will be regarded as the weight of all the skill properties while comparing to the time, space and pay properties of the task T. For instance, if T.time_requirement.weight is the highest, we will sort workers according to the value of worker.time in ascending order. Workers with the same value of the time property will be compared on the property with the second highest weight, etc. In particular, worker.score will be used as a criterion for comparison while comparing two workers on the skill property. Definitely, you can implement your own sorting algorithm adjusting to your specific requirement.

Note: the *Candidate* and *PreferCandidate* worker sets calculated by the matching algorithm will be saved and used in the team formation algorithm if the team formation process is performed.

3.4 Team Formation Algorithm

If we get an empty worker set for a task after performing the matching process, then the Task-Worker Matching Processor will invoke the Team Formation module to handle this issue. However, a task publisher getting a set of workers in the PreferCandidate may prefer a worker team that satisfies all the requirements of the task. In this case, the team formation process will also be performed. The notations we will use are listed below.

1) T: a task published by a client
2) W: a set of workers n Number of workers
3) I: a set of required properties of the task T m Number of required properties
4) W^j: jth worker in W
5) I^i: ith property of the task T
6) Q: team assigned to the task T
7) q: property profile of the team Q

Worker. We consider a set of workers $W = \{W^j; j = 1, 2, ..., n\}$. Each worker has a set of properties in his/her profile, these properties may or may not be in the required properties of the task T. We use $a_{ij} = 1$ to denote that the jth worker (W^j) has the ith property of I (I^i), while $a_{ij} = 0$ otherwise.

Team. If we cannot find a suitable worker meeting all requirements of the task, then the task needs to be assigned to a team of workers. We let $Q \subseteq W$ denote the team assigned to the task. We use $q_i = 1$ to denote that ith property of I (I^i) is covered by the team Q. For team Q, we compute its team profile q defining the expertise of the team as the (binary) sum of the properties of each individual:

$$x_j = \begin{cases} 1, \text{if jth worker belongs to team Q} \\ \\ 0, \text{otherwise} \end{cases} \quad \text{for } W^j \in W$$

$$q_i = \min\{\textstyle\sum_{W^j \in W} a_{ij} x_j, 1\} \quad i = 1,2,3 \dots m$$

In other words, a property is covered by the team if there exists at least one member who has that property. Given a team Q with profile q assigned to task T, we say that the team Q covers the task T if and only if $q_i \geq 1$, $\forall i = 1,2,3\dots$m. Note that this happens if every property required by the task is possessed by the team.

Therefore, the team formation problem can be formally formulated as a binary integer program as follows, where c_j represents the cost of choosing the worker w^j.

$$\text{Minimize} \sum_{W^j \in W} c_j x_j$$
$$\text{Subject to } \textstyle\sum_{W^j \in W} a_{ij} x_j \geq 1 \quad \text{for } I^i \in I$$
$$\text{and } x_j = 0 \text{ or } 1 \quad \text{for } W^j \in W$$

By now, the team formation problem has been modeled as a Set Covering Problem (SCP). Here we assume the costs c_j are equal for $\forall w^j \in W$ and set $c_j = 1$, since we think the cost of forming a team mainly related to the worker number. Thus the problem is referred to as the unit cost SCP in which the task properties I are considered as the rows to be covered, and the properties of a worker are regarded as the column with 0, 1 values.

Paper [18] introduces an effective and simple heuristic to solve the SCP by applying the meta-heuristic Meta-RaPS (Meta-heuristic for Randomized Priority Search). In Meta-RaPS, a feasible solution is generated by introducing random factors into a construction method. The Meta-RaPS-SCP-Construction procedure given in the paper [18] could construct a feasible solution for a SCP instance. While in the scenario of our team formation problem, a feasible solution is a worker team possessing all the required properties of the task.

However, it's not sufficient to simply find a team that covers the properties listed in the task, since the team may not meet the matching rules of the related properties. Therefore a validation on the formed worker team is needed. If a worker team found by Meta-RaPS-SCP-Construction is not feasible for the task, we will find another worker team and perform the validation process again. Actually, we'll get a different worker team each time we perform the Meta-RaPS-SCP-Construction procedure due to the randomness of its implementation algorithm. The %priority parameter determines the percentage of time that the best feasible basic element (which means a worker in this paper) will be chosen. The second parameter, %restriction, is used to determine whether a feasible basic element is acceptable and therefore should appear on the candidate list (CL). The smaller the %priority, the more randomness will be introduced. For a given %priority, the larger the %restriction, the more randomness will be introduced. Elements are added to the solution until a feasible solution is generated.

Let $W \leftarrow$ PreferCandidate $\cup$ Candidate; We get the updated PreferCandidate and Candidate from the matching process. So only the workers meeting some requirements of the task will be taken into consideration instead of all the workers while form a team, and solution space will be highly narrowed. An integer number preferCount is used to limit the size of the output team Set Qs. Sometimes there is no worker team feasible for the task or the amounts of feasible worker teams can not reach the predefined number, thus we introduce an integer variable maxLoops to limit the times our algorithm performed. Therefore the program exits normally instead of caught in an endless loop. Note, our algorithm doesn't aim to find the optimal team, but a set of near-optimal teams with a low time complexity.

Algoritm 2.Team formation

Input: Set<worker> W; task T; int preferCount; int maxLoops.
Output: Set<team> Qs; //a team is a set of workers

1. *function teamFormation(Set<worker> W, task T, int preferCount,int maxLoops):*
2. $\quad$ *Qs ← Ø; Set<Property> PSet ← Ø; int i = 0;*
3. $\quad$ *While Qs.size < preferCount && i ≤ maxLoops:*
4. $\qquad$ *Boolean isFeasible = true;*
5. $\qquad$ *team Q = Meta-RaPS-SCP-Construction*
   $\qquad\qquad$ *(T, W, %priority, %restriction);*
6. $\qquad$ *for each property p of task T:*
7. $\qquad\qquad$ *PSet = Ø;*
8. $\qquad\qquad$ *for all workers in team Q add p' to PSet;*
9. $\quad$ *//p' is the property of the worker in team Q with the same property name as p*
10. $\qquad\qquad$ *Property pt = p.composite(PSet);*
11. $\quad$ *//the composite function is given in the definition of p as shown in meta-model*
12. $\qquad\qquad$ *if p.match(pt) = false then*
13. $\qquad\qquad\qquad$ *isFeasible = false;*
14. $\qquad\qquad\qquad$ *break;*
15. $\qquad\qquad$ *endif*
16. $\qquad$ *endfor*
17. $\qquad$ *if isFeasible = true then*
18. $\qquad\qquad$ *Qs = Qs ∪ Q;*
19. $\qquad$ *endif*
20. $\qquad$ *i ++;*
21. $\quad$ *end while*
22. $\quad$ *return Qs;*
23. *end function*

---

4   Simulation Experiments

In order to demonstrate the effectiveness of the STWM, we grab the data of workers on upwork website including the available working time, space and the expected reward, especially the skills a worker possessing which are listed as labels of the workers. And we re-describe them with our meta-model to generate a set of properties, then we simulate 1000 workers with a certain number of properties random selected from the properties we constructed. We conduct three experiments to evaluate the effectiveness of our solution.

4.1   Experiment for Task-Worker Matching with Comparison

In this experiment, we construct two tasks A and B, both of which have requirements for language, database, and pay while the weight of the same property is different. Definitions of these two task are shown as follows (metadata Class for language property is given in Sect. 3.2):

task A{
    skill_requirement = {langOfA,dbOfA};
    skill_weight = 0.70;
    time_requirement = timeOfA;
    space_requirement = null;
    pay_give = payOfA;
}
	task B{
	    skill_requirement = {langOfB,dbOfB};
	    skill_weight = 0.70;
	    time_requirement = timeOfB;
	    space_requirement = null;
	    pay_give = payOfB;
	}

langOfA{
    value:<{Java,JavaScript},null>
    weight: 0.80
    skill_level:<{3.0,3.0},{>,>}>
    constraint: Java && JavaScript
    }
	langOfB{
	    value:<{Java,JavaScript},null>
	    weight: 0.20
	    skill_level:<{3.0,3.0},{>,>}>
	    constraint: Java && JavaScript
	    }

The definition of meta-model for property "database" is as follows:

databaseMetaData{
    name:database
    type:<t,String ǁ String[]>
    constraint: null
    match: include
    composite: ∪
    domain: skill
 	
}
	database{
	    value: <{v}, null>
	    weight: w
	    skill_level: <double[],constraint>
	}

dbOfA{
    value:<{mysql},null>
    weight: 0.20
    skill_level: <{3.0},{>}>
    constraint: null
    }
	dbOfB{
	    value:<{mysql},null>
	    weight: 0.80
	    skill_level: <{3.0},{>}>
	    constraint: null
	    }

The above meta-model shows that both task A and task B require for workers who know Java and JavaScript well and also are familiar with mysql database. While task A prefer programming skills, task B is more focus on the database skill. We do not give the complete definitions for timeOfA, timeOfB, payOfA, and payOfB since the objects of the same property for task A and task B are equal and will have no effects on our matching result. During the matching process, the searching space is narrowed to nearly 100 workers after performing the Cluster method in our matching function. Table 1a and b shows the top three workers returned by our matching algorithm. Numbers in the table are the skill_level values of the workers.

Table 1. Workers recommended for tasks A and B

a. Workers recommended for task A

Properties Workers	Language		Database	Worker.score
	Java	JavaScript		
A1	4.96	4.92	3.12	6.92
A2	4.90	4.80	4.20	6.87
A3	4.83	4.76	3.14	6.71

b. Workers recommended for task B

Properties Workers	Language		Database	Worker.score
	Java	JavaScript		
B1	4.03	3.21	4.98	3.49
B2	3.26	4.13	4.78	3.35
B3	3.58	4.47	4.72	3.30

From data in Table 1a and b, we can see, workers recommended for the tasks with the same skill requirements but different skill weights are completely different. For task A, "database" is not a necessary property, so a worker with a low skill_level on database but a high skill_level value on language can still be discovered and recommended to the clients. The same applies for task B. However, if we publish task A and task B on current crowdsourcing market, such as upwork website, these two tasks will be treated as the same one. Therefore the workers recommended will have no difference. Besides, on upwork, a worker who possesses one of the three skills – Java, JavaScript and mysql can be considered an appropriate candidate for task A, while in our approach, only those who exactly meet the customized matching rules of the task will be added to the final worker set of the task, which means only those who master Java and JavaScript programming languages and understanding mysql database well will be considered as a candidate. Experiment 1 evaluates the feasibility and flexibility of our meta-model as well as the effectiveness of our matching algorithm. Our solution can solve the problems of current task description and task-worker matching mentioned in the introduction part.

4.2   Experiment for Team Formation

In experiment 2, we construct task C as follows:

---

task C{   langOfC{
   skill_requirement = {langOfC,dbOfC};   value:<{Java,C++,JavaScript,Ruby},null>
   skill_weight = 0.70;   weight:0.60
   time_requirement = timeOfC;   skill_level: <{3.0,3.0,3.0,3.0},{>,>,>,>}>
   space_requirement = null;   constraint: Java ‖ C++ && JavaScript
   pay_give = payOfC;   && Ruby
}   }

---

dbOfC{   timeOfC{   payOfC{
   value:<{mysql,Oracle},null>   value:<100,inHours>   value:<500,inTotal>
   weight:0.40   weight:0.10   weight:0.20
   skill_level: <{3.0,3.0},{>,>}>   constraint: null   constraint: null
   constraint: mysql ‖ Oracle   }   }
}

We can see, task C is looking for workers who master Java or C++, and JavaScript, Ruby, besides knowing database (mysql or Oracle) well. And the time for accomplishing the task must be less than 100 h. The pay of the task is limited to \$500. However, the workers we simulated are given at most two values on the language property. Thus, our matching algorithm returns an empty worker set for task C since langOfC.weight > 0.50 which means it's a property must be satisfied. Then the team formation procedure will be performed, Table 2 is the worker team found by our team formation algorithm. We set preferCount = 2, maxLoops = 100, %priority = 80 % and %restriction = 60 %.

Table 2. Teams recommended for task C

		Language	Database	Time	Pay
Team 1	Worker1-1	Java(4.52), Ruby(4.26)	mysql(4.83)	90	321
	Worker1-2	C++(3.59), JavaScript(3.62)	mysql(3.61)	95	150
Team 2	Worker2-1	Java(4.17), JavaScript(3.21)	Oracle(3.77)	100	270
	Worker2-2	Ruby(3.87), JavaScript(3.58)	none	76	162

The teams given in Table 2 meet all the requirements of task C. Take team 1 as an instance, the composite function of language property is ∪, thus the values of the language property of team 1 are worker1-1.language ∪ worker1-2.language, which equals to {Java, C++, Ruby, JavaScript}, and the skill_level of each value is higher than 3.0. By the same rule, time.value of team 1 is 95 and pay.value of team 1 is 471, both of which satisfy the match function of the related property. The same applies to database property. Experiment 2 demonstrates the effectiveness of our team formation mechanism with the task requirements and worker skills described in our meta-model.

Then we set more restrict constraints on the property of task C. Let langOfC.value = {Java, JavaScript, Ruby, Html5} with a constraint: Java && JavaScript && Ruby && Html5. And payOfC.value = 50. The team formation algorithm returns us an empty set of teams with preferCount = 2, maxLoops = 100, %priority = 80 % and % restriction = 60 %. And we tried with different values assigned to these four parameters, but still get the same result. In this case, considering the applicability of this team formation algorithm for the real project, we'll inform the task publisher that there is no worker suitable for their task, neither the worker team. The task should be re-described.

5 Conclusion and Future Work

In this paper, we have presented a novel solution to self-adaptive task-worker matching in software crowdsourcing. We propose an extensible meta-model for the description of task requirements and worker skills. Based on this meta-model, we define a matching algorithm to match the task and workers adaptively according to the matching rules which are customized by task publishers. Besides, if there is no worker that satisfies the requirements of the task, our solution will select workers to form a team that is quite up to the task and recommend it to task publishers.

In the next work, we plan to conduct some experiments in a real crowdsourcing workplace to evaluate the practicability of our solution. We also expect to improve our meta model to support more complex constraints on task requirements such as the dependency between tasks.

Acknowledgements. This paper is supported by the program of University-Industry Cooperation of Shanghai under Granted No. Hu-CXY-2014-013 and the National Natural Science Foundation of China under Granted No. 61472242.

References

1. Howe, J.: The rise of crowdsourcing. Wired Mag. **14**(6), 1–4 (2006)
2. Wu, W., Tsai, W.T., Li, W.: An evaluation framework for software crowdsourcing. Front. Comput. Sci. **7**(5), 694–709 (2013)
3. Tsai, W.T., Wu, W., Huhns, M.N.: Cloud-based software crowdsourcing. IEEE Internet Comput. **3**, 78–83 (2014)
4. Yuen, M.C., King, I., Leung, K.S.: A survey of crowdsourcing systems. In: 2011 IEEE Third International Conference on Privacy, Security, Risk and Trust (PASSAT) and 2011 IEEE Third Inernational Conference on Social Computing (SocialCom), pp. 766–773. IEEE (2011)
5. Buhrmester, M., Kwang, T., Gosling, S.D.: Amazon's Mechanical Turk a new source of inexpensive, yet high-quality, data? Perspect. Psychol. Sci. **6**(1), 3–5 (2011)
6. Lakhani, K.R., Garvin, D.A., Lonstein, E.: Topcoder (a): developing software through crowdsourcing. Harv. Bus. Sch. Case **610**, 032 (2010)
7. Kittur, A., Nickerson, J.V., Bernstein, M., et al.: The future of crowd work. In: Proceedings of the 2013 Conference on Computer Supported Cooperative Work, pp. 1301–1318. ACM (2013)
8. Raddick, J., Lintott, C., Bamford, S., et al.: Galaxy zoo: motivations of citizen scientists. In: Bulletin of the American Astronomical Society, vol. 40, p. 240 (2008)

9. Chilton, L., Horton, J., Miller, R.C., Azenkot, S.: Task search in a human computation market. In: Proceedings of HCOMP 2010 (2010)

10. Ambati, V., Vogel, S., Carbonell, J.G.: Towards task recommendation in micro-task markets. In: Human Computation. pp. 1–4 (2011)

11. Snow, R., O'Connor, B., Jurafsky, D., et al.: Cheap and fast—but is it good?: evaluating non-expert annotations for natural language tasks. In: Proceedings of the Conference on Empirical Methods in Natural Language Processing, pp. 254–263. Association for Computational Linguistics (2008)

12. Sheng, V.S., Provost, F., Ipeirotis, P.G.: Get another label? improving data quality and data mining using multiple, noisy labelers. In: Proceedings of the 14th ACM SIGKDD International Conference on Knowledge Discovery and Data Mining, pp. 614–622. ACM (2008)

13. Yuen, M.C., King, I., Leung, K.S.: Task matching in crowdsourcing. In: 2011 International Conference on Internet of Things (iThings/CPSCom) and 4th International Conference on Cyber, Physical and Social Computing, pp. 409–412 (2011)

14. Anagnostopoulos, A., Becchetti, L., Castillo, C., et al.: Online team formation in social networks. In: Proceedings of the 21st International Conference on World Wide Web, pp. 839–848. ACM (2012)

15. Lappas, T., Liu, K., Terzi, E.: Finding a team of experts in social networks. In: Proceedings of the 15th ACM SIGKDD International Conference on Knowledge Discovery and Data Mining. ACM, pp. 467–476 (2009)

16. Dorn, C., Dustdar, S.: Composing near-optimal expert teams: a trade-off between skills and connectivity. In: Meersman, R., Dillon, T.S., Herrero, P. (eds.) OTM 2010. LNCS, vol. 6426, pp. 472–489. Springer, Heidelberg (2010)

17. Klyne, G., Carroll, J.J.: Resource description framework (RDF): concepts and abstract syntax (2006)

18. Lan, G., DePuy, G.W., Whitehouse, G.E.: An effective and simple heuristic for the set covering problem. Eur. J. Oper. Res. **176**(3), 1387–1403 (2007)

GroupDRM: Group-Based Dynamic Resource Management Model in Wireless Network

Zhipeng Tan$^{(\boxtimes)}$, Jie Cui, Dan Feng, and Wei Zhou

Wuhan National Laboratory for Optoelectronics, School of Computer Science,
Huazhong University of Science and Technology, Wuhan, China
zhipengtan@163.com

Abstract. In the field of wireless communications, Universal Mobile Tele communications System (UMTS) offers broadband data transmission for mobile computer and phone users. As a part of UMTS, the UMTS Terrestrial Radio Access Network (UTRAN) needs to deploy distributed resource management system to meet three key user operations: Apply, Locate and Release. The traditional resource management models are no longer suitable for the increasing user amount and dynamic these operations, and resource consumption is relatively large especially CPU. We propose a new group-based dynamic resource management model, called as GroupDRM, which can meet all demands. Comparing to the traditional static model and complete dynamic model, GroupDRM model greatly reduces the delay of apply. The model also shows its advantages over the traditional dynamic model on the performances of releasing, locating and resource consumption.

Keywords: Wireless network · URTAN · RNC · URNTI · Resource management model

1 Introduction

In the field of wireless communications, Universal Mobile Telecommunications System (UMTS) [1] is used to handle broadband, packet-based transmission of multimedia such like text, photo and video. UMTS enables mobile computer and phone users to transfer multimedia with high-speed no matter where they are. As a part of UMTS, the UMTS Terrestrial Radio Access Network (UTRAN) deploys Radio Network Controllers (RNC) to provide resource service for User Equipment (UE).

RNC supplies and manages resources. In the early period of system construction, there was only one centralized RNC. But with the rapid increase of user demands, the single RNC could hardly provide sufficient resources, and its poor process capacity was overwhelmed by high-frequency resource manage request. Meanwhile, the single point failure has a strong impact on system availability. Therefore, distributed resource management solution involving multiple RNCs is implemented to cope with the increasing user demands.

A distributed resource management scenario [2, 3] is shown in Fig. 1. When a UE finds a Base Station (BS) and builds a connection to RNC1, RNC1 will allocate resources and generates a fixed length integer called UTRAN Radio Network

© Springer International Publishing Switzerland 2015
G. Wang et al. (Eds.): ICA3PP 2015, Part I, LNCS 9528, pp. 399–414, 2015.
DOI: 10.1007/978-3-319-27119-4_28

Temporary Identity (URNTI) for UE. When UE moves to another geographic position and connects to RNC2, the previous service shouldn't be interrupted. Thus the system must be able to find the resources on RNC2 by the URNTI. Finally, when UE closes its connection, the resources on RNC1 and the URNTI can be recycled.

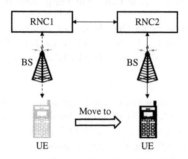

Fig. 1. A real application scenario in UTRAN

From the real scenario described above, a typical resource management problem can be abstracted as below: Firstly we define the RNC as Resource Server (RS), define the URNTI as Resource Identifier (RI) and UE as user, then the RS cluster must satisfy three kinds of requests:

(1) Apply: When a user sends a resource apply request to a RS, the RS must allocate a local resource and return a unique RI to the user;
(2) Locate:When a user sends a resource locate message (together with a RI) to a RS, the RS must use the RI to find out which RS provides the user's resource;
(3) Release:When a user sends a resource release request to the RS, the RS should free the corresponding resource and recycle the RI.

The target of this paper is to design and implement a new distributed resource management model which can efficiently manage the RIs and offer the Apply, Locate and Release interfaces transparently for users and reduce resource consumption obviously especially CPU. Our design goals are as follows:

(1) **High performance.** To reduce the delay of resource apply, locate and release request as much as possible.
(2) **High scalability.** The system should be able to expand its service ability by joining more RSs.
(3) **High availability.** The system should handle the leaving of RS due to hardware failure or software crash while keeping the minimum impact on current service. The RIs allocated on the leaved RS should be recycled to avoid the wasting of RIs.
(4) **Strong consistency.** Once a RI was allocated in a RS, all other RSs in the cluster cannot allocate the same RI until it is released.

2   Related Works

As far as we know, currently only the traditional static model [4, 5] is proposed to handle this resource management problem. As shown in Fig. 2, supposes a RI is a P-bits unsigned integer which can express 2P RIs in total. The top Q bits of a RI are used to save the ID of a RS in the cluster and the rest P-Q bits are used to save the local resource ID in a RS. A RS will combine its ID with an unallocated local resource ID to generate a RI and return it to the user. Any RS in the cluster could locate the target RS from the top Q bits and find the corresponding local resource by the rest P-Q bits. However, the static model has the following limitations:

(1) The RS ID is fixed at Q bits, which means the total amount of RSs in cluster couldn't exceed 2^Q. If the actual RS amount K is smaller than 2^Q, there will be $(2^Q\text{-}K) \times 2^{P-Q}$ RIs that cannot be allocated.
(2) The local resource ID is fixed at P-Q bits, which means a RS could only allocates 2^{P-Q} RIs at most. When the resource demand D on a RS is smaller than 2^{P-Q}, then $2^{P-Q}\text{-}D$ RIs will be unavailable. When the demand D is greater than 2^{P-Q}, the amount of RIs will be not enough.
(3) When a RS fails, the RIs belong to the RS are wasted.

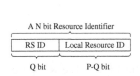

A N bit Resource Identifier

| RS ID | Local Resource ID |

Q bit   P-Q bit

Fig. 2. Static model

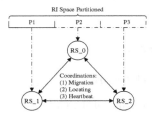

Fig. 3. Dynamic model

In our previous work [6], we designed a traditional dynamic model to improve the static model. As shown in Fig. 3, the RI space is initially partitioned and assigned to each RS in the cluster. Users can apply and release the RIs on each RS. When the amount of unallocated RIs on a RS is not enough to meet the demand of users, the RS will communicate with other RSs for RI migration. The migration paths are recorded on the RSs where the migration occurs. A RI can be located by querying the migration path in the cluster. However, the traditional dynamic model appeared the following problems: (1) If there are frequent RI migrations in the cluster, the migration path of typical RIs may become very long and it will greatly reduce the locating efficiency; (2) When the total amount of RIs in the system is very large, the time and space complexity of managing the RIs will be very high. (3) If there are too many RSs in the cluster, when a RS needs to find suitable amount of unallocated RIs on other RSs, the query overhead will be unaffordable since there is no efficient guidance.

The classical balls-into-bins problem [7] is similar to the problem of this paper. The RSs can be treated as bins, and the RIs can be treated as balls. We need to put adequate amount of balls into bins according to the bins' demand [8, 9]. Current studies on data distribution also have a strong relationship with the balls into bins model. The data items can be regarded as balls and the servers saving the data items can be treated as bins. Each server has a capacity (similar to the demand on RS). The data distribution strategies can be classified from two aspects: whether server capacities are uniform [10] and whether data items exist replications [11, 12].

Although these strategies described above can provide us many valuable insights, they can't completely solve the problem of this paper because of the following reasons:

(1) Each RS has a frequently changing demand. Scheduling RIs as soon as possible to meet the user demands is a key target of design. But for data distribution strategies, the server capacity won't be changed since a server joined the cluster. Even the data distribution methods dedicated for non-uniform capacities choose the fairness as their goal and save data items according to the server capacity ratio.

(2) The RIs which were allocated to users on a RS can't be migrated to other RS. But the data distribution methods didn't emphasize the problem that whether the data items can be migrated while they are being occupied by users.

(3) When a RS failed, the resource service offered by the RS will be interrupted. All the RIs allocated on the leaved RS can be recycled so there is no redundancy requirement. It is different from the data distribution strategies which treat the replication as an important factor.

3 Design

3.1 Architecture

The architecture of the GroupDRM model is shown in Fig. 4. The RI space is partitioned into many segments. Suppose a RI contains P bits, then the total amount of RIs is 2^P and an available RI is in the range of $[0, 2^P - 1]$. If the range is partitioned in granularity R ($2^P \% R = 0$), there will be $2^P/R$ segments. Number these segments from 0 consequently and the range of segment ID is $[0, 2^B/R - 1]$. All these segments will be used as the atomic units in the following algorithms of RI migration and location.

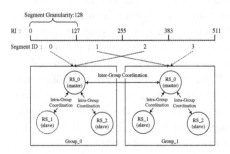

Fig. 4. The architecture of GroupDRM (2 Groups with 9 bit-RI)

Segment ID	Group ID	RS ID
...	...	...

Fig. 5. Structure of inner-group and outer-group segment locate table

The whole RS cluster is divided into several groups and each group has a centralized master RS. The dynamic user demand on each RS is satisfied by the intra-group and inter-group RI coordination. The motivation of grouping is to ensure the scalability of the RS cluster. The coordination overhead can be significantly reduced among large amounts of RSs by grouping. Because when the demands on the RSs in the same group have small fluctuation, the low overhead intra-group coordination can solve the problem. Only when large fluctuation happens, the high overhead inter-group coordination is needed. Besides, from the view of physical topology, the RSs with faster network communications can be deployed into one group to achieve better performance. The RSs across different failure domains can also be in one group to enhance the system reliability.

Suppose the RS amount in the cluster is N, and separate the cluster into M ($M \leq N$) groups. Number the groups from 0 consequently and the range of group ID is [0, $M - 1$]. The RS amount in each group can be different. Suppose the RS amount in group i is N_i and number the RSs in the group from 0 in sequence, the range of RS ID is [0, $N_i - 1$]. Where $N_i \geq 1$ and $N_0 + N_1 + ... + N_{M-1} = N$. The RSs in each group will elect a master RS by using the leader election algorithm. The master RS in each group plays an important role in the heartbeat mechanism and RI migration process while providing resource service as other slave RSs at the same time.

Next, all the segments will be assigned to each group. A RS can allocate all the corresponding RIs of the segments which have been assigned to it. In this way, the management of RI can be parallel and distributed. Figure 4 gives an example of 2 groups RSs with 9 bit-RI. First, the segment S will be assigned to the group S % M by using the hashing method. Since the system started, this kind of outer-group mapping won't be changed to guarantee the fast locating of which group manages a certain segment. The group amount stays the same so as to avoid recalculating all the mappings. Second, the master RS decides the segment assignment relationship inside each group. However, this kind of inner-group mapping shouldn't be fixed because the demand on each RS changes over time and a certain RS may also join or quit. In such a dynamic environment, we decide to employ table-based method to record the segment assignment information: an Inner-Group Segment Locate Table (IG-SLT) and an Outer-Group Segment Locate Table (OG-SLT) are created on each RS. The structures of the two tables are same. As shown in Fig. 5, a record (A, B, C) in the table indicates that segment A is assigned to RS C in group B. If the value of B, C is null, it means the segment A is unassigned. The IG-SLT on a RS is used to save the assignment information of all the segments which are assigned to the current RS's group and the IG-SLTs on the RSs within same group are updated synchronously. Unlike the IG-SLT, the OG-SLT on a RS maintains the assignment information of all the segments which are not assigned to the current RS's group. Each RS judges the invalidation of segment assignment information independently and updates the OG-SLT asynchronously. When the system is initialized, all the segments are not assigned to any RS in a group. Both IG-SLT and OG-SLT are null. Soon afterwards when there is demand on a certain RS, the RS begins to apply segment to the master RS in the group and the master RS is responsible to update the information in the related table.

3.2   Resource Apply

Each RS maintains a segment set which saves all the segments assigned to it. Suppose the granularity of a segment is R, each segment corresponds to R RIs. Each RI has a mapping relationship with a local resource and whether the RI is allocated is marked by a bitmap. For simplicity, define RS(i, j) represents the RS j in Group i. As shown in Fig. 6, the resource apply algorithm is below:

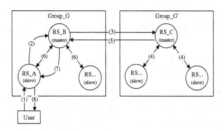

Fig. 6. The algorithm for resource apply

Resource Apply Algorithm

(1) When RS(G,A) receives a resource apply request from a user, it judges that whether an unallocated RI exists in local. If exists, directly goes to step (8);

(2) If there is no more unallocated RI, RS(G,A) needs to send a segment apply request to the master RS(G,B) in group G. After receiving the apply request, master RS(G,B) will look up the IG-SLT to judge whether unassigned segment exists. If exists, goes to step (6);

(3) If there is no more unassigned segment, segment migration process among different groups is required. Master RS(G,B) will send the segment apply requests to other groups' master RS one by one until a master RS(G',C) which has an unassigned segment S is found.

(4) Master RS(G',C) sends the updating IG-SLT messages to all the slave RSs in group G' to record that the segment S is assigned to RS(G,A);

(5) Master RS(G',C) returns a apply success message of segment S to Master RS(G,B).

(6) Master RS(G,B) sends the updating IG-SLT messages to all the slave RSs in group G to record that the segment S is assigned to RS(G,A);

(7) After the updating is finished, master RS(G,B) returns a apply success message of segment S to RS(G,A). And RS(G,A) adds the segment S into its own segment set.

(8) RS(G, A) finds a unallocated RI and set the bitmap of the RI as allocated. At last the RI is returned to the user.

The master RS will synchronize the IG-SLTs on all the slave RSs in the same group when the segment migration happens. There are two reasons below:

(1) The segment assignment information needs redundancy to ensure the system reliability. If the assignment information of a segment is saved in only one RS, the information will lost once the RS failed.
(2) All the RSs in the system have the demand of locating segments. The efficiency of locating will be improved if more RSs obtain the segment assignment information.

However, it may appear the chain reaction during the process of applying segment among different groups: A master RS(G,A) sends a segment apply message to another master RS(G',B) and master RS(G',B) sends a segment apply message to another master RS(G",C). To avoid this situation, we take measures that when a master RS obtains a segment apply request and there is no more unassigned segment on it, the master is allowed to apply segment to other group only when the applying RS and the master RS are in the same group.

The chain reaction will also happen during the segment migrating. Namely, a segment was migrated from group G to group G' and then from group G' to group G". This will reduce the efficiency of locating. Thus when a master RS is looking for unassigned segments, it should only search the segments belonging to its own group, but not the segments migrated from other group. In this way, the segment migration can only happen among two groups for higher locating efficiency.

3.3 Resource Locate

Because each RI belongs to a segment, the problem of locating a RI on any RS in the cluster can be transformed into the problem of locating a segment. The RS received the locate request will send several segment query messages to the RSs in the cluster to locate the correct RS and return the result to user. Before introducing the locating process, we first define that when a RS receives a segment S' query message, it will return two types of result:

(1) If the segment S belongs to the segment set in the current RS, returns the Query Hit message which contains the ID of current RS and the local resource index of the located RI.
(2) Otherwise looks up the IG-SLT to acquire the information that the segment S is assigned to another RS, and returns the Query Forward message which contains the ID of the forwarded RS. As shown in Fig. 7, the resource locate algorithm is below:

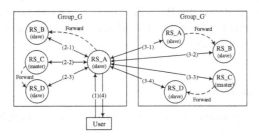

Fig. 7. The algorithm for resource locate

Resource Locate Algorithm

(1) When a RS(G,A) receives a locate request of a RI from a user, suppose the granularity of the segment is R, the corresponding segment ID can be calculated by S=RI/R. Furthermore, the ID of the group where the segment S is assigned can be calculated by G'=S%M from the group amount M. According to whether G' is equal to G, the locating process can be separated into two cases: the inner-group locating and the outer-group locating;

(2) When G'=G, inner-group locating is required;

(2-1) First RS(G,A) judges that whether the segment S belongs to the segment set on itself. If so, goes to step (4). Otherwise looks up the IG-SLT and sends a segment S's query message to the RS(G,B) recorded in the IG-SLT. If it gets the Query Hit message, goes to step (4). Otherwise goes to next step;

(2-2) RS(G,A) sends a query message to the master RS(G,C) in group G. If it gets the Query Hit message, goes to step (4). Otherwise if it gets the Query Forward message to RS(G,D), goes to next step;

(2-3) RS(G,A) sends a query message to RS(G,D). If it gets the Query Hit message, goes to step (4). Otherwise the locating process fails;

(3) When G'≠G, outer-group locating is required;

(3-1) Firstly RS(G,A) looks up the OG-SLT and sends a segment S's query message to the RS(G',A) recorded in the OG-SLT. If it gets the Query Hit message, goes to step (4). Otherwise if it gets the Query Forward message to RS(G',B), goes to next step;

(3-2) RS(G,A) sends a query message to RS(G',B). If it gets the Query Hit message, goes to step (4). Otherwise goes to next step;

(3-3) RS(G,A) sends a query message to the master RS(G',C) in group G'. If it gets the Query Hit message, goes to step (4). Otherwise if it gets the Query Forward message to RS(G',D), goes to next step;

(3-4) RS(G,A) sends a query message to RS(G',D). If it gets the Query Hit message, goes to step (4). Otherwise the locating process fails;

(4) RS(G,A) returns the locating result to the user.

Due to the processes of locating and migrating are asynchronous, the segment query messages may arrive at a certain RS during the process of synchronizing IG-SLTs. As a result, the locating information may expire. However, each synchronizing process is sponsored by the master RS in a group. So the master RS will always have the newest locating information. This is the reason why to send the query message to the master RS when a RS didn't get the Query Hit message. Similarly, the information saved in the OG-SLT on each RS may also expire due to segment migration. To address this problem, when locating the segment assigned to the outer group, it is necessary to send query message to the master RS in the outer group. Each time after the locating process is done, the RS will update its OG-SLT. From this view, the OG-SLT can be regarded as a cache table which is asynchronously updated and can improve the locating efficiency.

3.4 Resource Release

The resource release algorithm can be seen as an anti-process of applying and the logic is relatively simple:

Resource Release Algorithm

(1) When a RS(G,A) receives a RI release request from a user, it sets the bitmap of the RI and returns a release success message to the user.
(2) Particularly when RS(G,A) finds that all the corresponding RIs of a segment S are unallocated, it means the segment should be returned to the master RS in the same group for RI recycling. According to the group amount M, the ID of the group where the segment S is assigned can be calculated by G'=S%M. RS(G,A) sends a segment release request to master RS(G',B) in group G'.
(3) Master RS(G',B) sends the updating IN-SLT messages to all the slave RSs in group G' to record that the segment S is unassigned;
(4) After the updating is finished, master RS(G',B) returns a release success message of segment S to RS(G,A).
(5) RS(G,A) deletes the segment S from its own segment set.

---

4 Evaluation

We implement the GroupDRM model in Linux as well as the traditional static model and dynamic model for comparisons. A centralized test program is designed to generate all the user's behaviors so that workload of the entire RS cluster can be precisely controlled and data can be easily collected. The test program will send resource apply, locate and release requests to the cluster in typical workload. Message delay and RS CPU usage are used as the evaluation index. The performance of 3 models is tested under 5 kinds of RS amount and 11 kinds of workload level. The online joining and leaving of the RS are tested as well.

The 5 kinds of RS amount are 4, 8,12,16,20 separately. For the GroupDRM model, each group has 4 RSs and there will be 5 groups at most. The RS processes in the same group will run on the same test machine. And the test program will run on a test machine alone. Thus 6 test machines are needed in total. Each test machine is a dual-socket, 4-cores-per-socket, 2-threads-pers-core server equipped with Intel Xeon E5620 CPUs running at 2.40 GHz. The system includes 12 GB of memory and an Intel 82576 Gigabit Ethernet Controller. All servers are connected with Gigabit Ethernet switch.

4.1 Workload

The test program interacts with the RS cluster in the unit of user transaction. A user transaction contains the following operations:

(1) Sends a resource apply request to RS A;
(2) Waits RS A to return the apply success message which includes an allocated RI. Calculates the time interval between the current and previous message as the apply delay;
(3) Randomly selects a RS B in the cluster and sends a resource locate request of RI to RS B;

(4) Waits RS B to return the locate success message of RI. Calculates the time interval between the current and previous message as the locate delay;

(5) Waits T seconds. T is defined as the service time and the value of T will be random picked each time among the range of $[T_{min}, T_{max}]$.

(6) Sends a resource release request of the RI to RS A.

(7) Waits RS A to return a release success message of RI. Calculates the time interval between the current and previous message as the release delay;

If the test program interacts with a RS in the frequency of F user transactions per second, the average RI (resource) demand per second D can be calculated approximately as following:

$$D = F \times (T_{min} + T_{max}) \div 2 \tag{1}$$

In order to generate a random and dynamic workload and fully trigger the RI migration process under different models. We decide to employ the sine function to set the user transaction frequency on each RS. Suppose the total amount of the RSs in the cluster is N, the user transaction frequency of the i-th RS is:

$$F_i = M \times \sin(i \div N \times \pi \times (N \div 4 + 1)) + L \tag{2}$$

Consequently, the average RI demand per second D_i of the i-th RS can be obtained by combining Formulas (1) and (2):

$$D_i = (M \times \sin(i \div N \times \pi \times (N \div 4 + 1)) + L) \times (T_{min} + T_{max}) \div 2 \tag{3}$$

The values of the parameters in actual test are below:

$$M = 25, i \in [1, N], N \in [1, 5], L \in [30, 40], T_{min} = 5, T_{max} = 15$$

The total RI amount M of each model is proportional to the amount of RSs N in the cluster: $M = 512 \times NR = 512 \times N$. Each RS has 512 RIs in average. The reason why the range of L is set to [30, 40] is that we want to observe the influence of performance under different demand saturations. The demand saturation (DS) is defined as the percentage of the total amount of system's RIs which are being occupied by users:

$$DS = \sum_1^N D_i \div R \times 100\% \tag{4}$$

The sinusoidal demand waveforms generated by Formula (3) under different RS amounts can be seen in Fig. 8 intuitively. The demand saturations under different RS amounts are also calculated in Table 1.

Obviously, the demand on each RS shouldn't be static. Suppose the beginning of the test program is at time 0, the sinusoidal demand waveform rotates one RS unit to the right every 10 s. The average RI demand per second on the i-th RS at time t - D(i, t), can be expressed below,

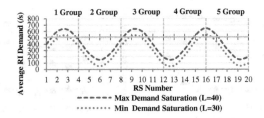

Fig. 8. Sinusoidal demand waveform under different RS amounts

Table 1. Demand saturation ranges under different RS amounts

RS amount	Total RI amount	Minimum demand saturation (L = 30)	Maximum demand saturation (L = 40)
4	2048	59 %	78 %
8	4096	67 %	87 %
12	6144	58 %	77 %
16	8192	63 %	83 %
20	10240	58 %	77 %

$$D_{(i,t)} = D_{((i-1+N-1)\%N+1,t-10)} \tag{5}$$

The duration of each test case of each model is 100 s. The granularity of each segment is 32. After a test case is over, the average data of all the user transactions are calculated.

4.2 Performance

The applying delay reveals the key performance of a model because it determines the service response time for the user. From Figs. 9, 10, 11, 12 and 13 display the average applying delay of the 3 models under 5 kinds of RS amounts and 11 kinds of demand saturations. It can be found that the average apply delay of the 3 models present different trends under different ranges of demand saturations.

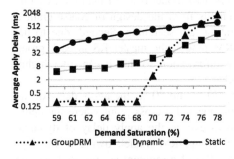

Fig. 9. Average apply delay of 4 RSs

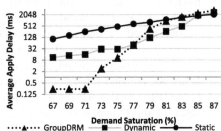

Fig. 10. Average apply delay of 8 RSs

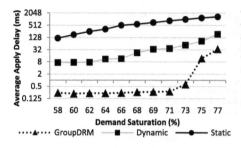

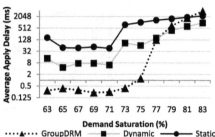

Fig. 11. Average apply delay of 12 RSs

Fig. 12. Average apply delay of 16 RSs

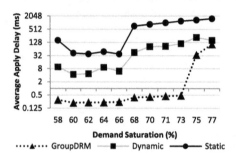

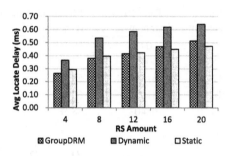

Fig. 13. Average apply delay of 20 RSs

Fig. 14. Average locate delay of all demand saturations

(1) When the demand saturation is under 70 %, compared to the static model, the GroupDRM model reduces 100 to 2000 times of apply delay. Compared to the dynamic model, the GroupDRM model reduces 25 to 125 times of apply delay. This demonstrated the effectiveness of the migration algorithms in the GroupDRM model. When the RIs in a RS were not enough to meet the demand of users, more RIs will be migrated to the RS so that the users' demand can be satisfied immediately. However, the static model wasn't able to migrate RI. A lot of users' resource apply requests began to queue up until the previous RIs were released. This greatly increase the apply delay. Besides, there are two reasons to explain why the apply delay of the GroupDRM model is lower than the dynamic model. First, the GroupDRM model benefits from the design of coarse-grained which has lower overhead in RI migrating and searching. Second, due to the "Group-Based" design of the GroupDRM model, the master RS in each group always have the newest RI assignment information so that it can offer higher efficient direction to the migrating of RI.

(2) When the demand saturation is between 70 % and 80 %, the apply delay of the GroupDRM model and dynamic model appeared a cross point where the apply delay of the GroupDRM model began to exceed the apply delay of dynamic model. This shows a limitation of the GroupDRM model: owing to the segmentation of RI space, only when all the RIs of a segment are released and the

segment can be migrated. But the service time of a user is random. Thus there may exist many fragments in a segment which intensify the lacking of RIs when the demand saturation is high. This leads to the increasing of apply delay. A possible optimization is to set lower segment granularity in the GroupDRM model.

(3) When the demand saturation is higher than 80 %, due to the lacking of RIs, the overhead of frequently RI migration cancel out the improvement. Thus the apply delay of the GroupDRM model and dynamic model come near to the static model. However, this situation is unusual in actual applications.

In the static model, the mapping relationship of RI is fixed and there is no RI migration. This determines that the static model will gain the best locating efficiency. However, in order to greatly decrease the apply delay, it is worth bringing in the RI migration mechanism which will inevitably increase the locating overhead slightly. In Fig. 14, the average locating delay of all demand saturations in GroupDRM model is about the same as the static model and is lower than the dynamic model. This is because the GroupDRM model locates the RIs in granularity of segment and the updates the IG-SLT and OG-SLT in different strategies. These advantages compensated the overhead caused by RI migration. However, due to the relative fine-grained and fully-distributed features of the dynamic model, it suffered the highest locate delay compared to other 2 models.

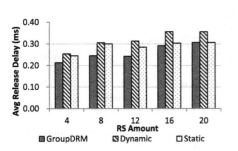

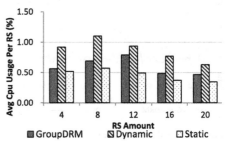

Fig. 15. Average release delay of all demand saturations

Fig. 16. Average CPU usage per RS of all demand saturations

Because the resource release process of the each model doesn't involve RI migration, the release delay is mainly affected by the searching algorithm of RI locally. As shown in Fig. 15, the GroupDRM model gains the lowest average release delay of all demand saturations for the reason that the RIs can be quickly searched in the unit of segment. However, since the dynamic model had to process the searching and migrating of RIs at the same time, it still suffered the highest release delay.

The test program collects the CPU usage of all the RSs in the cluster every 2 s and calculated the average value per RS after the test is over. From Fig. 16 we can observe that due to the extra searching operations and network messages caused by RI migration, the average CPU usage of all demand saturations in the GroupDRM model and dynamic model is higher than static model. The coarse-grained design of the GroupDRM model determines its lower migration overhead compared to the dynamic model. On the other hand, the CPU usage doesn't increase with the growing RS amount. This demonstrated the good scalability of the GroupDRM model.

Both the GroupDRM model and the dynamic model support the online joining and leaving RS. To measure the changes of performance when the RS is joining and leaving the cluster, we define the total amount of apply, locate and release messages which are returned from the RS cluster to the test program in a second as the total service frequency of the cluster.

In the online joining test, each model deployed 12 RSs to be divided into 4 groups while each group has 3 RSs. The total amount of RIs is 8192. Since the test program started, the average demand per second on each RS was kept at 250. And join a new RS into each group every 40 s one by one. The test program also began to send the user transactions to every new RS with the same demand as other RSs. It is shown in Fig. 17, both the GroupDRM model and dynamic model can migrate RIs to the new RSs so that the total service frequency of the cluster can be increased linearly with the growing of RS amount. The total service frequency of static model stays the same because it doesn't support the online joining of RS when the RS amount reaches a certain upper bound.

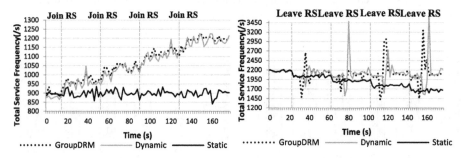

Fig. 17. Total service frequency of online RS leaving

Fig. 18. Total service frequency of online RS joining figure

In the online leaving test, each model deployed 16 RSs divided into 4 groups while each group has 4 RSs. The total amount of RIs is 8192 and each RS has 512 RIs in average. Since the test program started, the average demand per second on each RS was kept at 500. Leave a RS from each group every 40 s and the test program also shift the demand from the leaved RS to a surviving RS in each group at the same time. Because the demand saturation is closer to 100 %, the cluster can only maintain its previous total service frequency by recycling the RIs on the leaved RS. It can be seen in Fig. 18 that each time when a RS leaved, the total service frequency can return to the previous level after a jitter which is caused by heartbeat timeout. This demonstrates that both the GroupDRM model and dynamic model can recycle the RIs on the leaved RS and migrate the RIs to the RS which has the huge demand. However, the total service frequency of static model continued to drop down with the decreasing RS amount because it doesn't support the leaving of RS.

5 Conclusion

The paper is focused on a typical resource management problem in wireless communications, a new group-based dynamic distributed resource management model is proposed. The following conclusions can be drawn:

(1) The GroupDRM model can reduce 100 to 2000 times of apply delay compared to the static model. And reduce 25 to 125 times of apply delay compared to the dynamic model.

(2) The apply delay of the GroupDRM model and dynamic model become closer to the static model. This revealed a phenomenon that the overhead caused by frequent migration will eliminate the improvement brought by the migration.

(3) Due to the advantages of the coarse-grained and group-based design, the locating delay, releasing delay and CPU usage of the GroupDRM model are all superior to the dynamic model.

(4) The GroupDRM model supported the online joining of RS to linearly increase its service abilities and could handle the online leaving of RS to ensure the reliability of the system.

Acknowledgments. This work is supported by 973 project 2011CB302301, the National Basic Research 973 Program of China under Grant by National University's Special Research Fee (2015XJGH010).

References

1. Lescuyer, P., Bott, F.: UMTS: Origins Architecture and the Standard, pp. 208–210. Springer, London (2004)
2. Korhonen, J.: Introduction to 3G Mobile Communications, pp. 41–44. Artech House, America (2003)
3. Johnson, C.: Radio Access Networks for UMTS: Principles and Practice, p. 46. John Wiley and Sons, America, New Jersey (2008)
4. Tanner, R., Woodard, J.: WCDMA - Requirements and Practical Design, p. 232. UbiNetics Ltd, UK (2004)
5. Kaaranen, H., Ahtiainen, A., Laitinen, L., Naghian, S., Niemi, V.: UMTS Networks: Architecture, Mobility and Services, 2nd edn, pp. 139–142. Wiley, England (2005)
6. Jie, C.: Research on distributed resource management strategy in wireless network (in Chinese). M.S. thesis, Huazhong University of Science and Technology, Wuhan, Hubei, China (2014)
7. Gonnet, G.: Expected length of the longest probe sequence in hash code searching. J. ACM **28**(2), 289–304 (1981)
8. Raab, M., Steger, A.: "Balls into Bins"—a Simple and tight analysis. In: Luby, M., Rolim, J. D.P., Serna, M. (eds.) Randomization and Approximation Techniques in Computer Science. Lecture Notes in Computer Science, vol. 1518, pp. 159–170. Springer, Heidelberg (1998)
9. Mitzenmacher, M.: The power of two choices in randomized load balancing. Ph.D. thesis, Computer Science Department, University of California at Berkeley (1996)

10. Patil, S., Gibson, G.: Scale and concurrency of GIGA+: file system directories with millions of files. In: 9th USENIX Conference on File and Storage Technologies (2011)
11. Brinkmann, A., Effert, S.: Redundant data placement strategies for cluster storage environments. In: 12th International Conference on Principles of Distributed Systems (OPODIS) (2008)
12. Miranda, A., Effert, S., Kang, Y., Miller, E.L., Brinkmann, A., Cortes, T.: Reliable and randomized data distribution strategies for large scale storage systems. In: 18th International Conference on High Performance Computing (HiPC), pp. 1–10. IEEE Press (2011)

ESR: An Efficient, Scalable and Robust Overlay for Autonomic Communications

Jiaqi Liu[1], Guojun Wang[2], Deng Li[2(✉)], and Hui Liu[3]

[1] School of Software, Central South University, Changsha 410083, China
liujiaqi@csu.edu.cn
[2] School of Information Science and Engineering, Central South University,
Changsha 410083, China
{csgjwang,d.li}@csu.edu.cn
[3] Department of Computer Science, Missouri State University, Springfield, MO 65897, USA
huiliu@missouristate.edu

Abstract. Autonomic Communication (AC) refers to self-managing systems which are capable of supporting self-configuration, self-healing and self-optimization. However, information reflection and collection, lack of centralized control, non-cooperation and so on are just some of the challenges within AC systems. Since many self-* properties are achieved by a group of autonomous entities that coordinate in a peer-to-peer (P2P) fashion, thus, it has opened the door to migrating research techniques from P2P systems. Motivated by the challenges in AC and based on comprehensive analysis of popular P2P applications, we present a novel Efficient, Scalable and Robust (ESR) Peer-to-Peer (P2P) overlay, which is inspired by two other scientific areas (i.e. conditioning monkeys and prime meridian). Differing from current structured and unstructured, or meshed and tree-like P2P overlay, the ESR is a whole new three-dimensional structure to improve the efficiency of routing, while information exchanges take in immediate neighbors with local information to make the system scalable and fault-tolerant. Meanwhile, rather than a complex game theory or incentive mechanism, a simple but effective punish mechanism has been presented based on a new ID structure which can guarantee the continuity of each node's record in order to discourage negative behavior on a autonomous environment as AC. Large number of experiment results show the advantages of the ESR.

Keywords: P2P overlay · Super node · Information interaction · Autonomic communications

1 Introduction

The term Autonomic Communication (AC) [1] addresses such challenging issues as the continuous growth in ubiquitous and mobile network connectivity, together with the increasing number of networked devices populating our everyday environments (e.g., PDAs, sensor networks, tags, etc.), by trying to identify novel flexible network architectures, and by conceiving novel conceptual and practical tools for the design, development, and execution of "autonomic" communication services. It is used to enable

© Springer International Publishing Switzerland 2015
G. Wang et al. (Eds.): ICA3PP 2015, Part I, LNCS 9528, pp. 415–429, 2015.
DOI: 10.1007/978-3-319-27119-4_29

networks, associated devices and services to work in an unsupervised manner, to self-configure, self-monitor, self-adapt and self-heal - the so-called self-* properties. For such a highly distributed and heterogeneous environment, the classical, centralized client-server communication model seems to be inappropriate because of its inherent limitations in terms of scalability, fault-tolerance and ability to handle highly dynamic environments. The lack of global or central control implies the need for new techniques to design and verify self-* properties.

1.1 The Centric Characteristic of AC

The representative article [1] has presented challenges to theory and practice in ACs, including (1) interaction with strangers, (2) information reflection and collection, (3) lack of centralized goals and control. (4) meaningful adaptation, (5) cooperative behavior in the face of competition, as well as (6) heterogeneous services and semantics. By analyzing above challenges, we firstly present that the centric and most important characteristic in researches on AC is the Information Exchange (InfoEx). Any communication between any two nodes must have InfoEx. For example, nodes need when exchanging information about others' IDs. The InfoEx is necessary and basic in the (1), and the (3) just results from the lack of global InfoEx in fully distributed environments so that the (5) have to be guaranteed but so difficult. For the (4), the InfoEx is in bad need of so that the system will adapt correctly to given stimuli, maintain key behaviors and avoid deleterious ones. Moreover, designers also need the InfoEx to understand adaptation at a system level so that adaptations that optimize individual services do not cause undesirable interactions with those of other services, to say nothing of the importance of the InfoEx for the (2) and (6).

1.2 Exploiting P2P Overlay Structure

At the view of InfoEx, P2P networks in the Internet and ACs share many key characteristics such as self-* properties and decentralization due to the common nature of their distributed components: a P2P network consists of a dynamically changing set of nodes (or called peers) connected via the Internet, and a AC environment consists of nodes communicating with each other using various links (e.g. wired or wireless). These common characteristics lead to further similarities between the two types of networks.

The P2P is not an alternative of the AC and can not be directly applied to ACs. The concept of network overlays [2] makes it possible to provide a range of different networking abstractions, as an approach to the virtualization of the underlying network resource(s). Existing approaches to P2P overlays can be divided into two general classes [3]: (1) mesh-based P2P and (2) tree-based P2P. They will be introduced in detail in Sect. 2.

The paper presents an Efficient, Scalable and Robust (ESR) P2P overlay. Differing from current meshed and tree-like P2P overlay, the ESR is a whole new three-dimensional structure to improve the efficiency of routing, while InfoExes take in immediate neighbors with local information to make the system scalable and fault-tolerant. Meanwhile, a new cluster head organization mechanism called Tri-IC is presented.

The Tri-IC mechanism makes the overlay to be with the small world characteristic, solve the mismatching problems between logical and physical locations, and improve the performance and robustness.

The rest of the paper is organized as follows. Section 2 deals with the related work. We present the overlay structure with different issues in Sect. 3. In Sect. 4 we show the performance analysis and simulation results of the ESR. Finally, conclusions are made in Sect. 5.

2   Related Work

Most current researches combining the autonomic systems with P2P refer to the P2P-based framework for distributed network management including wired [4] and wireless [5], or the combination of autonomic computing and P2P [6, 7]. The latter is the main branch of those combining researches. Even there are many similar characteristics between ACs and P2P overlays, the challenges of ACs make it impossible to immigrate any P2P overlay to ACs.

2.1   Mesh-Based P2P Overlay vs. AC

Mesh-based approaches makes peers self-organize into a mesh in a distributed manner. Many P2P overlays usually organize networks into multi-dimensional (i.e. more than 2-dimensional) structures. There are many researchers proposing 3-dimensional [7], N-dimensional (N > 3) [8] or cross-layer [9] P2P networks.

The HyperCuP algorithm described in [7] is capable of organizing super-peers of a P2P network into a recursive graph structure called a hypercube that stems from the family of Cayley graphs, as shown in Fig. 1.

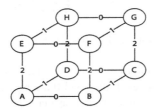

Fig. 1. HyperCup topology

To build overlay networks, it is very important that being aware of the underlying network infrastructure or providing physical network topology information. To guide the construction of overlay networks, researches increase the dimension of the coordinate space [10] to improve the distance prediction accuracy. Distance prediction uses $O(N)$ measurements of Round Trip Time (RTT) to predict the N^2 RTTs among N nodes. The prediction is used to guide the selection of nearby nodes However, it has been observed that, once beyond a certain threshold, the prediction cannot benefit from higher dimensions [11].

Compared with the unstructured mesh-based approach, the structured DHT-like overlay are unsuitable when the search key is similar, but not identical, to the key used to store the data item [12], which situation is often appeared in AC. Moreover, such a structured approach may make the overlay be much fragile if user machines are join/leave the system frequently.

From above analysis, the N-dimensional overlay is complicated, hard to understand and maintain especially for the highly dynamic environments as ACs. Furthermore, the heterogeneity characteristic is not fully considered in above multi-dimensional overlays [7].

2.2   Tree-Based P2P Overlay vs. AC

Tree-like structures are widely used in many research directions such as content distribution, file-sharing and application layer multicast and so on. Normally, there are two types of tree structures in abstraction.

Type I: grouping low level nodes to be the upper level node [13].
Each cluster can be treated as an abstract "super" node, and the resulting abstract nodes can be partitioned in the same way to form a higher-level cluster. An example network with three levels of hierarchy is shown in Fig. 2.

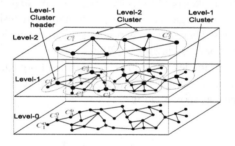

Fig. 2.   Tree-based structure I

Three levels of cluster hierarchy in a network. Each node in a physical network is treated as a level-0 cluster. Nodes in the level-0 are grouped to form level-1 clusters. The bigger dots in the level-1 denote cluster headers. Then level-1 clusters are further grouped into level-2 clusters. The solid lines denote abstract links among clusters. C_k^h denotes the kth cluster in the level h. The routing performance depends on the cluster structure generated by a clustering algorithm, which, in turn, is determined by three parameters: number of hierarchy levels, number of clusters, and cluster size distribution.

Type II: grouping low level cluster centers to be the upper level node [14]. Being different from Type I, only cluster centers rather than all nodes in each cluster can be the upper level node.

First all the nodes are grouped into clusters at the leaf level, level 0. Each cluster has a cluster center. Then, all cluster centers of the leaf level are grouped into clusters at level 1. Recursively, all cluster centers at level i are grouped into clusters at level $i + 1$;

in other words all nodes at level $i + 1$ are centers at level i. An example is illustrated in Fig. 3(a), which can be mapped to the tree structure in Fig. 3(b).

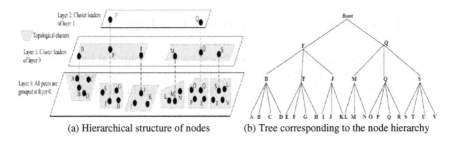

(a) Hierarchical structure of nodes   (b) Tree corresponding to the node hierarchy

Fig. 3. An example of Type II

Many tree-like structures belong to Type II, for example, Zigzag [15] (e.g. Figure 2) is similar with but better than [13].

Whatever the type of the structure is, nodes in the upper level are more important and storing more information. Therefore, the upper level nodes may be more vulnerable. There are large of researches concentrate on discussing the limitations of tree-like structures such as in [13, 16, 17]. Thus, we do not detailedly discuss it in this article.

2.3 Our Contributions

According to above analysis, we can draw a conclusion that neither the pure multi-dimension P2P structure nor the pure tree-like P2P structure is very adaptive to challenges of ACs.

To our knowledge, no related work has addressed the centric characteristic (i.e. InfoEx) of AC. **Our work, however, complements many pieces of recent work and firstly aims at satisfying all requirements**. The detailed key characteristics of our design are summarized below:

- **A loose coupled 3D overlay called ESR is presented, which has global view combined with limited state, and localized connection and InfoEx.** Current N-dimensional P2P overlays are either not suitable for highly dynamic environment with frequent node joining and leaving [16], or without consideration of heterogeneity of peers [17].**To our knowledge, there is no similar research with our overlay.**
- **A whole new tri-IC mechanism is presented to secure the efficiency and robustness.** It differs from most cluster head based mechanisms where cluster heads only backup each other. There are three cluster heads in each cluster called Information Center (IC), which is used as center for InfoEx. Besides the function of backup, each of those three ICs has different duties so as to lighten every IC's work load.
- **The unique and successive of peers' identities (IDs) without the need of global knowledge or hashing, even though both dynamic and random events like joins, leaves and crashes take place.** It is very important for the overlay to be maintained

effectively and autonomously so that the corresponding mechanisms (e.g. game theory) could be applied conveniently.

3   The Formation of Overlay Network Topology

The section presents a new Tri-IC scheme based on nodes' physical locations and the activity of nodes in InfoEx. Experiments show that the IC in ESR combines both merits of the consideration of nodes' distances [18] and nodes' capabilities [19].

3.1   The Selection of ICs

Unlike those mechanisms [20] which select super nodes by a single parameter, the paper comprehensively considers multi-dimensional parameters including the vector evaluation, the nodes' satisfaction degree of and the completion time of information interaction among nodes, the distance between any two nodes and nodes' mobility.

In the information interaction, a node will receive task requests from other nodes (such as requesting that node to search files, to transfer information, to compute, etc.). The efficiency (ef) of one node to finish other nodes' task requests (R_T) in the total time T mainly consists of two aspects: firstly, the satisfaction degree ($S(R_T)$) from those nodes which present task requests; secondly, the time for completing task requests ($L(R_T)$). Proportional relation among ef, $S(R_T)$ and $L(R_T)$ is $ef \propto S(R_T)/L(R_T)$, that is, the higher satisfaction degree for completing tasks and the less for costing time, the higher the efficiency of the information interaction is.

Make RN_{ti} as the set of those nodes which interact with the node p_h at a certain time t_i, $|RN_{ti}|$ means the number of nodes which interact with the p_h. In the process of information interaction, there are various task types from nodes. Make TN_{ti} as the set of all requested task types which are received from $|RN_{ti}|$ nodes at time t_i by node p_h. $|TN_{ti}|$ means the number of task types.

Rc_{ti}^h shows the requirements from tasks in TN_{ti} for resources in the node p_h as following:

$$Rc_{ti}^h = (rc_{h1}, rc_{h2}, \dots rc_{h|TN_{ti}|}) \tag{1}$$

Where rc_{hj} shows the resource requests for the node p_h by all type j ($j \in [1, |TN_{ti}|]$) tasks from $|RN_{ti}|$ nodes.

Pc_{ti} shows resources ability which is provided by node p_h for each type of tasks:

$$Pc_{ti} = (\sum_{j=1}^{|RN_{ti}|} pc_{j1}, \sum_{j=1}^{|RN_{ti}|} pc_{j2}, \dots \sum_{j=1}^{|RN_{ti}|} pc_{j|TN_{ti}|}) \tag{2}$$

where pc_{kj} shows the node p_h's ability provided for all type k tasks from the jth node which interact with the p_h. When satisfying the condition as formula (3), $S_h(R_{ti}) = 1$, that is, it is 1 that the satisfaction degree of the p_h for completing all tasks in the information interaction at a certain time t_i.

$$Rc_{ti}^h = \sum_{j=1}^{|TN_{ti}|} rc_{hj} \leq Pc_{ti}^h = \sum_{j=1}^{|TN_{ti}|} \sum_{k=1}^{|RN_{ti}|} pc_{kj} \tag{3}$$

The satisfaction degree of the p_h for completing all task requests within the total time T are defined as formula (4):

$$S_h(R_T) = \prod_{i=1}^{|T|} \left\{ 1 - [\sum_{j=1}^{|TN_{ti}|} \max(rc_{hj} - \sum_{k=1}^{|RN_{ti}|} pc_{kj}, 0)] \middle/ \sum_{j=1}^{||TN_{ti}|} rc_{ij} \right\} \tag{4}$$

Formula (4) describes the degree that how the node p_h can satisfy the resource requirements from nodes which send tasks to the p_h. Apparently, to task requests for the same resource requirements, the more the Pc is, the more the $S_h(R_T)$ is. That is to say, the satisfaction of the p_h about interactive information is the greater. If the Pc is greater than or equal to the resources ability needed by task requirements, the satisfaction degree is the greatest (i.e. it equals to 1).

The time $L_h(R_T)$ for completing requested tasks R_T by the p_h shows as formula (5):

$$L_h(R_T) = \sum_{i=1}^{|T|} \max_{k \in [1,|RN_{ti}|]} \sum_{r_m \in R_k, m=1}^{|R_k|} l(r_m) \tag{5}$$

R_k shows the task request set from the node k in the RN_{ti} to the p_h, $l(r_m)$ shows the execution time of the p_h for completing the mth task request from one of other nodes. In the process of information interaction, one node will accept different task requests from various other nodes at the same time. Thus, the node which accepted task requests will divide its resource ability into various parts, in order to be suitable for different types of task requests. Each task request node has a sum of completion time for its various task requests. The maximum of all sums is the total task completion time by the node p_h at the time t_i. To add up every t_i ($i \in [1, T]$)during total time T, the sum is the $L_h(R_T)$.

Based on the formulas (4) and (5), the paper defines the efficiency of node p_h (ef_h) during the information interaction within the total time T as the formula (6):

$$ef_h = \frac{S_h(R_T)}{L_h(R_T)} \tag{6}$$

In AC, due to the mobility of nodes, the distances among some nodes will change frequently even in the same AS. At any time t_i, it is possible that the distance between any two nodes will change. At the time t_i, a parameter Sd_{ti}^h is presented as formula (7):

$$Sd_{ti}^h = \max_{p_j \in RN_{ti}} d(p_h, p_j) - \min_{p_j \in RN_{ti}} d(p_h, p_j) \tag{7}$$

where $d(p_h, p_j)$ shows the distance between the node p_h and the node p_j. Sd_{ti}^h is used to show the difference between two distance values: one value is the distance between the node p_h with the farthest node to the p_h, and the other value is the distance between the node p_h with the nearest node to the p_h. Then, Sd_h is defined as the average of Sd_{ti}^h during a total time T, as formula (8):

$$Sd_h = \frac{\sum_{i=1}^{|T|} Sd_{ti}^h}{|T|} \tag{8}$$

Differing from mechanisms used a single parameter, this paper presents a comprehensive node capability assessment mechanism called measurement level mechanism, which considers both the efficiency and the distance among nodes during information interaction. The value M of the measurement level for every node in one AS is defined as formula (9).

$$M_h = \frac{ef_h}{Sd_h} \tag{9}$$

In every AS, the three nodes which have the highest measurement level will be chosen as ICs. Different duties of each IC will be introduced in detail in the next section.

3.2   The Logical Topology Structure of ESR

Before describing the logical structure of ESR, the section firstly introduces the definition of some relevant parameters required for.

Definition 1: The term Measurement Rank (MR) is used to evaluate the rank of one node's measurement level. Nodes according to their measurement levels in the information interaction are classified into different ranks.

There are 4 kinds of measurement levels of nodes, the three nodes with the ordinal highest measurement levels is respectively regarded as rank 1, rank 2 and rank 3 in one AS. $MR_1/MR_2/MR_3$ shows the nodes set whose measurement levels is 1/2/3 respectively. MR_3 is the highest level, and the measurement level of all other nodes is 0 (MR_0), which is the lowest level. $MR(p)$ means the rank of node p's measurement level. Any two nodes i and j which can directly connected each other must satisfy the situation $|MR(i) - MR(j)| \leq 1$, while the exception is the node k belonging to MR_3, the node k's permitted differences with any other node i in the same AS meet $|MR(k) - MR(i)| \leq 2$; If any two nodes i and j lie in two different ASs, anyone can not directly connect to the other until $|MR(i) - MR(j)| < 1$ is satisfied (i.e. $MR(i) = MR(j)$). All the lowest level (MR_0) nodes can not directly conct to each other.

Definition 2: Multilayer structure topology. *maxMR* shows the highest measurement level. A multilayer structure topology is defined as an undirected graph G: $< V, E >$, where V is the set of nodes, and E is the set of edges. The building and maintenance of the structure should obey a Connection Restriction Rule (CRR) and keep the Connectivity Preserving Rule (CPR). It needs to meet:

(1) $CRR: \forall (p, q) \in E$,   if $p, q \in AS^i$, $MR(p), MR(q) < maxMR$,   s.t.
    $|MR(p) - MR(q)| \leq 1$; if $(\exists MR \in \{MR(p), MR(q)\} = maxMR) \wedge MR(p) \neq MR(q)$,
    s.t. $|MR(p) - MR(q)| \leq 2$. if $p \in AS^i \wedge q \notin AS^i$, s.t. $|MR(p) - MR(q)| < 1$.
(2) CPR: $\forall p \in V$, if $MR(p) < maxMR$, then $\exists q \in V$ make $MR(q) = MR(p) + 1$, and
    $(p, q) \in E$.

CPR shows that in multilevel topology structure, if a node's MR is not the highest, the node must always have a connection to a node with the higher MR than itself.

Based on CRR and CPR, nodes according to their MRs interconnect each other in each AS. The highest grade three nodes directly connect to each other, and are regarded as ICs, which respectively called the IC of the layer (IC_{layer}), the IC of the level (IC_{level}) and the IC of the AS (IC_{inner}). The MR_0 nodes are called General Peers (GPs). In one AS, all GPs connected to the IC_{inner}. Any two AS connect with each other only through corresponding ICs, and hence only nodes with the same MR can establish direct relationship. Figure 4 shows a diagram of the ESR structure, where the black solid dot means the GP, the black solid square means the IC_{inner}, the blank dot means the IC_{level}, and the blank square means the IC_{layer}.

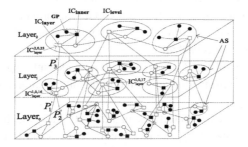

Fig. 4. Global overlay topology structure of

All nodes in the internetwork are divided into ASs in various scales as ellipse and form a logical structure as shown in the Fig. 4. In order to understand the structure of ESR more easily, one layer (i.e. the *layer₀* in the Fig. 4) is detailedly described as shown in Fig. 5.

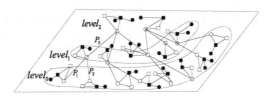

Fig. 5. Structure in the inner of layer

In Fig. 5, nodes in dotted circles belong to the same level, such as nodes in $level_0$ and $level_1$. A level consists of multiple ASs, and a layer consists of multiple levels. At $level_0$, the left 4 nodes make up of the first AS at this level. As described in definition 1 and 2, the black solid square shows the IC_{inner} (MR_1). Because of the regulation $|MR(i) - MR(j)| \leq 1$, the IC_{inner} connect with GPs (MR_0 which are the black solid dots), and the IC_{level} (MR_2 which is the blank dot). In the same way, the IC_{level} connect with the IC_{inner} (i.e. MR_1) and the IC_{layer} (i.e. MR_3 which is the blank square). Since the regulation to MR_3 nodes k is $|MR(k) - MR(i)| \leq 2$, the IC_{layer} can connect with the IC_{inner} and IC_{level}. Thus, the connection between IC_{inner} and IC_{layer} is an exception for IC_{inner}'s regulation $|MR(i) - MR(j)| \leq 1$. In Fig. 5, the left second 4 nodes is the second AS at $level_0$. It is clear that the first AS and the second AS in $level_0$ do not connect with each other directly. Furthermore, an AS do not connect with other ASs at the same level. Several levels make up of a layer. ASs with the same level number but in neighbor layers must linked together by their IC_{layer}s. For example, in Fig. 4, the AS^{16} at the $level_0$ in the $layer_1$ connects with the AS^{23} at the $level_0$ in the $layer_2$ via the $IC_{layer}^{1,0,16}$ and the $IC_{layer}^{1,0,23}$. The exception is the AS at the highest level u in every layer, which have to connect with the AS at a 1-lower level (i.e. level u-1) in the upper layer.

IC_{inner}: From previous constraint rules, all GPs in one AS adjoin to the IC_{inner} in the same AS. Moreover, every GP voluntarily submits its information to the IC_{inner} in the same AS. The function of IC_{inner} is to maintain GPs' information in the same AS, to assign ID for any new node, to copy all stored information in the IC_{inner} to the other two ICs (i.e. IC_{level} and IC_{layer}) as backup.

IC_{level}: The function of the IC_{level} is to report all nodes information in its AS to the superior IC_{level}. Those information are stored in the information table backed up from the IT_{inner}.

IC_{layer}: IC_{layer}s are used to connect ASs in different layers. One IC_{layer} can connect at most w the lower neighbor IC_{layer}s, and can connect to at most one the upper IC_{layer}. IC_{layer}'s function is to report all nodes information in its AS to the superior IC_{layer}. Those information are stored in the information table backed up from the IT_{inner}. Nodes can used those information to quickly restore the connection if several nodes or ASs are collapse.

4   Performance Analysis

This section will evaluate the performance of the ESR structure, mainly including the scalability, the stability and the fault-tolerance. Topology structures with different node scales are produced by GT-ITM generation tools [21], which is widely used to generate and analyze graphs using a wide variety of models for internetwork topology.

4.1   Scalability

This section uses parameters (including the maximum degree of nodes and the proportion of different degree nodes to total nodes) along with the change of the system's scales to evaluate the scalability of the system. The evaluation builds ESR network topological structures where total number of nodes is $N = 500$, $N = 1000$, $N = 1500$, $N = 2000$ respectively. For each size, GT-ITM produces 100 times topology respectively, so as to check the changes of nodes degree under various system scales.

Figure 6 shows the degree distribution of each node with N = 500 and N = 2000 in the system. From the Fig. 6, we can see that the degree of most nodes is 1, which obviously are GPs because they only connect with the ICinner. A small number of nodes with high degrees are the ICs. In two scale systems, the average degree of nodes is both around 2.5. That is to say, the average degree of nodes is almost not influenced by network scales. That should result from CRP and CRR. Figure 7 shows the proportion of various degree nodes to whole nodes when the size of N changes from 500 to 2000 every 500 nodes. X-axis shows the node degree d, namely the number of other nodes which connect with each node. Y-axis means the proportion of the degree d nodes to total nodes.

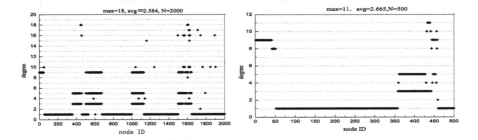

Fig. 6. Node degree in different scale system

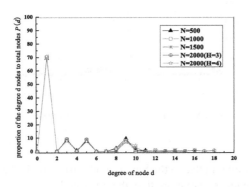

Fig. 7. Fraction of node with different degree

In Fig. 7, the number of layers and of levels are 3 respectively (i.e., $H = 3$) besides $N = 2000$. When $N = 2000$, another results when $H = 4$ are added in order to analyze the influence of different values of H on the distribution of degrees in ESR. It can be seen from the Fig. 7 that the number of high degree nodes is few, while the number of low degree nodes (e.g. nodes whose degree is 1) hold 70 %. Thus, the structure has the power-law characteristics. Networks with power-law characteristics, have stronger resistance to random attack. From the Fig. 7, it also can be seen that the degree has little change with the layers or the scale of the system increasing (e.g. H is changed from 3 to 4). We can draw a conclusion that the ESR structure can adaptively adjust topology structure to adapt to the change of the system's scale. The degree of ICs will not increase with the system's scale increase, but remain at a relatively stable state, so that the system has good scalability.

4.2   Stability

We regard following operations as the disturbed to nodes including querying, transferring messages, information interacting. For ACs with limited resources, the more times nodes are disturbed, the more likely to cause system instability or even collapse it is. That is, a good topology for information interaction should have the fewer disturbed times to nodes, so as to ensure the stability of the system. When querying resources, the paper chooses the flooding searching algorithm which is commonly used, to compare the average disturbed situations in the Super - node and the ESR structure. In order to facilitate reading and analysis, though doing experiments in a variety of scales ($N = 500$, $N = 1000$, $N = 1500$, $N = 2000$), Fig. 8 shows average times that every node is disturbed when query 120000 times only in the system size $N = 1000$.

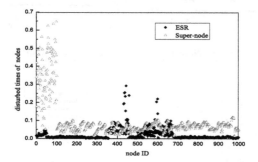

Fig. 8.   Average disturbed times of node

In Fig. 8, being similar to that in the Super - node structure, in the ESR, some nodes' average disturbed frequency are more than the other nodes.

By analysis, we can find out that those nodes are ICs (in the ESR) or super nodes (in the Super - node). Moreover, we can find that the disturbed frequency of ICs in the ESR is far less than that of super nodes in the Super node structure. In the ESR structure, the disturbed times of most nodes are very low, and some even are zero.

From characteristics of the ESR structure, we know that the three ICs assume different tasks respectively, and work together with each other. Thus, loads of a single IC or of GPs are reduced. It is reflected in the results so that the average disturbed frequency of nodes is generally less. The system has good stability.

4.3   Fault Tolerance

In this section, we evaluate fault tolerance in the way that how the whole system can still work normally when there are nodes exiting the system. Here uses the efficiency of completing tasks for file search (by the flooding searching algorithm) as a parameter to analyze fault tolerance of the ESR. Figure 9 gives the change of file search success rate in the ESR structure and the Super - node structure [20] along with the increase of the proportion of nodes leaving.

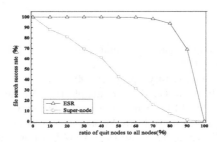

Fig. 9. File search success rate with node quit

In Fig. 9 we can see that when there are nodes to leave the system, the ESR structure can maintain the higher file search success rate than the Super-node. After about 70 % nodes exit, the file search success rate of the ESR structure begins to slow down. The ESR adopts distributed ICs, known from the analysis of its scalability, the structure has the typical nature of the power-law. Therefore, that greatly optimizes the system's performance, reduces large amount of redundant information which the information flooding leads to, and reduces the possibility of the collapse due to the heavy loads. On the other hand, a single super node is responsible for all tasks' loads in the Super - node structure, but three ICs in the ESR have different functions, and share each other's loads. Three nodes in the ESR share the loads of one node in the Super - node structure. Not only three ICs in one AS back up each other, but also the ICs in the upper neighbor level AS and the ICs in the upper neighbor layer AS back up.

5   Conclusion

(1) Combining with existing P2P overlay network structures' advantages based on Mesh (Mesh - -based) and Tree (Tree - -based), and comprehensively considering character-istics of ACs, the paper presents a kind of multi-layer and multi-level structure mobile overlay with triple ICs network called ESR.

(2) The ESR structure ensures the consistency of the underlying physical network and the logical network topology structure; At the point view of information interaction, considering node contribution ability, mobility information etc. comprehensively, choose the relatively stable three ICs; Three ICs back up each other, and undertake different functions, which avoid the emergence of network bottleneck, and ensure the stability of the structure and fault tolerance; Through different ICs to connect various

ASs, only need know the adjacent AS's information, information interaction only need through the local connection, low consumption of information update and process. Known through the experiment analysis, the ESR structure is good at the scalability, stability and fault tolerance.

Acknowledgments. This research is supported by the National Natural Science Foundation of China under Grant No. 61272149 and No. 61309001.

References

1. Dobson, S., et al.: A survey of autonomic communications. ACM Trans. Auton. Adapt. Syst. (TAAS) **1**(2), 223–259 (2006)
2. Herbert, A.: What happens to pastry, pp. 10–16 2007
3. Magharei, N., Rejaie, R., Yang, G.: Mesh or Multiple-Tree: A comparative study of live P2P streaming approaches. In: IEEE International Conference on Computer Communications (INFOCOM 2007), pp. 1424–1432. IEEE Piscataway, NJ (2007)
4. Kim, K.-H., Nam, H., Singh, V., Song, D.: DYSWIS: Crowdsourcing a home network diagnosis. In: 23rd International Conference on Computer Communication and Networks (ICCCN), Shanghai, pp. 1–10 (2014)
5. Tutschku, K., Tran-Gia, P., Andersen, F.-U.: Trends in network and service operation for the emerging future internet. AEU – Int. J. Electron. Commun. **62**(9), 705–714 (2008)
6. Movahedi, Z., Ayari, M., Langar, R., Pujolle, G.: A survey of autonomic network architectures and evaluation criteria. IEEE Commun. Surv. Tutorials **14**(2), 464–490 (2012)
7. Schlosser, M.T., Sintek, M., Decker, S., Nejdl, W.: HyperCuP - hypercubes, ontologies, and efficient search on peer-to-peer networks. In: Moro, G., Koubarakis, M. (eds.) AP2PC 2002. LNCS (LNAI), vol. 2530, pp. 112–124. Springer, Heidelberg (2003)
8. Cheng, B., Fan, J., Jia, X., Jia, J.: Parallel construction of independent spanning trees and an application in diagnosis on Möbius cubes. J. Supercomputing **65**(3), 1279–1301 (2013)
9. Kuo, J.-L., Shih, C.-H., Ho, C.-Y., Chen, Y.-C.: A cross-layer approach for real-time multimedia streaming on wireless peer-to-peer ad hoc network. Ad Hoc Netw. **11**(1), 339–354 (2013)
10. Rizk, R., Saber, W., Harb, H.: Conditional clustered matrix factorization based network coordinate system. J. Netw. Comput. Appl. **45**, 191–202 (2014)
11. Costa, M., Castro, M., A. Rowstron, A., Key, d P.: PIC: Practical internet coordinates for distance estimation. In: Proceedings of IEEE ICDCS, March 2004
12. Ben-Gal, I., Shavitt, Y., Weinsberg, E., Weinsberg, U.: Peer-to-peer information retrieval using shared-content clustering. Knowl. Inf. Syst. **39**(2), 383–408 (2014)
13. Lian, J., Naik, K., Agnew, G.: A framework for evaluating the performance of clustering algorithms for table-driven hierarchical networks. IEEE/ACM Trans. Networking **15**(6), 1478–1489 (2007)
14. Tran, D.A., Nguyen, T.: Hierarchical multidimensional search in peer-to-peer networks. Comput. Commun. **31**(2), 346–357 (2008)
15. Tran, D.A., Hua, K.A., Do, T.T.: A peer-to-peer architecture for media streaming. J. Sel. Areas Commun. **22**(1), 1–14 (2004)
16. Lin, J.W.: Message broadcast using multiple trees in DHT P2P networks. J. Internet Technol. **15**(4), 691–698 (2014)
17. Shen, H., Li, Z., Li, J.: A DHT-Aided chunk-driven overlay for scalable and efficient peer-to-peer live streaming. IEEE Trans. Parallel Distrib. Syst. **24**(11), 2125–2137 (2013)

18. Furno, A., Zimeo, E.: Self-scaling cooperative discovery of service compositions in unstructured P2P networks. J. Parallel Distrib. Comput. **74**(10), 2994–3025 (2014)
19. Hsiao, H.-C., Hong-Wei, S.: On optimizing overlay topologies for search in unstructured peer-to-peer networks. IEEE Trans. Parallel Distrib. Syst. **23**(5), 924–935 (2012)
20. Chandra, J., Mitra, B., Ganguly, N.: Effect of constraints on superpeer topologies. In: Proceedings IEEE INFOCOM, 2013, pp. 60–64 (2013)
21. Zegura, E.W., Calvert, K.L., Bhattacharjee, S.: How to model an internetwork. In: The Conference on Computer Communications (INFOCOM 1996), pp. 594–602. IEEE Computer Society, Washington (1996)

Energy Efficient Sleep Scheduling for Wireless Sensor Networks

Paul Chiedozie Uzoh, Jilong Li, Zhenbo Cao, Jinbae Kim,
Aamir Nadeem, and Kijun Han[✉]

Department of Computer Science and Engineering, Kyungpook National University,
Buk-gu, Daegu, 41566, South Korea
{Upaul,jllee,zbcao,jbkim,anadem}@netopia.knu.ac.kr,
kjhan@knu.ac.kr

Abstract. Recently, wireless sensor network (WSN) has become a formidable force in almost all areas of our everyday life. However, there are still many issues with wireless sensor networks among which is the energy problem. One of the numerous techniques that have been introduced as a way of solving the problem of energy deficit inherent in a WSN is sleep scheduling. Sleep scheduling allows sensor nodes to periodically take turns to sleep in order to minimize energy cost in a WSN. Apparently, Overemission in a WSN is one of the main causes of energy drainage in sensor nodes. Traditional schemes fail to take into consideration the sleeping timetable of other nodes; hence they let transmitter nodes repeatedly send RTS preamble packets and similar control packets to sleeping nodes. Our proposed sleep scheduling scheme addresses this problem from a whole new perspective using a system called Designated Sensor Node (DSN) mechanism. The DSN scheme significantly reduces flooding of the network with unnecessary control packets. The effect in turn leads to the minimization of unnecessary energy waste in a WSN.

Keywords: DSN · WSN · Sleep scheduling · Overemission · RTS packets · Control packets

1 Introduction

Recent advances in WSN have considerable impact in our everyday life. It is being used in the military to serve many purposes like, monitoring friendly forces, equipment and ammunition battlefield surveillance, reconnaissance of opposing forces and terrain, battle damage assessment nuclear, biological and chemical attack detection. It also has vast applications in environmental monitoring, health, manufacturing, agriculture, and so on. The proliferation and diversity of its usage could not have been without the development of Micro-Electro-Mechanical-Systems (MEMs) technologies. MEMs is the technology of very tiny devices. Large-scale deployment of wireless sensor networks is made possible today with the introduction of MEMs technology. Similarly, MEMs has made it possible for sensors that are smaller, cheaper and intelligent to be developed. These sensors are equipped with wireless interfaces to communicate with one another.

© Springer International Publishing Switzerland 2015
G. Wang et al. (Eds.): ICA3PP 2015, Part I, LNCS 9528, pp. 430–444, 2015.
DOI: 10.1007/978-3-319-27119-4_30

Sensor nodes generally have limited processing and computing resources. However, when compared to traditional sensors they are inexpensive. These sensor nodes can sense, measure, and gather information from the environment. Sensor devices are meant to be low power devices equipped with one or more sensors. Battery is the main power source in a wireless sensor node. There may be a need for a secondary power supply like the harvesting of power from the environment. Perhaps the greatest advantage of wireless sensor networks is the fact that it can be deployed in dangerous regions, even places that cannot be reached by humans who may want to explore those areas for some reasons. For this same reason, powering, recharging or replacement of wireless sensor nodes have proven problematic and have culminated into a very big issue. Therefore, to effectively utilize or maximize the network energy and extend its lifetime, researchers have developed lots of energy-efficient protocols like radio duty cycling to prolong the network lifetime [1–6].

Radio duty cycling introduces the problem of finding moment in time where both the sender and the receiver are active so that a link can be established. Traditionally, Medium Access Control (MAC) protocols use either synchronous or asynchronous approaches to handle challenges of radio duty cycling in WSN [2, 7, 8].

The issue of limited energy resources in WSN poses a performance problem in terms of the throughput of a network and also on the overall lifetime attainable by a network. Extending battery life of the wireless node and prolonging the overall network lifetime of a WSN is thus a foremost task in the design of practical WSNs [9–11].

A Network lifetime can be defined as the time till the first sensor node runs out of its battery capacity [3]. Network lifetime maximization involves all levels of sensor network hierarchy, from hardware/software design, to communication protocols. Recent efforts dealing with communication-related energy costs, mainly focus on two separate but equally important fronts which are energy-efficient routing and sleep scheduling [1].

Radio transceiver consumes more energy compared to other parts of a sensor node. The radio transceiver is controlled by a MAC protocol. MAC protocol also coordinates accesses among nodes that are competing for the shared medium and tries to reduce interference among transmitting nodes. There are several major sources of unnecessary energy consumptions in the MAC layer [2]. The first is idle listening. Idle listening occurs when a node leaves its radio transceiver on even though there is no data being transmitted or received at the time. Energy usage during idle listening state can be compared to that of receiving state energy consumption. Overhearing is yet another cause of energy waste in a wireless sensor network. This happens when a node intercepts a packet that is destined for another node. Since the intercepted packets also have to be decoded before the node realizes that it was meant for another node which leads to unnecessary power consumption. The third waste of energy is over-emission which happens when the transmitter node transmits a packet while the receiver node is not ready to receive.

In the proposed approach, we designed a DSN scheme where the designated node holds schedule information of nodes going into sleep mode. Although the DSN is responsible for the storage of the schedules of all the nodes going into sleep mode, it does not detect how the entire network work. Therefore, it is not entirely a centralized system. However, it is responsible for the effective functioning of the network. The DSN node stores the sleep schedule of all the neighboring nodes and must remain awake while all other nodes are sleeping. However, since the DSN does a lot of processing and controlling, it uses up a larger amount of energy in the process. Therefore, after a time threshold and depending on energy level and other criteria, the DSN selects another node to act as the replacement. This ensures balance of energy consumption between nodes in the same network. The active period of a node is not fixed. However, just like in [3], after a certain time threshold without any event activation, nodes randomly set a sleep schedule and share them with the DSN before going to sleep. Figure 1 shows the basic concept of a DSN-based network. This paper focuses on the introduction of an effective sleep scheduling scheme that helps to achieve energy maximization in a WSN through effective sleep scheduling scheme.

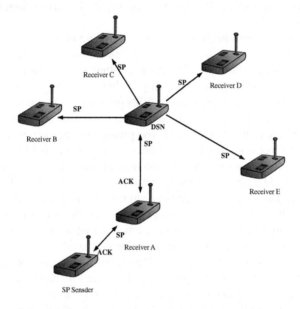

Fig. 1. Designated Sensor Node

The rest of the paper is presented as follows. In Sect. 2, related work is introduced. Section 3 introduces the proposed system model, and in Sect. 4 the scheme is compared to a related work through results and discussions. Finally, Sect. 5, concludes the paper.

2   Related Work

One of the proposed solutions for the reduction of unnecessary energy consumption on IEEE 802.11 is Sensor MAC(S-MAC) [2]. S-MAC protocol uses a periodic listen and sleep schedule scheme to minimize idle listening and ensure energy efficiency. In S-MAC, each node turns its radio transceiver off and goes into a sleep mode for a period of time. The node switches to a listening mode when it wakes up and then communicate with other nodes. The listen period is used for the exchange of control packets, such as RTS, CTS, SYNC, ACK packets, as well as data packets. In S-MAC, neighboring nodes form a virtual cluster and set up a common synchronized listen-sleep schedule. However, this method has some drawbacks as the uniform duty cycle of S-MAC can have a high end-to-end latency. The traffic load across the entire network is huge and S-MAC, having a fixed active time cannot adapt to this much traffic. Many other protocols have been designed to address the inefficiencies in S-MAC. Such protocols are DS-MAC and Time-out MAC (TMAC) [4, 7]. All these schemes have been proposed to enhance the performance of the S-MAC protocol. After a time threshold without any event activation in T-MAC, the listening period ends immediately and the node returns to sleep mode. This was not the case in S-MAC. On the other hand, DS-MAC aims at improving the latency performance of S-MAC by adjusting the duty cycle of the sensor node depending on the traffic condition. A similar work tries to find a way to maximize the lifetime of a WSN by a joint routing and sleep scheduling scheme [1]. Although their work is a theoretically based scheme, this paper follows a similar path with modifications to their proposed sleep scheduling mechanism. However, our work is restricted to only the technical aspect of sleep-wake scheduling mechanism. This work also focuses mainly on the sleep scheduling with a minimal interest in the routing aspect.

Joint Routing and Sleep Scheduling endeavors to jointly optimize energy consumption in a WSN. One of the advantages of this scheme is that it combines both sleep scheduling and routing to maximize the lifetime of a WSN. The combination makes it a more comprehensive approach to solving the issue of energy maximization. However, sleep scheduling mechanism in PS-MAC like most other mechanisms mentioned earlier in this paper fails to effectively tackle the problem of overemission. As shown in the paper, the authors assume a node which initializes its RF circuits as soon as it wakes up from sleep mode. This is shown in Fig. 2. The nodes take time T_{rf} and E_{rf} amount of energy to initialize its radio frequency. When a node has a packet to send after it has successfully initialized its RF, it first listens to the channel for a period of T_{lis}^i to see if any of its neighbors are transmitting.

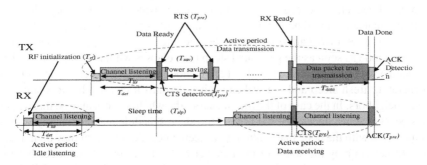

Fig. 2. Timing diagram in different active periods

The paper defines T_{det}^i as the total time from when a node wakes up to when it goes back to sleep. This is calculated as $T_{det}^i = T_{rf} + T_{lis}$. In the paper, if the channel is idle for T_{det}^i time, then the node can send an RTS preamble. If the target receiver is also in an active mode, and gets the RTS preamble, it replies with a clear to send (CTS) packet.

However, if the receiver happens to be in a sleep mode, the transmitter will resend the RTS preamble before going into a power saving mode for a short period of time T_{sav}. The process is repeated over and over again until the receiver node wakes up and captures the RTS preamble. Subsequently, to ensure that all transmitter-receiver pairs are sufficiently connected and that communication between other links within the same RF range is correctly detected, then T_{det}^i has to be long enough to cover at least two consecutive RTS preambles including the T_{sav} in-between them. The condition also has to be true for all sensor nodes within its RF range. Contrary to our proposed scheme, transmitters in [1] have no way of knowing the status of the receivers before sending an RTS. Therefore, if a sender has a packet to send to a receiver, it keeps sending an RTS over and over again until one is captured. Here, in the best case scenario, the T_{det}^i, must be long enough to cover at least two consecutive RTS preambles including the T_{sav} between them. One can therefore assume that in some cases, RTS could be sent more than two times before it can be captured by the intended receiver. This could happen when the intended receiver (j) goes into sleep mode just immediately before the first RTS arrives. In this case, the transmitter have longer time to wait and therefore more RTS preambles to send before the receiver wakes up. In some situations, extension of sleep duration of nodes may be necessary depending on some conditions like the characteristics of the event to be sensed. Hence, increasing the time a node requires to sleep T_{slp}^i, results in a proportional increase in the number of RTS preambles a transmitter has to send before the receiver wakes up and captures a packet.

Probability sensor MAC (PS-MAC) [3], uses a probabilistic method to guess the time a node wakes up. The advantage of PS-MAC is that it can closely guess the expected time to eradicate over-emission in a WSN. In PS-MAC, each sensor node makes use of a pseudo-random number generator to generate a pre-wakeup probability and seed number. When this is done, the node exchanges its pre-wakeup probability and seed numbers with its neighboring nodes to enable each node to know its neighbor's sleep schedule. However, This scheme fails to take into consideration one thing- there is a possibility that some or all neighboring nodes may either be busy or temporarily out of reach. In this case, there can be two possible outcome scenarios- (1) The node may go into sleep mode as soon as the generated sleep time elapses without being able to share its schedule with the neighboring nodes. (2) The node may have to keep cancelling and re-generating fresh sleep and pre-wakeup schedule until it can be able to share them with its neighbors. In the case of the first scenario, the whole system may be thrown into chaos because when nodes that did not get the sleep schedule may eventually want to communicate with the node that is already in sleep mode. At this point they do not have a way of determining the status of the receiver node. Therefore, these nodes have no option but to resort to sending RTS packets until one becomes acknowledged. This can lead back to over-emission energy waste in PS-MAC protocol. Similarly, in the second scenario where a node keeps re-generating fresh sleep schedule when its previously generated (but not shared) schedule time elapses. Since there is no guarantee if and when the node can be able to share its pre-wakeup schedule, the node can go on regenerating fresh schedule until it is able to share it with all its neighbors. This also can go on indefinitely and therefore, it can have serious effects on the whole scheme.

3 Proposed Scheme

Although the target of this work is mainly to reduce to the barest minimum the number of control packets, we still retain the idea of RTS preambles to avoid collision. However, this scheme reduces the number of RTS and other control packet like sync packets being sent by ensuring that these packets are only sent when the intended receiver is awake to receive them. In S-MAC, and other previous schemes, sync packets are sent whenever fresh sleep schedule is generated. However, in this proposed scheme, there is no need for the synchronization phase since it is always possible to obtain the schedule from the DSN node any time if needed.

For simplicity, we say that a node can either be in a sleep mode or in an active mode. The radio transceiver is switched off when in sleep mode. The sleep duration is fixed for all nodes in the network, so for any node i, the sleep duration is denoted by D_{slp}^i. The reason all the nodes have a fixed sleep period is so that the DSN can calculate and know exactly when a node is supposed to be awake. We refer to this as Expected Time of Awakening (ETA). This can be calculated using Eq. 1.

$$ETA_i = D_{slp} - T_{slpt}^i \tag{1}$$

Where, D_{slp} is the sleep duration of any node and T_{slpt}^i is how long any given node i has already been asleep.

A node initializes its radio frequency (RF) when it wakes up. When in active mode, a node can either be transmitting or receiving data using time slots. Thus, an active period is said to be a data transmission slot if the node transmits a packet in this time slot. Similarly, an active period is a data reception slot if the node receives a packet in this time slot.

After a certain threshold without event activation, a node randomly chooses a time to go to sleep. However, when a node randomly generates a sleep schedule, other nodes have no way of knowing about it, therefore the node has to send its new sleep schedule to the DSN and waits for and acknowledgement (ACK) from the DSN as illustrated in Fig. 3. The node only goes into sleep mode when it receives an ACK from the DSN.

At any given time, a node can get the schedule information and the status of another node from the DSN by sending a request packet (RP). The request packet specifies the ID of the node whose schedule is being requested as well as the ID of the requesting node. This helps the DSN to determine which schedule is going to which node. When the DSN node receives the request packet, it forwards the most recent schedules of all the nodes in sleep mode to the requesting node.

Naturally, nodes go in and out of the networks due to so many reasons. Some of these reasons are explained in [12]. Nodes transition from fully functional to partially functional and eventually to non-functional states as illustrated in Fig. 4. Nodes that are fully functional are nodes that have energy level above the energy threshold θ. Partially functional (PF) nodes have energy levels lower than θ while non-functional nodes are no longer part of the network hence their edges are deleted. PF nodes are still part of the network however, they may not be able to receive or transmit packets with their current

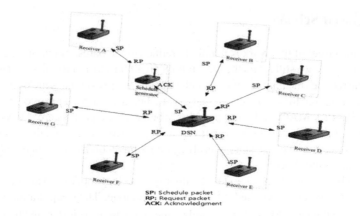

SP: Schedule packet
RP: Request packet
ACK: Acknowledgment

Fig. 3. Schedule generator generates SPs sends it to the DNS and receives and ACK, while other nodes send Request Packet (RP) whenever they need to know the status of a certain node.

energy level. In PS-MAC, PF neighboring nodes will continuously and unsuccessfully try to exchange schedule packets with them thereby causing over emission. However, this problem does not occur in the DSN network because if a node gets disconnected in the network due to low energy, the DNS purges its schedule from the list. Hence, when a node requests a none-functional node's sleep schedule, the DSN replies with a void packet which indicates that the requested node has been disconnected from the network.

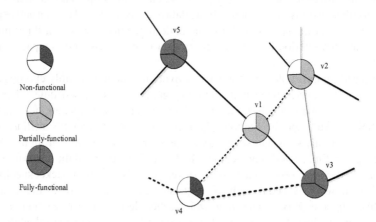

Fig. 4. (Color online) Fractional percolation on a network: the green nodes v3 and v5 remain intact (FF); the amber nodes v1 and v2 are under some nonfatal error (PF); the red node v4 suffers from some fatal error (NF). Dotted lines mean deleted edges [12].

DSN scheme addresses the shortcoming in PS-MAC. In the DSN scheme, each node has to receive an ACK from the DSN before they can go into sleep mode. After receiving the schedule, the DSN saves the schedule for future referencing and also shares this sleep schedule with all the nodes that are awake and ready to receive a packet. Similarly, since the DSN has the expected time of awakening of all the sleeping nodes, whenever a node rejoins the network after its sleep cycle is over, the DSN shares the sleep schedules of all neighboring nodes with the node that is re-entering active mode. When any node, for instance node B in Fig. 3 wants to communicate with a sleeping node C, then B can calculate the time node C will wake up and will add a randomly generated number (γ). I.e. ETA + γ. The random number is used to avoid collision at C when there are more than just one node waiting to communicate with it as soon as it re-enters active mode.

In DSN network, we use the parameters in Table 1. The assumption is that all packets including preambles are received at a constant power of p_{rx}, while it takes a transmitter a power of p_{tx} to transmit any packet. The duration of a data packet is denoted by T_{data} while assuming that all packets (RTS, CTS, ACK...), are of a fixed length T_{pre}. Similarly, energy for a potential transmitter to calculate the expected time of a potential receiver is denoted by p_{eta}. When a node wakes up from sleep, it takes that node a power of E_{rf} and time T_{rf} to initialize its RF circuits. There are two possible times that a node can receive a sleep schedule of its neighbors. (1) When it is fully active and (2) When it has just come out of sleep mode. In the first case scenario, RF initialization is not considered when calculating the amount of energy it takes to receive the schedule packet while, in the second case scenario, the RF initialization is taken into consideration when calculating the average amount of energy it takes a node to receive a schedule packet. Also, in DSN network, the amount of energy to receive a sleep schedule and transmit a data packet is separately dependent on three different characteristics of transmitters- (a) the DSN node, (b) a waking node and (c) an active node.

Table 1. SYSTEM PARAMETERS.

Peta	Power to calculate expected time of awakening	28 (mW)
Ptx	Transmission power	50 (mW)
Prx	Receiving power	30 (mW)
E*rf*	Energy to initialize RF circuits	15.05 (µJ)
Trf	Time to initialize RF circuits	2.1 (ms)
Tdata	Time to transmit one data packet	16 (ms)
Tpre	Time to transmit one RTS/CTS/ACK preamble	0.832 (ms)

3.1 The DSN

In the DSN scheme, the designated node deals with a lot of communications. Therefore, it uses up more energy than other nodes in the network. Also a DSN node cannot go into sleep mode while all the nodes in the network are sleeping. For this reason, the energy of the DSN node may dry up faster than all other nodes in the network. To avoid this problem and ensure that the energy consumption is balanced between all the nodes in the network, each node in the wireless sensor network (WSN) take turns to function as the DSN. However, before going into sleep mode, the current DSN has to share all the information it has with the new DSN. Unfortunately, when a new DSN is chosen, other nodes have no way of knowing the identity of this new DSN. Therefore, the new DSN has to broadcast its address to nodes in the network. As the DSN, the new designated node knows the ETA of all the nodes so it shares its ID together with the status of all other nodes with any node re-entering into active mode. This ensures that all nodes have their neighboring nodes' schedule and also know who the current DSN is at all times. When a new DSN has been successfully selected, then the old DSN (now an ordinary node in the network) can immediately generate a sleep schedule, share it with its neighbors as well as with the new DSN node before going into sleep mode. Unlike other nodes that have to wait for a certain threshold time before generating a sleep schedule, a node that has just finished acting as a DSN can immediately generate a sleep schedule. The next DSN node is chosen when the current DSN has used up a certain amount of energy from its initial energy (say $\frac{1}{N}$ of its initial energy). The initial energy here is the amount of energy it has prior to starting as the DSN. The current energy level (CEL) is given by.

$$CEL = \frac{\text{Initial Energy level}}{N} \tag{2}$$

The criteria for choosing the next DSN are- 1) the node must be free at the time the new DSN is being chosen. 2) Nodes being considered by the current DSN must possess and energy level greater than the threshold and the node with the highest energy level than others is chosen. When more than one nodes meet the above conditions, then random selection is used to select the next DSN. Figure 5 illustrates the process of determining the new DSN. The current DSN initiates the process of choosing the next DSN by broadcasting a status request packet to the nodes in the network. Each node then replies with their current energy status, current transmission status, and other relevant data. When the DSN receives these information, it then initiates the DSN choosing process. In the first stage, the process first determines nodes that are currently busy (some nodes may have just finished sending out CTS packets and are waiting for data transmission to commence) and these nodes are dropped. The next stage checks for the energy level of the nodes. Nodes that fall short of the minimum energy level threshold are dropped. The minimum energy level threshold is the energy level of the current DSN which is made available to the process from the start. At this stage, it is possible to have only one node with the required energy level threshold or a node that has greater amount of energy than other nodes. When this is the case, that node is automatically selected as the DSN. However, it is also possible to have more than one nodes that meet the above requirements and possess similar energy level. If there are more than 1 nodes at this stage, then the process uses random selection to choose the next DSN.

In the DSN scheme, only a DSN node has to transmit an ACK packet after receiving a sleep schedule, therefore the energy consumed by a DSN node to receive and transmit and ACK packet (R_{DSN}), is calculated as follows.

$$R_{DSN} = p_{rx} \left(T_{data} + T_{pre} \right) + p_{tx} \left(T_{data} + T_{pre} \right) \tag{3}$$

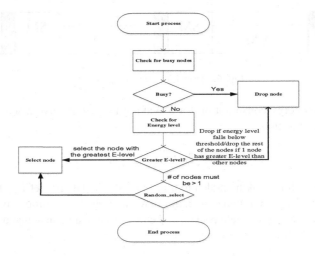

Fig. 5. Choosing the DSN.

Similarly, the energy required for a DSN node to transmit a data packet to node j in DSN is equal to.

$$T^j_{DSN} = 2R_{DSN} + P_{eta} \tag{4}$$

Where P_{eta} is the energy required to calculate the expected time of awakening of that receiver.

This mechanism looks like a centralized system where the absence of the DSN may lead to the total failure of the whole system. However, this is not entirely so. The work of the DSN is mainly to hold schedule information. It does not determine the functionality of the entire system. Moreover, a temporary DSN can assume the role of DSN if the current DSN remains inactive for a set period of time.

3.2 The Waking Node

A Waking node in a DSN network is considered to be the node that is transitioning from a sleep mode (SM) into an active mode (AM) see Fig. 6. A node that has just woken up needs time T_{rf} and energy E_{rf} to initialize its radio frequency (RF), this is denoted by the gray areas in-between SMs and AMs. These two factors are taken into consideration while calculating the energy consumption to receive and or transmit a single data packet. RF initialization is considered only for the waking node. This is because a node first initializes its RF when it wakes up and this is the only time RF initialization is required. Consequently, the additional energy required to do this (I_{rf}) is given by.

$$I_{rf} = T_{rf} \times E_{rf} \tag{5}$$

A waking node requires RF initialization. However, it does not require to send an Acknowledgement packet whenever it receives a schedule packet from the DSN.

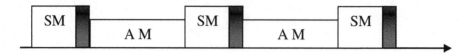

Fig. 6. Transition of waking node.

Therefore, the energy consumption for a Waking node to receive a schedule packet (R_{wn}), is calculated thus.

$$R_{wn} = I_{rf} + p_{rx} \left(T_{data} + T_{pre} \right) \tag{6}$$

Subsequently for a waking node i to transmit a single data packet T_{wn}, to a receiver j, the energy required to initialize its radio frequency, the ETA computational energy, the energy to receive a schedule packet, and energy to transmit an actual data packet is calculated as follows

$$T_{wn}^{ij} = R_{wn} + P_{eta} + p_{tx} \left(T_{data} + T_{pre} \right) \tag{7}$$

3.3 Active Node

An active node is considered to have an already initialized RF. This can be a node that has fully transitioned into an active mode or a node that has just finished communicating with other nodes and is now an active listener. Similar to the waking node in the previous section, this node does not require to transmit an ACK packet whenever it receives a schedule packet, therefore, the energy to receive a sleep schedule packet (R_{an}), is simply

$$R_{an} = p_{rx} \left(T_{data} + T_{pre} \right) \tag{8}$$

Subsequently, to know how much energy it takes a node i to transmit a single data packet to another node j then, the amount of energy to receive a sleep schedule, the energy to compute ETA of a particular receiver and the energy required to transmit an actual data packet to that receiver is calculated. Therefore, for an active node, the energy required to transmit a single data packet T_{an} is.

$$T_{an}^{ij} = R_{an} + P_{eta} + p_{tx} \left(T_{data} + T_{pre} \right) \tag{9}$$

4   Results and Discussions

In a DSN network, a transmitter avoids sending RTS preamble and other control packets repeatedly to the intended receiver who may either be temporarily out of reach or even disconnected from the network. Also, synchronization of sleep schedule is avoided since the DSN has all the information. The transmitter requires to know only the time when a node goes into sleep mode to be able to compute the ETA of that node. The transmitter already has or can obtain this information from the DSN node at any given time. Once the transmitter has this information, it can calculate when the receiver wakes up. Hence it only has to send one RTS to the receiver after it has re-entered active mode. Apparently, no RTS is sent while the receiving node is in sleep mode. In the proposed scheme, a node makes sure that the DSN receives its sleep schedule. The DSN keeps record of the sleep timetable of all the nodes in the network. DSN node hands over all its information to another node to act as the DSN when it has used up about $\frac{1}{N}$ of the initial energy as at the time it started acting as the DSN. This regulates the amount of time a node can act as the DSN. It is also an effective way to ensure balance of energy consumption among all nodes in a DSN-base network.

It is mentioned earlier that sleep duration of sensor nodes in the network may require to be extended depending on the situation. For example, sensor nodes that are deployed in an area were events to be studied happen periodically may opt for longer sleep duration to save the energy consumption that result from frequent turning on and off of the radio transmitter. In this work, we compared the energy consumed by a node in DSN with that in PS-MAC. In the proposed DSN scheme, the energy consumption based on the type of node is separately calculated owing to the fact that there can be three distinct nodes in the DSN network. The result in Fig. 7 below clearly shows that as the sleep duration of the sensors in the network increased, so did the average amount of RTS and control packets sent. This is attributed to the fact that some transmitters in PS-MAC scheme who want to communicate with nodes that just entered sleep mode potentially send more control packets before the intended receivers become active again. Similarly, when some neighboring nodes are busy or temporarily out of reach, some nodes in the PS-MAC either repeatedly try to share their sleep schedules with them, thereby causing them to regenerate new schedules when the time elapses.

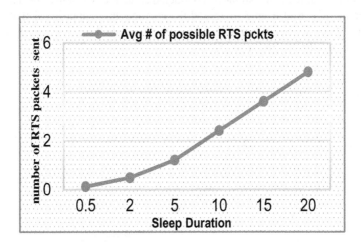

Fig. 7. Possible number of RTS packets sent with and interval of 4.16 ms.

In terms of energy consumption, Fig. 8 shows the average amount of energy consumed by each type of sensor node in a DSN network and PS-MAC respectively to initialize RF, receive and transmit data and control packets with respect to sleep duration. This proves that deploying sensor nodes equipped with PS_MAC protocol in a field where sensors require to go into sleep mode for a longer period of time is clearly not a good idea. However, DSN on the other proves to be much more efficient in this scenario because the transmitter only has to get the schedule of the intended receiver, calculate its ETA and transmits just once only when the node is awake and ready to communicate.

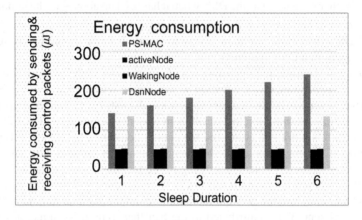

Fig. 8. Duty cycle-based average energy consumption of each node

The scenario in Fig. 7 does not only bring about a significant amount of energy waste, it also considerably impacts on the throughput and quality of service of the entire network. Figure 9 shows that the DSN has an edge over the PS-MAC in terms of the network throughput in an investigation conducted using the NS2 software. The number of sensors are increased from 5 to 35 and the average throughput is calculated which proves that DSN scheme can not only reduce energy waste but also outperform the PS-MAC in terms of the quality of service.

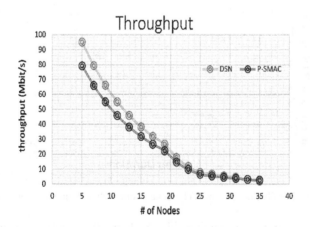

Fig. 9. Average throughput

However in the DSN scheme, as the number of nodes in the network is increased the average throughput becomes more and more similar to that of the PS-MAC. This is because as the number of sensors in the network increased, the number of processing the DSN has to deal with also increased. Since the DSN does a lot of work at this time, this means that it also uses up energy faster and therefore the change of the DSN happens more frequently. This drawback will be studied in our future work to sustain the throughput when the number of sensor increases.

5   Conclusion

A DSN scheme that enhances energy consumption of wireless sensor nodes through sleep scheduling for nodes in the network was proposed. This scheme adopts Designated Sensor Nodes that work not as a coordinator, but as a time schedule keeper in a WSN. It assures that all nodes know the status of all their neighboring nodes at all times. It also allows for them to calculate the ETA of any particular node. By doing so, possible flooding of the network with RTS preambles and other control packets while the intended receiver is in sleep mode is effectively avoided. DSN scheme also introduces an effective way to ensure that energy consumption of all nodes in the network is balanced by means of DSN role shift. It provides an effective way to rotate the job of a DSN among all the sensor nodes in the network by considering their energy levels. This effect ensures the extension of the network's lifetime.

Acknowledgments. This research was financially supported by the Ministry of Education (MOE) and National Research Foundation of Korea (NRF) through the Human Resource Training Project for Regional Innovation (no. 2014H1C1A1067126), the BK21 Plus project (SW Human Resource Development Program for Supporting Smart Life) funded by the Ministry of Education, School of Computer Science and Engineering, Kyungpook National University, Korea (21A20131600005), and the This work was supported by the IT R&D program of MSIP/KEIT. [10041145, Self-Organized Software platform (SoSp) for Welfare Devices].

References

1. Liu, F., Tsui, C.-Y., Zhang, Y.: Joint Routing and Sleep Scheduling for Lifetime Maximization of Wireless Sensor Networks. IEEE Trans. Wirel. Commun. 9(7), 2258–2267 (2010)
2. Ye, W., Heidemann, J., Estrin, D.: Medium access control with coordinated adaptive sleeping for wireless sensor networks. IEEE/ACM Trans. Networking 12(3), 493–506 (2004)
3. Choi, S.-C., Lee, J.-W., Kim Y., Chong, H.: An energy-efficient mac protocol with random listen-sleep schedule for wireless sensor networks. In: TENCON 2007 - 2007 IEEE Region 10 Conference, Taipei (2007)
4. Dam, V.T., Langendoen, K.: An adaptive energy-efficient mac protocol for wireless sensor networks. In: Proceedings of the 1st International Conference on Embedded Networked SenSys, California (2003)

5. Niu, J., Cheng, L., Gu, Y., Jun, J., Zhang, Q.: Minimum-delay and energy-efficient flooding tree in asynchronous low-duty-cycle wireless sensor networks. In: Wireless Communications and Networking Conference (WCNC), 2013 IEEE, Shanghai (2013)
6. Rasouli, H., Kavian, Y., Rashvand, H.: ADCA: adaptive duty cycle algorithm for energy efficient IEEE 802.15.4 beacon-enabled wireless sensor networks. Sens. J. IEEE **14**(11), 3893–3902 (2014)
7. Yuan, X., Bagga, S., Shen, J., Balakrishnan, M., Benhaddou, D.: DS-MAC: differential service medium access control design for wireless medical information systems. In: Engineering in Medicine and Biology Society, 2008, EMBS 2008, 30th Annual International Conference of the IEEE, Vancouver, BC (2008)
8. Cunha, F., Mini, R., Loureiro, A.: Sensor-MAC with dynamic duty cycle in wireless sensor networks. In Global Communications Conference (GLOBECOM), 2012 IEEE, Anaheim, CA (2012)
9. Raghunathan, V., Ganeriwal, S., Srivastava, M.: Emerging techniques for long lived wireless sensor networks. IEEE Commun. Mag. **44**(4), 108–114 (2006)
10. Li, J., AlRegib, G.: Network lifetime maximization for estimation in multihop wireless sensor networks. IEEE Trans. Sig. Process. **57**(7), 2456–2466 (2009)
11. Dagher, J., Marcellin, M., Neifeld, M.: A theory for maximizing the lifetime of sensor networks. IEEE Trans. Commun. **55**(2), 323–332 (2007)
12. Shang, Y.: Vulnerability of networks: fractional percolation on random graphs. Am. Phys. Soc. **89**(1), 012813-1–012813-4 (2014)

QoS Prediction in Dynamic Web Services with Asymmetric Correlation

Qi Xie[1]([✉]), Bing Tang[2], Zibin Zheng[3], and Mengtian Cui[1]

[1] College of Computer Science and Technology,
Southwest University for Nationalities, Chengdu 610041, China
qi.xie.swun@gmail.com
[2] School of Computer Science and Engineering,
Hunan University of Science and Technology, Xiangtan 411201, China
[3] School of Data and Computer Science, Sun Yat-sen University,
Guangzhou 510000, China

Abstract. Web services are the mainstream implementation of service-oriented architectures in which both functional and non-functional Quality of Service (QoS) is significantly considered by service users and providers. Although multiple QoS-based models to QoS prediction for Web services via collaborative filtering have been proposed, the accuracy of existing ones is not adequate, since these works rarely have considered the influence of asymmetric correlation among service users on prediction accuracy. This paper combines asymmetric correlation among service users and asymmetric correlation propagation into the deviation computation of different service items in QoS prediction. In this paper, a novel method for QoS prediction in dynamic Web services is proposed, which includes a framework consisting of asymmetric correlation model, asymmetric correlation propagation model and deviation computation algorithm with correlation. To study the QoS prediction performance of our method, a well-known dataset consisting of about 1.97 million real-world QoS records is used in the experiments. The experimental results demonstrate that our method achieves better prediction accuracy than other well-known methods.

Keywords: Services computing · QoS prediction · Collaborative filtering · Slope one · Asymmetric correlation

1 Introduction

Web services technologies are emerging as a powerful vehicle for organizations that need to integrate their applications within and across organizational boundaries [1–4]. The growing presence and adoption of Web services as the delivery mode in business have caused a wide range of attentions not only from industry but also academia. Due to the large number of Web services that meet the specific functional requirements of service users, its time and resource consuming for service users to choose appropriate services to satisfy their various needs.

© Springer International Publishing Switzerland 2015
G. Wang et al. (Eds.): ICA3PP 2015, Part I, LNCS 9528, pp. 445–459, 2015.
DOI: 10.1007/978-3-319-27119-4_31

To help service users find their desired services, there is urgently need to build effective methods of service selection and recommendation.

To facilitate effective Web service recommendation, the quality of candidate services needs to be assessed from non-functional properties [5]. Quality-of-Service (QoS), which is usually employed for representing the non-functional characteristic of Web services such as response-time, failure-rate and availability, has become an important differentiating point of different Web services [6]. And different Web service QoS properties can be divided into two parts: one is the user-independent QoS properties (e.g., price, popularity, etc.) and the other is the user-dependent QoS properties (e.g., response-time, failure-rate, throughput, etc.) [7]. Specially, the values of user-independent QoS properties are usually provided by service providers and equal for different users, while the values of user-dependent QoS properties can fluctuate widely for different service users since the values are highly related to the Internet conditions and the positions of the service users. Consequently, the same Web service may have very different QoS values for different service users, and methods where QoS values obtained by one user are straight used by other users are inappropriate. Instead, a personalized Web service prediction is needed, in which accurate values of the user-dependent QoS properties should be obtained immediately.

Some previous works [8–11] have employed collaborative filtering (CF) [12–15] to Web service recommendation. These methods can predict the QoS performance of a Web service for a user by employing historical QoS information from other similar service users, who have similar historical QoS experience on the same set of commonly-invoked Web services [5–7].

To improve the prediction accuracy, some hybrid prediction methods are proposed by combining of both memory-based CF method and model-based CF method [16] or user-based CF [17,18] method and item-based CF method [10,11,19,20]. Work [16] employs clustering model and item-based CF method to enhance the prediction accuracy. Zheng et al. [10,11] and Tang et al. [19,20] combine user-based CF method and item-based CF method to balance two different CF methods, then increase the prediction accuracy of the traditional CF methods.

However, there is still one problem of the previous works to be solved, which influences the performance of QoS prediction. That is to say, the current methods fail to recognize the importance of the asymmetric correlation among different service users. Through the experiments implemented on a real-world Web service dataset[1], which includes 1.97 million Web service invocation results of 339 Web services observed by 5825 service users, we conclude that the asymmetric correlation among service users is the same significant as the similarity of services for QoS prediction.

To address the absence of asymmetric correlation among service users, different from the above methods, we propose a novel method for QoS prediction in dynamic Web services. The proposed method systematically integrates asymmetric correlation among service users and asymmetric correlation propagation

---

[1] http://www.wsdream.net.

into the deviation computation of different service items in QoS prediction. In addition, this paper mainly focuses on the asymmetric correlation model for service users, asymmetric correlation propagation model and deviation computation method with asymmetric correlation.

The main contributions of this work are threefold:

- Firstly, the asymmetric correlation for service users is introduced into the QoS prediction in dynamic Web services, which has a significant effect on the prediction accuracy.
- Secondly, asymmetric correlation propagation model is also proposed to take into account of the propagation and attenuation of asymmetric correlation for service users.
- Finally, experiments are conducted to evaluate our method by employing a real-world QoS dataset which includes about 1.97 million invocations for Web services.

The remainder of this paper is organized as follows: Sect. 2 provides an overview on the proposed framework of QoS value prediction. Section 3 introduces the QoS value prediction method with asymmetric correlation in detail. Section 4 presents the experiments of our method. Section 5 concludes the paper with a summary and a description of future work.

2   Framework of QoS Value Prediction

To provide the optimal services for service users among functionally equivalent ones, the framework shown in Fig. 1 acts as a platform for service users to obtain optimal Web services with satisfying predicted QoS values by employing asymmetric correlation and asymmetric correlation propagation. Figure 1 shows the framework overview of QoS value prediction, which includes the following procedures.

(a) Asymmetric correlation (AC) modeling is the first crucial problem to be solved in our framework. Firstly, existing QoS values of Web services are collected and analyzed to build the correlation matrix (CM) for QoS values. And the correlation matrix records the numbers of Web services that have been invoked by each pair of service users. After that, asymmetric correlation matrix (ACM) for service users can be constructed by using correlation matrix, where each entry in the ACM matrix is related to not only the numbers of Web services invoked by each pair of service users but also the numbers of Web services invoked by the others. Finally, according to the asymmetric correlation matrix, asymmetric correlation graph for service users can be built.

(b) Asymmetric correlation propagation modeling is the second crucial problem to be attacked. In this step, the propagation of asymmetric correlation for service users in asymmetric correlation graph is taken into account adequately. Furthermore, it's very important to obtain the relation flow, which transfers the values of asymmetric correlation for a service user to others strongly connected to it.

(c) Deviation computation of Web services in QoS prediction framework will be built based on the values of asymmetric correlation propagation and the QoS dataset. Then the results of deviation computation can be used to find the different services for corresponding service users. In this step, traditional deviation computation employing SLOPEONE method [14] is modified and extended with the values of propagation.

(e) After finding the appropriate different services, the missing QoS values for service users can be predicted by employing the deviation character.

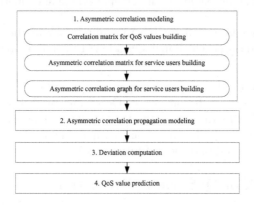

Fig. 1. Framework overview of QoS value prediction

3   QoS Value Prediction with Asymmetric Correlation

3.1   Preliminaries

In order to make an accurate prediction, some researchers employ collaborative filtering methods to provide personalized prediction of QoS values for service users [8–11]. Due to the great successes in modeling characteristics of service users and Web services, collaborative filtering techniques have been widely employed in famous commercial systems, such as Amazon, eBay, etc. [10]. In the QoS prediction scenario, CF methods can automatically predict QoS values of unused services for service users by collecting Web service QoS information from other users.

In a typical QoS prediction scenario [10,11], there is a user-item matrix which includes M service users and N Web service items. Every entry in this user-item matrix $r_{m,n}$ denotes a vector of QoS values (e.g., response-time, failure-rate, etc.), which is obtained by the service user m on the Web service item n. And if Web service item n is not invoked by service user m previously, then $r_{m,n} = 0$.

Item-based CF method can provide dramatically better performance than user-based method [10,15]. And Slope One method (named as SLOPEONE) is a typical item-based CF method which works on comparing the intuitive principle of a popular differential between service items rather than similarity between service items [15]. The typical deviation computation of service item i and j can be calculated by:

$$Dev(i,j) = \sum_{u \in U(i) \cap U(j)} \frac{r_{u,i} - r_{u,j}}{|U(i) \cap U(j)|}, \tag{1}$$

where every user u has invoked both service item i and service item j, and $|U(i) \cap U(j)|$ is the number of service users consisting of u. $r_{u,i}$ and $r_{u,j}$ represent the QoS values of service item i and service item j observed by user u, respectively.

In addition, the SLOPEONE method uses different service items to predict the QoS values by employing the following equation:

$$P(r_{u,i}) = \overline{r_u} + \frac{\sum\limits_{j \in R_u} Dev(i,j)}{|R_u|}, \tag{2}$$

where $P(r_{u,i})$ is a vector of predicted QoS values of entry $r_{u,i}$ in the user-item matrix using SLOPEONE method. $\overline{r_u}$ is a vector of average QoS values of different service items invoked by service user u. Furthermore, $R_u = \{j | j \in r_u, j \neq i, num(Dev(i,j)) > 0\}$ is the set of all relevant items, in which $num(Dev(i,j)) > 0$ represents the number of service user u, who invoked both service item i and service item j, should be larger than 0. And $|R_u|$ is the number of R_u. $Dev(i,j)$ can be calculated by Eq. (1).

3.2   Asymmetric Correlation Modeling

In this paper, asymmetric correlation is introduced to address the absence of correlations among service users, which have a significant effect on QoS value prediction. Furthermore, modeling of asymmetric correlation includes three steps which are described as follows.

Correlation Matrix (CM) for QoS Values Building. A necessary first step before correlation matrix (CM) building is to give the definition of CM, which is based on the assumption that the more items that have been rated by both user u_p and user u_q, the closer the users are [21]. Based on work [21], in which correlation rating matrix records the number of items that have been rated by each pair of users in MovieLens scenario, the CM in QoS value prediction for Web services can be defined by:

$$S(u_p, u_q) = \begin{cases} \{i_n : (r_{u_p,i_n} \neq \emptyset) \wedge (r_{u_q,i_n} \neq \emptyset)\} (u_p \neq u_q) \\ \emptyset \qquad\qquad\qquad\qquad\qquad\quad (u_p = u_q) \end{cases} n = 1, ..., N, \tag{3}$$

$$CM_{u_p,u_q} = |S(u_p, u_q)|, \qquad p = 1, ..., M, q = 1, ..., M, \tag{4}$$

where $S(u_p, u_q)$ is a set of Web services observed by both service user u_p and service user u_q, and $|S(u_p, u_q)|$ is the number of $S(u_p, u_q)$. r_{u_p,i_n} and r_{u_q,i_n} are the sets of QoS values of Web service in observed by service user u_p and service user u_q, respectively. Furthermore, M is the number of service users and N is the number of Web service items in user-item matrix.

Equations (3) and (4) show that CM is an M-by-M symmetric matrix. Taking into account the degrees of service user correlations, the values of correlations for service users, which invoked different number of Web services, should be different.

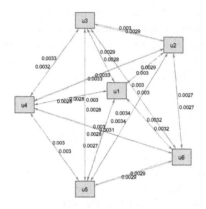

Fig. 2. Asymmetric correlation graph for service users

Asymmetric Correlation Matrix (ACM) for Service Users Building. According to [21], the correlation of service users is related to not only the numbers of Web services invoked by each pair of users but also the total numbers of Web services invoked by other users. Therefore, CM matrix can be improved and transformed to asymmetric correlation matrix (ACM). So, the ACM matrix for service users in our method can be calculated by:

$$
ACM_{u_p,u_q} = \begin{cases} \dfrac{|S(u_p,u_q)|}{\sum\limits_{\substack{l \in M \\ l \neq p}} |S(u_p,u_l)|}, & p \neq q, \\ 0, & p = q, \end{cases} \quad p = 1, ..., M, q = 1, ..., M, \tag{5}
$$

where u_p and u_q are the service users in user-item matrix, and u_l are the service users who are not equal to u_p.

From Eqs. (4) and (5), it can be observed that ACM matrix is different from CM matrix and ACM matrix is an asymmetric matrix.

Asymmetric Correlation Graph for Service Users Building. According to ACM matrix, the correlations of service users can be built as a directed graph as shown in Fig. 2, in which a node u_p expresses a service user and a directed edge e_{pq} from node u_p to node u_q expresses an asymmetric correlation from u_p to u_q. Therefore, the asymmetric correlation graph can be employed in asymmetric correlation propagation model to obtain the relation flow.

3.3   Asymmetric Correlation Propagation Modeling

In the step, we take into account not only asymmetric correlation among service users but also propagation and attenuation of asymmetric correlation. Observing from Fig. 2, we can intuitively see that the correlation among service users can spread throughout the graph and some users may obtain high correlation than others.

PageRank is an excellent way to prioritize the results of Web keyword searches, which counts the approximation of a pages importance or quality by not counting links from all pages equally, and by normalizing by the number of links on a page. And the PageRank for node n is defined as follows [22]:

$$PR(n) = a \cdot \sum_{q:(q,n)\in\varepsilon} \frac{PR(q)}{w_q} + (1-a) \cdot \frac{1}{|v|}, \qquad (6)$$

where $PR(n)$ is the importance score for every node $n \in v$ according to the graph connectivity. $|v|$ is the number of nodes in graph $G = (v, \varepsilon)$, in which ε is the set of directed connected edges among nodes. a is a decay factor which is usually set to 0.85. And w_q is the out-degree of node q.

Similar to PageRank [23], an asymmetric correlation propagation model is proposed which is based on the intuition that the correlation of service users can be effectively computed by employing a similar method as PageRank.

So, the following equation can be defined to compute the propagation of correlation among service users by modifying Eq. (6). And then, different correlation ranks for service users can be obtained.

$$PR(u_q) = a \cdot \sum_{p\in N(u_q)} PR(u_p)ACM(u_p, u_q) + (1-a) \cdot \frac{1}{M}, \qquad (7)$$

where $PR(u_q)$ is a vector of correlation ranks for service user u_q. $N(u_q)$ is a set of service users that connect to service user u_q. ACM is the asymmetric correlation matrix calculated by Eq. (5), and M is the number of service users in user-item matrix.

In vector form, Eq. (7) can be equivalently defined as:

$$\begin{bmatrix} PR(u_1) \\ \cdot \\ \cdot \\ \cdot \\ PR(u_M) \end{bmatrix} = a \cdot ACM^T \cdot \begin{bmatrix} PR(u_1) \\ \cdot \\ \cdot \\ \cdot \\ PR(u_M) \end{bmatrix} + \begin{bmatrix} (1-a)/M \\ \cdot \\ \cdot \\ \cdot \\ (1-a)/M \end{bmatrix}, \qquad (8)$$

where ACM^T is the transposed matrix of the ACM.

The correlation ranks for service users can be determined by calculate the eigenvector with eigenvalue 1 or by repeating the process until all correlation ranks become stable [23].

3.4   Deviation Computation and QoS Value Prediction

In traditional CF, Gao et al. [21] use different weights for users to represent the relationships. Different from this work which focuses on movie recommendation by using MovieLens dataset, our method employs about 1.7 million real-world QoS records (eg., response-time, throughput.) for Web services observed by service users to predict the missing QoS values for service users, and modifies the propagation model to suit the dynamic QoS prediction Scenario.

In this step, the asymmetric correlation and propagation among service users are combined into deviation computation of Web services for QoS value prediction in service-oriented architecture.

And then, the following equations are employed to compute the deviation and predict the QoS values by using enhanced SLOPEONE method respectively.

$$Dev'(i,j) = \frac{\sum\limits_{u \in U(i) \cap U(j)} (r_{u,i} - r_{u,j}) * PR(u)}{\sum\limits_{u \in U(i) \cap U(j)} PR(u)}, \tag{9}$$

$$P'(r_{u,i}) = \overline{r_u} + \frac{\sum\limits_{j \in R_u} Dev'(i,j)}{|R_u|}, \tag{10}$$

where $PR(u)$ is a set of correlation ranks for service user u which can be calculated by Eq. (8). $Dev'(i,j)$ is the new deviation value that is employed to predict the QoS values in Eq. (10). $P'(r_{u,i})$ is a new vector of predicted QoS of $r_{u,i}$ in user-item matrix, in which the asymmetric correlation and propagation have been took into account adequately.

4   Experiments

4.1   Dataset Description

To study the QoS value prediction performance of our method, we use a well-known dataset provided by Zheng et al. [7], which includes about 1.97 million invocations for Web services which are obtained from 339 service users on 5825 publicly available Web services. In addition, a 339 × 5825 user-service item matrix can be obtained by analyzing and processing the dataset, and each entry in the user-service item matrix represents a QoS value (i.e., response-time.).

In order to evaluate the performance of our method, we randomly choose different number of services from 5825 available Web services named as NS ranging from 1000 to 4000 with a step value of 1000. Then, a 339 × NS user-service item matrix is constructed. After that, all entries in the 339 × NS user-service item matrix are divided into two parts randomly, one as the training set and the other as the test set. A parameter $percent$ ($0 < percent \leq 1$) is employed to present the percentage of training set in whole user-service item matrix, and (1-$percent$) shows the percentage of test data. Furthermore, to simulate the real situation, entries in training set are removed randomly with $density$ ($0 < density \leq 1$).

4.2   Metrics

Mean Absolute Error (MAE) is employed to measure the prediction accuracy of our method in comparison with other well-known CF methods, such as the User-based method using Pearson Correlation Coefficient (named as UPCC), the Item-based method using Pearson Correlation Coefficient (named as IPCC), and WSRec method [10]. The MAE is defined as:

$$MAE = \frac{\sum_{u,i} |r_{u,i} - \hat{r}_{u,i}|}{N}, \tag{11}$$

where $r_{u,i}$ is the real QoS value of service item i invoked by user u, $\hat{r}_{u,i}$ denotes the predicted QoS value for service item i, and N is the number of predicted values. In addition, the Normalized Mean Absolute Error (NMAE) is also used to measure the prediction quality as follows.

$$NMAE = \frac{MAE}{\sum_{u,i} r_{u,i}/N}. \tag{12}$$

The lower the MAE, NMAE are, and the more effective the prediction methods are.

In order to study the prediction performance more completely, other metrics are introduced in this paper, which include Precision, Recall, and F-measure [24,25].

Precision is defined as the ratio of number of truly "high" ratings among these that were predicted to be "high" by a prediction method in this way [25]:

$$Precision = \frac{|R_{u,i} \cap T_{u,i}|}{|R_{u,i}|}, \tag{13}$$

where $R_{u,i}$ is a vector of predicted QoS values of $r_{u,i}$ with "high" QoS values and $T_{u,i}$ is a vector of true QoS values observed by users with "high" QoS values.

Recall is defined as the ratio of number of correctly predicted "high" ratings among all the ratings obtained to be "high" which is calculated by [25]:

$$Recall = \frac{|R_{u,i} \cap T_{u,i}|}{|T_{u,i}|}. \tag{14}$$

Larger Precision and Recall correspond to the better performances respectively. However, the values of Precision and Recall are usually conflictual. That is to say, the Precision can be improved by increasing the number of "high" QoS values with high efficiency, while the Recall is increasing correspondingly with high cost [26]. Due to the inconsistent performances between precision and recall, F-measure metric can be used to balance of above two competitive metrics [27].

$$F_\beta = \frac{(1 + \beta^2) \cdot (Precision \cdot Recall)}{\beta^2 \cdot Precision + Recall}, \tag{15}$$

where the parameter β is a regular certain value which is set to 0.5, 1, and 2 respectively.

4.3   Comparison

Since the user-service item matrix is usually very sparse in reality, the QoS value prediction methods always encounter the sparsity problem. Then, the parameter *density* is set to 0.1 to keep the consistency with the real-world data distribution. Table 1 shows the MAE and NMAE values of five different prediction methods on response-time with *percent = 0.8, density = 0.1* and *NS* from 1000 to 4000 with a step value of 1000. And the best performance result is shown with parameter $\lambda = 0.2$ in WSRec method [10]. The UPCC method and IPCC method are the famous CF methods which are widely studied. In addition, SLOPE-ONE method is defined in Eq. (2) and our method is named SLOPEONE-R which takes into account the asymmetric correlation and propagation adequately. Figure 3 includes three versions of Table 1. One version compares the MAE and NMAE values with different *NS* range from 1000 to 4000, the second version uses the bar graph to show the MAE and NMAE values with different methods while the last version employs curve graph to illustrate the five methods with different MAE and NMAE values under different experimental sets.

Table 1. MAE and NMAE comparison with basic methods

NS	Metric	Methods				
		UPCC	IPCC	WSRec	SLOPEONE	SLOPEONE-R
1000	MAE	0.8217	0.7047	0.6986	0.6560	0.6506
	NMAE	0.9172	0.7889	0.7820	0.7323	0.7217
2000	MAE	0.8268	0.6970	0.6934	0.6479	0.6478
	NMAE	0.9242	0.7833	0.7792	0.7242	0.7241
3000	MAE	0.8260	0.6952	0.6926	0.6476	0.6474
	NMAE	0.9232	0.7789	0.7760	0.7237	0.7236
4000	MAE	0.8422	0.7094	0.7049	0.6518	0.6517
	NMAE	0.9205	0.7797	0.7747	0.7123	0.7122

The experimental results for the five methods using the same error measure and over the same data set shown in Table 1 and Fig. 3 indicate that:

- Our SLOPEONE-R method improves the prediction performance, and out-performs other four methods for two different metrics-MAE and NMAE under all experimental settings.
- The SLOPEONE-based methods outperform the Pearson Correlation Coefficient (PCC)-based methods, which indicates that deviation computation is more important than similarity computation in QoS prediction.
- The SLOPEONE-R method obtains smaller MAE and NMAE values than SLOPEONE method. This observation shows that asymmetric correlation and propagation among service users have an important effect on QoS prediction accuracy.

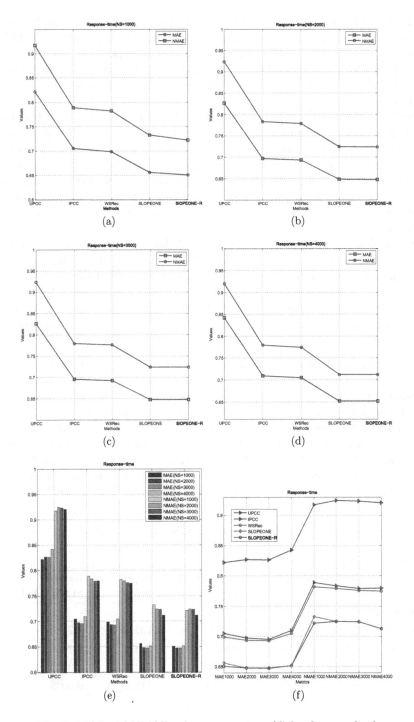

Fig. 3. MAE and NMAE values comparison (Color figure online)

- Fig. 3(a)–(d) show that the MAE and NMAE values have the similar downward trend of five different methods with different *NS*, which the MAE is smaller than NMAE consistently and the UPCC method obtains the largest MAE and NMAE values while SLOPEONE-R method always gains the smallest MAE and NMAE values. This illustrates the better prediction accuracy of our method.
- Both Fig. 3(e) and (f) illustrate that the MAE and NMAE values of five methods generally experience a downward trend with the rise of the Web service number from 1000 to 3000, indicating that more QoS values can improve the prediction accuracy. By contrast, the MAE values of five methods experience an upward trend when the Web service number is set to 4000, since the prediction accuracy is influenced not only by the Web service number, but also by the nature of datasets. Furthermore, too many QoS values may suffer from data over fitting.
- It can be seen from the Table 1 and Fig. 3 that the absolute values of MAE and NMAE of our method are improved with slight enhancement. The reason is that the number of service users in user-service item matrix is 339 and the mean rank for every user is about 0.002950 with a small value. Though with slight enhancement of MAE and NMAE values, our method can obtain better performance with other metrics which will be discussed in following paragraph.

As shown in Table 2, we compare our SLOPEONE-R method with WSRec method and SLOPEONE method by employing three metrics, such as Precision, Recall and F-measure with the parameter $\beta = 0.5$, $\beta = 1$ and $\beta = 2$ respectively. In the experiment, we set $NS = 1000$, $percent = 0.8$, and $density = 0.1$. In services computing, the "high" QoS values in Eqs. (13) and (14) are more than 0 in the experiment. In addition, the ratios of performance improved by using SLOPEONE-R method versus WSRec method and SLOPEONE method are also presented in Table 2. Furthermore, Fig. 4 illustrates the different levels of performance with seven metrics which are composed of Tables 1 and 2.

Table 2. Performance comparison of three methods

Metric	Methods				
	WSRec	SLOPEONE	SLOPEONE-R	Impro. vs. WSRec	Impro. vs. SLOPEONE
Precision	1	1	1	-	-
Recall	0.3805	0.8930	0.8996	136.43 %	0.74 %
F0.5	0.7543	0.9766	0.9782	29.68 %	0.16 %
F1	0.5512	0.9435	0.9471	71.83 %	0.38 %
F2	0.4343	0.9125	0.9180	111.37 %	0.60 %

Observing from Table 2 and Fig. 4, we draw the conclusion that:

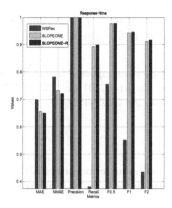

Fig. 4. Performance comparison with seven metrics (Color figure online)

- The SLOPEONE-R method outperforms other competitive methods steadily in all metrics except Precision, indicating that by using asymmetric correlation and propagation among service users, the prediction accuracy can be enhanced noticeably.
- It can be seen from the Table 2 that the prediction accuracy of SLOPEONE-R method obtains significant enhancement on average by 87.33 % versus WSRec, and by 0.47 % versus SLOPEONE for four different metrics (e.g., Recall, F0.5, F1, F2.), indicating better prediction accuracy of our method.
- In Table 2, the Precision values of three different methods are equal, since $R_{u,i}$ is the subset of $T_{u,i}$ in QoS prediction and the true and effective QoS values in $T_{u,i}$ are all larger 0, then the values of Precision for different methods are equal to 1.
- In Fig. 4, the same as the experimental results given in Table 1 and Fig. 4, the experimental results of three different methods are following the same trends, which SLOPEONE-based methods outperforms PCC-based methods and SLOPEONE-R method exceeds SLOPEONE method with high values of metrics-Recall, F0.5, F1 and F2.

5   Conclusion and Future Directions

In this paper, we leverage the correlations of service users, more specifically asymmetric correlation and asymmetric correlation propagation among service users, to discover relations among all service users involved in QoS prediction. Furthermore, our method combines asymmetric correlation and asymmetric correlation propagation into the deviation computation of different service items in QoS prediction, by using improved PageRank method and extended SLOPE-ONE method to improve the prediction accuracy. In addition, experiments are conducted in real-world dataset indicating the effectiveness and feasibility of our method. Future direction includes integrating more QoS properties in our method to predict QoS values. Moreover, experiments of proposed method will be enlarged under more different situations.

Acknowledgments. This work was supported by the National Natural Science Foundation of China under Grant No. 61502401 and No. 61379019, Guangdong Natural Science Foundation (Project No. 2014A030313151).

References

1. Zheng, Z., Michael, R.L.: Selecting an optimal fault tolerance strategy for reliable service-oriented systems with local and global constraints. J. IEEE Trans. Comput. **64**, 219–232 (2015)
2. Ikbel, G., Nawal, G., Tarak, C., Said, T., Mohamed, J.: Pruning based service selection approach under QoS and temporal constraints. In: 2014 IEEE International Conference on Web Services (ICWS), pp. 9–16. IEEE Computer Society, Washington, DC (2014)
3. Mustapha, A., Mohamed, Q., Zahi, J.: Leveraging formal concept analysis with topic correlation for service clustering and discovery. In: 2014 IEEE International Conference on Web Services (ICWS), pp. 153–160. IEEE Computer Society, Washington, DC (2014)
4. Zeng, L., Benatallah, B., Dumas, M., Kalagnanam, J., Sheng, Q.Z.: Quality driven web services composition. In: WWW, pp. 411–421, (2003)
5. He, P., Zhu, J., Zheng, Z., Xu, J., Lyu, M.R.: Location-based hierarchical matrix factorization for web service recommendation. In: 2014 IEEE International Conference on Web Services, pp. 297–304. IEEE (2014)
6. Menasce, D.: Qos issues in web services. J. IEEE Internet Comput. **6**, 72–75 (2002)
7. Zheng, Z., Zhang, Y., Michael R, L.: Distributed QoS evaluation for real-world web services. In: 8th International Conference on Web Services (ICWS 2010), pp. 83–90. IEEE Computer Society, Washington, DC (2010)
8. Rong, W., Liu, K., Liang, L.: Personalized web service ranking via user group combining association rule. In: International Conference on Web Services, pp. 445–452. IEEE Computer Society, Washington, DC (2009)
9. Shao, L., Zhang, J., Wei, Y., Zhao, J., Xie, B., Mei, H.: Personalized QoS prediction for web services via collaborative filtering. In: International Conference on Web Services, pp. 439–446. IEEE Computer Society, Washington, DC (2007)
10. Zheng, Z., Ma, H., Michael, R.L., King, I.J.: QoS-aware web service recommendation by collaborative filtering. IEEE Trans. Serv. Comput. **4**, 140–152 (2011)
11. Zheng, Z., Ma, H., Michael R.L., King, I.: WSRec: a collaborative filtering based web service recommender system. In: 7th IEEE International Conference on Web Services, pp. 437–444. IEEE Computer Society, Washington, DC (2009)
12. Burke, R.: Hybrid recommender systems: survey and experiments. J. User Model. User-Adap. Interact. **12**, 331–370 (2002)
13. Hofmann, T.: Latent semantic models for collaborative filtering. J. Acm Trans. Inf. Syst. **22**, 89–115 (2004)
14. Lemire, D., Maclachlan, A.: Slope one predictors for online rating-based collaborative filtering. In: SIAM Data Mining (SDM 2005), pp. 471–480 (2005)
15. Sarwar, B., Karypis, G., Konstan, J., Reidl, J.: Item-based collaborative filtering recommendation algorithms. In: 10th International Conference on World Wide Web, pp. 285–295 (2001)

16. Chen, X., Zheng, Z., Liu, X., Huang, Z., Sun, H.: Personalized QoS-aware web service recommendation and visualization. J. IEEE Trans. Serv. Comput. **6**, 35–47 (2013)
17. Resnick, P., Iacovou, N., Suchak, M., Bergstrom, P., Riedl, J.: GroupLens: an open architecture for collaborative filtering of netnews. In: Computer Supported Cooperative Work, pp. 175–186 (1994)
18. Breese, J. S., Heckerman, D., Kadie, C.: Empirical analysis of predictive algorithms for collaborative filtering. In: Uncertainty in Artificial Intelligence, pp. 43–52 (1998)
19. Jiang, Y., Liu, J., Tang, M., Liu X.: An effective web service recommendation method based on personalized collaborative filtering. In: 2011 IEEE International Conference on Web Services, pp. 211–218. IEEE Computer Society (2011)
20. Tang, M., Jiang, Y., Liu, J., Liu, X.: Location-aware collaborative filtering for qos-based service recommendation. In: 19th International Conference on Web Services (ICWS), pp. 202–209. IEEE (2012)
21. Gao, M., Wu, Z., Jiang, F.: Userrank for item-based collaborative filtering recommendation. J. Inf. Process. Lett. **111**, 444–446 (2011)
22. Gori, M., Pucci, A., Roma, V., Siena, I.: Itemrank: a random-walk based scoring algorithm for recommender engines. In: 20th International Joint Conference on Artificial Intelligence (IJCAI), pp. 778–781 (2007)
23. Zheng, Z., Michael R.L.: Component recommendation for cloud applications. In: 2nd International Workshop on Recommendation Systems for Software Engineering, pp. 323–345 (2010)
24. Esmaili, K.S., Neshati, M., Jamali, M., Abolhassani, H., Habibi, J.: Comparing performance of recommendation techniques in the blogsphere. In: ECAI 2006 Workshop on Recommender Systems, pp. 40–44 (2006)
25. Gao, M., Fu, Y., Chen, Y., Jiang, F.: User-weight model for item-based recommendation systems. J. Softw. **7**, 2133–2140 (2012)
26. Liu, R., Jia, C., Zhou, T.: Personal recommendation via modified collaborative filtering. J. Phys. A Stat. Mech. Appl. **388**, 462–468 (2009)
27. Gong, M., Xu, Z., Xu, L.: Recommending web service based on user relationships and preferences. In: 20th International Conference on Web Services (ICWS), pp. 380–386. IEEE Computer Society, Washington, DC (2013)

A Personalized Recommendation Approach Based on Content Similarity Calculation in Large-Scale Data

Huigui Rong[1,3]([✉]), Liang Gong[1], Zheng Qin[1], Yupeng Hu[1],
and Chunhua Hu[2]

[1] College of Computer Science and Electronic Engineering,
Hunan University, Changsha 410082, China
{ronghg,zqin}@hnu.edu.cn
[2] School of Computer and Information Engineering,
Hunan University of Commerce, Changsha 410205, China
[3] Department of Computer Science and Engineering,
Michigan State University, Michigan 48864, USA

Abstract. Recommendation algorithms are widely used to discover interesting content for users from massive data in many fields. However, with more diversification of user requirements, the recommended accuracy and efficiency become a serious concern for improving user satisfaction degree. In this paper, we redefine the concept of content similarity by combining search words with personalized search references and describing their dimensions, then propose the calculation method of content similarity by defining the Hamming distance among current keywords, classified items and historical keywords. Through the pretreatment of support vector data description (SVDD), we may find specific tendency from the personal preference of classified items and present the final recommendation results arranged from high similarity to low one. Simulation experiments show that our proposed approach improves recommendation performance over the other two classical algorithms by an average of 17.2 % and reduces the MAE by 6.3 % on our large-scale dataset. At the same time, our proposed approach has a better performance on recall rate and coverage rate, and user satisfaction degree is also improved at higher extent.

Keywords: Content similarity · Personalized recommendation · Support vector data description (SVDD)

1 Introduction

Recently, personalized recommendation has received much attention due to its accuracy properties, which offer important economic benefits and higher user satisfaction degree [1–3]. It helps finding desired information and commodities that users are interested in based on user characteristics and purchasing behavior from the rapid growth of data. Personalized algorithms are widely used to

© Springer International Publishing Switzerland 2015
G. Wang et al. (Eds.): ICA3PP 2015, Part I, LNCS 9528, pp. 460–477, 2015.
DOI: 10.1007/978-3-319-27119-4_32

discover interesting content for users from massive data in E-commerce and large data application fields. However, it has been found to be unsatisfactory in recommendation accuracy and efficiency, especially for large-scale data [4].

One better way to improve the accuracy and efficiency is to find hidden relation among user preferences, historical keywords and classified items and present right recommendation from these hidden links. For example, Bobadilla et al. [5] utilized a user-item rating data to estimate a particular item and give a recommendation list for target users. Yin H and Wei S [6,7] constructed a temporal context-aware model for user behavior modeling in social media systems and presented some approaches for improving recommendation efficiency. Zhang Y et al. [8] adopted the statistical strategy, machine learning and data mining methods to construct user profile by analyzing the historical data of target users(rate, purchase, browse, click, etc.), then made recommendations. However, although these two types of algorithms have considered the user rating data, ignore many characteristics of items and the user itself, such as a film's director, actor and release time, etc., what's more, the cold start and sparse problem are still not solved. For addressing these problems, Lops P proposed a content-based recommendation algorithm [9]. It constructs user preference profile according to historical information (such as evaluation, sharing and collected documents), calculates the similarity between recommended items and user preference profile, then recommends the most similar items to users. The feature of text item (blog, news, webpage, etc.) is relatively easy to be extracted; therefore, the content-based recommendation has been widely applied in the field of text item recommendation. Users-item matrix can be modeled as a bipartite graph [10]; nodes respectively represent users and items; edges represent user evaluation of the item. This algorithm offers users reasonable recommendation through analyzing the structure of bipartite graph.

As the hardware performance getting more and more powerful, Zhang J [11] proposed a recursive prediction algorithm from the dynamic network resource allocation process. This algorithm allows nearest neighbor users to join the prediction process, and predicts the recursion for users who don't need specific scores, which effectively alleviates the effect of sparse matrix on recommended quality and improves the recommendation accuracy. Pizzat-o L [12] deeply analyzed the characteristics of dating, recruitment and other websites, found user preferences by analyzing user personal information, and then made recommendation for users. Tian B [13] presented a new way of recommendation algorithm based on user credit rating and support vector data description (SVDD) model through in-depth analysis of the characteristics of user credit rating, which effectively improved the recommendation accuracy with a increase of complexity. Rong Hui-gui [14] redefined the attribute similarity and similarity composition and proposed a collaborative filtering recommendation algorithm based on user similarity, which improved recommendation efficiency and accuracy in social networks. Yang Y [15] put forward an improved clustering collaborative filtering combination recommendation algorithm based on client/item. Through using clustering technology and user-based collaborative filtering algorithm to predict the neighbor users, giving unscored target items final prediction scores to get the recommended lists, which solved the sparse problem and compensated the deficiency of collaborative filtering algorithm in recommending new items. Meanwhile the recommendation quality has been improved by giving a greater value of time and ensuring the new users have a larger weight in recommendation process.

Obviously, current algorithms mainly focus on item-user classification and ratings instead of mining more important relation among current user preferences, historical keywords and classified items. In our proposed approach, the SVDD pretreatment is introduced to make pre-classification, and then obtains classified items by using trained classifier to divide all candidate resource into N categories in server idle time. According to *Ebbinghaus* forgetting curve, recently searched records have greater impact on recommendation results than the previous ones. Based on the above two principles, the present paper proposes a composite approach with a linear fitting for the two sub similarity. Our contributions are summarized as follows:

(1) First, we redefine the concept of content similarity by combining with personalized search references and their attributes, and give a composite search approach for optimizing search accuracy and efficiency. This method allows us to find some search opportunities and design new classifiers and classified approaches.
(2) Second, by defining the Hamming distance among current keywords, classified items and historical keywords, we propose a personalized recommendation algorithm based on content similarity calculation.
(3) Third, we implemented our algorithms and conducted side-by-side comparisons with the popular ones. The experimental results show that our new algorithm has outperformed the popular ones with the same time complexity. In particular, on our large-scale dataset, our approach improves recommendation performance over the other two ones by an average of 17.2 % and reduces the MAE by 6.3 %.

2   Related Work and Background

The essence of item classification is dividing textual items into different categories, cutting off the irrelevant header files, format etc. retaining the core of the text part only. Now the mainstream classification methods include K-means, K-Nearest Neighbor (KNN), Gaussian mixture model (GMM) and SVDD, etc. Built on the basis of statistical theory, SVDD can obtain better classification results in cases of small sample, nonlinear and high dimension [16]. Therefore, SVDD is introduced as a strategy of text classification and pretreatment, preparing for content similarity calculation.

In this paper, we can directly calculate the similarity between current keywords and characteristic lexical items through item classification in advance, and then do top-N sequencing combined historical keywords and different weights, finally return the results to users. In this way, the entire pretreatment process is completed with idle time in servers, which not only reduces the time complexity, but also improves personalization and diversification.

2.1 Related Work of Feature Extraction

One item contains hundreds of lexical items, it is impossible to represent an item with all the lexical items, the most characteristic lexical item must be chosen to do the work. Since the frequency of each lexical item is different, the distribution of their weight is different too. This paper uses a recognized vector space model to represent item, in this model, each item R_T is represented by a vector $V(\rho)$ and each dimension of vector $V(\rho)$ says a unique lexical item in vector space model [17]. So item R_T can be taken as a set composed by many sequences such as lexical item τ and weight ω, and item R_T can be expressed by the following formula

$$V(\rho) = (\tau_1, \omega_1(\rho); \tau_2, \omega_2(\rho); \ldots; \tau_n, \omega_n(\rho)) \tag{1}$$

where $\tau_1, \tau_2, \ldots, \tau_n$ represent the feature lexical of the item R_T, $\omega_n(\rho)$ show the weight of feature lexical item $\tau_1, \tau_2, \ldots, \tau_n$.

As the frequency of each feature lexical item and their location are not the same, the importance of each feature lexical item is discriminatory, different weights should be assigned to each of them. The TF-ITF method [18] combines the frequency of feature lexical item with document frequency; it currently is the most widely used weight assignment method, which can be described by the following formula

$$\omega_i(\rho) = \frac{tf_i(\rho)log(\frac{N}{n_i})}{\sqrt{\sum_j tf_j(\rho)log(\frac{N}{n_j})^2}} \tag{2}$$

where $tf_i(\rho)$ represent the frequency of lexical item τ_i in item R_T, N express the total number of text in text corpus. n_i denotes the number of text containing lexical item τ_i in text corpus.

By importing user dictionary, word segmentation plug-in, formula (1), (2) quantize item R_T as equation (1) described. Owing to the high dimension of quantized item R_N and irrelevance between feature lexical items, this paper adopts SVDD (support vector data description) which was proposed by Ref [16] to classify item R_N.

2.2 Background of SVDD Model

The basic idea of support vector data description (SVDD) is establishing a non-linear mapping function ϕ, mapping data x in input space to point $\phi(x)$ in high-dimensional feature space, seeking support vector in the feature space, and constructing an optimal hyper-sphere with minimum radius while most of the points are contained. Each hyper-sphere is a category of model, so items are divided into several categories. Figure 1 is a sample of hyper-sphere schematic diagram in two-dimensional space. Yellow dots represent vector of this hyper-sphere; ξ_i is relaxation factor; x_i indicate sample data.   Model is described as:

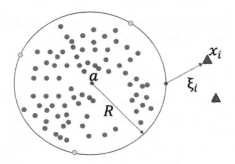

Fig. 1. Hyper-sphere schematic diagram (Color figure online)

for item R_N { $X|x_i \in R^d$,i=1,2,. . .,N } in high-dimensional space mapped, work out center a and radius R of the optimal hyper-sphere accommodates item R_N, and the problem is converted into optimization seeking:

$$\begin{cases} \min_{R,\xi} R^2 + C \sum_i = 1^N \xi_i, i = 1, 2, \dots l \\ s.t. (\pi(x_i) - a)(\pi(x_i) - a)^T \ll R^2 + \xi_i \end{cases} \qquad (3)$$

In this model a is the center; R is the radius; $(\phi(x_i) - a)(\phi(x_i) - a)^T$ is the distance between point x_i and center a. When $(\phi(x_i) - a)(\phi(x_i) - a)^T > 0$, we can determine that target points located outside of the hyper-sphere. Relaxation factor ξ_i is mainly used to deal with abnormal sample points which may appear in the training data set. After adding relaxation factor, the distance between all of the training samples and center need not be strictly limited within R, but it should be punished accordingly. C is a penalty factor, its value compromises between empirical error and generalization ability, it is the control parameter of training error and classifier complexity.

3   Content Similarity Definition and Calculation

We redefine the content similarity and its attributes from user search preferences, and it consists of two parts: the first part is the similarity between search keywords and classified item R_C, for measuring the distance D_{K-R} between search keywords and the elements, the smaller the distance, the higher similarity between them; the other Part is the similarity between classified item R_C and historical keywords. From *Ebbinghaus* forgetting curve, contents that users are interested in are most likely to be their recently searched content. Therefore, recently searched records have greater impact on recommendation results than the previous ones; that is to say, the more recent that the classified items correspond to historical keywords, the more similar to the current preferences should be recommended preferentially.

3.1 Similarity Calculation Between Current Keywords and Classified Items

Assume that the text classification method proposed above divides all the items into n categories, t items in each class. $S(i)$ indicates category $i, i = 1, 2, \ldots, n$. $S_{(i)}(x)$ denotes the xth item in the ith category, $x = 1, 2, \ldots, t$, such as $S_{(1)}(3)$ is the 3rd item in the 1st category. $K_i(x)$ says the similarity [19] between keywords and the xth item in the ith category. Adopting locality sensitive hashing algorithm LSH [20] to express keywords and feature lexical items in items as binary codes. For instance "I love China" expressed as "0100100100110101", "I love American" appeared as "0101100110110001". And then calculate the Hamming distance d_T between them,

If $0 \le d_T < 4, K_i(x) = 1$;
If $4 \le d_T < 8, K_i(x) = 2$;
If $8 \le d_T < 16, K_i(x) = 3$;
If $d_T \ge 16, K_i(x) = 4$;

$K_i(x)$ is smaller, shows the similarity between items and keywords is greater. The Hamming distance $d_T = 3 < 4$ in the example, so their similarity $K_i(x) = 1$.

$D_{K-R}(i)$ denotes the similarity between keywords and all items in the ith category, comes the following equation:

$$D_{K-R}(i) = \frac{1}{\sum_{i=1}^{n} K_i(x)} \tag{4}$$

$D_{K-R}(i)$ and similarity are positively related. The value of $D_{K-R}(i)$ is greater, the similarity between them is higher.

If taking the Hamming distance between keywords and feature lexical items in item R_T to measure the similarity between them, weights each category distributed are not the same. if $a(i)$ id defined as the weight of each category, the sum of all weights of categories is 1.

$$\sum_{i=1}^{n} a(i) = 1 \tag{5}$$

Due to the different similarity, different weights are assigned to each category, categories with higher similarity get greater weights, otherwise, the opposite.

$$a(i) = \frac{D_{K-R}(i)}{\sum_{i=1}^{n} D_{K-R}(i)} \tag{6}$$

Therefore, there comes a new equation when similarity between classified items and keywords takes weight into consideration.

$$d_{K-R}(i) = \frac{D_{K-R}(i)}{\sum_{i=1}^{n} D_{K-R}(i) \sum_{i=1}^{n} K_i(x)} \tag{7}$$

If two different categories have the same weight, formula (7) should be used to calculate the variance of similarity between items and keywords in the two categories, the item with smaller variance gains priority to be recommended.

$$
\begin{cases}
\overline{K_i(x)} = \dfrac{\sum_{x=1}^{t} K_i(x)}{t} \\[2mm]
S^2 = \dfrac{\sum_{x=1}^{t} (K_i(x) - \overline{K_i(x)})^2}{t-1}
\end{cases}
\tag{8}
$$

3.2   Similarity Calculation Between Classified Items and Historical Keywords

Every user has its own particular preferences in certain professional field, we can find specific tendency from historical keywords and take good advantage of it to improve the accuracy of recommendation. By the definition method mentioned before, we can get the other weight $\beta(i)$($\beta(i) = \frac{D_{K-R}(i}{\sum_{i=1}^{n} D_{K-R}(i)}$) and the similarity between keywords in users' historical keywords which assigned weight $\beta(i)$ and the ith category

$$
\widetilde{d_{K-R}}(i) = \frac{\widetilde{D_{K-R}}(i)}{\sum_{i=1}^{n} \widetilde{D_{K-R}}(i) \sum_{i=1}^{n} \widetilde{K_i(x)}}
\tag{9}
$$

3.3   Content Similarity Calculation

Content similarity calculation in this paper combines $D_{K-R}(i)$ and $\widetilde{D_{K-R}}(i)$ in linear fitting, then follows the calculation. Their effects on content similarity are different, the values of weight α and β are different too, and the settings can be changed according to the actual situation. Linear fitting for the two sub similarity calculated, compute the similarity $Sim_{K-R}(i)$ between item R_C and keywords. The magnitude of $Sim_{K-R}(i)$ describes the discretion of similarity between items and keywords.

$$
\widetilde{Sim}_{K-R}(i) = \frac{\alpha D_{K-R}(i)}{\sum_{i=1}^{n} D_{K-R}(i) \sum_{i=1}^{n} K_i(x)} + \frac{\beta \widetilde{D_{K-R}}(i)}{\sum_{i=1}^{n} \widetilde{D_{K-R}}(i) \sum_{i=1}^{n} \widetilde{K_i(x)}}
\tag{10}
$$

where α and β are the weights of two sub similarity in items similarity, satisfy $\alpha + \beta = 1$.

4   Approach Based on Content Similarity

We present the composite recommendation approach based on content similarity calculation with the support of SVDD pretreatment(CSC-SVDD), and this approach is composed of two parts, one part is to textualize and quantize the items returned from the typed keywords by users with the method of text classification, and then classify the item R_N with the method of SVDD. Another is to calculate the similarity of item R_C with the keywords typed by users and historical keywords for users, and then get a similarity between current keywords and classified items. Finally, return recommendation results to users through the linear fitting of the two sub similarities.

The main procedure of our proposed approach includes two sub-algorithms. Algorithm 1 describes the pretreatment process with SVDD and gives a complete procedure that includes removing excess irrelevant portions, texualizing, extracting the feature lexical items, distributing the weights of feature lexical items, quantizing item R_T, converting into item R_N, and classifying item R_N with the SVDD classification method. Finally, return n classified items to servers for Intermediate processing results in Algorithm 1.

Algorithm 1. K & R_C $(U_0, X, int$ $n)$

```
% textualize and quantize items
% classify item R_N by the method of SVDD
```
Input:
```
    user U_0 , typed keywords K;
```
Output:
```
    n classified items ;
 1: Acquire item
    User type in the search keywords K, and the server end will initially
    screen the eligible item R.
 2: Textual item
    We can get the item R_T by removing the irrelevant header files,
    formats, etc. and leaving the most important part of text.
 3: Quantize item
    Represent the item with the vector space model V(d), use segmentation
    tool to participle the item R_T, extract feature lexical items t_i and
    assign weights ω_i(d) with method of TF-IDF,we can get item R_N, that
    is V(ρ) = (τ_1,ω_1(ρ);τ_2,ω_2(ρ);...;τ_n,ω_n(ρ)).
 4: Train classifier
    Train SVDD classifier C by using artificial standard data sample X,
    and get the decision function f(x) and supporting vector in formula
    (7) .
 5: Classify result
    Calculate the items with different decision function f(x), handle the
    computational results, and then obtain n categories, in other words,
    a classifier C classify items into n categories .
 6: return n classified items;
```

The Algorithm 2 defines the content similarity and calculation method of the two composed sub-similarity and presents recommendation set procedure for user. Part one is the similarity between classified item R_C and current keywords, we measure the distance D_{K-R} between current keywords and classified items and obtain the value of similarity; part two is the similarity between classified item R_C and historical keywords. Therefor, we can get the linear fitting value of the two part similarity. Finally, return recommendation results to users according to the similarity in Algorithm 2.

Algorithm 2. S_N $(K, R, \widetilde{C_0})$
___
% calculate similarity between classified items and keywords
% finally recommend set $\widetilde{C_0}$ for user U_0
Input:
    user U_0, search keywords K, n classified items;
Output:
    recommended set $\widetilde{C_0}$;
1: Similarity calculation between classified items and keywords
    Calculate the similarity $d_{K-R}(i)$ between keywords typed by user and classified items based on $d_{K-R}(i) = D_{K-R}(i)a(i)$, If any two calculated similarity appears identical, we should take variance calculation based on formula (13) between these two similarities, the smaller one would have the priority to recommend.
2: Similarity calculation between classified items and searched records
    In the similar way, calculate the similarity $\widetilde{d_{K-R}}(i)$ between classified items and special needs by user based on $\widetilde{d_{K-R}}(i) = \widetilde{D_{K-R}}(i)b(i)$.
3: Calculation between keywords and total similarity of items
    Calculate the total similarity $Sim_{K-R}(i)$ between items and keywords based on $Sim_{K-R}(i) = \alpha d_{K-R}(i) + \beta \widetilde{d_{K-R}}(i)$.
4: Confirm the candidate set C_0
    Put the recommended class i into C_i with the method of Top-N algorithm based on $Sim_{K-R}(i)$, and then we can get the recommended set $C_1, C_2, \ldots, C_n$.
5: Produce the recommended set $\widetilde{C_0}$
    Transform the previous candidate set to the recommendation set $\widetilde{C_0}$ by the order of similarity, that is to say, $\widetilde{C_0} = \widetilde{C_1}, \ldots, \widetilde{C_n}$. Then put out the recommendation set $\widetilde{C_0} = \widetilde{C_1}, \ldots, \widetilde{C_n}$ for users U_0 .
6: **return** recommended set $\widetilde{C_0}$;

4.1   Complexity Analysis

Algorithm complexity is usually a measure of an algorithm performance, generally it covers time complexity and space complexity. From the above analysis, the execution process of our proposed algorithm needs to store historical keywords, recommend set, train set, textualized items and quantized items, which take up less storage space. With the historical keywords increasing, storage space also linearly increases without changes in magnitude. In addition, the current hardware can support a large storage capacity with less cost. In large-scale data analysis, time complexity deserves on a particular concern, and so, this paper focuses on time complexity analysis of our proposed approach.

The time overhead of algorithm execution $T(n)$ may be divided into two parts: the time $T_1(n)$ of classifying items in Algorithm 1 and similarity calculation of Algorithm 2, the time $T_2(n)$ of recommending results for users. In Algorithm 1, SVDD training that consumes server idle time will not be included in the algorithm execution time. If the classifier is trained to n categories, the items to be classified R_N have m, the average execution times of quantizing item is Y, the classifier could have n decision functions, then the maximum executions times of Algorithm 1 is below:

$$f(n) = Y \times m + m \times n = (Y + n) \times m$$

Where Y are constants, $m \gg n$, use the computing principles of time complexity, ignore the constants, low power and maximum power coefficients, we could calculate similarity calculation of time complexity:

$$T_1(n) = O(n) \times O(m) = O(mn)$$

The execution time $T_2(n)$ of the Algorithm 2 is mainly concentrated on the similarity calculation formula $Sim_{K-R}(i) = \alpha d_{K-R}(i) + \beta \widetilde{d_{K-R}}(i)$, obviously, time complexity of similarity calculation is composed of two parts. If the project is divided into n categories, the number of each items contained is $t_1, t_2, \ldots, t_n$, and $t_1 + t_2 + \ldots + t_n = m$, the user could have the historical keywords M, the recommended number for users was N_0, the required number for executing the Algorithm 2:

$$f(n) = (M + 1) \times m \times (n + 1)^2 + 2 \times (n + 1) + N_0$$

Where N_0, M are constants, $m \gg n$, use the computing principles of time complexity, ignore the constants, low power and maximum power coefficients, we could calculate similarity calculation of time complexity:

$$T_2(n) = T(mn^2) + T(n) + T(1)$$
$$= O(mn^2)$$

So the total time complexity of our approach is

$$T(n) = T_1(n) + T_2(n)$$
$$= O(mn^2) + O(mn)$$
$$= O(mn^2)$$

From the above analysis: the time complexity of our approach is $O(mn^2)$, and obviously, it depends on the number of items to be classified. In general, $m \gg n$, so the time complexity of the algorithm can approximate as $O(m)$. The quantity of items to be classified that returned by the servers largely determines the algorithm execution time.

5   Data Simulation

5.1   The Simulation Experiment Environment Settings

The proposed method covers the classification pretreatment mainly based on existing work of SVDD and content similarity calculation. So, the designed experiment may be divided into two parts: (1) Comparing selected classic classification algorithms of svm-light [21], libsvm [22] and svm-svdd [23], getting classification items returned by the servers; (2) Performing a series of similarity calculation based on proposed content similarity calculation method and returning recommended set.

The experimental environment is designed to close to the real and complex network environments to test the validity of our proposed algorithm in a real environment. The experimental operation platform parameters: Intel i5 3rd generation processor, memory 8 G, win7 ultimate 64-bit system, the traditional support vector machine adopts libsvm include SMO algorithm (Java code), svm-light and svm-svdd. The approximate solution ξ_i in 0.023 during whole simulation process and the experiment process is set up as follows:

(1) We adopt the classic recommendation dataset *MovesLens*, which contained 10 million movie ratings data on 10000 films from 20000 users. Randomly we select 1000 users, who made 476,543 evaluations for a total of 3138 films.

(2) Data set preprocess: remove the irrelevant parts of items textually, import the user dictionary, use segmentation tools for word, extract feature lexical items, assign the weights to the feature lexical items, and quantize the data set.

(3) Classifier generation: we train the classifier by the method of svm-svdd with the experimental training data sets (see Fig. 2(a)) normalized before.

(4) Classify items: use the trained classifier to classify the experimental test datasets (see Fig. 2(b)).

(5) Recommended items: assign weights according to the content similarity, which it is between users typed keywords and classified items and between historical keywords and classified items, then extract a certain percentage items of each category to return to the user, the one with the highest weights has the priority to return to the user.

In Fig. 2, bar chart represents distribution of items with the left Y-axis, while line chart says the percentage of items in total quantity corresponding the right Y-axis. 'unkwn' in Fig. 2(b) indicates a set which has not been successfully classified by classifier.

5.2   Analysis of Experimental Results

For better evaluating the recommendation algorithm performance and user satisfaction, we introduce several metric factors including MAE(Mean Absolute Error) [24], accuracy rate, recall rate and coverage rate.

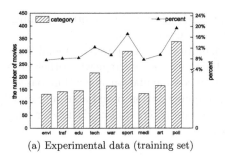

(a) Experimental data (training set)

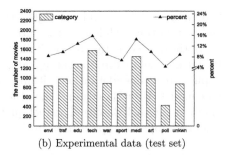

(b) Experimental data (test set)

Fig. 2. Experimental data

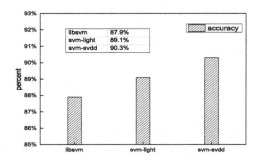

Fig. 3. Comparison of classification accuracy

For the experimental part of the classification, the three kinds of comparison methods all have two parameters (C, R) to be determined. Selecting parameters is very important, research [21] show that: it is an effective method to confirm the good parameters by using the group of exponential growth C and R. In this experiment, $C = [2^{-10}, 2^{-9}, \dots, 2^5$ and $R = [2^{-10}, 2^{-9}, \dots, 2^5]$, search on C and R to make the optimal classification accuracy. When the three classification methods (C, R) are sequentially taken (16, 0.015625), (32, 0.03125) and (1.25, 0.5), their classification accuracy compare as example shown in Fig. 3, the training time, test time and support vector comparison is shown in Table 1.

Table 1. Comparison of testing time, training time and support vector

Comparative item	libsvm algorithm	svm-svdd algorithm	svm-light algorithm
Testing time(s)	151.5	63.0	34.0
Training time(s)	415.6	198.7	140.6
Support vector(n)	326	218	138

Analysis of the experimental results above, we can find that svm-svdd algorithm produced the significantly less number of support vectors than the other two methods, libsvm and svm-light. And the svm-svdd required shorter training and testing time, while the recognition rate was almost equal.

In the experimental part of similarity calculation, we compared and analyzed the mean absolute error, accuracy rate, recalling rate and coverage with other two popular recommendation algorithms; one is recommendation algorithm based user model (User-Based) and the other is recommendation based attribute and interaction (A& I-Based). The real quality evaluations lay its foundation for our proposed approach application in this paper.

Table 2. Four possible cases to recommend items

Users need	Recommend	Don't recommend
Need	A	B
Not need	C	C

(1) Accuracy

Accuracy indicates the probability of users just interested in items recommended by the recommendation system. Table 2 summarizes the four possible cases, which A, B, C, D respectively represents a quantity of four cases. B_u is the quantity of items users U_0 needed, obviously $L = A + C$, $B_u = A + B$.

For a user U_0, the accuracy of recommendation system is proportion that the results user desired in the L results, that is

$$P_u(L) = \frac{A}{L} = \frac{A}{A + C} \tag{11}$$

(2) Recall rate

Recall rate of recommendation system is the probability that items user needed was recommended by system, defined as the ratio of the items user desired in the recommendation list and all items user desired in recommendation system. For a user U_0, that is

$$R_u(L) = \frac{A}{B_u} = \frac{A}{A + B} \tag{12}$$

F_1 index[3], considering the accuracy and recall. It defined as follows:

$$F_1(L) = \frac{2P(L)R(L)}{P(L) + R(L)} \tag{13}$$

(3) Coverage rate

Coverage rate indicates that the results recommended to users by system can account for the proportion of all search results, the index apparently related with the length L of recommendation list. It is defined as follows:

$$COV_R(L) = \frac{N_d(L)}{N} \qquad (14)$$

wherein, $N_d(L)$ denotes the number of different items from the all recommendation list for users. With higher recommended coverage, the more types of goods to the user recommend by system, the greater possibilities of novel to be recommended.

(4) MAE

In actual tests, the errors between the system recommended and the actual value of user evaluation can directly measure the recommendation quality. The smaller MAE is, the higher recommendation quality will be.

$$MAE_u = \frac{\sum_{i=1}^{n} |p_{u,i} - q_{u,i}|}{n} \qquad (15)$$

where n is the total number of Top-N items recommended, $p_{u,i}$ is the actual ratings, $q_{u,i}$ is the corresponding predicted ratings.

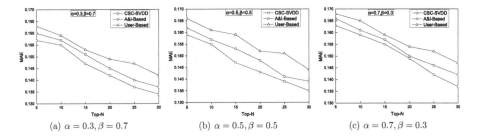

(a) $\alpha = 0.3, \beta = 0.7$ (b) $\alpha = 0.5, \beta = 0.5$ (c) $\alpha = 0.7, \beta = 0.3$

Fig. 4. Changes in MAE (Mean Absolute Error) of Top-N

As for this experiment, the two weights α and β, satisfy the condition: $\alpha + \beta = 1$, according to the least squares fitting of the actual test data and linear programming, we adjusted the values of α and β constantly to obtain the best experimental results. By iterating the value of α and β of (iteration pitch 0.01), we found that when $\alpha = 0.61$ and $\beta = 0.39$, the algorithm could achieve better recommendation performance, better accuracy rate and coverage rate.

In simulation experiments, the before-mentioned three algorithms are compared by MAE indicator and the curve graphs of MAE are showed in Fig. 4. Compared with $\alpha = 0.5$, the mean absolute error curve shows the tendency of download when $\alpha > 0.7$. As the value of α increases, the value of MAE will also increase. Through a large number of experiments, we found that when $\alpha = 0.61$ and $\beta = 0.39$, the algorithm achieved better recommendation results with higher mean absolute error and coverage rate.

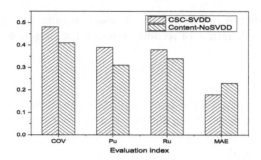

Fig. 5. The impact of SVDD pretreatment

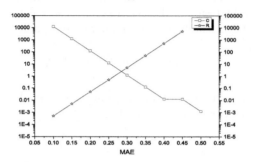

Fig. 6. The impact of C, R on MAE

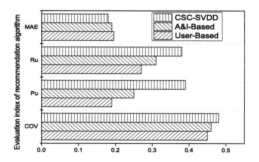

Fig. 7. Comparison of three algorithms

The experimental results in Fig. 5 shows the difference between our proposed CSC-SVDD approach and the other algorithm without SVDD pretreatment support, when $\alpha = 0.61, \beta = 0.39$. From Fig. 6, we can see the recommendation performance is almost improved of 10 % with the support of SVDD pretreatment. These recommendation results returned to users not only cover the similarity, the user historical keywords and weighted classification items are also included. Therefor, the coverage rate, accuracy rate and recall rate of the proposed algorithm were higher than those of traditional algorithms based on without SVDD pretreatment; while MAE is lower than those traditional ones. From the experimental results, the impact curves of the change of C, R on MAE may be obtained, as shown in Fig. 6, where Y-coordinate has been taken logarithm. We found the trend of two curves by C and R is totally different: the increase of C made smaller effect on MAE, while the increase of R made larger effect on MAE.

The other two algorithms of based on user (User-Based) and attribute and interaction (A& I-Based) are introduced for comparison with our proposed one in Fig. 7, From the comparison graph of three algorithms in MAE, recall rate, coverage rate and accuracy rate, the experimental results show that our proposed algorithm improves recommendation performance over the other two ones by an average of 17.2 % and reduces the MAE by 6.3 % and obviously, our proposed algorithm had a better performance on recall rate and coverage rate.

6   Conclusion

In this paper, we propose a new composite approach of personalized recommendation for large-scale data. This approach allows us to find some interesting search opportunities from a fresh angle, unify some seemingly different algorithms, and discover more unknown search opportunities from the interrelated large dataset. Our experimental results show that the proposed search algorithm gives insights that (1) significantly improve the accuracy of the personalized recommendation with almost the same time complexity and (2) lead to a higher coverage rate and lower MAE. More importantly, this combined approach opens another direction for further work on improving user salification at greater extent.

Acknowledgments. This work is partly supported by National Natural Science Foundation of China under under Grant No. 61273232, 61472131, 61272546, 61300218 and 61572181, by the Program for New Century Excellent Talents in University under Grant Number NCET-13-0785.

References

1. Wang, J., Li, G., Feng, J.: Can we beat the prefix filtering?: an adaptive framework for similarity join and search. In: Proceedings of the 2012 ACM SIGMOD International Conference on Management of Data, pp. 85–96. ACM (2012)
2. Kusumoto, M., Maehara, T., Kawarabayashi, K.I.: Scalable similarity search for simrank. In: Proceedings of the 2014 ACM SIGMOD International Conference on Management of Data, pp. 325–336. ACM (2014)
3. Yang, B., Zhao, P.F.: Review of the art of recommendation algorithms. J. Shanxi Univ. (Nat Sci Ed) **34**(3), 337–350 (2011)
4. Deng, D., Li, G., Feng, J.: A pivotal prefix based filtering algorithm for string similarity search. In: Proceedings of the 2014 ACM SIGMOD International Conference on Management of Data, pp. 673–684. ACM (2014)
5. Bobadilla, J., Ortega, F., Hernando, A., Arroyo, Á.: A balanced memory-based collaborative filtering similarity measure. Int. J. Intell. Syst. **27**(10), 939–946 (2012)

6. Yin, H., Cui, B., Chen, L., Hu, Z., Huang, Z.: A temporal context-aware model for user behavior modeling in social media systems. In: Proceedings of the 2014 ACM SIGMOD International Conference on Management of Data, pp. 1543–1554. ACM (2014)

7. Wei, S., Ye, N., Zhang, S., Huang, X., Zhu, J.: Collaborative filtering recommendation algorithm based on item clustering and global similarity. In: 2012 Fifth International Conference on Business Intelligence and Financial Engineering (BIFE), pp. 69–72. IEEE (2012)

8. Zhang, Y., Zhu, X., Shen, Q.: A recommendation model based on collaborative filtering and factorization machines for social networks. In: 2013 5th IEEE International Conference on Broadband Network & Multimedia Technology (IC-BNMT), pp. 110–114. IEEE (2013)

9. Lops, P., De Gemmis, M., Semeraro, G.: Content-based recommender systems: state of the art and trends. Recommender Systems Handbook, pp. 73–105. Springer, Heidelberg (2011)

10. Zhu, G., Lin, X., Zhu, K., Zhang, W., Yu, J.X.: Treespan: efficiently computing similarity all-matching. In: Proceedings of the 2012 ACM SIGMOD International Conference on Management of Data, pp. 529–540. ACM (2012)

11. Zhang, J., Pu, P.: A recursive prediction algorithm for collaborative filtering recommender systems. In: Proceedings of the 2007 ACM Conference on Recommender Systems, pp. 57–64. ACM (2007)

12. Pizzato, L., Rej, T., Chung, T., Koprinska, I., Kay, J.: Recon: a reciprocal recommender for online dating. In: Proceedings of the Fourth ACM Conference on Recommender Systems, pp. 207–214. ACM (2010)

13. Tian, B., Nan, L., Zheng, Q., Yang, L.: Customer credit scoring method based on the SVDD classification model with imbalanced dataset. In: Zaman, M., Liang, Y., Siddiqui, S.M., Wang, T., Liu, V., Lu, C. (eds.) CETS 2010. CCIS, vol. 113, pp. 46–60. Springer, Heidelberg (2010)

14. Huigui, R., Shengxu, H., Chunhua, H., Jinxia, M.: User similarity-based collaborative filtering recommendation algorithm. J. Commun. **35**(2), 16–24 (2014)

15. Yang, Y., Wang, X.R., Hu, Y.C.: Researches of collaborative filtering recommendation algorithm based on user and item clustering combination. J. Guangxi Univ. Technol. **4**, 019 (2011)

16. Yanhong, L., Anrong, X., Xiyun, S.: New classification algorithm k-means clustering combined with svdd. Appl. Res. Comput. **27**(3), 883–886 (2010)

17. Xiaopeng, H., Xianfeng, L., Jun, G., Ming, T.: Updated learning algorithm of support vector data description based on k-means clustering. Comput. Eng. **35**(17), 184–186 (2009)

18. Xiao, L., Xiangru, M., Zelong, C., Xuchun, Z.: Comprehensive evaluation for network survivability based on support vector data description. Appl. Res. Comput. **30**(3), 853–856 (2013)

19. Lu, J., Lin, C., Wang, W., Li, C., Wang, H.: String similarity measures and joins with synonyms. In: Proceedings of the 2013 ACM SIGMOD International Conference on Management of Data, pp. 373–384. ACM (2013)

20. Shizhe, S.: Research on the locality sensitive hashing. Master's thesis, Xidian University (2013)

21. Joachims, T.: Svmlight: support vector machine. SVM-Light Support Vector Machine, 19(4)U. University of Dortmund (1999). http:/svmlight.joachims.org/

22. Chang, C.C., Lin, C.J.: Libsvm: a library for support vector machines. ACM Trans. Intell. Syst. Technol. (TIST) **2**(3), 27 (2011)

23. Wang, Z., Zhao, Z.-S., Zhang, C.: SVM-SVDD: a new method to solve data description problem with negative examples. In: Guo, C., Hou, Z.-G., Zeng, Z. (eds.) ISNN 2013, Part I. LNCS, vol. 7951, pp. 283–290. Springer, Heidelberg (2013)
24. Herlocker, J.L., Konstan, J.A., Terveen, L.G., Riedl, J.T.: Evaluating collaborative filtering recommender systems. ACM Trans. Inf. Syst. (TOIS) **22**(1), 5–53 (2004)

A General Methodology to Design Deadlock-Free Routing Algorithms for Mesh Networks

Zhigang Yu[1]([✉]), Xinyu Wang[2], Kele Shen[1], and Haikuo Liu[2]

[1] Tsinghua National Laboratory for Information Science and Technology,
Department of Computer Science and Technology,
Tsinghua University, Beijing 100084, China
yuzg@live.com, shenkele@aliyun.com
[2] College of Management Science and Engineering,
Dongbei University of Finance and Economics, Dalian 116025, China

Abstract. This paper presents a general methodology to design deadlock-free routing algorithms for mesh networks. Classifying directions of the network channels, constructing deadlock-free zones, and arranging the produced deadlock-free zones in a specific order are the three fundamental steps that the proposed methodology takes to generate connected and deadlock-free routing algorithms. Applying the proposed methodology to 2-D mesh network, we generate eighty two routing algorithms: some of them (such as dimension order routing, turn model) have already been proposed in the literature; while most of them have not been proposed before. Furthermore, the methodology reveals the relation among the previously reported routing algorithms proposed in different papers. Extensive simulation experiments have been performed for nine selected routing algorithms, considering various traffic patterns, different network sizes, various buffer sizes, and a wide range of injection rates. Results show that for a given network the performance of a routing algorithm mainly depends on the traffic pattern.

Keywords: Mesh networks · Routing algorithm · Deadlock-free · Adaptive routing · Design methodology

1 Introduction

Interconnection networks are widely used for multi-computer interconnect, for processor memory interconnect, for I/O interconnect, for multi-core interconnect and as router and switch fabric [1–5]. Evolving technology and increasing processors/memory performance make the multi-computer interconnection networks become even more critical as they determine the overall system performance.

As an essential ingredient of interconnection networks, mesh networks belong to *k-ary n-cube* family that consists n dimensions with k nodes in each dimension [4–6]. Mesh networks have lots of superior architecture proprieties, such as

© Springer International Publishing Switzerland 2015
G. Wang et al. (Eds.): ICA3PP 2015, Part I, LNCS 9528, pp. 478–491, 2015.
DOI: 10.1007/978-3-319-27119-4_33

topology regularity, high path diversity, low node degree and linear scalability cost. Therefore, mesh networks are widely used in both off-chip and on-chip interconnection networks. In particular, two dimensional mesh (2-D mesh) is usually preferred for on-chip networks (OCNs) due to its layout on a 2-D surface. Examples includes Tile80 [1], NVIDIA Tegra K1 Mobile Processor and the router fabric in supercomputer Anton2 [7].

In order to efficiently route packets through a network, a routing algorithm must be used. Routing algorithm sets up a path for packet from its source node to destination node. In general, the choice of routing algorithm used in a network sets an upper-bound on the achievable throughput (ideal throughput) and a lower-bound on the packet latency (zero load latency). However, deadlock is prone to occur without a careful design for the routing algorithms. Therefore, deadlock-free routing algorithm plays a vital role in interconnection network design.

Plenty of routing algorithms have been proposed in the literature for mesh networks. According to the way used to prevent deadlock, we classify the previously proposed routing algorithms into two different classes: (1) turn-based routing algorithms [8–13] and (2) virtual channel-based routing algorithms [14–20, 23].

The turn-based routing algorithms eliminate cycle dependencies by prohibiting some turns. While the virtual channel-based routing algorithms employ virtual channels to prevent deadlock and improve performance. Examples of the first class are dimension order routing (DOR), direction order routing (DIR) [21], turn model [8], and odd-even turn model [9]. The second class includes virtual network partition [14], planar adaptive routing (PAR) [15], and virtual network partition with channel overlapping in [16]. Duato's protocol [6], which supports fully adaptive routing in adaptive virtual channels and prevents deadlock in escape virtual channels, lies in the second class.

The proposed methodology in this paper constructs a deadlock-free algorithm in three steps: (1) classifying directions of network channels according to dimension and +/-; (2) generating deadlock-free zones using these directions; (3) arranging these zones in an order. The methodology belongs to the first class as it prevents deadlock by prohibiting turns violating the predefined zone order. In addition to providing a simple approach to construct routing algorithms, the methodology can also reveal the relation among the previously reported routing algorithms proposed in different papers [22].

The switching technique we use in this paper is wormhole switching [4,25], however the design methodology proposed in this paper is also valid for packet switching and virtual cut-through [24,26,27].

The remainder of the paper is organized as follows. Section 2 gives the basic definitions to prepare the topology in order to deal with the proposed methodology, and also presents the preliminary definitions used in the rest of the paper. Our simple approach to generate deadlock-free routing algorithms is proposed in Sect. 3. The case study for two-dimensional mesh using proposed methodology is presented in Sect. 4. Using evaluation setup is described in Sect. 5. We present the simulation results for the routing algorithms obtained by the methodology in Sect. 6. Finally, Sect. 7 concludes this paper.

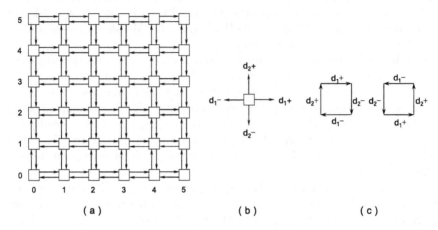

Fig. 1. A 6×6 mesh (a) the 4 directions, (b) and the deadlock configuration within zone $\{d_1+, d_1-, d_2+, d_2-\}$.

2   Preliminaries and Basic Definitions

Definition 1. An *n-dimensional mesh* is established as grid structure, it has $k_1 \times k_2 \times \cdots \times k_{n-1} \times k_n$ nodes, k_i nodes along dimension i. Each node is identified by n coordinates, $(x_1, x_2, \cdots, x_{n-1}, x_n)$, where $0 \leq x_i \leq k_i - 1$ for each dimension i. Two nodes $A(a_1, a_2, \cdots, a_{n-1}, a_n)$ and $B(b_1, b_2, \cdots, b_{n-1}, b_n)$ are neighbors if and only if $b_i = a_i$ for all i, except one, j, where $|b_j - a_j| = 1$. Figure 1(a) shows structure of a 6×6 mesh.

Definition 2. A channel along dimension i is termed a positive (negative) channel if its source node $A(a_1, ..., a_n)$ and sink node $B(b_1, ..., b_n)$ only differ in the ith coordinate such that $b_i = a_i + 1$ ($b_i = a_i - 1$). We label the positive (negative) channel in dimension i as d_i+ (d_i-).

Definition 3. The channels in an n-dimensional mesh can be further classified into $2n$ *directions*, that is, $d_1+, d_1-, d_2+, d_2-, \cdots, d_n+, d_n-$. Figure 1(b) shows the 4 directions in a 2-dimensional mesh.

Definition 4. A *zone* Z_i is defined as a set of channel directions, which can be used by the routing algorithm to direct the packets to their destinations without any restriction, that is, the packets are allowed to turn adaptively from one direction to others and vice versa. Therefore, for the aforementioned $2n$ directions $(d_1+, d_1-, d_2+, d_2-, \cdots, d_n+, d_n-)$, $2^{2n} - 1$ different zones may exist. For example, zone $Z_i = \{d_1+, d_2-\}$ contains two channel directions, in that the packets are allowed to turn from d_1+ to d_2- (and vice versa) adaptively.

Definition 5. A zone is *deadlock-free* if there is no cyclic dependency [4–6] among its channel directions.

Although there exist $2^{2n} - 1$ different zones, a few of them are deadlock-free. For example, Fig. 1(c) shows that a zone containing four directions $\{d_1+, d_1-, d_2+, d_2-\}$ induces cyclic dependencies. In order to generate deadlock-free zones, first it is necessary to determine the cyclic dependencies among all combinations of channel directions. Then, by placing cyclic-independent channel directions in the same zone, a deadlock-free zones is generated.

It is easy to know that zones containing just one channel direction are deadlock-free, as there is no cyclic dependency between channels of one direction. Otherwise, *the 180-degree turns are usually not allowed in deadlock-free zones.*

To exhaust all combinations of channel directions is extremely complicated and time-consuming. Here we just enumerate some combinations without cyclic dependencies:

$\{d_1+\}, \{d_2+\}, \cdots, \{d_n+\};$
$\{d_1+, d_2+\}, \{d_3+, d_4+\}, \cdots, \{d_{n-1}+, d_n+\};$

$\vdots$

$\{d_1+, d_2+, \cdots, d_n+\}, \{d_1-, d_2-, \cdots, d_n-\}.$

Definition 6. A *routing algorithm* can be defined as a sequence of zones, such as, $Z_1 \to Z_2 \to \cdots \to Z_i \to \cdots \to Z_m$. Within each zone, packets can use the channels adaptively; Among zones, packets must obey the predetermined order. That is, we first route packets with directions in Z_1, then route packets with directions in Z_2, and so on.

Deadlock-freedom and *connectivity* are the two most important aspects of routing algorithm design. Deadlock-freedom means that no cyclic dependencies are created, thus any packet can eventually reach its destination. Connectivity ensures that any packet has at least one path from source node to destination node. Here, we give two lemmas.

Lemma 1. *A routing algorithm is connected if and only if the union of its zones includes all 2n directions $(d_1+, d_1-, d_2+, d_2-, \cdots, d_n+, d_n-)$ in an n-dimensional mesh.*

Proof. $\Rightarrow$ We prove this lemma by contradiction. Suppose routing algorithm R: $Z_1 \to Z_2 \to \cdots \to Z_m$ is connected, and the union of all these zones $Z = Z_1 \cup Z_2 \cup \cdots \cup Z_m$, doesn't include $\{d_i+\}$. Therefore, the channels in d_i+ direction will never be provided by R. For any packet whose source node is $S(s_1, \cdots, s_i, \cdots, s_n)$ and destination node is $P(p_1, \cdots, p_i, \cdots, p_1)(s_i < p_i)$, it cannot get to destination using R. Thus R is not connected, contrary to the assumption that R is connected.

$\Leftarrow$ Suppose routing algorithm R: $Z_1 \to Z_2 \to \cdots \to Z_m$ and the union of all these zones includes all 2n directions. We need to prove that R is connected, i.e. R can provide at least one path for any packet from its source to destination node. Without loss of generality, suppose packet P need to traverse directions $d_i+, d_j-, d_k+, d_m-, d_p+, d_q-$ to reach its destination. We can first find the zone containing d_i+, then find the zone containing d_j-, and so on. We use $Z_{i'}, Z_{j'}, Z_{k'}, Z_{m'}, Z_{p'}$, and $Z_{q'}$ to represent the zones we have found in last step, respectively. Then we arrange these zones in an increasing order according to zones' ID (for example, $Z_{j'}, Z_{i'}, Z_{m'}, Z_{p'}, Z_{q'}, Z_{k'}$). With this zone order, accordingly we get the ordered directions $(d_j-, d_i+, d_m-, d_p+, d_q-, d_k+)$. To reach destination, P can traverse these directions in order. Thus we prove that if the union of a routing algorithm's zones include all directions, the routing algorithm is connected. ∎

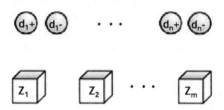

Fig. 2. The problem of putting $2n$ balls into m boxes (Ball stands for direction of channel, box stands for zone).

This lemma reveals that if we want to guarantee the connectivity of routing algorithm, all these $2n$ directions must be included in its zones. Then the problem of making routing algorithm connected becomes the problem of putting $2n$ balls into m boxes, at least one ball in each boxes (Fig. 2). Here, $2n$ balls stand for $2n$ directions in an n-dimensional mesh, m boxes stand for m zones in a routing algorithm. Obliviously, $m \leq n$. By this way, we can design lots of routing algorithms and also guarantee its connectivity. For example, $R_1 : Z_1 = \{d_1+, d_1-, d_2+, d_2-, \cdots, d_n+, d_n-\}$ is connected but not deadlock-free. *How to be deadlock-free?* We need the following lemma.

Lemma 2. *A routing algorithm is deadlock-free if it is made up of an ordered sequence of deadlock-free zones.*

Proof. The predefined zone order eliminates the potential cyclic dependency among channel directions of different deadlock-free zones. Additionally, there is no cyclic dependency among channel directions of the same deadlock-free zone. Thus, the whole routing algorithm is deadlock-free. ∎

With these two lemmas, we have the following theorem.

Theorem 1. *If a routing algorithm is made up of deadlock-free zones and the union of its zones covers all directions, then it must be deadlock-free and connected.*

Proof. With Lemmas 1 and 2, the correctness of this theorem is quite obvious. ∎

Consider the following two routing algorithms:

$$R_2 : \underbrace{d_1+, d_1-, d_2+, d_2-}_{Z_1} \rightarrow \underbrace{d_3+, d_4+, \cdots, d_n+}_{Z_2} \rightarrow \underbrace{d_3-, d_4-, \cdots, d_n-}_{Z_3}$$

$$R_3 : \underbrace{d_1-, d_2-, \cdots, d_n-}_{Z_1} \rightarrow \underbrace{d_1+, d_2+, \cdots, d_n+}_{Z_2}$$

In R_2, Z_2 and Z_3 are deadlock-free zones, while Z_1 is not deadlock-free. Therefore, R_2 is not deadlock-free. According to Lemma 1, R_2 is connected. R_3, made up of two deadlock-free zones, is connected and deadlock-free.

3 The Methodology

The proposed methodology uses the following steps to generate connected and deadlock-free routing algorithms.

Step 1. Classifying the directions of channels according to dimension number (1 to n) and direction information (positive or negative).
Step 2. Determining deadlock-free zones according to Lemma 2. All $2n$ directions must be used to generate deadlock-free zones according to Lemma 1.
Step 3. Placing the generated deadlock-free zones in a sequence that leads to a connected, deadlock-free routing algorithm according to Theorem 1.

In brief, the first step is preparatory work, the second step guarantees deadlock-freedom of the routing algorithm, and the third step provides connectivity between each source destination pair. These three steps give a general methodology to design connected and deadlock-free routing algorithm for mesh networks.

Applying the methodology directly, a list of routing algorithms are obtained:

$$R_1 : \underbrace{d_1+, d_1-}_{Z_1} \rightarrow \cdots \rightarrow \underbrace{d_n+, d_n-}_{Z_n}$$

(Already proposed as dimension-order routing in [4])

$$R_2 : \underbrace{d_1+}_{Z_1} \rightarrow \cdots \rightarrow \underbrace{d_n+}_{Z_n} \rightarrow \underbrace{d_1-}_{Z_{n+1}} \rightarrow \cdots \rightarrow \underbrace{d_n-}_{Z_{2n}}$$

(Already proposed as direction-order routing in [21])

$$R_3 : \underbrace{d_1-, d_2-, \cdots, d_n-}_{Z_1} \rightarrow \underbrace{d_1+, d_2+, \cdots, d_n+}_{Z_2}$$

(Already proposed as negative first routing in [8])

$$R_4 : \underbrace{d_1-, d_2+, d_3-, \cdots}_{Z_1} \rightarrow \underbrace{d_1+, d_2-, d_3+, \cdots}_{Z_2}$$

(New routing algorithm)

R_1 routes packets in one dimension, then moves on to the next dimension, until the final destination is reached. Its another name, dimension-order routing (DOR), is more familiar. Unlike R_1, R_2 requires packets to traverse the $2n$

directions in a fixed order $(d_1+, d_2+, \cdots, d_n+, d_1-, \cdots, d_n-)$. It was first proposed for torus [21], then adopted for mesh [7]. R_3 or negative-first routing (NF), routes a packet first adaptively in the negative directions, then adaptively in the positive directions. NF is a partially adaptive routing algorithm, and it can provide fully adaptive routing for packets only needs to traverse channels in negative directions (Z_0) or positive directions (Z_1). For other cases, channels in negative directions must be traversed first. R_4 is a new routing algorithm designed with the proposed methodology. R_4 differs from R_3 in that packets are routed first adaptively in some specific directions, then adaptively in the other directions. The directions in the zone are quite different.

With aforementioned three steps, we can design deterministic or partially adaptive routing algorithm without using virtual channels [4]. To improve performance or support fully adaptive routing, we should introduce virtual channels, we leave this discussion for future work.

4   Two-Dimensional Meshes

For two-dimensional (2-D) meshes, the terminology used in the definition of n-dimensional meshes can be simplified. Dimensions 0 and 1 become X and Y. We take 2-D meshes as example, with the proposed methodology we can construct lots of deadlock-free routing algorithms.

4.1   Constructing Deadlock-Free Routing Algorithms

There are only four kinds of channel directions $X+, X-, Y+, Y-$ in a 2-D mesh. According to the proposed methodology, we can first construct deadlock-free zones and then assign an order among these zones. As Lemma 2, all directions must be used to guarantee routing algorithms' connectivity. So the problem of constructing connected routing algorithms becomes the problem of putting 4 balls into m boxes, at least one ball in each boxes. Thus we have $2 \leq m \leq 4$.

Figure 3 shows the routing algorithms design with different m value. When $m = 4$, there are 4 zones and each zone contains one direction (We call this case "1+1+1+1" pattern). Obliviously, all zones are deadlock-free. Considering the order of zones, there are more than A_4^4 routing algorithms can be constructed. These kinds of routing algorithms were once proposed as direction order routing (DIR) in [21] and were further discussed in [7]. For simplicity, we only list one of them. Routing algorithm $\{X+\} \rightarrow \{Y+\} \rightarrow \{X-\} \rightarrow \{Y-\}$ means that packets must ordered traverse channels in order $X+, Y+, X-, Y-$.

When $m = 3$, there are 3 zones and one zone contains two direction, the other two each contains one direction ("1+1+2" pattern). There are more than $C_4^2 A_3^3$ routing algorithms can be constructed. These kinds of routing algorithms have not been proposed in literature yet. The example $\{X+\} \rightarrow \{Y+\} \rightarrow \{X-, Y-\}$ indicates that: for packets that need to traverse both $X-$ and $Y-$ channels, they can turn from $X-$ to $Y-$ (and vice versa) adaptively; for the other packets, the order $X+, Y+, X-, Y-$ must be obeyed.

"1+1+1+1" pattern	A_4^4=24
{X+}→{Y+}→{X−}→{Y−}	Direction order routing
"1+1+2" pattern	$C_4^2 A_3^3$=36
{X+}→{Y+}→{X−,Y−}	New1
"2+2" pattern	$C_4^2 A_2^2$=12
{X+,X−}→{Y−,Y+}	Dimension order routing
{X−,Y−}→{X+,Y+}	Negative first routing
{X+,Y−}→{X−,Y+}	New2
"1+3" pattern	$C_4^1 A_2^2$=8
{X−}→{X+,Y+,Y−}	West first routing
{X+,X−,Y−}→{Y+}	North last routing
Odd-even column/row	2
odd column: {X−}→{X+,Y+,Y−} even column:{X−,X+,Y−}→{X+}	Odd-Even Turn Model for column
odd row: {Y−}→{Y+,X+,X−} even row:{Y−,X+,X−}→{Y+}	Odd-Even Turn Model for row

Fig. 3. Design routing algorithms with proposed methodology in 2-D meshes.

When m comes to 2, there are 2 zones. Both "1+3" pattern and "2+2" pattern satisfy the requirement. There are more than $C_4^2 A_2^2 + C_4^1 A_2^2$ routing algorithms can be constructed. The popular dimension order routing algorithm (DOR), negative first routing (NF), west first routing (WF) and north last routing (NL) all belong to this case. Besides these reported routing algorithms, we list a new routing algorithm, named New2, $\{X+, Y−\} \to \{X−, Y+\}$. Unlike NF, WF, NL, it provide adaptiveness for transpose traffic[1].

In addition, if we employ different routing algorithms in odd or even columns, we get Odd-Even turn model (OE) proposed by Chiu in [9]. OE declares that SW and NW turn are not allowed in odd column, EN and ES turn are not allowed in even column. The following routing algorithm $\{X−\} \to \{X+, Y+, Y−\}$, $\{X−, X+, Y−\} \to \{X+\}$ reveal above two rules respectively. Extending OE to different rows is quite straightway.

4.2   Analysis on Routing Adaptivity

The adaptivity directly influences routing algorithm's ability to avoid congestion, and then influence overall system performance. In this section, we discuss the adaptivity of different routing algorithms. The constructed routing algorithms can be classified into two classes: deterministic (each zone contains only one direction) and partially adaptive routing algorithms (some zones contain more than one direction). Deterministic routing algorithms, such as DOR and DIR, provide single path for packet to reach its destination. With adaptive routing,

---

[1] See Sect. 6 for detail.

several routing options may be provided by a router to forward a packet. As the former does not offer adaptivity, we focus our discussion on the partially adaptive routing algorithms, that is, NF, WF, NL, New1 and New2.

For example, NF routing routes a packet first adaptively in the negative directions, then adaptively in the positive directions. NF is a partially adaptive routing algorithm, it can provide fully adaptive routing for packets only needs to traverse channels in negative directions (X-, Y-) or positive directions (X+, Y+). For other cases, channels in negative directions must be traversed first. Similarly, WF, NL and New2 routing algorithms support fully adaptive routing in two areas. New1 routing algorithm offers adaptive routing only in the (X-,Y-) area. All these adaptive routing algorithms have their own characteristics, with different traffic patterns, they give different performance.

Although higher routing adaptivity usually means better performance, the choice of routing algorithms always is a trade-off between implementation complexity and performance. The research in [7] shows that, for some specific applications, DIR is enough to provide the best performance while maintaining low implementation complexity. The authors use linear programming to find the optimal solution from the 24 direction order routing algorithms. The proposed methodology gives a general way to design deadlock-free routing algorithms. Given an application, we can find the optimal solution from these constructed deadlock-free routing algorithms.

5   Evaluation Setup

5.1   Simulation

Measurements are implemented in a cycle-accurate simulator Noxim developed by Palesi *et. al.* We consider 4×4 2-D mesh with bidirectional channels. Wormhole flow control is applied throughout our simulation. Each packet contains 2–10 flits and each virtual channel is 4 flits deep to cover the credit round-trip delay in credit-based flow control. Unless otherwise specified, parameters are the same as the baseline configuration shown in Table 1. Packets are injected into the network using a Bernoulli process. All contentions are resolved with age-based arbitration which means always giving high priority to older packets.

Table 1. Baseline configuration and variations

Characteristic	Baseline	Variations
Mesh	4×4	8×8, 16×16
Buffer size	4 flits	8, 16 flits

The *throughput* (flits/cycle/node) and *latency* (cycles) are the two most important metrics to evaluate the performance of routing algorithms. In our

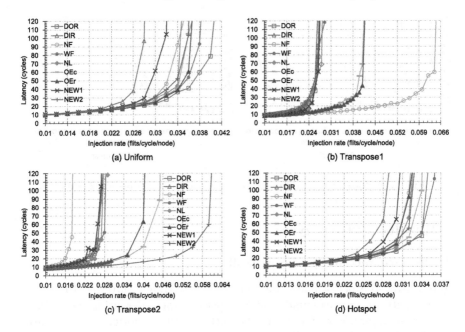

Fig. 4. Performance of different routing algorithms for different traffic patterns.

simulation, 10,000 cycles are used to warm up the network before collecting statistics, and another 50,000 cycles are used to capture the network steady state.

Nine routing algorithms are implemented, including two deterministic algorithms (dimension order routing (DOR), direction order routing (DIR)) and seven partially adaptive algorithms (negative first (NF), west first (WF), north last (NL), odd-even turn model for column (OEc), newly proposed odd-even turn model for row (OEr), NEW1 and New2). All these algorithms are deadlock-free and do not need any virtual channel.

5.2 Traffic Patterns

Uniform, transpose1, transpose2 and hotspot traffic patterns, have been used in the past to stress and evaluate routing algorithms [4,5,9]. We evaluate the methodology using these traffic patterns. With uniform, each node sends packets to randomly selected node. With transpose1, node (i, j) sends packets to node $(k-1-j, k-1-i)$ (k is number of nodes in each dimension). For transpose2 traffic, node (i, j) sends packets to node (j, i) and hotspot, one node is designated as the hotspot node, which receives additional 6 % traffic in addition to the regular uniform traffic.

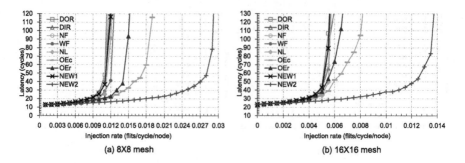

Fig. 5. Performance for different network sizes under transpose2 traffic.

6   Results and Analysis

6.1   Performance of Synthetic Traffic

Figure 4 gives the performance for four synthetic traffic patterns [19]. Across the four patterns, we can find that the performance of routing algorithm is highly traffic-aware. For different traffic patterns, the performance of a routing algorithm changes dramatically.

For uniform traffic, DOR performs best, DIR performs worst and all other partially adaptive routing algorithms fall midway. Although DOR doesn't offer any routing adaptivity for traffic, DOR benefits from its ability to incorporate more global, long-term information about the characteristics of uniform traffic, which may lead to more even distribution of traffic [9]. In contrast, the partially adaptive algorithms offer adaptivity, but suffer from network congestion. Among them, WF gives the second best performance. It is worth to note that the proposed OEr (Odd-Even turn model for row) outperforms the original OEc, indicating that applying Odd-Even turn model for row is better than for column under this traffic. Otherwise, New2 algorithm gives very similar performance to NF, NL, WF; all of them provide adaptivity in two areas.

Transpose1 sends packets from node (i, j) to node $(3 - j, 3 - i)$. NF offers adaptivity for all traffic and performs best. And then OEc (OEr) performs the second best, as it provides even routing adaptivity [9]. The other six routing algorithms give very similar performance, saturating at very low load. As for New2, traffic1 pattern is unfavorable, it can not offer any adaptivity and thus behaves just like a deterministic routing algorithm.

For traspose2, node (i, j) sends packets to node (j, i); then $\triangle x = j - i$, $\triangle y = i - j$; thus $\triangle x$ and $\triangle y$ will always have different symbols $(+/-)$. This traffic is favorable to New2: New2 can offer adaptivity for all packets in this traffic and is superior to all of the other algorithms. Similarly, the OE algorithms (OEc and OEr) still take up the second place, as their much even routing adaptivity. However, the once best algorithm for transpose1 traffic (NL) performs worst, even worse than deterministic algorithm without adaptivity. The other five algorithms have similar performance.

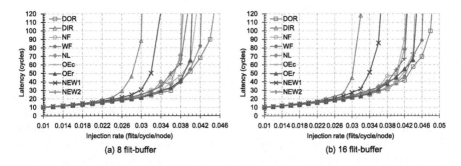

Fig. 6. Performance with different buffer sizes for uniform traffic.

Hotspot traffic pattern, in which the hotspot node receives extra 6 % traffic in addition to uniform traffic, is considered to be more realistic [9]. Similar to uniform, DOR works well. However, WF outperforms DOR and becomes the best algorithm in this traffic. This is mainly because: (1) under uniform traffic, WF has similar performance to DOR; (2) introducing hotspot node, WF benefits from its adaptivity to avoid hotspot node. the OE algorithms (OEc and OEr) still give medium performance. Otherwise, the gap between the best algorithm and the other algorithm becomes narrow.

6.2 Impact of Network Size

Figure 5 explores the scalability for 8×8 and 16×16 mesh under transpose2 traffic. A similar trend of proposed New2 performing best can be observed for all network sizes. With larger network, the gap between New2 and other algorithms become larger. The throughput improvement of New2 over OEc (the second best algorithm) is 75 % and 58 % for 16×16 and 8×8 mesh respectively, while it is 30 % in 4×4 mesh in Fig. 4(c), indicating an increased benefit of New2 over OEc for a larger network. In a larger network, packets have to pass through longer path to reach destination, increasing the possibility of encountering network congestion. Without proper adaptivity, the algorithm may suffer from performance degradation. For New2, it can offer adaptivity for all traffic. Therefore, the gap becomes more apparent in a larger network.

6.3 Impact of Buffer Size

In this subsection, we study the impact of buffer size on the performance of routing algorithm under uniform traffic. The buffer size is set to 8-flit, 16-flit. As can be seen from Fig. 6, all algorithms have similar trend for both two buffer sizes; with larger buffer size, the performance of each algorithm improves. The throughput improvement of DOR over WF (the seconde best algorithm) is 14 % and 15 % for 16-flit and 8-flit buffer respectively, while it is 17 % in 4-flit buffer in Fig. 4(a), indicating an decreased benefit of DOR over WF for a larger buffer. With larger buffer, more packets can be stored in the local buffer, the emergence of the congestion will be reduced, thus the differences among different algorithms decrease.

7   Conclusion

We proposed a general methodology to design deadlock-free routing algorithms for mesh networks. The proposed methodology provides a simple approach to construct deadlock-free routing algorithm, thus we can generate lots of new routing algorithms to meet the demand of applications. Additionally, the proposed methodology covers most well-known previously reported routing algorithms (such as dimension order routing, direction order routing, turn model) and reveals the implicit relation among them. Simulation results show that for a given network the performance of a routing algorithm mainly depends on the traffic pattern: one routing algorithm may perform best under one traffic pattern, while perform worst under another. For a specific application, the proposed methodology offers more alternatives when searching the routing algorithm that can provide the best performance. It is worth to note that the proposed New2 algorithm perform best under the transpose2 traffic pattern, i.e., New2 is suitable for the kind of applications (FFT, for example) with transpose2-like features.

Acknowledgements. We sincerely thank the anonymous reviewers for their helpful comments and suggestions. This work is supported by the National Science Foundation of China under grants 61171121, 61402086, 61572279 and Scientific Research Foundation of Liaoning Provincial Education Department (No. L2015165), and DUFE Excellent Talents Project (No. DUFE2015R06).

References

1. Vangal, S.R., Howard, J., Ruhl, G., Dighe, S., Wilson, H., Tschanz, J., Finan, D., Singh, A., Jacob, T., Jain, S., Erraguntla, V., Roberts, C., Hoskote, Y., Borkar, N., Borkar, S.: An 80-tile sub-100-W teraflops processor in 65-nm CMOS. IEEE J. Solid-State Circuits **43**(1), 29–41 (2008)
2. Bell, S., Edwards, B., Amann, J., Conlin, R., Joyce, K., Leung, V., MacKay, J., Reif, M., Bao, L.W., Brown, J., Mattina, M., Miao, C.C., Ramey, C., Wentzlaff, D., Anderson, W., Berger, E., Fairbanks, N., Khan, D., Montenegro, F., Stickney, J., Zook, J.: Tile64-processor: a 64-core SoC with mesh interconnect. In: International Solid-State Circuits Conference, pp. 88–89,598. IEEE Press, New York (2008)
3. Marculescu, R., Ogras, U.Y., Peh, L.S., Jerger, N.E., Hoskote, Y.: Outstanding research problems in NoC design: system, microarchitecture, and circuit perspectives. IEEE Trans. CAD Integr. Circ. Syst. **28**(1), 3–21 (2009)
4. Dally, W.J., Towles, B.: Principles and Practices of Interconnection Networks. Morgan Kaufmann, San Francisco (2004)
5. Duato, J., Yalamanchili, S., Ni, L.: Interconnection Networks: An Engineering Approach. IEEE Press, New York (1997)
6. Duato, J.: A new theory of deadlock-free adaptive routing in wormhole networks. IEEE Trans. Parallel Distrib. Syst. **4**(12), 1320–1331 (1993)
7. Towles, B., Grossman, J.P., Greskamp, B., Shaw, D.E.: Unifying on-chip and internode sitching within the Anton 2 network. In: International Symposium on Computer Architecuture (ISCA), pp. 1–12. IEEE Press, New York (2014)
8. Glass, C.J., Ni, L.: The turn model for adaptive routing. J. ACM **41**(5), 874–902 (1994)

9. Chiu, G.M.: The odd-even turn model for adaptive routing. IEEE Trans. Parallel Distrib. Syst. **11**(7), 729–738 (2000)
10. Boura, Y.M., Das, C.R.: Efficient fully adaptive wormhole routing in n-dimensional meshes. In: International Conference on Distributed Computing Systems, pp. 589–596. IEEE Press, New York (1994)
11. Palesi, M., Holsmark, R., Kumar, S., Catania, V.: Application specific routing algorithms for networks on chip. IEEE Trans. Parallel Distrib. Syst. **20**(3), 316–330 (2009)
12. Glass, C.J., Ni, L.M.: Maximally fully adaptive routing in 2D meshes. In: International Conference on Parallel Processing, pp. 101–104. IEEE Press, New York (1992)
13. Fu, B., Han, Y.H., Li, H.W.: An abacus turn model for time/space-efficient reconfigurable routing. In: International Symposium on Computer Architecture (ISCA), pp. 259–270. ACM Press, New York (2011)
14. Linder, D.H., Harden, J.C.: An adaptive and fault-tolerant wormhole routing strategy for k-ary n-cubes. IEEE Trans. Comput. **40**(1), 2–12 (1991)
15. Chien, A., Kim, J.H.: Planar-adaptive routing: low-cost adaptive networks for multiprocessors. J. ACM **42**(1), 91–123 (1995)
16. Xiang, D.: Deadlock-free adaptive routing in meshes with fault-tolerance ability using channel overlapping. IEEE Trans. Dependab. Sec. Comput. **8**(1), 74–88 (2011)
17. Luo, W., Xiang, D.: An efficient adaptive deadlock-free routing algorithm for torus networks. IEEE Trans. Parallel Distrib. Syst. **23**(5), 800–808 (2012)
18. Xiang, D., Zhang, Y.L., Pan, Y.: Practical deadlock-free fault-tolerant routing in meshes based on the planar network fault model. IEEE Trans. Comput. **58**(5), 620–633 (2009)
19. Ma, S., Wang, Z., Jerger, N.E., Shen, L., Xiao, N.: Novel flow control for fully adaptive routing in cache-coherent NoCs. IEEE Trans. Parallel Distrib. Syst. **25**(9), 2397–2407 (2014)
20. Alonso, M.G., Xiang, D., Flich, J., Yu, Z.G., Duato, J.: Achieving balanced buffer utilization with a proper co-design of flow control and routing algorithm. In: International Symposium on Networks-on-Chip, pp. 25–32. IEEE Press, New York (2014)
21. Scott, S., Thorson, G.: The cray T3E network: adaptive routing in a high performance 3D torus. In: High-performance Interconnects Symposium, Hot Interconnects IV, pp. 147–156. Stanford University (1996)
22. Moravejia, R., Sarbazi-Azadb, H., Zomayac, A.Y.: A general methodology for direction-based irregular routing algorithms. J. Parallel Distrib. Comput. **70**(5), 270–363 (2010)
23. Wang, X.Y., Xiang, D., Yu, Z.G.: TM: a new and simple topology for interconnection networks. J. Supercomput. **66**(1), 514–538 (2013)
24. http://www.top500.org/
25. Xie, M., Lu, Y., Wang, K., Cao, H., Yang, X.: Tianhe-1A interconnect and message-passing services. IEEE Micro **32**(1), 8–20 (2012)
26. Adiga, N.R., Blumrich, M.A., Chen, D., Coteus, P., Gara, A., Giampapa, M.E., Heidelberger, P., Singh, S., Steinmacher-Burow, B.D., Takken, T., Tsao, M., Vranas, P.: Blue gene/L torus interconnection network. IBM J. Res. Dev. **49**, 265–276 (2005)
27. Yu, Z.G., Xiang, D., Wang, X.Y.: Balancing virtual channel utilization for deadlock-free routing in torus networks. J. Supercomput. **71**(8), 3094–3115 (2015)
28. Verbeek, F., Schialtz, J.: On necessary and sufficient conditions for deadlock-free routing in wormhole networks. IEEE Trans. Parallel Distrib. Syst. **22**(10), 2022–2032 (2011)

Completion Time-Aware Flow Scheduling in Heterogenous Networks

Shiming He[1(✉)], Kun Xie[2,3], and Dafang Zhang[2]

[1] Hunan Provincial Key Laboratory of Intelligent Processing of Big Data on Transportation, School of Computer and Communication Engineering, Hunan Province Engineering Research Center of Electric Transportation and Smart Distributed Network, Changsha University of Science and Technology, Changsha 410114, China
heshiming_hsm@163.com
[2] College of Computer Science and Electronics Engineering, Hunan University, Changsha 410082, China
dfzhang@hnu.edu.cn
[3] Department of Electrical and Computer Engineering, State University of New York at Stony Brook, New York, USA
cskxie@gmail.com

Abstract. In China, the expressway isn't free. When a vehicle exits, the exit toll station needs to calculate the toll according to the vehicle trajectory obtained by sending a trajectory query task to the trajectory center remotely. For the accurate of toll and keep the exit smoothly, transmitting the trajectory result reliably and in time is a key issue. There are three heterogenous networks in expressway, Fibernet, Telecommunications Network and 3G. We concurrently exploit three heterogenous networks by allocating the trajectory result into three sub-flows where each sub-flow is transmitted in one kind of networks. But existing multipath transfer solution(FMTCP) doesn't consider the difference of completed time among all sub-flows and can't make sure the completed time in time. Therefore, we formulate the sub-flows schedule as a integer programming problem, which is proved to be NP-hard problem, and propose a Completion time-aware Flow Scheduling scheme (CaFS) which calculates the size of sub-flows. For the reliably, it exploits generation-based network coding. For the transmission in time, CaFS allocates the size of sub-flow into suitable generation and scheduling the generations. The simulation results demonstrate that, comparing with the FMTCP, CaFS improves 31.9 % in completion time and 30 % in task finished rate.

Keywords: Multi-network transmission · Sub-flows schedule · Network coding · MPTCP · Heterogenous networks

1 Introduction

In China, the expressway isn't free. Therefore, how to accurately calculate the fee of passing the expressway (named toll) is significantly important for the

G. Wang et al. (Eds.): ICA3PP 2015, Part I, LNCS 9528, pp. 492–507, 2015.
DOI: 10.1007/978-3-319-27119-4_34

driver and the company of expressway. If the toll is overestimated, the driver is extremely unwilling to pay any more than the real toll. If the toll is underestimated, it damages the interests and enthusiasms of expressway investors. Therefore, the trajectory of vehicle is the key basis for accurate toll.

The trajectory is recorded by the high speed cameras capturing photographic video or images of license plates along the expressway of vehicle, and is uploaded to the trajectory center. When a vehicle exits, the exit toll station needs the trajectory to calculate the toll which is not storied locally. Therefore, it sends a query task for the trajectory of vehicle to the trajectory center. The driver is extremely unwilling to wait for a long time for paying the toll. If the query time for the trajectory is too long, the exit may be congestion. Hence, to keep the exit smoothly, the exit toll station will give up the query for the trajectory and let the vehicle leave with the toll of the shortest trajectory, if the toll station can't obtain the real trajectory in a time limiter which is the deadline of query.

As shown in Fig. 1, a vehicle goes to location B from location A. Location C, D, E are on the expressway. There are cameras to capture the image of vehicle on location C, D, E. Because of a loop exits, there are three trajectories from A to B, such as $A \rightarrow C \rightarrow B$, $A \rightarrow D \rightarrow B$ and $A \rightarrow E \rightarrow B$. The real trajectory is $A \rightarrow C \rightarrow B$, but the toll is calculated according to the shortest trajectory $A \rightarrow D \rightarrow B$, if the query result completion time overruns the time limiter.

If the vehicle always exits with the toll of the shortest trajectory, a lot of toll loses, which damages the interests and enthusiasms of investors. According to the real trajectory, the toll will increase by 2.08 % (about RMB 130,000,000 every month) by estimating the loops in Beijing-Zhuhai Expressway Network area.

Therefore, in order to avoid toll calculation mistake, transmitting the trajectory query result from the trajectory center to the exit toll station reliably and in time is a key issue in expressway. Another solution is pre-distributing the trajectory to toll station. In pre-distribution, it's needed to estimate the possible exit toll station to pre-distribute the trajectory. Due to the huge vehicle traffic, the complex of estimation is high. There may be estimation mistake. If estimation is fail, the query between the exit toll station and the trajectory center is still needed in real time.

At present, the networks of expressway are heterogenous networks. There are three kinds of networks in expressway including Fibernet, Telecommunications

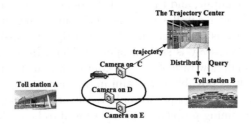

Fig. 1. The trajectory of vehicle

Network and 3G. Fibernet is unconnected in some area, delay and jitter are high. Telecommunications Network is stability, but the recovery time is uncertain. 3G shares the bandwidth, but is instability in remote regions. It has been demonstrated that multiple networks transmitting simultaneously can improve the throughput and reliably effectively [1–6]. Therefore, we consider concurrently exploiting multiple network and allocating the trajectory query result to three network for concurrent transmission.

There are several multipath transfer solutions proposed to transmit simultaneously over multiple networks, including pTCP(parallel TCP) [1], MTCP(Multi-path Transmission Control Protocol) [2], SCTP-CMT(Stream Control Transmission Protocol-Concurrent Multipath Transfer) [3], Multipath TCP (MPTCP) [4–6] which is standardized by IETF.

MPTCP enables multihomed devices to use several paths through multiple interfaces within a single TCP connection. In order to exploit the multiple networks resource, a single TCP consists of multiple TCP sub-flows. A sub-flow transmits through one kind of networks and all sub-flows share the same source and destination but with different interfaces. The protocol adds a new layer above the transport layer which provides packet scheduling across multiple TCP sub-flows and guarantees packet delivery through the use of a somewhat complex management scheme. MPTCP can improve the throughput and reliably effectively, which is applied to LTE network [7] and analyzed the security [8] and performance cost [9].

However, a sub-flow experiencing high delay and loss severely affects the performance of other sub-flows [10,11], thus becoming the bottleneck of the MPTCP connection and significantly degrading the aggregate goodput. To solve the bottleneck problem, several suggestions [12–15] on incorporating network coding [16] with MPTCP have been proposed. [12–14] compensate for the lost or delayed packets by network code packets. But both of them use fixed-rate coding scheme, which does not have good performance when the path quality decreases sharply. [15] proposes Fountain code-based Multipath TCP (FMTCP) which takes advantage of the random nature of the fountain code to flexibly transmit encoded symbols from the same or different data blocks over different sub-flows.

In expressway, the query for the trajectory must complete in the deadline. Otherwise, the query result is idle. The completed time of query is depended on the last sub-flow. Based on network coding, MPTCP [12–15] focus on the improvement of throughput, and they don't consider the significant difference of completion time among all sub-flows. Hence, they can't make sure the completion time of query as quick as possible. Therefore, multipath transfer over heterogenous networks of expressway is still an open problem. In order to improve the economic benefits, high flow rate of vehicle, completing the transmission of query reliably and as quick as possible is the aim in our paper.

To solve the problem, this paper formulates the problem of sub-flows schedule as an integer programming problem, which is proved to be an NP-hard problem. To solve the problem, we propose a Completion time-aware Flow Scheduling scheme (CaFS) which decomposes the problem to each task and calculates the size of sub-flows. For the reliably, CaFS exploits generation-based network coding. To complete the transmission as quickly as possible, CaFS allocates the size of each sub-flow into a suitable generation and scheduling the generations. The simulation results demonstrate that, compared with the FMTCP, our algorithm improves by 31.9 % in completion time and 30 % in task finished rate.

The rest of this paper is organized as follows. The System Model and Limitation of MPTCP and FMTCP are introduced in Sect. 2. After analyzing the constraints of the problem, we give the problem formulation in Sect. 3. Section 4 proposes the scheme. Section 5 discusses the performance of the new algorithm. Conclusion is drawn in Sect. 6.

2 System Model and Limitation of MPTCP and FMTCP

To record the trajectory of vehicle, vehicle license plate recognition [17] is exploited, as shown in Fig. 1. The expressway is deployed with high speed cameras to capture photographic video or images of license plates which are generated license plates information. The license plates information is uploaded to *the Trajectory Center*. The trajectory center pre-distributes the trajectory to toll station close to the vehicle. When a vehicle exits, the toll station firstly searches its local database for the trajectory of vehicle. If it can't search the trajectory locally, the toll station queries for the trajectory from the trajectory center remotely.

There are three kinds of networks between toll station and the trajectory center including Fibernet, Telecommunications Network and 3G.

As shown in Fig. 2, vehicle A and B exit. Assuming that the toll station can't search their trajectories in local database, the toll station send two queries task (query A and query B) to the trajectory center. The trajectory center searches its database and gets two query results A and B including their trajectories, tolls and the images of vehicle license plates, respectively. Three sub-flows are set up for each query result, where each sub-flow transmits in one of the three networks. Firstly, the query result is coded and is divided into three parts transmitted by sub-flow to the toll station. The toll station gets the whole query result from three sub-flows which is decoded to obtain the trajectory, tolls and the images of vehicle license plate. In Fig. 2, query result A is divided into tree parts (A1, A2 and A3), and query result B is divided into tree parts (B1, B2 and B3). A1 and B1 are transmitted by 3G with red, A2 and B2 are transmitted by Telecommunications Network with green, and A3 and B3 are transmitted by Fibernet with blue.

Before presenting our proposed scheme, we first provide some analysis on the limitation of MPTCP and FMTCP through simulation studies using ns-2. According the network setting in Table 2, we set up one query task from the toll station to the trajectory center in Fig. 2. We show the completion times of three sub-flows in MPTCP and FMTCP in Fig. 3. Noted that, the completion times of three sub-flows are significantly different, specially in MPTCP. It goes worse, when the number of query tasks increases.

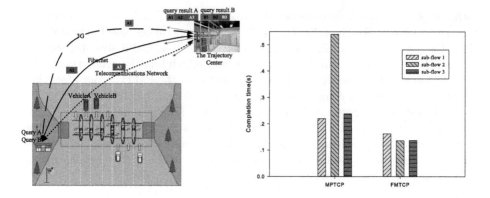

Fig. 2. Trajectory query

Fig. 3. Limitation of MPTCP and FMTCP

Firstly, three kinds of networks are totally different, and the differences in the bandwidth and delay are significant. Secondly, MPTCP and FMTCP focus on the improvement of throughput and minimizing the maximum completion time among sub-flows isn't considered. Hence, the completion time of sub-flows are different.

The completion time of query task is depended on the last sub-flow. The slower the last sub-flow completes, the longer the completion time of task is. If the last sub-flow completes after the deadline, the deadline of query is missed and the query result is idle. The received part of query result is wasted.

The performances of three kinds of networks differ considerably. The completion time of sub-flows may be very variable, which not only makes the missing of deadline and wastes the bandwidth and receive buffer, but also reduces the flow rate of vehicle and damages the economic benefits because of the shortest path toll. Therefore, in order to improve the economic benefits and high flow rate of vehicle, we should minimize the maximum sub-flow's completion time.

3 Problem Formulation

In this section, we give the problem formulation of scheduling problem. We define the query and query result transmission of a vehicle as a task. The full set of tasks is $T = \{t_0, t_1, ..., t_{n-1}\}$, and task t_i is described as $\{src_i, dst_i, len_i, d_i, f_{i,j} | j = 1, 2, ..., m\}$, in which src_i, dst_i, len_i, and d_i are the source, destination, size and deadline of task t_i. The number of networks m is three, therefore the task t_i is transmitted by three sub-flows $f_{i,1}$, $f_{i,2}$ and $f_{i,3}$. Sub-flow $f_{i,j}$ has the tuple $< l_{i,j}, e_{i,j} >$, $l_{i,j}$ is the size of sub-flow $f_{i,j}$, $e_{i,j}$ is the expected transferring time or completion time of sub-flow $f_{i,j}$. The sum of all sub-flows of task t_i equal to the size of task t_i, expressed as follows:

$$\sum_j l_{i,j} = len_i, \forall i \tag{1}$$

We define a binary variable c_i, which has value 1 if the task t_i completes in its deadline, that is, the completion time of all sub-flows is shorter than its deadline ($e_{max,i} = \max_{j} \{e_{i,j}\}$, $e_{max,i} \leq d_i$), and value 0 otherwise, expressed as follows:

$$e_{max,i} = \max_{j} \{e_{i,j}\}, \forall i \tag{2}$$

$$c_i = \begin{cases} 1, e_{max,i} \leq d_i \\ 0, otherwise \end{cases}, \forall i \tag{3}$$

If c_i equals to 1, the task t_i is an available task; otherwise, the task t_i is an unavailable task.

The bandwidths of three networks are $\{W_j\}$, where $j = \{1, 2, ..., m\}$ is the id of three networks. The delays of sub-flows are $\{RTT_{i,j}|i = \{0, 1, ..., n-1\}$, $j = \{1, 2, ..., m\}\}$. Since the three kinds of networks' packet loss rate is small enough, we set the packet loss rate to a small constant value in this paper.

Obviously, the completion time of sub-flow has a search algorithm time, in addition to network transmission time, expressed as Eq. (4). The search algorithm time is $query_i$ for computing the query result, the transmission time equals to the size of data $l_{i,j}$ divided by throughput $truc_{i,j}$.

$$e_{i,j} = query_i + l_{i,j}/truc_{i,j}, \forall i, j \tag{4}$$

In TCP protocol, for one TCP flow, if the bandwidth delay product ($W_j * RTT_{i,j}$) is larger than the windows of TCP (cw), the throughput depends on the windows of TCP and delay. Otherwise, it depends on the bandwidth delay product and delay. Throughput is calculated by Eq. (5).

$$tru_{i,j} = (min(cw, W_j * RTT_{i,j})/RTT_{i,j}), \forall i, j \tag{5}$$

For multiple TCP flows, if the sum of throughput of single TCP flows is smaller than the bandwidth of network, the throughput with multiple TCP flows equals to the throughput of single TCP flow; otherwise, the sum of throughput with multiple TCP flows equal to the bandwidth of network, calculated by Eq. (6).

$$\begin{cases} truc_{i,j} = tru_{i,j}, if \sum_{i} tru_{i,j} \leq W_j \\ \sum_{i} truc_{i,j} = W_j, truc_{i,j} <= tru_{i,j}, otherwise \end{cases}, \forall i, j \tag{6}$$

Our object is completing tasks as quickly as possible, that is, minimizing the sum of maximum sub-flow's completion time of tasks. According to Eqs. (1), (2), (3), (4), (5) and (6), We formulate the problem as the following system:

$$\begin{aligned} \text{minimize} \quad & \sum_{i \in [0, n-1]} e_{max,i} \\ \text{subject to} \quad & \sum_{j} l_{i,j} = len_i, \forall i \\ & e_{max,i} = \max_{j} \{e_{i,j}\}, \forall i \end{aligned}$$

$$c_i = \begin{cases} 1, e_{max,i} \le d_i \\ 0, otherwise \end{cases}, \forall i$$

$$e_{i,j} = query_i + l_{i,j}/truc_{i,j}, \forall i, j$$

$$tru_{i,j} = (min(cw, W_j * RTT_{i,j})/RTT_{i,j}), \forall i, j$$

$$\begin{cases} truc_{i,j} = tru_{i,j}, if \sum_i tru_{i,j} \le W_j \\ \sum_i truc_{i,j} = W_j, truc_{i,j} <= tru_{i,j}, otherwise \end{cases}, \forall i, j \qquad (7)$$

$$l_{i,j} \in [0, len_i], \forall i, j$$

$$l_{i,j} \in N, \forall i, j$$

$$i \in [0, n-1]$$

$$j \in [1, m]$$

where the variable is l . In order to transform the constraint Eq. (2) to linear constraint, we express Eq. (2) as Eq. 8).

$$e_{max,i} \ge e_{i,j}, \forall i, j \qquad (8)$$

The variables c_i are determined by the $e_{max,i}$, and they can't be considered in the final problem. Therefore, problem (3) can be formulated as problem (9).

$$\begin{aligned}
\text{minimize} \quad & \sum_{i \in [0, n-1]} e_{max,i} \\
\text{subject to} \quad & \sum_j l_{i,j} = len_i, \forall i \\
& e_{max,i} \ge e_{i,j}, \forall i, j \\
& e_{i,j} = query_i + l_{i,j}/truc_{i,j}, \forall i, j \\
& tru_{i,j} = (min(cw, W_j * RTT_{i,j})/RTT_{i,j}), \forall i, j \\
& \begin{cases} truc_{i,j} = tru_{i,j}, if \sum_i tru_{i,j} \le W_j \\ \sum_i truc_{i,j} = W_j, truc_{i,j} <= tru_{i,j}, otherwise \end{cases}, \forall i, j \\
& l_{i,j} \in [0, len_i], \forall i, j \\
& l_{i,j} \in N, \forall i, j \\
& i \in [0, n-1] \\
& j \in [1, m]
\end{aligned} \qquad (9)$$

where the variables is l. The problem (9) is NP-hard. We have the following theorem regarding the complexity of the problem (9).

Theorem 1. *The problem (9) is NP-hard.*

Proof. To prove that the problem is NP-hard, we reduce from the knapsack problem which is a well-known NP-hard problem. A special case of the problem (9) is that the sum of throughput of single TCP flow is smaller than the bandwidth of network, that is, $\sum_i tru_{i,j} \le W_j$. Then, this special case of the problem (9) can be decomposed to n sub-problems for each task formulated as:

$$\begin{aligned}
\text{minimize} \quad & e_{max,i} \\
\text{subject to} \quad & \sum_j l_{i,j} = len_i
\end{aligned}$$

$$\begin{aligned}
&e_{max,i} \geq e_{i,j}, \forall j \\
&e_{i,j} = query_i + l_{i,j}/truc_{i,j}, \forall j \\
&truc_{i,j} = (min(cw, W_j * RTT_{i,j})/RTT_{i,j}), \forall j \\
&l_{i,j} \in [0, len_i], \forall j \\
&l_{i,j} \in N, \forall j \\
&j \in [1, m]
\end{aligned} \tag{10}$$

where the variable $l_{i,j}$ represents how many packets in task t_i are allocated to the j-th network. The above formulation can be reduced to the knapsack problem.

The key difference between the general case of our problem and the knapsack problem is that the throughput of sub-flows in each task may share the bandwidth of network. That is, there may be needed another allocation of network's bandwidth to sub-flows throughput.

4   Completion Time-Aware Flow Scheduling Scheme

In this section, we propose an scheme named Completion time-aware Flow scheduling (CaFS). We calculate the size of all sub-flows according to the problem (9). Then, we exploit generation based network coding to code packet for reliably, calculate the generation size of each sub-flow and schedule packet sending in each generation.

4.1   Sub-flow Size Calculation

Firstly, we must calculate the size of each sub-flow according problem (9). There are two situations in problem (9). One is that the sum of throughput of single TCP flows is smaller than the bandwidth of network. The other is that the sum of throughput of single TCP flows is larger than the bandwidth of network.

In the first case, we can decompose the problem to each task. For each task, the object is $minimize\ e_{max,i}$. For three sub-flows of each task, when the completion time of three sub-flows are equal, expressed as Eq. (11), the maximum completion time is minimum. Hence, we can allocate the length of three sub-flows as the rate of throughput of three sub-flows.

$$e_{i,j} = e_{i,k}, \forall j \neq k, j, k \in [1, m] \tag{11}$$

In the second case, in order for simplicity, we decide that the network allocate the bandwidth to task averagely. That is, if the sum of throughput of single TCP flows is larger than the bandwidth of network, the throughput of multiple TCP flows equal to the bandwidth of network divided by the number of task, expressed as (12). Then, we can decompose the problem similarly as the first case.

$$truc_{i,j} = \begin{cases} tru_{i,j}, \sum_i tru_{i,j} \leq W_j \\ W_j/n, otherwise \end{cases}, \forall i, j \tag{12}$$

Therefore, we can design the Sub-flow Size Calculation algorithm, as shown in Algorithm 1.

Algorithm 1. Sub-flow Size Calculation algorithm

Input:
    $n, m, len, W, RTT, query$
Output:
    l, c
1: **for** each task t_i in T **do**
2:    **for** each network j in m **do**
3:      $tru_{i,j} = (min(cw, W_j * RTT_{i,j})/RTT_{i,j})$
4:      **if** $\sum_i tru_{i,j} \leq W_j$ **then**
5:        $truc_{i,j} = tru_{i,j}$
6:      **else**
7:        $truc_{i,j} = W_j/n$
8:      **end if**
9:    **end for**
10:   **for** each network j in m **do**
11:     $l_{i,j} = len_i * truc_{i,j}/(\sum_j truc_{i,j})$
12:     $l_{i,j} = [l_{i,j}]$
13:     $e_{i,j} = query_i + l_{i,j}/truc_{i,j}$
14:    **end for**
15:   **if** $\sum_j l_{i,j} \neq len_i$ **then**
16:     $l_{i,m} = len_i - \sum_{j,j \neq m} l_{i,j}$
17:     $e_{i,m} = query_i + l_{i,m}/truc_{i,j}$
18:    **end if**
19:   **if** $\max_j e_{i,j} > d_i$ **then**
20:     $c_i \leftarrow 0$
21:    **else**
22:     $c_i \leftarrow 1$
23:    **end if**
24: **end for**
25: **return** l, c;

The key idea of the CaFS algorithm is to minimize the completion time of each task $t_i \in T$ independently. For each task and each network, we calculate the throughput of single TCP flow at line 3. And according to the relationship of sum of throughput of single TCP flows and network's bandwidth, we get the throughput of multiple TCP flow at line 4–8. Then by solving the system of Eq. (13) including Eqs. (1), (4) and (11), we can get the size of sub-flow at line 11. Because the size of sub-flow is integer, we round it off at line 12. Then, according the size of sub-flow, we can obtain the completion time of sub-flow at line 13.

$$\begin{cases} \sum_j l_{i,j} = len_i, j \in [1,m] \\ e_{i,j} = e_{i,k}, \forall j \neq k, j, k \in [1,m] \\ e_{i,j} = query_i + l_{i,j}/truc_{i,j}, j \in [1,m] \end{cases} \tag{13}$$

After rounding, the sum of the size of sub-flows may not equal to the size of task. Hence, we recalculate the last sub-flow's size and completion time by the size of task minus the sum of above $m - 1$ sub-flows' size at line 15−18.

In the end, if the maximum completion time of sub-flows is bigger than the deadline, the task t_i is unavailable and c_i is set to 0. Otherwise, the task t_i is available and c_i is set to 1.

In the proposed algorithm, every task calculates the size and completion time of all sub-flows.

4.2   Network Coding-Based Scheduling

In Completion time-aware Flow scheduling scheme, we also exploit Generation-Based Random Linear Network Coding for reliably. In Generation-Based Random Linear Network Coding, the packets are divided into several generations. Only the packets in the same generation are coded together. We set the generation size of network coding to the size of TCP windows. Therefore, there are g generations which equal to $len_i * ps/cw$.

Although we obtain the size of sub-flows in above sub-section, how to schedule the packet of all generation into sub-flow still affects the completion time of task. Hence, we define the generation size of sub-flow $lg_{i,j,k}$, as expressed in Eq. (14).

$$lg_{i,j,k} = cw * l_{i,j}/len_i, \forall k \in [1, g] \tag{14}$$

As shown in Algorithm 2, we design the Generation Size of Sub-flow Calculation algorithm. For each task, each network and each generation, we can get generation size of sub-flow in line 4. But the generation size of sub-flow is integer, we round it. After rounding, the sum of the generation size of sub-flow may not equal to the size of sub-flow. Hence, we recalculate the last generation's size by the size of sub-flow minus the sum of above $g-1$ generations size at line 6−8.

In order to balance the completion time of sub-flow, for a sub-flow, if the packets of current generation are finished or the current the generation size is zero, it don't need to wait for other sub-flow and can transmit the next generation's packet, as shown in Algorithm 3.

5   Simulation

In this section, to demonstrate the properties of the proposed algorithm we present some simulation results which validate that our algorithm increases performance effectively.

5.1   Methodology

We use ns2 [18] to do the simulations. The network topology is a tree-topology. The root node is the trajectory center and leaf nodes are the toll stations. Actually, each toll station may include 2, 4, 6, or 8 exit lanes. For simplicity, we assume

Algorithm 2. Generation Size of Sub-flow Calculation

Input:
  n, m, len, l
Output:
  lg
1: **for** each task t_i in T **do**
2:   **for** each network j in m **do**
3:     **for** each generation k in g **do**
4:       $lg_{i,j,k} = [cw * l_{i,j}/len_i]$
5:     **end for**
6:     **if** $\sum\limits_{k} lg_{i,j,k} \neq l_{i,j}$ **then**
7:       $lg_{i,j,g} = l_{i,j} - \sum\limits_{k, k \neq g} lg_{i,j,k}$
8:     **end if**
9:   **end for**
10: **end for**
11: **return** lg;

Algorithm 3. Generation Scheduling

Input:
  lg
1: **for** each generation k in g **do**
2:   **while** $lg_{i,j,k} > 0$ **do**
3:     send a packet which belong to k-th generation
4:     $lg_{i,j,k} - -$
5:   **end while**
6: **end for**

that each toll station include only one exit lanes in our simulation. Therefore, the number of concurrent query task is no larger than the number of the toll stations.

There are three kinds of networks Fibernet, Telecommunications Network and 3G. The bandwidths of Fibernet, Telecommunications Network and 3G are 622 Mbps(STM-4), 100 Mbps and 2 Mbps, respectively, as shown in Table 1. The network delay depend on the distance between toll station and the trajectory center. The propagation velocity in fiber is $2.0 * 10^8\, m/s$ and that in Copper is $2.3 * 10^8\, m/s$. We assume that the delay in Fibernet is 30 ms and that in Telecommunications Network is 26 ms. The delay in 3G is 50 ms.

The traffic in expressway of Hunan province is 1 million vehicle everyday. According to the demand of expressway, the completion time of query is smaller than 0.35 s. Therefore we set the deadline of task (d_i) to 0.35 s. The search algorithm time $(query_i)$ is 0.005 s. The size of task (len_i) is 100 packets and packet size (ps) is 1000 byte. The windows of TCP (cw) sets to 32 KB. The block size of FMTCP (bs) is 20 packet. The parameters are shown in Table 2.

We implement two kinds of schemes in ns2.

Table 1. Network parameters

Network type	Bandwidth	RTT
Fibernet	622 Mbps(STM-4)	30 ms
Telecommunications network	100 Mbps	26 ms
3G	2 Mbps	50 ms

Table 2. Simulation parameters

Parameter	Value	Notes
n	10–50	The number of tasks
m	3	The number of networks
d_i	0.35 s	The deadline of task
$query_i$	0.005 s	Search algorithm time
len_i	100 packets	The size of task
cw	32 KB	The windows of TCP
ps	1000 byte	Packet size
bs	32 packets	The block size of FMTCP
gs	32 packets	The generation size of CaFS

(1) FMTCP: FMTCP [15] which is a network coding based algorithm is applied.

(2) CaFS: Our proposed scheme is applied.

Since the performance of MPTCP is worse than FMTCP [15], we focus on the comparison between FMTCP and our algorithm.

Three metrics are used to evaluate the performance. One is throughput which is the average throughput of all tasks. The other is completion time which is the maximum delay of task's sub-flows. Final metric is task finished rate which is the rate between the number of available tasks and all tasks, that is, $\sum_i c_i/n$. In each run, we examine two kinds of schemes sequentially with the same source-destination pairs.

Various factors affect the performance. We perform two set of simulations to analyse the effect of the number of tasks and RTT. As follow, we show the simulation results respectively.

5.2   Impact of the Number of Tasks

In our first set of simulations, we change the number of the toll stations from 10 to 50 and evaluate the end-to-end throughput and completion time from the toll stations to the trajectory center. That is, the number of concurrent tasks equals to the number of the toll stations.

Figures 4 and 5 present the average throughput and completion time, achieved by FMTCP and CaFS affected by the number of tasks. The error bars are the standard deviation of throughput and completion time of the tasks. CaFS always achieves the higher throughput and lower completion time than FMTCP in the evaluated cases. The average throughput of FMTCP and CaFS are 2.66 Mbps and 3.31 Mbps, respectively. The completion time of FMTCP and CaFS are 0.35 s and 0.27 s, respectively. The average gain of FMTCP/CaFS is 1.24 times in throughput, and 31.9 % in completion time.

The reason for CaFS to outperform the FMTCP is that CaFS minimizes the maximum sub-flows completion time by its flow scheduling and is able to allocate packet suitably to three kinds of networks.

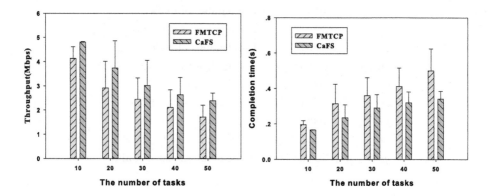

Fig. 4. Throughput with the number of tasks

Fig. 5. Completion time with the number of tasks

Figure 6 shows the task finished rate of FMTCP and CaFS with the different number of tasks. When the number of tasks is small (such as 10), the FMTCP and CaFS can make all the task finish within the deadline 0.35s. With the increase of the number of tasks, the task finished rate of FMTCP and CaFS decrease. In 50 tasks case, the task finished rate of FMTCP decreases to 20 %, however, the task finished rate of CaFS is still larger than 50 %. According to Fig. 5, the completion time of CaFS is smaller than that of FMTCP, therefore the available task number of CaFS should be larger than that of FMTCP.

5.3   Impact of RTT

In our second set of simulations, we set the number of task to 50 and change the RTTs of Fibernet, Telecommunications Network and 3G sequentially according to Table 3.

Figures 7 and 8 show the average throughput and completion time of FMTCP and CaFS in different scenarios. It is clear that the transmitted with FMTCP experience lower throughput and higher completion time than those transmitted by CaFS. In scenarios 2, 3 and 4, the RTTs decrease. When the RTT of

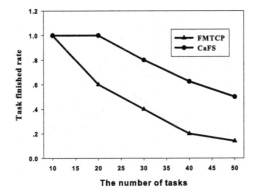

Fig. 6. Task finished rate with the number of tasks

Table 3. The RTT values of test case

Test case/RTT(ms)	1	2	3	4	5	6	7
Fibernet	30	30	30	10	30	30	50
Telecommunications network	24	24	4	24	24	44	24
3G	50	30	50	50	70	50	50

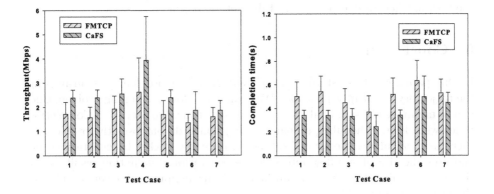

Fig. 7. Throughput with the different RTT

Fig. 8. Completion time with the different RTT

network with higher bandwidth increases, the throughput increase and completion time decreases sharply. In scenarios 5, 6 and 7, the RTTs increase. When the RTT of network with higher bandwidth increases, the throughput decrease and completion time increases sharply. The average throughput and completion time of FMTCP and CaFS are 1.78Mbps, 0.50s and 2.48Mbps, 0.36s, respectively. The average gain of FMTCP/CaFS is 1.39 times in throughput, and 39 % in completion time.

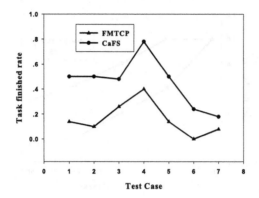

Fig. 9. Task finished rate with the different RTT

Generally, the performance of CaFS is better than that of FMTCP. This is because CaFS, with its flow scheduling, is able to allocate packet suitably to three kinds of network.

In Fig. 9, we present the task finished rate of FMTCP and CaFS in different scenarios. For 3G, the task finished rate independent with the RTT. For Telecommunications Network and Fibernet, the RTT plays a significant part in the task finished rate, especially in Fibernet.

6   Conclusion

In this paper, we have studied the Flow Scheduling problem of transmitting the trajectory result in expressway. We formulate Flow Scheduling problem that aim to minimize the sum of all task's completion time. We propose a Completion time-aware Flow Scheduling scheme (CaFS) which decomposes the problem to each task, calculates the size of sub-flows, code the packet by generation and allocates the size of sub-flow into suitable generation. Simulation results show that CaFS achieves higher task finished rate, throughput and lower completion time than existing FMTCP.

Acknowledgments. [This work was supported by National Natural Science Foundation of China (Key Program 71331001, 71420107027, 61303045, 61572184), the Prospective Research Project on Future Networks (Jiangsu Future Networks Innovation Institute) under Grant No. BY2013095-4-06.

References

1. Hsieh, H., Sivakumar, R.: pTCP: an end-to-end transport layer protocol for striped connections. In: The 10th IEEE International Conference on Network Protocols, pp. 24–33 (2002)

2. Park, K., Choi, Y., Kim, D., Park, D.: Mtcp: a transmission control protocol for multi-provider environment. Consum. Commun. Netw. Conf. **2**, 735–739 (2006)

3. Iyengar, J.R., Amer, P.D., Stewart, R.: Concurrent multipath transfer using sctp multihoming over independent end-to-end paths. IEEE/ACM Trans. Netw. **14**(5), 951–964 (2006)

4. Wischik, D., Raiciu, C., Greenhalgh, A., Handley, M.: Design, implementation and evaluation of congestion control for multipath tcp. In: 8th USENIX NSDI, pp. 1–14 (2011)

5. Barr, S., Paasch, C., Bonaventure, O.: Multipath tcp: from theory to practice. In: Network, pp. 444–457 (2011)

6. Ford, A., Raiciu, C., Handley, M., Bonaventure, O.: Tcp extensions for multipath operation with multiple addresses. In: RFC6824 (2013)

7. Zhou, D., Song, W., Wang, P., Zhuang, W.: Multipath tcp for user cooperation in lte networks. IEEE Netw. **29**(1), 18–24 (2015)

8. Pearce, C., Neohapsis, Zeadally, S.: Ancillary impacts of multipath tcp on current and future network security. IEEE Internet Comput. **19**(5), 58–65 (2015)

9. Secci, S., Pujolle, G., Nguyen, T.M.T., Nguyen, S.C.: Performance-cost trade-off strategic evaluation of multipath tcp communications. IEEE Trans. Netw. Serv. Manag. **11**(2), 250–263 (2014)

10. Li, M., Lukyanenko, A., Tarkoma, S., Cui, Y., Yla-Jaaski, A.: Tolerating path heterogeneity in multipath tcp with bounded receive buffers. Comput. Netw. **64**, 1–14 (2014)

11. Iyengar, J., Amer, P., Stewart, R.: Performance implications of a bounded receive buffer in concurrent multipath transfer. Comput. Commun. **30**(4), 818–829 (2007)

12. Zhuoqun, X., Zhigang, C., Hui, Y., Ming, Z.: An improved mptcp in coded wireless mesh networks. In: IC-BNMT, pp. 795–799 (2009)

13. Ming, L., Andrey, L., Yong, C.: Network coding based multipath tcp. In: IEEE INFOCOM, pp. 25–30 (2012)

14. Jason, C., Calmon, D.P., Flavio, Z., Weifei, P., Giovanni, Z.M.L., Mdard, M.: Multi-path tcp with network coding for mobile devices in heterogeneous networks. In: IEEE 78th Vehicular Technology Conference (2013)

15. Cui, Y., Wang, L., Wang, X., Wang, H., Wang, Y.: Fmtcp: a fountain code-based multipath transmission control protocol. IEEE/ACM Trans. Netw. **23**(2), 465–478 (2015)

16. Ahlswede, R., Cai, N., Li, Y.S.: Network information flow. IEEE Trans. Inform. Theor. **46**(4), 1204–1216 (2000)

17. For, W.K., Leman, K., Eng, H.L., Chew, B.F., Wan, K.W.: A multi-camera collaboration framework for real-time vehicle detection and license plate recognition on highways. In: Intelligent Vehicles Symposium, pp. 192–197. IEEE (2008)

18. VINT-Project, UC-Berkeley, LBL: Ns2 manual (2007). http://www.isi.edu/nsnam/ns/doc/

Towards VM Power Metering: A Decision Tree Method and Evaluations

Chonglin Gu[1], Shuai Shi[1], Pengzhou Shi[1],
Hejiao Huang[1,2(✉)], and Xiaohua Jia[1]

[1] Harbin Institute of Technology Shenzhen Graduate School,
Shenzhen 518055, China
[2] Shenzhen Key Laboratory of Internet Information Collaboration,
Shenzhen 518055, China
hjhuang@hitsz.edu.cn

Abstract. In recent years, a large number of cloud data centers have been built around the world. It brings new challenges in the power management of data centers such as power monitoring, and scheduling for energy saving. All these challenges can be conquered much more easily if we know the power consumption of each virtual machine. Since VM runs at software level, modeling methods have been adopted to measure its power. However, current methods are not accurate enough, especially when multiple VMs are interacting with each other. In this paper, we propose a decision tree method to measure the power consumption of each VM. The advantage of our method is that the collected dataset can be partitioned into easy-modeling pieces by a best selected resource feature with proper value. We also propose a novel but simple method to evaluate the accuracy in a more objective way. We use standard deviation of errors to evaluate the stability of our method. Experiments show that our method can measure the power consumption of VM with high accuracy and stability.

Keywords: VM · Virtual machine · Metering · Power · Cloud computing

1 Introduction

Cloud computing has been developing so fast that the number of data centers is increasing every year. A huge amount of power is consumed by modern servers with enhanced computing capacity. VM (Virtual Machine) power metering is very important in the power saving of data centers. Using the power consumption of each VM, the deployment and consolidation can be made more effectively to save as much power as possible. VM power metering is also significant for fair billing for VM users. IaaS providers such as Amazon charges users according to the running time and configuration of each VM. The problem is that the resource usage may be completely different for VMs of the same type in the same period.

© Springer International Publishing Switzerland 2015
G. Wang et al. (Eds.): ICA3PP 2015, Part I, LNCS 9528, pp. 508–523, 2015.
DOI: 10.1007/978-3-319-27119-4_35

VM power metering is just the solution, since power consumption can directly reflect how much resource is used by the VM.

There are basically three steps for VM power metering: information collection, modeling such as creating decision tree, evaluation and parameters adjusting. The last step is to refine the parameters of this model when error exceeds a certain threshold in real use. The modeling information includes server power and profiling features for resource. To get the information of server power consumption, we can use externally attached PDU (Power Distributed Unit) such as WattsUp series [1] and Scheleifenbauer power meter [2]. We can also use servers like Dell Power Series that integrate power sensors inside to collect information, which can be accessed through APIs. To get resource features for each VM, we can use black box method, which collects profiling features for each VM at host level [3]. For information collection, too frequent sampling will degrade the system performance. Otherwise, the accuracy of the model will decline [4,5]. We empirically select 2 s as our sampling rate. In modeling, most researches in literature adopt linear models, and the only difference is the selection of resource features for modeling. Kansal in [6] selects CPU utilization, LLCM (Last Level Cache Missing), and transfer time of IO. Krishnan in [7] selects instructions retired and LLCH (Last Level Cache Hits). Kim in [8] selects the number of active cores, retired instructions, and number of memory accesses. The number of active cores is taken into account by Bertran in [9]. Chen in [10] selects CPU and hard disk, while Bohra in [11] uses PMCs (Performance Monitoring Counters). As for non-linear models, Versick in [12] proposes a polynomial model with order six, while Xiao in [13] builds his polynomial model using PMCs. Yang in [14] proposes a machine learning method called ε-SVR for VM power metering. Quesnel in [15] proposes a method that fairly divides the idle server power into each VM. The shortcoming of linear model is that the resource features for modeling may not be always in rigorous linear relationship, and there may exist correlation between different resource features. Meanwhile, current nonlinear models are inefficient in real use. They need frequent adjusting parameters for different applications, because they are globally built on the whole dataset. Thus, the complexity may be aggravated by a frequent adjusting of parameters.

In this paper, we solve the above mentioned problems by trying to build a piecewise linear model using tree structure. In theory, piecewise modeling is a simple decision tree with very few leaves. Finally, we found that the decision tree can be built with high prediction accuracy by recursively partitioning the dataset into two subsets using a best selected resource feature with proper value. The commonly used evaluation method in literature always shrinks the real error between estimated and real server power. They use real error divided by server power for evaluation, which makes the relative error seem very small. Therefore, we propose a novel but simple evaluation method that can well reflect the extent of error changes in an objective way. We also propose to use standard deviation of error to evaluate the stability of our model. Experiments show that our method can measure the power consumption of each VM with high accuracy and stability. It also proves that our model is suitable for different applications such as CPU intensive, IO intensive, and distributed applications.

The rest of paper is organized as follows. In Sect. 2, the principle of VM power metering is introduced. In Sect. 3, decision tree method will be introduced to estimate the power consumption of physical server. In Sect. 4, VM power metering and evaluations will be given in detail. Section 5 discusses experiment setup and accuracy evaluation. Finally, Sect. 6 concludes this paper.

2   Principle for VM Power Metering

In this section, we will describe the basic principle for VM power metering. There are basically three steps for VM power metering: (1) information collection: collect modeling information such as physical server power, profiling features of resource for both host and each VM running on it. (2) modeling: build a proper model and train parameters using the collected information. (3) evaluation and adjusting: evaluate the accuracy of our model. When error exceeds a certain threshold, collect information again and update parameters of our model. For ease of understanding, the power consumption of VMs on the server is shown in Fig. 1 [3].

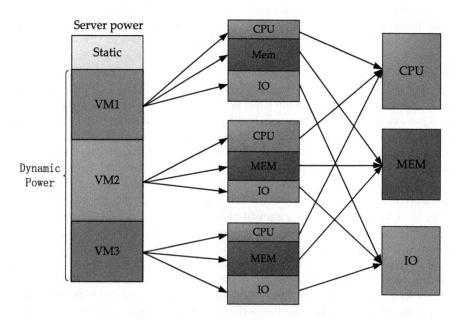

Fig. 1. The power consumption of VMs on the server.

As can be seen, server power is mainly composed of static power and dynamic power. Dynamic power is composed of the power consumption of components like CPU, memory and IO. The power consumption of each component can be divided into each VM according to the proportion used by each VM. Thus, the power consumption of each VM can be estimated easily if there is a model that can accurately estimate server power. In the following part, we will discuss how to build such a server power model, and how to apply this model to estimate the power consumption of each VM.

3 Decision Tree Methods for Physical Server Power

VM power metering is closely related to the power model of physical server. In this section, we will discuss how to estimate the power consumption of server in a piecewise modeling way using decision tree.

Given a dataset composed of server power with resource features, we need to find a model to predict server power for any new inputting resource features. This is a regression problem, and it can be formulated as follows: suppose there are n observations in the training dataset. Each observation has a vector of predictor variables R and a response variable $P_{Measured}$. $R=\{R_{CPU}, R_{memory}, R_{IO}\}$, where R_{CPU}, R_{memory}, and R_{IO} denote CPU utilization, LLCM, and IO throughput, respectively. $P_{Measured}$ is the real server power measured using PDU. Thus, the training samples can be denoted as $D = \{(R_1, P_1), ..., (R_n, P_n)\}$. Our goal is to find a proper model to estimate server power, denoted as $P_{Estimated}$, for any new predictor vector R.

3.1 Linear Model

Linear model is the commonly used model for power metering, and the parameters can be calculated using the ordinary least square method as follows.

Suppose the input vectors are stored in a matrix X, the corresponding values of the vectors can be stored in a vector y. The linear regression parameters is stored in vector w. For any new X_1, the predicted result is $Y_1 = X_1^T w$. The basic idea for linear model is to find a vector $\hat{w}$ so as to minimize the square error, denoted as:

$$min\{(y - Xw^T)^T(y - Xw^T)\} \tag{1}$$

Calculate the partial derivatives for this formula, so we have the best $\hat{w}$:

$$\hat{w} = (X^T X)^{-1} X^T y \tag{2}$$

This global modeling method is not accurate when the resource features for modeling are not in rigor linear relationship. Usually, a dataset in irregular curved shape can be modeled using several linear models in a piecewise way. Inspired by this, we try to improve accuracy by building a piecewise linear model using tree structure.

3.2 Piecewise Linear Model

Piecewise linear model is a modified linear model that partitions the whole training data into several pieces, for each there is a linear model fitted on it. The common criterion for partitioning is to divide the dataset into three disjoint pieces according to low, middle, and high in utilization for a resource feature like CPU, memory and IO, as is mentioned in [16]. It can be denoted as $S1$, $S2$, and $S3$, where $p0 \leq S1 \leq p1$, $p1 < S2 \leq p2$, $p2 < S3 \leq p3$. $p0$, $p1$, $p2$, and $p3$ are endpoints for each piece. Each piece can be further partitioned using another resource feature. For ease of understanding, this model can be illustrated using a decision tree, as shown in Fig. 2.

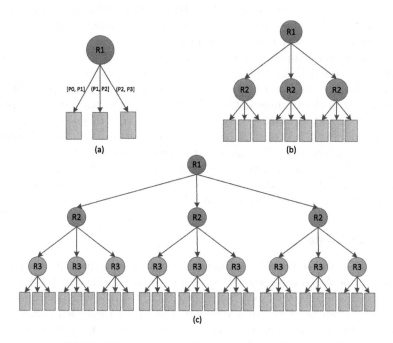

Fig. 2. Piecewise methods with different features.

Piecewise modeling is a decision tree method in theory, and the leaves of this tree are the partitioned subsets. In Fig. 2, it is built as a ternary tree. $R1$ denotes the resource feature for partitioning such as CPU utilization, LLCM, or IO throughput. In (a), it shows the dataset is partitioned into three disjoint pieces according to high, middle and low utilization of $R1$. In partitioning, $p0$ and $p3$ are the minimum and maximum value for R_i in the whole dataset. $p1$ and $p2$ are the $1/3$ and $2/3$ points between $p0$ and $p3$. For each piece, it can be further partitioned into three smaller pieces by using another feature $R2$, as is shown in (b). Likewise, the whole dataset can finally be partitioned into 27 pieces, as is shown in (c).

3.3   Decision Tree Model

There are some problems for the piecewise linear model: (1) the accuracy of a tree does not depend on the depth of tree, so that some partitioning is unnecessary if the accuracy could not be improved. (2) in each partition, the selection of resource features will have great impact on accuracy. In view of this, a decision tree method is proposed to solve the above mentioned problems.

The basic idea is to recursively partition the input dataset into pieces until the accuracy of the tree cannot be improved, or all the features are used up. The key in the creation of a decision tree is partition feature selection. A good feature selection will avoid unnecessary partitions while maximally enhancing the accuracy of decision tree. Here we mainly focus on how to select the best feature in each partition. For each feature, we try to use it to partition the dataset into three parts according to high, middle and low in utilization. The feature with maximum error reduction after partitioning will be selected. After partitioning, this feature will not be used for the subsets partitioned by it. If there is no feature for partitioning, this dataset is added to the tree as a leaf node, and a linear model will be fitted on it.

In prediction, the decision tree is used as a ternary search tree. The input is a vector of resource features. We search the tree by comparing the values of each partitioning resource feature, and finally find a leaf node. The output is calculated by taking the input into the fitted model of this leaf. Note that, some leaves may be generated as null, with no data partitioned to it. Our solution is that when encountering an empty leaf, select a nearest node, and go on searching from it until finding a nonempty leaf.

3.4   Regression Tree Model

There are some problems for the decision tree method mentioned above: (1) a resource feature could not be used for further partition once used. (2) it is blur to partition the dataset into high, middle and low in utilization, and it may cause inaccuracy using such partitioning criterion. In view of this, we propose to use regression tree to solve the problems. The following two algorithms show how the regression tree is created using collected data set as follows:

As can be seen in Algorithm 1, the regression tree is created by recursively partitioning dataset by a best selected resource feature with proper value, denoted as $(feature, value)$. The merit of regression tree is that its partitions rely on the characteristics of dataset rather than artificially setting in ternary tree. Regression tree is a binary tree with more flexibility, and any ternary tree can be represented by it with one more partition. The dataset is added to the tree as a leaf node when there is no proper partitioning feature to be selected any more for this dataset. In our implementation, each leaf node only stores the parameters of linear model fitted on the dataset of this leaf. Function $SplitData$ in this algorithm is to partition the training dataset into two parts by the $value$ of resource $feature$. Function $BestSplitSelection$ returns the best selected $(feature, value)$ pair for partition. If the dataset is not suitable for further partition, the returned $feature$ is null.

The main idea is to find the best $(feature, value)$ pair from the training data for splitting, so that the accuracy can be enhanced after partitioning. In Algorithm 2, there are two stopping conditions for partitioning. One is the minimum

---

Algorithm 1. CreateTree.

Input:
    The training dataset D;
Output:
    A tree T;
1: $(feature, value) = BestSplitSelection(D, s, t)$;
2: **if** $feature = null$ **then**
3:     **return** $value$;
4: **else**
5:     $T.feature = feature$;
6:     $T.value = value$;
7:     $(D_1, D_2) = SplitData(D, feature, value)$;
8:     $T.left = CreateTree(D_1)$;
9:     $T.right = CreateTree(D_2)$;
10: **end if**

---

size of partitioned subset s, which ensures that the leaf is modeled with enough data. The other is the threshold of error reduction t, which means partition happens only when error reduction is obvious and exceeds a certain threshold. The feature will be returned as null when any stopping condition is satisfied, or the accuracy cannot be further improved by partitioning. In this algorithm, the $Error$ function is calculated like this:

$$Error(D) = \sum (P_{Estimated} - P_{Measured})^2 \tag{3}$$

$Error(D)$ is the quadratic sum of the error between real server power and estimated power for each observation in the training data. $MakeLeaf(D)$ returns the parameters of linear model fitted on D. Thus, each leaf node stores modeling parameters. For any new observation, a leaf node can be searched by repeatedly comparing values of the tree. Thus, $P_{Estimated}$ of this observation can be calculated using the linear model obtained by fitting the dataset of this leaf.

Regression tree is one of the most important decision trees in supervised learning. It is a binary tree, created by recursively partitioning data into subsets until violating one of the constraints: the minimum size of node and the threshold of error reduction. Therefore, regression tree is more flexible and superior to ternary decision tree in our experiments, as can be seen in Sect. 4. Since the minimum size of each node is s, the complexity of $CreateTree$ can be obtained easily, which is $O(3nlog_2^{n/s})$.

4   VM Power Metering and Evaluations

4.1   Estimation of VM Power

In the Sect. 3, we have introduced decision tree methods for estimating the power consumption of server. In this part, we will discuss how to apply decision tree for

Algorithm 2. BestSplitSelection.

Input:
    The training dataset D;
    The minimum size of node s;
    Threshold of error reduction t;
Output:
    $(bestfeature, bestvalue)$;
1: $olderr = Error(D)$;
2: $newerr = 0$;
3: $besterr = Infinit$;
4: $bestfeature = nulls$;
5: $bestvalue = nulls$;
6: **for all** $d \in D$ **do**
7:    **for all** $feature \in \{CPU, memory, IO\}$ **do**
8:       $(D_1, D_2) = SplitData(D, feature, d.R_{feature})$;
9:       **if** $size(D_1) < s$ or $size(D_2) < s$ **then**
10:          continue;
11:       **end if**
12:       $newerr = Error(D_1) + Error(D_2)$;
13:       **if** $newerr < besterr$ **then**
14:          $besterr = newerr$;
15:          $bestfeature = feature$;
16:          $bestvalue = d.R_{feature}$;
17:       **end if**
18:    **end for**
19: **end for**
20: **if** $0 < olderr - besterr < t$ **then**
21:    **return** $(null, MakeLeaf(D))$;
22: **end if**
23: **if** $size(D_1) < s$ or $size(D_2) < s$ **then**
24:    **return** $(null, MakeLeaf(D))$;
25: **end if**
26: **return** $(bestfeature, bestvalue)$;

VM power metering. The input parameters s and t are determined by repeatedly trying. For each leaf node in regression tree, a separate linear model is built. In this paper, we collect the resource features from host level using black box method. The resource features are CPU utilization, LLCM (Last Level Cache Missing) and IO throughput, denoted as R_{CPU}, R_{LLCM}, and R_{IO}, respectively. Usually, server power, denoted as P_{Server}, consists of dynamic power and static power, which are denoted as $P_{Dynamic}$ and P_{Static}, respectively. P_{Static} is the basic power of server regardless running VMs or not, and $P_{Dynamic}$ is the dynamically changing power when there are VMs running on it. Thus, we have:

$$P_{Server} = P_{Static} + P_{Dynamic}, \tag{4}$$

$$P_{Dynamic} = \alpha R_{CPU} + \beta R_{LLCM} + \gamma R_{IO} + e, \tag{5}$$

where e is the adjusting bias in model, α, β, and γ are the parameters obtained using linear fitting, respectively. $P_{Dynamic}$ can be obtained when there is no VM or applications running on the server. Based on the parameters of server power model, we calculate the power consumption of each VM like this:

$$P_{VM_i} = \alpha R_{VM_i}^{CPU} + \beta R_{VM_i}^{LLCM} + \gamma R_{VM_i}^{IO} + e_i, \tag{6}$$

where $R_{VM_i}^{CPU}$, $R_{VM_i}^{LLCM}$, $R_{VM_i}^{IO}$ denote CPU, LLCM and IO throughput used by VM_i, respectively, n is the number of VMs on the server, e_i is the bias of each VM i, and it can be calculated as follows:

$$e_i = e*(\alpha R_{VM_i}^{CPU} + \beta R_{VM_i}^{LLCM} + \gamma R_{VM_i}^{IO})/ \sum_{j=1}^{n}(\alpha R_{VM_j}^{CPU} + \beta R_{VM_j}^{LLCM} + \gamma R_{VM_j}^{IO}) \tag{7}$$

4.2   Accuracy Evaluation

VM power is usually calculated through a fair dividing of the power consumption of server. In literature, the commonly used evaluation method for VM power metering is to directly evaluate server power model. It uses real error divided by server power measured using PDU for evaluation. Thus, accuracy using traditional evaluation method can be denoted as follows:

$$Accuracy1 = 1 - \frac{1}{n} \sum \frac{|P_{Estimated} - P_{Measured}|}{P_{Measured}}, \tag{8}$$

When P_{Static} accounts for a large part of server power, the relative error will be very small. For instance, suppose the measured server power is 200 W, in which static power accounts for 160 W. If the error between estimated and real server power is 10 W, then we will get a relative error about 5 %. This is in fact not as accurate as it seems. The real error shrinks after dividing it by such a big denominator in the formula (7). Meanwhile, other papers give real error within $1\sim 2$ W to show the goodness of their result. However, it is indeed a very big error if $P_{Dynamic}$ is just $3\sim 4$ W.

In view of these problems, we propose a novel but simple evaluation method as follows:

$$Accuracy2 = 1 - \frac{1}{n} \sum \frac{|P_{Estimated} - P_{Measured}|}{P_{Dynamic}} \tag{9}$$

The advantage of our evaluation is that it reflects the modeling errors against dynamic power, not using a big denominator. Therefore, our evaluation method is more objective in real use.

We also use stability to make evaluation, it reflects the fluctuation of errors. The lower, the better. In fact, users always hope our regression tree can behave stably, and the errors do not always change suddenly. Therefore, we define stability using standard deviation of real errors, denoted as Err. So we have:

$$E_{Stability} = \delta(Err) \tag{10}$$

5   Experiments

5.1   Experiments Setup

The configuration of server in our experiment is Lenovo T350 with CPU of 4 cores and 8GB memory. There are three VMs running on the host, each is configured with 2GB memory, and 2 vCPUs, which is implemented by virtualization to make one physical CPU be shared by many VMs by allocating different CPU time pieces to each VM. We use KVM as virtualization for our experiment, due to its light-weighted merit. Each VM will run as a separate process in the system, so we use tools like *perf*, *sysstat*, and *iostat* to collect profiling information. The power meter in this experiment is an externally attached PDU called HOPI 9800 that can be accessed through USB in real time. To evaluate our method, we choose benchmarks including CPU intensive, IO intensive, and distributed Hadoop benchmarks, as listed in Table 1. For UnixBench, there are 8 different testing instances. The CPU intensive dataset consists of the observations from these 8 instances running one after another, such that the samplings is sufficient for modeling in CPU intensive scenario. In total, we have 5 benchmarks, CPU intensive, IO intensive, and 3 Hadoop distributed benchmarks. To be objective, all experiment results are based on 100-fold crossing validation.

5.2   Result Analysis

In this paper, we first try modeling using linear regression method, and then try improving linear model by piecewise linear method. We use CPU, LLCM and IO to build piecewise linear modeling in ternary tree, respectively. We found piecewise modeling indeed works.

In Fig. 3, it shows real errors of the piecewise linear methods on different benchmarks, where Linear, CPU, LLCM, IO, and DTree denote linear method, piecewise linear method using CPU, LLCM, IO, and decision tree method. It can be seen that piecewise linear model using LLCM as partitioning resource feature is more accurate than other methods. While other features such as CPU utilization and IO throughput do not work well after partitioning into three pieces.

Table 1. Benchmarks

Benchmarks	Test instances	Descriptions
UnixBench	dhry2 whets	CPU intensive tests
	hanoi int	
	short long	
	float double	
IOZone	read write	IO intensive tests
Hadoop	pi sort	Distributed system tests
	randomwriter	

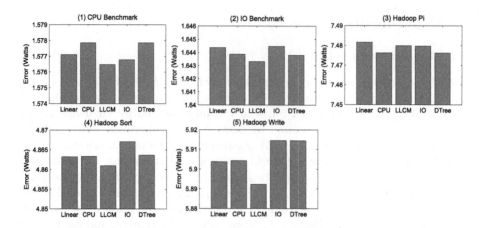

Fig. 3. Real errors of different piecewise linear methods on different benchmarks.

Inspired by this, we tried to build a more complex piecewise linear model using decision tree, hoping for enhancement in accuracy. Unfortunately, our decision tree method is not so accurate as expected, even bringing greater errors for some cases. One reason is that there are unnecessary partitions that bring very little enhancement in accuracy, even causing overfitting. Another reason is that the partitioning criterion into three pieces is too subjective rather than based on the characteristics of dataset. Therefore, we propose to use regression tree to conquer the shortcomings mentioned above. Since piecewise linear method using LLCM is a ternary tree method with highest accuracy, we use it on behalf of ternary tree methods to make comparison in the following part.

In our regression tree, each leaf node has a separate set of parameters α, β, γ, which are fitted using linear model on the data set of this leaf node. For error threshold t, we set it to be 5. Note that the accuracy will be affected if this value is too large, and it is inefficient for creating tree if it is too small, which needs more recursions in partitioning. For minimum partitioned size s, we have tried different values. In our experiment, the best parameter s for the five benchmarks are 185, 165, 15, 205, 75, respectively. Large value means the tree has many big leaf nodes, so that the partitioning times is limited and the tree is not high. It also means the relationship between resource features and power is a curve with very few separate linear pieces. For s with small value like 15, many more linear pieces are generated, which reflects the pattern of relationship varying frequently in ranges of resource feature values.

In Fig. 4, it shows comparisons of real errors for linear method, piecewise linear method using LLCM, and regression tree method (RegTree) on different benchmarks. It can be found that our regression tree has the smallest error in comparison, and it performs similarly to other methods on benchmark Hadoop Write. We also found that errors for distributed Hadoop benchmarks are higher than CPU intensive and IO intensive benchmarks, because complex virtualization is involved for the interactions of VMs. In spite of this, our regression tree

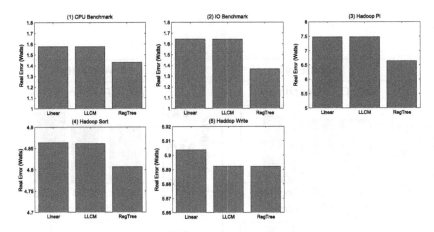

Fig. 4. Comparisons of real errors on different benchmarks.

method is still the most accurate in the power estimation on different benchmarks. Our regression tree avoids artificial partitioning, and it is modeled based on collected data set. The relationship between resource features and power is usually more of a curve rather than a rigorous line. Therefore, our regression tree using piecewise modeling idea is more accurate, and its binary tree structure is more flexible in real use.

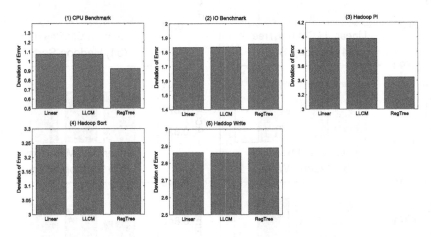

Fig. 5. Comparisons of error deviations on different benchmarks.

Figure 5 shows comparisons of standard deviations of error for linear method, piecewise linear method using LLCM, and regression tree method on different benchmarks. Note that standard deviation of error reflects the stability of method. From Fig. 5, it can be seen that our regression tree method is the most

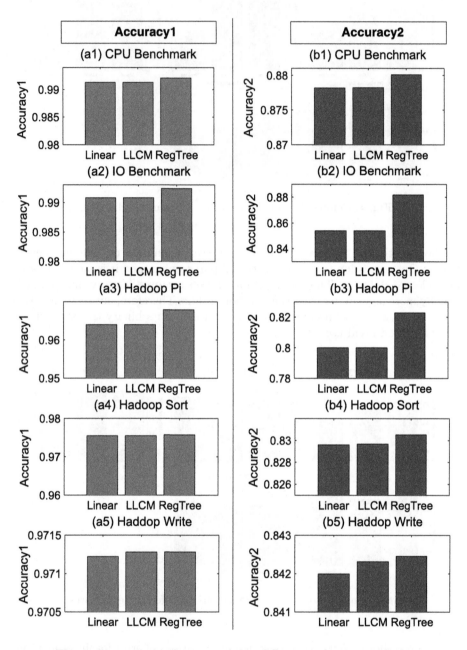

Fig. 6. Comparisons of accuracy using different evaluation methods.

stable among the three methods in general, although its deviation is slightly higher on benchmarks such as IO, Hadoop Sort and Write.

Figure 6 shows comparisons of accuracy using different evaluation methods. The left group (**Accuracy1**) uses traditional evaluation, and it shows that our regression tree method has an accuracy about 98 % on average, superior to other methods. However, it uses a big denominator P_{static} in the formula, such that the accuracy of different methods in comparison are so similar. Our proposed evaluation method can well solve this problem. As can be seen in the right group (**Accuracy2**), the accuracy of different methods can be distinguished more easily using our proposed evaluation. For example, (b2) and (b3) using our proposed evaluation method shows our regression tree method is superior to others in a much more distinguished way than that in (a2) and (a3). The main reason is that our evaluation formula does not use big denominator to weaken the extent of errors. It reflects the extent of errors against dynamic power very well, avoiding error shrinking in literature.

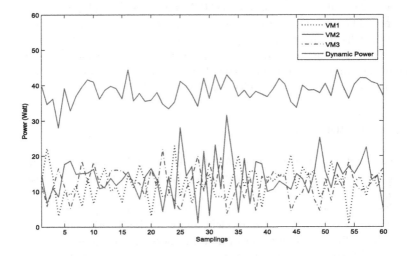

Fig. 7. The power consumption of VMs and server.

Figure 7 is an example showing the power consumption of each VM and server within 60 samplings. The whole server power is composed of the power consumption of each VM in real energy accounting, so we have:

$$P_{Server} = P_{VM1} + P_{VM2} + P_{VM3} \tag{11}$$

Based on the estimated power consumption, we can calculate the energy consumed by each VM and server as follows:

$$W = \sum_{i=1}^{n}(P_i * \Delta(t_i)), \tag{12}$$

where W denotes total energy consumed during n samplings, and its unit is **WH** (Watts Hour), $\Delta(t_i)$ denotes the sampling interval. P_i is the power consumption for the ith sampling interval. Similarly, we can calculate the electricity cost, denoted as $Cost$, for each VM and server as follows:

$$Cost = \sum_{i=1}^{n}(P_i * \Delta(t_i) * Pr_i), \tag{13}$$

where Pr_i is the electricity price during ith sampling interval.

For ease of understanding, here is an example to calculate energy consumption and electricity cost for each VM and its host. Suppose the price is 20 \$/MWH during our 60 samplings, and the samping interval is 2 s. Based on the estimated power in Fig. 7 during the period of 2 min, the energy consumption are 0.40 WH, 0.46 WH, 0.41 WH for each VM, and the server power is 6.8097 WH, in which static power accounts for a large part. Suppose all the VMs run in this pattern for an hour. Thus, we can roughly estimate the electricity expenditure for each VM are 0.024 cents, 0.028 cents, and 0.025 cents, respectively. The server costs 0.41 cents. The cheapest price for a EC2 VM with low configuration will cost 1.3 cents per hour, much more expensive than that of our server, because costs such as management, and cooling expenditure are all considered by Amazon. Through our analysis, we hope future IaaS will provide more fair charging for users based on energy or electricity cost of each VM.

6   Conclusion

VM power metering is very important for the power management of data centers. In this paper, we propose a regression tree method to estimate the power consumption of each VM. It recursively partition the dataset by a best selected feature and proper value using binary tree structure. It proved to be a perfect solution in piecewise linear models, more relying on the characteristics of dataset. In addition, a significant evaluation method is proposed, which reflects the extent of error in a more objective way. We also propose to use standard deviation of errors to evaluate stability of our method. Experiments show our regression tree can measure the power consumption of both VM and server with high accuracy and stability. It also proved that our evaluation method is currently the most objective as far as we know. For future work, one interesting direction is fair billing based on energy consumed by each VM. Another direction is how to deploy and schedule VMs for green data centers based on dynamic changing VM power and fluctuating electricity prices.

Acknowledgments. This work was financially supported by National Natural Science Foundation of China with Grant No. 11371004, and Shenzhen Strategic Emerging Industries Program with Grants No. ZDSY20120613125016389, No. JCYJ2012061315-1201451, No. JCYJ20130329153215152, and KQCX20150326141251370.

References

1. WattsUp Meter. https://www.wattsupmeters.com/secure/index.php. Accessed 29 May 2014
2. Public APIs of Schleifenbauer PDU. http://sdc.sourceforge.net/index.php. Accessed 29 May 2014
3. Gu, C., Huang, H., Jia, X.: Power metering for virtual machine in cloud computing-challenges and opportunities. IEEE Access **2**, 1106–1116 (2014)
4. McCullough, J.C., Agarwal, Y., Chandrashekar, J., Kuppuswamy, S., Snoeren, A.C., Gupta, R.K.: Evaluating the effectiveness of model-based power characterization. In: USENIX Annual Technical Conference (2011)
5. Yang, H., Zhao, Q., Luan, Z., Qian, D.: iMeter: an integrated VM power model based on performance profiling. Future Gener. Comput. Syst. **36**, 267–286 (2013)
6. Kansal, A., Zhao, F., Liu, J., Kothari, N., Bhattacharya, A.A.: Virtual machine power metering and provisioning. In: Proceedings of the 1st ACM Symposium on Cloud Computing, pp. 39–50. ACM (2010)
7. Krishnan, B., Amur, H., Gavrilovska, A., Schwan, K.: VM power metering: feasibility and challenges. ACM SIGMETRICS Perform. Eval. Revi. **38**(3), 56–60 (2011)
8. Kim, N., Cho, J., Seo, E.: Energy-based accounting and scheduling of virtual machines in a cloud system. In: 2011 IEEE/ACM International Conference on Green Computing and Communications (GreenCom), pp. 176–181. IEEE (2011)
9. Bertran, R., Becerra, Y., Carrera, D., Beltran, V., Gonzàlez, M., Martorell, X., Navarro, N., Torres, J., Ayguadé, E.: Energy accounting for shared virtualized environments under DVFS using pmc-based power models. Future Gener. Comput. Syst. **28**(2), 457–468 (2012)
10. Chen, Q., Grosso, P., van der Veldt, K., de Laat, C., Hofman, R., Bal, H.: Profiling energy consumption of VMs for green cloud computing. In: 2011 IEEE Ninth International Conference on Dependable, Autonomic and Secure Computing (DASC), pp. 768–775. IEEE (2011)
11. Bohra, A.E., Chaudhary, V.: VMeter: Power modelling for virtualized clouds. In: 2010 IEEE International Symposium on Parallel & Distributed Processing, Workshops and Phd Forum (IPDPSW), pp. 1–8. IEEE (2010)
12. Versick, D., Waßmann, I., Tavangarian, D.: Power consumption estimation of CPU and peripheral components in virtual machines. ACM SIGAPP Appl. Comput. Rev. **13**(3), 17–25 (2013)
13. Xiao, P., Hu, Z., Liu, D., Yan, G., Qu, X.: Virtual machine power measuring technique with bounded error in cloud environments. J. Netw. Comput. Appl. **36**(2), 818–828 (2013)
14. Yang, H., Zhao, Q., Luan, Z., Qian, D.: Uvmpm: A unitary approach for VM power metering based on performance profiling. In: 2012 41st International Conference on Parallel Processing Workshops (ICPPW), pp. 614–615, IEEE (2012)
15. Quesnel, F., Mehta, H.K., Menaud, J.M.: Estimating the power consumption of an idle virtual machine. In: IEEE International Conference on Green Computing and Communications (GreenCom), 2013 IEEE and Internet of Things (iThings/CPSCom), and IEEE Cyber, Physical and Social Computing, pp. 268–275. IEEE (2013)
16. Li, Y., Wang, Y., Yin, B., Guan, L.: An online power metering model for cloud environment. In: 2012 11th IEEE International Symposium on Network Computing and Applications (NCA), pp. 175–180. IEEE (2012)

A Dynamic State Estimation of Power System Harmonics Using Distributed Related Kalman Filter

Wei Sun[1], Chanjuan Zhao[1(✉)], Jianping Wang[1], Chenghui Zhu[1], Daoming Mu[1], Liangfeng Chen[2], Jie Li[3], and Qiyue Li[1]

[1] School of Electrical Engineering and Automation, Hefei University of Technology, Hefei 230009, China
wsun@hfut.edu.cn, jojo20061864@126.com
[2] Hefei Institutes of Physical Science, Chinese Academy of Sciences, Hefei 230000, China
[3] School of Computer and Information, Hefei University of Technology, Hefei 230009, China

Abstract. In order to improve the performance of measuring the harmonic state, a distributed related Kalman filter method for power system dynamic harmonic state estimation is presented. Firstly, the neighbor correlation coefficient is introduced into the distributed Kalman filtering. And then, a method for calculating the neighbor node fusion variables which suitable for power harmonic measurements is given based on the distributed related Kalman filter. Lastly, further distributed fusion processing among the neighbor nodes of estimated values is proposed. The algorithm is simulated on IEEE-14 bus power system. The results show that the proposed algorithm has less communication cost, better anti-disturbance performance, and more accurate estimation in comparison to the conventional Kalman filtering.

Keywords: Harmonic state estimation · Distributed related kalman filter · Correlation coefficient · IEEE-14 bus power system · Anti-disturbance

1 Introduction

In recent decades, with the development of power electronic technology, widely used nonlinear loads have led to a corresponding increase in harmonic levels in power systems worldwide. The existence of harmonics in power systems could cause serious problems such as voltage distortion, increased losses and heating, and malfunction of protective equipment [1]. Hence, accurate estimation of the power system harmonic levels is essential for reducing harmonics and improving the power quality.

Power system harmonic state estimation can be categorized into static estimation and dynamic estimation. Static estimation usually needs to collect a certain number of measured data and then calculates the estimated value of harmonics by statistical methods, such as the weighted least squares estimation algorithm [2] and the singular value decomposition algorithm [3]. However, due to the continuity of harmonic injection, harmonic levels in the power system are dynamic. Thus, static estimation inherits the constraints of estimated speed and accuracy because of the lagged calculation. On the other hand, dynamic estimation method can not only estimate the current harmonic

© Springer International Publishing Switzerland 2015
G. Wang et al. (Eds.): ICA3PP 2015, Part I, LNCS 9528, pp. 524–536, 2015.
DOI: 10.1007/978-3-319-27119-4_36

states but also predict the next time status by using the current measurements and the previous status information. Therefore, the dynamic estimation method is more suitable for harmonic state estimation of power gird.

In order to estimate harmonic levels, a lot of recently studies of dynamic estimation have been presented, e.g. wavelet transform algorithm [4], artificial neural network algorithm [5] and Kalman filter algorithm [6] etc. In which, the Kalman filter based method attracts many attentions. H. M. Beides and G. T. Heydt firstly applied the Kalman filter to the harmonic estimation problem in [6]. They defined the harmonic voltage magnitude and phase angle of the power system as state variables, and the harmonic apparent power and some bus voltage harmonics as measured variables. However, this would lead to the mistake of estimation results. Considering the uncertainty of the system noise covariance matrix Q in the large time varying system, Kent K. C. Yu et al. focused on an adaptive Kalman filter method for dynamic harmonic state estimation. They utilized statistical rules to switch between the two basic Q models for steady-state and transient estimation [7]. Based on different models and different covariance matrices, various improved Kalman filter algorithms have been applied to power system harmonic state estimation in [8–11].

In theory, these adaptive Kalman filter algorithms can achieve good performance by minimizing the square of the expected error between the values of the actual measurements and estimated system states. In practice, all of these algorithms use a centralized estimate method that requires a communication network connecting all the measuring points in power grid. This solution needs high communication bandwidth and short latency, and could cause serious impact on estimation results when data loss or sink node failure occurs. There are still many deficiencies in the application of practice.

In this paper, according to the characteristics of the power system harmonic voltage state, the concept of neighbor correlation coefficient ξ_{ij} is introduced to represent the degree of correlation between node i and neighbor node j. And then, a method to calculate the neighbor node fusion variables (the fused inverse-covariance matrices and the fused sensor data) which are suitable for power harmonic measurements is proposed. To simplify the calculations, we reconstruct the iterative process of the algorithm. Moreover, further distributed fusion processing among the neighbor nodes of estimated values is utilized to ensure the unanimous correlation of the estimation results between neighbors. Thus a distributed related Kalman filter algorithm is presented to power system harmonic estimation. The simulation results show that the proposed algorithm not only can improve the accuracy of the estimated values, but also have little communication cost and better anti-disturbance performance.

2　System Modeling

In the noise-free case, power system voltage sampling signal model with n harmonics can be expressed as the Eq. (1):

$$Z_k = \sum_{r=1}^{n} A_k^r \cos(r\omega k\Delta t + \theta_k^r) \; k = 0, 1, 2 \dots \tag{1}$$

where r is the harmonic order; k is the time sequence; ω represents the fundamental frequency; Δt is the two adjacent time interval; A_k^r refers to the amplitude of harmonic r at time k; θ_k^r refers to the phase angle of harmonic r at time k; There are a total of n harmonic levels.

In the approach of dynamic state estimation, the following assumptions of power system voltage sampling signal model have been used [6]:

1. In normal operation, the power system is under the quasi-static state.
2. The power system is linear.
3. All R, L, C components are frequency independent, and each harmonic level is independent.

Then the power system harmonic sampling signal model at the harmonic level r can be described by the following equation:

$$Z^r(k) = A^r(k)\cos(rwk\Delta t + \theta^r(k)) = A^r(k)\cos\theta^r(k)\cos rwk\Delta t - A^r(k)\sin\theta^r(k)\sin rwk\Delta t \tag{2}$$

where, $X^r(k) = \begin{bmatrix} X_1^r(k) \\ X_2^r(k) \end{bmatrix} = \begin{bmatrix} A^r(k)\cos\theta^r(k) \\ A^r(k)\sin\theta^r(k) \end{bmatrix}$ is the state vector of harmonic r. $X_1^r(k)$ represents the in-phase component while $X_2^r(k)$ represents the quadrature component of harmonic r with respect to its respective rotating reference. The state equation at the harmonic level r contaminated with noise is as follows:

$$X^r(k+1) = F(k, X^r(k)) + W^r(k) \tag{3}$$

where $F(k, X^r(k))$ is the state transition function.

When the power system is in the quasi-static state, harmonic voltage state $X(k)$ is an stationary random process. Thus, the amplitude of state variable oscillations is small. This model infers that the state at time $k+1$ will be the same at time k [12]. The state equation at any harmonic order can be expressed as follows:

$$X(k+1) = X(k) + W(k) \tag{4}$$

where $W(k)$ is model error, and it can be considered as Gaussian noise with zero mean [11].

System noise covariance matrix is given by the Eq. (5):

$$Q(k) = E(W(k)W^T(k)) \tag{5}$$

Since the power system state variables are orthogonal, $Q(k)$ is positive definite diagonal matrix. It can be obtained by off-line calculations based on historical data [13].

We can get the system measurement equation contaminated with noise from Eq. (2):

$$Z^r(k) = H^r(k)X^r(k) + V^r(k) \tag{6}$$

where the measurement vector of harmonic r at time k is $Z^r(k)$. $V^r(k)$ is measurement error that can be considered as Gaussian noise with zero mean [11]. $H^r(k)$ is the output matrix. It can be written as:

$$H^r(k) = [\cos(r\omega k \Delta t) \quad -\sin(r\omega k \Delta t)] \tag{7}$$

$H^r(k)$ is time-varying variable. It indicates the correlations between the measured variables and the state variables of the system without noise. System measurement covariance matrix is expressed as follows:

$$R(k) = E(V^r(k)V^r(k)^T) \tag{8}$$

$R(k)$ is generally considered to be a positive definite diagonal matrix.

By Eqs. (4) and (6), we can get the power system state equation and measurement equation at harmonic level r contaminated with noise as follows:

$$\begin{cases} X^r(k+1) = X^r(k) + W^r(k) \\ Z^r(k) = H^r(k)X^r(k) + V^r(k) \end{cases} \tag{9}$$

Power system harmonic amplitude $A(k)$ and phase angle $\theta(k)$ at time k can be expressed by the following equation:

$$\begin{cases} A(k) = \sqrt{[X_1(k)]^2 + [X_2(k)]^2} \\ \theta(k) = \arctan \frac{X_2(k)}{X_1(k)} \end{cases} \tag{10}$$

3   Distributed Related Kalman Filter

3.1   Kalman Filter

Considering that the power system state equation and measurement equation at any harmonic order is as follows:

$$\begin{cases} X(k+1) = A(k)X(k) + W(k) \\ Z(k) = C(k)X(k) + V(k) \end{cases} \tag{11}$$

References [6–9] adopted conventional Kalman Filter method to estimate power system dynamic harmonic state. The sequential recursive computation steps for the harmonic estimate by the Kalman filter are expressed as (12) [14].

$$\begin{cases} \bar{X}(k/k-1) = A(k-1)\hat{X}(k-1/k-1) \\ P(k/k-1) = A(k-1)P(k-1/k-1)A^T(k-1) + Q(k-1) \\ G(k) = P(k/k-1)C^T(k)(C(k)P(k/k-1)C^T(k) + R(k))^{-1} \\ \hat{X}(k/k) = \bar{X}(k/k-1) + G(k)(Z(k) - C(k)\bar{X}(k/k-1)) \\ P(k/k) = (I - G(k)C(k))P(k/k-1) \end{cases} \tag{12}$$

where $\bar{X}(k/k-1)$ is the state predictive value at time $k-1$; $\hat{X}(k/k)$ is the state estimated value at time k; $G(k)$ is the Kalman filter gain matrix; $P(k/k)$ represents estimate error covariance matrix; $P(k/k-1)$ refers to the estimate forecast error covariance matrix;

$Q(k)$ is the system noise covariance matrix and $R(k)$ is the system measurement covariance matrix; The initial states are set to $P(0/-1) = P(0)$ and $\bar{X}(0/-1) = X(0)$.

Although the Kalman filter algorithm can be well functioned in the power system harmonic voltage state estimation, this approach uses a centralized estimate method that requires a communication network connecting all the measuring points. This needs high communication bandwidth and short communication latency, and is not scalable for power grid which has large number of data acquisition nodes. In addition, when measurement data is lost at the time of calculating and transmitting, it will lead to serious errors on estimation results, which also indicates that the proposed algorithm shows poor anti-disturbance performance [6–8]. Hence, there still have many deficiencies of using Kalman filter algorithm in the application of practices. In order to solve those problems, we will introduce an improved distributed related Kalman filter in the following subsection.

3.2   Distributed Related Kalman Filter

Considering the correlations between the neighbor states, distributed Kalman filter proposes a distributed state estimation algorithm by exchanging measurements and estimates among neighboring nodes. And this algorithm reduces the communication cost comparing to the conventional Kalman filter algorithm. The distributed computing approach has better applicability [15, 16]. However distributed Kalman filter algorithm can only use multiple sensors to estimate the same target state. Since each bus power system harmonic voltage is not exactly the same, we need to use multiple sensor nodes to estimate multi-bus harmonic voltage state cooperatively.

Actually, power system harmonics at neighbor buses are correlated to some extent. As a consequence, we propose an adaptive distributed Kalman filter algorithm for dynamic harmonic state estimation. Consider a sub-network in power system consisting of n nodes interconnected as a network node system. Each bus is defined as a node, all the other buses directly connected to current bus is its neighbor nodes. If the system state equation and measurement equation are shown as Eq. (11), and let $Q(k) = E(W(k)W^T(k))$ and $R(k) = E(V(k)V^T(k))$, then the sequential recursive computation steps for the harmonic estimation by the information Kalman filter are expressed as (13) [17].

$$\begin{cases} \bar{X}(k/k-1) = A(k-1)\hat{X}(k-1/k-1) \\ P(k/k-1) = A(k-1)P(k-1/k-1)A^T(k-1) + Q(k-1) \\ G(k) = P(k/k)C^T(k)R^{-1}(k) \\ \hat{X}(k/k) = \bar{X}(k/k-1) + G(k)(Z(k) - C(k)\bar{X}(k/k-1)) \\ P(k/k) = (P^{-1}(k/k-1) + C^T(k)R^{-1}(k)C(k))^{-1} \end{cases} \tag{13}$$

In the network node system, we assume the neighbor nodes set of any node i as N_i $(J_i = N_i \cup \{i\})$, and the number of neighbor nodes of node i is m. In the general case, the power system harmonic measurement equation of node i can be written as (14).

$$Z_i(k) = C_i(k)X_i(k) + V_i(k) \tag{14}$$

Local Kalman filter results of node i can be obtained by Eq. (12):

$$\hat{X}_i(k/k) = \bar{X}_i(k/k - 1) + G_i(k)(Z_i(k) - C_i(k)\bar{X}_i(k/k - 1))$$
$$= \bar{X}_i(k/k - 1) + P_i(k/k)C_i^T(k)R_i^{-1}(k)(Z_i(k) - C_i(k)\bar{X}_i(k/k - 1)) \qquad (15)$$

Make $u_i(k) = C_i^T(k)R_i^{-1}(k)Z_i(k)$, $U_i(k) = C_i^T(k)R_i^{-1}(k)C_i(k)$, then $P_i(k/k)$ can be simplified as:

$$P_i(k/k) = (P_i^{-1}(k/k - 1) + C_i^T(k)R_i^{-1}(k)C_i(k))^{-1} = (P_i^{-1}(k/k - 1) + U_i(k))^{-1} \qquad (16)$$

The proposed local Kalman filter state estimation results are not global optimum. Actually, power system harmonic injections at neighbor buses are correlated to some extent. As a consequence, we introduce the neighbor correlation coefficient ξ_{ij} to represent the degree of correlation between node i and its neighbor node j. And then, a method to calculate the neighbor node fusion variables (the fused inverse-covariance matrices and the fused sensor data) which is suitable for power harmonic measurements is proposed. Namely the fused sensor data:

$$y_i'(k) = \frac{1}{m + 1}(\sum_{j \in N_i} \xi_{ij}u_j(k) + u_i(k)) \qquad (17)$$

and the fused inverse-covariance matrices:

$$S_i'(k) = \frac{1}{m + 1}\sum_{j \in J_i} U_j(k) \qquad (18)$$

According to the fusion consistency, we can use $y_i'(k)$, $S_i'(k)$ to replace $u_i(k)$ and $U_i(k)$ into the Eq. (15):

$$\hat{X}_i(k/k) = \bar{X}_i(k/k - 1) + P_i(k/k)(y_i'(k) - S_i'(k)\bar{X}_i(k/k - 1)) \qquad (19)$$

And the estimate error covariance matrix:

$$P_i(k/k) = (P_i^{-1}(k/k - 1) + S_i'(k))^{-1} \qquad (20)$$

To simplify the calculations, we reconstruct the original iterative process. Now we make the following substitutions:

$$y_i(k) = (m + 1)y_i'(k); S_i(k) = (m + 1)S_i'(k) \circ$$

Let $M_i(k) = \frac{1}{(m+1)}P_i(k/k) = ((m + 1)P_i^{-1}(k + 1/k) + S_i(k + 1))^{-1}$, then we can get:

$$\hat{X}_i(k + 1) = \bar{X}_i(k + 1/k) + M_i(k + 1)(y_i(k + 1) - S_i(k + 1)\bar{X}_i(k + 1/k)) \qquad (21)$$

$$P_i'(k + 1/k) = \frac{1}{m + 1}P_i(k + 1/k) = A(k)M_i(k)A^T(k) + Q(k) \qquad (22)$$

For the purpose of ensuring the unanimous correlation of the estimation results among neighbors, we use multiple sensor nodes to estimate multi-bus harmonic voltage state cooperatively. Considering the proposed reconstruction of the iterative process, we introduce ε as the estimate difference coefficient. It can be recognized as a correction coefficient among neighbors. By the fact that power system harmonic injections at neighbor buses are correlated to some extent and harmonic voltages of each bus are not exactly the same, we introduce correction term $\varepsilon M_i(k+1) \sum_{j \in N_i} (\xi_{ij} \bar{X}_j(k+1/k) - \bar{X}_i(k+1/k))$ to the harmonic estimated results. By adding the difference between the node i estimates and the neighbor j related estimates to the estimation results, we can ensure the unanimous correlation of the estimation results among neighbors. The improved estimation result is as follows:

$$\hat{X}_i(k+1) = \bar{X}_i(k+1/k) + M_i(k+1)(y_i(k+1) - S_i(k+1)\bar{X}_i(k+1/k))$$
$$+\varepsilon M_i(k+1) \sum_{j \in N_i} (\xi_{ij} \bar{X}_j(k+1/k) - \bar{X}_i(k+1/k)) \quad (23)$$

Thus, the above analysis results can be summarized as follows:

$$u_i = C_i^T R_i^{-1} Z_i, \ \forall i \in J_i, \ y_i = \sum_{j \in N_i} \xi_{ij} u_j + u_i \quad (24)$$

$$U_i = C_i^T R_i^{-1} C_i, \ \forall i \in J_i, \ S_i = \sum_{j \in J_i} U_j \quad (25)$$

The iterative equations of Distributed related Kalman filter algorithm are represented as follows:

$$M_i(k+1) = (P_i'^{-1}(k+1/k) + S_i(k+1))^{-1} \quad (26)$$

$$\hat{X}_i(k+1) = \bar{X}_i(k+1/k) + M_i(k+1)(y_i(k+1) - S_i(k+1)\bar{X}_i(k+1/k))$$
$$+ \varepsilon M_i(k+1) \sum_{j \in N_i} (\xi_{ij} \bar{X}_j(k+1/k) - \bar{X}_i(k+1/k)) \quad (27)$$

$$P_i'(k+1/k) = A(k)M_i(k)A^T(k) + Q(k) \quad (28)$$

$$\bar{X}_i(k+1/k) = A(k)\hat{X}_i(k) \quad (29)$$

4   Simulation Test

4.1   Simulation Model

In order to demonstrate the distributed related Kalman filter algorithm, this paper selects IEEE-14 bus system simulating on Matlab2012b as the scenario [13]. The simulation system topology is shown in Fig. 1. For illustrative purposes, the circuit model is equivalent to type Π model; load model is equivalent to three-phase RLC circuit model; generators are replaced by three-phase synchronous motor models. In this case, the rated power of the generator is 100 MVA, the rated voltage is 230 kV, and the rated frequency is 50 HZ. The simulation system includes a harmonic source at bus 3. In practice, three-phase power system is mainly affected by the odd harmonics, and odd harmonics cause greater harm than the even one. Actually many elements of the power system devices mainly produce 5th, 7th etc. odd harmonics. For example, three-phase rectifier loads mainly generate $6n \pm 1$ harmonics, such as 5th, 7th, 11th, 13th, 17th, and 19th etc. Frequency converter mainly produce 5th, 7th harmonics when it is at work [1, 18]. Therefore, we make the harmonic source at bus 3 mainly produce 5th, 7th harmonics, where the 5th harmonic current amplitude is approximately 100A, 7th harmonic current amplitude is approximately 60A. The specific parameters of the system are listed in [13].

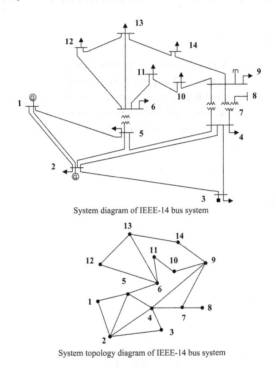

System diagram of IEEE-14 bus system

System topology diagram of IEEE-14 bus system

Fig. 1. System diagram and system topology diagram of IEEE-14 bus system.

Based on the preceding text, we select bus line voltage as the measured variable, and apply the Kalman filter method proposed by literature [6–9] and the distributed related Kalman filter method to estimate the power system harmonic state. Here we make a dynamic estimation of the 5th harmonic voltage at bus 12. The system state equation and measurement equation are expressed as $X(k + 1) = A(k)X(k) + W(k)$, and $Z(k) = C(k)X(k) + V(k)$. According to the above analysis, it can be obtained that

$A(k) = I, C(0) = [1\ 0]$, and the initial states are $P(0) = 50I, X(0) = Z(0)$. While the power system is under the quasi-static state [6], the measurement covariance matrix R and system covariance matrix Q are usually considered as constant matrix in the current literature about power system harmonic state estimation using Kalman filter [13]. Based on historical statistics, Q is set to unit matrix I and R is set to 1 in this paper. The simulation topology diagram of IEEE-14 bus system is shown in Fig. 1. From such figure, we observe that the neighbors of bus 12 (node 12) are bus 6(node 6) and bus 13(node 13). According to the statistics feature we take $\xi_{12-6} = 0.9$, $\xi_{12-13} = 0.98$, $\varepsilon = 0.25_{\circ}$.

As the actual power system harmonic injection is dynamic, this paper makes loads at buses 4, 5, 10, 13 switching to simulate the dynamic process of the power system. The simulation time is set to 6 s. The sampling frequency is set to 10 kHz. The data collected are used to estimate harmonic state. The estimation results are output every 0.06 s and there are totally 100 sets of data are collected for the purpose of comparison.

4.2 Data Analysis

4.2.1 Simulation Data Analysis in Normal Situation

In order to verify the superiority of the proposed algorithm, the conventional Kalman filter and the distributed related Kalman filter are used to estimate harmonics. Two error indexes namely relative tolerance and root-mean-square error are presented. Figure 2 and Fig. 3 show the harmonic voltage estimation results at bus 12 using the Eq. (12) and the Eqs. (26)–(29).

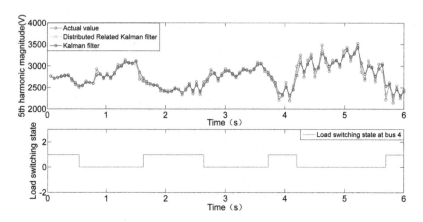

Fig. 2. Fifth harmonic voltage magnitude at bus 12 (*actual and estimated*) and load switching state at bus 4.

Figure 2 shows the 5th harmonic voltage estimation results at bus 12 using the conventional Kalman filter and the distributed related Kalman filter. It is obvious that both Kalman and distributed Kalman methods can track dynamic harmonics well in the power system. The lower part of Fig. 2 describes the load switching condition at bus 4, in which high-level represents load is incorporated in the simulation power systems,

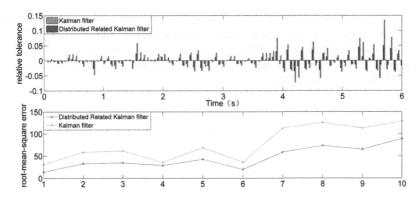

Fig. 3. Relative tolerance and root-mean-square error of fifth harmonic voltage magnitude estimation values at bus 12.

low-level represents load is disconnected from the grid. From Fig. 2, we can find out that the load switching has a significant impact on the power system harmonic voltage amplitude. So we can simulate the power system dynamic harmonic injection by load switching.

Figure 3 shows the relative tolerance and root-mean-square error of harmonic voltage estimation. In this paper, we divide 100 sets of simulation data into 10 groups, each group contains 10 sets of data, and then compute the root-mean-square error. Simulation results show that the distributed related Kalman filter method has a significant improvement in estimation performance compared to conventional Kalman filter method. The relative tolerance of harmonic estimation results at load switching point is significantly smaller when using distributed related Kalman filter method from Fig. 3. At time 1.56 s, relative tolerance of estimation results increase from 3 % using distributed related Kalman filter method to 7 % using Kalman filter method. At time 5.7 s, the relative tolerance of the former is only about 5 %, while the latter reached 14 %, and its root mean square error is significantly smaller than the latter one.

The above simulation results indicate that the distributed related Kalman filter method obtain higher estimation accuracy than Kalman filter method, distributed related Kalman filter method has better dynamic tracking performance.

4.2.2 Simulation Data Analysis in Abnormal Situation

In actual measurement process, data anomalies or data loss may occur due to many reasons such as measuring device damaged or communication failures. The distributed related Kalman filter method can show good stability and ability in estimating harmonics. Figure 4 shows the fifth harmonic voltage magnitude at bus 12 (*actual and estimated*) while such data loss condition. From Fig. 4, the measured value and the actual value have big difference during time 4.26 s ~ 4.56 s owing to data loss. We use historical estimates to replace bad data, and then the conventional Kalman filter and the distributed related Kalman filter are employed into harmonic state estimation. Simulation results indicate that the distributed related Kalman filter method has a significant improvement in estimation performance compared to conventional Kalman filter method. Figure 5 shows that relative tolerance of estimation results increase from less than 8 % using distributed related Kalman filter method to-16 % using Kalman filter method in bad data time segment; at the same time the root-mean-square error of the former is only about 130, while the latter reached 240.

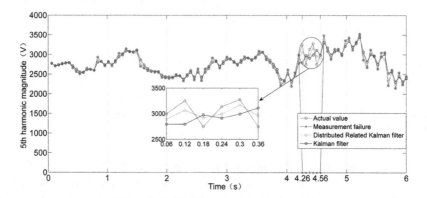

Fig. 4. Fifth harmonic voltage magnitude at bus 12 (*actual and estimated*) while bad data exist.

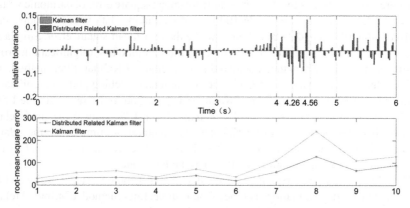

Fig. 5. Relative tolerance and root-mean-square error of fifth harmonic voltage magnitude estimation values at bus 12 (*bad data*).

The above simulation results indicate that the distributed related Kalman filter method obtain higher estimation accuracy than Kalman filter method when bad data occurs, distributed related Kalman filter method has better anti-disturbance performance.

Table 1 shows the estimation performance of 5th harmonic voltage magnitude at some bus in IEEE-14 bus system using Kalman filter method and distributed related Kalman filter method, respectively. The better dynamic estimation performance of the distributed related Kalman filter method can be found. From Table 1, we can see that the proposed method has lower estimation error about 43 % less in comparison to the Kalman filter method. The maximum estimation error using distributed related Kalman filter estimate is about 7 %, and it is almost the 39 % of the Kalman filter maximum estimation error. Thus, we can conclude that the distributed related Kalman filter method obtain higher estimation accuracy than Kalman filter method especially when collection data fluctuate wildly.

Table 1. Performance comparison of fifth harmonic voltage magnitude estimation at some bus using Kalman filter and distributed related Kalman filter.

Maximum relative tolerance (5th harmonic magnitude)	Kalman filter	Distributed Related Kalman filter
Bus 1	16 %	8 %
Bus 2	15 %	8 %
Bus 3	8 %	−7 %
Bus 4	13 %	6 %
Bus 5	14 %	5 %
Bus 13	10 %	5 %

5   Conclusion

This paper presents a dynamic state estimation of power system harmonics using distributed related Kalman Filter. In considering the characteristics of the power system harmonic voltage state, the concept of neighbor correlation coefficient is introduced into the distributed Kalman filter for the first time, furthermore this paper gives a new method to calculate the neighbor node fusion variables which suitable for power harmonic measurements. Thus we can use multiple sensor nodes to estimate multi-bus harmonic voltage state cooperatively. The simulation results show that the proposed algorithm has less communication cost, better anti-disturbance performance, and more accurate estimation in comparison to the conventional Kalman filtering. So that it can provide better data basis for harmonic compensation of power system.

Acknowledgments. This work was supported by the National Natural Science Foundation of China (51307041, 51304058 and 51177034). The authors would like to thank the anonymous reviewers for their invaluable comments for improving this work.

References

1. Arrillaga, J., Watson, N.R.: Power System Harmonics, 2nd edn. China Power Press, Beijing (2008)
2. Dugui, W., Zheng, X.: Power system harmonic state estimation based on phasor measurements (I). Trans. China Electrotech. Soc. **19**, 64–68 (2004)

3. Yu, K.K.C., Watson, N.R.: Three-phase harmonic state estimation using SVD for partially observable systems. In: 2004 International Conference on Power System Technology, POWERCON2004, pp. 29–34, Singapore (2004)
4. Pham, V.L., Wong, K.P.: Wavelet-transform-based algorithm for harmonic analysis of power system waveforms. IEE Proc. Gener. Transm. Distrib. **146**, 249–254 (1999)
5. Qun, W., Ning, W., Zhaoan, W.: An measuring approach of power harmonics based on artificial neural network. Autom. Electr. Power Syst. **22**, 35–39 (1998)
6. Beides, H.M., Heydt, G.T.: Dynamic state estimation of power system harmonics using Kalman filter methodology. IEEE Trans. Power Deliv. **6**, 1663–1670 (1991)
7. Yu, K.K.C., Watson, N.R.: An adaptive Kalman filter for dynamic harmonic state estimation and harmonic injection tracking. IEEE Trans. on Power delivery **20**, 1577–1584 (2005)
8. Ma, H., Girgis, A.A.: Identification and tracking of harmonic sources in a power system using a Kalman filter. IEEE Trans. Power Deliv. **11**, 1659–1665 (1996)
9. Kennedy, K., Lightbody, G.: Power system harmonic analysis using the Kalman filter. In: IEEE Power Engineering Society General Meeting, pp. 90–92. IEEE Press, New York (2003)
10. Saiz, V.M.M., Guadalupe, J.B.: Application of Kalman filtering for continuous real-time tracking of power system harmonics. IEE Proc. Gener. Transm. Distrib. **144**, 13–20 (1997)
11. Liu, Y.Z., Chen, S.: A wavelet based model for on-line tracking of power system harmonics using Kalman filtering. In: IEEE Power Engineering Society Summer Meeting, pp. 1237–1242. IEEE Press, New York (2001)
12. Debs, A.S., Larson, R.E.: A dynamic estimator for tracking the state of power system. IEEE Trans. Power Appar. Syst. **PAS-89**, 1670–1678 (1970)
13. Shihou, Z., Shiying, H.: Study on dynamic harmonic state estimation technology based on Kalman filter. Chongqing University (2008)
14. Chui, C.K.: Kalman Filtering with Real-Time Applications, 4th edn. Tsinghua University Press, Bejing (2014)
15. Olfati-Saber, R.: Distributed Kalman filtering for sensor networks. In: 46th IEEE Conference on Decision and Control, pp. 5492–5498. IEEE Press, New York (2007)
16. Olfati-Saber, R.: Distributed Kalman filter with embedded consensus filters. In: 44th IEEE Conference on Decision and Control, pp. 8179–8184. IEEE Press, New York (2005)
17. Speyer, J.L.: Computation and transmission requirements for a decentralized linear-quadratic-gaussian control problem. IEEE Trans. Autom. Control **24**, 266–269 (1979)
18. Xiyang, S.: Harmonic harm and elimination for power system. Electr. Technol. Intell. Build. **3**, 63–66 (2009)

An Efficient Cluster-Based Data Sharing Algorithm for Bidirectional Road Scenario in Vehicular Ad-hoc Networks

Junhua Wang[1], Kai Liu[1(✉)], Edwin H.M. Sha[1],
Victor C.S. Lee[2], and Sang H. Son[3]

[1] College of Computer Science, Chongqing University, Chongqing 400044, China
{jhua,liukai0807,edwinsha}@cqu.edu.cn
[2] Department of Computer Science,
City University of Hong Kong, Hong Kong, China
csvlee@cityu.edu.hk
[3] Department of Information and Communication Engineering,
DGIST, Daegu, Korea
son@dgist.ac.kr

Abstract. Efficient data sharing in vehicular ad hoc networks (VANETs) is one of the fundamental requirements to enable emerging intelligent transportation systems. Much research has focused on the routing algorithms and MAC protocols in VANETs. However, unique characteristics of data sharing for bidirectional road scenarios make it challenging to design an efficient scheduling algorithm. In this work, we present the data sharing model among vehicles driving in opposite directions, and investigate the potential interference caused by simultaneous vehicle-to-vehicle (V2V) communications. On this basis, we propose a cluster-based algorithm to implement efficient data sharing in bidirectional road scenarios. Specifically, we design a time slot division policy to assign the clusters with specific slots according to the driving directions and relative positions of vehicles. Then, based on certain required quality of services, we derive a theoretical model by analyzing the signal-to-interference-and-noise ratio (SINR) in V2V communications, which determines how to divide vehicles into different clusters. Finally, we build the simulation model and give an extensive performance evaluation, which demonstrates that the proposed algorithm is efficient in terms of enhancing data throughput under different traffic workloads.

Keywords: Data dissemination · Vehicle-to-vehicle communication · Bidirectional scenarios · Scheduling algorithm · Vehicular ad-hoc networks

1 Introduction

With the rapid development of vehicular wireless communication technologies, vehicles can communicate with roadside infrastructures via Vehicle-to-Infrastructure (V2I) communication and also with other vehicles via Vehicle-to-Vehicle (V2V) communication by installing roadside units (RSUs) and on-board

© Springer International Publishing Switzerland 2015
G. Wang et al. (Eds.): ICA3PP 2015, Part I, LNCS 9528, pp. 537–551, 2015.
DOI: 10.1007/978-3-319-27119-4_37

unit (OBU) devices. In VANETs, efficient information services via V2I and V2V communications are critical to enhance road safety, relieve traffic congestion and enable autonomous driving in near future.

Currently, most research on data dissemination in VANETs focused on the design of MAC protocols and routing algorithms [1–3]. These work mainly considered the timeliness and the reliability of message delivery by selecting proper forwarding nodes. Some of the work [4–6] considered that users on the road need to share different types of data, such as entertainment messages, location-based information or other commercial messages. These researches aim at maximizing the data throughput in VANETs and enhancing the information service. However, none of them has considered the data sharing in bidirectional road scenarios, where unique challenges as well as opportunities arise for providing efficient information services via V2I and V2V communications.

Previous work [7–9] has shown that vehicles are prone to traveling in clusters. Based on this observation, this work considers to alleviate broadcast interference and enhance data throughput by dividing vehicles into clusters and designing particular strategies for V2V communication. In this work, we investigate the scenario where the RSU is installed at each end of a bidirectional road segment. When vehicles passing through the RSU, they will be informed to join a cluster and assigned with a broadcast period. The cluster classification and the time slot assignment will be determined by analyzing signal-to-interference-and-noise ratio (SINR) [10] in V2V communication with the purpose of maximizing the chance of cooperatively sharing their information for vehicles driving in opposite directions and thus, improving the overall data throughput.

The main contributions of this paper are outlined as follows. First, we present an information service model in bidirectional road scenarios, where RSUs are used to enable vehicles driving on opposite directions to cooperatively share their information and improve the overall service performance. Second, based on theoretical analysis of the SINR model in such an environment, we propose an algorithm to divide vehicles into clusters with the purpose of alleviating V2V communication interference and guaranteeing certain quality of services. Third, we build the simulation model and demonstrate the efficiency of the proposed algorithm via a comprehensive performance evaluation.

The rest of this paper is organized as follows. Section 2 reviews the related work. Section 3 presents the system architecture. In Sect. 4, we formulate the problem and propose the cluster-based algorithm. In Sect. 5, we build the simulation model and give performance evaluation. Finally, we conclude this work and discuss future research directions in Sect. 6.

2   Related Work

In VANETs, great efforts have been put into investigating information service via V2I and V2V communications [6,11,12]. W. Z et al. [6] studied the multiple access modes downloading schemes: vehicles downloaded files from RSU directly, through relay vehicles and through other vehicles, and proposed the credit-based incentives for relay vehicle selection to guarantee the stability and quality of the link bandwidth. L. T et al. [11] proposed a novel approach for the vehicles to download a common content in mutually disjoint coalitions, and a distributed coalition formation algorithm was designed to obtain a stable coalition structure and minimize the total communication cost. A multiple-vehicle protocol was proposed [12] for collaborative data downloading by network coding, and derived the probability mass functions of the downloading completion time through multiple periods of V2I and V2V. However, these studies did not consider the data sharing among vehicles on opposite directions through cooperative V2I and V2V communications for information services in VANETs.

In bidirectional traffic scenarios, packet reachability in end-to-end (E2E) connections and store-carry-forward (SCF) connections was analyzed in [13]. Y. Liu et al. [14] studied on the insights of message delivery delay in VANETs towards the factors of message delivery distance and density of vehicles based on the bidirectional traffic model. In [15], an inter-vehicle ad-hoc routing metric called EFD (Expected Forwarding Delay) based on the density and velocities of vehicles was proposed, and the clusters in opposite directions were used as a bridge to propagate the massage for two co-directional clusters to reduce the delay. Nevertheless, the above work cannot well exploit the V2V communication for information services when vehicles on opposite directions meet with each other. The problem investigated in our work is distinguished from the above studies with respect to the following aspects. First, we consider both the bidirectional data sharing and the cluster classification when designing the cooperative V2V communication strategy. Second, RSUs are in charge of dividing vehicles into clusters, and appointing them with different broadcast time slots. Third, the cluster is derived based on the analysis of the SINR at the receivers to guarantee certain data throughput performance.

3   System Model

3.1   Service Model

In this model, we consider a segment of a bidirectional road with two RSUs installed at each end of the segment. In accordance with the WAVE architecture [16], one control channel and one service channel are adopted in this model. The RSU is aware of vehicles status including driving directions, velocities and locations via V2I communication in the control channel. Based on certain strategy, the RSU is able to classify vehicles into different clusters and determine the V2V communication period for each vehicle. The instructions will be broadcasted to vehicles via the control channel. After vehicles leaving the RSU's coverage, they will obey the timing instruction determined by the RSU and periodically broadcasts their cached data items via V2V communication in the service channel.

As shown in Fig. 1, there are two RSUs installed at each end of a bidirectional road segment. Generally, the RSU has to complete the following two tasks. (1) Collecting the vehicles' location information and dividing the vehicles into different clusters; (2) assigning each vehicle a certain broadcast period and the

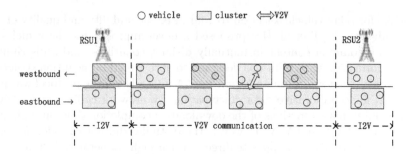

Fig. 1. Cluster-based V2V data sharing in a bidirectional road segment

corresponding broadcast time slot. With such instructions, vehicles driving in the opposite directions will exchange information with each other via V2V communication. Note that although only one road segment with two RSUs is considered in this model, it is straightforward to extend the system to larger areas with more RSUs cooperated for information services.

3.2   SINR Model

According to the service model, it is critical to well coordinate vehicles driving on opposite directions for data sharing via V2V communication, because the short meeting time between two vehicles and possible severe interference at the receiver may significantly degrade the service performance. To quantitatively measure the interference, the commonly adopted SINR model [10] is analyzed in this work. Consider the network with a set of senders $S = \{S_1, S_2, ..., S_{|S|}\}$ and and a set of receivers $R = \{R_1, R_2, ..., R_{|R|}\}$. For $1 \leq j \leq |R|$ and $1 \leq i \leq |S|$, the distance between R_j and S_i is denoted by $d(j, i)$. For a receiver R_j, its designated sender is denoted by $S_a(1 \leq a \leq |S|)$, and the distance between R_j and S_a is denoted by $d^a(j)$. We have $d^a(j) = d(j, i)$ when S_i is the designated sender for R_j. In this model, given a time slot, we consider that the two vehicles with the closest distance in opposite directions are a pair of sender and receiver. Other sender vehicles at this time slot will cause interference to this receiver. Therefore, given a receiver R_j and a sender S_a, the signal-to-interference-and-noise ratio (SINR) is computed by [10]:

$$SINR_{S_a \to R_j}^{S \backslash \{S_a\}} = \frac{P_{tx}|d^a(j)|^{-\alpha}}{N_0 + \displaystyle\sum_{S_i \in S \backslash \{S_a\}} P_{tx}|d(j, i)|^{-\alpha}} \tag{1}$$

where P_{tx} is the transmission power. N_0 is a background noise and α is the path-loss exponent.

As $d^a(j) = |S_a - R_j|$ and $d(j, i) = |S_i - R_j|$, we have

$$SINR_{S_a \to R_j}^{S \backslash \{S_a\}} = \frac{P_{tx}|S_a - R_j|^{-\alpha}}{N_0 + \displaystyle\sum_{S_i \in S \backslash \{S_a\}} P_{tx}|S_i - R_j|^{-\alpha}} \tag{2}$$

To let R_j receive data from S_a in the presence of the concurrent transmitters, it must satisfy the following constraint:

$$SINR_{S_a \to R_j}^{S \setminus \{S_a\}} \geq \beta \tag{3}$$

where β is the threshold.

3.3   An Example

Figure 2 gives an example to illustrate the SINR model for V2V data sharing in bidirectional road segment.   As shown in Fig. 2, $S = \{S_0, S_1, S_2, S_3, S_4\}$ is

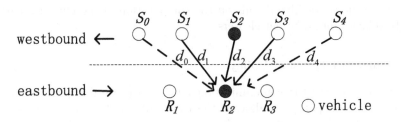

Fig. 2. An example SINR model for V2V data sharing in bidirectional road scenarios

the set of westbound vehicles, while $R = \{R_1, R_2, R_3\}$ represents the set of eastbound vehicles. For the receiver R_2, the distance between S_0, S_1, S_2, S_3, S_4 and R_2 are respectively d_0, d_1, d_2, d_3, d_4. Denote D_{ifer} as the maximum interference range in V2V communication. That is, when the distance between two vehicles is greater than D_{ifer}, the communication interference to each other can be ignored. Suppose that $d_2 \leq d_1 \leq d_3 \leq D_{ifer}$ and $d_4 \geq d_0 \geq D_{ifer}$, then the interference from sender S_0, S_4 is not considered. Assume that the target sender of R_2 is S_2, the SINR value from sender S_2 to the receiver R_2 in the presence of a set of concurrent transmitters $S \setminus \{S_2\} = \{S_0, S_1, S_3, S_4\}$ is computed by:

$$SINR_{S_2 \to R_2}^{\{S_0, S_1, S_3, S_4\}} = SINR_{S_2 \to R_2}^{\{S_1, S_3\}} = \frac{P_{tx}|S_2 - R_2|^{-\alpha}}{N_0 + P_{tx}|S_1 - R_2|^{-\alpha} + P_{tx}|S_3 - R_2|^{-\alpha}} \tag{4}$$

Suppose $P_{tx} = 1$, $N_0 = 0$, $\alpha = 2$, $\beta = 1$, and $d_2 = 100\,m$, $d_1 = d_3 = 150\,m$. According to Eq. 4, we have:

$$SINR_{S_2 \to R_2}^{\{S_0, S_1, S_3, S_4\}} = \frac{d_2^{-2}}{d_1^{-2} + d_3^{-2}} = \frac{100^{-2}}{150^{-2} + 150^{-2}} = 1.125 \tag{5}$$

As $\beta = 1$, it satisfies Eq. 3. Therefore, R_2 can successfully receive the data from S_2 in this case.

4 Proposed Solution

In this section, in order to guarantee certain quality of services for data sharing among vehicles driving in opposite directions, we propose a cluster-based algorithm to divide the vehicles in each direction into different clusters. The general idea is described as follows. First, we present a time slot division policy which assigns clusters with different time slots such that vehicles in different clusters will transmit data in turn. The purpose of such a policy is to alleviate interference when multiple vehicles are transmitting data at the same time. Second, we explore the relationship between the length of clusters and the number of effective data transmission between any two clusters in opposite directions, so as to determine the length of clusters according to a certain required quality of service. Finally, we give details on the computation of the cluster length to classify vehicles into different clusters.

4.1 Time Slot Division Policy

In order to alleviate the communication interference, we design the following time slot division policy to allocate the time slot for different clusters. First of all, since vehicles cannot transmit and receive information at the same time due to the half-duplex of OBUs [17], the clusters in opposite directions have to transmit data items alternately in different time slots. Second, to avoid vehicles in close proximity broadcasting data items simultaneously, we designate that the adjacent clusters on the same direction have to broadcast data items in different time slots. The above policy is formally described as follows. Denote τ as the duration of a time slot, and a broadcast period consists of 4 time slots, namely, $[0, \tau]$, $[\tau, 2\tau]$, $[2\tau, 3\tau]$ and $[3\tau, 4\tau]$. We label each cluster according to the sequence of their geographical positions and driving directions. Given the current time slot t, denote $C_{west}(t) = \{C_1, C_3, C_5, ..., C_{2(|C_{west}(t)|-1)}\}$ as the set of clusters on the westbound, and denote $C_{east}(t) = \{C_2, C_4, C_6, ..., C_{2|C_{east}(t)|}\}$ as the set of clusters on the eastbound. We classify the clusters into 4 sets according to the following rules.

(i) For cluster C_i, if $i\%4 = 1$, then C_i is classified into $S_{[0,\tau]}$, namely, $S_{[0,\tau]} = \{C_i|\ i\%4 = 1\}$;

(ii) For cluster C_i, if $i\%4 = 2$, then C_i is classified into $S_{[\tau,2\tau]}$, namely, $S_{[\tau,2\tau]} = \{C_i|\ i\%4 = 2\}$;

(iii) For cluster C_i, if $i\%4 = 3$, then C_i is classified into $S_{[2\tau,3\tau]}$, namely, $S_{[2\tau,3\tau]} = \{C_i|\ i\%4 = 3\}$;

(iv) For cluster C_i, if $i\%4 = 0$, then C_i is classified into $S_{[3\tau,4\tau]}$, namely, $S_{[3\tau,4\tau]} = \{C_i|\ i\%4 = 0\}$.

With the above rules, clusters on the westbound and the eastbound will be selected alternately, and any two adjacent clusters on the same direction will be selected in every other time slot. The time slot division policy is presented as follows.

- Denote $t\%4 = \omega$ $(\omega = 0, 1, 2, 3)$. If $\omega = 0$, then then the clusters in $S_{[3\tau, 4\tau]}$ will be selected;
- Otherwise, the clusters in $S_{[(\omega-1)\tau, \omega\tau]}$ will be selected.

For vehicles within each selected cluster, only one of them is allowed to broadcast data during the assigned time slot. With this designed policy, we analyze the relationship between the cluster length and the effect of interference below.

4.2   Minimum Number of Effective Data Transmission

To quantitatively measure the quality of data sharing, we define an *effective data transmission* as one instance of successful data transmission from a cluster in one direction to another cluster on the opposite direction. The number of effective data transmission between two clusters in opposite directions is denoted by K. The period during which the two clusters in opposite directions can successfully share data items is defined as *effective data sharing period*, and it is denoted by t_I. When the two clusters crossing with each other, due to the time slot division policy, the number of effective data transmission K may vary with different designated time slots of these two clusters.

In the following, given a certain value of t_I, we analyze the worst case, namely, the minimum number of effective data transmission, which is denoted by $K_{\min}$. Specifically, given t_I, it is possible that even though the two clusters could transmit data without interference, but the current time slot is not assigned to any one of them. Clearly, according to the time slot division policy, as long as there are more than 2 time slots, one of the two clusters will be selected to broadcast data. Therefore, $K_{\min}$ is derived when the two clusters need to wait for 2 time slots. During t_I, each broadcast period (i.e., 4τ) will have 2 times of effective data transmission. Denote $r = t_I\%4\tau$, $K_{\min}$ can be obtained based on the following two cases:

Case (1) $r = 0, 1, 2, K_{\min} = 2 \cdot \lfloor \frac{t_I}{4\tau} \rfloor$;
Case (2) $r = 3, K_{\min} = 2 \cdot \lfloor \frac{t_I}{4\tau} \rfloor + 1$

In the next part, given the minimum number of required effective data transmission (i.e., given $K_{\min}$), we derive the minimum cluster length $L_{\min}$.

4.3   Cluster Division

A. Theoretical Analysis on $L_{\min}$
The longer length of a cluster gives a longer distance between any two adjacent clusters in the same direction, and thus there will be less interference from the clusters in the same direction when sharing data with the clusters in the opposite direction. In the following, we derive $L_{\min}$ based on the SINR model such that a pre-determined minimum number of effective transmission between any two clusters in opposite directions (i.e., $K_{\min}$) can be satisfied. As shown in Fig. 3,

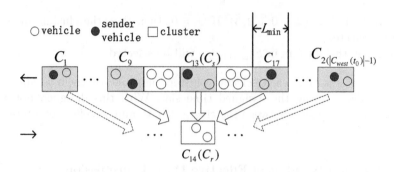

Fig. 3. SINR computation when C_r retrieving data from C_s at time t_0

suppose at t_0, we have the cluster set $S_{[0,\tau]} = \{C_1, C_5, C_9, ...\}$ and $t_0\%4 = 1$. Accordingly, any $C_i \in S_{[0,\tau]}$ will be selected to broadcast data at t_0. Given the sender cluster C_{13} (i.e. C_s), and its target receiver cluster C_{14} (i.e. C_r), then the clusters which may cause interferences at are $\{S_{[0,\tau]} - C_s\}$. According to the SINR model, the SINR at C_r is computed by:

$$SINR_{C_s \to C_r} = \frac{\frac{P_{tx}}{d^\alpha(C_s, C_r)}}{N_0 + \sum\limits_{\{C_i | C_i \in \{S_{[0,\tau]} - C_s\},\, d(C_i, C_r) < D_{ifer}\}} \frac{P_{tx}}{d^\alpha(C_i, C_r)}} \tag{6}$$

where D_{ifer} represents the maximum interference range of V2V communication.

Since a receiver cluster may consist of a number of vehicles which have different distances to the sender vehicles, to guarantee that any vehicle in the receiver cluster is able to successfully retrieve the data, we consider the worst case of data sharing. Specifically, when computing the distance between the target sender cluster and target receiver cluster, we consider the longest distance between two vehicles in the two clusters. In contrast, when computing the distance between an interference cluster and the receiver cluster, we consider the shortest distance between two vehicles in the two clusters. Thus, Eq. 6 can be presented as follows:

$$SINR_{C_s \to C_r} = \frac{\frac{P_{tx}}{d_{\max}{}^\alpha(C_s, C_r)}}{N_0 + \sum\limits_{\{C_i | C_i \in \{S_{[0,\tau]} - C_s\},\, d(C_i, C_r) < D_{ifer}\}} \frac{P_{tx}}{d_{\min}{}^\alpha(C_i, C_r)}} \tag{7}$$

where $d_{\max}(C_s, C_r)$ represents the longest distance between cluster C_s and C_r, $d_{\min}(C_i, C_r)$ represents the shortest distance between cluster C_i and C_r.

If the $SINR_{C_s \to C_r}$ in Eq. 7 is larger than the threshold β, C_r can successfully receive the data from C_s. Therefore, in the duration t_I, the $SINR_{C_s \to C_r}$ is expected to be always greater than β to keep C_s and C_r sharing data. Denote $\mu \in [0, \frac{t_I}{2}]$, and assume that the vehicles share a similar speed (the average speed is denoted as v). Then we can assume the shortest distance between the two clusters is obtained at $\frac{t_I}{2}$, then the communication scenarios in $[0, \frac{t_I}{2}]$, and $[\frac{t_I}{2}, t_I]$ are symmetric. Accordingly, we take the period $\mu \in [0, \frac{t_I}{2}]$ for analysis. Equation 7 can be transformed as follows (detailed calculation can be found in [18]):

$$SINR_{C_s \rightarrow C_r} = \frac{\frac{P_{tx}}{((vt_I - 2v\mu + L_{\min})^2 + H^2)^{\frac{\alpha}{2}}}}{N_0 + \sum_{i=0}^{M} \frac{P_{tx}}{((vt_I - 2v\mu + (2i+1)L_{\min})^2 + \varepsilon^2)^{\frac{\alpha}{2}}} + \sum_{j=0}^{N} \frac{P_{tx}}{(((2j+1)L_{\min} - vt_I + 2v\mu)^2 + \varepsilon^2)^{\frac{\alpha}{2}}}}$$

(8)

where $M = \left\lfloor \frac{\sqrt{D_{ifer}^2 - \varepsilon^2} - vt_I + 2vu}{2L_{\min}} - \frac{1}{2} \right\rfloor$, and $N = \left\lfloor \frac{\sqrt{D_{ifer}^2 - \varepsilon^2} + vt_I - 2vu}{2L_{\min}} - \frac{1}{2} \right\rfloor$.

Based on Eq. 8 and the analysis in Sect. 4.2, $L_{\min}$ can be computed when $K_{\min}, \tau, v$ are determined.

B. Computation of $L_{\min}$

For simplicity, we set the parameters in SINR model as $P_{tx} = 1, N_0 = 0, \alpha = 2$, and the $SINR_{C_s \rightarrow C_r}$ in Eq. 8 can be transformed to:

$$SINR_{C_s \rightarrow C_r} = \frac{\frac{1}{(vt_I - 2v\mu + L_{\min})^2 + H^2}}{\sum_{i=0}^{M} \frac{1}{(vt_I - 2v\mu + (2i+1)L_{\min})^2 + \varepsilon^2} + \sum_{j=0}^{N} \frac{1}{((2j+1)L_{\min} - vt_I + 2v\mu)^2 + \varepsilon^2}}$$

(9)

Firstly, in Eq. 9, $SINR_{C_s \rightarrow C_r}$ is a dynamic expression because of the variable μ. To make sure the two clusters can successfully transmit data in the duration of $[0, \frac{t_I}{2}]$, the minimum SINR value during the period must be greater than the threshold β. The Eq. 9 is proved to be monotonically increasing along with the variable μ (detailed proof can be found in [18]). Accordingly, the minimum value is obtained when $\mu = 0$. Let $\mu = 0$, and we get

$$SINR_{C_s \rightarrow C_r} = \frac{\frac{1}{(vt_I + L_{\min})^2 + H^2}}{\sum_{i=0}^{M} \frac{1}{(vt_I + (2i+1)L_{\min})^2 + \varepsilon^2} + \sum_{j=0}^{N} \frac{1}{((2j+1)L_{\min} - vt_I)^2 + \varepsilon^2}}$$

(10)

where $M = \left\lfloor \frac{\sqrt{D_{ifer}^2 - \varepsilon^2} - vt_I}{2L_{\min}} - \frac{1}{2} \right\rfloor$, and $N = \left\lfloor \frac{\sqrt{D_{ifer}^2 - \varepsilon^2} + vt_I}{2L_{\min}} - \frac{1}{2} \right\rfloor$.

Secondly, we release the constraint based on the following observations. In the worst case analysis, we use the shortest distance between each pair of the interference cluster and target receiver cluster, and use the longest distance between the target sender cluster and target receiver cluster, which may lead no feasible solutions to the constraints. Actually, it is unlikely to have such a worst scenario in reality. Therefore, to be demonstrated in our simulation analysis, it is reasonable to adopt the center distance between the sender cluster and the receiver clusters when computing the cluster length, and we have

$$SINR_{C_s \rightarrow C_r} = \frac{\frac{1}{(vt_I)^2 + H^2}}{\sum_{i=0}^{M} \frac{1}{(vt_I + (2i+1)L_{\min})^2 + \varepsilon^2} + \sum_{j=0}^{N} \frac{1}{((2j+1)L_{\min} - vt_I)^2 + \varepsilon^2}}$$

(11)

Table 1. Statistics in different traffic scenarios

Traffic scenarios	Mean arrival rate (vehicles/h)		Mean density (vehicles/km)	
	Lane1	Lane2	Lane1	Lane2
1	1198	1000	16.30	14.94
2	1612	1292	22.03	19.80
3	1990	1735	27.09	24.96
4	2322	2138	30.74	29.90
5	2728	2401	37.66	34.69

With Eq. 11, the L_{min} can be computed by setting $SINR_{C_s \to C_r} > \beta$, and then, the vehicles can be classified into different clusters based on the derived L_{min}.

5   Performance Evaluation

5.1   Simulation Model

The simulation model is built according to the system architecture described in Sect. 3.1 and it is implemented by CSIM19 [19]. Specifically, we simulate a segment of a bidirectional road with two RSUs installed at each end, and the length of the road segment is 1500m. There are two lanes in each direction, and without loss of generality, we consider a symmetric scenario of the two directions, including the vehicle arrival rate and the mean traffic velocity. In each direction, the arrival of vehicles in the two lanes follows the Poisson process with the parameters λ= 0.553 and 0.482 respectively. The mean velocity is set to 20 m/s. The parameters of SINR model are set as follows: $P_{tx} = 1$, $\alpha = 2$, $N_0 = 0$, and the threshold $\beta = 1$. The maximum interference range of V2V communication D_{ifer} is set to 500 m in this simulation.

In order to evaluate the algorithm performance under different traffic workloads, we give a comprehensive simulation study by varying the vehicle arrival rate in each lane. As the statistics shown in Table 1, the mean vehicle arrival rate increases from traffic scenarios 1 to 5, and it covers a wide range of traffic workload.

For performance comparison, we implement two alternative strategies for V2V data sharing. One is called "Broadcast_in_turn", which divides the broadcast period into 2 time slots, such that the vehicles on the two opposite directions will broadcast data items in turn in different time slots. The other alternative solution is called "Cluster_1", which is a simplified version of our proposed cluster-based solution by setting the cluster size to 1. In such a case, the broadcast period for each vehicle is 4 time slots.

To quantitatively analyze the algorithm performance, we consider the following metrics for performance evaluation. (1) Average data throughput, which is the amount of data sharing via V2V communication in each time slot. For the sake of emphasizing the generality of our analysis, in this simulation, we do not specify absolute values of the data size. Instead, we consider that each vehicle can transmit one data packet in a time slot, so that the data throughput is measured by the number of data packets transmitted in a time slot. Also, we only consider the data transmission among vehicles in the two opposite directions, so as to directly reflect algorithm performance regarding to the concerned system model. (2) The ratio of interference (r_{ifer}). Denote n_{ifer} as the number of receiver vehicles which did not retrieve the data due to interference, and denote n as the total number of receiver vehicles. The ratio of interference is defined as $r_{ifer} = n_{ifer}/n$. A lower value of the ratio implies a better performance of the algorithm in terms of alleviating interferences in V2V communication.

5.2 Simulation Results

The average data throughput under different traffic workloads is shown in Fig. 4. As noted, the average data throughput of the proposed cluster-based algorithm is always higher than the other two algorithms. Specifically, with an increasing of vehicle arrival rate, the traffic density is getting higher. Normally, a higher data throughput is expected when more vehicles participate into V2V communication. Nevertheless, as shown in Fig. 4, the performance of "Cluster_1" even drops in a heavier traffic workload environment. It implies that the severe interference dominate the algorithm performance when the traffic workload is getting higher. In contrast, for the cluster-based algorithm, the data throughput is significantly improved in a higher traffic workload environment, which demonstrates that the algorithm can well exploit the benefit of V2V communication by alleviating interference when the traffic density is getting higher.

Recall that the cluster-based algorithm determines the cluster length according a theoretical minimum number of effective data transmission $(K_{\min})$. In the simulation, we have collected the actual average number of effective data transmission given different values of $K_{\min}$. Figure 5 shows the average data throughput under different actual number of effective data transmission, which is denoted by K_{actual}. As noted, when the value of K_{actual} increases from 1 to 6, the average data throughput increases at the beginning, and then it decreases. In the default setting, the highest throughput is obtained when K_{actual} is around 4.4. The reason is explained below. According to the cluster-based algorithm, when the required number of effective data transmission is smaller, the derived cluster length will be shorter, which gives more clusters on the road. Accordingly, more vehicles are allowed to broadcast data simultaneously, which may give severe interference, resulting in a lower average data throughput. In contrast, if the number of effective data transmission is too large, the cluster length will be much longer, and there are few clusters on the road. Accordingly, there will be even fewer vehicles which can broadcast data at the same time, which leads to the decrease of data throughput. To sum up, observed from Fig. 5, there is a tradeoff when determining the cluster length to maximize the average data throughput. More details are analyzed below.

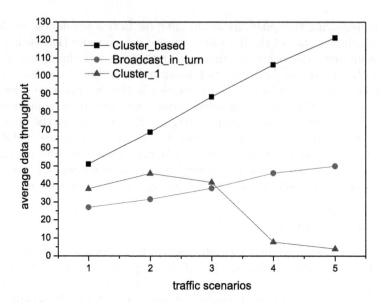

Fig. 4. Average data throughput of algorithms under different traffic workloads

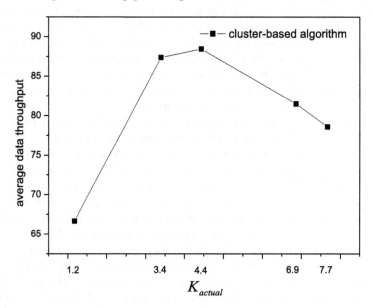

Fig. 5. Average data throughput under different actual number of effective data transmission

Table 2 summarizes the statistics of the proposed algorithm under different values of required minimum number of effective data transmission (i.e. $K_{\min}$). Specifically, $L_{\min}$ represents the theoretically derived cluster length when $K_{\min}$

Table 2. Statistics under different values of $K_{\min}$

$K_{\min}$	$L_{\min}(m)$	K_{actual}	$L_{actual}(m)$	Data throughput	r_{ifer}
	10	1.2	30.90	66.6	0.306
	60	2.0	91.14	87.0	0.061
1	130	3.4	149.79	87.4	0.036
2	170	4.4	189.92	88.5	0.008
3	290	6.9	306.21	81.5	0.000
4	330	7.7	347.94	78.6	0.000
5	445	9.2	463.42	73.0	0.000
6	485	9.4	503.43	66.1	0.000

is given. K_{actual} represents the actual mean number of effective data transmission collected in simulation, and L_{actual} represents the actually obtained cluster length. As shown, the value of K_{actual} is always greater than that of $K_{\min}$, which verifies the correctness of the theoretical model and demonstrates that the proposed solution can guarantee the required quality of services. In addition, we note that the actual cluster length L_{actual} is longer than the theoretical value $L_{\min}$. This is because in reality, the distance between adjacent vehicles varies with different traffic scenarios, giving different cluster lengths. The statistics of data throughput is consistent with that shown in Fig. 5, and we observe that a proper value of K_{actual} will give the highest data throughput. To give insights of the trade-off for determining K_{actual}, we further analyze the ratio of interference r_{ifer}. As shown, when the cluster length is short (e.g. around 30m), the ratio of interference is over 30 %, which significantly influences the system performance. With an increasing of K_{actual}, the value of r_{ifer} gradually decreases until reaches 0. Note that although a longer cluster length will help to alleviate interference, it will cause less efficient concurrent V2V communication because very few vehicles are allowed to broadcast data at the same time. Therefore, the data throughput decreases when L_{actual} keeps increasing.

6   Conclusions and Future Work

In this paper, we focus on efficient data sharing among vehicles driving in opposite directions. Specifically, we present the cluster-based data sharing model in a bidirectional road segment and examine the characteristics of V2V communication by analyzing the SINR in the concerned vehicular communication environment. On this basis, we propose a cluster-based algorithm to enable efficient data sharing based on V2V communication. In particular, a time slot division policy is developed to designate clusters into different time slots for the purpose of alleviating communication interference. Furthermore, given a required number of effective transmission between two clusters in opposite directions, we give a theoretical model to derive the cluster length to satisfy the requirement. Finally, we build the simulation model and implement the proposed algorithm as well as alternative solutions for performance evaluation. The comprehensive simulation results and analysis demonstrate the superiority of the proposed algorithm in terms of maximizing the average data throughput in such a system.

In our future work, the multi-hop V2V communication will be investigated to further enhance the system performance. Meanwhile, the data dissemination at the RSUs and the cooperation among multiple RSUs are expected to be explored. Finally, we will look into the impacts from MAC and PHY layers in vehicular communications to enhance the robustness of the solution in realistic wireless communication environments.

Acknowlegements. This work was supported in part by the Fundamental Research Funds for the Central Universities (Grant No. 106112015CDJZR185518); the NSFC 61472052; the ICT R&D program of MSIP/IITP (14-824-09-013, Resilient Cyber-Physical Systems Research) and the GRL Program (2013K1A1A2A02078326) through NRF.

References

1. Lee, J., Chen, W.: Reliably suppressed broadcasting for vehicle-to-vehicle communications. In: 2010 IEEE 71st Vehicular Technology Conference (VTC 2010-Spring), pp. 1–7 (2010)
2. Schmidt, R.K., Lasowski, R., Leinmüller, T., Linnhoff-Popien, C., Schafer, G.: An approach for selective beacon forwarding to improve cooperative awareness. In: 2010 IEEE Vehicular Networking Conference (VNC), pp. 182–188 (2010)
3. Sou, S.-I., Tonguz, O.K.: Enhancing vanet connectivity through roadside units on highways. IEEE Trans. Veh. Technol. **60**(8), 3586–3602 (2011)
4. Ye, F., Roy, S., Wang, H.: Efficient data dissemination in vehicular ad hoc networks. IEEE J. Sel. Areas Commun. **30**(4), 769–779 (2012)
5. Hao, Y., Tang, J., Cheng, Y.: Secure cooperative data downloading in vehicular ad hoc networks. IEEE J. Sel. Areas Commun. **31**(9), 523–537 (2013)
6. Zhao, W., Qin, Y., Cheng, Y., Yang, O.W.: An efficient downloading service of large popular files in vanet based on 802.11 p protocol. Int. J. Distrib. Sens. Netw. **2015**(824294), 10 (2015)
7. Wisitpongphan, N., Bai, F., Mudalige, P., Sadekar, V., Tonguz, O.: Routing in sparse vehicular ad hoc wireless networks. IEEE J. Sel. Areas Commun. **25**(8), 1538–1556 (2007)
8. Chai, R., Yang, B., Li, L., Sun, X., Chen, Q.: Clustering-based data transmission algorithms for vanet. In: 2013 International Conference on Wireless Communications Signal Processing (WCSP), pp. 1–6. IEEE (2013)
9. Maglaras, L., Katsaros, D.: Social clustering of vehicles based on semi-markov processes. IEEE Trans. Veh. Technol. **99**, 1–1 (2015)
10. Chau, C.-K., Zhang, J., Chen, M., Liew, S.C.: Interference-safe csma networks by local aggregate interference power measurement. In: 10th International Symposium on Modeling and Optimization in Mobile, Ad Hoc and Wireless Networks (WiOpt), vol. 2012, pp. 1–8. IEEE (2012)

11. Tong, L., Ma, L., Li, L., Li, M.: A coalitional game theoretical model for content downloading in multihop vanets. In: 2013 IEEE 11th International Conference on Dependable, Autonomic and Secure Computing (DASC), pp. 627–632. IEEE (2013)
12. Zhu, W., Li, D., Saad, W.: Multiple vehicles collaborative data download protocol via network coding. IEEE Trans. Veh. Technol. **64**(4), 1607–1619 (2015)
13. Fan, P., Li, Y., Zhang, G., Li, J., Mu, D.: Packet reachability of vanet in bidirectional road scenario. In: 2010 12th IEEE International Conference on Communication Technology (ICCT), pp. 80–83. IEEE (2010)
14. Liu, Y., Niu, J., Ma, J., Shu, L., Hara, T., Wang, W.: The insights of message delivery delay in vanets with a bidirectional traffic model. J. Netw. Comput. Appl. **36**(5), 1287–1294 (2013)
15. Akand, M., Rashid, M., Nayeem, M.T., Sumon, M., Zaman, R.U., Alam, M.M.: A probabilistic delay model for bidirectional vanets in city environments. In: 10th IEEE Conference on Vehicular Technology Society Asia Pacific Wireless Communications Symposium (IEEE APWCS 2013) (2013)
16. Li, Y.J.: An overview of the DSRC/WAVE technology. In: Zhang, X., Qiao, D. (eds.) QShine 2010. LNICST, vol. 74, pp. 544–558. Springer, Heidelberg (2012)
17. Xie, X., Wang, F., Li, K., Zhang, P., Wang, H.: Improvement of multi-channel mac protocol for dense vanet with directional antennas. In: Wireless Communications and Networking Conference, WCNC, pp. 1–6. IEEE (2009)
18. Wang, J., Liu, K., Sha, E.H., Lee, V.C., Son, S.H.: An efficient cluster-based data sharing algorithm for bidirectional road scenario in vehicular ad-hoc networks. Technical report (2015). http://cacs.cqu.edu.cn/wp-content/uploads/2015/02/appendix.pdf
19. Schwetman, H.: Csim19: a powerful tool for building system models. In: Proceedings of the 33nd Conference on Winter Simulation, pp. 250–255. IEEE Computer Society (2001)

A Distributed Joint Cooperative Routing and Channel Assignment in Multi-radio Wireless Mesh Network

Hong Qiao[1], Dafang Zhang[1]($\boxtimes$), Kun Xie[1], Ji Zhang[1], and Shiming He[2]

[1] College of Computer Science and Electronic Engineering,
Hunan University, Changsha 410082, China
{hqiao,dfzhang,xiekun,tosky1984}@hnu.edu.cn
[2] School of Computer and Communication Engineering,
Changsha University of Science and Technology, Changsha 410114, China
heshiming_hsm@163.com

Abstract. Cooperative communication is an effective method of alleviating fading and increasing wireless transmission capacity. However, interference will decrease the performance of cooperative communication in multi-hop wireless mesh network drastically. And the multi-radios technique can reduce interference effectively. In order to fully exploit advantage of cooperative communication, this paper studies the joint problem of cooperative routing and channel assignment in multi-radio wireless mesh network, and proposes a distributed algorithm for it. The algorithm is composed of two stages. In the first stage, a distributed cooperative routing algorithm based on a novel $RATC$(Reminder Available Transmission Capacity) metric is proposed to make flows pass through network evenly. In the second stage, a distributed channel assignment algorithm for both direct links and cooperative links is proposed to minimize the interference. The simulation result shows that our proposed algorithm can effectively promote overall network throughput in different network scenes.

Keywords: Cooperative routing · Multi-radio · Channel assignment · Wireless mesh network · Interference

1 Introduction

Cooperative communication obtains diversity gain by organizing single-antenna of multiple users into a virtual MIMO (Multi-Input Multi-Output) system. And cooperative routing is a cross-layer routing solution by combining cooperative communication in physical layer with routing selection in network layer. For Wireless Mesh Network (WMN) with stable power, cooperative routing can be used for improving wireless network throughput by choosing reasonable cooperative relay nodes for transmission links.

© Springer International Publishing Switzerland 2015
G. Wang et al. (Eds.): ICA3PP 2015, Part I, LNCS 9528, pp. 552–566, 2015.
DOI: 10.1007/978-3-319-27119-4_38

Relative research shows that cooperative routing has plenty of advantages of improving transmission capacity in single hop wireless network, but the performance in multi-hop wireless network may not better than that of traditionally direct routing due to extra interference of cooperative transmission [1]. In order to exploit advantage of cooperative communication in multi-hop wireless network, we need to absorb other technique to alleviate interference. Since Multi-Radios Multi-Channel(MRMC) can decrease interference evidently, it can be used to work with cooperative routing to obtain efficient diversity gain with less interference and promote network overall throughput finally.

In the multi-radio multi-channel WMN, cooperative routing and channel assignment strategy decides the network performance. However, for the cooperative routing, its performance is seriously undermined by interference among links, which can cause data conflict and retransmission. While existing cooperative routing [2–12,20] algorithms don't consider channel assignment with limited number of radios and channels and they can't take advantage of MRMC technique. For the channel assignment, existing methods [13–17] didn't consider characteristics of cooperative transmission, such as changes of transmission rate and interference range stemming from cooperative relay nodes, and they can't directly be extended to cooperative transmission network.

Compared with traditional direct routing, cooperative routing in MRMC WMN faces more challenges. On the one hand, cooperative routing needs to determine both the multi-hop node and the cooperative relay at each hop by considering the constraint of limited number of radios, while direct routing just needs to determine its next multi-hop node. On the other hand, there are multiple direct links in a cooperative transmission, including links from sender to receiver, from sender to cooperative relay and from cooperative relay to receiver. And the interference of cooperative transmission is more complex than that of direct transmission. Cooperative relay can improve the transmission capacity, but it also can brings extra interference. Different strategy of cooperative relay selection can result in different interference. And we need get a balance between diversity gain and interference in the cooperative transmission.

Therefore, in order to fully exploit cooperative communication in multi-hop MRMC WMN to improve network throughput, this paper studies the joint problem of cooperative routing and channel assignment, and design a distributed algorithm for it. The proposed algorithm is consist of two stages. In the first stage, a distributed cooperative routing algorithm based on a novel metric is proposed to make flows pass through network evenly. In the second stage, a distributed channel assignment algorithm based on graph coloring is proposed to assigning channel for both direct links and cooperative links. And the simulation result shows that our proposed algorithm can effectively promote overall network throughput.

The major advantages of the proposed algorithm can be summarized as follows:

(1) We propose a new cooperative routing metric $RATC$ (Reminder Available Transmission Capacity) by considering both available transmission capacity of

links and the number of radios on the node. Based on this metric, a cooperative routing algorithm is proposed to make flows evenly distributed in the network and transmit data with less interference.

(2) By considering the characteristic of cooperative links, we propose a channel assignment algorithm to assign channels to links by using local link information. Compared with traditional channel assign method, our method can be used for both cooperative links and direct links.

The rest of paper is organized as follow: In Sect. 2 describes the problem. Section 3 specifies the algorithm design. Section 4 presents performance evaluation results and the final Sect. 5 concludes the paper.

2   Problem Statement

2.1   Motivation

We consider a multi-radio multi-hop wireless network $G = \{V, E\}$,where V represents node set and E represent edge set. Each node is equipped with one or multiple wireless radios and each radio can use several orthogonal channels. And there are multiple concurrent sessions.

In single hop WMN, cooperative communication can obtain diversity gain by combining multiple copies of signal from different paths. While in multi-hop WMN, besides diversity gain, cooperative communication can also bring extra interference stemming from cooperative relay. And multi-radio technique can effectively decrease interference. If advantages of two techniques are adopted at the same time, the better wireless network services for flows could be offered.

However, by using the traditional cooperative routing algorithm, forwarding paths of flows may be concentrated and more nodes may be shared by multiple flows, which results in more interference among transmission links. Besides, if flows choose too many cooperative relays to help send data, interference among links will also increase. Although orthogonal channels can reduce contention interference, overall network throughput will still be constrained seriously for the limited number of radios.

Let's illustrate the problem by Fig. 1. In Fig. 1, each node is equipped with 2 radios and can use 5 orthogonal channels. And we assume that transmission range equals to interference range. The arrow line denotes links of flows cooperative routing. And the digital on the arrow line represents the channel assigned to the link. As Fig. 1(a) shows, there are two flows transmitted simultaneously in the network. Sources and destinations of flow 1 and flow 2 are S_1 and D_1, S_2 and D_2 respectively. By using traditional cooperative routing, S_1 will transmit data to A, then A and C cooperatively transmit the data to D, and then D transmit the data to G, finally G and F cooperatively send the data to D_1. That is to say, flow 1 chooses the path $S_1 \rightarrow (A, C) \rightarrow D \rightarrow (G, F) \rightarrow D_1$. Similarly, flow 2 chooses the path $(S_2, E) \rightarrow D \rightarrow (G, H) \rightarrow D_2$. From Fig. 1(a), link $(A, C) \rightarrow D, (S_2, E) \rightarrow D, (G, F) \rightarrow D_1, (G, H) \rightarrow D_2, D \rightarrow G$ can only transmit for flow 1 and flow 2 alternately by time division resulting from interference, which extremely decreasing network throughput.

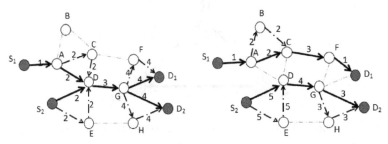

(a) Traditional cooperative routing   (b) Alternative cooperative routing

Fig. 1. Cooperative routing example

But, if forwarding paths of flows can be evenly distributed in the network and share same nodes as few as possible, higher throughput will be achieved. Like Fig. 1(b), the transmission capacity of some links may decrease, but the overall network throughput can be improved.

Therefore, this paper wants to solve the problem that how to choose cooperative routing for flows to make flows pass through network evenly and assign channels to links to minimize interference among forwarding links, resulting in better overall network throughput finally.

2.2 Cooperative Transmission Model

Cooperative communication can obtain diversity gain by receiving multiple copies of the same message from different forwarding paths. Figure 2 shows the classic three-node model of cooperative transmission. S, R and D represent sender, cooperative relay and receiver respectively. When S broadcasts signal to D, R will also overhear the same signal and then transmits it to D. Finally, D will receive two copies of the same signal and combine two copies together using maximum ratio combining to get a stronger signal.

Although a cooperative transmission can use multiple nodes as cooperative relays, [19] shows that the diversity gain of selecting the best relay is a little less than the diversity gain achieved by using multiple relay nodes. Therefore, we consider a cooperative transmission can at most select one cooperative relays in this paper.

Compared with traditional direct transmission, cooperative transmission has difference in transmission rate and interference range under the same condition.

Cooperative Transmission Rate. There are several existing cooperative transmission modes [3, 6, 18], and AF-RAKE proposed in [18] can maximize increasing transmission rate with less interference. And this paper discusses cooperative routing based on it and introduce it next.

According to [18], MAC layer transmission rate of AF-RAKE mode can be calculated as follow:

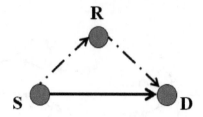

Fig. 2. Three node mode of cooperative transmission

$$C_{AF} = W \log_2(1 + SNR_{sd} + \frac{SNR_{sr} + SNR_{rd}}{SNR_{sr} + SNR_{rd} + 1}) \qquad (1)$$

where

$$SNR_{sd} = \frac{P_s}{\sigma_d^2}|h_{sd}|^2, SNR_{sr} = \frac{P_s}{\sigma_r^2}|h_{sr}|^2, SNR_{rd} = \frac{P_r}{\sigma_d^2}|h_{rd}|^2$$

represent signal-noise-ratio between nodes; and W represents the bandwidth; P_s and P_r represents transmission power of s and r; h_{sd}, h_{sr} and h_{rd} denotes path loss between s and d, s and r, r and d respectively; σ_d^2 and σ_r^2 denotes variance of zero-mean background noise at d and r.

If s transmits signal to d using direct transmission mode, the MAC layer rate is:

$$C_D = W \log_2(1 + SNR_{sd}) \qquad (2)$$

Cooperative Interference Range. Different from direct transmission, a cooperative transmission contains multiple direct links. In order to simplify the description, we treat links in a cooperative transmission as a cooperative link. Because cooperative relays take part in transmission, the interference range of cooperative link is different from direct transmission link. In direct transmission, only source node S and destination node D take part in the transmission, and the interference range of the link is union interference range of S and D, like Fig. 3(a). While interference of cooperative transmission link is union interference range of S, D and cooperative relay R, like Fig. 3(b). Thus, compared with direct transmission, interference range of cooperative transmission is larger in the same network environment.

In the next section, well express a distributed algorithm for cooperative routing and channel assignment.

3 Algorithm Description

In fact, the joint problem of direct routing and channel assignment without selecting cooperative relays in multi-radio multi-channel wireless network is

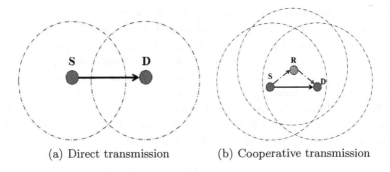

(a) Direct transmission   (b) Cooperative transmission

Fig. 3. Interference range of wireless transmission

already NP-hard. Meanwhile, the problem of joint flow routing and cooperative relays selection is also NP-hard. If the two NP-hard problems are put together to solve at the same time, it will be much more complicated. Hence, to reduce complexity of the joint problem of cooperative routing and channel assignment, we break it into two stages of cooperative route selection and channel assignment.

For the first stage, if too many nodes are shared by multiple flows, interference will be large. Although nodes can alleviate the interference by using orthogonal channels, network throughput will also be restrained because of limited number of radios. By considering both available transmission capacity of links and the number of radios, a cooperative routing algorithm is proposed to make flows pass through network more evenly and use same nodes for transmitting data as few as possible.

For the second stage, channel assignment should consider the characteristic of cooperative links. And a graph coloring algorithm is proposed to assign channels to both cooperative links and direct links to minimize interference.

3.1 Cooperative Routing

To uniformly describe routing selection, we use $\text{link}(x, y, m)$ to denote the cooperative link and direct link. If $m = 0$, it means a direct link $x \rightarrow y$. And if $m > 0$, it means a cooperative link $(x, m) \rightarrow y$. Define $Cap(i)$ as the transmission rate in MAC layer of link (x, y, m), and this can be calculated according to formula (1) or (2).

For either a cooperative link or a direct link, all nodes of the link have to use a common channel to transmit data. Hence, the radio's number of a direct link is the least number of radios on its sender and receiver. Similarly, the radio's number of a cooperative link is the least number of radios on its sender, receiver and relays. Define $RD(x, y, m)$ as the radio number of link (x,y,m), and CH as the set of available orthogonal channels for links, and $|CH| > RD(x, y, m)$. Thus, link (x, y, m) can transmit data simultaneously in $RD(x, y, m)$ orthogonal channels at most, and the largest transmission capacity of link(x,y,m) will be $RD(x, y, m) \times CAP(x, y, m)$.

In order to make flows pass through network evenly and decrease the interference, we use the $RATC$ (Reminder Available Transmission Capacity) to denote the available transmission capacity of links during routing process. Initially, the $RATC$ of each link is equal to its largest transmission capacity, that is, $RATC(x,y,m) = RD(x,y,m) \times Cap(x,y,m)$. During the routing process, if sender or receiver of link(x,y,m) has been selected as other flows' forwarding node, the link should allocate its transmission time to flows averagely. Hence, after providing forwarding service for k flows, the reminder available transmission capacity of link (x,y,m) should be calculated as:

$$RATC(x,y,m) = \frac{RD(x,y,m)Cap(x,y,m)}{k+1} \tag{3}$$

it means the transmission capacity of link(x,y,m) is divided into $k+1$ parts, k of them are allocated to the k flows, and the rest one is left as available transmission rate for other potential flows.

Denote $LC(x,y,m)$ as link(x,y,m)'s transmission cost,

$$LC(x,y,m) = \frac{1}{RATC(x,y,m)} \tag{4}$$

which can be regarded as effective time of transmitting unit data by using multiple channels; And define $PC((x,y,m),f)$ as transmission cost from link(x,y,m)'s receiver to flow f's destination:

$$PC((x,y,m),f) = min \sum_{l \in p} LC(x,y,m), \forall p, S_p = T_l, D_p = D_f \tag{5}$$

where T_l represents link(x,y,m)'s receiver, D_f represents flow f's destination, p represents any paths whose source is $T(x,y,m)$ and destination is D_f.

During the routing process, we will select one link for each flow with minimal cost at a certain time slot t, and formulate this problem as a integer linear programming as following:

$$\min_{X((x,y,m,f),t)} \sum_{i,f} (LC(x,y,m) + PC((x,y,m),f))X((x,y,m),f,t)$$

$$s.t. \sum_{(x,y,m) \in S_f} X((x,y,m),f,t) = 1, \forall f \in F \tag{6}$$

where $X((x,y,m),f,t)$ equals to 1 when at time slot t, link(x,y,m) is selected to transmit data for flow f, else $X((x,y,m),f,t)$ equals to 0. S_f is the link set whose transmitter nodes receive flow f at time slot $t-1$ and its a potential link set which may be selected for flow f at time t.

The objective of problem (6) is to minimize the sum of link cost and path cost of the links selected at time slot t within one constraints that each flow selects one link to transmit at time slot t. After solving the problem at each time slot, the available transmission capacity of selected link will be updated according to (3), and then each link cost LC and path cost PC will also be updated according to (4) and (5) respectively. By solving the problem (6) step and step, cooperative routing for all flows can be determined preliminarily.

In addition, in order to further reduce interference, the algorithm will adjust the preliminary cooperative routes to make them follow next two rules.

(a) If the node has been selected as some flows' multi-hop nodes, they can't be selected as cooperative relays.

(b) The number of cooperative transmission that the node participates in can't be larger than the number of radios on the node.

We'll adjust preliminary routes to obey these rules by using local link information.

After determining cooperative routes, we can assign orthogonal channels to links in the forwarding path without violating radio constraint in order to minimize interference.

3.2   Channel Assignment

The channel assignment problem can be transformed into a graph coloring problem that coloring vertices in the graph by using k colors to minimize the number of monochromatic edges of the graph.

And the only input is the network conflict graph, which can be obtained based on connection network to characterize the interference relation among links. The relationship between network connection graph and conflict graph can be expressed by Fig. 4. Figure 4(a) shows a connection graph, and each vertex represents a wireless route node, and an edge between a node pair represents a wireless transmission link. Figure 4(b) shows a conflict graph corresponding to Fig. 4(a). In Fig. 4(b), a vertex represents a transmission link in Fig. 4(a), and an edge between a node pair represents the two nodes are interfering each other. For example, the link$(A, B, 0)$ and (B, C, D) in Fig. 4(a) are corresponding to $l_{(A,B,0)}$ and $l_{(B,C,D)}$ in Fig. 4(b), and the edge between l_{AB} and l_{BC} means they have interference relation.

Different from traditional graph coloring method, our algorithm needs to consider the characteristic of cooperative links. A cooperative link is consider as a whole of three direct links. When assigning a channel to a cooperative link, all these direct links need to be assigned with the same channel under the constraint number of radios. In Fig. 5(b), when assigning a channel c_1 to link (B, C, D), link $(B, C, 0), (B, D, 0), (D, C, 0)$ should be also assigned with c_1. Conversely, when assigning a channel c_2 to link $(B, C, 0)$, it has to ensure that all direct links of link (B, C, D) can communicate with each other at least via one common channel. So, channel assignment for the cooperative link is more complex.

The graph coloring problem can be solved by a greedy approach. At the beginning, each vertex in the graph is colored with the same color 1. Consequently, we try to change the color of some vertex in a greedy manner without violating the degree constraint iteratively. In each iteration, we try to change the color of some vertex u from its former color to k. All possible u and k pairs will be considered except those violating degree constraint. And the (u, k) pair

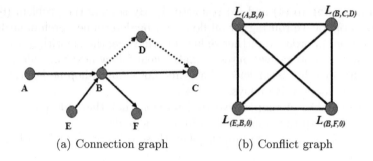

(a) Connection graph   (b) Conflict graph

Fig. 4. Connection and Conflict graph

resulting in minimal number of monochromatic edges will be selected at this iteration. The iteration will continue until the number of monochromatic edges can't decrease any more.

As for a MRMC WMN, we firstly construct the conflict graph according to its connection graph and then color the conflict graph by a greedy approach.

Let V_c denote the conflict graph. Initially, a uniform channel is assigned to each forwarding link $l_{(x,y,m)} \in V_c$. Then, each sender x of forwarding link $l_{(x,y,m)}$ selects a channel i replace its former channel. And this change should satisfy three conditions:

(a) changing the channel of $l_{(x,y,m)}$ does not violate the radio constraint at x,y and m if $m > 0$.

(b) $l_{(x,y,m)}$ has not select i before;

(c) selecting i for $l_{(x,y,m)}$ can result in the largest decrease in the local network interference.

Consequently, x notices its h-hop neighbor that it has changed the channel. Finally, after several iteration, all forwarding links will be assigned a channel.

In order to guarantee termination in a distribution setting, we impose additional restriction that each pair $(l_{(x,y,m)}, i)$ is picked at most once in the entire duration of the algorithm. Hence, the total iteration number is $|V_c| \times |CH|$, and each iteration can be completed in at most $|V_c| \times |CH|$ times. And the total time complexity of the greedy algorithm is $O(|V_c| \times |CH|)^2$.

3.3   Distributed Design

Similar to traditional direct network, nodes propagate connectivity and channel information with its neighbors to the whole network. The connectivity information includes the neighbor list, transmission rate to each neighbor node and receiving SNR from neighbor. Based on these information, the cooperative routing and channel assignment algorithm can be designed in a distributed manner.

The algorithm is consist of two stages. The first stage is finding cooperative routes for flows according to $RATC$ metric. And the second stage is to assign orthogonal channels to cooperative links and direct links in the routes. And the detail of the algorithm is described as follow.

Stage 1: Finding Cooperative Route

(1) Initially, all radios on each node is assigned with a same channel to communicate with each other. And LC and PC of each link can be obtained by using the traditional heuristic routing method according to periodic broadcasting message from network nodes.

(2) The source of each flows gathers the information of its outgoing links and other flows within 2-hops by broadcasting $RREQ(RouteRequest)$ message. According to formula (6), the source selects the best forwarding link. After this, the source updates LC and PC of its outgoing links.

(3) After receiving $RREQ$ from upstream, the next hop node will judge whether it is the destination of the flow and reply with $RREP(RouteReply)$. If it is, the node just needs to update its LC and PC of its outgoing links and stop further routing, else the node will repeat the step (2) until reaching the destination.

(4) After all flows finish their preliminary cooperative routing, all cooperative nodes in cooperative routes check their routing information. If the cooperative node is also selected as multi-hop node of other flows, it will send $RREQ$ message to its neighbors to cancel the role of cooperative relay. Suppose the cooperative node serves for k cooperative links and is equipped with n radios. If $k > n$, the node will select n cooperative links with biggest improvement from its cooperation, and send RREQ message to senders and receivers of the rest cooperative links to cancel its cooperation.

Stage 2: Assigning Channel

(5) Once finishing routing process, all nodes construct local conflict graph according to 2-hop network connectivity information.

(6) For a forwarding link $l_{(x,y,m)}$, its sender x changes one of its radio from c_i to c_j after waiting for a certain random delay, where the c_i is former channel corresponding to link $l_{(x,y,m)}$. And the change needs to satisfy above three conditions. Then, x sends a $RREQ$ message to notice y and m if $m > 0$.

(7) y and m change the channel of their radio corresponding to $l_{(x,y,m)}$, and reply x with a $RREP$ message.

(8) x broadcasts the update message to its 2-hops neighbors once receiving the reply.

(9) The node repeats the step (6), (7) and (8) until local network interference can't reduce anymore or the node has try every possible channel.

According to the distributed algorithm, we can find optimal cooperative routes for flows and assign channels to forwarding links with minimal interference.

4 Simulation Results

We randomly generate 49 nodes in an area of 600 m × 600 m evenly. The network uses the bandwidth of 2 MHz for each channel. The transmission of each node is 0.28 w and both transmission range and interference range are 150 m. We assume the line-of-sight (LOS) link between nodes and h_{sd} only include the propagation gain between node s and d and is given by $h_{sd} = \|s - d\|^{-4}$, where $\|s - d\|$ is the distance between nodes s and d and loss index is 4. For the AWGN channel, we assume the variance of noise is 10^{-10}W at all nodes.

To demonstrate the performance of our proposed algorithm, we evaluate the overall network throughput in different scenes and compare it with two other algorithms in various scenes.

(a) *uni_CCR*: Uniform channel assignment and Contention-aware Cooperative routing [3] algorithm is used.

(b) *color_CCR*: Traditional coloring channel assignment [21] and Contention-aware Cooperative routing algorithm is used.

We perform three set of simulations to analyze the effect of the number of flows, the number of channels, node density, the number of radios and the transmission range. As follows, we show the simulation results respectively.

Figure 5 illustrates the result of overall network throughput with increasing number of flows under three different algorithms. In this case, each node is equipped with 2 radios and can use 5 orthogonal channels. The number of flows varies from 10 to 20. The result shows that network throughput achieves about 40 % throughput gain compared with *uni_CCR*, and achieves from 70 % throughput gain compared with *color_CCR*. The reason is that the proposed algorithm consider available transmission capacity of links and the number of radios, and make flows pass through network more evenly, resulting in more balanced traffic and less interference among links.

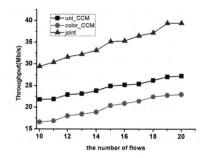

Fig. 5. Throughput vs. number of flows

Figure 6 shows the impact of channels number on throughput. In this case, each node is equipped with 2 radios, and there are 15 flows transmitting data. The number of channels varies from 2 to 7. From Fig. 6, we can see that the proposed algorithm brings about from 10 % to 66 % throughput gain compared with *uni_CCR*, and from 42 % to 117 % throughput gain in contrast with *color_CCR*. This is also because our algorithm makes flow pass through network more evenly and traffic load will be more balanced. In addition, we see that the throughput of *uni_CCR* and *color_CCR* changes little while the number of channels is increasing. For the *uni_CCR*, each nodes has only 2 radios, and each node can be only assigned 2 identical channels. So, the number of channels has no influence on the throughput. For the *color_CCR*, it assigns channels to links firstly, and then find the routing path. And in order to maintain connection between nodes, channel assignment for links has seldom change with increasing channels, also resulting from limited radio number of nodes. And this cause almost no change of flows routings and interference among forwarding links. Hence, the throughput of *uni_CCR* and *color_CCR* will unchanged little.

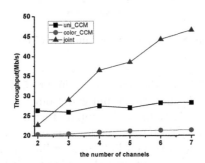

Fig. 6. Throughput vs. number of channels

Figure 7 shows the result of throughput with increasing node density. In this case, each node is equipped with 2 radios and can use 5 orthogonal channels. The number of flows is 15 and the number of nodes changes from 36 to 66. The result shows that the proposed algorithm obtain throughput gain about 40 % compared with *uni_CCR*, and from 85 % compared with *color_CCR*. Besides, with increasing number of node, more high-rate links exists under the higher node density and thus improves the throughput.

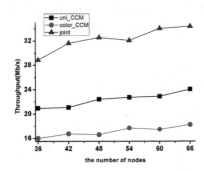

Fig. 7. Throughput vs. number of nodes

Figure 8 illustrates the result of throughput with different radios. In this case, there are 15 flows in the network and each node can use 5 orthogonal

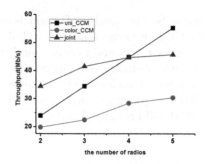

Fig. 8. Throughput vs. number of radios

channels. And the number of radios changes from 2 to 5. Figure 8 illustrates that the proposed algorithm obtains throughput gain from −17 % and 44 %, compared with *uni_CCR*, and from 50 % to 85 % compared with *color_CCR* respectively. With the increase of radios' number, nodes can use more orthogonal channel to transmit data independently, and links among links will become smaller and smaller. And at this time, the network throughput will be mainly determined by the distance of routes. Because our algorithm consider reminder available transmission capacity of links during routing, the distance of routes is longer than that of *uni_CCR* and *color_CCR*, since. Hence, the throughput gain of our algorithm will decrease.

Figure 9 shows the result of throughput with increasing transmission range. Each node is equipped with 2 radios and can use 5 orthogonal channels. The number of flows is 15 and the transmission range changes from 110 m to 170 m. The result shows that the proposed algorithm obtains throughput gain from 30 % and 50 %, compared with *uni_CCR*, and from 60 % to 100 % compared with *color_CCR* respectively. From the figure, we can see that with the increase of transmission range, the network throughput of three algorithms decrease. The reason is that although cooperative opportunity will increase with longer transmission range, the interference among forwarding links will also increase.

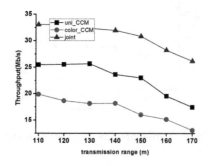

Fig. 9. Throughput vs. transmission range

And the drawback of interference increment overcomes the benefit of cooperative transmission.

5 Conclusion

In order to provide better service for flows in the WMN, this paper adopts both multi-radio multi-channel technique and cooperative communication technique at the same time to sufficiently exploit diversity gain of cooperative communication with least interference. After studying the joint problem of cooperative routing and channel assignment, a distributed cooperative routing and channel assignment algorithm is proposed to improve the overall network throughput. The simulation result shows that the proposed algorithm can improve network performance effectively under different network scene.

Acknowledgments. This work is supported by the National Basic Research Program of China (973) under Grant No. 2012CB315805, the National Natural Science Foundation of China under Grant No. 61472130 and 61173167.

References

1. Dehghan, M., Ghaderi, M., Goeckel, D.L.: On the performance of cooperative routing in wireless networks. In: IEEE Conference on Computer Communications Workshops, pp. 1–5. IEEE Press, San Diego (2010)
2. Sharma, S., Yi, S., Hou, Y.T., Sherali, H.D., Kompella, S., Midkiff, S.F.: Joint flow routing and relay node assignment in cooperative multi-hop networks. IEEE J. Sel. Areas Commun. **30**(2), 254–262 (2012)
3. Zhang, J., Zhang, Q. :Contention-aware cooperative routing in wireles mesh networks. In: IEEE International Conference on Communications, pp. 1–5. IEEE Press, Dresden (2009)
4. Ong, L., Motani, M.: Optimal routing for decode-forward in cooperative wireless networks. IEEE Trans. Commun. **58**(8), 2345–2355 (2010)
5. Xie, K., Wang, X., Wen, J.G., Cao, J.N.: Cooperative routing with relay assignment in multi-radio multihop wireless networks. In: IEEE/ACM Trans. Netw. (2015). doi:10.1109/TNET.2015.2397035
6. Elhawary, M., Haas, Z.J.: Energy-efficient protocol for cooperative networks. IEEE/ACM Trans. Netw. **19**(2), 561–574 (2011)
7. Zhang, J., Zhang,Q.: Cooperative routing in multi-source multi-destination multi-hop wireless networks. In: IEEE International Conference on Communications, pp. 2369–2377. IEEE Press, Phoenix (2008)
8. Xie, K., Cao, J.N., Wang, X., Wen, J.G.: Optimal resource allocation for reliable and energy efficient cooperative communications. IEEE Trans. Wirel. Commun. **12**(10), 4994–5007 (2013)
9. Lin, I.T., Iwao, S.: Distributed ad hoc cooperative routing in cluster-based multihop networks. In: IEEE 20th International Symposium on Personal, Indoor and Mobile Radio Communications, pp. 2643–2647. IEEE Press, Tokyo (2009)
10. Siam, M.Z., Krunz, M., Younis, O.: Energy-efficient clustering/routing for cooperative MIMO operation in sensor networks. In: IEEE International Conference on Computer Communications, pp. 621–629. IEEE Press, Rio de Janeiro (2009)

11. Shen, Z.G., Ding, Z.G., Dresden, K.K.: Distributed and power efficient routing in wireless cooperative networks. In: IEEE International Conference on Communications, pp. 1–5. IEEE Press, Dresden (2009)

12. Xu, H.L., Huang, L.S., Qiao, C.M., Zhang, Y.D., Quan, S.: Bandwidth-power aware cooperative multipath routing for wireless multimedia sensor networks. IEEE Trans. Wirel. Commun. 11(4), 1532–1543 (2012). doi:10.1109/TWC.2012.020812. 111265

13. Dhananjay, A., Zhang, H., Li, J.Y., Subramanian, L.: Practical, distributed channel assignment and routing in dual-radio mesh networks. ACM SIGCOMM Comput. Commun. Rev. 39(4), 99–110 (2009)

14. Ramachandran, K.N., Belding, E.M., Almeroth, K.C.: Interference-aware channel assignment in multi-radio wireless mesh networks. In: IEEE International Conference on Computer Communications, pp. 1–12. IEEE Press, Barcelona (2006)

15. Chieochan, S., Hossain, E.: Channel assignment for throughput optimization in multichannel multsiradio wireless mesh networks using network coding. IEEE Trans. Mob. Comput. 12(1), 118–135 (2013)

16. Zhao, W., Nishiyama, H., Fadlullah, Z., Kato, N., Hamaguchi, K.: DAPA: Capacity Optimization in Wireless Networks through a Combined Design of Density of Access Points and Partially Overlapped Channel Allocation. IEEE Trans. Veh. Technol.. (2015). doi:10.1109/TVT.2015.2437714

17. Xu, J., Zeng, K., Liu, W.: Online learning for unreliable passive monitoring in multi-channel wireless networks. In: IEEE International Conference on Communications, pp. 7257–7262. IEEE Press, London (2015)

18. Zhu, Y., Zheng, H.T.: Understanding the impact of interference on collaborative relays. IEEE Trans. Mob. Comput. 7(6), 724–736 (2008)

19. Zhao, Y., Adve, R., Lim, T.J.: Improving amplify-and-forward relay networks: optimal power allocation versus selection. IEEE Trans. Wirel. Commun. 6(8), 3114–3123 (2006)

20. Merlin, S., Vaidya, N., Zorzi, M.: Resource allocation in multi-radio multi-channel multi-hop wireless networks. In: IEEE Conference on Computer Communications, pp. 610–618. IEEE Press, Phoenix (2008)

21. Subramanian, A.P., Gupta, H., Das, S.R., Cao, J.: Minimum interference channel assignment in multiradio wireless mesh networks. IEEE Trans. Mob. Comput. 7(12), 1459–1473 (2008)

Improved Approximating Algorithms for Computing Energy Constrained Minimum Cost Steiner Trees

Nianchen Zou and Longkun Guo$^{(\boxtimes)}$

College of Mathematics and Computer Science, Fuzhou University,
Fuzhou 350108, China
longkun.guo@foxmail.com

Abstract. Nowadays, two issues in data transmission for networks are attracting considerable interest in the research community: energy efficiency and cost minimization, i.e., to minimize the energy consumed and resource occupied. This paper considers approximation algorithms for the energy constrained minimum cost Steiner tree (ECMST) problem which have applications in energy-efficient minimum cost multicast.

Let $G = (V, E)$ be a given undirected graph, $S \subseteq V$ be a terminal set, and $c : E \rightarrow \mathbb{Z}_0^+$ and $d : E \rightarrow \mathbb{Z}_0^+$ respectively be the cost function and energy consumption function for the edges. For a threshold D, ECMST is to compute a minimum cost tree spanning all specified terminals of S, with its total energy consumption bounded by D. This paper first shows that ECMST is pseudo-polynomial solvable when the number of the terminals are fixed. Then it presents a polynomial time factor-$(2(1 + \frac{1}{k}), 2(1 + k))$ approximation algorithm via Lagrangian Relaxation for any $k > 0$. Last but not the least, by a more sophisticated application of Lagrangian relaxation technique, we obtain an approximation algorithm with ratio $(2, 2 + \epsilon)$ for any fixed $\epsilon > 0$.

Keywords: Approximation algorithm · Multiple constraint · Steiner tree · Lagrangian relaxation · Energy efficiency

1 Introduction

In many networks applications, there are often two or more QoS constraints, say, cost and energy consumption, for determining a route, since a route is often required to achieve simultaneously efficient utilization of network resources and consumed energy. When considering data multicast against these two QoS constraints, provided that traditional data multicast is often accomplished via a Steiner tree, the energy constrained minimum cost Steiner tree (ECMST) problem arises. The ECMST problem is to find a minimum cost Steiner tree T that satisfies a given budget restriction D on its total energy consumption, i.e., $\sum_{e \in T} d_e \leq D$. Obviously, ECMST is a $\mathcal{NP}$-hard problem since it can be embedded into the minimum Steiner tree problem that is $\mathcal{NP}$-hard. So it is impossible

© Springer International Publishing Switzerland 2015
G. Wang et al. (Eds.): ICA3PP 2015, Part I, LNCS 9528, pp. 567–577, 2015.
DOI: 10.1007/978-3-319-27119-4_39

to find an exact solution for ECMST problem unless $\mathcal{P} = \mathcal{NP}$. In this paper, we focus on bifactor approximation algorithm, i.e., (α, β)-approximation, for the ECMST problem.

Definition 1. *An algorithm is an (α, β)-approximation for every instance of the ECMST problem, if and only if it computes in polynomial time a Steiner tree T for which the total cost is at most β times of that of an optimal solution, and $d(T) \leq \alpha D$ holds, where D is the energy consumption bound.*

1.1   Related Work

The ECMST problem is first discussed by Rosenwein et al. [24], where various problem formulations and decomposition based approaches were given. Later, Chen [6] presented a fully polynomial time approximation scheme for the problem in Halin networks. However, the fully polynomial time approximation scheme can not be applied to ECMST for the same ratio, since even the minimum Steiner tree problem is $\mathcal{APX}$-hard. Unlike special graphs, there exist few articles addressing approximation algorithms for ECMST for general undirected or directed graphs.

Though not many works exist on ECMST itself in literature, some special cases of the ECMST problem are well studied. The constrained minimum spanning tree (CMST) problem, the ECMST problem when $S = V$, is known $\mathcal{NP}$-hard [1]. Goemans and Ravi [22] presented a $(2, 1)$-approximation algorithm based on Lagrangian relaxation and then improved the ratio to $(1 + \epsilon, 1)$ but with a much higher time complexity. Marathe et al. [18] gave a $(1 + \epsilon, 1 + \frac{1}{\epsilon})$-approximation algorithm for the CMST problem. Hassin and Levin [15] presented an efficient polynomial time approximation scheme (EPTAS) for this problem based on Lagrangian relaxation and matroid intersection. Yen Hung Chen [7] presents two polynomial time approximation schemes (PTAS) for the CMST problem. Applying the second PTAS to Hassin and Levin's algorithm [15], the approximation ratio can be improved to $(1, 1 + 4\epsilon)$ for the CMST problem. When the energy consumption of each edge is set to zero, ECMST would be reduced to the minimum Steiner tree problem, one of the most fundamental $\mathcal{NP}$-hard problems [9], which is to compute a tree T spanning all terminals of S of minimum cost $\sum_{e \in T} c_e$. This problem has been studied by many researchers and a lot of algorithms have been developed [10,21,23], among which the current best approximation ratio is 1.39 [3].

Problems related to ECMST have also been well investigated. The shallow-light Steiner tree (SLST) problem is to compute a minimum cost Steiner tree that satisfies a fixed delay constraint between the root and every other terminal. On the heuristic algorithm side, Kompella et al. [16] proposed a heuristic approach for the problem. Kadaba and Jaffe [2] proposed an algorithm for the problem when the cost and energy consumption functions are identical. To improve the previous methods, Xu Ying presented a hybrid scatter search heuristic algorithms [25]. On the approximation algorithm side, Charikar et al. presented a quasi-polynomial time approximation algorithm with single factor ratio $O(\log^2 t)$

[5], while Hajiaghayi et al. proposed a polynomial time approximation algorithm with bifactor ratio $(O(\log^2 t), O(\log^4 t))$ [14]. The k disjoint bi-constrained path problem (kBCP) is another related bicriteria optimization problem, which targets k disjoint st-paths whose cost and delay both satisfy the given constraints. For kBCP, approximation algorithms with a bifactor of $(1 + \beta, 1 + \ln \frac{1}{\beta})$ and a single factor ratio of $O(\ln n)$ (i.e. bifactor approximation ratio $(1, O(\ln n))$ have been developed for general k in [12], where $1 > \beta > 0$ is any fixed positive real number. For the k restricted shortest path problem (kRSP), which is to compute k-disjoint shortest path satisfying a given delay constraint, Peng et al. [4] and Orda et al. [20] have achieved bifactor ratios of $(1 + \frac{1}{r}, r(1 + \frac{2(\log r+1)}{r})(1 + \epsilon))$ and $(1 + \frac{1}{r}, 1 + r)$ for $k = 2$, respectively. Based on LP-rounding technology, an approximation ratio $(2, 2)$ has been obtained in [11], and then been improved to ratio$(1 + \epsilon, 2 + \epsilon)$ in [13].

1.2   Our Results

The first result of this paper is that ECMST admits a pseudo-polynomial algorithm when the number of the terminals are fixed. The second is to reduce ECMST to CMST by constructing a complete multiple-graph. Then by using binary search and Lagrangian relaxation method following a similar line as in [4,18], we obtain a $(2(1 + \frac{1}{k}), 2(1 + k))$ approximation algorithm. Furthermore, based on Lagrangian relaxation and observations on the adjacency relations for matroids, we improve the ratio to $(2, 2 + \epsilon)$.

The remainder of this paper is organized as below: Sect. 2 gives a pseudo-polynomial time algorithm for ECMST when the terminal number is fixed; Sect. 3 gives an approximation algorithm with ratio $(2(1 + \frac{1}{k}), 2(1 + k))$ for ECMST; Sect. 3.3 further improves the ratio to $(2, 2 + \epsilon)$; Sect. 4 concludes this paper.

2   A Pseudo Polynomial Time Algorithm for ECMST with a Fixed Terminal Number

In this section, we shall extend the Dreyfus-Wagner algorithm to compute a minimum-cost Steiner tree with a given energy constraint D in pseudo-polynomial time. The Dreyfus-Wagner algorithm is an existing exact algorithm for computing minimum Steiner tree for any terminal subset (with size k) within a running time $O(3^k n + 2^k n^2 + n^3)$ [8].

We would like to give some notations before the technique paragraphs. We denote by $C_D(S)$ the optimal Steiner tree spanning S and satisfying the constraint D, and $P_D(u, v)$ the minimum-cost path between u and v that satisfies the constraint D. Our algorithm uses a dynamic programming method, which computes optimal trees $C_{D'}(S' \cup \{u\})$ for all $S' \subseteq S$ and $u \in V$ recursively. It uses the following recursion formulas:

Theorem 1. *Let $G = (V, E)$ be a given graph, $S \subseteq V$ be a terminal set. Then for any $S' \subseteq S$, $u \in V/S'$, we have*

$$C_{D'}(S' \cup \{u\}) = \min_{v \in V, \varnothing \neq S'' \subset S'} \{C_{D_1}(S'' \cup \{v\}) \cup C_{D_2}((S'/S'') \cup \{v\}) \cup P_{D_3}(u, v) : D_1 + D_2 + D_3 \leq D'\}.$$

Proof. For any $v \in V$, we have:

$$C_{D'}(S' \cup \{u\}) = \min\{C_{D_0}(S' \cup \{v\}) \cup P_{D_3}(u, v) : D_0 + D_3 \leq D'\}.$$

Then for any $S'' \subset S'$

$$C_{D_0}(S' \cup \{v\}) = \min\{C_{D_1}(S'' \cup \{v\}) \cup C_{D_2}((S'/S'') \cup \{v\}) : D_1 + D_2 \leq D_0\}.$$

This completes the proof.

The full layout of our algorithm is as depicted in Algorithm 1.

Algorithm 1. An exact algorithm for ECMST

Input: Graph $G = (V, E)$, a set of terminals $S \subseteq V$, cost $c : E \rightarrow \mathbb{Z}_0^+$, energy consumption $d : E \rightarrow \mathbb{Z}_0^+$, and an energy constraint D;
Output: $C_D(S)$.

1. Set $i := 2$;
2. **For each** $u \in V$, $v \in V$ and $D' \in \{0, 1, \ldots, D\}$ **do**
   Compute $P_{D'}(u, v)$ using the algorithm for computing a restricted shortest path in [17];
3. **For** $D' = 0$ to D **do**
   For each $S' \subseteq S$ with $|S'| = i$ and each $u \in V/S'$ **do**
   $C_{D'}(S' \cup \{u\}) =$

   $$\min_{v \in V, \varnothing \neq S'' \subset S'} \{C_{D_1}(S'' \cup \{v\}) \cup C_{D_2}((S'/S'') \cup \{v\}) \cup P_{D_3}(u, v) : D_1 + D_2 + D_3 \leq D'\};$$

4. **If** $i \leq |S| - 1$ **then** $i = i + 1$;
   Go to Step 3;
   else terminate.

Theorem 2. *Algorithm 1 will terminate in $O(mn^2 D^2 + mn^3 D \log \log n + 3^k \cdot D^4)$ time, where $|V| = n$, $|E| = m$ and $|S| = k$, respectively, are the numbers of the vertices, edges and terminals of the graph.*

Proof. In Algorithm 1, Step 2 takes at most $O(mD + mn \log \log n)$ time for using the algorithm of [17] for each $P_{D'}(u, v)$. The number of all $P_D(u, v)$ is $O(n^2 \cdot D)$, so the total running time of Step 2 is $O(mn^2 D^2 + mn^3 D \log \log n)$. Step 3 takes at most $O(2^i \cdot \binom{D'}{3})$ time for each $C_{D'}(S' \cup \{u\})$, where 2^i is the number of all possible combinations of S'' and $S' \setminus S''$ wrt a S' with $|S'| = i$, and $\binom{D'}{3}$ is the number of combinations of D_1, D_2 and D_3. Hence, the whole Step 3 runs in time

$O((\sum_{i=1}^{k} \binom{k}{i} 2^i) \cdot D^4) = O(3^k \cdot D^4)$. The other steps of algorithm takes trivial time comparing to Step 2 and 3. Therefore, the time complexity of Algorithm 1 is $O(mn^2D^2+mn^3D\log\log n)+O(3^k \cdot D^4) = O(mn^2D^2+mn^3D\log\log n+3^k \cdot D^4)$. This completes the proof.

3 Approximation Algorithms for ECMST

The key idea of our algorithms is to construct a complete multiple-graph $H = (S, F)$, in which a solution to the constrained minimum spanning tree problem (CMST) is an approximation solution to ECMST in the original G. The idea is based on the observation that CMST can be well approximated by using Lagrangian relaxation technique.

3.1 The Construction of the Auxiliary Graph H

The graph H is mainly composed by two parts: its vertices are exactly the terminal nodes in G, while its edges are the minimum cost paths satisfying different energy constraints. The construction is as below: For every pair of terminal nodes, say node i and j, find shortest paths $P_1(i, j)$, ..., $P_D(i, j)$ between i and j in G where $d(P_1(i, j)) \leq 1$, ..., $d(P_D(i, j)) \leq D$. The cost of edge $e_{i,j}^k \in F$, i.e., $c(e_{i,j}^k)$, equals the cost of the path $P_k(i, j)$, and its energy consumption $d(e_{i,j}^k)$ equals k. Besides, if there exists no path between i and j satisfying $d(e_{i,j}^k) \leq k$, the cost of the edge between i and j is set to infinity ($+\infty$). Therefore, there are $O(D|S|^2)$ edges in H in total, i.e., $|F| = O(D|S|^2)$. Note that parallel edges might arise, so H is a multi-graph. The detailed construction is as in Algorithm 2 (A simple example is as depicted in Fig. 1).

Algorithm 2. Construction

Input: Graph $G = (V, E)$, a set of terminals $S \subseteq V$, a cost function $c : E \to Z_0^+$, an energy consumption function $d : E \to Z_0^+$, an energy consumption constraint D;
Output: A graph H.

1. $F = ?$;
2. **For** each $i \in S$ **do**
       For each $j \in S/\{i\}$ **do**
           For each $1 \leq k \leq D$ **do**
               Compute the paths $P_k(i, j)$ between i and j;
               /* $P_k(i, j)$ is a minimum cost path with $d(P_k(i, j)) \leq k$.*/
               $e_{i,j}^k = P_k(i, j)$, $F = F \cup \{e_{i,j}^k\}$, $c(e_{i,j}^k) = c(P_k(i, j))$, $d(e_{i,j}^k) = k$;
           else $c(e_{i,j}^k) = +\infty$
3. Return $H = (S, F)$.

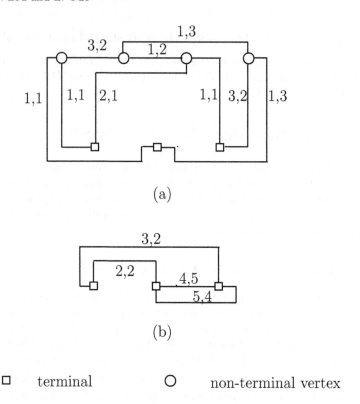

(a)

(b)

□   terminal   ○   non-terminal vertex

Fig. 1. A simple example for the construction of H: (a) The original graph G in which every edge has an energy consumption and a cost; (b) The auxiliary graph H.

The following lemma states the connection between graph G and H :

Lemma 1. *Let T^* be an optimum Steiner tree for S satisfying the total energy consumption constraint D in G and T_H^* be an optimum minimum cost spanning tree under constraint $2D$ in H, then $c(T_H^*) \leq 2c(T*)$.*

Proof. Consider the graph M with $V(M) = V(T^*)$. For any $u, v \in V(M)$, adding two copies of edge $e(u, v)$ into M if and only if $e(u, v) \in T^*$. Obviously, M is Eulerian since the degree of each vertex in M is even. Then there exists an Eulerian walk W in M and $d(W) = 2d(T^*) \leq 2 \cdot D$. Let $\{v_1, v_2, ..., v_{|S|}\}$ be the order of vertices in W. Assume that the energy consumption of $W(v_i, v_{i+1})$, the path between v_i and v_{i+1} along W, is D_i' for $1 \leq i \leq| S | -1$. Then all $e_{i,i+1}^{D_i'}(1 \leq i \leq |S| - 1)$ defines a tour W'in H, where $e_{i,i+1}^{D_i'}$ is for the restricted shortest path $P_{D_i'}(i, i+1)$ in G. Since $c(e_{i,i+1}^{D_i'}) \leq c(W(v_i, v_{i+1}))$, we have $c(W') \leq c(W) = c(M) = 2 \cdot c(T^*)$ and $d(W') = d(M) \leq 2 \cdot D$. Because $W'$is a tour, it contains a spanning tree of H. Therefore, we have $c(T_H^*) \leq c(W') \leq 2 \cdot c(T^*)$. This completes the proof.

3.2   A Simple Method

This subsection gives a simple method to compute in H a minimum cost spanning tree satisfying an energy consumption restriction $2D$. The key idea of our algorithm is to combine the Lagrangian Relaxation technique and binary search. The detailed algorithm is as depicted in [4].

Let T^* be an optimum Steiner tree for S satisfying the total energy consumption constraint D in G and T_H^* be an optimum minimum cost spanning tree under constraint $2D$ in H. Then we have the following Theorem:

Theorem 3. *Assume that the output of the algorithm is a Steiner tree T. Then $d(T) \leq 2(1 + \frac{1}{k})D$ and $c(T) \leq 2(1 + k)c(T^*)$, where $k > 0$;*

Proof. From [4], we have $c(T) \leq (1 + k)c(T_H^*)$ and $d(T) \leq 2(1 + \frac{1}{k})D$. And according to Lemma 1, we know that $c(T_H^*) \leq 2c(T^*)$ and $d(T_H^*) \leq 2D$. Then $d(T) \leq 2(1 + \frac{1}{k})D$ and $c(T) \leq 2(1 + k)c(T^*)$. This completes the proof.

Theorem 4. *Let T_c and T_d be the spanning trees with minimum total cost and minimum total energy consumption respectively in graph $H = (S, F)$, and let $|V| = n$, $|E| = m$. Algorithm terminates in $O((m+n\log n)(D|S|^2+\log\frac{(1+k)c(T_d)}{c(T_c)}))$ time.*

Proof. In Algorithm 2, since Step 2 of the algorithm will terminate in $O(D|S|^2)$ rounds and finding the paths between two nodes takes $O(m + n\log n)$ times, the time complexity of Algorithm 2 is within $O((D|S|^2)(m + n\log n))$. Computing in H a minimum cost spanning tree satisfying an energy consumption restriction $2D$ takes $O((|F| + |S|\log|S|)\log\frac{(1+k)c(T_d)}{c(T_c)})$ time [4]. Then this algorithm will end in $O((D|S|^2)(m + n\log n)) + O((|F| + |S|\log|S|)\log\frac{(1+k)c(T_d)}{c(T_c)}) = O((m + n\log n)(D|S|^2 + \log\frac{(1+k)c(T_d)}{c(T_c)}))$ time.

3.3   An Improved Approximation Algorithm

This subsection gives an improved approximation algorithm for CMST. In graph H, the constrained minimum spanning tree problem can be formulated by the following:

$$\min \sum_{e_{i,j}^k \in F} c(e_{i,j}^k) \cdot x_{i,j}^k$$

$$s.t. \sum_{e_{i,j}^k \in F} d(e_{i,j}^k) \cdot x_{i,j}^k \leq 2D$$

$$x \in X$$

where X denote the set of incidence vectors of spanning trees of H.

For any $\alpha \geq 0$,

$$f(\alpha) = \min \sum_{e_{i,j}^k \in F} (c(e_{i,j}^k) + \alpha \cdot d(e_{i,j}^k)) \cdot x_{i,j}^k - \alpha \cdot 2D$$

$$s.t. \, x \in X$$

For the CMST problem, we give an approximation algorithm that extends the method in [22]. Let $\alpha^* := \arg\max_{\alpha \geq 0} f(\alpha)$, $w(e_{i,j}^k) := c(e_{i,j}^k) + \alpha \cdot d(e_{i,j}^k)$. The key idea of the algorithm is using the Lagrangian Relaxation technique, and exploiting adjacency relations for matroids. In general, the algorithm is composed by 3 steps. Firstly, solve the Lagrangian relaxation and compute α^* by minimum spanning tree computations; Secondly, find a minimum tree T_0 with respect to the new cost $w_e^* = c_e + \alpha^* \cdot d_e$; Thirdly, repeat improving the tree by a greedy edge replacement until the energy consumption is below $2D$ (W.l.o.g. assuming that $d(T_0) > 2D$).

For the third step, assume that T_i is the tree computed in the ith iteration still with $d(T_i) > 2D$, we compute T_{i+1} by replacing an edge $e \in T_i$ with another edge $e' \in F \setminus T_i$, such that

$$\min_{\forall e \in T_i, \, e' \in F \setminus T_i} \left\{ \frac{d(T_i) - \max\{d(T_{i+1}), 2D\}}{c(T_i) - c(T_{i+1})} \right\} \tag{1}$$

is attained. Intuitively, the minimum in Formula (1) means that the algorithm decrease the energy consumption at the price of a minimum cost increase.

Formally, the algorithm is as depicted in Algorithm 3.

Algorithm 3. An improved approximation algorithm

Input: Graph $G = (V, E)$, a set of terminals $S \subseteq V$, cost $c : E \rightarrow Z_0^+$, energy consumption $d : E \rightarrow Z_0^+$, a total energy consumption constraint D, and a real number ϵ;

Output: A Steiner tree T of G;

1. Compute a complete multiple-graph $H = (S, F)$ by Algorithm 2;
2. Compute α^* according to the method by Megiddo in [19];
3. Compute T_0 with minimum $\sum_{e \in T_0} w_e^*$, where $w_e^* = c_e + \alpha^* \cdot d_e$; /*W.l.o.g., assume that $d(T_0) > 2D$. */
4. Set $i := 0$;
5. Find a pair of $e \in T_i$ and $e' \in F \setminus T_i$, such that $T_{i+1} := T_i \setminus \{e\} \cup \{e'\}$ is a tree attaining

$$\min_{\forall e \in T_i, \, e' \in F \setminus T_i} \left\{ \frac{d(T_i) - \max\{d(T_{i+1}), 2D\}}{c(T_i) - c(T_{i+1})} \right\};$$

6. **If** $d(T_{i+1}) > 2D$ **then** set $i := i + 1$ and go to Step 5;
   Else return T which is a Steiner tree in G corresponding to T_{i+1}.

Theorem 5. *The output of Algorithm 3 is a Steiner tree T in which the total energy consumption of the edges are bounded by 2 times of D and the total cost of the edges are bounded by $2 + \theta$ times of the optimum solution T^*, where $\theta = \frac{c_{max}}{c(T^*)}$.*

Proof. Assume that Algorithm 3 terminates in t iterations, i.e., $d(T_{t-1}) > 2D$ and $d(T_t) \leq 2D$.

Then we show that $c(T_{t-1}) \leq c(T_H^*)$ as below. From Algorithm 3, we know T_{t-1} is a tree with minimum $\sum w_e^*$. Then there exist a sequence $T_{t-1} = T_0$, T_1, ..., $T_l = T_H^*$ of minimum $\sum w_e^*$, such that T_i and T_{i+1} are adjacent for $i = 0, , 1, ..., l-1$. According to [22], there is a T with $\sum w_e^*$ such that $c(T) \leq c(T_H^*)$ if and only if $d(T) \geq 2D$. So there exist edges $e \in T_i$ and $e' \in T_{i+1}$, such that $c(e) - c(e') < 0$ and $d(e) - d(e') > 0$.

Assume that that T_{t-1} is obtained from T_0 by replacing a series of edges, say $e_1, e_2, ..., e_h \in T_{t-1}$ and $e_1^*, e_2^*, ..., e_h^* \in T_0$. Then $c(T_{t-1}) = c(T_0) + \sum_{i=1}^h [c(e_i^*) - c(e_i)]$ and $d(T_{t-1}) = d(T_0) + \sum_{i=1}^h [d(e_i^*) - d(e_i)]$. Since in every replacement we decrease the delay and increase the cost, then $c(e_i) - c(e_i^*) < 0$ and $d(e_i) - d(e_i^*) > 0$ for any $i \in \{1, 2, ..., h\}$. According to our algorithm, each edge replacement attains

$$\min_{\forall e \in T_i, \, e' \in F \setminus T_i} \left\{ \frac{d(T_i) - \max\{d(T_{i+1}), 2D\}}{c(T_i) - c(T_{i+1})} \right\};$$

From Ravi et al.'s result [22], there exists a tree $T_\leq$ with $\sum_{e \in T_\leq} w_e^*$ minimized and $d(T_\leq) \leq 2D$. That is, $c(T_{t-1}) \leq c(T_\leq) \leq c(T_H^*)$. Let $\theta := \frac{c_{max}}{c(T^*)}$, then

$$c(T_t) = c(T_{t-1}) - c(e) + c(e') \leq c(T_H^*) + c_{max} = c(T_H^*) + \theta \cdot c(T^*)$$

According to Lemma 1, we have $c(T_H^*) \leq 2c(T^*)$. Then $d(T_t) \leq 2D$ and $c(T_t) \leq (2+\theta)c(T^*)$, i.e., $d(T) \leq 2D$ and $c(T) \leq (2+\theta)c(T^*)$. This completes the proof.

From the technique of a Ravi et al.'s paper [22], the approximate ratio could improve to $(2, 2 + \epsilon)$, where $\epsilon > 0$.

Theorem 6. *Let $|V| = n$, $|E| = m$, then Algorithm 3 runs in $O((D|S|^2)(m + n\log n)) + O(|S|^{1+O(\frac{1}{\epsilon})}(D|S|\log^2|S| + \log^3|S|))$ time.*

Proof. Step 1 takes $O((D|S|^2)(m + n\log n))$ time, and Step 2 takes $O(\log^2|F|(|F| + |S|\log|S|)) = O(|F|\log^2|S| + |S|\log^3|S|)$ time by using the method in [19]. At last, the algorithm repeats Step 5 for at most $O(D)$ times, each of which takes $O(m^2)$ time to find the minimum. Therefore, this algorithm will end in $O((D|S|^2)(m + n\log n)) + O(|S|^{1+O(\frac{1}{\epsilon})}(D|S|\log^2|S| + \log^3|S|))$ time. This completes the proof.

4   Conclusion

In this paper, we first presented a pseudo-polynomial time exact algorithm for the energy constrained minimum cost Steiner tree (ECMST) problem, when the number of the terminals is fixed. Then we proposed two polynomial time approximation algorithms for ECMST. The first is with a bifactor ratio $(2(1 + \frac{1}{k}), 2(1 + k))$, that is, its output is with total energy consumption and cost receptively bounded by $2(1 + \frac{1}{k})D$ and $2(1 + k)$ times of that of an optimal solution of ECMST, where $k > 0$ is a real number. The second improves the ratio to $(2, 2 + \epsilon)$, where $\epsilon > 0$. In future, we shall investigate algorithms with better approximation ratio for ECMST.

Acknowledgments. This project was supported by National Science Foundation of China (#61300025), Doctoral Fund of Ministry of Education of China for Young Scholars (#20123514120013) and Natural Science Foundation of Fujian Province (#2012J05 115).

References

1. Aggarwal, V., Aneja, Y.P., Nair, K.P.K.: Minimal spanning tree subject to a side constraint. Comput Oper. Res. **9**(4), 287–296 (1982)
2. Bharath-Kumar, K., Jaffe, J.M.: Routing to multiple destinations in computer networks. IEEE Trans. Commun. **31**(3), 343–351 (1983)
3. Byrka, J., Grandoni, F., Rothvoss, T., Sanità, L.: Steiner tree approximation via iterative randomized rounding. J. ACM (JACM) **60**(1), 6 (2013)
4. Chao, P., Hong, S.: A new approximation algorithm for computing 2-restricted disjoint paths. IEICE Trans. Inf. Syst. **90**(2), 465–472 (2007)
5. Charikar, M., Chekuri, C., Cheung, T., Dai, Z., Goel, A., Guha, S., Li, M.: Approximation algorithms for directed steiner problems. J. Algorithms **33**(1), 73–91 (1999)
6. Chen, G., Burkard, R.E.: Constrained steiner trees in halin graphs. RAIRO-Oper. Res. **37**(03), 179–194 (2003)
7. Chen, Y.H.: Polynomial time approximation schemes for the constrained minimum spanning tree problem. J. Appl. Math. **1–8**, 2012 (2012)
8. Dreyfus, S.E., Wagner, R.A.: The steiner problem in graphs. Networks **1**(3), 195–207 (1971)
9. Garey, M.R., Graham, R.L., Johnson, D.S.: The complexity of computing steiner minimal trees. SIAM J. Appl. Math. **32**(4), 835–859 (1977)
10. Gilbert, E.N., Pollak, H.O.: Steiner minimal trees. SIAM J. Appl. Math. **16**(1), 1–29 (1968)
11. Guo, L.: Improved lp-rounding approximations for the k-disjoint restricted shortest paths problem. Front. Algorithmics **2014**, 94–104 (2014)
12. Guo, L., Shen, H., Liao, K.: Improved approximation algorithms for computing k disjoint paths subject to two constraints. J. Comb. Optim. **29**(1), 153–164 (2015)
13. Guo, L., Liao, K., Shen, H., Li, P.: Efficient approximation algorithms for computing k-disjoint restricted shortest paths. In: 27th ACM Symposium on Parallelism in Algorithms and Architectures, pp. 62–64 (2015)
14. Hajiaghayi, M.T., Kortsarz, G., Salavatipour, M.R.: Approximating buy-at-bulk and shallow-light k-Steiner trees. In: Díaz, J., Jansen, K., Rolim, J.D.P., Zwick, U. (eds.) APPROX 2006 and RANDOM 2006. LNCS, vol. 4110, pp. 152–163. Springer, Heidelberg (2006)
15. Hassin, R., Levin, A.: An efficient polynomial time approximation scheme for the constrained minimum spanning tree problem using matroid intersection. SIAM J. Comput. **33**(2), 261–268 (2004)

16. Kompella, V.P., Pasquale, J.C., Polyzos, G.C.: Multicast routing for multimedia communication. IEEE/ACM Trans. Network. (TON) **1**(3), 286–292 (1993)
17. Lorenz, D.H., Raz, D.: A simple efficient approximation scheme for the restricted shortest path problem. Oper. Res. Lett. **28**(5), 213–219 (2001)
18. Marathe, M.V., Ravi, R., Sundaram, R., Ravi, S.S., Rosenkrantz, D.J., Hunt III, H.B.: Bicriteria network design problems. J. Algorithms **28**(1), 142–171 (1998)
19. Megiddo, N.: Applying parallel computation algorithms in the design of serial algorithms. J. ACM **30**(4), 852–865 (1983)
20. Orda, A., Sprintson, A.: Efficient algorithms for computing disjoint QoS paths. IEEE INFOCOM **1**, 727–738 (2004)
21. Prömel, H.J., Steger, A.: A new approximation algorithm for the steiner tree problem with performance ratio 5/3. J. Algorithms **36**(1), 89–101 (2000)
22. Ravi, R., Goemans, M.X.: The constrained minimum spanning tree problem. In: Karlsson, R., Lingas, A. (eds.) SWAT 1996. LNCS, vol. 1097, pp. 66–75. Springer, Heidelberg (1996)
23. Robins, G., Zelikovsky, A.: Tighter bounds for graph steiner tree approximation. SIAM J. Discrete Math. **19**(1), 122–134 (2005)
24. Rosenwein, M.B., Wong, R.T.: A constrained steiner tree problem. Eur. J. Oper. Res. **81**(2), 430–439 (1995)
25. Ying, X., Rong, Q.: A hybrid scatter search meta-heuristic for delay-constrained multicast routing problems. Appl. Intell. **36**(1), 229–241 (2012)

A Hybrid Genetic Algorithm for Privacy and Cost Aware Scheduling of Data Intensive Workflow in Cloud

Congyang Chen[1,2,3(✉)], Jianxun Liu[1], Yiping Wen[1,2],
Jinjun Chen[1,2,3], and Dong Zhou[1,2]

[1] Key Laboratory of Knowledge Processing and Networked Manufacture,
Hunan University of Science and Technology,
Xiangtan 411100, China
chencongyangmm@gmail.com, ljx529@gmail.com,
ypwen81@gmail.com, jinjun.chen@gmail.com
[2] College of Computer Science and Engineering,
Hunan University of Science and Technology,
Xiangtan 411100, China
dongzhou1979@hotmail.com
[3] Faculty of Engineering and Information Technology,
University of Technology Sydney,
Ultimo, NSW 2070, Australia

Abstract. In the context of cloud computing and big data, the data of all walks of life has been obtained conveniently. Some information of users in the business process is in need of protection with the popularity of workflow applications, which will greatly affect the scheduling of workflow. Meanwhile, the amount of data is usually very large in workflow, the data privacy protection in workflow has also become an important research problem. In this paper, in order to satisfy the requirement of data privacy protection from user and minimize the total scheduling cost in workflow scheduling, we proposed a privacy and cost aware method based on genetic algorithm for data intensive workflow applications which takes into account computation cost, data transmission cost and data storage cost in cloud to solve this problem on finding the best scheduling solution. The proposed algorithm uses the summation of upward and downward rank values for prioritizing workflow tasks, then merges it to make an optimal initial population to obtain a good solution quickly. Besides, a series of operations like selection, crossover and mutation have been used to optimize the scheduling. In the workflow task scheduling, we assign the datacenter for tasks needing privacy protection, which data of these tasks cannot be moved or copied to other datacenter. Finally, we demonstrate the potential of proposed algorithm for optimizing economic cost with user privacy protection requirement. The experimental results show that proposed algorithm can help improve the scheduling and save the time and cost by an average of 3.6 % and 15.6 % respectively.

Keywords: Privacy protection · Cloud computing · Workflow scheduling · Genetic

© Springer International Publishing Switzerland 2015
G. Wang et al. (Eds.): ICA3PP 2015, Part I, LNCS 9528, pp. 578–591, 2015.
DOI: 10.1007/978-3-319-27119-4_40

1 Introduction

In recent years, more and more enterprises are migrating their own business system to the cloud with the constantly development of cloud computing technology and cloud infrastructure. For most enterprises, it is a common phenomenon to provide more convenient of application support for customer via the services of business process based on cloud computing. In this context, as a powerful support tool that supports business process automation, workflow technology combined with cloud computing technology has become a new trend. Cloud workflow has aroused wide attention from academic and industry at home and abroad now. Meanwhile, a series of research findings and some industrial products such as IBM Blueworks Live and other products have also sprung up.

Cloud workflow scheduling is a process that executes and manages tasks with mapping the interdependent tasks from workflow instances into the distributed resources in cloud, which is also very important for cloud users and cloud service providers. However, we find that how to give the utmost assurance of and manage the data privacy of user during execution of the cloud workflow task is still a neglected research blind spot now. In fact, the cross-organizational business collaboration process in the fields of emergency management, supply chain management and health care, etc., which are data intensive workflows with the size and/or quantity of data is large and are including the trade secrets or personal privacy data. For Example, it cannot move or copy the patient's personal information to others when the hospital seeking for other help. In the Tianchi Big Data competition, the players, at the time of final, cannot download the dataset and only can use these data in Tianchi Big Data Platform provided by Alibaba. If there are no good scheduling strategy to address the data privacy protection and management issues, these data will be accumulated a certain scale to larger data with repeated runs of the business, which most likely has detrimental effects on individuals, enterprises, even the whole society.

The rest of paper is organized as follows. In the next section we describe the related work. Section 3 defines the model, resource, and problem definition underneath our approach. Section 4 we present our proposed algorithm. In Sec. 5 the evaluating of performance of CP-GA is presented. Finally, we summaries the conclusions and the future work in Sec. 6.

2 Related Works

For service providers, it is a common phenomenon to collect their customers' information, like service requests. From large to small firms, they commonly use them to analyze customers' behaviors, habits, and other sensitive information. Pearson divided the user privacy information into three category, (1) personally identifiable information, such as name, age, etc.; (2) sensitive personal information, such as race, wage income, etc.; (3) the available data on line, including the user's video, article, pictures, etc. [1]. In terms of privacy protection technologies, there are 3 categories in existing technologies, they are perturbation of the data, data encryption and data anonymization technique [2].

In terms of cloud privacy protection, privacy protection scheme based on data encryption has always been the most common technique. Fabian et al. [3] used the attribute-based encryption method and proposed an architecture that protected the privacy and security of patient data in a semi-trusted and cross-cloud environment. In addition, according to the characteristics of cloud computing platforms and privacy features of the data itself, researchers at home and abroad have a study on the frameworks of cloud privacy protection. For example, Kamara et al. [4] put forward a cloud storage security framework that combined the data processor, the data confirmed, the token generator and the certificate generator to cooperate the encrypted storage services of user data in cloud. Yang et al. [5] researched the personal media data privacy protection problem with the storage service supplied by the third party cloud service providers and put forward a solution.

There are lots of research findings in workflow scheduling algorithms in cloud computing environment [6]. Min Zheng [7] et al. proposed a cloud workflow algorithm based on dynamic planning to solve the scheduling overhead optimization of cloud workflow in dynamic resource prices environment. S. Mukute [8] et al. proposed an algorithm based on Job Shop to solve the issue of dynamic scheduling in cloud computing with a special attention to the case of instance-intensive cost-constrained workflows. Juan et al. [9] proposed a multi-objective workflow scheduling method called Multi-Objective Heterogeneous Earliest Finish Time (MOHEFT) for multi-objective optimization problem in Amazon EC2 Cloud. Liu Ke et al. [10] presented a novel compromised-time-cost scheduling algorithm which focus on the trade-off of time and cost throughout the scheduling process.

Heuristic algorithms, Genetic Algorithm, Ant Colony Optimization, Particle Swarm Optimization and other meta-heuristic algorithms have been applied to the cloud workflow scheduling. Chen et al. [11] used ant colony optimization algorithm to optimize the scientific workflow scheduling and discussed the multi-objective scheduling optimization problem with Various QoS Requirements. In addition to optimizing execution time, the cost arising from data transmits between resources as well as execution costs must also be taken into account. Suraj Pandey et al. [12] proposed a particle swarm optimization (PSO) based scheduling heuristic for data intensive applications. In order to meet the requirements of instance aspect handling in practical workflow application. Wen Yiping et al. [13] proposed a method which utilizes the theory of ant colony optimization to achieving the objectives of minimum acidity instances' total dwelling time and minimum acidity instances' total cost with constraints. Guangzhen Lu et al. [14] proposed a novel heuristic workflow scheduling algorithm CLWS, which it distributes task levels by their concurrence and adopts the efficiency algorithm MDP to optimize the sequential tasks with time dependency. Mustafizur Rahman et al. [15] developed a hybrid heuristic that can effectively integrate most of the benefits of both heuristic and metaheuristic-based approaches to optimize execution cost and time as well as meet the user's requirements through an adaptive fashion. Arash et al. [16] proposed a hybrid heuristic method (HSGA) to find a suitable scheduling for workflow graph, based on genetic algorithm in order to obtain the response quickly moreover optimizes makespan, load balancing on resources and speedup ratio.

3 Problem Definition

Privacy and cost aware scheduling of data intensive workflow in cloud aims to make the usage cost minimization completing the application with the user privacy constraint of the premise. In order to address the problem of workflow scheduling with the user privacy protection in cloud. First of all, we define the workflow and resource model and the target needs to be solved.

3.1 Workflow Model

According to the characteristics of workflow applications, we can model a workflow application as a directed acyclic graph: $W = (T, CE, DE, D)$, where T represents a set of tasks; we can define $T = \{t_i | t_i = \langle name, L_i, O_i, W_i \rangle\}$, where name is the task name, L_i and O_i represent the input and the output dataset related to the task. W_i describes the task's computation; CE, which is a set of directed edges, which represents the inter-dependencies of control flow among tasks in workflow, can be defined as $CE = \{\langle t_i, t_j \rangle | \langle t_i, t_j \rangle \in T \times T\}$; DE describes the interdependencies of data flow among tasks in workflow defined as $CE = \{\langle t_i, t_j, data_{ij} \rangle | t_i, t_j \in T, data_{ij} \subseteq O_i$ and $data_{ij} \subseteq I_j\}$, where $data_{ij}$ represents the size of the data which needs to be transmitted from task t_i to task t_j; D is a set of data related to the workflow including input/output data, defined as $D = \{d_i | d_i = \langle i, sd_i, isprivate, ld_i \rangle\}$, where i is the unique identifier of data d_i, sd_i is the size of data d_i, $isprivate$ is the privacy attribute of data d_i and ld_i is the location where d_i belongs.

3.2 Resource Model

According to the characteristics of cloud resource, the available datacenter in cloud can be defined as:$DC = \{dc_i | dc_i = \langle space_i, \cos t_i \rangle\}$, where $space_i$ represents the currently available storage size of datacenter dc_i, $\cos t_i$ represents the storage rates of dc_i ($/MB).

At the same time, we assume that the cloud service providers can provide different rental prices and the configuration of virtual resources to carry out the task of workflow, These resources can be defined as $R = \{r_i | r_i = \langle rc_i, rt_i, rp_i, rl_i \rangle\}$, where rc_i represents computational capability of one type of virtual resources and different type of virtual resources have different computational capabilities; rt_i represents the time unit of price; rp_i represents the price function of virtual resource (here we use the price strategy in accordance with Amazon EC2) and rl_i represents the datacenter where a virtual resource belongs.

In terms of the communication bandwidth and the transmission rates, we can assume there be n datacenters. So communication bandwidth and transmit price among datacenters can be respectively represented by matrix BW and TC, where $BW_{p,q}(1 \leq p \leq n, 1 \leq q \leq n)$ represents the communication bandwidth which transmitted from d_p to d_q, the unit is MB/S and $TC_{p,q}(1 \leq p \leq n, 1 \leq q \leq n)$ represents the transmit price from datacenter dc_p to dc_q.

We define the scheduling solution as $S: T \times R \to \{0,1\}$, that is, Matrix S represents an effective mapping which from all tasks in workflow to virtual resources. $S_{i,j} = 1$, stands for the fact that task t_i is scheduled to virtual resource r_j.

The demand for privacy protection is based on the strong dependence or sensitivity of the data. It can greatly affect the process of workflow scheduling algorithm. So we can define the demand of privacy protection as $P: D \times DC \to \{0,1\}$, namely, Matrix P represents an effective mapping from user privacy data in workflow to the datacenter. If the value of $P_{i,j}$ is 1, it means that the user privacy data (the data of workflow tasks need to be protected) can only be placed and scheduled in datacenter dc_j, i.e., it cannot be moved or copied to other datacenters in all the process of scheduling optimization.

3.3   Cloud Resource Cost

The cloud resource cost is the cost of completing the workflow task, depending on three parts: the computation cost of executing tasks, the storage cost of task data and the transmission cost which transmits the input/output data between tasks.

In cloud workflow scheduling, if a task has more than one input data set, first of all, we must transmit the data set to the datacenter where the task will be executed. For ease of calculation, we set the predecessor set of task t_i as $pred(t_i)$, so we can define these three parts with given scheduling scheme S as follows.

In this paper we assume that cloud service providers take the form of pricing per unit charge the fee, that is, according to user's total amount of use, the total amount of service charge is calculated by multiplying the total use with the price per unit of resource. Hence, the computational cost formula for executing workflow with the virtual resource under a given scheduling scheme S can be defined by

$$Cost_{comp} = \sum_{r_k \in R} \left\lceil \frac{ET(t_e, r_k) - ST(t_s, r_k)}{rt_k} \right\rceil \times rt_k \times rp_k \tag{1}$$

where t_s and t_e are the first task and the last task which are respectively scheduled to the vm r_i; $ST(t_s, r_k)$ and $ET(t_e, r_k)$ are the start time of task t_s and the completion time of task t_e, respectively. the start time and end time of task t_i can be defined by

$$ST(t_j, r_k) = \max_{t_i \in pred(t_j)} \{ ET(t_i, r_k) + DT(t_i, t_j) \} \tag{2}$$

$$ET(t_i, r_k) = ST(t_i, r_k) + ExeTime(t_i, r_k) \tag{3}$$

where $DT(t_i, t_j)$ is the transmission time of these data from one of its predecessors t_i to task t_j $data_{ij}$ stands for the size of the data in MB and BW_{ij} represents the communication bandwidth between the executors of task t_i, and t_j.

$$DT(t_i, t_j) = data_{ij} / BW_{ij} \tag{4}$$

Then the transmission cost can be defined by

$$Cost_{tran} = \sum_{data_{ij} \in DE} C_{tran}\left(data_{ij}, r_m, r_n\right) \tag{5}$$

where $C_{tran}\left(data_{ij}, t_i, t_j\right)$ is the cost of transmitting $data_{ij}$ from resource r_m of t_i to resource r_n of t_j, and r_m, r_n belong to datacenter dc_p and dc_q respectively. $C_{tran}\left(data_{ij}, t_i, t_j\right)$ is defined as Eq. 6, where TC_{pq} is transmission price from datacenter dc_p to dc_q.

$$C_{tran}\left(data_{ij}, r_m, r_n\right) = data_{ij} \times TC_{pq} \tag{6}$$

The total storage cost can be defined by

$$Cost_{stor} = \sum_{t_i \in T, r_m \in R} C_{stor}(t_i, r_m) \tag{7}$$

where $Cost_{stor}$ is the storage cost when t_i is executed on resource r_m in datacenter dc_p. $C_{stor}(t_i, r_m)$ can be defined as Eq. 8, where sd_i is the input and output data size of task t_i. $Cost_p$ is the storage price of datacenter dc_p:

$$C_{stor}(t_i, r_m) = sd_i \times \cos t_p \tag{8}$$

Therefore, the privacy and cost aware scheduling problem of data intensive cloud workflow in this paper is seeking the lowest cost scheduling solution of cloud resources used with the premise of satisfying user demand for privacy.

4   CP-GA: Privacy and Cost-Aware Genetic Algorithm

In this section we describe the CP-GA as an extension to the standard genetic algorithm for optimizing workflow cost with the user privacy requirement.

4.1   Encoding

In GA method, every solution is encoded as a chromosome. Each chromosome has n genes (tasks). In workflow scheduling each schedule appears in a chromosome form. Each schedule contains the tasks of workflow and the related candidate virtual resources. Figure 1 depicts the encoding format of a chromosome in CP-GA method.

t_1	t_2	t_3	t_4	t_5	......	t_{39}	t_{40}
r_4	r_3	r_5	r_2	r_1	......	r_7	r_4

Fig. 1. A sample encoding of a schedule as a chromosome in CP-GA

Here, we make a serial of number to all available resources in the datacenters, the value of gene is the number of assigned virtual resource with the relevant task. The tasks of workflow are ordered on priority based on the summation of upward and downward rank values (B-Rank) [17] (the orders of tasks maybe change) according to Sect. 4.3, the tasks should mapped on the suitable resources from available virtual resources.

4.2   Initial Population

The target in our algorithm is designed to minimize cost with the user demand for privacy. Therefore, the initial population cannot be simply made randomly as normal genetic algorithm. First of all, we should use B-Rank method to sort the tasks according to interdependencies relationship between tasks in workflow. For each task, we select a candidate virtual resource with the lowest cost from current available virtual resource list. At this moment, we also have to take into account the user privacy protection issue, that is, for the task needed privacy protection, we must assign the specified datacenter to execute, such as $t_2 \rightarrow d_2$, $t_5 \rightarrow d_3$. Meanwhile, the task cannot be moved to other datacenter in the follow-up process of optimization.

Currently, for each chromosome, we must choose a set of cost-effective resources (except for privacy protection, assigning a specific datacenter to schedule the task). In this manner, the first task in first chromosome is assigned with the fittest virtual resource (always is the lowest cost) from virtual resource list, the second task in first chromosome is assigned the second-fittest resource (also probably is the best when it is idle). The fittest candidate-resources will be searched from the next point. This process continues to making a population. But in making each chromosome, if the counter of resources is finished, the resource selection will be continued from first place.

4.3   B-Rank

Since the data of each task, its parent task and its child task are not all the same. The different types of virtual resources and the user privacy protection demand, for the specified task, it can only be scheduled to the specified datacenter. Each scheduling cost of task has affected the total scheduling cost. In order to achieve goal of workflow scheduling, the rank of tasks is particularly important.

In our algorithms, the scheduling priorities are based on upward and downward ranking. The upward rank of a task t_i can be recursively defined by

$$rank_{u(t_i)} = \overline{C_{comp(t_i)}} + \max_{t_j \in succ(t_i)} \left(\overline{C_{tran}\left(data_{ij}, t_i, t_j\right)} + rank_u\left(t_j\right) \right) \tag{9}$$

where $succ(t_i)$ is the set of immediate successors of task t_i, $\overline{Cost_{comp(t_i)}}$ is the average computation cost of task t_i and $\overline{Cost_{tran}\left(data_{ij}, t_i, t_j\right)}$ is the average transmission cost which transmit the $data_{ij}$ from task t_i to task t_j. For the exit task t_{exit}, the upward rank value is equal to

$$rank_{u(t_{exit})} = \overline{C_{comp(t_{exit})}} \tag{10}$$

Generally, we set $rank_{u(ti)}$ as the length from task t_i to the exit task, including the computation cost of task t_i.

Similarly, the downward rank of a task t_i is recursively defined by

$$rank_{d(t_i)} = \max_{t_i \in pred(t_i)} \left(\overline{C_{comp(t_i)}} + \overline{C_{tran}\left(data_{ji}, t_j, t_i\right)} + rank_d\left(t_j\right) \right) \tag{11}$$

where $pred(t_i)$ is the set of immediate predecessors of task t_i. The downward ranks are computed recursively by traversing the task graph downward starting from the entry task of the graph. So for the entry task t_{entry}, the downward rank value is equal to zero.

4.4   Fitness Value

Because of our algorithm is designed to minimize cost completing workflow with the user demand for privacy, the fitness value of each solution can be computed through:

$$Fitness = \sum_{i=1}^{m} \left(cost_{comp} + cost_{tran} + cost_{stor} \right) \tag{12}$$

where $cost_{comp}$ is the computation cost, $cost_{tran}$ is the transmission cost and $cost_{stor}$ is the storage cost. So the target in our algorithm is:

$$Min(Fitness) \tag{13}$$

4.5   Reproduction

Firstly, we get the fitness of all individuals in the group according to the Sect. 4.4, and select the individual needs to be copied under a certain probability, and then determine the best individual by a specified method. Here, we use roulette selection method, and set the group sizes to n, set the fitness of individual i to f_i, so the probability of individual i is selected can be computed through:

$$P_{si} = \frac{f_i}{\sum_{j=1}^{n} f_j} \tag{14}$$

cumulative probability can be computed through:

$$q_i = \sum_{j=1}^{i} p_{sj} \tag{15}$$

Next, figuring out selection probability of each individual and cumulative probability of each individual according to the selection probability. We can generate a random number *random* between [0,1], if $random \leq q_1$, the individual 1 is selected, if $q_i < random \leq q_{i+1}$, the individual i is selected.

4.6   Crossover

In this section, we use partially matched crossover. First, one parent chromosome is randomly selected. Then two positions of genes are selected randomly and the positions are different (also, make sure the virtual resources got involved in privacy protection only can be selected with the same datacenter). For example, we selected the first and third position and the area between two points called match area. Then exchange the match area of parent A and parent B. So the match relation of $r_4 \leftrightarrow r_1$ and $r_2 \leftrightarrow r_6$ are obtained and replace the resource one by one according to the match relation except for the match area in *Parent A* and *Parent B*. Figure 2 illustrates the mentioned example.

Before Crossover

Parent A

t_1	t_2	t_3	t_4	t_5	t_6
r_4	r_3	r_5	r_2	r_2	r_8

Parent B

t_1	t_2	t_3	t_4	t_5	t_6
r_1	r_3	r_5	r_6	r_7	r_6

After Crossover

Child A

t_1	t_2	t_3	t_4	t_5	t_6
r_1	r_3	r_5	r_6	r_6	r_8

Child B

t_1	t_2	t_3	t_4	t_5	t_6
r_4	r_3	r_5	r_2	r_7	r_2

Fig. 2.   Crossover operation method in CP-GA

4.7   Mutation

Here, inversion is used for mutation operator. Firstly, two positions in the parent are selected randomly (also, be sure the resources involved in privacy protection only can be selected in the same datacenter), then make the data between these two positions inversion. For example, we selected the first and fifth position, then exchange r_1 and r_7. Figure 3 illustrates the before and after mutation in mentioned example.

Parent:

t_1	t_2	t_3	t_4	t_5	t_6
r_1	r_3	r_5	r_6	r_7	r_8

Child:

t_1	t_2	t_3	t_4	t_5	t_6
r_7	r_3	r_5	r_6	r_1	r_8

Fig. 3.   Mutation operation method in CP-GA

5 Performance Evaluation

5.1 The Experiment Environment

In order to test performance, we use CloudSim to finish the experiment and make up three datacenters and ten virtual resources with four different types (comply with the price strategy in Amazon EC2).

The parameters of workflow instance and resources model is shown in Fig. 4. The price rate for different kinds or types of resources are shown in Table 1. The algorithm parameters are listed in Table 2 and the workflow tasks details are listed in Table 3.

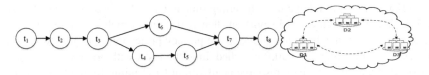

Fig. 4. The workflow and resource used in CP-GA

Table 1. The virtual resource parameters

On-demand Instance	Compute price($/h)	Storage price($/GB)	Transmit price($/GB)	MIPS(Hz)
m1_small	0.064	0.1	0.12	800
m1_medium	0.129	0.1	0.12	1612
m1_large	0.256	0.1	0.12	3200
m2_xlarge	0.514	0.1	0.12	6425

Table 2. The task parameters of workflow

Task number	Task lengths	Input data	Output data
t1	19365	15	36
t2	49809	20	28
t3	30218	24	44
t4	44157	37	17
t5	16754	45	34
t6	18336	16	43
t7	20045	58	28
t8	31493	78	54

Table 3. The values of SGA and CP-GA parameter

Parameter	Value
Population size	20
Iterations	1 ~ 200
Crossover rate	0.95
Mutation rate	0.75

Where task t_3 and task t_5 need to be scheduled to the specific datacenter because of the demand for privacy protection. In our experiment, task t_3 should be scheduled to datacenter D_2 and task t_5 should be scheduled to datacenter D_2.

5.2   The Experiment Results

5.2.1   The Influence on Algorithm with Different Evolutional Generation

Firstly, we respectively use SGA and CP-GA to schedule workflow with 200 workflow instances for privacy protection. Here, our completion time is different with makespan of others which is the time needed with all tasks of all workflow instances have finished (the same below). The detailed experimental results are shown as follow.

In Fig. 5, we can find that the scheduling time in CP-GA is less than SGA by about 3.75 %. The improvement is inapparent, that is the time which scheduling task with privacy protection maybe is long. Due to the privacy protection, it is not always select the best virtual resource in workflow scheduling, the tasks with privacy protection can be executed until the specified resource is idle. In order to minimize the final economic cost, CP-GA only can sacrifice some time for cost. While the scheduling cost obtained by CP-GA is much better than the scheduling cost obtained by SGA. It benefits from the selection operator, crossover operator and mutation, CP-GA can heavily increase the congruence speed and avoid involving local optimization as far as possible.

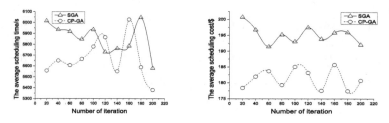

Fig. 5. The influence on results with 200 workflow instances

5.2.2   The Influence of SGA and CP-GA with (or Without) Privacy Protection

In this experiment, we schedule four types of workflow instance number with 20, 50, 100 and 200. The experimental results are shown in Figs. 6 and 7.

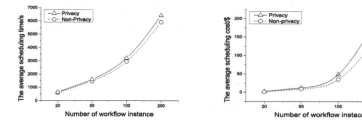

Fig. 6. Scheduling workflow with SGA

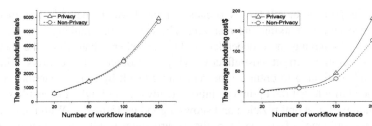

Fig. 7. Scheduling workflow with CP-GA

Above experimental results indicate that the scheduling time and cost with privacy protection are more than the scheduling without privacy protection, which is due to the privacy protection required scheduling the tasks with privacy protection to the specified virtual resources. Although there are more economic resources can be selected when scheduling the tasks with privacy protected, the broker only can schedule the task to the specified virtual resources (and the specified resource is probably busy, so the task will be scheduled has to wait until the resource is idle).

5.2.3 Scheduling Without Privacy Protection

Finally, we experiment with privacy protection and no privacy protection and evaluate the influence of time and cost with different workflow instance numbers. The results are shown in Figs. 8 and 9.

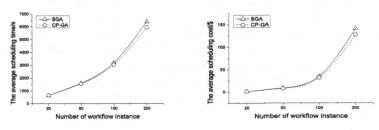

Fig. 8. The average scheduling cost and time without privacy protection

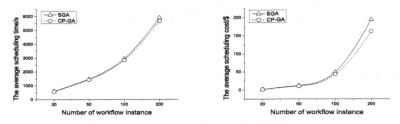

Fig. 9. The average scheduling cost and time with privacy protection

As it shown above, both the scheduling results of CP-GA is better than SGA with the amount increment of tasks, especially the cost. The completion time decreased in the scheduling process of CP-GA is because of the B-Rank method. The method consists of two phases: ranking and mapping. The idea of this ranking is to execute before those tasks having more dependent tasks than other. Meanwhile, the method prefers to select the current cost-effective virtual resource for the tasks will be scheduled and continuing to optimize the scheduling result by fitness function, which improves the ability to get the optimal solution greatly. Accordingly, the cost has been a certain amount of cost optimization and shows a good performance. With the privacy protection, the influence of cost is little, the experimental results show that our proposed algorithm CP-GA can reduce the required cost and additional scheduling time, saving on average by 15.6 % and 3.6 % respectively.

6 Conclusion

In this paper we proposed and analyzed a cost and privacy aware method based on genetic algorithm for data intensive workflow applications that takes into account both computation cost, data transmission cost and data storage cost in cloud. Our new method called CP-GA extends a well-known GA, which use the optimize characteristics B-Rank and partially matched crossover method, etc. In our algorithm we used B-Rank to sort tasks and initial population, then optimized by a series of operators to solve the problem with local optimum and privacy protection. In the workflow task scheduling process, we specified the datacenter for tasks in workflow needing privacy protection, which data of the tasks could not be moved or copied to other datacenter. CP-GA not only regarded minimization of cost with privacy protection as the goal but also took the average computation time as a reference amount. Finally, our algorithm could minimize user cost of cloud computing resource with meeting the user's privacy protection requirement by simulation experiments. In future work we intend to evaluate CP-GA for other objective functions. We will consider increasing the number of objectives to two or more and present a method that support prediction mechanism and meet the requirement of instance aspect handling-oriented optimal scheduling in practical workflow applications.

Acknowledgments. This paper was supported by Nature Science Fund of China, under grant number 61272063, 61402167, 61202111, 61402168, 61300129, the Planned Science and Technology Project of Hunan Province under grant number 13FJ4048, 2014GK3004, and Scientific Research Fund of Hunan Provincial Education Department under grant number 13C160.

References

1. Pearson, S.: Taking account of privacy when designing cloud computing services In: Proceeding s of the 2009 ICSE Workshop on Software Engineering Challenges of Cloud Computing, pp. 44–52. IEEE Computer Society, Washington DC (2009)
2. Liu, Y., Zhang, T., Jin, X., Cheng, X.: Personal privacy protection in the era of big data. J. Comput. Res. Dev. **52**(1), 229–247 (2015)

3. Fabian, B., Ermakova, T., Junghanns, P.: Collaborative and secure sharing of healthcare data in multi-clouds. Inf. Syst. **48**, 132–150 (2015)
4. Kamara, S., Lauter, K.: Cryptographic cloud storage. In: Sion, R., Curtmola, R., Dietrich, S., Kiayias, A., Miret, J.M., Sako, K., Sebé, F. (eds.) RLCPS, WECSR, and WLC 2010. LNCS, vol. 6054, pp. 136–149. Springer, Heidelberg (2010)
5. Yang, J., Li, J., Niu, Y.: A hybrid solution for privacy preserving medical data sharing in the cloud environment. Future Gener. Comput. Syst. **43–44**, 74–86 (2015)
6. Chen, C., Liu, J., Wen, Y., Chen, J.: Research on workflow scheduling algorithms in the cloud. In: Cao, J., Wen, L., Liu, X. (eds.) PAS 2014. CCIS, vol. 495, pp. 35–48. Springer, Heidelberg (2015)
7. Zheng, M., Cao, J., Yao, Y.: Cloud workflow scheduling algorithm oriented to dynamic pric changes. Comput. Integr. Manuf. Syst. **19**(8), 1849–1858 (2013)
8. Mukute, S., Hapanyengwi, G., Mapako, B., et al.: Scheduling in instance-intensive cost-constrained workflows in a cloud. Int. J. Sci. Eng. Res. **4**, 755–760 (2013)
9. Durillo, J.J., Prodan, R.: Multi-objective workflow scheduling in Amazon EC2. Cluster Comput. **17**(2), 169–189 (2014)
10. Liu, K., Yang, Y., Chen, J., et al.: A compromised-cost scheduling algorithm in SwinDeW-C for instance-intensive cost-constrained workflows on cloud computing platform. Int. J. High Perform. Comput. Appl. **24**(4), 445–456 (2010)
11. Chen, W., Zhang, J.: An ant colony optimization approach to a grid workflow scheduling problem with various QoS requirements. IEEE Trans. Syst. Man Cybern. Part C Appl. Rev. **39**(1), 29–43 (2009)
12. Pandey, S., Wu, L., Guru, S.M., Buyya, R.: A particle swarm optimization-based heuristic for scheduling workflow applications in cloud computing environments. In: Proceedings of the 24th IEEE International Conference on Advanced Information Networking and Applications (AINA), pp. 400–407 (2010)
13. Wen, Y., Liu, J., Chen, Z.: Instance aspect handling-oriented scheduling optimization in workflows. Ruan Jian Xue Bao J. Softw. **26**(3), 574–583 (2015)
14. Lu, G., Tan, W., Sun, Y., Zhang, Z., Tang, A.: QoS constraint based workflow scheduling for cloud computing services. J. Softw. **9**(4), 926–930 (2014)
15. Rahman, M., Hassan, M.R., Ranjan, R., Buyya, R.: Adaptive workflow scheduling for dynamic grid and cloud computing environment. Concurrency Comput. Pract. Experience **25**(13), 1816–1842 (2013)
16. Delavar, A.G., Aryan, Y.: HSGA: a hybrid heuristic algorithm for workflow scheduling in cloud systems. Cluster comput. **17**(1), 129–137 (2014)
17. Topcuoglu, H., Hariri, S., Wu, M.: Performance-effective and low-complexity task scheduling for heterogeneous computing. IEEE Trans. Parallel Distrib. Syst. **13**(3), 260–274 (2002)

A Metadata Management Strategy Based on Event-Classification in Intelligent Transportation System

Yayun Su and Yaying Zhang[✉]

Key Laboratory of Embedded System and Service Computing, Tongji University,
Shanghai 200092, China
suyayun21@163.com, yaying.zhang@tongji.edu.cn

Abstract. With the explosive growth of data information, the object-oriented storage system has been widely used. This paper proposed a metadata management strategy based on Distributed File System-Ceph in terms of event classification, taking advantage of the characteristics of data in urban traffic system. The large amount of data with a wide variety of sources and data types was first classified by machine learning, and a classification model was established. Then, improvements on load balancing were made to the existing Ceph Load Balancing Strategy of metadata partition. The metadata partitioning is to assign and migrate metadata obtained from the event classification model to the target server chosen by the fuzzy optimum method. Experimental results show that the proposed load balancing strategy based on event classification can not only make the overall load of the metadata servers in a relatively stable state but also make the migration times less than that of other algorithms. The extra overhead of the system is also reduced.

Keywords: Metadata management strategy · Ceph · Event classification · Traffic data · Load balancing

1 Introduction

In intelligent transportation system [1], various types of traffic data are continuously collected and captured every day, i.e., traffic incidents, accident events, video and other real-time traffic data. The size of data reaches the terabyte-scale or even petabyte-scale. Furthermore, large amounts of traffic data generated by cameras, sensors and geomagnetic coil etc. show their inherent special characteristics, such as multisource, heterogeneity, continuity, ever-expanding and spatial-temporal correlation [2].

Nowadays, massive data storage systems mostly adopt the object storage technology, in which data and metadata are stored separately, and metadata server (MDS) cluster was introduced. In the object-based storage [3] architecture of spatial data, accesses to metadata occupy about 50 % to 80 % of the total data accesses [4]. Statistics indicated that the metadata operations account for about 50 % of all files operations [5–8]. Thus, the performance of the metadata server becomes one of the key factors of system performance. Moreover, since the urban traffic data has characteristics of a wide variety of sources, a large size of data, diversity in demands as well as heterogeneity [9], the

© Springer International Publishing Switzerland 2015
G. Wang et al. (Eds.): ICA3PP 2015, Part I, LNCS 9528, pp. 592–605, 2015.
DOI: 10.1007/978-3-319-27119-4_41

existing metadata management strategies have weaknesses in load balance and data retrieval speed, eventually result in delays in responses to user requests. Therefore current strategies are not well applied in the intelligent transportation system.

With the above concerns, this paper combined the Ceph file system metadata management strategy with the characteristics of traffic data to build a classification model of traffic incidents through decision tree classification learning algorithm, and to optimize the metadata management strategy for the intelligent transportation surveillance systems.

2   Related Work

Metadata partition strategies mainly have two groups: directory subtrees partition and hashing partition.

Directory subtrees partition includes static subtrees partition and dynamic subtrees partition [5]. Static subtrees partition based metadata on file directory subtrees, which would not change the subtrees before modifying the system configuration. It is a simple method but has the problem of load imbalance. In dynamic subtree partition, different subtrees under directories were delegated to the different metadata servers. Subtrees migration and replication strategy is used to help keep load balance of metadata servers.

Hashing partition is mainly divided into static hash, lazy hybrid [10] and dynamic hybrid [11]. Static hash distributes the metadata according to the hash value of the file. It has the problems of data name repetition and data migration when removed. Lazy hybrid method combines the advantage of the directory tree partition and static hash with good scalability. But its metadata lookup table will become the bottleneck for concurrent access. Dynamic hybrid is based on the change of the MDS dynamic load balancing, which integrated directory subtrees partitioning policy and hash partitioning policy to implement dynamic metadata management. The major disadvantage is that a large amount of data will be migrated when it dynamically balance the loads of MDSs.

Most of the above works cannot deal with the conflicting objects well, i.e. heterogeneous environment and migration cost. We proposed a new strategy in this paper to address these problems.

3   Ceph File System Metadata Management Strategy

3.1   Ceph File System

Ceph [12] is a Linux petabytes distributed file system with excellent performance of high reliability and good scalability. Ceph ecosystem has four parts as shown in Fig. 1: the client, a near-POSIX file system interface that each instance of a host or process exposes; The metadata server [13], which is used to cache and synchronize the distributed metadata; An object storage cluster [11, 14], which is used to store all data and metadata jointly; Cluster monitors are used for performing monitoring functions.

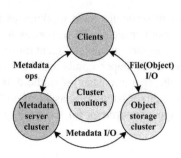

Fig. 1. The conceptual framework of Ceph ecosystem

The client uses the metadata server to perform metadata operations to locate data. The metadata server does not store data but only manages metadata, and so metadata server can be replicated by directory tree and use subtree migration strategies to achieve the metadata server cluster load balancing.

3.2   MDSs Load Balancing Strategy

The metadata server (MDS) [12] is to manage the file system namespace. Although both data and metadata are stored in the object storage cluster, they are managed separately to support scalability. Figure 2 presents the metadata server namespace management, which can be overlapped for redundancy and performance. Ceph dynamically maps subtrees of the directory hierarchy to metadata servers based on the current workload. Individual directories are hashed across multiple nodes only when they become hot spots [5].

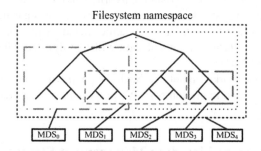

Fig. 2. The metadata server namespace management

MDS load balancing policy is defined as follows:

- Node load (L): The average CPU utilization over time.
- Metadata heat (p): When receiving client's request, MDS'metadata counter will increase a heat, and its ancestors metadata will be a corresponding increase (heat with the level index fell back structure). MDS cluster periodically send their load information overload so that each node can decide to migrate the local part of the load to the load lighter node; priority will be part of the tree node which migrated to the parent directory where the file level heat statistics with the decision to select the

appropriate size of the sub-tree migration. Each directory has a list of small capacity, and it records the recent visit to the directory of client information.

The Metadata node traffic can be calculated as follows [15]:

$$P_{new} = P_{old} \times f(\Delta t) + 1 \tag{1}$$

$$P_{a\_new} = P_{a\_old} \times f(\Delta t) + {}^{1}\!/_{2^n} \tag{2}$$

Where Δt is the time difference of two statistical node heat, P_{new} is the current node heat and P_{old} is the heat of the nodes last time, P_{a_new} is the current heat of the ancestor node and P_{a_old} is the heat of the ancestor node last time, f is the attenuation function, n is the difference of directory level between the ancestor node and current node.

4   Metadata Management Strategy Based on Ceph and Classified Events

The hot-spot is the metadata which might be accessed by thousands of the clients simultaneously or over a short period of time [16], and it will make the MDS where the corresponding metadata were stored becomes overloaded.

The Ceph metadata management strategy can well solve the problems of hot spots and imbalanced load, however, there are still several problems: (1). By default the processing capacity of all the MDSs is the same; (2). Only the efficiency of CPU is considered when evaluating the pressure of nodes; (3). It will lead to the phenomenon of system jitter when migrations among servers occur repeatedly. Aimed at these problems, the paper proposed the improved metadata management strategy based on Ceph in intelligent traffic systems. First of all, according to the feature of the traffic data, we build up the classified model of traffic event to get the potential hotspot. Then the target server of subtree is obtained to replicate and migrate by fuzzy optimum seeking method which considers the multiple indexes of the server in the heterogeneous environment.

4.1   Subtree Replicate Strategy Based on the Event Classified

To avoid the imbalanced load of servers caused by the hotspots, we classifies the traffic events by machine learning in advance, replicates the metadata of potential hotspots(traffic events), make the choice of the server by fuzzy optimum method, and then stores the copy in the server and try to make the load of each server under equilibrium state.

A. Selection of Classification Model.

According to the characteristics of traffic data, C4.5 decision tree is employed as the classify model for the traffic events in terms of the attributes such as the time of the accident occurs, the type of the accident, the location of the accident.

C4.5 decision tree is an approach that approximates discrete function and has good robustness to noise data, and can learn disjunctive expression. It classifies the data by the evaluation criterion of information entropy and information gain ratio.

With the decision tree, we can get many values when we handle continuous attributes such as *Time*. It will produce a great deal of branches if dealt with directly, which leads to the decision tree with huge structure and makes it difficult to be adopted into the classification issues. Therefore, we would partition the continuous attribute value *Time* into a discrete set of intervals at first. The discretization is done as follows:

1. Do the equal division of '*Time*' (the attribute of time) in an hour, which will be divided into K intervals.

2. Calculate the *Gini* coefficient of each interval: $GiniT = 1 - \sum_{i=1}^{m} p_i^2$, where m is class number, T is training sample set, p_i is the frequency of the class c_i in sample set T.

3. Merge the adjacent intervals, and then calculate the *Gini* coefficient, if $Gini\left(K'\right) < Gini(K)$, then stop merging.

The attribute of time can be divided into several intervals with the method above.

We can get multiple values and branches from the attribute of time. The less leaf nodes the decision tree have, the higher classification accuracy it will be. Too many branches will lead to overfitting, enlarge the scale of the decision tree and reduce the ability to predict. For this purpose, the branches need to be merged. Each attribute value of entropy is calculated. If the two differential absolute value of entropy is less than a certain threshold value (we adopt 0.001 in this paper), then merge the two branches.

According to the sample of the traffic data $S = \{x_1, x_2, x_3, \ldots, x_m\}$, the attribute set of the sample S will be divided into K intervals with the different values $C_1, \ldots, C_k$.

Attribute A will be divided to get information entropy according to the attribute of the set S.

$$infoS = -\sum_{i=1}^{k} p_i \log_2(p_i) \tag{3}$$

Where

$$P_i = \frac{|C_i|}{|S|}. \tag{4}$$

$$s.t. 1 \leq i \leq k \tag{5}$$

We define the expected value of the entropy after S is partitioned using attribute A:

$$info_A(S) = \sum_{j=1}^{t} \frac{|S_j|}{|S|} info\left(S_j\right) \tag{6}$$

Where S_j is the subset of S for which attribute A has value j (i.e., $S_j = \{s \in S | A(s) = j\}$)

According to (3) and (6), we have:

$$gain(A) = info(S) - info_A(S) \tag{7}$$

Define the calculation of information gain rate:

$$IGR\left(S, A_i\right) = \frac{gain\left(A\right)}{split_{info(S)}} \tag{8}$$

Where

$$split\_info = -\sum_{j=1}^{t} \frac{\left|S_j\right|}{\left|S\right|} \log_2(\frac{\left|S_j\right|}{\left|S\right|}) \tag{9}$$

Finally, we merge the leaf nodes with same values belonging to the same parent node.

B. Choice of Target Server

The replication and migration of the subtree as well as the choice of the target server can be regarded as the decision problem of the target server. A lot of factors should be taken into account when it comes to choose the target server. We should consider the self-load condition of the target server as well as the cost of the migration of files. The criterion between the two might conflict, so we should weigh the choices of the methods for multiple targets.

Chen and Zhao combined the system analysis with fuzzy set analysis and proposed the fuzzy optimum selecting theory [17]. The basic idea is to determine the membership degree of the solution sets about the target sets affiliated to the fuzzy concept "optimum". Then calculate the relative optimal membership degree of each solution according the fuzzy optimum formula. After that, we can get the best solution.

Hence, the implementation steps are as follows:

- First, we estimate the CPU utilization. When the CPU utilization is lower than 90 %, add the server into the set of candidate node servers (i.e., target set).

Take the following 6 indexes as eigenvalues into consideration:

- The total heat of the metadata $P(O_1)$;
- Movement cost(O_2):The cost of the data transmission between the two MDSs, it can be manually set directly;
- CPU utilization (O_3): average utilization of CPU in a period of time T;
- Memory utilization (O_4): average utilization of memory in a period of time T;
- Disk I/O utilization (O_5): average I/O in a period of time T;
- The network band width utilization (O_6): average utilization of broadband in a period of time T;
  - Establish relative membership degree matrix:

$$X = \begin{pmatrix} x_{11} & \cdots & x_{1n} \\ \vdots & \cdots & \vdots \\ x_{m1} & \cdots & x_{mn} \end{pmatrix} = (X_{ij})_{m \times n}, i = 1, 2, \ldots, m, j = 1, 2, \ldots, n \tag{10}$$

Where X_{ij} is the eigenvalue of the object j of target i. To eliminate the influence of m different target eigenvalues (i.e., $m = 6$), we need to do normalization of each target and convert to standard matrix $R = (r_{ij})_{m \times n}$. We choose the cost as the index, the relative membership degree formula is

$$r_{ij} = \frac{supX_{ij} - X_{ij}}{supX_{ij} - inf\left(X_{ij}\right)} \tag{11}$$

Where $supX_{ij}$ and $infX_{ij}$ are respectively for the index under different server parameters of the maximum and minimum values. r_{ij} is the membership degree of the object j of target i. The relative membership degree matrix of X is

$$R = \begin{pmatrix} r_{11} & \cdots & r_{1n} \\ \vdots & \cdots & \vdots \\ r_{m1} & \cdots & r_{mn} \end{pmatrix} = r_{ij}, \ i = 1, 2, \ldots, m, \ j = 1, 2, \ldots, n \tag{12}$$

- Calculate the corresponding weight vector of each index with entropy method.

1. Calculate the proportion of the index parameter values about the object j of index i

$$f_{ij} = \frac{1 + r_{ij}}{\sum_{j=1}^{n}(1 + r_{ij})}, \ i = 1, 2, .., m, \ j = 1, 2, .., n \tag{13}$$

2. Calculate the entropy of the index i

$$H_i = -\frac{\sum_{j=1}^{n}(f_{ij}lnf_{ij})}{lnn}, \ i = 1, 2.., m, \ j = 1, 2, .., n \tag{14}$$

3. Calculate the entropy weight of the index i

$$\omega_i = \frac{1 - H_i}{\sum_{j=1}^{m}(1 - H_i)}, \ j = 1, 2, \ldots, m \tag{15}$$

Then the target weight vector is obtained

$$\omega = (\omega_1, \omega_2, \omega_3, \omega_4, \omega_5, \omega_6)^T \tag{16}$$

- Calculate the weighted optimal target matrix based on the obtained optimal size of the matrix R and the target weight vector:

$$S = \begin{pmatrix} S_{11} & \cdots & S_{1n} \\ \vdots & \vdots & \vdots \\ S_{61} & \cdots & S_{6n} \end{pmatrix} = S_{6j}, \ j = 1, 2, .., n \tag{17}$$

Where

$$S_{ij} = \omega_i r_{ij} \tag{18}$$

- Define the relatively ideal solution and negative ideal solution of optimal relative vectors are as follows

Define the optimal relative membership degree:

$$g = (g_1, g_2, \dots g_6)^T = (1, 1, \dots, 1)^T \tag{19}$$

Take the weight of the target into consideration, the weight is considered as

$$g^{\omega+} = (g_1^{\omega+}, g_2^{\omega+}, \dots, g_6^{\omega+})^T = (\omega_1, \omega_2, \dots, \omega_6)^T \tag{20}$$

Define the worst relative optimal membership degree

$$b = (b_1, b_2, \dots, b_6)^T = (0, 0, \dots, 0)^T \tag{21}$$

The system have the target optimal membership matrix R, the target optimal membership vector of object j is

$$r_j = (r_{1j}, r_{2j}, \dots, r_{6j})^T \tag{22}$$

The corresponding optimal weighted vector is

$$s_j = (s_{1j}, s_{2j}, \dots, s_{6j})^T \tag{23}$$

Define the optimal distance of the weight distance

$$d\left(s_j, g_\omega^+\right) = u_j \left(\sum_{i=1}^{6} [d(s_{ij}, g_i^{\omega+})]^p \right)^{1/p} \tag{24}$$

Where p is the distance parameter, $p = 1$ is hamming distance, $p = 2$ is Euclidean distance.

Define the worst distance of the weight distance

$$d\left(s_j, b\right) = u_j \left(\sum_{i=1}^{6} [d\left(s_{ij}, 0\right)]^p \right)^{1/p} \tag{25}$$

Establish the target function to solve the optimal values of u_j in the system

$$min \left\{ F\left(u_j\right) = u_j^2 \left[d\left(s_{ij}, g_\omega^+\right) \right]^2 + u_j'^2 [d(s_{ij}, b)]^2 \right\} \tag{26}$$

To get the minimum sum of the square of the weight distance optimal distance and the square of the weight worst distance. The calculation formula of the optimal value of u_j is

$$u_j = \cfrac{1}{1 + [\cfrac{\sum_{i=1}^{m}[d(s_{ij}, g_\omega^+)]^p}{\sum_{i=1}^{m}[d(s_{ij}, 0)]^p}]^{2/p}}, j = 1, 2, \ldots, n \tag{27}$$

$$\text{s.t.}\frac{dF(u_j)}{du_j} = 0 \tag{28}$$

The relative membership vector is $u = (u_1, u_2, \ldots, u_n)$. Finally we can get the order of merit of the candidate servers.

4.2 Subtree Migration Strategy Based on the Event Classified

The classification accuracy of the decision tree would never be 100 %, error classification data will affect the result. Because of the request of arbitrariness, non-hot data obtained from the tree may become a hot spot in a short time. When the server load is overweight and any index reaches the threshold, the migration process of the subtree is launched:

- Select the target server for subtree migration according to the fuzzy optimum selection method;
- Determine the migrate subtree according to the heat of the MDS information reported by server itself;
- Migrate the subtree on overload server to the selected target server.

5   Test and Result Analysis

Experiments are divided into two parts. The first part is the classification of traffic data based on C4.5 decision tree and the second part is the metadata load balancing strategy.

The algorithm of the first part of the experiment is implemented in MATLAB7.0. The computer configuration is as follows: CPU Intel Core i5 (clocked at 3.1 GHz), memory 4G. The training set is divided into three attributes, namely property set $S = \{EventType, Location, Time\}$, respectively representing event type, event location, event time. There are two class labels $C = \{YES, NO\}$, respectively indicating hot and non-hot data.

Traffic event classification results are shown in Fig. 3:

The second part of the experiment using four heterogeneous servers to form a MDS cluster, named MDS1, MDS2, MDS3, MDS4, a monitor inspecting the cluster running situation and the clients use multiple threads simultaneously to request to MDS. The load information of each cycle per MDS is recorded. Define the cluster load balancing degree $SD = \sqrt{\sum_{i=1}^{n}(L_i - \bar{L})^2}$, where L_i represents the i-th MDS load information (CPU utilization), $\bar{L}$ is the average load.

Table 1 shows the specification of nodes on the cluster.

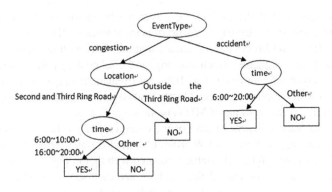

Fig. 3. The result of Events Classification

Table 1. Specification of nodes on cluster

	CPU	Memory	Hard disk	OS
MDS1	1.60 GHz	2 GB	100G	Ubuntu 14.0
MDS2	2.80 GHz	2 GB	250G	Ubuntu 14.0
MDS3	2.80 GHz	4 GB	250G	Ubuntu 14.0
MDS4	3.10 GHz	4 GB	500G	Ubuntu 14.0

MDSs with no load balancing strategy in the running state of different time are shown in Fig. 4. The cluster did not apply any load balancing strategy. The increasing of the number of connections will heavily increase load of metadata servers. At the same time, the CPU utilization of MDS1 is the highest because of its low configuration, and it became the first overloaded node. MDS4 performance is the best, so the growth rate of load is relatively slower than other MDSs.

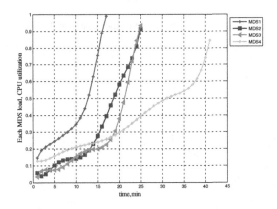

Fig. 4. The CPU utilization of the cluster with no load balancing strategy

CLBS presents that if the load of the server reaches a threshold, subtrees will be migrated spontaneously to decrease the load of heavily loaded MDSs. Figure 5 indicates that MDS1, MDS2 and MDS3 has a fluctuation at the different times respectively when increasing the nodes of clients, which may trigger the scheduling policy, the overloaded server MDS1 may transfer the load to the MDS4 with light load to adjust the load imbalance.

When the cluster applies metadata cluster load balancing strategy based on weights (WLBS) [18], the running status of MDSs is shown in Fig. 6.

When the imbalance degree of load of the entire cluster reaches a threshold, it will trigger load balancing strategy. And WLBS adjust the load by subtree migration policy. The entire cluster load is relatively stable compared with that in Fig. 5, there is no data in Fig. 6 with a high fluctuation from their neighbors, and each server's load is more evenly. In consequence this approach can achieve load balance between metadata servers.

When the proposed load balancing algorithm based on event classification of MDS is applied, the operating state over time as shown in Fig. 7. All the loads of MDSs are increasing steadily and slowly in 20 min compared with that in Figs. 4 and 5, after that MDS2, MDS3 and MDS1 has a fluctuation successively, as their loads may be heavy

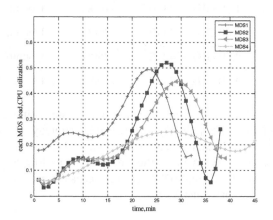

Fig. 5. The CPU utilization of the cluster with CLBS

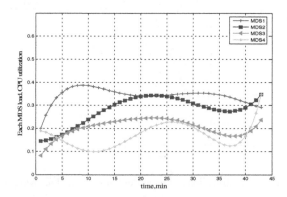

Fig. 6. The CPU utilization of the cluster with WLBS

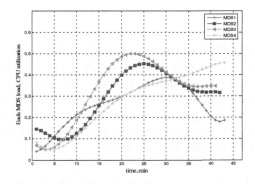

Fig. 7. CPU utilization of the cluster with load balancing strategy based on event classification

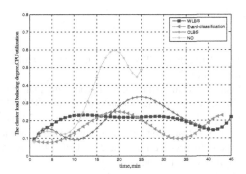

Fig. 8. Load balancing degree of each strategy

or reach the threshold, clients will access MDS4 instead, thus the load of MDS4 is still increasing steadily.

The comparison of load balancing degree of MDS cluster in different load balancing strategy (no load balancing strategy, CLBS, WLBS, load balancing strategy based on event classification) shown in Fig. 8.

In Fig. 8, the highest fluctuation shows that if we don't apply any strategies, the cluster is imbalance due to the heterogeneity of the cluster and the uncertainty of access. The stability of cluster is better when load balancing strategy based on event classification applied than that CLBS applied. Both WLBS and our method have good load balancing performance, but the number of migration between MDSs in WLBS is significantly more than other strategies, and also with more system overhead (see Table 2).

Table 2. Migration times of each strategy

Strategy	Migration times
NO	0
CLBS	5
WLBS	18
Based on event-classification	3

6 Conclusion

For large amounts of traffic data produced by traffic monitoring every day. The Ceph file system metadata management strategy and the characteristics of traffic data is combined to build a classification model of traffic incidents through decision tree classification learning algorithm, and the metadata management strategy is optimized for the intelligent transportation systems. The proposed method improves the metadata management strategy, which makes it alleviate the pressure of the server effectively and makes it convenient for users for fast accessing.

Acknowledgments. This research was supported by the International Science & Technology Cooperation Program of China (2012DFG11580).

References

1. Dimitrakopoulos, G., Demestichas, P.: Intelligent transportation systems. IEEE Veh. Technol. Mag. **5**(1), 77–84 (2010)
2. Zhao, Z., Fang, J., Ding, W., et al.: An integrated processing platform for traffic sensor data and its applications in intelligent transportation systems. In: 2014 IEEE World Congress on Services (SERVICES), pp. 161–168. IEEE Computer Society (2014)
3. Li, W., Xue, W., Shu, J., et al.: Dynamic hashing: adaptive metadata management for petabyte-scale file system. In: proceeding of the 23st IEEE/14th NASA Goddard Conference on Mass Storage System and Technologies (2006)
4. Lin, Y., Li, R., Xu, Z., et al.: A dynamic method for metadata partitioning based on intensive access of spatial data. In: 6th IEEE Joint International Conference on Information Technology and Artificial Intelligence (ITAIC), pp. 177–180. IEEE (2011)
5. Weil, S.A., Brandt, S.A., Miller, E.L., et al.: Ceph: A scalable, high-performance distributed file system. In: Proceedings of the 7th symposium on Operating systems design and implementation. USENIX Association, pp. 307–320 (2006)
6. Outerhout, J.K., Da Costa, H., Harrison, D., et al.: A Trace-driven analysis of the Unix 4.2 BSD file system. ACM (1985)
7. Roselli, D.S., Lorch, J.R., Anderson, T.E.: A comparison of file system workloads. In: USENIX Annual Technical Conference, General Track, pp. 41–54 (2000)
8. Yan, J., Zhu, Y., Xiong, H., et al.: A design of metadata server cluster in large distributed object-based storage. In: MSST, pp. 199–205 (2004)
9. Qin, M., Wang, Y., Cui, Z., et al.: The design and realization of an advance urban traffic surveillance and Management system. In: The 6th World Congress on Intelligent Control and Automation (2006)
10. Brandt, S.A., Miller, E.L., Long, D.D.E., Xue, L.: Efficient metadata management in large distributed storage systems. In: Proceedings of the 20th IEEE/the 11th NASA Goddard Conference on Mass Storage Systems and Technologies, IEEE Computer Society, Washington (2003)
11. Honicky, R.J., Miller, E.L.: Replication under scalable hashing: a family of algorithms for scalable decentralized data distribution. In: International Symposium on Parallel and Distributed Processing, vol. 96a. IEEE Computer Society (2004)
12. Ceph: A Linux PB-level distributed file system. https://www.ibm.com/developerworks/cn/linux/l-ceph/

13. Weil, S.A., Brandt, S.A., Miller, E.L., et al.: Intelligent metadata management for a petabyte-scale file system. In: 2nd Intelligent Storage Workshop (2004)
14. Xin, Q., Miller, E.L., Schwarz, T., Long, D.D.E., et al.: Reliability mechanisms for very large storage systems. In: Proceedings of the 20th IEEE/11th NASA Goddard Conference on Mass Storage Systems and Technologies (MSST), pp. 146–156 (2003)
15. Hua, Y., Zhu, Y., Jiang, H., et al.: Supporting scalable and adaptive metadata management in ultralarge-scale file system. IEEE Trans. Parallel Distrib. Syst. **22**(4), 580–593 (2011)
16. Zhou, G., Lan, Q., Chen, J.: A dynamic metadata equipotent subtree partition policy for mass storage system. In: FCST, pp. 29–34. IEEE Computer Society (2007)
17. Chen, S.: Optimum selecting theory and model for fuzzy design. Syst. Eng. **8**, 55–61 (1990)
18. Zhang, J., Qian, W., Xu, X., et al.: WLBS: a weight-based metadata server cluster load balancing strategy. Int. J. Adv. Comput. Technol. (IJACT) **14**(9), 77–85 (2012)

Internet of Things
and Cyber-Physical-Social Computing

NRLoc: Neighbor Relative RSS-Based Indoor Localization System

Xuefeng Sha, Kai Lin$^{(\boxtimes)}$, Wenjian Wang, and Jiming Luo

School of Computer Science and Technology,
Dalian University of Technology, Dalian 116024, China
{shaxuefeng,dlutwwj0boa}@mail.dlut.edu.cn, link@dlut.edu.cn,
logicluo@foxmail.com

Abstract. The popularity of smartphones has fostered a growing interest in Location Based Service (LBS). While indoor location information is imperative for the realization of mobile LBS applications, recently research on indoor localization systems that rely on received signal strength (RSS) fingerprint has been attracting much attention. In this paper, we propose a novel approach which utilizes the "neighbor relative" RSS(NR-RSS) to search the fingerprint database for positioning. Our proposed scheme can realize calibration-free positioning access different devices. With the assistance of NR-RSS, adjusted by directions, our efficient scheme can dampen the unpredictable signal fluctuation problem in indoor environment. We evaluated the proposed method in realistic environment and the results showed that our system could achieve a relative high level of accuracy where the device heterogeneity and Wi-Fi signals fluctuation problem exists.

Keywords: Indoor localization · Wi-Fi fingerprint · Smartphones · LBS · RSS

1   Introduction

As the explosive growth of smartphones, LBS [1] is gradually on the rise and prosper. However, the main issue for LBS is how to accurately gain the users' position information. With the assistance from Global Positioning System (GPS) [2], the location of people at outdoor regions can be easily determined with a certain level of precision. But indoor localization still remains a challenge.

Various positioning systems have been proposed in the last decade, employing various technologies, such as ultrasonic [3], infrared, radio frequency identification(RFID) [4], ultra-wideband(UWB) etc. However, the use of these systems requires large numbers of support devices and equipment to get high accuracy of localization, and the cost makes it unacceptable for most users. It is preferable to utilize the current existing wireless communication infrastructure to get users' position. Recently, received signal strength (RSS) fingerprint system based on Wi-Fi has begun to gain in popularity. However, the complexity and cost of

© Springer International Publishing Switzerland 2015
G. Wang et al. (Eds.): ICA3PP 2015, Part I, LNCS 9528, pp. 609–621, 2015.
DOI: 10.1007/978-3-319-27119-4_42

fingerprint map building require an extensive and thorough site-survey process. Moreover, the static radio map is also vulnerable to environmental dynamics and device heterogeneity. Some works have focused on the effective schemes of building the map fingerprint databases [5], and others aim at improving the location accuracy of the RSS fingerprint matching mechanism. To reduce the calibration effort, some researches concentrate on the signal wave propagation model-based techniques to estimate the RSS values at a given location. These systems build mathematical or theoretic models instead of manually tagging to calculate the given location RSS values [6–8]. A large number of studies also describe positioning systems based on inertial measurements [9]. However, the major flaw of this kind of systems is that the estimation error growths with time due to the typical drift of the inertial measurements [10]. For this reason, inertial measurements methods usually combine with other techniques to get high accuracy. In this paper, we propose NRLoc which mainly utilizes fingerprint-based technology. Moreover, we also exploit the inherent gyrometer in the smartphones which can obtain the information of the orientation and direction to assist positioning.

There are some major problems for traditional RSS fingerprint systems to consider. First, they have to deal with the situation that real RSS fingerprints at any location may change with times and circumstances. Secondly, since different smartphones may have different frameworks and hardware modules, for the same Wi-Fi RSS, different smartphones may get different measurement data. Finally, as for each time localization process, the RSS fingerprint localization system will query the RSS fingerprint databases which store a great deal of RSS fingerprint data. This query process will take a significant amount of time for each matching. Although some systems adopt clustering of map locations to reduce the computational requirements, clustering algorithm itself also introduces error and adds complexity to those systems.

In this paper, we present a quite scalable and accurate indoor localization system with low computational requirements. This paper makes the following contributions taking the three issues mentioned above into account:

1. We analyze the changes of RSS at a region over time. Based on our observations and records, we find that although the absolute values of the RSS at a region constantly change, the relative values of RSS of two locations do not change much.
2. We also make use of the orientation data to assist matching the RSS fingerprints at the localization phase.
3. We propose NRLoc, a novel indoor localization system that solves the matching problem caused by heterogeneous devices.
4. We have implemented NRLoc and evaluated it in real-world indoor areas using multiple smartphones.

The rest of this paper is organized as follows. Several preliminary questions are discussed in Sect. 2. Section 3 describes the system architecture and the proposed method. Section 4, we evaluated the performance of our system through real-world experiments. Section 5 draws conclusion from this work.

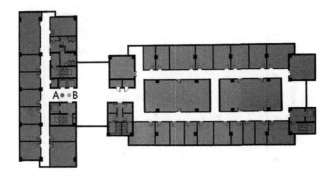

Fig. 1. Floor plan

2 Preliminary Questions Statement

For fingerprint-based indoor localization systems, to build up a robust and precise radio map is crucial. But there are two major issues limiting the accuracy of the radio map. The first one is that the RSS value of an Access Point(AP) may vary with the changes of environment over time. The other one is that for heterogeneous devices which are designed differently, the RSS measurement data may vary widely even when they are placed at the exactly the same location.

In order to display the impact of the two issues mentioned above on the accuracy of the fingerprint data, we used four different smartphones (Galaxy S3, MX2, Mi3, Ascend P6) to collect the RSS values of an AP at the same place throughout the day. Our experiment is carried on the ninth floor of a 16-storey building. The layout of the floor is shown in Fig. 1. For each RSS value, we collect ten times at A point and take the average as the RSS value to remove the chance element.

From the experiment results, as the Fig. 2 shows, we can easily reach two conclusions. (1) The RSS values collected by the same smartphone vary at different times of day; (2) At the same time, the RSS values of the AP differ across different smartphones; For Conclusion 1, the fluctuation of RSS values over time is caused by environmental dynamics. In [11] Yi-chao Chen et.al point out that RSS is mainly affected by following three dynamic factors: people presence and movements,relative humidity level, and open or close doors. The radio signal propagation from the APs to the smartphones can be interfered with these environment factors mentioned above. Besides, the instability of the Wi-Fi signal emitted by APs is another important factor. As for Conclusion 2, in the same circumstance, different smartphones getting different RSS values is due to the diversity of hardware and software architectures of different smartphones. We also do another experiment. This time we collect RSS values at A point and B point respectively in exactly the same way as before. A point and B point are both in the corridor of the building and their distance is about 3 m, as shown in Fig. 1. Then we can get the difference value of the two points RSS values at the i time:

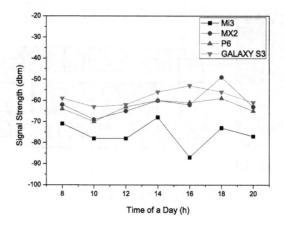

Fig. 2. Performance of heterogeneous device

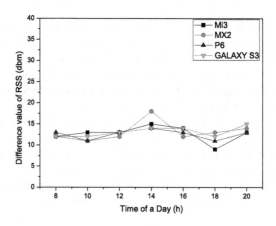

Fig. 3. RSS difference value variation

$$\Delta RSS_i = RSS_i^A - RSS_i^B \tag{1}$$

where RSS_i^A and RSS_i^B stand for the RSS values of A point and B point respectively at a certain time instant i. The relationship of ΔRSS_i and time is shown in Fig. 3, where different styles of line represent different smartphones collecting results respectively.

From the first experiment, we learn that the RSS values of a particular location can fluctuate throughout the day. But as Fig. 3 shows, the difference value of the RSS values of A and B points stays relatively stable during the day. This can be explained that even though there are various factors impacting the RSS of a particular position as discussed above, but as A and B point are very close, these environmental dynamics produce almost the same effect on them, so the

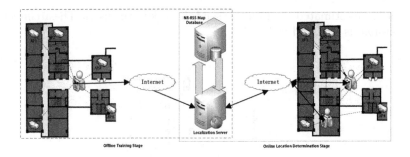

Fig. 4. System overview

RSS values of A and B points change almost synchronously. This results in the stability of the ΔRSS_i.

As shown in Fig. 3, we also can notice that the ΔRSS_i values of the four different smartphones are close while the four smartphones' RSS values at A or B point are quite different at the same moment, as shown in Fig. 2. For the same smartphone, the RSS values collected by it may be always higher or lower than the real values, but this kind of error trends to exist all the time. Therefore, the difference values of RSS values at the two points for different smartphones should be close to the same value. The result of Experiment 2 supports our assumption, as shown in Fig. 3.

Given the facts above, we can easily come to the conclusion that the difference value of the RSS values is more robust and stable against the fluctuation of RSS and the heterogeneity of devices. Here we call the difference value neighbor relative RSS, short for NR-RSS. In our system we use NR-RSSs as the fingerprint data to build up radio map instead of the absolute RSS values.

3   System Overview and Proposed Schemes

In this section, we present the overview of our systems and some main application modules are illustrated in the proposed indoor localization system. The system working mainly contains two stages: offline training stage and online location determination stage as shown in Fig. 4. In the offline stage, surveying-users use smartphones to collect RSS data at all designed locations and then send them to the remote localization server. The server processes these information to get NR-RSS for building up the NR-RSS fingerprint map database. All interested locations are kept inside this database. In the online location determination stage, the mobile users use smartphone to scan the Wi-Fi signals and the orientation information and periodically send these information to the localization server. The server combines the received RSS and orientation information with the history neighbor RSS information to obtain the NR-RSS, then the NR-RSS is compared with all entry locations in the NR-RSS fingerprint database. With our match algorithm and filtered by the orientation, the system returns the outcome as an estimated location and sends it back to the users. The architecture of the system is depicted in Fig. 5.

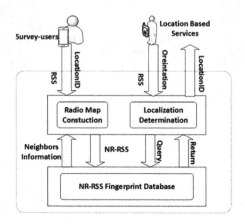

Fig. 5. The NRLoc architecture

3.1   Fingerprint Collection

Surveying-users equipped with smartphones measure RSS from the surrounding APs at the targeted indoor environment. These RSS values are used to calculate the NR-RSS, which are stored at the corresponding position in the NR-RSS fingerprint map. The map is divided into equally spaced grids. Each grid has its unique Location ID. The grid spacing is crucial in the performance of the system. For our method, it is the ideal situation that the mobile users receive the location information feedback from the server when they get to the next neighbor grid. In our work, the best grid spacing is empirically determined according to the normal walking speed of mobile users. The tuple M corresponding to each grid has such form:

$$M = (L, \boldsymbol{S}) \tag{2}$$

where L represents the Location ID of the grid, $\boldsymbol{S}$ is the RSS set collected by surveying-users at the real physical locations which are corresponding to the current grids. $\boldsymbol{S}$ is stores as

$$\boldsymbol{S} = \{(ID_1, MS_1), (ID_2, MS_2), \dots, (ID_n, MS_n)\} \tag{3}$$

Here, ID represents the MAC address of the APs, MS is the mean value of the RSS values measured by the surveying-users. n is the number of surrounding APs. Surveying-users should scan the Wi-Fi signals and send such tuple M information of each grid to the fingerprint server at the targeted location.

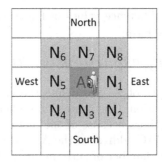

Fig. 6. Neighbor definition

3.2   NR-RSS Fingerprint Database Construction

Previous fingerprint-based localization systems build the fingerprint map radio using absolute RSS values (ARSS). These systems are vulnerable to the change of environment and heterogeneous devices. Unlike typical fingerprint-based localization systems, we devise a novel technique which makes use of neighbor relative RSS values to overcome the above weakness. Let us start with the basic scenario. At some moment a mobile user is located at A point as shown in Fig. 6. The user should arrive at one of the eight orientations next moment, regardless of the limitation factors of the real environment, such as walls and obstacles etc. $N_1, N_2, \ldots, N_8$ stand for the eight orientations respectively. At the training phase, survey-user scans the Wi-Fi signals at A point and its eight neighbor points. The server receives the information of A and its neighbors, processes the information to build the fingerprint data of Location A in the NR-RSS fingerprint database.

Table 1. Example of NR-RSS fingerprinting map

Lo	ARSS	NR-RSS							
ID	S	$\overrightarrow{RS_1}$	$\overrightarrow{RS_2}$	$\overrightarrow{RS_3}$	$\overrightarrow{RS_4}$	$\overrightarrow{RS_5}$	$\overrightarrow{RS_6}$	$\overrightarrow{RS_7}$	$\overrightarrow{RS_8}$

Table 1 is an example of the fingerprint data for Location A at our NR-RSS fingerprinting map. Loc stores the location ID values which are unique for each grid. ARSS stores the absolute RSS values. In order to improve the accuracy, we scan the Wi-Fi signals several times and calculate the mean value as ARSS at each position. For ARSS, S has the form in (3). Accounting for ARSS varying with the environmental dynamics, as discussed in Sect. 2, the ARSS in our fingerprint map will also be updated constantly at the localization phase. This scheme guarantees the high accuracy of our system, up to a certain extent. The last and most important part is the NR-RSS Column which reflects the main idea of our systems. We use the ARSS values of Location A and its eight neighbors to calculate the difference values of Location A and its neighbors as NR-RSS. $\overrightarrow{RS_i}$ has following form:

$$\overrightarrow{RS_i} = \{(ID_1, RS_1), (ID_2, RS_2), ..., (ID_n, RS_n)\} \tag{4}$$

where i is the ith neighbors of A. We define the east as the first neighbor, increasing in clockwise direction. One thing to note here is that a location does not always have eight neighbors because of the real structure of buildings limitation. ID represents the MAC address of the APs, RS is the difference value of A and its neighbor. n is the number of surrounding APs.

The fingerprint server handle the raw data received from mobile clients, building the NR-RSS fingerprint map, and store it in the map database server. This map has all the locations of the interest area stored. Each location information is stored in the form of Location A described above. Our fingerprint map are robust and stable against the change of environment and the heterogeneity of devices by using the NR-RSS and ARSS which can be updated constantly.

3.3   Localization

When mobile users equipped with smartphones initialize our indoor localization application, as there is no history data for the first time localization, our system uses the typical positioning solution RADAR [12] to obtain user initial location. We call this process Global Search Localization (GSL). Because GSL has to search all the locations in the fingerprint map, the time it takes will be a little longer. But this only happens at localizing the starting position, during the following localization phase, our system will utilize our NR-RSS match method to position and can return location information real time. At the GSL, orientation information collected by inertial sensors in the smartphone is also sent to the fingerprint server.

After initializing, our system will localize mobile users by our novel NR-RSS match solution. First, we use the acceleration sensor in the smartphone to judge whether the mobile user is in motion or stands still. If the mobile user stands still, his current location is the same as last localization outcome. Otherwise, when the mobile user goes to the next place, he sends the raw ambient RSS values to the fingerprint server with a Wi-Fi enabled smartphone. In addition, the user will also obtain the orientation information through the integrating angular velocity from gyroscope. Since the orientation measured by smartphones can be disturbed by many factors [13], the orientation information provides assistance for positioning.

Second, we come to the processing and matching stage. The first step is to calculate the difference value of the current local RSS fingerprint values and its last adjacent location (LAL) RSS fingerprint values. We call this difference value Current Neighbor Difference RSS (CND-RSS). LAL has corresponding NR-RSS stored in the NR-RSS fingerprint map. Therefore, the next thing to do is to determine which neighbor of LAL the mobile user arrives at. A metric and a search methodology are required to compare the neighbors and to pick out the one that best matches the observed current local RSS fingerprint values. Our solution is to compute the Eucildean distance of the CND-RSS to the pre-stored NR-RSSs of LAL in the fingerprint database, and then pick the neighbor location that minimizes the distance.

$$D_i = ||RS_i - CR|| \tag{5}$$

where RS_i is the NR-RSS of the ith neighbor of LAL stored in the database and CR is CND-RSS. The neighbor who has smallest D is chosen to be the location estimation and gives feedback to the mobile user. If there are two or more neighbors having the close smaller distance, namely these neighbors satisfy the following condition:

$$D_j < \varepsilon \tag{6}$$

Here, j is the number of LAL neighbors which have close smaller D and ε represents the threshold to determine that the j neighbors all have the possibility to be current location estimation. If there is only one neighbor of LAL with the D smaller than ε, the neighbor is the current location estimation. Otherwise, we utilize the orientation information of the LAL receiving from the mobile user to filter the j neighbors for further accurate location estimation. The orientation information indicates which direction the mobile users will go to from LAL. Among the j neighbors, we chose the one whose orientation (relative LAL) is close to the collecting orientation information as the current localization outcome. After successfully localizing the current position, we update ARSS values in the fingerprint database by the latest RSS values collected by the mobile user. This scheme guarantees our absolute RSS records in the database to be updated with the variation of the environment constantly. Therefore, our fingerprint map is robust against the environmental dynamics.

Our approach is based on the assumption that the mobile user will arrive at one of the neighbors from his last location. However, as the walking speed of mobile users is different, it is not possible that mobile users will exactly arrive at the center of next neighbors every time. So the errors of the estimated position increase over time, and at last mobile users might go to the other place instead of the neighbors at some moment. As Fig. 6 shown, a mobile user walks from A, and next moment he does not arrive at one of the neighbors, the shadow grids in the Figure. He may go to the some place outside the neighbors. Our algorithm determines such situation by the value of D.

$$D > \delta \tag{7}$$

where, δ stands for the threshold to determine whether the mobile user arrives at the one of the eight neighbors or other outside places. In the later situation, we start a search method which is similar with the GSL described above. Unlike GSL, instead of searching all the location items in the database, we set A and its neighbors as the center and match outward expansion grids, until the grid whose absolute RSS values and orientation (relative A) are close to the observed information. In this way, we only need to search a small amount of location records

---

Algorithm 1. Localization Algorithm

1: Initialize (GSL)
2: **loop**
3:     **if** movement **then**
4:         Compute CND-RSS
5:         Match CND-RSS with NR-RSS fingerprints
6:         **if** $D > \delta$ **then**
7:             PGSL
8:         **else**
9:             **if** $D_j < \varepsilon$ and $j > 1$ **then**
10:                 Filter by orientation
11:                 Localize
12:             **else**
13:                 Find out the minimum D
14:                 Localize
15:             **end if**
16:         **end if**
17:     **else**
18:         current location = the last location
19:     **end if**
20: **end loop**

---

and return the location estimation result real time. We term this process Pseudo Global Search Localization (PGSL). Algorithm 1 explains the entire process of our system working.

4 Evaluation

This section discusses the experiment results we have conducted to evaluate the performance of our proposed system.

4.1 Experimental Setup

NRLoc has both smartphone client and server components. To carry out a proper evaluation of our system in real environments, we implement the client system on four different smartphones(Galaxy S3, MX2, Mi3, Ascend P6), which are Android smartphones equipped with a 3 axis accelerometer, a magnetometer, and a gyroscope. The server is developed with JAVA at Window platform. We have collected realistic RSS and orientation data in a WLAN environment shown in Fig. 1 at different times of the day, and over multiple days, keeping the simulations as close to realistic scenarios as possible.

4.2 Preliminary Experiments

The accuracy of our localization system is significantly influenced by the various system parameters. To obtain an ideal result of location estimation, we should find out the optimal parameters value first, to be used for the subsequent experiments. These include the grid spacing, the threshold ε for direction filtering, the threshold δ for determining whether implementing PGSL.

Grid Spacing. As we localize the grid every time instead of specific geographic coordinates, the grid spacing will impact the location error and correct rate significantly. The floor plan is divided into many grids and a set of localization is performed by altering the grid length from 1 to 3 m while the user is walking at a speed of 1.4 m/s. The statistic results of the location error and the correct rate are shown in Table 2. With increased grid length, the correct rate becomes higher while location error also becomes bigger. The grid length of 1.5 m provides the best result in general with the correct rate of 68.9 %, and location error of 2.1 m. We use 1.5 m as the grid length for the subsequent experiments.

Table 2. Impact of grid spacing

Grid length	Location error	Correct rate
1	1.3	41.2 %
1.5	2.1	68.9 %
2	3.0	72.3 %
3	4.1	86.1 %
5	5.9	91.2 %

Threshold for Direction Filtering ε. As mentioned above, ε is used to determine when direction filtering should be performed. When two or more neighbors in the NR-RSS map have close small difference value of RSS with the last location, we use orientation to assist localizing. Here the small difference value is determined by ε. We empirically determine the value by collecting fingerprints of 20 different locations and their neighbors. We analyze the situations that the neighbor whose NR-RSS is closest to the CND-RSS was not the correct location estimation. If ε is too small, there will be no neighbors to filter and PGSL will be implemented frequently. This will result in low accuracy of our system. Conversely, if ε is too big, there will be several neighbors to filter each time, making the NR-RSS match meaningless. According to our experiment results, ε of 9 dBm has the best performance and this value is chosen throughout the experiments. By the way, δ can be determined based on the fingerprint map data.

4.3   Impact of Device Heterogeneity

The aim for this evaluation is to display the performance of our system with different devices to demonstrate our algorithm works well under heterogeneous

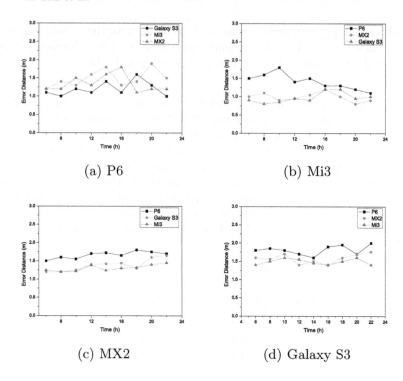

(a) P6   (b) Mi3

(c) MX2   (d) Galaxy S3

Fig. 7. Impact of device heterogeneity

devices. We use four different smartphones to build fingerprint map and localize. The same smartphone is never used for both constructing fingerprint map and for localization. Only one device was used for building fingerprint map while the other three smartphones are used to localize each time. We localized at different times of the day to check the performance of our system against environmental dynamics. The experiment results have been plotted in Fig. 7. The results indicate that the accuracy of our system does not degrade with device heterogeneity and our system can get the relative high accuracy of 1.5 m. This re-affirms our belief that our method will work well in complex real-world scenarios. In fact, our other experiments showed that our system works better in the building with complex structure than empty space as the former has quite different neighbors. Due to the lack of space, we do not display this part of evaluation experiments.

5   Conclusion

In this paper, we propose and evaluate NRLoc, a novel indoor localization scheme that uses existing Wi-Fi infrastructure. The proposed radio map building and localization techniques are based on the neighbor relationship. Our techniques provide robust and stable localization accuracy against device heterogeneity and environmental dynamics. Experiments using heterogeneous smartphones have confirmed that our system is feasible and reliable. NRLoc can achieve high localization accuracy with about 1.5 m error on the average. As NRLoc can localize real time with high accuracy, it has potential for large scale deployment.

Acknowledgment. This research is partially supported by the National Science Foundation of China (NSFC) under Grant No. 61103234 and No. 61272417

References

1. Mohammadi, M., Molaei, E., Naserasadi, A.: A survey on location based services and positioning techniques. Int. J. Comput. Appl. **24**(5), 1–5 (2011)
2. Kaplan, E.D., Hegarty, C.J. (eds.): Understanding GPS: Principles and Applications. Artech House, Boston (2005)
3. Priyantha, N.B., Chakraborty, A., Balakrishnan, H.: The cricket location-support system. In: Proceedings of the 6th Annual International Conference on Mobile Computing and Networking, pp. 32–43, ACM, August 2000
4. Jin, G.Y., Lu, X.Y., Park, M.S.: An indoor localization mechanism using active RFID tag. In: IEEE International Conference on Sensor Networks, Ubiquitous, and Trustworthy Computing 2006, vol. 1, p. 4, IEEE, June 2006
5. Swangmuang, N., Krishnamurthy, P.V.: On clustering RSS fingerprints for improving scalability of performance prediction of indoor positioning systems. In: Proceedings of the First ACM International Workshop on Mobile Entity Localization and Tracking in GPS-less Environments, pp. 61–66, ACM, September 2008
6. Castro, P., Chiu, P., Kremenek, T., Muntz, R.: A probabilistic room location service for wireless networked environments. In: Abowd, G.D., Brumitt, B., Shafer, S. (eds.) Ubicomp 2001: Ubiquitous Computing. LNCS, vol. 2201, pp. 18–34. Springer, Heidelberg (2001)
7. Brunato, M., Battiti, R.: Statistical learning theory for location fingerprinting in wireless LANs. Comput. Netw. **47**(6), 825–845 (2005)
8. Youssef, M., Agrawala, A.: The Horus location determination system. Wirel. Netw. **14**(3), 357–374 (2008)
9. Harle, R.: A survey of indoor inertial positioning systems for pedestrians. IEEE Commun. Surv. Tutor. **15**, 1281–1293 (2013)
10. Ladetto, Q.: On foot navigation: continuous step calibration using both complementary recursive prediction and adaptive Kalman filtering. In: Proceedings of ION GPS, vol. 2000, pp. 1735–1740, September 2000
11. Chen, Y.C., Chiang, J.R., Chu, H.H., Huang, P., Tsui, A.W.: Sensor-assisted wi-fi indoor location system for adapting to environmental dynamics. In: Proceedings of the 8th ACM International Symposium on Modeling, Analysis and Simulation of Wireless and Mobile Systems, pp. 118–125, ACM, October 2005
12. Bahl, P., Padmanabhan, V.N.: RADAR: an in-building RF-based user location and tracking system. In: Nineteenth Annual Joint Conference of the IEEE Computer and Communications Societies, INFOCOM 2000 Proceedings, vol. 2, pp. 775–784, IEEE (2000)
13. Roy, N., Wang, H., Choudhury, R.R.: I am a Smartphone and I can tell my user's walking direction. In: Proceedings of the 12th International Conference on Mobile Systems, Applications, and Services, ACM, June 2014

Social Attributes Based Cooperative Caching
in Ad Hoc Networks

Zhiwei Yang, Weigang Wu[⊠], and Zhenghao Zhu

Department of Computer Science, Sun Yat-Sen University, Guangzhou 51006, China
{yangzhw,zhuzhhao}@mail2.sysu.edu.cn, wuweig@mail.sysu.edu.cn

Abstract. Cooperative caching is an efficient technique to reduce data access cost in ad hoc networks. Although quite a lot of work has been done on cooperative caching, how to place and discover cache copies efficiently is still a challenging task. Motivated by the fast development of social networks, we propose to improve the efficiency of cooperative caching by considering the social attributes of network nodes. We include friendship, interest similarity and centrality in the design of cache placement metric and cache discovery metric. Cache placement metric is used to evaluate the significance of candidate data items while cache discovery metric is used to choose target nodes of cache query. Correspondingly, with the novel social attribute based metrics, cache copies can be placed more accurately and discovered more easily. To validate the performance of our design, we conduct extensive simulations via ns-3. The algorithm without consideration of social network is also simulated for comparison purpose. Simulation results show that social attribute based cooperative caching can significantly reduce data access time, while keeping the message cost similar.

Keywords: Cooperative caching · Network caching · Ad hoc network · Social network · Social attributes

1 Introduction

In a wireless ad hoc network, there is no support of any fixed infrastructure (e.g. the base stations in 3G networks or access points in wireless LANs), and network nodes communicates with each other through multi-hop paths. A network node can be any computing device, ranging from a mobile computer, e.g. smartphone, laptop, to a backbone network device, e.g. mesh routers, or even an embedded small sensor node. Due to the advantages in flexible deployment, low cost and easy maintenance, wireless ad hoc networks are especially suitable for the scenarios where the deployment of network infrastructure is too costly or even impossible, e.g. outdoor assemblies, disaster recovery and battlefield.

On the other hand, wireless ad hoc networks are resource constrained in terms of bandwidth, power, etc., so data access cost is a major concern. To cope with this challenge, cooperative caching has been proposed and studied. With multi-hop communication paths, caching data at intermediate nodes can significantly reduce message cost and consequently save various resources, from network bandwidth to battery power. Accessing data at cache node can also help reduce data access delay.

G. Wang et al. (Eds.): ICA3PP 2015, Part I, LNCS 9528, pp. 622–636, 2015.
DOI: 10.1007/978-3-319-27119-4_43

Quite a lot of work has been conducted for data caching in wireless ad hoc networks, including cache placement [1, 2], cache discovery [3, 4], and cache consistency [5]. Cache placement refers to determining where and what to cache; cache discovery refers to the mechanism to find and obtain a cached data item; and cache consistency means to ensure that content in cache copies is consistent with the source copy. The first two problems are so closely related that they are usually studied together.

The cache placement problem in ad hoc networks has been proved to be NP-hard, even if only one data item is considered [2]. Existing works on cache placement mainly focus on how to make use of the data access frequency information and network topology information in selecting cache nodes [2, 6–8]. For cache discovery, recent research has been focused on combining passive with active query approaches [3, 4, 9, 10] to obtain better performance.

In this paper, we introduce social attributes into the design of cooperative caching systems. In social wireless networks, individuals having similar interests or commonalities may converse and connect with one another using mobile devices. This type of networking has been attracting more and more attentions from both academia and industry. Especially, social network in ad hoc environments has been studied by quite a number of researchers [11].This motivates us to consider making use of social network analysis [12] to improve the efficiency of cooperative caching.

Intuitively, the friendship in social network can guide nodes in choosing data items to cache and choosing target node to query. Centrality and interest similarity are two major social attributes considered in our work. We introduce social attributes into both cache placement and cache discovery.

The design of placement metric is at the core of cache placement. In existing works [7, 8], the significance of a data item is simply represented by access frequency and/or access cost (the number of hops to get it). In social network, nodes prefer to share data with friends. Then, a data item should be significant if it is frequently requested by friend nodes. We design new metric of data significance which includes friendship and interest similarity.

In cache discovery phase, a node will query possible cache nodes to get data requested. Cache query in previous works is usually done based on physical neighborhood, i.e. hop-by-hop broadcasting [3, 4]. By considering social attributes, we propose to query the nodes with high centrality or similar interests because these nodes are more likely to have the data requested than others. Correspondingly, a metric is designed to select the possible cache nodes.

To evaluate the efficiency of our design, we conduct simulations using ns3. Social attributes such as friendship and social circles are established by trimming from a real social network [13]. A cooperative caching system without considering social attributes is also simulated for comparison purpose. The results clearly show that social attributes can help save data access time obviously.

The rest of the paper is organized as follows. Section 2 reviews existing solutions for cache placement and cache discovery in ad hoc networks. The system mode and assumptions involved in our work are presented in Sect. 3. In the following section, we define new metrics for cache placement and cache discovery, which are based on social attributes of network nodes. Based on the new metrics, Sect. 5 describes our new cache algorithm with detailed cooperative caching operations. Section 6 presents simulation results and analysis. Finally, Sect. 7 concludes the paper with future directions.

2   Related Work

Although quite a lot of work has been done on cooperative caching in wireless ad hoc networks, very few of existing algorithms consider social attributes in cache discovery and placement. In the following, we briefly review existing cache placement and discovery algorithms respectively.

Cache placement algorithms mainly differ in the metric to evaluate the significance of data items. In popularity based algorithms [6, 14], placement decision is made based on how "popular" the data item is. Popularity can be represented by access frequency, time interval from last access, etc. These algorithms differ in whether and how the access of a neighbor host is considered. The work of Yin and Cao [8] focuses on information cached at a node. Depending on the access frequency and cache space, a node may cache the data itself or the path to the nearest cache node.

On the other hand, in a benefit-based algorithm [2, 15], data items are selected according to how much "benefit", e.g. the reduction in message cost, query delay, energy consumption, etc., can be obtained by caching the data items. Nuggehalli et al. [2] formulated the cache placement problem with a single data item as a special case of the connected facility location problem and considered the tradeoff between the query delay and overall energy consumption. In [16], the placement metric is defined as the reduction of data access cost by caching a data item, where access cost is defined as the production of access frequency and distance (hop count) to get the data item.

Existing cache discovery approaches can be categorized into two classes: passive discovery and active discovery. In passive discovery systems [8, 16], the cache copy at one node is unknown to other nodes. The data requests are always destined to the data source. In active cache discovery [3, 15], a cache node proactively disseminate the cache information to other nodes so that each node can maintain a nearest cache table. Then a data request is destined to the nearest cache node rather than the source node. Hybrid approaches can be found in [4, 9, 10]. The solution in [4] imposes a cluster based hierarchy on a flat ad hoc network. It focuses on how to construct the hierarchy and how to discover the nearest cache node, inside and out-side of the clusters. In [9, 10], a node tries to find a cache by flooding within a predefined zone before sending the request to remote nodes.

The only work making use of social attributes in caching algorithm design is done by Zhuo et al. [17]. They exploited the social community structure to combat the unstable network topology in DTNs and proposed a centrality metric to evaluate caching capability of each node within a community. Since the authors focus on contact duration of network nodes, social attributes are not well studied in caching operations.

3   System Model

We consider a multi-hop wireless ad hoc network, which consists of n nodes, denoted as $N = \{N_1, N_2, N_3,..., N_n\}$. The network is connected to Internet via a gateway node, say N_n. Nodes communicate with each other via multi-hop wireless paths, and those paths are selected by routing protocols, e.g. OLSR. The network topology may change from time to time due to mobility or link failures. However, we assume that the network is always connected despite topology changes.

The network nodes need to access data items to serve users. We assume that there are m data items, denoted as D. $D = \{D_1, D_2, D_3, ..., D_m\}$. These data items are tagged based on its content, e.g. business, technology, music, sports, etc. Accordingly, data items can be classed into different categories: $C = \{C_1, C_2, C_3, ...\}$. Each data item is associated with one category. For ease of presentation, we denote the category of D_i as C_{Di}. The data items are owned and maintained by data sources. Network nodes access data items following requirements of users. To reduce data access cost, a node may cache the data item obtained for future access. Such data copies can be shared among network nodes, i.e. a node can request data from peer nodes besides the source nodes.

4   Design of Cache Metrics

Cache placement metric is the metric to determine whether a data item should be cached. Cache discovery metric is used to select proper target nodes to query. These metrics are at the core of a cooperative cache algorithm. Since the cache metrics are based on social attributes, we firstly introduce related social network concepts, and then define our social attribute based cache metrics.

4.1   Social Attributes and Concepts

(1) Interests

Each node may be interested in different types of data [18]. According to the category of data items, the interests of a network node can be defined as:

$$IS(N_i) = \{C_i \in C, Int(N_i, C_i) = 1\} \qquad (1)$$

where $Int(N_i, C_i)$ is the interest function:

$$Int(N_i, C_i) = \begin{cases} 1, & \text{if } N_i \text{ is interested in } C_i \\ 0, & \text{otherwise} \end{cases} \qquad (2)$$

(2) Friendship

Friendship is the basic relationship in social networks. Friendship network can be viewed as an overlay network represented by an undirected graph $G(N, E)$, where the set of vertices N represents the nodes in the network, and E is the set of edges indicating whether two nodes are friends.

The friendship among network nodes is predefined and unchangeable. Friendship is also symmetric, i.e. N_i is a friend of N_j iff N_j is friend of N_i. Each node has knowledge of its friends' interests. We define friendship function:

$$Fri(N_i, N_j) = \begin{cases} 1, & \text{if } N_i \text{ and } N_j \text{ are friends} \\ 0, & \text{otherwise} \end{cases} \tag{3}$$

Then, we have the friend set of N_i:

$$FS\left(N_i\right) = \left\{N_j | N_j \in N, Fri\left(N_i, N_j\right) = 1\right\} \tag{4}$$

Also the friends' interest set of N_i:

$$FIS\left(N_i\right) = \left\{C_i | N_j \in FS\left(N_i\right), C_i \in IS\left(N_j\right)\right\} \tag{5}$$

(3) Centrality

Centrality is commonly used in social network analysis, which indicates how "important" a node is. It can be defined differently in terms of measurement, e.g. by degree, by closeness, or by betweenness [12]. For simplicity, we adopt the centrality based degree in our design. In fact, other definition can also be used. The centrality of N_i is defined as:

$$Cen_i = \sum_k^n Fri(N_i, N_k) \tag{6}$$

(4) Social Circle

A social circle is a group of people tend to cluster together, due to similar friends and interests [19]. In this paper, we assume the nodes in one circle share the same set of interests. On the other hand, one node may appear in more than one circle.

(5) Social factor

Social factor reflects the closeness or trustiness between a pair of friends [20]. Social factor is a way to measure how a node is willing to cooperate with its friends. The higher social factor between them goes, the closer of these two nodes will be. Initially the value of social factor is set to be one. The social factor SF_{ij} increases by one when node Ni gets a requested data time from N_j; if N_j does not have the requested data, or is not willing to share its cached content, SF_{ij} decreases by one.

4.2   Cache Metrics

Two different metrics are used in our caching system. Cache discovery metric is used to select target node to query, while cache placement metric is used to determine whether a new data item should be cached and which cache item should be replaced if the cache space if full.

Upon a data access request, node N_i needs to discover possible cache copies. Querying the whole network is obviously unacceptable. N_i should query only nodes that have the requested data with high probability, so as to reduce communication cost and time cost. To do so, we design metric to select query targets, with social attributes aforementioned.

The underlying idea of our design is that, nodes with similar interests may have similar data access patterns and are likely to request same cache copies.

We define $SFS(N_i, C_{Di})$, the subset of friend set of N_i, i.e. $FS(N_i)$, in which nodes have the same interest C_{Di}:

$$SFS\left(N_i, D_{Ci}\right), = \left\{N_j | N_j \in FS\left(N_i\right), C_{Di} \in IS\left(N_j\right)\right\} \tag{7}$$

To avoid querying node too far away, we define the subset of $SFS(N_i, C_{Di})$, with distance constraint:

$$NSFS\left(N_i, C_{Di}\right) = \left\{N_j | N_j \in SFS\left(N_i, C_{Di}\right), Dis\left(N_i, N_j\right) < d\right\} \tag{8}$$

where $Dis(N_i, N_j)$ is the distance in terms of hops, and d is the distance limitation.

On the other hand, we would like to query nodes with high centrality because those nodes can help propagate query fast. Then, we define N_i's highest centrality friend node:

$$HCF\left(N_i\right) = N_j \tag{9}$$

s.t. $Cen_j = max\, Cen_k, N_k \in FS\left(N_i\right)$

Cache placement metric is in fact a metric to evaluate the significance of a data item. With social attributes considered, we define the significance of D_i at node N_i:

$$RplMtc(D_i, N_i) = \begin{cases} 0\ whenC_{D_i} \notin FIS(N_i), C_{D_i} \notin IS(N_i) \\ 0.5\ when\ C_{D_i} \in FIS(N_i), C_{D_i} \notin IS(N_i) \\ 1\ when\ C_{D_i} \notin FIS(N_i), C_{D_i} \in IS(N_i) \\ 1.5\ when\ C_{D_i} \in FIS(N_i), C_{D_i} \in IS(N_i) \end{cases} \tag{10}$$

When the cache space of node N_i is full, the cache copy with the lowest significance will be replaced with new cache copies.

5   The Social Based Cooperative Caching Algorithm

With the metrics defined in the previous section, we design our social attributes based cooperative caching algorithm. The algorithm consists of two parts: cache discovery and cache placement. The pseudo code of our algorithm is shown in Fig. 1.

To access a data item, the request node will first try to find out a cache copy by querying other nodes. To reduce the cost of query, only part of network nodes will be queried. In existing works, this is usually achieved by limiting the number of hops or time of the query propagation. In our algorithm, this is done by selecting target nodes according to the cache discovery metric.

Based on the response from target nodes, the request node will choose one of them as the reply node, and send data request. Then, the reply node will send back data copy

Algorithm – social cooperative caching

Upon request D_i at N_i

  send $QRY(D_i, N_k, C_{Di})$ to {

    the first nq nodes in $SFS(N_i, C_{Di})$ with high social factor.

    the node $HCF(N_i)$, the friend with the highest centrality.

  }

  set timeout for response.

  Upon timeout occurs:

send $RQS(D_i, N_i, N_j)$ to source node.

  Upon receiving $QRY(D_i, N_i, C_{Di})$ at N_j

if(D_i is in cache space)

    send $RSP(D_i, N_i, N_j)$ to N_i .

    else if(QRY is forwarded less than mh times)

    forward the query to $NSFS(N_j, C_{Di})$ w/t probability ff.

  Upon receiving$RSP(D_i, N_i, N_j)$ at N_i

if (this is the first response for D_i)

    send $RQS(D_i, N_i, N_j)$ to N_j

  Upon receiving $RQS(D_i, N_i, N_j)$ at N_j

    send $RPL(D_i, N_i, N_j, [Content])$

  Upon receiving $RPL(D_i, N_i, N_j, data)$ at N_i

if(cache space is full)

    remove the item with least $RplMtc$.

put D_i into cache space;

increase SF_{ij}

Fig. 1. Pseudo code of our algorithm

required. Upon receiving the data copy, the request node needs to do cache placement/ replacement. If the cache space is not full yet, the new copy will be put in cache space. Otherwise, the existing cache with lowest significance will be replaced. The significance of data items are calculated using cache placement metric.

In the following, we first define data structures and message types involved in our algorithm, and then describe the proposed algorithm. Since many operations and factors need to be varied and extended, we present a basic algorithm first, and then discuss variants of the basic algorithm.

5.1 Data Structure and Message Type

For each node N_i, besides its own status, i.e. interest set $IS(N_i)$, centrality Cen_i, it also maintains a list of friends and a table of caches.

Each entry of the friend list contains the following data:
N_j, the id of the friend;
$IS(N_j)$, the interest set of N_j;

Cen_j, centrality of N_j;

SF_{ij}, social factor of the friendship between N_i and N_j.

Each node keeps a cache table to record its local cache copies. Entries of cache table are identified by data id, each entry contains the information of source node id, a timestamp, size of the data item, and the actual cache data, etc.

Following are the message types involved in our algorithm:

$QRY(D_i,N_i,C_{Di})$, the message sent by N_i, querying for D_i.

$RSP(D_i,N_i,N_j)$, the message sent by N_j to respond to the query from N_i. This message indicates that D_i is available at N_j.

$RQS(D_i,N_i,N_j)$, the message sent by N_i to request data copy of D_i from N_j.

$RPL(D_i,N_i,N_j,data)$: the reply message sent by N_j carrying data copy N_i required.

5.2   The Basic Algorithm

When node N_i wants to access some data item, say D_i, it will first determine the category of D_i, then send query message to two classes of nodes: the friend nodes which are interested in C_{Di} and the node with the highest centrality. Since N_i may have many nodes with the same interest, N_i can select a number nq (short for number of queries) of them to save query cost. The node $HCF(N_i)$ is also queried because it has more friends and can help propagate the query easily. Obviously, the number nq must be carefully selected according to the node density and network scale.

Also, node N_i needs to set a timeout for possible response from target nodes. This is necessary to avoid block due to no response from target nodes. Of course, the value of the timeout must be carefully chosen based on the round trip time.

When some node, say N_j, receives the query from N_i, it will first check whether the requested data is cached. If N_j has the cache copy of the requested data, it simply sends a response message to N_i. Otherwise, N_j forward the query to all nodes in $NSFS$. The reason we use $NSFS$ rather than SFS in forwarding is to avoid querying long distance cache nodes.

To limit the cost of query forwarding, we set a limitation for each query message in terms of number of hops. This is similar to the TTL in routing operations, but in our social caching algorithm, one hop refers to one hop of friendship instead of physical neighbors. If a query has been forwarded for mh times (i.e. hops in friendship, mh means "max hop"), the receiver will not forward it anymore. Moreover, the forwarding can be further limited by probabilistic forwarding. That is, even within the mh hops, the receiver of query forward the message with a specific probability ff (short for forwarding factor). The value of ff can be determined based on the density of friends.

Once the response message from N_j is received, the request node N_i will send a request message to N_j. On the other hand, if no response is received before timeout occurs, N_i has to request data from the source node because no cache node is available.

After receiving the request message, the data source or cache node will send back the data D_i to N_i. Upon receiving the data copy, N_i will consume it and then try to cache it. If the cache space is full, victim cache will be selected using the metric $RplMtc$. N_i also needs to increase the social factor between N_i and N_j.

5.3   Variants and Extensions

(1) Querying one-hop neighbors

In a wireless ad hoc network, message is always transmitted via physical broadcasting, so one hop neighbors of a request node can receive the query message almost without additional cost. Then, we can include such neighbors as target nodes of query. This can help improve cache hit ratio with little overhead.

Please notice that, these neighbors will not forward the query message unless it is in the path of *SFS* nodes or *HCF* node.

(2) Two-step version

In the basic algorithm, there are four steps, i.e. query, response, request, and reply. To reduce steps, we can let target nodes of query send back the data packet directly rather than a response. Then, only two steps are necessary: query and response.

However, such light version may cause redundant data copies sent to the same request node and consequently waste network resource. Obviously, there is a tradeoff between control message cost and data message cost. Intuitively, the four-way version suits for environments with large data items while the two-way version is suitable for systems with small data items and sensitive to response time.

6   Simulation Results and Analysis

To evaluate the performance of our proposed algorithm, we have carried out extensive simulations using the ns-3 simulator. For comparison purpose, we also simulated a non-social cooperative caching algorithm, denoted as CMP. Our algorithm is denoted as SCC.

CMP is in fact a generalization of existing query based cache algorithms. In CMP, query message is propagated by hop-by-hop broadcasting. Same as in our SCC algorithm, the forwarding of query is limited to mh times. That is, a query message is propagated to all the mh-hop neighbors of the request node. The replacement of SCC is based on LRU. To be fair, the forwarding of a query in SCC is also constrained to mh times.

6.1   Simulation Setup

We simulated a wireless ad hoc network with 100 nodes, which are distributed in an area of 1000 m × 1000 m. The nodes are initially deployed randomly, and then move following the random walk model. The speed of the movement is set to approximate the speed of real walk of human beings. IEEE 802.11 and OLSR are adopted as the MAC protocol and routing protocol respectively.

There are totally 1000 data items, and they are randomly divided into 16 categories. One node is selected to act as data source node. To show the longer delay of getting data from data source, an additional delay of 100 ms is added to request to gateway. This is a reasonable (if not small) value of real Internet access delay. And we put the data source at the corner of the simulated area.

The social circle and friendship is simulated by applying the dataset of SNAP [18]. We used a subset of the ego-Facebook Social Networks Dataset to set social attributes. From the subset, we read friend relations and circle information. A circle is a group containing several nodes having similar interests. Nodes in a circle are very likely to be friends, and node may appear in more than one circle. We assign each circle with a particular interest, thus different nodes are interested in different data categories, and friends turn to have similar interests.

We have 14 circles, each of which is assigned with one category. To make the data access reasonable, we let a node request the data items in the associated category with a probability called "interest factor", denoted by *inf*. That is, when a node generates a request, with a probability of 1-*inf*, the node randomly chooses a data item which this node is not interested in. Of course, the node will randomly choose some data item in its associated category with a probability *inf*.

We vary the values of four key parameters to examine their effects. The data access rate is varied from 1/40 s to 1/5 s. The size of each data item is varied from 1 kB to 30 kB. The interest factor is in the scope of 0.7 to 1.0 and the size of cache space (i.e. cache capacity) is varied from 15 to 50 data items.

6.2   Performance Metrics

Like similar works, four metrics are used to measure the performance of caching algorithms.

Hit Ratio, the ratio of requests met by cache nodes over all the requests.

Success Ratio, the percentage of the requests that are replied before the timeout occurs.

Access Delay, the average time interval between sending a data request and receiving the corresponding reply.

Message Cost, the total packets transmitted in MAC layer by all nodes for data access, including all query, response, request and reply operations.

6.3   Simulation Results

(1) Cache hit ratio

The results of cache hit ratio are shown in Fig. 2. Both the algorithms can achieve higher hit ratio with higher access rate. This is easy to understand. With the increase of access rate, more data will be requested and cached. Consequently, more requests can be met by cache copies. Hit ratio is almost not affected by data item size, since the cache capacity is set in terms of number of data items and item size will not change the percentage of items in cache space over total data items.

Interest factor is varied from 0.7 to 1.0. Figure 2(c) shows that, a high interest factor is beneficial. With interest factor increases, the data requests will be more focused on specific interest and consequently cache copies can meet future requests with a higher possibility. The effect of cache capacity is simple. With larger capacity, more cache copies can be stored and more requests can be replied with cache copies.

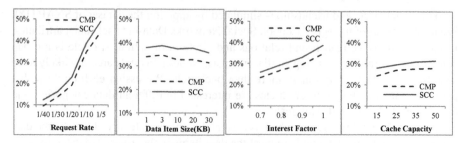

(a) interest factor 1.0, data size 3kB, (b) interest factor 1.0, request rate 1/10,
cache capacity 25   cache capacity 25
(c) request rate 1/10, data size 3kB, (d) interest factor 0.8, request rate 1/10,
cache capacity 25   data size 3kB

Fig. 2. Cache hit ratio

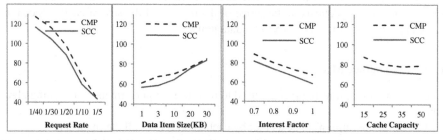

(a) interest factor 1.0, data size 3kB, (b)interest factor 1.0, request rate 1/10,
cache capacity 25   cache capacity 25
(c) request rate 1/10, data size 3kB, (d) interest factor 0.8, request rate 1/10,
cache capacity 25   data size 3kB

Fig. 3. Access delay

Now, let us compare our algorithm SCC with the non-social algorithm CMP. From all the four figures in Fig. 2, we can see that SCC can achieve higher hit ration in various cases, and the difference is obvious. Such advantage obviously indicates that social factors can benefit cooperative caching.

(2) Access Delay

Access delay decreases with the increase of request rate, as shown in Fig. 3(a). This is similar to hit ratio. With higher request rate, more cache copies are available. Since cached copies are nearer than source copies, access delay is reduced by cache copies. As shown in Fig. 3(b), access delay is enlarged with larger data item size. This is just because, larger data item needs more time to be transferred from cache node to request node, which is not related to the performance of caching algorithm itself.

With the increase of interest factor, access delay is decreased. This can be understood similar to the effect of interest factor on hit ratio. With a large interest factor, data requests present a small variety in interest. Then, cache hit ratio increases and access delay decrease. The decrease of access delay with increase of

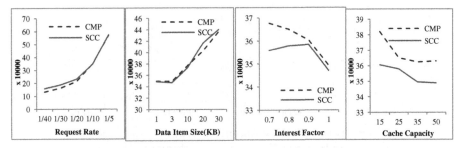

(a) interest factor 1.0, data size 3kB, (b) interest factor 1.0, request rate 1/10,
cache capacity 25   cache capacity 25
(c) request rate 1/10, data size 3kB, (d) interest factor 0.8, request rate 1/10,
cache capacity 25   data size 3kB

Fig. 4. Message cost

cache capacity can also be explained by change of hit ratio because getting data from cache nodes is faster than from the source node.

Compared with CMP, SCC can always get data faster, under all cases. This is consistent with the difference in hit ratio. High hit ratio will certainly result in shorter delay. However, the advantage of SCC is not so obvious as in hit ratio. This is because, besides cache hit ratio, access delay is also affected by many other factors, such as data item size.

(3) Message cost

The results of message cost are plotted in Fig. 4. With the increase of request rate, message cost increases, and this is expected. The effect of data item size and cache capacity is also straightforward. Larger items will cause more bytes to be transmitted. With larger cache capacity, more data items can be cached and communication coast is reduced.

The effect of interest factor is more interesting. Generally, with the increase of interest factor, the message cost of CMP decreases because the nodes in choose data with more focus. However, the effect of interest factor on SCC is complex. With the increase of interest factor, message cost of SCC increase a little and then decrease fast at $inf = 0.9$. This indicates the two-fold effect of interest factor in SCC. On the one hand, with interest factor increases, there is less random in choosing data to access and message cost is reduced as in CMP. On the other hand, with a higher interest factor, more nodes will be queried and then message cost increases.

Compare with CMP, SCC performs a little worse in message cost, although the difference is minor. This is because, in SCC, the message is sent to friend node via unicast, which is not so efficient as broadcast in CMP. Although the cost of broadcast is much less than unicast, the difference between SCC and CMP in message cost is ignorable. This indicates that the advantage of SCC in cache placement is more significant than the disadvantage in message cost.

(4) Success Ratio

Figure 5 shows the results of success ratio. Under various cases, SCC and CMP achieve very close success ratio. With request rate increases, success ratio also

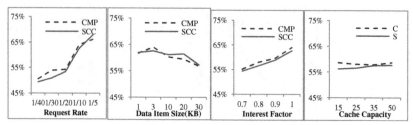

(a) interest factor 1.0, data size 3kB, (b) interest factor 1.0, request rate 1/10,
cache capacity 25   cache capacity 25
(c) request rate 1/10, data size 3kB, (d) interest factor 0.8, request rate 1/10,
cache capacity 25   data size 3kB

Fig. 5. Success ratio

increases. This should be the benefit of the increasing of cache hit ratio. With high request rate, more cache copies are available, and more requests can be met successfully because accessing cache copies is faster than accessing the source copies. The effect of data item size can be explained by traffic load. With larger data items, traffic load of the network will be heavier and the access delay will be longer (as shown in Fig. 3). Then, more reply will not be delivered in time thus more request cannot be met successfully.

Interest factor also affect success ratio significantly. With a larger interest factor, the diversity of data items requested by nodes in a circle will be reduced and then more data items can be obtained from cache. This is same as the performance in hit ratio. The effect of cache capacity is simple. With a larger cache space, more data items can be cached and certainly fewer requests will fail.

7   Conclusion and Future Work

In this paper, we propose a social attribute based cooperative caching algorithm for ad hoc networks. Data access interest and friendships among network nodes are considered in the design of cache placement and discovery mechanisms. Different from similar works on cooperative caching, where cache copies are discovered via hop-by-hop query, our algorithm uses social attributes to guide the discovery of cache copies desired. Such design can obviously improve the efficiency of cache discovery and improve cache hit ratio. The advantage of our social attribute based design is validated via extensive simulations with various parameters included. The results show that, with very similar success ratio and message cost, social based caching algorithm can achieve higher hit ratio and lower access delay.

Since social attributes are rarely considered in data caching, especially in caching for ad hoc networks, more efforts are absolutely desired for further study. Open problems include social attributes in cache consistency maintenance, relation between friendship and data popularity, etc.

Acknowledgments. This research is partially supported by National Natural Science Foundation of China (No. 61379157).

References

1. Fan, X., Cao, J., Wu, W.: Contention-aware data caching in wireless multi-hop ad hoc networks. J Para. Distrib. Comput. **71**(4), 603–614 (2011)
2. Nuggehalli, P., Srinivasan, V., Chiasserini, C.-F.: Energy-efficient caching strategies in ad hoc wireless networks. In: Proceedings of the ACM International Symposium on Mobile Ad Hoc Networking and Computing (MobiHoc 2003), New York, NY, USA, pp. 25–34 (2003)
3. Sailhan, F., Issarny, V.: Cooperative caching in Ad Hoc networks. In: Chen, M.-S., Chrysanthis, P.K., Sloman, M., Zaslavsky, A. (eds.) MDM 2003. LNCS, vol. 2574, pp. 13–28. Springer, Heidelberg (2003)
4. Chauhan, N., Awasthi, L.K., Chand, N., Joshi, R.C., Mishra, M.: A cooperative caching strategy in mobile ad hoc networks based on clusters. In: Proceedings of the 2011 International Conference on Communication, Computing & Security, pp. 17–20 (2011)
5. Huang, Y., Cao, J., Wang, Z., Jin, B., Feng, Y.: Achieving flexible cache consistency for pervasive internet access. In: The Fifth Annual IEEE International Conference on Pervasive Computing and Communications 2007, PerCom 2007, pp. 239–250 (2007)
6. Hara, T.: Effective replica allocation in ad hoc networks for improving data accessibility. In: Twentieth Annual Joint Conference of the IEEE Computer and Communications Societies, vol. 3, pp. 1568–1576 (2001)
7. Tang, B., Gupta, H., Das, S.R.: Benefit-based data caching in Ad Hoc networks. IEEE Trans. Mob. Comput. **7**(3), 289–304 (2008)
8. Yin, L., Cao, G.: Supporting cooperative caching in ad hoc networks. Presented at the INFOCOM 2004, Twenty-third Annual Joint Conference of the IEEE Computer and Communications Societies, vol. 4, pp. 2537–2547 (2004)
9. Chiu, G.-M., Young, C.-R.: Exploiting in-zone broadcasts for cache sharing in mobile ad hoc networks. IEEE Trans. Mob. Comput. **8**(3), 384–397 (2009)
10. Du, Y., Gupta, S.K., Varsamopoulos, G.: Improving on-demand data access efficiency in MANETs with cooperative caching. Ad Hoc Netw. **7**(3), 579–598 (2009)
11. Katsaros, D., Dimokas, N., Tassiulas, L.: Social network analysis concepts in the design of wireless ad hoc network protocols. IEEE Netw. **24**(6), 23–29 (2010)
12. Daly, E.M., Haahr, M.: Social network analysis for routing in disconnected delay-tolerant MANETs. In: Proceedings of the 8th ACM International Symposium on Mobile Ad Hoc Networking and Computing (Mobihoc 2007), New York, NY, USA, pp. 32–40 (2007)
13. Stanford large network dataset collection. http://snap.stanford.edu/data/. Accessed July 2014
14. Hara, T.: Cooperative caching by mobile clients in push-based information systems. In: Proceedings of the Eleventh International Conference on Information and Knowledge Management, pp. 186–193 (2002)
15. Tang, B., Gupta, H., Das, S.: Benefit-based data caching in Ad Hoc networks. In: The Proceedings of the 14th IEEE International Conference on Network Protocols (ICNP 2006), pp. 208–217 (2006)
16. Jianliang, X., Li, B., Lee, D.L.: Placement problems for transparent data replication proxy services. IEEE J. Sel. Areas Commun. **20**(7), 1383–1398 (2002)
17. Zhuo, X., Li, Q., Cao, G., Dai, Y., Szymanski, B., La Porta, T.: Social-based cooperative caching in DTNs: a contact duration aware approach. In: 2011 IEEE 8th International Conference on Mobile Adhoc and Sensor Systems (MASS), pp. 92–101 (2011)

18. Liu, L., Antonopoulos, N., Mackin, S.: Social peer-to-peer for resource discovery. In: 15th EUROMICRO International Conference on Parallel, Distributed and Network-Based Processing (PDP 2007), pp. 459–466 (2007)

19. Hui, P., Yoneki, E., Chan, S.Y., Crowcroft, J.: Distributed community detection in delay tolerant networks. In: Proceedings of 2nd ACM/IEEE International Workshop on Mobility in the Evolving Internet Architecture, New York, NY, USA, pp. 7:1–7:8 (2007)

20. Pan, D., Chen, W., Ruan, Z., Lu, K.: A transmission scheme for opportunistic networks with social selfish nodes. In: Proceedings of the 4th International Conference on Internet Multimedia Computing and Service, New York, NY, USA, pp. 15–19 (2012)

Entropy-Based Social Influence Evaluation in Mobile Social Networks

Sancheng Peng[1], Jian Li[1(✉)], and Aimin Yang[2(✉)]

[1] School of Computer Science, Zhaoqing University,
Zhaoqing 526061, Guangdong Province, People's Republic of China
zqlijian@qq.com
[2] School of Informatics, Guangdong University of Foreign Studies,
Guangzhou 510420, People's Republic of China
amyang18@163.com

Abstract. How to evaluate social influence of one user on other users in mobile social networks becomes increasingly important. It can help to identify the influential users in mobile social networks. In addition, it can also provide important insights into the design of social platforms and applications, such as viral marketing, domain expert finding, and advertising. In this paper, we present a framework to quantitatively measure social influence in mobile social networks. In the proposed framework, social influence is a measure of uncertainty with its value represented by entropy. We establish a social relationship graph based on the social network theory that addresses the basic understanding of social influence. Based on the social relationship graph, we present an evaluation model on social influence using information entropy to describe the complexity and uncertainty of social influence. We evaluate the performance of our solution using a customized program based on a real-world SMS/MMS-based communication data set. The numerical simulations and analysis show that the proposed influence evaluation strategies can characterize the social influence of mobile social networks effectively and efficiently.

Keywords: Mobile social networks · Social influence · Information entropy · Social relationship graph

1 Introduction

A mobile social network [1] is a social network extracted from a data set of mobile communication, where each cellular phone represents a node, and relations between any two cellular phones form the set of edges. With the rapid development and increasing popularity of mobile social networks, more and more interest has been made in leveraging information available from mobile social networks to promote the adoption of new products or services. For example, in a mobile social network, user A usually gathers information from his/her friends, when he/she contemplates purchasing products or services. A also shares his/her

G. Wang et al. (Eds.): ICA3PP 2015, Part I, LNCS 9528, pp. 637–647, 2015.
DOI: 10.1007/978-3-319-27119-4_44

opinions within a specific mobile social networks regarding to different products which he/she has recently purchased or he/she is familiar with.

Social influence [2] refers to the case when individuals change their behaviors under the influence of others. The strength of social influence depends on the relation among individuals, network distances, time effect, characteristics of networks and individuals, etc. Viral marketing, online advertising, recommendation, and other applications can benefit from social influence by qualitatively and quantitatively measuring the influence of individuals on others. In light of the increasing business applications, how to measure a user's social influence to other users in mobile social media becomes increasingly important.

However, there are still many challenges [3,4] need to be addressed: (1) It is difficult to accurately provide the physical meaning of social influence; (2) It is still very unclear what factors should be considered to describe social influence; (3) It also lacks an effective method to properly integrate those factors to evaluate each user's influence efficiently and effectively; (4) It is hard to characterize the uncertainty of social influence, as well as the complexity of the concept of social influence.

Our goal is to address the above challenges. In this paper, our focus is to explore the essential factors that should be considered to describe a user's social influence, to present a general evaluation model on social influence by integrating these factors, and to provide an effective approach to characterize the uncertainty of social influence. To evaluate the social influence of mobile users, the following most important questions are to be taken into account: (1) what factors may impact a user's influence? (2) how does the impact take place? and (3) how does the impact be quantified?

We present a novel entropy-based model to evaluate social influence of users. Our purpose is to design a general model, which shows what the social influence of each individual is on a given information entropy. Our contributions are summarized as follows:

- We establish a social relationship graph based on the social network theory. This graph is constructed using the actual SMS/MMS communication data from people's daily lives for social interactions. It is built to reveal the connections of social interaction and the spreading of SMS/MMS.
- We present an evaluation model on social influence using information entropy to describe the complexity and uncertainty of social influence. In this model, we provide two factors, such as friend entropy and interaction frequency entropy.
- We evaluate the performance of our solution using a customized program based on a real-world SMS/MMS-based communication data set. Through extensive numerical simulations and analysis, we confirm that our strategies can characterize the social influence of mobile social networks effectively and efficiently.

The remainder of this paper is organized as follows: In Sect. 2, we provide a survey of related work, and provide an overview of information entropy in

Sect. 3. In Sect. 4, we present an influence model based on information entropy, and describe the experimental evaluation in Sect. 5. Finally, we conclude this paper and suggest future work in Sect. 6.

2 Related Work

Domingos and Richardson [5] investigated social influence in the customer network. They proposed a model to identify customer's influence between each other in the customer network, and built a probabilistic model to mine the spread of influence for viral marketing. Dietz et al. [6] devised a probabilistic topic model to explain the generation of documents. This model incorporated the aspects of topical innovation and topical inheritance via citations to predict the citation influences. Anagnostopoulos et al. [7] exploited a statistical analysis method to identify and measure whether social influence is a source of correlation between the actions of individuals with social ties.

Tang et al. [8] proposed a Topical Affinity Propagation (TAP) method to model the topic-level social influence in social networks, and developed a parallel model learning algorithm based on the map-reduce programming model. Pal et al. [9] used topic-sensitive retweet information to quantify pairwise influence and to identify the topic authorities in Twitter. Rodriguez et al. [10] proposed a model to infer the influence propagation given a set of observed user actions and associated timestamps to produce a network that best explains the observed actions times. Xiang et al. [11] developed an unsupervised model to estimate relationship strength from interaction activity (i.e., communication, tagging) and user similarity. They formulated a link-based latent variable model, along with a coordinate ascent optimization procedure for the inference.

Liu et al. [12] proposed a generative graphical model which leveraged both heterogeneous link information and textual content associated with each user in the network to mine topic-level influence strength. Weng et al. [13] presented an algorithm called Twitter-Rank based on PageRank algorithm to measure the influence of users in Twitter. TwitterRank measures the influence taking both the topical similarity between users and the link structure into account. Ding et al. [14] measured the influence of users using random walks on the multi-relational data (i.e., the retweet, the reply, the reintroduce, and the read) in Micro-blogging.

Li et al. [15] proposed a probabilistic model to capture the dual effect of topic preference and to mine topic-level opinion influence in microblog. Tang et al. [16] proposed a model to compute the user influence by combining content-based and network-based approaches. They extended PageRank algorithm and proposed a UserRank algorithm to quantify user influence in a weighed social network. Sang and Xu [18] presented a multimodal topic-sensitive influence model, which enables simultaneous extraction of node topic distribution, topic-sensitive edge strength, and the topic space.

Peng et al. [17] introduced two factors to evaluate influence of each node. One factor is intimacy degree (ID), which is used to reflect the closeness between users. The other factor is activity degree (AD), which is used to determine which node is more active. Tang et al. [19] studied a problem of conformity influence analysis in large social networks. They defined three major types of conformities to formulate the problem of conformity influence analysis. Huang et al. [20] proposed a framework to quantitatively measure individuals' social influence by examining the number of their followers and their sensitivity of discovering good items. He et al. [21] introduced transfer entropy to identify peer influence in online social networks. Lee et al. [22] proposed a method to find influentials by considering both the link structure and the temporal order of information adoption in Twitter. They measured the influence of user i with the total count of the effective readers for all tweets of i, based on the node degree-centrality.

Although the existing models provide some valuable insights into the problem of social influence evaluation in mobile social networks, most algorithms fail to characterize the uncertainty. In this paper, we aim to find out how to characterize the uncertainty of social influence, and how to construct a comprehensive social influence evaluation model to reveal the relationship between social interactions and the strength of social influence.

3   Overview of Information Entropy

Information entropy was founded by Claude Elwood Shannon, an American mathematician, electronic engineer and cryptographer, in the work of "A Mathematical Theory of Communication" in 1948. It is a concept from information theory. It tells how much information there is in an event. In general, the more uncertain or random the event is, the more information it will contain. It has applications in many areas, including lossless data compression, statistical inference, cryptography, and recently in other disciplines as biology, physics or machine learning, privacy protection [23], and so on.

According to Shannon's theory, if a random variable X represents a set of possible events x_i whose probabilities of occurrence are p_i, $i = 1, ..., n$, then a measure $H(X)$ of the uncertainty of the outcome of an event given such distribution of probabilities should have the following three properties [24]:

- $H(x_i)$ should be continuous in p_i;
- If all probabilities are equal, it means that $p_i = 1/n$, then $H(X)$ should be a monotonically increasing function of n (if there are more choices of events, and then the uncertainty about one outcome should increase);
- If a choice is broken down into other choices, with probabilities $c_j, j = 1, ..., k$, then $H(X) = \sum_{j=1}^{k} c_j H_k$, where H_k is the value of the function $H(X)$ for each choice.

Thus, Shannon proved that the only function that satisfies all three properties is given by.

$$H(X) = -\sum_{i=1}^{N} p(x_i)\log_2 p(x_i) \tag{1}$$

where the sum is over all states (Shannon's definition had a constant k multiplied by it, which has been removed here). The base 2 for the logarithm is chosen so that the measure is given in terms of bits of information. As an example, a device with two positions (like a flip-flop circuit) can store one bit of information. The number of possible states for N such devices would then be 2^N, and $\log_2 2^N = N$, meaning that N such devices can store N bits of information, as should be expected. This definition bears a lot of resemblance to Gibbs' entropy, but is more general, as it can be applied to any system that carries information.

4   Modeling Social Influence Evaluation Using Information Entropy

4.1   Constructing Social Relationship Graph

We model a mobile social network by a directed, weighted graph, $G(V, E, W)$, where set V of vertices corresponds to the cellular phones in cellular networks, set E of directed edges corresponds to the traffic flow among cellular phones i to j, and set W of weight values corresponds to the total number of SMS/MMS messages sent from cellular phone i to j in a given time period. The degree of vertex i, d_i, is the number of cellular phones that its owner communicates with. The amount of messages initiated from i to j is denoted by C_{ij}.

From a real-world data set which we collected from one of the largest cellular networks in China, we can extract a smartphone social network. The network is huge and complex. In order to explain the idea of a smartphone social network, we take eleven users from the data set and use them as an example. The data of this sample social network is listed in Table 1.

According to Table 1, we treat each smartphone as a vertex, so a weighted social relationship graph can be obtained and is shown in Fig. 1.

In Fig. 1, we find that the social-interactions based SMS/MMS are in our everyday lives. If only the one-way behavior is presented, even if W is large, it is difficult to show that the relationship between these two users are very close. For example, if a smartphone user always sends advertising information to other people, it cannot show that their relationships are close. Thus, we take the smaller of the weight values of the two directed edges between two nodes to measure the strength of their social relationship. That is, the social graph weight between node i and j, denoted by W_{ij}, is given by

$$W_{ij} = \min\{C_{ij}, C_{ji}\} \tag{2}$$

where C_{ij} denotes the number of SMS/MMS messages sent from node i to j.

Thus, according to Eq. (2), we can obtain the effective interactions between two nodes in a week, as shown in Table 2.

In addition, the transition result of Fig. 1 is shown in Fig. 2. The behaviors of SMS/MMS-based social interactions between two smartphone users are characterized accurately by changing one directed weighted graph $G(V, E, W)$ into another undirected weighted graph $G'(V, E, W)$.

Table 1. The number of interactions between two cellular phone users in a week

Between two smartphones	The number of interactions	Between two smartphones	The number of interactions
$A \rightarrow B$	3	$F \rightarrow I$	7
$A \rightarrow C$	6	$G \rightarrow B$	7
$A \rightarrow D$	9	$G \rightarrow D$	8
$B \rightarrow A$	6	$G \rightarrow F$	8
$B \rightarrow D$	15	$G \rightarrow H$	21
$B \rightarrow F$	4	$G \rightarrow I$	0
$B \rightarrow G$	8	$G \rightarrow J$	5
$C \rightarrow A$	16	$H \rightarrow D$	3
$C \rightarrow D$	7	$H \rightarrow E$	11
$C \rightarrow E$	11	$H \rightarrow G$	13
$D \rightarrow A$	4	$H \rightarrow J$	7
$D \rightarrow B$	6	$H \rightarrow K$	3
$D \rightarrow C$	7	$I \rightarrow F$	6
$D \rightarrow E$	3	$I \rightarrow G$	7
$D \rightarrow G$	4	$I \rightarrow J$	12
$D \rightarrow H$	17	$J \rightarrow G$	9
$E \rightarrow C$	4	$J \rightarrow H$	22
$E \rightarrow D$	8	$J \rightarrow I$	11
$E \rightarrow H$	8	$J \rightarrow K$	6
$E \rightarrow K$	0	$K \rightarrow E$	4
$F \rightarrow B$	2	$K \rightarrow H$	0
$F \rightarrow G$	1	$K \rightarrow J$	2

4.2   Computing of Social Influence

In this paper, we measure the social influence of mobile users computing the entropy of friend nodes and the entropy of interaction frequency of mobile users.

(1) Entropy computation among friend nodes

Let $N_i(t)$ be the number of friend nodes of node i in time t. In general, the size of $N_i(t)$ is an important factor to measure the influence of a node in a social network. Thus, the entropy of friend nodes $I_i^f(t)$ for node i is described as follows.

$$I_i^f(t) = -\frac{1}{N_i(t) + \theta} \log_2 \frac{1}{N_i(t) + \theta} \tag{3}$$

where θ is an adjusted parameter used to satisfy the monotony decreasing characteristics of expression.

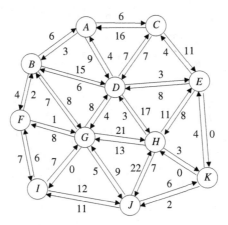

Fig. 1. A weighted social relationships graph (directed) based on the total number of SMS/MMS messages between two nodes in a week.

Table 2. The number of interactions between two cellular phone users in a week

Between two smartphones	The number of effective interactions	Between two smartphones	The number of effective interactions
A, B	3	E, H	8
A, C	6	E, K	0
A, D	4	F, G	1
B, D	6	F, I	6
B, F	2	G, H	13
B, G	7	G, I	0
C, D	7	G, J	5
C, E	4	H, J	7
D, E	3	H, K	0
D, G	4	I, J	11
D, H	3	J, K	2

(2) Entropy computation on interaction frequency among friend nodes

Let $C_{ij}(t)$ be the number of interactions between node i and j in time t. In general, the size of $C_{ij}(t)$ is also an important factor to measure the influence of a node in a social network. Thus, the entropy of interaction frequency $I_i^c(t)$ for node i is described as follows.

$$I_i^c(t) = -\frac{1}{\sum_{j=1}^{N_i(t)} C_{ij}(t) + \lambda} \log_2 \frac{1}{\sum_{j=1}^{N_i(t)} C_{ij}(t) + \lambda} \quad (4)$$

where λ is an adjusted parameter used to satisfy the monotony decreasing characteristics of expression.

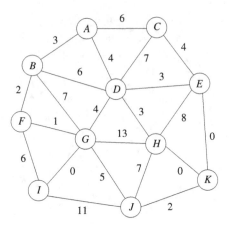

Fig. 2. A weighted social relationships graph (undirected) based on the number of effective interactions between two nodes in a week.

(3) Total social influence of node

According to the above analysis, the influence of i on its friend nodes is described as follows.

$$I_i(t) = \alpha I_i^f(t) + \beta I_i^c(t) \qquad (5)$$

where α and β denote $I_i^f(t)$ and $I_i^c(t)$ of weight, respectively, and $\alpha + \beta = 1$.

5   Simulations

To validate the effectiveness of the proposed model, we conduct experiments by using the message records collected by one of the largest cellular networks in China. The data set of 0.4 million users in this network exchanged about 20 million SMS/MMS messages over a three-week period in October 2012. To protect the privacy of users, the content of the message records is removed when we conduct the collection of the data set, and the uniqueness of the identifiers of the phone numbers involved are replaced by pseudocodes. In addition, we designed and developed a C++ simulator to implement our proposed mechanism, which is an extension of the proposed model. Due to the huge scale of the real-world data set, we took 5114 users for our experiments, rather than including all the users.

The influence diffusion is a metric to measure how many users can be influenced by the most influential k specific users (or called seed nodes). To test the influence spread, we use the model of worm propagation presented in our previous work [25] to propagate social influence. To obtain the influence spread of each model, we select top k=(10, 20, 30, 40) influential nodes as seeds. Besides node degree-centrality model, and entropy-based influence evaluation model, we also implement a random model as the baseline, which selects seeds randomly.

Figure 3 shows the influence spread of the entropy-based social influence evaluation model with different k at time t. As can be seen from the results, as the

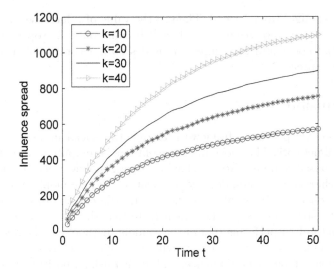

Fig. 3. A comparison of influence spread of the entropy-based social influence evaluation model with different k influential nodes.

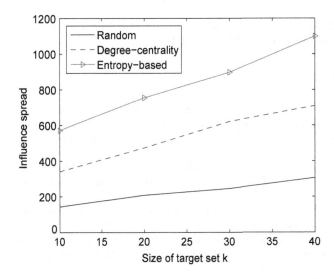

Fig. 4. A comparison of influence spread of different models with different k influential nodes.

value of k increases, the number of influence spread increases. The reason is because the more the most influential nodes, the more nodes can be influenced.

Figure 4 shows the influence spread of different models with different k influential nodes. From the results, it can be seen that the influence spread of the entropy-based social influence evaluation model is the better than the node degree-centrality model and random model. The influence spread increases slowly, as k changes from 1 to 10. Then as the value of k increases, the number of influence spread increases quickly. This is because only the top 1 to 10 nodes are influential nodes and the succeeding nodes do not contribute to increasing the influence spread.

6   Conclusion

In this paper, we present a framework to quantify social influence in a given mobile social network. The social influence of users is computed by analyzing the SMS/MMS-based communication behaviors among mobile users. In addition, we reveal and characterize the hidden social relations among mobile users through the analysis on the entropy of friend nodes and the entropy of interaction frequency. Extensive analysis results demonstrate that the influence spread of our proposed method outperforms that of the random method and the node centrality method. As for our further work, we will focus on characterizing the impact of casual relationship on social influence, and distinguishing positive influence and negative influence. In addition, how to quickly and effectively identify influential users in smartphone social networks is also worthy of further study.

Acknowledgments. This work is supported by the National Natural Science Foundation of China under Grant No. 61379041.

References

1. Peng, S., Wu, M., Wang, G., Yu, S.: Containing smartphone worm propagation with an influence maximization algorithm. Comput. Netw. **74**, 103–113 (2014)
2. Chen, M., Mao, S., Liu, Y.: Big data: a survey. Mob. Netw. Appl. **19**, 171–209 (2014)
3. Wang, G., Jiang, W., Wu, J., Xiong, Z.: Fine-grained feature-based social influence evaluation in online social networks. IEEE Trans. Parallel Distrib. Syst. **25**, 2286–2296 (2014)
4. Peng, S., Wang, G., Xie, D.: Social influence analysis in social networking big data: opportunities and challenges. In: IEEE Network (2015, to appear)
5. Domingos, P., Riehardson, M.: Mining the network value of customers. In: 7th ACM Conference on Knowledge Discovery and Data Mining, pp. 57–66. ACM Press, New York (2001)
6. Dietz, L., Bickel, S., Scheffer, T.: Unsupervised prediction of citation influences. In: 24th International Conference on Machine Learning (2007)
7. Anagnostopoulos, A., Kumar, R., Mahdian, M.: Influence and correlation in social networks. In: 14th ACM SIGKDD International Conference on Knowledge Discovery and Data Mining, pp. 7–15. ACM Press, New York (2008)
8. Tang, J., Sun, J., Wang, C., Yang, Z.: Social influence analysis in large-scale networks. In: 15th ACM SIGKDD International Conference on Knowledge Discovery and Data Mining, pp. 807–816. ACM Press, New York (2009)
9. Pal, A., Scott, C.: Identifying topical authorities in microblogs. In: 4th ACM International Conference on Web Search and Data Mining, pp. 45–54. ACM Press, New York (2011)

10. Rodriguez, M.G., Leskovec, J., Krause, A.: Inferring networks of diffusion and influence. In: 16th ACM SIGKDD International Conference on Knowledge Discovery and Data Mining, pp. 1019–1028. ACM Press, New York (2010)
11. Xiang, R., Neville, J., Rogati, M.: Modeling relationship strength in online social networks. In: 19th International World Wide Web Conference, pp. 981–990. ACM Press, New York (2010)
12. Liu, L., Tang, J., Han, J., Yang, S.: Learning influence from heterogeneous social networks. Data Min. Knowl. Dis. **25**, 511–544 (2012)
13. Weng, J., Lim, E.-P., Jiang, J., He, Q.: Twitterrank: finding topic-sensitive influential twitterers. In: 3rd ACM International Conference on Web Search and Data Mining, pp. 261–270. ACM Press, New York (2010)
14. Ding, Z., Jia, Y., Zhou, B., Han, Y.: Mining topical influencers based on the multi-relational network in micro-blogging sites. China Commun. **10**, 93–104 (2013)
15. Li, D., Shuai, X., Sun, G., Yang, J., Ding, Y., Luo, Z.: Mining topic-level opinion influence in microblog. In: 21st ACM International Conference on Information and Knowledge Management, pp. 1562–1566. ACM Press, New York (2012)
16. Tang, X., Yang, C.C.: Ranking user influence in healthcare social media. ACM Trans. Intell. Syst. Technol. **3**, Article No. 74 (2012)
17. Peng, S., Wang, G., Yu, S.: Mining mechanism of top-k influential nodes based on voting algorithm in mobile social networks. In: The 11th IEEE/IFIP International Conference on Embedded and Ubiquitous Computing (EUC 2013), pp. 2194–2199, IEEE Press (2013)
18. Sang, J., Xu, C.: Social influence analysis and application on multimedia sharing websites. ACM Trans. Multimed. Comput. Commun. Appl. **9**, Article No. 53 (2013)
19. Tang, J., Wu, S., Sun, J.: Confluence: conformity influence in large social networks. In: 19th ACM SIGKDD International Conference on Knowledge Discovery and Data Mining, pp. 347–355. ACM Press, New York (2013)
20. Huang, J., Cheng, X., Shen, H., Zhou, T., Jin, X.: Exploring social influence via posterior effect of word-of-mouth recommendations. In: 5th ACM International Conference on Web Search and Data Mining, pp. 573–582. ACM Press, New York (2012)
21. He, S., Zheng, X., Zeng, D., Cui, K., Zhang, Z., Luo, C.: Identifying peer influence in online social networks using transfer entropy. In: Wang, G.A., Zheng, X., Chau, M., Chen, H. (eds.) PAISI 2013. LNCS, vol. 8039, pp. 47–61. Springer, Heidelberg (2013)
22. Lee, C., Kwak, H., Park, H., Moon, S.: Finding influentials based on the temporal order of information adoption in Twitter. In: 19th International World Wide Web Conference, pp. 1137–1138. ACM Press, New York (2010)
23. Motahari, S., Ziavras, S., Jones, Q.: Online anonymity protection in computer-mediated communication. IEEE Trans. Inf. Forensics Secur. **5**(3), 570–580 (2010)
24. Sandoval Jr., L.: Structure of a global network of financial companies based on transfer entropy. Entropy **16**, 4443–4482 (2014)
25. Peng, S., Wu, M., Wang, G., Yu, S.: Propagation model of smartphone worms based on semi-Markov process and social relationship graph. Comput. Secur. **44**, 92–103 (2014)

An Energy Efficient Multi-hop Charging Scheme with Mobile Charger for Wireless Rechargeable Sensor Network

Shuo Li[1,2], Jian He[1], Xiaoyong Zhang[1(✉)], and Jun Peng[1]

[1] School of Information Science and Engineering, Central South University,
Changsha 410075, Hunan, China
hangxy@csu.edu.cn
[2] College of Electronic & Information Engineering, Changsha University
of Science and Technology, Changsha 410114, Hunan, China

Abstract. Traditional wireless sensor networks (WSNs) are constrained by limited battery energy that powers the sensor nodes, which impedes the sustainable operation of the whole network. Recent advancements in wireless charging technology provide a promising way to solve this challenge. It uses a mobile charger to traveling through the whole network fields to replenish energy for every sensor nodes to guarantee none of the nodes will run out the energy. But these algorithms only adapt to small-scale network and its' energy efficiency is very low. In fact, none of these algorithms have considered the multi-hop energy transmission, whose feasibility have been demonstrated recently. In this paper, we proposed an energy efficient mobile multi-hop charging strategies. By introducing optimal central point based polling point selection algorithm, we constructed the best arrest point of each partition for the mobile charger. And in each partition, we adopt multi-hop wireless charging way to replenish energy for these nodes. By jointly optimizing traveling path, relay routing, and charging time, we develop a charging efficiency function to analyze the energy efficiency. Experimental results demonstrate that our strategies have high charging efficiency.

Keywords: Mobile charging · Multi-hop wireless charging · Energy efficiency · Wireless rechargeable sensor network

1 Introduction

Wireless sensor networks (WSNs) have been widely used for military surveillance, environmental monitoring, scientific exploration, target tracking and home automation [1]. In spite of their widespread application, however, energy efficiency remains a critical challenge for long network lifetime. Currently, as most wireless sensor nodes are powered by batteries, which impedes the sustainable operation of the WSNs. To prolong the lifetime of WSNs, many approaches have been proposed to scavenge energy from surrounding energy sources such as solar energy [2], wind energy [3], temperature variations [4], biochemical processes [5], and passive human movement [6]. However, due to the time-varying nature of renewable energy resources, these methods are not very stable.

© Springer International Publishing Switzerland 2015
G. Wang et al. (Eds.): ICA3PP 2015, Part I, LNCS 9528, pp. 648–660, 2015.
DOI: 10.1007/978-3-319-27119-4_45

Recently, as the development of the wireless power transfer technology [7], which allow energy to be transferred from energy-rich sources to energy-hungry nodes. Since wireless recharging can guarantee the continuous power supply and its' demand is not high to the environment, it has found many related applications such as RFIDs [8], laptops [9], smart grids [10], and civil structures monitoring [11]. These applications mainly involves two methods: (1) through strongly coupled magnetic resonances [12], and (2) through radio frequency (RF) signals [13].

With the novel technology, recent studies propose to introduce a mobile charger (MC) to replenish energy for sensor nodes in wireless rechargeable sensor network (WRSNs) [10, 14, 15] so that none of them in the network will run out of energy. But when the network scale is larger, by using a MC to replenish energy for every node is very hard to finish and it's energy efficiency is also very low. This is because the MC may not carry sufficient energy and not have enough time to recharge every node. So it is unscientific to just use this way to replenish energy for larger sensor network.

In order to cover the above shortage of singer MC charging, some scholars has introduced partition algorithm in charging strategies [16]. The main idea is to divide the network into several parts for charging using some original partition algorithm, then it select a center node for each part as the arrest point of MC, and use the MC move to the arrest point to charge for every point in this part. However, these algorithms must guarantee the charging radius greater than the partition' radius, it greatly increases the difficulty of the partition, and reduces the charging efficiency.

As the same time, recent breakthroughs in wireless energy transfer are expected to increase the sustainability of WSN and make them operational forever [17]. The technique uses strongly coupled magnetic resonance to transmit power between devices without the need of any contact between the transmitter and the receiver. A step further, Watfa et al. [18] express that it is possible to transfer wireless energy over multi-hop. In such a system, a node can both transmit and receive energy, the node is several hops away from the charger and that neighboring nodes are able to exchange energy.

Inspired by this advance in multi-hop wireless energy transfer, in this paper, we proposed an energy efficient mobile multi-hop charging strategies. By introducing optimal central point based polling point selection algorithm, we constructed the best arrest point of each partition for the mobile charger. And in each partition, we adopt multi-hop wireless charging way to replenish energy for these nodes. By jointly optimizing traveling path, relay routing, and charging time, we develop a charging efficiency function to analyze the energy efficiency. The effectiveness of the proposed framework is validated by simulations.

The remainder of the paper is organized as follows. Section 2 describes the system model and problem formulation. Partition model and algorithm implementation are discussed in Sect. 3. Simulation results and analysis are given in Sect. 4, followed by concluding remarks work in Sect. 5.

2 System Model and Problem Formulation

In this section, we model our multi-hop wireless charging scheme with mobile charger for wireless rechargeable sensor network. We successively describe the network model, a one-hop energy transfer and multi-hop energy transfer with mobile charger.

2.1   Network Model

We consider a WRSN environment with a set N of sensor nodes and a stationary base station deployed at the center of the network. Each sensor $n_i \in N$ is equipped with a rechargeable battery. In our scenario, the only sources of energy in the network is the mobile charger which is charged from the base station, and each node play as intermediary transmitter to transfer the energy over multi-hop. So a transmitter of energy can be either a charger or a node. Then we assume that a node can receive energy from only one transmitter and that a transmitter can transmit energy to multiple neighbors. It means that is a tree structure, where a node can transmit energy to its sons, and a node receives energy from its unique parent.

As shown in the Fig. 1. There are some sensor nodes and a base station on the network, a mobile charger is a moving vehicle equipped with a powerful wireless charger and it can keep information synchronized with the base station via a long range radio. It starts from the base station and will choice the appropriate arrest point to charge the center node. Meanwhile, the center will transfer the energy to other nodes of this partition with the method of multi-hop. Until all of the nodes in this partition are charged at a threshold value, the mobile charger will move to next appropriate arrest point. When the mobile charger run out of the energy, it must return to the base station and replenish energy, then the mobile still return to previous arrest point and continue to charger for the nodes of this partition. There we assume that the movement time of the mobile charger is negligible compared with charging time.

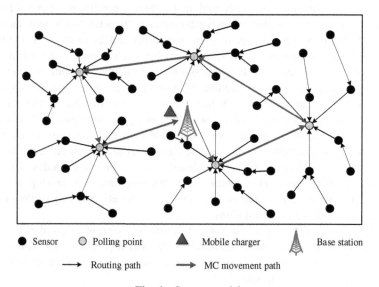

Fig. 1. System model.

2.2   Multi-hop Energy Transfer

In this network model, each sensor node is equipped with a rechargeable battery. When the center node are replenished energy by mobile charger, it will transfer energy to the nodes near to it. These nodes will store the energy by charging their batteries. Once their batteries are fully charged (or charge to a threshold value), these charged nodes will transfer the energy stored in their batteries to the next hop nodes which in sequence store this energy in their batteries and in the next round transmit it to the next hop nodes. Then cycle in turn until all nodes are charged.

When the energy is transmitted from a charger to other nodes through multi-hop path, energy is lost at each intermediate transmission along these path. We denote there a center node n_0, an intermediate node n_1 and a final node n_2, then the total power distribution is:

$$P_{total} = P_{work} + P_{n_0} + P_{n_1} + P_{n_2} \tag{1}$$

$$P_{work} = 2\lambda_{work}|A_{n_1}|^2, \quad P_{n_0} = 2\lambda_{n_0}|A_{n_0}|^2,$$
$$P_{n_1} = 4\lambda_{n_1}|A_{n_1}|^2 \quad , \quad P_{n_2} = 2\lambda_{n_2}|A_{n_2}|^2 \tag{2}$$

Where $P_{n_0}, P_{n_1}, P_{n_2}$ is the power lost due to absorption and radiation at nodes 0,1,2 and P_{work} is the useful power delivered to the final node. When the useful transmitted power is used to charge the battery, $\lambda_{work} = \lambda_{charge}$ which is the rate of energy consumed in charging the battery. There we assume that all the energy transmitted to the intermediate node will be used in the energy transfer from the intermediate node to the final node and that the nodes are identical. Then we think there are no energy losses from charging and discharging the batteries, and we can get the following formula:

$$\lambda_{charge}|A_{n_1}|^2 = \lambda_d|A_{n_1}|^2 + \lambda_d|A_{n_2}|^2 + \lambda_d|A_{n_2}|^2 \tag{3}$$

Then the energy efficiency is calculate as follows:

$$\eta_{work} = \frac{P_{work}}{P_{total}} = \frac{\lambda_{charge}|A_{n_2}|^2}{\lambda_d|A_{n_0}|^2 + 2\lambda_d|A_{n_1}|^2 + \lambda_d|A_{n_2}|^2 + \lambda_{charge}|A_{n_2}|^2} \tag{4}$$

After a series of logical derivations, we can conclude that:

$$\eta_{work} = \left[\frac{\lambda_d}{\lambda_{charge}}\left(1 + \frac{1}{fom^2}\left(1 + \frac{\lambda_{charge}}{\lambda_d}\right)^2\right)\right]^{-2} \tag{5}$$

Where *fom* is the distance-dependent figure-of-merit of the perturbed resonant energy-exchange system.

However, that part of the energy transmitted will be loss while charging and discharging the batteries, it means the nodes are not identical. By using Poynting's Theorem and after a series of equations we get the expression of the energy efficiency at h hop:

$$\eta_h = \left[\frac{\lambda_d}{\lambda_{charge}} \left(1 + \frac{1}{fom^2} \left(1 + \frac{\lambda_{charge}}{\lambda_d} \right)^2 \right) + 1 \right]^{-h} \tag{6}$$

2.3 Problem Formulation

In this network model, each sensor node is equipped with a rechargeable battery. When the center node are replenished energy by mobile charger, it will transfer energy to the nodes near to it. These nodes will store the energy by charging their batteries. Once their batteries are fully charged (or charge to a threshold value), these charged nodes will transfer the energy stored in their batteries to the next hop nodes which in sequence store this energy in their batteries and in the next round transmit it to the next hop nodes. Then cycle in turn until all nodes are charged.

In order to improve the energy efficiency of whole network, we consider the energy efficiency as the optimal objection function and formulate the optimization as follows:

$$\max \frac{1}{N} \sum_{h \in H} \eta_h C_h \tag{7}$$

Where H is the sets of hop, and C_h is the number at h hop. So we construct the energy efficiency problem as hop optimization problem.

3 Charging Scheme

In this section, we first construct network topology by using minimum connected dominating set algorithm. Then on the basis of this topology, we generate the sub-network based hop constraints. Finally, we introduce the optimal central point (OCP) based polling point selection algorithm to deal with the hop optimization problem.

3.1 Network Topology Construction

In this subsection, we use the minimum connected dominating set algorithm to construct network topology, the definition of minimum connected dominating set is shown as follows:

Definition 1: A connected dominating set of a graph G is a set D $(D \subseteq V(G))$ of vertices with two properties:

1. Any node in D can reach any other node in D by a path that stays entirely within D. That is, D induces a connected subgraph of G.
2. Every vertex in G either belongs to D or is adjacent to a vertex in D. That is, D is a dominating set of G.

A minimum connected dominating set of a graph G is a connecting dominating set with the smallest possible cardinality among all connected dominating sets of G. The connected domination number of G is the number of vertices in the minimum connected dominating set.

This paper adopt the minimum connected dominating set algorithm to construct network topology, the algorithm consists of two basic processes: tag process and streamlining the process. In the tag process, the sensor nodes will be tagged as True (flagged) or False (not flagged), and the initial state of all sensor nodes is tagged as False, then the nodes flagged will be considered as candidate nodes of the minimum connected dominating set. In the streamlining process, we streamline the candidate nodes according to the remaining energy priority rules, and make the number of candidate nodes are close to the minimum connected dominating set. The algorithm process show as follows.

Algorithm 1. Network topology construction algorithm based on minimum connected dominating set

---

Input:
   $V(G)$;
Output:
   Minimum connected dominating set D;
Tag process:
   Step 1: All sensor nodes $u \in V$ exchange neighbor node information set $H(v)$ with its neighbor nodes;
   Step 2: If the node v and node w is the neighbor node of node u, and satisfy: $(u,v) \in E$, $(u,w) \in E$, and $(v,w) \notin E$, then the node u will be tagged as True;
Streamlining process:
   Step 3: If $e_v < e_u$, node u send the control message packets to its neighbor node v;
   Step 4: Constructing the subgraph $G[V'_+]$ according to all control message packets b received, where $V'_+ = \{w \mid w \in (V' \cap N(u)) \wedge (e_u < e_w)\}$ is the neighbor node set of node u, and which have more remaining energy.
   Step 5: Calculating the strongly connected set's elements $\{V'_{c_1}, V'_{c_2}, ..., V'_{c_l}\}$ of $G[V'_+]$;
   Step 6: If exist $V'_{c_i}, 1 \leq i \leq l$, and satisfy: $N(u) - V'_{c_i} \subseteq N(V'_{c_i})$, then tag the node u as False;

3.2 Sub-network Generation

After network topology construction, due to the energy consumption of data forwarding is proportional to its hop, meanwhile the nodes' energy charging efficiency is inverse proportion to its hop, so it is necessary to decompose the connected network into several unconnected sub-network. In this paper, we propose a sub-network generation algorithm based on hop constraints to reduce the network energy consumption and improve the energy charging efficiency. The algorithm process is shown as follows.

Algorithm 2. Sub-network generation algorithm with hop constraints

---

Input:

h_{MAX}, V;

Variable:

i, $V_{hop(1)}$, $V_{hop(2)}$,...,$V_{hop(h_{MAX})}$;

Output:

n_{sub} sub-network: $G_{s\_1}, G_{s\_2},..., G_{s\_n_{sub}}$;

Process:

Step 1: Constructing end node set V_e, and tagging all the end node as False;

Step 2: Initializing the hop counter $i = 0$, and packaging it in control message packets (expressed as hop_num_msg);

Step 3: All the end nodes $u \in V_{hop(i)}$ broadcast the hop_num_msg concurrent to the neighbor nodes;

Step 4: When the backbone node (tagged as Ture) receives the hop_num_msg packets, updating the hop counter $i = i+1$, and constructing backbone node set $V_{hop(i)}$ corresponding to hop i;

Step 5: **If** $h \geq h_{MAX}$ & the source node of hop_num_msg packet is backbone node

> Current backbone node broadcast pp_msg, and regard it as polling point of the sub-network;

Else

> Iterating the Step 3 until the node stop sending hop_num_msg packet after time T_{delay};

End If

Step 6: **If** ($V / (V_{hop(0)} \cup V_{hop(1)} \cup ... \cup V_{hop(i)}) = \varnothing$)

> Finishing the sub-network generation with hop constraints, and the Algorithm is end;

Else

$$V = V / (V_{hop(0)} \cup V_{hop(1)} \cup ... \cup V_{hop(i)}), \textbf{goto Step 1;}$$

End If

3.3 OCP Based Polling Point Selection Algorithm

According to the analysis in the previous section, with the largest local network communication load sensor nodes for polling point is the optimal choice in WCSN. According to this conclusion, this paper quickly build the network topology by using the minimum connected dominating set, and propose a sub-network generation algorithm based on hop constraints. In this section, we transform the polling point selection problem of all subnets into optimal central point problem, so as to realize the optimal polling point selection.

In WSN, giving a graph $G = (V, E)$ and looking for a node $u \in G(V)$, then the node u have the biggest gathering communication load of the network G, namely the optimal central point problem.

Theorem 1: In subnet G_{s_i}, if the choice of the polling point p_i satisfy the following formula:

$$\text{MAX E}\left[\Lambda_{G_{s\_i}}(u)\right] \Leftrightarrow \text{MAX } \varepsilon(p_i) \tag{8}$$

Then we consider the polling point selection problem which aims at the balance of network energy consumption, and transform it into optimal central point problem which aims at maximizing the total energy consumption to solve the problem.

According to the Theorem 1, we can get the following inference.

Inference 1: In subnet G_{s_i}, when consider the biggest communication load node which is solved by optimizing the optimal central point problem as the polling point, the network average remaining energy is minimum at the end of network survival time, it means the energy consumption will reach to optimal equilibrium. Then the network survival time can be maximized.

By analyzing from the perspective of energy consumption, we know there have two factors that can affect the link cost: (1) the remaining energy of the sensor node, it shows the current state of nodes' energy; (2) the gathering communication load of the sensor node, which indicates that the change trend of nodes' energy. There we define the remaining energy-load factor for node u.

$$f_u = \frac{e_u}{\Lambda_{G_{s\_i}}(u)} \tag{9}$$

In the distributed polling algorithm based on the maximum load communication, the link cost between node u and v can be redefined as follows.

$$\omega_{uv} = \frac{\sigma}{\min(f_u, f_v)} \tag{10}$$

Where σ is constant. Then we can define the total energy consumption $\varepsilon(p_i)$ when p_i is the polling point.

$$\varepsilon(p_i) = \sum_{\forall u \in G_{s\_i}} \lambda_u \omega_{up_i} \tag{11}$$

Where λ_u is the probability of the node packet. So we can regularly update the link state and calculate $\varepsilon(p_i)$ according to formula (11). If $\varepsilon(p_1) < \varepsilon(p_1')$, we will chose p_1' as the new polling point, then we can consider $\varepsilon(p_1) < \varepsilon(p_1')$ as the update condition of polling point.

The Fig. 2 is the polling point selection algorithm based on OCP. Figure 2(a) is the initial state of the network node. As shown in Fig. 2(b), algorithm first construct network topology by using minimum connected dominating set, then form the connected network. In Fig. 2(c), algorithm construct subnets and set the root node of current subnet as the polling point. Figure 2(d) shows the changes of remaining energy and communication load after a period of running time, then the algorithm reselect polling point of each subnets to realize the optimization of energy efficiency.

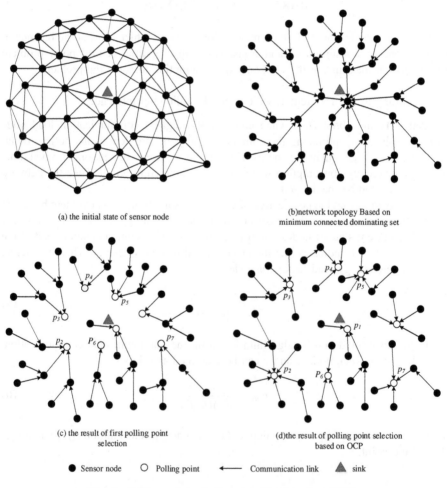

(a) the initial state of sensor node

(b) network topology Based on minimum connected dominating set

(c) the result of first polling point selection

(d) the result of polling point selection based on OCP

● Sensor node   ○ Polling point   ◀— Communication link   ▲ sink

Fig. 2. Polling point selection algorithm based on OCP.

3.4 Mobile Multi-hop Charging Strategies

After the selection of polling point, we use the mobile charger to visit the polling point and charge for it. When the center node are replenished energy by mobile charger, it will transfer energy to the nodes near to it. These nodes will store the energy by charging their batteries. Once their batteries are fully charged (or charge to a threshold value), these charged nodes will transfer the energy stored in their batteries to the next hop nodes which in sequence store this energy in their batteries and in the next round transmit it to the next hop nodes. Then cycle in turn until all nodes are charged.

4 Analytical and Simulation Result

Here we give the simulation scenario and simulation parameters. N sensor nodes are randomly distributed in the network, and in Table 1, we give out the specific scenarios. There we set the mobile charger located in the center of the network, and the mobile rate of MC is 1 m/s. The communication radius is 23 meters, and the size of packet is 100 bytes, the coding rate is 250 Kbps, and the initial energy is 200 J. Every five changing cycle, the OCP algorithm will reselect the polling point. There we do 100 times simulation and use the average results to validate the simulation performance.

Table 1. Parameter settings under different network scale

Node numbers	Network scale(m)	The largest mobile distance of MC(m)
25	50×50	40
50	70×70	80
100	100×100	150
200	150×150	280

The Fig. 3 is the simulation result of OPC based polling point selection algorithm at 70×70 network scale with 50 nodes. According to the simulation result, the distribution of polling point is reasonable. The MC local at the center of the network, and travel for polling point at the shortest path. Then charge the polling point nodes, and charge for nodes by adopting multi-hop way.

There we analyze the network performance of proposed algorithm compared with Rendezvous Design for Variable Tracks (RD-VT) [19], the basic idea of this algorithm is to find a sub-tree such that all the polling points on the sub-tree can be visited by a BS tour no longer than L, while the total edge length of the path tree is minimized. The Fig. 4 is the simulation result at 150×150 network scale with 200 nodes. After a charger cycle, the residual energy of OPC algorithm evenly distribute, but the central nodes' residual energy of RD-VT algorithm is very little, obvious, the energy efficiency of OPC algorithm is more well than RD-VT algorithm. Because the topology update frequency of OPC algorithm is lower, its can reduce the energy cost of network control message.

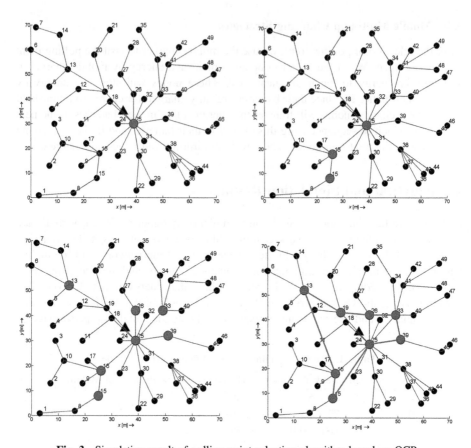

Fig. 3. Simulation result of polling point selection algorithm based on OCP.

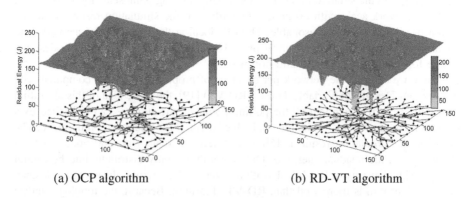

(a) OCP algorithm   (b) RD-VT algorithm

Fig. 4. The distribution of residual energy after a charger cycle.

5   Conclusion

Traditional wireless sensor networks (WSNs) are constrained by limited battery energy that powers the sensor nodes, which impedes the sustainable operation of the whole network. Recent advancements in wireless charging technology provide a promising way to solve this challenge. Inspired by this advance in multi-hop wireless energy transfer, in this paper, we proposed an energy efficient mobile multi-hop charging strategies. By introducing bounded relay hop based polling point selection algorithm, we constructed the best arrest point of each partition for the mobile charger. And in each partition, we adopt multi-hop wireless charging way to replenish energy for these nodes. By jointly optimizing traveling path, relay routing, and charging time, we develop a charging efficiency function to analyze the energy efficiency. The effectiveness of the proposed framework is validated by simulations.

Acknowledgments. The authors would like to acknowledge that this work was partially supported by the National Natural Science Foundation of China (Grant No. 61379111, 61003233 and 61202342) and Research Fund for the Doctoral Program of Higher Education of China (Grant No. 20110162110042)

References

1. Nakayama, H., Ansari, N., Jamalipour, A., Kato, N.: Fault-resilient sensing in wireless sensor networks. Comput. Comm. **30**(11/12), 2376–2384 (2007)
2. Raghunathan, V., Kansal, A., Hsu, J., Friedman, J., Srivastava, M.: Design considerations for solar energy harvesting wireless embedded systems. In: Proceedings of the 4th International Symposium on Information Processing in Sensor Networks, p. 64, IEEE Press (2005)
3. Park, C., Chou, P.: Ambimax: autonomous energy harvesting platform for multi-supply wireless sensor nodes. In: SECON (2006)
4. Stark, I.: Thermal energy harvesting with thermo life. In: Proceedings of International Workshop Wearable and Implantable Body Sensor Networks (2006)
5. Thomson, E.: Preventing forest fires with tree power: sensor system runs on electricity generated by trees (2008). http://www.physorg.com/news141291261.html
6. Starner, T.: Human-powered wearable computing. IBM Syst. J. **35**, 618–629 (1996)
7. Kurs, A., Karalis, A., Robert, M., Joannopoulos, J.D., Fisher, P., Soljacic, M.: Wireless power transfer via strongly coupled magnetic resonances. Science **317**(5834), 83–86 (2007)
8. http://www.seattle.intel-research.net/wisp/
9. http://www.laptopmag.com/reviews/laptops/dell-latitude-3330.aspx
10. Erol-Kantarci, M., Mouftah, H.: Suresense: sustainable wireless rechargeable sensor networks for the smart grid. IEEE Wirel. Commun. **19**(3), 30–36 (2012)
11. Mascareñas, D., Flynn, E., Todd, M., Park, G., Farrar, C.: Wireless sensor technologies for monitoring civil structures. Sound Vibr. **42**(4), 16–21 (2008)
12. Kurs, A., Karalis, A., Moffatt, R., Joannopoulos, J., Fisher, P., Soljacic, M.: Wireless power transfer via strongly coupled magnetic resonances. Science **9**(1), 64–76 (2001)

13. Yeager, D., Powledge, P., Prasad, R., Wetherall, D., Smith, J.: Wirelessly-charged UHF tags for sensor data collection. In: Proceedings of IEEE International Conference on Radio Frequency Identification (RFID 2008) (2008)

14. He, S., Chen, J., Jiang, F., et al.: Energy provisioning in wireless rechargeable sensor networks. IEEE Trans. Mob. Comput. **12**(10), 1931–1942 (2013)

15. Zhao, M., Li, J., Yang, Y.: Joint mobile energy replenishment and data gathering in wireless rechargeable sensor networks. In: Proceedings of the 23rd International Teletraffic Congress, pp. 238–245. International Teletraffic Congress (2011)

16. Dai, H., Wu, X., Chen, G., Xu, L., Lin, S.: Minimizing the number of mobile chargers for large-scale wireless rechargeable sensor networks. Comput. Commun. **46**, 54–65 (2014)

17. Kurs, A., Karalis, A., Moffat, R., Joannopoulos, J., Fisher, P., Soljacic, M.: Wireless power transfer via strongly coupled magnetic resonances. Science **317**, 83–86 (2007)

18. Watfa, M.K., Al-Hassanieh, H., Salmen, S.: The road to immortal sensor nodes. In: International Conference on Intelligent Sensors, Sensor Networks and Information Processing, pp. 523–528 (2008)

19. Xing, G., Wang, T., Jia, W., Li, M.: Rendezvous design algorithms for wireless sensor networks with a mobile base station. In: Proceedings of the 9th ACM International Symposium on Mobile Ad Hoc Networking and Computing, pp. 489–500. ACM, Hong Kong SAR, China (2008)

Distributed Compressive Sensing Based Data Gathering in Energy Harvesting Sensor Network

Weirong Liu, Gaorong Qin, Fu Jiang[(⊠)], Kaiyang Liu,
and Zhengfa Zhu

School of Information Science and Engineering, Central South University,
Changsha 410075, Hunan, China
weirong_liu@126.com, gaorong_q@163.com,
jiangfu@csu.edu.cn

Abstract. Wireless sensor networks are gaining popularity in practical monitoring and surveillance applications. One of the major challenges for designing sensor networks is to minimize the transmission cost. Distributed compressive sensing is a promising technique for energy efficient data gathering in wireless sensor networks. In this paper, we propose a distributed compressive sensing-based data gathering scheme in energy harvesting sensor networks, in which the sensor readings possess both inter-(spatial) and intra-(temporal) signal correlations to improve the recovery quality of sensory data and prolong the sensor network's lifetime as well. Besides, we also consider that the sensors operate with intermittently available energy that is harvested from the environment. A cluster-based routing strategy is exploited and a joint sparsity model is used for compressing the sensory data. Then the Simultaneous Orthogonal Matching Pursuit (SOMP) algorithm is designed to recover the sparse data. The simulation results show significant gain in terms of signal reconstruction accuracy and energy consumption.

Keywords: Wireless · Sensor network · Data gathering · Compressive sensing · Sparsity · Transmission cost

1 Introduction

Wireless Sensor Network (WSN), as an important information access technology, is a basic method to realize the fusion of physical world and information world [1, 2]. But it is inconvenient to replace batteries for sensor nodes as for the WSN's harsh deployment conditions. Energy harvesting from ambient energy such as solar, wind, thermal and piezoelectric, appears as a promising alternative to the fixed-energy battery and prolong the lifetime for WSN [3, 4]. Owing to the varying energy harvesting condition, sensors intermittently harvest ambient energy probabilistically.

In WSNs, the sensors periodically gather the sensory data, process and transmit data to the sink node. A major challenge for designing WSN is to propose schemes that minimize the cost of energy and bandwidth for the sensors. Considering the environment does not change frequently, it is not necessary to transmit all measurements in

© Springer International Publishing Switzerland 2015
G. Wang et al. (Eds.): ICA3PP 2015, Part I, LNCS 9528, pp. 661–673, 2015.
DOI: 10.1007/978-3-319-27119-4_46

case of high sampling frequently. Therefore, taking advantage of the spatial-temporal properties in sensory data from real deployments for in-network compression is an essential technique to reduce the amount of data transmission preserving relatively high recovery accuracy in the sink [5].

The compressive sensing (CS) techniques in [7] provide a promising sampling scheme to break Shannon sampling theorem and promise an accurate recovery of sensory data if the data are sparse in some domain. It is advantageous whenever signals are sparse in a known basis, measurements (computation at the sensor nodes) are expensive, and computations at the receiver end are cheap. These characteristics completely match WSNs. Employing CS in WSNs offers promising improvements as low power sensor nodes [6].

In recent years, CS has received much attention in the WSNs research community. In [8, 9], C. Chou et al. proposed CS based data gathering schemes to effectively reduce sensor nodes' transmission cost and prolong network lifetime. In [10], D. Ebrahimi et al. presented a decentralized method for the compressive data gathering problem. Based on forwarding trees. In [11], Tsung-Yi Tsai et al. proposed a distributed algorithm to efficiently construct a routing path suitable for CS-based data aggregation in large-scale WSNs without complete network topology information. However, these methods consider only temporal correlation among individual signals measured by single sensor, didn't consider both the temporal and spatial correlations among different signals. Besides, the multi-hop tree-type routing strategy can lead to high transmission cost in large-scale WSN's data gathering.

Considering a WSN monitoring a natural phenomenon, the sensory data obtained by the sensors are likely both intra-signal and inter-signal correlations. Leveraging these correlations, [12] proposed a new theory for distributed compressive sensing (DCS) that enables new distributed coding algorithms for multi-signal ensembles that exploit both intra- and inter-signal correlation structures.

In this paper, a modified HEED clustering algorithm is proposed to select cluster heads and partition the sensor network. Each node utilizes measurement matrix to obtain the sensory data. We also exploit the JSM-2 joint sparsity signal model and sparse random projections to compress sensory data, which can significantly reduce CS measurement transmission cost. Finally, Simultaneous Orthogonal Matching Pursuit (SOMP) based reconstruction algorithm is used to recover sensory data accurately.

2 Model and Preliminaries

Since sensor nodes have limited resources, it is essential to transfer and gather as few data as possible. To do so, we first use a modified HEED clustering approach to cluster the sensor network, then the distributed compressive sensing technique is employed to accurately reconstruct the state of the environment at the sink node using as few as possible measurements. The DCS-based data gathering framework is shown in Fig. 1. In this section, we give the network model and signal joint sparsity model, then present some preliminaries of distributed compressed sensing.

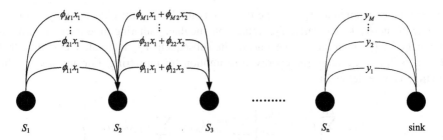

Fig. 1. Compressive data gathering scheme

2.1   Data Gathering Network Model

The routing strategy can affect the node's transmission cost and load balancing during the data gathering. Direct communication is the simplest routing strategy for small scale WSN. In this model, if the sensor node is far away from the sink node, it will require a large amount of transmission power. Therefore, direct communication model is not suitable to the large-scale WSN. The tree-type routing model is adopted in a lot of existing CS based data gathering schemes [7–11].

Clustered-based routing strategy is an efficient data gathering routing protocol [13], which partitions the WSN into multiple clusters and each cluster has a cluster head. The sensor nodes in each cluster send sensory data to its cluster head, then cluster head use tree-type routing strategy or single hop to relay the data to sink node. As for the sensor node is capable of harvesting ambient energy from environment, we improve the HEED approach on the node's probability of becoming a cluster head by taking both the residual energy and the harvesting energy into consideration.

2.2   Energy Consumption Model

We currently assume that node failures are primarily caused by energy depletion. As for the energy consumption for data transmission make up most of the total energy consumption. Thus, we first defined the energy consumption model for sensor node data transmitting and receiving as follows [14]:

$$E_{Tx}(k, d) = \begin{cases} kE_{elec} + k\xi_{fs}d^2 , & d < d_0 \\ kE_{elec} + k\xi_{amp}d^4, & d \geq d_0 \end{cases}$$

$$E_{Rx}(k) = kE_{elec}$$

(1)

where k is the amount of sensory data to be transmitting, E_{elec} denotes module circuit energy consumption for send 1 bit sensory data. d is the transmitting distance and d_0 is a threshold value. ξ_{fs} and ξ_{amp} is the energy consumption of node's transmission amplifier on symmetric channel.

We divided the node's work time into rounds. Each round is partitioned into clustering process time interval and data gathering time interval. Let the clustering process time, denoted as T_{CL}, be the time interval taken by the clustering algorithm to cluster the network. Similarly, T_{DG} represents the data gathering time interval between the end of a T_{CL} interval and the start of the subsequent T_{CL} interval. We assume that $T_{DG} >> T_{CL}$ to decrease the energy consumption for clustering. For any node i, the lifetime can be defined as:

$$E_0 + \sum_{r=0}^{LTi} E_{hr} = \sum_{r=0}^{LTi} \left\{ \sum_{j \in R_i^r} E_{Rx}^r(k_{ji}) + \sum_{h \in T_i^r} E_{Tx}^r(k_{ih}, d_{ih}) \right\} \tag{2}$$

where E_0 is the total battery energy, E_{hr} denotes the energy harvesting from the surround environment probabilistically in each round. R_i^r is the node set consisted of the nodes which send k_{ji} bits data to the ith node in the rth round. Similarly, T_i^r is the node set consisted of the nodes which receives k_{ih} bits data from the ith node in the rth round. Thus, the lifetime of the whole network can be represented as:

$$LT - 1 = \min\{LTi : i \in J\} \tag{3}$$

$$LT - 2 = \max\{LTi : i \in J\} \tag{4}$$

where LT-1 and LT-2 denotes the first dead sensor node and the latest dead sensor node respectively. In this paper, we defined the network lifetime as LT-1.

2.3 Compressive Sampling

The conventional sample-then-compress framework suffers from three inherent inefficiencies [16]. First, the initial number of samples N may be large even if the desired K is small. Second, the set of all N transform coefficients must be computed even though all but K of them will be discarded. Third, the locations of the large coefficients must be encoded, thus introducing an overhead. Compressive sampling solves these inefficiencies by directly acquiring a compressive signal representation without going through the intermediate stage of acquiring N samples [17]. It makes the sampling more efficient than conventional method.

Suppose that the measured data from all the network sensors at a given time form an N-dimensional vector $\mathbf{d} = [d_1, d_2, \ldots, d_N]^T$. Consider that d is K-sparse in a particular domain with transform basis Ψ. Then d can be represented as

$$\mathbf{d} = \Psi \mathbf{s} = \sum_{i=1}^{N} s_i \psi_i \tag{5}$$

where $\mathbf{s} = [s_1, s_2, \ldots, s_N]$ is the $N \times 1$ column vector of weighting coefficients $s_i = \langle s, \psi_i \rangle = \psi_i^T \mathbf{d}$ and $\bullet^T$ denotes transposition. $\Psi = [\psi_1, \psi_2, \ldots, \psi_N]$ is the representation basis with column vector $\{\psi_i\}$. s is sparse if the number of non-zero coefficients is small. More specifically, if the number of non-zero coefficients is less than K, we say that d is K-sparse.

With the CS theory, if the sensory data d is K-sparse in some transform basis such as Discrete Cosine Transform (DCT) [18], then d can be recovered from a small number of measurements by solving a programming optimization problem. In the practical implementation for WSNs, a sensor node transforms its sensory data to an M-dimensional measurement vector by the projections, and then sends out the measurements to the sink node. Mathematically, the projection can be represented as

$$\mathbf{y} = \Phi \mathbf{d} = \Phi \Psi \mathbf{s} = \Theta \mathbf{s} \tag{6}$$

where $\Theta = \Phi \Psi$ is an $M \times N$ projection matrix. The measurement process is not adaptive, meaning that Φ is fixed and does not depend on the signal. $\mathbf{y} = [y_1, y_2, \ldots, y_M]^T$ is the node's measurements.

In CS theory, the raw sensory data can d be recovered from the measurement vector y if the projection matrix Φ fulfill the Restricted Isometry Property (RIP) [19]:

$$M \geq c\mu^2(\Phi, \Psi)K \log N \tag{7}$$

where c is a positive constant, $\mu(\Phi, \Psi)$ is the coherence between transform basis and projection matrix denoted as follow [20]:

$$\mu(\Phi, \Psi) = \sqrt{n} \cdot \max_{1 \leq k, j \leq n} |\langle \phi_i, \psi_i \rangle| \tag{8}$$

As for the K-sparse signal, since M < N in (2), there are infinitely many $\mathbf{s}'$ that satisfy $\Theta \mathbf{s}' = \mathbf{y}$. Therefore, the signal recovered algorithm aims to find the signal's sparse coefficient vector. With a sufficient number of measurements, the raw sensory data can be recovered by the l_0 minimization problem as follow:

$$\hat{\mathbf{s}} = \arg \min \|\mathbf{s}'\|_0 \quad s.t. \ \Theta \mathbf{s}' = \mathbf{y} \tag{9}$$

however, l_0 minimization problem is both numerically unstable and NP-complete. Surprisingly, optimization based on l_1 norm can exactly recover K-sparse signals with high probability using only $M \geq cK \log(N/K)$ identically distributed Gaussian measurements [21]:

$$\hat{\mathbf{s}} = \arg \min \|\mathbf{s}'\|_1 \quad s.t. \ \Theta \mathbf{s}' = \mathbf{y} \tag{10}$$

This is a convex optimization problem that conveniently reduces to a linear program known as basis pursuit [21] whose computational complexity is about $O(N^3)$. With the solution $\hat{\mathbf{s}}$ given by (5), the estimation of the original data can be represented as

$$\hat{\mathbf{d}} = \Psi \hat{\mathbf{s}} \tag{11}$$

In this way, the raw sensory data is recovered and all the computation was done on the sink node which has a stable power supply.

2.4   Joint Sparsity Signal Model for DCS

The DCS theory builds on a concept termed as the joint sparsity signal model. Duarte et al. [10] proposed a general framework for joint sparsity models (JSMs) and three joint sparsity signal models that apply in different situations. According to JSM-2 model, the signal can be represented as:

$$\mathbf{d}_j = \Psi \mathbf{s}_j , \quad j \in [1, 2, \ldots, J] \tag{12}$$

where $\mathbf{d}_j$ is the sensory signal sensed by the jth sensor node, and $\mathbf{s}_j$ is in general different but having the common sparse supports of size K. It means that all signals are K-sparse and can be recovered from the same K transform basis vectors of Ψ, but with different coefficients. Each signal corresponds to a $M_j \times N$ measurement matrix Φ_j. Then the projection can be represented as

$$\mathbf{y}_j = \Phi_j \mathbf{d}_j = \Phi_j \Psi \mathbf{s}_j \tag{13}$$

where the measurement matrix Φ_j can be independent and identically distributed Gaussian random matrix, ± 1 Benoit/Radmacher matrix and so on. In this paper, we employ the identically distributed Gaussian random matrix for signal projection.

For simplicity, we redefine the measurement matrix and representation of sensory signal as follow: $\bar{M} = \sum_{j \in \Lambda} M_j$, $\mathbf{d} \in R^{j \times N}$, $\mathbf{y} \in R^{\bar{M}}$, $\Phi \in R^{\bar{M} \times N}$ where $j \in \Lambda$, $\Lambda = \{1, 2, \ldots, J\}$ is the index of the sensory signals. Eventually, we can represent the joint signal model gather by sink node as

$$\mathbf{d} = \begin{bmatrix} \mathbf{d}_1 \\ \mathbf{d}_2 \\ \vdots \\ \mathbf{d}_J \end{bmatrix}, \quad \mathbf{y} = \begin{bmatrix} \mathbf{y}_1 \\ \mathbf{y}_2 \\ \vdots \\ \mathbf{y}_J \end{bmatrix}, \quad \Phi = \begin{bmatrix} \Phi_1 & 0 & \cdots & 0 \\ 0 & \Phi_2 & \cdots & 0 \\ \vdots & \vdots & \ddots & \vdots \\ 0 & 0 & \cdots & \Phi_J \end{bmatrix} \tag{14}$$

where the value 0 denotes the zero matrix and $\mathbf{y} = \Phi \mathbf{d}$.

3   Proposed Data Gathering Scheme Using Distributed Compressive Sensing

In this section, a distributed spatial-temporal sensory data gathering scheme is proposed based on DCS theory. Firstly, the deployed WSN is clustered by using an energy efficient clustering algorithm. Then, the sensor node's reading will be gathering through the cluster heads to the sink node. Finally, the sink node runs the recovery algorithm to recover the sensory data.

3.1 Distributed Clustering Routing Strategy

The intuition behind compressive data gathering is that higher efficiency can be achieve by reducing the capacity of sensory data and thus decreases the transmission cost. It is an effective way to prolong the lifetime of WSN. However, the data routing strategy can also affect transmission cost and load balancing during the data gathering, especially for large-scale WSN. Luo et al. [23] have proposed a compressive data gathering (CDG) approach that utilizes CS technology to efficiently reduce communication cost. A chain-type routing strategy is considered, in which data sensed at a sensor node is relayed to the sink node through a chain of other nodes. In this model, depicted in Fig. 1, reading x_1 sensed at node s_1 is sent to the next node s_2. Then, node s_2 relays its own data x_2 while transmitting x_1 to the next node s_3. This process continues till the last node s_n routes readings $x_1, x_2, \cdots, x_n$ to the sink node. Therefore, in this scheme, all the nodes transmit M sensor readings and hence it is able to disperse the communication costs to all sensor nodes along a given sensory data gathering route chain. However, when the sensory data extend to N-dimensional, the readings relayed by each sensor node increase rapidly accordingly [24].

In this paper, against the background of energy harvesting WSN, we modify the HEED clustering approach method to partition WSN into clusters. Our goal is to select a set of cluster heads which cover the entire sensing field. Each node must be mapped exactly to one cluster and is able to directly communicate with its cluster head. Cluster heads use a routing strategy for multiple communication with the sink node. The communication cost is defined as

$$C_{amrp} = \frac{\sum_{i=1}^{M} P_{min}^{i}}{M} \qquad (15)$$

where P_{min}^{i} denotes the minimum power level required by the node i to communicate with a cluster head, M is the number of nodes within the cluster range. It provides a good estimate of the communication cost and is a measure of the expected intra-cluster communication energy consumption if this node becomes a cluster head.

With the background of energy harvesting WSN, the probability of one sensor node becoming a cluster head need to take the harvesting energy into consideration. Thus, each sensor node sets the probability as follows:

$$P_{CH} = P_{init} \times \frac{E_{residual}}{E_0 + \sum_{r=0}^{R} E_{hr}} \qquad (16)$$

where $E_{residual}$ is the estimated current residual energy in the node and $E_0 + \sum_{r=0}^{R} E_{hr}$ is a reference maximum energy, which corresponds to the sum of a fully charged battery and the harvesting energy in R rounds. P_{init} is the initial percentage of cluster heads among all nodes. It is only used to limit the initial cluster head announcements, and has no direct impact on the final clusters.

3.2   Sensory Data Recovery

Under the JSM-2 signal model, separate recovery of each signal via l_0-norm minimization would require K + 1 measurements, while separate recovery via l_1-norm minimization would require cK measurements. In practice, as for this signal model, the common sparse support among the signals enables a fast iterative algorithm to recover all of the signals jointly. Tropp and Gilbert [25] have proposed such an algorithm, Simultaneous Orthogonal Matching Pursuit (SOMP) algorithm, which can be readily applied in our DCS framework.

In [12], the original SOMP algorithm is extended to adapt the JSM-2 signal model, thus the DCS-tailored SOMP algorithm is called DCS-SOMP. DCS-SOMP employs the common structure information of all the signals, then effectively reduces the number of sensing per sensor. The DCS-SOMP based sensory data recovery algorithm can be described in Table 1. For the sake of simplicity, we assume that the sensed signal per sensor has the same sensing frequency $M_j = M$, then the measurement matrix can be represented as:

$$\Phi_j = [\phi_{j,1}, \phi_{j,2}, \ldots, \phi_{j,N}] \tag{17}$$

As the number of iterations approaches M, the norms of the residues of an orthogonal pursuit decrease faster than for a non-orthogonal pursuit. And that the algorithm only need to run for up to M iterations due to step 3. The computational complexity of this algorithm is $O(JNM^2)$, which matches that of separate recovery for each signal while reducing the required number of measurements.

4   Performance Analysis

In this section, we present numerical simulations to demonstrate the effectiveness of the proposed algorithm. The parameters are set in Table 2. The initial energy of sensor node is set as 0.5 J. If the residual energy of node is lower than 0.002 J, the sensor node is assumed to be dead. Once there is a dead node in the network, we assume that the network lifetime is the node's lifetime.

In order to evaluate the accuracy, we calculate normalised mean square error (NMSE) to denote the signal reconstruction error, which is calculated as

$$NMSE = \frac{\left\| \hat{\mathbf{d}}_j - \mathbf{d}_j \right\|_2}{\left\| \mathbf{d}_j \right\|_2} \tag{23}$$

where $\mathbf{d}_j$ is the initial signal, $\hat{\mathbf{d}}_j$ is the reconstruction signal.

In addition, after compressive sensing and signal reconstruction processing, the signal to noise ratio (SNR) for the output signal is different from the input signal. Here, we define the SNR for the output signal as

Table 1. The DCS-SOMP based sensory data recovery algorithm

Algorithm 1. Sensory Data Recovery

Step 1: Initialize

For each sensor node $j \hat{1}$ A, $A = [1, 2, \ldots, C]$, where C denotes the nodes in a cluster, the projection data is represented as $\mathbf{y}_j$, the iteration counter is set as $l = 1$ and initialize the set of selected index $W = \cancel{E}$ and the orthogonalized coefficient vectors $\hat{b}_j = 0, \hat{b}_j \hat{1}$ R^M. According to equation(13), define the residual of the measurement $\mathbf{y}_j$ remaining after the first l iterations as $r_{j,l}$, and initialize $r_{j,0} = \mathbf{y}_j, r = [\mathbf{y}_1, \mathbf{y}_2, \ldots, \mathbf{y}_C]$.

Step 2: Select

Select the dictionary vector that maximizes the value of the sum of the magnitudes of the projections of the residual, and add its index to the set of selected indices:

$$W = [W \ n_l]$$

where $f_{j,n}$ is the column vector of the measurement matrix Φ_j represented as equation(17) and $r_{j,l-1}$ is the residual of the measurement $\mathbf{y}_j$ remaining after j-l iterations.

Step 3: Orthogonalize

The selected basis vector against the orthogonalized set of previously selected dictionary vectors is orthogonalized:

Step 4: Iterate

Update the estimate of the coefficients for the selected vector and residuals:

$$\langle \quad \rangle$$
$$\| \ \|$$

$$r_{j,l} = r_{j,l-1} - \frac{\langle r_{j,l-1}, r_{j,l} \rangle}{\| r_{j,l} \|_2^2} r_{j,l}$$

Step 5: Check for convergence

If $\| r_{j,l} \|_2 > e \| \mathbf{y}_j \|_2$ for all j, then increment l and go to step 2. Otherwise, continue to step 6. The parameter determines the target error power level allowed for algorithm convergence.

Step 6: De-orthogonalize

Consider the relationship between $\Gamma_j = [r_{j,1}, r_{j,2}, \ldots, r_{j,M}]$ and the $\Phi_j = [\phi_{j,1}, \phi_{j,2}, \ldots, \phi_{j,N}]$ given by the QR factorization $\Phi_{j,\Omega} = \Gamma_j R_j$, where $\Phi_{j,\Omega} = [\phi_{j,n_1}, \phi_{j,n_2}, \ldots, \phi_{j,n_M}]$ is the mutilated basis[24]. Since $\mathbf{y}_j = \Gamma_j \beta_j = \Phi_{j,\Omega} \mathbf{s}_{j,\Omega} = \Gamma_j R_j \mathbf{s}_{j,\Omega}$, where $\mathbf{s}_{j,\Omega}$ is the mutilated coefficient vector, we can compute the signal estimates $\{\hat{s}_j\}$ as $\hat{\mathbf{s}}_{j,\Omega} = R_j^{-1} \hat{\beta}_j$, where $\hat{\mathbf{s}}_{j,\Omega}$ is the mutilated version of the sparse coefficient vector $\hat{\mathbf{s}}_j$.

Table 2. Simulation parameters for energy consumption analysis

Variables	Value
E_0	0.5 J
E_{elec}	50 $nJ/bits$
ξ_{fs}	10 $pJ/bits/m^4$
ξ_{amp}	0.0013 $pJ/bits/m^4$
Network size	150 × 150
Number of nodes	200
Length of signal	50

$$SNR = \frac{\sum\limits_{i=1}^{N} \frac{d_{j,i}^2}{N}}{\sum\limits_{i=1}^{N} \frac{\left(\hat{d}_{j,i}-d_{j,i}\right)^2}{N}} \tag{24}$$

where $d_{j,i}$ is the ith value of initial signal $\mathbf{d}_j$, similarly $\hat{d}_{j,i}$ denotes the ith value of reconstruction signal $\hat{\mathbf{d}}_j$. N is the length of the signal.

4.1 Probability of Exact Reconstruction

In order to present the probability of perfect recovery corresponding to various numbers of measurements M with $C = 20$ sensor nodes in a cluster, we fixed the signal lengths at $N = 50$ and change the sparsity of each signal $K = \{6, 7, 8\}$, over 1000 iterations in each case. With the DCS-SOMP reconstruction algorithm, the probability of perfect recovery increases as a function of M. As shown in Fig. 2, the smaller the sparsity K, the less measurement is required to reach a certain probability of perfect recovery. In addition, the convergence is faster. Therefore, with the increase of sparsity K, the required measurement increases to achieve the same probability of perfect recovery.

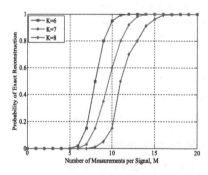

Fig. 2. A Probability of exact reconstruction versus measurement

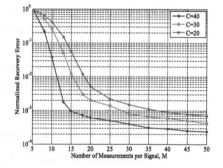

Fig. 3. Normalized recovery error versus measurement

4.2   Normalized Recovery Error

Normalized recovery error is calculated to measure the accuracy. By modeling the homogeneous SNR and fixed the signal sparsity $K = 6$, Fig. 3 compares the normalized recovery errors of different number of sensor nodes C in a cluster and 1000 iterations have been done for each case to obtain the results. The length of signal is set as $N = 50$. As it can be clearly shown in Fig. 3, the normalized recovery error decreases with the increase of measurement M per signal. Under the same number of measurement per signal, the more sensor nodes in a cluster, the better signal reconstruction performance.

4.3   Signal to Noise Ratio

In this subsection, the input noise is taken into consideration. The signal to noise ratio of output signal is presented in Fig. 4. The number of sensor nodes is set as $C = 30$, and the length of signal is $N = 50$. Figure 4 illustrates that how the SNR of output signal can be affected by the distributed compressive sensing with different SNR of input signal. As shown in Fig. 4, the SNR of output signal increases with the SNR of input signal. It is also shown that more measurement per signal can obtain better SNR for output signal.

4.4   Network Lifetime

In order to compare the proposed data gathering algorithm in terms of energy consumption, we use the network lifetime to present the energy consumption performance. The scenarios with J = 200, 250,

300 sensor nodes are taken into consideration, in which the sink node is located in the center of sensing field. The monitoring field is partitioned into several subareas. In order to simplify the discussion, we assume that the compressive ratio M/N per signal is identical in the whole network and as for each case with different sensor node J, 100 iterations are taken to avoid the error. As shown in Fig. 5, the network lifetime

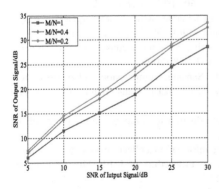

Fig. 4. SNR of output signal versus SNR of input signal

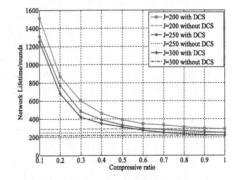

Fig. 5. Network lifetime versus compressive ratio

descends with the compressive ratio. Under the same compressive ratio, the less sensor nodes in the sensing field, the longer the network lifetime will be. When the compressive ratio is $M/N = 1$, the network lifetime is equal to the scenario without using the distributed compressive sensing.

5 Conclusion

In this paper, we investigated the distributed compressive sensing for data gathering in energy harvesting wireless sensor network. In order to energy efficiently gather sensory data in wireless sensor networks, we proposed a distributed compressive sensing-based data gathering scheme in which the sensor readings possess both inter-(spatial) and intra-(temporal) signal correlations to improve the recovery quality of sensory data and prolong the sensor network's lifetime as well. Besides, in order to balance the energy consumption, a cluster-based routing strategy is employed for routing the sensory data. Finally, the DCS-SOMP algorithm is used as the decoding method to recover the sparse data. The simulation results show significant gain in terms of signal reconstruction accuracy and energy consumption.

Acknowledgments. The authors would like to acknowledge that this work was partially supported by the National Natural Science Foundation of China (Grant No. 61379111, 61202342, 61402538, and 61403424) and Research Fund for the Doctoral Program of Higher Education of China (Grant No. 20110162110042).

References

1. Yick, J., Mukherjee, B., Ghosal, D.: Wireless sensor network survey. Comput. Netw. **52** (12), 2292–2330 (2008)
2. Corke, P. et al.: Environmental wireless sensor networks. In: Proceedings of the IEEE, pp. 1903-1917 (2009)
3. Ho, C.K., Zhang, R.: Optimal energy allocation for wireless communications with energy harvesting constraints. IEEE Trans. Signal Process. **60**, 4808–4818 (2012)
4. Erol-Kantarci, M., Mouftah, H.: Suresense: sustainable wireless rechargeable sensor networks for the smart grid. IEEE Wirel. Commun. **19**(3), 30–36 (2012)
5. Anastasi, G., Conti, M., Di Francesco, M., Passarella, A.: Energy conservation in wireless sensor networks: a survey. Ad Hoc Netw. **7**(3), 537–568 (2009)
6. Quer, Y.G., Masiero, R., Rossi, M., Zorzi, M.: Sensing, compression and recovery for wireless sensor networks: monitoring framework design. IEEE Trans. Wirel. Commun. **11**, 3447–3461 (2012)
7. Emmanuel, S., Candès, J., Wakin, M.B.: An introduction to compressive sampling. IEEE Signal Process. Mag. **25**(2), 21–30 (2008)
8. Chou, C.T., Rana, R., Hu, W.: Energy efficient information collection in wireless sensor networks using adaptive compressive sensing. In: Proceedins of IEEE 34th Conference Local Computer Networks, pp. 443–450 (2009)

9. Rana, R., Hu, W., Chou, C.T.: Energy-Aware Sparse Approximation Technique (EAST) for rechargeable wireless sensor networks. In: Silva, J.S., Krishnamachari, B., Boavida, F. (eds.) EWSN 2010. LNCS, vol. 5970, pp. 306–321. Springer, Heidelberg (2010)
10. Ebrahimi, D., Assi, C.: A distributed method for compressive data gathering in wireless sensor networks. IEEE Commun. Lett. **18**(4), 624–627 (2013)
11. Tsai, T.Y., Lan, W.C., Liu, C., et al.: Distributed compressive data aggregation in large-scale wireless sensor networks. J. Adv. Comput. Netw. **1**(4), 295–300 (2013)
12. Baron, D., Duarte, M.F., Wakin, M.B. et al.: Distributed compressive sensing[J]. arXiv preprint arXiv:0901.3403(2009)
13. Wu, X. et al.: Distributed spatial-temporal compressive data gathering for large-scale WSNs. In: Computing, Communications and IT Applications Conference (ComComAp) 2013
14. Tabassum, N., Urano, Y., Haque, A.K.M.A.: GSEN: an efficient energy consumption routing scheme for wireless sensor network. In: International Conference on Networking, International Conference on Systems and International Conference on Mobile Communications and Learning Technologies (ICNICONSMCL 2006), pp. 117–122. IEEE (2006)
15. Mallat, S.: A Wavelet Tour of Signal Processing. Academic, New York (1999)
16. Candès, E., Romberg, J., Tao, T.: Robust uncertainty principles: exact signal reconstruction from highly incomplete frequency information. IEEE Trans. Inform. Theor. **52**(2), 489–509 (2006)
17. Donoho, D.: Compressed sensing. IEEE Trans. Inform. Theor. **52**(4), 1289–1306 (2006)
18. Ahmed, N., Natarajan, T., Rao, K.R.: Discrete cosine transform. IEEE Trans. Comput. **23**(1), 90–93 (1974)
19. Candes, E.J., Tao, T.: Decoding by linear programming. IEEE Trans. Inf. Theor. **51**(12), 4203–4215 (2005)
20. Candès, E., Romberg, J., Tao, T.: Robust uncertainty principles: exact signal reconstruction from highly incomplete frequency information. IEEE Trans. Inform. Theor. **52**(2), 489–509 (2006)
21. Fornasier, M., Rauhut, H.: Compressive sensing. In: Scherzer, O. (ed.) Handbook of Mathematical Methods in Imaging, pp. 187–228. Springer, New York (2011)
22. Duarte, M.F., Sarvotham, S., Baron, D., Wakin, M.B., Baraniuk, R.G.: Distributed compressed sensing of jointly sparse signals. In: Proceedings of the 39th Asilomar Conference on Signals, Systems and Computation, Pacific Grove, CA, USA, pp. 1537–1541 (2005)
23. Luo, C., Wu, F., Sun, J., Chen, C.W.: Efficient measurement generation and pervasive sparsity for compressive data gathering. IEEE Trans. Wirel. Commun. **9**(12), 3728–3738 (2010)
24. Chetan, A., Ghosh, D.: Distributed compressive data gathering in wireless sensor networks. In: 2012 IEEE 11th International Conference on Signal Processing (ICSP), Vol. 3. IEEE (2012)
25. Tropp, J., Gilbert, A.C., Strauss, M.J.: Simulataneous sparse approximation via greedy pursuit. In: IEEE International Conference on Acoustics, Speech, Signal Processing (ICASSP), Philadelphia (2005)
26. Shapiro, J.: Embedded image coding using zerotrees of wavelet coefficients. IEEE Trans. Signal Proc. **41**, 3445–3462 (1993)

Feedback Mechanism Based Dynamic Fingerprint Indoor Localization Algorithm in Wireless Sensor Networks

Yu Liu, Juan Luo$^{(\boxtimes)}$, Qian Yang, and Jinyu Hu

College of Computer Science and Electric Engineering,
Hunan University, Changsha 410082, China
juanluo@hnu.edu.cn

Abstract. In location fingerprint based indoor localization system, the received signal strength (RSS) from a set of Wi-Fi access points are used as a unique fingerprint to identify a specific location. However, indoor environment is much more complex and changeable compared to outdoor environment, which leads to larger localization error brought by outdated RSS fingerprints. And re-measuring RSS fingerprints for all locations to maintain a dynamically changing fingerprint database will cause high cost and complexity. To solve this problem, this paper proposes a feedback mechanism based dynamic fingerprint indoor localization algorithm called FMDFLA, it makes RSS fingerprint update timely to cope with changes in the indoor environment. FMDFLA adds distance between grids matrix in offline database which used for scope judgment in online phase. In online phase, we update fingerprint to obtain the "update-point" and "non-update-point", feedback the RSS of "update-point" to "non-update-point" by using specific method. Furthermore, we update fingerprint for a number of times to obtain the best result of localization. Simulation results show that the localization accuracy and the stability of FMDFLA are higher than traditional CS based localization algorithm and fingerprint localization algorithm in dynamic indoor environment.

Keywords: Dynamic fingerprint · Feedback · Indoor localization · Location fingerprint

1 Introduction

Indoor localization technology is mainly divided into special equipment based localization technology, Wi-Fi signal ranging based localization technology and fingerprint based localization technology. Among them, the special equipment based localization technologies include optical tracking, RFID, Zigbee, Bluetooth, GPS(A-GPS), etc. Zhang *et al.* using RFID Tag Arrays for location sensing and frequent route detection [1]. This type of localization technologies have the advantages of high accuracy, which can mostly achieve centimeter-level accuracy, but it need to deploy special hardware device and the cost is high. Wi-Fi

© Springer International Publishing Switzerland 2015
G. Wang et al. (Eds.): ICA3PP 2015, Part I, LNCS 9528, pp. 674–687, 2015.
DOI: 10.1007/978-3-319-27119-4_47

signal ranging based localization technologies contain AOA, TOA, TDOA, and signal propagation models based localization. The disadvantages of these methods are that it is not easy to obtain feature information, and localization accuracy is low since it is extremely vulnerable to the impact of changes in indoor environment. Fingerprint based localization technology derived from database technology (DCM, Database Correction Method) [2]. This technology has the advantages of low cost, easy implementation and high accuracy. Therefore, fingerprint localization technology is a relatively popular and widespread indoor localization technology at present. However, there is a major problem for fingerprint localization. In the complex indoor environment, due to the interference of objects (such as the movement of people) and the impact of multipath fading, any position of the RSS fingerprints are dynamic changing while the offline fingerprint is fixed. This will lead to a deviated location match that is far away from the actual location of the fingerprint in online phase, resulting in larger positioning error. To solve this problem, the fingerprint must be adjusted to decrease the difference between the current RSS fingerprints and the offline fingerprints as small as possible. A method to achieve this target is to re-measure the RSS value at all reference positions. However, the more updated position, the greater the cost and complexity [3]. Some researchers have attempted to re-measure the RSS of a part of reference positions [4] to reduce cost, but this method can only adjust the RSS of updated location and not update the fingerprint effectively.

This paper proposes a feedback mechanism based dynamic fingerprint indoor localization algorithm called FMDFLA. FMDFLA adds the distance between grids matrix in offline phase, and preset a localization error threshold. In online phase, if the localization error exceeds this threshold, then re-measure the RSS of some reference location, which is called "update-point". We also define the "non-update-point" within specific region. Then we use the distance between grids matrix that has been established in offline phase within the specified scope to search "update-point" which nearby "non-update-point". By means of spatial correlation, we use linear interpolation method to calculate the RSS value of "non-update-point", so that the RSS of "non-update-point" can be updated too. Thus, we can achieve feedback of RSS values from "update-point" to "non-update-point" and execute positioning. We save those RSS values that have the best localization effect to the offline database, this mechanism will not only maintain a real-time fingerprint database, but also build a good foundation for the next positioning. The main contributions of this paper are as follows:

(1) In this paper, fingerprint is dynamic updated, which can effectively deal with the dynamic indoor environment, and improve the indoor localization accuracy.
(2) We divide the indoor region into horizontal and vertical grids, and add the distance between grids matrix in the offline database, which is different from most fingerprint localization algorithms.
(3) In this paper, "update-point" and "non-update-point" are proposed, and these points are selected in specific area, which can not only effectively adjust the fingerprint but reduce the cost and complexity of updating.

(4) In this paper, through judging whether the updated fingerprints are advantageous to improve accuracy to determine whether save these fingerprints to offline database or not, which makes the offline database optimal and useful to the next time positioning.

2   Related Work

The current researches on fingerprint database positioning method mainly concentrate in two categories: the first category is the research on localization algorithms, mainly for the purpose of improving the positioning accuracy. The representative of deterministic algorithm research is RADAR developed by Microsoft [5], in which the location matching methods including Nearest Neighbor in Signal Space and K-NNSS are proposed to infer user's location. The methods maintain the location fingerprint database made of signal strength from selected sites to different Aps. Measuring the signal strength during the online phase, finding out several coordinates from fingerprint database which most matches the measured signal strength, then calculate the average coordinates as the estimated location of the point to be tested. And Zhang *et al.* find that there is a strong correlation between the calling patterns and co-cell patterns of users and propose algorithm NextCell [6]. Literature [7] proposed Assemblage Analysis Method according to high correlation between the continuous samples, which can reduce the computation of the positioning algorithm but do not improve the positioning accuracy.

The second category is the construction of the location fingerprint database. Bolliger proposed re-measured RSS values among part reference positions [4] in order to update the fingerprint database while considering the complex indoor environment, but this scheme has limited reference point, while others are still in a non-updated reference point state.

To reduce cost, the fingerprint database is required to make a meaningful change. Gallagher *et al.* proposed a new method by using user's feedback [8]. And Fang *et al.* proposed a dynamic fingerprint combination (DFC) algorithm [9], which by dynamically weighting the spatial correlation from multiple location fingerprinting systems, improving the quality of mobile localization. Firstly, DFC algorithm extracts the complementary advantages of fingerprinting functions to construct a fusion profile, and then dynamically combines individual outputs based on the fusion profile surrounding the test sample. This algorithm improves the positioning accuracy while also reducing the risk of poor performance of the fingerprinting. And DFC algorithm was applied to the GSM network in this article. Experimental results show that DFC improves the positioning accuracy of base fingerprinting algorithms, including the Bayesian approach and a neural network model.

3   Dynamic Fingerprint Database Algorithm

3.1   The Process of Fingerprint Localization

The process of fingerprint localization has two phases: an offline phase and an online phase. The aim of offline phase is to build the offline database. The main work in this phase is collecting all RSS of reference points to build the location fingerprint database in localization area, each RSS corresponding to a specific location. In order to reduce the influence of interference to RSS, we collect the RSS for a period of time at each reference point. In online phase, measure the real-time RSS of target node location, and adopt matching algorithm to find out the most similar RSS in offline database, thus ensure the actual location of user.

Typical fingerprint localization still using static fingerprint database, the location performance of this technology is poor in dynamic changing indoor environment. So, dynamic adjust fingerprint database has very important significance to cope with the change of environment.

3.2 Dynamic Fingerprint Database Algorithm (FMDFLA)

Notations used in this paper are summarized in Table 1.

Table 1. Notations

Symbol	Description
N	Number of samples
Ψ	Sampling matrix
M	Number of measurements
ϕ	A measurement matrix
Θ	Number of update-points
D	Distances between grids matrix
R	Radius of Cut-off area
r	Communication radius of anchor
δ	Localization errors
L	Number of anchors
T	Localization error threshold
G	Fingerprint max update time
g	Current update time

The system architecture of FMDFLA is shown in Fig. 1. FMDFLA consists of an offline phase and an online phase. The offline phase mainly to build a complete database, and this database will be used to the localization of online phase.

Offline Phase. The main task of the offline phase is to build the complete database. We divide this task into 3 steps: (1) collecting offline RSS information; (2) associating RSS information with location; (3) building the distances between grids matrix; (4) getting the coordinates of anchors.

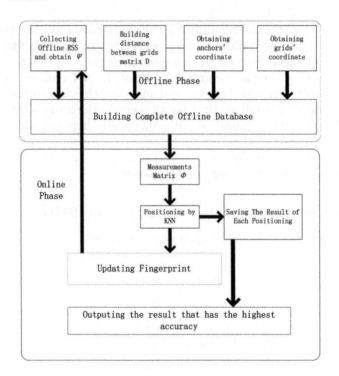

Fig. 1. The system architecture

In order to collect offline RSS, the indoor region is divided into horizontal and vertical grids. Assuming that the indoor region is divided into $n \times n$ grids, we define $N = n \times n$, the total number of grids. Reference point is deployed in a grid, and anchors are randomly deployed in the indoor region. Nodes can collect anchor's RSS within the scope of the anchor's communication, record the RSS value and store them to the offline database.

Online Phase. FMDFLA uses classical KNN(K Nearest Neighborhood) method as matching algorithm in online phase. When a target node enters the indoor region, we firstly use the KNN method to obtain the estimate location error δ, and compare δ to localization error threshold T that we predetermined, if δ is bigger than T, and then we update the RSS of some reference points. We call these updated reference points the "update-point", and call those not yet updated reference points the "non-update-point", using the spatial correlation [10] to calculate RSS of "non-update-point", the specific calculate method will explained at next section.

3.3   Grids Division

We divide the indoor region into many virtual square grids, and code these grids in the form of coordinate, as shown in Fig. 3.

Theorem 1. In a rectangular region, we define that r is the communication radius of an anchor, I is interference loss, r is communication ration, and α is interference loss coefficient. Grid number should meet $\frac{2S_{region}}{r^2} \leq N_{grid} \leq \frac{S_{region}}{(10^{\frac{\lg(I_{min})-\wedge}{\alpha}})}$ to make the cost of samples in offline phase varies in a certain range, where S_{region} is the area of the rectangular region, $\wedge$ is a constant; I_{min} is the smallest interference loss.

Proof. Suppose the coordinate of vertex of a rectangular area are (x_{left}, y_{buttom}), (x_{left}, y_{top}), (x_{right}, y_{buttom}) and (x_{right}, y_{top}) respectively. The area of it could be denoted by $S_{region}=(x_{right} - x_{left}) \times (y_{top} - y_{buttom})$.

We can get the number of grids N_{grid} in a rectangular area, as shown in Eq. (1),

$$N_{grid} = \frac{[(x_{right} - x_{left}) \times (y_{top} - y_{bottom})]}{d_{grid}^2} = \frac{S_{region}}{d_{grid}^2}, 0 \leq d_{grid} \leq d_{region} \quad (1)$$

where d_{grid} is the length of grid, d_{region} is the longest edge of the area. According to Eq. (1), N_{grid} is inversely proportional to the square of d_{grid}.

Assume that the premise of grids division is that each reference node in the grid can hear from anchors at any point in the same grid, which means that any reference node in a grid is within the communication range of anchors in this grid, then, $0 \leq d_{grid} \leq \frac{\sqrt{2}r}{2}$.

However, if the edge of a grid is too small, each node will produce strong interference when gathering RSS during offline phase. Therefore, we should find a lower limit for the length of grid edge to ensure the sampling node with minimum interference.

Classical transmission model is shown in Eq. (2),

$$P_R = \frac{P_t G_t G_R I}{d^\alpha}(h_t h_R)^2. \quad (2)$$

According to Eq. (2), we can get

$$\lg(I) = \alpha \lg(d) + \wedge, \quad (3)$$

where P_t is transmitting power, P_R is received power. G_t and G_R represent antenna gain of sending and receiving node respectively. h_t and h_R are the height of antenna for sending and receiving node respectively, and $\wedge$ is $\lg(\frac{P_R}{P_t G_t G_R (h_t h_R)^2})$, which is a constant. d is the distance between a couple of communication nodes. According to Eq. (3), we can get

$$d_{grid} = 10^{\frac{\lg(I)-\wedge}{\alpha}}. \quad (4)$$

Interference loss coefficient α is a fixed number in a certain environment. According to Eq. (4), we can get the minimum value of d_{min} when interference loss is the smallest, which is I_{min}. So, here comes the Eq. (5)

$$10^{\frac{lg(I_{min})-\wedge}{\alpha}} \le d_{grid} \le \frac{\sqrt{2}r}{2}. \tag{5}$$

According to Eqs. (5) and (1), we get

$$\frac{2S_{region}}{r^2} \le N_{grid} \le \frac{S_{region}}{(10^{\frac{lg(I_{min})-\wedge}{\alpha}})}. \tag{6}$$

This completes the proof of Theorem 1.

4   Algorithm Implementation

The localization process of FMDFLA consists of an offline phase and an online phase. As mentioned above, we build offline database in offline phase, and use the KNN method and our fingerprint update mechanism to locate target node. The target nodes and L anchors are randomly deployed in the indoor region, and communication radius of anchor is r.

4.1   Offline Phase

In order to build complete offline database, we should collect RSS information in the whole indoor area. However, it is difficult to obtain accurate RSS information in dynamic indoor environment. For example, settings in a laboratory, such as chairs, desks, equipment, and moving staffs can form a complex environment for signal propagation. The complex environment could lead to potential RSS outliers.

One way to solve this problem is to collect a large number of samples and get their average value. In order to get jth grid average RSS from anchor i, we place a node in jth grid. This node can receive RSS from anchor i. Assuming that the amount of RSS samples of node j is q. Then, the average RSS value for this node from anchor i is:

$$\varphi_{i,j} = \sum_{\tau=1}^{q} \varphi_{i,j}(\tau)/q, \tag{7}$$

where $\varphi_{i,j}(\tau)$ represents the τth RSS that jth grid received from anchor i. $\varphi_{i,j}$ represents the average RSS value for grid j from anchor i.

The original fingerprint database Ψ is shown in Eq. (8),

$$\Psi = \begin{bmatrix} \varphi_{1,1} & \varphi_{1,2} & \cdots & \varphi_{1,N} \\ \varphi_{2,1} & \varphi_{2,2} & \cdots & \varphi_{2,N} \\ \vdots & \vdots & \ddots & \vdots \\ \varphi_{L,1} & \varphi_{L,2} & \cdots & \varphi_{L,N} \end{bmatrix}. \tag{8}$$

If node j is beyond the communication range of anchor i, that is, node j cannot receive RSS information from anchor i, then $\varphi_{i,j} = 0$.

Building Distance Between Grids Matrix. In online phase, we must use the distance between grids to judge whether "update-point" is within the scope of Cut-off area. However, if we calculate the distance between grids in online phase, it will increase the complexity of algorithm and cause the additional calculate cost, and then increase the cost of algorithm. So, we skillfully build the distance between grids matrix in offline phase, in online phase, we only need to invoke this matrix to get the distance between grids.

Presently, the total number of grids is N, we define the distance between ith grid and jth grid is $d_{i,j}$, distance between grids matrix is shown in Eq. (9),

$$D = \begin{bmatrix} d_{1,1} & d_{1,2} & \cdots & d_{1,N} \\ d_{2,1} & d_{2,2} & \cdots & d_{2,N} \\ \vdots & \vdots & \ddots & \vdots \\ d_{L,1} & d_{L,2} & \cdots & d_{L,N} \end{bmatrix}. \tag{9}$$

If $i = j$, then $d_{i,j}=0$.

Building Complete Offline Database. As we conduct the experiment in two dimensions, the anchors' x-coordinates and y-coordinates are very important for localization of target node. So, each anchor's x-coordinate, y-coordinate, RSS value at each reference point in offline phase, and the distance between grids matrix are combined together to be the complete offline database, as shown in Eq. (10),

$$(x, y; \Psi; D), \tag{10}$$

where (x, y) is anchor's coordinate.

4.2   Online Phase

After building the complete offline database, a good foundation for online phase has established. In this subsection, we will explain the localization process of FMDFLA and our fingerprint update mechanism in detail.

Estimate RSS Fingerprint Using Linear Interpolation. Using the spatial correlation of adjacent position, if we want to calculate the RSS of "non-update-point", we only need to know the RSS of adjacent "update-point" that around it. This method uses the RSS of exactly three surrounding "update-point" and coordinate of their location as inputs, and the output is RSS of "non-update-point".

Utilizing RSS fingerprints of three "update-point" and corresponding coordinate $F_1(X_1, Y_1, RSS_1)$, $F_2(X_2, Y_2, RSS_2)$, $F_3(X_3, Y_3, RSS_3)$ as feedback information, we try to calculate $F_n(X_n, Y_n, RSS_n)$ that is surrounded by F_1, F_2 and F_3, and X_n, Y_n are known coordinates. We can represent F_n by using a vector B that is normal to F_1, F_2 and F_3, as shown in Eq. (11),

$$B = F_1 F_2 \times F_1 F_3, \tag{11}$$

where
$$F_1 F_2 = \begin{bmatrix} X_2 - X_1 \\ Y_2 - Y_1 \\ RSS_2 - RSS_1 \end{bmatrix}. \tag{12}$$

And
$$F_1 F_3 = \begin{bmatrix} X_3 - X_1 \\ Y_3 - Y_1 \\ RSS_3 - RSS_1 \end{bmatrix}. \tag{13}$$

From (11), (12), (13), we have

$$B = F_1 F_2 \times F_1 F_3 = \begin{vmatrix} i & j & k \\ W_1 & W_2 & W_3 \\ Z_1 & Z_2 & Z_3 \end{vmatrix}. \tag{14}$$

Rewrite Eq. (14), we get Eq. (15),

$$F_n = B = Ai + Bj + Ck + D = 0, \tag{15}$$

where A, B, C and D are all arbitrary constant, because X_n, Y_n are known, we have

$$F_n(X_n, Y_n, RSS_n) = AX_n + BY_n + CRSS_n + D = 0. \tag{16}$$

So far, according to Eq. (16), we can obtain the value of RSS_n, and then take this value as updated RSS and feedback to "non-update-point". This process only considers one anchor, if there are more than one anchors, repeat the same calculation process to all of them.

Cut-Off Area. We define Cut-off area is a circle region, radius R is arbitrary, as shown in Fig. 2(a). R is the radius of Cut-off area; yellow points are points that within Cut-off area, red points are points that outside Cut-off area; A represents "non-update-point" or current estimate location of target node.

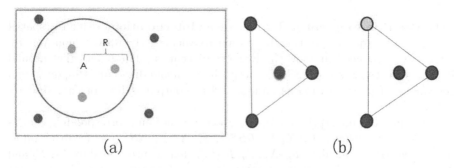

Fig. 2. Cut-off area and "update-point".

Update Fingerprint Effectively and Reliably. Dynamic fingerprint method is based on two assumptions as follows:

(1) Positions that are close to each other should get similar RSS fingerprint [3].
(2) The smaller distance between feedback and the points that needs to update is, the more credible the fingerprint from feedback will be.

We use linear interpolation to estimate the RSS of "non-update-point". According to assumption 1, if A represents the estimate location of target node, we only set these yellow points as "non-update-point", as shown in Fig. 4; According to assumption 2, if A represents "non-update-point", we only set these yellow points as the effective "update-point" while ignore those red "update-point", as shown in Fig. 3. Thus, we ensured that the fingerprint updated effectively and reliably.

As shown in Fig. 2(b), Red point represents "non-update-point"; blue points represent "update-point"; yellow point represents "non-update-point" that instead of "update-point". if there are exactly three "update-point" in Cut-off area, the RSS of "non-update-point" can be calculated directly; if there are more than three "update-point" in Cut-off area, we choose the nearest three "update-point"; if there are less than three "update-point" in Cut-off area, choose the "non-update-point" that most close to this "non-update-point" in Cut-off area instead, note that we should ensure that the RSS change frequency of the chosen "non-update-point" is low, since its RSS value is more reliable, therefore, this RSS can be used to feedback to "non-update-point".

Algorithm. FMDFLA

Input: Anchor's number L, anchor's communication radius r, number of "update-point" Θ, fingerprint max update time G, localization error threshold T.
Output: Target node coordinates P_x, P_y.

/* Initialization */
$i=1$, $g=0$.
/* Steps */
(1) Build sampling matrix Ψ and distance between grids matrix D, obtain coordinate of anchors and each grid, and combine them to be the complete offline database.
(2) In online phase, obtain measurement matrix Φ, and use KNN method to calculate the estimate location P_x, P_y.
(3) Obtain localization error δ_i, if $\delta_i<T$, go to (8) directly; if $\delta_i>T$, go to (4).
(4) Re-measure RSS of some reference points, obtain "update-point" and "non-update-point", and then make $g = g + 1$, $i = i + 1$, go to (5).
(5) if there are exactly three "update-point" in Cut-off area, the RSS of "non-update-point" can be calculated directly; if there are more than three "update-point" in Cut-off area, we choose the nearest three "update-point"; if there are

less than three "update-point" in Cut-off area, choose the "non-update-point" that most close to this "non-update-point" in Cut-off area instead.

(6) Obtain all RSS values of "update-point" and "non-update-point", return these values to online phase.

(7) Use updated RSS to estimate location and calculate δ_i, if $\delta_i < T$, go to (8); if $\delta_i > T$ and $g > G$, go to (8), otherwise go to (4). If $\delta_i < \delta_{i-1}$, save the updated RSS fingerprint to Ψ.

(8) Compare all localization results and return the coordinate P_x, P_y that have the smallest δ.

In step (4), "update-point" is randomly chosen from reference points.

In ith localization, we obtain the estimate coordinate (x_i, y_i), use Euclidian principle, its localization error δ_i is shown in Eq. (17),

$$\delta_i = \sqrt{(x_0 - x_i)^2 \times (y_0 - y_i)^2}. \tag{17}$$

Saving all localization errors, then we have Δ:

$$\Delta = [\delta_1, \delta_2, \ldots, \delta_G], \tag{18}$$

where G is fingerprint max update time. In step (8), find the coordinate P_x, P_y that have the smallest δ in Δ, and return this coordinate.

5   Simulation

5.1   Localization Environment

In our experiments, the maximum transmitting power is 20 dbm, and the minimum interval of the transmission is 1dbm. Each node works in the same channel, and each anchor has the same communication radius.

We select our laboratory whose size is 30 × 30m*m as the location region. And we select the WSN node that can transmit signal as anchor node, and each anchor node is distributed randomly. There are L anchor nodes in the laboratory, and the coordinate of these anchor nodes are known. We also choose the WSN node located in a grid as the reference node, and each reference node has a fixed position and can receive RSS from the anchor node. Moreover, we use a mobile phone as the target node which can receive RSS from the anchor node. We divide the indoor region into $N = 30 \times 30$ grids. L anchors are randomly deployed in the region, where $L = 30$. All target nodes receive RSS from perceived anchors to execute localization process. Simulation is about how does location accuracy changes with the number of target nodes, measurements, fingerprint max update time, the number of "update-point" and radius of Cut-off area. FMDFLA is compared with traditional CS [11] based localization, fingerprint localization algorithms [12] and LMAT [13].

In our simulation, sampling matrix Ψ is obtained by employing the indoor classical model defined by the IEEE 802.15.4 standard. It must be highlighted that our experiments are executed in dynamic indoor environment, that is, the received RSS of each reference node may change at any time, as well as the measured RSS of target node. So, our experimental environment is different from that of most localization algorithms.

We compare the localization results with different update time. First, we set "update-point" number $\Theta=100$. we find that the location error has reduced obviously with G increases from 1 to 5. But with G increase from 5 to 10, the location accuracy is almost invariable. Because the more time fingerprint update, the more cost FMDFLA will have, so we rule $G=5$ in later experiment.

5.2   Impact of "update-Point" Number

In the localization process of FMDFLA, we randomly select some reference points as "update-point" and re-measure RSS of these points. However, the more updated position, the greater the cost and complexity [10], so we should select "update-point" as less as possible. In experiment, we vary the size of Θ to observe the impact on localization results. As shown in Fig. 3(a), with Θ increasing from 100 to 500, the localization accuracy of each curve is also increasing, but with the increasing of Θ, the cost of FMDFLA will increase quickly. As shown in Fig. 4(a), when $\Theta=100$, the localization error of FMDFLA is still less than traditional CS and fingerprint localization, thus, we rule $\Theta=100$ in our experiment.

5.3   Impact of Cut-Off Area Radius

The size of Cut-off area radius R limits the chance of finding "update-point", the smaller radius of Cut-off area is, the fewer "update-point" will be found. In our experiment, R increases from 2 m to 10m. As shown in Fig. 3(b), when R increases to 5m, the localization accuracy has a great improvement, but when R is greater than 5, its impact on the localization accuracy is quite small.

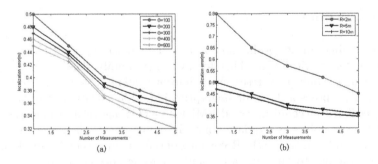

(a)   (b)

Fig. 3. Impact of update-point number Θ and Cut-off area radius R on localization error

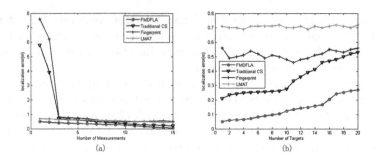

Fig. 4. Impact of measurements number and target node number on localization error of fingerprint, traditional CS and FMDFLA.

5.4   Impact of Measurements Number

As shown in Fig. 4(a), in dynamic indoor region, the localization error of traditional CS and fingerprint is quite large when measurements number is less than 3, while the localization accuracy of FMDFLA is still very high, so the stability of FMDFLA is higher than the two algorithms. In addition, the localization error of FMDFLA is below 0.2 m when measurements number reaches 15. Moreover, FMDFLA outperforms the other three algorithms in all measurements.

5.5   Impact of Target Node Number

Figure 4(b) depicts the localization performance of FMDFLA, LMAT, traditional CS and fingerprint algorithm with target node number ranging from 1 to 20 across 15 measurements. As shown in Fig. 4(b), the localization error of FMDFLA is much smaller than the other three algorithms in dynamic indoor region. Moreover, the localization error of FMDFLA is usually below 0.1 m when the number of target node is less than 8.

6   Conclusions

Traditional fingerprint localization is not enough to cope with the complex dynamic indoor environment. Therefore, we must modify Traditional fingerprint localization or apply new research to improve indoor localization technology. This paper proposes a dynamic fingerprint indoor localization algorithm based on the feedback mechanism called FMDFLA. This algorithm randomly selects some reference points as "update-point" in online phase when needs to update fingerprint, and re-measure the RSS values of these points, then feedback the RSS of "update-point" to "non-update-point" by using specific method, which not only adjusts fingerprint effectively but reduces cost and complexity in update. Moreover, we update fingerprint for a number of times to ensure that the current fingerprint is more close to the real-time indoor environment. In addition, we record localization results of each time update and return the estimate coordinate that has smallest localization error. FMDFLA can not only ensure the real-time character of fingerprint but make the localization results more optimal, and it is good for next positioning as well.

Acknowledgments. This work was partially supported by National Natural Science Foundation of China (61370094).

References

1. Zhang, D., Zhou, J., Guo, M., Cao, J., Li, T.: TASA: tag-free activity sensing using RFID tag arrays. IEEE Trans. Parallel Distrib. Syst. **22**(4), 558–570 (2011)
2. Juurakko, S.W.: Database correlation method with error correction for emergency location. Wirel. Pers. Commun. **30**(2–4), 183–194 (2004)
3. Pan, S.J., Kwok, J.T., Yang, Q., Pan, J.J.: Adaptive localization in a dynamic wifi environment through multi-view learning. In: Proceedings of the AAAI 2007, vol. 2, pp. 1108–1113 (2007)
4. Bolliger, P.: Redpin-adaptive, zero-configuration indoor localization through user collaboration. In: Proceedings of Location and Context Awareness, pp. 55–60 (2008)
5. Bahl, P., Padmanabhan, V.: Radar: an in-building RF-based user location and tracking system. In: Proceedings of the IEEE Nineteenth Annual Joint Conference of the IEEE Computer and Communications Societies, INFOCOM 2000, vol. 2, pp. 775–784 (2000)
6. Zhang, D., Xiong, H., Yang, L.T., Gauthier, V.: Nextcell: predicting location using social interplay from cell phone traces. IEEE Trans. Comput. **64**(2), 452–463 (2015)
7. Youssef, M., Agrawala, A.: Handling samples correlation in the horus system. In: Twenty-third AnnualJoint Conference of the IEEE Computer and Communications Societies, INFOCOM 2004, vol. 2, pp. 1023–1031, March 2004
8. Gallagher, T., Li, B., Dempster, A., Rizos, C.: Database updating through user feedback in fingerprint-based wi-fi location systems. In: Ubiquitous Positioning Indoor Navigation and Location Based Service (UPINLBS), pp. 1–8, October 2010
9. Fang, S.H., Hsu, Y.T., Kuo, W.H.: Dynamic fingerprinting combination for improved mobile localization. IEEE Trans. Wirel. Commun. **10**(12), 4018–4022 (2011)
10. Anton, H., Birens, I., Davis, S.: Three-dimensional space; vectors. In: Calculus, Chapter 12, Sect. 6, 8th edn., pp. 835–843. Wiley, New York (2005)
11. Feng, C., Valaee, S., Tan, Z.: Multiple target localization using compressive sensing. In: Global Telecommunications Conference, GLOBECOM 2009, pp. 1–6. IEEE, November 2009
12. Kushki, A., Plataniotis, K., Venetsanopoulos, A.: Kernel-based positioning in wireless local area networks. IEEE Trans. Mob. Comput. **6**(6), 689–705 (2007)
13. Jiang, J., Han, G., Xu, H., Shu, L., Guizani, M.: LMAT: localization with a mobile anchor node based on trilateration in wireless sensor networks. In: IEEE GLOBE-COM 2011 (2011)

A GPU Based Fast Community Detection Implementation for Social Network

Guo Li[1], Dafang Zhang[1]([✉]), Kun Xie[1], Tanlong Huang[1,2], and Yanbiao Li[1]

[1] College of Computer Science and Electronic Engineering,
Hunan University, Changsha 410082, China
{liguo,dfzhang,xiekun,lybmath_cs}@hnu.edu.cn
[2] PLA 95874, Nanjing 210016, China
htl2515941@163.com

Abstract. Community structure represents a group of nodes which have similar characteristics in social network, so community detection is an important and popular work. However, community detection algorithms face the problem of low efficiency, due to complicated community definition and large amount of calculation. In order to implement efficient community detecting, we design Inner Outer Ratio (IOR) community metric, and propose Neighbor Compare Bidirectional Iteration (NCBI) detecting algorithm on GPU platform. IOR metirc uses (InnerEdges/InnerNodes)/(OuterEdges/OuterNodes) ratio for community structure definition. IOR metric only needs local network information and has a balanced consideration on both edges and nodes, and it is suit for high-performance parallel computing on GPU. NCBI algorithm adopts quick initialization mechanism through neighbor comparison, and uses bidirectional iteration to detect most probable communities based on IOR metric. To certify our community metric, we compare with traditional metrics including modularity and normal conductance. Experiment results show IOR metric is accuracy and works well in parallel computing, NCBI detecting algorithm is faster based on GPU accelerating platform.

Keywords: GPU · Community metric · Community detection · Social network · Parallel computing

1 Introduction

Community is usually referred as a group of nodes in social network. The nodes in the group have strong connections while nodes between groups have weak connections [1]. Community detection has been widely used in social networks, such as advertisement and recommendation [1–5]. It attracts more and more interest recently [6–10].

Community detection is generally a NP-Hard problem, which confirmed in [11–15]. Traditional community metrics are complicated, it's difficult to guarantee the community detection efficiency, and hard to expand to parallel distributed computing.

ⓒ Springer International Publishing Switzerland 2015
G. Wang et al. (Eds.): ICA3PP 2015, Part I, LNCS 9528, pp. 688–701, 2015.
DOI: 10.1007/978-3-319-27119-4_48

Therefore, designing an appropriate community metric to fit for parallel and distributed computing platform is critical. GPU (graphics processing units) achieves great success in high-performance computing at many scientific research fields, such as gene engineering, data mining et al. Dedicating more resources on parallel computing makes GPU good at floating point calculation compared to CPU, especially on large scale data. To realize full potential of GPU hardware, needing parallelization data. However, it is not easy to do for the traditional community definition, because the degree of data dependency is high.

In order to overcome above problems and improve community detection efficient, we need to design a community metric, which should be a precise definition to fit for task decomposition and data parallelization, and can be applied to detection algorithm for parallel distributed computing. The challenges are converting data requirement from global information to local information, and transforming computation algorithm from serial to parallel.

This paper proposes a novel Inner Outer Ratio (IOR) metric to measure community structure with local network information, making less dependence between the data. In addition, IOR Metric has a balanced consideration on both edges and nodes which can improve measurement accuracy. Based on IOR metric, we propose neighbor compare bidirectional iteration (NCBI) detecting algorithm which utilizes both partition and aggregation methods to improve the search coverage concurrently. Meanwhile, adding a quick initialization mechanism through neighbor comparison, which makes detecting communities faster.

The contributions of this paper can be summarized as follows:

- We propose an accurate and practical Inner Outer Ratio Metric to give a quantification definition on community structure. Depending on only local information and considering network element in equilibrium, IOR metric calculation is lightweight and fits for GPU platform with parallel data.
- Based on IOR metric, we propose Neighbor Compare Bidirectional Iteration detecting algorithm to detect the communities in a network. The NCBI detecting algorithm obtains both the advantages of partition and aggregation for community detection, and can expand to high-performance GPU hardware platform. Therefore, it can detect communities quickly.
- We have carried out theoretical comparison and experimental verification to evaluate the performance of proposed metric and algorithm. The results show IOR metric is accuracy and practicability, NCBI algorithm is efficiency.

The rest of this paper is organized as follows. Section 2 presents related work of community metrics and detection algorithms, Sect. 3 gives problem statement in community metric. Our community metric is proposed in Sect. 4, Sect. 5 puts forward our detection algorithm. In Sect. 6, we conduct experiments and analyze the results. The paper is concluded in Sect. 7.

2   Related Work

2.1   Community Metrics and Detection Algorithms

Edge betweenness is a community metric proposed by Girvan and Newman [1]. Modularity community metric is adopted by Thang and Nam, et al. [2,11].

Modularity metric is most widely accepted in real social networks. Conductance is already a widely adopted metric in quantifying the goodness of a community structure, but it is biased towards large communities. Consequently, Bimal and Alan, et al. [16,17] propose normalized conductance. Traditional community detection algorithms are mainly based on above metrics. The community detection algorithms use segmentation or aggregation methods to detect community. For example, the QCA (Quick Community Adaptation) algorithm [2] based on modularity is from a previous known structure, updates the network communities along with inserting nodes adaptively. The community detection algorithm based on normalized conductance [17] selects seed node first of all, and then adding neighboring nodes greedily, until a sufficient strong community is found.

In summary, the algorithms in [1] are remove edges with a certain feature iteratively, the approaches in [3,12,16–18] are similar to greedy adding, the algorithms in [2,11] use dynamic mechanism to add or remove community element. They are all one-way iteration.

2.2   Community Detection Based on GPU in Social Network

Recently, GPU is applying to community detection and social network due to the high-performance parallel computing ability. In the processing flow on GPU, there has three important steps. Step 1, instructions transfer from main processor CPU to co-processor GPU, data transfer from host (CPU Memory) to device (GPU memory). Step 2, GPU launch a mass of threads for parallel computing. Step 3, the compute result will return back to host. The reason to transfer data between host and device is that GPU threads can not access host memory directly in generally, GPU only can operate its own memory due to the limitation of hardware [19]. [20] shown GPU has promising potential in accelerating computation on social network, due to its parallel processing capacity and ample memory bandwidth, GPU is able to scale up to large-scale social networks. [21] proposed hierarchical parallel algorithm on single-GPU and multi-GPU architectures and used modularity to measure community quality. [22] used GPU for high-performance computing in large-scale social network with data from Stanford Network Analysis Project. [23,24] improved the compute speed in GPU platform more than twice compared to CPU platform, their community detection algorithms both are based on Newman algorithm. [25] used modularity metric to detect communities based on GPU. [26] designed a novel parallel community detection algorithm based on weighted label propagation in GPU platform, and used modularity to measure community quality.

In Summary, GPU can speed up significantly on social network computing. However, traditional community metrics and algorithms are transferred from serial method, lack the parallelism in data and algorithm structure, which can not develop full potential on GPU platform.

3   Problem Statement

The existing community definitions are still ambiguous by adopting 'more', 'denser' and so on words. This brings a challenge problem, how to give a quantitative definition on community structure. To resolve this issue, community metric must be figured out firstly.

There are three traditional metrics to identify community: betweenness, modularity, and conductance [1,2,17].

(1) Edge betweenness metric [1]. The definition of edge betweenness is the number of shortest paths between pairs of vertices that run along the edge. There are several disadvantages. First, need global network information. Second, community metric is an indirect and complicated evaluation criteria. Third, the applied range is limited in the network where information flow follows the shortest available path.

(2) Modularity metric [2,11]. Modularity is defined as Formula 1.

$$Q = \sum_{C \in c} \left(\frac{m_c}{M} - \frac{d_c^2}{4M^2} \right) \tag{1}$$

m_c is the numbers of edges inside community, M is the total edges in network, d_c is the total degree of the nodes in community, the degree of a node is the number of edges connected to the node. This metric has some disadvantages. First, need an initial community structure. Second, community metric is non-locality and resolution limit.

(3) Conductance metric [16,17]. The definition of conductance metric is let $G = (V, E)$ denotes a network, V represents node and E indicates edge, $A \in V$ and A is a subset of the vertices that form a community, and let $B = V - A$. Then defines e_{AB} is the number of edges between A and B, e_{AA} is the number of edges with in A, as shown in Fig. 1(a).

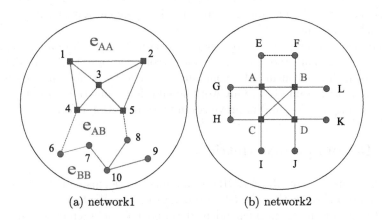

(a) network1   (b) network2

Fig. 1. Demo networks

The traditional conductance is e_{AA}/e_{AB}, but if all vertices are in a single community, the result would be 0. Hence, improved normalized conductance metric has proposed, as Formula 2, $e_A = e_{AA} + e_{BB}$, $e_B = e_{BB} + e_{AB}$.

$$C = \frac{e_{AA}}{e_{AA} + e_{AB}} - \frac{e_A e_A}{e_A e_A + e_A e_B} \tag{2}$$

This metric has some deficiencies. First, still the non-locality problem. Second, the normalized conductance metric focused on edges in networks and ignored nodes.

In summary, current mainstream community metrics exist two primary issues. Firstly, needing global information of network seems inevitable. Secondly, considering both edges and nodes scarcely in the same extent.

For instance, let's construct a community to compare different metrics, as shown in Fig. 1(b). Obviously, node A, B, C and D compose a community which inside connections are denser than outside. Edge betweenness is an indirect metric, so we take modularity and normalized conductance to measure. According to formula 1, the result Q value is -0.016. According to formula 2, the result C value is -0.06. However, if result is not positive, neither modularity metric nor normalized conductance metric indicates a community structure. Strangely, back to the network in Fig. 1(a) which community is (1, 2, 3, 4, 5) distinctly, the result Q is 0.16 and C is 0.13, both are positive and represent community structure normally.

There is no doubt that exist a question why modularity and normalized conductance metric work in network from Fig. 1(a), but failure in network from Fig. 1(b). The answer is these metrics place biased emphasis on edges, when the number of edges inside community is less than the number of community neighbor edges in the network, there exist mistake. That's the weakness of non-locality too. We can add irrelevant edges to the network arbitrarily, which has no effect on community, but could hit the community metric value, because the calculation need the number of edges in whole networks. In addition, GPU memory has hierarchy memory architecture, independent data have advantages in parallel computing.

Therefore, our key work is to design a novel metric which don't need global network information, and have a balanced consideration on both edges and nodes. Meanwhile, ensuring the community metric to fit for efficient parallel detection algorithm on GPU. Our work should figure out the inaccuracy problem in existing metrics, and improve community detection effectiveness.

4   IOR Community Metric

We propose Inner Outer Ratio (IOR) community metric, instead of trying to construct an optimized method based on previous metric. We focus on the requirement of local information, independent data, balance between edges and nodes, much of attention in our metric will be devoted to the property of parallel and distributed computing.

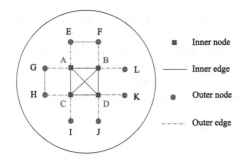

Fig. 2. Inner Outer Ratio community metric

In order to avoid the disadvantages of global information requirement, we introduce adjacency network to replace global network. We define four keywords:

Definition 1 (*InnerNodes*): Nodes in community.
Definition 2 (*OuterNodes*): Neighbor nodes of community.
Definition 3 (*InnerEdges*): Edges with two endpoints in community.
Definition 4 (*OuterEdges*): Edges with exactly only one endpoint in community.

The adjacency network is composed of InnerNodes, OuterNodes, InnerEdges and OuterEdges, it contains a community with neighbor nodes and edges. Such treatments can narrow down the scope form global network to local adjacency network effectively. Next, we consider the equilibrium between nodes and edges. We define three ratio notions:

Definition 5 (*InnerRatio*): InnerEdges/InnerNodes.
Definition 6 (*OuterRatio*): OuterEdges/OuterNodes.
Definition 7 (*InnerOuterRatio*): InnerRatio/OuterRatio.

$$IOR = (InnerEdges/InnerNodes) \,/\, (OuterEdges/OuterNodes) \qquad (3)$$

The IOR value compute formula is Formula 3. There are several design points of IOR community metric:

Point 1: InnerNodes must be more than 4, because too few nodes can't constitute community. Only if the nodes number is equal or greater than 4, the InnerEdges number is bigger than InnerNodes number.
Point 2: OuterNodes couldn't be 0, otherwise it means the community is the network.
Point 3: InnerEdges must be greater than 0, or it demonstrates no connections in the community.
Point 4: OuterEdges must be greater than 0, as OuterNodes could not be 0 and greater than or equal 1, the definition of OuterEdges suggests that if exists one outer node, there must at least exists one edge.

Accordingly, we arrange OuterNodes as the denominator, to prevent special circumstance that the community becomes whole network. Finally, the Inner

Outer Ratio must be greater than 0, on account of InnerRatio and OuterRatio both are positive.

In practical community detection, community has a limited number of sizes, and the community detection scale should be adjustable, so we give definition 8 and 9 to control community detecting scale.

Definition 8 (*MinCommunityScale*): The minimum nodes number in a community.

Definition 9 (*MaxCommunityScale*): The maximum nodes number in a community.

The *MinCommunityScale* should be equal or greater than 4. Obviously, the *MaxCommunityScale* should be less than network nodes number. Setting a reasonable community scale can increase detection speed.

Theorem 1: Suppose C is the combination of nodes and edges structure, if Inner Outer Ratio of the structure is equal or more than 1, C is community structure, and the more the better.

Proof: When Inner Outer Ratio $>= 1$, it means InnerRatio $>$ OuterRatio, which indicates a tighter connection inside community than the outside. Much more, the IOR value is the bigger the better, which depicts a powerful community structure with more connections inside. Through the simple ratio formula, we combine general community definition and mathematical formula together delicately.

Judging from compute process of IOR, our community metric is practical and suits for parallel computing, therefore can make full use of GPU performance.

5   NCBI Community Detection Algorithms

We propose Neighbor Compare Bidirectional Iteration (NCBI) Algorithm, it has two design points. First, comparing neighbor nodes number before detecting community. Second, detecting directions contain both add and remove. Through neighbor compare initialization, we detect most probable communities at the beginning instead of random search. Through bidirectional iterative, we improve accurate and search range compared to one-way iterative.

In fact, the most accurate detecting algorithm is not the iterative search, but the complete search based combination, which can cover all situations. However, nodes combination amount can be very huge even the number of nodes is not much. The community detecting algorithm based on combination is to list all nodes combination exhaustively. For instance, conducting a combination of 50 nodes from 100 nodes, the number is $C_{100}^{50} = 1.00891E + 29$, while a 64-bit unsigned integer only reaches $1.84467E + 19$, the exponent 29 is far outnumbered by exponent 19.

The reality makes us to seek a more practical algorithm [27,28]. As a complete search algorithm, detecting algorithm based on combination can avoid NP hard problem, but will occupy huge memory and need tremendous computing power that we can not afford, and the time complexity is $O(n!)$. Therefore, we have to use incomplete search algorithm, that is iterative search algorithm.

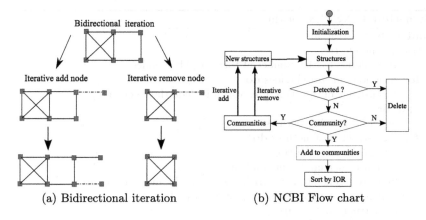

(a) Bidirectional iteration   (b) NCBI Flow chart

Fig. 3. NCBI algorithm

Most iterative search algorithms have a direction, search in increasing or decreasing. We find that the two directions can combine in social network community detecting, which can bring a more wider search range, we call it bidirectional iteration, as shown in Fig. 3(a).

Bidirectional iteration based on neighbor comparison initialization can replace the former one-way iteration and suit for parallel computing. Compared to detection algorithm based on combination, the time complexity drops to $O(nlog(n))$, and NCBI also suits for parallel computing on GPU. As shown in Algorithm 1, The initialization sorts all nodes in network by their neighbor nodes amount from most to least, then constructs a set of structures, each structure contains the node and its neighbor nodes. Afterwards, conducting bidirectional iteration search. One way is iterative adding the neighbor node, the other way is iterative removing the inner node, as depicted in Fig. 3(b).

It is important to be aware of the differences between serial and parallel thinking when programming on GPU hardware platform. In parallel computing, every thread has its own data space, and can access simultaneously, so allocating memory is important unlike serial computing.

6 Experiment

In this section, we validate NCBI community detection algorithms based on IOR Metric in CPU and GPU platform. Our data sets consists of two parts, one is test data for accuracy validation, coming from our demo networks Fig. 1(a) and (b). The other is real community data coming from popular community data sets, 'dolphin' data set contains an undirected social network of frequent associations between 62 dolphins [29], 'karate' data set contains the network of friendships between the 34 members of a karate club [30], these data sets also used in [1,12]. 'Adjnoun' data set contains the network of common adjective and noun adjacencies in the novel 'David Copperfield' [31]. The purpose of using real community data is to verify practicability and efficiency of our algorithm.

Algorithm 1. NCBI algorithm

Input: network structure
Output: communities
1: //sort all nodes by the number of their neighbor nodes
2: **for** each node in sorted.nodes **do**
3:     //construct initial structures which include their neighbours;
4: **end for**
5: //loop: each initial structures
6: **for** each struct in structures **do**
7:     if(struct is community)
8:         add to detected communities;
9:     //iterative: generate new structures from add and remove directions
10:    iterativeFunction(communities, structures) {
11:    if(newstructures == 0)
12:        return;
13:    **for** each node in neighbour nodes **do**
14:        add a neighbour node to generate a new structure;
15:    **end for**
16:    **for** each node in inner nodes **do**
17:        remove a node to generate a new structure;
18:    **end for**
19:    }
20:    refine(structures); //distinct, sort
21:    iterativeFunction(communities, structures);
22: **end for**
23: refine(communities); //distinct, sort

Our evaluating indicators are the accuracy of community metric, the best community detection time and the detected time proportion, the coverage of different algorithms, the computing time between CPU and GPU. Then, we expand experiments with these indicators on different data sets and heterogeneous hardware platform.

We compare NCBI with several existed community detection algorithms, including Quick Community Adaptation algorithm based on modularity metric [2,11], and greedy detect algorithm based on normalized conductance metric [16,17]. The results are shown in Table 1.

Table 1. The comparison of community metric

	Figure 1(a) Network	Figure 1(b) Network
Modularity	0.16	−0.016
Normalized conductance	0.13	−0.06
Inner Outer Ratio	1.6	1.5

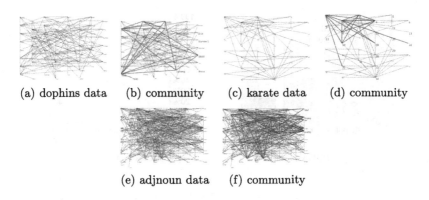

(a) dophins data   (b) community   (c) karate data   (d) community

(e) adjnoun data   (f) community

Fig. 4. Detected communities

We find out that under the special situation of the inner edges is less than outer edges in the network, the traditional community metrics can not work, while our IOR metric still valid. Besides, our algorithm result is more stable and accurate in community structure.

We perform several experiments using three different real-world dataset: dolphins, karate and adjnoun. Figure 4(a), (c) and (e) are the relations of nodes and edges in the community structure. The community detection experiment results are the best communities, which IOR value is highest, as shown in Fig. 4(b), (d) and (f), marked with bold lines.

The corresponding performance experiments are as follows:

First, we validate the advantage of neighbor comparison initialization. In Fig. 5(a), the left column represents initialization by sorting the amount of neighbor nodes, and the right column stands for initialization randomly. From the results, we notice that neighbor comparison initialization can find the best community earlier.

Second, we compare the proportion of the best community detect time in the total time. The results are shown in Fig. 5(b), the series 'NCBI' stands for our algorithm, the series 'IA' represents iterative add algorithm, and the series 'IR' indicates iterative remove algorithm. The experiments show NCBI algorithm achieves a better performance than the two traditional algorithms.

Third, we verify the advantage of NCBI algorithm compared to segmentation or aggregation algorithms, to validate our algorithm whether has a wider search range. The bidirectional iteration algorithm combines the removing edges algorithm and adding nodes algorithm, so it can coverage more range compared to a single search direction. A wider range can increase the prospects of getting a better community, the results are shown in Fig. 5(c). In the three data sets, the proportion of NCBI algorithm is all bigger than IA and IR algorithms.

Fourth, we compare the accuracy of our algorithm with traditional single direction iterative algorithms in Fig. 6. There are some points from different algorithms but have the same IOR value, that is normal, because in the same scale, the detected best IOR value is easy to overlap. The experiment results show

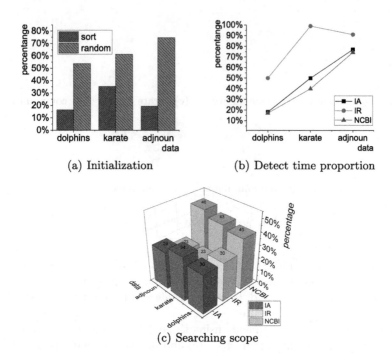

(a) Initialization   (b) Detect time proportion

(c) Searching scope

Fig. 5. Comparison experiments

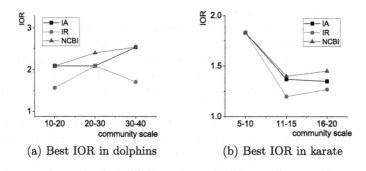

(a) Best IOR in dolphins   (b) Best IOR in karate

Fig. 6. The comparison of IOR values

NCBI algorithm has a better IOR value, that is because compare to traditional single direction iterative algorithms, our algorithm has a wider coverage.

Fifth, we compare computing performance between CPU and GPU platform. In Fig. 7(a), The X-axis is the number of communities for computing, the Y-axis is the computing time. We find that in large-scale computing of 50,000 communities, the performance improvement is noticeable based on GPU.

In Fig. 7(b), we compare the memory copy time and computing time during GPU internal processing. The X-axis and Y-axis are the same as Fig. 7(a), the column data can divide into three sections, section 'h2d' represents the time

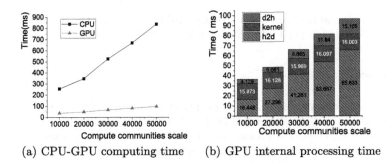

(a) CPU-GPU computing time   (b) GPU internal processing time

Fig. 7. GPU experiments

copying data from host memory to device memory, 'd2h' is device to host, and 'kernel' indicates the parallel executing time of multi-threads. It's obviously, data copy occupying a major proportion in the total processing time, showing the enormous potential of parallel computing, and data migration between CPU and GPU is worth to optimize in the future.

In summary, from the experiments of demo data, we verify the accuracy of IOR metric, from the experiments of real data, we compare the computing speed, computing time proportion, detecting range, and GPU parallel extensible ability, to prove the efficiency and practicability of NCBI algorithm.

7   Conclusion

In this paper, we solve the problem: how to detect community in social network quickly based on GPU parallel computing platform. To achieve the goal, we propose an innovative Inner Outer Ratio metric. IOR metric only needs local information instead of global information, and gives a balanced consideration both on nodes and edges. Moreover, IOR metric is lightweight, which needs less calculation and suits for parallel computing.

Afterwards, we design NCBI community defection algorithm based on IOR metric, and implement in high-performance parallel hardware platform GPU for accelerating. The NCBI algorithm has an initialization mechanism to ensure that detecting most probable communities at the beginning, then we combine the advantages of segmentation and aggregation algorithms, by expanding search range to improve detection efficiency.

Through experiments, we show that IOR metric has advantages of accuracy and practicability, NCBI algorithm is suits for high-performance parallel GPU computing, which can provide a fast and stable performance.

Acknowledgments. This work is supported by the National Science Foundation of China under Grant 61472130, the National Basic Research Program of China (973) under Grant 2012CB315805, the National Science Foundation of China under Grant 61572184, the Prospective Research Project on Future Networks of Jiangsu Future

700 G. Li et al.

Networks Innovation Institute under Grant BY2013095-1-05 and the Hunan Provincial Innovation Foundation For Postgraduate under Grant CX2014B150.

References

1. Girvan, M., Newman, M.E.J.: Community structure in social and biological networks. Proc. Natl. Acad. Sci. **99**, 7821–7826 (2002)
2. Nguyen, N.P., Dinh, T.N., Xuan, Y., Thai, M.T.: Adaptive algorithms for detecting community structure in dynamic social networks. In: Proceedings of IEEE INFOCOM, pp. 2282–2290 (2011)
3. Wu, J., Xiao, M., Huang, L.: Homing spread: community home-based multi-copy routing in mobile social networks. In: Proceedings of IEEE INFOCOM, pp. 2319–2327 (2013)
4. Wang, Y., Wu, J., Xiao, M., Zhang, D.: Heterogeneous community-based routing in opportunistic mobile social networks. In: 2014 IEEE 11th International Conference on Mobile Ad Hoc and Sensor Systems (MASS), pp. 600–605 (2014)
5. Zhang, D., Zhang, D., Xiong, H., Hsu, C.H., Vasilakos, A.V.: Basa: building mobile ad-hoc social networks on top of android. IEEE Netw. **28**(1), 4–9 (2014)
6. Nascimento, M.C.: Community detection in networks via a spectral heuristic based on the clustering coefficient. Discrete Appl. Math. **176**, 89–99 (2014)
7. Wu, Z., Zou, M.: An incremental community detection method for social tagging systems using locality-sensitive hashing. Neural Netw. **58**, 14–28 (2014)
8. Liu, R., Feng, S., Shi, R., Guo, W.: Weighted graph clustering for community detection of large social networks. Procedia Comput. Sci. **31**, 85–94 (2014)
9. Navakas, R., Dziugys, A., Peters, B.: A community-detection based approach to identification of inhomogeneities in granular matter. Phys. A Stat. Mech. Appl. **407**, 312–331 (2014)
10. Zhang, D., Hsu, C.H., Chen, M., Chen, Q., Xiong, N., Lloret, J.: Cold-start recommendation using bi-clustering and fusion for large-scale social recommender systems. IEEE Trans. Emerg. Top. Comput. **2**(2), 239–250 (2014)
11. Dinh, T.N., Nguyen, N.P., Thai, M.T.: An adaptive approximation algorithm for community detection in dynamic scale-free networks. In: Proceedings of IEEE INFOCOM, pp. 55–59 (2013)
12. Chang, C.S., Hsu, C.Y., Cheng, J., Lee, D.S.: A general probabilistic framework for detecting community structure in networks. In: Proceedings of IEEE INFOCOM, pp. 730–738 (2011)
13. Jaho, E., Karaliopoulos, M., Stavrakakis, I.: Iscode: a framework for interest similarity-based community detection in social networks. In: INFOCOM WKSHPS NetSciCom, pp. 912–917 (2011)
14. Olsen, M.: A general view on computing communities. Math. Soc. Sci. **66**(3), 331–336 (2013)
15. Xie, K., Wang, L., Wang, X., Xie, G., Zhang, G., Xie, D., Wen, J.: Sequential and adaptive sampling for matrix completion in network monitoring systems. In: 2015 IEEE Conference on Computer Communications (INFOCOM), pp. 2443–2451. IEEE (2015)
16. Viswanath, B., Post, A., Gummadi, K.P., Mislove, A.: An analysis of social network-based sybil defenses. In: Proceedings of SIGCOMM (2010)
17. Mislove, A., Viswanath, B., Gummadi, K.P., Druschel, P.: You are who you know: inferring user profiles in online social networks. In: Proceedings of WSDM (2010)

18. Hui, P., Yoneki, E., Chan, S.Y., Crowcroft, J.: Distributed community detection in delay tolerant networks. In: Proceedings of ACM SIGCOMM Workshop MOBIARCH (2007)
19. Wang, Y., Li, C., Tian, Y., Yan, H., Zhao, C., Zhang, J.: A parallel algorithm of Kirchhoff pre-stack depth migration based on GPU. In: Sun, X., Qu, W., Stojmenovic, I., Zhou, W., Li, Z., Guo, H., Min, G., Yang, T., Wu, Y., Liu, L. (eds.) ICA3PP 2014, Part II. LNCS, vol. 8631, pp. 207–218. Springer, Heidelberg (2014)
20. Liu, X., Li, M., Li, S., Peng, S.: IMGPU: GPU-accelerated influence maximization in large-scale social networks. IEEE Trans. Parallel Distrib. Syst. **25**(1), 136–145 (2014)
21. Cheong, C.Y., Huynh, H.P., Lo, D., Goh, R.S.M.: Hierarchical parallel algorithm for modularity-based community detection using GPUs. In: Wolf, F., Mohr, B., Mey, D. (eds.) Euro-Par 2013. LNCS, vol. 8097, pp. 775–787. Springer, Heidelberg (2013)
22. Seo, S.W., Kyong, J., Im, E.J.: Social network analysis algorithm on a many-core GPU. In: 2012 Fourth International Conference on Ubiquitous and Future Networks (ICUFN), pp. 217–218 (2012)
23. Yaduan, Z., Gang, L., Ying, Z., Lan, S.: Community mining algorithms for complex network based on GPU parallel computing. Appl. Res. Comput. **30**, 2426–2428 (2013)
24. Li, P.: Community structure discovery algorithm on GPU with CUDA. In: 2010 3rd IEEE International Conference on Broadband Network and Multimedia Technology (IC-BNMT), pp. 1136–1139 (2010)
25. Mrzek, M., Blazic, B.J.: Fast network communities visualization on massively parallel gpu architecture. In: 2013 36th International Convention on Information & Communication Technology Electronics & Microelectronics (MIPRO), vol. 264, no. 6, pp. 269–274 (2013)
26. Soman, J., Narang, A.: Fast community detection algorithm with gpus and multi-core architectures. In: 2011 IEEE International Parallel & Distributed Processing Symposium (IPDPS), pp. 568–579 (2011)
27. Xie, K., Wang, L., Liu, X.L., Wen, J., Cao, J.: Cooperative routing with relay assignment in multi-radio multi-hop wireless networks. In: 2014 IEEE 22nd International Symposium of Quality of Service (IWQoS), pp. 248–257 (2014)
28. Kun, X., Jiannong, C., Jigang, W.: Distributed load-balancing algorithm for fast tag reading. Int. J. Parallel Emergent Distrib. Syst. **28**(5), 434–448 (2013)
29. Lusseau, D., Schneider, K., Boisseau, O.J., Haase, P., Slooten, E., Dawson, S.M.: The bottlenose dolphin community of doubtful sound featuresa large proportion of long-lasting associations. Behav. Ecol. Sociobiol. **54**, 396–405 (2003)
30. Zachary, W.W.: An information flow model for conflict and fission in small groups. J. Anthropol. Res. **33**, 452–473 (1977)
31. Newman, M.E.J.: Finding community structure in networks using the eigenvectors of matrices. Phys. Rev. E **74**(3), 92–100 (2006)

An Efficient Privacy-Preserving Compressive Data Gathering Scheme in WSNs

Kun Xie[1,2], Xueping Ning[1(✉)], Xin Wang[3], Jigang Wen[4],
Xiaoxiao Liu[5], Shiming He[6], and Daqiang Zhang[7]

[1] College of Computer Science and Electronics Engineering,
Hunan University, Changsha 410082, China
ningxp@hnu.edu.cn
[2] The State Key Laboratory of Networking and Switching Technology,
Beijing University of Posts and Telecommmunications, Beijing 100876, China
xiekun@hnu.edu.cn
[3] Department of Electrical and Computer Engineering,
State University of New York at Stony Brook, New York 11790, USA
xwang@ece.sunysb.edu
[4] Institute of Computing Technology,
Chinese Academy of Sciences, Beijing 100080, China
wenjigang@ict.ac.cn
[5] State Grid HuNan Electric Power Company Research Insitute,
Changsha 410000, China
silverlxx@gmail.com
[6] School of Computer and Communication Engineering,
Changsha University of Science and Technology,
Changsha 410114, China
smhe@hnu.edu.cn
[7] School of Software Engineering, Tongji University, Shanghai 201804, China
dqzhang@tongji.edu.cn

Abstract. Due to the strict energy limitation and the common vulnerability of WSNs, providing efficient and security data gathering in WSNs becomes an essential problem. Compressive data gathering, which is based on the recent breakthroughs in compressive sensing theory, has been proposed as a viable approach for data gathering in WSNs at low communication overhead. Nevertheless, compressive data gathering is susceptible to various attacks due to the open wireless medium. To thwart traffic analysis/flow tracing and realize privacy preservation, this paper proposes a novel Efficient Privacy-Preserving Compressive Data Gathering Scheme which exploits homomorphic encryption functions in compressive data gathering. With homomorphic encryption on the compressive sensing encoded sensory reading messages, the proposed scheme offers two significant privacy-preserving features, message flow untraceability and message content confidentiality, for efficiently thwarting the traffic analysis attacks. Extensive performance evaluations and security analysis demonstrate the validity and efficiency of the proposed scheme.

Keywords: Homomorphic encryption function · Compressive sensing · Privacy-preserving · WSNs

© Springer International Publishing Switzerland 2015
G. Wang et al. (Eds.): ICA3PP 2015, Part I, LNCS 9528, pp. 702–715, 2015.
DOI: 10.1007/978-3-319-27119-4_49

1   Introduction

Wireless sensor networks (WSNs) are increasingly deployed in security critical applications such as environment monitoring [1,2], event detection [3–5], target counting and tracking [6–10]. However, WSNs usually consist of a large number of low-cost sensor nodes that have extremely limited sensing, computation, and communication capabilities. Moreover, as sensor nodes are prone to attacks in remote and hostile environments to gather sensitive information, security issues such as data confidentiality are extremely important. Such environments make efficient and security data gathering in WSNs very challenging.

Conventional data gathering in WSNs is done by in-network data compression in which the sensory readings are compressed by exploiting the spatial correlation of the sensed data at the sink node [11,12]. However, to gather data from N sources, in-network compression approaches need $O(N^2)$ single-hop transmissions in the worst case. Therefore, these approaches still suffer from high communication overhead.

As a ground-breaking signal processing technique developed in recent years, compressive sensing [13–17] can accurately reconstruct sparse signals with a relatively small number of random measurements. Compressive data gathering, which is based on the compressive sensing theory, has been proposed as a viable approach for data gathering in WSNs at low communication overhead [6,18]. The basic idea of compressive data gathering is to multiply each raw sensor reading with a random measurement vector of M random values and then simply sum the partial projected results at each non-leaf node along the routing paths (tree) to the sink, and the sink at last accurately reconstructs the original sensor readings based on the received small number of messages. The communication overhead is bounded by $O(MN)$, which is much smaller compared to $O(N^2)$ required in traditional in-network compression approaches.

Nevertheless, the security of compressive data gathering is generally overlooked in current work. Due to the open wireless medium, WSNs are susceptible to various attacks, such as eavesdropping and node compromising. These attacks may breach the security of WSNs, including confidentiality, integrity, and authenticity. Particularly, some advanced attacks, such as controllable event triggering attack (CETA), and random event triggering attack (RETA) aiming to obtain the measurement matrix of compressive sensing, can also to be launched in WSNs. These attacks seriously impact the privacy of compressive data gathering [19]. Despite many recent interests in applying CS theory in WSN, only the work in [19] tries to study secure compressive data gathering by protecting the measurement matrix of compressive sensing. The methods proposed may be vulnerable to the information leakage, which results in low confidentiality. Moreover, the computation and communication overhead involved to protect measurement matrix is very high.

In this paper, based on compressive sensing and Homomorphic Encryption Functions (HEFs) [20,21], we propose an Efficient Privacy-Preserving Compressive Data Gathering Scheme for WSNs. Our objective is to achieve the sensory readings confidentiality by preventing traffic analysis and flow tracing in WSNs.

To the best of our knowledge, this is the first research effort exploiting Homomorphic Encryption Functions in compressive data gathering to thwart traffic analysis/flow tracing and realize privacy preservation. We have made following contributions in the proposed scheme.

- With the employment of HEFs, the confidentiality of sensory readings transmitted in WSNs is effectively guaranteed, making it difficult for attackers to recover the plain text of sensory readings. Since only the sink knows the decryption key, the adversaries still cannot decrypt the sensory readings even if some intermediate sensor nodes are compromised, or when the adversaries obtain information on the CS measurement matrix or the routing paths (tree) for data gathering. Moreover, the coding/mixing feature of compressive data gathering can also be exploited naturally to satisfy the requirements of privacy preservation against traffic analysis and flow tracing.
- Due to the Homomorphism of HEFs, message recoding at intermediate sensor nodes can be directly performed on both the encrypted messages received and encoded sensory readings of themselves, without knowing the decryption keys or performing expensive decryption operations on each incoming message.
- We have done extensive performance evaluations and security analysis. The performance evaluations on computational complexity demonstrate the efficiency of the proposed scheme. Moreover, the security analysis demonstrates that the proposed scheme can not only resist attacks from both inside and outside the network, but also resist brute force attack. Moreover, the influence of HEFs on the recovery performance for compressive sensing is negligible. Thus, the compressive sensing feature can be kept in our Efficient Privacy-Preserving Compressive Data Gathering Scheme.

The rest of the paper is organized as follows. In Sect. 2, we present the fundamentals of compressive sensing and discuss the related work. Section 3 introduces the network model and attack model. The proposed Privacy-Preserving Compressive Data Gathering Scheme is described in Sect. 4. We present the security analysis of the proposed scheme in Sect. 5. Finally, Sect. 6 concludes the work.

2   Fundamentals and Related Work

2.1   Fundamentals

Compressive sensing (CS) is a ground-breaking signal processing theorem developed in recent years. According to the CS theory [13–17], a sparse signal can be recovered with a high probability by solving an optimization problem from non-adaptive linear projections which preserves the structure of sparse signals. Suppose $\mathbf{x} \in R^N$ is an unknown sparse vector where $\|\mathbf{x}\|_0 = K$ and $K \ll N$. We call K the sparsity level of $\mathbf{x}$. Then $\mathbf{x}$ can be reconstructed by a small number of measurements from the acquisition system by solving the following problem

$$\min_{\mathbf{x}} \|\mathbf{x}\|_0 \quad \text{subject to} \quad \mathbf{y} = \mathbf{\Phi}\mathbf{x} \tag{1}$$

where $\mathbf{\Phi}$ is an $M \times N$ measurement matrix and the number of measurements M satisfies:

$$M \geq cK \log \frac{N}{K} \tag{2}$$

where c is a constant value.

However, Eq. (1) is intractable because it is an NP-hard problem [22]. In recent research work [23,24], it has been proven that the signal $\mathbf{x}$ can be recovered by solving the following minimum l_1-norm optimization problem with a very high probability

$$\begin{align} \min_{\mathbf{x}} & \|\mathbf{x}\|_1 \\ \text{subject to} \quad & \mathbf{y} = \mathbf{\Phi x} \end{align} \tag{3}$$

with the measurement matrix $\mathbf{\Phi}$ satisfying the Restricted Isometry Property (RIP)[25], expressed as

$$(1 - \delta_s) \|\mathbf{x}\|^2 \leq \|\mathbf{\Phi x}\|^2 \leq (1 + \delta_s) \|\mathbf{x}\|^2 \tag{4}$$

where δ_s is a constant and $\delta_s \in [0, 1)$. From [26] and [27], we know that Bernoulli matrix and Gaussian random matrix satisfy the Restricted Isometry Property when M satisfies (2).

2.2   CS in WSNs

Compressive sensing is becoming a new paradigm for data gathering in WSNs as it can greatly improve the communication efficiency. In [28], a universal compressive wireless sensing scheme was proposed, in which sensed data are collected and sent by synchronized amplitude-modulated analog transmissions to the fusion center in a single hop network. In [14], the authors presented the first complete design to apply compressive sensing to data gathering for large-scale WSNs, which is shown to be able to reduce the global communication cost. Xiang et al. [15,16] aimed to minimize the energy consumption in data collection with compressive sensing and formulate a mixed integer programming for data recovering. Zhao et al. [17] proposed a CS-based data aggregation scheme which adopts Treelet as a sparse transformation tool to efficiently deal with unordered sensory data. In [29], an alternative solution for unreliable transmissions is to take more samples at the sources, so data recovery at the sink can still be performed in the face of data loss. The detection of data anomaly is formulated as a compressive sensing problem in [30].

Nevertheless, the security of compressive data gathering is generally overlooked in current work. Only one recent work [19] tries to study secure compressive data gathering in WSNs. Pengfei Hu etc. in [19] proposed two statistical inference attacks on compressive data gathering, which can estimate the measurement matrix $\mathbf{\Phi}$ when the eavesdroppers collect enough data in one or more nodes. They also proposed a new compressive data aggregation scheme SCDG to improve the data confidentiality.In every monitoring round, SCDG needs to generate new seeds sent from the sink to the sensor nodes, according to the seeds received, new measurement vectors are generated in sensor nodes. The computation and communication overhead is high. Moreover, the measurement vectors are individually generated in each node in every monitoring round, which results in a high error rate.

In contrast, this paper exploits Homomorphic Encryption Functions in compressive data gathering to thwart traffic analysis/flow tracing and realize privacy preservation. With lightweight Homomorphic Encryption Functions exploited, our scheme is efficient with low computational complexity. Moreover, the influence of HEFs on the recovery performance for compressive sensing is negligible. Thus, the good feature of compressive sensing can be kept in our Efficient Privacy-Preserving Compressive Data Gathering Scheme.

3   Network Model and Attack Model

3.1   Network Model

Consider a WSN which consists of one sink node and N randomly distributed sensor nodes. The ultimate goal of the WSN is to securely collect all data from sensor nodes at the sink with low cost. Without data aggregation, each node needs to send its sensory reading to the sink following a routing path, hence nodes around the sink will carry heavy traffic as they are supposed to relay the data from the downstream nodes. To alleviate the bottleneck problem, we adopt compressive data gathering in which the compressive sensing is applied to the data collection and the sink node collects data from various sensors along aggregation paths which forms a tree topology.

Let $\mathbf{x}(t)$ denote the sensory reading of the tth-round of the WSN with $\mathbf{x}(t) = (x_1(t), x_2(t), \cdots, x_N(t))^T$, where $x_i(t)$ ($i \in [1, N]$) corresponds to the reading of sensor S_i. Let $\mathbf{\Phi}$ denote an $M \times N$ measurement matrix, with the column vector ϕ_i assigned to sensor S_i. After all nodes obtain their readings at the tth-round, each node S_i multiplies its reading $x_i(t)$ by its coefficient column vector ϕ_i to expand its reading to a M-dimension vector $\phi_i x_i(t)$. Then S_i transmits this encoded vector $\phi_i x_i(t)$ in M messages rather than the raw data $x_i(t)$ to its upstream node. The aggregation is done by summing the coded vectors whenever they meet, therefore, the traffic load on the aggregation path is always M. After the sink collects the aggregated M-dimension vector (denote $\mathbf{y} \in R^{M \times 1}$ the aggregated M-dimension vector) rather than N raw sensory readings, a compressive sensing recovery algorithm can be utilized as a decoding algorithm to recover the original N sensory readings. The communication overhead is low and bounded by $O(MN)$.

Let us utilize Fig. 1 to illustrate the basic idea of compressive data gathering. S_1 multiplies its reading $x_1(t)$ with the coefficient vector ϕ_1, and sends encoded vector to S_2. Upon receiving the messages, S_2 multiplies its reading $x_2(t)$ with coefficient vector ϕ_2 and then sends sums $\phi_{j1} x_1(t) + \phi_{j2} x_2(t)$ ($j \in [1, M]$) to S_4. Similarly, each node S_i contributes to the relayed messages and recoded the messages by adding its own encoded data. Finally, the sink will receive a vector $\sum_{i=1}^{N} \phi_i x_i(t)$, M weighted sums of all the readings.

In the compressive data gathering scheme, the encoding process is done in a distributed fashion on each node, where each node simply performs some multiplications and summations whose computational cost can be negligibly small.

Without loss of generality, anonymous secure routing protocol [1] is deployed to assist sensor nodes to determine forwarding paths. The secure routing paths are only required to be established at the beginning and the secure routing paths are not required to change or re-established for each new monitoring round. The monitoring round of a packet can be hidden in the secure routing scheme and the attackers cannot identify the monitoring round of a packet for their further analysis.

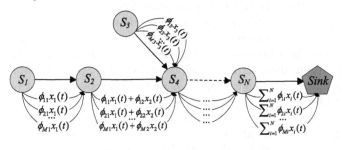

But this aggregation procedure may cause potential information leakage in network because the coefficient matrix Φ can be estimated by an adversary through statistical inference. With a good estimation of the coefficient matrix, attacker can easily recover the original sensory readings.

Fig. 1. Compressive data gathering

3.2   Attack Model

We consider following two attack models (as shown in Fig. 2) which attack the confidentiality of data.

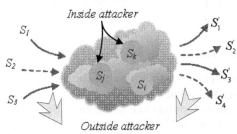

Fig. 2. Attack-model

An outside attacker can be considered as a global passive eavesdropper which has the ability to observe all network links and thus all messages transmitted in the WSN. By analyzing and comparing the messages of link outgoing packets with incoming packets, it is possible for a global outside attacker to trace flow packets in the WSNs. An inside attacker may compromise several intermediate nodes. If the intermediate nodes have the decryption keys, the message plaintext can be easily recovered.

We assume that the attacker has sufficient resources (e.g., in storage, computation and communication) to perform these advanced attacks. Both outside and inside attackers may perform more advanced traffic analysis/flow tracing techniques such as time correlation, size correlation, content correlation, and brute force.

4   Detailed Solution

Due to the typically remote and hostile deployment environment, it is difficult to provide an effective physical protection to sensors. Rather than requiring more external protection, it is essential to enforce secure compressive data gathering along the aggregation paths for high data fidelity.

There are two typical secure data aggregation categories: hop-by-hop encrypted data aggregation and end-to-end encrypted data aggregation.

In hop-by-hop encrypted data aggregation, security and data aggregation are achieved together in a hop-by-hop fashion. That is, data aggregators must decrypt every message received, aggregate the messages according to the corresponding aggregation function, and encrypt the aggregation result before forwarding it. If the inside attacker compromises the intermediate aggregators, the data confidentiality is breached because the aggregators has the decrypt key. Therefore, hop-by-hop secure data aggregation protocols cannot provide data confidentiality at data aggregators and result in higher latency because of the decryption/encryption process.

To mitigate the drawbacks of hop-by-hop secure data aggregation, end-to-end encrypted data aggregation exploits symmetric cryptography or asymmetric key cryptography functions to provide end-to-end data confidentiality. The data aggregators do not have to decrypt sensory data to perform aggregation which results in less latency and energy consumption compared to hop-by-hop secure data aggregation.

Therefore, to reduce the transmission delay and energy consumption, our Privacy-Preserving Compressive Data Gathering Scheme follows the end-to-end encrypted data aggregation. Particularly, we exploit homomorphic encryption function (HEFs) to enhance the security in the compressive data gathering. Before we give the detailed solution in Sect. 4.2, we first introduce the fundamental of Homomorphic Encryption Function.

4.1   Homomorphic Encryption Function

Homomorphic encryption is a form of encryption that allows operations on plaintext to be performed by operating on corresponding ciphertext. Let $E(x)$ denote the encryption of the message x. $E(\cdot)$ needs to satisfy the following properties:

(1) Additivity: Given the ciphertext, $E(x)$ and $E(y)$, there exists a computationally efficient algorithm $Add(\cdot, \cdot)$ such that $E(x + y) = Add(E(x), E(y))$

(2) Scalar Multiplicativity: Given $E(x)$ and a scalar t, there exists a computationally efficient algorithm $Mul(\cdot, \cdot)$ such that $E(t \cdot x) = Mul(E(x), t)$.

Benaloh [20] and Paillier [21] cryptosystems are such two additive HEFs, where the addition on plaintext can be achieved by performing a multiplicative operation on the corresponding ciphertext, i.e., $E(x_1+x_2) = E(x_1).E(x_2)$. Based on $E(t \cdot x) = E(\sum_{i=1}^{t} x)$, the following two equations can be easily derived.

$$E(t \cdot x) = E^t(x)$$
$$E(\sum_i t_i \cdot x_i) = \prod_i E^{t_i}(x) \tag{5}$$

As Paillier cryptosystem [21] is one of the few practical homomorphic public-key cryptosystems, in this paper, we employ the Paillier cryptosystem as the HEF to apply encryption to enhance the security of compressive data gathering. In the Paillier cryptosystem, given a message m and the public $key(n, g)$, the encryption function can be described as follows.

$$E(m) = g^m \cdot r^n (mod\ n^2), \tag{6}$$

where r is a random factor in the Paillier cryptosystem. It satisfies the following homomorphic property:

$$
\begin{aligned}
E(m_1) \cdot E(m_2) &= g^{m_1+m_2} \cdot (r_1 \cdot r_2)^n (mod\ n^2) \\
&= E(m_1 + m_2).
\end{aligned}
\tag{7}
$$

4.2 Operations at Sensor Nodes and Sink

Our scheme is designed based on HEF with public-key encryption. Without loss of generality, the sensory readings would be encrypted by a public key which is known for all nodes including eavesdroppers. We assume that each sink acquires two keys, the encryption key ek (public key) and the decryption key dk (private key), from an offline Trust Authority (TA) and the encryption key ek is published to all the other nodes. For security, the sink is required to negotiate the key pair in advance [31]. During the message transmission, we also assume that the encryption key ek and the monitoring round of a packet are hidden by the secure routing scheme [32], and only authenticated intermediate nodes can obtain the information.

From Fig. 1, we know that the aggregated M-dimension vector obtained at the sink utilizing traditional compressive data gathering can be written as follows:

$$\mathbf{y}(t) = \sum_{i=1}^{N} \phi_i x_i(t), (\mathbf{y}(t) \in R^{M \times 1}). \tag{8}$$

which can be further written as follows.

$$
\begin{pmatrix} y_1(t) \\ y_2(t) \\ \cdots \\ y_M(t) \end{pmatrix} = \begin{pmatrix} \phi_{11} & \phi_{12} & \phi_{13} & \cdots & \phi_{1N} \\ \phi_{21} & \phi_{22} & \phi_{23} & \cdots & \phi_{2N} \\ \cdots & \cdots & \cdots & \cdots & \cdots \\ \phi_{M1} & \phi_{M2} & \phi_{M3} & \cdots & \phi_{MN} \end{pmatrix} \begin{pmatrix} x_1(t) \\ x_2(t) \\ x_3(t) \\ \cdots \\ x_N(t) \end{pmatrix} \tag{9}
$$

$$
\Rightarrow \begin{cases} \phi_{11}x_1(t) + \phi_{12}x_2(t) + \phi_{13}x_3(t) + \cdots + \phi_{1N}x_N(t) = y_1(t) \\ \phi_{21}x_1(t) + \phi_{22}x_2(t) + \phi_{23}x_3(t) + \cdots + \phi_{2N}x_N(t) = y_2(t) \\ \cdots \\ \phi_{M1}x_1(t) + \phi_{M2}x_2(t) + \phi_{M3}x_3(t) + \cdots + \phi_{MN}x_N(t) = y_M(t) \end{cases} \tag{10}
$$

For secure compressive data gathering, we expect the sink to receive encrypted aggregated messages instead of the raw aggregating messages, that is,

$$\begin{cases} E_{ek}(\phi_{11}x_1(t) + \phi_{12}x_2(t) + \phi_{13}x_3(t) + \cdots + \phi_{1N}x_N(t)) = y_1'(t) \\ E_{ek}(\phi_{21}x_1(t) + \phi_{22}x_2(t) + \phi_{23}x_3(t) + \cdots + \phi_{2N}x_N(t)) = y_2'(t) \\ \qquad\qquad\qquad\qquad \cdots \\ E_{ek}(\phi_{M1}x_1(t) + \phi_{M2}x_2(t) + \phi_{M3}x_3(t) + \cdots + \phi_{MN}x_N(t)) = y_M'(t) \end{cases} \qquad (11)$$

where $E_{ek}()$ is the HEF encryption function using the public key ek, $y_j'(t)$ is the expected cryptal aggregating message value of $y_j(t)$ received at the sink. According to the properties of HEFs, Eq. (11) can be further written as

$$\begin{cases} E_{ek}(\phi_{11}x_1(t)) \cdot E_{ek}(\phi_{12}x_2(t)) \cdots E_{ek}(\phi_{1N}x_N(t)) = y_1'(t) \\ E_{ek}(\phi_{21}x_1(t)) \cdot E_{ek}(\phi_{22}x_2(t)) \cdots E_{ek}(\phi_{2N}x_N(t)) = y_2'(t) \\ \qquad\qquad\qquad\qquad \cdots \\ E_{ek}(\phi_{M1}x_1(t)) \cdot E_{ek}(\phi_{M2}x_2(t)) \cdots E_{ek}(\phi_{MN}x_N(t)) = y_M'(t) \end{cases} \qquad (12)$$

$$\Rightarrow \begin{cases} E_{ek}^{\phi_{11}}(x_1(t)) \cdot E_{ek}^{\phi_{12}}(x_2(t)) \cdots E_{ek}^{\phi_{1N}}(x_N(t)) = y_1'(t) \\ E_{ek}^{\phi_{21}}(x_1(t)) \cdot E_{ek}^{\phi_{22}}(x_2(t)) \cdots E_{ek}^{\phi_{2N}}(x_N(t)) = y_2'(t) \\ \qquad\qquad\qquad\qquad \cdots \\ E_{ek}^{\phi_{M1}}(x_1(t)) \cdot E_{ek}^{\phi_{M2}}(x_2(t)) \cdots E_{ek}^{\phi_{MN}}(x_N(t)) = y_M'(t) \end{cases} \qquad (13)$$

According to the Eq. (13), our Privacy-Preserving Compressive Data Gathering Scheme can be designed as follows. During the transmission, each node i needs to encrypt its own readings and obtain $E_{ek}(x_i(t))$, and then performs the exponential operation on encrypted values with the exponent being the measurement vector ϕ_i. During data forwarding in intermediate nodes, the node just needs to multiply the received data vector and its own encrypted data vector, and then forwards the new data vector to the next upstream node.

Figure 3 illustrates an example of the proposed scheme. In this figure, node S_1 first encrypts the message generated by itself, i.e. $E_{ek}(x_1(t))$, then performs the exponential operation on $E_{ek}(x_1(t))$ with the exponents being the M values in vector $\phi_1 = (\phi_{11}, \phi_{21}, \cdots, \phi_{M1})^T$. We can then have a vector of M encrypted data $(E_{ek}^{\phi_{11}}(x_1(t)), E_{ek}^{\phi_{21}}(x_1(t)), \cdots, E_{ek}^{\phi_{M1}}(x_1(t)))^T$. After the node S_2 receives the encrypted data vector from S_1, it should perform a multiplying operation on corresponding data in two vectors and obtain a new vector, i.e. $(E_{ek}^{\phi_{11}}(x_1(t)) \cdot E_{ek}^{\phi_{12}}(x_2(t)), E_{ek}^{\phi_{21}}(x_1(t)) \cdot E_{ek}^{\phi_{22}}(x_2(t)), \cdots, E_{ek}^{\phi_{M1}}(x_1(t)) \cdot E_{ek}^{\phi_{M2}}(x_2(t)))^T$, then forward this new vector to S_4. Finally, the sink node will receive the data vector encrypted with $y_j'(t) = \prod_{i=1}^{N} E_{ek}^{\phi_{ji}}(x_i(t)))$

With HEFs, intermediate nodes are allowed to directly perform multiplication on the encrypted messages. In other words, due to the homomorphism of the HEF, encryption on the summation of messages in each node can be achieved by performing a multiplication operation on the corresponding ciphertext, data forwarding can be achieved by operating on the encrypted messages without the need of knowing the decryption keys or performing the decryption operations.

After receiving the aggregated messages of a monitoring round, the sink node can follow below two steps to recover the raw sensory readings.

- **Step 1** Decrypt the received message using the corresponding decryption key dk, that is

$$y_j(t) = D_{dk}(y_j'(t))), (1 \leq j \leq M))$$ (14)

where $D_{dk}(\cdot)$ denotes the Decryption function.
- **Step 2** Solve the following compressive sensing recovery problem to recover the original sensory reading vector $\mathbf{x}(t)$ from the decrypted data $\mathbf{y}(t)$

$$\min_{\mathbf{x}(t)} \|\mathbf{x}(t)\|_1$$
$$\text{subject to} \quad \mathbf{y}(t) = \mathbf{\Phi}\mathbf{x}(t)$$ (15)

through Orthogonal Matching Pursuit (OMP) [33].

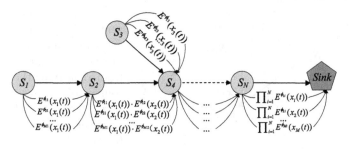

Fig. 3. Encryption model

From above steps, we can conclude that the influence of HEFs on the recovery performance for compressive sensing is negligible. Thus, the compressive sensing feature can be kept in our Efficient Privacy-Preserving Compressive Data Gathering Scheme.

5   Security Analysis

5.1   Preventing Inside Attacks

To prevent inside attacks, the first is to protect the monitoring round number. If an adversary attempts to launch a traffic-analysis attack, the adversary should first identify the packet's monitoring round number. However, in our scheme, the monitoring round number is hidden in the secure routing scheme.

The second is to resist attacks from analyzing the size correlation and content correlation, the two widely-used techniques in traffic analysis. In our scheme, the message received by an immediate node is the product of its previous nodes in topology, so adversaries cannot obtain the size of message. To launch the message content correlation attack, the adversary must intercept messages of the same monitoring round and determine if an intercepted message in some downstream link is a linear combination of some known messages. But in our scheme, it is impossible for adversary to achieve the content correlation between messages.

5.2   Preventing Outside Attacks

Our scheme can prevent timing attacks and protect route. According to [34], timing attack needs to record the set of messages coming in and going out of the network as well as the arrival and departure time respectively. As shown in Fig. 4, S_1 and S_2 are the nodes where messages come from, S_6 and S_7 are the nodes where messages go to. But in our scheme, messages in every node are encrypted, and every receiving and forwarding message in the intermediate node is the mixed message of its previous hops. In Fig. 4, the messages received in node S_6 and S_7 are just vectors, and they are the products of unknown nodes to adversary. So it is impossible for adversaries to obtain the correlated route timing information by analyzing the messages in the two sets. So attackers cannot obtain the path of source messages and their next hop from collecting messages from outside or recording the time of message forwarding. Then we can prevent the attackers from inferring the route information of message forwarding and the topology of network by timing attack.

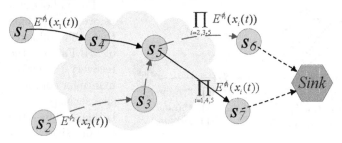

Fig. 4. Route protection

Except for preventing timing attack, we can also prevent adversaries from identifying the source of a message. For global adversary, it is easy to trace the forwarding path of a message if the encrypted message remains the same during its forwarding. In our scheme, the encrypted message is changed after getting through every node, so its hard to trace the path or to find the source of a message for adversaries.

5.3   Brute Force Attack

When adversaries adopt brute force attack to obtain the sensory readings in our scheme, the computational complexity in the brute force attack should include three parts.

First, one should know the monitoring round number of messages. Assume that we have collected the messages from W monitoring rounds, then the complexity of judging there are M messages from one monitoring round is $O(C_{MW}^M)$.

Second, because the data gathering in our scheme is along aggregation paths, to obtain the measurement matrix to further recover the original sensory data, one should infer the topological structure. Based on the messages found from the same monitoring round, if one wants to infer the topological structure to build the measurement matrix with N columns (where N is the number of sensor nodes), the complexity of identifying the first column is $O(N)$. And similarly, after identifying the first column, the complexity to identify the second column is $O(N-1)$. For a WSN consisting of N sensor nodes, the overall complexity to infer the correct topological structure to build the measurement matrix required in compressive sensing theory is $O(N!)$.

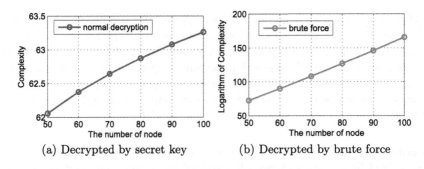

(a) Decrypted by secret key   (b) Decrypted by brute force

Fig. 5. Complexity of decryption when $K=4$, $W=5$, $q=10$, $M=8$ and $n=1000$

Third, one should compute the real message under the condition of not knowing the secret key. Attackers can collect data from a compromised node, but the data on every node is the product of encrypted data from compromised node and its previous nodes. If attackers want to infer messages of compromised node and its former nodes from the attacked node while not knowing the messages from former nodes, they need to estimate the maximum value of messages, and find out the real data in the range of zero and the maximum. The number of node in network topological structure is usually large, so it is impossible for an attacker to compromise every node to collect data, but can only estimate the real message from part of compromised nodes. Assume $q = max(x_i(t))$ is the estimated maximum, the complexity of finding correct data of one node in the range of 0 and q is $O(q+1)$. There are N nodes in our topological structure, then the complexity of finding all the plaintext on every node is $O((q+1)^N)$.

Based on the analysis above, the overall complexity for attacker to infer message by brute force is $O(C_{MW}^M(N!+(q+1)^N))$, its in factorial and exponential order. So if one wants to infer our message by brute force attack, it is impossible with the huge computation power needed.

The complexities of decryption by secret key at the sink and brute force are related to the number of nodes in the topological structure. With the increase of node number, the complexity increases almost linearly when decrypted by the secret key, and increases exponentially when decrypted by the brute force. As shown in Fig. 5, when the node number increases from 50 to 100, the complexity of normal decryption on the sink increases from 62 to 63.3, and the logarithm of complexity of brute force increases from 72 to 165.

6   Conclusion

In this paper, we propose an Efficient Privacy-Preserving Compressive Data Gathering Scheme against traffic analysis and flow tracing in WSNs. With the lightweight homomorphic encryption exploited, the proposed scheme offers two significant privacy preserving features, packet flow untraceability and message content confidentiality, which can efficiently thwart traffic analysis/flow tracing attacks. Moreover, with homomorphic encryption, the proposed scheme keeps the essence of compressive data gathering, and each sink can recover the original sensory reading through CS reconstruction algorithm after the sink decrypts the messages received. We have done extensive performance evaluations and security analysis, which demonstrates that our scheme not only has good security feature to protect the privacy, but also has low computation and communication overhead.

Acknowledgments. The work is supported by the open Foundation of State key Laboratory of Networking and Switching Technology (Beijing University of Posts and Telecommunications) under Grant No. SKLNST-2013-1-04, the Prospective Research Project on Future Networks (Jiangsu Future Networks Innovation Institute) under Grant No. BY2013095-4-06, the National Natural Science Foundation of China under Grant Nos. 61572184, 61472283, 61271185, 61173167, and 61472131, U.S. National Science Foundation under Grant Nos. ECCS-1231800 and CNS 1247924.

References

1. Xing, K., Cheng, X., Liu, F.: Location-centric storage for safety warning based on roadway sensor networks. J. Parallel Distrib. Comput. **67**(3), 336–345 (2007)
2. Xie, K., Wang, L., Wang, X.: Learning from the past: intelligent on-line weather monitoring based on matrix completion. In: ICDCS, pp. 176–185. IEEE (2014)
3. Liu, F., Cheng, X., Chen, D.: Insider attacker detection inwireless sensor networks. In: Infocom, pp. 1937–1945 (2007)
4. Wu, W., Cheng, X., Ding, M.: Localized outlying and boundary data detection in sensor networks. Knowl. Data Eng. **19**(8), 1145–1157 (2006)
5. Ding, M., Cheng, X.: Robust event boundary detection in sensor networks - a mixture model based approach. In: INFOCOM 2009, pp. 2991–2995. IEEE (2009)
6. Zhang, B., Cheng, X., Zhang, N.: Sparse target counting and localization in sensor networks based on compressive sensing. In: INFOCOM, pp. 2255–2263 (2011)
7. Wu, D., Chen, D., Xing, K.: A statistical approach for target counting in sensor-based surveillance systems. INFOCOM **131**(5), 226–234 (2012)
8. Cheng, X., Chen, D., Cheng, W.: A monte carlo method for mobile target counting. In: ICDCS, pp. 750–759 (2011)
9. Tian, X., Zhu, Y.H., Zhang, D.: Reliable and energy-efficient data forwarding in industrial wireless sensor networks. IEEE Syst,J. **PP**(99), 1–11 (2015)
10. Xie, K., Luo, W., Wang, X.: Road condition gathering with vehicular dtn. In: INFOCOM WKSHPS, pp. 576–581. IEEE (2015)
11. Tang, Y., Zhang, B., Jing, T.: Robust compressive data gathering in wireless sensor networks. Wireless Commun. **12**(6), 2754–2761 (2013)
12. Li, Y., Xie, K., Wang, X.: Pushing towards the limit of sampling rate: adaptive chasing sampling. In: MASS (2015)
13. Dl, D.: Compressed sensing. IEEE Trans. Inform. Theor. **52**(4), 1289–1306 (2006)
14. Luo, C., Wu, F., Sun, J.: Compressive data gathering for large-scale wireless sensor networks. In: Mobile computing and networking, pp. 145–156. ACM (2009)
15. Xiang, L., Luo, J., Vasilakos, A.: Compressed data aggregation for energy efficient wireless sensor networks. In: SECON, pp. 46–54 (2011)

16. Xiang, L., Luo, J., Rosenberg, C.: Compressed data aggregation: energy-efficient and high-fidelity data collection. Networking **21**(6), 1722–1735 (2013)
17. Zhao, C., Zhang, W., Yang, X.: A novel compressive sensing based data aggregation scheme for wireless sensor networks. In: ICC, pp. 18–23 (2014)
18. Kaneko, M., Agha, A.K.: Compressed sensing based protocol for interfering data recovery in multi-hop sensor networks. Commun. Lett. **18**(1), 42–45 (2014)
19. Hu, P., Xing, K., Cheng, X.: Information leaks out: attacks and countermeasures on compressive data gathering in wireless sensor networks. In: 2014 Proceedings IEEE INFOCOM, pp. 1258–1266 (2014)
20. Benaloh, J.: Dense probabilistic encryption. In: Proceedings of the Workshop on Selected Areas of Cryptography (1994)
21. Paillier, P.: Public-key cryptosystems based on composite degree residuosity classes. In: Stern, J. (ed.) EUROCRYPT 1999. LNCS, vol. 1592, pp. 223–238. Springer, Heidelberg (1999)
22. Chen, S.S., Donoho, D.L.: Atomic decomposition by basis pursuit. SIAM Rev. **43**(1), 33–61 (2001)
23. Candes, E., Romberg, J., Tao, T.: Stable signal recovery from incomplete and inaccurate measurements. Commun. Pure Appl. Math. **59**(8), 1207–1223 (2006)
24. Iwen, M.A.: Simple deterministically constructible rip matrices with sublinear fourier sampling requirements. In: CISS, pp. 870–875 (2009)
25. Emmanuel, J., Cands, T.T.: Decoding by linear programming. IEEE Trans. Inf. Theory **34**(4), 435–443 (2004)
26. Candes, E.J., Tao, T.: Near-optimal signal recovery from random projections: universal encoding strategies. Inf. Theory **52**(12), 5406–5425 (2006)
27. Candes, E.J., Tao, T.: Decoding by linear programming. Inf. Theory **51**(12), 4203–4215 (2005)
28. Bajwa, W., Haupt, J., Sayeed, A.: Compressive wireless sensing. In: IPSN, pp. 134–142 (2006)
29. Charbiwala, Z., Chakraborty, S., Zahedi, S.: Compressive oversampling for robust data transmission in sensor networks. In: INFOCOM, pp. 1–9 (2010)
30. Wang, J., Tang, S., Yin, B.: Data gathering in wireless sensor networks through intelligent compressive sensing. In: INFOCOM, pp. 603–611 (2012)
31. Challal, Y., Seba, H.: Group key management protocols: a novel taxonomy. Int. J. Inf. Technol. **2**(1), 105–118 (2005)
32. Lin, X., Lu, R., Zhu, H.: Asrpake: an anonymous secure routing protocol with authenticated key exchange for wireless ad hoc networks. In: Communications, pp. 1247–1253 (2007)
33. Joel, A., Tropp, A.C.G.: Signal recovery from random measurements via orthogonal matching pursuit. IEEE Trans. Inform. Theory **53**(12), 4655–4666 (2007)
34. Raymond, J.-F.: Traffic analysis: protocols, attacks, design issues, and open problems. In: Federrath, H. (ed.) Designing Privacy Enhancing Technologies. LNCS, vol. 2009, pp. 10–29. Springer, Heidelberg (2001)

A Group XOR-ing Coding Strategy Based on Wireless Network Overhearing

Zuoting Ning, Dafang Zhang$^{(\boxtimes)}$, and Kun Xie

College of Computer Science and Electronic Engineering,
Hunan University, Changsha 410082, China
{b12100023,dfzhang,xiekun}@hnu.edu.cn

Abstract. In the overhearing research of wireless network, the network coding theory is attracted by more and more scholars. However, the existing research based on wireless network coding, either designate a certain network topology or network scenarios, or are based on pair XOR-ing coding, which are lack of network structure adaptability and security. In two-hop wireless network, an overhearing management strategy based on group XOR-ing is proposed in this paper. Firstly, coding node receives packets from different source nodes, and encodes the packets in coding queue by the way of group XOR-ing according to the packets' information in overhearing buffer. Secondly, the sink nodes decode the received packets by using these packets in overhearing buffer, so that, sink nodes get the intended packets that are sent from corresponding source node. Finally, sink nodes delete these packets, which have been used for decoding, to hold newly overheard ones. We first make research on two-flow wireless network, when the network topology changes dynamically, we make further research on the applicability and scalability on our proposed scheme in case of single-flow and multi-flow network topology. What's more, we analyze the security of this strategy. Based on experiment and theory analysis, it is demonstrated that our scheme has higher throughput gains and lower delay than traditional schemes. Moreover, the scheme in this paper is well scalable, adaptable and secure.

Keywords: Wireless network coding · Overhearing · Group XOR-ing · Adaptive · Throughput · Delay

1 Introduction

Network coding [1] has been proved to improve network throughput, reduce network congestion, balance network overload and decrease network latency [2], and was widely recognized by the academic and industry area.

In wireless network, due to the weakness of wireless link, the packets are sometimes lost, which has deteriorated performance in network throughput, security and network latency [3–9]. Wireless overhearing is based on the broadcast nature of wireless link, nodes within the transmission range can receive the packets sent by source nodes. Combined with network coding theory, some scholars

© Springer International Publishing Switzerland 2015
G. Wang et al. (Eds.): ICA3PP 2015, Part I, LNCS 9528, pp. 716–729, 2015.
DOI: 10.1007/978-3-319-27119-4_50

have proposed wireless overhearing strategies based on network coding [10], and proved that these strategies can further improve network performance in wireless network, such as reducing the delay, improving network throughput and enhancing security. Therefore, the research on network coding overhearing management strategies [11–15] becomes a hotspot in wireless network, more and more researchers focus on how to improve the network performance and security in wireless overhearing research. Interested by this topic, we devote ourselves into wireless network coding.

Subsequently, many researchers made deep research on network coding from different aspects. From the perspective of the data stream, network coding is divided into inter-flow coding and intra-flow coding [16]; Through the linear relationship between input and output of nodes, it can be categorized into linear network coding and non-linear network coding [17]; Also, it can be divided into deterministic and random network coding [18] according to the network topology, while from its application, there are researches on distributed storage system [19] and security [20], etc.

Katti [15] and etc. proposed COPE based on inter-flow network coding, this protocol adopted lightweight XOR-ing operation to carry out network coding within two hops, and improve the network throughput by opportunistic overhearing. Based on COPE, Chachulski [21] proposed MORE protocol, which aimed at solving the routing problem of intermediate nodes in opportunistic network coding. By sending packets to multiple assistant nodes, it extended network coding from two-hop to multi-hop, which increased the network throughput. Le [22] and Omiwade [23] etc. made detailed discussion on multi-hop network coding, allowing the intermediate nodes to forward the coded packets. Literatures [24–27] proposed new network coding protocols based on packet-level layer, but there are still some complexity problems on how to apply these protocols in real scenarios. Therefore, it posed great difficulties in actual deployment of wireless network coding. Li [28] and etc. proposed a random wireless network coding method, which revealed the fact that only a few nodes get a lot of coding opportunities in stochastic network environment. The P. Mannersalo et al. [29], from the perspective of coding performance, proposed a method of reducing the number of intermediate nodes in order to improve network performance. Georgios [30] and others proposed network coding overhearing methods within two-hop model from the perspective of overhearing wireless network channel. Sink nodes sent overheard packets to achieve network throughput gain by adopting NACK mechanism. Wang [31] and etc. proposed the best-effort service and historical information based network coding strategies, in the case that capacity of overhearing buffer is less than that of the virtual queue. Best-effort service strategy was carried out to perform packets management in wireless network, which was based on the condition that overheard packets were all used for decoding. While historical-information strategy is based on decoding contribution ratio of different flows to carry out overhearing management policies.

In this paper, we propose an overhearing strategy based on group XOR-ing network coding (short for GX-Coding), which mainly focuses on coding approaches on packets, moreover, it accomplishes accurate decoding operation according to packets in overhearing buffer. Our scheme is self-adaptive, and can be applied in different network topologies. Compared with the existing network coding overhearing policies, this scheme has better network performance and security. Specifically, our contributions are as following.

Group XOR-ing Strategy. We propose the group XOR-ing coding strategy. According to the size relationship between overhearing buffer and flow virtual queue, we research out an adaptive network coding overhearing strategy that can adaptively adjust group coding approaches. For example, the strategy can choose out the fundamental packet set, according to the packets' amount from different flows or the size relation between overhearing buffer and flow virtual queue. Thus, sink nodes can successfully decode the received packets. It needs to be clear that, our strategy is based on two hops topology.

Security Enhancement. Existing strategies rarely refer the security analysis and comparison, network coding, especially, random network coding is somewhat weak in security. As to lightweight XOR-ing coding, how to ensure the security of network coding, as well as reducing the coding complexity. This paper makes detailed discussion and demonstration on security, and proves that our proposed scheme is secure, particularly in calculation.

Scalability Supporting. Firstly, in the "X" topology, we research out overhearing strategy based on group XOR-ing coding; then, when the network reduces to single-flow structure, the group XOR-ing coding is still applicable? At last, suppose the network topology evolves into multi-stream model, namely, the "Wheel" topology, whether the scheme can be applied? To single flow model in this paper, our coding scheme evolves into intra-flow group XOR-ing coding; While for the "Wheel" model, the coding scheme turns into inter-flow group XOR-ing coding. No matter what kind of network structure is, our scheme can be applied.

The paper is organized as follows. In Sect. 2, we make detailed description of the underlying network topology of this research, and elaborate researching questions of this paper; Sect. 3 focuses on our scheme, namely algorithm thoughts; Sect. 4 carries out detailed analysis and demonstration, which is primarily composed by complexity analysis, and security analysis; The Sect. 5 is experiment implementation, we perform various of experiments on our scheme, and compare the results with other methods; Finally, we conclude this paper and prospect the future work.

2   Network Topology and Problem Description

2.1   Base Model

Consider a broadcast network with a coding node R and two sink nodes D_A, D_B, as shown in Fig. 1. In this topology, there are two flows A and B, the number of network flow is denoted as Flow-num which is equal to 2, corresponding to $S_A \rightarrow D_A$ and $S_B \rightarrow D_B$, S_A and S_B represent two source node, D_A and D_B

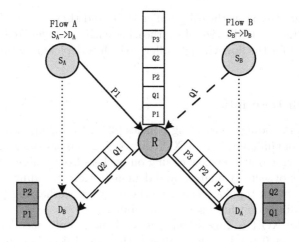

Fig. 1. Network topology.

indicate two sink nodes. P represents the packet which source node S_A send to the sink node D_A through the relay node R, while Q denotes the packet that source node S_B send to the sink node D_B via node R. Two dotted arrows represent that the sink nodes D_B, D_A can overhear the packets that source nodes S_A, S_B send to the relay node R respectively.

Each broadcast time is divided by slots, and the interval for each time slot occupies $[t, t+1)$. In each time slot, a number of data packets are transmitted through the node R. We assume that all the packets are composed of L bits, and satisfy uniform distribution.

Data rate. When r is less than r_i, $i = 1, 2$, the sink node i correctly receive all data packets transmitted over R. Receiving packets is carried out in the physical layer, such as demodulation operation. For ease of simplicity, we assume $r \in \{r1, r2\}$, and the encoding node selects $\max\{r1, r2\}$ coded packets to send directly to the two sink nodes. Thus, for each sink node, the maximum number of packets are transmitted in given time slot.

XOR-ing. To simplify the problem, we take two packets $x1, x2$ for example, XOR-ing operations are the process that two packets are summed after modulus operation by-bit, it is denoted as $x1 \oplus x2$. When the sink nodes have the original data packets participating encoding, they can accurately decode the received encoded packets; for example, when sink node D_2 has the side packet $x1$, it can carry out XOR-ing operation on received packet, namely $x1 \oplus x2$, and yields packet $x2$ by calculating $x1 \oplus (x1 \oplus x2)$.

Packet arrival. Source packets have the following properties during transmission: any packets sent to the node R can be overheard by sink nodes $D_2(D_1)$ with probability $p1(p2)$, and become side packets of the sink nodes. This probability corresponds to random overhearing and are independent. Packets are transmitted with rate $\lambda1$ and $\lambda2$ respectively.

Suppose the size of overhearing buffer is D, and that of virtual queue is M for each flow. In Fig. 1, the size of overhearing cache is 2, denoted by the green part, and it is 3 for the flow virtual buffer , which is depicted by the transparent rectangle.

2.2 Problem Description

Existing network coding overhearing policies [8, 11, 21, 24], either are carried out with packets from different flow by XOR-ing coding in pairs, or are generally performed by carrying out inter-flow coding on packets from different flows. Meanwhile, they lack of security analysis and demonstration on coding schemes, especially, when network topology changes, the existing overhearing policies based on network coding don't have good adaptability.

For pairwise XOR coding scheme, as each node only encodes the packets from two different flows, therefore, after each turn of decoding, it only can get one packet, which leads to many circles of decoding operation to get the native packets for sink nodes. Especially when the overhearing cache is available, the sink nodes need many rounds to request packets from source node, resulting in the decrease of link utilization and the increase of network latency. Using inter-flow network coding, which is performed on packets from different flows, is likely to cause difficulties to sink nodes in decoding operation, and the sink nodes need to receive enough packets from the coding node, which leads to a sharp increase of network latency. As to the encoding performance analysis, existing methods do not have good property in security, and lack security analysis. Moreover, existing researches aim at specified network topology, and are not well adapted when the network topology changes dynamically.

3   Scheme

This section puts forward the scheme of the group XOR-ing coding in wireless overhearing, it works as following: coding node gets the fundamental packet set according to the packet's number relation among different flows. Then, makes modulo and division operation among packets' amount from different flows in coding queue, and gets the coding rounds and the remainder packets quantity, according to which, coding node performs group XOR-ing operation on packets in coding queue. Meanwhile, the sink nodes choose the corresponding overheard original packets to decode received packets step-by-step, and finally obtain the corresponding data packet sent by the source node. Corresponding coding and decoding algorithm is described as follows.

Intermediate Node: Group Coding. Firstly, the relay node receives data packets from different flows i ($i = 1,$ 2) and makes statistic on the amount of packets from different flows, then executes a comparison in the quantity of packets between different flows to get minimum packet quantity Min, then do module and dividing operation between Min and the packet's amount of other flows, getting respective multiples C_n and remainder Re_n. The multiples C_n

determines the group coding rounds between flow n and i, while the remainder Re_n denotes the surplus packets quantity of flow i that participate in coding.

Algorithm 1.

00: FUNCTION GROUP-CLUSTER_CODING_PACKETS($Pcd_{i,t}$)
01: receive($pkt_{id,n}$) //receive packets from two different flows
02: count($pkt_{id,n}$) $\to N_{id}$ //makes statistic on packets amount of each flow
03: min($pkt_{j,n}$, min, j) //obtains the minimum packet number and flow id
04: **for** $i \in$ flow $[1, id]$ **do**
05:    $N_{id}/$ min $\to C_i$, N_{id} mod min $\to Re_i$; //obtains multiples and remainder
06: **for** $i \in [1, C_i]$ **do** //outer loop, determined by the multiples of another flow
07:    **for** $t \in [1, \text{min}]$ **do** //inner loop, determined by the minimum   flow
08:       $pkt_{i,1} \oplus pkt_{j,1} \oplus pkt_{i,2} \oplus pkt_{j,2} \oplus \ldots \oplus pkt_{i,t} \oplus pkt_{j,t}$ $\to p_{i,t}$;
09:       $p_{i,t} \to Pcd_{i,t}$;
10:    **end for**
11: **end for**
12: **for** $i \in [1, Re_i]$ **do**//remained packets
13:    $pkt_{id,1} \oplus pkt_{j,1} \oplus pkt_{id,2} \oplus pkt_{j,2} \oplus \ldots \oplus pkt_{id,i} \oplus pkt_{j,i}$ $\to p_{id,i}$;
14:    $p_{id,i} \to Pcd_{id,i}$;
15: **end for**
16: return;

Secondly, the relay node selects Min packets in flow n, as well as the same amount of packets in flow i, carries out group XOR-ing operation to form new coded packet $P_{n,Min}$ that is the XOR-ing result of respective Min packets from flow n and flow i. Then, makes XOR-ing operation among $P_{n,Min}$, the first packet in flow i and that of flow n to obtain packet $P_{n,Min-1}$, together with the second packet in flow i and n, packet $P_{n,Min-2}$ is obtained. By such analogy, the relay node finally gets packet $P_{n,1}$.

Thirdly, for the remained data packets in flow n, the relay node selects Re_n packets from flow i, and makes XOR-ing operation with the surplus packets in flow n, and in the same manner as described in step 2, the corresponding packet $P_{n,Ren}$, $P_{n,Ren-1}$, ..., $P_{n,1}$ can be obtained.

Finally, relay node multicasts all coded packets to the sink nodes. The process is depicted in Algorithm 1.

Sink Nodes: Group Decoding. Firstly, the nodes receive coded packets from the relay node and get the information that how many original packets are included in the coded packet.

Secondly, the sink nodes choose packets whose IDs are also contained in the header of coded packets, and carry out group XOR-ing operation between received packets and selected overheard packets, then get the original packets' ID and corresponding XOR-ed packets from the intended flow. By this way, the sink nodes obtain the series of coded packets that are combinations of packets by one tolerance from the same source node.

Thirdly, the sink nodes carry out XOR-ing operation between the packets that we finally get by step 2 according to their IDs which are contained in coded packets header. Therefore, sink nodes sequentially get every original packet sent by the corresponding source nodes.

Finally, the sink nodes delete the packets having been used for decoding from overhearing cache, and go into the next round. The decoding process is described in Algorithm 2.

Algorithm 2.

00: FUNCTION PACKET_DECODING(Pde_i, t)
01: receive($pkt[id, n]$) //receive packets from intermediate node
02: record($pkt[id, n]$) $\rightarrow$ Arr[id, num] //gets the coded packets set
03: **for** $i \in [1, num]$ **do**
04:    Pac[$id', Arr[id', 1]$] $\oplus$ Pac[$id', Arr[id', 2]$] $\oplus \ldots \oplus$
       Pac[$id', Arr[id', i]$] $\oplus pk_t \rightarrow$
05:       Pac[$id, Arr[id, 1]$] $\oplus$ Pac[$id, Arr[id, 2]$] $\oplus \ldots \oplus$
       Pac[$id, Arr[id, i]$] $\rightarrow P_i$
06:    $P_i \oplus P_{i+1} \rightarrow Pac[id, Arr[id, i]]$;
07:    **while**(Pac[$id,$]] == $Arr[id,]$) **do**//decoded packets agree with intended
       ones
08:       delete(Pac[$id', Arr[id',]$]); //deletes packets having been used for
          decoding
09: **end for**
10: **return** Pac;

---

4   Scheme Analysis

4.1   Amount of Coded Packets

In this paper, the intermediate node encodes received packets in the buffer by group XOR-ing coding. The total amount of coded packets can be represented as follows.

Theorem 1. *The sum of coded packets depends on the data flow which has the maximum packets in the buffer.*

Proof. Assume there are N data flows in the network, and the packets set of each data flow is denoted as P_i ($i = 1, 2, 3 \ldots, N$). The packets of the i-th data flow can be denote as $P_{i,j}$, $j = (1, 2, 3 \ldots, M_i)$, where M_i denotes the total number of packets in the i-th data flow. According to the principle of group XOR-ing coding, the basic packets-set is determined by the data flow which sends the fewest packets. Therefore, we firstly need to obtain the divisible and residual relations between the basic data flow $P_{\min}$ and other flows P_i. Then we can obtain the multiple C_i and reminder Re_i. The number of packets of the base data flow is $M_{\min}$, and the total rounds of encoding process will be C_i. The number of new encoded packets each round is the same as the base packets-set size, namely M_{min}. Hence, the total number of encoded packets after C_i runs is $M_{min} \times C_i$, and Re_i encoded packets will be generated by group encoding with Re_i reminder packets. Therefore, the total number of encoded packets generated by the intermediate node Num is given by

$$Num = M_{min} \times C_i + \text{Re}_i \tag{1}$$

From the equation (1), due to $\text{Re}_i < M_{min}$, the larger C_i is, the more encoded packets will be generated. Hence, the number of packets of the data flow which has the maximum value C_i is the largest.

4.2 Security

Assuming the eavesdroppers can obtain the encoded packets without knowing the encoding strategy. In this case, he cannot get any meaningful information about the original packets. Therefore, the group encoding strategy is secure.

Table 1. Factorials under different values

n	30	40	50	60	70
$n!$	2.65×10^{32}	8.16×10^{47}	3.04×10^{64}	8.32×10^{81}	1.19×10^{100}

However, if the eavesdropper knows the encoding strategy, namely, it knows that the encoded packets are generated by gradually group-encoding, but without knowing the corresponding original packets of each coded packets. In this case, the eavesdropper can only apply the method of exhaustion, and we demonstrate that the computation overhead is very huge. Suppose that the intermediate sends n packets within a given time, the eavesdropper needs to perform $O(n!)$ times to get the original information successfully, namely, the computation complexity is $O(n!)$. Table 1 shows the Factorials under different numbers of encoded packets being sent by intermediate node.

For example, if the number of encoded packets $n = 40$, and the eavesdropper can compute 10^{20} times per second, the average time of decoding the encoded packets to obtain the original packets is given by

$$T = \frac{8.16 \times 10^{47}}{365 \times 24 \times 3600 \times 10^{20}} = 2.5875 \times 10^{20} \quad \text{(years)}$$

5 Experimental Results

This paper reproduces the current popular wireless overhearing management strategies based on network coding, such as FIFO, best-effort service and historical information based strategy, and makes comparison with these three methods.

5.1 Experiment Condition

(a) **Scenarios:** We have a 9-node wireless test-bed in which one node acts as relay in circle center, while the other 8 nodes uniformly lie in the circle. The experiments described in this paper run on 802.11a with a bit-rate of 6Mb/s. Running the test-bed on 802.11b is impractical because of a high level of interference from the local wireless networks.

(b) **Software:** Nodes in the test-bed run Linux. Our implementation runs as a user space daemon, and sends and receives raw 802.11 frames from the wireless device using a libpcap-like interface. The implementation exports a network interface to the user that can be treated like any other network device (e.g., eth0).

(c) **Hardware:** Each node in the test-bed is a PC equipped with an 802.11 wireless card attached to an omni-directional antenna. The cards are based on the NETGEAR 2.4 & 5GHz 802.11a/g chip-set.

5.2 Metrics

Our experiment uses the following metrics.

(a) *Network Throughput:* The measured total end-to-end throughput, i.e., the sum of the throughput of all flows in the network as seen by their corresponding applications.

(b) *Delay:* Data transmission time in the network media, that is, the time that packets cost from entering the network to leave it.

5.3 Result Analysis

We want to realize our scheme, described in Sect. 3, in real circumstance, and form the comparison with the existing overhearing strategies based on network

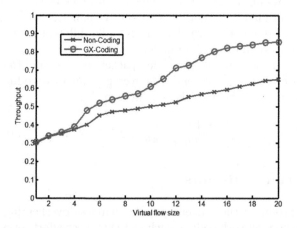

Fig. 2. Throughput gain in single direction "Alice-Bob" topology

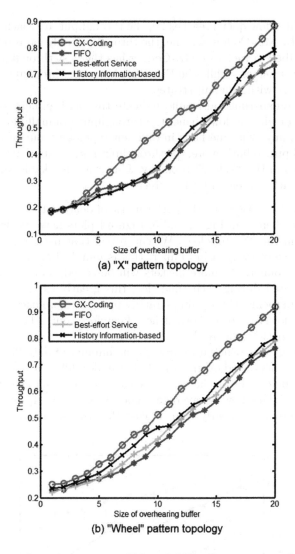

Fig. 3. Throughput gain in "X" and "Wheel" pattern topologies

coding. We focus on the throughput and delay performances over different over-hearing buffer size.

Throughput Gain. We run the overhearing strategies in different topologies, single direction "Alice-Bob", the "X" and the "Wheel" topologies depicted in previous sections. In the single direction "Alice-Bob" topology, we carry out group XOR-ing and Non-Coding strategies, and form the results showed in Fig. 2. Then, we get the results under the "X" and the "Wheel" topologies depicted in Fig. 3. As to the single direction Alice-Bob topology, our scheme has better performance in throughput, compared with Non-Coding scheme. Especially as the size of virtual flow queue reaches 20, the throughput approaches 0.85 by our scheme, while by Non-Coding scheme, the throughput only gains 0.65. As in "X" topology described in Fig. 3(a), GX-Coding has the best throughput gains than the other three schemes. While the Fig. 3(b) shows the throughput gains for the "wheel" topology with different strategies.

These above experimental results indicate that as the increase of the over-hearing buffer or virtual flow queue, the throughput gradually arises. However, compared with any other methods in different topologies, our scheme performs best in throughput. What's more, the throughput goes to above 0.9 by using GX-Coding schemes in the "Wheel" topology. This is a remarkable improvement in throughput, nearly increased by 15 percent.

Delay. We set about assessing the performance of delay in the "X" and "Wheel" topologies, and then form Figs. 4 and 5. Figure 4 plots network delay for different strategies in the "X" topology. We can reveal that network delay decreases with the increase of overhearing buffer, this is mainly because that the larger the overhearing buffer, the more packets will be coded, and then more packets will be propagated during each time slot, this greatly saves the transmission time. As to our scheme, GX-Coding strategy prompts more packets to be coded, which sharply lowers the network delay. Therefore, our scheme has the best performance in network delay than any others.

Similarly, Fig. 5, in which n represents the number of data flows, reveals the relation between delay and overhearing buffer under different number of flows in the "Wheel" topology. From the figure, we can conclude that the delay increases with the sum of data flow on average. When n equals to 4, our scheme gains least delay, approaching nearly 65ms in case that the overhearing buffer is 20.

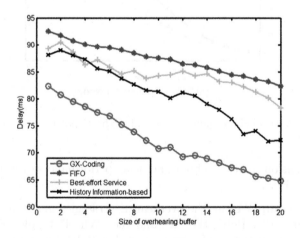

Fig. 4. Delay performance in the "X" topology

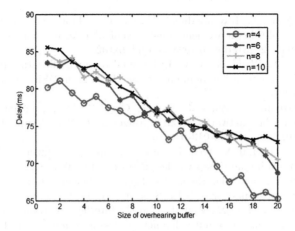

Fig. 5. Delay performance in the "Wheel" topology by GX-Coding scheme

6   Conclusion and Future Work

In two-hop network, we propose a new wireless overhearing management strategy which is based on group XOR-ing network coding. This strategy has a good feature of security, especially in computation security; Moreover, the proposed scheme has good characteristic of scalability from single flow to multi-flow. Experimental results demonstrate that, compared with other existing methods, this approach has the best performance in network throughput and delay.

In the future work, as every sink node in our group XOR-ing coding scheme has to wait until all coded packets are received, we focus on how to reduce the waiting time for these sink nodes that are meant to receive few packets.

Acknowledgments. Authors gratefully thank the anonymous reviewers for their valuable comments on this manuscript. This work is supported by the National Natural Science Foundation (NNSF) of China under Grants No. 61472130 and No. 61173167. Any opinions, findings, and conclusions or recommendations expressed in this material are those of the authors and do not necessarily reflect the views of the NNSF.

References

1. Ahlswede, R., Cai, N., Li, S.Y.R., et al.: Network information flow. IEEE Trans. Inf. Theor. **46**(4), 1204–1216 (2000)
2. Ji, L., Xiao Song, W., Cheng-ke, W.U.: Opportunistic network coding based delay-sensitive broadcast transmission algorithm. Acta Electronica Sinica **39**(5), 1214–1219 (2011)
3. Xie, K., Wang, L., Liu, X., Wen, J., Cao, J.: Cooperative routing with relay assignment in multi-radio multihop wireless networks. IEEE/ACM Trans. Networking (TON) (2015)

4. Zhang, D., Yang, Z., Raychoudhury, V., Chen, Z., Lloret, J.: An energy-efficient routing protocol using movement trend in vehicular Ad-hoc networks. Comput. J. **56**(8), 938–946 (2013). doi:10.1093/comjnl/bxt028

5. Xie, K., Cao, J., Wang, X., Wen, J.: Optimal resource allocation for reliable and energy efficient cooperative communications. IEEE Trans. Wirel. Commun. **12**(10), 4994–5007 (2013)

6. Zhang, D., Huang, H., Zhou, J., Xia, F., Chen, Z.: Detecting hot road mobility of vehicular ad hoc networks. ACM/Springer Mob. Netw. Appl. **18**(6), 803–813 (2013). doi:10.1007/s11036-013-0467-6

7. Xie, K., Wang, L., Liu, X., Wen, J., Cao, J.: Cooperative routing with relay assignment in multi-radio multi-hop wireless networks. In: IWQoS (2014)

8. Chi, K., Zhu, Y., Zhang, D.: Reliable and energy-efficient data forwarding in industrial wireless sensor networks. IEEE Syst. J. 1–11 (2015, accepted)

9. Xie, K., Wang, X., Liu, X., Wen, J., Cao, J.: Interference-aware cooperative communication in multi-radio multi-channel wireless networks. IEEE Trans. Comput. (2015)

10. Chaporkar, P., Proutiere, A.: Adaptive network coding and scheduling for maximizing throughput in wireless networks. In: ACM Mobicom (2007)

11. Paschos, G., Fragiadakis, C., Georgiadis, L., Tassiulas, L: Wireless network coding with partial overhearing information. In: Proceedings of the IEEE Infocom, pp. 2337–2345 (2013)

12. Khreishah, A., Wang, C.-C., Shroff, N.B.: Rate control with pairwise intersession network coding. IEEE/ACM Trans. Netw. **18**(3), 816–829 (2010)

13. Paschos, G.S., Georgiadis, L., Tassiulas, L.: Scheduling with pairwise XORing of packets under statistical overhearing information and feedback. Queueing Syst., special issue for Communications. Networks **72**, 361–395 (2012)

14. Georgiadis, L., Tassiulas, L.: Broadcast erasure channel with feedback capacity and algorithms. In: Workshop on Network Coding, Theory and Applications (NetCod) (2009)

15. Athanasiadou, S., Gatzianas, M., Georgiadis, L., Tassiulas, L.: XOR based coding algorithms for the 3-user broadcast erasure channel with feedback. In: RAWNET Workshop: Workshop on Resource Allocation and Cooperation in Wireless Networks, WiOPT (2012)

16. Katti, S., Rahul, H., Hu, W., et al.: XORs in the air: practical wireless network coding. IEEE/ACM Trans. Netw. **16**(3), 497–510 (2008)

17. Li, S.Y.R., Yeung, R.W., Cai, N.: Linear network coding. IEEE Trans. Inf. Theor. **49**(2), 371–381 (2003)

18. Ho, T., Karger, D., Medard, M., et al.: The benefits of coding overrouting in a randomized setting. In: IEEE International Symposium on Information Theory, Yokohama, Japan, p. 442 (2003)

19. Dimakis, G., Godfrey, P.B., Wainwright, M., et al.: Network coding for distributed storage systems. In: The 26th Annual IEEE Conference on Computer Communications, Anchorage, AK, USA (2007)

20. Ho, T., Leong, B., Koetter, R., et al.: Byzantine modification detection in multicast networks with random network coding. IEEE Trans. Inf. Theor. **54**(6), 2798–2803 (2008)

21. Chachulski, S., Jennings, M., Katti, S., et al.: Trading structure for randomness in wireless opportunistic routing. ACM SIGCOMM Comput. Commun. Rev. **37**(10), 169–180 (2007)

22. Jilin, L., Lui, J.C.S., Ming, C.D.: DCAR: Distributed codingaware routing in wireless networks. In: Proceedings of 28th IEEE International Conference on Distributed Computing Systems, pp. 462–469. IEEE Computer Society, Beijing (2008)
23. Omiwade, S., Zheng, R., Hua, C.: Practical localized network coding in wireless mesh networks. In: Fifth Annual IEEE Communications Society Conference on Sensor, Mesh and Ad Hoc Communications and Networks, pp. 332–340. IEEE Computer Society, Crowne Plaza (2008)
24. Chaporkar, P., Proutiere, A.: Adaptive network coding and scheduling for maximizing throughput in wireless networks. In: ACM MobiCom (2007)
25. Rayanchu, S., Sen, S., Wu, J., Banerjee, S., Sengupta, S.: Loss-Aware network coding for unicast wireless sessions: design, implementation, and performance evaluation. In: ACM SIGMETRICS (2008)
26. Chachulski, S., Jennings, M., Katti, S., Katabi, D.: Trading structure for randomness in wireless opportunistic routing. In: ACM SIGCOMM (2007)
27. Scheuermann, B., Hu, W., Crowcroft, J.: Near-Optimal co-ordinated coding in wireless multihop networks. In: ACM CoNEXT (2007)
28. Jilin, L., Lui, J., Dah, M.: How many packets can we encode? An analysis of practical wireless network coding. In: IEEE INFOCOM, pp. 371–375, April 2008
29. Mannersalo, P., Paschos, G.S., Gkatzikis, L.: Performance of wireless network coding: motivating small encoding numbers. arXiv: 1010.0630v1 (2010)
30. Paschos, G.S., Fragiadakis, C., Georgiadis, L., Tassiulas, L.: Wireless network coding with partial overhearing information. In: Proceedings IEEE INFOCOM, pp. 2337–2345 (2013)
31. Wang, Y., Han-cheng, L., Lin, H.P., Ping, X.K.: Overhearing management policies on network coding. Acta Electronica Sinica 1(40), 47–52 (2012)

An Energy-Balanced WSN Algorithm
Based on Active Hibernation
and Data Recovery

Changming Liu, Cai Fu[(⊠)], Deliang Xu, Lin Sun, and Lansheng Han

School of Computer, Huazhong University of Science and Technology,
Wuhan 430074, China
liuchangming@hust.edu.cn, stand_fucai@126.com

Abstract. Nowadays, many algorithms are brought up to elect the optimal nodes as head nodes for WSNs, but the network lifetime may not be optimal because of the lack of maintenance for cluster heads'(CHs) energy. Based on the above consideration, we come up with the CHs' active hibernation algorithm for dynamic clustering network. First we propose that after the CHs' energy reaches its threshold, instead of becoming the non-CHs directly, they will enter a FIFO queue in which they can hibernate. Second, in order to avoid the effect that the hibernation has on data collection and network coverage, a data recovery mechanism is designed. Third, a theoretical model is formed to analyze the effect and efficiency improvement of the CHs' hibernation work. The theoretical analysis and experiments show that without the influence of the redundant nodes, CHs' hibernation algorithm has better performance in network lifetime and energy balancing.

Keywords: Wireless sensor networks · Energy balancing · Active hibernation · Data recovery · Network lifetime

1 Introduction

Wireless sensor networks consist of many tiny, inexpensive and battery-powered wireless sensor devices that organize themselves into multihop radio networks. As the batteries of most sensor nodes are non-rechargeable. One key issue is to optimize the energy consumption of the network.

In this research field, LEACH provided an important idea to divide the nodes into different clusters which reduced the energy wastage sharply by cutting long-distance data transmission and apportioning energy consumption to every node. Much progress has been made since then on the basic of LEACH.

What energy efficient WSN routing algorithms essentially do mostly can be concluded into two aspects. One aspect is minimizing the energy consumption of the whole network and the other one is apportioning it to every node as even as possible.

As for former, the energy used in collecting and computing data is low which owes to the development in the hardware technology. So the main problem is reducing the energy used in data transmission. Many researches were made such as [1] proposed that energy was wasted when the nodes were kept in listening state but not receiving data in

G. Wang et al. (Eds.): ICA3PP 2015, Part I, LNCS 9528, pp. 730–743, 2015.
DOI: 10.1007/978-3-319-27119-4_51

data collection process. So sleeping scheduling was introduced. [4] came up with the idea that the transmission of redundant data can be reduced if it had the same hash value as it of the head node. [5] proposed an idea that the relative information entropy can be used to measure the similarity of two data, so we can calculate the relative information entropy between different data before sending it. If the similarity was beyond limit, then it would not be sent. [7] came up with a routing protocol based on position response to reduce the energy used in routing process. [8] proposed a method that enabled the CHs to notice the failure of the non-CH nodes by adding fault-tolerant mechanism so that these non-CH nodes wouldn't have to use the time division multiple access scheme which is an energy-consuming process to send data. So the energy was saved. [11] designed a new protocol to reduce the listening time and the chance of collisions to save energy. [15] proposed a node selection algorithm to further reduce the number of active node, so the energy was saved.

As for latter, there exist two aspects. (1) The energy imbalance between different clusters. (2) The energy imbalance between different nodes within a cluster. As for former, it is determined by the cluster's relative physical location, and the latter is mainly because the heavy task of the CHs. Some papers such as [3] brought up the idea that we can determine the scale of every cluster to make them equal in energy consumption. And we can find another node apart from header to share the transmitting task. [2] worked out a new election algorithm to find the optimal head node. [6] proposed that we can base header's election and clustering algorithm on the nodes' distribution density to balance the energy within the cluster. [9] brought up the problem that the single-hop communication among clusters caused serious imbalance in the energy of the cluster heads. And the optimum choice of the CHs must be made by comprehensive consideration of the remaining energy and many other information. [10] proposed that when nodes chose their routing by multihop, the residual energy and the energy of communication must be considered to balance the energy by choosing one path.

From above we can see that in order to balance the energy within a cluster, nowadays, many efforts have been made to work out new election algorithm which can find the optimal node to be the head node. Or sharing the task of header with another one which reflects the idea that sharing the huge energy consumption with the normal node. But they are not good enough to solve the problem which is brought by the heavy task of head nodes. And when a cluster is settled, the ideal physical location for the head node is also determined. Once deviating from its ideal position, the wastage in energy will increase obviously. In conclusion, certain privilege for head nodes is needed. Based on above considerations, we propose that the CHs will enter a queue and hibernate after a new header is elected, so that they can recover from their heavy task to some extent. On the one hand, it helps balancing the residual energy between the CHs and the non-CHs. On the other hand, it is conducive to keeping the CHs at their optimal location which helps the network run more efficiently. In order to reduce the influence to the integrity of data collection which is caused by CHs' hibernation, certain data recovery mechanism is designed. During the CHs' hibernation process, their data will be recovered by the correlation between the CHs and their neighbors.

2 System Model

Based on some basic research hypotheses that is often used in other studies, in this section we present the system models consisting of a network model and an energy model to formalize how this WSN works and use it as basis for our proposed algorithm.

2.1 Network Model

As is used in paper [1], we assume that a WSN has n static sensor nodes, which are all equipped with single omni-directional antennas, and the communication link between nodes is symmetric and there exists a sink node to collect the data from other sensor nodes. The network is represented as a communication graph $G = (V, E)$, where $V = \{v1, v2,..., vn\}$ denotes the set of nodes, and E denotes the set of edges referred to the communication links. And once determined, the physical location of the sensor nodes will not change, and every node has its own ID to identify each other.

2.2 Energy Model

In energy model, we assume that all the sensor nodes have the same initial energy. And each node operates in 2 physical states: active state, sleeping state. And theoretically there is another transient state. But given the situation that the energy used in switching states is negligible compared to the energy used for regular purpose. And energy used in sleeping state is extreme low [1] that it is often overlooked. So we adopt the same energy model as the one used in paper [8].

And energy model are:

When receiving data:

$$E_{Rx}(k) = E_{elec} * k \tag{1}$$

When transmitting data:

$$\begin{aligned} E_{Tx}(k, d) &= E_{elec} * k + \varepsilon_{fs} * k * d \wedge 2 (\text{if } d < d_0) \\ &= E_{elec} * k + \varepsilon_{amp} * k * d \wedge 4 (\text{if } d < d_0) \end{aligned} \tag{2}$$

k denotes the length of message in bit. d denotes the distance between two nodes in meters. d_0 is a constant.

3 Algorithm Description

This algorithm is mainly aiming at solving the problem brought by the heavy task of the head node. Through hibernation, the head node can recover from the heavy task. By data recovery, the data collection will be little effected. And by adding the data recovery task to head's neighbor nodes, it helps balancing the energy between those neighbor nodes and those nodes which are far from the head node. And this algorithm helps to make the head node work in a more stable state according to the result of experiments.

3.1   Introduction of Thinking

As we all know, in a normal dynamic election process, nodes switch in two main different statuses. When elected, one or two nodes will become the CHs. If not, it continues to be a normal node, collecting data and transmitting it to the head node. With election algorithm, it can be ensured that, to a certain extent, the cluster head is the optimal node within the cluster which helps to make the network run more efficiently. But with the operation of the network, the head node will deviate from its ideal location, and efficiency will be effected according to many experiments.

From Fig. 1, we can see that with hibernation, what is different from what is introduced above is that when the head node finishes its task, or its energy reaches a certain threshold, instead of becoming normal node directly, it will hibernate for a period of time and run at an extremely low cost. To make sure that the hibernating nodes won't be too many, the hibernating time is calculated according to the networks' current situation. In the meantime, some of its neighbor nodes will run certain data recovery algorithm to recover its data by the correlation of their data.

When the hibernation ends, the node will become a non-CHs. And its data recovery nodes will notice this event at a low cost and stop recovering data for it.

From above introductions, we can conclude that the whole hibernation process can be appropriately described as a FIFO structure, the queue, as we see in Fig. 2. When a head node reaches its threshold energy and a new head node is elected, the old one will enqueue and hibernate, and at the same time, if the queue's length is beyond limit which is calculated according to the current situation, the hibernating node at the queue's head will dequeue and become a non-CH.

3.2   Algorithm Description

Network Initialization. After completing deploying the WSN nodes, all the nodes are divided into different clusters according to certain clustering algorithm. Nodes can acquire their physical position and their distance from the sink node. And the headers of every cluster can be appointed by the sink node or through election algorithm.

Data Transmission. After the cluster is formed, normal nodes start collecting data and transmitting it to the head node. In the meantime, apart from receiving aggregating and transmitting data, the head node will collect its own data and transmit to its neighbors at a certain low frequency for data recovery purpose. When receiving the data from head, the neighbors will compare it with what he collected and work out the relative information entropy. In the meantime if they are the same, then the data could not be sent for the purpose of cutting transmission of redundant data.

Once the header reaches its energy threshold, it will commence a certain election algorithm and appoint a node as new head node.

Dynamic Election Process. When head node commences election algorithm, all the members send a basic message E_Msg(IDs,Ers,L(xs,ys)) which denotes its ID to identify itself, its residual energy and its physical location to the head. And head will

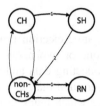

Fig. 1. Status switching process with head's hibernation.

find out the optimal one according to a certain standard, then broadcasts this message to form a new cluster.

Head's Hibernation. After the head node selects a new head, it will hibernate for a period of time whose length is determined according to the network's current situation to make sure that it will not affect the data's collection and the network's coverage and connectivity. But in the meantime, hibernation must save as much energy as it can. Then the neighbor nodes will recover the old head's data through data recovery mechanism.

When waking up, the node will collect and transmit data by itself. Its neighbor nodes will notice this event at a low cost and stop recovering data for it.

Algorithm 1. Head Node
_____

Input: 1. A communication graph G=(V,E)

2. Frequency of sending data, a

3. The current round, r

Output: A new head node N

2: if (energy>=threshold)

3:     r ++

4:         Receive, aggregate data and transmit to sink node

5:     if (r %a == 0)

6:         collect and send its data to neighbor nodes.

7:     end

8:else

9:     Run election algorithm, and find the optimal node N

10:    Broadcast the message of the elected node.

11:    Initial Timer = $ceil(\alpha * n * l)$. n denotes the scale of

        the cluster. α restrain the length of the queue and l denotes the workload of
        the head node.

12:    hibernate

13:end
_____

Algorithm 2. Header's Hibernation

    Input: Timer t
    Output: void
1: if (t > 0)
2:    t - -
3: else
4:    Start collecting and transmitting data and run normal node algorithm
 5: end

Algorithm 3. Normal Node

    Input: void
    Output: void
1: if (election starts)
2:    send E_Msg (IDs,Ers,L(xs,ys) to head node and wait for result
3:    if(elected)
4:            commence Head Node algorithm
5:    else
6:            join new head
7:        end
8: else
9:    collect and transmit data
    10:end

Algorithm 4. Recovery Node

    Input: void
    Output: void
1: collect and transmit regular data D1 to head node
2: if(D2 received)
3:    calculate $D(D1\|D2)^{[13]}$, ID = head's ID
4: end
5: if(ID hibernates)
6:    transmit D1 = D1 || D(D1 || D2) || ID to the new head
7:    if(ID wakes)
8:        run normal node algorithm
9:    end
10:end

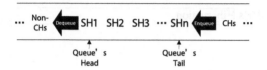

Fig. 2. Queue of the sleeping heads

3.3 Process of Data Recovery

When a neighbor node receives data m1 from the head node and what it collects is m2. It can work out D(m1‖m2) which denotes the relative information entropy of these two data and represents the similarity of information between them and transmit it when recovery work commence. And when recovery work starts, all the neighbor nodes will send D(m1‖m2) along with the ID of the hibernating node they are recovering data for and the normal data they collect. Then the new head can work out the data of the hibernating node by using the relative information entropy to the data which the recovery node collects. With all the recovery nodes' data and relative information entropy calculated, the data of the hibernating node can be recovered.

4 Algorithm Performance

It can be concluded that the time complexity of this algorithm is $O(n)$, n is the number of the nodes. Because that all the algorithms introduced above are linear in time complexity. And it is obvious that the speed of the queue's moving is depending on the energy threshold of the CHs which is determined by the election algorithm (Table 1).

Table 1. Symbol Definition

Symbols	Meaning
E_0	Initial energy
n	Number of nodes
l_0	Data packet length
l_1	Data recovery packet length
α	Ratio the hibernating nodes takes in all alive nodes
θ	Data compression rate
n_0	Average number of neighbor nodes
d_0	Average distance from non-CHs to CHs
d_1	Distance from CH to next hop
d_2	Distance from a node to its neighbor
b	Number of rounds

If the CHs don't hibernate after their task is finished. In b rounds, the total energy consumption will be E.

$$E = b[(n - 1) * E_{elec} * l_0] + (n - 1) * b * (E_{elec} * l_0 + \varepsilon_{fs} * l_0 * d_0^2)$$
$$+ b(1 - \theta)(n - 1)(E_{elec} * l_0 + \varepsilon_{fs} * l_0 * d_1^2) \tag{3}$$

If the CHs hibernate and send its data to their neighbor nodes a times in b rounds for data recovery purpose, the energy consumption will be E'.

$$E' = b * [(n - 1 - \alpha n - \alpha n n_0) * E_{elec} * l_0 + \alpha n n_0 * E_{elec} * (l_0 + l_1)]$$
$$+ b(1 - \theta)(n - 1)(E_{elec} * l_0 + \varepsilon_{fs} * l_0 * d_1^2)$$
$$+ a * (E_{elec} * l_0 + \varepsilon_{fs} * l_0 * d_2^2)$$
$$+ (n - 1 - \alpha n - \alpha n n_0 - n_0) * b * (E_{elec} * l_0 + \varepsilon_{fs} * l_0 * d_0^2) \tag{4}$$
$$+ n_0[b(E_{elec} * l_0 + \varepsilon_{fs} * l_0 * d_0^2) + a * E_{elec} * l_0]$$
$$+ \alpha n n_0 * b * [E_{elec} * (l_0 + l_1) + \varepsilon_{fs}(l_0 + l_1)d_2^2]$$

By bringing some practical parameters to these equations, we can work out some conclusions through theoretical calculation. First of all, the efficiency mentioned in the Figs. 4–6 equals (E-E')/E in numbers and we suppose that, on the basis of many simulation experiments, the regular data packet length l0 is 2000 bits long, and data recovery packet l1 is 200 bits long, both networks run 15 rounds, and in hibernation algorithm 2 rounds for the header to send its data, α is equal to 0.3 which represents the maximum ratio that the hibernating nodes takes in the whole cluster. The number of nodes in the cluster n is equal to 35, and every node has 3 nodes as their neighbor.

Conclusion 1. The upper bound of the queue's length is determined by the network's coverage strategy, the length's lower bound is zero.

Proof. If E equals E', we can calculate that α equals 0, which means if a CHs reaches its energy threshold, it will become a non-CH directly, there will be no difference. So by calculation we can find that

$$efficiency = k * \alpha * n \tag{5}$$

$$k = (b * E_{elec} * l_0 - n_0 * (b * E_{elec} * (l_0 + l_1)$$
$$+ (1 + * n_0) * b * (E_{elec} * l_0 + \varepsilon_{fs} * l_0 * d_0^2) - *n_0 * E_{elec} * b))/E \tag{6}$$

On the other hand, through certain network coverage strategy, there must be enough non-hibernating nodes to ensure the coverage of the area, and the correctness of the routing protocol must be verified as was introduced in [14].

As was proposed in [12]

$$R = 2 * M\sqrt{\frac{1 - (1 - p)^{\frac{1}{N-1}}}{\pi}} \tag{7}$$

R denoted the perceived radius of the nodes, M denoted the side length of the square area, p denoted coverage ratio, N is the number of the nodes that is needed to cover the square area. To guarantee certain coverage ratio, we can work out the upper bound of the number of hibernating nodes.

Conclusion 2. On the one hand, the upper bound of the number of round that the CHs use for data recovery can be no more than (k1-k2)/k3 of the number of the total rounds, which means a <= (k1− k2)/k3 * b. On the other hand as (a/b) decrease to 0, efficiency will have its upper bound.

Proof. Through calculation we can find that

$$efficiency = 1 - \frac{k2}{k1} - \frac{k3}{k1} * \frac{a}{b} \tag{8}$$

$$k1 = (2 - \theta)(n - 1)(E_{elec} * l_0 + \varepsilon_{fs} * l_0 * d_0^2) + (n - 1)E_{elec} * l_0 \tag{9}$$

$$\begin{aligned} k2 = &((1 - \theta) * (n - 1) + 2(n - 1 - \alpha n(1 + n_0))) * E_{elec} * l_0 \\ &+ 2\alpha * n * n_0 * E_{elec}(l_0 + l_1) + (1 - \theta)(n - 1)\varepsilon_{fs} * l_0 * d_1^2 \\ &+ (n - 1 - \alpha n(1 + n_0)) * \varepsilon_{fs} * l_0 * d_0^2 + \alpha n n_0(l_1 + l_0)d_2^2 \end{aligned} \tag{10}$$

$$k3 = E_{elec} * l_0 + \varepsilon_{fs} * l_0 * d_2^2 \tag{11}$$

And with a and b growing, efficiency will have its upper bound under this situation. As we can see from Fig. 3.

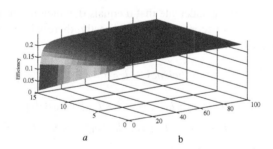

Fig. 3. The influence of the number of rounds for efficiency

As we can see, when b is greater than 15, the influence of the number of rounds is extremely slight (curved surface is close to be horizontal). And it is based on the fact that b denotes the number of rounds for the cluster's regular operation, and a denotes the number of rounds for the CHs to broadcast their data, so a is much less than b which means the number of rounds for the cluster's operations has little effect on efficiency which is approximate to be 23.6 %.

As is the case with conclusion 2, there is also a conclusion for the influence of the packet length to efficiency.

Conclusion 3. The upper bound of the length of packet which is sent for data recovery can be no more than (k1-k2)/k3 of the length of regular data packet, which means l1 <= (k1- k2)/k3 * l2. And as (l1/l2) decrease to zero, efficiency will have its upper bound.

Proof. Similar to Conclusion 2, it can be found that

$$efficiency = 1 - \frac{k5}{k4} - \frac{k6}{k4} * \frac{l_1}{l_0} \tag{12}$$

$$k4 = b(n-1)E_{elec} + \varepsilon_{fs} * d_0^2 + b(1-\theta)(n-1)(E_{elec} + \varepsilon_{fs} * d_1^2) \tag{13}$$

$$k5 = (b(2n - 2 - 2\alpha n + (1 - \theta)(n - 1)) + n_0 a) * E_{elec}$$
$$+ b(1 - \theta)(n - 1)\varepsilon_{fs} * d_1^2 + (a + \alpha n n_0 b)\varepsilon_{fs} * d_2^2 \tag{14}$$
$$+ (n - 1 - \alpha n - \alpha n n_0) * b * \varepsilon_{fs} * d_0^2$$

$$k6 = \alpha n n_0 * b(E_{elec} + \varepsilon_{fs} * d_1^2) \tag{15}$$

There is a obvious tendency that the efficiency grows as (l1/l0) decreases. But its growth rate declines when (l1/l0) is close to 0. By calculation, when l0 which denoted the length of regular data grows further to 6500 bits, the maximum of efficiency is 28.3 % and won't grow no more and the minimum is 24.6 %. And when (l1/l0) increases, efficiency will drop below zero and when (l1/l0) equals 0.4469, E = E' which means the length of the data that a recovery node sends for the purpose of recovering data for the hibernating head cannot be more than 44.69 % of the length of the regular data.

As we can see from Fig. 5, when the number of the whole cluster is less than 40, the number of the neighbor nodes that every node has in average has effect on the efficiency. It varies from 17.1 % (when $n_0 = n$) to 24.3 % (when $n_0 = 1$). But as n increases from 40, the efficiency remains unchanged which means the number of the nodes in the cluster won't have effect on the efficiency. The maximum remains 23.3 % and the minimum is 20.4 % as n_0 varies.

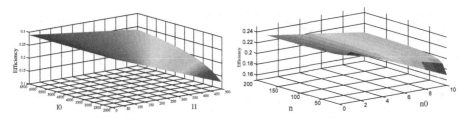

Fig. 4. The influence of the length of data.   **Fig. 5.** The influence of the number of nodes

5 Experiment and Results

Experiment compares hibernation algorithm with LEACHM, DEEC, GL-DC to prove efficiency. Nodes are randomly distributed. Network lifetime, total residual energy, the standard deviation of the cluster head's energy and average residual energy are evaluated. To avoid the influence of the redundant nodes, we adopt an environment where redundant nodes are few.

5.1 Experiment Environment

In this section, we evaluate the performance of our algorithms using environment built in MATLAB. The parameters are as followed (Table 2).

Table 2. Experiment parameters

Parameter	Value
Number of nodes	100
Area (in square meters)	200*200
Sink node's location	(100,250)
Initial energy (in joule)	3
$E_{elec}(10^{\wedge}(-9)$J/bit)	50
$E_{fs}(10^{\wedge}(-12)$J/bit/square meter)	10
$E_{amp}(10^{\wedge}(-12)$J/bit/biquadratic meter)	0.00013
DataPacket length (bit)	2000
ControlPacket length(bit)	50

5.2 Experiment Results

As we can see in Fig. 6, the number of dead nodes of DEEC and LEACHM increase linearly.GL-DC has a massive death after the beginning period, and heads hibernation algorithm's growth's rate is low in the beginning and middle period, and it increases significantly when reaching the end. This shows that hibernation algorithm is better at putting off the massive death which means that the network runs in a more efficient and stable way. This is mainly because that hibernation helps the CHs recover from their

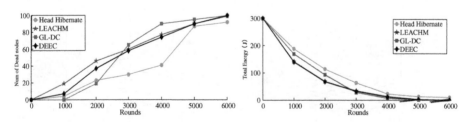

Fig. 6. Network lifetime   **Fig. 7.** Total residual energy

heavy work, so the early death which is mainly caused by the massive workload of the CHs is put off significantly.

Figure 7 shows that hibernation algorithm's energy consumption is more linear and cost less than LEACHM, DEEC and GL-DC which means that the network runs in a more stable and efficient way. This is mainly because hibernation is better at keeping the CHs at their optimal physical location, so the optimal CHs work longer that the other which makes the networks run more efficiently. And it also helps balancing the residual energy between the CHs and the non-CHs which contributes to the efficiency development of the whole network.

Figure 8 presents the standard deviation of the head's residual energy. As we can see, the differences of the CHs' energy are huge in DEEC and LEACHM compared to GL-DC and hibernation algorithm. Which means the energy of the CHs are varying a lot in DEEC and LEACHM. And the CHs in hibernation and GL-DC run in a more stable way. By saving energy for these heads, the gap of residual energy between old and new head is decreased. The chance of appearance of those which have big gap in energy is lower. So the CHs work in a more stable and efficient way.

Figure 9 shows that when that hibernation algorithm has more average residual energy than others in most of the time. While hibernation's algorithm has more survival of nodes, it has more average energy also.

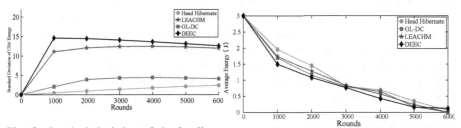

Fig. 8. Standard deviation of the head's energy

Fig. 9. Average residual energy

6 Conclusion and Future Work

6.1 Summary of the Study

This paper introduces an energy balanced algorithm for WSN combining dynamic election and hibernation. Unlike the other ways to work out new election algorithm, we propose that based on certain election algorithm, we can make the headers recover from its heavy task so that energy consumption is balanced between the CHs and the non-CHs. To avoid influencing data collection, certain data recovery mechanism is adopted.

The contributions of this novel mainly are:

- We use FIFO structure to combine dynamic election process and hibernation in order to balance the energy between the CHs and the non-CHs which is proved to be efficient and also keep the elected header at their ideal location longer than only with election process.

- During header's hibernation period, we adopt data recovery mechanism so that the influence to data collection can be reduced. And by adding data recovery task to CHs' neighbors, we can balance the energy consumption between the header's neighbors and those are far from the header to certain extent.
- The effect of this CHs' hibernation algorithm can be ensured to an appropriate level because of the fact that, as we can conclude from theoretical analysis, the referred parameters' practical values which are often adopted in many experiments are amongst the lower bound and upper bound of the theoretical calculation which means CHs' hibernation algorithm is more efficient under normal circumstances.
- By using this FIFO structure we can always adopt this CHs' hibernation algorithm to different CHs' election process. As we can see, CHs' election and CHs' hibernation are complementary to each other. Efficiency can be improved when either of these is optimized.

6.2   Future Work

To further improve the efficiency, efforts should be made to find a more scientific method to calculate the queue length. And the number of the nodes that a hibernating node uses for data recovery can be determined more optimally because that although adding more nodes to recover data for the hibernating node can improve the accuracy of the data that is recovered in this data recovery mechanism, but the growth rate will increase slowly and the energy wastage will increase slowly. And to improve the efficiency of the network, we can adopt a more advanced data recovery mechanism or CHs' election algorithm.

Acknowledgments. The paper is supported by China NSF(61572222, 61272405, 60903175, 61272033, 61272451) and University Innovation Foundation (2013TS102, 2013TS106).

References

1. Ma, J., Lou, W., Li, X.-Y.: Contiguous link scheduling for data aggregation in wireless sensor networks. IEEE Trans. Parallel Distrib. Syst. **25**(7), 1691–1701 (2014)
2. Lee, S., Lee, J., Sin, H.:An energy-efficient distributed unequal clustering protocal for wireless sensor networks. In: World Academy of Science (2008)
3. Aslam, N., Phillips, W., Robertson, W., Sivakumar, S.: A multi-criterion optimization technique for energy efficient cluster formation in wireless sensor networks. In: Information Fusion (2011)
4. Villas, L.A., Guidoni, D.L., Araújo, R.B., Boukerche, A., Loureiro, A.A.F.: A scalable and dynamic data aggregation aware routing protocol for wireless sensor networks. In: Proceedings of the 13th ACM International Conference on Modeling, Analysis, and Simulation of Wireless and Mobile Systems (2010)

5. Qiang, Z., Xiao, L., Xiaochen, C.: Research on the scheme of data aggregation based on clustering for wireless sensor network. Chin. J. Sens. Actuators **23**(12), 1163–1167 (2010)
6. Singh, B., Lobiyal, D.K.: An energy-efficient adaptive clustering algorithm with load balancing for wireless sensor network. Int. J. Sensor Netw. **12**(1), 37–52 (2012)
7. Zaman, N., Low, T.J., Alghamdi, T.: Energy efficient routing protocol for wireless sensor network. In: 2014 16th International Conference on Advanced Communication Technology (ICACT) (2014)
8. Karim, L., Nasser, N., Sheltami, T.: A fault-tolerant energy-efficient clustering protocol of wireless sensor network. Wirel. Commun. Mob. Comput. **14**(2), 175–185 (2014)
9. Li, X., Gang, W., Zhongqi, L., Yanyan, Z.: An energy-efficient routing protocol based on particle swarm clustering algorithm and inter-cluster routing algorithm for WSN. In: Control and Decision Conference (CCDC) (2013)
10. Yessad, S., Tazarart, N., Bakli, L., Medjkoune-Bouallouche, L., Aissani, D.: Balanced energy efficient routing protocol for WSN. In: Communication and Information Technology International Conference (2012)
11. Jha, M.K., Pandey, A.K., Pal, D., Mohan, A.: An energy-efficient multi-layer MAC (ML-MAC) protocol for wireless sensor networks. AEU-Int. J. Electron. Commun. **65**(3), 209–216 (2011)
12. Yannis, M., Katsaros, D., Alexis, D.: Topology control algorithm for wireless sensor networks, a critical survey[c]. In: 11th International Conference on Computer System and Technology, pp. 1–10 (2010)
13. Yager, R.R.: On the entropy of fuzzy measures. IEEE Trans. Fuzzy Syst. **8**(4), 453–461 (2000)
14. Chen, Z., Zhang, D., Zhu, R., Ma, Y., Yin, P., Xie, F.: A review of automated formal verification of ad hoc routing protocols for wireless sensor networks. Sensor Lett. **11**(5), 752–764 (2013)
15. Cheng, H., Su, Z., Zhang, D., Lloret, J., Yu, Z.: Energy-efficient node selection algorithm with correlation optimization in wireless sensor networks. Int. J. Distrib. Sensor Netw. **2014** (576573), 14 (2014)

MN-ALG: A Data Delivery Algorithm for Large Scale Wireless Electronic Shelf Label System

Yingzhuang Chen[1], Qifei Zhang[1(✉)], Chaofan Tu[1], Yuchang Zhang[1],
Fan Bai[2], Yinchao Xue[1], and Sheng Zhang[3]

[1] School of Software Technology, Zhejiang University, Ningbo 315048, China
zhangqf@cst.zju.edu.cn
[2] Department of Electrical and Electronic Engineering,
University of Nottingham, Nottingham, UK
[3] Chinese People's Liberation Army 73610 Army, Nanjing, Jiangsu, China

Abstract. Electronic Shelf Labeling System (ESLs) can be used in various application scenes such as in warehouses and supermarkets, it significantly improves the management efficiency. In this paper, we propose a data delivery algorithm called "MN-ALG", on the purpose to fulfill: the ability of building large-scale networks; the requirement of label nodes using "Sleep/Waken" working mode; achieving efficient transmission of data. MN-ALG broadcasts notification messages to destination nodes via an auxiliary channel, achieves data delivery and notification process in parallel, and by controlling notified number, the problem of channel congestion could be avoided. We implement MN-ALG in real-world environment. Experimental data show, implementing the proposed MN-ALG algorithm would help enlarge the scale as well meets the latency constraints performance of the system in comparison with other data delivery algorithms.

Keywords: WSN · ESLs · Data delivery algorithm · Large-scale · Real-time · Sleep/Waken

1 Introduction

The rapid development of wireless sensor networks (WSN) [1] has brought a profound impact to all areas of people's life. Wireless electronic shelf label system (ESLs) [12] is a specific application of WSN. It can be applied to a wide range of application scenarios such as warehouse management [2] and supermarket merchandise management [3−5]. Label nodes' downstream data released from upper software system and upstream data of the label cluster generated are delivered through a wireless gateway (which is commonly called as "Access Point", "AP", or "sink node"). Downstream data, mainly about application data such as screen updating data, LED indicating command and so on, while upstream data, including the running states report, event executed feedback etc.

As it's shown in Fig. 1(a), wireless ESLs is a network made up of a wireless AP and a numerous of label nodes. AP maintains the network and is responsible for

© Springer International Publishing Switzerland 2015
G. Wang et al. (Eds.): ICA3PP 2015, Part I, LNCS 9528, pp. 744–754, 2015.
DOI: 10.1007/978-3-319-27119-4_52

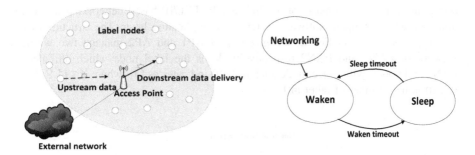

(a). A working state of ESLs system   (b). Label node's logical ruing state machine

Fig. 1 (a). A working state of ESLs system, (b). Label node's logical ruing state machine

delivering the label nodes' task data. In Fig. 1(a), the "Access Point" is doing a downstream data delivery to a label.

Figure 1(b) illustrates the flow chart of how the label nodes run. Firstly, all of the nodes shall join in a network maintained by a gateway (AP). Then the nodes are periodically switched between "waken" and "sleep" state. By letting nodes entering to "sleep" mode when they having no task event to deal with, the overall power consumption of the system can be significantly reduced [1, 12]. Only in "waken" state do labels handle their task events. The system has the following requirements to fulfill:

(1) Real-time. After entering the "waken" state, nodes' task data should be timely delivered in the cycle;
(2) Large-scale network capacity. In some scenarios, the system may consist of thousands of label nodes [11], which may lead to data delivery congestion in short sleep cycle. In order to guarantee the Quality of Service (QoS) for delivery, the congestion problem [13, 14] should be effectively handled with.

All of the ESL systems mentioned in [2–5] have their own characters. However, most of them are mainly focus on the aspects of low power, system architecture and application use, while the study for large-scale networks with good data delivery performance is rare but it is of great importance for application requirement. On the requirements of large-scale network, low-power, short data delivery delay, many typical algorithms for delivery are not suit well for meeting them. For those concerns, the paper proposes a data-delivery algorithm called "MN-ALG" and applied to an actual system. Test results show that the algorithm is perfectly suit for real application environment with real-time data delivery as well as its inherent advantage for supporting large-scale networking.

2 System Design

2.1 Topology

The ESL system is star-topology based [1]. In accordance with the IOT hierarchical division manner [6], the system's sensing layer is composed of wireless electronic label nodes, network layer consists of a wireless AP, TCP/IP based networking and communicating server, upper software system is in application layer. The structure of the system as is shown in Fig. 2, the gateway of AP1 and AP2 manage two wireless network of PAN1 and PAN2 respectively, T_X is the label node which affiliated to PAN1 and bound with object node(such a shelf) indicates as O_X, where $X \in \{1,2,3, \dots , m\}$, m is the number of label in PAN1.

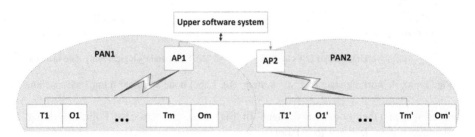

Fig. 2. Architecture of ESL system

2.2 Running requirements

Wireless Label system should meet the following running requirements:

(1) Low power consumption. In order to extend the lifetime of the system and reduce maintenance costs, energy-saving strategy such as with working mode of "sleep/waken" should be applied to the system.

(2) High QoS needs to be guaranteed for data delivery. This mainly includes two aspects: one is the quality of message transmission. Since the network is large-scale, concerns about the problem of channel congestion and the success rate of delivery should be made; the other one is delay factor of the data delivery. The communicating channel shall be as clear as possible, once the node becomes awaken, the delivery process is should be carried on as soon as possible if there is data to delivery.

In a summary, in order to meet the above-mentioned requirements, the following two problems are concerned: ① how to make the label node to be capable of delivering data when it is in the "waken" state; ② how to synchronize the cluster accessing the channel to avoid the problem of channel congestion. In this paper, a synchronization strategy is proposed to solving them.

2.3 System Model

The paper studies single network and the topology of the system is tree topology (while it also easily extended to any multi-level structures), the number of the node cluster is noted as Tnu, the Access point is noted as S, the nodes set is noted as N, that is $N = \{T_X\}$, $X \in \{1, 2, \cdots, Tnu\}$.

- T_{si}: T_i's sleep time, where $i \in \{1, 2, \cdots, T_{nu}\}$ (as the same in the followings);
- T_{ai}: T_i's waken up time;
- T_{nu}: Number of nodes of network, $T_{nu} = |M|$;
- RT_i: The real-time measurement for T_i's downstream data delivery. When Ti wakes up from T_{si} cycle to T_{ai} cycle, its data shall be delivered during that cycle, rather than the next T_{ai} cycle.

Nodes of T_x shall be pushed to their own T_{ax} state when T_i is in T_{si} state, where $X \in \{1, 2, \cdots, T_{nu}\}$, $x \neq i$, as to ensure during which time other nodes can do delivering when T_i is sleeping, avoiding channel traffic jam with T_i. As shown on Fig. 3, at time point of a, Ti's downstream data Ed released to S, while T_i is in sleep state, the data cannot be delivered immediately until it enters the next waken state. At time point of b, where T_i firstly enters the waken state, the process of data delivery carries on. It can be inferred that $|RT_i| \approx |b - a|$.

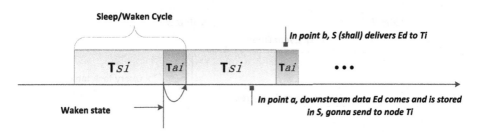

Fig. 3. Synchronization schema for Ti's data delivery

T_i's task data Ed is comes from upper-ware, Ed is temporarily stored in S. when T_i enters T_{ai} (waken period) from T_{si} (the sleep cycle), Ed shall be delivered to T_i by S. Assuming Eu is the upstream data, its generation and report process are in its waken state, the delivery process of Ed is using a CSMA/CA procedure and is of good real-time performance.

Key issues to solve. To design and implement an algorithm which can synchronize S and T_i to delivers Ed and satisfies:

(1) Delivering data in the first T_{ai} period, that's to say that $|RT_i| \leq |T_{si}| + |T_{ai}|$;
(2) Achieving large-scale network capacity.

3 Nodes Monitor Notification Algorithm

3.1 Two typical Synchronization algorithms

Node Wakes Up and Query-Response Algorithm. Let $\phi(t)$ as the nodes set readying to use the channel at time point of t, and γ as the node of getting the right to access channel. $y = Fc(t)$, where Fc is the solving procedure to access the channel for a node which is y, normally, it includes the execution process of $CSMA/CA$ in MAC layer. The steps of the algorithm basically are as the following:

- α enters to waken state, where $\alpha \in \{Tx \mid x \in \{1, 2, 3 \ldots, Tnu\}\}$, node α is added to $\phi(t)$, $\phi(t) \cup \{a\} \rightarrow \phi(t)$
- $\alpha = Fc(t)$, α get the access right for the channel, and $\phi(t) - \{a\} \rightarrow \phi(t)$
- S receives the query message of α, queries task table of α, ready to response to α
- $S = Fc(t)$, S replies the task data to α

As shown in Fig. 4, label A periodically transmits query request using the CSMA/CA mechanism after waking up, AP returns a query response in a period of time, A is waiting for the task data to reply, after doing the assignment operation, the node reenters the sleep/query process.

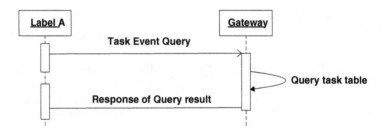

Fig. 4. Query-Response algorithm

The algorithm is used in the systems of both [3, 5]. In a small-scale network, the algorithm works well and it can achieve the good performance of the data delivery [3]. However, it also has the following challenges:

(1) A plurality of nodes may wake up and send a query message at the same time, which results in intensive competition for channel accessing. As a result, the competitor nodes will perform a back-off window which prolongs the delay of data delivery. Meanwhile, the energy consumption increase;
(2) The load capacity of the channel is positively correlated with the nodes scale of the network.

De Mil P *et al.* [5] used the algorithm to deploy a system which had 12,000 nodes, the delivery success rate was just about 75 % while Tsi was set up to 5 minutes. It can be inferred that the scale of the network is limited and the goal for real-time is difficult to guarantee by using the protocol [16].

Sleep Cycle Synchronization Algorithm Based on Time Slot. The main principle of this algorithm is to synchronize each node's wake-up time point. By using the assigned time, each node wakes up intermittently and communicates with the AP for data transfer in a predefined time slice, while during which time other nodes are in sleep state [15]. As shown in Fig. 5, AP synchronizes the sleep time and slot time for each

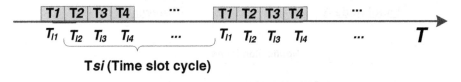

Fig. 5. Sleep cycle synchronization algorithm

node, T_{si} and T/i is the sleep time cycle and time slice assigned by AP to node T_i respectively, AP and T_i will do a communication process in a slice of T/i.

The algorithm can control the nodes' wake up time points, however, with the high requirement of achieving expected synchronization effect, the nodes' crystal stability are very essential. The setting of the sleep cycle is not only concerned about the max supported number of nodes, but also matters the application data size, data transfer timing issues and other factors. It may require multiple slots in total when it comes to deliver the long data.

3.2 Nodes Monitor Notification Algorithm (MN-ALG)

In this paper, MN-ALG algorithm is proposed, similar to [8], which employs a radio frequency waking up (Wake-Up Radio) mechanism. The main characteristic of MN-ALG is that AP can send a message to the cluster to notice the wanted labels (activate the node) to retrieve data from AP. AP has a notification module, and each label node has a counterpart of monitoring module. The monitoring module periodically wakes up for a short time to listen notification. When the listening node detects its notification for activating, it will be activated (to work state) and it will send a handshake message to the AP, and start receiving application data.

Monitor module periodically monitors notice messages. Notification module sends notification messages until the target labels have been activated (by receiving handshake message). After monitoring module receives the notification broadcast, it resolves and checks the notification message. Once the nodes detect they own wake-up notification, they will turn to a functioning state and try to get the task data from the gateway as the timing diagram shown in Fig. 6.

The synchronization schematic of AP's notification module and label's monitor module is shown in Fig. 7, where the parameters' meaning as:

- *TC*: the cycle of monitor module entering to listen;
- *T1*: the size of monitor module listening time slice;
- *T2*: the cycle of notification module sends each notification frame;

To ensure the integrated reception of each notice frame, here it shall satisfy $T1 > 2T2$. In time point of ①, the AP generates a notification command, after which it sends the command to its sub-module of "MN" designating to notice node A (listen module A in Fig. 7). MN module adds and assembles the item to wake-up frame and sends it with *T2* interval by each notification frame. In time point of ②, node A enters into listen time, after receiving frames F3 (in this figure, the label has missed frame F2),

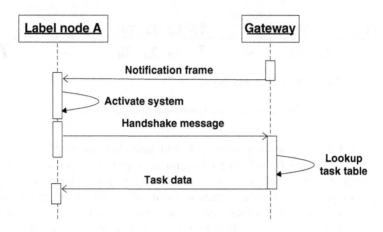

Fig. 6. MN-ALG algorithm

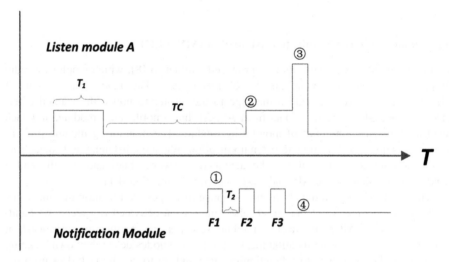

Fig. 7. MN-ALG schematic algorithm

node A resolves F3 and recognizes its wake-up command, in time point ③, node A activates the system and sends a "handshake" message to AP, which indicating node A has been waken up. And begin to do the following logic procedure. On MN module sides, it stops sending Node A's notification (in time ④).

In order to improve data delivery efficiency, notice frame is designed to contain a plurality of wake-up items. the gateway RF module is designed as two separate sub-modules, the notification and data delivery module, the 2 modules use separate channels, notification module is responsible to wake up labels, data delivery module is responsible for the data delivery. By separating the 2 modules, the notification and business data delivery work can be achieved in parallel.

AP will send notification broadcast to destination nodes if AP received task data from upper-ware. Once the destination nodes are activated, their work channel will be switched from the listening channel to the delivery channel, after which each of them will send a handshake message with a CSMA/CA procedure to inform the AP that "I have been notified and activated" and start performing data transmission process.

Compared with the query-response algorithm, the label node in MN-ALG does not send a query message, which can avoid channel contention with other waken nodes. The AP controls the simultaneous number of label nodes to wake up by sensing the channel busy status, thus it can improve the data delivery efficiency and avoid the channel congestion significantly; most importantly, the channel resources is almost idle if there is no application data to transmit, channel resource are not having constrained relationship with the number of the network, that is to say it has the ability to build large-scale network in the sense of channel resource.

Through the introduction of the three kinds of algorithms mentioned above, Table 1 provides a brief comparison of them.

Table 1. Summary comparison of the mentioned algorithms

Algorithm	Relations between real-time requirement and network capacity	Requirement for implement
Query-response	The more the network number of nodes has, the more serious of channel congestion will be, which causes data delivery success rate reduced, the performance of real-time worsen, system power consumption increased	Relatively low
Sleep synchronization	Time slices are relatively fixed, also the number of time slots and network capacity are limited.	Synchronization deviating and correction process is complex; Time slice allocation mechanism is complex
MN-ALG	Could easily reach the goal of real-time and build a large-scale network	An extra module is introduced as notification module

4   Experiments and Analysis

The system was implemented in real-world. In order to test its good performance in large scale nodes environment, constrained by limited test resources, we deployed 1200 labels, all of the nodes' sleep cycle (TC) is set to 4s, listening module listening period is 16ms, the maximum number set for simultaneously waking up (tMa) is 5, which means that the nodes accessing the channel at the same time is utmost to 5 by the notification module. The sending interval of each notification frame is 7ms. This paper designs four different test groups as following, let tCa as the number of simultaneously wakes up items of each test group. The test groups are:

(A) test group 1, 1 label node for waking up test (t Ca = 1), runs 6 test cases;
(B) test group 2, 3 label nodes for simultaneously waking up (t Ca = 3), runs 4 test cases;
(C) test group 3, 5 label nodes for simultaneously waking up (t Ca = 5), runs 5 test cases;
(D) test group 4, 8 label nodes for simultaneously waking up (t Ca = 8), runs 5 test cases;

Test results are as shown in Tables 2, 3, 4, 5. Each data item is (t A /t W, the units are in seconds), where t A represents the interval between AP receives destination node's application data and AP receives the node's activated handshake message. t W represents the interval between AP receives destination node's application data and notification module starts sending notice message to the destination node(s).

Table 2. Test group 1(t Ca = 1)

Test case	Node 1
1	2.2/0
2	1.5/0
3	3.1/0
4	4.1*/0
5	3.8/0

Table 3. Test group 2(t Ca = 3)

Test case	Node 1	Node 2	Node 3
1	1.4/0	2.5/0	2.4/0
2	3.2/0	2.7/0	1.9/0
3	2.2/0	1.3/0	3.6/0
4	1.9/0	4.2/0	2.3/0

Table 4. Test group 3(t Ca = 5)

Test case	Node 1	Node 2	Node 3	Node 4	Node 5
1	3.8/0	2.9/0	2.8/0	1.9/0	3.2/0
2	2.1/0	4.1/0	2.3/0	2.8/0	3.1/0
3	2.7/0	2.3/0	3.0/0	3.8/0	1.9/0
4	3.3/0	4.2/0	2.8/0	1.6/0	2.0/0
5	1.4/0	2.6/0	1.9/0	2.7/0	1.4/0

From the above test tables, conclusions could draw as the followings:
① When t Ca ≤ t Ma, then t W is zero. AP immediately pushes wake-up command to notification module without hold-on time;
② When t Ca > t Ma, then t W > 0. Gateway controls the maximum wakes up number in order to control the channel accessing of label nodes;

Table 5. Test group 4(t Ca = 8)

Test case	Node 1	Node 2	Node 3	Node 4	Node 5	Node 6	Node 7	Node 8
1	3.8/0	2.9/0	2.8/0	1.9/0	3.2/0	4.8/1.9	3.9/2.8	4.2/2.9
2	2.1/0	4.1/0	2.3/0	2.8/0	3.1/0	3.3/2.1	4.6/2.3	5.1/2.8
3	2.7/0	2.3/0	3.0/0	3.8/0	1.9/0	3.3/1.9	4.1/2.3	6.8/2.7
4	3.3/0	4.2/0	2.8/0	1.6/0	2.0/0	3.0/1.6	5.4/2.0	6.0/3.3
5	1.4/0	2.6/0	1.9/0	2.7/0	1.4/0	3.4/1.4	5.2/1.4	3.8/1.9

③ It $A - t$ M ≈ TC, it is nothing to do with t Ma. Regardless of how many labels are set for maximum waking up simultaneously, as long as notification message has been sending, the destination node(s) can always be activated within the range of sleep time (In some cases, it is slightly larger than nodes actual sleep time, such as in test case where marked with "*", the reason is that the process of sending notification frame and reentering to sleep cycle of the destination node are concurrent, causes listening missing).

④ Real-time measurement is by tA, AP Delivery time is determined (TC-related) when the channel is not busy.

5   Conclusion

The paper analyzes and implements the MN-ALG algorithm for large scale electronic shelf label system. The system uses an auxiliary channel to wake up the targeted label nodes to retrieve application data.

Once notification message has been sent out, the destination node(s) could be awakened after the node's first listening period. The activation process such as simultaneously waking up number is controlled by the AP, when downstream data are intensive, the AP controls the activated nodes to access the channel thus can meet the potential QoS requirement of application data delivery.

The paper also introduced other 2 typical algorithms. Both Query-response and Sleep synchronization algorithms work well in a small-scale network with real-time data delivery. Query-response is easy to use compared to the other 2, while it doesn't effectively meet the requirement of building a large network with the real-time requirement of application task delivery, in a dense network, query message will significantly affect the data delivery process and its success rate. Sleep synchronization algorithm is relatively hard to implement both in hardware and software senses for achieving high synchronizing effect, and when it comes to a large-scale network, other strategies need to introduce to guarantee good data delivery performance, which may bring about the design focus shifts to the synchronizing strategies.

The proposed MN-ALG algorithm can guarantee real-time data delivery, and can meet the large-scale requirement of network, which provides a good reference for similar systems.

Acknowledgments. This work is supported by the National Key Technology Support Program of China (NO. 2013BAH01B06), the Environmental Charity Project of China (NO. 2013467065) and the Ningbo Natural Science Foundation (No. 2013A610064).

References

1. Gholamzadeh, B., Nabovati, H.: Concepts for designing low power wireless sensor network. J. Proc. World Acad. Sci. Eng. Technol. **45**, 560 (2008)
2. Tee, K.X., Chew, M.T., Demidenko, S.: An intelligent warehouse stock management and tracking system based on silicon identification technology and 1-wire network communication. In: 6th IEEE International Workshop on Electronic Design, Test and Applications, pp. 110–115, IEEE (2011)
3. Ying, W., Yu, H.: Design of electronic shelf label systems based on ZigBee. In: 4th IEEE International Conference on Software Engineering and Service Science (ICSESS) (2013)
4. Xu, J., Li, W., Xu, J., et al.: Design of electronic shelf label based on electronic paper display. In: 3rd International Conference on Consumer Electronics, Communications Networks, pp. 250–253, IEEE (2013)
5. De Mil, P., Jooris, B., Tytgat, L., et al.: Design and implementation of a generic energy-harvesting framework applied to the evaluation of a large-scale electronic shelf-labeling wireless sensor network. EURASIP J. Wirel. Commun. Netw. **2**, 50 (2010)
6. Yang, Z., Peng, Y., Yue, Y., et al.: Study and application on the architecture and key technologies for IOT. In: International Conference on Multimedia Technology, pp. 747–751, IEEE (2011)
7. Zigbee Alliance. http://www.zigbee.org/
8. Boaventura, A.S., Carvalho, N.B.: A low-power wakeup radio for application in WSN-based indoor location systems. Int. J. Wirel. Inf. Netw. **20**(1), 67–73 (2013)
9. Feng, Y.J., Li, Z., Zhang, H.X., et al.: Sleep method of wireless electronic shelf labels using relative time. J. Guangdong Univ. Technol. **31**(3), 130–136 (2014)
10. Yick, J., Mukherjee, B., Ghosal, D.: Wireless sensor network survey. J. Comput. Netw. Int. J. Comput. Telecommun. Netw. **52**(12), 2292–2330 (2008)
11. Horvat, G., Zagar, G., Vinko, D.: Influence of node deployment parameters on QoS in large-scale WSN. In: 3rd Mediterranean Conference on Embedded Computing MECO 2014, pp. 202–205 (2014)
12. Hongsheng, L., Sumin, L., Bing, H.: Research on node sleep/wake-up mechanism in WSN based on energy threshold setting. In: 5th International Conference on Wireless Communications, Networking and Mobile Computing. WiCom 2009, pp. 1–4, IEEE (2009)
13. Ju, H., Li, C., Huang, A.: EasiCC: a congestion control mechanism for WSN. J. Comput. Res. Dev. (2008)
14. Cao, J., Xin, Y.U.: Congestion control algorithm for WSN in traffic information collection. Comput. Mod. **4**, 59–63 (2014)
15. Yedage, S.L., Mehetre, D.C.: A survey on different wake-up scheduling in WSN. Int. Adv. Comput. Res. **4**, 14 (2014)
16. Rajesh, S.L., Desai, S.C.: Nature inspired energy efficient wireless sensor networks: using duty-cycled wake-up scheduling swarm intelligence. Int. J. Comput. Trends Technol. **10**, 5 (2014)

The Optimization and Improvement of MapReduce in Web Data Mining

Changqing Yin[1(✉)], Shichao Zhang[1], Shukun Liu[1], Shangwei Song[2],
Guangyu Gao[1], and Xiyuan Zhou[1]

[1] School of Software Engineering, Tongji University, Shanghai 201800, China
yinchangqing@tongji.edu.cn
[2] College of Design and Innovation, Tongji University, Shanghai 201800, China

Abstract. Extracting and mining social networks information from massive Web data is of both theoretical and practical significance. However, one of definite features of this task was a large scale data processing, which remained to be a great challenge that would be addressed. MapReduce is a kind of distributed programming model. Just through the implementation of map and reduce those two functions, the distributed tasks can work well. Nevertheless, this model does not directly support heterogeneous datasets processing, while heterogeneous datasets are common in Web. This article proposes a new framework which improves original MapReduce framework into a new one called Map-Reduce-Merge. It adds merge phase that can efficiently solve the problems of heterogeneous data processing. At the same time, some works of optimization and improvement are done based on the features of Web data.

Keywords: Cloud computing · Web data · Mapreduce · Map-Reduce-Merge · Web data mining

1 Introduction

How to implement a Web mining based on the core computing model MapReduce of cloud computing is still a problem to be solved. As we all know, MapReduce is efficient when deals with isomorphic data, but the performance faced with heterogeneous data is often less than ideal.

In this paper, the general concepts and definitions of MapReduce are provided, and introduce an improved model in Web data mining named Map-Reduce-Merge, merge the heterogeneous data produced by Reduce end effectively by increasing the Merge stage. In the meantime, it enhances the efficiency of Web data mining through optimizing the scheduling strategy, Map and Reduce tasks.

© Springer International Publishing Switzerland 2015
G. Wang et al. (Eds.): ICA3PP 2015, Part I, LNCS 9528, pp. 755–762, 2015.
DOI: 10.1007/978-3-319-27119-4_53

2   Map-Reduce

2.1   Overview

MapReduce is a programming model proposed by Google [1], it combines file system GFS [2] to implement parallel computing for large data set on massive scale distributed servers system. The concepts of "Map" and "Reduce", and their basic thoughts come from the features of functional program language and vector program language. MapReduce makes it greatly available for developers to deploy their programs on distributed system without knowledge of parallel programming.

2.2   Programming Model

MapReduce is a simple programming model for data processing.

- When a job is submitted, according to the distribution of file blocks in distributed systems, jobs are divided into several sub-tasks and processed by Mappers (the worker execute Map tasks). Generally tasks will be assigned to the machine contains data or the machine in the same rack to improve the processing speed, which is so-called "code find data" mode.
- Each Mapper executes on different file block, according to the Map execution program, to transform data into key/value pairs. And as for each key/value pair, it executes the Map function provided by users to process. This stage is the massive parallel execution stage.
- When Map task is completed, there will be Shuffle and Sort stage in the framework. It will distribute and sort the data produced by the Mappers and write them into local file system for the next stage, which improve the efficiency of Reduce.
- Reduce tasks obtain their own data from the output of Map tasks, download to the local and merge them.

3   Map-Reduce-Merge

3.1   Programming Model

Map-Reduce-Merge model can handle multiple heterogeneous data sets, and its basic characteristics are as follows (α, β, γ represent different data set, k represent key and v represent value entity):

In this model, the map function will convert a key/value input (k1, v1) to an intermediate key/value pairs [(k2, v2)]. Reduce function will make value of [v2] whose key is k2 gathered together, to produce a value of [v3], which is associated with k2. Noted here, the input and output of the two functions are in the same data set α. Another pair of map and reduce functions produce intermediate output (K3 [v4]) from another dataset beta. Based on the keys: K2 and K3, merge function can merged into a key/value results (k4, v5) from the two output of Reduced function by different data sets. This ultimately results generate a new data set γ (Fig. 1). If $\alpha = \beta$, then the merge function will do a self-merge, similar to the self-join in relational algebra.

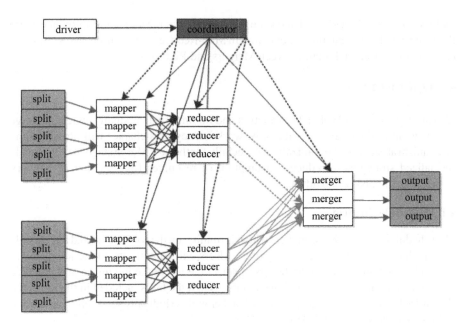

Fig. 1. Map-Reduce-Merge model.

The characteristics of Map and Reduce in new model are almost the same as its original MapReduce. The only difference is that here Reduce output is a key/value pairs, not just values. This change is introduced because the merge function needs the input of data set consisting of key/value. In the Google MapReduce, the result of Reduce is the final result, users can package any required data into [V3], and there is no need to pas k2 to the next stage.

In order to build the merge function to read data from multiple data sets, design emphasizes to pass the key: k2 from the Map to Reduce, and then to the merge function. This can ensure that the data is divided into the areas and classified by keys before the Merge.

3.2 Model Implementation

So far has already implemented a Map-Reduce-Merge framework, whose Map and Reduce module has some trivial changes from MapReduce of Google. Merge is similar to Map and Reduce, developers can implement the user-defined logic of data processing. Calling mapper will produce one key/value pair. Calling Reducer will produce a set of value classified by key. Merger will process two key/value pairs which come from different sources.

At the Merge stage, users would adopt different data processing logic according to data resource. After the mission of Map and Reduce is completed, the Coordinator of Map-Reduce-Merge will start Mergers on a cluster of Nodes. When Merger starts, a Merger ID will be assigned to it. With this ID, Partition Selector can decide from which Render can Merge get input data. Similarly, Mappers and Reducers are also assigned an ID. As for Mappers, this ID stands for Input File Split. As for Reducers, this ID stands for Input Bucket. Mappers split and store their output. For the users of MapReduce, there IDs is the detail of system implementation. In Map-Reduce- Merge, users associate these IDs with the output and input between Mergers and Reducers.

4   Optimization

Aim at the features of Web data extraction and mining, such as small single data, large total amount of data, the existence of network latency, this chapter will provide some mechanism about model optimization, especially for the new Merge stage, it will provide specialized strategies to reduce consumption of resources (like number of network connection and disk bandwidth).

4.1   Schedule Strategy

The scheduler is the decision-makers which is running on the JobTracker and responsible for scheduling the jobs submitted by users. Users will submit jobs to the job queue to wait to be scheduled, the scheduler firstly select the job in the job queue and initialize it, then depending on the scheduling strategy, assign the tasks included in the job to the slot on TaskTracker to execute [3]. (TaskTracker will periodically send heartbeat request to Job- Tracker to acquire tasks).

Because schedule strategy has significant impact on the efficient use of the cluster, load balancing, job execution efficiency [4], it has a great significance to provide an efficient scheduling execution environment to MapReduce Merge programming model framework. In order to better fulfill the requirement of Web data, the schedule strategy should be improved as follows:

- Using the multi-queue to process jobs submitted by users. Like Capacity scheduler, every queue correspond to a user group, administrator can manage the users and their queue. Queue has priority according to that of user group. The group of the queue can submit jobs with different priority, which correspond to the urgency of the task, such as real-time operating can have higher job priority data whereas analysis jobs correspond to a lower priority, multi-queue scheduling support preemption.
- Classify the type of tasks. Job type is the result of refinement for requirement of job resource. So far job type is divided into CPU-intensive and disk-intensive which is similar to three queue scheduler [5, 11]. Allocate a certain amount of computing resource for different job type and compute parallel can enhance the utilization of cluster. The multi-type of job scheduling policy is a best-effort scheduling under the premise of ensuring the multi-queue scheduling. Finally, introduce competition mechanism for resources among multi-user queue.

4.2   Map

In the process of Map task, the intermediate key/value pair $< k2, v2 >$ outputted by map function is written to a circular cache in logic, rather than immediately written to the local file system. When the circular cache is full, it will continue to receive the output from map function while write intermediate file to disk at the same time [6, 12].

This intermediate file organization is not compact enough, so it can be optimized. Increase one thread to merge the output of multiple Map tasks. This thread is started by the TaskTracker and will periodically check the number of Map output files of each task on the node. When the number of map output files of a certain task reaches the default size of configuration, the files will be merged. The file merge is the same way as the merge of multiple spill file, which is a merge on the disk to save the memory consumption of the node.

By this merge operation, reduce the number of intermediate files can be reduced, which makes the output data of the same the Map task on a node more compact. This compact organizational structure has two advantages:

- The less output file can reduce the overhead of establishing a network connection in the Reduce task Shuffle stage, to improve the speed of data transmission on the network.
- The merge operation of Map end reduces the workload of the Reduce task merge phase. In the download and merge stage of Reduce task, it will merge the Map intermediate data several times until get a complete Reduce input and then call reduce function. Merge in the node contains Map can reduce the number of intermediate files, and then reduce the round of merge, finally reduce the execution time.

4.3   Reduce

Reduce end can be improved in the following two aspects.
1. Unbalance of Reduce tasks.
   The reasons for unbalanced data can be summarized into two categories [7, 8]:

- Intermediate results are key dispersed, while after partition too is aggregation. Although the number of different key is large, but after mapping, too many key gathered in the same Reduce task.
- Intermediate results are key single, while result is diverse. The type of key number is relatively small, but the number of records corresponding to the key is large. According to the principle that the records with same key is mapping to the same Reduce, one Reduce can process all the records of one key.

Aim at the unbalance in the data, the improvement target is to make the data be evenly distributed to each Reduce task to ensure that each amount of Reduce task can be roughly equal. To avoid some nodes to deal with too much data "exhausting", while others node have no data processing "starve to death".

Improvement program will start twice MapReduce Job. Firstly, use the Reduce in first MapReduce to merge locally, to ensure Reduce operation data in the second reduce operation is balanced and the records with same key can be processed in the same Reduce task.

For the first input of the Reduce stage, it is not necessary to ensure that each key corresponding to the record must be mapped to the same Reduce. On the contrary, each record should be randomly mapped to a reduce records having the same key which is uniformly dispersed, but need to ensure that the amount of calculation in each Reduce should be substantially equal. Reduce operating merged the records with same key record into one, after the local polymerization data is greatly reduced, and there is only one record corresponding to one key in each Reduce output. At this point the data as the second input of MapReduce, map function have nothing to do, directly regard the input data as output, the data is mapped to Reduce task in accordance with the original partition. Reduce do one operation, the same data is combined to give the final output of each key corresponding to a result.

However this does not mean that all the calculations need local polymerization, if Map output can reach Reduce equilibrium requirements, this program will be executed. So need to develop a strategy to determine under what circumstances local data aggregation should be operated. At the beginning of Map firstly attempts to do Hash mapping, if the mapping of the different number of records/Try to certain records the number of records is greater than a given threshold, then it means the Map output data and input to the Reduce task is balanced, so just execute the original MapReduce process. Otherwise launch another MapReduce Job and operate local polymerization in the first Reduce.

2. The I/O problem in shuffle phase of Reduce.

To optimize I/O in shuffle phase, firstly reduce the number of connections to establish, for each download thread in its life cycle, only to establish a long connection to the same node. When the output of the MAP can be downloaded, then download it from this link, after all output complete downloading, then close the connection. This is effective for jobs with many maps.

Because http is based on the TCP connection to transfer files, TCP slow start-up characteristics determine the data transfer rate cannot immediately reach the network bandwidth. The proposed method to merge Map output file can increase the amount of once data transmitted, which can improve the transmission rate [5, 13].

Map output merger changed the organizational form of the intermediate data. Shuffle download thread will not necessarily be able to directly download a Map output file according to file information get from JobTracker It may get the output file, which may be obtained by combined Map output file. In this regard, solution is to keep the original Map task progress reporting mode and Shuffle stage download access to information the same way. Only make minor modifications in the implementation process of the download, as far as possible through the merger of the intermediate output file, making a large amount of data transferred.

For example, the map A task execution is complete and report to the JobTracker. Then Reduce tasks query to JobTracker for the completion of Map A, and try to communicate to the node contains map A and download the output data of Map A. At the same time, Map B is completed in the same node as Map A, and the output of Map A and Map B has been merged into an output file. The node will send combined output to the Reduce node, and inform that the transferred data is a result of the merger of A and B tasks. After Reduce tasks have received the data, it will mark Map A and MAP B as received, and do not further access to the node for the output data of the task B.

For a special case, the completion information of Map A and Map B has been acquired by Reduce separately, downloaded by two download threads. The nodes will receive one of the download requests, and send the merge of A and B. Reduce take retreat, does not immediately re-attempt when the download request of connection to the same node is refused, the download will not restart until all the threads connected to the node are completed and not able to obtain the desired output data.

4.4 Workflow

The MapReduce program strictly abides by the two-stage process, the first Map and the second Reduce. The user can change the default configuration. However, some basic operations, such as Partition and Sort are built-in, and must be executed. It is a little troublesome for the users just want to perform Map or Reduce tasks. Although such restrictions make MapReduce simple, but it cannot meet the needs of advanced users, who more often want to customize the entire workflow. So it should be possible to optimize the interface of the framework to allow advanced users to have greater freedom to define the workflow to meet their own requirements.

5 Conclusions

Firstly, this paper simply introduces the concept and programming model of MapReduce. The MapReduce has many important features, such as high-throughput, high-performance, fault tolerance and ease of manageability [9, 10]. Among them, the most important features is the parallel programming abstraction for two simple primitives, Map and Reduce, so developers can easily work in the real-world data processing converted into parallel programs.

However, MapReduce cannot directly support the handling of heterogeneous data sets, this is a fatal flaw for the non-standardization of Web data processing. It can be solved effectively by Adding Merge stage on the basis of the original model. And the new programming framework of the Map-Reduce-Merge inherited the original MapReduce characteristics. Finally, for some of the features for Web data, do further optimization and improvement on the part of the Map-Reduce-Merge model scheduling policy, workflow, and load balancing to enhance the framework operating efficiency while also expanded its versatility.

References

1. Dean, R., Ghemawat, A.: MapReduce: implified data processing on large cluster. In: SDI, pp. 137–149 (2004)
2. Ghemawat, N., Gobioff, H., Leung, S.T.: The google file system. In: Operating Systems Principles, pp. 29–43 (2003)
3. Fei, X., Lu, S., Lin, C.: A MapReduce-Enabled scientific workflow composition framework. In: Proceedings of the IEEE International Conference on Web Services, Los Angeles, pp. 663–670 (2009)
4. Hadoop 0.20 Documentation, Capacity Scheduler
5. Lammel, R.: Google's MapReduce programming model—revisited. Draft, p. 26 (2006)

6. Tian, C., Zhou, H., He, Y., Zha, L.: A dynamic mapreduce scheduler for heterogeneous workloads. In: Proceedings of the 8th International Conference on Grid and Cooperative Computing, Lanzhou, pp. 218–224 (2009)
7. Dean, J., Ghemawat, S.: MapReduce: simplified data processing on large clusters. In: OSDI, pp. 137–150 (2004)
8. Pike, R., Dorward, S., Griesemer, R.: Interpreting the data: parallel analysis with sawzall. Sci. Program. **13**, 227–298 (2005). doi:10.1155/2005/962135
9. Kim, K., Jeon, K., Han, H., Kim, S., Jung, H., Yeom, H.Y., Bench, M.R.: A benchmark for MapReduce framework. In: Proceedings of the 2008 14th IEEE International Conference on Parallel and Distributed Systems, Victoria, pp. 11–18 (2008). http://dx.doi.org/10.1109/ICPADS.2008.70
10. Zhang, D., Zhou, J., Guo, M., Cao, J.: TASA: tag-free activity sensing using RFID tag arrays. IEEE Trans. Parallel Distrib. Syst. (TPDS) **22**, 558–570 (2011)
11. Zhang, D., Chen, M., Guizani, M., Xiong, H., Zhang, D.: Mobility prediction in telecom cloud using mobile calls. IEEE Wirel. Commun. **21**(1), 26–32 (2014)
12. Chen, Q., Zhang, D., Guo, M.: SAMR: a self-adaptive Map-Reduce scheduling algorithm in heterogeneous environments. In: Proceedings of the 10th IEEE International Conference on Scalable Computing and Communications (ScalCom 2010), pp. 2736–2743. Bradford, UK (2010)
13. Zhang, D., Yang, L.T., Chen, M., Zhao, S., Guo, M., Zhang, Y.: A real-time locating system using active RFID for internet of things. IEEE Syst. J. doi:10.1109/JSYST.2014.2346625

An Intimacy-Based Algorithm for Social Network Community Detection

Yi Zheng, Dafang Zhang$^{(\boxtimes)}$, and Kun Xie

College of Computer Science and Electronic Engineering,
Hunan University, Changsha 410083, China
{zy19830814,dfzhang,xiekun}@hnu.edu.cn

Abstract. Community detection is a crucial way to understand social network, and it reflects the structural characteristics of the network and the interesting features of community. We introduce the intimacy among nodes to detect community in social network. By reducing the degree of intimacy matrix between the communities, we approached the accurate community detection firstly. Then, in order to reduce the algorithm complexity, the intimacy-based algorithm for community merger is proposed. At last, compared with the existing algorithms in the theoretical and experimental respectively, we obtain that our algorithm drops the time complexity, reduces the iterations and cuts down the realization time based on the precise community detection.

Keywords: Social network · Community · Community detection · Intimacy · Intimacy matrix

1 Introduction

Complex networks [1] in reality, such as social networks (SNs) [2], often evolve heavily over time and frequently experience topological changes during their evolution. In the sense of online social networks OSNs [3], such as Facebook, Twitter or Google+, these changes are often introduced by users joining in or leaving a particular group or community [4]. For example, friends and friends connecting together, or new people making friend with each other. In social network, community is consist of social members who have closely relationship. People tend to be friend with others in the same community, based on the basic assumption that a network system consists of a number of communities, among which the connections are much fewer than those inside the same community.

Community detection, as a result, is the classification of network nodes into communities so that the networks natural structure is properly displayed. Detecting this special structure finds itself extremely useful in deriving social-based solutions for many network problems, such as forwarding and routing strategies in communication networks [5–7], or sybil defense [8,9].

There have existed many community detection algorithms [10,12,13] and some of them can be transplanted to the dynamic weighted graph, but they

© Springer International Publishing Switzerland 2015
G. Wang et al. (Eds.): ICA3PP 2015, Part I, LNCS 9528, pp. 763–776, 2015.
DOI: 10.1007/978-3-319-27119-4_54

have many problems. For example, some modularity-based algorithms [10] have the problems of resolution limit and extreme degeneracy [11]. Some algorithms [12,13] designed for dynamic social networks, which solve the problem in unweighted graph and weighted graph.

In this paper, we propose a new metric, called intimacy, to describe the relationship among nodes. Comparing with the popular community detection algorithm [13], our method can achieve 39.06 % lower iterations, 47.09 % lower implementation time under lower time complexity. To the best of our knowledge, our work is the first one to achieve community detection with intimacy.

The rest of the paper is organized as follows. In Sect. 2, we provide the basic network model and problem statement. In order to obtain community detection, Sect. 3 presents the intimacy-based dynamic community detection algorithm. Section 4 proposes the algorithm analysis for IDCD. In Sect. 5, we establish our simulation environment and contrast IDCD with other existing methods in community detection performance. Finally, we conclude the paper in Sect. 6.

2   Network Model and Problem Statement

2.1   Dynamic Social Network

As depicted in Fig. 1(a), it shows the social construction for SNs. It is well known that SNs consists of people and relationship between people. And in the network graph, we utilize nodes and lines instead of people and the relationship. A dynamic social network which can be defined as a time sequence of network graph. We denote it by $G = \{G_1, G_2, \cdots, G_t, \cdots, G_n\}$, where $G_t = \{N_t, E_t\}$ represents a time dependent network recorded at time t. $N_t = \{n_1^t, n_2^t, \cdots, n_m^t\}$ denotes the set of nodes at time t, $E_t = \{e_1^t, e_2^t, \cdots, e_f^t\}$ denotes the edge set at time t. Nodes and lines keep changing over time. No matter how they change, we can divide them into four communities by the intimacy of them as shows in Fig. 1(b). Our research is based on the dynamic social network.

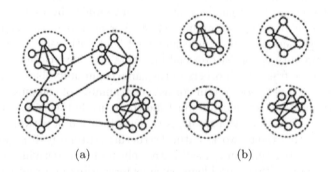

(a)   (b)

Fig. 1. Figure (a) and (b) are the SNs at time t

2.2   Problem Statement

In the dynamic social network, people will change time by time, e.g. the number and the location. The relationship of people will also change with them. Under this circumstance, we should solve these problems: 1. how to describe the relationship between nodes? 2. how to divide the communities by intimacy of nodes? 3. how to give the efficient community detection scheme?

Denotes L_t as the connection matrix at time t, described as

$$L_t = [l_{ij}^t] \qquad (1)$$

l_{ij}^t denotes the relationship between node i and j at time t. If $l_{ij}^t = 0$, node i has no relation with node j; otherwise node i has relations with node j.

In order to further research internal relationship in SNs, we present the definition of intimacy. Specifically, we utilize the value to describe the intimate relation between nodes and the intimate relation between communities. It expresses the degree of close relationship among them. To obtain the precise refinement of relationship among each other, we add several factors of close relation to traditional weighted value. Two nodes have closer relations if they have bigger intimacy.

We can obtain the intimacy matrix by intimacy, it can be expressed as

$$A_t = [a_{ij}^t]_{m \times m} \qquad (2)$$

A_t denotes the intimacy matrix at time t, a_{ij}^t denotes the intimacy value between node i and j at time t, m denotes the number of nodes.

Intimacy describes the relationship among nodes, it consists of family affection, friendship and hobby similarity. Firstly, we obtain the intimacy matrix A_t by using family affection matrix, friendship matrix and hobby similarity matrix between initial nodes in mobile social network. By previous studies, family affection degree matrix [14], friendly degree matrix [15] and hobby similarity matrix [16] in mobile social network are obtained, we can acquire the expression of intimacy matrix by

$$A_t = \mu T_t + \phi F_t + \gamma H_t \qquad (3)$$

A_t denotes the intimacy degree matrix, T_t denotes the family affection degree matrix, F_t denotes the friendly degree matrix, H_t denotes the hobby similarity matrix. We will analysis the influence to community division with different μ, ϕ and γ in the simulation experiment.

Then, based on nodes information, we combine the nodes which have higher intimacy value by distributing to several nodes at the same time. With k small communities, establish intimacy matrix M_t for community. Detect and merge the intimated community by intimacy matrix. After combining, we should judge community structure whether it can not change or only have one community. If it is, terminate the partition and obtain the community; then, on the basis of intimacy matrix, the intimacy value is updated by distributing to several nodes simultaneously, and proceed with combining until it suit to the condition.

Finally, we obtain the dynamic community partition after updating the intimacy matrix M_t. IDCD algorithm is a distributed algorithm as it can be distributed to several nodes simultaneously, it only needs know neighbour nodes information and need not know the overall information. Intimacy can show the relationship between nodes whether digraph or undigraph. Therefore, this algorithm is suitable to both digraph and undigraph. We focus on undigraph in this paper.

In the following, we present our method in detail.

3   Intimacy-Based Dynamic Community Detection Algorithm

Definition 1. *For a graph G which has m nodes and f edges, the measurement of graph denseness is called edge density, denoted by δ_G. An expression of edge density is*

$$\delta_G = f/m \tag{4}$$

$\Re_a$ denotes the added nodes set and $\Re_r$ denotes the reduced nodes set. We obtain the intimacy value with change of node and time.

(1) We consider n_a nodes add to this SNs at time t_1 and get the change of nodes' intimacy value by

$$\begin{cases} m_{ij}^{t_1} = m_{ij}^{t_0}, \ i \notin \Re_a, \ j \notin \Re_a \\ m_{ij}^{t_1} = m_{ij}^{t_1}, \ i \in \Re_a, \ j \notin \Re_a \\ m_{ij}^{t_1} = m_{ij}^{t_1}, \ i \in \Re_a, \ j \in \Re_a \end{cases} \tag{5}$$

$m_{ij}^{t_0}$ denotes intimacy value between node i and j at time t_0, $m_{ij}^{t_1}$ denotes intimacy value between node i and j at time t_1.

(2) We consider n_r nodes leave from this SNs at time t_1, get the change of nodes' intimacy value and can be written as

$$\begin{cases} m_{ij}^{t_1} = m_{ij}^{t_0}, \ i \notin \Re_r, \ j \notin \Re_r \\ m_{ij}^{t_1} = 0, \ i \in \Re_r, \ j \notin \Re_r \\ m_{ij}^{t_1} = 0, \ i \in \Re_r, \ j \in \Re_r \end{cases} \tag{6}$$

$m_{ij}^{t_0}$ denotes intimacy value between node i and j at time t_0, $m_{ij}^{t_1}$ denotes intimacy value between node i and j at time t_1.

Then, we will obtain the method of community merging, intimacy matrix updating and the criterion of terminating community detection.

3.1   Community Merging

The main idea of community merging is to get satisfactory communities together by intimacy value among nodes and edge density. All of community merging will be done under this circumstance of $m_{max}^t > \alpha$ (m_{max}^t denotes intimacy value between community I and other communities).

We obtain the maximum intimacy value of community m_{max}^t and the minimum intimacy value of community m_{min}^t, the method of community merging by

(1) For community I at time t, as $m_{max}^t > \delta_G m_{min}^t$, merge the community whose intimacy value is great than or equal to $\delta_G m_{min}^t$, it can be expressed as

$$C_u^t = \{C_I^t, C_1^t, C_2^t, \cdots, C_J^t\} \tag{7}$$

C_u^t denotes a community after merging, $C_I^t, C_1^t, C_2^t, \cdots, C_J^t$ denote communities which intimacy value to community I is great than or equal to $\delta_G m_{min}^t$.

(2) For community I, as $m_{max}^t < \delta_G m_{min}^t$, merge the community which has the maximum intimacy value to it.

$$C_u^t = \{C_I^t, C_J^t\} \tag{8}$$

C_u^t denotes a community after merging, C_J^t denotes a community whose intimacy value to it is equal to m_{max}^t.

There is a special circumstances: if a node has only one edge with other nodes, we will judge it belong or not to this community with adjacent node by threshold value. If its intimacy value is greater than threshold value, it belongs to this community and merge it; otherwise not.

3.2 Intimacy Matrix Updating

After merging community, we provide the process of updating intimacy matrix. As the communities merged, the intimacy value between them is changed. Therefore, the intimacy matrix is changed too. Through distributing to every element in the intimacy matrix, we will obtain the real time updating of the intimacy value step by step. Intimacy value is a metric to measuring the intimacy between nodes. Intimacy can be divided into affection, friendship and hobby. Therefore, merging is the process of acquiring intersection. The intimacy value after merging is the common part of their intimacy relationship. For example, we take the same part of common family relations, friendly relations and interests. Taking the minimum of intimacy value between merged members is the main method of updating intimacy matrix. There are two cases in the intimacy matrix renewing: one is between the community and node, the other is between the communities.

Under the condition of the community and node, I denotes the set of communities $I_1, I_2, \cdots, I_n$. The method of obtaining intimacy value between community and node can be provided as

$$m_{Ii}^t = min(m_{I_1 i}^t, m_{I_2 i}^t, \cdots, m_{I_n i}^t) \tag{9}$$

m_{Ii}^t denotes an intimacy value after updating, $m_{I_1 i}^t, m_{I_2 i}^t, \cdots, m_{I_n i}^t$ denote the intimacy value of two parts which need to be merged.

Under the situation of communities, We obtain the method of updating intimacy value between communities by setting

$$m_{jK}^t = min(m_{JK_1}^t, m_{JK_2}^t, \cdots, m_{JK_n}^t) \tag{10}$$

J denotes the set of communities $J_1, J_2, \cdots, J_n$, K denotes the set of communities $K_1, K_2, \cdots, K_n$. m_{jK}^t denotes an intimacy value after updating. $m_{JK_n}^t$

denote the intimacy value of two communities which need to be merged and can calculate through formula (9).

At last, the updated matrix M'_t at time t is derived by

$$M'_t = [m'_{ij}]_{k' \times k'} \tag{11}$$

m'_{ij} denotes an intimacy value of community after updating, k' denotes a number of communities after updating.

3.3   Judgment of Terminating Community Detection

IDCD algorithm is a process of loop iteration, we need an index to control the process. This index can be a judgment of terminating community detection. In this paper, this index is the judgment of community structure can not change or only have one community. As the intimacy value of adjacent community is less than or equal to threshold value, the process of detecting community will be ended. If there is only one community, it means through repeatedly consolidation, the whole SNs forms one community. It needs not to merge community and terminate community detection.

3.4   The Description of IDCD

The description of IDCD algorithm is presented in Algorithm 1. In Algorithm 1, L denotes connection matrix which need to processed, and $Comm$ denotes the community set after calculating.

Algorithm 1. $Comm$=IDCD(L)

00: **Input:**   Connection Matrix L
    Output: Community Set $Comm$
01: $A_t = \mu T_t + \phi F_t + \gamma H_t$
02: $m^t_{max} \leftarrow max(C^t)$; $m^t_{min} \leftarrow min(C^t)$
03: **if** $m^t_{max} \geq \delta_G m^t_{min}$ **then**
04:     $C^t_u \leftarrow combine\{C^t_I, C^t_1, C^t_2, \cdots, C^t_J\}$
05:       $m_{C_I C_1}, m_{C_I C_2}, \cdots, m_{C_I C_J} \geq \delta_G m^t_{min}$
06: **else**
07:     $C^t_u \leftarrow combine\{C^t_I, C^t_J\}$
08:       $m_{C_I C_1} = m^t_{max}$ and proceed step 10
09: **end if**
10: **if** community structure can not change or only have one community **then**
11:     Proceed step 16
12: **else**
13:     $m^t_{Ii} \leftarrow min(m^t_{I_1 i}, m^t_{I_2 i}, \cdots, m^t_{I_n i})$ and proceed step 15
14: **end if**
15: Repeat proceed step 2 to 14
16: Save the dividing community to $Comm$ and back

As depicted in Algorithm 1, we regard the connection matrix as input value. Firstly, we obtain the intimacy matrix A_t by using family affection matrix, friendship matrix and hobby similarity matrix between initial nodes in mobile social network. Then, small community is obtained by bigger intimacy value of nodes and compute the maximum and minimum of intimacy value between small communities. If $m_{max}^t \geq \delta_G m_{min}^t$, we combine the communities $C_I^t, C_1^t, C_2^t, \cdots, C_{J-1}^t$ and C_J^t which $m_{C_I C_1}, m_{C_I C_2}, \cdots, m_{C_I C_J} \geq \delta_G m_{min}^t$. Otherwise, combine the communities C_I^t with C_J^t and proceed step 10. If community structure can not change or only have one community, proceed step 16. Otherwise, update the intimacy matrix and proceed step 15. Repeat proceed step 2 to 14. Finally, we obtain the community set $Comm$.

4   Algorithm Analysis

IDCD algorithm aims to degrade the order of intimacy matrix. The astringency of algorithm is introduced in the following.

Theorem 1. *IDCD algorithm is convergent.*

Proof. The main idea of IDCD algorithm is the process of matrix reduce gradually ($M_{n \times n} \longrightarrow M'_{n' \times n'}$). The order n is changing as

$$f(x) = x - \sum_{i=1}^{\Omega} (J_i) \tag{12}$$

x denotes the order of intimacy matrix, $f(x)$ denotes the mapping from n to n', Ω denotes the number of community merging and updating, J_i denotes the number of merging communities.

In iterative processes, $f(x)$ is recursion relation and the judgment of terminating community detection is the control of the iteration ends.

1. The people in SNs is limited and the order of intimacy matrix is bounded, therefore the function $f(x)$ is bounded.

2. By Eq. (12), if $N \geq x_1 > x_2$,

$$f(x_1) \geq f(x_2) \tag{13}$$

The function $f(x)$ is monotonic function based on Eq. (13).

3. Assume that advisable range for members in SNs is $[a, b]$, the ultimate intimacy matrix ranging from a to b by $f(x)$ is bounded. The process of dividing is intimacy matrix reduced or unchanged through Eq. (13). Then function $f(x)$ meets two conditions as follow

(1) If $x \in [a, b]$, then $f(x) \in [a, b]$;

(2) For any $x_1, x_2 \in [a, b]$, it exists constant ξ and makes $|f(x_1) - f(x_2)| \leq \xi |x_1 - x_2|$.

Then, the function $f(x)$ meets Lipschitzian condition.

In conclusion, $f(x)$ is monotonic, bounded and continuous function, which is convergent function. Therefore, IDCD is convergent algorithm.

5   Performance Evaluation

In our paper, we implemented the proposed new scheme IDCD. Extensive simulations on a real-world social network datasets illustrate the performance of IDCD. To compare the performance of IDCD to that of the existing algorithm, we utilize other classic methods, such as SAWD [13], AFOCS [12] and CMD-WDG [10]. The comparative results show that our approach is efficient.

5.1   Zachary's Karate Club

The evaluation of IDCD is based on seven datasets. The first one is by Zachary's karate club network [17]. This is a social network of friendships between 34 members of a karate club at an American university in the 1970. It is an undirected, unweighted network having 34 nodes and 78 edges. Due to some reason their was a dispute between the administrator and instructor and the network was divided into two groups. Node 1 and 33 represents the administrator and instructor respectively.

We utilize NMI overlapping version [18] as metrics to make sure μ, φ and γ in intimacy and threshold value. It is one of the most important entropy measures in information theory. The higher the NMI score is, the more similar the two community partitions are. If it equals 1, it means the two kinds of community partitions are exactly coincident.

Firstly, we get the intimacy coefficient through NMI score by Fig. 2.

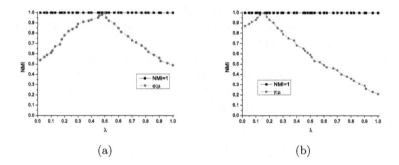

(a)   (b)

Fig. 2. Parameter choosing for μ, φ and γ

λ(the specific value of coefficient in intimacy) in Fig. 2(a) shows the value of $\varphi : \mu$, λ in Fig. 2(b) shows the value of $\gamma : \mu$. NMI score changes as the parameter λ changes. When $\varphi : \mu = 0.5$, $\gamma : \mu = 0.166$, NMI score reach the maximum 1 respectively. Therefore, as $\mu : \varphi : \gamma = 6 : 3 : 1$, NMI score attain the maximum 1. We confirm μ, φ and γ in intimacy.

Then, from large numbers of tests, we obtain the combining threshold α ranging from 0–0.42. We select the representative values 0.30–0.39 to analyze an

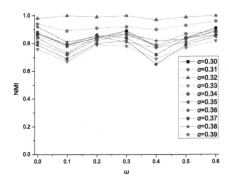

Fig. 3. Parameter choosing for threshold value

appropriate value for α. Because in this scope, the NMI score shows better than in other scopes. The simulation results are shown in Fig. 3.

NMI score changes as the parameter ω changes (the larger the ω is, the weaker the node strength is in its community). As $\alpha = 0.32$, NMI score will level off to 1, we confirm the threshold value in this SNs. We obtain all of the parameters based on numerous simulations and find the communities by our IDCD algorithm.

As intimacy and threshold value are determined, we obtain intimacy matrix through club's family affection, friendship and hobby similarity. Through two times iterations, the intimacy matrix is changing from Fig. 4(a) (the black cell denotes it has relationship between nodes or communities and the white cell denotes it has no relationship) to Fig. 4(c) through Fig. 4(b).

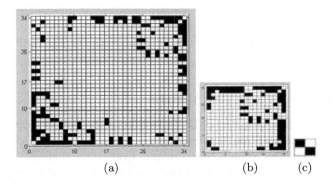

(a)   (b)   (c)

Fig. 4. The change of intimacy matrix

On the basis of the partition result, two communities are formed as blue square and red circle, which are shown in Fig. 5. The partition result is same to the previous studies.

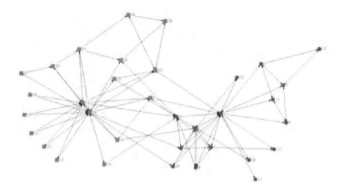

Fig. 5. Communities in Zachary's Karate Club Network

5.2 The Social Evolution

As a further test of our algorithm, we turn to MIT Social Evolution dataset [19]. The Social Evolution dataset is closely track the everyday life of a whole undergraduate dormitory with mobile phones, so that social scientists can validate their models against the spatio-temporal patterns and behavior-network co-evolution as contained in this data. The Social Evolution dataset covered the locations, proximities, and phone calls of more than 80 % of residents who lived in the dormitory used in our simulation, as captured by their cell phones from October 2008 to May 2009. This dormitory has a population of approximately 30 freshmen, 20 sophomores, 10 juniors, 10 seniors and 10 graduate student tutors.

In Fig. 6, we give a visual presentation about social graphs founded on the Social Evolution Dataset. Two pictures are obtained at different network snapshots. The dense parts are the potential community structures.

By our IDCD algorithm, we detect 12 communities in Fig. 6(a) and 10 communities in Fig. 6(b).

5.3 Simulation Results and Analysis

We test the other five datasets by IDCD. Dolphin social network [20].—An undirected social network of frequent associations between 62 dolphins in a community living off Doubtful Sound, New Zealand. College Football [21].—A network of American football games between Division IA colleges during regular season Fall 2000, where 115 nodes denote football teams and 613 edges represent regular season games. Yeast PPI [22].—A protein-protein interaction network where each node represents a protein. It owns 2631 nodes and 7182 edges. Netscience [23].— A coauthorship network of scientists working on condensed matter physics. The simplification network consist of 7343 nodes and 11898 edges. PGP network.—It is a web based on trust, and the comprehension of trust networks is, nowadays, crucial to understand the complexity of the information society. There are

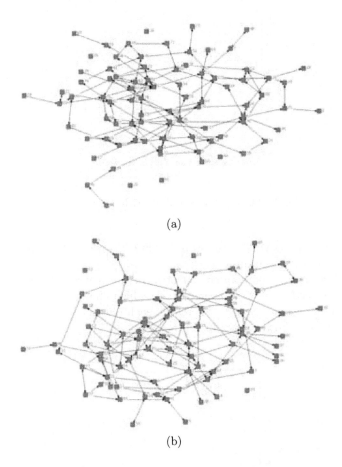

(a)

(b)

Fig. 6. Figure (a) and (b) captured at 2009-01-09 and 2009-01-16 respectively

10680 users generate 24340 records for secure information exchange. All of accurate detect results can obtained by IDCD. Our method can obtain the exactly result without calculating modularity.

After above simulations, our algorithm is compared with existing algorithms through theoretical analysis and experimental analysis.

Firstly, we compare IDCD with existing algorithms for time complexity. Time complexity of IDCD, SAWD, AFOCS and CMDWDG is $O(m + mt)$, $O(n^2)$, $O(mn)$ and $O(m^2n)$ respectively. Because of $O(m + mt) < O(n^2) < O(mn) < O(m^2n)$, our algorithm is lower than other algorithms in time complexity by contrastive analysis.

Then, the comparison of algorithms' iterations is depicted in Fig. 7.

The algorithm's iterations increase as the number of nodes increase under same community detection result (the same modularity) in Fig. 7. Obviously, the iterations of IDCD performs better than other algorithms. On average, our

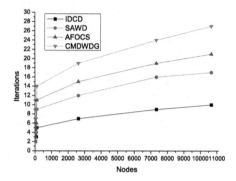

Fig. 7. The comparison of algorithms' iterations

method is lower than SAWD with 39.06 %, AFOCS with 51.27 % and CMDWDG with 62.49 % on the iterations.

At last, we obtain the comparison of algorithms' implementation time. In this paper, we record the fired time of CPU which changes as the achievement of algorithm's program changes. Therefore, each dataset be tested for 10 times by each algorithm and averaged in Fig. 8.

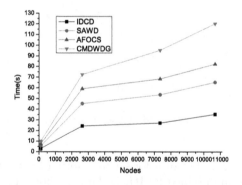

Fig. 8. The comparison of algorithms' implementation time

In Fig. 8, the implementation time of IDCD, SAWD, AFOCS and CMD-WDG are increasing as the number of nodes increasing. We do our best to measuring the relation of nodes, the implementation time of our algorithm is lower than other algorithms. We have measured that IDCD is lower than SAWD with 47.09 %, AFOCS with 58.69 % and CMDWDG with 69.88 % on the implementation time.

In conclusion, our method performs better than other algorithms. It can achieve 39.06 % lower iterations, 47.09 % lower implementation time under lower time complexity.

6   Conclusions

In this paper, we propose a new community detection scheme for SNs based on intimacy. It presents a new metric to describe the relationship among nodes. We utilize intimacy matrix and community merging to handle the problem. We conduct simulations on the UCINET analysis platform to evaluate IDCD performance. Extensive simulations on the several datasets show that our method can achieve a very good community detection performance in an efficient way.

Acknowledgments. This work is supported by The National Basic Research Program of China (2012CB315805); The National Natural Science Foundation of China (61173167, 61472130).

References

1. Watts, D.J., Strongate, S.H.: Collective dynamics of small-world networks. Nature **393**, 440–442 (1998)
2. Palla, G., Barab'asi, A.L., Vicsek, T.: Quantifying social group evolution. Nature **446**(7136), 664–667 (2007)
3. Amin, R., Muthucumaru, M.: Using sommunity structure to control information sharing in online social networks. Comput. Commun. **41**, 11–21 (2014)
4. Barber, M.J., Clark, J.W.: Detecting network communities by propagating labels under constraints. Phys. Rev. E. **80**(2), 026129 (2009)
5. Dinh, T.N., Xuan, Y., Thai, M.T.: Towards social-aware routing in dynamic communication networks. In: 28th IEEE International Performance Computing and Communications Conference, pp. 161–168. IEEE Press, Phoenix (2009)
6. Nguyen, N., Dinh, T., Xuan, Y., Thai, M.: Adaptive algorithms for detecting community structure in dynamic social networks. In: 30th IEEE International Conference on Computer Communications, pp. 2282–2290. IEEE Press, Shanghai (2011)
7. Hui, P., Crowcroft, J., Yoneki, E.: Bubble rap: social-based forwarding in delay-tolerant networks. IEEE T. Mob. Comput. **10**(11), 1576–1589 (2011)
8. Wei, W., Xu, F.Y., Tan, C.C., Li, Q.: SybilDefender: a defense mechanism for sybil attacks in large social networks. IEEE T. Parall. Distr. **24**(12), 2492–2502 (2013)
9. Viswanath, B., Mislove, A., Cha, M., Gummadi, K.P.: A survey of techniques to defend against sybil attacks in social networks. Int. J. Adv. Res. Comput. Commun. Eng. **3**(5), 6577–6580 (2014)
10. Duan, D.S., Li, Y.H., Jin, Y.N., Lu, Z.D.: Community mining on dynamic weighted directed graphs. In: 1st ACM International Workshop on Complex Networks Meet Information & Knowledge Management, pp. 11–18. ACM Press, Hong Kong (2009)
11. Khadivi, A., Rad, A., Hasler, M.: Network community-detection enhancement by proper weighting. Phys. Rev. E. **83**(4), 046104 (2011)
12. Nguyen, N.P., Dinh, T.N., Tokala, S., Thai, M.T.: Overlapping communities in dynamic networks: their detection and moibile applications. In: 17th Annual International Conference on Mobile Computing and Networking, pp. 85–96. ACM Press, Las Vegas (2011)
13. Li, Z., Wang, C., Yang, S.Q., Jiang, C.J., Li, X.Y.: LASS: local-activity and social-similarity based data forwarding in mobile social networks. IEEE T. Parall. Distr. **26**(1), 174–184 (2014)

14. Fan, J., Chen, J., Du, Y., Gao, W., Wu, J., Sun, Y.: Geocommunity-based broadcasting for data dissemination in mobile social networks. IEEE T. Parall. Distr. **24**(4), 734–743 (2013)
15. Jiang, J., Wang, X., Sha, W.P., Huang, P., Dai, Y.F., Zhao, B.Y.: Understanding latent interactions in online social networks. ACM TWEB **7**(10), 18–57 (2013)
16. Obradovic, D., Baumann, S., Dengel, A.: A social network analysis and mining methodology for the monitoring of specific domains in the blogosphere. Soc. Netw. Anal. Min. **3**(2), 221–232 (2013)
17. Zachary, W.W.: An information flow model for conflict and fission in small groups. J. Anthropol. Res. **33**, 452–473 (1977)
18. Lancichinetti, A., Fortunato, S., Kertesz, J.: Detecting the overlapping and hierarchical community structure in complex networks. New J. Phys. **11**(3), 033015 (2009)
19. Madan, A., Cebrian, M., Moturu, S., Farrahi, K., Pentland, A.: Sensing the "Health State" of a community. Pervasive Comput. **11**(4), 36–45 (2012)
20. Lusseau, D., Newman, M.E.J.: Identifying the role that animals play in their social networks. Proc. Biol. Sci. **271**(6), 477–481 (2004)
21. Girvan, M., Newman, M.E.J.: Community structure in social and biological networks. Proc. Natl. Acad. Sci. **99**, 7821–7826 (2002)
22. Von Merging, C., Krause, R., Snel, B.: Comparative assessment of large-scale data sets of protein-protein interactions. Nature **417**(6998), 399–403 (2002)
23. Xiang, B., Chen, E.H., Zhou, T.: Finding community structure based on subgraph similarity. Complex Netw. **207**, 73–81 (2009)

A Method for Detection of Anomaly Node in IOT

Zhenguo Chen[1,2(✉)], Liqin Tian[2], and Chuang Lin[3]

[1] School of Information Science & Engineering, Northeastern University,
Shenyang 110819, China
zhenguo_chen@126.com
[2] Department of Computer Science and Technology, North China Institute
of Science and Technology, East Yanjiao, Beijing 101601, China
[3] Department of Computer Science and Technology, Tsinghua University,
Beijing 100084, China

Abstract. Perceived data would be affected by the node status in the Internet of things. If the status of node was abnormal, the perception data would not reliable. In order to guarantee the reliability of the perception data in the Internet of things, a method for detecting the anomaly of nodes is proposed. Detection unit was constructed firstly. Each detection unit included working node, associated node and decision node. The detection unit can realize self-detection, which can detect the abnormal nodes in time. The task of the working node was to perceive the data and submit it to the data center. It would always be in working status until it was abnormal. When the work node has an exception, the alarm information would be issued. Then, the work node will be replaced by the associated node. Data perception of monitoring area would be responsible for the associated nodes. In each detection unit, three levels of detection can be completed. The first level is the work node self-check. The second stage is the auxiliary detection of associated nodes. The third level is the final decision of the node. Using the simulation tool Matlab7.0, the results show that our method is effective.

Keywords: Internet of things · Nodes detection · Perception data · Reliability · Anomaly node

1 Introduction

Internet of things (IOT) is called the third wave of world information industry after the computer and the Internet. Technically, the Internet of Things integrates multiple wired and wireless communication, control, and IT technologies, which connect various terminals or subsystems under a unified management platform that employs open and standardized data presentation technologies such as XML/web services/ SOA. At present, many applications have been proposed and studied based on the Internet of things [1, 2]. Internet of things (IOT) has changed the way of communication. The communication between people and people is extended to the remote and real time communication between objects and objects, people and objects [3]. In the process of development and application of the Internet of things, how to ensure the reliable of data is one of the key technologies that we must face and solve. In view

© Springer International Publishing Switzerland 2015
G. Wang et al. (Eds.): ICA3PP 2015, Part I, LNCS 9528, pp. 777–784, 2015.
DOI: 10.1007/978-3-319-27119-4_55

of the important form of the perception and recognition of the Internet of things, the reliability evaluation and selection mechanism of the nodes are studied by using the perception data. A method that can detect the abnormal nodes in time and ensure the reliable data is proposed.

The Internet of Things is also known as wireless sensor network (WSNs). It is new information collection platforms that can be used to monitor and collect the real-time information of various target things within the region, and the real-time information will be send to gateway node to monitor and track the status of things in the specified range. In the process of monitoring and data transmission, it is an important problem to ensure the credibility and reliability. Due to wireless sensor network has its own characteristics, making the vulnerable to such as passive eavesdropping, active intrusion, and fake information, information obstruction of various forms of attack, which makes the perception of data cannot be guaranteed to be correct and reliable. Therefore, it is necessary to detect the abnormal nodes in time and ensure the data is reliable.

2   Related Work

In order to detect the abnormal node in time and improve the IOT security, credibility and reliability, many researchers were studied, and give some effective methods, such as Li et al. proposes a block-sparse signal reconstruction algorithm based on the adaptive step. Then, the abnormal node will be predicted based on the algorithm at the Sink node [4]. Wang et al. proposed a mechanism for detecting abnormal reading based on compressed sensing (CS) and self regression model, which can distinguish the abnormal data and the abnormal data [5]. In literature [6], the anomaly detection problem is modeled as a weighted L1 norm minimization problem, and then the OMP algorithm is used to solve the problem. In addition, in order to ensure the safety and reliability of the Internet of things, more scholars have studied the defense and security algorithms. Su presented a hash chain random key pre distribution based on schema in the plan node just needs less key information, can higher probability to establish pair wise key, guarantees in the presence of a large number of damaged nodes of network survivability [7]. Ma proposed key management scheme for heterogeneous region, make full use of node deployment knowledge and the known region information to construct key pre distribution scheme and improve the performance of the key management, and enhance the anti-attack ability of network [8]. Kong presents a based on EBS (exclusion basis system) suitable for in large-scale cluster based wireless sensor network dynamic key management scheme, significantly improve the network of anti-capture ability [9]. Wang aiming at the problems of low efficiency of key management and authentication mechanism, and using the threshold secret sharing mechanism proposed a lightweight security system and algorithm, removed the participation of the third party certification center, reduces the overhead and ensure the secure communication between nodes [10]. Lin proposed a new bandwidth efficient collaborative authentication mechanism, only need to add very little additional overhead can be achieved in the intermediate routing nodes filter injects false data attacks, greatly reducing the burden to the sink node [11]. Challal use unital design theory proposed enhancement based on unital key pre distribution mechanism, to ensure high security connection increase the scale of network coverage and the overall performance of the premise, and in the same size of the network conditions reduce the storage overhead [12]. The traditional key and authentication mechanism based solution can be implemented for external attacks, but it can do nothing about the internal attack of the network.

In the research of network security in wireless sensor networks, in order to solve the internal network attack, researchers were also studied, such as Li using a specific key deployment with the supervision of collaboration between neighbor nodes; good realized network false packets filtering [13]. Rasheed describes a allows arbitrary double key pre distribution mechanism as a basic component of the three layer general framework, this new architecture requires two new key pool, a mobile sink is used to access the network, a used to establish inter sensor key pair in dealing with mobile sink replication attacks than the polynomial pool based mechanism has more high elasticity of the network [14].Tian etc. presents an effective mechanism and quantitative analysis method for guaranteeing the reliability of monitored region and remote main trunk [15].

From the analysis, it can be seen that there are some research results in the aspects of abnormal nodes and data reliability, but the research is not deep, and there is no relevant research results in the field of self-check using perception data.

3   Basic Concepts

In order to detect the abnormal nodes, this paper introduces the concept of the detection unit and the three functional nodes.

3.1   Detection Unit

The detecting unit is the basic unit for self-inspection, and every detecting unit needs to include three kinds of monitoring nodes, namely, the working node, the associated node, and the decision node. Depending on the application scenario, the size of the detection unit is stable. Through the characteristics of the three types of nodes in the detection unit, the decision of whether the work node is abnormal.

3.2   Three Functional Nodes

Assume that the three types of nodes have certain storage and computing power, and can be used as a data transceiver.

The working node is a node that is completing the perception task and data transmission. The frequency of data perception is fixed or adjustable, and it is assumed to be N. The node can sense data of monitoring area. The working node can store the mean of the perceived data and a small amount of configuration information.

The associated node function is similar to working node. Its working frequency is one of the M points of the working node. The data of associated node is transmitted to the working node, and it is completed by the working node to determine the status of the working node.

The decision node is a passive node default in sleeping. When the work node and the associated node are not consistent, the active message is sent by the working node to activate the decision node. It should sense data after being activated and the perceived data sent to the working node, the final decision in the working node.

4   Proposed Algorithm

We propose a method for detecting node anomaly, which includes three levels, and the implementation mechanism of these three levels is as follows. Taking into account the characteristics of the node resource constraints, the design algorithm in this paper is simple in the premise of ensuring the effect.

4.1   Decision Algorithm

According to the three stages of the algorithm, this paper presents three detection processes. Figure 1 shows the process of the work node self-detection. The algorithm is named **WNSelf-Check**. Figure 2 shows the algorithm for the detection of the associated nodes. The algorithm is named **AN_CHECK**. Figure 3 shows the algorithm of the final judgment. The algorithm is named **DN_CHECK**.

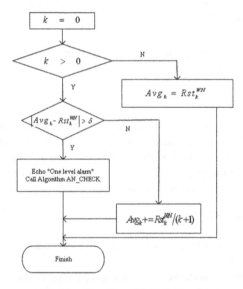

Fig. 1. Algorithm WNSelf-Check

In algorithm **WNSelf-Check**, k is counter. Avg_k represents the mean of the data before the k collection. Rst_k^{WN} represents the data of working nodes for the k collection. δ represents the absolute value of the difference between the current acquisition data and the average of historical data.

The algorithm **AN_CHECK** is used to complete the linkage mechanism between the associated nodes and the working nodes, and the second levels of the algorithm are realized. First need according to the working frequency of the node combined with

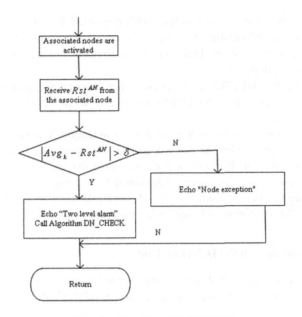

Fig. 2. Algorithm AN_CHECK

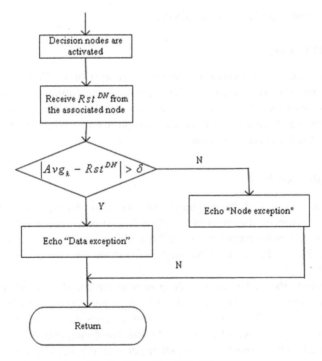

Fig. 3. Algorithm DN_CHECK

empirically determined associated nodes working frequency, and on the one hand to ensure the conservation of resource nodes, on the other hand to ensure timely detection of abnormal conditions of nodes. In this paper, the frequency of the associated nodes is 1/10 of the working frequency.

In algorithm **AN_CHECK**, Rst^{AN} represents the data of associated nodes.

The final decision will be carried out by decision node. In fact, the idea is similar to the associated nodes.

The final decision algorithm is the last parts of detection. Therefore, if the data of decision node are not matched with the historical data mean it is considered that the monitoring area is abnormal; otherwise it is considered that the node is abnormal.

In order to realize the coordination between detection units, this paper will make each detection unit as an independent unit, and participate in the whole IOT. Trust evaluation between detection units is based on Bayesian estimation method.

4.2 Trust Evaluation in the Detection Unit

Specific implementation method, please refer to the literature [16]. So it won't cover those again. In order to compare, the simulation results will be finish in the same environment.

5 Simulation and Result Analysis

5.1 Algorithm Analysis

This algorithm takes full account of the characteristics of IOT nodes have limited resources, in terms of decision rules, the number of computing and communication traffic were considered, due to storage only mean and current monitoring is stored required, therefore storage without increased significantly. While the unit detection results can be used for node selection.

5.2 Simulation Analysis

The algorithm is a part of the evaluation of IOT trust. Through the simulation in Matlab 7.0 environment, the effect of the algorithm on node state detection is investigated. The experimental parameters are set, the working frequency of the N is 1, network node number 243, and the trust evaluation of the detection unit is conducted by the method of [16].

Figure 4 shows the convergence of the trust after the introduction of the algorithm. As can be seen, the convergence rate of the abnormal nodes is much faster.

As a result, the algorithm can find the abnormal nodes more quickly and complete the adjustment of the degree of trust. In addition, the communication of the method introduced in this paper is mostly confined to the detection unit, so the energy consumption caused by the introduction of data sending and receiving is completely negligible. Energy consumption is shown in Fig. 5.

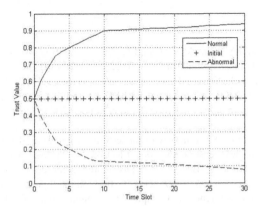

Fig. 4. The convergence of the trust

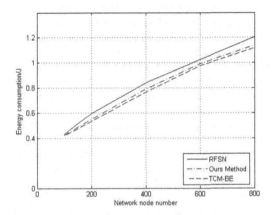

Fig. 5. Energy consumption comparison

6 Conclusions

In this paper, a mechanism for detecting node anomaly is proposed. In the mechanism, the detection unit is constructed which comprises a working nodes, associated nodes, decision nodes. The three detection levels based on three nodes can detect the abnormal state of the node effectively.

We introduce the mechanism into the trust evaluation method of IOT. The results show that the proposed algorithm can improve the convergence rate of the abnormal nodes under the condition that the energy consumption is not significantly improved.

Acknowledgements. The work was supported by the Fundamental Re-search Funds for the Central Universities (3142014125, 3142015022, 3142013098, and 3142013070) and Natural Science Foundation of Hebei Province (F2014508028) and National Natural Science Foundation of China (61163050, 61472137).

References

1. Zhang, D.Q., Zhou, J.Y., Guo, M.Y., Cao, J.N.: TASA: tag-free activity sensing using RFID tag arrays. IEEE Trans. Parallel Distrib. Syst. **22**, 558–570 (2011)
2. Zhang, D.Q., Zhao, S.J., Yang, T.R., Chen, M., Wang, Y.S., Liu, H.Z.: Next Me: localization using cellular traces in internet of things. IEEE Trans. Ind. Inform. **11**(2), 302–312 (2015)
3. International Telecommunication Union: Internet Reports 2005: The Internet of Things. ITU, Geneva (2005)
4. Li, P., Wang, J.X., Cao, J.N.: Abnormal event detection scheme based on compressive sensing and GM (1, 1) in wireless sensor networks. J. Electron. Inf. Technol. **37**(7), 1586–1590 (2015)
5. Wang, J., Tang, S.J., Yin, B.C., et al.: Distributed compressive sampling for lifetime optimization in dense wireless sensor networks through intelligent compressive sensing. In: IEEE International Conference on Computer Communications, pp. 603–611. IEEE Press, Orlando, FL, USA (2012)
6. Xia, Y., Zhao, Z.F., Zhang, H.G.: Distributed anomaly event detection in wireless networks using compressed sensing. In: 2011 11th International Symposium on Communications and Information Technologies, pp. 250–255, Hangzhou, China(2011)
7. Su, Z., Lin, C., Ren, F.Y.: Hash chain based random keys pre-distribution scheme in wireless sensor networks. J. Comput. **32**(1), 30–41 (2009)
8. Ma, C.G., Shang, Z.G., Wang, H.Q.: Domain-based key management for heterogeneous wireless sensor networks. J. Commun. **30**(5), 74–81 (2009)
9. Kong, F.R., Li, C.W.: Dynamic key management scheme for wireless sensor network. J. Softw. **21**(7), 1679–1691 (2010)
10. Wang, C., Hu, G.Y., Zhang, H.G.: Lightweight security architecture design for wireless sensor network. J. Commun. **33**(2), 30–35 (2012)
11. Liu, X.D., Zhu, H.J., Liang, X.H., Shen, X.M.: BECAN: a bandwidth-efficient cooperative authentication scheme for filtering injected false data in wireless sensor networks. IEEE Trans. Parallel Distrib. Syst. **23**(1), 32–43 (2012)
12. Challal, Y., Bouabdallah, A., Tarokh, V.: A highly scalable key pre-distribution scheme for wireless sensor networks. IEEE Trans. Wirel. Commun. **12**(2), 948–959 (2013)
13. Li, J.Z., Yu, L., Gao, H., Xiong, S.G.: Grouping-enhanced resilient probabilistic en-route filtering of injected false data in WSNs. IEEE Trans. Parallel Distrib. Syst. **23**(5), 881–889 (2012)
14. Rasheed, A., Mahapatra, R.N.: The three-tier security scheme in wireless sensor networks with mobile sinks. IEEE Trans. Parallel Distrib. Syst. **23**(5), 958–965 (2012)
15. Tian, L.Q., Lin, C., Zhang, Q., Chen, Z.G.: Topological reliability design and optimal analysis to remote monitoring based on internet of things with uniform clustering. J. Softw. **25**(8), 1625–1639 (2014)
16. Liu, T., Xiong, Y., Huang, W.C., Lu, Q.W., Guang, Y.W.: Trust computation model of nodes based on bayes estimation in wireless sensor networks. Comput. Sci. **40**(10), 61–64 (2013)

Author Index